Question Help consists of homework and practice questions to give students unlimited opportunities to master concepts. **Learning aids** walk students through the problem—giving them assistance when they need it most.

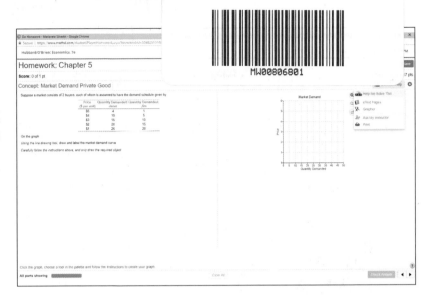

"I love the 'Help Me Solve This' feature. It really helped me figure out what I was doing wrong and how to fix a problem rather than just saying 'wrong' or 'right'."

— Student, Illinois State University

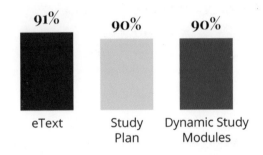

91%	90%	90%
eText	Study Plan	Dynamic Study Modules

% of students who found learning aids helpful

Dynamic Study Modules use the latest developments in cognitive science and help students study chapter topics by adapting to their performance in real time.

Pearson eText enhances student learning. Worked examples, videos, and interactive tutorials bring learning to life, while algorithmic practice and self-assessment opportunities test students' understanding of the material.

The **Gradebook** offers an easy way for you and your students to see their performance in your course.

89%

of students would tell their instructor to keep using MyLab Economics

For additional details visit: www.pearson.com/mylab/economics

Symbols Used in This Book

Δ [capital delta] = a change in the following variable— for example, the change in p between Periods 1 and 2 is $\Delta p = p_2 - p_1$, where p_i is the price in Period i)

ε [epsilon] = the price elasticity of demand

π [pi] = profit = revenue − total cost = $R - C$

θ = proportion or probability or share

Abbreviations, Variables, and Function Names

AFC = average fixed cost = fixed cost divided by output = F/q

AVC = average variable cost = variable cost divided by output = VC/q

AC = average cost = total cost divided by output = C/q

AP_i = average product of input i—for example, AP_L is the average product of labor

C = total cost = variable cost + fixed cost = $VC + F$

CS = consumer surplus

D = market demand curve

DWL = deadweight loss

F = fixed cost

i = interest rate

I = indifference curve

K = capital

L = labor

LR = long run

m = constant marginal cost

MC = marginal cost

MP_i = marginal (physical) product of input i—for example, MP_L is the marginal product of labor

MR = marginal revenue

MRS = marginal rate of substitution

$MRTS$ = marginal rate of technical substitution

n = number of items such as firms in an industry

p = price

PS = producer surplus

Q = market (or monopoly) output

q = firm output

R = revenue = pq

r = price of capital services

s = per-unit subsidy

S = market supply curve

SR = short run

t = specific or unit tax

T = tax revenue (tQ)

TS = total surplus

U = utility

VC = variable cost

w = wage

Y = income or budget

Managerial Economics and Strategy

THIRD EDITION

Managerial Economics and Strategy

THIRD EDITION

Jeffrey M. Perloff
University of California, Berkeley

James A. Brander
Sauder School of Business,
University of British Columbia

FOR JACKIE, LISA, BARBARA, AND CATHY

Vice President, Business, Economics, and UK Courseware:
  Donna Battista
Director of Portfolio Management: Adrienne D'Ambrosio
Specialist Portfolio Manager: Chris DeJohn
Editorial Assistant: Aly Grindall
Vice President, Product Marketing: Roxanne McCarley
Senior Product Marketer: Carlie Marvel
Product Marketing Assistant: Marianela Silvestri
Manager of Field Marketing, Business Publishing:
  Adam Goldstein
Field Marketing Manager: Ashley Bryan
Vice President, Production and Digital Studio, Arts and Business:
  Etain O'Dea
Director, Production and Digital Studio, Business and Economics:
  Ashley Santora
Managing Producer, Business: Alison Kalil
Content Producer: Carolyn Philips

Operations Specialist: Carol Melville
Design Lead: Kathryn Foot
Manager, Learning Tools: Brian Surette
Senior Learning Tools Strategist: Emily Biberger
Managing Producer, Digital Studio and GLP: James Bateman
Managing Producer, Digital Studio: Diane Lombardo
Digital Studio Producer: Melissa Honig
Digital Studio Producer: Alana Coles
Digital Content Team Lead: Noel Lotz
Digital Content Project Lead: Courtney Kamaouf
Full Service Project Management: Pearson CSC, Nicole Suddeth
  and Kathy Smith
Interior Design: Pearson CSC
Cover Design: Pearson CSC
Cover Art: Arsgera/Shutterstock
Printer/Binder: LSC Communications, Inc.
Cover Printer: LSC Communications, Inc.

ISBN 10: 0-13-518378-2
ISBN 13: 978-0-13-518378-6

Brief Contents

Contents

Preface

What's New in the Third Edition

We have substantially revised the third edition based in large part on the very helpful suggestions of instructors and students who used the second edition. We have updated and revised every chapter. Key revisions include:

- Spreadsheet-based Q&A Exercises are a new feature in Chapters 3, 6–10, and 12–16. This major innovation helps students learn how to address real-world business problems using spreadsheets, which is an increasingly important skill in today's business world.

- Chapters 1, 5, 6, 7, 9, and 14 have a new theme on *disruptive innovations*: innovations, such as online retailing, 3D printing, and social media, that dramatically change consumer options or the way an industry is structured, possibly creating new industries and destroying old ones.

- A new feature is the 21 *Common Confusions*, which explain why a widely held belief is incorrect.

- Over three-quarters of the Mini-Cases (brief applications of the theory) are new (22) or revised (48).

- Of the 655 end-of-chapter questions, 150 are new or revised.

- Nearly a quarter of the Managerial Implications (brief discussions of how to use economic theory to improve managerial decisions) are new or substantially revised.

- This edition is even more user-friendly. It drops some of the more technical material from Chapters 2, 4, 6, 7, 8, and 11, and adds more emphasis on current managerial issues in both the main text and the features.

- Because instructors and students enjoyed the cartoons in the second edition, this edition has 45% more cartoons. In addition to providing entertainment, these cartoons convey important economic points in a memorable way.

The Managerial Economics Program

This book differs from other managerial economics books in three main ways:

1. **Modern Theories.** We place greater emphasis than other texts on modern theories that are increasingly useful to managers. These include:
   - Modern contract theory to show students how to write contracts to avoid or minimize problems
   - Behavioral economics to explain why people deviate from rational behavior

- Game theory to help students think about business strategies and choose strategies that maximize profits
- Analysis of real-world pricing tools.

2. **Real-world Examples.** We make more extensive use of real-world business examples to illustrate how to use economic theory in making business decisions. To illustrate important economic concepts, we use calculations, graphs, and spreadsheets based on actual markets and real data.

3. **Problem-based Learning.** We employ a problem-based learning approach to demonstrate how to apply economic theory to specific business decisions. In each chapter, we solve problems using a step-by-step approach to model good problem-solving techniques, and each end of chapter section includes an extensive set of questions.

These innovative hallmarks are woven throughout the text.

To improve student results, we recommend pairing the text content with **MyLab Economics,** which is the teaching and learning platform that empowers instructors to reach every student. By combining trusted author content with digital tools and a flexible platform, MyLab personalizes the learning experience and will help students learn and retain key course concepts while developing skills that future employers are seeking in their candidates. MyLab Economics allows professors increased flexibility in designing and teaching their courses. Learn more at www.pearson.com/mylab/economics.

Solving Teaching and Learning Challenges

As teachers, we understand the challenges of managerial economics courses. Our experience teaching managerial economics at the Wharton School (University of Pennsylvania) and the Sauder School of Business (University of British Columbia) as well as teaching a wide variety of students at the Massachusetts Institute of Technology; Queen's University; and the University of California, Berkeley, has convinced us that students do best with an emphasis on problem solving and real-world issues and examples from actual markets. In the features of the book and MyLab Economics, we show how to apply economic theory to managerial decisions using actual business examples and real data.

We demonstrate that economics is practical and useful to managers by examining real markets and actual business decisions. Successful managers make extensive use of economic tools to reduce the cost of production, to choose pricing structures or output levels to maximize profit, and to make many other managerial decisions. We highlight applications of these tools in the *Managerial Problems, Mini-Cases, Managerial Implications,* and *Q&As* throughout the book, and the videos in MyLab Economics.

Managerial Problems

After the introductory chapter, each chapter starts with a *Managerial Problem* that motivates the chapter by posing a real-world managerial question. At the end of each chapter, we answer this question in the *Managerial Solution* using the economic principles discussed in that chapter. Thus, each Managerial Problem–Managerial Solution pair combines the essence of a Mini-Case and a Q&A.

Managerial Problem

Paying Employees to Relocate

When Google wants to transfer an employee from its Washington, D.C., office to its London branch, it must decide how much compensation to offer the worker to move. International firms are increasingly relocating workers throughout their home countries and internationally.

As you might expect, workers are not always enthusiastic about being relocated. In a survey by Runzheimer International, 79% of firms' relocation managers responded that they experienced resistance from employees who were asked to relocate to high-cost locations. A survey of some of their employees found that 81% objected to moving because of fear of a lowered standard of living.

One possible approach to enticing employees to relocate is for the firm to determine the goods and services consumed by employees in the original location and then pay those employees enough to allow them to consume essentially the same items in the new location. According to a survey by Mercer, 79% of international firms reported that they provided their workers with enough income abroad to maintain their home lifestyle.

However, economists who advise on compensation packages point out that such an approach will typically overcompensate employees by paying them more than they need to obtain the same level of economic well-being they have in the original city. How can a firm's human resources (HR) manager use consumer theory to optimally compensate employees who are transferred to other cities?

Mini-Cases

The *Mini-Cases* apply economic theory to interesting and important managerial problems. For example, Mini-Cases demonstrate how price increases on iTunes affect music downloads using actual data, how to estimate Crocs' production function for shoes using real-world data, why top-end designers limit the number of designer bags customers can buy, the effect of cyberattacks, how Pfizer used limit pricing to slow the entry of rivals, why advertisers pay so much for Super Bowl commercials, and how managers of auto manufacturing firms organize production and trade to avoid taxes and tariffs.

Mini-Case

Apple's IPad

Apple's iPad was the first commercially successful tablet. Users interact with the iPad using Apple's multi-touch, finger-sensitive touchscreen (rather than the pressure-triggered stylus that most previous tablets used) and a virtual onscreen keyboard (rather than a physical one). Most importantly, the iPad offers an intuitive interface and is well integrated with Apple's iTunes, eBooks, and various application programs.

People loved the original iPad. Even at $499 for the basic model, Apple had a virtual monopoly in its first year in 2010, with 87% of the tablet market. Moreover, the other tablets available in 2010 were not viewed by most consumers as close substitutes. Apple reported that it sold 25 million iPads worldwide in its first full year.

Unfortunately for Apple, its monopoly was short lived. Within a year of the iPad's introduction, over a hundred iPad want-to-be tablets were available. Apple's share of the tablet market fell to 29% by early 2018.

Managerial Implications

The *Managerial Implications* feature provides bottom-line statements of economic principles that managers can use to make key managerial decisions. For example, we describe how managers can assess whether they are maximizing profit. We also show how they can structure discounts to maximize profits, promote customer loyalty, design auctions, prevent gray markets, and use important insights from game theory to make good managerial decisions.

> **Managerial Implication**
>
> Taking Advantage of Limited Strategic Thinking
>
> Managers should consider the level of strategic sophistication of customers (and rivals). For example, successful managers of Hollywood movie studios anticipate limited strategic thinking by moviegoers. Normally Hollywood studios release movies for prescreening by critics before general release to generate buzz through positive reviews. This technique works well for good movies, but has the opposite effect for movies that get poor reviews.
>
> If a studio is not confident about a movie's quality it can use a *cold opening*, releasing the movie with no prescreenings for movie critics. A fully rational moviegoer understands this tactic and is less likely to go to movies with cold opens. Thus, if everyone were rational, studios wouldn't use cold openings.
>
> However, Brown, Camerer, and Lovallo (2012) found that while some moviegoers instantly understand the system, some never catch on to this pattern. As a result, cold opens generate more revenue and more profit on average than comparable not-very-good movies that are prescreened. And, on average, moviegoers are disappointed by cold opens relative to other movies. Thus, a manager should not overestimate the reasoning ability of the general movie-going public.

Q&As and End-of-Chapter Questions

The largest challenge facing students is learning how to apply economics concepts to solve problems. To help them learn this crucial skill, we provide three to five *Q&As* (Questions & Answers) in each chapter after the introductory chapter. Each *Q&A* poses a qualitative or quantitative problem and then uses a step-by-step approach to solve the problem. The *Q&As* focus on important managerial issues such as how a cost-minimizing firm should adjust to changing factor prices, how a manager prices bundles of goods to maximize profits, how to determine Intel's and AMD's profit-maximizing quantities and prices using their estimated demand curves and marginal costs, and how to allocate production across plants internationally.

> **Q&A 3.1**
>
> In 2018, Amazon raised the annual subscription fee for its Prime membership service, which provides free two-day shipping on many goods and other benefits, from \$99 to \$119. Piper Jaffray, an investment bank, estimated that before the price increase, Prime had 77 million U.S. subscribers.[3] The bank speculated that the number of members would fall to about 62 million. If so, what is the arc elasticity of demand for a Prime membership?
>
> **Answer**
>
> *Use Equation 3.2 to calculate the arc elasticity.* The change in the price is $\Delta p = \$119 - \$99 = \$20$, and the change in quantity is $\Delta Q = 62 - 77 = -15$. The average price is $\bar{p} = (\$99 + \$119)/2 = \$109$, and the average quantity is $\bar{Q} = (77 + 62)/2 = 69.5$ million. Plugging these values into Equation 3.2, we find that the arc price elasticity of demand for Prime memberships is
>
> $$\varepsilon = \frac{\Delta Q/\bar{Q}}{\Delta p/\bar{p}} = \frac{-15/69.5}{20/109} \approx -\frac{0.216}{0.183} \approx -1.18.$$
>
> When price rose by 18.3%, the quantity demanded was estimated to fall by 21.6%, so the arc elasticity of demand is $\varepsilon = -1.18$. Based on this elasticity, a 1% rise in price would cause the quantity demanded to fall by 1.18 percent.

At the end of the book, we provide solutions to selected end-of-chapter questions. In addition, detailed answers to all the end-of-chapter questions are provided in MyLab Economics so that students can confirm their understanding without having to contact a professor and also be better prepared for exams.

MyLab Economics Videos

Today's students learn best when they analyze and discuss topics in the text outside of class. To further students' understanding of what they are reading and discussing in the classroom, we provide a set of videos in MyLab Economics. In these videos, Tony Lima presents key figures, tables, Excel applications and concepts in step-by-step animations with audio explanations that discuss the economics behind each step. For example, some of these show students how to use Excel to run regressions, analyze different pricing strategies, cover applications of game theory, address risk and diversification, and choose contracts that reduce moral hazard in principal-agent relationships.

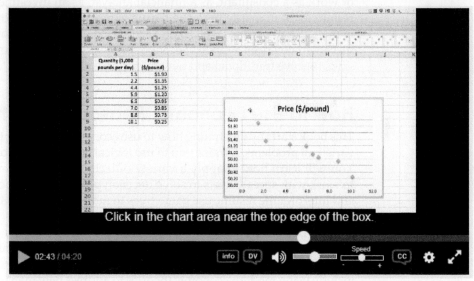

Using Calculus Sections and *Calculus Exercises*

Some students learn economics best using verbal or graphical explanations. However, others find mathematical explanations clearer. Consequently, some managerial economics courses use calculus while others do not. Both types of course can use this book effectively due to the optional *Using Calculus* sections in the text. Non-calculus courses can omit these short sections with no loss of continuity. For courses that require calculus, *Using Calculus* sections reinforce the graphical, verbal, and algebraic treatment of major topics.

In contrast, many other books relegate calculus to appendices, mix calculus in with other material where it cannot easily be skipped, or avoid calculus entirely. Our approach has proven effective in courses that use no calculus and have very limited mathematical prerequisites, and in courses with significant calculus content. End-of-chapter questions that require calculus are clearly indicated.

Using Calculus

Profit Maximization
with a Specific Tax

We can use calculus to solve the problem in Q&A 8.1. After the government imposes the specific tax t, the competitive firm's profit is

$$\pi = pq - [C(q) + tq],$$

where $C(q)$ is the firm's before-tax cost and $C(q) + tq$ is its after-tax cost. We obtain a necessary condition for the firm to maximize its after-tax profit by taking the first derivative of profit with respect to quantity and setting it equal to zero:

$$\frac{d\pi}{dq} = \frac{d(pq)}{dq} - \frac{d[C(q) + tq]}{dq} = p - \left[\frac{dC(q)}{dq} + t\right] = p - [MC + t] = 0.$$

Thus, the competitive firm maximizes its profit by choosing q such that its after-tax marginal cost, $MC + t$, equals the market price.

Developing Career Skills

You may be asking yourself, why study economics if I want to manage a business or work as a consultant, as a financial analyst, as an investment banker, in human resources, or in marketing? The reason is that employers know that you need economic skills to perform well. To get a great job upon graduation and have a successful career, you need a range of economic skills and need to know how to apply these skills to solve traditional and new managerial challenges.

How to Use Economic Reasoning on the Job

This book starts by illustrating how to use economic reasoning to analyze and solve a variety of problems. It trains you to use logical analysis based on empirical evidence. You will learn how to apply a variety of techniques that firms value such as how to work with spreadsheets to solve decision problems, conduct regression analyses and interpret the results, use game trees to map strategic decisions, and analyze the effects of pricing decisions.

The book shows you how to approach problems that you are likely to encounter on the job. These applications include using basic economic tools to predict the effects of input price changes or government actions on a market. But they also include using modern economic theories to address new managerial challenges such as

- developing strategies to compete in oligopolistic markets,
- structuring stock options to motivate executives,
- using online platforms (two-sided markets) that bring buyers and sellers together, such as eBay,
- responding to cyberattacks and to potentially disruptive innovations such as 3D printing.

Spreadsheet Exercises

In contrast to other managerial economics textbooks, a major feature of this book helps you develop a facility in using spreadsheets and shows how to use them to solve real-world managerial problems.

Managers increasingly rely on spreadsheets. Spreadsheets make it easier than ever to apply economic principles to managerial decisions. Earlier editions of this book included spreadsheet-based end-of-chapter questions. In this edition, we've added 11 spreadsheet *Q&As*, which train you by taking you step-by-step through spreadsheets to solve a managerial problem. These *Q&As* show how to use spreadsheets to calculate elasticities, determine the effect of price changes on revenue and profit, calculate present values, assess the benefits of dynamic pricing, simplify decision-making under uncertainty, and analyze other important questions.

Q&A 6.2

Suppose that a small guitar firm has experimented with the cost of producing different quantities of output per hour by varying the number of workers, holding the size of the plant fixed and using just one CNC machine. It has estimated its cost function as $C = 125 + 10q - 5q^2 + q^3$ where q is quantity produced per hour and C is measured in dollars. The corresponding marginal cost function is $MC = 10 - 10q + 3q^2$.[4] Use an Excel spreadsheet to show the fixed cost, and to calculate variable cost, total cost, average cost, and marginal cost for output levels from 1 to 10 in one-unit increments. Use the spreadsheet to find the output level at which average cost is minimized and verify that $AC = MC$ at this output level.

Answer

1. *Open an Excel spreadsheet and put titles* Quantity, Fixed Cost, Variable Cost, Total Cost, Average Cost, *and* Marginal Cost *in cells A1 through F1.* Fill in the numbers 1 through 10 in one-unit increments in cells A2–A11 and enter the number 125 (fixed cost) in each cell from B2 through B11.

2. *Fill in the other columns using appropriate formulas.* Enter "=10*A2−5*A2^2+A2^3" in cell C2 and copy this formula into the remaining cells in column C. Enter "=B2+C2" in cell D2, then copy that formula into the rest of column D up to cell D11. Enter "=D2/A2" into cell E2 and copy that formula

into the rest of column E. Enter "=10−10*A2+3*A2^2" into cell F2 and also copy that formula into the rest of column F. The formulas are shown in the screenshot.

	A	B	C	D	E	F
1	Quantity	Fixed Cost	Variable Cost	Total Cost	Average Cost	Marginal Cost
2	1	125	=10*A2-5*A2^2 +A2^3	=B2+C2	=D2/A2	=10-10*A2+3*A2^2
3	2	125	=10*A3-5*A3^2 +A3^3	=B3+C3	=D3/A3	=10-10*A3+3*A3^2
4	3	125	=10*A4-5*A4^2 +A4^3	=B4+C4	=D4/A4	=10-10*A4+3*A4^2
5	4	125	=10*A5-5*A5^2 +A5^3	=B5+C5	=D5/A5	=10-10*A5+3*A5^2
6	5	125	=10*A6-5*A6^2 +A6^3	=B6+C6	=D6/A6	=10-10*A6+3*A6^2
7	6	125	=10*A7-5*A7^2 +A7^3	=B7+C7	=D7/A7	=10-10*A7+3*A7^2
8	7	125	=10*A8-5*A8^2 +A8^3	=B8+C8	=D8/A8	=10-10*A8+3*A8^2
9	8	125	=10*A9-5*A9^2 +A9^3	=B9+C9	=D9/A9	=10-10*A9+3*A9^2
10	9	125	=10*A10-5*A10^2 +A10^3	=B10+C10	=D10/A10	=10-10*A10+3*A10^2
11	10	125	=10*A11-5*A11^2 +A11^3	=B11+C11	=D11/A11	=10-10*A11+3*A11^2

3. *Look in the Average Cost column to identify the output at which average cost is minimized.* Average cost reaches its lowest level in cell E6, where the quantity produced is 5 and average cost is 35. At this output level, marginal cost is also equal to 35, as the screenshot shows. (The average cost column has been formatted to show two digits after the decimal point.)

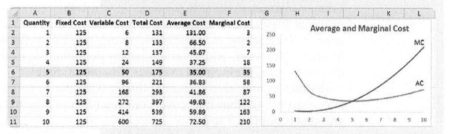

	A	B	C	D	E	F	G	H	I	J	K	L
1	Quantity	Fixed Cost	Variable Cost	Total Cost	Average Cost	Marginal Cost						
2	1	125	6	131	131.00	3						
3	2	125	8	133	66.50	2						
4	3	125	12	137	45.67	7						
5	4	125	24	149	37.25	18						
6	5	125	50	175	35.00	35						
7	6	125	96	221	36.83	58						
8	7	125	168	293	41.86	87						
9	8	125	272	397	49.63	122						
10	9	125	414	539	59.89	163						
11	10	125	600	725	72.50	210						

Note: It is possible to use Excel to draw any of the cost curves by inserting a scatterplot. The screenshot shows the average and marginal cost curves.

In addition to these *Q&As*, each chapter except the first has three end-of-chapter spreadsheet exercises addressing topics such as choosing the profit-maximizing level of advertising and designing compensation contracts to motivate employees. All spreadsheet exercises are available in MyLab Economics as static exercises, and select exercises (marked with an ✗ in the text) are available in an auto-graded format. Using proven, field-tested technology, auto-graded Excel Projects let professors seamlessly integrate Microsoft® Excel® content into the course without having to manually grade spreadsheets. Students can practice important skills in Excel, helping you master key concepts and gain proficiency with the program. Simply download a spreadsheet, work live on a problem in Excel, and then upload that file back to MyLab Economics. Within minutes, you will receive a report that provides personalized, detailed feedback and, if necessary, pinpoints where you went astray in the problem. This feedback helps nurture your understanding of the key topics in the course while building confidence in your Excel skills, preparing you for success in class and in your career.

8. MyLab Economics Spreadsheet Exercises[23]

8.1 A monopolist's inverse demand function is $p = 100 - 2Q$, so its marginal revenue is $MR = 100 - 4Q$. Its cost function is $C = 25 + 4Q + 2Q^2$ and its marginal cost is therefore $MC = 4 + 4Q$.

a. Create a spreadsheet with column headings Q, p, MR, MC, R, C, profit, and CS (consumer surplus). Enter the values 1 to 25 in one-unit increments in the quantity column and enter the appropriate formulas in all the other cells. Determine the profit maximizing output and price for an unregulated monopoly. What is the monopoly's profit and the consumer surplus at this output and price?

b. Now use your spreadsheet to determine the price, quantity, profit, and consumer surplus if the regulator imposes a price cap (ceiling) of 70.

c. Which of the two pricing structures yields the highest total surplus? If the regulator wants to use price cap regulation *and* wants to maximize total surplus, what price cap should the regulator choose?

Table of Contents Overview

Because instructors differ in the order in which they cover material and in the range of topics they choose to teach, this text allows for flexibility. The most common approach to teaching managerial economics is to follow the sequence of the chapters in order. However, many variations are possible. For example, some instructors choose to address empirical methods (Chapter 3) first.

Instructors may skip consumer theory (Chapter 4) without causing problems in later chapters. Or, they may cover consumer theory after the chapters on production and cost (Chapters 5 and 6).

Chapter 7, "Firm Organization and Market Structure," provides an overview of the key issues that are discussed in later chapters, such as types of firms, profit maximization and its alternatives, and the structure of markets. We think that presenting this material early in the course is ideal, but an instructor can cover all of this material except for the section on profit maximization later.

An instructor may teach pricing with market power (Chapter 10) at any point after discussing monopoly (Chapter 9). Because game theory is introduced in two chapters (Chapters 12 and 13), instructors can conveniently choose how much game theory to present. Although Chapter 11 on oligopoly and monopolistic competition precedes the game theory chapters, a course could cover the game theory chapters first.

A common variant is to present Chapter 14 on uncertainty earlier in the course. A course could present asymmetric information (Chapter 15) at any point after the uncertainty chapter. Thus, a course could cover both the uncertainty and information chapters early.

Chapter 16 on government and business discusses market failures, government regulation, externalities, public goods, and intellectual property. A course could cover this material earlier. For example, the regulation and intellectual property material could follow monopoly. The externality and public good treatment could be presented at any point after Chapter 8 on competitive firms and markets.

The final chapter, Global Business (Chapter 17), is valuable in a course that stresses international issues. An instructor could cover this chapter at any point after the competition and monopoly chapters.

Instructor Teaching Resources

This book has a full range of supplementary materials that support teaching and learning. This program comes with the following teaching resources:

Supplements available to instructors at www.pearsonhighered.com	Features of the Supplement
Instructor's Manual Authored by Matt Roelofs of Western Washington University	• *Chapter Outlines* include key terminology, teaching notes, and lecture suggestions. • *Teaching Tips* and *Additional Discussion Questions* provide tips for alternative ways to cover the material and brief reminders on additional help to provide students. • *Solutions* are provided for all problems in the book.
Test Bank Authored by Todd Fitch of the University of California, Berkeley	• Multiple-choice problems of varying levels of complexity, suitable for homework assignments and exams • Many of these draw on current news and events
Computerized TestGen	TestGen allows instructors to: • Customize, save, and generate classroom tests • Edit, add, or delete questions from the Test Item Files • Analyze test results • Organize a database of tests and student results.

PowerPoints
Authored by Nelson Altamirano of National University
	• Slides include all the graphs, tables, and equations in the textbook, as well as lecture notes.
	• PowerPoints meet accessibility standards for students with disabilities. Features include, but not limited to:
	  • Keyboard and Screen Reader access
	  • Alternative text for images
	  • High color contrast between background and foreground colors

Acknowledgments

Our greatest debt is to our very patient students at MIT; the University of British Columbia; the University of California, Berkeley; and the University of Pennsylvania for tolerantly dealing with our various approaches to teaching them economics. We appreciate their many helpful (and usually polite) suggestions.

We also owe a great debt to our editors for the first edition, Adrienne D'Ambrosio and Jane Tufts. Adrienne D'Ambrosio, Editorial Director, was involved in every stage in designing the book, writing the book, testing it, and developing supplemental materials. Jane Tufts, our developmental editor, reviewed each chapter of this book for content, pedagogy, and presentation. By showing us how to present the material as clearly and thoroughly as possible, she greatly strengthened this text. For the second edition, we thank Christina Masturzo for guiding us as our Portfolio Manager on the print and digital resources.

We are also grateful to Satyajit Ghosh, University of Scranton, for doing most of the work on the end-of-chapter spreadsheet exercises in the first two editions and in MyLab Economics. We benefitted greatly from his creative ideas about using spreadsheets to teach managerial economics. Our other major debt is to Tony Lima for his outstanding work creating MyLab Economics videos and for valuable comments on the text.

We thank our teaching colleagues who provided many helpful comments and from whom we have shamelessly borrowed ideas. We particularly thank Tom Davidoff, Isaac Holloway, Stephen Meyer, Nate Schiff, Ratna Shrestha, Mariano Tappata, James Vercammen, and Lanny Zrill for using earlier versions of the textbook and for making a wide range of helpful contributions. We are also grateful to our colleagues Jen Baggs, Michael Brar, Dennis Carlton, Jean-Etienne de Bettignies, Keith Head, Larry Karp, John Ries, Juliana Rogo, Tom Ross, Leo Simon, Scott Templeton, Chloe Tergiman, and Ralph Winter for many helpful comments. We thank Sophie Endl, Evan Flater, Kai Rong Gan, Albina Gibadullina, Guojun He, Joyce Lam, WeiYi Shen, Yihang Xu, Louisa Yeung, and Maddison Zapach for their valuable work as research assistants on the book.

We are very grateful to the many reviewers who spent untold hours reading and commenting on our original proposal and several versions of each chapter. Many of the best ideas in this book are due to them.

We'd especially like to thank Matthew Roelofs for carefully reviewing the accuracy of the entire manuscript for the first two editions and for many contributions to the end-of-chapter questions in this edition, along with other helpful comments. We also thank Gordon Lenjosek for checking the accuracy of this edition and suggesting useful changes.

We also thank the following reviewers and others, who provided valuable comments at various stages:

Laurel Adams, *Northern Illinois University*

James C. W. Ahiakpor, *California State University, East Bay*

Nelson Altamirano, *National University*

Ariel Belasen, *Southern Illinois University, Edwardsville*

Bruce C. Brown, *California State Polytechnic University, Pomona*

Donald Bumpass, *Sam Houston State University*

James H. Cardon, *Brigham Young University*

Jihui Chen, *Illinois State University*

Ron Cheung, *Oberlin College*

Abdur Chowdhury, *Marquette University*

George Clarke, *Texas A&M International University*

Kristen Collett-Schmitt, *Notre Dame University*

Douglas Davis, *Virginia Commonwealth University*

Christopher S. Decker, *University of Nebraska, Omaha*

Craig A. Depken, II, *University of North Carolina, Charlotte*

Jed DeVaro, *California State University, East Bay*

Casey DiRienzo, *Elon University*

David Ely, *San Diego State University*

Asim Erdilek, *Case Western Reserve University*

John Fizel, *Penn State University*

Satyajit Ghosh, *University of Scranton*

Rajeev Goel, *Illinois State University*

Abbas P. Grammy, *California State University, Bakersfield*

Clifford Hawley, *West Virginia University*

Cary Heath, *University of Louisiana*

Matthew John Higgins, *Georgia Institute of Technology*

Jack Hou, *California State University, Long Beach*

Andrew Hussey, *University of Memphis*

Timothy James, *Arizona State University*

Charles Johnston, *Baker College*

Michael Jones, *University of Cincinnati*

Peter Daniel Jubinski, *St. Joseph's University*

Chulho Jung, *Ohio University*

David E. Kalist, *Shippensburg University*

Barry Keating, *University of Notre Dame*

Daniel Lee, *Shippensburg University*

Tom K. Lee, *California State University, Northridge*

Dale Lehman, *Alaska Pacific University*

Tony Lima, *California State University, East Bay*

Albert Loh, *University of North Florida*

Vincent J. Marra Jr., *University of Delaware*

Scott McGann,. *San Diego State University*

Sheila J. Moore, *California Lutheran University*

Thomas Patrick, *The College of New Jersey*

Anita Alves Pena, *Colorado State University*

Troy Quast, *Sam Houston State University*

Jack Reardon,. *Hamline University*

Barry Ritchey, *Anderson University*

Matthew Roelofs, *Western Washington University*

Charles Sebuharara, *Binghampton University*

Amit Sen, *Xavier University*

Stephanie Shayne, *Husson University*

Maura Shelton, *University of Washington*

Nancy Sowers, *Berea College*

Caroline Swartz, *University of North Carolina, Charlotte*

Scott Templeton, *Clemson University*

Xiahua (Ken) Wei, *University of Washington*

Keith Willett, *Oklahoma State University*

Douglas Wills, *University of Washington, Tacoma*

Mark L. Wilson, *Troy University*

David Wong, *California State University, Fullerton*

It was a pleasure to work with the highly skilled people at Pearson and Pearson CSC, who were incredibly helpful in producing this book. Carolyn Philips, Kathy Smith, and Nicole Suddeth did a wonderful job of supervising the production process, assembling the extended publishing team, and managing the schedule. We also want to acknowledge, with appreciation, the efforts of Melissa Honig, Courtney Kamauf, and Noel Lotz, in developing the MyLab Economics online assessment and tutorial system for the book.

Finally, we thank our wives, Jackie Persons and Barbara Spencer, for their great patience and support during the nearly endless writing process. We apologize for misusing their names—and those of our other relatives and friends—in the book!

J. M. P.

J. A. B.

Introduction

An Economist's Theory of Reincarnation: If you're good, you come back on a higher level. Cats come back as dogs, dogs come back as horses, and people—if they've been very good like George Washington—come back as money.

If all the food, clothing, entertainment, and other goods and services we wanted were freely available, no one would study economics, and we would not need managers. However, most of the good things in life are scarce. We cannot have everything we want. Consumers cannot consume everything but must make choices about what to purchase. Similarly, managers of firms cannot produce everything and must make careful choices about what to produce, how much to produce, and how to produce it. Studying such choices is the main subject matter of economics. **Economics** is the study of decision making in the presence of scarcity.[1]

Managerial economics is the application of economic analysis to managerial decision making. It focuses on how managers make economic decisions by allocating the scarce resources at their disposal. To make good decisions, a manager must understand the behavior of other decision makers, such as consumers, workers, other managers, and governments. In this book, we examine decision making by such participants in the economy, and we show how managers can use this understanding to be successful.

Learning Objectives

1. Describe the major business decisions managers face.
2. Explain how economic models are useful in managerial decision making.
3. Illustrate how a knowledge of economics can help your career.

1.1 Managerial Decision Making

A firm's managers allocate the limited resources available to them to achieve the firm's objectives. The objectives vary for different managers within a firm but each managerial task is constrained by resource scarcity. At any moment in time, a production manager has to use the existing factory and a marketing manager has a limited marketing budget. Such resource limitations can change over time, but managers always face constraints.

---

[1]Many dictionaries define economics as the study of the production, distribution, and consumption of goods and services. However, professional economists think of economics as applying more broadly, including any decisions made subject to scarcity.

Profit

The main objective of most private-sector firms is to maximize *profit*, which is the difference between revenue and cost. Senior managers of a firm might have other concerns as well, including social responsibility and personal career objectives. However, the primary responsibility of senior managers to the owners of the firm is to focus on the *bottom line*: maximizing profit.

Managers have a variety of roles in the profit maximization process. The production manager seeks to minimize the cost of producing a particular good or service. The market research manager determines how many units of any particular product can be sold at a given price, which helps to determine how much output to produce and what price to charge. The research and development (R&D) manager supervises the development of new products that will be attractive to consumers. The most senior manager, usually called the *chief executive officer* (CEO), coordinates the firm's managerial functions and sets its overall strategy.

Trade-Offs

People and firms face trade-offs because they can't have everything. Managers must focus on the trade-offs that directly or indirectly affect profits. Evaluating trade-offs often involves *marginal* reasoning: considering the effect of a small change. Key trade-offs include:

- **How to produce:** To produce a given level of output, a firm trades off inputs, deciding whether to use more of one and less of another. Car manufacturers choose between metal and plastic for many parts, which affects the car's weight, cost, and safety.

- **What prices to charge:** Some firms, such as farms, have little or no control over the prices at which their goods are sold and must sell at the price determined in the market. However, many other firms set their prices. When a manager of such a firm sets the price of a product, the manager must consider whether raising the price by a dollar increases the profit margin on each unit sold by enough to offset the loss from selling fewer units. Consumers, given their limited budgets, buy fewer units of a product when its price rises. Thus, ultimately, the manager's pricing decision is constrained by the scarcity under which consumers make decisions.

- **Whether to innovate:** One of the major trade-offs facing managers is whether to maximize profit in the short run or in the long run. For example, a forward-looking firm may invest substantially in innovation—designing new products and better production methods—which lowers profit in the short run, but may raise profit in the long run.

Other Decision Makers

It is important for managers of a firm to understand how the decisions made by consumers, workers, managers of other firms, and governments constrain their firm. Consumers purchase products subject to their limited budgets. Workers decide on which jobs to take and how much to work given their scarce time and limits on their abilities. Rivals may introduce new, superior products or cut the prices of existing products. Governments around the world may tax, subsidize, or regulate products.

Interactions between economic decision makers take place primarily in markets. A **market** is an exchange mechanism that allows buyers to trade with sellers. A market may be a town square where people go to trade food and clothing, or it may be an international telecommunications network over which people buy and sell financial securities. When we talk about a single market, we refer to trade in a single good or group of goods that are closely related, such as soft drinks, movies, novels, or automobiles. The primary participants in a market are firms that supply the product and consumers who buy it, but government policies such as taxes also play an important role in the operation of markets.

Strategy

When competing with a small number of rival firms, senior managers consider how their firm's products are positioned relative to those of its rivals. The firm uses a strategy—a battle plan that specifies the *actions* or *moves* that the firm will make to maximize profit. A strategy might involve choosing the level of output, the price, or the type of advertising now and possibly in the future. For example, in setting its production levels and prices, Pepsi's managers must consider what choices Coca-Cola's managers will make. One tool that is helpful in understanding and developing such strategies is *game theory*, which we use in several chapters.

1.2 Economic Models

Economists use economic models to explain how managers and other decision makers make decisions and to interpret the resulting market outcomes. A **model** is a description of the relationship between two or more variables. Models are used in many fields. For example, astronomers use models to describe and predict the movement of comets and meteors, medical researchers use models to describe and predict the effect of medications on diseases, and meteorologists use models to predict weather.

Business economists construct models dealing with economic variables and use such models to describe and predict how a change in one variable will affect another variable. Such models are useful to managers in predicting the effects of their decisions and in understanding the decisions of others. Models allow managers to consider hypothetical situations—to use a *what-if analysis*—such as "What would happen if we raised our prices by 10%?" or "Would profit rise if we phased out one of our product lines?" Models help managers predict answers to what-if questions and to use those answers to make good decisions.

According to the *income threshold model*, people whose incomes are below a threshold do not buy a particular consumer durable, while many people whose income exceeds that threshold buy it.

If this theory is correct, we predict that, as most people's incomes rise above the threshold in lower-income countries, consumer durable purchases will increase from near zero to large numbers virtually overnight. This prediction is consistent with evidence from Malaysia, where the income threshold for buying a car is about $4,000.

In China, incomes have risen rapidly and now exceed the threshold levels for many types of durable goods. In response to higher incomes, Chinese car purchases have taken off.

For example, Li Rifu, a 46-year-old Chinese farmer and watch repairman, thought that buying a car would improve the odds that his 22- and 24-year-old sons would find girlfriends, marry, and produce grandchildren. Soon after Mr. Li purchased his Geely King Kong for the equivalent of $9,000, both sons met girlfriends, and his older son got married.

Given the rapid increase in Chinese incomes in the past couple of decades, four-fifths of all new cars sold in China are bought by first-time customers. An influx of first-time buyers was responsible for Chinese car sales increasing by a factor of nearly 18 between 2000 and 2017. In 2005, China produced fewer than half as many cars as the United States. In 2017, China was by far the largest producer of cars in the world. It produced nearly three times as many cars as the United States—the second largest producer—as well as 39% more than the entire European Union. One out of every three cars in the world is produced in China.[2]

Simplifying Assumptions

Everything should be made as simple as possible, but not simpler. —Albert Einstein

A model is a simplification of reality. The objective in building a model is to include the essential issues, while leaving aside the many complications that might distract us or disguise those essential elements. For example, the income threshold model focuses on only the relationship between income and purchases of durable goods. Prices, multiple car purchases by a single consumer, and other factors that might affect durable goods purchases are left out of the model. Despite these simplifications, the model—if correct—gives managers a good general idea of how the automobile market is likely to evolve in countries such as China.

We have described the income threshold model in words, but we could have presented it using graphs or mathematics. Representing economic models using mathematical formulas in spreadsheets has become very important in managerial decision making. Regardless of how the model is described, an economic model is a simplification of reality that contains only its most important features. Without simplifications, it is difficult to make predictions because the real world is too complex to analyze fully.

[2]The sources for Mini-Cases are available at the back of the book.

Economists make many *assumptions* to simplify their models. When using the income threshold model to explain car purchasing behavior in China, we *assume* that factors other than income, such as the color of cars, do not have an important effect on the decision to buy cars. Therefore, we ignore the color of cars that are sold in China in describing the relationship between income and the number of cars consumers want. If this assumption is correct, by ignoring color, we make our analysis of the auto market simpler without losing important details. If we're wrong and these ignored issues are important, our predictions may be inaccurate. Part of the skill in using economic models lies in selecting a model that is appropriate for the task at hand.

Testing Theories

Blore's Razor: When given a choice between two theories, take the one that is funnier.

Economic *theory* refers to the development and use of a model to formulate *hypotheses*, which are proposed explanations for some phenomenon. A useful theory or hypothesis is one that leads to clear, testable predictions. A theory that says "If the price of a product rises, the quantity demanded of that product falls" provides a clear prediction. A theory that says "Human behavior depends on tastes, and tastes change randomly at random intervals" is not very useful because it does not lead to testable predictions.

An alternative theory.

Economists test theories by checking whether the theory's predictions are correct. If a prediction does not come true, they might reject the theory—or at least reduce their confidence in the theory. Economists use a model until it is refuted by evidence or until a better model is developed for a particular use.

A good model makes sharp, clear predictions that are consistent with reality. Some very simple models make sharp or precise predictions that are incorrect. Some more realistic and therefore more complex models make ambiguous predictions, allowing for any possible outcome, so they are untestable. Neither incorrect models nor untestable models are helpful. The skill in model building lies in developing a model that is simple enough to make clear predictions but realistic enough to be accurate. Any model is only an approximation of reality. A good model is one that is a close enough approximation to be useful.

Although economists agree on the methods they use to develop and apply testable models, they often disagree on the specific content of those models. One model might present a logically consistent argument that prices will go up next quarter. Another, using a different but equally logical theory, may contend that prices will fall next quarter. If the economists are reasonable, they will agree that pure logic alone cannot resolve their dispute. Indeed, they

I ADMIT, THIS DISCOVERY DOES SEEM TO SUPPORT THE ASTEROID THEORY.

will agree that they'll have to use empirical evidence—facts about the real world—to find out which prediction is correct. One goal of this book is to teach managers how to think like economists so that they can build, apply, and test economic models to deal with important managerial problems.

Positive and Normative Statements

Economic analysis sometimes leads to predictions that seem undesirable or cynical. For instance, an economist doing market research for a producer of soft drinks might predict that "if we double the amount of sugar in this soft drink we will significantly increase sales to children." An economist making such a statement is not seeking to undermine the health of children by inducing them to consume excessive amounts of sugar. The economist is only making a scientific prediction about the relationship between cause and effect: More sugar in soft drinks is appealing to children.

Such a scientific prediction is known as a **positive statement**: a testable hypothesis about matters of fact such as cause-and-effect relationships. *Positive* does not mean that we are certain about the truth of our statement; It indicates only that we can test the truth of the statement.

An economist may test the hypothesis that the quantity of soft drinks demanded decreases as the price increases. Some may conclude from that study that "The government should tax soft drinks so that people will not consume so much sugar." Such a statement is a value judgment. It may be based on the view that people *should* be protected from their own unwise choices, so the government *should* intervene.

This judgment is *not* a scientific prediction. It is a **normative statement**: a belief about whether something is good or bad. A normative statement cannot be tested because a value judgment cannot be refuted by evidence. A normative statement concerns what somebody believes *should* happen; a positive statement concerns what *is* or what *will* happen. Normative statements are sometimes called *prescriptive* statements because they prescribe a course of action, while positive statements are sometimes called *descriptive* statements because they describe reality. Although a normative conclusion can be drawn without first conducting a positive analysis, a policy debate will be better informed if a positive analysis is conducted first.[3]

Good economists and managers emphasize positive analysis. This emphasis has implications for what we study and even for our use of language. For example, many economists stress that they study people's *wants* rather than their *needs*. Although people need certain minimum levels of food, shelter, and clothing to survive, most people in developed economies have enough money to buy goods well in excess of the minimum levels necessary to maintain life. Consequently, in wealthy countries, calling something a "need" is often a value judgment. You almost certainly have been told by someone that "you *need* a college education." That person was probably making a value judgment—"you *should* go to college"—rather than a scientific prediction that you will suffer terrible economic deprivation if you do not go to college. We can't test such value judgments, but we can test a (positive) hypothesis such as "Graduating from college or university increases lifetime income."

---

[3]Some argue that, as (social) scientists, we economists should present only positive analyses. Others argue that we shouldn't give up our right to make value judgments just like the next person (who happens to be biased, prejudiced, and pigheaded, unlike us).

New Theories

One of the strengths of economics is that it is continually evolving, for two reasons. First, economists—like physicists, biologists, and other scientists—are always trying to improve their understanding of the world around them.

For example, traditional managerial textbooks presented theories based on the assumption that decision makers always optimize: They do the best they can with their limited resources. While we cover these traditional theories, we also present another recently developed approach referred to as *behavioral economics*, which is the study of how psychological biases and cognitive limits can prevent managers and others from optimizing.[4]

Second, economic theory evolves out of necessity. Unlike physical and biological scientists, economists and managers also have to develop new ways to think about *disruptive innovations*. Although most innovations are incremental, some are sufficiently disruptive to dramatically change the way an industry is structured—or even to create new industries and destroy old ones.

The internet is an example of a disruptive innovation. Internet-based online retailing has displaced much traditional brick-and-mortar retailing, online payment systems have largely replaced cash and checks, and online media, especially social media, have changed the way most people acquire and transmit information.

To analyze the economic effects of the internet and other disruptive innovations, economists have extended established theories and developed new ones. For example, the internet has given rise to many services that allow two groups of users to interact—such as auction services, dating sites, job matching services, and payment services. In response, economists have developed the theory of such *two-sided* markets, which has been important to the ongoing evolution of these markets and to government policy toward them.[5] This book describes economic theories of the internet and of two-sided markets, along with other recent developments in economics.

1.3 Using Economic Skills in Your Career

This book will help you develop skills in economic analysis that are crucial in business decision-making. Some readers will get jobs that use economic analysis intensively, as in assessing financial investment options for financial institutions. Others may work in setting prices or planning other actions based on formal analyses, such as spreadsheet-based economic modeling. Other students will get jobs that emphasize different skills, but economic decisions come up everywhere in business.

All readers will benefit from familiarity with the applications of economics presented in this book. Many managers as well as concerned citizens regularly use these skills to predict the likely outcomes from government actions and other events. Readers will also find that much of the analysis in the book is relevant to their own personal decisions, such as investment or educational choices.

---

[4]The 2017 Nobel Prize in Economic Sciences was awarded to Richard H. Thaler "for his contributions to behavioral economics."

[5]For example, economist Hal Varian used two-sided market theory to help Google develop its auction-based approach to selling ads. Courts have relied on economic analyses of two-sided markets in credit card, merger, and other cases.

SUMMARY

1. **Managerial Decision Making.** Economic analysis helps managers develop strategies to pursue their objectives effectively in the presence of scarcity. Various managers within a firm face different objectives and different constraints, but the overriding objective in most private-sector firms is to maximize profits. Making decisions subject to constraints implies making trade-offs. To make good managerial decisions, managers must understand how consumers, workers, other managers, and governments will act. Economic theories normally (but not always) assume that all decision makers attempt to maximize their well-being given the constraints they face.

2. **Economic Models.** Managers use models based on economic theories to help make predictions and decisions, which they use to run their firms. A good model is simple to use and makes clear, testable predictions that are supported by evidence. Economists use models to construct *positive* hypotheses such as causal statements linking changes in one variable, such as income, to its effects, such as purchases of automobiles. These positive propositions can be tested. In contrast, *normative* statements, which are value judgments, cannot be tested.

3. **Using Economic Skills in Your Career.** A knowledge of economics will be valuable to you in a career in management, economics, or other fields. It will also be useful in your everyday life.

Supply and Demand

2

Talk is cheap because supply exceeds demand.

Managerial Problem

Carbon Taxes

Burning fossil fuels such as gasoline, coal, and heating oil releases gases containing carbon into the air.[1] These "greenhouse" gases are widely believed to contribute to global warming. To reduce this problem and raise tax revenues, many environmentalists and political leaders have proposed levying a *carbon tax* on the carbon content in fossil fuels.[2]

When governments impose carbon taxes on gasoline, managers of firms that sell gasoline need to think about how much of the tax they have to absorb and how much they can pass through to firms and consumers who buy gasoline. Similarly, managers of firms that purchase gasoline must consider how any pass-through charges will affect their costs of shipping, air travel, heating, and production. This pass-through analysis is critical in making managerial decisions concerning how much to produce, how to set prices, whether to undertake long-run capital investments, and whether to operate or shut down.

Finland and Sweden implemented the first broad-based carbon taxes on fuels containing carbon (such as gasoline) in the early 1990s. Various other countries followed suit, including Ireland and India in 2010 and the United Kingdom in 2013. However, strong opposition to carbon taxes has limited adoption in other parts of the world.

The first North American carbon tax was introduced in 2006 in Boulder, Colorado (where it was applied to only electricity generation), and this tax was renewed in 2012. In 2007 and 2008, the Canadian provinces of Quebec and British Columbia became the first provinces or states in North America to impose a broad-based carbon tax. Canada is set to impose a national carbon tax in 2018.

Such carbon taxes harm some industries and help others. The tax hurts owners and managers of gasoline retailing firms, who need to consider whether they can stay in business in the face of a significant carbon tax. Shippers and manufacturers that use substantial amounts of fuel in production, as well as other firms, would also see their operating costs rise.

In contrast, a carbon tax creates opportunities for other firms and industries. For example, wind and solar power, which are alternatives to fossil fuels in generating electricity, would become

---

[1]Starting with this chapter, each chapter begins with a Managerial Problem that contains a specific question, which is answered at the end of the chapter using the theories presented in the chapter. Sources for the Managerial Problems, Mini-Cases, and Managerial Implications appear at the back of the book.

[2]Their political opponents object, claiming that fears about global warming are exaggerated and warning of large price increases from such taxes.

much more attractive. Anticipating greater opportunities in this market in the future, PacifiCorp, a utility owned by Warren Buffett, announced a plan in 2017 to spend $3.5 billion over three years to bring hundreds of new wind turbines online. It also plans to greatly expand its use of solar power. In 2018, the Solar Corporation of India (SECI) called for bids ("tenders") to build two large solar power projects.

Managers in the motor vehicle industry would need to consider whether to change their product mix in response to a carbon tax, perhaps focusing more on fuel-efficient vehicles. Even without a carbon tax, when gas prices rise, many consumers switch from sports utility vehicles (SUVs) to smaller cars. A carbon tax would favor fuel-efficient vehicles even more.

At the end of this chapter, we will return to this topic and answer a question of critical importance to managers in the motor vehicle industry and in other industries affected by gasoline prices: What would be the effect of imposing a carbon tax on the price of gasoline?

To analyze the effects of carbon taxes on gasoline prices and other variables, managers use an economic tool called the *supply-and-demand model*. Managers who use this model to anticipate the effects of events make more profitable decisions. The supply-and-demand model provides a good description of many markets and applies particularly well to those with many buyers and many sellers, as in most agricultural markets, much of the construction industry, many retail markets (such as gasoline retailing), and several other major sectors of the economy. In markets where this model is applicable, it allows us to make clear, testable predictions about the effects of new taxes or other shocks on prices and additional market outcomes.

Learning Objectives

1. Explain how the quantity of a good or service that consumers want depends on its price and other factors.
2. Describe how the quantity of a good or service that firms want to sell depends on its price and other factors.
3. Show how the interaction between consumers' demand curve and producers' supply curve determines the market price and quantity of a good or service.
4. Predict how an event that affects consumers or firms changes the market price and quantity.
5. Analyze the market effects of government policy using the supply-and-demand model.
6. Discuss when to use the supply-and-demand model.

2.1 Demand

Consumers decide whether to buy a particular good or service and, if so, how much to buy based on its price and on other factors, including their incomes, the prices of other goods, their tastes, and the information they have about the product. Government regulations and other policies also affect buying decisions. Before concentrating on the role of price in determining quantity demanded, let's look briefly at some other factors.

Income plays a major role in determining what and how much to purchase. People who suddenly inherit great wealth might be more likely to purchase expensive Rolex watches or other luxury items and would probably be less likely to buy inexpensive Timex watches and various items targeted toward lower-income consumers. More broadly, when a consumer's income rises, that consumer will often buy more of many goods.

The *price of a related good* might also affect consumers' buying decisions. Related goods can be either *substitutes* or *complements*. **Substitutes** are a pair of goods or services for which an increase in the price of one causes a consumer to demand a larger quantity of the other. Before deciding to go to a movie theater, a consumer considers the price of a substitute, such as streaming a movie online. The more expensive a trip to a movie theater is, the more likely that the consumer purchases a streamed movie to watch at home instead. Different brands of a good are often close substitutes. Before buying a pair of Levi's jeans, a customer might check the prices of other brands and substitute one of those brands for Levi's if its price is sufficiently attractive.

Complements are a pair of goods or services for which an increase in the price of one causes a consumer to demand a smaller quantity of the other. Smartphones, such as the iPhone and Samsung Galaxy, and music purchased online and downloaded to the smartphone are complements. A decline in the price of smartphones increases the demand for online music.

Consumers' *tastes* are important in determining their demand for a good or service. Consumers do not purchase foods they dislike or clothes they view as unfashionable or uncomfortable. The importance of fashion illustrates how changing tastes affect consumer demand. Clothing items that have gone out of fashion often languish in discount sections of clothing stores even though they commanded high prices a couple of years (or even a few weeks) earlier when they were in fashion. Firms devote significant resources to trying to change consumer tastes through advertising.

Similarly, *information* about the effects of a good has an impact on consumer decisions. In recent years, positive health outcomes linked to various food items have created greater demand for these healthy foods (such as soy products and high-fiber breads) when the information became well known.

Government rules and regulations affect demand. If a city government bans the use of skateboards on its streets, demand for skateboards in that city falls. Governments might also restrict sales to particular groups of consumers. For example, many political jurisdictions do not allow children to buy tobacco products, which reduces the quantity of cigarettes consumed.

Other factors might also affect the demand for specific goods. For example, consumers are more likely to use Facebook if most of their friends use Facebook. This *network effect* arises from the benefits of being part of a network and from the potential costs of being outside the network.

Although many factors influence demand, economists focus most on how a good's *own* price affects the quantity demanded. The relationship between price and quantity demanded plays a critical role in determining the market price and quantity in supply-and-demand analysis. To determine how a change in price affects the quantity demanded, economists ask what happens to quantity when price changes and other factors affecting demand, such as income and tastes, are held constant.

The Demand Curve

The amount of a good that consumers are *willing* to buy at a given price, holding constant the other factors that influence purchases, is the **quantity demanded**. The quantity demanded of a good or service can exceed the quantity *actually* sold. For example, as a promotion, a local store might sell Ghirardelli dark chocolate bars for $1 each today only. At that low price, you might want to buy 10 chocolate bars, but because the store has only 5 remaining, you can buy at most 5 chocolate bars at this price. The quantity you demand at this price is 10 chocolate bars—it's the amount you want—even though the amount you actually buy is only 5.

Using a diagram, we can show the relationship between price and the quantity demanded. A **demand curve** shows the quantity demanded at each possible price, holding constant the other factors that influence purchases. Figure 2.1 shows the estimated annual world demand curve, D^1, for coffee, which is one of the world's most valuable traded commodities. The internationally traded commodity is unroasted ("green") coffee beans. These unroasted beans are sold to Starbucks, Folgers, Maxwell House, and other firms that roast and sell coffee to retail consumers.[3] In this section, we analyze the market for unroasted coffee beans, which we call *coffee*. Although this demand curve is a straight line, demand curves may also be smooth curves or wavy lines. By convention, the vertical axis of the graph measures the price, p, per unit of the good. We measure the price of coffee in dollars per pound (abbreviated *lb*). The horizontal axis measures the quantity, Q, of the good, which is usually a *physical measure per time period*. This figure measures the quantity of coffee in millions of tons (2,000 lb) per year.

The demand curve hits the vertical axis at $12, indicating that the quantity demanded is zero when the price is $12 per lb or higher. The demand curve hits the horizontal (quantity) axis at 12 tons, the quantity of coffee buyers would want each year if the price were zero. To find out how much consumers demand at a price between zero and $12, say, $6, we draw a horizontal line from that price on the vertical axis until we hit the demand curve, and then we draw a vertical line down to the horizontal quantity axis. As the figure shows, the quantity demanded at a price of $6 per lb is 6 million tons per year.

FIGURE 2.1 A Demand Curve

The estimated global demand curve, D^1, for coffee shows the relationship between the quantity demanded per year in millions of tons and the price per lb. The downward slope of the demand curve shows that, holding other factors that influence demand constant, consumers demand a smaller quantity of a good when its price is high and a larger quantity when the price is low. A change in price causes a *movement along the demand curve*. For example, an increase in the price of coffee causes consumers to demand a smaller quantity of coffee.

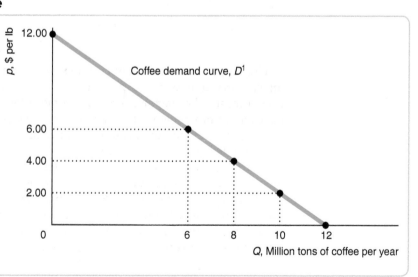

---

[3]We estimated the demand curve using data from the Food and Agriculture Organization, Commodity Review and Outlook and the International Coffee Organization, **www.ico.org**, and World Bank, World Development Indicators. We rounded the numbers for simplicity.

One of the most important things to know about a demand curve is what it does *not* show. All relevant economic variables that the demand curve graph does not explicitly display—income, prices of related goods (such as tea or sugar), tastes, information, and so on—are held constant. Thus, the demand curve shows how quantity varies with price but not how quantity varies with income, the prices of related goods, tastes, information, or other variables.

Effects of a Price Change on the Quantity Demanded. One of the most important results in economics is the **Law of Demand**: Consumers demand more of a good if its price is lower, holding constant income, the prices of other goods, tastes, and other factors that influence the amount they want to consume. According to the Law of Demand, *demand curves slope downward*, as in Figure 2.1.

A downward-sloping demand curve illustrates that consumers demand a larger quantity of this good when its price is low and a smaller quantity when its price is high. What happens to the quantity of coffee demanded if the price of coffee drops and all other variables remain constant? If the price falls from $6 per lb to $4 per lb in Figure 2.1, the annual quantity buyers want to purchase increases from 6 million tons to 8 million tons per year. Similarly, if the price drops from $4 to $2 per lb, the quantity buyers demand increases from 8 to 10 million tons.[4]

These changes in the quantity demanded in response to changes in price are *movements along the demand curve*. Thus, the demand curve is a concise summary of the answer to the question "What happens to the quantity demanded as the price changes, when all other factors are held constant?"

Although we generally expect demand curves to have a clear downward slope, as the coffee demand curve does, a vertical or horizontal demand curve is possible. We can think of horizontal and vertical demand curves as being extreme cases of downward-sloping demand. The Law of Demand rules out demand curves that have an upward slope.

The Law of Demand is an empirical claim—a claim about what actually happens. It is not a claim about general theoretical principles. It is theoretically possible that a demand curve could slope upward. However, the available empirical evidence strongly supports the Law of Demand.

Effects of Other Factors on Demand. If a demand curve shows how a price change affects the quantity demanded, holding constant all other factors that affect demand, how can we use demand curves to show the effects of a change in one of these other factors, such as income? One approach is to draw the demand curve in a three-dimensional diagram with the price of coffee on one axis, income on a second axis, and the quantity of coffee on the third axis. But just thinking about drawing such a diagram probably makes your head hurt.

Economists use a simpler approach to show the effect of factors other than a good's own price on demand. A change in any relevant factor other than the price of the good causes a *shift of the demand curve* rather than a *movement along the demand curve*. We illustrate such a shift in Figure 2.2. This figure shows that the coffee demand curve shifts *to the right* from the original demand curve D^1 to a new demand curve D^2 if average annual household income in high-income countries, which consume most of the world's coffee, increases by $15,000, from $35,000 to $50,000. On the new

---

[4]From now on, we will not state the physical and time period measures unless they are particularly relevant. Thus, we say that the price is $2 (with the "per lb" understood) and the quantity is 10 (with the "million tons per year" understood).

FIGURE 2.2 **A Shift of the Demand Curve**

The global demand curve for coffee shifts to the right from D^1 to D^2 as average annual household income in high-income countries rises by $15,000, from $35,000 to $50,000. As a result of the increase in income, more coffee is demanded at any given price.

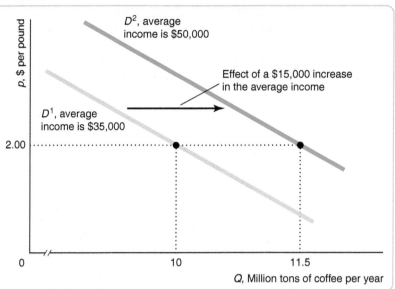

demand curve, D^2, consumers demand more coffee at any given price than on D^1 because income has risen, encouraging consumers to buy more coffee. At a price of $2 per lb, the quantity of coffee demanded goes from 10 million tons on D^1, before the increase in income, to 11.5 million tons on D^2, after the increase.

The prices of related goods—substitutes and complements—also affect the quantity of coffee demanded. Consumers who view tea and coffee as substitutes demand more coffee at any given price of coffee as the price of tea rises. That is, their demand curve for coffee shifts to the right.

Complements have the opposite effect. Consumers who view sugar and coffee as complements demand less coffee at any given price of coffee as the price of sugar rises. That is, their demand curve for coffee shifts to the left.

In addition, changes in other factors that affect demand, such as information, can shift a demand curve. Reinstein and Snyder (2005) found that movie reviews affect the demand for some types of movies, but not others. Holding price constant, they determined that if a film received "two-thumbs-up" reviews on a popular movie-review television program, the opening weekend demand curve shifted to the right by 25% for a drama, but the demand curve did not significantly shift for an action film or a comedy.

To properly analyze the effects of a change in some variable on the quantity demanded, we must distinguish between a *movement along a demand curve* and a *shift of a demand curve*. A change in the *good's own price* causes a *movement along a demand curve*. A change in *any other relevant factor besides the good's own price* causes a *shift of the demand curve*.

The Demand Function

The demand curve shows the relationship between the quantity demanded and a good's own price, holding other relevant factors constant at some particular levels. We illustrate the effect of a change in one of these other relevant factors by shifting the demand curve. We can also represent the same information—information about how price, income, and other variables affect quantity demanded—using a mathematical relationship called the *demand function*. This function shows the effect of a good's own price and other relevant factors on the quantity demanded. Any factors not explicitly listed in the demand function are assumed to be irrelevant or held constant. For example, we could specify the demand for coffee as a function of the price of coffee, income, the price of tea, the price of sugar, the prices of other related goods, and possibly other factors as well. However, if we hold constant all potentially relevant factors except the price of coffee, p, the price of sugar, p_s, and income, Y, the demand function is

$$Q = D(p, p_s, Y), \tag{2.1}$$

where Q is the quantity of coffee demanded, D is the demand function, p is the price of coffee, and Y is income. This expression shows how the quantity of coffee demanded varies with the price of coffee and the income of consumers.

Equation 2.1 is a general functional form—it does not specify a particular form for the relationship between quantity, Q, and the explanatory variables, p and Y. The estimated demand function that corresponds to the demand curve D^1 in Figures 2.1 and 2.2 has the specific (linear) form

$$Q = 8.56 - p - 0.3p_s + 0.1Y, \tag{2.2}$$

where Q is the quantity of coffee in millions of tons per year, p is the price of coffee in dollars per lb, p_s is the price of sugar in dollars per lb, and Y is the average annual household income in high-income countries in thousands of dollars.

When we draw the demand curve D^1 in Figures 2.1 and 2.2, we set p_s and Y at specific values, $p_s = \$0.20$ per lb and $Y = \$35$ thousand per year. By substituting these values for p_s and Y in Equation 2.2, we can express the quantity demanded as a function of only the price of coffee:

$$\begin{aligned} Q &= 8.56 - p - 0.3p_s + 0.1Y \\ &= 8.56 - p - (0.3 \times 0.2) + (0.1 \times 35) \\ &= 12 - p. \end{aligned} \tag{2.3}$$

The demand function in Equation 2.3 corresponds to the straight-line demand curve D^1 in Figure 2.1 with $Y = 35$. The constant term, 12, in Equation 2.3 is the quantity demanded (in millions of tons per year) if the price is zero. Setting the price equal to zero in Equation 2.3, we find that the quantity demanded is $Q = 12 - 0 = 12$. Figure 2.1 shows that $Q = 12$ where D^1 hits the quantity axis—where price is zero.

Equation 2.3 also shows us how quantity demanded varies with a change in price: a movement *along* the demand curve. If the price falls from p_1 to p_2, the change in price, Δp, equals $p_2 - p_1$. (The Δ symbol, the Greek letter delta, means "change in" the variable following the delta, so Δp is the "change in the price.") If the price of coffee falls from $p_1 = \$4$ to $p_2 = \$2$, then $\Delta p = \$2 - \$4 = -\$2$. Quantity demanded changes from $Q_1 = 8$ at a price of $\$4$ to $Q_2 = 10$ at a price of $\$2$, so $\Delta Q = Q_2 - Q_1 = 10 - 8 = 2$ million tons per year, as Figure 2.1 shows.

More generally, the quantity demanded at p_1 is $Q_1 = D(p_1)$, and the quantity demanded at p_2 is $Q_2 = D(p_2)$. The change in the quantity demanded, $\Delta Q = Q_2 - Q_1$, in response to the price change (using Equation 2.3) is

$$\begin{aligned} \Delta Q &= Q_2 - Q_1 \\ &= D(p_2) - D(p_1) \\ &= (12 - p_2) - (12 - p_1) \\ &= -(p_2 - p_1) \\ &= -\Delta p. \end{aligned}$$

Thus, the change in the quantity demanded, ΔQ, is $-\Delta p$ in this case.

For example, if $\Delta p = -\$2$, then $\Delta Q = -1\Delta p = -1(-2) = 2$. That is, a \$2 decrease in price causes the quantity demanded to rise by 2 million tons per year. The change in quantity demanded is positive—the quantity demanded increases—when the price falls. This effect is consistent with the Law of Demand. Similarly, raising the price would cause the quantity demanded to fall.

<table>
<tr>
<td>

Using Calculus

Deriving the
Slope of a
Demand Curve

</td>
<td>

We can use calculus to determine how the quantity changes as the price increases. Given the demand function for coffee of $Q = 12 - p$, the derivative of the demand function with respect to price is $dQ/dp = -1$. Therefore, the slope of the demand curve in Figure 2.1, which is $dp/dQ = 1/(dQ/dp)$, is also -1. More generally, the Law of Demand states that the derivative of the demand function with respect to price is negative, $dQ/dp < 0$.

</td>
</tr>
</table>

Summing Demand Curves

The overall demand for coffee is composed of the demand of many individual consumers. If we know the demand curve for each of two consumers, how do we determine the total demand curve for the two consumers combined? The total quantity demanded *at a given price* is the sum of the quantity each consumer demands at that price.

We can use individual demand functions to determine the total demand of several consumers. Suppose that the demand function for Consumer 1 is

$$Q_1 = D^1(p)$$

and the demand function for Consumer 2 is

$$Q_2 = D^2(p).$$

At price p, Consumer 1 demands Q_1 units, Consumer 2 demands Q_2 units, and the total quantity demanded by both consumers is the sum of these two quantities:

$$Q = Q_1 + Q_2 = D^1(p) + D^2(p).$$

We can generalize this approach to look at the total demand for three, four, or more consumers, or we can apply it to groups of consumers rather than just to individuals. It makes sense to add the quantities demanded only when all consumers face the same price. Adding the quantity Consumer 1 demands at one price to the quantity Consumer 2 demands at another price would not be meaningful for this purpose—the result would not show us a point on the combined demand curve.

<table>
<tr>
<td>

Mini-Case

Summing Corn
Demand Curves

</td>
<td>

We illustrate how to sum individual demand curves to get a summed or combined demand curve graphically, using estimated demand curves for corn (McPhail & Babcock, 2012). The figure shows the U.S. feed demand (the use of corn to feed animals) curve, the U.S. food demand curve, and the summed demand curve from these two sources.[5]

</td>
</tr>
</table>

---

[5]For graphical simplicity, we do not show the other major sources of U.S. demand for corn: export, storage, and use in biofuels (ethanol). Thus, this summed demand curve is not the total demand curve for corn.

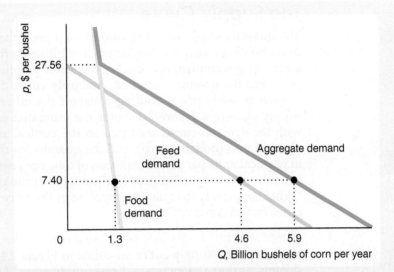

To derive the sum of the quantity demanded for these two uses at a given price, we add the quantities from the individual demand curves at that price. That is, we add the demand curves horizontally. At a price for corn of $7.40, the quantity demanded for food is 1.3 billion bushels per year and the quantity demanded for feed is 4.6 billion bushels. Thus, the summed quantity demanded at that price is $Q = 1.3 + 4.6 = 5.9$ billion bushels.

When the price of corn exceeds $27.56 per bushel, farmers stop using corn for animal feed, so the quantity demanded for this use equals zero. As a result, the summed demand curve is the same as the food demand curve at prices above $27.56.

2.2 Supply

Knowing how much consumers want to buy at any given price is not enough by itself to tell us the market price and quantity. We also need to know how much firms want to supply at any given price. Firms determine how much of a good to supply given the price of that good and other factors, including the costs of producing the good. Usually, we expect firms to supply more at a higher price. Before concentrating on the role of price in determining supply, we describe the role of some other factors.

Costs of production (how much the firm pays for factors of production such as labor, fuel, and machinery) affect how much of a product firms want to sell. As a firm's cost falls, it is usually willing to supply more, holding price and other factors constant. Conversely, a cost increase will often reduce a firm's willingness to produce. If the firm's cost exceeds what it can earn from selling the good, the firm will produce nothing. Thus, factors that affect costs also affect supply. If a *technological advance* allows a firm to produce its good at lower cost, the firm supplies more of that good at any given price, holding other factors constant.

Government rules and regulations can also affect supply directly without working through costs. For example, in some parts of the world, retailers may not sell most goods and services on particular days of religious significance. Supply on those days is constrained by government policy to be zero.

The Supply Curve

The **quantity supplied** is the amount of a good that firms *want* to sell at a given price, holding constant other factors that influence firms' supply decisions, such as costs and government actions. We can show graphically the relationship between price and the quantity supplied. A **supply curve** displays the quantity supplied at each possible price, holding constant the other factors that influence firms' supply decisions. Figure 2.3 shows the estimated supply curve, S^1, for coffee. As with the demand curve, the price on the vertical axis is measured in dollars per physical unit (dollars per lb), and the quantity on the horizontal axis is measured in physical units per period (millions of tons per year). Because we hold fixed other variables that may affect supply, the supply curve concisely answers the question "What happens to the quantity supplied as the price changes, holding all other relevant factors constant?"

Effects of Price on Supply. We illustrate how price affects the quantity supplied using the supply curve for coffee in Figure 2.3. The supply curve is upward sloping. As the price increases, firms supply more. If the price is $2 per lb, the quantity supplied by the market is 10 million tons per year. If the price rises to $4, the quantity supplied rises to 11 million tons. An increase in the price of coffee causes a *movement along the supply curve*: firms supply more coffee.

Although the Law of Demand states that the demand curve slope downward, *no* corresponding "Law of Supply" states that the supply curve must slope in a particular way. We observe supply curves that are vertical, horizontal, or downward sloping in particular situations. However, supply curves are commonly upward sloping. Accordingly, if we lack specific information about the slope, we usually draw upward-sloping supply curves. Along an upward-sloping supply curve, the higher the price, the larger the quantity that firms supply, holding other factors constant.

Effects of Other Variables on Supply. A change in a relevant variable other than the good's own price causes the entire *supply curve to shift*. One such variable is the price of cocoa (which is a major component in chocolate). The land

FIGURE 2.3 A Supply Curve

The estimated supply curve, S^1, for coffee shows the relationship between the quantity supplied per year and the price per lb, holding constant cost and other factors that influence supply. The upward slope of this supply curve indicates that firms supply more coffee when its price is high and less when the price is low. An increase in the price of coffee causes firms to supply a larger quantity of coffee; any change in price results in a movement *along* the supply curve.

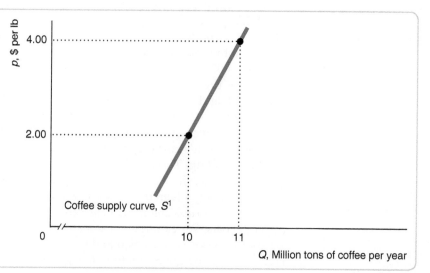

on which coffee is grown can also grow cocoa. When the price of cocoa rises, many coffee farmers switch to producing cocoa. Therefore, when the price of cocoa rises, the amount of coffee produced at any given price for coffee falls.

In Figure 2.4, when the cocoa price increases from $3 per lb to $6 per lb, the supply curve for coffee shifts leftward from S^1 to S^2. At a price of $2 per lb for coffee, the quantity supplied falls from 10 million tons on S^1 to 9.4 million tons on S^2.

It is important to distinguish between a *movement along a supply curve* and a *shift of the supply curve*. When the price of coffee changes, the change in the quantity supplied reflects a *movement along the supply curve*. When the price of cocoa or other variables that affect supply change, the entire *supply curve shifts*.

The Supply Function

We can write the relationship between the quantity supplied and price and other factors as a mathematical relationship called the *supply function*. Using a general functional form, we can write the coffee supply function, S, as

$$Q = S(p, p_c), \tag{2.4}$$

where Q is the quantity of coffee supplied, p is the price of coffee, and p_c is the price of cocoa. The supply function, Equation 2.4, might also incorporate other factors such as wages, transportation costs, and the state of technology, but by leaving them out, we are implicitly holding them constant.

Our estimated supply function for coffee is

$$Q = 9.6 + 0.5p - 0.2p_c, \tag{2.5}$$

where Q is the quantity in millions of tons per year, p is the price of coffee in dollars per lb, and p_c is the price of cocoa in dollars per lb. If we hold the cocoa price fixed at $3 per lb, we can rewrite the supply function in Equation 2.5 as solely a function of the coffee price. Substituting $p_c = \$3$ into Equation 2.5, we find that

$$Q = 9.6 + 0.5p - (0.2 \times 3) = 9 + 0.5p. \tag{2.6}$$

FIGURE 2.4 A Shift of a Supply Curve

A $3 per lb increase in the price of cocoa, which farmers can grow instead of coffee, causes the supply curve for coffee to shift leftward from S^1 to S^2. At a coffee price of $2 per lb, the quantity supplied falls from 10 on S^1 to 9.4 on S^2.

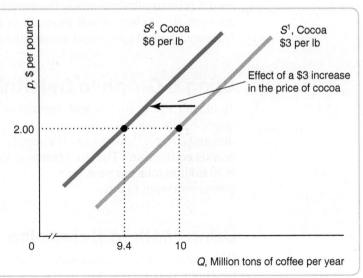

What happens to the quantity supplied if the price of coffee increases by $\Delta p = p_2 - p_1$? As the price increases from p_1 to p_2, the quantity supplied goes from Q_1 to Q_2, so the change in quantity supplied is

$$\Delta Q = Q_2 - Q_1 = (9 + 0.5p_2) - (9 + 0.5p_1) = 0.5\,(p_2 - p_1) = 0.5\Delta p.$$

Thus, a \$1 increase in price ($\Delta p = 1$) causes the quantity supplied to increase by $\Delta Q = 0.5$ million tons per year. This change in the quantity of coffee supplied as p increases is a *movement along the supply curve*.

Summing Supply Curves

The total supply curve shows the total quantity produced by all suppliers at each possible price. The overall amount of coffee supplied at any given price is the sum of the quantity supplied by Brazilian, Vietnamese, Colombian, and other producers in various countries.

2.3 Market Equilibrium

The supply and demand curves jointly determine the price and quantity at which a good or service is bought and sold. The demand curve shows the quantities consumers want to buy at various prices, and the supply curve shows the quantities firms want to sell at various prices. Unless firms set the price so that consumers want to buy exactly the same amount that suppliers want to sell, some consumers cannot buy as much as they want or some sellers cannot sell as much as they want.

When all market participants are able to buy or sell as much as they want, we say that the market is in **equilibrium**: a situation in which no participant wants to change its behavior. A price at which consumers can buy as much as they want and sellers can sell as much as they want is the *equilibrium price*. At this price, the quantity demanded equals the quantity supplied. This quantity is the *equilibrium quantity*. Thus, if the government does not intervene in the market, the supply-and-demand model is in equilibrium when the *market clears* in the sense that buyers and sellers are both able to buy or sell as much as they want at the market price—no one is frustrated and all goods that are supplied to the market are sold.

Using a Graph to Determine the Equilibrium

To illustrate how supply and demand curves determine the equilibrium price and quantity, we use the coffee example. Figure 2.5 shows the supply curve, S^1, and demand curve, D^1, for coffee. The supply and demand curves intersect at point e, the market equilibrium. The equilibrium price is \$2 per lb, and the equilibrium quantity is 10 million tons per year, which is the quantity firms want to sell *and* the quantity consumers want to buy.

Using Math to Determine the Equilibrium

We can determine the coffee equilibrium mathematically, using supply and demand functions that correspond to the supply and demand curves. We use these two

FIGURE 2.5 Market Equilibrium

The intersection of the supply curve, S^1, and the demand curve, D^1, for coffee determines the market equilibrium point, e, where $p = \$2$ per lb and $Q = 10$ million tons per year. At the lower price of $p = \$1$, the quantity demanded is 11, but the quantity supplied is only 9.5, so the excess demand is 1.5. At $p = \$3$ the price exceeds the equilibrium price. As a result, the market has an excess supply of 1.5 because the quantity demanded, 9, is less than the quantity supplied, 10.5. With either excess demand or excess supply, market forces drive the price back to the equilibrium price of $2.

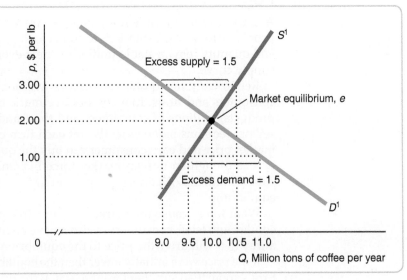

equations to solve for the equilibrium price at which the quantity demanded equals the quantity supplied (the equilibrium quantity). The demand function, Equation 2.3, is the relationship between the quantity demanded, Q_d, and the price:[6]

$$Q_d = 12 - p.$$

The supply function, Equation 2.6, is the relationship between the quantity supplied, Q_s, and the price:

$$Q_s = 9 + 0.5p.$$

We want to find the equilibrium price, p, at which $Q_d = Q_s = Q$. Thus, we set the right sides of these two equations equal,

$$12 - p = 9 + 0.5p,$$

and solve for the price.

Adding p to both sides of this expression and subtracting 9 from both sides, we find that $3 = 1.5p$. Dividing both sides of this last expression by 1.5, we learn that the equilibrium price is $p = \$2$. We can determine the equilibrium quantity by substituting this p into either the supply function or the demand function. Using the demand function, we find that the equilibrium quantity is

$$Q = 12 - 2 = 10$$

million tons per year. We can obtain the same quantity by using the supply function:

$$Q = 9 + (0.5 \times 2) = 10.$$

---

[6]Usually, we use Q to represent both the quantity demanded and the quantity supplied. However, for clarity in this discussion, we use Q_d and Q_s.

Forces That Drive the Market to Equilibrium

A market equilibrium is not just an abstract concept or a theoretical possibility.[7] Economic forces cause markets to adjust to the equilibrium. At the equilibrium, price and quantity remain stable until some new event occurs that shifts the demand or supply curve.

Remarkably, an equilibrium occurs without any explicit coordination between consumers and firms. In a competitive market such as that for most agricultural products, millions of consumers and thousands of firms make their buying and selling decisions independently. Yet each firm can sell the quantity it wants at the market price and each consumer can buy the quantity he or she wants at that price. It is as though an unseen market force like an *invisible hand* (a phrase coined by Adam Smith in 1776) directs people and firms to coordinate their activities to achieve equilibrium.

What forces cause the market to move to equilibrium? If the price is not at the equilibrium level, consumers or firms have an incentive to change their behavior in a way that will drive the price to the equilibrium level, as we now illustrate.

If the price were initially lower than the equilibrium price, consumers would want to buy more than suppliers want to sell. If the price of coffee is $1 in Figure 2.5, firms are willing to supply 9.5 million tons per year but consumers demand 11 million tons. At this price, the market is in *disequilibrium*: the quantity demanded is not equal to the quantity supplied. This market has **excess demand**—the amount by which the quantity demanded exceeds the quantity supplied at a specified price. If the price is $1 per lb, the market has an excess demand of $11 - 9.5 = 1.5$ million tons per year.

Some consumers are lucky enough to buy the coffee at $1 per lb. Other consumers cannot find anyone who is willing to sell them coffee at that price. What can they do? Some frustrated consumers may offer to pay suppliers more than $1 per lb.

Alternatively, suppliers, noticing these disappointed consumers, might raise their prices. Such actions by consumers and producers cause the market price to rise. As the price rises, the quantity that firms want to supply increases and the quantity that consumers want to buy decreases. This upward pressure on price continues until it reaches the equilibrium price, $2, which eliminates the excess demand.

If, instead, the price is initially above the equilibrium level, suppliers want to sell more than consumers want to buy. For example, at a price of $3, suppliers want to sell 10.5 million tons per year but consumers want to buy only 9 million tons, as Figure 2.5 shows. This market has an **excess supply**—the amount by which the quantity supplied exceeds the quantity demanded at a specified price—of $1.5 (= 10.5 - 9)$ million tons at a price of $3. Not all firms can sell as much as they want. Rather than allow their unsold coffee to get stale, firms lower the price to attract additional customers. As long as the price remains above the equilibrium price, some firms cannot sell as much coffee as they want, so they lower the price further. The price falls until it reaches the equilibrium level, $2, which eliminates the excess supply and hence removes the pressure to lower the price further.

Not all markets reach equilibrium through the independent actions of many buyers or sellers. In institutionalized or formal markets, such as the Chicago Mercantile Exchange—where coffee and other agricultural commodities, financial instruments,

---

[7]**MyLab Economics** has games (called *experiments*) for the Managerial Economics and Strategy course. These online games allow you to play against the computer. The *Market Experiment* illustrates the operation of the supply-and-demand model, allowing you to participate in a simulated market. To play, go to **MyLab Economics** Multimedia Library, Single Player Experiment, and set the Chapter field to "All Chapters."

energy, and metals are traded—buyers and sellers meet at a single location (or on a single website). Often in these markets certain individuals or firms, sometimes referred to as *market makers*, act to adjust the price and bring the market into equilibrium very quickly.

In summary, at any price other than the equilibrium price, either consumers or suppliers are unable to trade as much as they want. These disappointed market participants act to change the price, driving the price to the equilibrium level. The equilibrium price is called the *market clearing price* because no buyers or sellers are frustrated at this price—the market eliminates or clears any excess demand or excess supply.

Mini-Case

Speed of Adjustment to New Information

Most markets adjust quickly, especially formal markets, such as the Chicago Board of Trade corn futures market. Corn *futures* are contracts to deliver a fixed amount of corn at a specified future date. The price in this market is the *futures price* and the quantity is the number of contracts.

The U.S. Department of Agriculture (USDA) provides information about the corn market, which influences sellers and buyers, shifting the market supply and demand curves. The most important types of information that the USDA announces are its forecasts about corn production, changes in conditions that affect the crop while it is growing, and estimates of world supply and demand quantities.

The USDA made its announcements electronically two hours before the start of trading on a given day. Lehecka, Wang, and Garcia (2014) studied how these announcements affect futures prices and the number of contracts minute by minute. They found that the price changed rapidly in the first minute after trading started compared to the last minute of the previous day. The price adjustments diminished with each subsequent minute and died out within 10 minutes. Thus, this market adjusts very quickly.

2.4 Shocks to the Equilibrium

Once a market achieves equilibrium, the equilibrium can persist indefinitely because no one applies pressure to alter the price. The equilibrium changes only if a shock occurs that shifts the demand curve or the supply curve. These curves shift if one of the variables we were holding constant changes. If tastes, income, government policies, or costs of production change, the demand curve or the supply curve or both shift, and the equilibrium changes.

Effects of a Shift in the Demand Curve

Suppose that the average income in high-income countries increases by $15,000, from $35,000 to $50,000. As a result, consumers purchase more coffee at any given price. Reflecting this change, the demand curve for coffee shifts to the right from D^1 to D^2 in panel a of Figure 2.6. At the initial equilibrium price of $2, consumers now want to purchase 11.5 million tons of coffee per year. However, at that price, suppliers want to sell only 10 million tons, so the market has an excess demand of $11.5 - 10 = 1.5$ million tons.

FIGURE 2.6 Equilibrium Effects of a Shift of a Demand or Supply Curve

(a) A $15,000 increase in average annual household income causes the demand curve for coffee to shift to the right from D^1 to D^2. At the original equilibrium (e_1) price of $2, initially the market has excess demand of 1.5 million tons per year. Market pressures drive up the price. The equilibrium moves along the supply curve to e_2, where the new equilibrium price is $3.

(b) A $3 per pound increase in the price of cocoa causes some producers to shift from coffee production to cocoa production, reducing the quantity of coffee supplied at every price. The supply curve shifts to the left from S^1 to S^2, causing the market equilibrium to move from e_1 to e_2, where the new equilibrium price is $2.40.

(a) Effect of a $15,000 Increase in Income

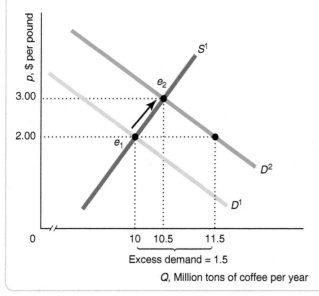

(b) Effect of a $3 Increase in the Price of Cocoa

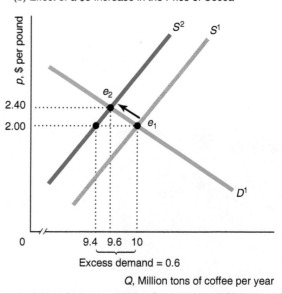

This excess demand creates market pressure, which drives the price up until it reaches a new equilibrium price of $3. At that price, firms want to sell 10.5 million tons and consumers want to buy 10.5 million tons, the new equilibrium quantity. The increase in income causes a *shift of the demand curve*, which in turn causes a *movement along the supply curve* from e_1 to e_2.

Q&A 2.1

The estimated global supply function for coffee is $Q = 9 + 0.5p$. The estimated demand function is $Q = 8.56 - p - 0.3p_s + 0.1Y$, where p_s is the price in dollars per lb of sugar, and Y is the average income in high-income countries in thousands of dollars. The initial price of sugar is $0.20 per lb. The initial income is $Y = 35$ ($35,000). Using algebra, determine the initial equilibrium price and quantity of coffee, and then determine how price and quantity change if the average income increases by 15 to $Y = 50$ and the price of sugar remains constant.

Answer

1. *Substitute the initial value of Y into the demand function to obtain quantity demanded purely as a function of p.* As we derived in Equation 2.3, if $Y = 35$, then

$$Q = 8.56 - p - 0.3p_s + 0.1Y = 8.56 - p - (0.3 \times 0.2) + (0.1 \times 35)$$
$$= 12 - p.$$

2. *Equate the supply and demand functions to determine the initial equilibrium.* The equilibrium price is determined by equating the right sides of these supply and demand functions:

$$9 + 0.5p = 12 - p.$$

Solving this equation for p, we find that $1.5p = 3$, or $p = \$2$. We calculate the equilibrium quantity by substituting this price into the supply or demand function: $Q = 9 + (0.5 \times 2) = 10$ or $Q = 12 - 2 = 10$ million tons per year.

3. *Repeat steps 1 and 2 using $Y = 50$ instead of $Y = 35$.* The new demand function is

$$Q = 8.56 - p - 0.3p_s + 0.1Y = 8.56 - p - (0.3 \times 0.2) + (0.1 \times 50)$$
$$= 13.5 - p.$$

Equating this expression to the right-hand side of the supply function, we obtain $9 + 0.5p = 13.5 - p$. Solving for p, we find that $1.5p = 4.5$ or $p = \$3$. We calculate the equilibrium quantity by substituting this price into the supply or demand function: $Q = 9 + (0.5 \times 3) = 10.5$ or $Q = 13.5 - (1 \times 3) = 10.5$.

4. *Show how the equilibrium price and quantity of coffee change by subtracting the original values from the new ones.* The change in the equilibrium price is $\Delta p = \$3 - \$2 = \$1$. The change in the equilibrium quantity is $\Delta Q = 10.5 - 10 = 0.5$ million tons per year. Panel a of Figure 2.6 illustrates these changes in the equilibrium price and quantity.

Effects of a Shift in the Supply Curve

We now consider how a shift in the supply curve affects the coffee market equilibrium. Assume that income remains at its original level of \$35,000 but the price of cocoa rises from \$3 per lb to \$6 per lb. This increase in the price of cocoa causes some coffee producers to switch to cocoa production. As a result, the supply curve for coffee shifts to the left from S^1 to S^2 in panel b of Figure 2.6. At any given price, producers want to supply less coffee than they did before the price of cocoa increased. At the original equilibrium price of coffee of \$2 per lb, consumers still want 10 million tons, but producers are now willing to supply only 9.4 million tons, so the market's excess demand is 0.6 million tons. Market pressure forces the price of coffee up until the market reaches a new equilibrium at e_2, where the equilibrium price is \$2.40 and the equilibrium quantity is 9.6. Here, a *shift of the supply curve* results in a *movement along the demand curve.*

In summary, a change in an underlying factor, such as income, the price of a related good, land use, or the cost of production, shifts the demand curve or the supply curve. As a result, the equilibrium changes. To describe the effect of this change, we compare the original equilibrium price and quantity to the new equilibrium values.

Well, there goes the price of lobsters!

Mini-Case

The Opioid
Epidemic Reduces
Labor Market
Participation

Opioids are drugs that act on the nervous system to relieve pain. They include heroin, fentanyl, and pain relievers that are available legally by prescription, such as oxycodone (OxyContin), hydrocodone (Vicodin), codeine, and morphine.

Although patients can safely use opioid pain relievers for a short period, many patients continue to use them for longer periods because these drugs produce euphoria in addition to pain relief. Unfortunately, continued use can result in dependence, and excessive use can cause death. Every day, 90 Americans die from opioid overdoses.

Opioid prescriptions per capita rose 350% nationwide between 1999 and 2015. The use and abuse of opioids are responsible for fewer people working due to premature deaths, an inability to pass a job-drug test, or an unwillingness to work due to sedation and other effects of the drug.

The labor-force participation rate of men—the ratio of employed working-age men to all working-age men—was 3.2 percentage points lower during 2014–2016 than during 1999–2001. According to Krueger (2017), labor-force participation fell more in areas where doctors prescribe relatively more opioid pain medication. He calculated that 0.6 percentage points of the decline for men, a fifth of the total, was due to opioid prescriptions. Similarly, the study estimated that about one-quarter of the decline in women's labor-force participation was attributable to the growth in opioid prescriptions.

Q&A 2.2

As the preceding Mini-Case discusses, opioid use reduces labor-force participation. Use a supply-and-demand diagram to show the effects of opioid use on the labor market equilibrium quantity, which is the number of workers, L, and the equilibrium price, which is the wage, w.

Answer

1. *Determine the original labor market equilibrium before the epidemic.* The intersection of the labor demand curve, D, and the original labor supply curve, S^1, determines the original equilibrium, e_1, where the quantity is L_1 and the wage is w_1.

2. *Show how the opioid epidemic affects the labor supply curve.* The opioid epidemic does not affect the labor demand curve, but it causes the labor supply curve to shift to the left from S^1 to S^2. At any given wage, fewer people are willing to work.

3. *Determine the new labor market equilibrium.* The new equilibrium occurs where the demand curve, D, intersects the new supply curve, S^2, at e_2. The new equilibrium quantity is L_2, and the new equilibrium wage is w_1.

4. *Discuss the effect of the epidemic on the labor market.* The equilibrium quantity falls from L_1 to L_2. The equilibrium wage rises from w_1 to w_2 for workers who remain employed.

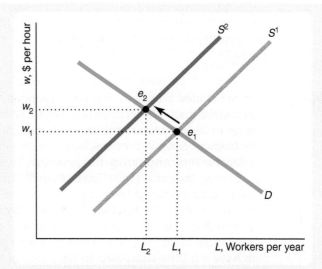

Managers can use the supply-and-demand model to anticipate how shocks to supply or demand will affect future business conditions and can take advantage of that knowledge. For example, Mars, one of the world's largest producers of chocolate products, is often among the first companies to learn about events that affect cocoa production, most of which occurs in Africa. Using their cocoa supply-and-demand model, Mars managers (called *Martians*) predict how much prices will change in the near future. If they expect prices to increase substantially, they immediately buy a great deal of cocoa at relatively low prices directly from suppliers in Africa. Alternatively, if they expect prices to fall, they may hold off buying now and then buy later at a lower price from organized markets such as ICE Futures U.S. or the London International Financial Futures and Options Exchange.

2.5 Effects of Government Interventions

Often governments are responsible for changes in market equilibrium. We examine three types of government policies. First, some government actions shift the supply curve, the demand curve, or both curves, which causes the equilibrium to change. Second, the government may use price controls that cause the quantity demanded to differ from the quantity supplied. Third, the government may tax or subsidize a good, which results in a gap between the price consumers pay and the amount sellers receive.

Policies That Shift Curves

Government policies may cause demand or supply curves to shift. Governments often limit who can buy goods. For example, many governments forbid selling alcohol to young people, which decreases the quantity demanded at each price and thereby shifts the demand curve to the left. Similarly, a government may restrict the amounts of foreign products that can be imported, which decreases the quantity supplied of imported goods at each price and shifts the importing country's supply curve to the left. Or, the government could start buying a good, which increases the quantity demanded at each price for the good and shifts the demand curve to the right.

In the United States, in many occupations, working without a license is illegal. More than 800 occupations require licensing at the local, state, or federal level, including animal trainers, dietitians and nutritionists, doctors, electricians, embalmers, funeral directors, hairdressers, librarians, nurses, psychologists, real estate brokers, respiratory therapists, and teachers (but not economists).

During the early 1950s, fewer than 5% of U.S. workers were in occupations covered by licensing laws at the state level. Since then, the share of licensed workers has grown, reaching nearly 18% by the 1980s, at least 20% in 2000, and 26% in 2015. Licensing is more common in occupations that require extensive education: More than 40% of workers with post-college education are required to have a license compared to only 15% of those with less than a high school education.

A worker must pass a test to obtain a license in some occupations. Frequently, licensed members of the occupation design these tests. By making the exam difficult, current workers can limit entry. For example, only 50% of people taking the California State Bar Examination in July 2017 passed it and only 27% passed the February 2018 exam, although all of them had law degrees.

To the degree that testing is objective, licensing may raise the average quality of the workforce. However, it restricts the number of workers in an occupation, which affects wages. To analyze the wage effect of licensing, we can use a graph similar to panel b of Figure 2.6, where the wage is on the vertical axis and the number of workers per year is on the horizontal axis. Licensing shifts the occupational supply curve to the left, reducing the equilibrium quantity of workers and raising the wage.

On average, licensing raises occupational wages by 11% in the United States (Kleiner and Vorotnikov, 2017) and 4% in the European Union (Koumenta and Pagliero, 2018). Kleiner (2015) estimates that occupational licensing costs consumers $203 billion annually.

Price Controls

Government policies that directly control the price of a good may alter the market outcome even though they do not affect the demand or supply curves of the good. Such a policy may lead to excess supply or excess demand if the price the government sets differs from the unregulated equilibrium price. We illustrate this result with two types of price control programs. When the government sets a *price ceiling* at $\bar{p}$, no goods may be sold at a price higher than $\bar{p}$. When it sets a *price floor* at $\underline{p}$, no goods may be sold at a price below $\underline{p}$.[8]

Price Ceilings.   Price ceilings have no effect if they are set above the equilibrium price that would be observed in the absence of price controls. If the government says

---

[8]MyLab Economics has a *Price Floors Experiment* and a *Price Ceilings Experiment* that illustrate the operation of price controls. To participate go to the **MyLab Economics** Multimedia Library, Single Player Experiment, and set the Chapter field to "All Chapters."

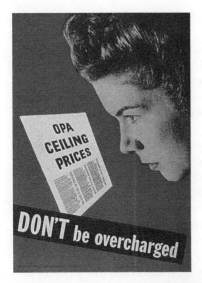

that firms may charge no more than $\bar{p} = \$6$ per gallon of gas and firms are actually charging $p = \$4$, the government's price control policy is irrelevant. However, if the unregulated equilibrium price, p, were above the price ceiling $\bar{p}$, the price that is actually observed in the market is the price ceiling. For example, if the equilibrium price of gas were $4 and a price ceiling of $3 is imposed, then the ceiling price of $3 is charged.

Currently, Canada and many European countries set price ceilings on pharmaceuticals. The United States used price ceilings on many goods during both world wars, the Korean War, and in 1971–1973 during the Nixon administration, among other times. Hawaii limited the price of wholesale gasoline from 2005 to 2006. New Jersey has a state law that prohibits raising prices on essential goods by more than 10% within 30 days of a declared state of emergency. In the aftermath of Hurricane Sandy in 2012, many businesses received fines as a result of this law.

The U.S. experience with gasoline illustrates the effects of price controls. In the 1970s, the Organization of Petroleum Exporting Countries (OPEC) reduced supplies of crude oil (which is converted into gasoline) to Western countries. As a result, the total supply curve for gasoline in the United States shifted to the left from S^1 to S^2 in Figure 2.7. Because of this shift, the equilibrium price of gasoline would have risen substantially, from p_1 to p_2. In an attempt to protect consumers by keeping gasoline prices from rising, the U.S. government set price ceilings on gasoline in 1973 and 1979.

The government told gas stations that they could charge no more than $p_1 = \bar{p}$. Figure 2.7 shows the price ceiling as a solid horizontal line extending from the price axis at $\bar{p}$. The price control is binding because $p_2 > \bar{p}$. The observed price is the price ceiling. At $\bar{p}$, consumers *want* to buy $Q_d = Q_1$ gallons of gasoline, which is the equilibrium quantity they bought before OPEC acted. However, firms supply only Q_s, which is determined by the intersection of the price control line with S^2. The binding price control resulted in excess demand of $Q_d - Q_s$.

Were it not for the price controls, market forces would drive up the market price to p_2, the price at which the excess demand would be eliminated. The government

FIGURE 2.7 A Price Ceiling on Gasoline

Reduced crude oil production (the major input in producing gasoline) causes the supply curve of gasoline to shift from S^1 to S^2. In an unregulated market, the equilibrium price would increase to p_2 and the equilibrium quantity would fall to Q_2. Suppose the government imposes a price control so that gasoline stations may not charge a price above the price ceiling, $p_1 = \bar{p}$. At this price, producers are willing to supply only Q_s, which is less than the amount $Q_1 = Q_d$ that consumers want to buy. The result is excessive demand, or a shortage of gasoline of $Q_d - Q_s$.

price ceiling prevents this adjustment. As a result, an enforced price ceiling causes a **shortage**: a persistent excess demand.

At the time of the controls, some government officials argued that the shortages resulted from OPEC's cutting off its supply of oil to the United States, but that's not true. Without the price controls, the new equilibrium would be e_2. In this equilibrium, the price, p_2, is much higher than before, p_1, but it eliminates the shortage. Moreover, without controls, the quantity sold, Q_2, is greater than the quantity sold under the control program, Q_s.

With a binding price ceiling, the supply-and-demand model predicts an *equilibrium with a shortage*. In this equilibrium, the quantity demanded does not equal the quantity supplied. The reason that we call this situation an equilibrium, even though a shortage exists, is that buyers and sellers who abide by the law do not change their behavior. Without the price controls, consumers facing a shortage would try to get more output by offering to pay more, or firms would raise prices. With effective government price controls, both firms and consumers know that they can't drive up the price, so they live with the shortage.

What happens? Some lucky consumers get to buy Q_s units at the low price of $\bar{p}$. Other potential customers are disappointed: They would like to buy at that price, but they cannot find anyone willing to sell gas to them. In addition, consumers spend a lot of time waiting in line—a pure waste that adds considerably to the cost of such government interventions.

What determines which consumers are lucky enough to find goods to buy at the low price with price controls? With enforced price controls, sellers use criteria other than price to allocate the scarce commodity. Firms may supply their friends, long-term customers, or people of a certain race, gender, age, or religion. They may sell their goods on a first-come, first-served basis. Or they may limit everyone to only a few gallons.

Another possibility is that firms and customers will try to evade the price controls. A consumer could go to a gas station owner and say, "Let's not tell anyone, but I'll pay you twice the price the government sets if you'll sell me as much gas as I want." If enough customers and gas station owners behaved that way, no shortage would occur. However, in cities such as Chicago, Hartford, New York, Portland, and Tucson, potential customers waited in line at the pump for an hour or more.[9] Deacon and Sonstelie (1989) estimated that for every dollar consumers saved due to the 1979 gasoline price controls, they lost $1.16 in waiting time and other factors.

Mini-Case **Venezuelan Price Ceilings and Shortages**	Venezuela was one of the richest countries in Latin America. A leading oil producer, it also has many other agricultural and nonagricultural industries. So why do people start lining up to buy groceries in Venezuela at 4 a.m., when shops open at 8 a.m.? Strict price ceilings on food and other goods create shortages throughout the country. According to a university study in 2018, one-quarter of Venezuelans eat two or fewer meals a day, 60% reported waking up hungry, and people reported losing 24 lb of weight on average during the previous year. Venezuelans also suffer from condom, birth control pill, and toilet paper shortages.

---

[9]See MyLab **Economics** Chapter Resources, Chapter 2, "Gas Lines," for a discussion of the effects of the 1973 and 1979 gasoline price controls.

Because Venezuela regulates the prices of many goods such as gasoline and corn flour, while Colombia, its direct neighbor to the west, does not, smuggling occurs. Given that gasoline sells for about 4¢ a gallon in Venezuela, and the price is over $3 a gallon in most of Colombia, the temptation to smuggle is great. Venezuela's Táchira state is adjacent to the Colombian border. Its government says that as much as 40% of the food sent to Táchira is smuggled into Colombia. Why sell corn flour at an artificially low price in Venezuela if you can sell it at a higher, market price in Colombia?

Venezuela's populist President Hugo Chávez and his handpicked successor, Nicolás Maduro, imposed strict price ceilings, purportedly to rein in inflation and make the goods more affordable for the poor. Do the ceilings help the poor?

For many Venezuelans, the answer is "No!" As Nery Reyes, a restaurant worker, said, "Venezuela is too rich a country to have this. I'm wasting my day here standing in line to buy one chicken and some rice."

Demonstrators have taken to the streets to protest persistent economic and social problems, including shortages. Many have died in these violent clashes with the National Guard. Hundreds of thousands of people have left Venezuela, and more than half of those between the ages of 15 and 29 say they want to leave the country.

The ultimate irony is that President Nicolás Maduro has advised Venezuelans to consume less to alleviate the shortages.

Price Floors. Governments also commonly use price floors. One of the most important examples of a price floor is a minimum wage in a labor market. A minimum wage law forbids employers from paying less than the minimum wage, $\underline{w}$.

Minimum wage laws date from 1894 in New Zealand, 1909 in the United Kingdom, and 1912 in Massachusetts. The Fair Labor Standards Act of 1938 set a federal U.S. minimum wage of 25¢ per hour. The U.S. federal minimum hourly wage rose to $7.25 in 2009 and remained at that level through early 2018, but 29 states and a number of cities set higher minimum wages.[10] As of 2019, the highest minimum wage is in Washington, D.C. ($14.00), followed by Washington State ($11.50), California ($12.00 for large firms),[11] and Massachusetts ($11.00). The minimum wage in Canada differs across provinces, ranging from C$14.00 to C$10.96 (where C$ stands for Canadian dollars) in 2018. If the minimum wage is *binding*—that is, if it exceeds the equilibrium wage, w^*—it creates *unemployment*: a persistent excess supply of labor.

---

[10]See **www.dol.gov** for U.S. state and federal minimum wages. See **www.fedee.com/pay-job -evaluation/minimum-wage-rates/** for minimum wages in European countries.

[11]According to California government website the minimum wage for large employers (> 25 employees) is $11.00 and for small companies is $10.50. See **www.dir.ca.gov/dlse/faq_minimum-wage.htm**. It is scheduled to go to $12 and $11 as of January 2019. According to **www.ncsl.org/ research/labor-and-employment/state-minimum-wage-chart.aspx**, the current Washington D.C. minimum wage is $13.25 and is scheduled to go to $14 on July 1, 2019.

FIGURE 2.8 The Minimum Wage: A Price Floor

In the absence of a minimum wage, the equilibrium wage is w^* and the equilibrium number of hours worked is L^*. A minimum wage, $\underline{w}$, set above w^*, leads to unemployment—persistent excess supply—because the quantity demanded, L_d, is less than the quantity supplied, L_s.

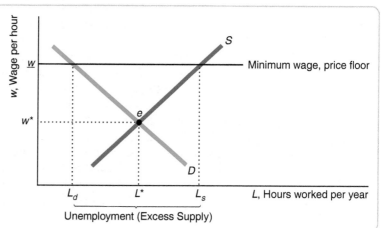

We illustrate the effect of a minimum wage law in a labor market in which everyone is paid the same wage. Figure 2.8 shows the supply and demand curves for labor services (hours worked). Firms buy hours of labor service by hiring workers. The horizontal axis shows the quantity of hours worked per year, and the vertical axis shows the hourly wage, which is the price of labor hours.

With no government intervention, the market equilibrium is e, where the wage is w^* and the number of hours worked is L^*. The minimum wage creates a price floor, a horizontal line, at $\underline{w}$. At that wage, the quantity demanded falls to L_d and the quantity supplied rises to L_s. As a result, the market has an excess supply of labor of $L_s - L_d$. The minimum wage prevents market forces from eliminating this excess supply, so it leads to an equilibrium with unemployment.

The original 1938 U.S. minimum wage law, which was set much higher than the equilibrium wage in Puerto Rico, created substantial unemployment there. It is ironic that a law designed to help workers by raising their wages may harm some of them by causing them to lose their jobs. A minimum wage law benefits only those workers who remain employed.[12]

Why Supply Need Not Equal Demand. The price ceiling and price floor examples show that the quantity supplied does not necessarily equal the quantity demanded in a supply-and-demand model. The quantity supplied need not equal the quantity demanded because of the way we define these two concepts. The quantity supplied is the amount sellers *want to sell* at a given price, holding other factors that affect supply, such as the price of inputs, constant. The quantity demanded is the quantity that buyers *want to buy* at a given price, if other factors that affect demand are held constant. The quantity that sellers want to sell and the quantity that buyers want to buy at a given price need not equal the *actual* quantity that is bought and sold.

When the government imposes a binding price ceiling of $\bar{p}$ on gasoline, the quantity demanded is greater than the quantity supplied. Despite the lack of equality between

---

[12]The minimum wage could raise the wage enough that total wage payments, wL, rise despite the fall in demand for labor services. If the workers could share the unemployment—everybody works fewer hours than he or she wants—all workers could benefit from the minimum wage. Card and Krueger (1995) have argued, based on alternatives to the simple supply-and-demand model, that minimum wage laws raise wages in some markets (such as fast foods) without significantly reducing employment. In contrast, Neumark and Wascher (2008) conclude, based on an extensive review of minimum wage research, that increases in the minimum wage often have negative effects on employment.

the quantity supplied and the quantity demanded, the supply-and-demand model is useful in analyzing this market because it predicts the excess demand that is observed.

We could have defined the quantity supplied and the quantity demanded so that they must be equal. If we were to define the quantity supplied as the amount firms *actually* sell at a given price and the quantity demanded as the amount consumers *actually* buy, supply must equal demand in all markets because the quantity demanded and the quantity supplied are *defined* to be the same quantity.

This distinction is important because many people, including politicians and newspaper reporters, are confused on this point. Someone who insists that "demand *must* equal supply" must be defining supply and demand as the *actual* quantities sold.

Because we define the quantities supplied and demanded in terms of people's *wants* and not *actual* quantities bought and sold, we view the statement "supply equals demand" as a theory, not a definition. This theory says that the intersection of the supply curve and the demand curve determines the price and quantity in a market, and the market clears *if the government does not intervene*. However, the theory also tells us that government intervention can prevent market clearing. For example, the supply-and-demand model predicts that excess demand will arise if the government imposes a price ceiling below the market clearing price or excess supply will result if the government imposes a price floor above the market clearing price.

Sales Taxes

New Jersey's decision to eliminate the tax on Botox has users elated. At least we think they're elated—we can't really tell.

Governments frequently impose sales taxes on goods, such as the carbon tax discussed at the beginning of the chapter.[13] Sales taxes typically raise the price that consumers pay for a good and lower the price that firms receive for it.

One type of sales tax is a *specific tax*, in which the government collects a specified dollar amount, t, per unit of output. For example, the federal government collects $t = 18.4$¢ on each gallon of gas sold in the United States.[14]

In this section, we examine two questions about the effects of a specific tax:

1. What effect does a specific tax have on the equilibrium price and quantity?
2. Is it true, as many people claim, that firms pass the entire tax through to their customers—the price that consumers pay rises by the full amount of the tax?

Equilibrium Effects of a Specific Tax. To answer these two questions, we must extend the standard supply-and-demand analysis to take account of taxes. We can illustrate the effect of a specific tax—our first question—using estimated supply and demand functions for the U.S. corn market.[15]

Many nutritionists argue that to fight obesity, we should reduce the amount of corn syrup (sugar) we consume. One way to do that would be to tax corn. Suppose that the government collects a specific tax of $t = \$2.40$ per bushel of corn from sellers (farms). If a customer pays p to a firm, the government takes $t = \$2.40$, so the firm keeps $p - t = p - \$2.40$.

[13]MyLab Economics has a *Taxes Experiment* that illustrates the effect of sales taxes. To participate go to the MyLab Economics Multimedia Library, Single Player Experiment, and set the Chapter field to "All Chapters."

[14]The other major type of sales tax is an *ad valorem tax*, in which the government collects a percentage of the price that consumers pay. The analysis of ad valorem taxes is similar to the analysis of specific taxes.

[15]Our linear curves are based on Roberts and Schlenker (2013).

FIGURE 2.9 Effect of a $2.40 Specific Tax on Corn Collected from Producers

The specific tax of $t = \$2.40$ per bushel of corn collected from producers shifts the pre-tax corn supply curve, S^1, up to the post-tax supply curve, S^2. The tax causes the equilibrium to shift from e_1 (determined by the intersection of S^1 and D^1) to e_2 (intersection of S^2 with D^1). The equilibrium price—the price consumers pay—increases from $P_1 = \$7.20$ to $P_2 = \$8.00$. The government collects tax revenues of $T = tQ_2 = \$27.84$ billion per year.

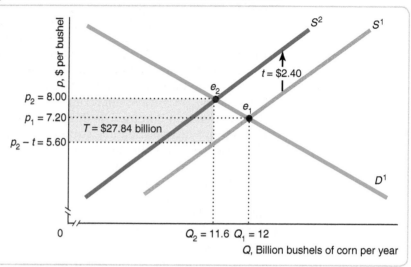

Before the tax, the intersection of the before-tax corn demand curve D^1 and the before-tax corn supply curve S^1 in Figure 2.9 determines the before-tax equilibrium, e_1, where the equilibrium price is $p_1 = \$7.20$, and the equilibrium quantity is $Q_1 = 12$ billion bushels of corn per year.

The tax causes the supply curve to shift. Before the tax, firms were willing to supply 11.6 billion bushels of corn per year at a price of $5.60 per bushel, as the pre-tax supply curve S^1 shows. After the tax, if customers pay $5.60, firms keep only $5.60 − $2.40 = $3.20, so they are not willing to supply as much corn as before the tax. For firms to be willing to sell 11.6 units after the tax, customers must pay $8.00 so that the firms receive $8.00 − $2.40 = $5.60 after paying the tax. As a result, the after-tax supply curve, S^2, is $t = \$2.40$ above the original supply curve S^1 at every quantity, as the figure shows.

The intersection of S^2 and the demand curve D^1 determines the after-tax equilibrium e_2, where consumers pay $p_2 = \$8.00$, firms receive $p_2 − t = p_2 − \$2.40 = \$5.60$, and $Q_2 = 11.6$. Thus, the answer to our first question is that the specific tax causes the equilibrium price consumers pay to rise, the net price that firms receive (after paying the tax) to fall, and the equilibrium quantity to fall.

Although customers pay a higher price and producers receive less because of the tax, the government acquires new tax revenue of $T = tQ_2 = \$2.40$ per bushel × 11.6 billion bushels per year = $27.84 billion per year. The length of the shaded rectangle is $Q_2 = 11.6$ billion per year, and its height is $t = \$2.40$ per bushel, so the area of the rectangle equals the tax revenue.

Pass-Through. Our second question concerns whether customers bear the entire burden of a tax, as many politicians and news stories assert.

Common Confusion Businesses pass through any sales tax to consumers, so that the price that consumers pay increases by the amount of the tax.

This belief is not accurate in general. Full pass-through can occur, but partial pass-through is more common.

As we just showed for the corn market in Figure 2.9, the price consumers pay rises from $7.20 to $8.00 after a $2.40 specific tax is imposed on firms. Thus, the firms shift only $0.80 of the $2.40 tax to consumers. The firms absorb $1.60 of the tax, because the price that firms receive falls from $7.20 to $5.60. Thus, the fraction of the tax that consumers pay is $0.80/$2.40 = $\frac{1}{3}$ and the fraction that firms absorb is $1.60/$2.40 = $\frac{2}{3}$.

However, in one special case, firms do pass the full amount of the tax to consumers, as the following Q&A shows.

| **Q&A 2.3** | If the supply curve is horizontal and the demand curve is linear and downward sloping, what is the effect of a $1 specific tax collected from producers on equilibrium price and quantity, and what share of the tax do consumers pay? Why? |

Answer

1. *Determine the equilibrium in the absence of a tax.* Before the tax, the perfectly elastic supply curve, S^1 in the graph, is horizontal at p_1. The downward-sloping linear demand curve, D, intersects S^1 at the pre-tax equilibrium, e_1, where the price is p_1 and the quantity is Q_1.

2. *Show how the tax shifts the supply curve and determine the new equilibrium.* A specific tax of $1 shifts the pre-tax supply curve, S^1, upward by $1 to S^2, which is horizontal at $p_1 + 1$. The intersection of D and S^2 determines the after-tax equilibrium, e_2, where the price consumers pay is $p_2 = p_1 + 1$, the price firms receive is $p_2 - 1 = p_1$, and the quantity is Q_2.

3. *Compare the before- and after-tax equilibria.* The specific tax causes the equilibrium quantity to fall from Q_1 to Q_2, the price firms receive to remain at p_1, and the equilibrium price consumers pay to rise from p_1 to $p_2 = p_1 + 1$. Thus, the firms pass the entire tax, $1, on to consumers.

4. *Explain why.* The reason consumers must absorb the entire tax is that firms will not supply the good at a price that is any lower than they received before the tax, p_1. Thus, the price must rise enough that the price suppliers receive after tax is unchanged. As consumers do not want to consume as much at a higher price, the equilibrium quantity falls.

Managers should use pass-through analysis to predict the effect on their price and quantity from not just a new tax but from *any per unit increase in costs*. Suppose that the cost of producing corn rises $2.40 per bushel because of an increase in the cost of labor or other factors of production, rather than because of a tax. Then, the same analysis as in Figure 2.9 would apply, so a manager would know that only 80¢ of this cost increase could be passed through to consumers.

2.6 When to Use the Supply-and-Demand Model

As we have seen, the supply-and-demand model can help us to understand and predict real-world events in many markets. As with many models, the supply-and-demand model need not be perfect to be useful. It is much like a map. A map can leave out many details and still be valuable—indeed, maps are useful in large part because they simplify reality. Similarly, the supply-and-demand model gains much of its power from its simplicity. The main practical question concerns whether the model is close enough to reality to yield useful predictions and conclusions. We have learned that the supply-and-demand model provides a very good description of actual events in highly competitive markets. It is precisely accurate in *perfectly competitive* markets, which are markets in which all firms and consumers are *price takers*: no market participant can affect the market price.

Perfectly competitive markets have five characteristics that result in price taking by firms: (1) many buyers and sellers transact in a market, (2) all firms produce identical products, (3) all market participants have full information about price and product characteristics, (4) transaction costs are negligible, and (5) firms can easily enter and exit the market over time.

In a market with a very large number of sellers, no single producer or consumer is a large enough part of the market to affect the price. The more firms in a market, the less any one firm's output affects total market output and hence the market price. If one of the many thousands of wheat farmers stops selling wheat, the price of wheat will not change. Similarly, no individual buyer of wheat can cause price to change through a change in buying patterns.

If consumers believe all firms produce identical products, consumers do not prefer one firm's good to another's. Thus, if one firm raised its price, consumers would all buy from the other firm.

If consumers know the prices that all firms charge and one firm raises its price, that firm's customers will buy from other firms. If consumers have less information about product quality than a firm, the firm can take advantage of consumers by selling them inferior-quality goods or by charging a much higher price than that charged by other firms. In such a market, the observed price may be higher than that predicted by the supply-and-demand model, the market may not exist at all (consumers and firms cannot reach agreements), or different firms may charge different prices for the same good.

If it is cheap and easy for a buyer to find a seller and make a trade, and if one firm raises its price, consumers can easily arrange to buy from another firm. That is, perfectly competitive markets typically have very low **transaction costs**: the expenses, over and above the price of the product, of finding a trading partner and making a trade for the product. These costs include the time and money spent gathering information on quality and finding someone with whom to trade. The costs of traveling and the value of the consumer's time are transaction costs. Other transaction costs may include the costs of writing and enforcing a contract, such as the cost of a lawyer's time. If transaction costs are very high, no trades at all might occur. In less extreme cases individual trades may occur, but at a variety of prices.

The ability of firms to enter and exit a market freely leads to a large number of firms in a market and promotes price taking. Suppose a firm could raise its price and make a higher profit. If other firms could not enter the market, this firm would not be a price taker. However, if other firms can enter the market, the higher profit will encourage entry until the price reverts to the original level.

In markets without these characteristics, firms may not be price takers. For example, in a market with only one seller of a good or service—a *monopoly*—the seller is a *price setter* and can affect the market price. Because demand curves slope downward, a monopoly can increase the price it receives by reducing the amount of a good it supplies. Firms are also price setters in an *oligopoly*—a market with only a small number of firms. In markets with price setters, the market price is usually higher than that predicted by the supply-and-demand model. That does not make the model wrong. It means only that the supply-and-demand model might not be the right tool to analyze markets with a small number of buyers and/or sellers. In such markets, we use other models.

As a practical matter, it is rare to find a market that fully and completely satisfies all the conditions needed for perfect competition. The practical issue concerns whether the market is "competitive enough" for the supply-and-demand model to be useful in the sense that it accurately describes the market and predicts the effects of changes to the equilibrium. Experience has shown that the supply-and-demand model is reliable in a wide range of markets, such as those for agriculture, financial products, labor, construction, many services, real estate, wholesale trade, and retail trade.

Managerial Solution

Carbon Taxes

We conclude our analysis of the supply-and-demand model by returning to the managerial problem posed in the introduction of this chapter: What will be the effect of imposing a carbon tax on the price of gasoline?

The primary targets of carbon taxes are fossil fuels such as oil, natural gas, and coal. These fuels release carbon-based pollutants—including greenhouse gases that contribute to global warming—into the environment. Typically, a carbon tax is a specific tax on the amount of carbon produced by consuming fuels or other products. Currently, the carbon tax in Sweden is about $150 per ton of carbon. Because the amount of carbon in a gallon or liter of gasoline is fixed, effectively, a carbon tax is a specific tax on gasoline. Consequently, we can analyze the impact of a carbon tax on gasoline in the same way that we analyzed the effect of a specific tax on corn.

A good manager considers the short-run and long-run price effects of a tax, which are likely to differ. As we've already seen, the degree to which a tax is passed through to consumers depends on the shapes of the demand and supply curves. Typically, short-run supply and demand curves differ from the long-run curves.

In particular, the long-run supply curve of gasoline differs substantially from the short-run curve. In the long run, the supply curve is upward sloping, as in our typical figure. However, the U.S. short-run supply curve of gasoline is very close to vertical. The U.S. refinery capacity has fallen over the past few decades. Currently, the 141 U.S. refineries can process a maximum of only 18.3 million barrels of crude oil per day, compared to 1981, when 324 refineries could process 18.6 million barrels per day. Refineries operate at almost full capacity during the summer, when the gasoline demand curve shifts to the right because families take long car trips during vacation. Consequently, refineries cannot increase their output in the short run, and the supply curve for gasoline is nearly vertical at the maximum capacity, $\overline{Q}$. That is, even if the price of gasoline rises, producers sell no more gasoline than $\overline{Q}$.

From empirical studies, we know that the U.S. federal gasoline specific tax of $t = 18.4¢$ per gallon is shared roughly equally between gasoline companies and consumers in the long run. However, we expect most of the tax to fall on firms that sell gasoline in the short run.

We contrast the long-run and short-run effects of a carbon tax in the figure. In both panels, the carbon tax is equivalent to a specific gasoline tax of t per gallon. If the government collects this tax from consumers, the before-tax demand curve D^1 shifts down by t to the after-tax demand curve D^2. Also, in both panels, the equilibrium shifts from e_1—the intersection of D^1 and the relevant supply curve—to e_2—the intersection of D^2 and the relevant supply curve (though these equilibrium points are not the same across the two panels).

Panel a shows the effect of the tax in the long run, where the long-run supply curve is upward sloping. The price that firms receive falls from p_1 to p_2, and the price that consumers pay rises from p_1 to $p_2 + t$. As the figure illustrates, the tax is shared roughly equally by consumers and firms in the long run.

In the short run in panel b, the upward-sloping short-run supply curve becomes vertical at full capacity, $\overline{Q}$. The price that consumers pay, p_1, is the same before the tax and after the tax. That is, the price that gasoline firms receive, p_2, falls by the full amount of the tax.

Manufacturing and other firms that ship goods are consumers of gasoline. They can expect to absorb relatively little of a carbon tax when it is first imposed, but half of the tax in the long run.[16]

(a) Long-Run Gasoline Market

(b) Short-Run Gasoline Market

---

[16]An alternative approach to using a carbon tax to control pollution is for the government to restrict emissions directly. The government gives each firm a fixed number of emission permits, each of which allows the owner to release a given quantity of emissions. A market-based variant allows firms to buy or sell these emission permits in a market. The resulting price of an emission permit acts much like a tax on emissions. See Chapter 16.

SUMMARY

1. **Demand.** The quantity of a good or service demanded by consumers depends on the price of a good, the price of goods that are substitutes and complements, consumers' incomes, the information they have about the good, their tastes, government regulations, and other factors. The *Law of Demand*—which is based on observation—says that *demand curves slope downward*: the higher the price, the less quantity of the good demanded, holding constant other factors that affect demand. A change in price causes a *movement along the demand curve*. A change in income, tastes, or another factor that affects demand other than price causes a *shift of the demand curve*. To get a total demand curve, we horizontally sum the demand curves of individuals or other subgroups of consumers. That is, we add the quantities demanded by each individual at a given price to get the total quantity demanded.

2. **Supply.** The quantity of a good or service supplied by firms depends on the price, costs of inputs, the state of technology, government regulations, and other factors. The market supply curve usually, but not always, slopes upward. A change in price causes a *movement along the supply curve*. A change in the price of an input or in technology causes a *shift of the supply curve*. The total supply curve is the horizontal sum of the supply curves for individual firms.

3. **Market Equilibrium.** Equilibrium arises when no market participant has an incentive to change its behavior. In an unregulated supply-and-demand model, the market equilibrium is a point: a price and a quantity. The intersection of the supply curve and the demand curve determines the market equilibrium. At the equilibrium price, the market for the good clears in the sense that the quantity of the good demanded by consumers exactly equals the quantity of the good that suppliers

supply to the market, which is the equilibrium quantity. The actions of buyers and sellers put pressure on price and quantity to move toward equilibrium levels if the market price is initially too low or too high.

4. **Shocks to the Equilibrium.** A change in an underlying factor other than a good's own price causes a shift of the supply curve or the demand curve, which alters the equilibrium. For example, if the price of coffee rises, we would expect the demand for tea, a substitute, to shift outward, putting upward pressure on the price of tea and leading to an increase in the quantity of tea sold.

5. **Effects of Government Interventions.** Some government policies—such as restrictions on who can buy a product—cause a shift in the supply or demand curves, thereby altering the equilibrium. Other government policies, such as price controls, can cause the quantity supplied to be greater or less than the quantity demanded, leading to persistent excesses or shortages. A specific tax, a type of sales tax, typically lowers the equilibrium quantity, raises the price paid by consumers, and lowers the price received by sellers, so firms are unable to pass the entire tax through to consumers.

6. **When to Use the Supply-and-Demand Model.** The supply-and-demand model is a powerful tool used to explain what happens in a market and to make predictions about what will happen if an underlying factor changes. This model accurately predicts what occurs in some markets but not others. The supply-and-demand model performs best in explaining and predicting the behavior of markets with many buyers and sellers, with identical or at least very similar products provided by different producers, with free entry and exit by producers, with full information about price and other market characteristics, and with low transaction costs.

QUESTIONS

All exercises are available on **MyLab Economics**; * = *answer at the back of this book;* ✗ = *this exercise is available in Excel Grader in* **MyLab Economics.**

1. Demand

*1.1 Does an increase in average income cause a shift of the demand curve for coffee or a movement along the demand curve? Explain briefly.

1.2 Given the estimated demand function, Equation 2.2, for coffee, $Q = 8.56 - p - 0.3p_s + 0.1Y$, use algebra (or calculus) to show how the demand curve shifts as per capita income, Y, increases by $10,000 a year. Illustrate this shift in a diagram.

1.3 Using the coffee demand function, $Q = 8.56 - p - 0.3p_s + 0.1Y$, show that sugar is a complement for

coffee. You can use a numerical example, algebra, or calculus.

1.4 Assume that both the U.S. and Canadian demand curves for lumber are linear. The Canadian demand curve lies inside the U.S. curve (the Canadian demand curve hits the axes at a lower price and a lower quantity than the U.S. curve). Draw the individual country demand curves and the combined (summed) demand curve for the two countries. Explain the relationship between the country and summed demand curves in words. (*Hint*: See the Mini-Case "Summing Corn Demand Curves.")

*1.5 The demand function for a truckload of firewood for college students in a small town is $Q_c = 400 - p$. It is sometimes convenient to rewrite a demand function with price on the left side. We refer to such a relationship as the *inverse demand function*. Therefore, the inverse demand function for college students is $p = 400 - Q_c$. The demand function for other town residents is $Q_r = 400 - 2p$.

 a. What is the inverse demand function for other town residents?

 b. At a price of $300, will college students buy any firewood? What about other town residents? At what price is the quantity demanded by other town residents zero?

 c. Draw the total demand curve, which sums the demand curves for college students and other residents. (*Hint*: See the Mini-Case "Summing Corn Demand Curves.")

2. Supply

2.1 The estimated supply function for avocados is $Q = 58 + 15p - 20p_f$, where p_f is the price of fertilizer. Determine how much the supply curve for avocados shifts if the price of fertilizer rises by $1.10 per lb. Illustrate this shift in a diagram.

*2.2 Explain why a change in the price of fertilizer causes a shift in the supply curve for avocados rather than a movement along the supply curve for avocados.

*2.3 Holding the price of fertilizer constant, by how much would the price of avocados need to rise to cause an increase of 60 million lb per month in the quantity of avocados supplied?

2.4 Assume that the total U.S. supply curve for frozen orange juice is the sum of the supply curve from Florida and the imported supply curve from Brazil. In a diagram, show the relationship between these three supply curves and explain it in words.

3. Market Equilibrium

*3.1 A large number of firms are capable of producing chocolate-covered cockroaches. The linear, upward-sloping supply curve starts on the price axis at $6 per box. A few hardy consumers are willing to buy this product (possibly to use as gag gifts). Their linear, downward-sloping demand curve hits the price axis at $4 per box. Draw the supply and demand curves. Does an equilibrium occur at a positive price and quantity? Explain your answer.

3.2 The demand function is $Q = 5,000 - 10p$, and the supply function is $Q = 200 + 6p$. Determine the equilibrium price and quantity.

3.3 Using the demand function, Equation 2.2, $Q = 8.56 - p - 0.3p_s + 0.1Y$, and the supply function,

Equation 2.5, $Q = 9.6 + 0.5p - 0.2p_c$, for coffee, determine the equilibrium price and quantity of coffee if $Y = \$55,000$, $p_s = 0.20$, and $p_c = \$5$. Draw the demand and supply curves and illustrate this equilibrium in a diagram.

*3.4 Using the demand function $Q = 8.56 - p - 0.3p_s + 0.1Y$ and supply function $Q = 9.6 + 0.5p - 0.2p_c$, determine the amount of any excess demand or excess supply at a price of $4 and explain the mechanism that would cause the equilibrium price to be reached.

4. Shocks to the Equilibrium

4.1 Using supply-and-demand diagrams, illustrate and explain the effect of an outward shift in the demand curve on price and quantity if

 a. The supply curve is horizontal.

 b. The supply curve is vertical.

 c. The supply curve is upward sloping.

4.2 Use supply-and-demand diagrams to illustrate the qualitative effect of the following possible shocks on the world coffee market.

 a. A new study shows significant health benefits from drinking coffee.

 b. An important new use for cocoa is discovered.

 c. A recession causes a decline in per capita income.

 d. A new coffee plant that allows for much greater output or yield without increasing cost is introduced into the market.

*4.3 The United States is increasingly *outsourcing* jobs to India: having the work done in India rather than in the United States. For example, the Indian firm Tata Consultancy Services, which provides information technology services, increased its workforce by 70,000 workers in 2010 ("Outsourcing Firm Hiring 60,000 Workers in India," *San Francisco Chronicle*, June 16, 2011). As a result of increased outsourcing, wages of some groups of Indian skilled workers have increased substantially over the years. Use a supply-and-demand diagram to explain this outcome.

4.4 The estimated monthly U.S. demand function for avocados is $Q = 144 - 40p + 20p_t$ where p is the price of avocados and p_t is the price of tomatoes, a substitute for avocados. The estimated supply function is given in Question 2.1, where the price of fertilizer, p_f, is $0.40, so the supply function can be written as $Q = 50 + 15p$. The initial price of tomatoes is 80¢ per lb. Using algebra, determine the initial equilibrium price and quantity of avocados, and then determine how price and quantity change if the price of tomatoes increases by 55¢ to $1.35. (*Hint*: See Q&A 2.1.)

4.5 President Trump introduced several policy measures designed to curb immigration. Use a supply-and-demand diagram to illustrate the effect of such policies on wages and employment if the policies shift the labor supply curve to the left but have no effect on the labor demand curve.

*4.6 Given that the U.S. supply of frozen orange juice comes mainly from Florida and Brazil, what effect would a freeze that damages oranges in Florida have on the price and quantity of frozen orange juice sold in the United States? What effect would the freeze have on the price of grapefruit juice? Use supply-and-demand diagrams in your answer.

4.7 Ethanol, a fuel, is made from corn. Ethanol production in 2014 was approximately 17 times what it was in 1990 (**www.ethanolrfa.org**, June 2015). What effect did this increased use of corn for producing ethanol have on the price of corn and the consumption of corn as food? Illustrate using a supply-and-demand diagram.

4.8 The major BP oil spill in the Gulf of Mexico substantially reduced the harvest of shrimp and other seafood in the Gulf, but had limited impact on the prices that U.S. consumers paid in 2010 (Emmeline Zhao, "Impact on Seafood Prices Is Limited," *Wall Street Journal*, June 20, 2010). The reason was that the United States imports about 83% of its seafood and only 2% of domestic supplies come from the Gulf. Use a supply-and-demand diagram to illustrate what happened.

4.9 For years, Chinese parents bought imported baby formula because of their concerns about the safety of domestic formula. However, in 2013, a major foreign producer announced that its concentrate might contain botulism. In 2014, the Chinese government yanked production permits for a third of the country's infant formula manufacturers due to safety concerns. Many worried parents stopped buying any formula. The price of formula rose from 350 to 450 yuan (the Chinese currency). Use a supply-and-demand diagram to explain why the price rose. Show the effect on equilibrium quantity.

*4.10 Increases in the price of petroleum affect the demand curve for aluminum. Petroleum-based chemicals (petrochemicals) are the main raw material used for plastic. Manufacturers use plastics to make many products, including beverage containers, auto parts, and construction materials. An alternative to plastic in these (and other) uses is aluminum. Thus, plastic and aluminum are substitutes. An increase in petroleum prices increases the cost of petrochemicals. Petroleum prices also affect the supply curve for aluminum. Increases in petroleum prices tend to raise energy prices, including electricity prices. Electricity is a very important input in producing aluminum. Therefore, increasing petroleum prices tend to increase the cost of electricity. In a supply-and-demand diagram, show how an increase in petroleum prices affects the demand curve and supply curve for aluminum. If the price of petroleum rises, would the price of aluminum rise, fall, or remain unchanged, or is the result indeterminate? Would the quantity of aluminum sold rise, fall, or remain unchanged, or is the result indeterminate? Explain your answers.

4.11 Use a figure to explain the fisher's comment about the effect of a large catch on the market price in the cartoon in this chapter about catching lobsters. What is the supply shock?

4.12 Bentonite clay, which consists of ancient volcanic ash, has many uses, including manufacturing kitty litter and clarifying wine. A major use is for drilling mud, a material pumped down oil and gas wells during drilling to keep the drilling bit cool. When oil drilling decreases, less bentonite is demanded at any given price. The price of crude oil was about $50 a barrel in 2016–2017. However, by 2018, it was over $70, causing drilling to increase. Use a supply-and-demand diagram to show the effect on the bentonite market and explain in words what happened.

5. Effects of Government Interventions

5.1 New York City has licensed street vendors for more than a century. It currently provides only a small number of general vending licenses. The waiting list is very long and, aside from military veterans, someone trying to get a license today has no chance. One popular item for street vendors is handbags. Use a supply-and-demand model to show how this licensing affects the market price and quantity of handbags sold by New York street vendors. (*Hint*: See the Mini-Case on "Occupational Licensing" and Q&A 2.2.)

*5.2 After Katrina, a major hurricane, damaged many U.S. gasoline refineries in 2005, the price of gasoline shot up around the country. The Federal Trade Commission announced that it would investigate price gouging—charging "too much"—and several members of Congress called for price controls on gasoline. What would have been the likely effect of such a law had it been passed?

5.3 Usury laws place a ceiling on interest rates that lenders such as banks can charge borrowers. Why would we expect low-income households in states with usury laws to have significantly lower levels of consumer credit (loans) than comparable households in states without usury laws? (*Hint*: The interest rate is the price of a loan, and the amount of the loan is the quantity measure.)

5.4 Some cities impose rent control laws, which are price controls or limits on the price of rental accommodations (apartments, houses, and mobile homes). As of 2015, New York City alone had approximately one million apartments under rent control. Show the effect of a rent control law on the equilibrium rental price and the quantity of New York City apartments. Show the amount of excess demand on your supply-and-demand diagram.

5.5 If the minimum wage raises the market wage, w, but hours worked, L, fall as a result, total wage payments, wL, may rise or fall. Use supply and demand curves to show that either outcome is possible depending on the shapes (slopes) of the supply and demand curves. (*Hint*: With the wage on the vertical axis and hours worked, L, on the horizontal axis, wage payments equal the area of the box with a height of the equilibrium wage and length of the equilibrium hours worked.)

5.6 Use the demand function and the supply function for the avocado market (given in Question 4.4) to determine how the equilibrium price and quantity change when a 55¢ per lb specific tax is imposed on this market. (*Hint*: See Figure 2.9.)

5.7 If the government collects a $1 specific tax, what share of the tax is paid by consumers and firms in each of the following cases? Explain why. (*Hint*: See Q&A 2.3.)

   a. The demand curve is vertical at quantity Q and the supply curve is upward sloping.

   b. The demand curve is horizontal at price p and the supply curve is upward sloping.

   c. The demand curve is downward sloping and the supply curve is horizontal at price p.

5.8 In Figure 2.9, the government imposes a specific tax on sellers, which causes the supply curve to shift up. At any given price paid by consumers, sellers supply less than before. Now suppose that the tax is imposed on buyers. Illustrate this effect by shifting the demand curve inward. Is the resulting equilibrium quantity the same as in Q&A 2.3? Explain briefly.

5.9 In 2012, voters in the state of Washington approved a ballot measure legalizing the recreational use of marijuana. The measure required that consumers pay a 37% tax on sales of recreational marijuana. For what slopes of the supply or demand curves will this tax substantially reduce the equilibrium quantity of marijuana?

5.10 Since 2014, Quebec, Canada, has offered a per-child subsidy (which is a negative tax) on day care for young children that lowers the price to $7 per child.

   a. What is the effect of this subsidy on the equilibrium price and quantity?

   b. Show the incidence of the subsidy on day care providers and parents using a supply-and-demand diagram.

6. When to Use the Supply-and-Demand Model

6.1 List as many industries as you can for which the supply-and-demand model is likely to be appropriate.

7. Managerial Problem

7.1 During the spring and summer of 2008, when gasoline prices were rising quickly, politicians in several countries proposed a moratorium on some or all gasoline taxes to help consumers. In the United States, John McCain, the Republican candidate for president, proposed suspending the federal gasoline tax of 18.4¢ for the summer, when demand tends to be high. (Hillary Clinton, while an active candidate for the Democratic nomination for president, also pushed this plan.) In the United Kingdom, Prime Minister Gordon Brown proposed delaying a two pence per liter rise in a fuel tax until the fall. How would these short-run policies have affected the prices consumers would pay in these countries if the policies had been enacted?

8. MyLab Economics Spreadsheet Exercises[17]

8.1 Suppose that the market for video games is competitive with demand function $Q_d = 130 - 4p + 2Y + 3p_m - 2p_c$, where Q_d is the quantity demanded, p is the market price, Y is the monthly budget that an average consumer has available for entertainment, p_m is the average price of a movie, and p_c is the price of a controller that is required to play these games.

   a. Given that $Y = \$100$, $p_m = \$30$, and $p_c = \$30$, use Excel to calculate quantity demanded for $p = \$10$ to $p = \$80$ in $5 increments. Use Excel's charting tool to draw the demand curve.

   b. Now, Y increases to $120. Recalculate the demand schedule in part a. Use Excel's charting tool to draw the new demand curve in the same diagram.

   c. Let $Y = \$100$ and $p_c = \$30$ again, but let p_m increase to $40. Recalculate the demand

---

[17]The spreadsheet exercises in this chapter are based on the work of Satyajit Ghosh in cooperation with the authors. The answers are available on MyLab Economics.

schedule in part a. Use Excel's charting tool to draw the graph of the new demand curve.

d. Let $Y = \$100$, $p_m = \$30$, and p_c increase to $40. Recalculate the demand schedule in part a and use Excel to draw the new demand curve.

8.2 In Smalltown, Pennsylvania, the demand function for men's haircuts is $Q_d = 500 - 30p + 0.08Y$, where Q_d is quantity demanded per month, p the price of a haircut, and Y the average monthly income in the town. The supply function for men's haircuts is $Q_s = 100 + 20p - 20w$, where Q_s is the quantity supplied and w the average hourly wage of barbers.

a. If $Y = \$5,000$ and $w = \$10$, use Excel to calculate quantity demanded and quantity supplied for $p = \$5, \$10, \$15, \$20, \$25,$ and $\$30$. Calculate excess demand for each price. (Note that an excess supply is negative excess demand.) Determine the equilibrium price and quantity. Use Excel's charting tool to draw the demand and supply curves.

b. Assume that Y increases to $\$6,875$ and w increases to $\$15$. Use Excel to recalculate quantity demanded, quantity supplied, and excess demand for $p = \$5, \$10, \$15, \$20, \$25,$ and $\$30$. Determine the new equilibrium price and quantity. Use Excel to draw the new demand and supply curves. How can you explain the change in equilibrium?

8.3 The demand and supply functions for oil in a small isolated country are $Q_d = 210 - 1.5p$ and $Q_s = -140 + 2p$, where p is the price per barrel and quantities are in millions of barrels per year.

a. Use Excel to calculate the quantity demanded and quantity supplied for $p = \$70, \$75, \$80, \dots, \$140$ (in $5 increments). Determine the equilibrium price and quantity.

b. Use Excel's charting tool to draw the demand and supply curves you derived in part a and graphically determine the equilibrium calculated in part a.

c. Now, assume that the government imposes a price ceiling of $80 per barrel. Use the spreadsheet from part a to determine the amount of any excess demand or excess supply. How much oil is sold?

d. The government abandons the price ceiling described in part c and imposes a price floor of $110 per barrel instead. Use your spreadsheet to determine any excess demand or excess supply now. How much oil is sold?

3

Empirical Methods for Demand Analysis

98% of all statistics are made up.

Managerial Problem

Estimating the Effect of an iTunes Price Change

When Apple launched iTunes, it charged 99¢ for each song on its U.S. site. Later, Apple reconsidered its pricing strategy. Music producers wanted Apple to charge more, but price competition from rivals such as Amazon created pressure on Apple to lower its price. In April 2009, Apple switched to a new U.S. pricing scheme: 69¢ a song for the older catalog, 99¢ for most new songs, and $1.29 for the most popular tracks.

In June 2015, Apple introduced a streaming audio service, Apple Music, which allows customers to play as many songs as they want as often as they want for $9.99 per month. This service competes with traditional music downloads, but Apple decided not to change the price of those downloads, keeping a price of $1.29 for hit songs, and that price remains in force.

Before Apple managers change an iTunes price, they predict the likely effect of the price change on sales. Rather than run a potentially costly experiment of trying different possible prices to see how the quantity demanded changes, iTunes managers could ask a focus group consisting of a random sample of music buyers how they would react to a price hike. After collecting their responses, the managers could analyze the data to predict the likely effects of a price change. How could the managers use the data to estimate the demand curve facing iTunes? How could the managers determine if a price increase would be likely to raise revenue, even though the quantity demanded would fall?

Managers commonly use data to estimate economic relationships, such as that between price and quantity shown by a demand curve, or to examine whether a particular economic theory applies in their markets. Data-based analysis of economic relationships is often referred to as *empirical* analysis. This chapter discusses empirical methods that can be used to analyze economic relationships, emphasizing particularly the empirical analysis of demand.

In Chapter 2, we focused on market demand curves in highly competitive markets, such as most agricultural markets. In highly competitive markets with many firms selling identical products, each individual firm is a *price taker*. In such markets, no one firm can significantly influence the market price. Any firm that tried to raise its price above the market equilibrium price would lose all of its sales. However, many firms, such as Apple, operate in markets that are not as competitive. Such firms are *price setters* that can raise their prices without losing all their sales. In the market for music downloads, Apple is a price setter.

A price-setting firm is concerned about the demand curve facing the firm rather than a market demand curve. In particular, the manager of a price-setting firm often wants to know how responsive its quantity demanded is to changes in its price or in other variables that affect demand. For example, in deciding whether to raise the price of iTunes songs by 30¢, an Apple manager would want to know how the number of iTunes downloads would fall in response to a 30¢ increase in price. This responsiveness can be measured empirically using the *price elasticity of demand*.

A manager might also wish to estimate the entire demand function to decide how to set the firm's profit-maximizing price, plan an advertising campaign, or choose how large a plant to build. In Chapter 2, we used estimated demand (and supply) functions to determine the equilibrium price and to analyze the effects of government policies on the market. This chapter describes how to estimate demand functions using *regression analysis*, which is an empirical method used to estimate a mathematical relationship between a dependent variable, such as quantity demanded, and explanatory variables, such as price and income.

Further, managers often wish to use data to forecast the future value of an important economic quantity such as future sales. This chapter describes major forecasting methods, focusing particularly on the role of regression analysis in forecasting.

Learning Objectives

1. Calculate elasticities and apply them to managerial problems.
2. Use regression analysis to estimate business relationships.
3. Determine the confidence we can place in a regression analysis.
4. Explain how to choose an appropriate regression specification.
5. Forecast important business variables using regression analysis.

3.1 Elasticity

Managers commonly summarize the responsiveness of one variable—such as the quantity demanded—to a change in another—such as price—using a measure called an **elasticity**, which is the percentage change in one variable divided by the associated percentage change in the other variable. In particular, a manager can use the elasticity of demand to determine how the quantity demanded varies with price.

The Price Elasticity of Demand

In making critical decisions about pricing, a manager needs to know how a change in price affects the quantity sold. The **price elasticity of demand** (or simply the *elasticity of demand* or the *demand elasticity*) is the percentage change in quantity demanded, Q, divided by the percentage change in price, p. That is, the price elasticity of demand (which we represent by ε, the Greek letter epsilon) is

$$\varepsilon = \frac{\text{percentage change in quantity demanded}}{\text{percentage change in price}} = \frac{\Delta Q/Q}{\Delta p/p}. \tag{3.1}$$

The symbol Δ (the Greek letter delta) indicates a change, so ΔQ is the change in the quantity demanded; $\Delta Q/Q$ is the percentage change in the quantity demanded;

Δp is the change in price; and $\Delta p/p$ is the percentage change in price. According to Equation 3.1, if a 1% increase in the price of a product results in a 3% decrease in the quantity demanded of that product, the elasticity of demand is $\varepsilon = -3\%/1\% = -3$.

The elasticity of demand is a pure number: It is not measured in any particular units like dollars or tons. A useful way to think about elasticity is to consider the effect of a 1% change. If the price elasticity of demand is -2, a 1% decrease in price would cause quantity demanded to increase by 2%.

Arc Elasticity.

Very often, a manager has observed the quantity demanded at two different prices. The manager can use this information to calculate an *arc price elasticity of demand*, which is a price elasticity of demand calculated using two distinct price-quantity pairs.[1]

Suppose a manager observes that when the price of coffee rises from $p_1 = \$1.80$ to $p_2 = \$2.20$, the global quantity of coffee demanded falls from $q_1 = 10.2$ million tons to $q_2 = 9.8$ million tons per year. To use Equation 3.1, the manager must determine the percentage change in the quantity, $\Delta Q/Q$, and the percentage change in price, $\Delta p/p$.

The change in the quantity demanded as the price falls is $\Delta Q = q_2 - q_1 = 9.8 - 10.2 = -0.4$ million tons. To determine the percentage change in quantity, the manager needs to divide this change by a quantity, Q. Should the manager use the initial quantity, 10.2, the final quantity, 9.8, or something else? When calculating a percentage change, this choice of the base quantity makes a difference. If the manager uses the initial quantity as the base, then the percentage change in quantity is $-0.4/10.2 \approx -3.9\%$ (where $\approx$ means "approximately equal to"). If the manager uses the final quantity as the base, the percentage change is $-0.4/9.8 \approx -4.1\%$.

Another approach is to use the average quantity as the base. The average quantity is $(9.8 + 10.2)/2 = 10$, so the associated percentage change is $-0.4/10 = -4.0\%$. Many analysts use the average quantity because the elasticity is the same regardless of whether we start at a quantity of 10.2 and move to 9.8 or start at 9.8 and move to 10.2. If, instead, the manager consistently uses the initial quantity as the base, or consistently uses the final quantity as the base, then the percentage change would vary depending on the direction of movement.

The percentage change in price can also be calculated by using the average price as the base. The price change is $\Delta p = p_2 - p_1 = \$2.20 - \$1.80 = \$0.40$. The average price is $(\$1.80 + \$2.20)/2 = \$2.00$. Thus, the percentage change in price is $\$0.40/\$2.00 = 20\%$.

An **arc price elasticity** is an elasticity that uses the average price and average quantity as the denominator for percentage calculations.[2] Using Equation 3.1, the arc price elasticity is

$$\varepsilon = \frac{\text{percentage change in quantity demanded}}{\text{percentage change in price}} = \frac{\Delta Q/\overline{Q}}{\Delta p/\overline{p}}, \tag{3.2}$$

where the bars over Q and p indicate average values. In our example, the arc price elasticity is $-(\Delta Q/\overline{Q})/(\Delta p/\overline{p}) = -4\%/20\% = -0.2$.

---

[1] In mathematics an arc is any segment of a smooth curve, so the arc price elasticity of demand is the elasticity along some segment of the demand curve.

[2] Because the arc elasticity of demand uses the average price and quantity as the base for percentage calculations it is sometimes called the *midpoint* elasticity.

Managerial Implication

Changing Prices to Calculate an Arc Elasticity

One of the easiest and most straightforward ways for a manager to determine the elasticity of demand for a firm's product is to conduct an experiment. If the firm is a *price setter* and can vary the price of its product—as Apple, Toyota, Kraft Foods, and many other firms can—the manager can change the price and observe how the quantity sold varies. Armed with two observations—the quantity sold at the original price and the quantity sold at the new price—the manager can calculate an arc elasticity. Depending on the size of the calculated elasticity, the manager may continue to sell at the new price or revert to the original price. It is often possible to obtain useful information from an experiment in a few markets or even just one small submarket—in one country, in one city, or even in one supermarket. Managers of price-setting firms should consider using such experiments to assess the effect of price changes on quantity sold.

Q&A 3.1

In 2018, Amazon raised the annual subscription fee for its Prime membership service, which provides free two-day shipping on many goods and other benefits, from $99 to $119. Piper Jaffray, an investment bank, estimated that before the price increase, Prime had 77 million U.S. subscribers.[3] The bank speculated that the number of members would fall to about 62 million. If so, what is the arc elasticity of demand for a Prime membership?

Answer

Use Equation 3.2 to calculate the arc elasticity. The change in the price is $\Delta p = \$119 - \$99 = \$20$, and the change in quantity is $\Delta Q = 62 - 77 = -15$. The average price is $\bar{p} = (\$99 + \$119)/2 = \$109$, and the average quantity is $\bar{Q} = (77 + 62)/2 = 69.5$ million. Plugging these values into Equation 3.2, we find that the arc price elasticity of demand for Prime memberships is

$$\varepsilon = \frac{\Delta Q/\bar{Q}}{\Delta p/\bar{p}} = \frac{-15/69.5}{20/109} \approx -\frac{0.216}{0.183} \approx -1.18.$$

When price rose by 18.3%, the quantity demanded was estimated to fall by 21.6%, so the arc elasticity of demand is $\varepsilon = -1.18$. Based on this elasticity, a 1% rise in price would cause the quantity demanded to fall by 1.18 percent.

Point Elasticity. An arc elasticity is based on a discrete change between two distinct price-quantity combinations on a demand curve. If we let the distance between these two points become infinitesimally small, we are effectively evaluating the elasticity at a single point. We call an elasticity evaluated at a specific price-quantity combination a *point elasticity*.

If a manager knows only two specific price-quantity points on a demand curve, then the manager's best summary of how quantity demanded responds to price changes is the arc elasticity of demand for the movement between these two points. If, in contrast, the manager has information about the entire demand curve, it is possible to calculate the point elasticity of demand at any point on the demand curve.

---

[3]Jaclyn Cosgrove and Abha Bhattarai, "Amazon Prime's Price Is Jumping to $119 a Year," *Los Angeles Times*, April 27, 2018.

The point elasticity indicates the effect on the quantity demanded arising from a very small change in price.

To calculate a point elasticity, we first rewrite the price elasticity formula, Equation 3.1, as

$$\varepsilon = \frac{\Delta Q/Q}{\Delta p/p} = \frac{\Delta Q}{\Delta p}\frac{p}{Q} \tag{3.3}$$

where we are evaluating the elasticity at the point (Q, p) and $\Delta Q/\Delta p$ is the ratio of the change in quantity to the change in price.

Holding other variables that affect demand fixed, we can use Equation 3.3 to calculate the elasticity of demand for a general linear demand curve. The mathematical function corresponding to a linear demand curve is

$$Q = a + bp, \tag{3.4}$$

where a and b are parameters or coefficients. We assume that a is a positive constant and b is a negative constant. The parameter a is the quantity demanded if the price is zero. The parameter b shows how much the quantity demanded falls if the price is increased by one unit (such as a dollar). As we showed in Chapter 2, if the price changes from p_1 to p_2, then

$$\Delta Q = Q_2 - Q_1 = (a + bp_2) - (a + bp_1) = b(p_2 - p_1) = b\Delta p, \tag{3.5}$$

so if $\Delta p = 1$, the change in the quantity demanded, $\Delta Q = b$, is negative.

Rearranging Equation 3.5, we see that $\Delta Q/\Delta p = b$. Thus, the elasticity of demand for a linear demand curve is

$$\varepsilon = \frac{\Delta Q}{\Delta p}\frac{p}{Q} = b\frac{p}{Q}. \tag{3.6}$$

As we discussed in Chapter 2, our estimated linear demand function for coffee is

$$Q = 12 - p,$$

where Q is the quantity of coffee in millions of tons and p is the price in dollars per lb. For this specific linear demand function, $a = 12$ and $b = -1$. Substituting these values into Equation 3.6, we find that the point elasticity of demand for coffee is

$$\varepsilon = -1\frac{p}{Q}. \tag{3.7}$$

Equation 3.7 allows us to determine the elasticity of demand at any point (any price-quantity combination) on the demand curve. In particular, we can find the point elasticity of demand at $p = \$2.20$, where the quantity demanded is $Q = 12 - (1 \times 2.20) = 9.8$, by substituting these values into Equation 3.7:

$$\varepsilon = -b\frac{p}{Q} = -\frac{2.20}{9.8} \approx -0.22.$$

We previously used the estimated demand function for coffee to calculate the arc elasticity of demand for a price change from $2.20 to $1.80. That elasticity was -0.2, which is different from the point elasticity of -0.22 just calculated. Although these two elasticities are different, neither is incorrect. Both are appropriate measures—they are just measuring different elasticities. The arc elasticity correctly measures the elasticity associated with a discrete change from a price of $2.20 to a price of $1.80, while the point elasticity correctly measures the elasticity at a price of $2.20 for an infinitesimal change in the price. Both elasticity measures are useful. To keep our discussion as short and clear as possible, the subsequent analysis will deal just with point elasticities unless explicitly stated otherwise.

Mini-Case	The Apple App Store (iOS) had about 2.1 million apps (mobile applications for smartphones and tablets) available as of 2018. Google Play (Android) had even more, about 3.7 million. How price sensitive are consumers of apps (mobile applications)? Are Apple aficionados more or less price sensitive than people who use Android devices?
Demand Elasticities for Google Play and Apple Apps	Ghose and Han (2014) estimated the demand for an app in the Apple App Store as −2.0. That is, a 1% increase in price causes a 2% drop in the quantity demanded for an Apple app. Thus, demand is elastic in the Apple App Store. The estimated demand elasticity for an app in Google Play is −3.7. Thus, the demand elasticity of a typical Android app is nearly twice that of an Apple app. Google Play consumers are more price sensitive than are Apple App consumers.

Using Calculus	As the change in price becomes very small, $\Delta p \to 0$, the ratio $\Delta Q / \Delta p$ converges to the derivative dQ/dp. Thus, the point elasticity of demand in Equation 3.3 may be written as
The Point Elasticity of Demand	

$$\varepsilon = \frac{dQ}{dp}\frac{p}{Q}. \qquad (3.8)$$

Elasticity Along the Demand Curve

The elasticity of demand is different at every point along a downward-sloping linear demand curve. However, horizontal and vertical demand curves, which are extreme cases of a linear demand curve, have the same elasticity at every point.

Downward-Sloping Linear Demand Curves. The elasticity of demand is different at every point along a downward-sloping linear demand curve. According to Equation 3.6, the elasticity of demand on a linear demand curve is $\varepsilon = b(p/Q)$. Although b is a constant, the price-quantity ratio, p/Q, varies as we move along the demand curve, so the elasticity must also vary. The higher the price, the lower the quantity, so the ratio p/Q is a more negative number, and the elasticity must be more negative. A 1% increase in price causes a larger percentage fall in quantity near the top (left) of the demand curve than near the bottom (right).

We use the linear coffee demand curve in Figure 3.1 to illustrate how the elasticity varies with price. At the lower right corner of Figure 3.1, where the coffee demand curve hits the quantity axis ($p = 0$ and $Q = 12$), the elasticity of demand for coffee, Equation 3.7, is $\varepsilon = -1(p/Q) = -1(0/12) = 0$. At a point where the elasticity of demand is zero, we say that the demand curve is *perfectly inelastic*.

For quantities between the midpoint of the linear demand curve and the lower end where $p = 0$, the demand elasticity lies between zero and negative one: $0 > \varepsilon > -1$.

FIGURE 3.1 The Elasticity of Demand Varies Along the Linear Coffee Demand Curve

With a linear demand curve, such as the coffee demand curve, the higher the price, the more elastic the demand curve (ε is larger in absolute value: it becomes a more negative number as we move up the demand curve). The demand curve is perfectly inelastic ($\varepsilon = 0$) where the demand curve hits the horizontal axis, is perfectly elastic where the demand curve hits the vertical axis, and has unitary elasticity at the midpoint of the demand curve.

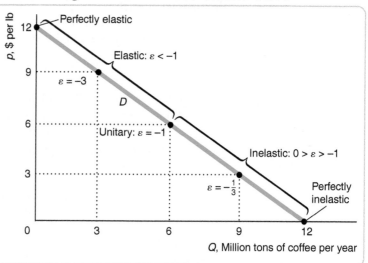

A point along the demand curve where the elasticity is between 0 and −1 is *inelastic* (but not perfectly inelastic): a 1% increase in price leads to a fall in quantity of less than 1%. For example, when the coffee price is $3 and the quantity demanded is 9, the elasticity of demand is $\varepsilon = -(3/9) = -\frac{1}{3}$, so a 1% increase in price causes quantity to fall by one-third of a percent.

Rearranging the elasticity formula in Equation 3.1, the percentage change in Q is ε times the percentage change in price: $\Delta Q/Q = \varepsilon\,(\Delta p/p)$. If the elasticity ε lies between 0 and −1, the percentage change in quantity is smaller than the percentage change in price. Thus, demand is inelastic in the sense that it changes little in response to a price change. As a physical analogy, if you try to stretch a rope, it stretches only slightly. The change in price is the force pulling at demand, just as your effort provides the force pulling at the rope. If the quantity demanded does not change much in response to this force, we say that the demand curve is inelastic.

At the midpoint of the linear demand curve, a 1% increase in price causes a 1% fall in quantity, so the elasticity equals −1, which we refer to as *unitary elasticity*.[4] At prices higher than at the midpoint of the demand curve ($6 on the coffee demand curve), the elasticity of demand is less than negative one, $\varepsilon < -1$. That is, the elasticity is a more negative number because it is larger in absolute value. In this range, the demand curve is *elastic*. A physical analogy is a rubber band that stretches substantially when you pull on it. A 1% increase in price causes a more than 1% fall in quantity. Figure 3.1 shows that the coffee demand elasticity is −3 where the price is $9 and 3 million tons are demanded: a 1% increase in price causes a 3% drop in quantity.

Where the demand curve hits the price axis at $p = \$12$ and $Q = 0$, the elasticity of demand is $\varepsilon = -(12/0)$, which is not defined. As Q approaches zero, the elasticity becomes a larger and larger negative number that approaches negative infinity, $-\infty$. The demand curve is *perfectly elastic* at the point where $Q = 0$. Because quantity is zero at $p = 12$, if we lower the price even slightly so that the quantity demanded becomes positive, the percentage increase in quantity demanded is infinite.

---

[4]At the midpoint of a general linear demand curve, $Q = a/2$ and $p = -a/(2b)$, so, using Equation 3.6, $\varepsilon = bp/Q = -b(a/[2b])/(a/2) = -1$.

Q&A 3.2

An estimated linear equation for the U.S. corn demand function is[5]

$$Q = 15.6 - 0.5p,$$

where p is the price in dollars per bushel and Q is the quantity demanded in billion bushels per year. Use Excel to calculate the price elasticity of demand for every price between \$2 and \$10 in one-dollar increments. Round the elasticity to three digits after the decimal point. Is the demand curve more elastic or less elastic at higher prices?

Answer

1. *Open an Excel spreadsheet; put titles "Price," "Quantity," and "Elasticity" in cells A1, B1, and C1; and put prices 2 through 10 in one-dollar increments in cells A2 through A10.*

2. *Use the corn demand function to fill in quantities in column B. Enter "=15.6−0.5*A2" in cell B2. Then copy cell B2 and paste it into cells B3 through B10. The quantity associated with each price in column A should appear in column B.*

3. *Use the elasticity formula for a linear demand function given by Equation 3.6 to fill in column C. Using Equation 3.6, $\varepsilon = bp/Q = -0.5p/Q$, because $b = -0.5$ in the corn demand function. Therefore, enter "=−0.5*A2/B2" in cell C2. Copy cell C2 and paste it into cells C3 through C10. The elasticity associated with each price in column A should appear in column B. Use Excel's format feature to round to three digits after the decimal point.*

4. *The spreadsheet shows that higher prices are associated with elasticities that are "more negative" (negative numbers that are larger in absolute value).*

	A	B	C
1	Price	Quantity	Elasticity
2	2	14.6	-0.068
3	3	14.1	-0.106
4	4	13.6	-0.147
5	5	13.1	-0.191
6	6	12.6	-0.238
7	7	12.1	-0.289
8	8	11.6	-0.345
9	9	11.1	-0.405
10	10	10.6	-0.472

Horizontal Demand Curves. Horizontal demand curves have constant elasticity (as do vertical demand curves). The demand curve that is horizontal at p^* in panel a of Figure 3.2 implies that people are willing to buy as much as firms want to sell at any price less than or equal to p^*. If the price increases even slightly above p^*,

---

[5]This demand curve is a linearized version of the estimated demand curve in Roberts and Schlenker (2013).

FIGURE 3.2 Vertical and Horizontal Demand Curves

(a) A horizontal demand curve is perfectly elastic at p*.
(b) A vertical demand curve is perfectly inelastic at every price.

(c) The demand curve for insulin of an individual with diabetes is perfectly inelastic below p* and perfectly elastic at p*, which is the maximum price the individual can afford to pay.

however, demand falls to zero. Thus, a small increase in price causes an infinite drop in quantity, so the demand curve is perfectly elastic.[6]

A horizontal demand curve is an extreme case of a linear demand curve: it is the flattest possible linear demand curve. Unlike downward-sloping linear demand curves, a horizontal demand curve does not have the property that the elasticity changes along the demand curve. For a horizontal demand curve, the elasticity is negative infinity at every point.

Why would a good's demand curve be horizontal? One reason is that consumers view this good as identical to another good and do not care which one they buy. If consumers regard Gala apples grown in Washington and Gala apples grown in Oregon as identical, they won't buy Washington apples if these sell at a higher price than those from Oregon. Similarly, they won't buy Oregon apples if their price is higher than that of Washington apples. If the two prices are equal, consumers do not care which type of Gala apple they buy. Thus, the demand curve for Oregon apples is horizontal at the price of Washington apples.

Vertical Demand Curves. A vertical demand curve, as in panel b in Figure 3.2, is perfectly inelastic everywhere. Such a demand curve is an extreme case of a linear demand curve—the opposite extreme from the horizontal demand curve. A vertical demand curve has an infinite (vertical) slope. A vertical demand function is also a special case of the constant-elasticity demand function. If ε takes on the value 0, then the demand function is $Q = Ap^0 = A$, so the demand curve is a vertical line at quantity A. If the price goes up, the quantity demanded is unchanged, so $\Delta Q = 0$. The elasticity of demand as given by Equation 3.1 must be zero: $(\Delta Q/\Delta p)(p/Q) = (0/\Delta p)(p/Q) = 0$.

A demand curve is vertical for *essential goods*—goods that people feel they must have and will pay anything to get. Because Jerry has diabetes, his demand curve for insulin could be vertical at a day's dose, Q^*. Panel c of Figure 3.2 assumes that the maximum feasible price is p^* and illustrates that the quantity demanded is unchanged at Q^* for all possible prices less than p^*.

---

[6]Using the constant-elasticity demand function, as ε becomes a very large negative number, the demand curve becomes increasingly flat and approaches a horizontal line.

Other Types of Demand Elasticities

In addition to the price elasticity of demand, we can also use elasticities to summarize how quantity demanded changes in response to changes in variables other than the good's price. Two such elasticities are the income elasticity of demand and the cross-price elasticity of demand.

The **income elasticity of demand** is the percentage change in the quantity demanded divided by the percentage change in income, Y:

$$\frac{\text{percentage change in quantity demanded}}{\text{percentage change in income}} = \frac{\Delta Q/Q}{\Delta Y/Y} = \frac{\Delta Q}{\Delta Y}\frac{Y}{Q}.$$

We say a good is a **normal good** if the quantity demanded increases as income rises. That is, a normal good has a positive income elasticity of demand. Goods like coffee or music downloads are normal goods: people buy more of them when their incomes rise. Conversely, a good is an **inferior good** if the quantity demanded falls as income rises. Inferior goods have negative income elasticities. For many college students, Kraft Macaroni & Cheese (food in a box) is an inferior good—they buy it when their incomes are low but switch to more appealing and expensive foods when their incomes rise.

The **cross-price elasticity of demand** is the percentage change in the quantity demanded divided by the percentage change in the price of another good, p_o:

$$\frac{\text{percentage change in quantity demanded}}{\text{percentage change in other price}} = \frac{\Delta Q/Q}{\Delta p_o/p_o} = \frac{\Delta Q}{\Delta p_o}\frac{p_o}{Q}.$$

The cross-price elasticity of demand determines whether goods are complements, substitutes, or unrelated goods. When the cross-price elasticity is negative, people buy less of the good if the price of the other good rises. Such goods are *complements*. For example, if some people insist on having sugar in their coffee, then, as the price of sugar rises, they consume less coffee. The cross-price elasticity of coffee demanded with respect to the price of sugar is therefore negative and coffee and sugar are complements.

If, alternatively, the cross-price elasticity is positive, the goods are *substitutes*. As the price of one good rises, people buy more of the substitute good. For example, cotton and wool are substitutes, and so the quantity of cotton demanded increases if the price of wool rises. If the cross-price elasticity is zero, then the goods are unrelated. Coffee and wool are unrelated goods. An increase in the price of wool has no effect on the quantity of coffee demanded (see Chapter 2).

Mini-Case Anti-Smoking Policies May Reduce Drunk Driving	Anyone who has seen bar scenes in old movies will know that smoking and drinking apparently go together: they're complements. Recent research has examined this relationship more rigorously, showing clearly that cigarettes and alcohol are complements. When the price of cigarettes rises or when smoking becomes more difficult (due to smoking bans, for example) people smoke less *and* drink less. The cross-elasticity of demand for alcohol with respect to cigarette prices is substantial. Krauss et al. (2014) found that a 1% increase in the price of cigarettes gives rise to almost a 1% decline in alcohol consumption. That is, the cross-price elasticity between alcoholic beverages and cigarettes is almost −1. Over the past two decades, smoking bans in workplaces, restaurants, bars, and other public places have become increasingly common. In 1995, California

introduced one of the United States' first statewide bans on smoking in public places, including bars and restaurants. Many other states followed suit, mostly about a decade later, although some, such as Texas and Alaska, still do not have statewide bans on smoking in public places. Smoking bans are common in much of the world, including in Australia, Canada, and most of Europe. China introduced a nationwide ban on smoking in enclosed public spaces in 2011, although enforcement is apparently very inconsistent. The Netherlands banned separate smoking rooms in hospitality facilities in 2018.

The complementarity between smoking and drinking implies that tobacco taxes (which raise the price of cigarettes) and restrictions on smoking have two health benefits. First, the tax reduces the negative health effects of smoking. Second, the tax reduces the negative effects of excessive drinking, including the very serious health risks created by drunk driving.

Demand Elasticities over Time

The shape of a demand curve depends on the period under consideration. Often consumers substitute between products in the long run but not in the short run. The price of U.S. gasoline in May 2018 was nearly one-third higher than in the previous year. However, most consumers did not change their consumption demand very much in the short run. Someone who drives 27 miles to and from work every day in a Ford Explorer did not suddenly start using less gasoline. However, if gas prices were to remain high in the long run, people would reduce their consumption of gasoline. Many people would buy smaller, more fuel-efficient cars; some would take jobs closer to home; and some would even move closer to their work or to convenient public transportation.

Liddle (2012) estimated the gasoline demand elasticities across many countries and found that the short-run elasticity for gasoline was −0.16 and the long-run elasticity was −0.43. Thus, a 1% increase in price lowers the quantity demanded by only 0.16% in the short run but by more than twice as much, 0.43%, in the long run.

Other Elasticities

We can summarize the relationship between any two related variables using an elasticity. In addition to the various demand elasticities that we've mentioned, others are also important. For example, just as we might measure the price elasticity of demand, we might also measure the **price elasticity of supply**, which is the percentage change in quantity supplied divided by the percentage change in price. It shows the percentage increase in quantity supplied arising from a 1% increase in price. A manager might be interested in the elasticity of cost with respect to output, which shows the percentage increase in cost arising from a 1% increase in output. Or, during labor negotiations, a manager might cite the elasticity of output with respect to labor, which would show the percentage increase in output arising from a 1% increase in labor input, holding other inputs constant.

Estimating Demand Elasticities

Price, income, and cross-price demand elasticities are important managerial tools. With these tools, managers can predict how the quantity demanded will respond to changes in consumer income, the product's own price, or the price of a related good. Managers use this information to set prices, as in the iTunes example, and in many other ways.

Managers use data to calculate or estimate elasticities. For example, Q&A 3.1 shows how a manager can observe the quantity effect of a change in price to determine the elasticity of demand for Amazon Prime memberships. Such a before-and-after price change calculation uses data from before the price change and after the price change to calculate an arc elasticity. By comparing quantities just before and just after a price change, managers can be reasonably sure that other variables that might affect the quantity demanded, such as income, have not changed appreciably.

Managers at iTunes could do such calculations for many songs and obtain an estimate of how the iTunes price change affected overall sales. They could then use this information to make other decisions about iTunes—such as how quickly to expand and upgrade server capacity or whether to charge different prices for various songs.

However, it may not always be feasible or desirable for a manager to calculate a before-and-after arc elasticity. To avoid a potentially expensive mistake, a manager often wants an estimate of the demand elasticity before actually making a price change. Similarly, a manager may fear a reaction by a rival firm in response to a pricing experiment. A manager wants to know the effect on demand of many possible price changes rather than focusing on just one price change. Such information enables the manager to select the best possible price rather than simply choosing between two particular prices. In effect, the manager would like an estimate of the entire demand curve. Regression analysis is an empirical technique that managers can use to estimate an entire demand curve or other important economic relationships.

3.2 Regression Analysis

Regression analysis is a statistical technique used to estimate the mathematical relationship between a *dependent variable*, such as quantity demanded, and one or more *explanatory variables*, such as price and income. The **dependent variable** is the variable whose variation is to be explained. The **explanatory variables** are those factors thought to affect the value of the dependent variable.

We focus on using regression analysis to estimate demand functions. However, regression analysis is a powerful tool that managers can also use to estimate many other important relationships, such as between cost and output or between wages and productivity. The use of regression analysis and related statistical methods in economics and business is called *econometrics*.

A Demand Function Example

To illustrate the use of regression, we estimate a demand function, where the dependent variable is the quantity demanded. In general, a demand function may include a number of explanatory variables. However, we initially focus on the case with only *one explanatory variable*, the price. We assume that other factors possibly affecting the quantity demanded, such as income and prices of related goods, remain constant during the relevant period. A demand function with price as the only explanatory variable defines a demand curve.

We also assume initially that the demand function is *linear*. That is, the demand curve is a straight line, as in Figure 3.1.

The Demand Function and the Inverse Demand Function. We can write the relationship between the quantity demanded and the price in two ways. Quantity is a function of price in a *demand function*, whereas price is a function of quantity in an *inverse demand function*.

An example of a linear demand function with only one explanatory variable is Equation 3.4: $Q = a + bp$. We can use algebra to rearrange this linear demand equation so that the price is on the left side and the quantity is on the right side. By subtracting a from both sides to obtain $Q - a = bp$, dividing both sides of the equation by b to obtain $(1/b)Q - a/b = p$, and rearranging the terms in the equation, we obtain

$$p = -\frac{a}{b} + \frac{1}{b}Q = g + hQ, \tag{3.9}$$

where $g = -a/b > 0$ and $h = 1/b < 0$, because b is negative. This equation, with p on the left side, is the *inverse demand function*. If a demand function is a linear function of p, as in Equation 3.4, then the inverse demand function, Equation 3.9, is a linear function of Q with constant coefficients g and h.

The inverse demand function and the demand function contain exactly the same information. Both versions of the demand relationship yield the same straight line when plotted on a diagram, and analysts commonly use both versions. Indeed, many people ignore the distinction between the inverse and direct forms and use the term *demand function* to describe both.

However, when doing regression analysis it is necessary to be clear about which version of the demand function we are estimating. In regression analysis, we put the dependent variable on the left side of the equation and the explanatory variable on the right side.

For example, suppose that Bill, the manager of the only lawn care firm in town, surveys customers about how many lawn treatments they will buy at various prices. He views the price as the explanatory variable and the quantity as the dependent variable, so he uses the survey to estimate a demand function. If instead his survey asked how much customers were willing to pay for various numbers of lawn treatments, he would estimate the inverse demand function.

Random Errors. For illustrative purposes, we have so far treated the estimated coffee demand function, $Q = 12 - p$, as if it were precisely accurate. This demand function tells us that if price is $2, then the quantity demanded is 10 (million tons), and if price rises to $3, then quantity demanded falls to 9. The real world is not that precise. When we look at actual data, we might see that in a year when price was $2, quantity demanded was slightly less than 10, while in a year when price was $3, quantity demanded was slightly more than 9. In practical terms, an estimated demand function is only an approximation; it does not necessarily match actual data perfectly. The imperfection in our estimate arises because we can never hold constant all the possible non-price factors that affect demand.

For example, if a new study reporting that coffee has previously unknown health benefits appeared during the period covered by our data, it might have caused the quantity demanded to increase for reasons unrelated to price. Conversely, another study suggesting negative health effects might have had the opposite effect. Many other factors, including random changes in consumer tastes, might also play a role. Or the data may contain errors. For instance, one year someone may have failed to record a large coffee shipment, so that it never showed up in the official data. Thus, the quantity demanded from year to year may vary in the data for many reasons aside from price changes.

If these other factors that affect demand are observed, such as consumers' income, we can include these variables as explanatory variables when we estimate our demand function. However, some relevant factors are not observable, and hence we cannot include them. When we estimate a demand function using regression analysis, we capture the effect of these unobserved variables by adding a *random error term*, e, to the demand equation:

$$Q = a + bp + e. \tag{3.10}$$

The **random error term** captures the effects of unobserved influences on the dependent variable that are not included as explanatory variables. The error is called *random* because these factors that might affect demand are unpredictable or even unknowable from the manager's point of view.

Regression analysis seeks to estimate the underlying straight line showing the true effect of price on the quantity demanded by estimating a and b in Equation 3.4 while taking account of the random error term. If we could somehow hold e constant at zero, we could obtain various combinations of Q and p and trace out the straight line given by Equation 3.4, $Q = a + bp$. However, if e does not equal zero, then the observed Q is not on this line. For example, if e takes on a positive value for one year, corresponding to some positive random effect on demand, then the actual Q is larger than the value implied by the linear demand curve $Q = a + bp$.

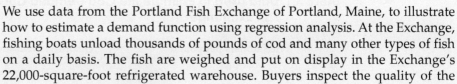

Mini-Case

The Portland Fish Exchange

We use data from the Portland Fish Exchange of Portland, Maine, to illustrate how to estimate a demand function using regression analysis. At the Exchange, fishing boats unload thousands of pounds of cod and many other types of fish on a daily basis. The fish are weighed and put on display in the Exchange's 22,000-square-foot refrigerated warehouse. Buyers inspect the quality of the day's catch. At noon, an auction takes place in a room overlooking the fish in the warehouse. Fleece-clad buyers representing fish dealers and restaurants sit facing a screen, an auctioneer, and representatives of the sellers. A screen at the front of the room shows bid information. Thousands of pounds of fish sell rapidly.

The quantity of fish delivered each day, Q, varies due to fluctuations in weather and other factors. Because fish spoils rapidly, all the fish must sell immediately. Therefore, the daily auction price for cod adjusts to induce buyers to demand the amount of cod available on that particular day. The price-quantity combination for cod on any particular day represents a point on the cod demand curve.

For each day it operates, the Portland Fish Exchange reports the quantity (in pounds) of each particular type of fish sold and the price for that type of fish. For example, on June 8, 2015, 2,946 lb of large white hake sold for \$0.97 per lb. A collection of such observations provides a data set that can be used for demand analysis using regression.

Here, quantity is the explanatory variable. Whatever quantity comes to market sells that day. Price adjusts to ensure that the amount of fish available meets the buyers' demand. As the quantity brought to market "explains" the price, we estimate an inverse demand curve.

Regression Analysis Using Microsoft Excel.

We illustrate how to estimate a linear regression based on data for cod from the Portland Fish Exchange, using Microsoft Excel. Table 3.1 shows a data set (or *sample*) based on reports published online by the Portland Fish Exchange. Each data point is a pair of numbers: the price (dollars per pound) and the quantity of cod (thousands of pounds) bought on a particular day. Our analysis uses eight daily observations. We have ordered the data from the smallest quantity to the largest to make the table easy to read.

Figure 3.3 shows the data points in this sample. Estimating this linear regression is equivalent to drawing a straight line through these data points such that the data points are as close as possible to the line. To fit this line through the quantity-price observations for cod, we estimate the linear inverse demand function, Equation 3.9, with an error term attached:

$$p = g + hQ + e. \tag{3.11}$$

The error term, e, captures random fluctuations in factors other than quantity that affect the price on a given day, such as random variations in the number of buyers who show up from day to day.[7] We expect that the error term averages zero in large samples.[8]

TABLE 3.1   Data Used to Estimate the Cod Demand Curve at the Portland Fish Exchange

Price, dollars per pound	Quantity, thousand pounds per day
1.90	1.5
1.35	2.2
1.25	4.4
1.20	5.9
0.95	6.5
0.85	7.0
0.73	8.8
0.25	10.1

---

[7]The cod supply curve each day is vertical at Q and largely determined by weather and government regulations on fishing. Because the quantity is determined independent of the price, it is said to be *exogenous*. As a result, we can use quantity to help explain the movement of the dependent variable, price, in our regression equation. Where the supply curve intersects the demand curve determines the equilibrium price for that day. Thus, fluctuations in the quantity—shifts in the vertical supply curve—trace out the demand curve. The dependent variable, price, is *endogenous*: it is determined inside the system by quantity and by the unobserved variables incorporated into the error term. If quantity and price are simultaneously determined—that is, both are endogenous variables—the demand curve should be estimated using different techniques than those we discuss here.

[8]We use a small data set in this and later examples to keep the presentation short and clear. In practice, regression analysis would normally involve many more observations. Although some studies use only 30 or 40 observations, most regression studies would normally involve hundreds or even thousands of observations, depending on the availability of data.

FIGURE 3.3 Observed Price-Quantity Data Points for the Portland Fish Exchange

Each dot indicates a particular price and the quantity of cod demanded at that price on a particular day at the Portland Fish Exchange.

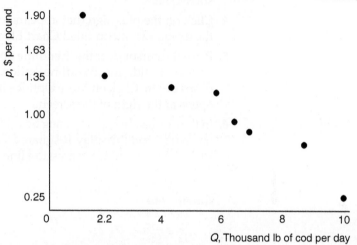

In Equation 3.11, g and h are the true coefficients, which describe the actual relationship between price and quantity along the cod inverse demand function. The regression provides us with estimates of these coefficients, $\hat{g}$ and $\hat{h}$, which we can use to predict the expected price, $\hat{p}$, for a given quantity:

$$\hat{p} = \hat{g} + \hat{h}Q. \tag{3.12}$$

One way to estimate $\hat{g}$ and $\hat{h}$ is to use the Microsoft Excel Trendline option for scatterplots.[9]

1. Enter the quantity data in column A and the price data in column B.

2. Select the data, click on the Insert tab, and select the "Insert Scatter (X, Y) or Bubble Chart" option in the Chart area of the toolbar. A menu of scatterplot types will appear, as the following screenshot shows.

[9]The following screenshots and detailed instructions are for the Windows version of Excel 2016. The Macintosh versions and other Windows versions of Excel are similar. Helpful instructions can be found in the Excel *Help* facility. Or search online for "Help Excel Trendline."

3. Click on the first scatterplot type, which is "Scatter." A chart appears in the spreadsheet.

4. Click on the plus sign that appears just outside the upper right corner to obtain the dropdown menu titled Chart Elements.

5. Place the cursor over the Trendline option in the Chart Elements menu. An arrow appears beside the Trendline option. Click on this arrow. An additional menu drops down. Click on More Options in this menu. A Format Trendline dialog box opens at the right of the screen.

6. In the Format Trendline dialog box select the options "Linear," "Display Equation on chart," and "Display R-squared value on chart," as the following screenshot shows. The estimated regression line appears in the diagram.

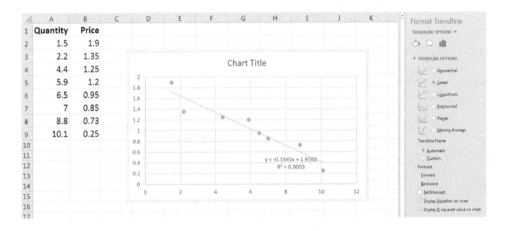

By default, Excel refers to the variable on the vertical axis as y (which is our p) and the variable on the horizontal axis as x (which is our Q). Rounding the coefficient estimates to two decimal places, we obtain the estimated inverse demand function

$$\hat{p} = 1.96 - 0.15Q, \qquad (3.13)$$

where $\hat{g} = 1.96$ and $\hat{h} = -0.15$ are the estimated coefficients.

The estimated inverse function implies a demand curve that hits the price axis at $\hat{g} = 1.96$, where the price is high enough to drive the quantity demanded to zero. The estimated coefficient $\hat{h} = -0.15$ is the slope of the demand curve. As the quantity increases by one unit (that is, by 1,000 pounds), the estimated change in price needed to induce buyers to purchase this larger quantity is $\hat{h} = -\$0.15 = -15¢$.[10]

Ordinary Least Squares Regression.

How does the regression routine in Excel estimate the parameters $\hat{g}$ and $\hat{h}$? The objective of the regression procedure is to select a regression line that *fits* the data well in the sense that the line is as close as possible to all the observed points.

---

[10]The price is $\hat{p}_1 = \hat{g} + \hat{h}Q$ when quantity is Q and $\hat{p}_2 = \hat{g} + \hat{h}(Q + 1)$ when quantity is $Q + 1$. Thus, the change in price is $p_2 - p_1 = (\hat{g} + \hat{h}[Q + 1]) - (\hat{g} + \hat{h}Q) = \hat{h}$. Similarly, using calculus, $d\hat{p}/dQ = \hat{h}$.

As Figure 3.4 shows, it would be impossible to draw a single straight line that fits the data perfectly by going through all eight points. Figure 3.4 shows that the actual prices and the prices predicted by the regression line differ. The second data point from the left ($p = \$1.35$ and $Q = 2.2$) has the largest gap between the actual and predicted prices. The predicted price, given by Equation 3.13, for $Q = 2.2$ is $\hat{p} = 1.96 - 0.15Q = 1.96 - (0.15 \times 2.2) = 1.63$.

The gap between the actual value of the dependent variable (price) and the predicted value is called a *residual*. For this observation, the residual is $\$1.35 - \$1.63 = -\$0.28$, indicating that the actual price is 28¢ below the estimated price.

The objective of a regression method is to fit the line to the data such that the residuals are collectively small in some sense. However, different criteria might be used to measure the quality of the fit, leading to different regression methods.

The most commonly used regression method is *ordinary least squares* (OLS). Excel uses this method in its scatterplot Trendline option. The OLS regression method fits the line to minimize the sum of the squared residuals. If $\hat{e}_1$ is the residual for the first data point, $\hat{e}_2$ is the residual for the second data point, and so on, then OLS minimizes the sum $\hat{e}_1^2 + \hat{e}_2^2 + \cdots + \hat{e}_8^2$.[11]

FIGURE 3.4 An Estimated Demand Curve for Cod at the Portland Fish Exchange

The dots show the actual quantity-price pair data points. The line is the estimated regression line of the linear relationship between the price and the quantity: $\hat{p} = \hat{g} + \hat{h}Q = 1.96 - 0.15Q$. The gap between the actual price, p, at a given quantity and the estimated price, $\hat{p}$, is the residual for Day i, $\hat{e}_i = p_i - \hat{p}_i$. The figure shows the residual for the second day, where $Q = 2.2$, the observed price is $p_2 = \$1.35$, and the estimated price is $\hat{p}_2 = \$1.63$, so the residual is $\hat{e}_2 = -\$0.28 = \$1.35 - \$1.63$.

---

[11]If we have a regression equation of the form $Y = a + bX + e$, the formulas used by spreadsheets and statistical programs to determine the OLS parameters are

$$\hat{b} = \frac{\sum_{i=1}^{n}(X_i - \overline{X})(Y_i - \overline{Y})}{\sum_{i=1}^{n}(X_i - \overline{X})^2}, \text{ and } \hat{a} = \overline{Y} - \hat{b}\overline{X},$$

where the observations are indexed by i, the data set has n observations, a bar above a variable indicates the average value of that variable, and the symbol $\sum_{i=1}^{n}$ indicates that the following expression should be summed from observation 1 through observation n.

Multivariate Regression

We call a regression with two or more explanatory variables a **multivariate regression** or *multiple regression*. In our cod example, if the price consumers are willing to pay for a given quantity increases with income, Y, then we would estimate an inverse demand function that incorporates both quantity and income as explanatory variables as

$$p = g + hQ + iY + e, \tag{3.14}$$

where g, h, and i are coefficients to be estimated, and e is a random error.

Using OLS, we would estimate the regression line:

$$\hat{p} = \hat{g} + \hat{h}Q + \hat{i}Y,$$

where $\hat{g}$, $\hat{h}$, and $\hat{i}$ are the estimated coefficients and $\hat{p}$ is the *predicted value* of p for any given levels of Q and Y. The objective of an OLS multivariate regression is to fit the data so that the sum of squared residuals is as small as possible, where the residual for any data point is the difference between actual price, p, and predicted price, $\hat{p}$.

A multivariate regression is able to isolate the effects of each explanatory variable, holding the other explanatory variables constant. We estimated a linear demand function for the U.S. avocado market, using the price of avocados and income as explanatory variables:

$$\hat{Q} = 120 - 40p + 0.01Y, \tag{3.15}$$

where quantity is measured in millions of lb per month, price is measured in dollars per lb, and Y is the average monthly household income in dollars. According to this estimated equation, if average income rises by $200 per month and the price of avocados stays constant, then the estimated quantity would rise by $0.01 \times 200 = 2$ million lb per month. The regression equation allows us to estimate the effect of changing only one variable, like income, while holding other explanatory variables constant. Similarly, if income remains constant and the price increases by $0.05 ($ = 5¢$) per lb, then the estimated quantity demanded changes by $-40 \times 0.05 = -2$ million lb per month.

Q&A 3.3

The manager of a trucking company that specializes in avocado transport uses the estimated demand function, Equation 3.15, to predict the quantity of avocados demanded at a price of $2.70 and a monthly income level of $6,000. What is the predicted quantity? If the actual quantity turns out to be 76 (million lb) what is the residual? Why would the predicted quantity differ from the actual quantity?

Answer

1. *Use the estimated demand function, Equation 3.15, to predict the quantity of avocados demanded.* Substitute the price of $2.70 and the income of $6,000 into the estimated demand function to obtain the predicted quantity demanded:

$$\hat{Q} = 120 - 40(2.70) + 0.01(6,000) = 72.$$

2. *Take the difference between the actual and the predicted quantity demanded to determine the residual.* Given that the actual quantity is 76, the residual is $76 - 72 = 4$. The actual quantity differs from the predicted quantity because of the random error reflecting other variables not explicitly included in the regression equation.

Goodness of Fit and the R^2 Statistic

Because an estimated regression line rarely goes through all the data points, managers want some measure of how well the estimated regression line fits the data. One measure of the *goodness of fit* of the regression line to the data is the R^2 (R-squared) statistic. The R^2 *statistic* is the share of the dependent variable's variation that is "explained by the regression"—that is, accounted for by the explanatory variables in the estimated regression equation. The highest possible value for R^2 is 1, which indicates that 100% of the variation in the dependent variable is explained by the regression. Such an outcome occurs if the dependent variable lies on the regression line for every observation.

If some observations do not lie on the regression line, as in Figure 3.4, then the R^2 is less than 1. The variation in the dependent variable that is not explained by the regression line is due to the error term in the regression. The lowest possible value for R^2 is zero, where the estimated regression explains none of the variation in the dependent variable. The R^2 is zero if we try to fit a line through a cloud of points with no slope. Thus, the R^2 statistic must lie between 0 and 1.

For example, Mai owns bakeries in two different small towns, where she faces no competition. She wants to know how many fewer pies she will sell if she raises her price, so she runs experiments in each town. At each bakery, she sets a new price each week for 14 consecutive weeks, so that she observes 14 weekly price-quantity combinations for each town. She then runs a regression to estimate the weekly demand function, $Q = a + bp$, Equation 3.4, in each town, where we expect that a is positive and b is negative.

Figure 3.5 illustrates these two regressions based on different data sets. In panel a, all the data points are very close to the estimated demand curve. That is, almost all variation in the number of pies demanded is explained by the regression. The R^2 statistic is 0.98, which is close to 1, indicating that the regression line provides very good

FIGURE 3.5 Two Estimated Apple Pie Demand Curves with Different R^2 Statistics

Mai, a bakery owner, changes the price of apple pie every Friday for 14 weeks to determine the weekly demand curve for apple pie. The observed price-quantity data points lie close to the estimated demand curve in panel a, where $R^2 = 0.98$. In panel b, where $R^2 = 0.54$, the data points are more widely scattered around the estimated demand curve.

(a) $R^2 = 0.98$

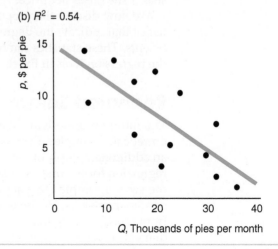

(b) $R^2 = 0.54$

predictions of the amount demanded at any given price. (As the Portland cod regression screenshot illustrates, Excel's Trendline includes an option to calculate the R^2.)

In contrast, the regression line in panel b does not fit the data as well. This panel shows some large divergences between data points and the predicted values on the regression line due to large random errors, and the R^2 statistic is only 0.54. Thus, Mai is more confident that she can predict the effect of a price change in the first town than in the second.

Managerial Implication	*A recent survey of North American males found 41% were overweight, 32% were critically obese, and 7% ate the survey. —Banksy*

Focus Groups

Managers interested in estimating market demand curves often can obtain data from published sources, as in our Portland Fish Exchange example. However, if Mai, the baker, wants to estimate the demand function for her firm, she must collect the relevant data herself. To estimate her firm's demand curve, she needs information about how many units customers would demand at various prices.

To obtain this information, Mai can hire a specialized marketing firm to recruit and question a *focus group*, which consists of a number of her actual or potential consumers. The marketing firm asks members of the group how many pies per week they would want to buy at various prices. Alternatively, the marketing firm might conduct an online or written survey of potential customers designed to elicit similar information, which can be used to estimate a demand curve. Mai should use a focus group if it's the least costly method of learning about the demand curve she faces.

3.3 Properties and Statistical Significance of Estimated Coefficients

Mai is particularly concerned about how close the estimated coefficients of the demand function Equation 3.4, $\hat{a}$ and $\hat{b}$, are to the true values. She cares because she wants to know how reliably she can predict the reduction in the number of pies she sells if she raises her price.

We now discuss the properties of these estimated coefficients and describe statistics that indicate the degree of confidence we can place in these estimated coefficients. These statistics can be obtained using most regression software, including the regression tools in Excel.

Repeated Samples

The intuition underlying statistical measures of confidence and significance rests on repeated samples. For example, Mai could use another focus group to generate an additional sample of data. She could then run a new regression and compare the regression for the first sample to that from this new focus group. If the results from the second sample were similar to those from the first, she would be more confident in the results. However, if the results of the second sample were very different from those of the first, she might have serious doubts about whether the estimated demand parameters $\hat{a}$ and $\hat{b}$ from either focus group were close to the true values.

Often it is costly, difficult, or impossible to gather repeated samples to assess the reliability of regression estimates. However, we can do something similar—we can divide a large data set into two subsamples and treat each subsample like a separate experiment. We can use each subsample to calculate regression parameter estimates. For that matter, we can take many random subsamples of the data set and generate estimates for each one. We can then assess whether the different parameter estimates for the different subsamples tend to be similar or widely dispersed.

Although analysts sometimes run regressions on random subsets of the data and use them to construct a set of parameter estimates, it may be unnecessary. Given certain (usually reasonable) assumptions, we can use statistical formulas to determine how much we would expect the parameter estimates to vary across samples. The nature of this potential variation allows us to assess how much confidence to place in particular regression results.

Desirable Properties for Estimated Coefficients

We would like our regression estimation method to have two properties. First, we would like the estimation technique to be *unbiased* in the sense that the estimated coefficients are not systematically lower or systematically higher than the true coefficients. An estimation method is **unbiased** if it produces an estimated coefficient, $\hat{b}$, that equals the true coefficient, b, on average. The ordinary least squares regression method is unbiased under mild conditions.[12]

The second property we would like an estimation technique to have is that the estimates should not vary greatly if we repeat the analysis many times using other samples. If we have two proposed unbiased estimation methods, we prefer the method that yields estimates that are consistently closer to the true values rather than a method that produces widely dispersed estimates in repeated samples. An important theoretical result in statistics is that under a wide range of conditions, the ordinary least squares estimation method produces estimates that vary less than other relevant unbiased estimation methods.

For each estimated coefficient, the regression program calculates a standard error. The *standard error* is a measure of how much each estimated coefficient would vary if we re-estimated the same underlying true demand relation with many different random samples of observations. The smaller the standard error of an estimated coefficient, the smaller the expected variation in the estimates obtained from different samples. A small standard error means that the various estimated coefficients would be tightly bunched around the true coefficient. If the standard error is large, the estimated coefficients are imprecise indicators of the true values.

A Focus Group Example

Consumers are statistics. Customers are people. —Stanley Marcus (early president of Neiman Marcus)

To illustrate these ideas, suppose that Toyota has asked us to conduct a focus group to predict how the number of Toyota Camry vehicles demanded would change if the

---

[12]One important condition for OLS estimation to be unbiased is that the equation be properly specified so that all relevant explanatory variables are included and the functional form is appropriate.

price changes. We arrange a focus group of 50 prospective car buyers to illustrate how Toyota could answer this question. We ask members of the group if they would be willing to buy a Camry at various prices. As a result, for each of eight prices ranging from $5,000 to $40,000, we have information on how many Camry vehicles this group would demand.

We estimate a linear demand function of the form $Q = a + bp + e$ and obtain standard errors to assess the reliability of the estimated parameters. The Excel Trendline does not provide standard errors. However, Excel's Regression tool provides them.[13] We demonstrate how to use this tool in an Excel Screenshot and corresponding step-by-step instructions.

	A	B	C	D	E	F	G
1	**Quantity**	**Price**					
2	1	40					
3	2	35					
4	7	30					
5	16	25					
6	24	20					
7	35	15					
8	40	10					
9	47	5					

Data Analysis

Analysis Tools

Fourier Analysis
Histogram
Moving Average
Random Number Generation
Rank and Percentile
Regression
Sampling
t-Test: Paired Two Sample for Means
t-Test: Two-Sample Assuming Equal Variances
t-Test: Two-Sample Assuming Unequal Variances

OK   Cancel   Help

1. Enter the data in an Excel spreadsheet, as shown in the screenshot. Title the columns *Quantity* and *Price* and put the quantities in cells A2 through A9 and the prices (in thousands of dollars) in cells B2 through B9.

2. Click on the *Data* tab, then on the *Data Analysis* icon at the upper right of the spreadsheet.[14] The Data Analysis dialog box displays as shown. Select the *Regression* tool and click *OK*.

3. In the Regression dialog that displays, fill in the *Input Y Range* field (the dependent variable) by selecting cells A2 through A9 or by typing **A2:A9** into the box.

4. Fill in the *Input X Range* field (the explanatory variable) by selecting the cells containing the prices or by typing **B2:B9**.

5. Click the *Output Range* button, enter A12 in the associated box, and then click *OK*.

Excel displays the regression results. The coefficients indicate that the estimated regression line is $Q = 53.857 - 1.438p$. We can use this estimated demand function to predict the quantity demanded at any given price. According to our estimated demand function, if the price is 27 ($27,000), we expect the focus group consumers to buy $\hat{Q} = 53.857 - 1.438p = 15.03$ Camrys. We would round this estimate to 15 cars, given that cars are sold in discrete units. However, if this focus group

---

[13]The Regression tool uses ordinary least squares to estimate the regression line and can accommodate multiple explanatory variables. This tool is available in all Windows versions of Excel and in Excel for the Mac as of the 2016 version. See Excel *Help* for information.

[14]If you do not see the *Data Analysis* icon, the Analysis Toolpak is not installed in your version of Excel. See Excel *Help* for installation instructions. (Select the File tab, then click on the question mark in the upper right corner to reach *Help*.)

represented a large group, perhaps a thousand times larger (50,000 consumers), our estimate of quantity demanded would be 15,030 vehicles.

The Regression tool also displays other regression output. The R^2 statistic (called *R Square* by Excel) is 0.977, which is close to the maximum possible value. This high R^2 indicates that the regression line explains almost all the variation in the observed quantity. Excel also displays standard errors and confidence intervals.

Confidence Intervals

We know that an estimated coefficient is not likely to equal the true value exactly. Therefore, it is useful to construct a *confidence interval*, which provides a range of likely values for the true value of a coefficient, centered on the estimated coefficient. For example, a 95% confidence interval is a range of coefficient values constructed using a method such that the true value of the coefficient would lie in the specified interval 95% of the time in repeated samples.

The length of a confidence interval depends on the estimated standard error of the coefficient and the number of *degrees of freedom*, which is the *sample size* (number of observations) minus the number of coefficients estimated. In our Camry example, we have eight observations and estimate two coefficients, so we have six degrees of freedom.

In regressions with a large sample size, the lower end of a 95% confidence interval is (approximately) the estimated coefficient minus twice its estimated standard error, and the upper end of the interval is the estimated coefficient plus twice its estimated standard error.

With smaller sample sizes, the confidence interval is larger.[15] With the six degrees of freedom of the Camry demand function regression, the confidence interval is the estimated coefficient plus or minus 2.447 times the standard error. In this regression, the slope coefficient, $\hat{b}$, on the price is -1.438 and its standard error is 0.090. Therefore, the 95% confidence interval for $\hat{b}$ is centered on -1.438 and goes approximately from $-1.658 (= -1.438 - [2.447 \times 0.090])$ to $-1.218 (= -1.438 + [2.447 \times 0.090])$.

If the confidence interval is small, then we are reasonably sure that the true parameter lies close to the estimated coefficient. If the confidence interval is large, then we believe that parameter is not very precisely estimated. Typically, the more observations we have, the smaller the estimated standard errors and the tighter the confidence interval. Thus, having a larger data set tends to increase our confidence in our results.

Hypothesis Testing and Statistical Significance

There are two possible outcomes: if the result confirms the hypothesis, then you've made a measurement. If the result is contrary to the hypothesis, then you've made a discovery. —Enrico Fermi

A manager can use estimated coefficients and standard errors to test important hypotheses. Very often, the crucial issue for a manager is to determine whether a certain variable really influences another. For example, suppose a firm's manager runs a regression where the demand for the firm's product is a function of the product's

---

[15]The relevant number can be found in a *t*-statistic distribution table.

price and the prices charged by several possible rivals. If the true coefficient on a rival's price is zero, then the potential rival's product is not in the same market as the manager's product, and the manager can ignore that firm when making decisions. Thus, the manager wants to formally test the *null* hypothesis that the rival's coefficient is equal to zero.

One approach is to determine whether the 95% confidence interval for that coefficient includes zero. If the entire confidence interval for the coefficient on a rival's price contains only positive values, the manager can be confident that the explanatory variable has a positive effect: the higher the rival's prices, the greater the demand for the manager's product.

Equivalently, the manager can test the *null hypothesis* that the coefficient is zero using a *t*-statistic. Such a test is called a *t-test*. The Excel Regression tool reports *t*-statistics automatically. The *t*-statistic equals the estimated coefficient divided by its estimated standard error. That is, the *t*-statistic measures whether the estimated coefficient is large relative to the standard error. In the Camry example, the *t*-statistic for the constant or intercept coefficient is $53.857/2.260 \approx 23.8$, and the *t*-statistic on the price coefficient is $-1.438/0.0895 \approx -16.1$.

If the absolute value of the *t*-statistic is larger than a *critical value*, then we know that the confidence interval does not include zero, so our *t*-test tells us to reject the null hypothesis that the coefficient is zero. For large samples, this critical value is about 2, while in our Camry example it is 2.447.

That is, our rule is that we reject the null hypothesis at a 95% level of confidence if the absolute value of the *t*-statistic exceeds the critical value. An equivalent statement is that, given a *t*-statistic with a magnitude exceeding the critical value, we will be wrong less than 5% of the time if we reject the hypothesis that the explanatory variable has no effect. The chance that we are wrong when we use a test statistic to reject the null hypothesis is often referred to as the *significance level* of the hypothesis test. Thus, in a large sample, if the (absolute value of the) *t*-statistic is greater than about 2, we reject the null hypothesis that the proposed explanatory variable has no effect at the 5% significance level or 95% confidence level. Rather than use this somewhat convoluted formal statement, many analysts say simply that the explanatory variable is "statistically significant" or "statistically significantly different from zero."

3.4 Regression Specification

Far better an approximate answer to the right question, which is often vague, than an exact answer to the wrong question, which can always be made precise.
—John Tukey

The first step in a regression analysis is to select a regression equation. We must determine the **regression specification**, which includes the choice of the dependent variable, the explanatory variables, and the functional relationship between them (such as linear, quadratic, or exponential). For example, in the Camry demand function regression, the dependent variable is the quantity of Camrys demanded; the only explanatory variable is price, measured in thousands of dollars; and the functional relationship between the variables is linear: $Q = a + bp + e$.

A regression analysis is valid only if the regression equation is correctly specified. In particular, the specification should include the appropriate explanatory variables, it must closely approximate the true functional form, and the underlying assumptions about its error term should be correct.

Selecting Explanatory Variables

When selecting variables to include in a regression, we must take care in choosing which explanatory variables to include. We should use all the observable variables that are likely to have a meaningful effect on the dependent variable. We use our understanding of causal relationships, including those that derive from economic theory, to select explanatory variables. In the Camry focus group example, we used our knowledge of demand theory to conclude that the price was likely to affect the quantity demanded.

Mini-Case Determinants of CEO Compensation	*It is unfortunate we can't buy many business executives for what they are worth and sell them for what they think they are worth.* —Malcolm Forbes

Human resources managers often use regression studies to determine if their employees are paid comparably to individuals in similar positions in other firms.[16] The very high compensation that chief executive officers (CEOs) of many major corporations receive is a source of much controversy, and many large corporations are under pressure to provide evidence to justify their payments. We use multivariate regression to analyze the determinants of CEO compensation. We use economic theory and previous studies to choose the variables that we believe are important determinants of CEO compensation. Then, we test whether these variables belong in the equation.

In our regression analysis, we use data on CEO compensation from Standard & Poor's Execucomp database for the 1992–2017 period for corporations in the S&P 500, which is Standard & Poor's list of 500 large corporations whose shares are traded on the two major U.S. stock exchanges, the New York Stock Exchange (NYSE) and the NASDAQ. We have more than 9,300 observations in our data set, where the dependent variable in each observation is the CEO's annual compensation in a particular S&P 500 corporation in a particular year, along with the values of the proposed explanatory variables. Well over half of this compensation was in the form of stock options, which give the holder the right to buy stock in the company, typically at an attractive price far below the market value. The rest consisted primarily of salary and bonuses.

In our multivariate regression, the dependent variable, Y, is CEO compensation in thousands of dollars. We expect the compensation to be greater for CEOs who manage large firms because that requires more work and responsibility. We use two measures of firm size: assets, A (in \$ billions), which are related to the firm's capital input, and employees, L (thousands of workers). Presumably, a CEO receives more pay when the company does well. One measure of

---

[16]Another use is in union negotiations. A large firm retained one of us to perform a regression analysis to determine how its unionized employees' wages compared to wages of comparable unionized and nonunionized workers in other firms. The firm used this study to bargain with its union.

a company's success is shareholders' average return over the previous three years, S (in percentage points per year). This return includes dividends, which are direct payments to shareholders, and capital gains, which are increases in the value of the shares of the shareholders. A CEO may also be worth more to a firm as the CEO's experience, X (the number of years that the CEO has held this job), rises.

We use ordinary least squares to estimate a multivariate regression equation that relates a CEO's salary to these explanatory variables:

$$Y = a + bA + cL + dS + fX + e,$$

where a is a constant and the other coefficients show how much a one-unit increase in the corresponding explanatory variable affects CEO compensation. For example, one extra unit of employees (1,000 employees) raises the CEO salary by c. The estimated compensation as a function of the explanatory variables is $\hat{Y} = 7{,}063.7 + 10.2A + 12.6L + 35.7S + 73.9X$, as the following table of regression results shows.

CEO Compensation Regression Results

Explanatory Variable	Coefficient	Standard Error	t-Statistic
Constant	7,063.7	217.0	32.6*
Assets ($billions), A	10.2	0.9	11.3*
Employees (000s), L	12.6	1.3	9.5*
Shareholder return, S	35.7	5.9	6.1*
Experience (years), X	73.9	19.9	3.7*

*indicates that we can reject the null hypothesis that the coefficient is zero at the 5% significance level.

Based on these t-statistics, we reject the null hypothesis that the coefficients on our four variables are zero at the 5% significance level. Each of these four t-statistics is larger than 2. For example, the t-statistic on the total assets coefficient is 11.3, which is substantially larger than 2. Thus, we conclude that these variables belong in our specification.

The estimated effect of increasing total assets by $1 billion is to raise the CEO's compensation by $10,200 ($10.2 thousand). If the average annual shareholder return over three years increases by one percentage point (say, rising from 6% to 7% per year), we estimate that a CEO's annual compensation is higher by $35.7 thousand.

Although these variables are *statistically significantly different than zero*, not all of them are *economically significant*. That is, they do not have a large impact on CEO compensation. For example, the effect of the company's financial performance—shareholders' average return—on CEO salary is relatively small. Most S&P 500 companies have equity values of several billion dollars or more. An increase in shareholder return of one percentage point would apply to the overall equity value and would therefore imply additional returns to shareholders of tens of millions of dollars. However, the difference in CEO salary would be about $36,000 per year. Although $36,000 is a significant amount to most of us, CEOs of S&P 500 companies have annual compensation well into the millions of dollars. Thus, although the shareholder return variable is statistically significant, it has only a modest effect on a CEO's compensation.

Q&A 3.4

In the preceding Mini-Case, what is the estimated effect of more employees on CEO compensation? Is this effect statistically significant?

Answer

1. *Use the regression coefficient in the estimated CEO compensation function to identify the estimated effect of more employees.* The regression table in the CEO compensation Mini-Case shows that if a firm's workforce increases by 1,000 employees, the CEO's compensation is estimated to rise by about $12,600 per year.

2. *Use the t-statistic in the regression table to assess statistical significance.* The t-statistic for the employees coefficient is 9.47. The asterisk in the table indicates that this coefficient is significantly different from zero at the 5% significance level, which is the normal standard applied to infer that a coefficient is statistically significant. Thus, we can say that the number of employees is estimated to have a statistically significant effect on CEO compensation.

Correlation and Causation. When selecting explanatory variables, it is important to distinguish between correlation and causation. We say that two variables, X and Y, are *correlated* if they move together. The quantity demanded and price are negatively correlated: when price goes up, quantity goes down. This correlation is *causal*, as changes in price directly affect the quantity demanded.

However, correlation does not necessarily imply causation. For example, monthly sales of gasoline and the monthly incidence of sunburn have a strong positive correlation in U.S. data. Both are relatively high in the summer months of July and August and low in winter months.

Does this correlation mean that a sunburn somehow increases a consumer's demand for gasoline? Should we use the incidence of sunburn as an explanatory variable for gasoline demand? The answer to both these questions is no. A third variable—sunshine—is the main cause of the correlation between gasoline sales and sunburn. During sunny summer months people drive more, in part because they take more vacations that involve driving. They also spend more time in the sun and are therefore more likely to get sunburned. If our gasoline demand regression equation included the incidence of sunburn as an explanatory variable, we would find a high R^2 statistic and a statistically significant positive coefficient on sunburn. However, these results would be *spurious*. Any interpretation that getting sunburned increases the demand for gasoline would be incorrect.

Thus, it is critical that we do not include explanatory variables that have only a spurious relationship to the dependent variable in a regression equation. In estimating gasoline demand we would include price and income as explanatory variables, and we might include sunshine hours or temperature, but we would not include sunburn incidence as an explanatory variable.

Correlation does not imply causation. Correlations often result when two variables are both caused by a third variable, as when sunshine makes people more likely to get sunburn and more likely to go for long drives.

> **Common Confusion** If two variables move together, one of the variables must have a causal effect on the other.

If two variables have a causal relationship, we should treat the causal variable as the explanatory variable. Suppose that a store selling umbrellas collects weekly data on rainfall and on umbrella sales. It would be incorrect to run a regression with umbrella sales as the explanatory variable and rainfall as the dependent variable. Although such a regression would likely yield a statistically significant coefficient on umbrella sales, it makes no sense to think of umbrella sales as affecting rainfall.[17] Because rainfall increases the demand for umbrellas, rainfall should be the explanatory variable and the demand for umbrellas should be the dependent variable.

Omitted Variables. Often, a manager has an otherwise appropriately specified regression but lacks information about one or more potential explanatory variables. Because these variables are not included in the regression specification, they are called *omitted variables*. If a key explanatory variable is missing, then the resulting coefficient estimates and hypothesis tests may be unreliable.

Suppose Jacob and Santiago are managers in the same firm. Jacob wants to estimate the effect of price on quantity demanded and therefore experiments with the price over some time interval, starting with a low price and trying successively higher prices as time proceeds. However, Santiago is interested in the effect of advertising on demand and—without telling Jacob—varies the advertising level over the same time interval, starting with a low advertising level and moving to a high level as time passes. As the higher prices offset the increased advertising activity, the quantity demanded stays fairly stable.

Because Jacob does not know about the advertising experiment, after he regresses quantity on price, he is amazed to discover that price increases have no effect on demand. Clearly, a regression of quantity demanded on price alone would be highly misleading in this situation, steering Jacob to an incorrect conclusion about the firm's demand function. If only the price increase occurred, the quantity demanded would have fallen. In this example, it is important to include both price and advertising as explanatory variables.

Functional Form

If at first it doesn't fit, fit, fit again. —John McPhee

So far, we have assumed that our regression equations were linear. However, we cannot assume that demand functions or other economic relationships are always linear.

Choosing the correct functional form may be difficult. One useful step, especially with a regression involving only one explanatory variable, is to plot the data and the estimated regression line for each functional form under consideration. We illustrate this approach with an advertising example. A large food manufacturing firm sells its products in many cities throughout the country. To determine the importance of

---

[17]Of course, many people believe that the failure to carry an umbrella causes rain.

advertising, it holds its price constant across cities but varies the number of commercials per week on local television in each city.[18]

Figure 3.6 shows the relationship between the quantity demanded and advertising, holding price and other relevant explanatory variables constant. Both panels contain the same data points. The vertical axis shows the quantity demanded per family per week, and the horizontal axis is the number of commercials per week on local television.

The two panels have different estimated regression lines based on different functional form specifications. Panel a shows an estimated linear regression, which is based on the assumption that the relationship between the quantity demanded and advertising is linear: $Q = a + bA + e$, where Q is quantity demanded, A is a measure of the amount of advertising, e is a random error term, and a and b are the parameters to be estimated.

Panel b shows an estimate based on a quadratic regression specification:

$$Q = a + bA + cA^2 + e.$$

The only difference between this specification and the linear specification is that we have added an extra term, the coefficient c times the advertising index squared: cA^2. If $c \neq 0$, the plot of the relationship between Q and A is curved. If $c = 0$, this extra quadratic term drops out and the equation reverts to a linear form. Therefore, the test of whether c is statistically significantly different from zero can be used as a test of whether the quadratic form is better than the linear form.

Table 3.2 shows OLS estimates of both the linear and quadratic specifications. The estimation of the linear specification does not look bad when considered by itself. The coefficient on advertising is statistically significantly different from zero, and the R^2 is 0.85, which implies that the line "explains" most of the variation in quantity. However, the data points in panel a of Figure 3.6 are not randomly distributed

FIGURE 3.6 **The Effect of Advertising on Demand**

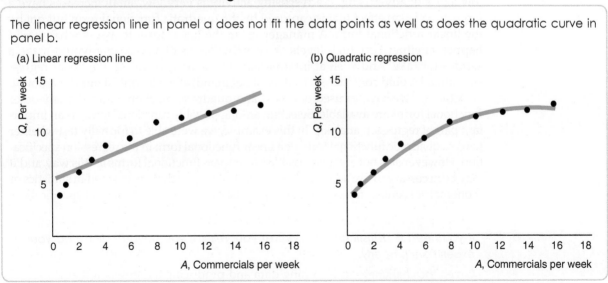

The linear regression line in panel a does not fit the data points as well as does the quadratic curve in panel b.

(a) Linear regression line

(b) Quadratic regression

[18]For example, Campbell Soup Company has conducted these types of experiments (Eastlack and Rao, 1989).

TABLE 3.2 **Regressions of Quantity on Advertising**

	Linear Specification			Quadratic Specification		
	Coefficient	Standard Error	t-Statistic	Coefficient	Standard Error	t-Statistic
Constant	5.43	0.54	10.05*	3.95	0.30	13.18*
Adverting, A	0.53	0.06	8.47*	1.20	0.10	12.18*
Advertising, A^2				−0.04	0.01	−7.05*

*indicates that we can reject the null hypothesis that the coefficient is zero at the 5% significance level.

around the regression line. Instead, they are first below the line, then above the line, and then below the line again. This pattern of residuals signals that the linear model is not the proper specification.

The estimated quadratic specification fits the data much better than the linear model: $R^2 = 0.99$. All the coefficients are statistically significantly different from zero. In particular, $\hat{c}$, the estimated coefficient on A^2, is statistically significant, so we reject the linear specification.

The data points appear randomly distributed around the quadratic regression curve in panel b of Figure 3.6, as they should for an appropriate specification. Because the quadratic functional form allows for a curved relationship between quantity and advertising, it captures two important phenomena that the linear specification misses. First, at high levels of advertising intensity, it becomes increasingly difficult to generate more demand, as virtually all potential consumers have purchased the product. The market becomes saturated: No more consumers can be convinced to buy the product. This saturation effect is captured by the declining slope of the regression line in panel b. The linear specification misses this effect.

Second, the linear form overstates the amount of demand that would occur at very low levels of advertising. If advertising activity is very low, small increases have a large payoff—an effect that is captured by the quadratic functional form but not by the linear functional form. A manager using the linear form to assess what would happen at either very high levels or very low levels of advertising would make a serious mistake. And even at intermediate levels of advertising, the linear regression model would consistently understate demand, albeit by only a modest amount.

Although we have focused on linear and quadratic functional forms, many other functional forms are available. Selecting among possible functional forms is an important part of regression analysis. In this example, we were able to formally test whether to use a quadratic functional form or a linear functional form in the regression specification. However, it is not always possible to compare functional forms in this way, and it may be necessary to use advanced statistical techniques that are covered in statistics or econometrics courses to assist in making decisions about functional form specification.

Managerial Implication

Experiments

If you need a statistician to interpret your results, you haven't designed your experiment properly.

Given the challenges in obtaining data and producing a regression that is properly specified, many firms use controlled experiments. For example, a firm can vary its price and observe how consumers react. Unfortunately, firms cannot control all important elements of an experiment as is done in a chemistry or physics lab. As a result, firms often use regressions to hold constant some variables that they could not control explicitly and to analyze their results.

Harrah's Entertainment relies on randomized tests of various hypotheses to design its marketing. It might send an attractive hotel offer for a Tuesday night to a randomly selected group of customers and compare the responses of that *test* group to those of other customers who received the usual offer and who serve as a *control* group.

In 1994, the credit card company Capital One was founded with the plan to apply experimental methods to all aspects of its business. For example, if the company wanted to know whether a credit card solicitation would be more successful if mailed in a blue envelope or in a white one, it ran an experiment. By 2017, Capital One was running tens of thousands of experiments per year.

Other companies such as Amazon, Facebook, Google, and Netflix also use experiments. These companies run many experiments on the internet, which allows them to conduct very low-cost experiments involving tens of thousands of customers.

Google shows on its website how a firm can run randomized experiments on the effectiveness of advertising while controlling for geographic or other differences. In an associated article, Google illustrates one such experiment and the linear regression models to analyze it and conduct hypothesis tests.[19] These examples show that managers can benefit from running experiments, particularly if they can make use of low-cost internet experiments.

3.5 Forecasting

We often refer to predictions about the future as *forecasts*. Managers frequently seek forecasts of important variables related to demand, such as sales or revenues. Large banks and other financial institutions commonly make forecasts regarding macroeconomic variables such as interest rates, gross domestic product, unemployment, and inflation. Governments make forecasts of revenues, expenditures, and budget balances, among other things, and we are all familiar with weather forecasts.

Managers use many different methods to forecast. We concentrate on two commonly used regression-based methods of forecasting: extrapolation and theory-based econometric forecasting.[20]

Extrapolation

Extrapolation seeks to forecast a variable of interest, like revenue or sales, as a function of time. Extrapolation starts with a series of observations collected over time, referred to as a *time series*. For example, a firm might have monthly sales data for

---

[19]See **http://services.google.com/fh/files/blogs/geo_experiments_final_version.pdf**.

[20]An alternative approach is to rely on subjective judgments. One judgment-based approach is the *Delphi technique*. A group of experts make initial forecasts, which are then made known to the group, who discuss the reasoning behind them. The experts then make new forecasts, and the process repeats until broad consensus is reached or until the differences in opinion have converged as much as reasonably possible. The resulting forecasts reflect the collective judgment of the group.

a new product for several years and be interested in projecting future sales based on these historical data. In extrapolation, the time series is *smoothed* in some way to reveal the underlying pattern, and this pattern is then extended or extrapolated into the future to forecast future sales. This type of forecasting is called *pure* time-series analysis because it seeks to forecast future values of some variable, like sales, purely on the basis of past values of that variable and the passage of time.

Trends.   Most of us automatically use our eyes to fit a trend line when we look at a plot of data points over time. Instead, a manager can use a regression technique to plot such a trend line more reliably.

Figure 3.7 shows quarterly revenue (= price times quantity) for Nike, a leading producer of athletic footwear and clothing.[21] Nike's quarters are December–February, March–May, June–August, and September–November, corresponding to winter, spring, summer, and fall in the Northern Hemisphere, where the vast majority of Nike sales occur. The first quarter in the figure is December 2008–February 2009 (the "winter of 2009"). The figure labels the winter, spring, summer, and fall quarters q1, q2, q3, and q4, respectively.

Nike could estimate its worldwide revenue (in billions of dollars) as a linear function of time, t, which equals 1 in the first quarter (winter 2009), 2 in the spring of 2009, and so on, up to 37 for the winter quarter of 2018, which is the final period in our sample. The linear regression equation is *Revenue* = $a + bt + e$, where e is the error term and a and b are the coefficients to be estimated. The estimated trend line is *Revenue* = $4.189 + 0.134t$, and the coefficient on the time trend is statistically significant at the 0.05 level. This line is plotted in Figure 3.7. Based on this regression, Nike

FIGURE 3.7 Nike's Quarterly Revenue: 2009–2018

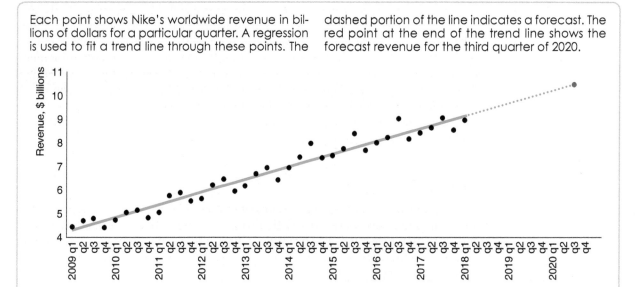

Each point shows Nike's worldwide revenue in billions of dollars for a particular quarter. A regression is used to fit a trend line through these points. The dashed portion of the line indicates a forecast. The red point at the end of the trend line shows the forecast revenue for the third quarter of 2020.

[21]The data are from Nike annual reports provided by Compustat. These data refer to worldwide revenues, about half of which come from North America.

could forecast its sales in the summer quarter of 2020, which is quarter 47, as $4.189 + (0.134 \times 47) = \$10.5$ billion, which is the red point at the right end of the trend line. Of course, the further into the future we forecast, the less reliable is the forecast.

Seasonal Variation. If we look at the trend line through the data in Figure 3.7, we notice a distinct pattern of the observations around the trend line. If this variation were purely random, we could not do much about it except to note that our forecasts have potential random errors associated with them. However, because this pattern looks systematic, we may be able to adjust for it. Revenue in virtually every spring and summer quarter is above the trend line, while revenue in almost every fall and winter quarter is below the trend line. Thus, it appears that the demand for Nike products varies *seasonally*. This pattern is not surprising, as we expect higher athletic footwear and clothing sales in the spring and summer than in the fall or winter.

In making forecasts, we should adjust for these seasonal effects. We can add variables to our regression that capture the seasonal effects. These variables, often called *seasonal dummy variables*, equal one in the relevant season and zero otherwise. For example, the winter dummy variable equals one in the winter quarter of the year and zero in all other quarters. We include these indicator variables only for winter, spring, and summer quarters. The fall quarter is then interpreted as the base case, and the coefficient on each of the other quarters shows us the difference between that quarter and the base case.

We estimate $Revenue = a + bt + c_1W + c_2S + c_3M + e$, where W, S, and M are quarterly dummy variables for winter, spring, and summer, respectively, and a, b, c_1, c_2, and c_3 are the coefficients we want to estimate. The new estimated equation is $Revenue = 3.847 + 0.135t + 0.179W + 0.452S + 0.675M$, and all the coefficients are statistically significant.

Our failure to include the seasonal dummy variables in our original regression may have led to a biased estimate. Based on this new regression model, the forecast value for the summer quarter of 2020 is $3.820 + (0.135 \times 47) + (0.179 \times 0) + (0.452 \times 0) + (0.675 \times 1) = \$10.84$ billion. This adjusted forecast is \$340 million (about 3.2%) more than our previous forecast that ignored seasonal effects. Properly incorporating seasonal effects allows us to adjust for the fact that revenues tend to be relatively high in the summer quarter.

Nonlinear Trends. Although Nike's revenue follows a linear trend, not all time trends are linear. In particular, the revenue growth of new products is often nonlinear. After a new product first reaches the market, its market share often grows slowly, as consumers need some time to become familiar with the product. At some point, a successful product takes off and sales grow very rapidly. Then, when the product eventually approaches market saturation, sales grow slowly in line with underlying population or real income growth. Ultimately, if other products displace this product, its sales will fall sharply. For example, the revenue of early generation mobile phones experienced exponential growth until smartphones began to dominate the market.

Theory-Based Econometric Forecasting

The consumers' demand function determines revenue. We know that variables such as income, population, and advertising affect the quantity demanded. Yet our forecast based on extrapolation (pure time-series analysis) ignored these variables. The role of such variables may be implicit in an extrapolation. For example, one reason why revenue may have grown smoothly over some period is that population increased smoothly over that period.

As a first approximation, extrapolation often proves useful, especially if we have properly addressed seasonal effects. However, the problem with such forecasts is that they are not based on an understanding of how other variables *cause* or determine the variable of interest. As a result, it is difficult for the forecaster to understand the underlying causal relationship that determines revenue and to anticipate the effects of changes in causal variables such as income or population. If we are interested in underlying economic structure, we need to use a different approach.

An alternative forecasting approach uses economic theory, such as a demand framework, to derive the causal relationships between economic variables. For example, in forecasting Nike's sales or revenue, we could estimate the effect of changes in income on demand for Nike's products and then take the expected pattern of income growth into account in forecasting sales.

Forecasting using a regression specification that incorporates underlying causal explanatory variables is called *causal econometric forecasting* or *theory-based econometric forecasting*. Such forecasting methods incorporate both extrapolation and estimation of causal or explanatory economic relationships. Thus, to forecast sales, we might use both previous values of sales and time as explanatory variables, and we would also use causal variables such as income. That is, with theory-based (causal) econometric forecasting, we predict the dependent variable based on the underlying causal factors—not just on the time-series pattern of the dependent variable.

We use these estimates to make *conditional forecasts*, where we base our forecast on specified values for the explanatory variables. For example, a manager might make one conditional forecast of sales based on the assumption that income will be 5% higher next year than this year and another conditional forecast based on the assumption that income next year will be the same as this year.

In our extrapolation analysis, we assumed that Nike's revenue would grow steadily over time. However, it is possible that underlying causal or structural factors affect its revenue. We would expect Nike's revenue to deviate from the trend line if a rival entered the business, if Nike added a new major product to its product line or acquired another large company, if the cost of transportation changed dramatically, or if a major recession occurred. Nike could regress its revenue on these economic factors. It could then use that regression to make forecasts that are conditional on how it expects these other factors to evolve over time.

Forecasting using theory-based econometric modeling is more difficult than using extrapolation. However, it often provides a better chance of identifying sudden deviations from a simple trend line, and it may contribute more to a firm's understanding of the underlying business interactions.

Managerial Solution

Estimating the Effect of an iTunes Price Change

How could Apple use a focus group to estimate the demand function for iTunes to determine if raising its price would raise or lower its revenue? To answer this question, we asked a focus group of 20 Canadian college students how many popular tracks they would download from iTunes at various prices, assuming that their incomes and the prices of other goods remained constant. The responses were

Price, $ per song	Quantity, Songs per year
1.49	441
1.29	493
1.19	502
1.09	536
0.99	615
0.89	643
0.79	740
0.69	757
0.49	810

The iTunes managers would first estimate a linear demand function of song downloads on price, obtaining demand coefficient estimates, the R^2 statistic, and standard errors, and then calculate the t-statistics (dividing each coefficient by its standard error).

Based on these results, the estimated linear demand function is $\hat{Q} = 1{,}024 - 413p$, where $\hat{Q}$ is our estimate of the number of downloads per year, and price p is the price in dollars per song. The price coefficient is -413, which means that a $1 increase in price would reduce estimated quantity demanded by 413 downloads. Converting this result to cents, a 1¢ increase in price would reduce estimated quantity demanded by 4.13 downloads per year. The t-statistic is -12.6, so this coefficient is significantly different from zero. The R^2 statistic is 0.96, indicating that the regression line fits the data closely.

Apple's manager could use such an estimated demand function to determine how revenue, R, which is price times quantity ($R = p \times Q$), varies with price. Panel a of Figure 3.8 shows the estimated iTunes demand curve. At $p = 99$¢, 615 songs were downloaded by the focus group according to this estimated demand curve. The corresponding revenue is the rectangle consisting of areas $A + B$. The height of this rectangle is the price, $p = 99$¢. The length of the rectangle is the quantity of songs downloaded, $Q = 615$, so the area of the rectangle equals $R = p \times Q = \$0.99 \times 615 \approx \$609$.

If the price were increased to $1.24, the quantity demanded would drop to 512. The corresponding revenue would be the rectangle $= A + C$, where the height is $1.24 and the length is 512. According to the focus group's responses, Apple would lose revenue equal to area B but gain the revenue equal to area C. Area B shows how much Apple loses from selling 103 ($= 615 - 512$) fewer units at the original price. Area C is the extra amount it makes on the 512 units it sells, because it sells each song for $0.25 ($= \$1.24 - \$0.99$) more than it did originally.

An increase in price has two offsetting effects on revenue. Revenue tends to fall because the price increase causes fewer units to be sold. However, revenue tends to rise because a higher price is collected on every unit that is sold. Because these two effects have opposite effects on revenue, management would not know in general whether a particular price increase would raise or lower revenue.

FIGURE 3.8 iTunes Focus Group Demand and Revenue Curves

Based on a focus group's responses, we estimate the iTunes demand curve and calculate a revenue (= price × quantity) curve. (a) According to the estimated demand curve, if the price were 99¢, the focus group would download 615 songs per year and revenue would be areas $A + B = \$507 + \$102 = \$609 = p \times Q = \$0.99 \times 615$. At a price of $1.24, the songs demanded would fall to 512, and the revenue would be areas $A + C = \$507 + \$128 = \$635 = p \times Q = \$1.24 \times 512$. (b) According to the corresponding revenue curve, revenue is greatest for this focus group at $p = \$1.24$, where $R = \$635$.

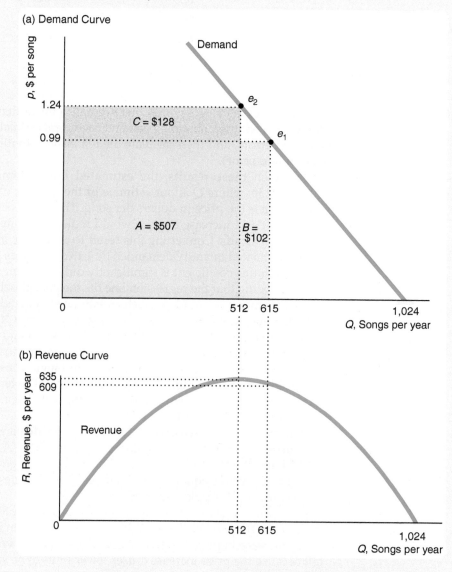

(a) Demand Curve

(b) Revenue Curve

However, because we have estimated the demand curve, we can calculate the size of these two effects and determine the net effect of a price increase on iTunes's revenue. The lost revenue from fewer sales is area *B*, which is $102. The revenue gain due to the higher price on the units sold is area *C*, which is $128. Therefore, revenue increases by $26 (= $128 − $102).

Panel b corresponds to panel a. Its horizontal axis measures quantity as in panel a, but its vertical axis measures revenue (rather than price as in panel a). Panel b shows the revenue curve, which relates revenue to the quantity sold.[22] At the original price of 99¢, where $Q = 615$, the revenue curve shows that revenue is $609, consistent with panel a. This curve shows that the revenue curve reaches its maximum where $Q = 512$ and $p = \$1.24$.

Given that the cost to Apple of selling an extra song is probably very close to zero, it seems that Apple would like to maximize its revenue. If the general population shares similar tastes with the focus group, then Apple's revenue would increase if it raised its price to $1.24 per song.[23]

SUMMARY

1. **Elasticity.** An elasticity shows how responsive one variable is to changes in another variable. The price elasticity of demand, ε, summarizes how much the quantity demanded changes when the price changes. The responsiveness of quantity is related to the shape of a demand curve at a particular point or over a particular interval. Specifically, the price elasticity of demand is the percentage change in the quantity demanded divided by an associated percentage change in price. For example, a 1% increase in price causes the quantity demanded to fall by ε%. Downward-sloping demand curves have a negative elasticity.

   The demand curve is perfectly inelastic if $\varepsilon = 0$, is inelastic if ε is between 0 and −1, has unitary elasticity if $\varepsilon = -1$, is elastic if $\varepsilon < -1$, and becomes perfectly elastic as ε approaches negative infinity. The quantity demanded varies less than in proportion to a 1% change in the price if the demand curve is inelastic, but varies more than in proportion if the demand curve is elastic. The elasticity of demand varies along a downward-sloping linear demand curve. A vertical demand curve is perfectly inelastic, and a horizontal demand curve is perfectly elastic.

2. **Regression Analysis.** Regression analysis fits an economic relationship to data. It explains variations in a dependent variable, such as the quantity demanded, using explanatory variables, such as price and income. A linear regression with just one explanatory variable corresponds to putting the dependent variable on the vertical axis and the explanatory variable on the horizontal axis, plotting the data points, and drawing the "best possible" straight line through these points. One method for finding a suitable estimated relationship is ordinary least squares (OLS), which chooses parameter estimates or "draws the regression line" such that the sum of squared deviations of the data points from the regression line is as small as possible. To help assess the fit of the regression line to the data, statistical packages report the R^2 statistic, which is the fraction of the actual variation in the dependent variable explained by the estimated regression equation.

3. **Properties and Statistical Significance of Estimated Coefficients.** A good estimation method should yield coefficient estimates that are unbiased—that would average out to the true value in repeated samples. It is also desirable that an estimation method not produce very different coefficient estimates in different random samples. Regression software produces statistics that can be used to assess how much confidence to place in regression coefficient estimates. Standard errors tell us how much we might expect coefficient estimates to differ from their true values. We use a *t*-test to assess whether an estimated regression coefficient is different from zero. We obtain a *t*-statistic for each coefficient by dividing the coefficient by its standard error. If the *t*-statistic exceeds a critical value that is approximately equal to 2, we can be confident that the coefficient differs from zero.

---

[22]Because the estimated demand function is $Q = 1{,}024 - 413p$, the corresponding inverse demand function is $p \approx 2.48 - 0.00242Q$. Thus, the revenue function is $R = p \times Q \approx 2.48Q - 0.00242Q^2$.

[23]See the Mini-Case "Available for a Song" in Chapter 10 for a larger-scale, more detailed study of Apple's pricing.

4. **Regression Specification.** Regression analysis is reliable only if the equation to be estimated is properly specified. One important aspect of specification is that the equation should include all relevant explanatory variables. A second specification issue is that a regression equation must have an appropriate functional form. Excluding relevant explanatory variables, including inappropriate explanatory variables, or using the wrong functional form can lead to misleading results.

5. **Forecasting.** One method of forecasting is to extrapolate a time series into the future. As a first step in extrapolation, a manager can regress the variable to be forecast, such as sales, on a time-trend variable. Next, using the estimated trend line, a manager can forecast the future value by substituting future times into the estimated regression equation. When extrapolating, it is often necessary to adjust for seasonal or other patterns. A second method of forecasting uses causal economic relationships, where the manager includes economic variables as explanatory variables instead of or in addition to a time trend. Here, forecasting the dependent variable may require the manager to use expected values of the explanatory variables.

QUESTIONS

All exercises are available on **MyLab Economics**; * = *answer at the back of this book;* **C** = *use of calculus may be necessary;* **X** = *this exercise is available in Excel Grader in* **MyLab Economics**.

1. Elasticity

1.1 The U.S. Tobacco Settlement between the major tobacco companies and 46 states caused the price of cigarettes to jump 45¢ (21%) in November 1998. Levy and Meara (2005) found only a 2.65% drop in prenatal smoking 15 months later. What is the elasticity of demand for this group?

1.2 When Apple raised the price of iTunes from 99¢ to $1.29, GS Boyz's "Stanky Legg" sales dropped from 22,686 units to 19,692 units (Glenn Peoples, "iTunes Price Change: Sales Down, Revenue Up in Week 1," *Billboard*, April 15, 2009). What was the song's arc elasticity of demand? (*Hint*: See Q&A 3.1.)

*1.3 The demand function for a good is $Q = 100 - 2p$. What is the elasticity at the point $p = 10$ and $Q = 80$?

*1.4 The only type of downward-sloping demand curve that has the same elasticity at every price is given by the *constant elasticity functional form* $Q = Ap^\varepsilon$, where A and ε are constants. Show, by differentiating this demand function with respect to p, that the elasticity of demand is ε in this case. **C**

1.5 The demand curve for a good is $Q = 500 - 4p^2$. What is the elasticity at the point $p = 5$ and $Q = 400$? Is the demand curve elastic or inelastic at this point? **C**

1.6 Which section of a straight-line demand curve is elastic? Which section is inelastic?

*1.7 According to Duffy-Deno (2003), when the price of broadband access capacity (the amount of information one can send over an Internet connection) increases 10%, commercial customers buy about 3.8% less capacity. What is the elasticity of demand for broadband access capacity for these firms? Is demand at the current price inelastic?

1.8 Suppose that the demand curve for wheat in each of six countries is perfectly inelastic up to some "choke" price p^*—a price so high that nothing is bought—so that the demand curve is vertical at Q^* at prices below p^* and horizontal at p^*. If p^* and Q^* vary across countries, what does the world's demand curve look like? Discuss how the elasticity of demand varies with price along the world's demand curve.

*1.9 Calculate the price and cross-price elasticities of demand for coconut oil. The coconut oil demand function (Buschena and Perloff, 1991) is

$$Q = 1,200 - 9.5p + 16.2p_p + 0.2Y,$$

where Q is the quantity of coconut oil demanded in thousands of metric tons per year, p is the price of coconut oil in cents per pound, p_p is the price of palm oil in cents per pound, and Y is the income of consumers. Assume that p is initially 45¢ per pound, p_p is 31¢ per pound, and Q is 1,275 thousand metric tons per year.

1.10 Using the coconut oil demand function from Question 1.9, calculate the income elasticity of demand for coconut oil at the prices and quantity given. Is coconut oil a normal good at that price and quantity combination?

1.11 The Mini-Case "Anti-Smoking Policies May Reduce Drunk Driving" describes how the equilibrium changed in the market for alcoholic beverages when tobacco taxes rose. Use a supply-and-demand diagram to illustrate what happened.

1.12 Ghose and Han (2014) found that the elasticity of demand for Google Play apps is −3.7. (See the Mini-Case "Demand Elasticities for Google Play and Apple Apps.") This elasticity applies to a small college town where consumers buy approximately 1,000 apps per month. If price rises by 5%, what would be the effect on quantity demanded? Would revenue rise or fall? What is the percentage change in revenue (= price × quantity)?

2. Regression Analysis

2.1 At the Portland Fish Exchange, each day fishers deliver some amount of cod to market. Supply is perfectly inelastic at that amount. The quantity of cod caught and brought to market varies day to day. Assuming the demand curve does not vary over time, use the supply-demand framework to illustrate how the price is determined on different days. Explain how this process allows us to identify different points on the demand curve.

2.2 Suppose that a restaurant uses a focus group of regular customers to determine how many customers would buy a proposed new menu item at various prices. Can this information be used to estimate an inverse demand function? A demand function? Explain briefly. Would it be possible to use a focus group to generate data that could be used to estimate a demand function that includes both price and income as explanatory variables?

*2.3 The estimated demand function for popsicles on a particular beach on a sunny summer day is given by $Q = 130 - \$3.5\,p$, where p is measured in dollars. What is the predicted quantity if $p = \$2.00$? If the actual quantity demanded is 129, what is the residual? Suggest at least two unobserved variables incorporated into the random error. (*Hint*: See Q&A 3.3.)

2.4 A producer of outdoor clothing used a focus group to obtain information about the demand for fleece jackets with built-in, battery-operated warming panels. At prices of $100, $90, $80, $70, $60, and $50, the focus group demanded 23, 31, 40, 44, 48, and 60 jackets, respectively. Use the Excel Trendline option to estimate a linear demand function and to determine the associated R^2 statistic. (*Hint*: Put price in the first column. Price will appear on the horizontal axis in this case.)

2.5 Purdue University provides monthly data on Florida electricity consumption online (**https://engineering.purdue.edu/LASCI/research-data/energy**). We can use these data to estimate monthly residential electricity demand as a function of price and the average monthly temperature. Using a linear regression equation, the estimated demand function is $E = 2400 - 25p + 84F$ where E is residential energy consumption in gigawatt hours (GWH), p is price in cents per kilowatt hour (KWH), and F is temperature in Fahrenheit degrees.

    a. What is the estimated residential electricity demand if the price is 8¢ per KWH and the average monthly temperature is 80 degrees?

    b. What has a larger estimated effect on quantity demanded, a one-cent decline in price or a one-degree fall in temperature? Explain, using calculations.

    c. In Florida, electricity use rises with temperature because air conditioning is a very important source of demand. What sign would you expect on the temperature variable in Canada and the northern U.S. states? Explain briefly.

2.6 In Figure 3.5 two estimated demand curves are shown. These demand curves result from regression equations in which Mai estimates quantity demanded as a function of price and no other variables. However, Mai recognized that other variables, such as sunshine or temperature, may affect the demand for pie. Collecting this data requires effort. In which town should collecting such data be a higher priority for Mai if she is trying to improve her ability to predict pie demand? Explain.

3. Properties and Statistical Significance of Estimated Coefficients

3.1 Using the data in Table 3.1, estimate the cod demand function if we use only the first seven observations.

3.2 How sensitive are your regression results in Question 3.1 to small changes in the data? In particular, how do your regression results change if

    a. The quantity in the first row of Table 3.1 were 2.0 instead of 1.5?

    b. The quantity in the second row of Table 3.1 were 2.7 instead of 2.2?

*3.3 In the Camry focus group analysis in this chapter, we use a regression to estimate the demand for Camrys. Using that equation, how many fewer Camrys would the focus group buy if the price were increased by $1,000? How many Camrys would we expect the focus group to purchase if the price is $20,000? What is the elasticity of demand if the price is $20,000?

3.4 Using the data in Question 2.4, determine the standard error and t-statistic for the price coefficient. Is price statistically significantly different from zero at the 0.05 level of significance? (*Hint*: Use Excel's Regression tool.)

4. Regression Specification

4.1 According to the regression results for CEO compensation, is the effect of experience on CEO compensation statistically significant? Is it economically significant? Explain. (*Hint*: See Q&A 3.4.)

4.2 Suppose that you believe the demand function has a constant-elasticity: $Q = Ap^\varepsilon$, where A is a positive constant and ε is the constant elasticity of demand. You have some data and want to estimate the constant-elasticity demand function $Q = Ap^\varepsilon u$, where A is a positive constant, ε is the constant elasticity of demand, and u is an error term. Take logarithms of both sides of this equation and show that you get an equation that is linear in logarithmic terms (called a log-linear equation). Explain how you can estimate this equation in Excel or other programs using the OLS techniques that we have discussed.

*4.3 You work for a firm producing fitness equipment. The firm tells you that the demand curve for the firm's main product—a multi-station home gym—is linear. You have in hand price and quantity data obtained from focus groups and instructions to run a regression of revenue on price. Should you use a linear functional form—with revenue as a linear function of price—or something else? Explain.

4.4 A medical clinic that surveys patients with a history of heavy drinking is likely to find that patients who have started to experience serious liver problems are more likely to cut back their drinking than others with a history of heavy drinking. An enthusiastic doctor uses data from this population and regresses current liver function, L, on current alcohol consumption, A. The regression specification is $L = a + bA$. The doctor is likely to get a positive estimate for b: Within the population of people with a history of heavy drinking, those who drink more currently tend to have healthier livers. What is wrong with this specification? (*Hint*: Think about factors that affect the demand for alcohol in this population.)

5. Forecasting

5.1 Heinz makes most of its money from ketchup and other prepared, packaged foods that are substitutes for fresh foods. Its revenue tends to be low in the summer quarter and high in the winter quarter. Can you provide a possible reason for this pattern? (*Hint*: Fresh fruits and vegetables are substitutes for many of Heinz's prepared foods.)

5.2 As reported in the text, we estimated Nike's quarterly revenue (in billions of dollars) function as $Revenue = 3.847 + 0.135t + 0.179W + 0.452S + 0.675M$. What does this estimated equation tell us about Nike's spring quarter revenues compared to the revenue in other quarters? (The spring quarter dummy variable is represented by S in the estimated regression equation.)

5.3 Recessions (when consumers' incomes fall) strongly affect FedEx's revenue, but have less of an effect on Heinz's revenue. Both firms' revenues vary seasonally. What regression specifications would you suggest using to forecast revenue for FedEx and for Heinz? Why might these specifications differ?

5.4 Here are annual revenue data in billions of dollars for the 10-year period 2008–2017 for two well-known retailers:

Amazon: 19.1; 24.5; 32.4; 48.1; 61.1; 74.5; 89.0; 107.9; 136.0; 177.9.

Walmart: 402.2; 406.1; 420.0; 445.0; 467.2; 474.5; 483.5; 480.0; 482.2; 496.8.

a. For each company, use linear extrapolation in Excel to forecast revenue in the year 2021. (*Hint*: Use either the Trendline option or the Regression tool.)

b. Based on these extrapolations, when would Amazon be predicted to equal Walmart in revenue?

c. Why has Amazon been growing faster than Walmart? Is the slow growth of Walmart related to the rapid growth of Amazon?

6. Managerial Problem

6.1 In the Managerial Solution, we estimated a focus group's demand function for iTunes downloads. The estimated coefficient on price is -413, and the t-statistic is -12.6.

a. Using these values, what is the standard error of this estimated coefficient?

b. Suppose we had another focus group sample, ran a regression on that sample, and obtained the same coefficient on price but with a standard error 10 times as large. What can you say about the statistical significance of the price coefficient in this second sample?

*6.2 Using Excel or another program, estimate the linear OLS demand regression for the iTunes focus group data in the Managerial Solution. What is the R^2? What are the coefficient estimates, the standard errors, and the t-statistics for each coefficient? Using a 95% confidence criterion, would you reject the hypothesis that the price coefficient is zero? (You can compare most of your answers to those in the Managerial Solution.)

7. MyLab Economics Spreadsheet Exercises[24]

7.1 The marketing department of Acme Inc. has estimated the following demand function for its popular carpet deodorizer, Freshbreeze: $Q = 100 - 5p$, where Q is the quantity of an 8-ounce box (sold in thousand units) and p the price of an 8-ounce box. Using Excel, calculate the point price elasticity of

---

[24]The spreadsheet exercises in this chapter are based on the work of Satyajit Ghosh in cooperation with the authors. The answers are available on **MyLab Economics**.

demand, ε, for price, $p = 1, 2, 3, \ldots, 19$. Describe the pattern of price elasticity of demand that you have calculated along the demand curve.

7.2 The ice cream store Cool Stuff sells exotic ice creams, including Tropical Cream and Green Mango. Cool Stuff has been varying the prices of these two flavors over the past 12 weeks and has recorded the sales data. The table shows the quantity sold of Tropical Cream, Q, given the price of a half-gallon of Tropical Cream, p, and the price of the other flavor, Green Mango, p_0. Use these data to estimate the demand function for Tropical Cream. Are the coefficients on the two prices statistically significantly different from zero at the 5% significance level? What is the R^2?

7.3 Bob Kehoe runs a small business clearing snow in the winter and cutting grass in the other seasons. For the past three years he has kept his prices constant but has experienced an upward trend in his income as new households move into his growing

community and seek his services. However, Bob's income is subject to seasonal fluctuations. Dividing the year into four seasons, the following data show Bob's seasonal income in thousands of dollars for the past three years.

Bob's Income
(in thousands of dollars)

Year	Jan–Mar	Apr–Jun	Jul–Sep	Oct–Dec	Total
1	22	20	25	13	80
2	24	21	24	16	85
3	30	22	22	17	91

Bob is still happy to take on more work. Assuming his prices remain unchanged and his community continues to grow, use Excel's Regression tool to forecast Bob's income in the four seasons of the next year and his total income for the year. Use seasonal dummy variables in your analysis.

Excercise 7.2

Q	84	82	85	83	82	84	87	81	82	79	82	78
p	8.50	9.00	8.75	9.25	9.50	9.25	8.25	10.00	10.00	10.50	9.50	10.25
p_0	5.25	6.00	6.00	6.50	6.25	6.25	5.25	7.00	7.25	7.25	6.75	7.25

APPENDIX 3A   The Identification Problem

Managers often want to know how much the quantity demanded will fall if they raise the price. That is, the manager wants a reliable estimate of the price coefficient in a demand function regression. Unfortunately, it is not always possible to estimate a demand function in which the price coefficient is identified. An **identification problem** arises if it is not possible to obtain a unique estimate of a particular parameter.

Two Examples

To illustrate the nature of the identification problem, we consider two examples. A manager can identify the price coefficient in the first example and cannot do so in the second example.

In both examples, the manager of the market research division of a large retail bakery chain wants to estimate how the quantity demanded of hard red winter wheat changes as the price rises. The manager has data on the price and quantity of the wheat, which change from week to week.

We say that the manager can *identify the demand function* if all the coefficients are identified. Whether the manager can identify the demand function—and, in particular, the price coefficient—depends on what causes the prices and quantities to vary over time. In any given week, the intersection of the demand and supply curves determines the observed price-quantity equilibrium pair. Shifts in either the demand or supply curve cause the price-quantity pair to change over time.

In our first example, we suppose that the factors other than price that affect the demand curve, such as income, remain constant, so that the demand curve does not shift. However, weather, which affects the supply curve, changes over time. Therefore, the supply curve shifts repeatedly.

(a) Identification

(b) Identification Problem

In panel a of the figure, the supply curve shifts from S^1 to S^2 to S^3 over time. The resulting price-quantity equilibrium pairs—(p_1, Q_1), (p_2, Q_2), and (p_3, Q_3)—lie on the demand curve, D. That is, the shifting supply curve traces out the demand curve. The demand function's price coefficient is identified: Because the observed price-quantity pairs lie on the demand curve, they show how the quantity demanded changes as the price changes.

In our second example, panel b of the figure, the manager cannot identify the price coefficient. The identification problem arises because both weather and income change over time, so that both the supply curve and the demand curve shift. The resulting equilibrium price-quantity pairs—(p_1, Q_1), (p_2, Q_2), and (p_3, Q_3)—do not lie on either a demand curve or a supply curve. Indeed, the line through them, labeled X, has no economic meaning. Interpreting the slope of X as the slope of the actual demand curve would be a mistake. Here, the manager cannot identify the demand function's price coefficient.

Avoiding the Identification Problem

If we knew that the demand curve was stable and that shifts in the supply curve generated the changes in price and quantity, then the observed data would trace out the demand curve and the price coefficient would be identified as in panel a. Our earlier estimate of the Portland Fish Exchange demand function was identified for this reason.

There are other possible ways to avoid the identification problem. One approach is to use a focus group, as in the Camry example. We could ask potential buyers about their buying intentions at particular prices. This process does not involve a supply curve. Respondents report points on their demand curves. The process traces out the demand curve, and there is no identification problem.

Another way to avoid an identification problem is to use an experiment, as in Mai's pie shop example. Mai generated data by running experiments: changing the price of her pies and seeing how many pies she sold. Again, this approach involves no supply curve. The experimenter exogenously determines the price and observes changes in quantity demanded, and is able to trace out the demand curve for each bakery.

Additional information may also be helpful. If we have data about factors that shift the supply and demand curves, managers can use more sophisticated regression techniques to separately identify and estimate the supply and demand functions.

Consumer Choice

4

If this is coffee, please bring me some tea; but if this is tea, please bring me some coffee.

When Google wants to transfer an employee from its Washington, D.C., office to its London branch, it must decide how much compensation to offer the worker to move. International firms are increasingly relocating workers throughout their home countries and internationally.

As you might expect, workers are not always enthusiastic about being relocated. In a survey by Runzheimer International, 79% of firms' relocation managers responded that they experienced resistance from employees who were asked to relocate to high-cost locations. A survey of some of their employees found that 81% objected to moving because of fear of a lowered standard of living.

One possible approach to enticing employees to relocate is for the firm to determine the goods and services consumed by employees in the original location and then pay those employees enough to allow them to consume essentially the same items in the new location. According to a survey by Mercer, 79% of international firms reported that they provided their workers with enough income abroad to maintain their home lifestyle.

However, economists who advise on compensation packages point out that such an approach will typically overcompensate employees by paying them more than they need to obtain the same level of economic well-being they have in the original city. How can a firm's human resources (HR) manager use consumer theory to optimally compensate employees who are transferred to other cities?

Economists use the theory of consumer choice to analyze consumers' decisions and to derive demand curves. To answer questions about individual consumer choice (or any kind of individual decision making) we need a model of individual behavior. The standard economic model of consumer behavior makes the following assumptions.

- Individual *tastes* or *preferences* determine the pleasure or satisfaction people derive from the goods and services they consume.
- Consumers face *constraints* or limits on their choices, particularly because their budgets limit how much they can buy.
- Consumers seek to *maximize* the level of satisfaction they obtain from consumption, subject to the constraints they face. People seek to "do the best they can with what they have."

Consumers spend their money on the bundles of products that give them the most pleasure or satisfaction. Someone who likes music and does not have much of a sweet tooth might spend a lot of money on concerts and relatively little on sweet desserts. By contrast, a consumer who loves chocolate and has little interest in music might spend a significant amount on gourmet chocolate and never go to a concert.

Consumers must make choices about which goods to buy. Limits on the amount they can spend (called "budget constraints") prevent them from buying everything that catches their fancy. Other constraints, such as legal restrictions on items like alcohol and recreational drugs, may also restrain their choices. Therefore, consumers buy the bundles of goods they like best, subject both to their budget constraints and to legal or other relevant constraints.

In economic analysis designed to explain behavior, economists assume that *the consumer is the boss* (sometimes referred to as *consumer sovereignty*). If Jason derives pleasure from smoking, an economist does not confuse the economic analysis of Jason's choices by interjecting his or her own personal judgment that smoking is undesirable. Economists accept the consumer's tastes and seek to predict the resulting behavior. Accepting each consumer's tastes is not the same as condoning the resulting behaviors. An economist might reasonably believe that consumers should avoid smoking. However, if the economist wants to know whether Jason will smoke more next year if the price of cigarettes decreases by 10%, any prediction is unlikely to be correct if the economist says, "He should not smoke; therefore, we predict he will stop smoking next year." A prediction based on Jason's actual tastes is more likely to be correct: "Given that Jason likes cigarettes, he is likely to smoke more next year if the price of cigarettes falls."

This chapter provides an analysis of consumer choice, focusing on how consumer tastes or preferences give rise to consumer demand.

Learning Objectives

1. Predict consumer choices using underlying properties of consumer preferences.
2. Summarize a consumer's preferences using a *utility function*.
3. Explain how prices and income limit what a consumer can purchase.
4. Show how consumers maximize their utility given prices and limited income.
5. Derive demand curves from underlying consumer preferences.
6. Discuss the role of behavioral biases in consumer choice.

4.1 Consumer Preferences

I have forced myself to contradict myself in order to avoid conforming to my own taste. —Marcel Duchamp, Dada artist

We start our analysis of consumer behavior by examining consumer preferences. Once we know about these, we will combine that knowledge with information about the constraints consumers face so that we can answer many questions such as the managerial problem posed at the beginning of this chapter.

A consumer faces choices involving many goods. Does the consumer prefer to buy ice cream or cake? Is it better to rent a large apartment or rent a single room and use the savings to pay for trips and concerts? A consumer must allocate his or her budget to buy a *bundle* (also called a *market basket* or combination) of goods.

How do consumers choose the bundles of goods they buy? One possibility is that consumers behave randomly and blindly choose one good or another without any thought. However, consumers appear to make systematic choices. For example, most consumers buy very similar items each time they visit a grocery store. A consumer typically ignores most items and buys a few specific items repeatedly. A consumer who likes apple juice and dislikes orange juice buys apple juice on a regular basis and rarely, if ever, buys orange juice. In contrast, a consumer who chose randomly would be as likely to buy apple juice as orange juice. By observing a consumer's consistent purchase of apple juice rather than orange juice, we can reject the hypothesis of random choices.

To explain consumer behavior, economists assume that consumers have a set of tastes or preferences they use to guide them in choosing between goods. These tastes differ substantially among individuals. Let's start by specifying the underlying assumptions in the economist's model of consumer behavior.

Properties of Consumer Preferences

Do not do unto others as you would that they should do unto you. Their tastes may not be the same. —George Bernard Shaw

Economists make three critical assumptions about the properties of consumers' preferences. For brevity, they refer to these properties as *completeness*, *transitivity*, and *more is better* (or *nonsatiation*).

Completeness. The completeness property holds that, when facing a choice between any two bundles of goods, a consumer can rank them so that one and only one of the following three relationships is true.

1. The consumer prefers the first bundle to the second.
2. The consumer prefers the second bundle to the first.
3. The consumer likes the two bundles equally and therefore is indifferent between the two bundles.

The completeness property rules out the possibility that the consumer cannot rank the bundles. Indifference is allowed, but indecision is not.

Transitivity. We assume that preferences are transitive. More specifically, we say that if a consumer *weakly prefers* Bundle *a* to Bundle *b*—likes *a* at least as much as *b*—and weakly prefers Bundle *b* to Bundle *c*, the consumer also weakly prefers Bundle *a* to Bundle *c*.

Transitivity of weak preference implies that indifference is also transitive: if a consumer is indifferent between Bundle *a* and Bundle *b*, and is indifferent between Bundle *b* and Bundle *c*, then the consumer must also be indifferent between Bundle *a* and Bundle *c*. Strict preference must also be transitive: If the consumer strictly prefers *a* to *b* and *b* to *c*, it follows that the consumer must strictly prefer *a* to *c*. Also, if the consumer prefers *a* to *b*, and is indifferent between *b* and *c*, then the consumer must also prefer *a* to *c*.

Transitivity is a necessary condition for what most people view as *rational behavior*. Suppose Amy told you she would prefer a scoop of ice cream to a piece of cake but

Mackenzie and Chase are Civilization's greatest threat.

would prefer a piece of cake to a chocolate bar, and then added that she would prefer a chocolate bar to a scoop of ice cream. You might reasonably accuse her of being irrational or inconsistent. At the very least, it would be difficult to know which dessert to serve her.

More Is Better. The more-is-better property holds that, all else being the same, more of a good is better than less. This property is really just a statement of what we mean by a **good**: a commodity for which more is preferred to less, at least at some levels of consumption. In contrast, a **bad** is something for which less is preferred to more, as with pollution (which we study in Chapter 16). Because managers primarily care about goods, we will concentrate on them.

The more-is-better property is not essential for the following analysis of consumer preferences—our most important results would hold even without this property. These results would, if properly interpreted, apply to bads and to items we do not care about one way or the other, as well as for goods. However, the more-is-better assumption greatly simplifies the analysis.

Mini-Case

You Can't Have Too Much Money

Not surprisingly, studies based on data from many nations find that wealthier people are happier on average than poorer people (Gere and Schimmack, 2017). But, do people become satiated? Can people be so rich that they can buy everything they want such that additional income does not increase their feelings of well-being? Using data from many countries, Stevenson and Wolfers (2013) found no evidence of a satiation point beyond which wealthier countries or wealthier individuals have no further increases in subjective well-being. Moreover, they found a clear positive relationship between average levels of self-reported feelings of happiness or satisfaction and income per capita within and across countries, although this effect is small at very high income levels.

Less scientific, but perhaps more compelling, is a survey of wealthy U.S. citizens who were asked, "How much wealth do you need to live comfortably?" On average, those with a net worth of over $1 million said they needed $2.4 million to live comfortably, those with at least $5 million in net worth said they needed $10.4 million, and those with at least $10 million wanted $18.1 million. Apparently, most people never have enough.

Preference Maps

Surprisingly, with just the completeness, transitivity, and more-is-better properties, we can tell a lot about a consumer's preferences. One of the simplest ways to summarize information about a consumer's preferences is to create a graphical interpretation—sometimes called a *preference map*. For graphical simplicity, we concentrate on choices between only two goods, but the model can be generalized algebraically to handle any number of goods.

Each semester, Lisa, who lives for fast food, decides how many pizzas and burritos to eat. The various bundles of pizzas and burritos she might consume are shown in panel a of Figure 4.1, with (individual-size) pizzas per semester on the horizontal axis and burritos per semester on the vertical axis.

At Bundle e, for example, Lisa consumes 25 pizzas and 15 burritos per semester. The more-is-better property implies that Lisa prefers all the bundles that lie above and to the right (area A) to Bundle e because they contain at least as much or more

FIGURE 4.1 Bundles of Pizzas and Burritos That Lisa Might Consume

Pizzas per semester are on the horizontal axis, and burritos per semester are on the vertical axis.
(a) Lisa prefers more to less, so she prefers Bundle e to any bundle in area B, including d. Similarly, she prefers any bundle in area A, including f, to e.

(b) The indifference curve, I^1, shows a set of bundles (including c, e, and a) among which she is indifferent: She likes all three bundles on this curve equally.
(c) The three indifference curves, I^1, I^2, and I^3, are part of Lisa's preference map, which summarizes her preferences.

of both pizzas and burritos as Bundle e. Thus, she prefers Bundle f (30 pizzas and 20 burritos) in that region.

By using the more-is-better property, we know that Lisa prefers Bundle e to all the bundles that lie in area B, below and to the left of Bundle e, such as Bundle d (15 pizzas and 10 burritos). All the bundles in area B contain fewer pizzas or fewer burritos or fewer of both than does Bundle e.

From panel a, we do not know whether Lisa prefers Bundle e to bundles such as b (30 pizzas and 10 burritos) in area D, which is the region below and to the right of e, or c (15 pizzas and 25 burritos) in area C, which is the region above and to the left of Bundle e. We can't use the more-is-better property to determine which bundle she prefers because each of these bundles contains more of one good and less of the other than e does. To be able to state with certainty whether Lisa prefers particular bundles in areas C or D to Bundle e, we have to know more about her tastes for pizza and burritos.

Preferences and Indifference Curves.   Suppose we asked Lisa to identify all the bundles that give her the same amount of pleasure she gets from consuming Bundle e. In panel b of Figure 4.1, we use her answers to draw curve I^1 through all bundles she likes as much as she likes e. Curve I^1 is an **indifference curve**: the set of all bundles of goods that a consumer views as being equally desirable.

Indifference curve I^1 includes Bundles c, e, and a, so Lisa is indifferent about consuming Bundles c, e, and a. From this indifference curve, we also know that Lisa prefers Bundle e (25 pizzas and 15 burritos) to Bundle b (30 pizzas and 10 burritos). How do we know that? Bundle b lies below and to the left of Bundle a, so Bundle a is preferred to Bundle b due to the more-is-better property. Both Bundle e and Bundle a are on indifference curve I^1, so Lisa likes Bundle e as much as Bundle a. Because Lisa is indifferent between e and a and she prefers a to b, she must prefer e to b by transitivity.

If we asked Lisa many, many questions, we could, in principle, draw an entire set of indifference curves through every possible bundle of burritos and pizzas. We summarize Lisa's preferences in an **indifference map** or *preference map*, which is a complete set of indifference curves that summarize a consumer's tastes. We refer to it as a *map* because it uses the same principle as a topographical or contour map, in which each line shows all points with the same height or elevation. With an indifference map, each line shows points (combinations of goods) with the same utility or well-being. Panel c of Figure 4.1 shows three of Lisa's indifference curves: I^1, I^2, and I^3. In this figure, the indifference curves are parallel, but they need not be.

We can demonstrate that all indifference curve maps must have the following four properties.

1. Bundles on indifference curves farther from the origin are preferred to those on indifference curves closer to the origin.
2. An indifference curve goes through every possible bundle.
3. Indifference curves cannot cross.
4. Indifference curves slope downward.

First, we show that bundles on indifference curves farther from the origin are preferred to those on indifference curves closer to the origin. By the more-is-better property, Lisa prefers Bundle f to Bundle e in panel c of Figure 4.1. She is indifferent among all the bundles on indifference curve I^3 and Bundle f, just as she is indifferent among all the bundles, such as Bundle c, on indifference curve I^2, and Bundle e. By the more-is-better property, she prefers Bundle f to Bundle e, which she likes as much as Bundle c, so she also prefers Bundle f to Bundle c. By this type of reasoning, she prefers all bundles on I^3 to all bundles on I^2.

Second, we show that an indifference curve goes through every possible bundle. This property is a consequence of the completeness assumption: The consumer can compare any bundle to another. Compared to a given bundle, some bundles are preferred to it, some are enjoyed equally, and some are inferior to it. Connecting the bundles that give the same well-being produces an indifference curve that includes the given bundle.

Third, we show that indifference curves cannot cross. If two indifference curves did cross, the bundle at the point of intersection would be on both indifference curves. But a given bundle cannot be on two indifference curves. Suppose that two indifference curves crossed at Bundle e, as in panel a of Figure 4.2. Because Bundles e and a lie on the same indifference curve I^1, Lisa is indifferent between e and a. Similarly, she is indifferent between e and b because both are on I^2. By transitivity, if Lisa is indifferent between e and a, and she is indifferent between e and b, she must be indifferent between a and b. But that's impossible! Bundle b is above and to the right of Bundle a, which means it contains more of both goods. Thus, Lisa *must* prefer b to a because of the more-is-better property. Because preferences are transitive and consumers prefer more to less, indifference curves cannot cross.

Finally, we show that indifference curves must be downward sloping. Suppose, to the contrary, that an indifference curve sloped upward, as in panel b of Figure 4.2. The consumer is indifferent between Bundles a and b because both lie on the same indifference curve, I. But the consumer must prefer b to a by the more-is-better property: Bundle a lies below and to the left of Bundle b. Because of this contradiction—the consumer cannot both be indifferent between a and b and strictly prefer b to a—indifference curves cannot be upward sloping. For example, if Lisa views pizza and burritos as goods, she cannot be indifferent between a bundle of one pizza and one burrito and another bundle with two of each.

Willingness to Substitute Between Goods. Lisa is willing to make some trade-offs between goods. The downward slope of her indifference curves shows that Lisa is willing to give up some burritos for more pizza or vice versa. She is indifferent

FIGURE 4.2 Impossible Indifference Curves

(a) Suppose that the indifference curves cross at Bundle e. Lisa is indifferent between e and a on indifference curve I^1 and between e and b on I^2. If Lisa is indifferent between e and a and she is indifferent between e and b, she must be indifferent between a and b by transitivity. But b has more of both pizzas and burritos than a, so she *must* prefer a to b. Because of this contradiction, indifference curves cannot cross. (b) Suppose that indifference curve I slopes upward. The consumer is indifferent between b and a because they lie on I but prefers b to a by the more-is-better assumption. Because of this contradiction, indifference curves cannot be upward sloping.

between Bundles a and b on her indifference curve I in panel a of Figure 4.3. If she initially has Bundle a (eight burritos and three pizzas), she could get to Bundle b (five burritos and four pizzas) by trading three burritos for one more pizza. She is indifferent as to whether or not she makes this trade.

The **marginal rate of substitution** (MRS) measures Lisa's willingness to trade one good for another. The MRS shows the rate at which a consumer can substitute one good for another while remaining on the same indifference curve. Graphically, the MRS is the slope of the indifference curve.[1] If pizza lies on the horizontal axis, Lisa's marginal rate of substitution of burritos for pizza is

$$MRS = \frac{\Delta B}{\Delta Z},$$

where ΔB is the number of burritos Lisa will give up to get ΔZ more pizzas while staying on the same indifference curve. Roughly speaking, we can say that the MRS is the amount of one good a consumer will sacrifice to obtain one more unit of another good while staying on the same indifference curve. If ΔZ is 1, then the associated value of ΔB is the MRS. Thus, if Lisa is willing to give up three burritos ($\Delta B = -3$) to get one more pizza ($\Delta Z = 1$), then the MRS is $-3/1 = -3$. We can illustrate why the MRS is negative by moving from Bundle a to Bundle b in panel a of Figure 4.3. The negative sign shows that Lisa is willing to give up some of one good to get more of the other: Her indifference curve slopes downward.

FIGURE 4.3 Marginal Rate of Substitution

(a) At Bundle a, Lisa is willing to give up three burritos for one more pizza; at b, she is willing to give up only two burritos to obtain another pizza. That is, the relatively more burritos she has, the more she is willing to trade for another pizza.
(b) An indifference curve of this shape is unlikely to be observed. Lisa would be willing to give up more burritos to get one more pizza, the fewer the burritos she has. Moving from Bundle c to b, she will trade one pizza for three burritos, whereas moving from b to a, she will trade one pizza for two burritos, even though she now has relatively more burritos to pizzas.

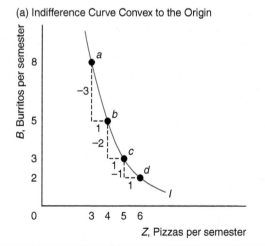
(a) Indifference Curve Convex to the Origin

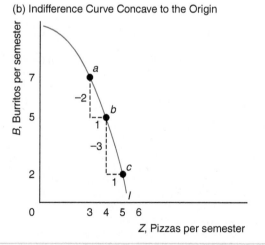
(b) Indifference Curve Concave to the Origin

---

[1]The *slope* of a straight line is "the rise over the run": It describes how much we move along the vertical axis (rise) as we move along the horizontal axis (run). The slope of an indifference curve at a particular point is the slope of a straight line that is tangent to the indifference curve at that point.

We are out of tickets for Swan Lake. Do you want tickets for Wrestlemania?

In specifying the *MRS*, we must be clear about which good is on the horizontal axis. Because pizza is on the horizontal axis in our figure, the *MRS* of "burritos for pizza" is −3, which is the slope of the indifference curve. If we were to switch axes so that burritos were on the horizontal axis, we could calculate the *MRS* of "pizza for burritos," which measures how much pizza Lisa would give up to get one more burrito while staying on the same indifference curve. In this case, the *MRS* of pizza for burritos would be $\Delta Z / \Delta B$, which is $-\frac{1}{3}$. From Lisa's point of view, one pizza is worth 3 burritos (the *MRS* of burritos for pizza is −3) or, equivalently, 1 burrito is worth about $\frac{1}{3}$ of a pizza (the *MRS* of pizza for burritos is $-\frac{1}{3}$).

Curvature of Indifference Curves. The indifference curves we have used so far, such as *I* in panel a of Figure 4.3, are *convex* to the origin of the graph: that is, the indifference curves are "bowed in" toward the origin.

Because the indifference curve in panel a is convex, when Lisa has a large number of burritos, *B*, she is willing to give up more of that good to get one more pizza, *Z*, than she would if she had only a small number of burritos. Starting at Bundle *a* in panel a of Figure 4.3, Lisa is willing to give up three burritos to obtain one more pizza. If she has Bundle *b*, she is willing to trade only two burritos for a pizza. If she has Bundle *c*, she is even less willing to trade; she will give up only one burrito for another pizza. This willingness to trade fewer burritos for one more pizza as we move down and to the right along the indifference curve reflects a *diminishing marginal rate of substitution*.

An indifference curve doesn't have to be convex, but casual observation suggests that most people's indifference curves over most pairs of products are convex. It is unlikely, for example, that Lisa's indifference curves would be *concave*, as in panel b of Figure 4.3. If her indifference curve were concave, Lisa would be willing to give up more burritos to get one more pizza when she has fewer burritos. In panel b, she trades one pizza for three burritos moving from Bundle *c* to *b*, and she trades one pizza for only two burritos moving from Bundle *b* to *a*, even though her ratio of burritos to pizza is greater.

Two extreme types of indifference curves are plausible: straight-line indifference curves and right-angle indifference curves. Straight-line indifference curves reflect **perfect substitutes**, which are goods that are essentially equivalent from the consumer's point of view. The consumer is completely indifferent between the two goods. For example, if Bill cannot taste any difference between Coca-Cola and Pepsi-Cola, he views them as perfect substitutes: he is indifferent between one additional can of Coke and one additional can of Pepsi. His indifference curves for these two goods are straight, parallel lines with a slope of −1 everywhere along the curve, as in panel a of Figure 4.4. Thus, Bill's marginal rate of substitution is −1 at every point along these indifference curves.

The slope of indifference curves of perfect substitutes need not always be −1; it can be any constant rate. For example, Helen knows from reading the labels that Clorox bleach is twice as strong as a generic brand, but otherwise no different. As a result,

FIGURE 4.4 Perfect Substitutes, Perfect Complements, Imperfect Substitutes

(a) Bill views Coke and Pepsi as perfect substitutes. His indifference curves are straight, parallel lines with a marginal rate of substitution (slope) of −1. Bill is willing to exchange one can of Coke for one can of Pepsi.
(b) Cathy likes pie à la mode but does not like pie or ice cream by itself: She views ice cream and

pie as perfect complements. She will not substitute between the two; she consumes them only in equal quantities.
(c) Lisa views burritos and pizza as imperfect substitutes. Her indifference curve lies between the extreme cases of perfect substitutes and perfect complements.

(a) Perfect Substitutes

(b) Perfect Complements

(c) Imperfect Substitutes

she is indifferent between one cup of Clorox and two cups of the generic bleach. If the generic bleach is on the vertical axis, the slope of her indifference curve is −2.[2]

The other extreme case is **perfect complements**: goods that an individual wants to consume only in fixed proportions. Cathy doesn't like pie by itself or vanilla ice cream by itself, but she loves pie à la mode (a slice of pie with a scoop of vanilla ice cream on top). Her indifference curves have right angles in panel b of Figure 4.4. Bundle *a* consists of one piece of pie and one scoop of ice cream, combining to make one serving of pie à la mode. If she gets an additional scoop of ice cream but no pie to go with it (Bundle *d*) she remains on the same indifference curve: the extra scoop of ice cream by itself provides no additional benefit to Cathy. Adding a third scoop of ice cream (shown as Bundle *e*) is also a matter of indifference to Cathy. She gets no extra benefit and remains on the same indifference curve. Similarly, if Cathy has only one scoop of ice cream, additional pieces of pie beyond the first leave her on the same indifference curve.

With preferences like this, Cathy consumes only bundles like *a*, *b*, and *c*, in which pie and ice cream are in equal proportions. She would never want to pay for any additional ice cream that was not matched by a piece of pie, and she would never want to pay for a piece of pie without a scoop of ice cream to go with it. She consumes ice cream and pie only in equal proportions.

With a bundle like *a*, *b*, or *c*, she will not substitute a piece of pie for an extra scoop of ice cream. For example, if she were at *b*, she would be unwilling to give up an extra slice of pie to get, say, two extra scoops of ice cream, as at point *e*. Indeed, she wouldn't give up the slice of pie even for a virtually unlimited amount of extra ice cream because the extra ice cream is worthless to her.

---

[2]Sometimes it is difficult to guess which goods are close substitutes. According to Harper's Index 1994, flowers, perfume, and fire extinguishers rank 1, 2, and 3 among "appropriate" Mother's Day gifts. Few would guess that perfume and fire extinguishers are substitutes.

The standard-shaped, convex indifference curve in panel c of Figure 4.4 lies between these two extreme examples. Convex indifference curves show that a consumer views two goods as imperfect substitutes.

4.2 Utility

Underlying our model of consumer behavior is the belief that consumers can compare various bundles of goods and decide which one gives them the greatest pleasure or satisfaction. It is possible to summarize a consumer's preferences by assigning a numerical value to each possible bundle to reflect the consumer's relative ranking of these bundles.

Following Jeremy Bentham, John Stuart Mill, and other nineteenth-century British economist-philosophers, economists apply the term **utility** to this set of numerical values that reflect the relative rankings of various bundles of goods. The statement that "Lorna prefers Bundle x to Bundle y" is equivalent to the statement that "consuming Bundle x gives Lorna more utility than consuming Bundle y." For example, Lorna prefers x to y if Bundle x gives Lorna a utility level of 10 and Bundle y gives her a utility level of 8.

Utility Functions

If we knew the **utility function**—the relationship between utility measures and every possible bundle of goods—we could summarize the information in indifference maps succinctly. Lisa's utility function, $U(B, Z)$, tells us how much utility she gets from B burritos and Z pizzas. Given that her utility function reflects her preferences, if Lisa prefers Bundle 1, (B_1, Z_1), to Bundle 2, (B_2, Z_2), then the utility she gets from the first bundle exceeds that from the second bundle: $U(B_1, Z_1) > U(B_2, Z_2)$.

For example, suppose that the utility, U, that Lisa gets from burritos and pizzas is

$$U = \sqrt{BZ}.$$

From this function, we know that the more she consumes of either good, the greater the utility she receives. Using this function, we can determine whether Lisa would be happier if she had Bundle x with 9 burritos and 16 pizzas or Bundle y with 13 of each. The utility she gets from x is 12 $(=\sqrt{9 \times 16})$. The utility she gets from y is 13 $(=\sqrt{13 \times 13})$. Therefore, she prefers y to x.

The utility function is a concept that economists use to help them think about consumer behavior; utility functions do not exist in any fundamental sense. If you asked your mother what her utility function is, she would be puzzled—unless, of course, she is an economist. But if you asked her enough questions about choices of bundles of goods, you could construct a function that accurately summarizes her preferences. For example, by questioning people, Rousseas and Hart (1951) constructed indifference curves between eggs and bacon, and MacCrimmon and Toda (1969) constructed indifference curves between French pastries and money (which can be used to buy all other goods).

Typically, consumers can easily answer questions about whether they prefer one bundle to another, such as, "Do you prefer a bundle with one scoop of ice cream and two pieces of cake to another bundle with two scoops of ice cream and one piece of cake?" But they have difficulty answering questions about how much more they prefer one bundle to another because they don't have a measure to describe how their pleasure from two goods or bundles differs. Therefore, we may know a consumer's rank-ordering of bundles even if we do not have a good idea of how much that consumer prefers one bundle to another.

Ordinal and Cardinal Utility

The term *ordinal* is used to describe a measure that contains information only about rankings or orderings. For example, a movie critic might give a movie between one and four stars. However, a 4-star movie is not necessarily "twice as good" as a 2-star movie or four times as good as a 1-star movie. All we can say is that the critic likes the 4-star movie better than the 2-star movie, which in turn the critic prefers to the 1-star movie: We know only the critic's relative rankings. Thus, movie rankings are an ordinal measure, even though numbers (the number of stars) might be used to represent the rankings. With utility, if we know only a consumer's relative rankings of bundles, our measure of utility is *ordinal*.

A *cardinal* measure allows us to make absolute numerical comparisons, as with length or weight. Cardinal measures contain more information than ordinal measures. For example, money is a cardinal measure. If Sofia has $100 and Hu has $50, we know not only that Sofia has more money than Hu (an ordinal comparison), but that she has precisely twice as much as Hu (a cardinal comparison).

Economists sometimes treat utility as a cardinal measure, allowing for statements like "Bundle *A* is twice as good as Bundle *B*," instead of just saying that Bundle *A* is preferred to Bundle *B*. However, most of our discussion of consumer choice in this chapter holds if utility has only ordinal properties. If utility is an ordinal measure, we should not put any weight on the absolute difference between the utility associated with one bundle and another. We care only about the relative utility or ranking of the two bundles.

Marginal Utility

Using Lisa's utility function over burritos and pizza, we can show how her utility changes if she gets to consume more of one of the goods. Suppose that Lisa has the utility function in Figure 4.5. The curve in panel a shows how Lisa's utility rises as she consumes more pizzas while we hold her consumption of burritos fixed at 10. Because pizza is a *good*, Lisa's utility rises as she consumes more pizza.

If her consumption of pizzas increases from $Z = 4$ to 5, $\Delta Z = 5 - 4 = 1$, and her utility increases from $U = 230$ to 250, $\Delta U = 250 - 230 = 20$. The extra utility ($\Delta U$) that she gets from consuming one more unit of a good ($\Delta Z = 1$) is the **marginal utility** from that good. Thus, marginal utility is the slope of the utility function as we hold the quantity of the other good constant.

$$MU_Z = \frac{\Delta U}{\Delta Z}.$$

Lisa's marginal utility from increasing her consumption of pizza from 4 to 5 is

$$MU_Z = \frac{\Delta U}{\Delta Z} = \frac{20}{1} = 20.$$

FIGURE 4.5 Utility and Marginal Utility

As Lisa consumes more pizza, holding her consumption of burritos constant at 10, her total utility, U, increases and her marginal utility of pizza, MU_Z, decreases (though it remains positive).

(a) If she increases her consumption of pizza from 4 to 5 per semester while holding her consumption of burritos fixed at 10, her utility increases from 230 to 250. Her marginal utility is the extra utility she gets, $\Delta U = 250 - 230 = 20$ from an extra pizza, $\Delta Z = 1$, which is $MU_Z = \Delta U / \Delta Z = 20/1 = 20$.
(b) At $Z = 5$, the height of Lisa's marginal utility curve is 20.

Panel b in Figure 4.5 shows that Lisa's marginal utility from consuming one more pizza varies with the number of pizzas she consumes, holding her consumption of burritos constant. Her marginal utility of pizza curve falls as her consumption of pizza increases, but the marginal utility remains positive: Each extra pizza gives Lisa pleasure, but it gives her less pleasure relative to other goods than did the previous pizza.

Using Calculus

Marginal Utility

The marginal utility from a particular good is the partial derivative of the utility function with respect to that good, which measures how utility changes as we change one good while holding consumption of other goods constant. Thus, if Lisa's utility function is $U(B, Z)$, her marginal utility from Z is the partial derivative of U with respect to Z: $MU_Z = \partial U(B, Z)/\partial Z$.

Marginal Rates of Substitution

Earlier we learned that the marginal rate of substitution (MRS) is the slope of the indifference curve. The marginal rate of substitution depends on marginal utilities. If Lisa has 10 burritos and 4 pizzas in a semester and gets one more pizza, her utility rises. That extra utility is the marginal utility from the last pizza, MU_Z. Similarly, if she receives one extra burrito instead, her marginal utility from the last burrito is MU_B.

Suppose that Lisa trades from one bundle on an indifference curve to another by giving up some burritos to gain more pizza. She gains marginal utility from the extra pizza but loses marginal utility from fewer burritos. We can show that the marginal rate of substitution can be written in terms of the marginal utilities:

$$MRS = \frac{\Delta B}{\Delta Z} = -\frac{MU_Z}{MU_B} \qquad (4.1)$$

Equation 4.1 tells us that the MRS, which is the slope of the indifference curve at a particular bundle, depends on the negative of the ratio of the marginal utility of pizza to the marginal utility of burritos. (We derive Equation 4.1 using calculus in Appendix 4A.)

An example illustrates the logic underlying Equation 4.1. Suppose that Lisa gains one unit of utility (one *util*) if she eats one more burrito, $MU_B = 1$, and two utils if she has one more pizza, $MU_Z = 2$. That is, one more pizza gives her as much extra pleasure as two burritos. Thus, her utility stays the same—she stays on the same indifference curve—if she exchanges two burritos for one pizza, so her $MRS = -MU_Z/MU_B = -2$.

4.3 The Budget Constraint

Knowing an individual's preferences is only the first step in analyzing that person's consumption behavior. Consumers maximize their well-being subject to constraints. The most important constraint most of us face in deciding what to consume is our personal budget constraint.

If we cannot save and borrow, our budget is the income we receive in a given period. If we can save and borrow, we can save money early in life to consume later, such as when we retire, or we can borrow money when we are young and repay those sums later in life. Savings are, in effect, a good that consumers can buy. For simplicity, we assume that each consumer has a fixed amount of money to spend now, so we can use the terms *budget* and *income* interchangeably.

For graphical simplicity, we assume that consumers spend their money on only two goods. If Lisa spends all her budget, Y, on pizza and burritos, then her budget constraint is

$$p_B B + p_Z Z = Y, \qquad (4.2)$$

where p_B is the price of burritos, p_Z is the price of pizza, $p_B B$ is the amount she spends on burritos, and $p_Z Z$ is the amount she spends on pizzas, Equation 4.2 shows that her expenditures on burritos and pizza use up her entire budget.

How many burritos can Lisa buy? Subtracting $p_Z Z$ from both sides of Equation 4.2 and dividing both sides by p_B, we determine the number of burritos she can purchase to be

$$B = \frac{Y}{p_B} - \frac{p_Z}{p_B} Z. \qquad (4.3)$$

According to Equation 4.3, Lisa can afford to buy more burritos only if

- her income (Y) increases,
- the price of burritos (p_B) or pizza (p_Z) falls, or
- she purchases fewer pizzas (Z).

For example, if Lisa has one more dollar of income (Y), she can buy $1/p_B$ more burritos.

If $p_Z = \$1$, $p_B = \$2$, and $Y = \$50$, Equation 4.3 is

$$B = \frac{\$50}{\$2} - \frac{\$1}{\$2}Z = 25 - \tfrac{1}{2}Z. \tag{4.4}$$

As Equation 4.4 shows, every two pizzas cost Lisa one burrito. How many burritos can she buy if she spends all her money on burritos? She can buy 25 burritos: By setting $Z = 0$ in Equation 4.3, we find that $B = Y/p_B = \$50/\$2 = 25$. Similarly, if she spends all her money on pizza, she can buy 50 of them: Setting $B = 0$, we can solve for $Z = Y/p_Z = \$50/\$1 = 50$.

Instead of spending all her money on pizza or all on burritos, she can buy some of each. Table 4.1 shows four possible bundles she could buy. For example, she can buy 20 burritos and 10 pizzas with $50.

Equation 4.4 is plotted in Figure 4.6. This line is called a **budget line** or *budget constraint*: the bundles of goods that can be bought if the entire budget is spent on those goods at given prices. This budget line shows the combinations of burritos and pizzas that Lisa can buy if she spends all of her $50 on these two goods. The four bundles in Table 4.1 are labeled on this line.

Lisa could, of course, buy any bundle that costs less than $50. The **opportunity set** is all the bundles a consumer can buy, including all the bundles inside the budget constraint and on the budget constraint (all those bundles of positive Z and B such that $p_B B + p_Z Z \le Y$). Lisa's opportunity set is the shaded area in Figure 4.6. She could buy 10 burritos and 15 pieces of pizza for $35, which falls inside the constraint. Unless she wants to spend the other $15 on some other good, though, she might as well spend all of it on the food she loves and pick a bundle on the budget constraint rather than inside it.[3]

TABLE 4.1 Allocations of a $50 Budget Between Burritos and Pizza

Bundle	Burritos, $2 each	Pizza, $1 each
a	25	0
b	20	10
c	10	30
d	0	50

[3]The budget line in Figure 4.6 is a smooth, continuous line, which implies that Lisa can buy fractional numbers of burritos and pizzas. Is that true? Will a restaurant sell you half a burrito? Maybe not. Why, then, don't we draw the budget line and opportunity set as discrete points (bundles) of whole numbers of burritos and pizzas instead of a continuous line? One reason is that Lisa can buy a burrito at a *rate* of one-half per time period. If Lisa buys one burrito every other week, she buys an average of one-half burrito every week. Thus, it is plausible that she could purchase fractional amounts over a particular time period.

FIGURE 4.6 The Budget Line

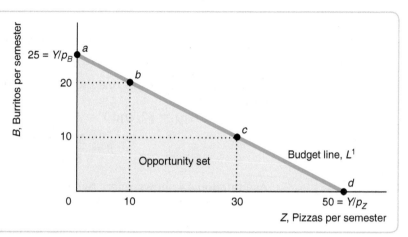

If $Y = \$50$, $p_Z = \$1$, and $p_B = \$2$, Lisa can buy any bundle in the opportunity set, the shaded area, including points on the *budget line*, L^1, $B = Y/p_B - (p_Z/p_B)Z = \$50/\$2 - (\$1/\$2)Z$. If Lisa buys one more unit of Z, she must reduce her consumption of B by $-(p_Z/p_B) = -\frac{1}{2}$ to stay within her budget. Thus, the slope, $\Delta B/\Delta Z$, of her budget line, which is also called the marginal rate of transformation (MRT), is $-(p_Z/p_B) = -\frac{1}{2}$.

Slope of the Budget Line

The relative prices of the two goods determine the slope of the budget line. According to the budget line, Equation 4.3, $B = Y/p_B - (p_Z/p_B)Z$, so every extra unit of Z that Lisa purchases reduces B by $-p_Z/p_B$. That is, the slope of the budget line is $\Delta B/\Delta Z = -p_Z/p_B$. Thus, the slope of the budget line depends on only the relative prices.

Lisa faces prices of $p_Z = \$1$ and $p_B = \$2$, so the slope of her budget line is $-p_Z/p_B = -\$1/\$2 = -\frac{1}{2}$. For example, if we reduce the number of pizzas from 10 at point b in Figure 4.6 to 0 at point a, the number of burritos that Lisa can buy rises from 20 at point b to 25 at point a, so $\Delta B/\Delta Z = (25 - 20)/(0 - 10) = 5/(-10) = -\frac{1}{2}$.

The slope of the budget line is called the **marginal rate of transformation** (MRT): the trade-off the market imposes on the consumer in terms of the amount of one good the consumer must give up to purchase more of the other good:

$$MRT = \frac{\Delta B}{\Delta Z} = -\frac{p_Z}{p_B}. \tag{4.5}$$

Because Lisa's $MRT = -\frac{1}{2}$, she can "trade" an extra pizza for half a burrito or, equivalently, she has to give up two pizzas to obtain an extra burrito.

Using Calculus

The Marginal Rate of Transformation

By differentiating the budget constraint, Equation 4.3, $B = Y/p_B - (p_Z/p_B)Z$, with respect to Z, we confirm that the slope of the budget constraint, or marginal rate of transformation, is $MRT = dB/dZ = -p_Z/p_B$, as in Equation 4.5.

Effects of a Change in Price on the Opportunity Set

If the price of pizza doubles but the price of burritos remains unchanged, the budget line swings in toward the origin in panel a of Figure 4.7. If Lisa spends all her money on burritos, she can buy as many burritos as before, so the budget line still hits the burrito axis at 25. If she spends all her money on pizza, however, she can now buy

FIGURE 4.7 Changes in the Budget Line

(a) If the price of pizza increases from $1 to $2 a slice, Lisa's budget line rotates from L^1 to L^2 around the intercept on the burrito axis. The slope or *MRT* of the original budget line, L^1, is $-\frac{1}{2}$, while the *MRT* of the new budget line L^2 is -1. The shaded area shows the combinations of pizza and burritos that Lisa can no longer afford.

(b) If Lisa's budget doubles from $50 to $100 and prices don't change, her new budget line moves from L^1 to L^3. This shift is parallel: both budget lines have the same slope or *MRT* of $-\frac{1}{2}$. The new opportunity set is larger by the shaded area.

(a) Price of Pizza Doubles

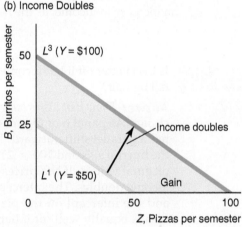

(b) Income Doubles

only half as many pizzas as before, so the budget line intercepts the pizza axis at 25 instead of at 50.

The new budget line is steeper and lies inside the original one. As the price of pizza increases, the slope of the budget line, *MRT*, changes. The original line, L^1, at the original prices, $MRT = -\frac{1}{2}$, shows that Lisa could trade half a burrito for one pizza or two pizzas for one burrito. The new line, L^2, $MRT = p_Z/p_B = -\$2/\$2 = -1$, indicates that she can now trade one burrito for one pizza, due to the increase in the price of pizza.

Unless Lisa wants to eat only burritos, she is unambiguously worse off due to this increase in the price of pizza because she can no longer afford the combinations of pizza and burritos in the shaded "Loss" area.

A decrease in the price of pizza would have the opposite effect: The budget line would rotate outward, pivoting around the intercept on the burrito axis. As a result, Lisa's opportunity set would increase.

Effects of a Change in Income on the Opportunity Set

If the consumer's income increases, the consumer can buy more of all goods. Suppose that prices remain at their original levels ($p_Z = \$1$ and $p_B = \$2$), but Lisa's income increases by $50 per semester to $Y = \$100$. Her budget line shifts outward—away from the origin—and is parallel to the original constraint in panel b of Figure 4.7. Why is the new constraint parallel to the original one? The intercept of the budget line on the burrito axis is Y/p_B, and the intercept on the pizza axis is

Y/p_Z. Thus, holding prices constant, the intercepts shift outward in proportion to the change in income. Originally, if she spent all her money on pizza, Lisa could buy $50 = \$50/\$1$ pizzas; now she can buy $100 = \$100/\$1$. Similarly, the burrito axis intercept goes from $25 = \$50/\$2$ to $50 = \$100/\$2$. Initially, if she consumed 25 burritos, Lisa could not consume any pizza; now if she consumes 25 burritos she can also consume 50 pizzas.

A change in income affects only the position and not the slope of the budget line, because the relative prices of pizza and burritos determine the slope. A decrease in the prices of both pizzas and burritos in the same proportion has the same effect as an increase in income, as the next Q&A shows.

Q&A 4.1

Is Lisa better off if her income doubles or if the prices of both the goods she buys fall by half?

Answer *Show that Lisa's budget line and her opportunity set are the same with either change.* As panel b of Figure 4.7 shows, if her income doubles, her budget line has a parallel shift outward. The new intercepts at $50 = 2Y/p_B = (2 \times 50)/2$ on the burrito axis and $100 = 2Y/p_Z = (2 \times 50)/1$ on the pizza axis are double the original values. If the prices fall by half, her budget line is the same as if her income doubles. The intercept on the burrito axis is $50 = Y/(p_B/2) = 50/(2/2)$, and the intercept on the pizza axis is $100 = Y/(p_Z/2) = 50/(1/2)$. Therefore, Lisa is equally well off if her income doubles *or* if prices fall by half.

Mini-Case

Rationing

During emergencies, governments frequently ration food, gas, and other staples rather than let their prices rise, as the United States and the United Kingdom did during World War II. Cuban citizens receive a ration book that limits their purchases of staples such as rice, legumes, potatoes, bread, eggs, and meat.

Water rationing is common during droughts. In recent years, water quotas have been imposed in parts of Australia, Brazil, Egypt, Honduras, India, Kenya, New Zealand,

Pakistan, South Africa, United States, Venezuela, and elsewhere. Rationing affects consumers' opportunity sets because they cannot necessarily buy as much as they want at market prices.

Q&A 4.2

A government rations water, setting a quota on how much a consumer can purchase. If a consumer can afford to buy 12 thousand gallons a month but the government restricts purchases to no more than 10 thousand gallons a month, how does the consumer's opportunity set change?

Answer

1. *Draw the original opportunity set using a budget line between water and all other goods.* In the graph, the consumer can afford to buy up to 12 thousand gallons of water a month if not constrained. The opportunity set, areas *A* and *B*, is bounded by the axes and the budget line.

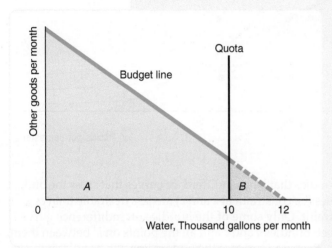

2. *Add a line to the figure showing the quota, and determine the new opportunity set:* A vertical line at 10 thousand on the water axis indicates the quota.

   The new opportunity set, area *A*, is bounded by the axes, the budget line, and the quota line.

3. *Compare the two opportunity sets:* Because of the rationing, the consumer loses part of the original opportunity set: the triangle *B* to the right of the 10 thousand gallons line. The consumer has fewer opportunities because of rationing.

4.4 Constrained Consumer Choice

Were it not for the budget constraint, consumers who prefer more to less would consume unlimited amounts of all goods. Well, they can't have it all! Instead, consumers maximize their well-being subject to their budget constraints. Now, we have to determine the bundle of goods that maximizes well-being subject to the budget constraint.

The Consumer's Optimal Bundle

My problem lies in reconciling my gross habits with my net income. —Errol Flynn

Given information about Lisa's preferences (as summarized by her indifference curves) and how much she can spend (as summarized by her budget line), we can determine Lisa's optimal bundle. Her optimal bundle is the bundle out of all the bundles she can afford that gives her the most pleasure. Here, we use graphical techniques to find her optimal bundle.

We first show that Lisa's optimal bundle must be on the budget line in Figure 4.8. Bundles that lie on indifference curves above the constraint, such as those on I^3, are not in her opportunity set. Although Lisa prefers Bundle *f* on indifference curve I^3 to *e* on I^2, she cannot afford to purchase *f*. Even though Lisa could buy a bundle inside the budget line, she does not want to do so, because more is better than less: For any bundle inside the constraint (such as *d* on I^1), another bundle on the constraint has more of at least one of the two goods, and hence she prefers that bundle. Therefore, the optimal bundle must lie on the budget line.

FIGURE 4.8 **Consumer Maximization, Interior Solution**

Lisa's optimal bundle is e (10 burritos and 30 pizzas) on indifference curve I^2. Indifference curve I^2 is tangent to her budget line at e. Bundle e is the bundle on the highest indifference curve (highest utility) that she can afford. Any bundle that is preferred to e (such as points on indifference curve I^3) lies outside the opportunity set, so she cannot afford them. Bundles inside the opportunity set, such as d, are less desirable than e because they lie on lower indifference curves.

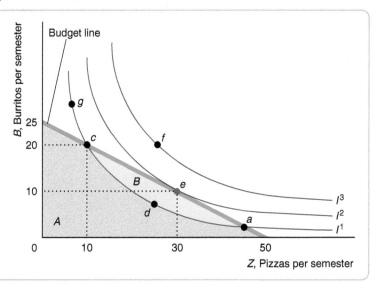

We can also show that bundles that lie on indifference curves that cross the budget line (such as I^1, which crosses the constraint at a and c) are less desirable than certain other bundles on the constraint. Only some of the bundles on indifference curve I^1 lie within the opportunity set: Bundles a and c and all the points on I^1 between them, such as d, can be purchased. Because I^1 crosses the budget line, the bundles between a and c on I^1 lie strictly inside the constraint, so bundles in area B of the opportunity set are preferable to these bundles on I^1 and are affordable. By the more-is-better property, Lisa prefers e to d because e has more of both pizza and burritos than d. By transitivity, e is preferred to a, c, and all the other points on I^1—even those, like g, that Lisa can't afford. Because indifference curve I^1 crosses the budget line, area B contains at least one bundle that is preferred to—lies above and to the right of—at least one bundle on the indifference curve.

Thus, the optimal bundle—the *consumer's optimum*—must lie on the budget line and be on an indifference curve that does not cross it. If Lisa is consuming this bundle, she has no incentive to change her behavior by substituting one good for another.

So far, we've shown that the optimal bundle must lie on an indifference curve that touches the budget line but does not cross it. This condition can hold in two ways. The first is an *interior solution*, in which the optimal bundle has positive quantities of both goods and lies between the ends of the budget line. The other possibility, called a *corner solution*, occurs when the optimal bundle is at one end of the budget line, where the budget line forms a corner with one of the axes.

Interior Solutions. In Figure 4.8, Bundle e on indifference curve I^2 is the optimal bundle. It is in the interior of the budget line away from the corners. Lisa prefers consuming a balanced diet, e, of 10 burritos and 30 pizzas, to eating only one type of food or the other.

For the indifference curve I^2 to touch the budget line but not cross it, it must be *tangent* to the budget line at point e. At the point of tangency, the budget line and the indifference curve have the same slope at the point e where they touch. The slope of the indifference curve, the marginal rate of substitution, measures the rate at which

Lisa is *willing* to trade burritos for pizza: $MRS = -MU_Z/MU_B$, Equation 4.1. The slope of the budget line, the marginal rate of transformation, measures the rate at which Lisa *can* trade burritos for pizza in the market: $MRT = -p_Z/p_B$, Equation 4.5. Thus, Lisa's utility is maximized at the bundle where the rate at which she is willing to trade burritos for pizza equals the rate at which she can trade:

$$MRS = -\frac{MU_Z}{MU_B} = -\frac{p_Z}{p_B} = MRT. \tag{4.6}$$

(Appendix 4B uses calculus to derive Equation 4.6.)

Rearranging terms, this condition is equivalent to

$$\frac{MU_Z}{p_Z} = \frac{MU_B}{p_B}. \tag{4.7}$$

Equation 4.7 says that the marginal utility of pizza divided by the price of a pizza (the amount of extra utility from pizza per dollar spent on pizza), MU_Z/p_Z, equals the marginal utility of burritos divided by the price of a burrito, MU_B/p_B. Thus, Lisa maximizes her utility if the last dollar she spends on pizza gets her as much extra utility as the last dollar she spends on burritos. If the last dollar spent on pizza gave Lisa more extra utility than the last dollar spent on burritos, Lisa could increase her happiness by spending more on pizza and less on burritos.

Q&A 4.3

Nate's utility function over raspberry jelly, J, and peanut butter, N, is $U = JN$. Nate's marginal utility from jelly is $MU_J = N$, and his marginal utility from peanut butter is $MU_N = J$.[4] The raspberry jelly Nate buys is $5 per jar and peanut butter is $10 per jar. Nate has a budget of $100 to allocate to these two items. If Nate maximizes his utility, how much of each good will he consume?

Answer

1. *Derive Nate's budget line by setting his expenditure equal to his available budget.* The expenditure on each item is its price times the amount consumed, so Nate's budget, 100, equals the sum of the expenditures on these two goods: $100 = 5J + 10N$.

2. *Use Equation 4.7 to find the relationship between N and J.* Equation 4.7 states that Nate maximizes his utility if he equalizes his marginal utility per dollar across jelly and peanut butter: $MU_J/5 = MU_N/10$. That is, $N/5 = J/10$ or $N = J/2$.

3. *Substitute this utility-maximizing condition into the budget equation to determine J and N.* Substituting this optimality condition into the budget constraint, we learn that $100 = 5J + 10N = 5J + 10(J/2) = 10J$. Solving this expression for J, we find that $J = 10$.

4. *Substitute the solution for J into the budget line to solve for N.* Substituting $J = 10$ into the budget constraint, we learn that $100 = 5J + 10N = 50 + 10N$, or $50 = 10N$, or $N = 5$. Thus, Nate's utility-maximizing bundle is $J = 10$ and $N = 5$.

---

[4]The marginal utility with respect to J, MU_J, is $\partial U/\partial J = \partial(JN)/\partial J = N$. Similarly, $MU_N = \partial(JN)/\partial N = J$.

Corner Solutions. Some consumers choose to buy only one of the two goods: a corner solution. They so prefer one good to another that they only purchase the preferred good.

Spenser's indifference curves in Figure 4.9 are flatter than Lisa's in Figure 4.8. That is, he is more willing than Lisa to trade pizza for an extra burrito. Spenser's optimal Bundle *e*, where he buys 25 burritos and no pizza, lies on an indifference curve that touches the budget line only once, at the upper-left corner. It is on the highest indifference curve that touches the budget line.

<table>
<tr><td>

Mini-Case

Why Americans Buy More E-Books Than Do Germans

</td><td>

Are you reading this text electronically? E-books are appearing everywhere in the English-speaking world. Thanks to the popularity of the Kindle, iPad, and other e-book readers, e-books accounted for about 11.5% of the U.K. market and close to 20% of the U.S. market, but only about 4.5% of the German market in 2017.

Why are e-books more successful in the United States than in Germany? Jürgen Harth of the German Publishers and Booksellers Association attributed the difference to tastes or what he called a "cultural issue." More than others, Germans love printed books. After all, a German invented printing. As Harth said, "On just about every corner there's a bookshop. That's the big difference between Germany and the United States."

An alternative explanation concerns government regulations and taxes that affect prices in Germany. Even if Germans and Americans had the same tastes, Americans would be more likely to buy e-books because they are less expensive than printed books in the United States. However, e-books are more expensive than printed books in Germany. Unlike in the United States, where publishers and booksellers are free to set prices, Germany regulates book prices. To protect small booksellers, Germany's fixed-price system requires all booksellers to charge the same price for new printed books and for e-books. However, the tax on e-books is higher than on print books, raising the after-tax price of an e-book relative to that of a print book. Is a difference in taste the only reason why U.S. consumers buy relatively more e-books than Germans do, or can different relative prices in the two countries explain this phenomenon?

</td></tr>
</table>

FIGURE 4.9 Consumer Maximization, Corner Solution

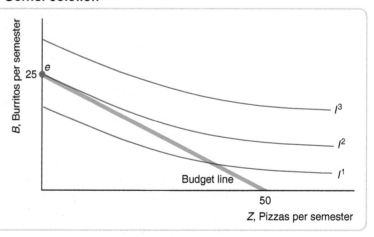

Spenser's indifference curves are flatter than Lisa's indifference curves in Figure 4.8. That is, he is willing to give up more pizzas for one more burrito than is Lisa. Spenser's optimal bundle occurs at a corner of the opportunity set at Bundle *e*: 25 burritos and 0 pizzas.

Q&A 4.4

Must we appeal to variations in taste to explain why Germans and Americans read different types of books, or can taxes and price disparities account for this difference? Suppose that Max, a German, and Bob, an American, are avid readers with identical incomes and tastes. Both are indifferent between reading a novel in a traditional printed book or on an e-reader. The after-tax price of e-books in Germany is higher than that of print books, but e-books cost less than print books in the United States. Use an indifference-curve/budget-line analysis to explain why Bob is more likely to buy e-books than is Max.

Answer

1. *Describe their indifference curves.* Both Max and Bob view e-books and printed books as perfect substitutes, so their indifference curves have a slope of -1. One such indifference curve is I in the figure.

2. *Describe the slopes of their budget line.* With printed books on the vertical axis, Max faces a budget line, L^M, that is relatively steep—steeper than his indifference curve—because the German taxes make e-books relatively expensive. Bob has a budget line that is flatter than his indifference curve.

3. *Use an indifference curve and a budget line to show why Max and Bob make different choices.* As the figure shows, Bob maximizes his utility by spending his entire book budget on e-books. He chooses the Bundle e_B, where his indifference curve I hits his budget line L^B on the e-book axis. In contrast, Max spends his entire book budget on printed books, at point e_M.

   If Bob and Max viewed the two types of books as imperfect substitutes and had the usual convex indifference curves, they would each buy a mix of e-books and printed books. However, because of the relatively lower price of e-books in the United States, Bob would buy relatively more e-books.

Promotions

Managers often use promotions to induce consumers to purchase more units. Two of the most frequently used promotions are *buy one, get one free* (BOGO) and *buy one, get the second one at half-price*. Such deals create kinks in the consumer's budget line. Consequently, consumers' responses to such offers depend on their tastes (the shape of their indifference curves).

Buy One, Get One Free. In a BOGO promotion, a customer gets a free unit of the product after buying one unit (or some other number of units) at the regular price. For example, a supermarket might offer a fifth fruit drink for free if the customer buys four at the regular price. Promotions of this type are often used for items like CDs, restaurant meals, movie tickets, and other relatively inexpensive consumer products. A 2018 search of Google for "buy one get one free" found 285 million Web sites. Remarkably, even a realty company, Michael Crews Development, made a BOGO offer: If you bought a home at $1.6 million or more, you would get a second $400,000 house at no additional charge.

In 2018, the Four Seasons Resort in the Bahamas offered one free night at its five-star hotel to customers who paid for three nights at the normal rate. The effect of such promotions on purchasing behavior can be illustrated using indifference curves and budget lines. Before the promotion was announced, Angela and Betty were separately planning to stay at the hotel for two nights each this month. Each has the same income and allocates the same budget to her vacation.

Figure 4.10 shows that Angela takes advantage of the promotion and Betty does not because their tastes differ. Both panels of the figure show the same budget lines. The horizontal axis shows the nights spent at the hotel per month, and the vertical axis measures all other goods per month. Their initial budget line before the promotion, L^1, is a standard downward-sloping line, where the slope depends on the ratio of the full price of a hotel room to the price of other goods.

The new BOGO budget line, L^2, is the same as the initial budget line for stays of fewer than three nights. However, if Angela or Betty pays for three nights, she gets an extra night for free. That is, she can get a fourth night with no reduction in her consumption of other goods. Therefore, her new budget line has a horizontal segment one night wide starting at three nights. For additional nights (beyond four) she would pay the regular price, so L^2 resumes its same downward slope for stays exceeding four nights.

FIGURE 4.10 **BOGO Promotion**

Angela and Betty are separately deciding how many nights to stay at the resort. Without the promotion, both Angela and Betty have an initial budget line of L^1. With the BOGO promotion where if either stays three nights, she gets the fourth night for free, the new budget line is L^2.
(a) Without the promotion, Angela's indifference curve I^1 is tangent to L^1 at point x, so she chooses to spend two nights at the resort. With the BOGO promotion, Angela prefers to purchase three nights and get an extra night for free with the promotion than pay for and stay only two nights: because her indifference curve I^1 cuts the new budget line L^2, she has a higher indifference curve, I^2, that touches L^2 at point y, so that she chooses to stay four nights. (b) Without the promotion, Betty chooses to stay two nights at x where her indifference curve I^3 is tangent to L^1. Because I^3 does not cut the new budget line L^2, no higher indifference curve can touch L^2, so Betty stays only two nights, at x, and does not take advantage of the BOGO promotion.

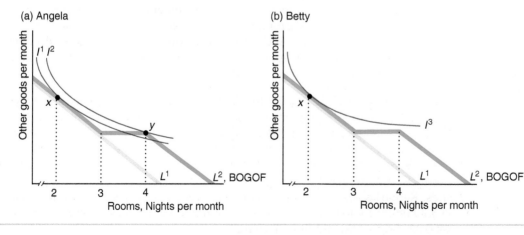

In panel a, Angela's indifference curve I^1 is tangent to L^1 at point x, which is located at two nights on the horizontal axis. Because I^1 is the highest indifference curve that touches her pre-promotion budget line, she chooses to spend two nights at the resort. However, her indifference curve I^1 cuts the new budget line L^2, so she can do better. A higher indifference curve, I^2, touches L^2 at point y, where she chooses to stay four nights. That is, Angela would prefer to purchase three nights and get an extra night for free with the promotion than pay for and stay only two nights.

Betty's indifference curves in panel b differ from Angela's. Again, we assume that initially Betty chooses to stay two nights at Bundle x, where her indifference curve I^3 is tangent to L^1. Because I^3 is flatter than Angela's I^1 in panel a (Betty is willing to give up fewer other goods for another night at the resort than is Angela), I^3 does not cut the new budget line L^2. Thus, no higher indifference curve can touch L^2, so Betty stays only two nights, at x, and does not take advantage of the promotion.

Managerial Implication Designing Promotions	When deciding whether to use a BOGO promotion, a manager should compare the benefit to the cost. For example, offering such a promotion is more likely to raise the hotel's profit if it has excess capacity, so that the cost of providing a room for an extra night's stay is very low. The manager also needs to determine whether it has more customers like Angela or more like Betty. To design an effective promotion, a manager should use experiments to learn about customers' preferences. For example, a manager could offer each promotion for a short period and keep track of how many customers respond to each promotion, how many nights they choose to stay, and by how much the promotion increases the firm's profit.

4.5 Deriving Demand Curves

We use consumer theory to show how much the quantity demanded of a good falls as its price rises. An individual chooses an optimal bundle of goods by picking the point on the highest indifference curve that touches the budget line. A change in a price causes the budget line to rotate, so that the consumer chooses a new optimal bundle. By varying one price and holding other prices and income constant, we determine how the quantity demanded changes as the price changes, which is the information we need to draw the demand curve.

We derive a demand curve using the information about tastes from indifference curves. To illustrate how to construct a demand curve, we estimated a set of indifference curves between recorded music—primarily tracks or songs purchased from iTunes, Amazon, Rhapsody, or other similar sources—and live music (at clubs, concerts, and so forth) using data for British young people (ages 14–24). Of these young people, university students spend about £18 per quarter on live music and £12 per quarter on music tracks, for a total budget of £30 for music.[5]

---

[5]Data on total expenditures are from *The Student Experience Report, 2007*, **www.unitestudents.com**, while budget allocations between live and recorded music are from the 2008 survey into the *Music Experience and Behaviour in Young People* produced by the British Music Rights and the University of Hertfordshire.

Panel a of Figure 4.11 shows three of the estimated indifference curves for a typical British university student, whom we call Jack.[6] These indifference curves are convex to the origin: Jack views live music and tracks as imperfect substitutes. We can construct Jack's demand curve for music tracks by holding his budget, his tastes, and the price of live music constant at their initial levels and varying the price of tracks.

FIGURE 4.11 Deriving an Individual's Demand Curve

If the price of recorded songs—tracks of music—rises, holding constant the price of live music (at £1 per unit), the music budget (at £30 per quarter), and tastes, the typical British university student, Jack, buys fewer tracks. This figure is based on our estimate of the typical student's utility function.

(a) On budget line L^3, the price of a track is £0.5. Jack's indifference curve I^3 is tangent to L^3 at Bundle e_3, where he buys 18 units of live music and 24 tracks per quarter. If the price of a track doubles to £1, the new budget line is L^2, and Jack reduces the number of tracks he demands to 12 per quarter.
(b) By varying the price of a track, we trace out Jack's demand curve, D^1. The tracks price-quantity combinations E_1, E_2, and E_3 on the demand curve for tracks in panel b correspond to optimal Bundles e_1, e_2, and e_3 in panel a.

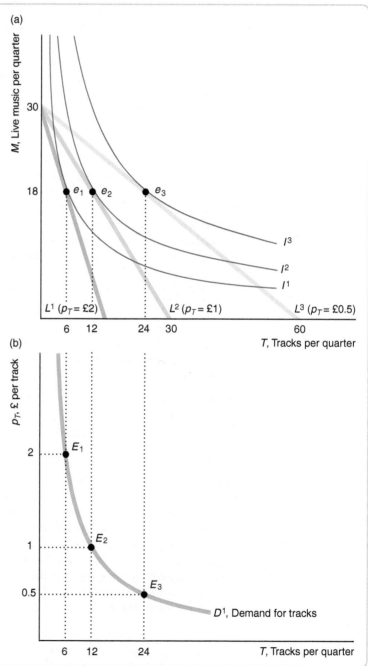

---

[6]The estimated utility function is $U = M^{0.6}T^{0.4}$, where M is the units of live music and T is the number of tracks.

The vertical axis in panel a measures the amount of live music that Jack consumes each quarter, and the horizontal axis measures the number of tracks he buys per quarter. Jack spends $Y = £30$ per year on live music and tracks. We set the price of live music, p_m, at £1 by choosing the units appropriately (so the units do not correspond to a concert or visit to a club). The price of tracks, p_t, is £0.5 per track. Jack can buy 30 (= Y/p_m = 30/1) units of live music if he spends all his money on that, or up to 60 (= Y/p_t = 30/0.5) tracks if he buys only tracks. The slope of his budget line, L^3, is $-p_t/p_m = -0.5/1 = -0.5$. Given budget line L^3, Jack consumes 18 units of live music per quarter and 24 tracks per quarter, Bundle e_3, which is determined by the tangency of indifference curve I^3 and budget line L^3.

Now suppose that the price of tracks doubles to £1 per track while the price of live music and Jack's budget remain constant. If he were to spend all his money on live music, he could buy the same 30 units as before, so the intercept on the vertical axis of L^2 is the same as for L^3. However, if he were to spend all his money on tracks, he could buy only half as many as before (30 instead of 60 tracks), so L^2 hits the horizontal axis half as far from the origin as L^3. As a result, L^2 has twice as steep a slope, $-p_t/p_m = -1/1 = -1$, as does L^3. The slope is steeper because the price of tracks has risen relative to the price of live music.

Because tracks are now relatively more expensive, Jack buys relatively fewer of them. He chooses Bundle e_2, where his indifference curve I^2 is tangent to L^2. He now buys only 12 tracks per quarter (compared to 24 at e_3).[7]

If the price of a track doubles again to £2, Jack consumes Bundle e_1, 6 tracks per quarter. The higher the price of tracks, the less happy Jack is because he consumes less music on the same budget: he is on indifference curve I^1, which is lower than I^2 or I^3.

We can use the information in panel a to draw Jack's demand curve for tracks, D^1, in panel b. Corresponding to each possible price of a track on the vertical axis of panel b, we record on the horizontal axis the number of tracks that Jack chooses in panel a.

Points E_1, E_2, and E_3 on the demand curve in panel b correspond to Bundles e_1, e_2, and e_3 in panel a. Both e_1 and E_1 show that when the price of a track is £2, Jack demands 6 tracks per quarter. When the price falls to £1, Jack increases his consumption to 12 tracks, point E_2. The demand curve, D^1, is downward sloping, as predicted by the Law of Demand.

4.6 Behavioral Economics

So far, we have assumed that consumers are rational, maximizing individuals. A rapidly growing field of study, **behavioral economics**, adds insights from psychology and empirical research on human cognitive and emotional biases to the rational economic model to better predict economic decision making.[8] We discuss three applications of behavioral economics in this section: tests of transitivity, the endowment effect, and salience. Later in this book, we examine the psychology of decision making in networks (Chapter 9), strategic interactions (Chapter 13), and under uncertainty (Chapter 14).

---

[7]The figure shows that he buys the same amount of live music, 18 units, when the price of tracks rises. This property is due to the particular utility function (a Cobb-Douglas) that we use in this example. With most other utility functions, the quantity of live music would change.

[8]The introductory chapter of Camerer, Lowenstein, and Rabin (2004) and DellaVigna (2009) provide excellent surveys of the major papers in this field and heavily influenced the following discussion.

Tests of Transitivity

In our presentation of the basic consumer choice model at the beginning of this chapter, we assumed that consumers make transitive choices. But do consumers actually make transitive choices?

A number of studies of both humans and animals show that preferences usually are transitive and hence consistent with our assumption. However, in some situations, people do not make transitive choices. Weinstein (1968) used an experiment to determine how frequently people fail to respond transitively. In the experiment, the subjects were given choices between 10 goods, offered in pairs, in every possible combination, and were told that each good had a value of $3. (None of the subjects knew the purpose of the experiment.) Weinstein found that 93.5% of the responses of adults—people over 18 years old—were transitive. However, only 79.2% of children aged 9–12 gave transitive responses.

Based on these results, one might conclude that it is appropriate to assume that adults exhibit transitivity for most economic decisions. However, one might modify the theory when applying it to children or when novel goods are introduced.

Economists normally argue that rational people should be allowed to make their own consumption choices so as to maximize their well-being. However, some might conclude that children's lack of transitivity or rationality provides one justification for political and economic restrictions and protections placed on young people.

Endowment Effects

Experiments show that people have a tendency to stick with the bundle of goods they currently possess. One important reason for this tendency is called the **endowment effect**, which occurs when people place a higher value on a good if they own it than if they are considering buying it.

We normally assume that an individual can buy or sell goods at the market price. Rather than rely on income to buy some mix of two goods, an individual who was *endowed* with several units of one good could sell some and use that money to buy units of another good.

We assume that a consumer's endowment does not affect the indifference curve map. In a classic buying and selling experiment, Kahneman, Knetsch, and Thaler (1990) challenged this assumption. In an undergraduate law and economics class at Cornell University, 44 students were divided randomly into two groups. Members of one group were given coffee mugs that were available at the student store for $6. Those students *endowed* with a mug were told they could sell it and were asked the minimum price they would accept for the mug. The subjects in the other group, who did not receive a mug, were asked how much they would pay to buy the mug. Given the standard assumptions of our model and that the subjects were chosen randomly, we would expect no difference between the selling and buying prices. However, the median selling price was $5.75 and the median buying price was $2.25. Sellers wanted more than twice what buyers would pay. This type of experiment has been repeated many times with many variations and consistently demonstrates an endowment effect.

However, some economists believe that this result has to do with the experimental design. Plott and Zeiler (2005) argued that if we take adequate care to train the subjects in the procedures and make sure they understand them, we no longer find this result. List (2003) examined the actual behavior of sports memorabilia collectors and found that amateurs who do not trade frequently exhibited an endowment effect, unlike professionals or amateurs who traded a lot. Thus, experience may reduce or even eliminate the endowment effect, and people who buy goods for resale may be less likely to become attached to these goods.

Others accept the results and have considered how to modify the standard model to reflect the endowment effect (Knetsch, 1992). One implication of these experimental results is that people will trade away from their endowments only if prices change substantially. This resistance to trade could be captured with a kink in the indifference curve at the endowment bundle. (We showed indifference curves with 90° kink in panel b of Figure 4.4.) Such indifference curves could have an angle greater than 90°, and an indifference curve could be curved at points other than at the kink. If the indifference curve has a kink, the consumer does not shift to a new bundle in response to a small price change, but may shift if the price change is large.

One practical implication of the endowment effect is that consumers' response may differ depending on how a choice is posed. However, that's not the common belief.

Common Confusion People respond the same way to equivalent questions.

The following Mini-Case shows that this belief is not always true.

| Mini-Case | Traditionally, electricity customers in Sacramento, California, paid a single price for each kilowatt of electricity all day. However, the cost of producing electricity is greatest when daily demand peaks during certain hours. Thus, the power company considered charging a higher than traditional price during those hours and a lower rate during the rest of the day. By doing so, they hoped to encourage households to run dishwashers and other appliances during low-production-cost periods. |

How You Ask the Question Matters

To find out whether customers would voluntarily agree to switch to time-based pricing, the electric utility ran an experiment. One group of electricity customers was invited to sign up for (*opt in*) a new time-based pricing structure. Another group was told that they would be put into the new pricing program unless they *opt out*. Fowlie et al. (2017) reported that only 20% of the first group chose to switch to time-based pricing. However, 90% of the second group stuck with the default choice of time-based pricing. This difference in response demonstrates the power of the endowment effect.

Salience

We often use economic theories based on the assumption that decision makers are aware of all relevant information. In this chapter, we assume that consumers know their own income, relevant prices, and their own tastes, and hence they make informed decisions.

Behavioral economists and psychologists have demonstrated that people are more likely to consider information if it is presented in a way that grabs their attention or if it takes relatively little thought or calculation to understand. Economists use the term *salience*, in the sense of *striking* or *obvious*, to describe this idea. For example, *tax salience* is awareness of a tax.

If a store's posted price includes the sales tax, consumers observe a change in the price as the tax rises. In contrast, if a store posts the pre-tax price and collects the tax at the cash register, consumers are less likely to note that the post-tax price has increased when the tax rate increases. Chetty et al. (2007) compared consumers' response to a rise in an *ad valorem* sales tax on beer (called an *excise tax*) that is included in the posted price to an increase in a general *ad valorem* sales tax, which is collected at the cash register but not reflected in the posted price. An increase in either tax has the same effect on the final price, so an increase in either tax should have the same effect on purchases if consumers pay attention to both taxes.[9] However, a 10% increase in the posted price, which includes the excise tax, reduces beer consumption by 9%, whereas a 10% increase in the price due to a rise in the sales tax that is not posted reduces consumption by only 2%. Chetty et al. also conducted an experiment in which they posted tax-inclusive prices for 750 products in a grocery store and found that demand for these products fell by about 8% relative to control products in that store and comparable products at nearby stores.

Why might a tax have no effect on consumer behavior? One explanation is consumer ignorance. For example, Furnham (2005) found that even at the age of 14 or 15, young people do not fully understand the nature and purpose of taxes. Similarly, unless the store posts the tax-inclusive price, many consumers ignore or forget about taxes.

An alternative explanation for ignoring taxes is **bounded rationality**: People have a limited capacity to anticipate, solve complex problems, or enumerate all options. To avoid having to perform hundreds of calculations when making purchasing decisions at a grocery store, many people choose not to calculate the tax-inclusive price. However, when post-tax price information is readily available to them without the need to do calculations, consumers make use of it. One way to modify the standard model to incorporate bounded rationality is to assume that people incur a cost in making calculations—such as the time taken or the mental strain—and that deciding whether to incur this cost is part of their rational decision-making process.

People incur this calculation cost only if they think the gain from a better choice of goods exceeds the cost. More people pay attention to a tax when the tax rate is high or when their demand for the good is elastic (they are sensitive to price). Similarly, some people are more likely to pay attention to taxes when making large, one-time purchases—such as for a computer or car—rather than small, repeated purchases—such as for a bar of soap. Thus, inattention due to bounded rationality is rational: Consumers are doing the best they can given their limited calculation abilities.

Managerial Implication

Simplifying Consumer Choices

Today's consumers often feel overwhelmed by choices. Cable TV subscribers must select from many possible channels, most of which they have never seen. Because consumers have bounded rationality, most dislike considering all the possibilities and making decisions. To avoid making decisions, many consumers do not buy these services and goods even though they would greatly benefit from such purchases.

To avoid this problem, good managers make decision making easier for consumers. For example, they may offer default bundles so that consumers don't have to make a large number of difficult decisions. Cable TV companies package groups of channels by content. Instead of choosing between possibly hundreds of individual channels, a consumer can opt for the sports package or the movie package. Rather than thinking through each option, the customer can make a much easier decision, such as "I like sports" or "I like movies," and is more likely to make a purchase.

---

[9]The final price consumers pay is $p^* = p(1 + \beta)(1 + \alpha)$, where p is the pre-tax price, α is the general sales tax, and β is the excise tax on beer.

Managerial Solution

Paying Employees to Relocate

We conclude our analysis of consumer theory by returning to the managerial problem posed in the introduction of this chapter: How can a firm's human resources manager use consumer theory to optimally compensate employees who are transferred to other cities?

Relocation managers use government sources to find information about the cost of living in various cities around the world (U.S. Defense Department, U.S. Government Services Administration, U.S. Office of Personnel Management, U.S. State Department), publications (*Money Magazine*, *Monthly Labor Review*), websites (**bestplaces.net**, **citymayors.com**, **homefair.com**, **moving.com**), and data and human resources consulting firms (such as EIU Data Services, Mercer Consulting, and Runzheimer International).[10] From this information, managers know that it is more expensive to buy the same bundle of goods in one city than another and that the relative prices of goods differ across cities.

As we noted in the Managerial Problem, most firms say they pay their employees enough in their new city to buy the same bundle of goods as in their original city. We want to investigate whether such firms are paying employees more than they have to for them to relocate. We illustrate our reasoning with an example using an employee who cares about only two goods.

Alexx's firm wants to transfer him from its Seattle office to its London office, where he will face a different cost of living with varying prices for goods and services. Alexx, who doesn't care whether he lives in Seattle or London, spends his money on housing and entertainment. Like most firms, his employer will pay him an after-tax salary in British pounds such that he can buy the same bundle of goods in London that he is currently buying in Seattle. Will Alexx benefit by moving to London? Could his employer have induced him to relocate for less money?

Alexx's optimal bundle, s, in Seattle is determined by the tangency of his indifference curve I^1 and his Seattle budget line L^S in the figure. It cost 53% more to live in London than in Seattle, on average, in 2011. If the prices of all goods are exactly 53% higher in London than in Seattle, the relative costs of housing and entertainment are the same in both cities. In that case, if his firm raises Alexx's income by 53%, his budget line does not change and he buys the same bundle, s, and his level of utility is unchanged.

However, relative prices are not the same in both cities. Controlling for quality, housing is relatively more expensive, and entertainment—concerts, theater, museums, zoos—is relatively less expensive in London than in Seattle. Thus, if Alexx's firm adjusts his income so that Alexx can buy the same bundle, s, in London as he did in Seattle, his new budget line in London, L^L, must go through s but have a different slope. Because entertainment is relatively less expensive than housing in London compared to Seattle, if Alexx spends all his money on entertainment,

[10]An international calculator that compares the cost of living in different cities around the world is available at **www.numbeo.com/cost-of-living/**.

he can buy more in London than in Seattle. Similarly, if he spends all his money on housing, he can buy less housing in London than in Seattle. As a result, L^L hits the vertical axis at a higher point than the L^S line and cuts the L^S line at Bundle s.

Alexx's new optimal bundle, l, is determined by the tangency of I^2 and L^L. Thus, because relative prices are different in London and Seattle, Alexx is better off with the transfer after receiving the firm's 53% higher salary. He was on I^1 and is now on I^2. Alexx could buy his original bundle, s, but chooses to substitute toward entertainment, which is relatively inexpensive in London, thereby raising his utility.

Consequently, his firm could have induced him to move with less compensation. If the firm lowers his income, the London budget line he faces will be closer to the origin but will have the same slope as L^L. The firm can lower his income until his lower-income London budget line, L^*, is tangent to his Seattle indifference curve, I^1, at Bundle l^*. Alexx still substitutes toward the relatively less expensive entertainment in London, but he is only as well off as he was in Seattle (he remains on the same indifference curve as when he lived in Seattle). Thus, his firm can induce Alexx to transfer to London for less than what it would have to pay so that Alexx could buy his original Seattle consumption bundle in London. ·

SUMMARY

Rational consumers maximize their utility (well-being) subject to constraints based on their income and the prices of goods.

1. **Consumer Preferences.** To predict consumers' responses to changes in constraints, economists use a theory about individuals' preferences. One way of summarizing a consumer's preferences is with a family of indifference curves. An indifference curve consists of all bundles of goods that give the consumer a particular level of utility. On the basis of observations of consumers' behavior, economists assume that consumers' preferences have three properties: completeness, transitivity, and more is better (nonsatiation). Given these three assumptions, indifference curves have the following properties:

   • Consumers get more utility or satisfaction from bundles on indifference curves that are farther from the origin.

   • An indifference curve goes through any given bundle.

   • Indifference curves cannot cross.

   • Indifference curves slope downward.

2. **Utility.** Economists use the term *utility* to describe the set of numerical values that reflect the relative rankings of bundles of goods. By comparing the utility a consumer gets from each of two bundles, we know that the consumer prefers the bundle with the higher utility. The marginal utility, MU, from a good is the extra utility a person gets from consuming one more unit of that good, holding the consumption of all other goods constant. The rate at which a consumer is willing to substitute Good 1 for Good 2, the marginal rate of substitution, MRS, depends on the relative amounts of marginal utility the consumer gets from each of the two goods.

3. **The Budget Constraint.** The amount of goods consumers can buy at given prices is limited by their income. As a result, the greater a consumer's income or the lower the prices of goods, the more the consumer can buy. The consumer has a larger opportunity set. The marginal rate of transformation (MRT) shows how much of one good the consumer must give up in trade for one more unit of another good. The MRT depends on the relative prices of the two goods.

4. **Constrained Consumer Choice.** Each person picks an affordable bundle of goods that maximizes his or her utility. If an individual consumes both Good 1 and Good 2 (an interior solution), the individual's utility is maximized when the following four equivalent conditions hold:

   • The indifference curve for Goods 1 and 2 is tangent to the budget line.

   • The consumer buys the bundle of goods that is on the highest obtainable indifference curve.

   • The consumer's marginal rate of substitution (the slope of the indifference curve) equals the marginal rate of transformation (the slope of the budget line).

- The last dollar spent on Good 1 gives the consumer as much extra utility as the last dollar spent on Good 2.

Sometimes, consumers choose to buy only one of the two goods (corner solutions). The last dollar spent on the good that is purchased gives more extra utility than would spending a dollar on the other good, which the consumer chooses not to buy.

5. **Deriving Demand Curves.** Individual demand curves can be derived by using the information about preferences contained in a consumer's indifference curve map. By varying the price of one good while holding other prices and income constant, we find out how the quantity demanded varies as its own price changes, which is the information we need to draw the good's demand curve. Consumers' preferences, which

are captured by the indifference curves, determine the shape of the demand curve.

6. **Behavioral Economics.** Using insights from psychology and empirical research on human cognition and emotional biases, economists are starting to modify the rational economic model to better predict economic decision making. Some decision makers, particularly children, fail to make transitive choices in certain circumstances. Some consumers exhibit an endowment effect: They place a higher value on a good if they own it than if they are considering buying it. Consequently, they are less sensitive to price changes and hence less likely to trade than would be predicted by the standard economic model. Consumers are more inclined to take into account information that is readily available to them (salient), while ignoring other information.

QUESTIONS

All exercises are available on **MyLab Economics**; * = *answer at the back of this;* ✘ = *this exercise is available in Excel Grader in* **MyLab Economics.**

1. Consumer Preferences

1.1 Give as many reasons as you can why we believe that economists assume that the more-is-better property holds, and explain how these explanations relate to the results in the Mini-Case "You Can't Have Too Much Money."

*1.2 Arthur spends his income on bread and chocolate. He views chocolate as a good but is neutral about bread, in that he doesn't care if he consumes it or not. Draw his indifference curve map.

1.3 Show that an indifference curve
   a. Cannot be thick (cannot have positive thickness, rather than being just a line).
   b. Cannot bend backward (forming a "hook" at the end).
   c. Cannot intersect another indifference curve.

1.4 Which of the following pairs of goods are complements and which are substitutes? Are the goods that are substitutes likely to be perfect substitutes for some or all consumers?
   a. An e-book version and audiobook version of the same novel.
   b. A smartphone and smartphone apps
   c. A bag of dog food and a coffee mug
   d. Tide laundry detergent and Cheer laundry detergent

1.5 Give as many reasons as you can why we believe that indifference curves are convex to the origin.

2. Utility

*2.1 William eats hot dogs only with mustard and consumes mustard only with hot dogs. He puts one unit of mustard on each hot dog he eats. Show his preference map. What is his utility function?

2.2 If Porsha views 3 glasses of juice as a perfect substitute for one cup of soda and vice versa, what is her marginal rate of substitution between juice and soda?

2.3 Javier consumes large pepperoni pizzas (Z) and boxes of graham crackers (G). Each of his indifference curves reflects strictly diminishing marginal rates of substitution (MRS). If $Z = 4$ and $G = 4$, his MRS between pizzas and boxes of graham crackers equals $-1\left(= -\frac{MU_P}{MU_G}\right)$. Will he prefer a bundle with 5 pizzas and 3 boxes of graham crackers to the bundle with 4 of each? Why?

*2.4 Sanghoon has a utility function over audiobooks, A, and movie downloads, M, given by $U = \sqrt{AM}$. Linh has a utility function given by $U = AM$. Explain why Sanghoon and Linh have the same ordering over any two bundles and therefore have the same ordinal preferences.

*2.5 Andy purchases only two goods, apples (a) and kumquats (k). He has an income of $40 and can buy apples at $2 per pound and kumquats at $4 per pound. His utility function is $U(a, k) = 3a + 5k$. That is, his constant marginal utility for apples is 3 and his constant marginal utility for kumquats is 5.

What bundle of apples and kumquats should Andy purchase to maximize his utility? Why?

3. The Budget Constraint

3.1 Yuka consumes mangos and oranges. She is given four mangos and three oranges. She can buy or sell mangos for $2 each. Similarly, she can buy or sell an orange for $1. If Yuka has no other source of income, draw her budget line and write the equation.

3.2 If the budget line is $Y = 500 = p_B B + p_Z Z = 5B + 10Z$, what is the marginal rate of transformation, MRT, between B (burritos) and Z (pizza)?

3.3 Change Q&A 4.1 so that Lisa's budget and the price of pizza double, but the price of burritos remains constant. Show how her budget constraint and opportunity set change. Is Lisa necessarily better off than before these changes? (*Hint*: What happens to the intercepts of the budget line?)

*3.4 Dale goes to the opera and ice hockey games. Draw a budget line for Dale. If the government imposes a 25% income tax on her, what happens to her budget line and opportunity set? (*Hint*: See Q&A 4.2.)

3.5 Sophia spends all her money on gummy worms and apps for her smartphone. A pound of gummy worms and a smartphone app each cost $2. Sophia's parents give her an allowance of $80 and 2 pounds of gummy worms each month. Draw her opportunity set, assuming that she cannot sell the gummy worms to her friends. How does her opportunity set change if she can sell the gummy worms at the market price of $2?

4. Constrained Consumer Choice

4.1 Linda loves buying shoes and going out to dance. Her utility function for pairs of shoes, S, and the number of times she goes dancing per month, T, is $U(S, T) = 2ST$, so $MU_S = 2T$ and $MU_T = 2S$. It costs Linda $50 to buy a new pair of shoes or to spend an evening out dancing. Assume that she has $500 to spend on shoes and dancing. (*Hint*: See Q&A 4.3.)

   a. What is the equation for her budget line? Draw it (with T on the vertical axis), and label the slope and intercepts.

   b. What is Linda's marginal rate of substitution? Explain.

   c. Use math to solve for her optimal bundle. Show how to determine this bundle in a diagram using indifference curves and a budget line.

*4.2 Nadia likes spare ribs, R, and fried chicken, C. Her utility function is $U = 10R^2C$. Her marginal utilities are $MU_R = 20RC$ and $MU_C = 10R^2$. Her weekly income is $90, which she spends on only ribs and chicken.

   a. If she pays $10 for a slab of ribs and $5 for a chicken, what is her optimal consumption bundle? Show her budget line, indifference curve, and optimal bundle, e_1, in a diagram.

   b. Suppose the price of chicken doubles to $10. How does her optimal consumption of chicken and ribs change? Show her new budget line and optimal bundle, e_2, in your diagram.

4.3 Lucas chooses between water and all other goods. If he spends all his money on water, he can buy 15 thousand gallons per week. At current prices, his optimal bundle is e_1, where he buys both types of goods. Show e_1 in a diagram. During a drought, the government limits the number of gallons per week that he may purchase to 10 thousand. Using diagrams, discuss under which conditions his new optimal bundle, e_2, will be the same as e_1. If the two bundles differ, can you state where e_2 must be located relative to e_1?

*4.4 Gasoline is typically less expensive in the United States than across the border in Canada, but now suppose that the U.S. gasoline price rises above that in Canada due to a change in taxes. How would the gasoline-purchasing behavior of a person who lives equally close to gas stations in both countries change? Answer using an indifference-curve and budget-line diagram.

4.5 Suppose we change Q&A 4.4 so that Max and Bob have indifference curves that are convex to the origin. Use a figure to discuss how the different slopes of their budget lines affect the choices they make. Can you make any unambiguous statements about how many total books each can buy? Can you make an unambiguous statement if you know that Bob's budget line goes through Max's optimal bundle?

4.6 Ralph usually buys one pizza and two colas from the local pizzeria. The pizzeria announces a special: All pizzas after the first one are half-price. Show the original and new budget lines. What can you say about the bundle Ralph will choose when faced with the new constraint?

4.7 Until 2012, California, Texas, and Pennsylvania required firms to collect sales taxes for online sales if the chain had a physical presence (a "brick" store as opposed to a "click" store) in those states. Thus, those states collected taxes on Best Buy's online sales, because it had stores in each of those states, but they did not collect taxes from Amazon.com because it did not have physical locations in those states. Starting in 2012, Amazon had to pay taxes in these states. After the tax was imposed on Amazon,

Best Buy had a 4% to 6% increase in its online sales in those states relative to the rest of the chain (**www.bizjournals.com/twincities/news/2013/01/11/best-buys-online-sales-up-in-states.html**). Use an indifference-curve/budget-line diagram to show why Best Buy's sales rose after taxes were imposed on Amazon. (*Hint*: Start by drawing a typical consumer's indifference curve between buying a good from Amazon or from Best Buy.)

4.8 The local swimming pool charges nonmembers $10 per visit. If you join the pool, you can swim for $5 per visit but you have to pay an annual fee of F. Use an indifference-curve diagram to find the value of F such that you are indifferent between joining and not joining. Suppose that the pool charged you exactly that value of F. Would you go to the pool more or fewer times than if you did not join? For simplicity, assume that the price of all other goods is $1.

4.9 Based on panel a in Figure 4.10, show that Angela would accept the BOGO promotion or the half-price promotion. Show that she may choose to stay either three or four nights with the half-price promotion, depending on the exact shape of her indifference curves.

5. Deriving Demand Curves

5.1 Some of the largest import tariffs (taxes on only imported goods) are on shoes. Strangely, the tariff is higher on cheaper shoes. The highest U.S. tariff, 67%, is on a pair of $3 canvas sneakers, while the tariff on $12 sneakers is 37%, and that on $300 Italian leather imports is 0%. (Adam Davidson, "U.S. Tariffs on Shoes Favor Well-Heeled Buyers," National Public Radio, June 12, 2007, **www.npr.org/templates/story/story.php?storyId=10991519**.) Laura buys either inexpensive canvas sneakers ($3 before the tariff) or more expensive gym shoes ($12 before the tariff) for her many children. Use an indifference curve and budget line figure to show how imposing these unequal tariffs affects the bundle of shoes that she buys compared to what she would have bought in the absence of tariffs. Can you confidently predict whether she'll buy relatively more expensive gym shoes after the tariff? Why or why not?

5.2 Draw diagrams similar to Figure 4.11 but with different shape indifference curves to show that as the price of tracks rises, the amount of live music Jack will buy may rise or fall.

5.3 Derive and plot Olivia's demand curve for pie if she eats pie only à la mode and does not eat either pie or ice cream alone (pie and ice cream are complements).

5.4 At large employers, 48% of employees earning between $10,000 and $24,999 a year participated in a voluntary retirement savings program, compared to 91% who earned more than $100,000 (**www.towerswatson.com/**). We can view savings as a good. In a figure, plot savings versus all other goods. Show why people might be more likely to "buy" some savings (put money in a retirement account) as their incomes rise.

5.5 Ajay and Florencia each have a budget of $80 per month to spend on downloaded music tracks and live concerts. At the initial prices, Ajay consumes both goods but Florencia buys only downloaded music and does not go to live concerts. Now the price of live concerts falls. Use figures to show that Ajay's utility must increase and that Florencia's utility may increase or stay the same but cannot fall. (*Hint*: Look at Figure 4.9.)

6. Behavioral Economics

*6.1 Northwestern University neuroscientist Moran Cerf has a simple approach to ordering food at restaurants. Whenever he goes out, he looks at the restaurant's list of specials and always picks the second item on the list (**www.businessinsider.com/neuroscientist-decision-making-hack-restaurants-2017-7**). Show that this approach can lead to choices that are not transitive if a restaurant varies the ordering of menu items from time to time.

6.2 Illustrate the logic of the endowment effect using a kinked indifference curve. Let the angle be greater than 90°. Suppose that the prices change, so the slope of the budget line through the endowment changes. Use the diagram to explain why an individual whose endowment point is at the kink will trade from the endowment point only if the price change is substantial.

*6.3 Why would a consumer's demand for a product change when the product price is quoted inclusive of taxes rather than before tax? Do you think fewer people would apply for a job if the salary were quoted after deducting income tax rather than in pre-tax form? Explain briefly.

7. Managerial Problem

7.1 In the Managerial Problem, suppose that entertainment is relatively more expensive in London than in Seattle so that the L^L budget line cuts the L^S budget line from below rather than from above, as in the figure in the Managerial Solution. Show that the conclusion that Alexx is better off after his move if his new income allows him to buy bundle s still holds. Explain the logic behind the following statement: "The analysis holds as long as the relative prices differ in the two cities. Whether both prices, one price, or neither price in London is higher than in Seattle is irrelevant to the analysis."

8. MyLab Economics Spreadsheet Exercises[11]

8.1 Lucy's company has just promoted her to a managerial position and given her a new office. She is very fond of small Persian carpets and Native American paintings and wants to get some carpets and paintings for her office. Her utility function for carpets (x) and paintings (y) is given by

$$U(x, y) = \sqrt{xy}.$$

Using Excel's charting tool, draw an indifference curve for $U = 4$ and another one for $U = 6$, where both indifference curves contain 1, 2, 4, and 8 carpets on a graph, with carpets on the horizontal axis and paintings on the vertical axis.

8.2 As described in Exercise 8.1, Lucy wants carpets and paintings for her office. Her company has given her a budget of $7,200 for this purpose. Persian carpets of the size that she wants can be purchased for $900 each and paintings from a local Native American artist cost $400 each.

   a. Using Excel's charting tool, draw Lucy's budget constraint if her budget is $5,000. Use 0, 1, 2, 3, 4, and 5 carpets as possible quantities. Put carpets on the horizontal axis and paintings on the vertical axis.

   b. Combining the information in the previous exercise with this exercise, use Excel to illustrate Lucy's utility-maximizing solution given that her budget is $5,000, the price of a carpet is $1,000, and the price of a painting is $500.

8.3 Sam's utility function over iced coffee, C, and tacos, T, is $U = min\ (C, T)$, where min denotes the minimum value. For example, if $C = 2$ and $T = 3$, $U = min\ (2, 3) = 2$. Sam spends his entire budget of $12 on coffee and tacos.

   a. Which of the panels in Figure 4.4 has indifference curves with the same shape as Sam's indifference curves over iced coffee and tacos? Explain.

   b. In Sam's favorite restaurant, Taco Corner, the price of iced coffee is $2 per cup, and the price of a taco is $1. Using Excel, create a column titled C and enter the values 1, 2, . . . , 6. Those numbers represent different possible numbers of cups of iced coffee Sam might purchase. For each of those values, calculate the number of tacos that Sam can buy if he spends the rest of his $12 budget on tacos. Calculate the resulting utility level for each consumption bundle and determine the combination of iced coffee and tacos that maximizes Sam's utility. (*Hint:* Use the *min* function in Excel.)

   c. Taco Corner reduces the price of iced coffee to $1.50 and raises the price of tacos to $1.50. Using Excel, re-do the calculations in part b and determine Sam's utility-maximizing consumption bundle now.

APPENDIX 4A   The Marginal Rate of Substitution

We can derive Equation 4.1 using calculus. Lisa's utility function is $U(B, Z)$. Along an indifference curve, we hold utility fixed at $\overline{U} = U(B, Z)$. If we increase Z, we would have to lower B to keep her on the same indifference curve. Let $B(Z)$ be the implicit function that shows how much B it takes to keep Lisa's utility at $\overline{U}$ given that she consumes Z. Thus, we can write her indifference curve as $\overline{U} = U(B(Z), Z)$, which is solely a function of Z.

    We want to know how much B must change if we increase Z, dB/dZ, given that we require her utility to remain constant by staying on the original indifference curve. To answer this question, we differentiate $\overline{U} = U(B(Z), Z)$ with respect to Z and set this derivative to zero because $\overline{U}$ is constant along an indifference curve:

$$\frac{d\overline{U}}{dZ} = 0 = \frac{\partial U(B(Z), Z)}{\partial B}\frac{dB}{dZ} + \frac{\partial U(B(Z), Z)}{\partial Z}$$
$$= MU_B\frac{dB}{dZ} + MU_Z.$$

The partial derivatives show how utility changes as we change either B or Z, holding the other constant. We know that $d\overline{U}/dZ = 0$ because $\overline{U}$ is a constant along the indifference curve. Rearranging terms in this expression, we obtain Equation 4.1 (where dB/dZ replaces $\Delta B/\Delta Z$): $MRS = dB/dZ = -MU_Z/MU_B$.

---

[11]The spreadsheet exercises in this chapter are based largely on the work of Satyajit Ghosh in cooperation with the authors. The answers are available on **MyLab Economics.**

For example, the Cobb-Douglas utility function (named after its inventors) is $U = B^a Z^{1-a}$. The marginal utilities are $MU_B = aB^{a-1}Z^{1-a} = aU/B$ and $MU_Z = (1-a)B^a Z^{-a} = (1-a)U/Z$. Thus,

$$MRS = -\frac{MU_Z}{MU_B} = -\frac{(1-a)U/Z}{aU/B} = -\frac{(1-a)}{a}\frac{B}{Z}. \qquad (4A.1)$$

APPENDIX 4B   The Consumer Optimum

We can derive Equation 4.6 using calculus. Lisa's objective is to maximize her utility, $U(B, Z)$, subject to (s.t.) a budget constraint:

$$\max_{B,\, Z} U(B, Z)$$

$$\text{s.t.} \quad Y = p_B B + p_Z Z, \qquad (4B.1)$$

where B is the number of burritos she buys at price p_B, Z is the number of pizzas she buys at price p_Z, Y is her income, and $Y = p_B B + p_Z Z$ is her budget constraint. This mathematical statement of her problem shows that her *choice variables* are B and Z, which appear under the "max" term in the equation.

Because we cannot directly solve a constrained maximization problem, we want to convert Equation 4B.1 into an unconstrained problem by substituting the budget constraint into the utility function. Using algebra, we rearrange her budget constraint so that B is a function of Z: $B(Z) = (Y - p_Z Z)/p_B$. Substituting this expression for $B(Z)$ into the utility function, we rewrite her problem as

$$\max_Z U(B(Z), Z) = U\left(\frac{Y - p_Z Z}{p_B},\, Z\right). \qquad (4B.2)$$

Because Equation 4B.2 is unconstrained, we can use standard maximization techniques to solve it. We derive the first-order condition by setting the derivative of Lisa's utility function with respect to Z equal to zero:

$$\frac{dU}{dZ} = \frac{\partial U}{\partial B}\frac{dB}{dZ} + \frac{\partial U}{\partial Z} = \left(-\frac{p_Z}{p_B}\right)\frac{\partial U}{\partial B} + \frac{\partial U}{\partial Z}$$

$$= \left(-\frac{p_Z}{p_B}\right)MU_B + MU_Z = 0, \qquad (4B.3)$$

where $MU_B(B, Z) = \partial U(B, Z)/\partial B$. Rearranging the terms in Equation 4B.3, we obtain the condition in Equation 4.6 that her utility is maximized if the slope of the indifference curve, MRS, equals the slope of the budget line, MRT:

$$MRS = -\frac{MU_Z}{MU_B} = -\frac{p_Z}{p_B} = MRT. \qquad (4B.4)$$

If the utility function is Cobb-Douglas, the MRS is given by Equation 4A.1, so Equation 4B.4 becomes

$$MRS = -\frac{MU_Z}{MU_B} = -\frac{(1-a)}{a}\frac{B}{Z} = -\frac{p_Z}{p_B},$$

or

$$(1-a)p_B B = ap_Z Z. \qquad (4B.5)$$

Rearranging the budget constraint, $p_Z Z = Y - p_B B$. Substituting $Y - p_B B$ for $p_Z Z$ in Equation 4B.5, we obtain $(1-a)p_B B = a(Y - p_B B)$. Thus, $B = aY/p_B$. Similarly, by substituting $p_B B = Y - p_Z Z$ in Equation 4B.5, we find that $Z = (1-a)Y/p_Z$.

5 Production

Hard work never killed anybody, but why take a chance?

Managerial Problem

Labor Productivity During Recessions

Why has a measure of labor productivity—the output produced per worker—risen for many firms during recent recessions (Lazear, Shaw, and Stanton, 2016)? During the Great Recession (fourth quarter of 2007 through the third quarter of 2009), labor productivity rose by 3.2% in nonfarm businesses. In contrast, in the two years before the Great Recession, labor productivity rose by only 2.2%.

Firms produce less output during recessions as demand for their products falls. Managers must consider whether to reduce production by laying workers off and, if so, how many workers to lay off. To make this decision, they face a managerial problem: How much will the output produced per worker rise or fall with each additional layoff?

In the Managerial Solution to this problem, we will examine whether the productivity of a beer bottling plant rises or falls. If we know the firm's production process, can we predict whether output produced per worker will rise or fall with each additional layoff?

This chapter looks at an important set of decisions that managers have to face. First, the firm must choose its production process, selecting how much labor and capital to use. Second, if a firm wants to expand its output, it must decide how to do that in both the short run and the long run. In the short run, a firm can usually expand output by hiring extra workers or extending the workweek (more shifts per day or more workdays per week) and using extra materials. To expand output even further, the firm may need to install more equipment or build a new plant, which takes more time. Third, given its ability to change its output level, a firm must determine how large to grow based on its expectations about future demand and costs.

Firms and the managers who run them perform the fundamental economic function of producing output—the goods and services that consumers want. The main lesson of this chapter is that firms are not black boxes that mysteriously transform inputs (such as labor, capital, and materials) into outputs. Economic theory explains how firms make decisions about production processes, the types of inputs to use, and the volume of output to produce.

In this chapter, we examine five main topics:

Learning Objectives

1. Use a production function to describe the relationship between inputs and output.
2. Predict the effects of short-run changes in labor on output.
3. Explain the long-run trade-off between labor and capital in production.
4. Determine whether a production function has decreasing, constant, or increasing returns to scale.
5. Describe the effects of innovation on production.

5.1 Production Functions

A firm uses a *production process* to transform *inputs* or *factors of production* into *outputs*. Firms use many types of inputs. Most of these inputs can be grouped into three broad categories:

- **Capital (K).** Services provided by long-lived inputs such as land, buildings (such as factories and stores), and equipment (such as machines and trucks)
- **Labor (L).** Human services such as those provided by managers, skilled workers (such as architects, economists, engineers, and plumbers), and less-skilled workers (such as custodians, construction laborers, and assembly-line workers)
- **Materials (M).** Natural resources and raw goods (e.g., oil, water, and wheat) and processed products (e.g., aluminum, plastic, paper, and steel)

The output can be a *service*, such as an automobile tune-up by a mechanic, or a *physical product*, such as a computer chip or a potato chip.

Firms can transform inputs into outputs in many different ways. Companies that manufacture candy differ in the skills of their workforce and the amount of equipment they use. While all employ a chef, a manager, and some relatively unskilled workers, many candy firms also use skilled technicians and modern equipment. In small candy companies, the relatively unskilled workers shape the candy, decorate it, package it, and box it by hand. In slightly larger firms, relatively unskilled workers may use conveyor belts and other equipment that was invented decades ago. In modern, large-scale plants, the relatively unskilled laborers work with robots and other state-of-the-art machines, which are maintained by skilled technicians. Before deciding which production process to use, a firm needs to consider its various options.

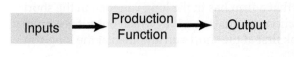

The different ways in which inputs can be transformed into output are summarized in the **production function**: the relationship between the quantities of inputs used and the *maximum* quantity of output that can be produced, given current knowledge about technology and organization.

The production function for a firm that uses only labor and capital is

$$q = f(L, K), \tag{5.1}$$

where q units of output (such as wrapped candy bars) are produced using L units of labor services (such as hours of work by assembly-line workers) and K units of capital (such as the number of conveyor belts).

The production function shows only the *maximum* amount of output that can be produced from given levels of labor and capital, because the production function includes only efficient production processes. A firm engages in **efficient production** (achieves *technical efficiency*) if it cannot produce its current level of output with fewer inputs, given existing knowledge about technology and the organization of production. A profit-maximizing firm is not interested in production processes that are inefficient and waste inputs: Such firms do not want to use two workers to do a job that can be done just as well by one worker.

A firm can more easily adjust its inputs in the long run than in the short run. Typically, a firm can vary the amounts of materials and relatively unskilled labor it uses comparatively quickly. However, it needs more time to find and hire skilled workers, order new equipment, or build a new manufacturing plant.

The more time a firm has to adjust its inputs, the more factors of production it can alter. The **short run** is a period so brief that at least one factor of production cannot be varied practically. A factor that cannot be varied practically in the short run is called a **fixed input**. In contrast, a **variable input** is a factor of production whose quantity can be changed readily by the firm during the relevant period. The **long run** is a lengthy enough period that all relevant inputs can be varied. Thus, in the long run, no inputs are fixed.

Suppose that a painting company's customers all want their homes painted by the end of the day. With its current inputs, the firm cannot complete all the jobs today. To do so, it needs to use more inputs. However, the firm does not have time to buy or rent an extra truck and purchase another compressor to run a power sprayer; these inputs are fixed in the short run. To get the work done that afternoon, the firm uses the company's one truck to pick up and drop off temporary workers, each equipped with only a brush and paint, at the last job. In the long run, however, the firm can adjust all its inputs. If the firm wants to paint more houses every day, it can hire more full-time workers, get a second truck, purchase more compressors to run the power sprayers, and buy a computer to track its projects.

How long it takes for all inputs to be variable depends on the factors a firm uses. For a janitorial service whose only major input is workers, the short run is brief. In contrast, an automobile manufacturer may need several years to build a new manufacturing plant or to design and construct a new type of assembly machine. A pistachio farmer needs the better part of a decade before newly planted trees yield a substantial crop of nuts.

For many firms, materials and often labor are variable inputs over a month. However, labor is not always a variable input. Finding additional highly skilled workers may take substantial time. Similarly, capital may be a variable or a fixed input. A firm can rent small capital assets (such as trucks or office furniture) quickly, but it may take the firm years to obtain larger capital assets (buildings and large, specialized pieces of equipment).

To illustrate the greater flexibility that a firm has in the long run than in the short run, we examine the production function in Equation 5.1, in which output is a function of only labor and capital. We look first at the short-run and then at the long-run production processes.

5.2 Short-Run Production

The short run is a period in which at least one input is fixed. Focusing on a production process in which capital and labor are the only inputs, we assume that capital is the fixed input and labor is variable. The firm can therefore increase output only by increasing the amount of labor it uses. In the short run, the firm's production function, Equation 5.1, becomes

$$q = f(L, \overline{K}), \tag{5.2}$$

where q is output, L is the amount of labor, and $\overline{K}$ is the firm's fixed amount of capital.

To illustrate the short-run production process, we consider a firm that assembles computers for a manufacturing firm that supplies it with the necessary parts, such as computer chips and disk drives. If the assembly firm wants to increase its output in the short run, it cannot do so by increasing its capital (eight workbenches fully equipped with tools, electronic probes, and other equipment for testing computers). However, it can increase output in the short run by hiring extra workers or paying current workers extra to work overtime.

The Total Product Function

The exact relationship between *output* or *total product* and *labor* can be illustrated by using a particular function, Equation 5.2, a table, or a figure. Table 5.1 shows the relationship between output and labor when a firm's capital is fixed. The first column lists the fixed amount of capital: eight fully equipped workbenches. The second column shows how much of the variable input, labor, the firm uses. In this example, the labor input is measured by the number of workers, as all work the same number of hours. Total output—the number of computers assembled in a day—is listed in the third column. As the number of workers increases, total output first increases and then decreases.

With zero workers, no computers are assembled. One worker with access to the firm's equipment assembles 5 computers in a day. As the number of workers

TABLE 5.1 Total Product, Marginal Product, and Average Product of Labor with Fixed Capital

Capital, $\overline{K}$	Labor, L	Output, Total Product of Labor q	Marginal Product of Labor, $MP_L = \Delta q / \Delta L$	Average Product of Labor, $AP_L = q/L$
8	0	0		
8	1	5	5	5
8	2	18	13	9
8	3	36	18	12
8	4	56	20	14
8	5	75	19	15
8	6	90	15	15
8	7	98	8	14
8	8	104	6	13
8	9	108	4	12
8	10	110	2	11
8	11	110	0	10
8	12	108	−2	9
8	13	104	−4	8

Labor is measured in workers per day. Capital is fixed at eight fully equipped workbenches.

increases, so does output: 1 worker assembles 5 computers in a day, 2 workers assemble 18, 3 workers assemble 36, and so forth. The maximum number of computers that can be assembled with the capital on hand, however, is limited to 110 per day. That maximum can be produced with 10 or 11 workers. If the firm were to use 12 or more workers, the workers would get in each other's way and production would be lower than with 11 workers. The dashed line in the table indicates that a firm would not use more than 11 workers, because it would be inefficient to do so. We can show how extra workers affect the total product by using two additional concepts: the marginal product of labor and the average product of labor.

The Marginal Product of Labor

Before deciding whether to employ more labor, a manager wants to determine how much an extra unit of labor, $\Delta L = 1$, will increase output, Δq. That is, the manager wants to know the **marginal product of labor (MP_L)**: the change in total output resulting from using an extra unit of labor, holding other factors (capital) constant. If output changes by Δq when the amount of labor increases by ΔL, the change in output per unit of labor is

$$MP_L = \frac{\Delta q}{\Delta L}.$$

As Table 5.1 shows, if the number of workers increases from 1 to 2, $\Delta L = 1$, output rises by $\Delta q = 13 = 18 - 5$, so the marginal product of labor is 13.

Using Calculus

Calculating the
Marginal Product
of Labor

The short-run production function, $q = f(L, \overline{K})$, can be written as solely a function of L because capital is fixed: $q = g(L)$. The calculus definition of the marginal product of labor is the derivative of this production function with respect to labor: $MP_L = dg(L)/dL$.

In the long run, when both labor and capital are free to vary, the marginal product of labor is the partial derivative of the production function, Equation 5.1, $q = f(L, K)$, with respect to labor:

$$MP_L = \frac{\partial q}{\partial L} = \frac{\partial f(L, K)}{\partial L}.$$

We use the symbol $\partial q/\partial L$ instead of dq/dL because we are taking a partial derivative.[1] We use partial derivatives when we want to change only one explanatory variable in a function that has more than one such variable. Here, q is a function of both labor, L, and capital, K. To obtain a partial derivative with respect to one variable, say L, we differentiate as usual where we treat the other variables (here just K) as constants.

---

[1]Above, we defined the marginal product as the extra output due to a discrete change in labor, such as an additional worker or an extra hour of work. In contrast, the calculus definition of the marginal product—the partial derivative—is the rate of change of output with respect to the labor for a very small (infinitesimal) change in labor. As a result, the numerical calculation of marginal products can differ slightly if derivatives rather than discrete changes are used.

Q&A 5.1

For a linear production function $q = f(L, K) = 2L + K$ and a multiplicative production function $q = LK$, what are the short-run production functions given that capital is fixed at $\overline{K} = 100$? What are the marginal products of labor for these short-run production functions?

Answer

1. *Obtain the short-run production functions by setting* $\overline{K} = 100$. The short-run linear production function is $q = 2L + 100$ and the short-run multiplicative function is $q = L \times 100 = 100L$.

2. *Determine the marginal products of labor by differentiating the short-run production functions with respect to labor*. The marginal product of labor is $MP_L = \mathrm{d}(2L + 100)/\mathrm{d}L = 2$ for the short-run linear production function and $MP_L = \mathrm{d}(100L)/\mathrm{d}L = 100$ for the short-run multiplicative production function.

The Average Product of Labor

Before hiring extra workers, a manager may also want to know whether output will rise in proportion to this extra labor. To answer this question, the firm determines how extra labor affects the **average product of labor** (AP_L): the ratio of output to the amount of labor used to produce that output,

$$AP_L = \frac{q}{L}.$$

Table 5.1 shows that 9 workers can assemble 108 computers a day, so the average product of labor for 9 workers is 12 ($= 108/9$) computers a day. Ten workers can assemble 110 computers in a day, so the average product of labor for 10 workers is 11 ($= 110/10$) computers. Thus, increasing the labor force from 9 to 10 workers lowers the average product per worker.

Graphing the Product Curves

Figure 5.1 and Table 5.1 show how output (total product), the average product of labor, and the marginal product of labor vary with the number of workers. (The figure's curves are smooth because the firm can hire a "fraction of a worker" by employing a worker for a fraction of a day.) The curve in panel a of Figure 5.1 shows the relationship between the amount of labor and *total product*, which is the amount of output that can be produced by a given amount of labor. Output rises with labor until it reaches its maximum of 110 computers at 11 workers at point B. Using additional workers beyond this maximum reduces the number of computers assembled.

Panel b of the figure shows how the average product of labor and marginal product of labor vary with the number of workers. We can line up the figures in panels a and b vertically because the units along the horizontal axes of both figures, the number of workers per day, are the same. The vertical axes differ, however. The vertical axis is total product in panel a and the average or marginal product of labor in panel b.

The Effect of Extra Labor. In most production processes, the average product of labor first rises and then falls as labor increases. One reason the AP_L curve initially rises in Figure 5.1 is that it helps to have more than two hands when assembling a

FIGURE 5.1   Production Relationships with Variable Labor

(a) The total product of labor curve shows how many computers, q, can be assembled with eight fully equipped workbenches and a varying number of workers, L, who work eight-hour days (see columns 2 and 3 in Table 5.1). Where extra workers reduce the number of computers assembled (beyond point B), the total product curve is a dashed line, which indicates that such production is inefficient and is thus not part of the production function. The slope of the line from the origin to point A is the average product of labor for six workers. (b) Where the marginal product of labor ($MP_L = \Delta q / \Delta L$, column 4 of Table 5.1) curve is above the average product of labor ($AP_L = q/L$, column 5 of Table 5.1) curve, the AP_L must rise. Similarly, if the MP_L curve is below the AP_L curve, the AP_L must fall. Thus, the MP_L curve intersects the AP_L curve at the peak of the AP_L curve, point b, where the firm uses six workers.

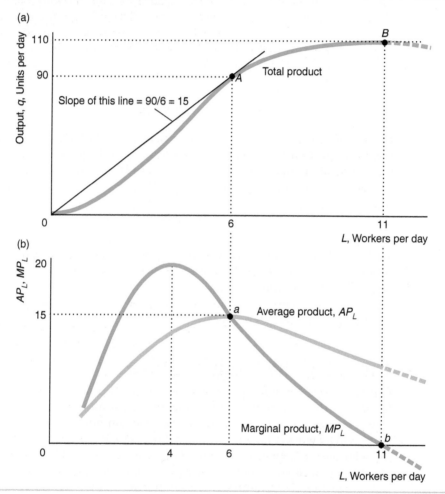

computer. One worker holds a part in place while another one bolts it down. As a result, output increases more than in proportion to labor, so the average product of labor rises. Doubling the number of workers from one to two more than doubles the output from 5 to 18 and causes the average product of labor to rise from 5 to 9, as Table 5.1 shows.

Similarly, output may initially rise more than in proportion to labor because of greater specialization of activities. With greater specialization, workers are assigned to tasks at which they are particularly adept, and time is saved by not having workers move from task to task.

As the number of workers rises further, however, output may not increase by as much per worker because workers might have to wait to use a particular piece of equipment or they might get in each other's way. In Figure 5.1, when the number of workers exceeds 6, total output increases less than in proportion to labor, so the average product falls.

If more than 11 workers are used, the total product curve falls with each extra worker as the crowding of workers gets worse. Because that much labor is not efficient, that section of the curve is drawn with a dashed line to indicate it is not part of the production function, which includes only efficient combinations of labor and capital. Similarly, the dashed portions of the average and marginal product curves are irrelevant because no firm would hire additional workers if doing so meant that output would fall.

Relationships Among Product Curves. The three curves are geometrically related. First we use panel b to illustrate the relationship between the average and marginal product of labor curves. Then we use panels a and b to show the relationship between the total product of labor curve and the other two curves.

An extra hour of work increases the average product of labor if the marginal product of labor exceeds the average product. Similarly, if an extra hour of work generates less extra output than the average, the average product falls. Therefore, the average product rises with extra labor if the marginal product curve is above the average product curve, and the average product falls if the marginal product curve is below the average product curve. Consequently, the average product curve reaches its peak, point a in panel b of Figure 5.1, where the marginal product and average product are equal: where the curves cross.

The geometric relationship between the total product curve and the average and marginal product curves is illustrated in panels a and b of Figure 5.1. We can determine the average product of labor using the total product of labor curve. The average product of labor for L workers equals the slope of a straight line from the origin to a point on the total product of labor curve for L workers in panel a. The slope of this line equals output divided by the number of workers, which is the definition of the average product of labor. For example, the slope of the straight line drawn from the origin to point A ($L = 6$, $q = 90$) is 15, which equals the "rise" of $q = 90$ divided by the "run" of $L = 6$. As panel b shows, the average product of labor for 6 workers at point a is 15.

The marginal product of labor also has a geometric relationship to the total product curve. The slope of the total product curve at a given point equals the marginal product of labor. That is, the marginal product of labor equals the slope of a straight line that is tangent to the total output curve at a given point. For example, at point *B* in panel a, where the firm uses 11 workers, the line tangent to the total product curve is flat so the marginal product of labor is zero (point *b* in panel b): A little extra labor has no effect on output. The total product curve is upward sloping when the firm uses fewer than 11 workers, so the marginal product of labor is positive. If the firm is foolish enough to hire more than 11 workers, the total product curve slopes downward (dashed line), so the MP_L is negative: Extra workers lower output.

When the firm uses 6 workers, the average product of labor equals the marginal product of labor. The line from the origin to point *A* in panel a is tangent to the total product curve, so the slope of that line, 15, is the marginal product of labor and the average product of labor at point *a* in panel b, which is the peak of the AP_L curve.

The Law of Diminishing Marginal Returns

Next to *supply equals demand*, the most commonly used economic phrase is that there are **diminishing marginal returns**: If a firm keeps increasing an input, holding all other inputs and technology constant, the corresponding increases in output will eventually become smaller (diminish). As most observed production functions have this property, this pattern is often called the *law of diminishing marginal returns*. This law determines the shape of the marginal product of labor curves: If only one input is increased, *the marginal product of that input will diminish eventually*.

In Table 5.1, if the firm goes from 1 to 2 workers, the marginal product of labor of the second worker is 13. If 1 or 2 more workers are used, the marginal product rises: The marginal product for the third worker is 18, and the marginal product for the fourth worker is 20. However, if the firm increases the number of workers beyond 4, the marginal product falls: The marginal product of a fifth worker is 19, and that of the sixth worker is 15. Beyond 4 workers, each extra worker adds less and less extra output, so the total product of labor curve rises by smaller increments. At 11 workers, the marginal product is zero. This diminishing return to extra labor might be due to crowding, as workers get in each other's way.

Instead of referring to the *law of diminishing marginal returns*, some people talk about the *law of diminishing returns*—leaving out the word *marginal*. Making this change invites a misunderstanding, as it is not clear if the phrase refers to marginal returns or total returns. If the marginal return falls but remains positive as labor increases, the total return rises. In panel b of Figure 5.1, marginal returns start to diminish when the labor input exceeds 4, but total returns rise, as panel a shows, until the labor input exceeds 11, where the marginal returns become negative.

In addition, many people misstate the law of diminishing returns.

Common Confusion An input's marginal product must eventually fall as a firm uses more of the input.

This claim is true only if as we add more of an input, we hold technology and other inputs constant. If we increase labor while simultaneously increasing other factors or adopting superior technologies, the marginal product of labor may rise indefinitely.

Mini-Case

Malthus and the Green Revolution

[W]hoever makes two ears of corn, or two blades of grass, to grow upon a spot of ground where only one grew before, would deserve better of mankind, and do more essential service to his country, than the whole race of politicians put together. —Jonathan Swift, Gulliver's Travels

In 1798, Thomas Malthus—a clergyman and professor of political economy—predicted that (unchecked) population would grow more rapidly than food production because the quantity of land was fixed. The problem, he believed,

was that the fixed amount of land would lead to a diminishing marginal product of labor, so output would rise less than in proportion to the increase in farm workers, possibly leading to widespread starvation and other "natural" checks on population, such as disease and violent conflict. Brander and Taylor (1998) argue that such a disaster might have occurred on Easter Island about 500 years ago.

Today the earth supports a population about eight times as large as when Malthus made his predictions. Why haven't most of us starved to death? The answer is that a typical agricultural worker produces vastly more food today than was possible when Malthus was alive. The output of a U.S. farm worker today is more than double that of an average worker just 50 years ago. We have not seen diminishing marginal returns to labor because the production function has changed due to dramatic improvements in agricultural production methods and because farmers make greater use of other inputs such as fertilizers and capital.

Two hundred years ago, most of the world's population had to work in agriculture to feed themselves. Today, less than 1% of the U.S. population works in agriculture. Over the past century, food production grew substantially faster than the population in most developed countries.

Of course, the risk of malnutrition and even starvation remains significant in many low-income countries. Fortunately, agricultural production in these nations increased dramatically during the second half of the twentieth century, saving an estimated one *billion* lives. This increased production resulted from a set of innovations called the *Green Revolution*. These innovations, including drought- and insect-resistant crop varieties, improved irrigation, better use of fertilizer and pesticides, scientific crop rotation, and improved equipment, were introduced primarily in the third quarter of the twentieth century, although progress has continued.

Norman Borlaug, the most important contributor to the Green Revolution, won the Nobel Peace Prize in 1970. However, as he noted in his Nobel Prize speech, superior science is not the complete answer to preventing starvation. A sound economic system and a stable political environment are also needed.

Economic and political failures such as the breakdown of economic production and distribution systems due to wars have caused widespread starvation and malnutrition, particularly in parts of sub-Saharan Africa. Environmental problems such as shifting rainfall patterns caused by global warming and soil degradation have also become a major concern. According to the 2017 annual report on food insecurity of the United Nations Food and Agriculture Organization, about 11% of the world's population suffers from significant undernourishment, with a particularly high concentration in sub-Saharan Africa.

5.3 Long-Run Production

We started our analysis of production functions by looking at a short-run production function in which one input, capital, was fixed, and the other, labor, was variable. In the long run, however, both of these inputs are variable. With both factors variable, a firm can usually produce a given level of output by using a great deal of labor and very little capital, a great deal of capital and very little labor, or moderate amounts of both. That is, the firm can substitute one input for another while continuing to produce the same level of output, in much the same way that a consumer can maintain a given level of utility by substituting one good for another.

Typically, a firm can produce in a number of different ways, some of which require more labor than others. For example, a lumberyard can produce 200 planks an hour with 10 workers using hand saws, with 4 workers using handheld power saws, or with 2 workers using bench power saws.

We illustrate a firm's ability to substitute between inputs in Table 5.2, which shows the amount of output per day the firm produces with various combinations of labor per day and capital per day. The labor inputs are along the top of the table, and the capital inputs are in the first column. The table shows four combinations of labor and capital that the firm can use to produce 24 units of output (numbers in bold): The firm may employ (a) 1 worker and 6 units of capital, (b) 2 workers and 3 units of capital, (c) 3 workers and 2 units of capital, or (d) 6 workers and 1 unit of capital.

Isoquants

These four combinations of labor and capital are labeled $a, b, c,$ and d on the "$q = 24$" curve in Figure 5.2. We call such a curve an **isoquant**, which is a curve that shows the efficient combinations of labor and capital that can produce the same (*iso*) level of output (*quantity*). The isoquant shows the smallest amounts of inputs that will

TABLE 5.2 **Output Produced with Two Variable Inputs**

Capital, K	Labor, L					
	1	2	3	4	5	6
1	10	14	17	20	22	**24**
2	14	20	**24**	28	32	35
3	17	**24**	30	35	39	42
4	20	28	35	40	45	49
5	22	32	39	45	50	55
6	**24**	35	42	49	55	60

FIGURE 5.2 A Family of Isoquants

These isoquants show the combinations of labor and capital that produce 14, 24, or 35 units of output, q. Isoquants farther from the origin correspond to higher levels of output. Points a, b, c, and d are various combinations of labor and capital the firm can use to produce q = 24 units of output. If the firm holds capital constant at 2 and increases labor from 1 (point e on the q = 14 isoquant) to 3 (c), its output increases to q = 24 isoquant. If the firm then increases labor to 6 (f), its output rises to q = 35.

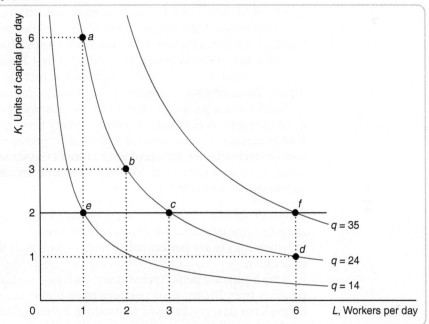

produce a given amount of output. That is, if a firm reduced either input, it could not produce as much output. If the production function is $q = f(L, K)$, then the equation for an isoquant where output is held constant at $\bar{q}$ is

$$\bar{q} = f(L, K).$$

An isoquant shows the flexibility that a firm has in producing a given level of output. Figure 5.2 shows three isoquants corresponding to three levels of output. These isoquants are smooth curves because the firm can use fractional units of each input.

We can use these isoquants to illustrate what happens in the short run when capital is fixed and only labor varies. As Table 5.2 shows, if capital is constant at 2 units, 1 worker produces 14 units of output (point e in Figure 5.2), 3 workers produce 24 units (point c), and 6 workers produce 35 units (point f). Thus, if the firm holds one factor constant and varies another factor, it moves from one isoquant to another. In contrast, if the firm increases one input while lowering the other appropriately, the firm stays on a single isoquant.

Properties of Isoquants. Isoquants have most of the same properties as indifference curves. The biggest distinction between indifference curves and isoquants is that an isoquant holds quantity constant, whereas an indifference curve holds utility constant. We now discuss three major properties of isoquants. These properties result from firms producing efficiently.

First, *the farther an isoquant is from the origin, the greater is the level of output.* That is, the more inputs a firm uses, the more output it gets if it produces efficiently. At point e in Figure 5.2, the firm is producing 14 units of output with 1 worker and 2 units of capital. If the firm holds capital constant and adds 2 more workers, it produces at point c. Point c must be on an isoquant with a higher level of output—here, 24 units—if the firm is producing efficiently and not wasting the extra labor.

Second, *isoquants do not cross*. Such intersections are inconsistent with the requirement that the firm always produces efficiently. For example, if the $q = 15$ and $q = 20$ isoquants crossed, the firm could produce at either output level with the same combination of labor and capital. The firm must be producing inefficiently if it produces $q = 15$ when it could produce $q = 20$. So that labor-capital combination should not lie on the $q = 15$ isoquant, which should include only efficient combinations of inputs. Thus, efficiency requires that isoquants do not cross.

Third, *isoquants slope downward*. If an isoquant sloped upward, the firm could produce the same level of output with relatively few inputs or relatively many inputs. If an isoquant sloped upward, the firm could produce the same level of output with a set of relatively few inputs or with more of the same inputs. Producing with more inputs would be inefficient. Virtually the same argument can be used to show that isoquants must be thin.

Shapes of Isoquants.   The curvature of an isoquant shows how readily a firm can substitute one input for another. The two extreme cases are production processes in which inputs are perfect substitutes or in which they cannot be substituted for each other.

If the inputs are perfect substitutes, each isoquant is a straight line. Suppose either potatoes from Maine, x, or potatoes from Idaho, y, both of which are measured in pounds per day, can be used to produce potato salad, q, measured in pounds. The production function is

$$q = x + y.$$

We can produce 1 pound of potato salad by using 1 pound of Idaho potatoes and no Maine potatoes, 1 pound of Maine potatoes and no Idaho potatoes, or any combination that adds up to 1 pound in total. Panel a of Figure 5.3 shows the $q = 1$, 2, and 3 isoquants. These isoquants are straight lines with a slope of -1 because we need to

FIGURE 5.3 Substitutability of Inputs

(a) If inputs are perfect substitutes, each isoquant is a straight line.
(b) If the inputs cannot be substituted at all, the isoquants are right angles (the dashed lines show that the isoquants would be right angles if we included inefficient production).

(c) Typical isoquants lie between the extreme cases of straight lines and right angles. Along a curved isoquant, the ability to substitute one input for another varies.

(a)

(b)

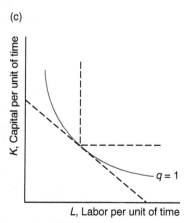

(c)

q = outputs

L = labor units

K = units of capital

$q = f(L, K)$

We can show why isoquants curve away from the origin by deriving an isoquant for trucking.

Self-driving trucks are poised to have a major impact on long-haul trucking. Otto (owned by Uber), Tesla, Embark, Peloton, and over 50 other companies are investing more than $1 billion on developing self-driving trucks and other high-tech trucking technologies.

Autonomous trucks are starting to hit the road. In 2016, an Otto self-driving truck carried 2,000 cases of Budweiser beer from Fort Collins, Colorado, to Colorado Springs along Interstate 25. In 2017, Embark autonomous trucks started hauling Frigidaire refrigerators 650 miles along the I-10 freeway from El Paso, Texas, to Palm Springs, California. Uber predicts that between 500,000 and 1.5 million self-driving trucks will be on the road by 2028.

Soon, a company that wants to transport a given amount of goods from one city to another will choose between two technologies:

- *Traditional*: A trucker drives the entire route.
- *Self-driving*: A trucker drives the first and last few miles through complex urban roads, but an autonomous truck drives the highway portion unattended.

A driver is legally restricted to 11 hours of driving a day and 60 hours a week. Given that big rigs cost $150,000 or more, leaving them idle for part of the day is wasteful. A self-driving truck can operate around the clock, with various human drivers handling the short distances at either end of a route. The alternative is to have the traditional big rig driven by several drivers.

The diagram shows the isoquant for 10 trips between Los Angeles and Phoenix. The vertical axis measures the amount of capital, and the horizontal records the amount of labor. Both technologies use labor and capital in fixed proportions. The diagram shows the two right-angle isoquants corresponding to each of these technologies.

The traditional truck contains less capital, K_1, than does the self-driving truck, K_2, which also includes artificial intelligence (AI). However, the traditional technology uses more labor, L_1, than does the self-driving technology.

A truck company could use a combination of traditional and self-driving trucks. By doing so, the firm can produce using intermediate combinations of labor and capital, as the solid-line, kinked isoquant illustrates.

With the introduction of new processes in the future, the isoquant will have more and more kinks (one for each new, efficient process) and will begin to resemble the smooth, convex isoquants we've been drawing.

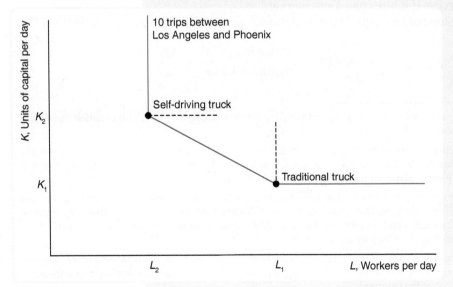

use an extra pound of Maine potatoes for every pound fewer of Idaho potatoes used.[2]

Sometimes it is impossible to substitute one input for the other: Inputs must be used in fixed proportions. Such a production function is called a *fixed-proportions production function*. For example, the inputs needed to produce 12-ounce boxes of cereal are cereal (in 12-ounce units per day) and cardboard boxes (boxes per day). If the firm has one unit of cereal and one box, it can produce one box of cereal. If it has one unit of cereal and two boxes, it can still make only one box of cereal. Thus, in panel b, the only efficient points of production are the large dots along the 45° line.[3] Dashed lines show that the isoquants would be right angles if isoquants could include inefficient production processes.

Other production processes allow imperfect substitution between inputs. These processes have isoquants that are convex to the origin (so the middle of the isoquant is closer to the origin than it would be if the isoquant were a straight line). They do not have the same slope at every point, unlike the straight-line isoquants. Most isoquants are smooth, slope downward, curve away from the origin, and lie between the extreme cases of straight lines (perfect substitutes) and right angles (fixed proportions), as panel c illustrates.

Substituting Inputs

The slope of an isoquant shows the ability of a firm to replace one input with another while holding output constant. Figure 5.4 illustrates this substitution using an estimated isoquant for a "personal and other service" firm (such as gardening, hairdressers, and laundries), which uses labor, L, and capital, K, to produce q units of service.[4] The isoquant shows various combinations of L and K by which the firm can produce 10 units of output.

The firm can produce 10 units of output using the combination of inputs at a or b. At point a, the firm uses 2 workers and 16 units of capital. The firm could produce the same amount of output with $\Delta K = -6$ fewer units of capital if it used one more worker, $\Delta L = 1$, point b. If we drew a straight line from a to b, its slope would be $\Delta K / \Delta L = -6$. Thus, this slope tells us how many fewer units of capital (6) the firm can use if it hires one more worker.[5]

The slope of an isoquant is called the *marginal rate of technical substitution (MRTS)*:

$$MRTS = \frac{\text{change in capital}}{\text{change in labor}} = \frac{\Delta K}{\Delta L}.$$

[2]The isoquant for $\bar{q} = 1$ pound of potato salad is $1 = x + y$, or $y = 1 - x$. This equation shows that the isoquant is a straight line with a slope of -1.

[3]This fixed-proportions production function is the minimum of g and b, $q = \min(g, b)$, where g is the number of 12-ounce measures of cereal, b is the number of boxes used in a day, and the min function means "the minimum number of g or b." For example, if g is 4 and b is 3, q is 3.

[4]The isoquant for $q = 10$ is based on the estimated "personal and other service" production function $q = 2.35L^{0.5}K^{0.4}$ (Devine, Doan, and Stevens, 2012), where a unit of labor, L, is a worker-day. Because capital, K, includes various types of machines, and output, q, reflects different types of service, their units cannot be described by any common terms.

[5]The slope of the isoquant at a point equals the slope of a straight line that is tangent to the isoquant at that point. Thus, the straight line between two nearby points on an isoquant has nearly the same slope as that of the isoquant.

The **marginal rate of technical substitution** tells us how many units of capital the firm can replace with an extra unit of labor while holding output constant. Because isoquants slope downward, the *MRTS* is negative. That is, the firm can produce a given level of output by substituting more capital for less labor (or vice versa).

Substitutability of Inputs Varies Along an Isoquant. The *MRTS* varies along a curved isoquant, as in Figure 5.4. If the firm is initially at point *a* and it hires one more worker ($\Delta L = 1$), the firm can give up six units of capital ($\Delta K = -6$) and yet remain on the same isoquant (at point *b*), so the *MRTS* is $\Delta K/\Delta L = -6$. If the firm hires another worker, the firm can reduce its capital by three units and stay on the same isoquant, moving from point *b* to *c*, so the *MRTS* is -3. This decline in the *MRTS* (in absolute value) along an isoquant as the firm increases labor illustrates a *diminishing MRTS*. The more labor and less capital the firm has, the harder it is to replace remaining capital with labor and the flatter the isoquant becomes.

   In the special case in which isoquants are straight lines, isoquants do not exhibit diminishing marginal rates of technical substitution because neither input becomes more valuable in the production process: The inputs remain perfect substitutes. Q&A 5.2 illustrates this result.

Q&A 5.2	A manufacturer produces a container of potato salad using 1 pound of Idaho potatoes, 1 pound of Maine potatoes, or 1 pound of a mixture of the two types of potatoes. Does the marginal rate of technical substitution vary along the isoquant? What is the *MRTS* at each point along the isoquant?

Answer

1. *Determine the shape of the isoquant.* As panel a of Figure 5.3 illustrates, the potato salad isoquants are straight lines because the two types of potatoes are perfect substitutes.

2. *On the basis of the shape, conclude whether the MRTS is constant along the isoquant.* Because the isoquant is a straight line, the slope is the same at every point, so the *MRTS* is constant.

3. *Determine the MRTS at each point.* Earlier, we showed that the slope of this isoquant was -1, so the *MRTS* is -1 at each point along the isoquant. That is, because the two inputs are perfect substitutes, 1 pound of Idaho potatoes can be replaced by 1 pound of Maine potatoes.

Substitutability of Inputs and Marginal Products. The marginal rate of technical substitution is equal to the ratio of marginal products. The marginal product of labor, $MP_L = \Delta q/\Delta L$, is the increase in output from an extra unit of labor, holding capital fixed. If the firm hires ΔL more workers, its output increases by $MP_L \times \Delta L$. For example, if the MP_L is 2 and the firm hires one extra worker, its output rises by 2 units.

   Similarly, the marginal product of capital, $MP_K = \Delta q/\Delta K$, is the increase in output from an extra unit of capital, holding other inputs fixed. Thus, a decrease in capital, holding labor fixed, causes output to fall by $MP_K \times \Delta K$. If the firm increases labor and decreases capital to keep output constant ($\Delta q = 0$), the fall in output caused by reducing capital must exactly equal the increase in output from increasing labor:

$$(MP_L \times \Delta L) + (MP_K \times \Delta K) = 0.$$

Rearranging these terms, we find that

$$-\frac{MP_L}{MP_K} = \frac{\Delta K}{\Delta L} = MRTS. \tag{5.3}$$

Thus, the ratio of marginal products equals the *MRTS* (in absolute value).

We can use Equation 5.3 to explain why marginal rates of technical substitution diminish as we move to the right along the isoquant in Figure 5.4. As we replace capital with labor (moving down and to the right along the isoquant), the marginal product of capital increases—if each firm has few pieces of equipment, each remaining piece is more useful—and the marginal product of labor falls, so the $MRTS = -MP_L/MP_K$ falls in absolute value.

Cobb-Douglas Production Functions.   We can illustrate how to determine the *MRTS* for a particular production function, the Cobb-Douglas production function. It is named after its inventors, Charles W. Cobb, a mathematician, and Paul H. Douglas, an economist and U.S. Senator. Through empirical studies, economists have found that the production processes in a large number of industries can be accurately summarized by the Cobb-Douglas production function, which is

$$q = AL^aK^b, \tag{5.4}$$

where A, a, and b are all positive constants. For example, we used the estimated "personal and other service" Cobb-Douglas production function, $q = 2.35L^{0.5}K^{0.4}$, to draw Figure 5.4, where $A = 2.35$, $a = 0.5$, and $b = 0.4$.

The constants a and b determine the relationships between the marginal and average products of labor and capital. The marginal product of labor is a times the average product of labor, $AP_L = q/L$. That is, $MP_L = aq/L = aAP_L$ (as we show in the following *Using Calculus* section). By dividing both sides of the expression by AP_L, we find that a equals the ratio of the marginal product of labor to the

FIGURE 5.4 How the Marginal Rate of Technical Substitution Varies Along an Isoquant

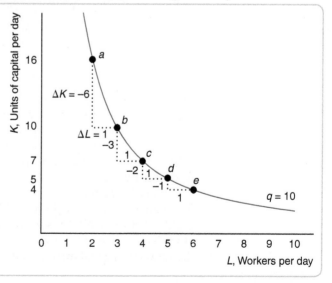

Moving from point a to b, a U.S. printing firm (Hsieh, 1995) can produce the same amount of output, $q = 10$, using six fewer units of capital, $\Delta K = -6$, if it uses one more worker, $\Delta L = 1$. Thus, its $MRTS = \Delta K/\Delta L = -6$. Moving from point b to c, its *MRTS* is -3. If it adds yet another worker, moving from c to d, its *MRTS* is -2. Finally, if it moves from d to e, its *MRTS* is -1. Thus, because the isoquant is convex to the origin, it exhibits a diminishing marginal rate of technical substitution. That is, each extra worker allows the firm to reduce capital by a smaller amount as the ratio of capital to labor falls.

average product of labor: $a = MP_L/AP_L$. Similarly, the marginal product of capital is $MP_K = bq/K = bAP_K$, and $b = MP_K/AP_K$.

The marginal rate of technical substitution along an isoquant that holds output fixed at $\bar{q}$ is

$$MRTS = -\frac{MP_L}{MP_K} = -\frac{a\bar{q}/L}{b\bar{q}/K} = -\frac{a}{b}\frac{K}{L}. \tag{5.5}$$

For example, given the personal and other service production function, $q = 2.35L^{0.5}K^{0.4}$, its $MP_L = aAP_L = 0.5AP_L$, and its $MRTS = -(0.5/0.4)K/L = -1.25K/L$. The $MRTS$ tells the firm's managers the rate at which they can substitute capital for labor without reducing output.

Using Calculus

Cobb-Douglas Marginal Products

To obtain the marginal product of labor for the Cobb-Douglas production function, Equation 5.4, $q = AL^aK^b$, we partially differentiate the production function with respect to labor, holding capital fixed:

$$MP_L = \frac{\partial q}{\partial L} = aAL^{a-1}K^b = a\frac{AL^aK^b}{L} = a\frac{q}{L}.$$

We obtain the last equality by substituting $q = AL^aK^b$. Similarly, we can derive the marginal product of capital by partially differentiating the production function with respect to K:

$$MP_K = \frac{\partial q}{\partial K} = bAL^aK^{b-1} = b\frac{AL^aK^b}{K} = b\frac{q}{K}.$$

5.4 Returns to Scale

So far, we have examined the effects of increasing one input while holding the other input constant (shifting from one isoquant to another) or decreasing the other input by an offsetting amount (moving along an isoquant). We now turn to the question of *how much output changes if a firm increases all its inputs proportionately*. The answer helps a firm determine its *scale* or size in the long run.

In the long run, a firm can increase its output by building a second plant and staffing it with the same number of workers as in the first one. Whether the firm chooses to do so depends in part on whether its output increases less than in proportion, in proportion, or more than in proportion to its inputs.

Constant, Increasing, and Decreasing Returns to Scale

If, when all inputs are increased by a certain proportion, output increases by that same proportion, the production function is said to exhibit **constant returns to scale** (CRS). A firm's production process, $q = f(L, K)$, has constant returns to scale if, when the firm doubles its inputs—by, for example, building an identical second plant and using the same amount of labor and equipment as in the first plant—it doubles its output:

$$f(2L, 2K) = 2f(L, K) = 2q.$$

We can check whether the potato salad production function has constant returns to scale. If a firm uses x_1 pounds of Idaho potatoes and y_1 pounds of Maine potatoes, it produces $q_1 = x_1 + y_1$ pounds of potato salad. If it doubles both inputs, using $x_2 = 2x_1$ Idaho and $y_2 = 2y_1$ Maine potatoes, it doubles its output:

$$q_2 = x_2 + y_2 = 2x_1 + 2y_1 = 2(x_1 + y_1) = 2q_1.$$

Thus, the potato salad production function exhibits constant returns to scale.

If output rises more than in proportion to an equal proportional increase in all inputs, the production function is said to exhibit **increasing returns to scale** (*IRS*). A technology exhibits increasing returns to scale if doubling inputs more than doubles the output:

$$f(2L, 2K) > 2f(L, K) = 2q.$$

Why might a production function have increasing returns to scale? One reason is that although it could build a copy of its original small factory and double its output, the firm might be able to more than double its output by building a single large plant, thereby allowing for greater specialization of labor or capital. In the two smaller plants, workers have to perform many unrelated tasks, such as operating, maintaining, and fixing the machines they use. In the large plant, some workers may specialize in maintaining and fixing machines, thereby increasing efficiency. Similarly, a firm may use specialized equipment in a large plant but not in a small one.

If output rises less than in proportion to an equal proportional increase in all inputs, the production function exhibits **decreasing returns to scale (*DRS*)**. A technology exhibits decreasing returns to scale if doubling inputs causes output to rise less than in proportion:

$$f(2L, 2K) < 2f(L, K) = 2q.$$

One reason for decreasing returns to scale is that the difficulty of organizing, coordinating, and integrating activities increases with firm size. An owner may be able to manage one plant well but may have trouble running two plants. In some sense, the decreasing returns to scale stemming from the owner's difficulties in running a larger firm may reflect our failure to take into account some factor such as management skills in our production function. If a firm increases various inputs but does not increase the management input in proportion, the "decreasing returns to scale" may occur because one of the inputs to production, management skills, is fixed.

This'll save a lot of time!

Another reason is that large teams of workers may not function as well as small teams, in which each individual takes greater personal responsibility.

Q&A 5.3

Under what conditions does a Cobb-Douglas production function, Equation 5.4, $q = AL^aK^b$, exhibit decreasing, constant, or increasing returns to scale?

Answer

1. *Show how output changes if both inputs are doubled.* If the firm initially uses L and K amounts of inputs, it produces $q_1 = AL^aK^b$. After the firm doubles the amount of both labor and capital it uses, it produces

$$q_2 = A(2L)^a(2K)^b = 2^{a+b}AL^aK^b = 2^{a+b}q_1. \tag{5.6}$$

That is, q_2 is 2^{a+b} times q_1. If we define $g = a + b$, then Equation 5.6 tells us that

$$q_2 = 2^g q_1. \tag{5.7}$$

Thus, if the inputs double, output increases by 2^g.

2. *Give a rule for determining the returns to scale.* If $g = 1$, we know from Equation 5.7 that $q_2 = 2^1 q_1 = 2q_1$. That is, output doubles when the inputs double, so the Cobb-Douglas production function has constant returns to scale. If $g < 1$, then $q_2 = 2^g q_1 < 2q_1$ because $2^g < 2$ if $g < 1$. That is, when input doubles, output increases less than in proportion, so this Cobb-Douglas production function exhibits decreasing returns to scale. Finally, the Cobb-Douglas production function has increasing returns to scale if $g > 1$ so that $q_2 > 2q_1$. Thus, the rule for determining returns to scale for a Cobb-Douglas production function is that the returns to scale are decreasing if $g < 1$, constant if $g = 1$, and increasing if $g > 1$.

Comment: One interpretation of g is that, as all inputs increase by 1%, output increases by g%. Thus, for example, if $g = 1$, a 1% increase in all inputs increases output by 1%.

Mini-Case

Returns to Scale for Crocs

Crocs, a foam-resin shoe manufactured by Crocs, Inc., took the shoe market by storm over the past dozen years. Popular with both children and their parents, these light, colorful, and inexpensive shoes are sold in 90 countries around the world.

We used regression analysis to estimate a Cobb-Douglas production function for Crocs.[6] The estimated production function is $q = AL^aK^b = 22.7L^{0.88}K^{0.48}$. That is, $A = 22.7$, $a = 0.88$, and $b = 0.48$. Because $a + b = 0.88 + 0.48 = 1.36 > 1$, Croc production exhibits increasing returns to scale. Labor is measured in thousands of employees; capital is an index of plant, property, and equipment (PPE); and one unit of output is a million dollars' worth of shoes, which is about 40,000 pairs of shoes.

The graph uses isoquants to illustrate Crocs' increasing returns to scale. A combination of

---

[6]The data are from the Crocs, Inc., annual reports from 2004 through 2017, as reported in Compustat.

2 units of labor and 7 units of capital produces 107 units of output and is one point on the $q = 107$ isoquant: $q = 22.7(2^{0.88})(7^{0.48}) \approx 107$. That is, 2 (thousand) workers and 7 units of capital produce about 107 million dollars' worth of shoes. If the firm doubles both of its inputs to 4 units of labor and 14 units of capital, it is operating on the 276-unit isoquant, which is *more* than double the initial output.

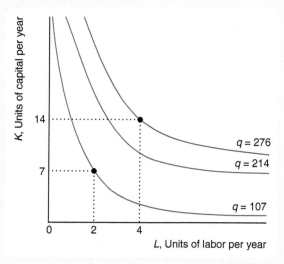

Varying Returns to Scale

For a Cobb-Douglas production function, the returns to scale are the same at all levels of output. However, for other production functions, the returns to scale may vary as the output level changes. Many production functions have increasing returns to scale for small amounts of output, constant returns for moderate amounts of output, and decreasing returns for large amounts of output. When a firm is small, increasing labor and capital allows for gains from cooperation between workers and greater specialization of workers and equipment—*returns to specialization*—so the production function exhibits increasing returns to scale. As the firm grows, returns to scale are eventually exhausted, so the production process has constant returns to scale. If the firm continues to grow, the owner starts having difficulty managing everyone, so the firm suffers from decreasing returns to scale.

We show such a pattern in Figure 5.5. The spacing of the isoquants reflects the returns to scale. Initially, the firm has one worker and one piece of equipment, point *a*, and produces 1 unit of output on the $q = 1$ isoquant. If the firm doubles its inputs, it produces at *b*, where $L = 2$ and $K = 2$, which lies on the dashed line through the origin and point *a*. Output more than doubles to $q = 3$, so the production function exhibits increasing returns to scale in this range. Another doubling of inputs to *c* causes output to double to 6 units, so the production function has constant returns to scale in this range. Another doubling of inputs to *d* causes output to increase by only a third, to $q = 8$, so the production function has decreasing returns to scale in this range.

FIGURE 5.5 Varying Scale Economies

The production function that corresponds to these isoquants exhibits varying returns to scale. Initially, the firm uses one worker and one unit of capital, point *a*. Point *b* has double the amount of labor and capital that *a* has. Similarly, *c* has double the inputs of *b*, and *d* has double the inputs of *c*. All these points lie along the dashed 45° line. The first time the inputs are doubled, *a* to *b*, output more than doubles from *q* = 1 to *q* = 3, so the production function has increasing returns to scale. The next doubling, *b* to *c*, causes a proportionate increase in output, constant returns to scale. At the last doubling, from *c* to *d*, the production function exhibits decreasing returns to scale.

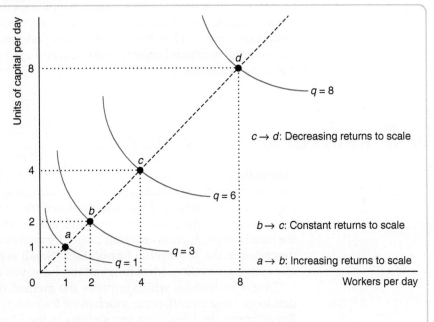

$c \rightarrow d$: Decreasing returns to scale

$b \rightarrow c$: Constant returns to scale

$a \rightarrow b$: Increasing returns to scale

Managerial Implication

Small Is Beautiful

Over the years, the typical factory has grown in size to take advantage of increasing returns to scale. However, three-dimensional (3D) printing may reverse this trend by making input requirements per unit to manufacture one item as low as when making thousands.

With 3D printing, an employee gives instructions—essentially a blueprint—to the machine, presses *print*, and the machine builds the object from the ground up, either by depositing material from a nozzle or by selectively solidifying a thin layer of plastic or metal dust using drops of glue or a tightly focused beam.

Until recently, firms primarily used 3D printers to create prototypes in the aerospace, medical, and automotive industries. Then, they manufactured the final products using conventional techniques. However, 3D printing has improved so much so that it can now be used for manufacturing final products, particularly in industries that need small numbers of customized parts. Nike is using 3D printers to produce the Zoom Superfly Skyknit running shoe. These printers are useful in creating customized prostheses for people with amputations.

Biomedical and aerospace companies make use of 3D printing for just-in-time manufacturing. With this technique, companies can fabricate small, highly customized batches of products as end-users need them. By 2018, Boeing and Airbus were each using thousands of different printed parts in their aircraft. The printers produce lighter parts, which lower the weight of planes (saving fuel) and can be quickly redesigned. Perhaps more striking, Airbus introduced the world's first entirely 3D-printed aircraft, a drone, in 2016.

Managers should use this technology to experiment. They can produce small initial runs to determine the size of the market and consumers' acceptance of the product. Based on information from early adopters, managers can determine if the market warrants further production and can quickly modify designs to meet end-users' desires.

5.5 Innovation

Innovation—a new idea, device, or method—affects markets in many ways. Over the past century, *new product innovations* such as antibiotics, television, jet aircraft, personal computers, and the internet have transformed the way we live and do business. Innovations that have dramatic effects on the products we consume or on the nature of production are often called *disruptive innovations*. Possibly 3D printing, described in the Managerial Implication "Small Is Beautiful," will turn out to be a disruptive innovation. Most innovations, however, are incremental.

Process innovations, which improve the method of production for existing products to increase output, occur much more frequently than new product innovations. For example, the life-saving innovations in the Mini-Case "Malthus and the Green Revolution" include process innovations such as irrigation and optimal crop rotation that greatly increased food production.

Organizational innovations—new ways of organizing firms—also increase output. For example, the Zappos online shoe retailer is experimenting with a new organizational structure, *holacracy*, in which workers are arranged in groups (circles) without top-down supervisors.

A successful process innovation or organizational innovation is an advance in knowledge that allows more output to be produced with the same level of inputs and is often called **technical progress**. Technical progress may be a matter of engineering, such as improving the design of robotic arms used in assembling cars. But such innovations may also be organizational or managerial, such as improving the way managers interact with workers.

Process Innovation

A process innovation changes the production function. Last year a firm produced

$$q_1 = f(L, K)$$

units of output using L units of labor services and K units of capital service. Due to technical progress from a process innovation, this year's production function differs from last year's. For example, if this technical progress allows a firm to produce 10% more output with the same inputs, the production function becomes

$$q_2 = 1.1f(L, K).$$

Flath, (2011) estimated the annual rate of technical progress in Japanese manufacturing firms to be 0.91% for electric copper, 0.87% for medicine, 0.33% for steel pipes and tubes, 0.19% for cement, and 0.08% for beer.

This type of technical progress reflects *neutral technical progress*, in which more output is produced using the same ratio of inputs. However, technical progress may be *nonneutral*. Rather than increasing output for a given mix of inputs, technical progress could be *capital saving*, whereby the firm can produce the same level of output as before, using less capital and the same amount of other inputs.

Alternatively, technical progress may be *labor saving*. The development of self-driving trucks is an example of labor-saving technical progress. Basker (2012) found that the introduction of barcode scanners in grocery stores increased the average product of labor by 4.5%, on average, across stores. Amazon makes extensive use of robots to move items in its warehouses, partially replacing workers. Other robots help doctors perform surgery more quickly and reduce patients' recovery times.

Mini-Case

Robots and the Food You Eat

Robots have been used in manufacturing for many years. They are now gaining a foothold in agriculture. Well over half the wine grapes in California are picked by robots, and robots are also used to harvest strawberries, tomatoes, lettuce, and other crops. The Hackney Nursery in Florida uses robots to assess whether flowers have adequate room for optimal growth and to move the flowers around accordingly. And fully autonomous cow-milking robots are widely used.

Not just the farming end of the food business is using robots. The Dalu Robot Restaurant in Jinan, China, uses robots to wait on tables, greet customers, and provide entertainment. Each robot serving food has a motion sensor that tells it to stop when someone is in its path so customers can reach for dishes they want. But perhaps the most popular employee is a female robot, complete with batting eyelashes, who greets people with an electronic "welcome." First-time customer Li Xiaomei praised the robots, claiming that "they have a better service attitude than humans."

Organizational Innovation

Organizational innovation may also alter the production function and increase the amount of output produced by a given amount of inputs. In the early 1900s, Henry Ford revolutionized the mass production of automobiles through two organizational innovations. First, he introduced interchangeable parts, which cut the time required to install parts because workers no longer had to file or machine individually made parts to get them to fit.

Second, Ford introduced a conveyor belt and an assembly line to his production process. Before this change, workers walked around the car, and each worker performed many assembly activities. In Ford's plant, each worker specialized in a single activity, such as attaching the right rear fender to the chassis. A conveyor belt moved the car at a constant speed from worker to worker along the assembly line. Because his workers gained proficiency from specializing in only a few activities and because the conveyor belts reduced the number of movements workers had to make, Ford could produce more automobiles with the same number of workers. These innovations reduced the ratio of labor to capital used. In 1908, the Ford Model T sold for $850, while rival vehicles sold for $2,000. By the early 1920s, Ford had increased production from fewer than a thousand cars per year to two million per year.

Mini-Case

A Good Boss Raises Productivity

Does a good supervisor make workers more productive? To answer this question, Lazear, Shaw, and Stanton (2015) looked at a large service-oriented company. Supervisor quality varied substantially as measured by the boss's effect on worker productivity. Replacing one of the 10% worst bosses with one of the 10% best ones raised a team's output by about the same amount as adding one worker to a nine-member team. Thus, differences in managers can cause one firm to be more productive than another.

Managerial Implication

Technical Progress and Competitive Advantage

In some industries, an important part of being a good manager involves adopting new technologies and looking for better ways to organize the firm. A firm that achieves a successful process or organizational innovation can produce more output with the same input levels than its rivals, which gives it a competitive advantage.

Managerial Solution

Labor Productivity During Recessions

During a recession, a manager of a Japanese beer bottling plant has to reduce output and decides to lay off workers. Will the firm's labor productivity—average product of labor—go up and improve the firm's situation or go down and harm it?

Layoffs have the positive effect of freeing up machines to be used by remaining workers. However, if layoffs force the remaining workers to perform a wide variety of tasks, the firm will lose the benefits from specialization. When the firm has many workers, the advantage of freeing up machines is important and increased multitasking is unlikely to be a problem. When the firm has only a few workers, freeing up more machines does not help much (some machines might stand idle some of the time), while multitasking becomes a more serious problem.

Holding capital constant, a change in the number of workers affects a firm's average product of labor. Labor productivity could rise or fall. For example, in panel b of Figure 5.1, the average product of labor rises as L increases up to 6 workers per day and then falls as the number of workers increases further. The average product of labor falls if the firm has six or fewer workers and lays one off, but rises if the firm initially has seven or more workers and lays off a worker.

Consider a Cobb-Douglas production function, $q = AL^aK^b$, where $AP_L = q/L = q = AL^{a-1}K^b$. The rate of change of the AP_L with respect to labor (its derivative) is $(a-1)AL^{a-2}K^b$. Thus, if a is less than one, so that $a - 1$ is negative, the AP_L falls with extra labor.

For example, for the beer firm's estimated Cobb-Douglas production function (Flath, 2011), $q = AL^{0.6}K^{0.4}$, $a = 0.6$ is less than 1, so the AP_L curve slopes downward at every quantity. We can illustrate how much the AP_L rises with a layoff for this particular production function. If $A = 1$ and $L = K = 10$ initially, then the firm's output is $q = 10^{0.6} \times 10^{0.4} = 10$, and its average product of labor is $AP_L = q/L = 10/10 = 1$. If the number of workers is reduced by one, then output falls to $q = 9^{0.6} \times 10^{0.4} \approx 9.39$, and the average product of labor rises to $AP_L \approx 9.39/9 \approx 1.04$. That is, a 10% reduction in labor causes output to *fall* by 6.1%, but causes the average product of labor to *rise* by 4%. The firm's output falls less than 10% because each remaining worker is more productive.

Until recently, most large Japanese firms did not lay off workers during downturns. Thus, in contrast to U.S. firms, their average product of labor fell during recessions because their output fell while labor remained constant. Similarly, European firms have 30% less employment volatility over time than do U.S. firms, at least in part because many European firms that fire workers are subject to a tax. Consequently, with other factors held constant in the short run, recessions might be more damaging to the profit of a Japanese or European firm than to the profit of a comparable U.S. firm. However, retaining *good* workers over short-run downturns might be a good long-run policy.

SUMMARY

1. **Production Functions.** A production function summarizes how a firm combines inputs such as labor, capital, and materials to produce output using the current state of knowledge about technology and management. A production function shows how much output can be produced efficiently from various levels of inputs. A firm produces efficiently if it cannot produce its current level of output with less of any one input, holding other inputs constant.

2. **Short-Run Production.** In the short run, a firm cannot adjust the quantity of some inputs, such as capital. The firm varies its output in the short run by adjusting its variable inputs, such as labor. If all factors are fixed except labor, and a firm that was using very little labor increases its use of labor, its output may rise more than in proportion to the increase in labor because of greater specialization of workers. Eventually, however, as more workers are hired, the workers get in each other's way or must wait to share equipment, so output increases by smaller and smaller amounts. This latter phenomenon is described by the law of diminishing marginal returns: The marginal product of an input—the extra output from the last unit of input—eventually decreases as more of that input is used, holding other inputs fixed.

3. **Long-Run Production.** In the long run, when all inputs are variable, firms can substitute between inputs.

An isoquant shows the combinations of inputs that can produce a given level of output. The marginal rate of technical substitution is the absolute value of the slope of the isoquant and indicates how easily the firm can substitute one factor of production for another. Usually, the more of one input the firm uses, the more difficult it is to substitute that input for another input. That is, the marginal rate of technical substitution diminishes as the firm uses more of an input.

4. **Returns to Scale.** When a firm increases all inputs in proportion and its output increases by the same proportion, the production process is said to exhibit constant returns to scale. If output increases less than in proportion to the increase in inputs, the production process has decreasing returns to scale; if it increases more than in proportion, it has increasing returns to scale. All three types of returns to scale are common. Many production processes exhibit first increasing, then constant, and finally decreasing returns to scale as the size of the firm increases.

5. **Innovation.** Using process innovation or organizational innovations, firms achieve technical progress: They can produce more output than before with the same inputs. This technical progress changes the production function.

QUESTIONS

All exercises are available on **MyLab Economics;** * = *answer at the back of this book;* ✖ = *this exercise is available in Excel Grader in* **MyLab Economics.**

1. Production Functions

1.1 What are the main types of capital and labor that can be used to produce candy?

*1.2 Suppose that for the function $q = f(L, K)$, if $L = 3$ and $K = 5$ then $q = 10$. Is it possible that $L = 3$ and

$K = 6$ also yields $q = 10$ for this production function? Why or why not?

1.3 As in Question 1.2, suppose that the production function shows that if $L = 3$ and $K = 5$ then $q = 10$. Is it possible that $L = 3$ and $K = 6$ yields $q = 11$ for this production function? Explain briefly.

1.4 Consider Boeing (a producer of jet aircraft), General Mills (a producer of breakfast cereals), and Wacky Jack's (which claims to be the largest U.S. provider of singing telegrams). For which of these firms is the *short run* the longest period? For which is the long run the shortest? Explain.

2. Short-Run Production

*2.1 If each extra worker produces an additional unit of output, how do the total product of labor, average product of labor, and marginal product of labor vary with labor? Plot these curves in a graph similar to Figure 5.1.

2.2 Each extra worker produces an additional unit of output up to six workers. As more workers are added, no additional output is produced. Draw the total product of labor, average product of labor, and marginal product of labor curves in a graph similar to Figure 5.1.

*2.3 Suppose that the production function is $q = L^{0.75}K^{0.25}$. (*Hint*: See Q&A 5.1.)

   a. What is the average product of labor, holding capital fixed at $\overline{K}$?

   b. What is the marginal product of labor?

   c. How is the marginal product of labor related to the average product of labor?

2.4 In the short run, a firm cannot vary its capital and operates with $K = 9$. It can, however, vary the amount of labor (L) that it uses. For each production function below, explain why the firm will or will not experience diminishing marginal returns to labor in the short run.

   a. $q = 35L + 40K$

   b. $q = L^{0.5}K^{0.5}$

   c. $q = min\{3L, 2K\}$

2.5 Based on the information in the Mini-Case "Malthus and the Green Revolution," how did the average product of labor in food production change over time?

*2.6 The 2017 report of the United Nations Food and Agriculture Organization (FAO) notes that the share of world population that is undernourished rose between 2014 and 2016, following a long period of decline. This increase occurred even though agricultural output per acre rose between 2014 and 2016. What factors might cause undernourishment to rise even though agricultural land productivity rose?

3. Long-Run Production

3.1 Why must isoquants be thin?

3.2 Set up by a former University of North Carolina (UNC) student, Morris Gelblum, the firm Sweeps uses UNC, Duke, North Carolina State, and other college students to perform a variety of short-term jobs, such as cleaning, yard work, painting, tech help, tutoring, and moving. A customer describes the work desired on the firm's website, and the firm provides workers. For one job, they provide "21 guys dressed up like Frankenstein." The firm's motto is "College Students, On-Demand." What input(s) does the firm use in the long run?

3.3 The isoquant in the Mini-Case "Self-Driving Trucks" is based on two technologies. Suppose that a company develops a third technology that assists but does not replace a human driver. It uses more labor and less capital than the fully self-driving technology, but less labor and more capital than the traditional technology. In the isoquant diagram, the input combination needed to produce 10 trips lies below the straight line joining the input combinations for the traditional and self-driving technologies. Illustrate the resulting isoquant.

3.4 Using the information given in Table 5.2, draw the isoquant corresponding to an output level of 20. Starting from $L = 4$ and $K = 1$, how much extra capital is needed to keep output constant if the labor is reduced by one unit to $L = 3$? How much extra capital is needed to keep output constant if labor is reduced by one more unit to $L = 2$?

*3.5 To produce a recorded DVD, $q = 1$, a firm uses one blank disk, $D = 1$, and the services of a recording machine, $M = 1$, for one hour. (*Hint*: See Q&A 5.2.)

   a. Draw the isoquants for this production function and explain its shape.

   b. What is the *MRTS* at each point along the isoquant corresponding to $q = 100$?

   c. Draw the total product, average product, and marginal product of labor curves for this production function. Use two diagrams, as in Figure 5.1.

3.6 The production function at Ginko's Copy Shop is $q = 1{,}000 \times min(L, 3K)$, where q is the number of copies per hour, L is the number of workers, and K is the number of copy machines. As an example, if $L = 4$ and $K = 1$, then the minimum of L and $3K$, $min(L, 3K) = 3$, and $q = 3{,}000$.

   a. Draw the isoquants for this production function.

   b. Draw the total product, average product, and marginal product of labor curves for this production function for some fixed level of capital.

3.7 Using the figure in the Mini-Case "Self-Driving Trucks," show that as the firm employs additional fixed-proportion technologies, the firm's overall isoquant approaches a smooth curve similar to that in panel c of Figure 5.3.

*3.8 A laundry cleans white clothes using the production function $q = B + 2G$, where B is the number of cups of Clorox bleach, G is the number of cups of a generic bleach that is half as potent, and q is the basketfuls of clothes that are cleaned. Draw an isoquant for one basketful of clothes. What is the marginal product of B? What is the marginal rate of technical substitution at each point on an isoquant?

*3.9 At $L = 4$, $K = 4$, the marginal product of labor is 2 and the marginal product of capital is 3. What is the marginal rate of technical substitution ($MRTS$)?

*3.10 Consider a Cobb-Douglas production function $q = 10L^{0.5}K^{0.5}$. If $L = 16$ and $K = 25$, calculate output, q, the marginal product of labor, and the marginal product of capital? (*Hint*: Use the marginal product formulas in Using Calculus "Cobb-Douglas Marginal Products.")

4. Returns to Scale

4.1 To speed relief to isolated South Asian communities that were devastated by the December 2004 tsunami, the U.S. government doubled the number of Navy helicopters from 45 to 90 in early 2005. The Navy admiral in charge indicated that doubling the number of helicopters would provide "close to twice as much" relief. Identify the outputs and inputs, and describe the production process. Is the admiral discussing a production process with nearly constant returns to scale, or is he referring to another property of the production process?

*4.2 The production function for the automotive and parts industry is $q = L^{0.27}K^{0.16}M^{0.61}$, where M is energy and materials (based on Klein, 2003). What kind of returns to scale does this production function exhibit? What is the marginal product of materials?

4.3 Under what conditions do the following production functions exhibit decreasing, constant, or increasing returns to scale? (*Hint*: See Q&A 5.3.)
    a. $q = L + K$.
    b. $q = L + L^aK^b + K$.

4.4 A production function has the property that $f(xL, xK) = x^2f(L, K)$ for any positive value of x. What kind of returns to scale does this production function exhibit? If the firm doubles L and K, show that the marginal product of labor and the marginal product of capital also double.

*4.5 Show in a diagram that a production function can have diminishing marginal returns to a factor and constant returns to scale.

4.6 Is it possible that a firm's production function exhibits increasing returns to scale while exhibiting diminishing marginal productivity of each of its inputs? To answer this question, calculate the marginal productivities of capital and labor for the production of Crocs using the production $q = AL^aK^b = 22.7L^{0.88}K^{0.48}$ given in the Mini-Case "Returns to Scale for Crocs."

*4.7 The Crocs production function is $q = 22.7L^{0.88}K^{0.48}$, where L is labor and K is capital. Epple, Gordon, and

Sieg (2010) estimated that the production function for U.S. housing is $q = 1.38L^{0.144}M^{0.856}$, where L is land and M is an aggregate of all other mobile, non-land factors, which we call materials. Haskel and Sadun (2012) estimated the production function for U.K. supermarkets is $q = L^{0.23}K^{0.10}M^{0.66}$, where L is labor, K is capital, and M is materials. Are the returns to scale decreasing, constant, or increasing for each of these production functions?

4.8 Michelle's business produces ceramic cups using labor, clay, and a kiln. She uses labor and clay in a fixed proportion, but has only one kiln. She can manufacture 25 cups a day with one worker and 35 with two workers.

    a. Does this information illustrate decreasing returns to scale or a diminishing marginal product of labor? What is the likely explanation for why output doesn't increase proportionately with the number of workers?

    b. Michelle believes that if she could use two kilns and two workers, she could produce 55 cups a day. If so, what can you say about returns to scale?

4.9 Does it follow that because we observe that the average product of labor is higher for Firm 1 than for Firm 2, Firm 1 is more productive in the sense that it can produce more output from a given amount of inputs? Why?

5. Innovation

5.1 Over the past 10 years, cloud storage services such as Dropbox, Google Drive, Apple's iCloud, and Microsoft's OneDrive have taken over computer storage. In addition, many major corporations have adopted "flatter" organizational structures, with fewer layers of middle management. At the same time, major corporations have greatly increased their use of online meeting technologies such as Cisco's WebEx, GoToMeeting, Google+ Hangouts, and others. Which of these innovations is a new product innovation, which is a process innovation, and which is an organizational innovation. Explain.

*5.2 Firm 1 and Firm 2 use the same type of production function, but Firm 1 is only 90% as productive as Firm 2. That is, the production function of Firm 2 is $q_2 = f(L, K)$, and the production function of Firm 1 is $q_1 = 0.9f(L, K)$. At a particular level of inputs, how does the marginal product of labor differ between the firms?

5.3 In a manufacturing plant, workers use a specialized machine to produce belts. A new labor-saving machine is introduced. With the new machine, the firm uses fewer workers to produce the same number of belts as it did using the old machine. In the long run, both labor and capital (the machine) are variable. From what you know, what is the effect of this invention on the AP_L, MP_L, and returns to scale?

If you require more information to answer this question, specify what you need to know.

5.4 Until the mid-eighteenth century, when spinning became mechanized, cotton was an expensive and relatively unimportant textile (Virginia Postrel, "What Separates Rich Nations from Poor Nations?" *New York Times*, January 1, 2004). Where it used to take a hand-spinner 50,000 hours to hand-spin 100 pounds of cotton, an operator of a 1760s-era hand-operated cotton mule-spinning machine could produce 100 pounds of stronger thread in 300 hours. When the self-acting mule spinner automated the process after 1825, the time dropped to 135 hours, and cotton became an inexpensive, common cloth. In a figure, show how these process innovations affected isoquants. Explain briefly.

5.5 A firm initially has a linear production function $q = 10L + 12K$. The firm undertakes an organizational innovation that doubles the marginal product of labor but does not affect the marginal product of capital. What is the new production function?

6. Managerial Problem

6.1 If a firm lays off workers during a recession, how will the firm's marginal product of labor change? (*Hint*: See Figure 5.1.)

*6.2 During recessions, U.S. firms lay off a larger proportion of their workers than Japanese firms do. (It has been claimed that Japanese firms continue to produce at high levels and store the output or sell it at relatively low prices during the recession.) Assuming that the production function remains unchanged over a period that is long enough to include many recessions and expansions, would you expect the average product of labor to be higher in Japan or the United States? Why?

7. MyLab Economics Spreadsheet Exercises[7]

7.1 Labor, L, and capital, K, are the only inputs in each of the following production functions:

a. $q_1 = (L + K)^2$.

b. $q_2 = (\sqrt{L} + \sqrt{K})^2$

c. $q_3 = (20 + \sqrt{L} + \sqrt{K})^2$

For each production function, use a spreadsheet to find the output associated with the following output combinations: $L = 2, K = 2; L = 4, K = 4;$ and $L = 8, K = 8$. Determine whether each production function exhibits increasing returns to scale, decreasing returns to scale, constant returns to scale, or variable returns to scale over this range.

7.2 The Green Revolution (see the Mini-Case "Malthus and the Green Revolution") was based in part on extensive experimentation. The following data illustrate the relationship between nitrogen fertilizer (in pounds of nitrogen) and the output of a particular type of wheat (in bushels). Each observation is based on one acre of land, and all other relevant inputs to production (such as water, labor, and capital) are held constant. The fertilizer levels are 20, 40, 60, 80, 100, 120, 140, and 160, and the associated output levels are 47, 86, 107, 131, 136, 148, 149, and 142.

a. Use Excel to estimate the short-run production function showing the relationship between fertilizer input and output. (*Hint*: As described in Chapter 3, use the Trendline option to regress output on fertilizer input. Try a linear function and try a quadratic function and determine which function fits the data better.)

b. Does fertilizer exhibit the law of diminishing marginal returns? What is the largest amount of fertilizer that should ever be used, even if it is free?

7.3 Summit Farms hires unskilled daily workers to pick strawberries in their fields. Output depends on the number of workers and on random factors such as weather. Summit Farms wishes to estimate its short-run production function and has collected the following data over 15 days on the number of workers, L, and output, q, measured in pounds of strawberries.

a. Use Excel's Regression tool to estimate a production function of the form $q = aL^2 + bL^3$ for Summit Farms. (*Hint*: This production function implies that output is zero when $L = 0$. Therefore, you should set the constant term in the regression to zero, which is an option in the Regression tool.)

b. Use the estimated function and Excel's charting tool to plot the estimated total product, average product of labor, and marginal product of labor curves. (*Hint*: See Figure 5.1.)

Question 7.3

Day	1	2	3	4	5	6	7	8	9	10	11	12	13	14	15
L	5	7	8	6	6	8	10	11	12	9	10	10	8	7	8
q	250	385	442	331	324	442	500	478	432	490	480	494	317	399	448

---

[7]The spreadsheet exercises in this chapter are based largely on the work of Satyajit Ghosh, in cooperation with the authors. The answers are available on MyLab Economics.

Costs

6

Too caustic? To hell with the costs, we'll make the picture anyway.—Samuel Goldwyn

Managerial Problem

Technology Choice at Home Versus Abroad

The manager of a semiconductor manufacturing firm, who can choose from many different production technologies, must determine whether to use the same technology in its foreign plant that it uses in its domestic plant. U.S. semiconductor manufacturing firms have been moving much of their production abroad since 1961, when Fairchild Semiconductor built a plant in Hong Kong. According to the Semiconductor Industry Association, worldwide semiconductor sales from the Americas dropped from 66% in 1976 to 34% in 1998, and to 17% in 2011, and then rose slightly to 22% in 2018.

Semiconductor firms moved their production abroad because of lower taxes, lower labor costs, and capital grant benefits. Capital grants are funds provided by a foreign government to firms to induce them to produce in that country. Such grants can reduce the cost of owning and operating an overseas semiconductor fabrication facility by as much as 25%, compared to the costs of running a U.S.-based plant. However, starting in 2012, China, Thailand, and other Asian countries substantially raised their minimum wages, which reduced the incentive of U.S. firms to move production to those locations.

The semiconductor manufacturer can produce a chip using either sophisticated equipment and relatively few workers or many workers and less complex equipment. In the United States, firms use a relatively capital-intensive technology, because doing so minimizes their cost of producing a given level of output. Will that same technology be cost minimizing if they move their production abroad?

Afirm uses a two-step procedure to determine the most efficient way to produce a certain amount of output. First, the firm ascertains which production processes are *technically efficient* so that it can produce the desired level of output without any wasted or unnecessary inputs. As we saw in Chapter 5, the firm uses engineering and other information to determine its production function, which summarizes the many technically efficient production processes available. A firm's production function shows the maximum output that can be produced with any specified combination of *inputs* or *factors of production*, such as labor, capital, energy, and materials.

The firm's second step is to pick from these technically efficient production processes the one that is also **economically efficient**, minimizing the cost of producing a specified output level.[1] To find out which process minimizes its cost of production, the firm uses information about the production function and the cost of inputs.

Managers and economists need to understand the relationship between costs of inputs and production to determine the least costly way to produce. By minimizing the cost of producing a given level of output, a firm can increase its profit.

Learning Objectives

1. Explain why managers should use opportunity costs in decision making.
2. Draw marginal cost, average cost, and other cost curves.
3. Explain how to choose inputs to minimize cost.
4. Predict how experience-based learning reduces costs.
5. Describe when it pays to produce two or more goods simultaneously.

6.1 The Nature of Costs

Making sound managerial decisions about investment and production requires information about the associated costs. Legally required financial accounting statements provide some cost information. However, such statements do not provide sufficient cost information for good decision making. Financial accounting statements correctly measure costs for tax purposes and to meet other legal requirements, but good managerial decisions require a different perspective on costs.

To produce a particular amount of output, a firm incurs costs for the required inputs, such as labor, capital, energy, and materials. A firm's manager (or accountant) determines the cost of labor, energy, and materials by multiplying the price of the factor times the number of units used. If workers earn $20 per hour and the firm hires 100 hours of labor per day, then the firm's cost of labor is $20 \times 100 = \$2,000$ per day. The manager can easily calculate these *explicit costs*, which are its direct, out-of-pocket payments for inputs to its production process during a given period. While calculating explicit costs is straightforward, some costs are implicit in that they reflect only a foregone opportunity rather than explicit, current expenditure. Properly taking account of foregone opportunities requires especially careful attention when dealing with durable capital goods, as past expenditures for an input may be irrelevant to current cost calculations if that input has no current, alternative use.

Opportunity Costs

An economist is a person who, when invited to give a talk at a banquet, tells the audience "There's no such thing as a free lunch."

A fundamental principle of managerial decision making is that managers should focus on *opportunity costs*. The **opportunity cost** of a resource is the value of the best alternative use of that resource. Explicit costs are opportunity costs. If a firm

---

[1]Similarly, economically efficient production implies that the quantity of output is maximized for any given level of cost.

purchases an input in a market and uses that input immediately, the input's opportunity cost is the amount the firm pays for it, the market price. After all, if the firm did not use the input in its production process, its best alternative would be to sell the input to someone else at the market price. The opportunity cost concept is particularly useful when the firm uses an input that it cannot purchase in a market or that was purchased in a market in the past.

An important example of such an opportunity cost is the value of a manager's time. For example, Maoyong owns and manages a firm. He pays himself only a small monthly salary of $1,000 because he also receives the firm's profit. However, Maoyong could work for another firm and earn $11,000 a month. Thus, the opportunity cost of his time is $11,000—from his best alternative use of his time—not the $1,000 he actually pays himself.

A financial statement may not include such an opportunity cost, but Maoyong needs to take account of this opportunity cost to make decisions that maximize his profit. Suppose that the explicit cost of operating his firm is $40,000, including the rent for work space, the cost of materials, the wage payments to an employee, and the $1,000 a month he pays himself. The full, opportunity cost of the firm is $50,000, which includes the extra $10,000 in opportunity cost for Maoyong's time beyond the $1,000 that he already pays himself. If his firm's revenue is $49,000 per month and he considers only his explicit costs of $40,000, it appears that his firm makes a profit of $9,000. In contrast, if he takes account of the full opportunity cost of $50,000, his firm incurs a loss of $1,000.

Another example of an opportunity cost is captured in the well-known phrase "There's no such thing as a free lunch." Suppose your parents come to town and offer to take you to lunch. Although they pay the explicit cost—the restaurant's tab—for the lunch, you still incur the opportunity cost of your time. No doubt the best alternative use of your time is studying this text book, but you could also consider working at a job for a wage or surfing the internet as possible alternatives. In considering whether to accept the "free" lunch, you need to compare this true opportunity cost against the benefit of dining with your parents.

At one point or another, most of us have held the following false belief:

Common Confusion I can save money by doing things myself rather than buying goods and services from firms.

The fallacy in this belief is that we have ignored the opportunity cost of our time. Have you ever tried to fix a plumbing problem and ended up taking hours to make a repair that a professional plumber could have done in a few minutes? Fixing the problem yourself only makes sense if the opportunity cost of your time is very low or the plumber's fee is very high. Similarly, growing our own food would cost most of us much more than buying it from a store once we take into account the value of our time.

Mini-Case

The Opportunity Cost of an MBA

During major economic downturns, do applications to MBA programs fall, hold steady, or rise? Knowledge of opportunity costs helps us answer this question.

The biggest cost of attending an MBA program is often the opportunity cost of giving up a well-paying job. Someone who leaves a job paying $6,000 per month to attend an MBA program is, in effect, incurring a $6,000 per month opportunity cost, in addition to the tuition and cost of textbooks (though this one is well worth the money).

Thus, it is not surprising that MBA applications rise in bad economic times when outside opportunities decline. People thinking of going back to school face a reduced opportunity cost of entering an MBA program if they think they might be laid off or might not be promoted during an economic downturn. As Stacey Kole, deputy dean for the MBA program at the University of Chicago's Graduate School of Business, observed, "When there's a go-go economy, fewer people decide to go back to school. When things go south, the opportunity cost of leaving work is lower."

During the Great Recession in 2008, when U.S. unemployment rose sharply and the economy was in poor shape, the number of people seeking admission to MBA programs also rose sharply. Applications continued to rise as unemployment remained high for several years. The U.S. unemployment rate peaked at 10% in late 2009 and did not fall below 8% until 2012. However the U.S. unemployment rate dropped below 5% by late 2015, and continued to fall. Correspondingly, U.S. MBA applications fell in the 2015, 2016, and 2017 admission years.

Q&A 6.1

Meredith's firm has sent her to a conference for managers and paid her registration fee. Included in the registration fee is free admission to a class on how to price derivative securities, such as options. She is considering attending, but her most attractive alternative opportunity is to attend a talk given at the same time by Warren Buffett on his investment strategies. She would be willing to pay $100 to hear his talk, and the cost of a ticket is $40. Given that attending either talk involves no other costs, what is Meredith's opportunity cost of attending the derivatives talk?

Answer

To determine her opportunity cost, determine the benefit that Meredith would forego by attending the derivatives class. Because she incurs no additional fee to attend the derivatives talk, Meredith's opportunity cost is the foregone benefit of hearing the Buffett speech. Because she values hearing the Buffett speech at $100, but only has to pay $40, her net benefit from hearing that talk is $60 (= $100 − $40). Thus, her opportunity cost of attending the derivatives talk is $60.

Costs of Durable Inputs

Determining the opportunity cost of capital such as land, buildings, or equipment is more complex than calculating the cost of inputs that are bought and used in the same period, such as labor services, energy, or materials. Capital is a **durable good**: a product that is usable for a long period, perhaps for many years. Two problems may arise in measuring the cost of a firm's capital. The first is how to allocate the initial purchase cost over time. The second is what to do if the value of the capital changes over time.

We can avoid these two measurement problems if capital is rented instead of purchased. For example, suppose a firm can rent a pick-up truck for $500 a month or buy it outright for $25,000. If the firm rents the truck, the rental payment is the relevant opportunity cost per month. The truck is rented month by month, so the firm does not have to worry about how to allocate the purchase cost of a truck over time. Moreover, the rental rate would adjust if the cost of trucks changes over time. Thus, if the firm can rent capital for short periods, it calculates the cost of this capital in the same way that it calculates the cost of nondurable inputs such as labor services or materials.

The firm faces a more complicated problem in determining the opportunity cost of the truck if it purchases the truck. The firm's accountant may *expense* the truck's purchase price by treating the full $25,000 as a cost when the truck is purchased, or the accountant may *amortize* the cost by spreading the $25,000 over the life of the truck, following rules set by an accounting organization or by a relevant government authority such as the Internal Revenue Service (IRS).

A manager who wants to make sound decisions about operating the truck should not focus on these cost accounting conventions but should use opportunity cost instead. The firm's opportunity cost of using the truck is the amount that the firm would earn if it rented the truck to others. Thus, even though the firm owns the truck, the manager should view the opportunity cost of this capital good as a rent per time period. If the value of an older truck is less than that of a newer one, the rental rate for the truck falls over time.

If no rental market for trucks exists, we must determine the opportunity cost in another way. Suppose that the firm has two choices: It can choose not to buy the truck and keep the truck's purchase price of $25,000, or it can use the truck for a year and sell it for $22,000 at the end of the year. If the firm did not purchase the truck, it would deposit the $25,000 in a bank account that pays, for example, 2% per year, earning $500 in interest and therefore having $25,500 at the end of the year. Thus, the opportunity cost of capital of using the truck for a year is $25,500 − $22,000 = $3,500.[2] This $3,500 opportunity cost equals the depreciation of the truck of $3,000 (= $25,000 − $22,000) plus the $500 in foregone interest that the firm could have earned over the year if the firm had invested the $25,000.

The value of trucks, machines, and other equipment declines over time, leading to declining rental values and therefore to declining opportunity costs. In contrast, the value of some land, buildings, and other forms of capital may rise over time. To maximize its economic profit, a firm must properly measure the opportunity cost of a piece of capital even if its value rises over time. If a beauty parlor buys a building when similar buildings in that area rent for $1,000 per month, then the opportunity cost of using the building is $1,000 a month. If land values rise, causing rents in the area to rise to $2,000 per month, the beauty parlor's opportunity cost of its building increases to $2,000 per month.

Sunk Costs

An opportunity cost is not always easy to observe but should always be taken into account in deciding how much to produce. In contrast, even though a **sunk cost**—a past expenditure that cannot be recovered—is easily observed, it is not relevant to a manager when deciding how much to produce now. If an expenditure is sunk, it is not an opportunity cost. Nonetheless, a cost paid for a specialized input should still be deducted from income before paying taxes even if that cost is sunk, and must therefore appear in financial accounts.

---

[2]The firm would also pay for gasoline, insurance, and other operating costs, but these items would all be expensed as operating costs and would not appear in the firm's accounts as capital costs.

If a firm buys a forklift for $30,000 and can resell it for the same price, then the expenditure is not sunk, and the opportunity cost of using the forklift is $30,000. If instead the firm buys a specialized piece of equipment for $30,000 and cannot resell it, then the original expenditure is a sunk cost—it cannot be recovered. Because this equipment has no alternative use—it cannot be resold—its opportunity cost is zero, and hence should not be included in the firm's current cost calculations. If the specialized equipment that originally cost $30,000 can be resold for $20,000, then only $10,000 of the original expenditure is sunk, and the opportunity cost is $20,000.

Managerial Implication Ignoring Sunk Costs	A manager should ignore sunk costs when making current decisions. To see why, consider a firm that paid $300,000 for a parcel of land for which the market value has fallen to $200,000, which is the land's current opportunity cost. The $100,000 difference between the $300,000 purchase price and the current market value of $200,000 is a sunk cost that has already been incurred and cannot be recovered. The land is worth $240,000 to the firm if it builds a plant on this parcel. Is it worth carrying out production on this land or should the land be sold for its market value of $200,000? A manager who uses the original purchase price in the decision-making process would incorrectly conclude that using the land for production will result in a $60,000 loss: the value of using the land of $240,000 minus the purchase price of $300,000. Instead, the firm should use the land because it is worth $40,000 more as a production facility than the firm's next best alternative of selling the land for $200,000. Thus, in making its decisions, the firm should use the land's opportunity cost and ignore the land's sunk cost—in short, "no use crying over spilt milk," "what's done is done," and "don't throw good money after bad."

6.2 Short-Run Costs

When making short-run and long-run production and investment decisions, managers must take the relevant costs into account. As noted in Chapter 5, the short run is the period over which some inputs, such as labor, can be varied while other inputs, such as capital, are fixed. In contrast, in the long run, the firm can vary all its inputs. For simplicity in our graphs, we concentrate on firms that use only two inputs, labor and capital. We focus on the case in which labor is the only variable input in the short run, and both labor and capital are variable in the long run. However, we can generalize our analysis to examine a firm that uses any number of inputs.

We start by examining various measures of cost and cost curves that can be used to analyze costs in both the short run and the long run. Then we show how the shapes of the short-run cost curves are related to the firm's production function.

Mini-Case Costs of Building a Guitar	What are the short-run costs of building an electric guitar? Online guitar seller Reverb described the cost of building a base-level, generic slab-body, two-pickup, T-style guitar with a bolt-on neck. For an inexpensive guitar, a computer numeric control (CNC) router is used to cut, carve, machine, and mill the wood. A CNC router can make a guitar

body in minutes that would take a craftsman hours to produce. A desktop CNC machine for a small shop costs about $10,000. These machines and the shop are the capital used to make a basic guitar.

A guitar also requires materials, particularly wood, and components such as tuners, pickups, wiring, and switches. These items are readily available. Labor is by far the most costly factor of production in making guitars. Enormous amounts of handwork go "into sanding, fitting, and finishing every nook and cranny on a body and a neck" of a guitar. Quality work on the fit and finish, including paint and fret work, requires yet more labor.

Labor's share of producing the hardshell case for a guitar is particularly large. The cost is $45 to $50. However, the cost of a mandolin case, which is one-quarter the size of a guitar case, is only $2 less. Labor is 95% of the cost, and the labor is the same for both cases.

In the short run, labor and materials are variable inputs and capital is fixed. The firm can increase production only by using more labor. In the long run, the firm can also increase its capital by buying more CNC machines and expanding its shop size.

Common Measures of Cost

All firms use the same basic cost measures for making both short-run and long-run decisions. The measures should be based on the opportunity costs of inputs.

Fixed Cost, Variable Cost, and Total Cost.
A **fixed cost** (F) does not vary with the level of output. Fixed costs, which include expenditures on land, office space, production facilities, and other *overhead* expenses, cannot be avoided by reducing output and must be incurred as long as the firm stays in business.

Fixed costs are often sunk costs, but not always. For example, a restaurant rents space for $2,000 per month on a month-to-month lease. This rent does not vary with the number of meals served (its output level), so it is a fixed cost. Because the restaurant has already paid this month's rent, this fixed cost is a sunk cost: The restaurant cannot get the $2,000 back even if it goes out of business. Next month, if the restaurant stays open, it will have to pay the fixed, $2,000 rent. If the restaurant has a month-to-month rental agreement, next month's fixed cost of $2,000 is an *avoidable cost*, not a sunk cost. The restaurant can shut down, cancel its rental agreement, and avoid paying this fixed cost. Therefore, in planning for next month, the restaurant should treat the $2,000 rent as a fixed cost but not as a sunk cost. The $2,000 per month rent is a fixed cost in both the short run (this month) and the long run. However, it is a sunk cost only in the short run.

Fixed   *Variable*

A **variable cost** (VC) changes as the quantity of output changes. Variable costs are the costs of *variable inputs*, which are inputs that the firm can adjust to alter its output level, such as labor and materials.

A firm's **cost** or **total cost** (*C*) is the sum of a firm's variable cost and fixed cost:

$$C = VC + F.$$

Because variable costs change as the output level changes, so does total cost. For example, in Table 6.1, if the fixed cost is *F* = $48 and the firm produces 5 units of output, its variable cost is *VC* = $100, so its total cost is *C* = $48 + $100 = $148.

Average Cost. Managers use three average cost measures corresponding to fixed, variable, and total costs. The **average fixed cost** (*AFC*) is the fixed cost divided by the units of output produced: *AFC* = *F*/*q*. The average fixed cost falls as output rises because the fixed cost is spread over more units. The average fixed cost falls from $48 for 1 unit of output to $4 for 12 units of output in Table 6.1.

The **average variable cost** (*AVC*), or variable cost per unit of output, is the variable cost divided by the units of output produced: *AVC* = *VC*/*q*. Because the variable cost increases with output, the average variable cost may either increase or decrease as output rises. In Table 6.1, the average variable cost is $25 at 1 unit, falls until it reaches a minimum of $20 at 6 units, and then rises.

The **average cost** (*AC*)—or *average total cost*—is the total cost divided by the units of output produced: *AC* = *C*/*q*. Because total cost is *C* = *VC* + *F*, if we divide both sides of the equation by *q*, we find that average cost is the sum of the average fixed cost and the average variable cost:

$$AC = \frac{C}{q} = \frac{F}{q} + \frac{VC}{q} = AFC + AVC.$$

In Table 6.1, *AFC* falls with output and *AVC* eventually rises with output. Average cost, the sum of *AFC* and *AVC*, falls until output is 8 units and then rises.

TABLE 6.1 How Cost Varies with Output

Output, q	Fixed Cost, F	Variable Cost, VC	Total Cost, C	Marginal Cost, MC	Average Fixed Cost, AFC = F/q	Average Variable Cost, AVC = VC/q	Average Cost, AC = C/q
0	48	0	48				
1	48	25	73	25	48	25	73
2	48	46	94	21	24	23	47
3	48	66	114	20	16	22	38
4	48	82	130	16	12	20.5	32.5
5	48	100	148	18	9.6	20	29.6
6	48	120	168	20	8	20	28
7	48	141	189	21	6.9	20.1	27
8	48	168	216	27	6	21	27
9	48	198	246	30	5.3	22	27.3
10	48	230	278	32	4.8	23	27.8
11	48	272	320	42	4.4	24.7	29.1
12	48	321	369	49	4.0	26.8	30.8

Marginal Cost. A firm's **marginal cost** (*MC*) is the amount by which a firm's cost changes if the firm produces one more unit of output. The marginal cost is

$$MC = \frac{\Delta C}{\Delta q},$$

where ΔC is the change in cost when the change in output, Δq, is 1 unit in Table 6.1. If the firm increases its output from 2 to 3 units ($\Delta q = 1$), its total cost rises from \$94 to \$114, so $\Delta C = \$20$. Thus its marginal cost is $\Delta C / \Delta q = \$20/1 = \$20$.

Because only variable cost changes with output, marginal cost also equals the change in variable cost from a one-unit increase in output:

$$MC = \frac{\Delta VC}{\Delta q}.$$

As the firm increases output from 2 to 3 units, its variable cost increases by $\Delta VC = \$20 = \$66 - \$46$, so its marginal cost is $MC = \Delta VC / \Delta q = \$20/1 = \$20$. A firm takes account of its marginal cost curve to decide whether it pays to change its output level.

Using Calculus

Calculating
Marginal Cost

Using calculus, marginal cost is $MC = dC/dq$, which is the rate of change of cost as we make an infinitesimally small change in output. Given that $C = VC + F$, it follows that $MC = dVC/dq + dF/dq = dVC/dq$, because fixed costs do not change as output changes: $dF/dq = 0$.

For example, suppose that the variable cost is $VC = 4q + 6q^2$ and the fixed cost is $F = 10$, so the total cost is $C = VC + F = 4q + 6q^2 + 10$. Using the variable cost, the marginal cost is $dVC/dq = d(4q + 6q^2)/dq = 4 + 12q$. We get the same expression for marginal cost if we use the total cost: $dC/dq = d(4q + 6q^2 + 10)/dq = 4 + 12q$.

Cost Curves

We illustrate the relationship between output and the various cost measures in Figure 6.1. Panel a shows the variable cost, fixed cost, and total cost curves that correspond to Table 6.1. The fixed cost, which does not vary with output, is a horizontal line at \$48. The variable cost curve is zero at zero units of output and rises with output. The total cost curve, which is the vertical sum of the variable cost curve and the fixed cost line, is \$48 higher than the variable cost curve at every output level, so the variable cost and total cost curves are parallel.

Panel b shows the average fixed cost, average variable cost, average cost, and marginal cost curves. The average fixed cost curve falls as output increases. It approaches zero as output gets large because the fixed cost is spread over many units of output. The average cost curve is the vertical sum of the average fixed cost and average variable cost curves. For example, at 6 units of output, the average variable cost is 20 and the average fixed cost is 8, so the average (total) cost is 28.

The relationships between the average and marginal cost curves and the total cost curve are similar to those between the average and marginal product curves and the total product curve (as discussed in Chapter 5). The average cost at a particular output level is the slope of a line from the origin to the corresponding point on the

FIGURE 6.1 Cost Curves

(a) Because the total cost differs from the variable cost by the fixed cost, F, of \$48, the total cost curve, C, is parallel to the variable cost curve, VC.
(b) The marginal cost curve, MC, cuts the average variable cost, AVC, and average cost, AC, curves at their minimums. The height of the AC curve at point a equals the slope of the line from the origin to the cost curve at A. The height of the AVC at b equals the slope of the line from the origin to the variable cost curve at B. The height of the marginal cost is the slope of either the C or VC curve at that quantity.

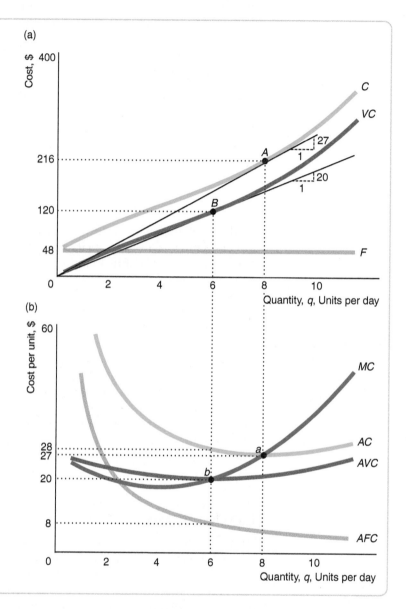

total cost curve. The slope of that line is the rise (the cost at that output level) divided by the run (the output level), which is the definition of the average cost. In panel a, the slope of the line from the origin to point A is the average cost for 8 units of output. The height of the cost curve at A is 216, so the slope is $216/8 = 27$, which is the height of the average cost curve at the corresponding point a in panel b.

Similarly, the average variable cost is the slope of a line from the origin to a point on the variable cost curve. The slope of the thin black line from the origin to B in panel a is 20 (the height of the variable cost curve, 120, divided by the number of units of output, 6), which is also the height of the average variable cost curve at 6 units of output, point b in panel b.

The marginal cost is the slope of either the cost curve or the variable cost curve at a given output level. Because the total cost and variable cost curves are parallel, they have the same slope at any given output. The difference between total cost and variable cost is fixed cost, which does not affect marginal cost.

The thin black line from the origin is tangent to the cost curve at A in panel a. Thus, the slope of the thin black line equals both the average cost and the marginal cost at point a (8 units of output). This equality occurs at the corresponding point a in panel b, where the marginal cost curve intersects the average cost.

Where the marginal cost curve is below the average cost, the average cost curve declines with output. Table 6.1 shows that the average cost of producing the first two units is 47. Because this average cost for 2 units is greater than the marginal cost of the third unit, 20, the average cost for 3 units falls to 38.[3] Where the marginal cost is above the average cost, the average cost curve rises with output. At 8 units, the marginal cost equals the average cost (at point a in panel b, the minimum point of the average cost curve), so the average is unchanging.

Because the thin black line from the origin through point B in panel a is tangent to the variable cost curve at B, the marginal cost equals the average variable cost at the corresponding point b in panel b. Again, where marginal cost is above average variable cost, the average variable cost curve rises with output; where marginal cost is below average variable cost, the average variable cost curve falls with output. Because the average cost curve is above the average variable cost curve everywhere and the marginal cost curve is rising where it crosses both average curves, the minimum of the average variable cost curve, b, is at a lower output level than the minimum of the average cost curve, a.

| Q&A 6.2 | Suppose that a small guitar firm has experimented with the cost of producing different quantities of output per hour by varying the number of workers, holding the size of the plant fixed and using just one CNC machine. It has estimated its cost function as $C = 125 + 10q - 5q^2 + q^3$ where q is quantity produced per hour and C is measured in dollars. The corresponding marginal cost function is $MC = 10 - 10q + 3q^2$.[4] Use an Excel spreadsheet to show the fixed cost, and to calculate variable cost, total cost, average cost, and marginal cost for output levels from 1 to 10 in one-unit increments. Use the spreadsheet to find the output level at which average cost is minimized and verify that $AC = MC$ at this output level. |

Answer

1. *Open an Excel spreadsheet and put titles* Quantity, Fixed Cost, Variable Cost, Total Cost, Average Cost, *and* Marginal Cost *in cells A1 through F1.* Fill in the numbers 1 through 10 in one-unit increments in cells A2–A11 and enter the number 125 (fixed cost) in each cell from B2 through B11.

2. *Fill in the other columns using appropriate formulas.* Enter "=10*A2−5*A2^2+A2^3" in cell C2 and copy this formula into the remaining cells in column C. Enter "=B2+C2" in cell D2, then copy that formula into the rest of column D up to cell D11. Enter "=D2/A2" into cell E2 and copy that formula

---

[3]The average cost of the first two units is 47. If we add a third unit with a marginal cost of 20, the new average can be calculated by adding the average values of the first two units plus the marginal cost of the third unit and dividing by 3: $(47 + 47 + 20)/3 = 38$. Thus, if we add a marginal cost that is less than the old average cost, the new average cost must fall.

[4]You could approximate the marginal cost by determining the change in total cost as output increases by one unit. However, this formula is exact and should be used here.

into the rest of column E. Enter "=10−10*A2+3*A2^2" into cell F2 and also copy that formula into the rest of column F. The formulas are shown in the screenshot.

	A	B	C	D	E	F
1	Quantity	Fixed Cost	Variable Cost	Total Cost	Average Cost	Marginal Cost
2	1	125	=10*A2-5*A2^2 +A2^3	=B2+C2	=D2/A2	=10-10*A2+3*A2^2
3	2	125	=10*A3-5*A3^2 +A3^3	=B3+C3	=D3/A3	=10-10*A3+3*A3^2
4	3	125	=10*A4-5*A4^2 +A4^3	=B4+C4	=D4/A4	=10-10*A4+3*A4^2
5	4	125	=10*A5-5*A5^2 +A5^3	=B5+C5	=D5/A5	=10-10*A5+3*A5^2
6	5	125	=10*A6-5*A6^2 +A6^3	=B6+C6	=D6/A6	=10-10*A6+3*A6^2
7	6	125	=10*A7-5*A7^2 +A7^3	=B7+C7	=D7/A7	=10-10*A7+3*A7^2
8	7	125	=10*A8-5*A8^2 +A8^3	=B8+C8	=D8/A8	=10-10*A8+3*A8^2
9	8	125	=10*A9-5*A9^2 +A9^3	=B9+C9	=D9/A9	=10-10*A9+3*A9^2
10	9	125	=10*A10-5*A10^2 +A10^3	=B10+C10	=D10/A10	=10-10*A10+3*A10^2
11	10	125	=10*A11-5*A11^2 +A11^3	=B11+C11	=D11/A11	=10-10*A11+3*A11^2

3. *Look in the Average Cost column to identify the output at which average cost is minimized.* Average cost reaches its lowest level in cell E6, where the quantity produced is 5 and average cost is 35. At this output level, marginal cost is also equal to 35, as the screenshot shows. (The average cost column has been formatted to show two digits after the decimal point.)

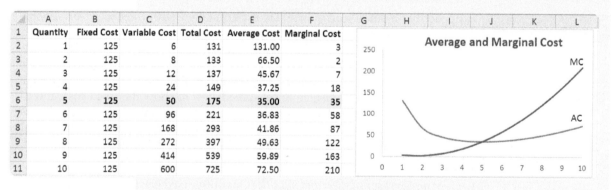

	A	B	C	D	E	F
1	Quantity	Fixed Cost	Variable Cost	Total Cost	Average Cost	Marginal Cost
2	1	125	6	131	131.00	3
3	2	125	8	133	66.50	2
4	3	125	12	137	45.67	7
5	4	125	24	149	37.25	18
6	5	125	50	175	35.00	35
7	6	125	96	221	36.83	58
8	7	125	168	293	41.86	87
9	8	125	272	397	49.63	122
10	9	125	414	539	59.89	163
11	10	125	600	725	72.50	210

Note: It is possible to use Excel to draw any of the cost curves by inserting a scatterplot. The screenshot shows the average and marginal cost curves.

Production Functions and the Shapes of Cost Curves

The production function determines the shape of a firm's cost curves. This function shows the amount of inputs needed to produce a given level of output (Chapter 5). The firm calculates its variable cost by multiplying the quantity of each input by its price and summing the costs of the variable inputs.

In this section, we focus on cost curves in the short run. If a firm produces output using capital and labor, and its capital is fixed in the short run, the firm's variable cost is its cost of labor. Its labor cost is the wage per hour, w, times the number of hours of labor, L, employed by the firm: $VC = wL$.

In the short run, when the firm's capital is fixed, the only way the firm can increase its output is to use more labor. If the firm increases its labor enough, it reaches the point of *diminishing marginal returns to labor*, at which each extra worker increases output by a smaller amount. We can use this information about the relationship between labor and output—the production function—to determine the shape of the variable cost curve and its related curves.

The Variable Cost Curve. If input prices are constant, the firm's production function determines the shape of the variable cost curve. We illustrate this relationship in Figure 6.2. The firm faces a constant input price for labor, the wage, of $20 per hour.

The total product of labor curve in Figure 6.2 shows the firm's short-run production function relationship between output and labor when capital is held fixed. At point *a*, the firm uses 5 hours of labor to produce 1 unit of output. At point *b*, it takes 20 hours of labor to produce 5 units of output. Here, output increases more than in proportion to labor: Output rises 5 times when labor increases 4 times. In contrast, as the firm moves from *b* to *c*, output increases less than in proportion to labor. Output doubles to 10 as a result of increasing labor from 20 to 46—an increase of 2.3 times. The movement from *c* to *d* results in an even smaller increase in output relative to labor. This flattening of the total product curve at higher levels of labor reflects diminishing marginal returns to labor.

This curve shows both the production relation of output to labor and the variable cost relation of output to cost. Because each hour of work costs the firm $20, we can relabel the horizontal axis in Figure 6.2 to show the firm's variable cost, its cost of

FIGURE 6.2 Variable Cost and Total Product

The firm's short-run variable cost curve and its total product curve have the same shape. The total product curve uses the horizontal axis, measuring hours of work. The variable cost curve uses the horizontal axis, measuring labor cost, which is the only variable cost.

labor. To produce 5 units of output takes 20 hours of labor, so the firm's variable cost is $400. By using the variable cost labels on the horizontal axis, the total product of labor curve becomes the variable cost curve.

As output increases, the variable cost increases more than proportionally due to the diminishing marginal returns. Because the production function determines the shape of the variable cost curve, it also determines the shape of the marginal, average variable, and average cost curves. We now examine the shape of each of these cost curves in detail, because when making decisions, managers rely more on these per-unit cost measures than on total variable cost.

The Marginal Cost Curve. The marginal cost is the change in variable cost as output increases by one unit: $MC = \Delta VC / \Delta q$. In the short run, capital is fixed, so the only way the firm can produce more output is to use extra labor. The extra labor required to produce one more unit of output is $\Delta L / \Delta q$. The extra labor costs the firm w per unit, so the firm's cost rises by $w(\Delta L / \Delta q)$. As a result, the firm's marginal cost is

$$MC = \frac{\Delta VC}{\Delta q} = w \frac{\Delta L}{\Delta q}.$$

The marginal cost equals the wage times the extra labor necessary to produce one more unit of output. To increase output by one unit from 5 to 6 units takes 4 extra hours of work in Figure 6.2. If the wage is $20 per hour, the marginal cost is $80.

How do we know how much extra labor we need to produce one more unit of output? That information comes from the production function. The marginal product of labor—the amount of extra output produced by another unit of labor, holding other inputs fixed—is $MP_L = \Delta q / \Delta L$. Thus, the extra labor we need to produce one more unit of output, $\Delta L / \Delta q$, is $1/MP_L$, so the firm's marginal cost is

$$MC = \frac{w}{MP_L}. \tag{6.1}$$

Equation 6.1 says that the marginal cost equals the wage divided by the marginal product of labor. If the firm is producing 5 units of output, it takes 4 extra hours of labor to produce 1 more unit of output in Figure 6.2, so the marginal product of an hour of labor is $\frac{1}{4}$ unit of output. Given a wage of $20 an hour, the marginal cost of the sixth unit is $20 divided by $\frac{1}{4}$, or $80.

Equation 6.1 shows that the marginal product of labor and marginal cost move in opposite directions as output changes. At low levels of labor, the marginal product of labor commonly rises with additional labor because extra workers help the original workers and they can collectively make better use of the firm's equipment. As the marginal product of labor rises, the marginal cost falls.

Eventually, however, as the number of workers increases, workers must share the fixed amount of equipment and may get in each other's way. As more workers are added, the marginal product of each additional worker begins to fall and the marginal cost of each additional unit of product rises. As a result, the marginal cost curve slopes upward because of diminishing marginal returns to labor. Thus, the marginal cost first falls and then rises.

The Average Cost Curves. Because they determine the shape of the variable cost curve, diminishing marginal returns to labor also determine the shape of the average variable cost curve. The average variable cost is the variable cost divided by output: $AVC = VC/q$. For the firm we've been examining, whose only variable input is labor, variable cost is wL, so average variable cost is

$$AVC = \frac{VC}{q} = \frac{wL}{q}.$$

Because the average product of labor, AP_L, is q/L, average variable cost is the wage divided by the average product of labor:

$$AVC = \frac{w}{AP_L}. \tag{6.2}$$

In Figure 6.2, at 6 units of output, the average product of labor is $\frac{1}{4}$ ($=q/L = 6/24$), so the average variable cost is \$80, which is the wage, \$20, divided by the average product of labor, $\frac{1}{4}$.

With a constant wage, the average variable cost moves in the opposite direction of the average product of labor in Equation 6.2. As we discussed in Chapter 5, the average product of labor tends to rise and then fall, so the average cost tends to fall and then rise, as in panel b of Figure 6.1.

The average cost curve is the vertical sum of the average variable cost curve and the average fixed cost curve, as in panel b of Figure 6.1. If the average variable cost curve is U-shaped, adding the strictly falling average fixed cost makes the average cost fall more steeply than the average variable cost curve at low output levels. At high output levels, the average cost and average variable cost curves differ by ever smaller amounts, as the average fixed cost, F/q, approaches zero. Thus, the average cost curve is also U-shaped.

In Appendix 6A we derive the average, marginal, and variable cost functions arising from a Cobb-Douglas production function (Chapter 5).

Short-Run Cost Summary

We use cost curves to illustrate three cost level concepts—total cost, fixed cost, and variable cost—and four cost-per-unit cost concepts—average cost, average fixed cost, average variable cost, and marginal cost. Understanding the shapes of these curves and the relationships among them is crucial to the analysis of firm behavior in the rest of this book. Fortunately, we can derive most of what we need to know about the shapes and the relationships between the short-run curves using four basic concepts:

1. In the short run, the cost associated with inputs that cannot be adjusted is fixed, while the cost from inputs that can be adjusted is variable.

2. Given that input prices are constant, the shapes of the variable cost and the cost-per-unit curves are determined by the production function.

3. Where a variable input exhibits diminishing marginal returns, the variable cost and cost curves become relatively steep as output increases, so the average cost, average variable cost, and marginal cost curves rise with output.

4. Because of the relationship between marginal values and average values, both the average cost and average variable cost curves fall when marginal cost is below them and rise when marginal cost is above them. Thus, the marginal cost cuts both these average cost curves at their minimum points.

6.3 Long-Run Costs

In the long run, the firm adjusts all its inputs so that its cost of production is as low as possible. The firm can change its plant size, design and build new machines, and otherwise adjust inputs that were fixed in the short run.

Although firms may incur fixed costs in the long run, these fixed costs are *avoidable* (rather than *sunk*, as they are in the short run). The rent of F per month that a restaurant pays is a fixed cost because it does not vary with the number of meals (output) served. In the short run, this fixed cost is sunk: The firm must pay F even if the restaurant does not operate. In the long run, this fixed cost is avoidable because the restaurant need not renew its rental agreement. The firm does not have to pay this rent if it shuts down. This cost is still a fixed cost, even in the long run, but it is not sunk in the long run.

To simplify our long-run analysis, we use examples with no long-run fixed costs ($F = 0$). Consequently, average cost and average variable cost are identical.

To produce a given quantity of output at minimum cost, our firm uses information about its production function and the price of labor and capital. In the long run when capital is variable, the firm chooses how much labor and capital to use; in the short run when capital is fixed, the firm chooses only how much labor to use. As a consequence, the firm's long-run cost of production is lower than its short-run cost if it has to use the "wrong" level of capital in the short run. In this section, we show how a firm picks the cost-minimizing combination of inputs in the long run.

Mini-Case

Short Run Versus Long Run in the Sharing Economy

Construction companies traditionally view workers' earnings as a variable cost and the capital that the firm owns—particularly heavy equipment such as bulldozers—as a fixed cost. The sharing economy is changing that.

When Platinum Pipeline Inc., a firm that installs water and sewer lines, won a new job, it needed a third bulldozer. Rather than buy one, the firm's president, Manuel de Freitas, merely called up an app on his phone and found a Caterpillar D6T dozer that he could rent for two months at $7,500 a month. The rental firm, Yard Club Inc., finds idle heavy equipment and rents it—much as Airbnb Inc. does with spare bedrooms. Often, rental companies own this equipment.

Renting construction equipment is catching on. In 2014, rental companies owned 54% of U.S. construction equipment, up from 40% a decade earlier. According to one forecast, the share could top 60% within the next 5 to 10 years. In 2018, Global Market Insights predicted that the construction equipment rental market will grow at over 4% a year from 2018 to 2024.

If construction firms can rent heavy equipment, their long run may be much shorter than if they have to buy the equipment.

Input Choice

A firm can produce a given level of output using many different *technically efficient* combinations of inputs, as summarized by an isoquant (see Chapter 5). From among these technically efficient combinations of inputs, a firm wants to choose that bundle of inputs with the lowest cost of production, which is the *economically efficient* combination of inputs. To do so, the firm combines information about technology from the isoquant with information about the cost of production.

The Isocost Line. The cost of producing a given level of output depends on the price of labor and capital. The firm hires L hours of labor services at a constant wage of w per hour, so its labor cost is wL. The firm rents K hours of machine services at a constant rental rate of r per hour, so its capital cost is rK. (If the firm owns the capital, r is the implicit rental rate.) The firm's total cost is the sum of its labor and capital costs:

$$C = wL + rK. \tag{6.3}$$

A firm can hire as much labor and capital as it wants at these constant input prices from competitive labor and capital markets.

The firm can use many combinations of labor and capital that cost the same amount. Suppose that the wage rate, w, is $20 an hour and the rental rate of capital, r, is $40. Five of the many combinations of labor and capital that the firm can use that cost $200 are listed in Table 6.2. These combinations of labor and capital are plotted on an **isocost line**, which represents all the combinations of inputs that have the same (*iso-*) total cost. Figure 6.3 shows three isocost lines. The $400 isocost line represents all the combinations of labor and capital that the firm can buy for $400, including the combinations a through e in Table 6.2.

Along an isocost line, cost is fixed at a particular level, $\overline{C}$, so by setting cost at $\overline{C}$ in Equation 6.3, we can write the equation for the $\overline{C}$ isocost line as

$$\overline{C} = wL + rK.$$

Using algebra, we can rewrite this equation to show how much capital the firm can buy if it spends a total of $\overline{C}$ and purchases L units of labor:

$$K = \frac{\overline{C}}{r} - \frac{w}{r}L. \tag{6.4}$$

By substituting $\overline{C} = \$400$, $w = \$20$, and $r = \$40$ in Equation 6.4, we find that the $400 isocost line is $K = 10 - \frac{1}{2}L$. We can use Equation 6.4 to derive three properties of isocost lines.

TABLE 6.2 Bundles of Labor and Capital That Cost the Firm $400

Bundle	Labor, L	Capital, K	Labor Cost, $wL = \$20L$	Capital Cost, $rK = \$40K$	Total Cost, $wL + rK$
a	20	0	$400	$0	$400
b	14	3	$280	$120	$400
c	10	5	$200	$200	$400
d	6	7	$120	$280	$400
e	0	10	$0	$400	$400

FIGURE 6.3 A Family of Isocost Lines

An isocost line shows all the combinations of labor and capital that cost the firm the same amount. The greater the total cost, the farther from the origin the isocost lies. All the isocosts have the same slope, $-w/r = -\frac{1}{2}$. The slope shows the rate at which the firm can substitute capital for labor holding total cost constant: For each extra unit of capital it uses, the firm must use two fewer units of labor to hold its cost constant.

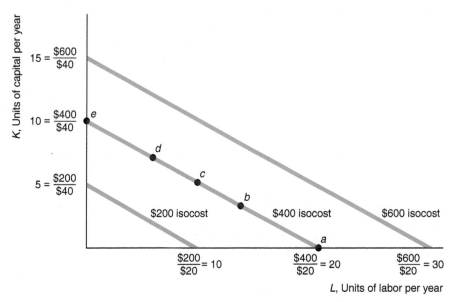

First, the points at which the isocost lines hit the capital and labor axes depend on the firm's cost, $\overline{C}$, and on the input prices. The $\overline{C}$ isocost line intersects the capital axis where the firm is using only capital. Setting $L = 0$ in Equation 6.7, we find that the firm buys $K = \overline{C}/r$ units of capital. In Figure 6.3, the $400 isocost line intersects the capital axis at $400/$40 = 10 units of capital. Similarly, the intersection of the isocost line with the labor axis is at $\overline{C}/w$, which is the amount of labor the firm hires if it uses only labor. In the figure, the intersection of the $400 isocost line with the labor axis occurs at $L = 20$, where $K = 10 - \frac{1}{2} \times 20 = 0$.

Second, isocost lines that are farther from the origin have higher costs than those closer to the origin. Because the isocost lines intersect the capital axis at $\overline{C}/r$ and the labor axis at $\overline{C}/w$, an increase in the cost shifts these intersections with the axes proportionately outward. The $200 isocost line hits the capital axis at 5 and the labor axis at 10, whereas the $400 isocost line intersects at 10 and 20.

Third, the slope of each isocost line is the same. From Equation 6.4, if the firm increases labor by ΔL, it must decrease capital by

$$\Delta K = -\frac{w}{r}\Delta L.$$

Dividing both sides of this expression by ΔL, we find that the slope of an isocost line, $\Delta K/\Delta L$, is $-w/r$. Thus, the slope of the isocost line depends on the relative prices of the inputs. The slope of the isocost lines in the figure is $-w/r = -$20/$40 = -\frac{1}{2}$. If the firm uses two more units of labor, $\Delta L = 2$, it must reduce capital by one unit,

$\Delta K = -\frac{1}{2}\Delta L = -1$, to keep its total cost constant. Because all isocost lines are based on the same relative prices, they all have the same slope, so they are parallel.

The isocost line plays a similar role in the firm's decision making as the budget line does in consumer decision making. Both an isocost line and a budget line are straight lines with a slope that depends on relative prices. However, they differ in an important way. The consumer has a single budget line that depends on the consumer's income. The firm faces many isocost lines, each of which corresponds to a different level of expenditure the firm might make. A firm may incur a relatively low cost by producing relatively little output with few inputs, or it may incur a relatively high cost by producing a relatively large quantity.

Combining Cost and Production Information. By combining the information about costs contained in the isocost lines with information about efficient production summarized by an isoquant, a firm chooses the lowest-cost way to produce a given level of output. We illustrate how a Japanese beer manufacturer picks the combination of labor and capital that minimizes its cost of producing 100 units of output. Figure 6.4 shows the isoquant for 100 units of output (based on the estimates of Flath, 2011, $q = 100 = 1.52L^{0.6}K^{0.4}$) and the isocost lines for which the rental rate of a unit of capital is $8 per hour and the wage rate is $24 per hour.

The firm minimizes its cost by using the combination of inputs on the isoquant that is on the lowest isocost line that touches the isoquant. The lowest possible isocost line that will allow the beer manufacturer to produce 100 units of output is the $2,000 isocost line. This isocost line touches the isoquant at the bundle of inputs x,

FIGURE 6.4 Cost Minimization

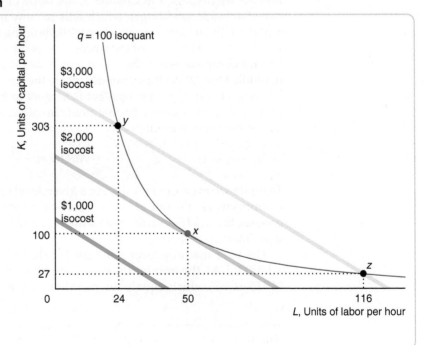

The beer manufacturer minimizes its cost of producing 100 units of output by producing at x (L = 50 and K = 100). This cost-minimizing combination of inputs is determined by the tangency between the q = 100 isoquant and the lowest isocost line, $2,000, that touches that isoquant. At x, the isocost is tangent to the isoquant, so the slope of the isocost, −w/r = −3, equals the slope of the isoquant, which is the negative of the marginal rate of technical substitution. That is, the rate at which the firm can trade capital for labor in the input markets equals the rate at which it can substitute capital for labor in the production process.

where the firm uses $L = 50$ workers and $K = 100$ units of capital.

How do we know that x is the least costly way to produce 100 units of output? We need to demonstrate that other practical combinations of input produce less than 100 units or produce 100 units at greater cost.

If the firm spent less than $2,000, it could not produce 100 units of output. For example, each combination of inputs on the $1,000 isocost line lies below the isoquant, so the firm cannot produce 100 units of output for $1,000.

The firm can produce 100 units of output using other combinations of inputs besides x; however, using these other bundles of inputs is more expensive. For example, the firm can produce 100 units of output using the combinations y ($L = 24$, $K = 303$) or z ($L = 116$, $K = 27$), but both of these combinations cost the firm $3,000.

At the minimum-cost bundle, x, the isoquant is *tangent* to the isocost line: The slopes of the isocost line and the isoquant are equal and the isocost line touches the isoquant at only one point. Suppose that an isocost line hits the isoquant but is not tangent to it. Then the isocost line must cross the isoquant twice, as the $3,000 isocost line does at points y and z. However, if the isocost line crosses the isoquant twice, then part of the isoquant must lie below the isocost line. Consequently, another lower isocost line also touches the isoquant. Only if the isocost line is tangent to the isoquant—so that it touches the isoquant only once—can we conclude that we are on the lowest possible isocost line.

At the point of tangency, the slope of the isoquant equals the slope of the isocost line. As we discussed in Chapter 5, the slope of the isoquant is the firm's *marginal rate of technical substitution*, which tells us how many units of capital the firm can replace with an extra unit of labor while holding output constant given its production function. The slope of the isocost line is the negative of the ratio of the wage to the cost of capital, $-w/r$, the rate at which the firm can trade capital for labor in input markets. Thus, at the input bundle where the firm minimizes its cost of producing a given level of output, the isoquant is tangent to the isocost line. Therefore, the firm chooses its inputs so that the marginal rate of technical substitution equals the negative of the relative input prices:

$$MRTS = -\frac{w}{r}. \tag{6.5}$$

To minimize the cost of producing a given level of output, the firm picks the bundle of inputs where the rate at which it can substitute capital for labor in the production process, the *MRTS*, exactly equals the rate at which it can trade capital for labor in input markets, $-w/r$.

The beer manufacturer's marginal rate of technical substitution is $MRTS = -1.5K/L$.[5] At the minimum-cost input bundle x, $K = 100$ and $L = 50$, so its $MRTS$ is -3, which equals the negative of the ratio of the input prices it faces,

---

[5]The production function is $q = 1.52L^{0.6}K^{0.4}$, so the marginal product of labor is $MP_L = \partial q/\partial L = (0.6)1.52L^{-0.4}K^{0.4}$, and $MP_K = \partial q/\partial K = (0.4)1.52L^{0.6}K^{-0.6}$. Thus, $MRTS = -MP_L/MP_K = -1.5K/L$.

$-w/r = -24/8 = -3$. In contrast, at y, the isocost cuts the isoquant so the slopes are not equal. At y, the $MRTS$ is -18.9375, which is greater in magnitude than the negative of the ratio of the input prices, -3. Because the slopes are not equal at y, the firm can produce the same output at lower cost. As the figure shows, the cost of producing at y is \$3,000, whereas the cost of producing at x is only \$2,000.

We can interpret the condition in Equation 6.5 in another way. We showed in Chapter 5 that the marginal rate of technical substitution equals the negative of the ratio of the marginal product of labor to that of capital: $MRTS = -MP_L/MP_K$. Thus, the cost-minimizing condition in Equation 6.5 (multiplying both sides by -1) is[6]

$$\frac{MP_L}{MP_K} = \frac{w}{r}. \tag{6.6}$$

Equation 6.6 may be rewritten as

$$\frac{MP_L}{w} = \frac{MP_K}{r}. \tag{6.7}$$

Equation 6.7 states the *last-dollar rule*: Cost is minimized if inputs are chosen so that the last dollar spent on labor adds as much extra output as the last dollar spent on capital.

The beer firm's marginal product of labor is $MP_L = 0.6q/L$, and its marginal product of capital is $MP_K = 0.4q/K$.[7] At Bundle x in Figure 6.4, the beer firm's marginal product of labor is 1.2 ($= 0.6 \times 100/50$) and its marginal product of capital is 0.4. The last dollar spent on labor gets the firm

$$\frac{MP_L}{w} = \frac{1.2}{24} = 0.05$$

more units of output. The last dollar spent on capital also gets the firm

$$\frac{MP_K}{r} = \frac{0.4}{8} = 0.05$$

more units of output. Thus, spending one more dollar on labor at x gets the firm as much extra output as spending the same amount on capital. Equation 6.7 holds, so the firm is minimizing its cost of producing 100 units of output.

If instead the firm uses more capital and less labor, producing at y, its MP_L is 2.5 ($= 0.6q/L = 0.6 \times 100/24$) and the MP_K is approximately 0.13 ($\approx 0.4q/K = 0.4 \times 100/303$). As a result, the last dollar spent on labor yields $MP_L/w \approx 0.1$ more output, whereas the last dollar spent on capital yields only a fourth as much extra output, $MP_K/r \approx 0.017$. At y, if the firm shifts one dollar from capital to labor, the reduction in capital causes output to fall by 0.017 units. Offsetting that reduction, the increase in labor causes output to increase by 0.1 units. Thus, the net gain is 0.083 units of output at the same cost. The firm should shift even more resources from capital to labor—which increases the marginal product

---

[6]See Appendix 6B at the end of this chapter for a calculus derivation of this cost-minimizing condition.

[7]Because the beer manufacturer's production function is $q = 1.52L^{0.6}K^{0.4}$, the marginal product of labor is $MP_L = (0.6)1.52L^{(0.6-1)}K^{0.4} = 0.6q/L$. Similarly, $MP_K = (0.4)1.52L^{0.6}K^{(0.4-1)} = 0.4q/K$.

of capital and decreases the marginal product of labor—until the firm is operating with the capital-labor bundle x, where Equation 6.7 holds and the last dollar spent on labor increases output just as much as the last dollar spent on capital.

To summarize, a manager can use three equivalent rules to pick the lowest-cost combination of inputs to produce a given level of output when isoquants are smooth: the lowest-isocost rule, the tangency rule (Equation 6.6), and the last-dollar rule (Equation 6.7).

Managerial Implication

Cost Minimization by Trial and Error

How can a manager minimize cost if the manager does not know the firm's production function? The manager can use the last-dollar rule to determine the cost-minimizing combination of inputs through trial and error. The manager can experiment by adjusting each input slightly, holding other inputs constant, to learn how production and cost change, and then use that information to choose a cost-minimizing bundle of inputs.

That is, managers don't draw isoquants and isocost lines to make decisions. Instead, they use an insight from such an analysis to employ the last-dollar rule.

Factor Price Changes. Once the beer manufacturer determines the lowest-cost combination of inputs to produce a given level of output, it uses that method as long as the input prices remain constant. How should the firm change its behavior if the cost of one of the factors changes? Suppose that the wage falls from $24 to $8 but the rental rate of capital stays constant at $8.

The firm minimizes its new cost by substituting away from the now relatively more expensive input, capital, toward the input whose price has fallen, labor. The change in the wage does not affect technological efficiency, so it does not affect the isoquant in Figure 6.5. However, because of the wage decrease, the new isocost lines

FIGURE 6.5 Effect of a Change in a Factor Price

Originally, the wage was $24 and the rental rate of capital was $8, so the lowest isocost line ($2,000) was tangent to the q = 100 isoquant at x (L = 50, K = 100). When the wage fell to $8, the isocost lines became flatter: Labor became relatively less expensive than capital. The slope of the isocost lines falls from −w/r = −24/8 = −3 to −8/8 = −1. The new lowest isocost line ($1,032) is tangent at v (L = 77, K = 52). Thus, when the wage falls, the firm uses more labor and less capital to produce a given level of output, and the cost of production falls from $2,000 to $1,032.

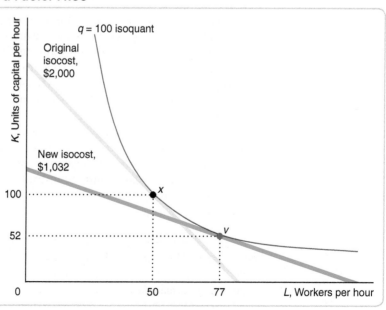

have a flatter slope, $-w/r = -8/8 = -1$, than the original isocost lines, $-w/r = -24/8 = -3$.

The relatively steep original isocost line is tangent to the 100-unit isoquant at Bundle x ($L = 50$, $K = 100$). The new, flatter isocost line is tangent to the isoquant at Bundle v ($L = 77$, $K = 52$). Thus, the firm uses more labor and less capital as labor becomes relatively less expensive. Moreover, the firm's cost of producing 100 units falls from \$2,000 to \$1,032 because of the fall in the wage. This example illustrates that a change in the relative prices of inputs affects the mix of inputs that a firm uses.

<table>
<tr><td>**Mini-Case**

The Internet and Outsourcing</td><td>To start a children's pajama business, Philip Chigos and Mary Domenico designed their products, chose fabrics, and searched for low-cost workers in China or Mexico from an office in the basement below their San Francisco apartment. Increasingly, such mom-and-pop operations are sending their clothing, jewelry, and programming work to Sri Lanka, China, India, Mexico, and Eastern Europe.</td></tr>
</table>

A firm *outsources* if it retains others to provide services that the firm had previously performed itself. Firms have always used outsourcing. For example, restaurants buy goods such as butter and flour or finished products such as bread and pies from other firms. Outsourcing increases profits if others can produce a good or service for less than the firm's own cost.

Many news outlets and politicians in high-wage countries have been wringing their hands about outsourcing to other countries. The different factor prices that firms face in low-wage countries may allow them to produce at lower cost.

In the past, most small firms could not practically outsource to other countries because of the high transaction costs of finding partners abroad and communicating with them. Now they can use the internet and e-mail to inexpensively communicate with foreign factories.

Mr. Chigos used the internet to find potential Chinese and Mexican manufacturers for the pajamas that Ms. Domenico designed. Hiring foreign workers is crucial. Mr. Chigos claims, "We'd love it to say 'Made in the U.S.A.' and use American textiles and production." However, if they did so, their cost would rise four to ten times, and "We didn't want to sell our pajamas for \$120." One result of easy access to cheap manufacturing, he said, is that more American entrepreneurs may be able to turn an idea into a product.

The would-be pajama tycoons plan to outsource to U.S. firms as well. They will use a Richmond, California, freight management company to receive the shipments, check the quality of the merchandise, and ship it to customers. They will market their clothes on the internet and through boutique retailers. They have no manufacturing plant, storefront, or warehouse. As Mr. Chigos notes, "With the technology available today, we'll never touch the product." Lower communication costs have made it feasible to take advantage of low foreign costs for outsourced activities.

If relative factor prices (and hence slopes of isocost lines) are different abroad than at home, the manager of a firm with smooth isoquants should use a different factor mix when producing abroad, as Figure 6.5 illustrates. However, Q&A 6.3 shows that if all foreign prices for capital and labor are proportionally lower than domestic prices so that relative factor prices are the same, the firm should use the same technology as at home.

Q&A 6.3

If a firm manufactures at home, it faces input prices for labor and capital of w and r and produces q units of output using L units of labor and K units of capital. Abroad, the wage and cost of capital are both half as much as at home. If the firm manufactures abroad, will it change the amount of labor and capital it uses to produce q? What happens to its cost of producing quantity q?

Answer

1. *Determine whether the change in factor prices affects the slopes of the isoquant or the isocost lines.* The change in input prices does not affect the isoquant, which depends only on technology (the production function). Moreover, cutting both the input prices in half does not affect the slope of the isocost lines. The original slope was $-w/r$, and the new slope is $-(w/2)/(r/2) = -w/r$.

2. *Using a rule for cost minimization, determine whether the firm changes its input mix.* A firm minimizes its cost by producing where its isoquant is tangent to the lowest possible isocost line. That is, the firm produces where the slope of its isoquant, $MRTS$, equals the slope of its isocost line, $-w/r$. Because the slopes of the isoquant and the isocost lines are unchanged after input prices are cut in half, the firm continues to produce using the same amount of labor, L, and capital, K, as originally.

3. *Calculate the original cost and the new cost and compare them.* The firm's original cost of producing q units of output was $wL + rK = C$. Its new cost of producing the same amount of output is $(w/2)L + (r/2)K = C/2$. Thus, its cost of producing q falls by half when the input prices are halved. The isocost lines have the same slope as before, but the cost associated with each isocost line is halved.

The Shapes of Long-Run Cost Curves

The shapes of the long-run average cost and marginal cost curves depend on the shape of the long-run total cost curve. The long-run cost curve in panel a of Figure 6.6 corresponds to the long-run average and marginal cost curves in panel b. The long-run cost curve of this firm rises less than in proportion to increases in output at outputs below q^* and then rises more rapidly. The corresponding long-run average cost curve first falls and then rises.

The explanation for why the long-run average cost curve is U-shaped differs from the explanation for why the short-run average cost curves are U-shaped. A key reason why the short-run average cost is initially downward sloping is that the average fixed cost curve is downward sloping: Spreading the fixed cost over more units of output lowers the average fixed cost per unit. In the long run, fixed costs are less important than in the short run, and may be absent altogether, as we have assumed in this section. Therefore, we cannot rely on fixed costs to explain the initial downward slope of the long-run average cost curve.

A major reason why the short-run average cost curve slopes upward at higher levels of output is diminishing marginal returns. In the long run, however, all factors can be increased, so diminishing marginal returns do not explain the upward slope of a long-run average cost curve.

As with the short-run curves, the shape of the long-run curves is determined by the production function relationship between output and inputs. In the long run, returns to scale play a major role in determining the shape of the average cost curve and other cost curves.

FIGURE 6.6 Long-Run Cost Curves

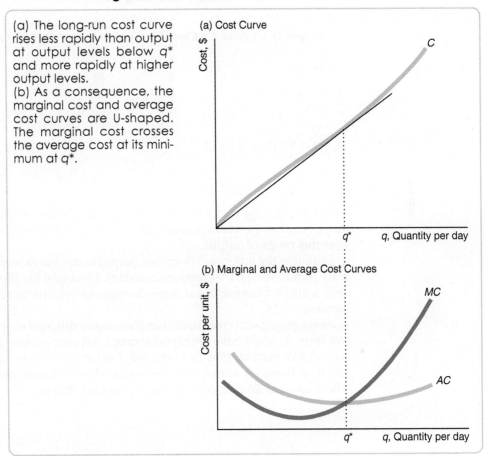

(a) The long-run cost curve rises less rapidly than output at output levels below q* and more rapidly at higher output levels.
(b) As a consequence, the marginal cost and average cost curves are U-shaped. The marginal cost crosses the average cost at its minimum at q*.

A cost function exhibits **economies of scale** if the average cost of production falls as output expands. If input prices are constant, increasing returns to scale is a sufficient condition for economies of scale. If a production function has increasing returns to scale, then the corresponding cost function has economies of scale: Doubling inputs more than doubles output, so average cost falls with higher output. However, even with constant input prices, it might be cost effective to use different factor proportions (such as using more robots and fewer workers) as the firm increases output. If so, the cost function might exhibit economies of scale even if the production function does not have increasing returns to scale.

If an increase in output has no effect on average cost, the production process has *no economies of scale*. We sometimes refer to such a cost function as exhibiting *constant costs*, because average cost does not change with output. Finally, a firm suffers from **diseconomies of scale** if average cost rises when output increases. To illustrate the relationship between returns to scale and long-run average cost, we use the returns-to-scale data in Table 6.3, which shows the cost-minimizing method of producing various quantities. The firm produces one unit of output using a unit each of labor and capital. Given a wage and rental cost of capital of $12 per unit, the total cost and average cost of producing this unit are both $24. Doubling both inputs causes output to increase more than in proportion to

TABLE 6.3 **Returns to Scale and Long-Run Costs**

Output, Q	Labour, L	Capital, K	Cost, C = wL + rK	Average Cost, AC = C/q	Returns to Scale
1	1	1	24	24	
3	2	2	48	16	Increasing
6	4	4	96	16	Constant
8	8	8	192	24	Decreasing

$w = r = \$12$ per unit.

3 units, reflecting increasing returns to scale. Because cost only doubles while output triples, the average cost falls and the cost function has economies of scale over this range of output.

Doubling the inputs again causes output to double as well—constant returns to scale—and average cost remains constant. Doubling the inputs once more causes only a small increase in output—decreasing returns to scale—so average cost increases.

Average long-run cost curves can have many different shapes. Perfectly competitive firms typically have U-shaped average cost curves. Average cost curves in noncompetitive markets may be U-shaped, L-shaped (average cost at first falls rapidly and then levels off as output increases), everywhere downward sloping, or everywhere upward sloping, or they may have other shapes.

Mini-Case

Economies of Scale at Google

Google has become a leader in data storage, offering access to what it calls Google Cloud Storage. People access their data from Google's massive data storage devices using the internet, as though from a cloud in the sky. By operating at a gigantic size and using a new approach, Google is able to lower its average cost and achieve economies of scale.

In the past, a firm would buy as many large hard disk units as it needed. Once the firm was buying the largest possible unit, to get more storage it would just buy more such hard disk units and its costs would rise in proportion to the number of units it needed.

Rather than buying off-the-shelf completed hard-disk units, Google buys raw computer parts in massive quantities, and assembles custom units on open racks without unnecessary components such as individual cases and fans. Google automatically backs up data on multiple hard disks. Thus, when a disk fails, a worker quickly yanks it out and replaces it with a new unit without spending time on a tedious manual backup. By sharing cooling and labor costs over many units, it lowers its average cost of storing data.

These lower costs that derive from greater economies of scale have allowed Google, Amazon, and a few other firms to create a new, disruptive industry. These firms provide disk storage with excellent backup in the cloud to individuals and firms who no longer have to buy relatively expensive, smaller hard drives and rely on themselves to back up their data.

Q&A 6.4

What is the shape of the long-run cost function for a fixed-proportion production function (see Chapter 5) in which it takes one unit of labor and one unit of capital to produce one unit of output? What is the shape of the average cost curve? Does it have economies or diseconomies of scale?

Answer

1. *Because no substitution is possible with a fixed-proportion production function, multiply the inputs (= the number of units of output) by their prices, and sum to determine total cost.* The long-run cost of producing q units of output is $C(q) = wL = rK = wq + rq = (w + r)q$. Cost rises in proportion to output. The long-run cost curve is a straight line with a slope of $w + r$.

2. *Divide the total cost function by q to get the average cost function.* The average cost function is $AC(q) = C(q)/q = [(w + r)q]/q = w + r$. Because the average cost for any quantity is $w + r$, the average cost curve is a horizontal straight line at $w + r$. Moreover, because the average cost does not change when the quantity of output changes, the cost function has constant costs: it does not have either economies or diseconomies of scale.

6.4 The Learning Curve

Average cost may fall *over time* for three reasons. First, operating at a larger scale in the long run may lower average cost due to increasing returns to scale (IRS). Second, technological progress (Chapter 5) may increase productivity and thereby lower average cost. Third, a firm may benefit from **learning by doing**: the productive skills and knowledge that workers and managers gain from experience. Workers who are given a new task may perform it slowly the first few times they try, but their speed increases with practice. Managers may learn how to organize production more efficiently, discover which workers to assign to particular tasks, and determine where more inventories are needed and where they can be reduced. Engineers may optimize product designs by experimenting with various production methods. For these and other reasons, the average cost of production tends to fall over time, and the effect is particularly strong with new products.

In some firms, learning by doing is a function of the time elapsed since a particular product or production process was introduced. However, more commonly, learning is a function of *cumulative output*: the total number of units of output produced since the product was introduced. The **learning curve** is the relationship between average costs and cumulative output. The learning curve for Intel central processing units (CPUs) in panel a of Figure 6.7 shows that Intel's average cost fell very rapidly with the first few million units of cumulative output, but then dropped relatively slowly with additional units (Salgado, 2008).

If a firm is operating in the economies of scale section of its average cost curve, expanding output lowers its cost for two reasons. Its average cost falls today because of economies of scale, and for any given level of output, its average cost is lower in the next period due to learning by doing.

In panel b of Figure 6.7, the firm is producing q_1 units of output at point A on average cost curve AC^1 in the first period. We assume that each period is long enough that the firm can vary all factors of production. If the firm expands its

FIGURE 6.7 **Learning by Doing**

(a) As Intel produced more cumulative CPUs, the average cost of production fell (Salgado, 2008). (b) In any one period, extra production reduces a firm's average cost due to economies of scale: because $q_1 < q_2 < q_3$, A is higher than B, which is higher than C. Extra production in one period reduces average cost in the future because of learning by doing. To produce q_2 this period costs B on AC^1, but to produce that same output in the next period

would cost only b on AC^2. If the firm produces q_3 instead of q_2 in this period, its average cost in the next period is AC^3 instead of AC^2 because of additional learning by doing. Thus, extra output in this period lowers the firm's cost in two ways: It lowers average cost in this period due to economies of scale and lowers average cost for any given output level in the next period due to learning by doing.

(a) Learning Curve for Intel Central Processing Units

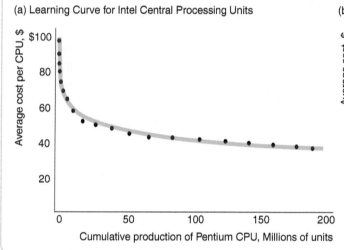

(b) Economies of Scale and Learning by Doing

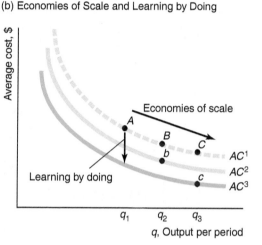

output to q_2 in Period 1, its average cost falls to B because of economies of scale. The learning by doing in Period 1 results in a lower average cost curve, AC^2 in Period 2. If the firm continues to produce q_2 units of output in Period 2, its average cost falls to b on AC^2.

If instead of expanding output to q_2 in Period 1, the firm expands to q_3, its average cost is even lower in Period 1 (C on AC^1) due to even greater economies of scale. Moreover, its average cost curve, AC^3, in Period 2 is even lower due to the extra experience gained from producing more output in Period 1. If the firm continues to produce q_3 in Period 2, its average cost is c on AC^3. Thus, all else being the same, if learning by doing depends on cumulative output, firms have an incentive to produce more in any one period than they otherwise would to lower their costs in the future.

Mini-Case

Solar Power Learning Curves

Learning by doing substantially reduces the cost of installing solar photovoltaic systems, which makes installation much less expensive in some countries than in others. If you want solar power for your home, you need to buy the module, which converts sunlight to electricity, and install the system by paying for labor and components, such as cables, inverters, and mounts. Modules are sold globally. However, the installation costs vary by country due to labor and other differences, as well as how many systems have been installed in the country.

Elshurafa et al. (2018) estimated learning curves for residential solar system installations, showing how the marginal cost varies with cumulative residential and commercial installations. On average, the global learning curve is 89%, which means that every time cumulative quantity doubles, the cost of installation falls to 89% of the previous level. The table shows these learning curve numbers for various countries or regions.

Country or Region	Learning Curve (%)
Sweden	74
United Kingdom	84
Japan	87
Europe	91
Australia	93
Canada	93
Mexico	93
United States	93
China	96

6.5 The Costs of Producing Multiple Goods

If a firm produces two or more goods, the cost of one good may depend on the output level of another. Outputs are linked if a single input is used to produce both of them. For example, cattle provide beef and hides (for leather), and petroleum supplies both heating fuel and gasoline. It is less expensive to produce beef and hides together than separately. If the goods are produced together, a single animal yields one unit of beef and one hide. If beef and hides are produced separately (throwing away the unused good), the same amount of output requires two animals and more labor.

A cost function exhibits **economies of scope** if it is less expensive to produce goods jointly than separately (Panzar and Willig, 1977, 1981). All else the same, if a firm has such a cost function, it can lower its total cost by producing its products together (say, at one plant) rather than separately (at two plants).

A measure of the degree of economies of *scope* (*SC*) is

$$SC = \frac{C(q_1, 0) + C(0, q_2) - C(q_1, q_2)}{C(q_1, q_2)},$$

where $C(q_1, 0)$ is the cost of producing q_1 units of the first good by itself, $C(0, q_2)$ is the cost of producing q_2 units of the second good, and $C(q_1, q_2)$ is the cost of producing both goods together. If the cost of producing the two goods separately, $C(q_1, 0) + C(0, q_2)$, is the same as producing them together, $C(q_1, q_2)$, then SC is zero. If it is cheaper to produce the goods jointly, SC is positive. A production process has *diseconomies of scope* if it is less expensive to produce the two goods separately, so SC is negative.

Empirical studies show that some medical production processes have economies of scope, others have none, and some have diseconomies of scope. Is it cost effective to separate outpatient and inpatient surgical procedures in a general hospital, or should outpatient surgeries be provided separately? Carey, Burgess, and Young (2015) estimate small scope economies ($SC = 0.12$) at the median for-profit hospital.

Gonçalves and Barros (2013) examined whether providing auxiliary clinical services in Portuguese hospitals is cost effective. They did not find economies of scope between the clinical chemistry service and other medical services, so outsourcing that service would not raise costs. However, in medical imaging, computed tomography exhibits scope economies with most other services, which suggests that outsourcing computed tomography would raise the costs of producing those other outputs.

Freeman, Savva, and Scholtes (2018) found significant diseconomies of scope between emergency admissions and non-emergency admissions in English hospitals. However, within the emergency category, there are positive economies of scope between the different major specialties. Non-emergency admissions do not exhibit economies of scope across specialties. The authors conclude that significant gains would arise from concentrating emergency care in hospitals focusing on emergency services.

If a U.S. semiconductor manufacturing firm shifts production from the firm's home plant to one abroad, should it use the same mix of inputs as at home? The firm may choose to use a different technology because the firm's cost of labor relative to capital is lower abroad than in the United States.

If the firm's isoquant is smooth, the firm uses a different bundle of inputs abroad than at home given that the relative factor prices differ (as Figure 6.5 shows). However, semiconductor manufacturers have kinked isoquants. Firms can use three different technologies to produce semiconductors. One technology is based on machines called *aligners*. This technology requires a relatively large amount of labor to reach any particular output level. The *stepper* technology uses more sophisticated machines and less labor, and advanced steppers called *wafer-handling steppers* represent an even larger capital input and correspondingly require less labor to reach any target output. Figure 6.8 shows a firm's $q = 200$ semiconductor chips isoquant. In its U.S. plant, the semiconductor manufacturing firm uses a wafer-handling stepper technology because the C^1 isocost line, which is the lowest isocost line that touches the isoquant, hits the isoquant at that technology.

The firm's cost of both inputs is less abroad than in the United States, and its cost of labor is relatively less than the cost of capital at its foreign plant than at its U.S. plant. The slope of its isocost line is $-w/r$, where w is the wage and r is the rental cost of the manufacturing equipment. The smaller w is relative to r, the less steeply sloped is its isocost curve. Thus, the firm's foreign isocost line is flatter than its domestic C^1 isocost line.

If the firm's isoquant were smooth, the firm would certainly use a different technology at its foreign plant than in its home plant. However, its isoquant has kinks, so a small change in the relative input prices does not necessarily lead to a change in production technology. The firm could face either the C^2 or C^3 isocost curves, both of which are flatter than the C^1 isocost. If the firm faces the C^2 isocost line, which is only slightly flatter than the C^1 isocost, the firm still uses the capital-intensive wafer-handling stepper technology in its foreign plant. However, if the firm faces the much flatter C^3 isocost line, which hits the isoquant at the stepper technology, it switches technologies. (If the isocost line were even flatter, it could hit the isoquant at the aligner technology.)

Even if the wage change is small so that the firm's isocost line is C^2 and the firm does not switch technologies abroad, the firm's cost will be lower abroad with the same technology because C^2 is less than C^1. However, if the wage is low enough that it can shift to a more labor-intensive technology, its costs will be even lower: C^3 is less than C^2.

Thus, whether the firm uses a different technology in its foreign plant than in its domestic plant turns on the relative factor prices in the two locations and whether the firm's isoquant is smooth. If the isoquant is smooth, even a slight difference in relative factor prices will induce the firm to shift along the isoquant and use a different technology with a different capital-labor ratio. However, if the isoquant has kinks, the firm will use a different technology only if the relative factor prices differ substantially.

FIGURE 6.8 Technology Choice

In the United States, the semiconductor manufacturer produces using a wafer-handling stepper on isocost C^1. At its plant abroad, the wage is lower, so it faces a flatter isocost curve. If the wage is only slightly lower, so that its isocost is C^2, it produces the same way as at home. However, if the wage is much lower so that the isocost is C^3, it switches to a stepper technology.

SUMMARY

From all technically efficient production processes, a cost-minimizing firm chooses the one that is economically efficient. The economically efficient production process is the technically efficient process for which the cost of producing a given quantity of output is lowest.

1. **The Nature of Costs.** In making decisions about production, managers need to take into account the opportunity cost of an input, which is the value of the input's best alternative use. For example, if the manager is the owner of the company and does not receive a salary, the amount that the owner could have earned elsewhere—the foregone earnings—is the opportunity cost of the manager's time and is relevant in deciding whether the firm should produce or not. A durable good's opportunity cost depends on its current alternative use. If the past expenditure for a durable good is sunk—that is, it cannot be recovered—then that input has no opportunity cost and the sunk cost should not influence current production decisions.

2. **Short-Run Costs.** In the short run, the firm can adjust some factors, such as labor, while other factors, such as capital, are fixed. Consequently, total cost is the sum of variable costs and fixed costs. Average cost is total cost divided by the number of units of output produced. Similarly, average variable cost is variable cost divided by output. Marginal cost is the amount by which a firm's cost changes if the firm produces one more unit of output. At quantities where the marginal cost curve is below the average cost curve, the average cost curve is downward sloping. Where the marginal cost curve is above the average cost curve, the average cost curve is upward sloping. Thus, the marginal cost curve cuts the average cost curve at its minimum point. Given that input prices are constant, the shapes of the variable cost and the cost-per-unit curves are determined by the production function. If labor is

the only variable factor in the short run, the shape of short-run cost curves reflects the marginal product of labor.

3. **Long-Run Costs.** Over a long-run planning horizon, the firm can adjust all inputs. Therefore all costs are avoidable in the long run. The firm uses the combination of inputs that minimizes its cost. To produce a given output level, the firm chooses the lowest isocost line that touches the relevant isoquant, which is tangent to the isoquant. Equivalently, to minimize cost, the firm adjusts inputs until the last dollar spent on any input increases output by as much as the last dollar spent on any other input. If the firm calculates the cost of producing every possible output level given current input prices, it knows its cost function: Cost is a function of the input prices and the output level. If the firm's average cost falls as output expands, its production process has economies of scale. If its average cost rises as output expands, its production process has diseconomies of scale.

4. **The Learning Curve.** A firm that introduces a new product or service often benefits from increased productivity as it gains experience and learns how to produce at lower cost, a process called learning by doing. Workers who are given a new task will typically speed up and make fewer mistakes with practice. The learning curve describes the relationship between average cost and cumulative output over time. This curve typically slopes downward, reflecting the decline in cost that arises from learning by doing.

5. **The Costs of Producing Multiple Goods.** If it is less expensive for a firm to produce two goods jointly rather than separately, its production process exhibits economies of scope. If diseconomies of scope exist, it is less expensive to produce the goods separately. The presence of economies of scope is important in determining the goods that the firm produces.

QUESTIONS

All exercises are available on **MyLab Economics;** * = *answer at the back of this book;* C = *use of calculus may be necessary;*
✗ = *this exercise is available in Excel Grader in* **MyLab Economics.**

1. The Nature of Costs

1.1 Executives at Leonesse Cellars, a premium winery in Southern California, were surprised to learn that shipping wine by sea to some cities in Asia was less expensive than sending it to the East Coast of the United States, so they started shipping to Asia (David Armstrong, "Discount Cargo Rates Ripe for the Taking," *San Francisco Chronicle*, August 28, 2005). Because of the large U.S. trade imbalance with major Asian nations, cargo ships arrive at West Coast seaports fully loaded but return to Asia half to completely empty. Use the concept of opportunity cost to help explain the differential shipping rates.

1.2 Ming lives in Seattle and recently bought a $375 ticket to attend a Seattle Seahawks game. He is a huge fan, so even though the ticket is pricey it is well below his willingness to pay of $600. However, as game day approaches, Ming receives an invitation from his friend, Cassandra, to spend the day at the Museum of Pop Culture touring a big exhibit on Marvel superheroes. The museum visit would only cost $75, but Ming (being a big Marvel fan too) would be willing to pay $250. What is his opportunity cost of going to the museum? (*Hint*: See Q&A 6.1.)

1.3 Many corporations allow CEOs to use the firm's corporate jet for personal travel. The Internal Revenue Service (IRS) requires that the firm report personal use of its corporate jet as taxable executive income, and the Securities and Exchange Commission (SEC) requires that publicly traded corporations report the value of this benefit to shareholders. An important issue is determining the value of this benefit. The IRS values a CEO's personal flight at or below the price of a first-class ticket. The SEC values the flight at the "incremental" cost of the flight: the additional costs to the corporation of the flight. The third alternative is the market value of chartering an aircraft. Of the three methods, the first-class ticket is least expensive and the chartered flight is most expensive.

    a. What factors (such as fuel) determine the marginal explicit cost to a corporation of an executive's personal flight? Does any one of the three valuation methods correctly determine the marginal explicit cost?

    b. What is the marginal opportunity cost to the corporation of an executive's personal flight?

*1.4 A firm purchased copper pipes a few years ago at $10 per pipe and stored them, using them only as the need arises. The firm could sell its remaining pipes in the market at the current price of $9. What is the opportunity cost of each pipe and what is the sunk cost?

1.5 You won a ticket to a hockey playoff game by having your name drawn from a hat at a charity event. You were excited about going, but on the day of the game, a major snowstorm has hit and conditions are miserable. Would you be more likely to go if you had bought the ticket yourself instead of winning it? Relate your answer to opportunity costs and sunk costs.

2. Short-Run Costs

*2.1 Nicolas has purchased a streaming audio service for $8.00 per month. As he listens to more songs in a month, he spreads this fixed cost over a larger quantity, q. Derive an algebraic formula for his average fixed cost per song and draw it in a diagram. One of his friends says to Nicolas, "The more music you

listen to, the less you pay per song so you should spend all your time listening to music." What is wrong with this reasoning?

2.2 Platinum Pipeline Inc. needs a Caterpillar D6T dozer to install water and sewer lines. How does its fixed cost change if it can rent a dozer rather than buy one? (*Hint*: See Mini-Case "Short-Run Versus Long-Run in the Sharing Economy.")

2.3 In the twentieth century, department stores and supermarkets largely replaced smaller specialty stores, as consumers found it more efficient to go to one store rather than many. In the early part of this century, many shoppers changed their behavior again and began to favor online shopping over visiting a brick-and-mortar store. Consumers incur a transaction or search cost to shop, primarily the opportunity cost of their time. This transaction cost consists of a fixed cost of traveling to and from the store and a variable cost that rises with the number of different types of items the consumer tries to find on the shelves. By shopping online a consumer can avoid some of the fixed transaction costs of traveling to a physical store. Use math to explain why a shopper's average costs may be lower when buying online rather than from a physical store and then explain why online shopping hasn't eliminated brick-and-mortar stores altogether.

2.4 Give the formulas for and plot AFC, MC, AVC, and AC if the cost function is

    a. $C = 10 + 10q$,

    b. $C = 10 + q^2$, or

    c. $C = 10 + 10q - 4q^2 + q^3$. **C**

2.5 In 1796, Gottfried Christoph Härtel, a German music publisher, calculated the cost of printing music using an engraved plate technology and applied these estimated cost functions in making production decisions. Härtel figured that the fixed cost of printing a musical page—the cost of engraving the plates—was 900 pfennigs. The marginal cost of each additional copy of the page is 5 pfennigs (Scherer, 2001).

    a. Graph the total cost, average cost, average variable cost, and marginal cost functions.

    b. Is cost lower if only one music publisher prints a given composition? Why?

    c. Härtel used his data to do the following type of analysis. Suppose he expects to sell exactly 300 copies of a composition at 15 pfennigs per page of the composition. What is the greatest amount the publisher is willing to pay the composer per page of the composition?

2.6 Gail works in a flower shop, where she produces 10 floral arrangements per hour. She is paid $15 an hour for the first eight hours she works and

$20 an hour for each additional hour she works. What is the firm's cost function? What are its *AC*, *AVC*, and *MC* functions? Draw the *AC*, *AVC*, and *MC* curves.

*2.7 A firm builds shipping crates out of wood. How does the cost of producing a 1-cubic-foot crate (each side is 1-foot square) compare to the cost of building an 8-cubic-foot crate if wood costs $1 a square foot and the firm has no labor or other costs? More generally, how does cost vary with volume?

2.8 The only variable input a janitorial service firm uses to clean offices is workers who are paid a wage, *w*, of $16 an hour. Each worker can clean four offices in an hour. Use math to determine the variable cost, the average variable cost, and the marginal cost of cleaning one more office. Draw a diagram like Figure 6.1 to show the variable cost, average variable cost, and marginal cost curves.

2.9 A firm has a Cobb-Douglas production function, $q = 2L^{0.5}K^{0.5}$. If it faces factor prices of $w = 20$ and $r = 40$ and its capital is fixed at $\bar{K} = 100$, what are its short-run average fixed cost, average variable cost, and marginal cost functions? Plot these curves. (*Hint*: See Appendix 6A.)

2.10 A firm has two plants that produce identical output. The cost functions are $C_1 = 10q - 4q^2 + q^3$ and $C_2 = 10q - 2q^2 + q^3$.

    a. At what output levels does the average cost curve of each plant reach its minimum?

    b. If the firm wants to produce four units of output, how much should it produce in each plant? C

3. Long-Run Costs

3.1 A newly invented machine serves as a mobile station for receiving and accumulating packed flats of strawberries close to where they are picked, which reduces workers' time and burden of carrying full flats of strawberries. According to Rosenberg (2004), a machine-assisted crew of 15 pickers produces as much output, *q**, as that of an unaided crew of 25 workers. In a 6-day, 50-hour workweek, the machine replaces 500 worker-hours. At an hourly wage cost of $10, a machine saves $5,000 per week in labor costs, or $130,000 over a 26-week harvesting season. The cost of machine operation and maintenance expressed as a daily rental is $200, or $1,200 for a six-day week. Thus, the net savings equal $3,800 per week, or $98,800 for 26 weeks.

    a. Draw the *q** isoquant, assuming that only two production methods are available (pure labor and labor-machine). Label the isoquant and axes as thoroughly as possible.

    b. Add an isocost line to show which technology the firm chooses (be sure to measure wage and rental costs on a comparable time basis).

    c. Draw the corresponding cost curves (with and without the machine), assuming constant returns to scale, and label the curves and the axes as thoroughly as possible.

*3.2 A bottling company uses two inputs to produce bottles of the soft drink Sludge: bottling machines (*K*) and workers (*L*). The isoquants have the usual smooth shape. The machine costs $1,000 per day to run and the workers earn $200 per day. At the current level of production, the marginal product of the machine is an additional 200 bottles per day, and the marginal product of labor is 50 more bottles per day. Is this firm producing at minimum cost? If it is minimizing cost, explain why. If it is not minimizing cost, explain how the firm should change the ratio of inputs it uses to lower its cost. (*Hint*: Examine the conditions for minimizing cost in Equations 6.5, 6.6, and 6.7.)

3.3 Suppose that the government subsidizes the cost of workers by paying for 25% of the wage (the rate offered by the U.S. government in the late 1970s under the New Jobs Tax Credit program). What effect will this subsidy have on the firm's choice of labor and capital to produce a given level of output? What happens if both capital and labor are subsidized at 25%? (*Hint*: See Q&A 6.3.)

*3.4 The all-American baseball is made using cork from Portugal, rubber from Malaysia, yarn from Australia, and leather from France, and it is stitched (108 stitches exactly) by workers in Costa Rica. To assemble a baseball takes one unit each of these inputs. Ultimately, the finished product must be shipped to its final destination—say, Cooperstown, New York. The materials used cost the same anywhere. Labor costs are lower in Costa Rica than in a possible alternative manufacturing site in Georgia, but shipping costs from Costa Rica are higher. What production function is used? What is the cost function? What can you conclude about shipping costs if it is less expensive to produce baseballs in Costa Rica than in Georgia?

3.5 California's State Board of Equalization imposed a higher tax on "alcopops," flavored beers containing more than 0.5% alcohol-based flavorings, such as vanilla extract (Guy L. Smith, "On Regulation of 'Alcopops,'" *San Francisco Chronicle*, April 10, 2009). Such beers are taxed as distilled spirits at $3.30 a gallon rather than as beer at 20¢ a gallon. In response, manufacturers reformulated their beverages to avoid the tax. By early 2009, instead of collecting a predicted $38 million a year in new taxes, the state collected only about $9,000. Use an isocost-isoquant diagram to explain the firms' response. (*Hint*: Alcohol-based flavors and other flavors may be close to perfect substitutes.)

3.6 A U.S. electronics firm is considering moving its production to a plant in Mexico. Its estimated production function is $q = L^{0.5}K^{0.5}$ (based on Hsieh, 1995). The U.S. factor prices are $w = r = 10$. In Mexico, the wage is half that in the United States, but the firm faces the same cost of capital: $w^* = 5$ and $r^* = r = 10$. What are L and K, and what is the cost of producing $q = 100$ units in both countries?

3.7 The Mini-Case "Economies of Scale at Google" describes economies of scale for Google Cloud Storage. The cost function for this service is well approximated by $C = F + cq$, where C is total cost, F is fixed cost, c is a constant, and q is output. What is marginal cost for this cost function? What are the average fixed cost, average variable cost, and average cost? Over what range of output does Google have economies of scale?

*3.8 What is the long-run cost function for a fixed-proportions production function for which it takes two units of labor and one unit of capital to produce one unit of output as a function of the wage, w, and the price of capital, r? What is the cost function if the production function is $q = L + K$? (*Hint*: See Q&A 6.4.)

3.9 Trader Joe's sells very cheap and popular wine produced by Bronco Wine (Hayley Peterson, "The Real Reasons Trader Joe's Wine Is So Cheap," *Business Insider*, May 6, 2017). When asked why the wine is so cheap, Bronco winemaker Ed Moody emphasizes the volume of output, stating that it is easier to make wine "in a 700,000-gallon tank than . . . in a 700-gallon one because there is less exposure to air and oxygen is the enemy in winemaking." Wine educator Keith Wallace emphasizes the role of machines: "The company uses machines to harvest the grapes, which helps keep labor costs low, but also increases the chances that bad grapes end up in the wine." One of these reasons is based on choosing input proportions to minimize cost and one is based on economies of scale. State which is which and explain.

4. The Learning Curve

4.1 In what types of industry would you expect to see substantial learning by doing? Why?

*4.2 A firm's learning curve, which shows the relationship between average cost and cumulative output (the sum of its output since the firm started producing), is $AC = a + bN^{-r}$, where AC is its average cost; N is its cumulative output; a, b, and r are constants; and $0 \leq r < 1$.

   a. What is the firm's AC if $r = 0$? What can you say about the firm's ability to learn by doing?

   b. If r exceeds zero, what can you say about the firm's ability to learn by doing? What happens to its AC as its cumulative output, N, gets extremely large? Given this result, what is your interpretation of a?

4.3 Panel a of Figure 6.7 shows that Intel's average cost in a given year falls with the quantity it produces. In addition, extra production this year lowers the average cost curve next year. For example, in year 1, $AC = 50$ if quantity is 20 and $AC = 40$ if quantity is 60. If Intel produces 20 in year 1 and 40 in year 2, the average cost in year 2 will be 40. However, for every extra 10 units it produces in year 1, its AC for any given quantity in year 2 falls by 10%.

   a. What is the total cost and the average cost over the two years combined if the firm produces 20 in year 1 and 40 in year 2?

   b. What is the total cost and average cost over the two years combined if the firm produces 60 in year 1 and 40 in year 2?

   c. Over the two years combined, what is the true additional cost of producing 60 instead of 20 in year 1?

4.4 In the Mini-Case "Solar Power Learning Curves," the cost of solar power installations fell as the installed base (cumulative experience) in a given country rose. If N represents cumulative national experience, would an average cost curve $AC = a + bN^{-r}$ exhibit such learning by doing? Explain. (*Note: a, b*, and r are all positive constants.)

5. The Costs of Producing Multiple Goods

5.1 The United Kingdom started regulating the size of grocery stores in the early 1990s, and today the average size of a typical U.K. grocery store is roughly half the size of a typical U.S. store and two-thirds the size of a typical French store (Haskel and Sadun, 2012). What implications would such a restriction on size have for a store's average costs? Discuss in terms of economies of scale and scope.

5.2 Conner runs a rafting company on a local river. He runs two kinds of trips – a wild whitewater experience and a more mellow wildlife tour. If he spends the day only doing whitewater trips, he can do 3 trips per day; if he spends the day only doing wildlife trips, he can do 4 trips. If he does some of each, however, he can do more total trips: 2 whitewater trips and 3 wildlife trips. Suppose that Conner's time is valued at $20 an hour. What can you say about his economies of scope? That is, what is the sign of his measure of economies of scope, SC?

*5.3 A refiner produces heating fuel and gasoline from crude oil in virtually fixed proportions. What can you say about economies of scope for such a firm? What is the sign of its measure of economies of scope, SC?

5.4 Many hospitals have regularly scheduled surgery and active emergency departments. Based on the information in the Mini-Case "Medical Economies of Scope," could it be more cost effective to have separate emergency centers? What do you think are the reasons for these economies or diseconomies of scope?

6. Managerial Problem

*6.1 In Figure 6.8, show that for some wages and capital rental costs the firm is indifferent between using the wafer-handling stepper technology and the stepper technology. How does this wage-cost of capital ratio compare to those in the C^2 and C^3 isocost lines?

7. MyLab Economics Spreadsheet Exercises[8]

7.1 The production function for a firm is

$$q = -0.6L^3 + 18L^2K + 10L,$$

where q is the amount of output, L is the number of labor hours per week, and K is the amount of capital. The wage is $100 and the rental rate is $800 per time period.

a. Using Excel, calculate the total short-run output, $q(L)$, for $L = 0, 1, 2, \ldots, 20$, given that capital is fixed in the short run at $\overline{K} = 1$. Also, calculate the average product of labor, AP_L, and the marginal product of labor, MP_L. (You can estimate the MP_L for $L = 2$ as $q(2) - q(1)$, and so on for other levels of L.)

b. For each quantity of labor in (a), calculate the variable cost, VC; the total cost, C; the average variable cost, AVC; the average cost, AC; and the marginal cost, MC. Using Excel, draw the AVC, AC, and MC curves in a diagram. (*Hint:* See Q&A 3.2.)

c. For each quantity of labor in (a), calculate w/AP_L and w/MP_L and show that they equal AVC and MC, respectively. Explain why these relationships hold.

7.2 A furniture company has opened a small plant that builds tables. Jill, the production manager, knows the fixed cost of the plant, $F = 78 per day, and includes the cost of the building, tools, and equipment. Variable costs include labor, energy costs, and wood. Jill wants to know the cost function. She conducts an experiment in which she varies the daily

production level over a 10-day period and observes the associated daily cost. The daily output levels assigned are 1, 2, 4, 5, 7, 8, 10, 12, 15, and 16. The associated total costs for these output levels are 125, 161, 181, 202, 207, 222, 230, 275, 390, and 535, respectively.

a. Use the Trendline tool in Excel to estimate a cost function by regressing cost on output (Chapter 3). Try a linear specification ($C = a + bq$), a quadratic specification ($C = a + bq + dq^2$), and a cubic specification ($C = a + bq + dq^2 + eq^3$). Based on the plotted regressions, which specification would you recommend that Jill use? Would it make sense to use the *Set Intercept* option? If so, what value would you choose? (*Hint:* Put output in column A and cost in column B. To obtain quadratic and cubic cost specifications, select the *Polynomial* option from the *Trendline* menu and set *Order* at 2 for the quadratic specification and at 3 for the cubic function.)

b. Generate the corresponding average cost data by dividing the known cost by output for each experimental output level. Estimate an average cost curve using the Trendline tool.

7.3 A Korean electronic chip manufacturer has a production function given by $q = L^{0.5}K^{0.5}$.

a. Use Excel to determine the amount of capital, K, needed to produce 10 units of output for each value of labor, L, starting from $L = 2$ and going to $L = 20$ in increments of 1. Plot this isoquant. (*Hint:* The formula for that isoquant is $10 = L^{0.5}K^{0.5}$. Squaring both sides of this equation, we obtain $100 = LK$. Dividing both sides of the equation by L, we learn that $K = 100/L$.)

b. Use Excel to determine the cost of each of these combinations of labor and capital if the wage rate, w, and the cost of capital, r, are each $30 per unit. Which combination of inputs minimizes the cost of producing 10 units of output?

c. The slope of the isoquant is $-100/L^2$. Calculate the slope of the isoquant for each combination of inputs. The slope of the isocost line is $-w/r = -30/30 = -1$. Verify that the cost-minimizing input combination occurs where the slope of the isoquant equals the slope of the isocost line. Draw the isoquant and the isocost line and show that they are tangent at the cost-minimizing combination of inputs.

---

[8]The spreadsheet exercises in this chapter are based on the work of Satyajit Ghosh in cooperation with the authors. The answers are available on MyLab Economics.

APPENDIX 6A Calculating Cost Curves

If we know the production function for a product (Chapter 5) and the factor prices, we can use math to derive the various cost functions. Based on the estimates of Flath (2011), the Cobb-Douglas production function of a typical Japanese beer manufacturer (Chapter 5) is

$$q = 1.52L^{0.6}K^{0.4},$$

where labor, L, is measured in hours, K is the number of units of capital, and q is the amount of output.

We assume that the firm's capital is fixed at $\overline{K} = 100$ units in the short run. If the rental rate of a unit of capital is \$8, the fixed cost, F, is \$800, and the average fixed cost is

$$AFC = F/q = 800/q,$$

which falls as output increases.

We can use the production function to derive the variable cost. Given that capital is fixed in the short run, the short-run production function is solely a function of labor:

$$q = 1.52L^{0.6}100^{0.4} \approx 9.59L^{0.6}.$$

Rearranging this expression, we can write the number of workers, L, needed to produce q units of output as a function solely of output:

$$L(q) = \left(\frac{q}{9.59}\right)^{\frac{1}{0.6}} = \left(\frac{1}{9.59}\right)^{1.67}q^{1.67} \approx 0.023q^{1.67}. \tag{6A.1}$$

Now that we know how labor and output are related, we can calculate variable cost directly. The only variable input is labor, so if the wage is \$24, the firm's variable cost is

$$VC(q) = wL(q) = 24L(q). \tag{6A.2}$$

Substituting for $L(q)$ using Equation 6A.1 into the variable cost Equation 6A.2, we see how variable cost varies with output:

$$VC(q) = 24L(q) = 24(0.023q^{1.67}) \approx 0.55q^{1.67}. \tag{6A.3}$$

Using this expression for variable cost, we can construct the other cost measures.

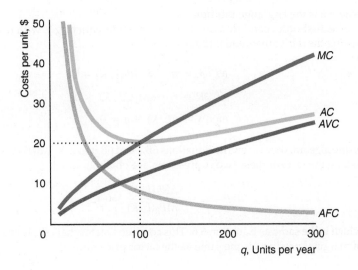

To obtain the equation for marginal cost as a function of output, we differentiate the variable cost, $VC(q)$, in Equation 6A.3 with respect to output:

$$MC(q) = \frac{dVC(q)}{dq} \approx \frac{d(0.55q^{1.67})}{dq}$$

$$= 1.67 \times 0.55q^{0.67} \approx 0.92q^{0.67}.$$

We can also calculate total cost, $C = F + VC$, average cost, $AC = C/q$, and average variable cost, $AVC = VC/q$, using algebra. The figure plots the beer firm's AFC, AVC, AC, and MC curves.

APPENDIX 6B   Long-Run Cost Minimization

We can use calculus to derive the tangency rule, cost-minimization condition, Equation 6.6. The problem the firm faces in the long run is to choose labor, L, and capital, K, to minimize the cost of producing a particular level of output, $\bar{q}$, given a wage of w and a rental rate of capital of r.

The firm's production function is $q = f(L, K)$, so the marginal products of labor and capital are $MP_L(L, K) = \partial f(L, K)/\partial L > 0$ and $MP_K = \partial f(L, K)/\partial K > 0$. The firm's problem is to minimize its cost of production, C, through its choice of labor and capital,

$$\min_{L,K} C = wL + rK,$$

subject to the constraint that a given amount of output, $\bar{q}$, is to be produced:

$$f(L, K) = \bar{q}. \tag{6B.1}$$

Equation 6B.1 is the formula for the $\bar{q}$ isoquant.

We can change this constrained minimization problem into an unconstrained problem by using the Lagrangian technique. The corresponding Lagrangian, $\mathcal{L}$, is

$$\mathcal{L} = wL + rK - \lambda[f(L, K) - \bar{q}],$$

where λ is the Lagrange multiplier.

The first-order conditions are obtained by differentiating $\mathcal{L}$ with respect to L, K, and λ and setting the derivatives equal to zero:

$$\partial \mathcal{L}/\partial L = w - \lambda MP_L(L, K) = 0, \tag{6B.2}$$

$$\partial \mathcal{L}/\partial K = r - \lambda MP_K(L, K) = 0, \tag{6B.3}$$

$$\partial \mathcal{L}/\partial \lambda = f(L, K) - \bar{q} = 0. \tag{6B.4}$$

Using algebra, we can rewrite Equations 6B.2 and 6B.3 as $w = \lambda MP_L(L, K)$ and $r = \lambda MP_K(L, K)$. Taking the ratio of these two expressions, we obtain

$$\frac{MP_L(L, K)}{MP_K(L, K)} = \frac{w}{r}, \tag{6B.5}$$

which is the same as Equation 6.6. This condition states that cost is minimized when the ratio of marginal products is the same as the factor price ratio, w/r.

Firm Organization and Market Structure

7

I won't belong to any organization that would have me as a member. —Groucho Marx

Managerial Problem

Amazon's Delivery Services

Amazon has a problem: It's too successful. It controls 44% of the U.S. e-commerce market, has well over $200 billion in annual sales; ships more than 1.2 billion packages a year; and has more than 100 warehouses, 7,500 truck trailers, and 40 airplanes. However, its rapid growth has made quick and inexpensive delivery of packages crucial to its operations. In 2017, it spent nearly $22 billion on shipping globally, or about 12% of its overall revenue.

Amazon has relied on shipping using United Parcel Service (UPS), FedEx, and the U.S. Postal Service (USPS). Amazon worries that these delivery services are relatively expensive and have trouble delivering on time, especially during heavy shipping periods, such as near the holidays in December. Consequently, Amazon says that it needs to develop its own delivery services.

It is using or considering three approaches. First, its Flex service contracts with individuals who drive their own cars to deliver packages for "the last mile." Second, it is developing a new service in which it would also contract with individuals to deliver packages for the last mile; however, these persons would use Amazon's new gray-and-blue delivery vans and wear black hats and blue-collared shirts with an Amazon logo.

A third option is for Amazon to create a shipping service to compete with UPS, FedEx, and USPS. Starting initially in Los Angeles, Shipping With Amazon (SWA) will pick up packages from businesses and deliver them to customers. However, to develop such a service able to compete with the large shipping companies would require an investment of many billions of dollars. FedEx has 650 aircraft, 150,000 trucks, 400,000 employees, and 4,800 operating facilities globally. UPS planned to spend $7 billion to upgrade its delivery network in 2018 alone.

What issues should Amazon consider in deciding whether to rely primarily on other delivery services or develop its own capabilities? Given that the up-front investment in SWA will cause Amazon to lose money for the first few years before turning a profit, how should Amazon decide whether this investment is worthwhile?

Having examined firms' production and cost decisions in earlier chapters, we now turn to some of the firm's other crucial decisions. We start by describing the organization and governance of firms.

Next, we consider the firm's objectives, starting with profit maximization. We show how managers can choose output to maximize profit, and we describe the firm's decision of when to shut down. We then examine firms that pursue social objectives. However, we point out two market forces that lead most firms to maximize profits.

We next use the concept of *present value* to address how managers make decisions when profits vary over time, such as when firms make investments that have short-term costs but lead to longer-term gains.

In pursuing a firm's objectives, such as profit maximization, managers must decide on the *vertical* structure of the firm—whether the firm produces needed inputs internally or buys them. Whether the firm makes or buys an input depends on the relative costs of these two approaches. The size of the market affects these costs, and thereby affects the make or buy decision. We show that as a market grows, firms typically change from producing their own inputs to buying them from others, but as the market grows even larger, firms may revert to producing the inputs themselves.

The size of the market affects not only individual firms' organizational structure but also the overall structure of the market. A market's structure depends on the number of firms, how easily they can enter or exit the market, their ability to set prices, whether they differentiate their products, and how the firms interact. And sometimes managers must cope with *disruptive innovations* that may dramatically change market structure or other factors that affect managerial decision making.

Learning Objectives

1. Explain how firms differ by type of ownership and organization.
2. Determine a firm's profit-maximizing output.
3. Use present values to compare costs and revenues that occur at different times.
4. Discuss profit-maximizing vertical organization.
5. Describe the four main types of market structure.

7.1 Ownership and Governance of Firms

A firm may be owned by a government, by other firms, by private individuals, or by some combination. A country's legal and governmental system affects whether firms are privately owned, how owners run firms, and whether or not they pursue profits.

Private, Public, and Nonprofit Firms

Atheism is a non-prophet organization. —George Carlin

Firms operate in the private sector, the public sector, or the nonprofit sector. The *private sector*—sometimes referred to as the *for-profit private sector* or *for-profit sector*—consists of firms that are owned by individuals or other nongovernmental entities and whose owners may earn a profit. Most of the firms that we discuss throughout this book—such as Apple, Nike, and Toyota—belong to the private sector. In almost every country, this sector provides most of that country's *gross domestic product* (GDP), which is a measure of the value of a country's total output.

The *public sector* consists of firms and other organizations that are owned by governments or government agencies, called *state-owned enterprises*. An example of a public-sector firm is the National Railroad Passenger Corporation (Amtrak), which is owned primarily by the U.S. government. The armed forces and the court system are also part of the public sector, as are most schools, colleges, and universities.

In most countries, the government produces between 10% and 20% of the country's GDP. Examples include the United States (11%), India (11%), Australia (16%), Germany (18%), Canada (17%), South Africa (19%), and the United Kingdom (19%).[1] The government's share is higher in a few countries that provide a high level of government services—such as Sweden (23%)—or maintain a relatively large army, such as Israel (23%).

The *nonprofit sector* consists of organizations that are neither government-owned nor intended to earn a profit, but typically pursue social or public interest objectives. Literally, this sector should be called the *nongovernment, not-for-profit sector*, but this term is normally shortened to just the *nonprofit sector*. Well-known examples include Greenpeace and Alcoholics Anonymous, along with many other charitable, educational, health, and religious organizations.

In 2018, the private sector created 76% of the U.S. gross domestic product, while nonprofits and households produced about 13%, and the government sector accounted for the remaining 11%.[2]

Sometimes all three sectors play an important role in the same industry. For example, in the United States, Canada, the United Kingdom, and many other countries, for-profit, nonprofit, and government-owned hospitals coexist. Similarly, while most schools and other educational institutions are government-owned, many are not, including some of the most prominent U.S. universities, such as Harvard, Stanford, and the Massachusetts Institute of Technology (MIT). These universities are often referred to as *private* universities. Most private universities are nonprofit organizations. However, some educational institutions, such as the University of Phoenix, are intended to earn profits and are part of the for-profit private sector.

A single enterprise may be partially owned by a government and partially owned by private interests. For example, during the 2007–2009 Great Recession, the U.S. government took a partial ownership position in many firms in the financial and automobile industries. If the government is the dominant owner, it is normal to view the enterprise as part of the public sector. Conversely, if the government has only a small ownership interest in a for-profit enterprise, that enterprise would be viewed as part of the private sector. Organizations or projects with significant government ownership and significant private ownership are sometimes referred to as *mixed enterprises* or *public-private partnerships*.

Mini-Case

Chinese State-Owned Enterprises

Before 1978, virtually all Chinese industrial firms were state-owned enterprises (SOEs). Since then, China has been transitioning to a market-based economy, gradually increasing the role of private-sector firms. It has dramatically reduced the number of SOEs, keeping mainly the largest ones.

By 1999, SOEs comprised only about 36% of Chinese industrial firms but still controlled nearly 68% of industrial assets (capital). Since 2000, the Chinese

[1]The data in this paragraph are from Version 9.0 of the Penn World Table as of October 2017, available for download at **www.rug.nl/ggdc/productivity/pwt/**. For a description of this data, see Feenstra, Inklaar, and Timmer (2015).

[2]**https://fred.stlouisfed.org/release/tables?rid=53&eid=13416&snid=13423**.

government has allowed many small SOEs to be privatized or go bankrupt, while it continues to subsidize many large SOEs. In 2017, SOEs accounted for 29% of industrial assets, and still accounted for 30% to 40% of China's GDP. China is also creating mixed enterprises by selling shares in state-owned enterprises to private investors. For example, in 2017, the giant state-owned mobile carrier China Unicom announced a plan to sell $11.7 billion in shares, corresponding to about one-third of the company, to private sector investors.

Ownership of For-Profit Firms

In this textbook, we focus on the private sector. The private sector has three main types of organizations: the sole proprietorship, the partnership, and the corporation.

Sole proprietorships are firms owned and controlled by a single individual.

Partnerships are businesses jointly owned and controlled by two or more people operating under a partnership agreement.

Corporations are owned by *shareholders*, who own the firm's *shares* (also called *stock*). Each share (or unit of stock) is a unit of ownership in the firm. Therefore, shareholders own the firm in proportion to the number of shares they hold. The shareholders elect a board of directors to represent them. In turn, the board of directors usually hires managers who manage the firm's operations. Some corporations are very small and have a single shareholder, often an owner-manager who owns and runs the business. Others are very large and have thousands of shareholders. The legal name of a corporation often includes the term Incorporated (Inc.) or Limited (Ltd.) to indicate its corporate status.

Publicly Traded and Closely Held Corporations.

Corporations may be either publicly traded or closely held. The term *public* in this context has a different meaning than its use in the term *public sector*. A publicly traded corporation is a corporation whose shares can be readily bought and sold by the general public. The shares of most of these corporations trade on major organized stock exchanges, such as the New York Stock Exchange, the NASDAQ (National Association of Securities Dealers Automated Quotations), the Tokyo Stock Exchange, the Shanghai Stock Exchange, the Toronto Stock Exchange, or the London Stock Exchange. For example, IBM shares can be readily bought and sold on the New York Stock Exchange.

The stock of a closely held corporation, sometimes referred to as *private equity*, is not available for purchase or sale on an organized exchange. Typically, a small group of individuals own this stock. The transition from closely held to publicly traded status is often an important step in the evolution of a corporation.

In making the transition from privately held to publicly traded status, the closely held firm will make an *initial public offering* (or IPO) of its shares on an organized stock exchange. This IPO is a way to raise money for the firm. For example, the 2018 IPO of Dropbox, a file-sharing and storage platform, raised over $750 million.[3] This ability to raise money by issuing stock is one major advantage of going public. However, a major disadvantage from the point of view of the original owners is that ownership of the firm becomes broadly distributed, possibly causing the original owners to lose control of the firm.

---

[3]Alex Barinka, "Dropbox Raises $756 Million After Pricing IPO Above Range," Bloomberg, March 22, 2018.

It is also possible for a publicly traded firm to go private and become closely held. Such a change occurs when a group of investors buys all or most of the shares held by the general public and takes the corporation out of any organized exchanges where its stock previously traded. Sometimes senior managers of the corporation are among the buyers. Commonly, the buyers include *private equity firms* that specialize in taking firms private, often in combination with other outside investors. One of the best-known private equity firms is KKR, which has taken many publicly traded firms private. For example, in 2018 KKR announced its purchase of Envision Healthcare Corporation in a deal valued at over $5.5 billion.[4]

Traditionally, the owners of sole proprietorships and partnerships were fully liable, individually and collectively, for any debts of the firm. In contrast, the owners of a corporation are not personally liable for the firm's debts; they have **limited liability**: The personal assets of the corporate owners cannot be taken to pay a corporation's debts even if it goes into bankruptcy. Because of the limited liability of corporations, the most that shareholders can lose is the amount they paid for their stock, which typically becomes worthless if the corporation goes bankrupt.

Changes in the laws in many countries have allowed a sole proprietorship or a partnership to obtain the advantages of limited liability by becoming a *limited liability company* (LLC).[5] These LLC firms can otherwise do business as usual and need not adopt other aspects of the corporate form such as filing corporate tax returns. The precise regulations that apply to LLCs vary from country to country, and from state to state within the United States. Adopting the LLC form has some costs that many firms are not willing to incur, including registration fees, and firms in some industries are not eligible. Therefore, traditional sole proprietorships and partnerships with unlimited personal liability for the owners remain very common. However, the LLC form has significantly extended the availability of limited liability.[6]

Firm Size. The purpose of limiting the liability of owners of corporations was to allow firms to raise funds and grow larger than was possible when owners risked everything they owned on any firm in which they invested. Consequently, most large firms were (and still are) corporations. According to the latest available Internal Revenue Service (IRS) statistics, U.S. corporations are responsible for 81% of business receipts and 58% of net business income even though they are only 18% of all nonfarm firms. Nonfarm sole proprietorships are 72% of firms but make only 4% of the sales revenue and earn 15% of net income. Partnerships are 10% of firms, account for 15% of revenue, and make 27% of net income.

As these statistics illustrate, larger firms tend to be corporations and smaller firms are often sole proprietorships. This pattern reflects a natural evolution in the life cycle of the firm, as an entrepreneur may start a small business as a sole proprietorship and then incorporate as the firm's operations expand.

---

[4]Aparajita Saxena, "KKR to Take Envision Private for $5.57 Billion in Healthcare Push," Reuters, June 11, 2018.

[5]In the United States, a few states had longstanding provisions for LLCs. National acceptance and standardization of this form dates from the Uniform Limited Liability Company Act of 1996.

[6]Forming a *limited partnership* has become an alternative method for a partnership to gain the advantages of limited liability. Such firms are owned in whole or in part by *limited partners,* whose financial liability is limited in the sense that they cannot lose more than the amount of their investment. Limited partnerships may also have one or more *general partners* who, like sole proprietors, are personally responsible for the firm's debts.

Indeed, successful corporations typically expand, and a relatively small number of corporations account for most of the revenue and income in the U.S. economy. According to the IRS, 81% of all corporations earn less than $1 million a year, and they account for only 3% of corporate revenue. In contrast, less than 1% of all corporations earn over $50 million, but they make 77% of total corporate revenue. In 2017, the U.S. corporation with the largest worldwide revenue was Walmart. Its revenue of $500 billion exceeded the annual GDP of fairly large countries, such as Austria ($478 billion) and Thailand ($483 billion).[7]

Firm Governance

In a small private-sector firm with a single owner-manager, the governance of the firm is straightforward: The owner-manager makes the important decisions for the firm. In contrast, governance in a large modern publicly traded corporation is more complex.

The shareholders own the corporation. However, most shareholders do not play an important role in day-to-day decision making or even in long-range planning in the firm and therefore do not control the firm in any meaningful sense. They are *passive shareholders*. Many people own shares in corporations like Microsoft and Sony, but virtually none of these individuals influence or even have knowledge about these firms' day-to-day managerial decisions.

Many of the ownership rights of shareholders are delegated to a board of directors that is elected by the shareholders, often referred to simply as the *board*. The board of a large publicly traded corporation normally includes outside directors, who are not employed as managers by the corporation, and inside directors, such as the chief executive officer (CEO) of the corporation and other senior executives. Some corporations have former politicians and other prominent people as outside directors, such as former U.S. Vice President Al Gore (Apple), but most directors are people with relevant business experience, particularly former CEOs. For example, former Hewlett Packard CEO Meg Whitman serves as a director for Procter & Gamble and for Dropbox.

7.2 Profit Maximization

The managers of all types of firms pursue goals. Managers of government agencies, charitable organizations, and other nonprofit organizations are supposed to take actions that benefit specific groups of people. Economists assume that most owners of private-sector firms want to maximize their profits. One reason for this belief is that owners and managers often state that profit maximization is their objective. Indeed, that's why private-sector firms are called *for-profit businesses*.

Profit

A firm's **profit**, π, is the difference between a firm's revenues, R, and its cost, C:

$$\pi = R - C.$$

If profit is negative, $\pi < 0$, the firm makes a *loss*.

---

[7]Fortune magazine annually provides a list of the largest corporations: **http://fortune.com/ fortune500**. GDP data are from the International Monetary Fund for 2017.

Measuring a firm's revenue is straightforward: It is the proceeds from selling the firm's products. Measuring cost is more challenging. For an economist, the correct measure of cost is the economic cost or *opportunity cost*: the value of the best alternative use of any input the firm employs. As discussed in Chapter 6, the opportunity cost of inputs often exceeds the explicit or out-of-pocket costs recorded in financial accounting statements. This distinction is important because a firm may make a serious mistake if it ignores some relevant opportunity costs.

Economic profit is revenue minus opportunity cost. When we refer to just *profit*, we mean economic profit. Economic profit is often different from the profit reported in a firm's financial accounting statements. For tax requirements and for other reasons, these *accounting profits* are often calculated using only explicit costs, leaving out important implicit opportunity costs. If implicit costs are left out, then a firm's accounting profit may be larger than its economic profit. An example illustrates the difference in the two profit measures and the importance of this distinction in dispelling a misconception:

> **Common Confusion** You should operate your firm if you are making an accounting profit.

That conclusion may not follow if accounting profit ignores implicit opportunity costs.

For small firms owned and managed by one person, the main difference between explicit costs and the opportunity cost is often the implicit cost of the owner-manager's time. Kahlil owns and manages a small restaurant with monthly revenues of $50,000 and has explicit monthly costs (rent, materials, and labor) of $45,000 a month. Thus, his accounting profit is $50,000 − $45,000 = $5,000 per month.

However, the best alternative use of his time is to work at another job where he could earn $6,000 a month. Thus, the opportunity cost of Kahlil's time spent running his restaurant is $6,000 per month. As a result, his opportunity cost of operating the restaurant is $45,000 + $6,000 = $51,000, so his firm's economic profit is $50,000 − $51,000 = −$1,000, which is negative—he is making a loss. Kahil can earn more money by shutting down his restaurant and working for someone else.

The owners of a firm may put other resources into a firm in addition to their own labor. The opportunity cost of these resources should also be included when calculating economic profit. In large corporations, the owners of the firm are shareholders who may provide no labor to the firm but still incur an opportunity cost: They cannot use the money they invested in the firm elsewhere. To be willing to invest in the firm, the owners must receive payments at least equal to the opportunity cost of their investment. This necessary payment to the owners is an implicit cost of doing business. If a firm earns an accounting profit of $100,000 but must pay $40,000 to the firm's owners to cover their opportunity cost, the firm has an economic profit of only $60,000. Businesses often refer to the amount that must be earned to cover the implicit costs of the owners as *normal profit* and call economic profit *above-normal* profit.

Two Steps to Maximizing Profit

Because both the firm's revenue and cost vary with its output, q, the firm's profit also varies with output:

$$\pi(q) = R(q) - C(q), \tag{7.1}$$

where $R(q)$ is its revenue function and $C(q)$ is its cost function. A firm decides how much output to sell to maximize its profit, Equation 7.1. To maximize its profit, any firm must answer two questions:

- **Output decision**: If the firm produces, what output level, q, maximizes its profit or minimizes its loss?

- **Shutdown decision**: Is it more profitable to produce q or to shut down and produce no output?

The profit curve in Figure 7.1 illustrates these two basic decisions. This firm makes losses at very low and very high output levels and positive profits at moderate output levels. The profit curve first rises and then falls, reaching a maximum profit of π^* when its output is q^*. As this profit level is positive, the firm chooses to produce output q^* rather than shut down and earn no profit.

Output Rules.   A firm can use one of three equivalent rules to choose how much output to produce. These rules are just three different ways of stating essentially the same thing. The most straightforward rule is:

Output Rule 1: The firm sets its output where its profit is maximized.

If the firm knows its entire profit curve in Figure 7.1, it sets its output at q^* to maximize its profit at π^*.

Even if the firm does not know the exact shape of its profit curve, it may be able to find the maximum by experimenting. The firm slightly increases its output. If profit increases, the firm increases the output more. The firm keeps increasing output until profit does not change. At that output, the firm is at the peak of the profit curve. If profit falls when the firm first increases its output, the firm tries decreasing its output. It keeps decreasing its output until it reaches the peak of the profit curve.

What the firm is doing is experimentally determining the slope of the profit curve. The slope of the profit curve is the firm's **marginal profit**: the change in the profit the firm gets from selling one more unit of output, $\Delta\pi/\Delta q$, where $\Delta q = 1$. In Figure 7.1, the marginal profit or slope of the profit curve is positive when output is less than q^*, zero when output is q^*, and negative when output is greater than q^*. Thus,

Output Rule 2: A firm sets its output where its marginal profit is zero.

FIGURE 7.1 **Maximizing Profit**

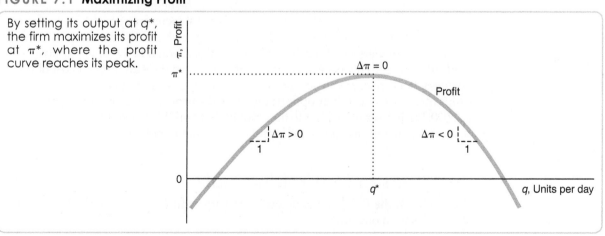

By setting its output at q^*, the firm maximizes its profit at π^*, where the profit curve reaches its peak.

A third way to express this profit-maximizing output rule is in terms of cost and revenue. The marginal profit depends on a firm's *marginal cost* and *marginal revenue*. A firm's **marginal cost** (**MC**) is the amount by which a firm's cost changes if it produces one more unit of output: $MC = \Delta C / \Delta q$, where ΔC is the change in cost when $\Delta q = 1$. Similarly, a firm's **marginal revenue** (**MR**) is the change in revenue it gets from selling one more unit of output: $\Delta R / \Delta q$, where ΔR is the change in revenue when $\Delta q = 1$. Provided *MR* is positive at output q, the firm earns more revenue by selling more units of output, but the firm also incurs an additional cost, $MC(q)$, which must be deducted from $MR(q)$ to determine the net effect on marginal profit. The change in the firm's profit is

$$\text{Marginal profit}(q) = MR(q) - MC(q).$$

Does it pay for a firm to produce one more unit of output? If the marginal revenue from this last unit of output exceeds its marginal cost, $MR(q) > MC(q)$, the firm's marginal profit is positive, $MR(q) - MC(q) > 0$, so it pays to increase output. The firm keeps increasing its output until it is producing the q, where its marginal profit $(q) = MR(q) - MC(q) = 0$. That is, the firm picks the q where its marginal revenue equals its marginal cost: $MR(q) = MC(q)$. Were the firm to produce more output so that its marginal cost exceeded its marginal revenue, $MR(q) < MC(q)$, the extra output would reduce the firm's profit. Thus, a third, equivalent rule is:

Output Rule 3: A firm sets its output where its marginal revenue equals its marginal cost:

$$MR(q) = MC(q). \tag{7.2}$$

Using Calculus

Maximizing Profit

We can use calculus to derive the condition that marginal revenue must equal marginal cost at the output level that maximizes profit. Using calculus, we define marginal revenue as the derivative of revenue with respect to output:

$$MR(q) = \frac{dR(q)}{dq}.$$

The derivative $dR(q)/dq$ is the limit of $\Delta R(q)/\Delta q$ as Δq gets very small. Our earlier definition of marginal revenue, $\Delta R(q)/\Delta q$ for $\Delta q = 1$, is nearly equivalent to the calculus definition if $\Delta q = 1$ is a "very small" change. Similarly, marginal cost is the derivative of cost with respect to output, $MC(q) = dC(q)/dq$ (Chapter 6).

To maximize profit in Equation 7.1, $\pi(q) = R(q) - C(q)$, the firm operates at the quantity q where the derivative of profit with respect to quantity is zero:

$$\frac{d\pi(q)}{dq} = \frac{dR(q)}{dq} - \frac{dC(q)}{dq} = MR(q) - MC(q) = 0. \tag{7.3}$$

The left side of Equation 7.3, $d\pi/dq$, is the firm's marginal profit. This result shows that marginal profit equals the difference in marginal revenue and marginal cost. Because this profit-maximizing condition requires that $MR(q) - MC(q) = 0$, it follows that the firm maximizes its profit when it chooses output such that $MR(q) = MC(q)$, which is the same condition as in Equation 7.2.[8]

Q&A 7.1

If a firm's revenue function is $R(q) = 120q - 2q^2$ and its cost function is $C(q) = 100 + q^2$, what output level maximizes its profit?

Answer

1. *Determine the marginal revenue and marginal cost by differentiating the revenue and cost functions.* The firm's marginal revenue is $dR(q)/dq = 120 - 4q$. Its marginal cost is $dC(q)/dq = 2q$.

2. *Equate the marginal revenue and marginal cost expressions to determine the output that maximizes profit.* Setting the marginal revenue equal to the marginal cost, we find that $120 - 4q = 2q$. Solving for q, we learn that the profit-maximizing output is $q = 20$.

3. *Alternatively, determine the profit function and then differentiate the profit function to find the maximum.* The profit function is $\pi(q) = R(q) - C(q) = [120q - 2q^2] - [100 + q^2] = 120q - 3q^2 - 100$. Taking the derivative of the profit function with respect to quantity (the marginal profit) and setting it equal to zero, we learn that $d\pi(q)/dq = 120 - 6q = 0$. Consequently, the profit-maximizing output is $q = 20$.

Managerial Implication

Marginal Decision Making

One of the most important implications of economics is that marginal analysis is very valuable to managers. If a manager knows the entire profit function (as in Figure 7.1), then it's easy to choose the profit-maximizing output. However, many managers are uncertain about what profit would be at output levels that differ significantly from the current level.

Such a manager can use marginal reasoning to maximize profit. By experimenting, the manager can determine if increasing output slightly raises profit—that is, the firm's marginal profit is positive (or, equivalently, its marginal revenue is greater than its marginal cost). If so, the manager should continue to increase output until the marginal profit is zero (marginal revenue equals marginal cost). Similarly, if marginal profit is negative, the manager should decrease output until marginal profit is zero.

Shutdown Rules. Producing the output level q such that $MR(q) = MC(q)$ is a necessary condition to maximize profit if the firm produces a positive output level. However, the firm might make losses even at the best possible positive output (although a smaller loss than at other positive outputs).

---

[8]For the quantity determined by the marginal condition, $MR = MC$ or $d\pi/dq = 0$, to maximize profit, a second-order condition must also hold: $d^2\pi/dq^2 < 0$. It is possible to have more than one *local* profit maximum, each of which satisfies the marginal condition. If the marginal condition holds at more than one quantity, the one with the highest profit is the *global* profit maximum.

Should the firm shut down if its profit is negative? Surprisingly, the answer is "It depends." The general rule, which holds for all types of firms in both the short run and the long run, is:

Shutdown Rule 1: The firm shuts down only if it can reduce its loss by doing so.

In the short run, the firm has variable costs, such as for labor and materials, and fixed costs, such as from plant and equipment (Chapter 6). If the fixed cost is *sunk*, this expense cannot be avoided by stopping operations—the firm pays this cost whether it shuts down or not. Thus, the sunk fixed cost is irrelevant to the shutdown decision. By shutting down, the firm stops receiving revenue and stops paying the avoidable costs (Chapter 6), but it is still stuck with its fixed cost. Thus, it pays for the firm to shut down only if its revenue is less than its avoidable cost.

Suppose that a firm's weekly revenue is $R = \$2,000$, its variable cost is $VC = \$1,000$, and its fixed cost is $F = \$3,000$, which is the price it paid for a machine that it cannot resell or use for any other purpose. This firm is making a short-run negative profit π (a loss):

$$\pi = R - VC - F = \$2,000 - \$1,000 - \$3,000 = -\$2,000.$$

If the firm shuts down, it still has to pay its fixed cost of $3,000, and hence it loses $3,000, which is a greater loss than the $2,000 it loses if it operates. Because its fixed cost is sunk, the firm should ignore it when making its shutdown decision. Ignoring the fixed cost, the firm sees that its $2,000 revenue exceeds its $1,000 avoidable, variable cost by $1,000, so it does not shut down. The extra $1,000 can be used to offset some of the fixed cost, reducing the firm's loss from $3,000 to $2,000.

However, if its revenue is only $500, it cannot cover its $1,000 avoidable, variable cost and loses an additional $500. When it adds this $500 loss to the $3,000 it must pay in fixed cost, the firm's total loss is $3,500. Because the firm can reduce its loss from $3,500 to $3,000 by ceasing operations, it shuts down. (Remember the shutdown rule: The firm shuts down only if it can reduce its loss by doing so.)

The firm's variable costs are always *avoidable*: The firm pays the variable costs only if it operates. In contrast, the firm's short-run fixed cost is usually *unavoidable*: The firm incurs the fixed cost whether or not it shuts down. Therefore, if the firm shuts down in the short run it incurs a loss equal to its fixed cost because it has no revenue ($R = 0$) or variable cost ($VC = 0$), so its profit is negative: $\pi = R - VC - F = 0 - 0 - F = -F$. If the firm operates and its revenue more than covers its variable cost, $R > VC$, then the firm does better by operating because $\pi = R - VC - F > -F$. Thus, the firm shuts down only if its revenue is less than its avoidable, variable cost: $R < VC$.

In conclusion, the firm compares its revenue to only its avoidable, variable costs when deciding whether to stop operating. If the fixed cost is sunk, the firm pays this cost whether it shuts down or not. The sunk fixed cost is irrelevant to the shutdown decision.

We usually assume that a fixed cost is sunk. However, if a firm can sell its capital for as much as it paid, its fixed cost is avoidable and should be taken into account when the firm is considering whether to shut down. A firm with a fully avoidable fixed cost always shuts down if it makes a short-run loss. If a firm buys a specialized piece of machinery for $1,000 that can be used only in its business but can be sold for scrap metal for $100, then $100 of the fixed cost is avoidable and $900 is sunk. Only the avoidable portion of fixed cost is relevant for the shutdown decision.

All capital and other inputs are adjustable in the long run, so all costs are avoidable. Thus, the firm can eliminate all costs by shutting down—it has no sunk fixed costs. In the long run, it pays to shut down if the firm faces any loss at all. As a result, we can restate the shutdown rule, which holds for all types of firms in both the short run and the long run, as:

Shutdown Rule 2: The firm shuts down only if its revenue is less than its avoidable cost.

Social Responsibility

Some managers pursue social objectives rather than maximize profit. Most enterprises in the nonprofit sector such as charities and religious organizations have social rather than financial objectives. Public-sector enterprises are often required by law to provide public services at prices below the profit-maximizing level. In the United States, public-sector corporations such as the Export-Import Bank and the Federal Deposit Insurance Corporation exist to support private-sector activity, not to maximize profit. Government-owned garbage companies may provide services at prices below what a profit-maximizing firm would charge.

Even some private-sector firms give up profit to achieve certain social goals. However, Milton Friedman, a Nobel Prize–winning economist, objected to such behavior. He argued that the sole responsibility of managers is to the owners of the firm, so managers should maximize profit.[9]

The philosopher and business professor R. Edward Freeman (1984) disagreed. According to his *stakeholder theory*, managers have obligations to several groups in addition to shareholders, including workers, customers, and the communities in which firms reside and operate. He contended that corporations should not use child labor in poor countries; they should provide safe working conditions and safe products; and they should not contaminate communities where they operate with toxic waste, even if such corporate policies reduce profit.

The pursuit of social objectives by corporations is called *corporate social responsibility* (CSR). However, as social responsibility is also relevant for unincorporated firms and for other types of organizations, many people refer to the *environmental, social, and governance* (ESG) objective.[10]

ESG has become increasingly important in managerial decision making, especially in large corporations. Most large corporations such as Exxon and Sony provide annual ESG reports.

Charitable Activities. ESG decisions are made by a firm's CEO and other senior managers, who often commit the firm to providing large contributions to hospitals, universities, environmental projects, disadvantaged groups, and other

---

[9]Milton Friedman, "The Social Responsibility of Business Is to Increase Its Profits," *New York Times Magazine*, September 13, 1970: 32–33.

[10]The world's largest developer of voluntary international standards, the International Organization for Standardization (ISO), has attempted to provide standards for social responsibility (**www.iso .org/iso/home/standards/management-standards/iso26000.htm**). The ISO defines social responsibility as "acting in an ethical and transparent way that contributes to the health and welfare of society." It identifies several major areas of social responsibility for business organizations, including the environment (or sustainability), governance, and other social issues such as treatment of employees, consumer safety, and charitable giving.

causes. A well-known example of corporate philanthropy is Ronald McDonald House Charities. It provides temporary housing and other support in over 50 countries for families of children who are hospitalized for extended periods.

However, such contributions may reduce returns to shareholders. These causes might seem worthy but, after all, as Friedman argued, if shareholders want to donate money for a new hospital or a new building on a university campus, they can do so directly. Shareholders might not want managers of the firms they invest in making such decisions for them.

Nonetheless, corporate shareholders sometimes propose ESG initiatives at shareholder meetings. Such ESG-related shareholder activism has been growing in frequency and raises the issue that different groups of shareholders might have different objectives.

In such circumstances, just what are the legal and ethical obligations of managers to shareholders? This topic has been the subject of much litigation. Courts have increasingly decided that businesses have implicit obligations to various stakeholders that often go beyond what is explicitly covered in formal contracts.

Strategic ESG. Purely *altruistic* ESG activities are costly to shareholders. However, some costly ESG activities may provide shareholders with significant benefits that more than offset the costs. For example, if consumers are willing to pay more for environmentally friendly products, then producing such products may raise a firm's profits. Similarly, a firm that acquires a reputation for treating its workers fairly may increase its sales or may be able to charge a higher price for its products.[11]

ESG activities that are intended to increase profits are called *strategic ESG* and are often described as "doing well by doing good." For example, McDonald's receives extensive, favorable media exposure and other reputational benefits from its Ronald McDonald Houses. ESG expenditures can often be more effective than conventional advertising in building consumer goodwill. In addition, some corporations believe that ESG activities prevent potentially costly government interventions.

Mini-Case	In the past few years, several trends in social responsibility have emerged. Not all of these activities reduce profits, but all are potentially important for the success of firms and society.
Trends in Social Responsibility	

1. *End of Workplace Harassment*: Susan Fowler published a whistle-blower essay in 2017 about sexism during her time at Uber. By 2018, the #MeToo movement was running strong, telling companies that women should not have to deal with sexual harassment any longer. As a result, founders, senior management, and others resigned or were fired at Uber, Fox, and other corporations.

2. *Increase Diversity*: Companies are under increasing pressure to hire and promote women, minorities, and other workers whom they have largely ignored or discriminated against in the past.

---

[11]Several fair trade labeling organizations, including Fairtrade International, designate certain products as *fair trade* products. The designation implies that certain standards of sustainability and treatment of workers have been met. Some consumers are willing to pay more for fair trade products (De Pelsmacker, Driesen, and Rayp, 2005).

3. *Involvement in Politics*: Corporations have always lobbied for special treatment, but, increasingly, heads of firms such as Facebook and Microsoft are speaking out on issues of social justice, such as border enforcement of immigration laws and anti-discrimination laws.

4. *Protect the Environment*: Many corporations, such as Google and Nike, are trying to slow global warming by reducing their carbon footprints and are lobbying for pro-environment policies.

5. *Brand Strategies Based on Philanthropy*: Some firms commit to making charitable contributions for each item consumers buy. For example, TOMS Shoes "Buy One, Give One" marketing strategy involves giving a poor child a pair of shoes for each pair purchased. Firms hope that some socially concerned consumers will buy from these companies rather than from their competitors for this reason.

Forcing Firms to Maximize Profit: The Survivor Principle and Competition for Corporate Control

Not all private-sector managers try to maximize profits. As we've seen, some have social objectives. Others fail to maximize profits through incompetence. Finally, some managers have selfish objectives that are inconsistent with owners' desire to maximize profits. They may want to gain personal prestige, to avoid working hard, or to maximize their own income.[12]

Why, then, do economists assume that most private-sector firms maximize profit? The two key reasons are the survivor principle and competition for corporate control.

Survivor Principle. According to the *survivor principle*, in perfectly competitive markets, the only firms that survive are those that maximize profit. Firms that fail to maximize profit lose money and are driven out of business.

The Struggle for Corporate Control. Managers who fail to maximize profit can be disciplined through *competition for corporate control*, where outside investors use the stock market to buy enough shares to take over control of an underperforming publicly traded corporation. An outsider may profit by seizing control of a company in which the current managers fail to maximize profits. After acquiring a controlling interest in an underperforming firm's stock, the acquirer can replace the current board and the current management, improve the profitability of the firm, and realize an attractive return on investment. Even if outside investors do not acquire full control of the firm, they can demand that the board replace current senior managers or that current managers pursue different policies. Such activist investors made demands on 805 companies in 2017, up from 570 in 2013.[13]

Of course, managers who fear losing their jobs resist such a takeover. For example, Sophia, the manager of an underperforming company, is worried because a

---

[12]For example, if a manager's compensation is based on sales, which are easy for owners to observe, rather than profit, which owners may not be able to observe, a manger may maximize revenue rather than profit. In Chapter 15, we analyze such conflicts between owners and managers and describe how to reduce their negative impact.

[13]Schulte, Roth, and Zabel, *The Activist Investing Annual Review*, 2018.

well-known corporate raider (such as Carl Icahn, Kirk Kerkorian, or T. Boone Pickens) is buying many shares of her firm.[14] She fears that the raider is planning a hostile takeover and will replace the current managers with new managers to turn around the underperforming firm. How does Sophia keep her job? If she can't instantly improve the firm's performance, she may hire the cleverest corporate lawyer she can find to construct takeover defenses.

Common defenses in the United States include a *shareholder rights plan*, which is better known as a *poison pill*. (See Table 7.1 for a list of takeover defense terminology.) A poison pill is a provision that a corporate board adds to its bylaws or charter that makes the firm a less attractive takeover target.

The law on the use of poison pills is evolving, with many countries limiting their use, including the United Kingdom and many other European countries. In Canada, regulatory authorities can remove provisions deemed to be poison pills from takeover bids, and they frequently do.

Poison pills do not always work in preventing a takeover, but they frequently cause some of the profits arising from the takeover to go to the original managers or

TABLE 7.1 Some Takeover Defense Terms

back-end plan: Provision that gives shareholders the right to cash or debt securities at an above-market price previously defined by the company's board in the event of a hostile takeover.

dead-hand: Provision that allows only the directors who introduce the poison pill to remove it for a fixed period after they have been replaced, thereby delaying a new board's ability to sell the firm.

flip-in: Provision that gives current shareholders of the firm other than the hostile acquirer the right to purchase additional shares of stocks at a discount price after the acquirer obtains a certain percentage of the firm's shares (usually between 20% and 50%).

flip-over: Provision that allows shareholders to buy the acquiring firm's shares at a discount price after a merger or takeover.

golden handcuffs: Employment clauses that require top employees to give back lucrative bonuses or incentives if they leave the firm within a specified period. As a poison pill, these clauses cease to hold after a hostile takeover so that the employees may quit immediately after cashing their stock options.

macaroni defense (similar to a flip-over): The issuance of many bonds with the condition they must be redeemed at an above-market price if the company is taken over.

poison pill, porcupine provision, shareholder rights plan, or shark repellent: Defensive provisions that corporate boards include in the firm's corporate charter or bylaws that make a takeover less profitable.

poison puts: The issuance of bonds that investors may cash before they mature in the event of a hostile takeover attempt.

---

[14]Corporate raiders are large investors who make hostile takeovers bids—seeking to buy a controlling interest in a firm despite the opposition of senior management. Sometimes, however, a raider will engage in *greenmail*, buying enough shares to credibly threaten a takeover, but agreeing to sell those shares back to the firm at a premium to end the takeover attempt.

boards of directors, so that they do not fight the takeover. The use of poison pills in the United States has declined significantly over the past two decades. Part of this decline resulted from requirements that shareholders vote on poison pills.

7.3 Profits Over Time

The rules for profit maximization described in the previous section apply when a firm's owners want the firm to maximize profit in the current period. This approach makes sense if actions today do not affect future profits, so the firm can ignore the future for now.

However, for many firms, their actions today affect future profits. A firm might make a costly investment today that will yield large profits in the future. For example, internet retailing giant Amazon lost money for years, investing much of the revenue it earned in improving its technology to increase its profits in future years. Such a firm should not necessarily shut down when incurring losses in early periods.

Managers must have some way of comparing early losses with later gains. They use interest rates to make these comparisons.

Interest Rates

Virtually everyone believes that a dollar today is more valuable than a dollar in the future. Consequently, a bank will only agree to loan you $1,000 for a year if you agree to return the $1,000 at the end of the year plus some additional amount. This additional amount, called *interest*, is determined by an **interest rate**: the percentage more that must be repaid to borrow money for a fixed period.[15]

Suppose a firm borrows $10,000 from a bank for one year at an annual interest rate of 5% (= 0.05). That is, the firm promises to repay the bank $1.05 one year from now for every dollar that it borrowed. At the end of the year, the firm must pay the bank $10,500 (= $10,000 × 1.05), which is the amount it borrowed, $10,000, plus the interest it owes, $10,000 × 0.05 = $500.

More generally, the amount of money the firm borrows today is the *present value* (*PV*) and the amount it must repay is the *future value* (*FV*). At an interest rate of i, at the end of the first year, the firm must repay

$$FV = PV(1 + i). \tag{7.4}$$

Compounding. Now suppose that the firm borrows the $10,000 for two years. Because it didn't pay the $500 interest it owed at the end of the first year, it is essentially borrowing $10,500 for the second year. Thus, for the second year, it owes interest on the $10,000 initial amount and on the $500 deferred interest payment. That is, it owes "interest on the interest." This accumulation of interest is called *compounding*. At the end of the second year, the firm owes

$$\$1,102.50 = (\$10,000 \times 1.05) \times 1.05 = \$10,000 \times 1.05^2.$$

[15]For simplicity, we refer to *the* interest rate throughout this chapter, but there are many interest rates. For example, a firm will usually have to pay a higher interest rate if it wants to borrow money for a longer period.

Generalizing, if the firm were to borrow for t years, it would owe $\$10,000 \times 1.05^t$ at the end of the last year.

Using Interest Rates to Connect Present and Future Values. Interest rates connect the value of money that a firm borrows today, the *present value* (PV), with the *future value* (FV) that it must repay later. The *FV* is the present value plus interest. As we've just seen, if the firm borrows PV today and allows the interest to compound for t years at an interest rate of i, then the future value, FV, it must repay is

$$FV = PV(1 + i)^t. \tag{7.5}$$

Similarly, if a firm is to receive a payment, FV, t years from now, the present value is

$$PV = \frac{FV}{(1 + i)^t}. \tag{7.6}$$

We obtain this last equation by dividing both sides of Equation 7.5 by $(1 + i)^t$. For example, if the interest rate is 5% and the firm will receive a payment of $\$10,500$ with certainty one year from now, the present value of this future payment is $PV = \$10,500/(1.05) = \$10,000$.

At high interest rates, money significantly in the future is worth very little today. Using Equation 7.6, we can calculate that a $\$1,000$ payment 25 years from now is worth only slightly more than $\$10$ today at a 20% interest rate: $PV = 1,000/(1.2)^{25} \approx 10,000/95.4 \approx \$10.50$.

Sometimes we want to calculate the present value of a stream of payments, such as the firm's annual profits over the next 15 years. We can generalize the relationships we have already developed to determine the present value of the stream of payments by calculating the present value of each future payment and then summing them.

Suppose an investor has a share of stock that pays $\$10$ in dividends at the end of each year for three years and nothing thereafter. If the interest rate is 10%, the present value of this series of payments is

$$PV = \frac{\$10}{1.1} + \frac{\$10}{1.1^2} + \frac{\$10}{1.1^3} \approx \$24.87.$$

More generally, a stream of payments of Y per year for t years given interest rate i has a present value of

$$PV = Y\left[\frac{1}{(1 + i)} + \frac{1}{(1 + i)^2} + \cdots + \frac{1}{(1 + i)^t}\right]. \tag{7.7}$$

If these payments are made at the end of each year forever, Equation 7.7 can be simplified. If the firm invests PV at i per year forever, it receives a payment of $Y = PV \times i$ each year forever. Dividing both sides of this equation by i, we find that

$$PV = \frac{Y}{i}. \tag{7.8}$$

Therefore, for a perpetual income flow of Y per period, the present value is simply the amount of the flow divided by the interest rate.

Investing and Profit Maximizing Over Time

How does a firm profit maximize over time? It maximizes the present value of the flow of its profits over time. Using interest rates, a firm can determine the present value of its profits over time. For example, if the interest rate is i, and the firm expects its profit to be π_1 in the first year, π_2 in the second year, π_3 in the third year, and zero thereafter, then the present value of this stream of profits is

$$PV = \frac{\pi_1}{1+i} + \frac{\pi_2}{(1+i)^2} + \frac{\pi_3}{(1+i)^3}.$$

We can use this approach to consider whether firms should make investments. Suppose that a firm makes a large investment this year, which lowers its profit this year, so that it will make a larger profit next year. The firm makes the investment if doing so raises the present value of its profits over the two years. For example, if the firm does not make the investment, it expects to make a $100,000 profit at the end of this year and at the end of next year. At an interest rate of 5%, its present value is

$$\$185{,}941.04 = \frac{\$100{,}000}{1.05} + \frac{\$100{,}000}{1.05^2}.$$

However, if it makes a $50,000 investment this year, its profit this year falls to $50,000, but its profit next year is $175,000. The present value of this stream of profits is

$$\$206{,}349.19 = \frac{\$50{,}000}{1.05} + \frac{\$175{,}000}{1.05^2}.$$

Q&A 7.2

You are the owner of a small building. You are considering two possibilities. First, you can sell the building for $550,000. Second, a major retail chain agrees to rent the property for the next five years, paying you an annual rent of $25,000, at the end of each of the five years. Then, at the end of the fifth year, it will buy the store from you for $600,000, so the final payment at the end of the fifth year is $625,000, including the last year's rent.

Use a spreadsheet to determine the present value of the second, rental option for interest rates of 3%, 5%, and 7%. What decision would you make for each interest rate?

Answer

1. *Open an Excel spreadsheet and put titles in the first row.* Put Year in cell A1, Payment in cell B1, 3% rate in cell C1, 5% rate in cell D1, and 7% rate in cell E1.

2. *Fill in columns A and B using the numbers given in the question.* Enter numbers 1 through 5 in cells A2 through A6, enter 25,000 in cells B2 through B5, and enter 625,000 in cell B6. Note that cell B6 incorporates the final rental payment of 25,000 and the sale price of 600,000.

3. *Enter the appropriate formulas to determine the present value of each payment in columns C through E.* Enter "=B2/(1.03)^A2" in cell C2, then copy this cell into cells C3 through C6. Enter "=B2/(1.05)^A2" in cell D2, then copy this cell into cells D3 through D6. And enter "=B2/(1.07)^A2" in cell C2, then copy this cell into cells E3 through E6.

4. *Calculate present values.* Put the title Present Value in cell A7. Then enter "=sum(C2:C6)" in cell C7 and copy this cell into cells D7 and E7.

After formatting, your spreadsheet should look as shown in the screenshot.

	A	B	C	D	E
1	Year	Payment	3% rate	5% rate	7% rate
2	1	25,000	24,272	23,810	23,364
3	2	25,000	23,565	22,676	21,836
4	3	25,000	22,879	21,596	20,407
5	4	25,000	22,212	20,568	19,072
6	5	625,000	539,130	489,704	445,616
7	Present Value		632,058	578,353	530,297

5. *Determine which of your two options has a higher present value for each interest rate.* Compare the present value under each interest rate with the present value of the first option to sell now, which is $550,000. If the interest rate is 3%, yielding a present value of $632,058, or 5%, yielding a present value of $578,353, you should opt for the rental option. If the interest rate is 7%, where the present value is $530,297, you should sell now.

Comment: The higher the rate, the lower the present value of a large payment that occurs five years from now.

Managerial Implication

Stock Prices Versus Profit

Many newspaper articles and business shows focus almost exclusively on the price of a share of the firm's stock rather than on its annual profit. Should a manager be more concerned about a firm's stock price than its profit?

It makes no difference whether the manager maximizes the stock price or profit if the stock price reflects the firm's profit, in which case the cumulative value of the firm's stock is the present value of owning the firm. The owner of stock in a corporation receives a share in the current and future profits of the firm. Therefore, the stock price should reflect current and future profits. The sum of the value of all the shares is the present value investors place on the flow of current and future profits.

If the firm earns an annual profit of π per year forever, the present value of that profit stream is π/i, where i is the interest rate (Equation 7.8). For example, if the firm earns $10 million a year forever and the interest rate is 5%, then the present value is $10/0.05 = $200 million. If shareholders expect this level of profit and the same interest rate to continue in the future and the firm issued one million shares of stock, then each share would sell for $200.

If the firm's profit were higher, then its present value would also be higher. For example, if the annual profit were expected to be $11 million per year forever (instead of $10 million), then the firm's present value would be $220 million and the value of each share would be $220. Thus, maximizing a constant profit flow maximizes the value of the firm and is therefore equivalent to maximizing the stock price.

However, if a firm's profit flow varies over time, then the link between a firm's profit and its stock price is more complex, and the stock price might be more relevant to managers than the current profit. Consider a firm that makes a major investment that causes it to suffer a loss this year but that results in higher profits in the future. If investors understand that the investment will pay off in the long run, the stock price rises after the investment is made. Thus, a manager who is concerned about a firm's long-run profit stream may try to maximize the present value of profit or, equivalently, maximize the firm's stock value, rather than concentrate on the profit this period. However, if investors are not well informed about the firm's current and expected future profits, so that the stock price does not closely track the present value of profits, then maximizing the stock price is not equivalent to maximizing the present value of profits.

7.4 The Make or Buy Decision

Managers make many decisions that affect the horizontal and vertical dimensions of a firm's organization. The *horizontal* dimension refers to the size of the firm in its primary market, while the *vertical* dimension refers to the various stages of the production process in which the firm participates.

To produce a good and sell it to consumers involves many sequential stages of production, marketing, and distribution activities. A manager must decide how many stages the firm itself will undertake. At each stage, a manager chooses whether to carry out the activity within the firm or to pay for it to be done by others. Deciding which stages of the production process to handle internally and which to buy from others is part of what is referred to as *supply chain management*.

Stages of Production

The turkey sandwich you purchase at your local food stand is produced and delivered through the actions of many firms and individuals. Farmers grow wheat and raise turkeys using inputs they purchase from other firms; processors convert these raw inputs into bread and turkey slices; wholesalers transfer these products from the food processors to the food stand; and, finally, employees at the food stand combine various ingredients to make a sandwich, wrap it, and sell it to you.

Figure 7.2 illustrates the sequential or *vertical* stages of a relatively simple production process. At the top of the figure, firms use raw inputs (such as wheat) to produce semi-processed materials (such as flour). Then the same or other firms use the semi-processed materials and labor to produce the final good (such as bread). In the last stage, the final consumers buy the product.

In the nineteenth century, production often took place along a river. Early stages of production occurred upstream, and then the partially finished goods were shipped by barge downstream—going with the flow of the river—to other firms that finished the product. These anachronistic river terms are still used to indicate the order of production: *Upstream* refers to earlier stages of production and *downstream* refers to later stages.

Vertical Integration

The number of separate firms involved in producing your turkey sandwich depends on how many steps of the process each firm handles. One possibility is that the food stand carries out many steps itself: making the sandwich, wrapping it, and selling it to you. An alternative is that one firm makes and wraps the sandwich and delivers it to another firm that sells it to you.

FIGURE 7.2 Vertical Organization

Raw inputs produced upstream are combined using a production process, $q = f(M, L)$, downstream to produce a final good.

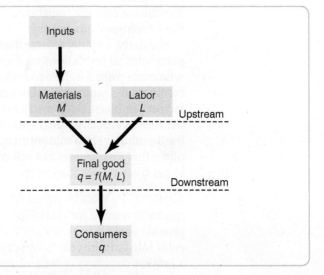

A firm that participates in more than one successive stage of the production or distribution of goods or services is **vertically integrated**. A firm may vertically integrate backward or *upstream* and produce its own inputs. For example, after years of buying its unique auto bodies from Fisher Body, General Motors purchased Fisher in a *vertical merger*. Or a firm may vertically integrate forward or *downstream* and buy its former customer. At different times, the car manufacturers General Motors and Ford have owned Hertz, the first car-rental company.[16]

The alternative to a firm producing an input or activity itself is to buy it. Firms may buy inputs from a market (such as buying corn on the Chicago Board of Trade or copper in the London Metal Exchange). Increasingly, many firms reach agreements with other firms to buy services from them on a continuing basis, a practice called *outsourcing*. For example, many U.S. computer manufacturing firms retain firms located in the United States, India, and elsewhere to provide services such as giving technical advice to their customers.

A firm can be partially vertically integrated. It may produce a good but rely on others to market it. Or it may produce some inputs itself and buy others from the market.

Quasi-Vertical Integration.

Some firms buy from a small number of suppliers or sell through a small number of distributors. These firms often control the actions of the firms with whom they deal by writing contracts that restrict the actions of those other firms. These contractual *vertical restraints* approximate the outcome from vertically merging. Such tight relationships between firms are referred to as *quasi-vertical integration*.

For example, a franchisor and a franchisee have a close relationship that is governed by a contract. Some franchisors such as Kentucky Fried Chicken (KFC) sell a proven method of doing business to individual franchisees, who are owners of

---

[16]Hertz, founded in 1918, was purchased by General Motors in 1926, which subsequently sold it. In 1954, Hertz went public. It was sold to a Ford Motor subsidiary in 1987 and became a fully owned Ford subsidiary in 1994. Hertz went public again in 2006.

KFC outlets. Such a fast-food franchisor may dictate the types of raw products its franchisees buy, the franchisees' cooking methods, the restaurants' appearance, and the franchisees' advertising.

Similarly, a manufacturer that contracts with a distributor to sell its product may place vertical restrictions on the distributor's actions beyond requiring it to pay the wholesale price for the product. These vertical restrictions are determined through contractual negotiations between the manufacturer and the distributor. The manufacturer imposes these restrictions to approximate the outcome that would occur if the firms vertically integrated. Examples of restrictions include requirements that the distributor sell a minimum number of units, that distributors not locate near each other, that distributors not sell competing products, and that distributors charge no lower than a particular price.

Contracts Versus Spot Markets.   Even if a company does not use the detailed contracts needed for quasi-vertical integration, it may sign long-term contracts that provide some features of vertical integration. For example, a furniture maker might enter into a multi-year contract to buy some specific annual quantity of wood from a lumber company at a fixed price. The furniture maker can then rely on a steady supply of wood at an affordable price, just as it would if it produced its own lumber in a vertically integrated structure.

If the furniture firm does not sign a long-term contract and does not vertically integrate, it buys lumber as it needs it at the current price from a variety of lumberyards or in a *spot market* or *cash market*: an organized market that sells commodities for immediate delivery (such as the Chicago Mercantile Exchange).

Degrees of Vertical Integration.   We see a spectrum of vertical integration ranging from full integration through quasi-integration and long-term contracts, to relying on spot markets. All firms are vertically integrated to some degree, but they differ substantially as to how many successive stages of production they perform internally. At one extreme, we have firms that perform only one major task and rely on markets and outsourcing for all others. For example, some retailers, such as computer retailers, buy products from a variety of manufacturers or markets, sell them to final consumers, and have any related service such as technical support for customers provided by other firms through outsourcing arrangements.

At the other extreme, we have firms that perform most stages of the production process. The leading broiler chicken producers, such as Tyson, Purdue, and Foster Farms, have integrated or quasi-vertically integrated (through the use of contracts) into virtually every production stage except the final stage of distribution to consumers.

The vertically integrated firms provide supplies to breeder farms that produce eggs. The breeder farms send eggs to a hatchery and the hatched chicks are sent to grow-out farms, where the birds grow to market weight. From there, the chickens go to the processing plant to be slaughtered and packed (either frozen or chilled). Packed chicken is then shipped to another company-owned plant for further processing into products such as frozen nuggets and chicken dinners. Finally, the products are sold to other firms such as fast-food restaurants and grocery stores for sale to final consumers (Martinez, 1999). By vertically integrating, these firms are able to take advantage of very large economies of scale at virtually every stage of the production process.

However, no firm is completely integrated: It would have to run the entire economy. Even Foster Farms buys some inputs, such as its equipment, from outside markets. As Carl Sagan observed, "If you want to make an apple pie from scratch, you must first create the universe."

Profitability and the Supply Chain Decision

Firms decide whether to vertically integrate, quasi-vertically integrate, or buy goods and services from markets or other firms, depending on which approach is the most profitable.[17] Although at first glance this profitability rule seems very simple, it has a number of tricky aspects. First, the firm has to take into account all relevant costs, including some that are not easy to quantify, such as transaction costs. Second, the firm must ensure a steady and timely supply of needed inputs to its production process. Third, the firm may vertically integrate, even if doing so raises its cost of doing business, so as to avoid government regulations.[18]

However, by vertically integrating and becoming larger and more complex, the firm may increase its managerial costs. Thus, firms do not always vertically integrate to avoid transaction costs and opportunistic behavior.

As a consequence of these complexities, firms in the same industry may reach different decisions about the optimal level of integration. We observe that such firms handle the supply chain in different ways. In the auto industry, Toyota is known as a leader in successful outsourcing and is less vertically integrated than its rivals such as General Motors and Ford.

Firms in some markets differ in how much they integrate because their managers have different strengths or the firms face different costs (such as costs that vary across countries). However, some of these firms could be making a mistake by being more or less integrated than other firms, if it lowers their profits and may drive them out of business.

Transaction Costs and Opportunistic Behavior. Among the most important reasons to integrate is to reduce transaction costs and to avoid **opportunistic behavior**: taking advantage of someone when circumstances permit.

By integrating, a firm can avoid the transaction costs of negotiating contracts. Instead of regularly negotiating deals with independent supply companies, a manager of a vertically integrated firm simply directs the input-producing section of the company to send the supplies. It can also minimize communication problems and better handle the timing of deliveries by vertically integrating.

Firms also vertically integrate to avoid opportunistic behavior. A firm may try to interpret the terms of a contract to its advantage, especially when terms are vague or missing. Such behavior is particularly likely when a firm deals with only one other firm: a classic principal-agent problem. If an electronic game manufacturer can buy computer chips from only one firm, it is at the mercy of that chip supplier. The supplier could take advantage of the situation by increasing its price substantially just before the holiday buying season. The game manufacturer may vertically integrate—manufacturing the chip itself—to avoid such opportunistic behavior.

Security and Flexibility of Supply. A common reason for vertical integration is to ensure supply of important inputs. Having inputs available on a timely basis is critical in many, if not most, industries. Costs would skyrocket if a car manufacturer

---

[17]For a more detailed analysis of the pros and cons of vertical integration, see Perry (1989) and Carlton and Perloff (2005). Two classic articles on vertical integration are Coase (1937) and Williamson (1975).

[18]Firms may also vertically integrate for reasons related to market power, allowing the firm to charge higher prices than it otherwise would or to reduce prices it would otherwise pay for its inputs. We discuss market power issues in later chapters.

had to stop assembling cars while waiting for a part. Backward (upstream) integration to produce the part itself may help to ensure timely arrival of parts. Alternatively, this problem may be eliminated through quasi-vertical integration, in which the buyer and seller agree to a contract whereby the supplier is rewarded for prompt delivery and penalized for delays. Toyota and other Japanese manufacturers pioneered the *just-in-time* system of having suppliers deliver inputs at the time needed to process them, thus minimizing inventory costs and avoiding bottlenecks.

Similarly, it is often important that a firm be able to vary its production quickly. If the demand curve shifts to the left during a recession, a firm may want to cut output, and hence temporarily reduce its use of essential inputs. By vertically integrating, firms may gain greater flexibility. PepsiCo Inc. offered to buy its two largest bottlers, Pepsi Bottling Group and PepsiAmericas, because, as PepsiCo Chairwoman and Chief Executive Officer Indra Nooyi said, "We could unlock significant cost synergies, improve the speed of decision making and increase our strategic flexibility."[19]

Mini-Case

Netflix

Netflix, a movie and television show distributor, disrupted the television industry. It currently has about 118 million streaming subscribers in 190 countries.

Netflix's chief executive, Reed Hastings, was asked whether Netflix was interested in vertically integrating forward into internet service provision or backward into producing its own shows. He replied,

> Vertical integration to the data transmission layer, no. In terms of content, we're now producing a lot of content ourselves. So that is a form of vertical integration that's been very successful for us.

He noted that Netflix works with about 600 internet service providers around the world, and that "Netflix is an application on top of the internet." Netflix benefits from letting subscribers connect to Netflix using whichever provider they prefer.

In contrast, vertically integrating into content provision works for them for three reasons: obtaining unique content, flexibility, and avoiding opportunistic behavior by film studios.

Although Netflix has 55 million U.S. subscribers, the average length of a subscription is only 43 months. In developing greater loyalty among its customers by providing high-quality, unique shows, such as *Stranger Things*, Netflix can keep subscribers longer.

With a steady stream of content, Netflix has flexibility in releasing films and a reliable pipeline.

By producing its own content, Netflix can avoid being the victim of opportunism. Netflix benefits from producing its own programming globally. For example, its globally popular show

---

[19]"PepsiCo Bids to Buy Its Bottlers," MarketWatch, April 20, 2009, **www.marketwatch.com/story/ pepsico-bids-buy-bottlers-reports**.

Narcos was produced for Netflix by a French company in Bogotá, Colombia, with a Brazilian star. Thus, Netflix is no longer dependent on a relatively small number of Hollywood production companies. These firms previously could subject Netflix to opportunistic behavior, threatening to cut off the supply of movies and shows with little notice unless Netflix paid them large sums.

Government Regulations. Firms may also vertically integrate to avoid government price controls, taxes, and regulations. A vertically integrated firm avoids *price controls* by selling to itself. For example, the U.S. government has set a maximum price for steel products on several occasions since World War II. Under such price controls, steel producers did not want to sell as much steel as before the controls took effect. Consequently, they rationed steel, selling their long-time customers only a fraction of what they had sold before the controls went into effect.

Because transactions within a company were unaffected by price controls, a buyer who really desired more steel could purchase a steel company and obtain all the steel it wanted (and at least one firm did so). Thus, purchasing a steel company allowed firms to avoid price controls. Were it not for the high transaction costs, firms could completely avoid price controls by vertically integrating.

More commonly, firms integrate to lower their taxes. Tax rates vary by country, state, and type of product. A vertically integrated firm can shift profit from one of its operations to another simply by changing the *transfer price* at which it sells its internally produced materials from one division to another. By shifting profits from a high-tax state or country to a low-tax state or country, a firm can increase its after-tax profits. The Internal Revenue Service tries to restrict such behavior by requiring that firms use market prices for internal transfers where possible.

Government regulations create additional incentives for a firm to integrate vertically (or horizontally) when the profits of only one division of a firm are regulated. When the government restricts the profit that a local telephone company earns on local services but not its profit on other services, such as selling telephones in competition with other suppliers, the telephone company tries to shift profits from its regulated division to its unregulated division.

Mini-Case

The Gig Economy

Traditionally, most firms vertically integrated by hiring workers instead of contracting with others to provide labor. The gig economy is disrupting this labor-employer relationship. In a *gig economy*, temporary jobs are common and firms contract with independent workers for short-term activities. For example, delivery services such as FedEx and UPS contract with extra temporary workers during the December holiday rush. Other gig jobs include driving for Lyft or Uber, freelance writing, and employment through temporary work agencies. The Federal Reserve reported in 2018 that nearly one-third of adults participate in gig work, either as their primary employment or to supplement other sources of income.

Part of the reason for the recent growth of the gig economy is that computers and smartphone apps have greatly reduced the transaction costs of short-term contracting, as when someone orders a Lyft ride. By contracting with temporary workers as needed, firms achieve greater flexibility and are able to avoid overhead costs such as providing work space and human resources services.

In addition, a major reason firms like using independent contractors is that the firms avoid having to pay half of the Social Security and Medicare taxes, which are 15% of income, as they must for full-time employees. They also avoid paying for unemployment insurance and workers' compensation in case of injury. Thus, government insurance requirements that apply only to full-time workers are a major cause of the trend toward gig employment.

Market Size and the Life Cycle of a Firm

Why do workers commonly engage in highly specialized activities? They do so because it is generally more efficient to divide production processes into several small steps in which workers specialize, with each worker becoming skilled in a certain activity.

Adam Smith, writing in Scotland at the time of the American Revolution, gave an example of a pin factory in *The Wealth of Nations* to illustrate that the division of labor can have important advantages in the "very trifling manufacture" of pins:

> [A] workman not educated to this business . . . nor acquainted with the use of machinery employed in it . . . could scarce, perhaps, with his utmost industry, make one pin a day, and certainly could not make twenty. But in the way in which this business is now carried on, not only the whole work is a peculiar trade, but it is divided into a number of branches, of which the greater part are likewise peculiar trades. One man draws out the wire, another straightens it, a third cuts it, a fourth points it, a fifth grinds it to the top for receiving the head; to make the head requires two or three distinct operations; to put it on, is a peculiar business, to whiten the pins is another; it is even a trade by itself to put them into the paper; and the important business of making a pin is, in this manner, divided into about eighteen distinct operations, which, in some manufactories, are all performed by distinct hands, though in others the same man will sometimes perform two or three of them. I have seen a small manufactory of this kind where ten men only were employed, and where some of them consequently performed two or three distinct operations. . . . [T]hey could, when they exerted themselves, make among them about twelve pounds of pins in a day [or] upward of forty-eight thousand pins in a day.

Using this insight about specialization, Henry Ford became the largest and probably the most profitable automobile manufacturer in the early 1900s by developing mass production techniques. He adapted the conveyor belt and assembly line so that he could produce a standardized, inexpensive car in a series of tasks in which individual workers specialized. By doing so, he achieved cost savings despite paying wages that were considerably above average.

Specialization is just as important in the modern economy as it was in Adam Smith's eighteenth-century pin factory or on Henry Ford's early twentieth-century assembly line. Recent research shows that surgeons who specialize in just a few procedures—performing each of those procedures many times—have much better results than surgeons who are less specialized. The value of specialization varies depending on the procedure and, not surprisingly, is greater for more complex procedures.[20]

---

[20]Melanie Evans, "A New Factor in Choosing a Surgeon," *Wall Street Journal*, September 19, 2016.

Despite the advantages of specialization, many workers and many firms do not specialize. Why? According to Adam Smith, the answer is that "the division of labor is limited by the extent of the market." That is, a firm can take advantage of specialization and economies of scale only if it produces a sufficiently large amount of output, which it produces only if enough consumers are willing to buy it.

Stigler (1951) and Williamson (1975) showed that Adam Smith's insight provides a theory of the life cycle of firms. They explain why firms rely on markets during certain periods, while during other periods, they vertically integrate. The key insight is that the degree of integration depends on the size of the market. If demand for a product at the current price is low so that the collective output of all the firms in the industry is small, each firm must undertake all the activities associated with producing the final output itself.

Why don't some firms specialize in making one of several inputs that they then sell to another firm to use in assembling the final product? The answer is that when the industry is small, it does not pay for a firm to specialize in one activity even given increasing returns to scale. A specialized firm may have a large setup or fixed cost. If the specialized firm produces large quantities of output, the average fixed cost per unit is small. In contrast, the average fixed cost is large in a small industry. Therefore, if specialized firms are to earn a profit, the sum of the specialized firms' prices must be higher than the cost of a firm that produces everything for itself.

As the industry expands, it may become profitable for a firm to specialize, because the per-unit transaction costs fall. That is, as the industry grows, firms *vertically disintegrate*. When the industry was small, each firm produced all successive steps of the production process, so that all firms were *vertically integrated.* In the larger industry, each firm does not handle every stage of production itself but rather buys services or products from specialized firms.

As an industry matures further, new products often develop and reduce much of the demand for the original product, so that the industry shrinks. As a result, firms again vertically integrate.

7.5 Market Structure

When making their horizontal and vertical decisions, managers need to take account of the behavior of actual and potential rival firms, which affect the profit function the manager's firm faces. So far, we have implicitly ignored the role of other firms. However, a firm's manager must take into account how its profit is affected by rival firms' output levels, the prices rivals set, or whether additional firms are likely to enter the market if the firm makes a large profit.

How rivals behave depends on the organization of the industry in which the firms operate. A firm will behave differently if it is one of a very large number of firms rather than the only one in the market. The behavior of firms depends on the **market structure**: the number of firms in the market, the ease with which firms can enter and leave the market, and the ability of firms to differentiate their products from those of their rivals.

The Four Main Market Structures

Most industries fit into one of four common market structures: perfect competition, monopoly, oligopoly, and monopolistic competition.

Perfect Competition. When most people talk about *competitive firms*, they mean firms that are rivals for the same customers. By this interpretation, any market that has more than one firm is competitive. However, economists often use the term *competitive* to refer to markets that satisfy the conditions for perfect competition (Chapter 2) or that closely approximate perfect competition.

Economists say that a market is perfectly competitive if each firm in the market is a *price taker*: a firm that cannot significantly affect the market price for its output or the prices at which it buys its inputs. Firms are likely to be price takers in markets where all firms in the market sell identical products, firms can freely enter and exit the market in the long run, all buyers and sellers know the prices charged by firms, and transaction costs are low. If any one of the 26,000 tomato producers in the United States were to stop producing or to double its production, the market price of tomatoes would not change appreciably. Similarly, by stopping production or doubling its production, a producer would have little or no effect on the price for fertilizer, labor, or other inputs.

Because firms can enter freely, firms enter whenever they see an opportunity to make a profit. This entry continues until the profit of the last firm to enter—the *marginal firm*—is zero.

Monopoly. A *monopoly* is the only supplier of a good that has no close substitute. De Beers, until recently, controlled the global diamond market. Monsanto has a monopoly in many genetically modified (GM) seeds. Many local public utilities such as cable television companies are local monopolies. Patents give monopoly rights to sell inventions, such as particular pharmaceuticals or GM seeds. A firm may be a monopoly if its costs are substantially below those of other potential firms.

A monopoly can *set* its price—it is not a price taker like a competitive firm. A monopoly's output is the market output, and the demand curve a monopoly faces is the market demand curve. Because the market demand curve is downward sloping, the monopoly—unlike a competitive firm—doesn't lose all its sales if it raises its price. As a consequence, the monopoly typically charges relatively high prices—much higher than the price set in a perfectly competitive market.

Oligopoly. An *oligopoly* is a market with only a few firms and with substantial barriers to entry, which prevent other firms from entering. A barrier to entry could be a government licensing law that limits the number of firms or patents that prevent other firms from using low-cost technologies. Nintendo, Microsoft, and Sony are oligopolistic firms that dominate the video game market. Only a handful of firms control the automobile, television, and aircraft manufacturing markets.

Because relatively few firms compete in an oligopolistic market, each can influence the price. One reason why oligopolies are price setters is because many oligopolies differentiate their products from those of their rivals. Because consumers perceive differences between a Honda Accord and a Toyota Camry, Toyota can raise the price of its Camry above the price of an Accord without losing all its sales. Some customers who prefer the Camry to the Accord will buy a Camry even if it costs more than an Accord.

Moreover, because an oligopoly has few firms, the actions of each firm affect its rivals. An oligopoly firm that ignores or inaccurately predicts its rivals' behavior is likely to lose profit. For example, as Toyota produces more cars, the price Honda can get for its cars falls. If Honda underestimates how many cars Toyota will produce, Honda may produce too many automobiles and lose money.

The need to consider the strategies of rival firms makes analyzing an oligopoly firm's profit-maximization decision more difficult than that of a monopoly or a competitive firm. A monopoly has no rivals, and a perfectly competitive firm ignores the behavior of individual rivals—it considers only the market price and its own costs in choosing its profit-maximizing output.

Oligopolistic firms may act independently or may coordinate their actions. A group of firms that explicitly agree (collude) to coordinate their activities is called a *cartel*. These firms may agree on how much each firm will sell or on a common price. By cooperating and behaving like a monopoly, the members of a cartel seek to earn the monopoly profit collectively—the maximum possible profit. In most developed countries, cartels are illegal. If oligopolistic firms do not collude, they earn lower profits than a monopoly, but usually earn higher profits than do firms in a competitive industry.

Monopolistic Competition. *Monopolistic competition* is a market structure in which firms are price setters but entry is easy. As in a monopoly or oligopoly, the market has few enough firms that each can affect the price. Indeed, monopolistically competitive firms often differentiate their products, which facilitates their ability to be price setters. However, as in competition, firms can freely enter, so the marginal firm earns zero profit.

Comparison of Market Structures

Table 7.2 summarizes the major features of these four market structures. The first row notes that perfectly competitive firms are price takers, whereas monopolies, oligopolies, and monopolistically competitive firms are price setters. Typically, monopolies charge higher prices than oligopolies and monopolistically competitive firms, while competitive firms charge lower prices.

In the long run in both competitive and monopolistically competitive markets, entry occurs until no new firm can profitably enter, so the marginal firm earns zero

TABLE 7.2 Properties of Monopoly, Oligopoly, Monopolistic Competition, and Perfect Competition

	Monopoly	Oligopoly	Monopolistic Competition	Perfect Competition
1. Ability to set price	Price setter	Price setter	Price setter	Price taker
2. Price level	Very high	High	High	Low
3. Entry conditions	No entry	Limited entry	Free entry	Free entry
4. Number of firms	1	Few	Few or many	Many
5. Long-run profit	≥ 0	≥ 0	0	0
6. Strategy dependent on individual rival firms' behavior	No (has no rivals)	Yes	Yes	No (cares only about market price)
7. Products	Single product	May be differentiated	May be differentiated	Undifferentiated
8. Example	Producer of patented drug	Automobile manufacturers	Plumbers in a small town	Apple farmers

economic profit. Monopolistically competitive markets typically have fewer firms than perfectly competitive markets do. Barriers to entry in a market result in a monopoly with one firm or an oligopoly with few firms. Monopolies and oligopolies may earn positive economic profits.

Oligopolistic and monopolistically competitive firms must pay attention to rival firms' behavior, in contrast to monopolistic or competitive firms. A monopoly has no rivals. A competitive firm ignores the behavior of individual rivals in choosing its output because the market price tells the firm everything it needs to know about its competitors. Oligopolistic and monopolistically competitive firms may produce differentiated products in contrast to monopolies and competitive firms.

Disruptive Innovations and the Evolution of Market Structure

Market structure is not static and can be affected by technological or organizational innovation. Most innovations are incremental, but some are sufficiently disruptive to dramatically change the way an industry is structured—or even to create new industries and destroy old ones. Trying to anticipate, join, or react to such *disruptive innovations* is an important challenge for modern managers.

Joseph Schumpeter (1942) referred to this process as *creative destruction*, while Clayton Christensen (1997) called it *disruptive innovation*. Christensen described the disruptive role of initially small innovators who displace large incumbents, often opening up a product class to a large group of new consumers. He noted that disruptive innovations need not be based on sophisticated advances in technology. Rather, a market disruption often arises from using "off-the-shelf" technologies in new and creative ways.

Small start-up companies often have a stronger incentive to innovate than incumbents precisely because they do not have an established position. An established firm that develops a new product that is better or cheaper than its existing product line runs the risk of cannibalizing its traditional business. A new start-up is free from such concerns.

Apple founders Steve Jobs and Steve Wozniak provide a classic example of such a disruption. They created the first commercially successful personal computer while working in the garage of Steve Jobs's parents with parts scavenged from nearby electronics stores. Ultimately, personal computers forced most of the traditional computer producers out of business, although IBM survived by quickly embracing the new technology. This innovation also brought the power of computing to the mass market, transforming many other industries along the way. This disruptive innovation of personal computers initially changed an oligopoly into a more competitive market (although later Apple and a few other personal computer companies formed a new oligopoly).

In contrast, a disruptive innovation might transform a competitive industry into a concentrated market. For example, the taxi industry has traditionally been competitive, but the disruptive innovation created by Uber in providing rides to passengers has given Uber an unprecedented level of market power in the industry. Amazon's innovations in e-commerce have already driven many "bricks and mortar" stores out of business and have allowed Amazon to develop an increasingly dominant position.

Road Map to the Rest of the Book

In Chapters 8 through 13, we examine the market outcomes under perfect competition, monopoly, oligopoly, and monopolistic competition. We start by examining competitive and monopoly firms, which can ignore the behavior of other firms.

Then we turn to oligopolies and other markets where firms need to develop strategies to compete with rival firms. In these chapters, we maintain the assumption that firms seek to maximize profits. In contrast, in Chapters 14 through 16 we return to the realistic issues introduced in this chapter concerning uncertainty, unequal information, and government regulation, which lead to agency problems. In Chapter 17, many of the issues raised in this chapter, such as outsourcing, are considered in a global context.

Managerial Solution

Amazon's Delivery Services

What issues should Amazon consider in deciding whether to rely primarily on other delivery services or develop its own capabilities? Given that the up-front investment in Shipping with Amazon (SWA) would cause Amazon to lose money for the first few years before turning a profit, how should Amazon decide whether this investment is worthwhile?

The answer to the first question turns on whether it is cost effective to rely on markets or to vertically integrate or quasi-vertically integrate. Initially, Amazon used markets, contracting with UPS, FedEx, USPS, and others to deliver its package. Now, Amazon believes that relying solely on those services results in high shipping costs, reduces its flexibility, results in unreliable services during periods of peak demand, and leaves it open to opportunistic behavior by these companies.

Amazon's first response, Flex, was to contract with individuals, which lowers its costs; increases its flexibility; and decreases its reliance on the major delivery services, reducing the possibility of opportunistic behavior. Its second option of contracting with individuals to use its trucks for delivery is a form of quasi-vertical integration. It is similar to the Flex program.

The third option, SWA, is a form of vertical integration. It requires a major investment initially, with a payoff in the future. This investment cannot pay unless its present value is positive. To simplify the story, we consider a two-year planning horizon. Suppose that the large investment causes Amazon's profit to be negative in year 1, $\pi_1 < 0$, so it is making a loss. However, its profit in year 2 is a large positive number, $\pi_2 > 0$. Thus, at an interest rate of i, the present value of this investment is $PV = \pi_1 + \pi_2/(1 + i)$. If this amount is greater than the present value of Amazon's profits over the two years if it does not make this investment, then the investment pays.

SUMMARY

1. **Ownership and Governance of Firms.** For-profit firms are normally organized as sole proprietorships, partnerships, or corporations. Owners may manage small companies (particularly sole proprietorships and partnerships) themselves, but owners of larger firms (particularly corporations) typically hire managers to run such firms. Most firms and most economic activity are in the for-profit sector, but government-owned firms and nonprofit firms are also important.

2. **Profit Maximization.** Most firms maximize economic profit, which is revenue minus opportunity cost. A firm

earning zero economic profit is making as much as it could if its resources were devoted to their best alternative uses. To maximize profit, a firm must make two decisions. First, the firm determines the quantity at which its profit is highest. Profit is maximized when marginal profit is zero or, equivalently, when marginal revenue equals marginal cost. Second, the firm decides whether to produce at all. It shuts down if doing so reduces a loss (negative profit) it would otherwise suffer. Nonprofit firms do not maximize profit, such as non-profit hospitals. In addition, some for-profit firms may forego some profits to pursue social objectives. However, market pressures make it difficult for most firms to deviate substantially from profit-maximizing behavior.

3. **Profits Over Time.** Interest rates reflect how much more people value a dollar today than a dollar in the future. To compare a future payment to one made today, we calculate the present value of the future payments using the relevant interest rate. A firm chooses between two options with different cash flows over time by picking the one with the higher present value.

4. **The Make or Buy Decision.** A firm may engage in many sequential stages of production itself; perform only a few stages itself and rely on markets for others; or use contracts or other means to coordinate its activities with those of other firms, depending on which approach is most profitable. A firm may vertically integrate (participate in more than one successive stage of the production or distribution of goods or services); quasi-vertically integrate (use contracts or other means to control firms with which it has vertical relations); or buy from others, depending on which is more profitable. Key incentives to vertically integrate include lowering transaction costs, ensuring a steady supply, and avoiding government restrictions.

5. **Market Structure.** A firm's profit depends in large part on the market structure, which reflects the number of firms in the market, the ease with which firms can enter and leave the market, and the ability of firms to differentiate their products from those of their rivals. The major market structures are perfect competition, monopoly, oligopoly, and monopolistic competition. Competitive firms are price takers, whereas others are price setters. Oligopolies and monopolistically competitive firms, unlike competitive firms and monopolies, must take account of rivals' strategies and may differentiate their products. Competitive and monopolistically competitive firms are in markets where entry by potential rivals is easy, so economic profit is driven to zero.

QUESTIONS

All exercises are available on **MyLab Economics**; * = *answer at the back of this book;* C = *use of calculus may be necessary;* ✗ = *this exercise is available in Excel Grader in* **MyLab Economics**.

1. Ownership and Governance of Firms

1.1 What types of firms would not normally maximize profit?

*1.2 Describe three important consequences of "going public" by selling shares in an initial public offering.

1.3 What types of firm organization allow owners of a firm to obtain the advantages of limited liability?

1.4 Has Chinese government control of industrial production declined significantly over the past several decades? Quantify your answer. (*Hint*: See the Mini-Case "Chinese State-Owned Enterprises.")

2. Profit Maximization

2.1 A firm has three different production facilities, all of which produce the same product. While reviewing the firm's cost data, Jasmin, a manager, discovers that one of the plants has a higher average cost than the other plants and suggests closing this plant. Another manager, Joshua, notes that the high-cost plant has high fixed costs but that the marginal cost in this plant is lower than in the other plants. He says that the high-cost plant should not be shut down but should expand its operations. Who is right?

*2.2 A firm has revenue given by $R(q) = 100q - 3q^2$ and its cost function is $C(q) = 100 + 10q$. What is the profit-maximizing level of output? What profit does the firm earn at this output level? (*Hint*: See Q&A 7.1.) C

2.3 Should a firm ever produce if it is losing money? Why or why not?

*2.4 Should a firm shut down if its weekly revenue is $1,000, its variable cost is $500, and its fixed cost is $800, of which $600 is avoidable if it shuts down? Why?

2.5 A firm has to pay a tax equal to 25% of its revenue. Give a condition that determines the output level at which it maximizes its after-tax profit. (*Hint*: See "Using Calculus: Maximizing Profit" and Q&A 7.1.) C

2.6 Milton Friedman argued that managers should try to maximize profit. Does his view conflict with the actions taken by senior executives of McDonald's to use corporate resources to support Ronald McDonald House projects? Explain.

2.7 According to *stakeholder theory*, what are the social responsibilities of managers?

2.8 The Mini-Case "Trends in Social Responsibility" lists several themes related to social responsibility in business that have generated recent attention. Is it possible that efforts made by managers to address some of these themes would increase profits? Explain briefly.

2.9 Why does competition for corporate control encourage firms to maximize profits?

2.10 Give examples of steps taken by corporate management to avoid takeovers that are not in shareholders' best interests.

2.11 An acquiring firm, *A*, seeks to buy a target firm, *T*. The acquiring firm has better managers. The value of the target firm, if acquired by *A*, is $100 million. The value of the target firm under its current management is only $80 million. However, the managers of *T* can impose a poison pill that would reduce the value of firm *T* to the acquirer by amount *P* without providing any benefit to shareholders of *T*. What is the minimum value of *P* that would prevent *A* from acquiring *T*? What is the cost of this poison pill to shareholders of the two firms?

3. Profits Over Time

3.1 Many retirement funds charge an administrative fee equal to 0.25% on managed assets. Suppose that Alexx and Spenser each invest $5,000 in the same stock this year. Alexx invests directly and earns 5% a year. Spenser uses a retirement fund and earns 4.75%. At the end of one year, how much will Alexx and Spenser have?

3.2 Using the information from the previous question, if Alexx and Spenser leave their investments in place for 30 years, with annual compounding of the interest, how much more will Alexx have than Spenser at the end of the 30-year period? (*Hint*: You can answer this question using a spreadsheet as in Q&A 7.2.)

3.3 A local pizzeria buys a used car to make pizza deliveries. It pays $2,000 down and $2,000 a year for two more years. What is the present value of these payments at a 5% interest rate?

3.4 A firm that owns and manages rental properties is considering buying a building that would cost $800,000 this year, but would yield an annual revenue stream of $50,000 per year for the foreseeable future. For interest rates smaller than what value would this purchase increase the present value of the firm?

3.5 At the time of its initial public offering (initial sale of stock), Groupon, an internet company that provides discount coupons, used unusual measures of its business performance (Michael J. de la Merced, "Abracadabra! Magic Trumps Math at Web Start-Ups," **dealbook.nytimes.com**, June 17, 2011). One such measure used by Groupon was *acsoi* (pronounced "ack-soy" or, alternatively, "ack-swa") for "adjusted consolidated segment operating income." Acsoi is operating profit before subtracting the year's online marketing and acquisition expenses. The firm's profit was negative, but its acsoi was positive. Groupon argued that acsoi marketing and acquisition expenses were an investment that would build future business and whose costs should therefore be amortized (spread out over time). If shareholders care about the stock price or the present value of the company, is acsoi an appropriate measure?

3.6 You work for a large mineral exploration company and propose buying new state-of-the-art equipment. The equipment is expensive and so is training employees to use it, but it will increase the yield of exploration activities in the future. The CEO of the company says that because your plan has high current costs it will depress the stock market value of the company. Does an investment that lowers current profit but increases future profit necessarily lower current stock prices? Explain briefly. (*Hint*: See the Managerial Implication "Stock Prices Versus Profit").

4. The Make or Buy Decision

*4.1 In 2012, the Campbell Soup Company acquired Bolthouse Farms for $1.55 billion. This acquisition increased the level of vertical integration in Campbell, as Bolthouse Farms owned and operated extensive farming operations where it produced many food items used in Campbell's products. Suppose that the value of produce provided by these farms after the acquisition would be $75 million per year for Campbell and that, in addition, Campbell could save $10 million per year in costs it would otherwise spend in searching for and negotiating over equivalent produce. However, the transaction cost of the acquisition (lawyers' fees, relocating some production facilities, paying severance to unnecessary employees, etc.) required a one-time payment of $50 million. If the interest rate used to discount future earnings is 5%, what is the gain to Campbell's from the acquisition?

4.2 Katie's Quilts is a small retailer of quilts and other bed linen products. Katie currently purchases quilts from a large producer for $100 each and sells them in her store at a price that does not change with the number of quilts she sells. Katie is considering vertically integrating by making her own quilts. If the fixed cost of vertically integrating is $10,000 and she can produce quilts at $50 per quilt, her total cost of producing quilts, *q*, herself is $C = 10,000 + 50q$. How many quilts does Katie need to sell for vertical integration to be a profitable decision?

4.3 A producer of ballpoint pens has been purchasing ink from an ink supplier and is considering acquiring the ink supplier. Would the pen company be more or less likely to vertically integrate by buying the ink manufacturer if the government taxes ink?

4.4 Based on the Mini-Case "NetFlix," did NetFlix undertake backward or forward integration? What were the primary benefits from the integration strategy that it chose?

4.5 As described in the Mini-Case "The Gig Economy," has the gig economy increased or decreased the extent of vertical integration? Explain briefly. What is the role of technological progress and what is the role of government policy in the growth of the gig economy?

4.6 When the western part of the United States was sparsely populated, many small towns had a single schoolhouse in which one teacher taught all subjects to students of all ages. Now, in large cities, teachers are often highly specialized, teaching a single subject, such as mathematics, to just one grade level. Explain why this change occurred by making reference to Adam Smith's famous description of a pin factory.

4.7 What are some of the major reasons that firms vertically integrate? Why don't these factors cause all firms to vertically integrate?

5. Market Structure

5.1 Which market structure best describes (a) airplane manufacturing, (b) electricians in a small town, (c) farms that grow tomatoes, and (d) cable television in a city? Explain your reasoning.

5.2 Describe the effects of the internet on the empirical relevance of perfect competition. Focus specifically on how the internet has affected the availability of price and product information, whether it has increased or decreased search costs and other transaction costs, and whether it has increased the ability of large numbers of buyers and sellers to interact.

5.3 The development of mini-mills was a disruptive innovation in the steel industry. Before mini-mills, steel production had substantial economies of scale and steel companies had to be very large to take full advantage of those economies. Mini-mills eliminated the advantage of large size in steel production. What effect do you think mini-mills had on market structure in the steel industry?

6. Managerial Problem

6.1 Would an increase in interest rates make the Shipping With Amazon (SWA) option more attractive or less attractive to Amazon? Show formally using an equation involving interest rates to explain your answer

7. MyLab Economics Spreadsheet Exercises[21]

*7.1 A firm's revenue function is $R(q) = 90q - 2q^2$. Its cost function is $C(q) = 104 + 6q + 1.5q^2$.

a. Using Excel, calculate the levels of revenue, total cost, and profit for the firm for $q = 0, 1, 2, \ldots, 24$. Determine the profit-maximizing output and the maximum profit for the firm.

b. Using Excel, draw the graph of the profit curve and determine the profit-maximizing level of output.

c. The firm's marginal revenue function is $MR = 90 - 4q$ and the marginal cost function is $MC = 6 + 3q$. Using Excel, calculate MR and MC for $q = 0, 1, 2, \ldots, 24$. Verify that the "$MR = MC$" rule determines the same profit-maximizing output as you found in part a.

7.2 A firm has the same revenue and cost function as in Spreadsheet Exercise 7.1.

a. The shareholders of the firm hire a manager on a profit-sharing basis whose payment, M, is 25% of the firm's profit: $M = 0.25(R - C)$. The shareholders receive the remaining 75%, so their income is $S = 0.75(R - C)$. Add columns for M and S to the spreadsheet in part a of Spreadsheet Exercise 7.1 and calculate the manager's payment and the shareholders' income for $q = 0, 1, 2, \ldots, 20$. Determine the amount of output that the manager will produce if the manager's objective is to maximize his or her own compensation.

b. Now suppose that the manager receives compensation equal to 10% of revenue, so that the return to the owners is $S = 0.9R - C$. Use Excel to determine the return to the manager and the return to the owners for $q = 0, 1, 2, \ldots, 20$.

*7.3 Second Look Enterprises (SLE) buys old computers, fixes them up, and resells them. Its weekly revenue function is $R = 40q - 2q^2$, so its marginal revenue is $MR = 40 - 4q$. Its weekly cost function is $C = 10q + 0.5q^2$, so its marginal cost is $MC = 10 + q$.

a. Use Excel to calculate SLE's revenue, cost, and profit for $q = 1$ to $q = 20$ in increments of 1. SLE's manager wants to maximize profit. Based on these calculations, what output does the manager choose? Create columns in your spreadsheet for MR and MC and verify that $MR = MC$ at the profit-maximizing output level.

b. Now assume that SLE is run by a manager who is paid 10% of the revenue and therefore wants to maximize revenue. How much output does the firm produce now? What is marginal revenue at this output level?

c. Now suppose that SLE is acquired and managed by a philanthropist who wants to promote recycling of used computers and therefore produces as much output as possible as long as the firm does not make losses. What output does SLE produce now?

---

[21]The spreadsheet exercises in this chapter are based largely on the work of Satyajit Ghosh, in cooperation with the authors. The answers are available on **MyLab Economics**.

Competitive Firms and Markets

8

The love of money is the root of all virtue.
—George Bernard Shaw

Managerial Problem

The Rising Cost of Keeping On Truckin'

To plan properly, managers need to be able to predict the impact of new government regulations on their firms' costs, their sales, and their probability of surviving. Managers complain constantly about the costs and red tape that government regulations impose on them. The highly competitive U.S. trucking industry has a particular beef. In recent years, federal and state fees have increased substantially and truckers have had to adhere to many new regulations.

The Federal Motor Carrier Safety Administration (FMCSA), along with state transportation agencies in 41 states, administers interstate trucking licenses through the Unified Carrier Registration Agreement. According to FMCSA's website in 2018, it has 40 different areas of regulation, each of which contains multiple specific items, including regulations on noise, drivers, hazardous materials, preserving records, and transporting migrant workers. A trucker must also maintain minimum insurance coverage, pay registration fees, and follow policies that differ across states before the FMCSA will grant permission to operate. The registration process is so complex and time consuming that firms pay substantial amounts to brokers who expedite the application process and take care of state licensing requirements.

For a large truck, the annual federal interstate registration fee can exceed $8,000. To operate, truckers and firms must pay for many additional fees and costly

regulations. These largely lump-sum costs—which are not related to the number of miles driven—have increased substantially in recent years. In 2017, regulations took effect requiring each truck to have an electronic onboard recorder, which documents travel time and distance, with an annualized cost of several hundred dollars per truck.

What effect do these new fixed costs have on the trucking industry's market price and quantity? Are individual firms providing more or fewer trucking services? Does the number of firms in the market rise or fall? (As we'll discuss at the end of the chapter, the answer to one of these questions is surprising.)

To answer questions about industry price and quantity, we need to combine our understanding of demand curves with knowledge about firm and market supply curves. We start our analysis of firm behavior by addressing the fundamental question: "How much should a firm produce?" To pick a level of output that maximizes its profit, a firm must consider its cost function and how much it can sell at a given price. The amount the firm thinks it can sell depends on the market demand of consumers and on its beliefs about how other firms in the market will behave. As described in Chapter 7, how a firm should approach such issues depends on the market's structure. We identified four primary market structures—monopoly, oligopoly, monopolistic competition, and perfect competition—that differ based on such attributes as the number of firms in the market, the control firms have over market prices, the ease with which firms can enter and leave the market, and the ability of firms to differentiate their products from those of their rivals.

This chapter focuses on *perfect competition*, a market structure in which there are so many buyers and sellers that each market participant is a *price taker*, who cannot affect the market's equilibrium price. Perfect competition is an important market structure for two main reasons. First, a significant part of the economy—including much of agriculture, finance, construction, real estate, wholesale and retail trade, and many service industries—is highly competitive and is well described by the model of perfect competition. Second, a competitive market is the only market structure that maximizes a commonly used measure of economic well-being (*total surplus*) and thus serves as a baseline against which to compare the economic outcomes of other market structures.

Learning Objectives

1. Describe the characteristics of perfect competition.
2. Graphically identify the competitive equilibrium and derive the short-run supply curve.
3. Contrast the short-run and long-run competitive equilibria and supply curves.
4. Use the concept of surplus to show the main advantage of perfect competition.

8.1 Perfect Competition

Perfect competition is a market structure in which buyers and sellers are price takers. A price-taking firm cannot affect the market price for the product it sells. A firm is a price taker if it faces a demand curve for its product that is horizontal at the market price. That is, it can sell as much as it wants at the market price, so it has no incentive to lower its price to gain more sales. If it raises its price even slightly, it sells nothing, as consumers can buy the product for less elsewhere. Thus, the firm sells its product at the market price. In this section, we discuss how the characteristics of a perfectly competitive market lead to price taking and how much a market can deviate from these characteristics and still be regarded as a competitive market.

Characteristics of a Perfectly Competitive Market

Perfectly competitive markets have five characteristics that force firms to be price takers:

1. The market consists of many small buyers and sellers.
2. All firms produce identical products.
3. All market participants have full information about price and product characteristics.
4. Transaction costs are negligible.
5. Firms can freely enter and exit the market in the long run.

Large Numbers of Buyers and Sellers. If the sellers in a market are small and numerous, no single firm can raise or lower the market price. The more firms in a market, the less any one firm's output affects the market output and hence the market price.

For example, the 316,000 U.S. corn farmers are price takers. If a typical grower were to drop out of the market, market supply would fall by only $1/316,000 = 0.00032\%$, so the market price would not be noticeably affected. Each corn farm can sell as much output as it can produce at the prevailing market equilibrium price, so each farm faces a demand curve that is a horizontal line at the market price.

Similarly, perfect competition requires that buyers be price takers as well. In contrast, if firms sell to only a single buyer—such as producers of weapons that are allowed to sell to only the government—then the buyer can set the price and the market is not perfectly competitive.

Identical Products. Firms in a perfectly competitive market sell *identical* or *homogeneous* products. Consumers do not ask which farm grew a particular Granny Smith apple because they view all Granny Smith apples as essentially identical products. If the products of all firms are identical, it is difficult for any single firm to raise its price above the going price charged by other firms.

In contrast, in the automobile market, which is not perfectly competitive, the characteristics of a Ferrari and a Honda Civic differ substantially. These products are *differentiated* or *heterogeneous*. Competition from Civics is not in itself a very strong force preventing Ferrari from raising its price.

Full Information. If buyers know that different firms are producing identical products and they know the prices charged by all firms, no single firm can unilaterally raise its price above the market equilibrium price. If it tried to do so, consumers would buy the identical product from another firm. However, if consumers are unaware that products are identical or they don't know the prices charged by other firms, a single firm may be able to raise its price and still make sales.

Negligible Transaction Costs. Perfectly competitive markets have very low transaction costs. Buyers and sellers can easily find each other and can trade without hiring lawyers to write contracts. If transaction costs are low, it is easy for a customer to buy from a rival firm if the customer's usual supplier raises its price.

In contrast, if transaction costs are high, customers may absorb a price increase from their traditional supplier to avoid incurring a substantial transaction cost in finding and contracting with a new supplier. Because some consumers prefer to buy a carton of milk at a local convenience store rather than travel several extra miles to a supermarket, the convenience store can charge slightly more than the supermarket without losing all its customers.

In some perfectly competitive markets, many buyers and sellers are brought together in a single room or online so that transaction costs are virtually zero. Transaction costs are very low at Flora Holland's daily plant and cut flower auctions in the Netherlands, which attract 7,000 suppliers and 4,500 buyers from around the world. The auction has about 125,000 transactions every day, with 12 billion cut flowers and 1.3 billion plants trading in a year.

Free Entry and Exit. The ability of firms to enter and exit a market freely in the long run leads to a large number of firms in a market and promotes price taking. Suppose a firm could raise its price and make a higher profit. If other firms can quickly and easily enter the market, the higher profit encourages entry by new firms until the price is driven back to the original level. Free exit is also important: If firms can freely enter a market but cannot quickly exit if prices decline, they are reluctant to enter the market in response to a possibly temporary profit opportunity.[1]

Perfect Competition in the Chicago Mercantile Exchange. The Chicago Mercantile Exchange, where buyers and sellers can trade wheat and other commodities, exhibits the characteristics of perfect competition, including a very large number of buyers and sellers who are price takers. Anyone can be a buyer or a seller. Indeed, a trader might buy wheat in the morning and sell it in the afternoon. They trade virtually *identical products*. Buyers and sellers have *full information* about products and prices, which is posted for everyone to see. Market participants waste no time finding someone who wants to trade and they can easily place buy or sell orders in person, over the telephone, or electronically without paperwork, so *transaction costs are negligible*. Finally, *buyers and sellers can easily enter this market and trade wheat*. These characteristics lead to an abundance of buyers and sellers and to price-taking behavior by these market participants.

Deviations from Perfect Competition

Many markets possess some, but not all, the characteristics of perfect competition. Such markets are still highly competitive, so that buyers and sellers are, for all practical purposes, price takers. For example, a government may limit entry into a market, but if the market has many buyers and sellers, they may still be price takers. Many cities use zoning laws to limit the number of certain types of stores or motels, yet such cities still have a large number of these firms. Other cities impose moderately large transaction costs on entrants by requiring them to buy licenses, post bonds, and deal with a slow-moving city bureaucracy, yet a significant number of firms still enter the market. Similarly, even if only some customers have full information, that may be sufficient to prevent firms from deviating significantly from price taking. For example, tourists do not know the prices at various stores, but, because locals know, no store can stay in business if it charges unusually high prices.

Economists use the terms *competition* and *competitive* more restrictively than do others. To an economist, a competitive firm is a price taker. In contrast, when most people talk about competitive firms, they mean that firms are rivals for the same customers. Even in an oligopolistic market (Chapter 7) with only a few firms, the firms compete for the same customers so they are competitive in this broader sense. From now on, we will use the terms *competition* and *competitive* to refer to all markets in which no buyer or seller can significantly affect the market price—they are price takers—even if the market is not perfectly competitive.

8.2 Competition in the Short Run

In this section, we examine the profit-maximizing behavior of competitive firms, derive their supply curves, and determine the competitive equilibrium in the short run. In the next section, we examine the same issues in the long run.

---

[1]For example, some governments, particularly in Europe, require firms to give workers six months' warning before they can exit the market.

The *short run* is a period short enough that at least one input cannot be varied (Chapter 5). Because a firm cannot quickly build a new plant or make other large capital expenditures, a new firm cannot enter a market in the short run. Similarly, a firm cannot fully exit in the short run. It can choose not to produce—to shut down—but it is stuck with some fixed inputs such as a plant or other capital that it cannot quickly sell or assign to other uses. In the long run, all inputs can be varied so firms can enter and fully exit the industry.

We treat the short run and the long run separately for two reasons. First, profit-maximizing firms may choose to operate at a loss in the short run, whereas they do not do so in the long run. Second, a firm's long-run supply curve typically differs from its short-run supply curve.

Economists usually assume that *all* firms—not just competitive firms—want to maximize their profits. This assumption is reasonable for at least two reasons (Chapter 7). First, many owners and managers of firms say that their objective is to maximize profits. Second, firms—especially competitive firms—that do not maximize profit are likely to lose money and be driven out of business. As we showed in Chapter 7, all firms—not just competitive firms—use a two-step decision-making process to determine how to maximize profit:

1. **How much to produce.** A firm first determines the output that maximizes its profit or minimizes its loss.

2. **Whether to produce.** Given that it has determined its profit-maximizing output, the firm decides whether to produce this quantity or shut down, producing no output.

How Much to Produce

As Chapter 7 shows, any operating firm—not just a competitive firm—maximizes its profit or minimizes its loss by setting its output where its marginal profit is zero or, equivalently, where its marginal revenue equals its marginal cost: $MR(q) = MC(q)$.[2] A competitive firm can easily determine its marginal revenue. Because it faces a horizontal demand curve, a competitive firm can sell as many units of output as it wants at the market price, p. Thus, a competitive firm's revenue, $R = pq$, increases by p if it sells one more unit of output, so its marginal revenue is p. For example, if the firm faces a market price of \$1 per unit, its revenue is \$5 if it sells 5 units and \$6 if it sells 6 units, so its marginal revenue for the sixth unit is \$1 = \$6 − \$5, which is the market price.[3] Thus, because a competitive firm's marginal revenue equals the market price, *a profit-maximizing competitive firm produces the amount of output, q, at which the market price, p, equals its marginal cost, MC:*

$$p = MC(q). \tag{8.1}$$

----

[2]As explained in Chapter 7, if $MR > MC$, then a small increase in quantity causes revenue to rise by more than cost, so maximizing profit requires an increase in output. If $MR < MC$, then maximizing profit requires a decrease in quantity as the reduction in cost exceeds the reduction in revenue. Only if $MR = MC$ is the firm maximizing profit.

[3]We can use calculus to show that marginal revenue equals price for a competitive firm. Because p is constant and $R(q) = pq$, $MR(q) = dR(q)/dq = d(pq)/dq = p$. Therefore, to maximize profit, a competitive firm must produce the quantity such that $p = MC$. In calculus, this is the called the *first order condition*. To make sure that we have found a maximum, a *second order condition* must also be satisfied. For a competitive firm, the second order condition implies that the marginal cost curve must be upward-sloping at the profit maximizing quantity.

To illustrate how a competitive firm maximizes its profit, we examine a representative firm in the highly competitive Canadian lime manufacturing industry. Lime is a nonmetallic mineral used in mortars, plasters, cements, bleaching powders, steel, paper, glass, and other products. The lime plant's estimated average cost curve, AC, first falls and then rises in panel a of Figure 8.1.[4] As always, the marginal cost curve, MC, intersects the average cost curve at its minimum point.

FIGURE 8.1 **How a Competitive Firm Maximizes Profit**

(a) A competitive lime manufacturing firm maximizes its profit at $\pi^* = \$426{,}000$ where its marginal revenue, MR, which is the market price, $p = \$8$, equals its marginal cost, MC.

(b) The corresponding profit curve reaches its peak at 284 units of lime. Estimated cost curves are based on Robidoux and Lester (1988).

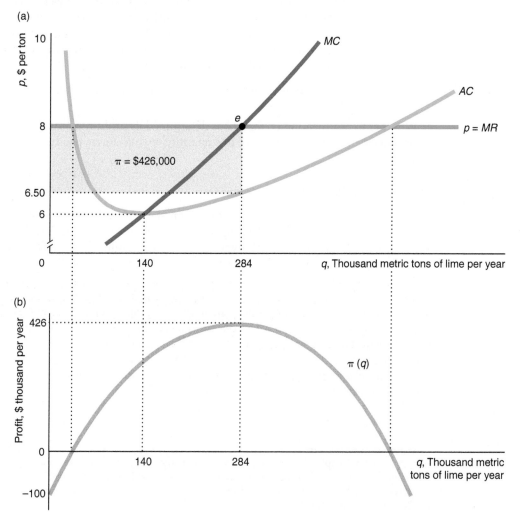

[4]The figure is based on Robidoux and Lester's (1988) estimated variable cost function. In the figure, we assume that the minimum of the average variable cost curve is $5 at 50,000 metric tons of output. Based on information from Statistics Canada, we set the fixed cost so that the average cost is $6 at 140,000 tons.

If the market price of lime is $p = \$8$ per metric ton, the competitive firm faces a horizontal demand curve (marginal revenue curve) at $8. The MC curve crosses the firm's demand curve (or price or marginal revenue curve) at point e, where the firm's output is 284 units (where a unit is a thousand metric tons).

Thus, at a market price of $8, the competitive firm maximizes its profit by producing 284 units. If the firm produced fewer than 284 units, the market price would be above its marginal cost. As a result, the firm could increase its profit by expanding output because the firm earns more on the next ton, $p = \$8$, than it costs to produce it, $MC < \$8$. If the firm were to produce more than 284 units, the market price would be below its marginal cost, $MC > \$8$, and the firm could increase its profit by reducing its output. Thus, the competitive firm maximizes its profit by producing that output at which its marginal cost equals its marginal revenue, which is the market price.[5]

At that 284 units, the firm's profit is $\pi = \$426,000$, which is the shaded rectangle in panel a. The length of the rectangle is the number of units sold, $q = 284,000$ (or 284 units). The height of the rectangle is the firm's average profit per unit. Because the firm's profit is its revenue, $R(q) = pq$, minus its cost, $\pi(q) = R(q) - C(q)$, its average profit per unit is the difference between the market price (or average revenue), $p = R(q)/q = pq/q$, and its average cost, $AC = C(q)/q$:

$$\frac{\pi(q)}{q} = \frac{R(q) - C(q)}{q} = \frac{R(q)}{q} - \frac{C(q)}{q} = p - AC. \tag{8.2}$$

At 284 units, the lime firm's average profit per unit is $\$1.50 = p - AC(284) = \$8 - \$6.50$, and the firm's profit is $\pi = \$1.50 \times 284,000 = \$426,000$. Panel b shows that this profit is the maximum possible profit because it is the peak of the profit curve.

Q&A 8.1

If a competitive firm's cost increases due to an increase in the price of a factor of production or a tax, the firm's manager can quickly determine by how much to adjust output by calculating how the firm's marginal cost has changed and applying the profit-maximization rule. Suppose that the Canadian province of Manitoba imposes a specific (per-unit) tax of t per ton of lime produced in the province. No other provincial government imposes such a tax. Manitoba has only one lime-producing firm, so the tax affects only that firm and hence has virtually no effect on the market price. Given the tax, how should the Manitoba firm change its output level to maximize its profit, and how does its maximum profit change?

Answer

1. *Show how the tax shifts the marginal cost and average cost curves.* The firm's before-tax marginal cost curve is MC^1 and its before-tax average cost curve is AC^1. Because the specific tax adds t to the per-unit cost, it shifts the after-tax marginal cost curve up to $MC^2 = MC^1 + t$ and the after-tax average cost curve to $AC^2 = AC^1 + t$.

---

[5]The firm chooses its output level to maximize its *total profit* rather than its *average profit* per ton. If the firm were to produce 140 units, where its average cost is minimized at $6, the firm would maximize its average profit at $2, but its total profit would be only $280,000. Although the firm gives up 50¢ in profit per ton when it produces 284 units instead of 140 units, it more than makes up for that lost profit per ton by selling an extra 144 units. At $1.50 profit per ton, the firm's total profit is $426,000, which is $146,000 higher than it is at 140 units.

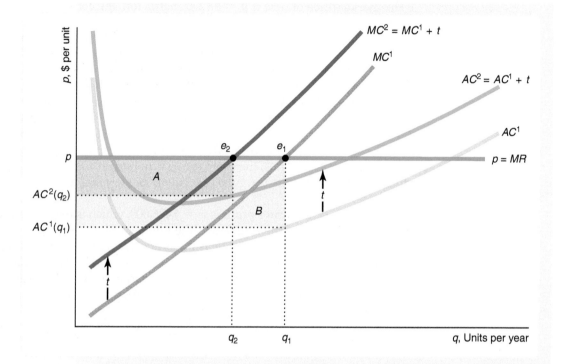

2. *Determine the before-tax and after-tax equilibria and the amount by which the firm adjusts its output.* Where the before-tax marginal cost curve, MC^1, hits the horizontal demand curve, p, at e_1, the profit-maximizing quantity is q_1. The after-tax marginal cost curve, MC^2, intersects the demand curve, p, at e_2, where the profit-maximizing quantity is q_2. Thus, in response to the tax, the firm produces $q_1 - q_2$ fewer units of output.

3. *Show how the profit changes after the tax.* Because the market price is constant but the firm's average cost curve shifts upward, the firm's profit at every output level falls. The firm sells fewer units (because of the increase in MC) and makes less profit per unit (because of the increase in AC). The after-tax profit is area $A = \pi_2 = [p - AC^2(q_2)]q_2$, and the before-tax profit is area $A + B = \pi_1 = [p - AC^1(q_1)]q_1$, so profit falls by area B due to the tax.

Using Calculus

Profit Maximization with a Specific Tax

We can use calculus to solve the problem in Q&A 8.1. After the government imposes the specific tax t, the competitive firm's profit is

$$\pi = pq - [C(q) + tq],$$

where $C(q)$ is the firm's before-tax cost and $C(q) + tq$ is its after-tax cost. We obtain a necessary condition for the firm to maximize its after-tax profit by taking the first derivative of profit with respect to quantity and setting it equal to zero:

$$\frac{d\pi}{dq} = \frac{d(pq)}{dq} - \frac{d[C(q) + tq]}{dq} = p - \left[\frac{dC(q)}{dq} + t\right] = p - [MC + t] = 0.$$

Thus, the competitive firm maximizes its profit by choosing q such that its after-tax marginal cost, $MC + t$, equals the market price.

Whether to Produce

Once a firm determines the output level that maximizes its profit or minimizes its loss, it must decide whether to produce that output level or to shut down and produce nothing. This decision is easy for the lime firm in Figure 8.1 because, at the output that maximizes its profit, it makes a positive profit. However, the question remains whether a firm should shut down if it is making a loss in the short run.

Most people's intuition is wrong about this decision:

> **Common Confusion** A firm should shut down if it is making a loss.

This intuition holds if the firm is making a loss in the long run, but it may be wrong in the short run. In the short run, a firm should operate if it can more than cover its variable cost, even if it cannot fully cover its unavoidable fixed cost.

In Chapter 7, we showed that all firms—not just competitive firms—use the same shutdown rule: The firm shuts down only if it can reduce its loss by doing so. Equivalently, the firm shuts down only if its revenue is less than its avoidable variable cost (VC): $R < VC$. If the firm shuts down, it does not incur the variable cost, so its only loss is its fixed cost (F), which we assume is unavoidable.

For a competitive firm, this rule is $R = pq < VC$. Dividing both sides of this inequality by output, we find that *a competitive firm shuts down only if the market price is less than its average variable cost*: $p < AVC = VC/q$.

We illustrate the logic behind this rule using our lime firm example. We look at three cases where the market price is (1) above the minimum average cost (AC), (2) less than the minimum average cost but at least equal to or above the minimum average variable cost, or (3) below the minimum average variable cost.

The Market Price Is Above Minimum AC. If the market price is above the firm's average cost at the quantity that it's producing, the firm makes a profit and so it operates. In panel a of Figure 8.1, the competitive lime firm's average cost curve reaches its minimum of $6 per ton at 140 units. Thus, if the market price is above $6, the firm makes a profit of $p - AC$ on each unit it sells and operates. In the figure, the market price is $8, and the firm makes a profit of $426,000.

The Market Price Is Between the Minimum AC and the Minimum AVC. The tricky case is when the market price is less than the minimum average cost but is at least as great as the minimum average variable cost. If the price is in this range, the firm makes a loss, but it reduces its loss by operating rather than shutting down.

Figure 8.2 (which reproduces the marginal and average cost curves from panel a of Figure 8.1 and adds the average variable cost curve) illustrates this case for the lime firm. The lime firm's average cost curve reaches a minimum of $6 at 140 units, while its average variable cost curve hits its minimum of $5 at 50 units. If the market price is between $5 and $6, the lime firm loses money (its profit is negative) because the price is less than its AC, but the firm does not shut down.

For example, if the market price is $5.50, the firm minimizes its loss by producing 100 units where the marginal cost curve crosses the price line. At 100 units, the average cost is $6.12, so the firm's loss is $-62¢ = p - AC(100) = \$5.50 - \$6.12$ on each unit that it sells.

Why does the firm produce given that it is making a loss? The reason is that the firm reduces its loss by operating rather than shutting down because its revenue exceeds its variable cost—or equivalently, the market price exceeds its average variable cost.

FIGURE 8.2 **The Short-Run Shutdown Decision**

The competitive lime manufacturing plant operates if the market price is above the minimum of the average variable cost curve, point a, at $5. With a market price of $5.50, the firm produces 100 units because that price is above $AVC(100) = \$5.14$, so the firm more than covers its out-of-pocket, variable costs. At that price, the firm makes a loss of area $A = \$62,000$ because the price is less than the average cost of $6.12. If it shuts down, its loss is its fixed cost, area $A + B = \$98,000$. Thus, the firm does not shut down.

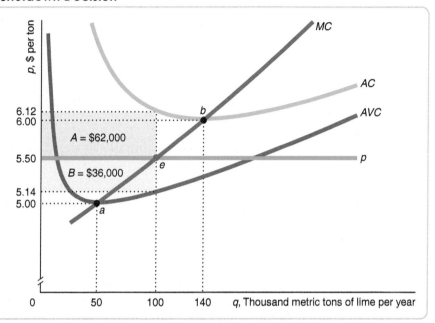

If the firm shuts down in the short run, it incurs a loss equal to its fixed cost of $98,000, which is the sum of rectangles A and B.[6] If the firm operates and produces $q = 100$ units, its average variable cost is $AVC = \$5.14$, which is less than the market price of $p = \$5.50$ per ton. It makes $36¢ = p - AVC = \$5.50 - \$5.14$ more on each ton than its average variable cost. The difference between the firm's revenue and its variable cost, $R - VC$, is the rectangle $B = \$36,000$, which has a length of 100 thousand tons and a height of 36¢. Thus, if the firm operates, it loses only $62,000 (rectangle A), which is less than its loss if it shuts down, $98,000. The firm makes a smaller loss by operating than by shutting down because its revenue more than covers its variable cost and hence helps to reduce the loss from the fixed cost.

The Market Price Is Less Than the Minimum AVC. If the market price dips below the minimum of the average variable cost, $5 in Figure 8.2, then the firm should shut down in the short run. Thus, the minimum of the average variable cost curve is the firm's *shutdown point*. At any price less than the minimum average variable cost, the firm's revenue is less than its variable cost, so it makes a greater loss by operating than by shutting down because it loses money on each unit sold in addition to the fixed cost that it loses if it shuts down.

In summary, a competitive firm uses a two-step decision-making process to maximize its profit. First, the competitive firm determines the output that maximizes its profit or minimizes its loss when its marginal cost equals the market price (which is its marginal revenue): $p = MC$. Second, the firm chooses to produce that quantity

---

[6]From Chapter 6, we know that the average cost is the sum of the average variable cost and the average fixed cost, $AC = AVC + F/q$. Thus, the gap between the average cost and the average variable cost curves at any given output is $AC - AVC = F/q$. Consequently, the height of the rectangle $A + B$ is $AC(100) - AVC(100) = F/100$, and the length of the rectangle is 100 units, so the area of the rectangle is F, or $\$98,000 = \$62,000 + \$36,000$.

unless it would lose more by operating than by shutting down. The competitive firm shuts down in the short run only if the market price is less than the minimum of its average variable cost, $p < AVC$.

Mini-Case Fracking and Shutdowns	Oil production starts and stops in the short run as the market price fluctuates. In 1998–1999 when oil prices were historically low, U.S. oil-producing firms shut down or abandoned 74,000 of 136,000 oil wells. History repeats itself. From 2011 through the first half of 2014, oil prices were above $100 per barrel—nearly hitting $130 at one point—which was above the shutdown point for virtually all U.S. wells. However, when oil prices fell below $50 a barrel in 2015 and below $30 a barrel in 2016, many U.S. wells shut down. From 2014–2016, 1,764 wells under development were left incomplete.

Conventional oil wells—which essentially stick a pipe in the ground and pump oil—have low enough shutdown points that they operated in 2014 and 2015. Some Middle Eastern oil wells break even at a price as low as $10 a barrel. Older Texas wells often have a break-even point at $20 to $30 per barrel.

Most new U.S. oil wells use hydraulic fracturing (fracking). Fracking pumps pressurized liquid consisting of water, sand, and chemicals to fracture oil shale (rock containing oil), which releases natural gas and oil.[7] Current fracking operations have a shutdown point at between $50 and $77 per barrel, with an average of about $65. Thus, fracking operations were more likely to shut down than were conventional wells during the recent period of low prices.

By mid-2018, the price of oil exceeded $65, and many fracking wells were operating again. In addition, oil companies had almost 7,000 wells that had been drilled but not fracked that were starting to come online.

---

[7]The first fracking experiment took place in 1947. At first, fracking wells had a minimum average variable cost that was too high to operate profitably. However, in recent years, technological innovation substantially lowered this cost, and the global price of oil was often high enough for fracking to be widely used. Due to fracking, U.S. oil production rose from 5.6 million barrels a day in 2010 to 9.3 million in 2015. Fracking is controversial because opponents fear it will create environmental problems and trigger earthquakes.

Q&A 8.2

A competitive firm has a cost function $C = 80 + 70q - 12q^2 + q^3$. Its fixed cost of 80 is sunk (unavoidable) in the short run. The corresponding marginal cost is $MC = 70 - 24q + 3q^2$. For prices $p = 34$, $p = 49$ and $p = 70$, use a spreadsheet to calculate the profit for each quantity between 4 and 10 and identify the profit-maximizing quantity. Show that price equals marginal cost at the profit-maximizing quantity. Would the firm choose to shut down in the short run at any of these prices?

Answer

1. *Open an Excel spreadsheet and put titles* Quantity, Cost, MC, Profit (p = 34), Profit (p = 49), *and* Profit (p = 70) *in cells A1 through F1.*

2. *Enter the quantities in column A and the cost formulas in columns B and C. In cells A2 though A8 enter the numbers 4 through 10. In cell B2 enter the cost formula "= 80+70*A2−12*A2^2+A2^3", then copy and paste this formula into cells B3 through B8. In cell C2, enter the marginal cost (MC) formula "= 70−24*A2+3*A2^2". Copy and paste this MC formula into cells C3 through C8.*

3. *Enter the profit formulas into columns D through F. For column D, price is 34. Revenue is 34q, so profit, which is revenue minus cost, should be entered in cell D2 as "= 34*A2−B2". Copy and paste this formula into cells D3 through D8. Follow the same procedure for columns E and F using prices 49 and 70 respectively instead of 34.*

The screenshot shows what your spreadsheet should look like.

	A	B	C	D	E	F
1	Quantity	Cost	MC	Profit (p = 34)	Profit (p =49)	Profit (p = 70)
2	4	232	22	-96	-36	48
3	5	255	25	-85	-10	95
4	6	284	34	-80	10	136
5	7	325	49	-87	18	165
6	8	384	70	-112	8	176
7	9	467	97	-161	-26	163
8	10	580	130	-240	-90	120

4. *For each price (columns D through F), determine the maximum profit (or minimum loss).* For the prices 34, 49, and 70, we have highlighted the maximum profit in the screenshot. Cell D4 shows a minimum loss and the other two highlighted cells show positive profits. The corresponding quantities are 6, 7, and 8.

5. *For each price, confirm that the maximum profit or minimum loss occurs where MC equals that price.* By inspection, we see that the maximum profit occurs where MC equals the price. For example, at a price of 49, the maximum profit of 18 occurs where $MC = 49$ (and quantity is 7).

6. *Decide whether the firm should shut down at any of these prices.* At the prices 49 and 70, the firm makes a profit, so it does not shut down. However, at a price of 34, it makes a loss, so it should check the shutdown condition. At this price, the firm just covers its variable cost and makes no contribution toward its fixed cost. It is indifferent between shutting down and operating in the short run.

When making shutdown decisions, good managers *ignore* unavoidable (sunk) fixed costs (Chapter 6). The manager of a competitive firm should continue operating if price at least equals average variable cost even if revenue is not sufficient to fully cover the sunk fixed costs. As long as price exceeds average variable cost, the firm at least partially offsets the sunk fixed costs by operating instead of absorbing the entire amount as a loss.

The Short-Run Firm Supply Curve

We just demonstrated how a competitive firm chooses its output for a given market price in a way that maximizes its profit or minimizes its losses. By repeating this analysis at different possible market prices, we can show how the amount the competitive firm supplies varies with the market price.

As the market price increases from $p_1 = \$5$ to $p_2 = \$6$ to $p_3 = \$7$ to $p_4 = \$8$, the lime firm increases its output from 50 to 140 to 215 to 285 units per year, as Figure 8.3 shows. The profit-maximizing output at each market price is determined by the intersection of the relevant demand curve—market price line—and the firm's marginal cost curve, as equilibria e_1 through e_4 illustrate. That is, as the market price increases, the equilibria trace out the marginal cost curve. However, if the price falls below the firm's minimum average variable cost at $5, the firm shuts down. Thus, the competitive firm's short-run supply curve is its marginal cost curve above its minimum average variable cost.

The firm's short-run supply curve, S, is a solid red line in the figure. At prices above $5, the short-run supply curve is the same as the marginal cost curve. The supply is zero when price is less than the minimum of the AVC curve of $5. (From now on, to keep the graphs as simple as possible, we will not show the supply curve at prices below the minimum AVC.)

FIGURE 8.3 How the Profit-Maximizing Quantity Varies with Price

As the market price increases, the lime manufacturing firm produces more output. The change in the price traces out the marginal cost (MC) curve of the firm. The firm's short-run supply (S) curve is the MC curve above the minimum of its AVC curve (at e_1).

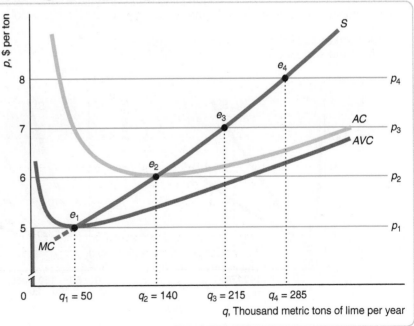

The Short-Run Market Supply Curve

The market supply curve is the horizontal sum of the supply curves of all the individual firms in the market. In the short run, the maximum number of firms in a market, n, is fixed because new firms need time to enter the market. If all the firms in a competitive market are identical, each firm's costs are identical, so their supply curves are identical, and the market supply at any price is n times the supply of an individual firm. If the firms have different costs functions, their supply curves and shutdown points differ. Consequently, the market supply curve reflects a different number of firms operating at various prices even in the short run. We examine competitive markets first with firms that have identical costs and then with firms that have different costs.

Short-Run Market Supply with Identical Firms. To illustrate how to construct a short-run market supply curve, we suppose, for graphical simplicity, that the lime manufacturing market has $n = 5$ competitive firms with identical cost curves. Panel a of Figure 8.4 plots the short-run supply curve, S^1, of a typical firm—the MC curve above the minimum AVC—where the horizontal axis shows the firm's output, q, per year. Panel b illustrates the competitive market supply curve, the dark line S^5, where the horizontal axis is market output, Q, per year. The price axis is the same in the two panels.

If the market price is less than $5 per ton, no firm supplies any output, so the market supply is zero. At $5, each firm is willing to supply $q = 50$ units, as in panel a. Consequently, the market supply is $Q = 5q = 250$ units in panel b. At $6 per ton, each firm supplies 140 units, so the market supply is 700 $(= 5 \times 140)$ units.

Suppose the market has fewer than five firms in the short run. The light-color lines in panel b show the market supply curves for various other numbers of firms.

FIGURE 8.4 Short-Run Market Supply with Five Identical Lime Firms

(a) The short-run supply curve, S^1, for a typical lime manufacturing firm is its MC above the minimum of its AVC.
(b) The market supply curve, S^5, is the horizontal sum of the supply curves of each of the five identical firms. The curve S^4 shows what the market supply curve would be with only four firms in the market.

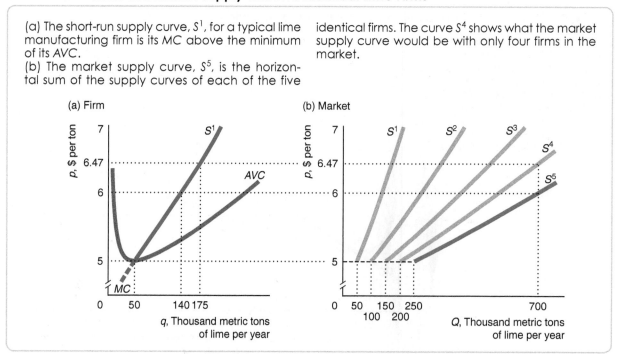

The market supply curve is S^1 if there is one price-taking firm, S^2 with two firms, S^3 with three firms, and S^4 with four firms. The market supply curve flattens as the number of firms in the market increases because the market supply curve is the horizontal sum of more and more upward-sloping firm supply curves.[8] Thus, *the more identical firms producing at a given price, the flatter the short-run market supply curve at that price.*

The flatter the supply curve is at a given quantity, the more elastic is the supply curve. As a result, the more firms in the market, the less the price has to increase for the short-run market supply to increase substantially. Consumers pay $6 per ton to obtain 700 units of lime if the market has five firms, but they must pay $6.47 per ton to obtain that much with only four firms. As the number of firms grows very large, the market supply curve approaches a horizontal line at $5.

Short-Run Market Supply with Firms That Differ.   If the firms in a competitive market have different minimum average variable costs, then not all firms produce at every price, a situation that affects the shape of the short-run market supply curve. Suppose that the only two firms in the lime market are our typical lime firm with a supply curve of S^1 and a second firm with a higher marginal and minimum average cost and the supply curve of S^2 in Figure 8.5. The first firm produces if the market price is at least $5, whereas the second firm does not produce unless the price is $6 or more. At $5, the first firm produces 50 units, so the quantity

FIGURE 8.5 Short-Run Market Supply with Two Different Lime Firms

The supply curve S^1 is the same as for the typical lime firm in Figure 8.3. A second firm has an MC that lies to the left of the original firm's cost curve and a higher minimum of its AVC. Thus, its supply curve, S^2, lies above and to the left of the original firm's supply curve, S^1. The market supply curve, S, is the horizontal sum of the two supply curves. When price is $6 or higher, both firms produce, and the market supply curve is flatter than the supply curve of either individual firm.

[8]In the figure, if the price rises by $\Delta p = 47$¢ from $6 to $6.47 per ton, each firm increases its output by $\Delta q = 35$ tons, so the slope (measured in cents per ton) of its supply curve over that range is $\Delta p / \Delta q = 47/35 \approx 1.34$. With two firms, $\Delta q = 70$, so the slope is $47/70 \approx 0.67$. Similarly, the slope is $47/105 \approx 0.45$ with three firms, 0.34 with four firms, and 0.27 with five firms. Although not shown in the figure, the slope is 0.13 with 10 firms and 0.013 with 100 firms.

on the market supply curve, S, is 50 units. Between $5 and $6, only the first firm produces, so the market supply, S, is the same as the first firm's supply, S^1. At and above $6, both firms produce, so the market supply curve is the horizontal summation of their two individual supply curves. For example, at $7, the first firm produces 215 units, and the second firm supplies 100 units, so the market supply is 315 units.

As in a market with identical firms, where both firms are producing, the market supply curve is flatter than that of either firm. Because the second firm does not produce at as low a price as the first firm, the short-run market supply curve has a steeper slope (less elastic supply) at relatively low prices than it would if the firms were identical.

When the firms differ, only the low-cost firm supplies goods at relatively low prices. As the price rises, the other, higher-cost firm starts supplying, creating a stair-like market supply curve. The more suppliers with differing costs, the more steps in the market supply curve. As price rises and more firms supply the good, the market supply curve flattens, so it takes a smaller increase in price to increase supply by a given amount. Stated the other way, the more firms differ in costs, the steeper the market supply curve is at low prices. Differences in costs are one explanation for why some market supply curves are upward sloping.

Short-Run Competitive Equilibrium

By combining the short-run market supply curve and the market demand curve, we can determine the short-run competitive equilibrium. We first show how to determine the equilibrium in the lime market, and we then examine how taxes change the equilibrium.

Suppose the lime manufacturing market has five identical firms in the short-run equilibrium. Panel a of Figure 8.6 shows the short-run cost curves and the supply curve, S^1, for a typical firm, and panel b shows the corresponding short-run competitive market supply curve, S.

In panel b, the initial demand curve D^1 intersects the market supply curve at E_1, the market equilibrium. The equilibrium quantity is $Q_1 = 1,075$ units of lime per year, and the equilibrium market price is $7.

In panel a, each competitive firm faces a horizontal demand curve at the equilibrium price of $7. Each price-taking firm chooses its output where its marginal cost curve intersects the horizontal demand curve at e_1. Because each firm is maximizing its profit at e_1, no firm wants to change its behavior, so e_1 is the firm's equilibrium. In panel a, each firm makes a short-run profit of area $A + B = \$172,000$, which is the average profit per ton, $p - AC = \$7 - \$6.20 = 80¢$, times the firm's output, $q_1 = 215$ units. The equilibrium market output, Q_1, is the number of firms, n, times the equilibrium output of each firm: $Q_1 = nq_1 = 5 \times 215$ units $= 1,075$ units (panel b).

Now suppose that the demand curve shifts to D^2. The new market equilibrium is E_2, where the price is only $5. At that price, each firm produces $q = 50$ units, and market output is $Q = 250$ units. In panel a, each firm loses $98,500, area $A + C$, because it earns $(p - AC) = (\$5 - \$6.97) = -\$1.97$ per unit and it sells $q_2 = 50$ units. However, such a firm does not shut down because price equals the firm's average variable cost, so the firm is covering its out-of-pocket expenses.

FIGURE 8.6 Short-Run Competitive Equilibrium in the Lime Market

(a) The short-run supply curve is the marginal cost above the minimum average variable cost of $5. At a price of $5, each firm makes a short-run loss of $(p - AC)q = (\$5 - \$6.97) \times 50,000 = -\$98,500$, area $A + C$. At a price of $7, the short-run profit of a typical lime firm is $(p - AC)q = (\$7 - \$6.20) \times 215,000 = \$172,000$, area $A + B$.

(b) If the lime market has five firms in the short run so that the market supply is S and the market demand curve is D^1, then the short-run equilibrium is E_1, the market price is $7, and market output is $Q_1 = 1,075$ units. If the demand curve shifts to D^2, the market equilibrium is $p = \$5$ and $Q_2 = 250$ units.

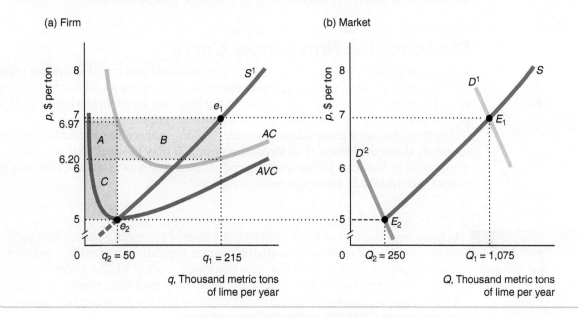

8.3 Competition in the Long Run

Originally one thought that if there were a half dozen large computers in this country, hidden away in research laboratories, this would take care of all requirements we had throughout the country. —Howard H. Aiken, a computer pioneer, 1952

In the long run, competitive firms can vary inputs that were fixed in the short run and firms can enter and exit the industry freely, so the long-run firm and market supply curves differ from the short-run curves. After briefly looking at how a firm determines its long-run supply curve to maximize its profit, we examine the relationship between short-run and long-run market supply curves and competitive equilibria.

Long-Run Competitive Profit Maximization

The firm's two profit-maximizing decisions—how much to produce and whether to produce at all—are simpler in the long run than in the short run because, in the long run, all costs are avoidable.

The firm chooses the quantity that maximizes its profit using the same rules as in the short run. The firm picks the quantity that maximizes long-run profit, which is the difference between revenue and long-run cost. Equivalently, it operates where long-run marginal profit is zero—where marginal revenue (price) equals long-run marginal cost.

After determining the output level, q^*, that maximizes its profit or minimizes its loss, the firm decides whether to produce or shut down. The firm shuts down if its revenue is less than its avoidable cost. Because all costs are avoidable in the long run, the firm shuts down if it would make an economic loss by operating.

The Long-Run Firm Supply Curve

A firm's long-run supply curve is its long-run marginal cost curve above the minimum of its long-run average cost curve (because all costs are avoidable in the long run). The firm is free to choose its capital in the long run, so the firm's long-run supply curve may differ substantially from its short-run supply curve.

The firm chooses a plant size to maximize its long-run economic profit in light of its beliefs about the future. If its forecast is wrong, it may be stuck with a plant that is too small or too large for its level of production in the short run. The firm acts to correct this mistake in plant size in the long run.

Mini-Case

The Size of Ethanol Processing Plants

When a large number of firms initially built ethanol processing plants, they built relatively small ones. When the ethanol market took off in the first few years of the twenty-first century, with the price reaching a peak of $4.23 a gallon in June 2006, many firms built larger plants or greatly increased their plant size. From 1999 to 2006, the number of plants nearly doubled and the average plant capacity nearly tripled (36 to 106 million gallons per year).

However, since then, the ethanol market price has collapsed. The price was generally below $3 and often below $1.50 from 2007 through 2018, hitting a low of $1.26 in January 2016. As a result, many firms closed plants or reduced their size. The average plant capacity fell by a third from 2006 to 2017 (106 to 78 million gallons per year).

The Long-Run Market Supply Curve

The competitive market supply curve is the horizontal sum of the supply curves of the individual firms in both the short run and the long run. Because the maximum number of firms in the market is fixed in the short run, we add the supply curves of a known number of firms to obtain the short-run market supply curve. The only way for the market to supply more output in the short run is for existing firms to produce more.

However, in the long run, firms can enter or leave the market. Thus, before we can add all the relevant firm supply curves to obtain the long-run market supply curve, we need to determine how many firms are in the market at each possible market price.

We now look in detail at how market entry affects long-run market supply. To isolate the role of entry, we derive the long-run market supply curve, assuming that the price of inputs remains constant as market output increases.

Entry and Exit. The number of firms in a market in the long run is determined by the *entry* and *exit* of firms. In the long run, each firm decides whether to enter or exit depending on whether it can make a long-run profit.

In some markets, firms face significant costs to enter, such as large start-up costs, or barriers to entry, such as a government restriction. For example, many city governments limit the number of cabs, creating a barrier that prevents additional taxis from entering. Similarly, patent protection prevents new firms from producing the patented product until the patent expires.

However, in perfectly competitive markets, firms can enter and exit freely in the long run. For example, many construction firms that provide only labor services enter and exit a market several times a year. In the United States, an estimated 213,000 new firms began operations and 187,000 firms exited in the first quarter of 2014.[9] The annual rates of entry and exit of such firms vary from year to year depending on the business cycle, but both normally exceed 10% of the underlying population of firms.

In such markets, a shift of the market demand curve to the right attracts firms to enter. For instance, without government regulations, the market for taxicabs would have free entry and exit. Car owners could enter or exit the market quickly. If the demand curve for cab rides shifted to the right, the market price would rise, and existing cab drivers would make unusually high profits in the short run. Seeing these profits, other car owners would enter the market, causing the market supply curve to shift to the right and the market price to fall. Entry would continue until the last firm to enter—the *marginal firm*—makes zero long-run profit.

Similarly, if the demand curve shifts to the left so that the market price drops, firms suffer losses. Firms with minimum average costs above the new, lower market price exit the market. Firms continue to leave the market until the next firm that considers leaving, the marginal firm, is again earning a zero long-run profit.

Thus, in a market with free entry and exit:

- A firm enters the market if it can make a long-run profit, $\pi > 0$.
- A firm exits the market to avoid a long-run loss, $\pi < 0$.

If firms in a market are making zero long-run profit, they are indifferent between staying in the market and exiting. We presume that if they are already in the market, they stay in the market when they are making zero long-run profit.

Mini-Case	Firms can easily enter or exit most transportation markets unless governments regulate them. Trucking and shipping firms may serve a particular route, but entry is easy. Other firms quickly enter and serve a route as soon as a profit opportunity appears. Entrants shift their highly mobile equipment—trucks or ships—from less profitable routes to more profitable ones.
Industries with High Entry and Exit Rates	The annual entry and exit rates in construction were 10% in 2015. However, many construction firms enter and exit the market repeatedly over the year. When home construction booms during the spring and summer, the number of home construction firms in a market is large. During the slow winter months, many of these firms shut down, only to reenter the market when the weather improves.

---

[9]Business Employment Dynamics, Bureau of Labor Statistics **www.bls.gov/bdm/** (viewed August 9, 2015).

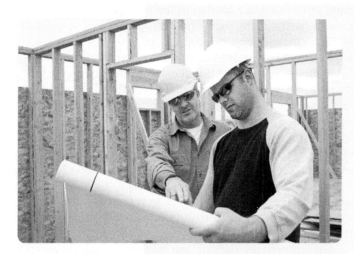

Even in agriculture, where it often takes firms substantial time to enter, about 7.5% of U.S. agricultural firms enter every year and about 8.5% exit. Solar energy firms rapidly entered and exited the California market (which has half of all solar energy systems). The number of firms went from 603 firms in 2008 to 1,057 in 2010 and 1,499 in 2018.

Long-Run Market Supply with Identical Firms and Free Entry. The long-run market supply curve is flat at the minimum of long-run average cost if firms can freely enter and exit the market, an unlimited number of firms have identical costs, and input prices are constant. This result follows from our reasoning about the short-run supply curve, in which we showed that the market supply curve is flatter, the more firms in the market. With a large number of firms in the market in the long run, the market supply curve is effectively flat.

The long-run supply curve of a typical vegetable oil mill, S^1 in panel a of Figure 8.7, is the long-run marginal cost curve above a minimum long-run average cost of $10. Because each firm shuts down if the market price is below $10, the long-run market supply curve is zero at a price below $10. If the price rises above $10, firms are making positive profits, so new firms enter, expanding market output until profits are driven to zero, where price is again $10. The long-run market supply curve in panel b is a horizontal line at the minimum long-run average cost of the typical firm, $10. At a price of $10, each firm produces $q = 150$ units (where one unit equals 100 metric tons). Thus, the total output produced by n firms in the market is $Q = nq = n \times 150$ units. Extra market output is obtained by new firms entering the market.

In summary, the long-run market supply curve is horizontal if the market has free entry and exit, an unlimited number of firms have identical costs, and input prices are constant. As we show next, when these strong assumptions do not hold, the long-run market supply curve typically slopes upward but may slope downward. We examine two reasons why a long-run market supply curve is not flat: limited entry and differences in cost functions across firms. In addition, although we do not demonstrate this result, a third reason why long-run supply curves may slope up (or down) is that input prices rise (or fall) when output increases.

Long-Run Market Supply When Entry Is Limited. If the number of firms in a market is limited in the long run, the long-run market supply curve slopes upward. The number of firms is limited if the government restricts that number, if all firms need a scarce resource, or if entry is costly. An example of a

FIGURE 8.7 **Long-Run Firm and Market Supply with Identical Vegetable Oil Firms**

(a) The long-run supply curve of a typical vegetable oil mill, S^1, is the long-run marginal cost curve above the minimum average cost of $10.

(b) The long-run market supply curve is horizontal at the minimum of the long-run minimum average cost of a typical firm. Each firm produces 150 units, so market output is 150n, where n is the number of firms.

scarce resource is the limited number of lots in Miami on which a luxury beach-front hotel could be built. High entry costs restrict the number of firms in a market because firms enter only if the long-run economic profit is greater than the cost of entering.

The only way to get more output if the number of firms is limited is for existing firms to produce more. Because individual firms' supply curves slope upward, the long-run market supply curve is also upward sloping. The reasoning is the same as in the short run, as panel b of Figure 8.4 illustrates, given that no more than five firms can enter. The market supply curve is the upward-sloping S^5 curve, which is the horizontal sum of the five firms' upward-sloping marginal cost curves above minimum average cost.

Long-Run Market Supply When Firms Differ. A second reason why some long-run market supply curves slope upward is that firms differ. Firms with relatively low minimum long-run average costs are willing to enter the market at lower prices than others, resulting in an upward-sloping long-run market supply curve (similar to the short-run example in Figure 8.5).

Suppose that a market has a number of low-cost firms and other higher-cost firms. If lower-cost firms can produce as much output as the market wants, only low-cost firms produce, and the long-run market supply curve is horizontal at the minimum of the low-cost firm's average cost curve. The long-run supply curve is upward sloping *only* if lower-cost firms cannot produce as much output as the market demands because each of these firms has a limited capacity and the number of these firms is limited.

Many countries produce cotton. Production costs differ among countries because of differences in the quality of land, amount of rainfall, costs of irrigation, costs of labor, and other factors.

The length of each step-like segment of the long-run supply curve of cotton in the graph is the quantity produced by the labeled country. The amount that the low-cost countries can produce is limited, so we observe production by the higher-cost countries if the market price is sufficiently high.

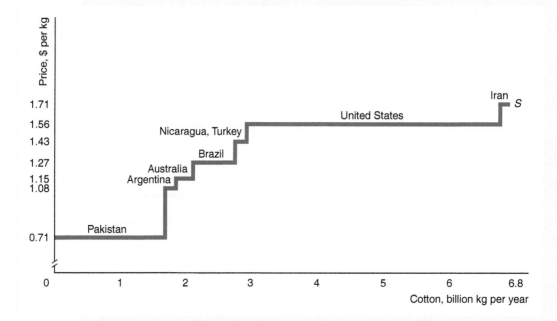

The height of each segment of the supply curve is the typical minimum average cost of production in that country. The average cost of production in Pakistan is less than half that in Iran. The supply curve has a step-like appearance because we are assuming that average cost is constant within a given country, up to capacity.

As the market price rises, the number of countries producing increases. At market prices below $1.08 per kilogram, only Pakistan produces. If the market price is below $1.50, the United States and Iran do not produce. If the price increases to $1.56, the United States supplies a large amount of cotton. In this range of the supply curve, supply is elastic. For Iran to produce, the price has to rise to $1.71. Price increases in that range result in only a relatively small increase in supply. Thus, the supply curve is relatively inelastic at prices above $1.56.

Long-Run Competitive Equilibrium

The intersection of the long-run market supply and demand curves determines the long-run competitive equilibrium. With identical firms, free entry and exit, and constant input prices, the long-run competitive market supply is horizontal at minimum long-run average cost, so the equilibrium price equals long-run average cost. A shift in the demand curve affects only the equilibrium quantity and not the equilibrium price, which remains constant at the minimum of long-run average cost. Because the market supply curve is different in the short run than in the long run, the long-run competitive equilibrium differs from the short-run equilibrium.

Q&A 8.3

A perfectly competitive industry is in long-run equilibrium. Each of the identical firms has a long-run cost function $C = 100 + q^2$. As a result, a firm's marginal cost function is $MC = 2q$. In the long-run competitive equilibrium, how much does the firm produce, and what is the equilibrium price? If the market quantity demanded at the equilibrium price is $Q = 2,500$, how many firms are in the market?

Answer

1. *Determine the AC curve.* $AC = C/q = 100/q + q$.

2. *Solve for the equilibrium quantity.* Because a profit-maximizing firm operates where $p = MC$ and free entry by firms into the market ensures that $p = AC$, it follows that $MC = AC$. Therefore, $MC = 2q = 100/q + q = AC$. Simplifying yields $q = 100/q$ or $q^2 = 100$ so $q = 10$.

3. *Use either the marginal cost curve or the average cost curve to determine the price.* Substituting $q = 10$ into the marginal cost function, we know that $p = MC = 2q = 20$. Similarly, $p = AC = 100/q + q = 20$.

4. *To obtain the number of firms, n, in the market, divide total output by the output per firm.* Because total market output is 2,500, $n = Q/q = 2,500/10 = 250$.

Comment: Firms in this industry have fixed costs of 100 even in the long run. This cost is avoidable in the long run if a firm exits the industry but does not vary with output if the firm operates. An example is rent on a building.

Zero Long-Run Profit with Free Entry

The long-run supply curve is horizontal if firms are free to enter the market, firms have identical cost, and input prices are constant. All firms in the market are operating at minimum long-run average cost. That is, they are indifferent between shutting down or not because they are earning zero economic profit.

In a competitive market with identical firms and free entry, if most firms are profit-maximizing, profits are driven to zero at the long-run equilibrium. Any firm that does not maximize profit—that is, any firm that sets its output so that the market price does not equal its marginal cost or does not use the most cost-efficient methods of production—loses money. Thus, *to survive in a competitive market in the long run, a firm must maximize its profit.* That only firms that maximize their profits operate is called the *survivor principle* (Chapter 7).

8.4 Competition Maximizes Economic Well-Being

We have two main reasons to study competition in a managerial economics course. First, many sectors of the economy are highly competitive, including agriculture, parts of the construction industry, many labor markets, and much retail and whole-sale trade. Second, and perhaps more important, perfect competition serves as an ideal or benchmark for other industries. This benchmark is widely used by econo-mists and widely misused by politicians.

Most U.S. politicians have at one point or another in their careers stated (with a hand over their heart), "I believe in the free market." While we're not about to bash free markets, we find this statement to be, at best, mysterious. What do the politi-cians mean by "believe in" and "free market?" Hopefully they realize that whether a free market is desirable is a scientific question rather than one of belief. Possibly when they say they "believe in," they are making some claim that free markets are desirable for some unspecified reason. By "free market," they might mean a market without government regulation or intervention.

We believe that this statement is a bad summary of what is probably the most important theoretical result in economics: *A perfectly competitive market maximizes an important measure of economic well-being.* Adam Smith, the father of modern economics, in his book *An Inquiry into the Nature and Causes of the Wealth of Nations*, published in 1776, was the first to observe that firms and consumers acting independently in their own self-interest generate a desirable outcome. This insight is called the *invisible hand theorem*.[10]

Because a competitive market is desirable, government intervention in a perfectly competitive market reduces a society's economic well-being. However, government intervention may increase economic well-being in markets that are not perfectly competitive, as with monopoly. In other words, freedom from government intervention does not guarantee that society's well-being is maximized in markets that are not perfectly competitive. In the rest of this section, we first describe widely accepted measures of consumer well-being, *consumer surplus*, and producer well-being, *producer surplus* (a concept close to that of profit). Next, we define a measure of a society's economic well-being, *total surplus*, as the sum of the consumer and producer measures of well-being. Then, we demonstrate why perfect competition maximizes total surplus. Finally, we discuss why a government action that causes a deviation from the perfectly competitive equilibrium reduces total surplus.

Consumer Surplus

The monetary difference between what a consumer is willing to pay for the quantity of the good purchased and what the consumer actually pays is called **consumer surplus** (*CS*). Consumer surplus is a dollar-value measure of the extra economic benefit the consumer receives from a transaction over and above the good's price. By measuring how much more a consumer is willing to pay than the consumer actually paid, we know how much the consumer gained from this transaction. For example, if Jane is willing to pay up to $500 for a ticket to a Bruno Mars concert, but only has to pay $150, her consumer surplus is $350.

We use this monetary measure to answer questions such as "What effect does a price increase have on consumers' well-being?" or "How much does a government quota on the number of items each consumer may buy hurt consumers?" or "What is the harm to consumers from one firm monopolizing a market?"[11]

---

[10]The term *invisible hand* was coined by Smith. He expressed the basic theorem as ". . .every individual . . . intends only his own security; and by directing that industry in such a manner as its produce may be of the greatest value, he intends only his own gain, and he is in this, as in many other cases, led by an invisible hand to promote an end which was no part of his intention. . . . By pursuing his own interest he frequently promotes that of the society more effectually than when he really intends to promote it."

[11]If we knew a consumer's utility function (Chapter 4), we could directly answer the question of how an economic event, such as a price change, affects a consumer's well-being. However, we do not know individual utility functions. Even if we did, we could not compare the utility levels of different individuals. If Mei says that she got 1,000 utils (units of utility) from watching a movie, while Alan reports that he got 872 utils, we would not know if Mei enjoyed the movie more than Alan. She might just be using a different subjective scale. Because of these and other difficulties in comparing consumers' utilities, we use a monetary measure.

Measuring Consumer Surplus Using a Demand Curve. Because consumer surplus is the difference between what a consumer is willing to pay for a unit of a good and the price of that good, it is a measure of what the consumer gains from trade: from exchanging money for the good. We can use the information stored in a demand curve and the market price to determine consumer surplus. The demand curve reflects a consumer's *marginal willingness to pay*: the maximum amount a consumer will spend for an extra unit. The consumer's marginal willingness to pay is the *marginal value* the consumer places on the last unit of output.

For example, David's demand curve for magazines per week, panel a of Figure 8.8, indicates his marginal willingness to buy various numbers of magazines. David places a marginal value of $5 on the first magazine. As a result, if the price of a magazine is $5, David buys one magazine, point *a* on the demand curve. His marginal willingness to buy a second magazine is $4, so if the price falls to $4, he buys two magazines, *b*. His marginal willingness to buy three magazines is $3, so if the price of magazines is $3, he buys three magazines, *c*.

David's consumer surplus from each additional magazine is his marginal willingness to pay minus what he pays to obtain the magazine. His marginal willingness to pay for the first magazine, $5, is area $CS_1 + E_1$. If the price is $3, his expenditure to obtain the magazine is area $E_1 = \$3$. Thus, his consumer surplus on the first magazine is area $CS_1 = (CS_1 + E_1) - E_1 = \$5 - \$3 = \$2$. Because his marginal willingness to pay for the second magazine is $4, his consumer surplus for the second magazine is the smaller area $CS_2 = \$1$. His marginal willingness to pay for the third

FIGURE 8.8 Consumer Surplus

(a) David's demand curve for magazines has a step-like shape. When the price is $3, he buys three magazines, point c. David's marginal value for the first magazine is $5, areas $CS_1 + E_1$, and his expenditure is $3, area E_1, so his consumer surplus is $CS_1 = \$2$. His consumer surplus is $1 for the second magazine, area CS_2, and is $0 for the third (he is indifferent between buying and not buying it). Thus, his total consumer surplus is the shaded area $CS_1 + CS_2 = \$3$.
(b) Steven's willingness to pay for trading cards is the height of his smooth demand curve. At price p_1, Steven's expenditure is $E (= p_1q_1)$, his consumer surplus is CS, and the total value he places on consuming q_1 trading cards per year is $CS + E$.

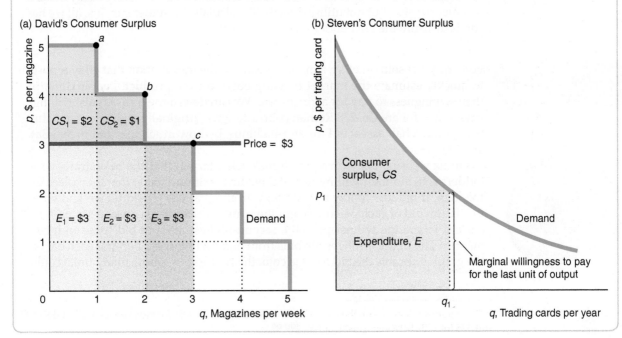

(a) David's Consumer Surplus

(b) Steven's Consumer Surplus

magazine is $3, which equals what he must pay to obtain it, so his consumer surplus is zero, $CS_3 = \$0$. He is indifferent between buying and not buying the third magazine.

At a price of $3, David buys three magazines. His total consumer surplus from the three magazines he buys is the sum of the consumer surplus he gets from each of these magazines: $CS_1 + CS_2 + CS_3 = \$2 + \$1 + \$0 = \$3$. This total consumer surplus of $3 is the extra amount that David is willing to spend for the right to buy three magazines at $3 each. Thus, *an individual's consumer surplus is the area under the demand curve and above the market price up to the quantity the consumer buys.*

David is unwilling to buy a fourth magazine unless the price drops to $2 or less. If David's mother gives him a fourth magazine as a gift, the marginal value that David puts on that fourth magazine, $2, is less than what it cost his mother, $3.

We can determine consumer surplus for smooth demand curves in the same way as with David's unusual stair-like demand curve. Steven has a smooth demand curve for baseball trading cards, panel b of Figure 8.8. The height of this demand curve measures his willingness to pay for one more card. This willingness varies with the number of cards he buys in a year. The total value he places on obtaining q_1 cards per year is the area under the demand curve up to q_1, the areas CS and E. Area E is his actual expenditure on q_1 cards. Because the price is p_1, his expenditure is $p_1 q_1$. Steven's consumer surplus from consuming q_1 trading cards is the value of consuming those cards, areas CS and E, minus his actual expenditures E to obtain them, or CS. Thus, his consumer surplus, CS, is the area under the demand curve and above the horizontal line at the price p_1 up to the quantity he buys, q_1.

Just as we measure the consumer surplus for an individual using that individual's demand curve, we measure the consumer surplus of all consumers in a market using the market demand curve. *Market consumer surplus is the area under the market demand curve above the market price up to the quantity consumers buy.*

To summarize, consumer surplus is a practical and convenient measure of consumers' economic benefits from market transactions. Consumer surplus has two advantages over utility as a measure of economic benefit. First, we can easily compare or combine the dollar-denominated consumer surplus of several individuals, but not the utilities of various individuals. Second, we can relatively easily measure consumer surplus, but not utility directly. To calculate consumer surplus, all we have to do is measure the area under a demand curve.

Managerial Implication

Willingness to Pay on eBay

For a product sold on eBay, a manager can use the information that eBay reports to quickly estimate the market demand curve for the product. People differ in their willingness to pay for a given item. We can determine individuals' willingness to pay for an A.D. 238 Roman coin, a sesterce (originally equivalent in value to two and a half asses) of Emperor Balbinus, by how much they bid in an eBay auction.

On its website, eBay correctly argues (Chapter 12) that the best strategy for bidders is to bid their willingness to pay: the maximum value that they place on the item. If bidders follow this strategy, from what eBay reports, we know the maximum bid of each person except the winner because eBay uses a *second-price auction*, where the winner pays the second-highest amount bid (plus an increment).[12] The figure arranges the bids from highest to lowest. Because each bar on the graph indicates the bid for one coin, the figure shows how many units could

---

[12] The increment depends on the size of the bid. For example, it is $1 for bids between $25 and $99.99 and $25 for bids between $1,000 and $2,499.99.

have been sold to this group of bidders at various prices (assuming each bidder wants only one coin). That is, it is the market demand curve.

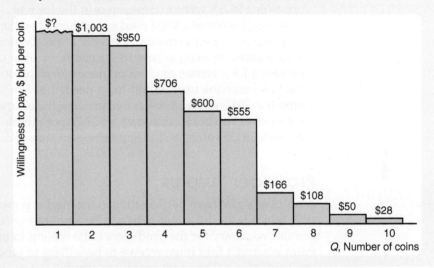

Effects of a Price Change on Consumer Surplus. If the supply curve shifts upward or a government imposes a new sales tax, the equilibrium price rises, causing the consumer surplus to fall. We illustrate the effect of a price increase on market consumer surplus using estimated supply and demand curves for sweetheart and hybrid tea roses sold in the United States.[13] We then discuss which markets are likely to have the greatest loss of consumer surplus due to a price increase.

Suppose that the introduction of a new tax causes the wholesale price of roses to rise from the original equilibrium price of 30¢ to 32¢ per rose stem, a movement along the demand curve in Figure 8.9. The consumer surplus at the initial price of 30¢ is area $A + B + C = \$173.74$ million per year.[14] At a higher price of 32¢, the consumer surplus falls to area $A = \$149.64$ million. Thus, the loss in consumer surplus from the increase in price is $B + C = \$24.1$ million per year.

Mini-Case

Digital Surplus

According to the U.S. Bureau of Economic Analysis, the information sector's contribution to gross domestic product (GDP), the value of national output, of about 4% to 5% has not changed in the past 35 years. Part of the reason is that many information goods have zero prices, such as social networking sites, search engines, Spotify, YouTube, and Wikipedia, which contribute to consumer surplus but are not fully captured in GDP. When people went from buying music in the form of CDs, records, and other physical products to streaming songs digitally, the price associated with music dropped and hence its recorded contribution to GDP fell by 40% even though people listened to more music than ever. Consumer surplus rose despite the drop in contribution to GDP.

---

[13]We estimated this model using data from the *Statistical Abstract of United States, Floriculture Crops, Floriculture and Environmental Horticulture Products,* and **usda.mannlib.cornell.edu**. The prices are in real 1991 dollars.

[14]The height of triangle A is 25.8¢ = 57.8¢ − 32¢ per stem and the base is 1.16 billion stems per year, so its area is $\frac{1}{2} \times \$0.258 \times 1.16$ billion = \$149.64 million per year. Rectangle B is $\$0.02 \times 1.16$ billion = \$23.2 million. Triangle C is $\frac{1}{2} \times \$0.02 \times 0.09$ billion = \$0.9 million.

Nordhaus (2005) estimated that of the returns from technological advances made between 1948 and 2001, only 3.7% were retained by corporations and the remaining 96.3% went to consumers in the form of consumer surplus.

Brynjolfsson et al. (2018) used experiments to determine consumers' willingness to pay for digital goods. A sample of Facebook users were asked whether they wanted to keep access to Facebook or give up access for a month in exchange for a certain amount of money. Brynjolfsson et al. estimated that the median Facebook user would have needed $37.76 to give up Facebook for a month in 2017. As Facebook is free to users, the estimated consumer surplus for the median Facebook consumer is $37.76 per month. Given that Facebook had 218 million U.S. users in 2018, it produces billions of dollars of consumer surplus.

Producer Surplus

A supplier's gain from participating in the market is measured by **producer surplus** (*PS*), which is the difference between the amount a good sells for and the minimum amount necessary for the producers to be willing to produce the good. The minimum amount a firm must receive to be willing to produce is the firm's avoidable production cost. Therefore, producer surplus is a measure of what the firm gains from trade.

Measuring Producer Surplus Using a Supply Curve. To determine a competitive firm's producer surplus, we use its supply curve: its marginal cost curve above its minimum average variable cost. The firm's supply curve in panel a of Figure 8.10 looks like a staircase. The marginal cost of producing the first unit is $MC_1 = \$1$, which is the area under the marginal cost curve between 0 and 1. The marginal cost of producing the second unit is $MC_2 = \$2$, and so on. The variable cost, *VC*, of producing four units is the sum of the marginal costs for the first four units:

FIGURE 8.9 Fall in Consumer Surplus from Roses as Price Rises

As the price of roses rises 2¢ per stem from 30¢ to 32¢ per stem, the quantity demanded decreases from 1.25 to 1.16 billion stems per year. The loss in consumer surplus from the higher price, areas *B* and *C*, is $24.1 million per year.

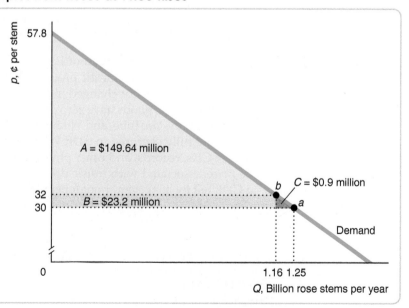

FIGURE 8.10 Producer Surplus

(a) The firm's producer surplus, $6, is the area below the market price, $4, and above the marginal cost (supply curve) up to the quantity sold, 4. The area under the marginal cost curve up to the number of units actually produced is the variable cost of production.

(b) The market producer surplus is the area above the supply curve and below the line at the market price, p^*, up to the quantity produced, Q^*. The area below the supply curve and to the left of quantity produced by the market, Q^*, is the variable cost of producing that level of output.

(a) A Firm's Producer Surplus

(b) A Market's Producer Surplus

$$VC = MC_1 + MC_2 + MC_3 + MC_4 = \$1 + \$2 + \$3 + \$4 = \$10.$$

If the market price, p, is $4, the firm's revenue from the sale of the first unit exceeds its cost by $PS_1 = p - MC_1 = \$4 - \$1 = \$3$, which is its producer surplus on the first unit. The firm's producer surplus is $2 on the second unit and $1 on the third unit. On the fourth unit, the price equals marginal cost, so the firm just breaks even. As a result, the firm's total producer surplus, PS, from selling four units at $4 each is the sum of its producer surplus on these four units:

$$PS = PS_1 + PS_2 + PS_3 + PS_4 = \$3 + \$2 + \$1 + \$0 = \$6.$$

Graphically, the total producer surplus is the area above the supply curve and below the market price up to the quantity actually produced. This same reasoning holds when the firm's supply curve is smooth.

A firm's producer surplus is revenue, R, minus variable cost, VC:

$$PS = R - VC.$$

In panel a of Figure 8.10, revenue is $4 \times 4 = \$16$ and variable cost is $10, so the firm's producer surplus is $6.

Q&A 8.4

If a firm has unavoidable fixed costs of F, how is its producer surplus related to its profit?

Answer

1. *Express the formula for profit in terms of variable and fixed cost.* A firm's profit is its revenue, R, minus its total cost, C, which equals variable cost plus fixed cost, F:

$$\pi = R - C = R - (VC + F).$$

2. *Take the difference between producer surplus and profit.* The difference is

$$PS - \pi = (R - VC) - (R - VC - F) = F.$$

Thus, the difference between a firm's producer surplus and profit is the fixed cost, F. If the fixed cost is zero (as often occurs in the long run), producer surplus equals profit.

Using Producer Surplus.   Even in the short run, we can use producer surplus to study the effects of a shock that affects the variable cost of production, such as a change in the price of a substitute or a variable input. Such shocks change profit by exactly the same amount as they change producer surplus because fixed costs do not change.

A major advantage of producer surplus is that we can use it to measure the effect of a shock on *all* the firms in a market without having to measure the profit of each firm in the market separately. We can calculate market producer surplus using the market supply curve in the same way as we calculate a firm's producer surplus using its supply curve. The market producer surplus in panel b of Figure 8.10 is the area above the supply curve and below the market price, p^*, up to the quantity sold, Q^*. The market supply curve is the horizontal sum of the marginal cost curves of each of the firms. As a result, the variable cost for all the firms in the market of producing Q is the area under the supply curve between 0 and the market output, Q^*.

Q&A 8.5

We estimated the supply curve for roses, which is the upward-sloping line in the following figure. How much producer surplus is lost if the price of roses falls from 30¢ to 21¢ per stem (so that the quantity sold falls from 1.25 billion to 1.16 billion rose stems per year)?

Answer

1. *Draw the supply curve, and show the change in producer surplus caused by the price change.* The figure shows the estimated supply curve for roses. Point a indicates the quantity supplied at the original price, 30¢, and point b reflects the quantity supplied at the lower price, 21¢. The loss in producer surplus is the sum of rectangle D and triangle E.

2. *Calculate the lost producer surplus by adding the areas of rectangle D and triangle E.* The height of rectangle D is the difference between the original and the new price, 9¢, and its base is 1.16 billion stems per year, so the area of D (not all of which is shown in the figure because of the break in the quantity axis) is $0.09 per stem × 1.16 billion stems per year = $104.4 million per year. The height of triangle E is also 9¢, and its length is 90 million stems per year, so its area is $\frac{1}{2}$ × $0.09 per stem × 90 million stems per year = $4.05 million per year. Thus, the loss in producer surplus from the drop in price is $108.45 million per year.

	Original Price, 30¢	Lower Price, 21¢	Change ($ millions)
Producer Surplus	$D + E + F$	F	$-(D + E) = -108.45$

Competition Maximizes Total Surplus

One of the most important results in economics is that perfect competition maximizes the sum of consumer surplus and producer surplus, which we call **total surplus** (*TS*):[15]

$$TS = CS + PS.$$

Total surplus is a measure of the total benefit to all market participants from market transactions, which are market participants' gains from trade. Total surplus implicitly weights the gains to consumers and producers equally. By using this measure to assess policies that affect market transactions, we are making a value judgment that the well-being of consumers and that of producers are equally important.

While most economists and many other people accept total surplus as a reasonable objective for society to try to maximize, not everyone agrees. Groups of producers commonly argue for legislation that helps them even if it hurts consumers by more than the amount producers gain—as though only producer surplus matters. Similarly, some consumer advocates argue that we should care only about consumers, so social well-being should include only consumer surplus.

A demonstration that perfect competition maximizes total surplus requires showing that (1) producing less than the competitive output lowers economic benefit as measured by total surplus, and (2) producing more than the competitive output lowers total surplus.

---

[15]Many economists call this sum *welfare*. We do not use that term because it has many different meanings in common language.

We show that reducing output from the competitive level reduces consumer surplus, producer surplus, and total surplus. (In Question 4.5 at the end of the chapter, you are asked to use a similar analysis to show that producing more than the competitive equilibrium quantity reduces total surplus.)

At the competitive equilibrium in Figure 8.11, e_1, where output is Q_1 and price is p_1, consumer surplus, CS_1, equals areas $A + B + C$, producer surplus, PS_1, is $D + E$, and the total surplus is $TS_1 = A + B + C + D + E$. Now suppose that we reduce output slightly from the competitive equilibrium quantity Q_1 to Q_2. As a result, price rises to p_2 at e_2, consumer surplus falls to $CS_2 = A$, producer surplus changes to $PS_2 = B + D$, and total surplus falls to $TS_2 = A + B + D$.

The change in consumer surplus is

$$\Delta CS = CS_2 - CS_1 = A - (A + B + C) = -B - C.$$

Consumers lose B because they have to pay $p_2 - p_1$ more than at the competitive price for the Q_2 units they buy. Consumers lose C because they buy only Q_2 rather than Q_1 at the higher price.

FIGURE 8.11 **Reducing Output from the Competitive Level Lowers Total Surplus**

Reducing output from the competitive level, Q_1, to Q_2 causes price to increase from p_1 to p_2. Consumers suffer: Consumer surplus is now A, a fall of $\Delta CS = -B - C$. Producers may gain or lose: Producer surplus is now $B + D$, a change of $\Delta PS = B - E$. Overall, the change in total surplus is $\Delta TS = -C - E$, which is negative. Therefore, total surplus falls by $C + E$, which is a deadweight loss (*DWL*) to society.

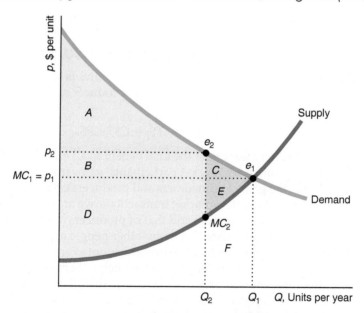

	Competitive Output, Q_1 (1)	Smaller Output, Q_2 (2)	Change (2) – (1)
Consumer Surplus, CS	$A + B + C$	A	$-B - C = \Delta CS$
Producer Surplus, PS	$D + E$	$B + D$	$B - E = \Delta PS$
Total Surplus, $TS = CS + PS$	$A + B + C + D + E$	$A + B + D$	$-C - E = \Delta TS = -DWL$

The change in producer surplus is

$$\Delta PS = PS_2 - PS_1 = (B + D) - (D + E) = B - E.$$

Producers gain B because they now sell Q_2 units at p_2 rather than p_1. They lose E because they sell $Q_2 - Q_1$ fewer units.

The change in total surplus, $\Delta TS = TS_2 - TS_1$, is[16]

$$\Delta TS = \Delta CS + \Delta PS = (-B - C) + (B - E) = -C - E.$$

The area B is a transfer from consumers to producers—the extra amount consumers pay for the Q_2 units goes to the sellers—so it does not affect total surplus. Total surplus drops because the consumer loss of C and the producer loss of E benefit no one. This change in total surplus, $\Delta TS = -C - E$, is a **deadweight loss** (DWL): the net reduction in total surplus from a loss of surplus by one group that is not offset by a gain to another group from an action that alters a market equilibrium.

The deadweight loss results because consumers value extra output by more than the marginal cost of producing it. At each output between Q_2 and Q_1, consumers' marginal willingness to pay for another unit—the height of the demand curve—is greater than the marginal cost of producing the next unit—the height of the supply curve. For example, at e_2, consumers value the next unit of output at p_2, which is much greater than the marginal cost, MC_2, of producing it. Increasing output from Q_2 to Q_1 raises firms' variable cost by area F, the area under the marginal cost (supply) curve between Q_2 and Q_1. Consumers value this extra output by the area under the demand curve between Q_2 and Q_1, area $C + E + F$. Thus, consumers value the extra output by $C + E$ more than it costs to produce it.

Society would be better off producing and consuming extra units of this good than spending this amount on other goods. In short, *the deadweight loss is the opportunity cost of giving up some of this good to buy more of another good.*

Just how much did Nicholas enjoy the expensive lime green woolen socks with the dancing purple teddy bears that his Aunt Fern gave him for the holidays? Often the cost of a gift exceeds the value that the recipient places on it.

Until the advent of gift cards, only 10% to 15% of holiday gifts were monetary. A gift of cash typically gives at least as much pleasure to the recipient as a gift that costs the same. (So what if giving cash is tacky?) Of course, it's possible that a gift can give more pleasure to the recipient than it cost the giver—but how often has that happened to you?

An *efficient gift* is one that the recipient values as much as the gift costs the giver, or more. The difference between the price of the gift and its value to the recipient is a deadweight loss. Joel Waldfogel (1993, 2009) asked Yale undergraduates just how large this deadweight loss is. He estimated that the deadweight loss is between 10% and 33% of the value of gifts. Waldfogel (2005) found that consumers value their own purchases at 10% to 18% more, per dollar spent, than items received as gifts.

---

[16]The change in total surplus is $\Delta TS = TS_2 - TS_1 = (CS_2 + PS_2) - (CS_1 + PS_1) = (CS_2 - CS_1) + (PS_2 - PS_1) = \Delta CS + \Delta PS.$

Waldfogel found that gifts from friends and "significant others" are most efficient, while non-cash gifts from members of the extended family are least efficient (one-third of the value is lost).[17] Luckily, grandparents, aunts, and uncles are most likely to give cash.

Waldfogel concluded that a conservative estimate of the deadweight loss of holidays with gift-giving rituals is about $12 billion. (And that's not counting about 2.8 billion hours spent shopping.) However, if givers get pleasure from picking the "perfect" gift, accounting for that pleasure would reduce this estimated deadweight loss.

Effects of Government Intervention

A government policy that limits trade in a competitive market reduces total surplus. For example, in some markets the government imposes a *price ceiling*, which sets a limit on the highest price that a firm can legally charge. If the government sets the ceiling below the precontrol competitive price, consumers want to buy more than the precontrol equilibrium quantity, but firms supply less than that quantity. (For example, see Chapter 2's Mini-Case "Disastrous Price Controls.") Thus, due to the price ceiling, consumers can buy the good at a lower price but cannot buy as much of it as they'd like. Because less is sold than at the precontrol equilibrium, society suffers a deadweight loss: Consumers value the good more than the marginal cost of producing extra units. Producer surplus must fall because firms receive a lower price and sell fewer units.

Q&A 8.6   What is the effect on the equilibrium and consumer, producer, and total surplus if the government sets a price ceiling, $\overline{p}$, below the unregulated competitive equilibrium price?

Answer

1. *Show the initial unregulated equilibrium.* The intersection of the demand curve and the supply curve determines the unregulated, competitive equilibrium, e_1, where the equilibrium quantity is Q_1.

---

[17]People may deal with a disappointing present by "regifting" it. Some families have been passing the same fruitcake among family members for decades. According to one survey, 33% of women and 19% of men admitted that they pass on an unwanted gift (and 28% of respondents said that they would not admit it if asked whether they had done so).

2. *Show how the equilibrium changes with the price ceiling.* Because the price ceiling, $\bar{p}$, is set below the equilibrium price of p_1, the ceiling binds. At this lower price, the quantity consumers demand increases to Q_d while the quantity firms are willing to supply falls to Q_s, so only $Q_s = Q_2$ units are sold at the new equilibrium, e_2. Thus, the price control causes the equilibrium quantity and price to fall, but consumers have excess demand of $Q_d - Q_s$.

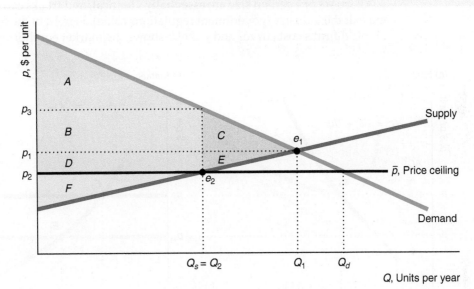

	No Ceiling	Price Ceiling	Change
Consumer Surplus, CS	$A + B + C$	$A + B + D$	$D - C = \Delta CS$
Producer Surplus, PS	$D + E + F$	F	$-D - E = \Delta PS$
Total Surplus, $TS = CS + PS$	$A + B + C + D + E + F$	$A + B + D + F$	$-C - E = \Delta TS = -DWL$

3. *Describe the effects on consumer, producer, and total surplus.* Because consumers are able to buy Q_s units at a lower price than before the controls, they gain area D. Consumers lose consumer surplus of C, however, because they can purchase only Q_s instead of Q_1 units of output. Thus, consumers gain net consumer surplus of $D - C$. Because they sell fewer units at a lower price, firms lose producer surplus $-D - E$. Part of this loss, D, is transferred to consumers because of lower prices, but the rest, E, is a loss to society. The deadweight loss to society is at least $C + E$.

Comment: This measure of the deadweight loss may *underestimate* the true loss. Because consumers want to buy more units than are sold, they may spend time searching for a store that has units for sale. This unsuccessful search activity is wasteful and hence a deadweight loss to society. Another possible inefficiency is that consumers who buy the good may value it less than those who are unable to find a unit to purchase. For example, someone might purchase the good who values it at p_2, while someone who values it at p_3 cannot find any to buy.

We return to the Managerial Problem at the beginning of the chapter: What effect do the government's higher annual fees and other lump-sum costs have on the trucking industry's market price and quantity? Are individual firms providing more or fewer trucking services? Does the number of firms in the market rise or fall? Because firms may enter and exit this industry in the long run, such higher lump-sum costs can have a counterintuitive effect on the competitive equilibrium.

All trucks of a certain size are essentially identical, and trucks can easily enter and exit the industry (government regulations aside). Panel a of the figure shows a typical firm's cost curves and panel b shows the market equilibrium.

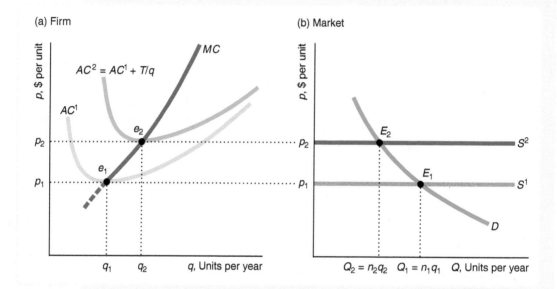

The new, higher fees and other lump-sum costs raise the fixed cost of operating by T. In panel a, a lump-sum, franchise tax shifts the typical firm's average cost curve upward from AC^1 to $AC^2 = AC^1 + T/q$, but does not affect the marginal cost. As a result, the minimum average cost rises from e_1 to e_2.

Given that an unlimited number of identical truckers are willing to operate in this market, the long-run market supply is horizontal at minimum average cost. Thus, the market supply curve shifts upward in panel b by the same amount as the minimum average cost increases. Given a downward-sloping market demand curve D, the new equilibrium, E_2, has a lower quantity, $Q_2 < Q_1$, and higher price, $p_2 > p_1$, than the original equilibrium, E_1.

As the market price rises, the quantity that a firm produces rises from q_1 to q_2 in panel a. Because the marginal cost curve is upward sloping at the original equilibrium, when the average cost curve shifts up due to the higher fixed cost, the new minimum point on the average cost curve corresponds to a larger output than in the original equilibrium. Thus, any trucking firm still operating in the market produces at a larger volume.

Because the market quantity falls but each firm remaining in the market produces more, the number of firms in the market must fall. At the initial equilibrium, the number of firms was $n_1 = Q_1/q_1$. The new equilibrium number of firms, $n_2 = Q_2/q_2$, must be smaller than n_1 because $Q_2 < Q_1$ and $q_2 > q_1$. Therefore, an increase in fixed cost causes the market price to rise and the total quantity and number of trucking firms to fall, as most people would have expected. However, it also has the surprising effect that it causes output per firm to increase for the firms that continue to produce.

SUMMARY

1. **Perfect Competition.** Perfect competition is a market structure in which buyers and sellers are price takers. Each firm faces a horizontal demand curve. A firm's demand curve is horizontal because perfectly competitive markets have five characteristics: the market has many small buyers and sellers, firms produce identical (homogeneous) products, buyers have full information about product prices and characteristics, transaction costs are negligible, and the market has free entry and exit in the long run. Many markets are highly competitive—firms are very close to being price takers—even if they do not strictly possess all five of the characteristics associated with perfect competition.

2. **Competition in the Short Run.** To maximize its profit, a competitive firm (like a firm in any other market structure) chooses its output level where marginal revenue equals marginal cost. Because a competitive firm is a price taker, its marginal revenue equals the market price, so it sets its output so that price equals marginal cost. New firms cannot enter in the short run. In addition, firms that are in the industry have some fixed inputs that cannot be changed and whose costs cannot be avoided. In this sense firms cannot exit the industry in the short run. However, a profit-maximizing firm shuts down and produces no output if the market price is less than its minimum average variable cost. Thus, a competitive firm's short-run supply curve is its marginal cost curve above its minimum average variable cost. The short-run market supply curve is the sum of the supply curves of the fixed number of firms producing in the short run. The short-run competitive equilibrium is determined by the intersection of the market demand curve and the short-run market supply curve.

3. **Competition in the Long Run.** In the long run, a competitive firm sets its output where the market price equals its long-run marginal cost. It shuts down if the market price is less than the minimum of its long-run average cost, because all costs are avoidable in the long run. Consequently, the competitive firm's long-run supply curve is its long-run marginal cost above its minimum long-run average cost. The long-run supply curve of a firm may have a different slope than the short-run curve because it can vary its fixed inputs in the long run. The long-run market supply curve is the horizontal sum of the supply curves of all the firms in the market. If all firms are identical, entry and exit are easy, and input prices are constant, then the long-run market supply curve is flat at minimum average cost. If firms differ, entry is difficult or costly, or input prices increase with output, the long-run market supply curve has an upward slope. The long-run market equilibrium price and quantity may be different from the short-run price and quantity.

4. **Competition Maximizes Economic Well-Being.** Perfect competition maximizes a commonly used measure of economic well-being, total surplus. Total surplus is the monetary value of the gain from trade. It is the sum of consumer surplus and producer surplus. Consumer surplus is the economic benefit or well-being obtained by a consumer in excess of the price paid. It equals the area under the consumer's demand curve above the market price up to the quantity that the consumer buys. Producer surplus is the amount producers are paid over and above the minimum amount needed to induce them to produce a given output level. A firm's producer surplus is its revenue minus the variable cost of production. Thus, if a firm has no fixed costs, as often occurs in the long run, a firm's producer surplus is the same as profit. In the short run, a firm's producer surplus is greater than profit by an amount equal to unavoidable fixed cost. Producer surplus is the area below the price and above the supply curve up to the quantity that the firm sells.

QUESTIONS

*All exercises are available on **MyLab Economics**; * = answer at the back of this book; **C** = use of calculus may be necessary;*
X = *this exercise is available in Excel Grader in* **MyLab Economics.**

1. Perfect Competition

1.1   According to Bustle.com, San Francisco has the most coffee shops of any American city (as of April 2016) with 2,613, with new shops opening regularly as the population grows. Suppose the city decides to stop issuing new business licenses for coffee shops so that the industry is capped at its current number of establishments. Which characteristics of this market are consistent with perfect competition and which are not? Is the coffee shop market likely to be nearly perfectly competitive? Why or why not?

*1.2   Why would high transaction costs or imperfect information tend to prevent price-taking behavior?

1.3   Economists often use the model of perfect competition to analyze the effect of economic shocks in particular industries. Which of the following industries is best approximated by perfect competition: agriculture, aircraft manufacturing, and social media (such as Facebook and Twitter)? Explain briefly.

2. Competition in the Short Run

2.1   A firm claims on its website that it has been in the same location for over 50 years and has lower overhead than other firms because it bought the land 50 years ago when it was inexpensive. It also claims that it charges lower prices than competitors because of its lower overhead. Discuss the logic of these claims.

*2.2   Many marginal cost curves are U-shaped. As a result, it is possible that the MC curve hits the demand or price line at two output levels. Which is the profit-maximizing output? Why?

2.3   Initially, the market price was $p = \$50$, and the competitive firm's minimum average variable cost was $42 while is minimum average cost was $54. Should it shut down? Why or why not? Now suppose the firm's average variable cost increases by $9 at every quantity, while other firms in the market are unaffected. What happens to its average cost? Should the firm shut down now? Why or why not?

2.4   Should a firm shut down if its revenue is $R = \$1,500$ per week and:

    a. its variable cost is $VC = \$1,100$ and its sunk fixed cost is $F = \$800$?

    b. its variable cost is $VC = \$1,600$ and its sunk fixed cost is $F = \$600$?

    c. its variable cost is $VC = \$1,100$ and its fixed cost is $F = \$1000$ ($800 of which is avoidable if it shuts down?

*2.5   The cost function for Acme Laundry is $C(q) = 10 + 10q + q^2$, so its marginal cost function is $MC = 10 + 2q$, where q is tons of laundry cleaned. Derive the firm's average cost and average variable cost curves. What q should the firm choose so as to maximize its profit if the market price is p? How much does it produce if the competitive market price is $p = 50$?

2.6   Beta Laundry's cost function is $C(q) = 50 + 10q + 2q^2$.

    a. What quantity maximizes Beta's profit if the market price is p? How much does it produce if $p = \$70$?

    b. If the government imposes a specific tax of $t = \$4$, what quantity maximizes Beta's after-tax profit? Does it operate or shut down? (*Hint:* See Q&A 8.1.) **C**

2.7   If the pre-tax cost function for John's Shoe Repair is $C(q) = 100 + 10q - q^2 + \frac{1}{3}q^3$, and it faces a specific tax of $t = 10$, what is its profit-maximizing condition if the market price is p? Can you solve for a single, profit-maximizing q in terms of p? (*Hint:* See Q&A 8.1.) **C**

2.8   If a specific subsidy (negative tax) of s is given to only one competitive firm, how should that firm change its output level to maximize its profit, and how does its maximum profit change? Use a graph to illustrate your answer. (*Hint:* See Q&A 8.1.)

2.9   In 2015, the average variable cost of producing wheat in Canada was close to $5.00 per bushel. Suppose that technological progress reduces the average variable cost to $4.00 per bushel. Use a figure to show how this change affects the supply curve of a typical competitive firm and the supply curve of all the firms in the market.

2.10   Fierce storms in October 2004 caused TomatoFest Organic Heirlooms Farm to end its tomato harvest two weeks early. According to Gary Ibsen, a partner in this small business (Carolyn Said, "Tomatoes in Trouble," *San Francisco Chronicle*, October 29, 2004, C1, C2), TomatoFest lost about 20,000 pounds of tomatoes that would have sold for about $38,000; however, because he did not have to hire pickers and rent trucks during these two weeks, his net loss was about $20,000. In calculating the revenue loss, he used the post-storm price, which was double the pre-storm price.

    a. Draw a diagram for a typical firm next to one for the market to show what happened as a result of the storm. Assume that TomatoFest's experience was typical of that of many small tomato farms.

b. Did TomatoFest suffer an economic loss? What extra information (if any) do you need to answer this question? How do you define "economic loss" in this situation?

2.11 The internet is affecting holiday shipping. In years past, the busiest shipping period was Thanksgiving week. Now, as people have become comfortable with e-commerce, they purchase later in the year and are more likely to have gifts shipped (rather than purchasing locally). FedEx, along with Amazon and other e-commerce firms, hires extra workers during this period, and many regular workers log substantial overtime hours.

a. Are the marginal and average costs of internet retailers likely to rise or fall with this extra business? (Discuss economies of scale and the slopes of marginal and average cost curves.)

b. Use side-by-side firm-market diagrams to show the effects on the number of firms, equilibrium price and output, and profits of such a seasonal shift in demand for e-retailers in both the short run and the long run. Explain your reasoning.

2.12 What is the effect on the short-run equilibrium of a specific subsidy of s per unit that is given to all n firms in a market?

3. Competition in the Long Run

3.1 Customers at California grocery and drug stores must pay an extra 10¢ for every paper bag the store provides (the store keeps this fee). Does such a charge affect the marginal cost of any particular good? If so, by how much? Is this fee likely to affect the overall amount that consumers pay for groceries?

*3.2 What are the short-run and long-run effects on firm and market equilibrium of the U.S. law requiring a firm to give its workers six months' notice before it can shut down its plant?

3.3 The Mini-Case "An Upward-Sloping Long-Run Supply Curve for Cotton" shows a supply curve for cotton. Discuss the equilibrium if the world demand curve crosses this supply curve in either (a) a flat section labeled Brazil or (b) the vertical section that follows it. What do cotton farms in the United States do?

3.4 Chinese art factories are flooding the world's generic art market (Keith Bradsher, "Own Original Chinese Copies of Real Western Art!" *New York Times*, July 15, 2005). The value of bulk shipments of Chinese paintings to the United States nearly tripled from slightly over $10 million in 1996 to $30.5 million in 2004 (and early 2005 sales were up 50% from the corresponding period in 2004). A typical artist earns less than

$200 a month, plus modest room and board, or $360 a month without food and housing. Using a step-like supply function (similar to the one in the Mini-Case "An Upward-Sloping Long-Run Supply Curve for Cotton"), show how the entry of the Chinese producers affects the world supply curve and how this change affects the equilibrium (including who produces art). Explain.

3.5 Oil spills such as BP's huge 2010 oil spill in the Gulf of Mexico and the 2015 Plains All American Pipeline oil spill into the ocean near Santa Barbara, California, led to clean-up efforts that greatly increased purchases of boat services, various oil-absorbing materials, and other goods and services to minimize damage from the spill. Use side-by-side firm and market diagrams to show the effects (number of firms, price, output, profits) of such a shift in demand in one such industry, such as boat services, in both the short run and the long run. Explain how your answer depends on whether the shift in demand is expected to be temporary or permanent.

3.6 In late 2004 and early 2005, the price of raw coffee beans jumped as much as 50% from the previous year. In response, the price of roasted coffee rose about 14%. Similarly, in late 2014 and early 2015, the price of raw beans fell by about 25%, yet the price of roasted coffee fell by only a few percentage points. Why did the roasted coffee price change less than in proportion to the rise in the cost of raw beans?

3.7 When the voters of Oakland, California, passed a measure to tax medical marijuana, effectively legalizing it, its City Council adopted regulations permitting industrial-scale marijuana farms with no size limits but requiring each to pay a $211,000 per year fee. One proposal called for a 100,000 square foot farm, the size of two football fields. Prior to this legalization, only individuals could grow marijuana. These small farmers complained bitterly, arguing that the large firms would drive them out of the industry they helped to build due to economies of scale. Draw a figure to illustrate the situation. Under what conditions (concerning relative costs, characteristics of the demand curve, number of low-cost firms, or other) would the smaller, higher-cost growers be driven out of business?

3.8 A typical firm in long-run equilibrium in an industry with identical firms has a cost function given by $C = 800 + 2q^2$ and has a marginal cost function of $MC = 4q$. The fixed cost of 800 is avoidable if the firm shuts down. What is the equilibrium price? (*Hint*: See Q&A 8.3.)

3.9 Given the cost information in the previous question and a demand function of $Q = 2,400 - 5p$, how many firms are in this industry in the long-run equilibrium?

4. Competition Maximizes Economic Well-Being

4.1 Using the information in panel a of Figure 8.8, determine what happens to David's quantity demanded and consumer surplus if price falls to $p = \$1$.

*4.2 If the inverse demand function for toasters is $p = 60 - Q$, what is the consumer surplus when the price is 30?

4.3 Access to Twitter is free, but Brynjolfsson et al. (2018) found that many Twitter users would be willing to pay for access. Draw a demand curve for Twitter. Show the consumer surplus at the current price of zero. (*Hint*: See the Mini-Case "Digital Surplus.")

4.4 For a firm, how does the concept of *producer surplus* differ from that of *profit* if it has no fixed costs? (*Hint*: See Q&A 8.4.)

*4.5 Using a graph similar to Figure 8.11, show that increasing output beyond the competitive level decreases total surplus because the cost of producing this extra output exceeds the value consumers place on it.

4.6 If the supply function is $Q = -50 + 5p$, what is the producer surplus if the price is \$40? (*Hint*: See Q&A 8.5.)

4.7 Nicholas owned no green sweaters, so his Aunt Fern gave him one for his 21st birthday. However, the market price of the sweater was higher than his willingness to pay for it. Draw a diagram showing Nicholas's demand curve for green sweaters and identify and explain the deadweight loss. (*Hint*: See the Mini-Case "The Deadweight Loss of Holiday Gifts.")

4.8 The government sets a minimum wage above the current equilibrium wage. What effect does the minimum wage have on the market equilibrium? What are its effects on consumer surplus, producer surplus, and total surplus? Who are the consumers and who are the producers? (*Hint*: See Q&A 8.6.)

4.9 Suppose that the demand curve for wheat is $Q = 100 - 10p$ and the supply curve is $Q = 10p$. The government imposes a price ceiling of $p = 3$. (*Hint*: See Q&A 8.6.)

   a. Describe how the equilibrium changes.

   b. What effect does this price ceiling have on consumer surplus, producer surplus, and deadweight loss?

5. Managerial Problem

5.1 The North American Free Trade Agreement provides for two-way, long-haul trucking across the U.S.–Mexican border. U.S. truckers have objected, arguing that the Mexican trucks don't have to meet the same environmental and safety standards as U.S. trucks. They are concerned that the combination of these lower fixed costs and lower Mexican wages will result in Mexican drivers taking business from them. Their complaints have delayed implementation of this agreement (except for a small pilot program during the Bush administration, which ended during the Obama administration). What would be the short-run and long-run effects of allowing entry of Mexican drivers on market price and quantity and on the number of U.S. truckers?

5.2 In the Managerial Solution, would it make a difference to the analysis whether the government collects lump-sum costs such as registration fees annually or only once when the firm starts operation? How would each of these franchise taxes affect the firm's long-run supply curve? Explain your answer.

5.3 Give an answer to the Managerial Problem for the short run rather than for the long run. (*Hint*: The answer depends on where the demand curve intersects the original short-run supply curve.)

5.4 In a perfectly competitive market, all firms are identical, firms can freely enter and exit, and the market has an unlimited number of potential entrants. Now, the government starts collecting a specific tax t. What is the effect on the long-run equilibrium market quantity, market price, and the quantity for an individual firm?

6. MyLab Economics Spreadsheet Exercises[18]

6.1 A competitive firm's cost of producing q units of output is $C = 18 + 4q + q^2$. Its corresponding marginal cost is $MC = 4 + 2q$.

   a. The firm faces a market price $p = \$24$. Create a spreadsheet with $q = 0, 1, 2, \ldots, 15$, where the columns are q, R, C, VC, AVC, MC, and profit. Determine the profit-maximizing output for the firm and the corresponding profit. Should the firm produce this level of output or should it shut down? Explain briefly. (*Hint*: See Q&A 8.2.)

   b. Suppose the competitive price declines to $p = \$12$. Repeat the calculations of part a. Should the firm shut down?

6.2 The long-run average cost curve for a competitive firm is $AC = 35 - 10q + q^2$.

   a. Use the Excel *Solver* tool to find the cost-minimizing quantity. Enter the labels q and AC in cells A1 and B1. Enter the formula for AC in

---

[18]The spreadsheet exercises in this chapter are based largely on the work of Satyajit Ghosh, in cooperation with the authors. The answers are available on MyLab Economics.

cell B2. Select the *Data* tab, then select the *Solver* tool.[19] A dialog box will appear. Enter B2 in the *Set Objective* row, select *Min*, and enter A2 in the *"By Changing Variable Cells"* row. Then select *Solve*. What is the cost-minimizing quantity? What is AC at this quantity?

b. This firm is one of many identical firms in a competitive industry that is in long run equilibrium. The market demand function for this industry is $Q = 620 - 8p$. Use Excel to determine the industry quantity. (*Hint*: The long-run supply curve is horizontal at the minimum of the average cost of a typical firm.)

c. How many firms are in this industry in the long-run competitive equilibrium?

6.3 In a competitive market, the market demand curve is $Q = 28 - 2p$ and the market supply curve is $Q_s = -8 + 2p$. Use a spreadsheet to answer the following questions.

a. Determine the quantity demanded and quantity supplied for $p = \$4, 5, 6, \dots, 14$. Determine the equilibrium quantity and price.

b. For prices $p = \$4, 5, 6, \dots, 14$, determine the consumer surplus. How does an increase in price affect the consumer surplus?

c. For prices $p = \$4, 5, 6, \dots, 14$, determine the producer surplus. How does an increase in price affect the producer surplus?

d. Suppose the government limits the quantity traded in the market to 6 units. Calculate the resulting deadweight loss.

---

[19]If you do not see the *Solver* tool, you need to load it first. Look up *Solver* in the Excel help facility for instructions.

9 Monopoly

Monopoly: one parrot.

A firm that creates a new drug may receive a patent that gives it the right to be the monopoly or sole producer of that drug for up to 20 years. As a result, the firm can charge a price much greater than its marginal cost of production. For example, one of the world's best-selling drugs, the heart medication Plavix, sold for about $7 per pill, though it cost only about 3¢ per pill to produce. A new drug to treat hepatitis C, Harvoni, sells for over $1,000 a pill or over $84,000 for a 12-week course of treatment. In 2015, Martin Shkreli, then the head of Turing Pharmaceuticals, raised the price of Daraprim, used to treat infections that are common in HIV/AIDS patients, from $13.50 to $750 per pill. Its price rose to as high at $800 by 2018. Shkreli acknowledged that the drug costs "very little money" to make.

Every year, many pharmaceuticals lose their patent protection, as Plavix has. In 2018, patents for Apidra (diabetes), Ampyra (multiple sclerosis), Lyrica (nerve and muscle pain), and many other high-revenue drugs expired. In 2019, patent protection for Avastin (cancer), Azasite (bacterial eye infections), Ranexa (heart disease), and others end.

Generally, when a patent for a highly profitable drug expires, competing firms enter the market and sell generic (equivalent) versions of the brand-name drug. Generics' share of all U.S. prescriptions rose from about 18% in 1984 to nearly 80% currently.

When the U.S. Congress originally passed a law permitting generic drugs to quickly enter a market after a patent expires, it expected that patent expiration would subsequently lead to sharp declines in drug prices.[1] If consumers view the generic product and the brand-name product as perfect substitutes, both goods will sell for the same price, and entry by many firms will drive the price down to the competitive level. Even if consumers view the goods as imperfect substitutes, one might expect the price of the brand-name drug to fall.

---

[1]Under the 1984 Hatch-Waxman Act, the U.S. government allows a firm to sell a generic product after a brand-name drug's patent expires if the generic-drug firm can prove that its product delivers the same amount of active ingredient or drug to the body in the same way as the brand-name product. Sometimes the same firm manufactures both a brand-name drug and an equivalent generic drug, so the two have identical ingredients. Generics produced by other firms usually have a different appearance and name than the original product and may have different nonactive ingredients, but they have identical amounts of the active ingredients.

However, the prices of many brand-name drugs have increased after their patents expired and generics entered the market. The generic drugs are relatively inexpensive, but the brand-name drugs often continue to enjoy a significant market share and sell for high prices. Regan (2008) studied the effects of generic entry on post-patent price competition for 18 prescription drugs, and found an average 2% increase in brand-name prices. Studies based on older data have found up to a 7% average increase. Why do some brand-name prices rise after the entry of generic drugs?[2]

Why can a firm with a patent-based monopoly charge a high price? Why might a brand-name pharmaceutical's price rise after its patent expires? To answer these questions, we need to understand the decision-making process for a **monopoly**: the sole supplier of a good that has no close substitute.[3]

Monopolies have been common since ancient times. In the fifth century B.C., the Greek philosopher Thales gained control of most of the olive presses during a year of exceptionally productive harvests. The ancient Egyptian pharaohs controlled the sale of food. In England, until Parliament limited the practice in 1624, kings granted monopoly rights called royal charters to court favorites. Particularly valuable royal charters went to companies that controlled trade with North America, the Hudson Bay Company, and with India, the British East India Company.

In modern times, government actions continue to play an important role in creating monopolies. Governments grant patents that allow the inventor of a new product, such as a new drug, to be the sole supplier of that product for up to 20 years, and sometimes grant monopoly rights for other reasons as well. Many utilities—water, gas, and electricity—are government-owned or government-protected monopolies.[4]

Some firms are able to gain monopoly power without government help. When first introduced, Apple's iPad had a near monopoly in the tablet market.

Unlike a competitive firm, which is a price taker (Chapter 8), a monopoly can *set* its price. A monopoly's output is the market output, and the demand curve a monopoly faces is the market demand curve. Because the market demand curve is downward sloping, the monopoly (unlike a competitive firm) doesn't lose all its sales if it raises its price. As a consequence, a profit-maximizing monopoly sets its price above marginal cost, the price that would prevail in a competitive market. Consumers buy less at this relatively high monopoly price than they would at the competitive price.

---

[2]The sources for this Challenge and the Applications in this chapter are listed at the end of this chapter.

[3]Analogously, a *monopsony* is the only *buyer* of a good in a given market.

[4]Whether the law views a firm as a monopoly depends on how broadly the market is defined. Is the market limited to a particular drug or the pharmaceutical industry as a whole? The manufacturer of the drug is a monopoly in the former case, but just one of many firms in the latter case. Thus, defining a market is critical in legal cases. A market definition depends on whether other products are good substitutes for those in that market.

Learning Objectives

1. Show how a monopoly chooses an output level to maximize its profit.
2. Calculate the extent of a monopoly's market power.
3. Describe how monopoly causes a market failure.
4. List the causes of monopoly.
5. Explain how a monopoly uses advertising to increase its profit.
6. Discuss the sources of market power for internet firms.

9.1 Monopoly Profit Maximization

All firms, including competitive firms and monopolies, maximize their profits by setting quantity such that *marginal revenue equals marginal cost* (Chapter 7). Chapter 6 demonstrates how to derive a marginal cost curve. We now derive the monopoly's marginal revenue curve and then use the marginal revenue and marginal cost curves to examine how the manager of a monopoly sets quantity to maximize profit.

Marginal Revenue

A firm's marginal revenue curve depends on its demand curve. We will show that a monopoly's marginal revenue curve lies below its demand curve at any positive quantity because its demand curve is downward sloping.

Marginal Revenue and Price. A firm's demand curve shows the price, p, it receives for selling a given quantity, q. The price is the *average revenue* the firm receives, so a firm's revenue is $R = pq$.

A firm's *marginal revenue*, MR, is the change in its revenue from selling one more unit. A firm that earns ΔR more revenue when it sells Δq extra units of output has a marginal revenue of

$$MR = \frac{\Delta R}{\Delta q}.$$

If the firm sells exactly one more unit ($\Delta q = 1$), then its marginal revenue, MR, is $\Delta R(= \Delta R/1)$.

The marginal revenue of a monopoly differs from that of a competitive firm because the monopoly faces a downward-sloping demand curve, unlike the competitive firm. The competitive firm in panel a of Figure 9.1 faces a horizontal demand curve at the market price, p_1. Because its demand curve is horizontal, the competitive firm can sell another unit of output without reducing its price. As a result, the marginal revenue it receives from selling the last (and every) unit of output is the market price.

Initially, the competitive firm sells q units of output at the market price of p_1, so its revenue, R_1, is area A, which is a rectangle that is $p_1 \times q$. If the firm sells one more unit, its revenue is $R_2 = A + B$, where area B is $p_1 \times 1 = p_1$. The competitive firm's marginal revenue equals the market price:

$$\Delta R = R_2 - R_1 = (A + B) - A = B = p_1.$$

FIGURE 9.1 Average and Marginal Revenue

The demand curve shows the average revenue or price per unit of output sold. (a) The competitive firm's marginal revenue, area B, equals the market price, p_1.

(b) The monopoly's marginal revenue is less than the price p_2 by area C, the revenue lost due to a lower price on the Q units originally sold.

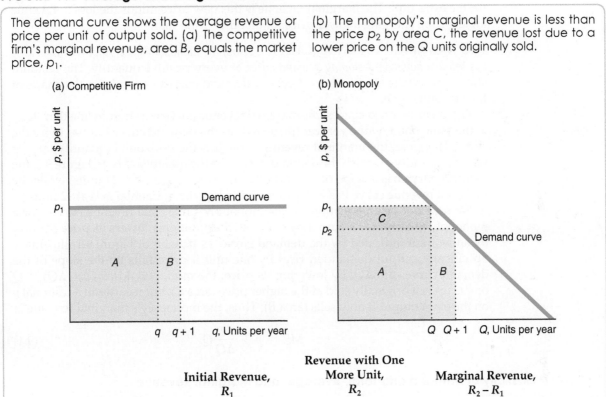

	Initial Revenue, R_1	Revenue with One More Unit, R_2	Marginal Revenue, $R_2 - R_1$
Competition	A	$A + B$	$B = p_1$
Monopoly	$A + C$	$A + B$	$B - C = p_2 - C$

A monopoly faces a downward-sloping market demand curve, as in panel b of Figure 9.1. So far, we have used q to represent the output of a single firm and Q to represent the combined market output of all firms in a market. Because a monopoly is the only firm in the market, q and Q are identical, so we use Q to describe both the firm's output and market output.

The monopoly, which initially sells Q units at p_1, can sell one extra unit only if it lowers its price to p_2 on *all* units. The monopoly's initial revenue, $p_1 \times Q$, is $R_1 = A + C$. When it sells the extra unit, its revenue, $p_2 \times (Q + 1)$, is $R_2 = A + B$. Thus, its marginal revenue is

$$\Delta R = R_2 - R_1 = (A + B) - (A + C) = B - C.$$

The monopoly sells the extra unit of output at the new price, p_2, so its extra revenue is $B = p_2 \times 1 = p_2$. The monopoly loses the difference between the original price and the new lower price, $\Delta p = (p_1 - p_2)$, on the Q units it originally sold: $C = \Delta p \times Q$. Therefore the monopoly's marginal revenue, $B - C = p_2 - C$, is less than the price it charges by an amount equal to area C.

Because the competitive firm in panel a can sell as many units as it wants at the market price, it does not have to cut its price to sell an extra unit, so it does not have to give up revenue such as area C in panel b. It is the downward slope of the monopoly's demand curve that causes its marginal revenue to be less than its price. For a monopoly to sell one more unit in a given period, it must lower the price on all the units it sells that period, so its marginal revenue is less than the price obtained for the extra unit. The marginal revenue is this new price minus the loss in revenue arising from charging a lower price for all other units sold.

The Marginal Revenue Curve. Thus, *the monopoly's marginal revenue curve lies below a downward-sloping demand curve* at every positive quantity. The relationship between the marginal revenue and demand curves depends on the shape of the demand curve.

For linear demand curves, the marginal revenue curve is a straight line that starts at the same point on the vertical (price) axis as the demand curve but has twice the slope. Therefore, the marginal revenue curve hits the horizontal (quantity) axis at half the quantity at which the demand curve hits the quantity axis. In Figure 9.2, the demand curve has a slope of −1 and hits the horizontal axis at 24 units, while the marginal revenue curve has a slope of −2 and hits the horizontal axis at 12 units.

We now derive an equation for the monopoly's marginal revenue curve. For a monopoly to increase its output by one unit, the monopoly lowers its price per unit by an amount indicated by the demand curve, as panel b of Figure 9.1 illustrates. Specifically, output demanded rises by one unit if price falls by the slope of the demand curve, $\Delta p / \Delta Q$. By lowering its price, the monopoly loses $(\Delta p / \Delta Q) \times Q$ on the units it originally sold at the higher price (area C), but it earns an additional p on the extra output it now sells (area B). Thus, the monopoly's marginal revenue is

$$MR = p + \frac{\Delta p}{\Delta Q}Q. \tag{9.1}$$

FIGURE 9.2 Elasticity of Demand and Total, Average, and Marginal Revenue

The demand curve (or average revenue curve), $p = 24 - Q$, lies above the marginal revenue curve, $MR = 24 - 2Q$. Where the marginal revenue equals zero, $Q = 12$, the elasticity of demand is $\varepsilon = -1$. For larger quantities, the marginal revenue is negative, so the MR curve is below the horizontal axis.

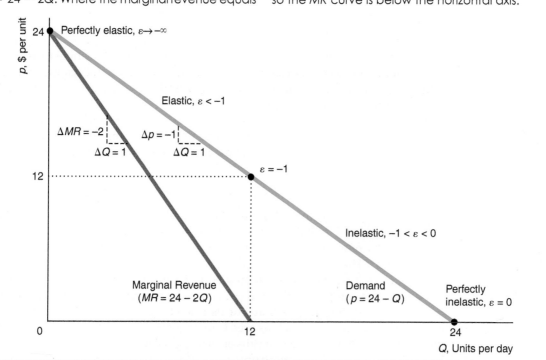

Because the slope of the monopoly's demand curve, $\Delta p / \Delta Q$, is negative, the last term in Equation 9.1, $(\Delta p / \Delta Q)Q$, is negative. Equation 9.1 confirms that the price the monopoly charges is greater than the marginal revenue, which equals p plus a negative term and must therefore be less than the price.

We now use Equation 9.1 to derive the marginal revenue curve when the monopoly faces the linear inverse demand function (Chapter 3)

$$p = 24 - Q \tag{9.2}$$

that Figure 9.2 illustrates. Equation 9.2 shows that the price consumers are willing to pay falls \$1 if quantity increases by one unit. More generally, if quantity increases by ΔQ, price falls by $\Delta p = -\Delta Q$. Thus, the slope of the demand curve is $\Delta p / \Delta Q = -1$.

We obtain the marginal revenue function for this monopoly by substituting into Equation 9.1 the actual slope of the demand function, $\Delta p / \Delta Q = -1$, and replacing p with $24 - Q$ (using Equation 9.2):

$$MR = p + \frac{\Delta p}{\Delta Q}Q = (24 - Q) + (-1)Q = 24 - 2Q. \tag{9.3}$$

Figure 9.2 shows a plot of Equation 9.3. The slope of this marginal revenue curve is $\Delta MR / \Delta Q = -2$, so the marginal revenue curve is twice as steep as the demand curve.

Using Calculus

Deriving a Monopoly's Marginal Revenue Function

Using calculus, if a firm's revenue function is $R(Q)$, then its marginal revenue function is

$$MR(Q) = \frac{dR(Q)}{dQ}.$$

For our example, where the inverse demand function is $p(Q) = 24 - Q$, the revenue function is

$$R(Q) = p(Q)Q = (24 - Q)Q = 24Q - Q^2. \tag{9.4}$$

By differentiating Equation 9.4 with respect to Q, we obtain the marginal revenue function, $MR(Q) = dR(Q)/dQ = 24 - 2Q$, which is the same as Equation 9.3.

Q&A 9.1

Given a general linear inverse demand function $p(Q) = a - bQ$, where a and b are positive constants, use calculus to show that the marginal revenue curve is twice as steeply sloped as the demand curve. (*Hint*: Recall that this linear inverse demand function corresponds to a linear demand curve with a price intercept a and a slope equal to the derivative of the inverse demand function with respect to quantity.)

Answer

1. *Differentiate the inverse linear demand function with respect to Q to determine its derivative, which is the slope of the demand curve.* The derivative of the linear inverse demand function with respect to Q is

$$\frac{dp(Q)}{dQ} = \frac{d(a - bQ)}{dQ} = -b.$$

2. *Differentiate the monopoly's revenue function with respect to Q to obtain the marginal revenue function; then differentiate the marginal revenue function with respect to Q to determine its slope.* The monopoly's revenue function is $R(Q) = p(Q)Q = (a - bQ)Q = aQ - bQ^2$. Differentiating the revenue function with respect to quantity, we find that the marginal revenue function is linear,

$$MR(Q) = dR(Q)/dQ = a - 2bQ.$$

The marginal revenue curve that corresponds to this marginal revenue function has a slope of

$$\frac{dMR(Q)}{dQ} = -2b,$$

which is twice the slope of the demand curve, $dp/dQ = -b$.

Comment: Note that the vertical axis intercept is a for both the demand curve and the *MR* curve and that the marginal revenue curve, like the demand curve, is linear. The marginal revenue curve is twice as steep as the demand curve.

Marginal Revenue and Price Elasticity of Demand.

The marginal revenue at any given quantity depends on the demand curve's height (the price) and shape. The shape of the demand curve at a particular quantity is described by the price elasticity of demand (Chapter 3), $\varepsilon = (\Delta Q/Q)/(\Delta p/p) < 0$, which tells us the percentage by which quantity demanded falls as the price increases by 1%.

At a given quantity, the marginal revenue equals the price times a term involving the elasticity of demand (Chapter 3):[5]

$$MR = p\left(1 + \frac{1}{\varepsilon}\right). \tag{9.5}$$

According to Equation 9.5, marginal revenue is closer to price as demand becomes more elastic. Where the demand curve hits the price axis ($Q = 0$), the demand curve is perfectly elastic, so the marginal revenue equals price: $MR = p$.[6] Where the demand elasticity is unitary, $\varepsilon = -1$, marginal revenue is zero: $MR = p[1 + 1/(-1)] = 0$. Marginal revenue is negative where the demand curve is inelastic, $-1 < \varepsilon \leq 0$.

With the inverse demand function in Equation 9.2, $\Delta Q/\Delta p = -1$, so the elasticity of demand is $\varepsilon = (\Delta Q/\Delta p)(p/Q) = -p/Q$. Table 9.1 shows the relationship among quantity, price, marginal revenue, and elasticity of demand for this linear example. As Q approaches 24, ε approaches 0, and marginal revenue is negative. As Q approaches zero, the demand becomes increasingly elastic, and marginal revenue approaches the price.

---

[5]By multiplying the last term in Equation 9.1 by p/p ($= 1$) and using algebra, we can rewrite the expression as

$$MR = p + p\frac{\Delta p}{\Delta Q}\frac{Q}{p} = p\left[1 + \frac{1}{(\Delta Q/\Delta p)(p/Q)}\right].$$

The last term in this expression is $1/\varepsilon$, because $\varepsilon = (\Delta Q/\Delta p)(p/Q)$.

[6]As ε approaches $-\infty$ (perfectly elastic demand), the $1/\varepsilon$ term approaches zero, so $MR = p(1 + 1/\varepsilon)$ approaches p.

TABLE 9.1 Quantity, Price, Marginal Revenue, and Elasticity for the Linear Inverse Demand Function $p = 24 - Q$

Quantity, Q	Price, p	Marginal Revenue, MR	Elasticity of Demand, $\varepsilon = -p/Q$	
0	24	24	$-\infty$	↑ more elastic
1	23	22	-23	
2	22	20	-11	
3	21	18	-7	
4	20	16	-5	
5	19	14	-3.8	
6	18	12	-3	
7	17	10	-2.43	
8	16	8	-2	
9	15	6	-1.67	
10	14	4	-1.4	
11	13	2	-1.18	
12	**12**	**0**	**-1**	
13	11	-2	-0.85	
$\vdots$	$\vdots$	$\vdots$	$\vdots$	↓ less elastic
23	1	-22	-0.043	
24	0	-24	0	

Choosing Price or Quantity

Any firm maximizes its profit by operating where its marginal revenue equals its marginal cost. Unlike a competitive firm, a monopoly can adjust its price, so it has a choice of setting its price *or* its quantity to maximize its profit. (A competitive firm sets its quantity to maximize profit because it cannot affect the market price.)

Whether the monopoly sets its price or its quantity, the other variable is determined by the market demand curve. Because the demand curve slopes down, the monopoly faces a trade-off between a higher price and a lower quantity or a lower price and a higher quantity. A profit-maximizing monopoly chooses the point on the demand curve that maximizes its profit. Unfortunately for the monopoly, it cannot set both its quantity and its price, such as at a point that lies above its demand curve. If it could do so, the monopoly would choose an extremely high price and an extremely large output and would earn a very high profit. However, the monopoly cannot choose a point that lies above the demand curve.

If the monopoly sets its price, the demand curve determines how much output it sells. If the monopoly picks an output level, the demand curve determines the price. Because the monopoly wants to operate at the price and output at which its profit is maximized, it chooses the same profit-maximizing solution whether it sets the price or quantity. Thus, setting price and setting quantity are equivalent for a monopoly. In the following discussion, we assume that the monopoly sets quantity.

Two Steps to Maximizing Profit

All profit-maximizing firms, including monopolies, use a two-step analysis to determine the output level that maximizes their profit (Chapter 7). First, the firm determines the output, Q^*, at which it makes the highest possible profit (or minimizes its loss). Second, the firm decides whether to produce Q^* or shut down.

Profit-Maximizing Output. In Chapter 7, we saw that profit is maximized where *marginal profit equals zero*. Equivalently, because *marginal profit equals marginal revenue minus marginal cost* (Chapter 7), marginal profit is zero where *marginal revenue equals marginal cost*.

To illustrate how a monopoly chooses its output to maximize its profit, we use the same linear demand and marginal revenue curves as above and add a linear marginal cost curve in panel a of Figure 9.3. Panel b shows the corresponding profit curve.

The marginal revenue curve, *MR*, intersects the marginal cost curve, *MC*, at 6 units in panel a. The corresponding price, 18, is the height of the demand curve, point *e*, at 6 units. The profit, π, is the gold rectangle. The height of this rectangle is the average profit per unit, $p - AC = 18 - 8 = 10$. The length of the rectangle is 6 units. Thus, the area of the rectangle is the average profit per unit times the number of units, which is the profit, $\pi = 60$.

FIGURE 9.3 **Maximizing Profit**

(a) At Q = 6, where marginal revenue, *MR*, equals marginal cost, *MC*, profit is maximized. The rectangle shows that the profit is $60, where the height of the rectangle is the average profit per unit, $p - AC = \$18 - \$8 = \$10$, and the length is the number of units, 6.
(b) Profit is maximized at Q = 6 (where marginal revenue equals marginal cost).

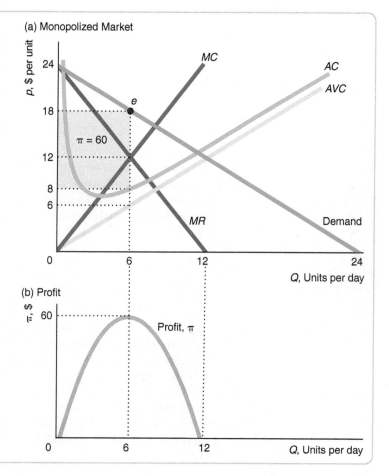

The profit at 6 units is the maximum possible profit: The profit curve in panel b reaches its peak, 60, at 6 units. At the peak of the profit curve, the marginal profit is zero, which is consistent with the marginal revenue equaling the marginal cost.

Why does the monopoly maximize its profit by producing where its marginal revenue equals its marginal cost? At smaller quantities, the monopoly's marginal revenue is greater than its marginal cost, so its marginal profit is positive—the profit curve is upward sloping. By increasing its output, the monopoly raises its profit. Similarly, at quantities greater than 6 units, the monopoly's marginal cost is greater than its marginal revenue, so its marginal profit is negative, and the monopoly can increase its profit by reducing its output.

As Figure 9.2 illustrates, the marginal revenue curve is positive where the elasticity of demand is elastic, is zero at the quantity where the demand curve has a unitary elasticity, and is negative at larger quantities where the demand curve is inelastic. Because the marginal cost curve is never negative, the marginal revenue curve can only intersect the marginal cost curve where the marginal revenue curve is positive, in the range in which the demand curve is elastic. That is, *a monopoly's profit is maximized in the elastic portion of the demand curve.* In our example, profit is maximized at $Q = 6$, where the elasticity of demand is -3. *A profit-maximizing monopoly never operates in the inelastic portion of its demand curve.*

The Shutdown Decision.

A monopoly shuts down to avoid making a loss in the short run if its price is below its average variable cost at its profit-maximizing (or loss-minimizing) quantity (Chapter 7). In the long run, the monopoly shuts down if the price is less than its average cost.

In the short-run example in Figure 9.3, the average variable cost, $AVC = 6$, is less than the price, $p = 18$, at the profit-maximizing output, $Q = 6$, so the monopoly chooses to produce. Because the price is also above the average cost at $Q = 6$, the average profit per unit, $p - AC$, (the height of the gold profit rectangle), is positive, so the monopoly makes a positive profit.

Using Calculus

Solving for the Profit-Maximizing Output

We can also solve for the profit-maximizing quantity mathematically. We already know the demand and marginal revenue functions for this monopoly. We need to determine its cost curves.

The monopoly's cost is a function of its output, $C(Q)$. In Figure 9.3, we assume that the monopoly faces a short-run cost function of

$$C(Q) = 12 + Q^2, \tag{9.6}$$

where Q^2 is the monopoly's variable cost as a function of output and 12 is its fixed cost. Given this cost function, Equation 9.6, the monopoly's marginal cost function is

$$\frac{dC(Q)}{dQ} = MC(Q) = 2Q. \tag{9.7}$$

This marginal cost curve in panel a is an upward sloping straight line through the origin with a slope of 2. The average variable cost is $AVC = Q^2/Q = Q$, so it is an upward sloping straight line through the origin with a slope of 1. The average cost is $AC = C/Q = (12 + Q^2)/Q = 12/Q + Q$, which is U-shaped.

Using Equations 9.4 and 9.6, we can write the monopoly's profit as

$$\pi(Q) = R(Q) - C(Q) = (24Q - Q^2) - (12 + Q^2).$$

By setting the derivative of this monopoly's profit function with respect to Q equal to zero, we have an equation that determines the profit-maximizing output:

$$\frac{d\pi(Q)}{dQ} = \frac{dR(Q)}{dQ} - \frac{dC(Q)}{dQ}$$

$$= MR - MC$$

$$= (24 - 2Q) - 2Q = 0.$$

Thus, $MR = 24 - 2Q = 2Q = MC$. To determine the profit-maximizing output, we solve this equation and find that $Q = 6$. Substituting $Q = 6$ into the inverse demand function (Equation 9.2), we learn that the profit-maximizing price is

$$p = 24 - Q = 24 - 6 = 18.$$

Mini-Case

Apple's iPad

Apple's iPad was the first commercially successful tablet. Users interact with the iPad using Apple's multi-touch, finger-sensitive touchscreen (rather than the pressure-triggered stylus that most previous tablets used) and a virtual onscreen keyboard (rather than a physical one). Most importantly, the iPad offers an intuitive interface and is well integrated with Apple's iTunes, eBooks, and various application programs.

People loved the original iPad. Even at $499 for the basic model, Apple had a virtual monopoly in its first year in 2010, with 87% of the tablet market. Moreover, the other tablets available in 2010 were not viewed by most consumers as close substitutes. Apple reported that it sold 25 million iPads worldwide in its first full year.

Unfortunately for Apple, its monopoly was short lived. Within a year of the iPad's introduction, over a hundred iPad want-to-be tablets were available. Apple's share of the tablet market fell to 29% by early 2018.

Q&A 9.2

When the iPad was introduced, Apple's constant marginal cost of producing its top-of-the-line iPad was about $220, its fixed cost was $2,000 million (= $2 billion), and we estimate that its inverse demand function was $p = 770 - 11Q$, where Q is the millions of iPads purchased.[7] What was Apple's average cost function? What was its marginal revenue function? What were its profit-maximizing price and quantity? What was its profit? Show Apple's profit-maximizing solution in a figure.

---

[7]See the Mini-Case "Apple's iPad" in the Sources at the end of this book for details on these estimates.

Answer

1. *Derive the average cost function using the information about Apple's marginal and fixed costs.* Given that Apple's marginal cost was constant, its average variable cost, AVC, equaled its marginal cost, $220. Its average fixed cost, AFC, was its fixed cost divided by the quantity produced, $2,000/Q$. Thus, its average cost was $AC = AVC + AFC = 220 + 2,000/Q$.

2. *Derive Apple's marginal revenue function using the information about its demand function.* Given that Apple's inverse demand function is linear, $p = 770 - 11Q$, its marginal revenue function has the same intercept and twice the slope: $MR = 770 - 22Q$.[8]

3. *Derive Apple's profit-maximizing quantity and price by equating the marginal revenue and marginal cost functions and solving.* Apple maximized its profit where $MR = MC$:

$$770 - 22Q = 220.$$

Solving this equation for the profit-maximizing output, we find that $Q = 25$ million iPads. By substituting this quantity into the inverse demand function, we determine that the profit-maximizing price was $p = \$495$ per unit as the figure shows.

4. *Calculate Apple's profit using the profit-maximizing price and quantity and the average cost.* At $Q = 25$, the firm's average cost was $AC = 220 + 2,000/25 = \$300$. The firm's profit was $\pi = (p - AC)Q = (495 - 300)25 = \$4,875$ million. The figure shows that the profit is a rectangle with a height of $(p - AC) = \$195$ and a length of $Q = 25$ million.

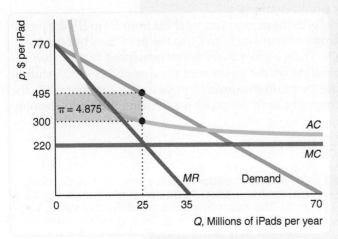

Effects of a Shift of the Demand Curve

Shifts of the demand curve or marginal cost curve affect the profit-maximizing monopoly price and quantity and can have a wider variety of effects with a monopoly than with a competitive market. In a competitive market, the effect of a shift in demand on a competitive firm's output depends only on the shape of the marginal cost curve. In contrast, the effect of a shift in demand on a monopoly's output depends on the shapes of both the marginal cost curve and the demand curve.

As we saw in Chapter 8, a competitive firm's marginal cost curve tells us everything we need to know about the amount that the firm is willing to supply at any given market price. The competitive firm's supply curve is its upward-sloping

---

[8]Alternatively, we can use calculus to derive the marginal revenue curve. We multiply the inverse demand function by Q to obtain Apple's revenue function, $R = 770Q - 11Q^2$. Then, we derive the marginal revenue function by differentiating the revenue function with respect to quantity: $MR = dR/dQ = 770 - 22Q$.

marginal cost curve above its minimum average variable cost. A competitive firm's supply behavior does not depend on the shape of the market demand curve because it always faces a horizontal demand curve at the market price. Thus, if we know a competitive firm's marginal cost curve, we can predict how much that firm will produce at any given market price.

In contrast, a monopoly's output decision depends on the shapes of its marginal cost curve and its demand curve. Unlike a competitive firm, *a monopoly does not have a supply curve.* Knowing the monopoly's marginal cost curve is not enough for us to predict how much a monopoly will sell at any given price.

Figure 9.4 illustrates that the relationship between price and quantity is unique in a competitive market but not in a monopolistic market. If the market is competitive, the initial equilibrium is e_1 in panel a, where the original demand curve D^1 intersects the supply curve, MC, which is the sum of the marginal cost curves of a large number of competitive firms. When the demand curve shifts to D^2, the new competitive equilibrium, e_2, has a higher price and quantity. A shift of the demand curve maps out competitive equilibria along the marginal cost curve, so every equilibrium quantity has a single corresponding equilibrium price.

For the monopoly in panel b, as the demand curve shifts from D^1 to D^2, the profit-maximizing monopoly outcome shifts from E_1 to E_2, so the price rises but the quantity stays constant, $Q_1 = Q_2$. Thus, *a given quantity can correspond to more than one profit-maximizing price*, depending on the position of the demand curve. A shift in the demand curve may cause the profit-maximizing price to stay constant while the quantity changes. More commonly, both the profit-maximizing price and quantity change.

FIGURE 9.4 Effects of a Shift of the Demand Curve

(a) A shift of the demand curve from D^1 to D^2 causes the competitive equilibrium to move from e_1 to e_2 along the supply curve (which is the horizontal sum of the marginal cost curves of all the competitive firms). Because the competitive equilibrium lies on the supply curve, each quantity (such as Q_1 and Q_2) corresponds to only one possible equilibrium price.

(b) With a monopoly, this same shift of demand causes the monopoly optimum to change from E_1 to E_2. The monopoly quantity stays the same, but the monopoly price rises. Thus, a shift in demand does not map out a unique relationship between price and quantity in a monopolized market. The same quantity, $Q_1 = Q_2$, is associated with two different prices, p_1 and p_2.

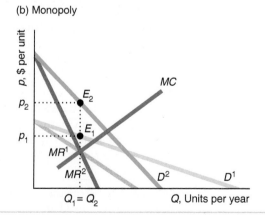

(a) Competition

(b) Monopoly

Q&A 9.3

A monopoly faces an inverse demand function $p = 40 - 2Q$ and has a cost function $C(Q) = 12 + 10Q + Q^2$. It follows that $MR = 40 - 4Q$ and $MC = 10 + 2Q$. The price elasticity of demand is $-0.5p/Q$ (see Equation 3.6 in Chapter 3). Use an Excel spreadsheet to calculate revenue, cost, profit, marginal revenue, marginal cost, and the demand elasticity for each quantity from 1 through 11 in one-unit increments. Find the profit-maximizing quantity and price. Verify that $MR = MC$ at this quantity. What quantity and price maximize revenue? What is the profit at the revenue-maximizing quantity? What are the price elasticities of demand at the profit-maximizing and revenue-maximizing quantities?

Answer

1. *Open an Excel spreadsheet; put the titles* Quantity, Price, Revenue, Cost, Profit, MR, MC, *and* Elasticity *in cells A1 through H1 and list the quantities in the first column.* Enter the quantities 1 through 11 in one-unit increments in cells A2 through A12.

2. *Fill in the correct formulas in cells B2 through H2.* Enter "$= 40-2*A2$" in cell B2, "$=A2*B2$" in cell C2, "$=12+10*A2+A2\wedge2$" in cell D2, "$=C2-D2$" in cell E2, "$=40-4*A2$" in cell F2, "$=10+2*A2$" in cell G2, and "$=-0.5*B2/A2$" in cell H2.

3. *Copy the formulas in row 2 and paste them into rows 3 through 12.* Copy cell B2 and paste it into cells B3 through B12, then do the same for each column from C2 through H2. Format column H to show two digits after the decimal point.

4. *Find the quantity and price where profit is greatest.* Scan the profit column to find the largest profit. This maximum profit of 63 is highlighted in yellow. The profit-maximizing quantity is 5 and the corresponding price is 30.

5. *Check whether marginal revenue equals marginal cost at the profit-maximizing quantity.* At the profit-maximizing quantity, 5, the marginal revenue and marginal cost are both 20.

	A	B	C	D	E	F	G	H
1	Quantity	Price	Revenue	Cost	Profit	MR	MC	Elasticity
2	1	38	38	23	15	36	12	-19.00
3	2	36	72	36	36	32	14	-9.00
4	3	34	102	51	51	28	16	-5.67
5	4	32	128	68	60	24	18	-4.00
6	5	30	150	87	63	20	20	-3.00
7	6	28	168	108	60	16	22	-2.33
8	7	26	182	131	51	12	24	-1.86
9	8	24	192	156	36	8	26	-1.50
10	9	22	198	183	15	4	28	-1.22
11	10	20	200	212	-12	0	30	-1.00
12	11	18	198	243	-45	-4	32	-0.82

6. *Through inspection, show that the profit maximum occurs at a smaller quantity than the revenue maximum.* The revenue maximum occurs at a quantity of 10, while the profit maximum occurs at a quantity of 5. We have highlighted the maximum revenue in blue.

7. *Determine the profit at the revenue maximum.* The profit is −12 at the revenue-maximizing output, so maximizing revenue does not maximize profit.

8. *Determine the elasticities where profit and revenue reach their maximums.* At the profit maximum, where quantity is five, the demand curve is elastic, with an elasticity of −3. Revenue always reaches its maximum at a price elasticity of demand of −1.0. We have highlighted these elasticities in green.

Mini-Case

Taylor Swift Concert Pricing

Taylor Swift's 2015 concert tour was a huge success, breaking the Rolling Stones' North American tour revenue record. Her 2018 "Reputation" tour is poised to be even more successful, opening to rave reviews and enthusiastic crowds. But not all her 2018 concerts are selling out. Why would the exceptionally popular pop music icon have empty seats at her concerts?

The main reason for the empty seats is high prices. Ms. Swift can earn more profit by charging high prices and selling fewer tickets. We examine why in the following Q&A.

Q&A 9.4

Illustrate why charging a higher price, p_1, than the price that causes the concert to sell out, p_2, increases profit. For simplicity, assume that the marginal cost of selling tickets is constant at m until the stadium's capacity is reached, and that fixed cost is zero. Explain why setting a price high enough that the show does not sell out increases profit.

Answer

1. *Draw the marginal cost curve and explain its shape.* The marginal cost curve is horizontal at m until capacity is reached at Q_2. Because no more than Q_2 seats are available, the marginal cost of providing an additional seat becomes infinite at Q_2. That is, the marginal cost curve is vertical at Q_2.

2. *Add the demand curve and marginal revenue curve to the diagram, and show the profit-maximizing price and quantity.* The intersection of the marginal revenue and marginal cost curve determines the profit-maximizing quantity, Q_1. The corresponding price on the demand curve at point a is p_1.

3. *Show the profit at Q_1.* Without a fixed cost, the average cost equals the marginal cost, m. Thus the profit is $\pi_1 = (p_1 - m)Q_1$, which is area $A + B$.

4. *Show the price such that ticket sales reach full capacity and the corresponding profit.* To reach capacity by selling Q_2 tickets, the price must fall to p_2 at point b on the demand curve. The corresponding profit is $\pi_2 = (p_2 - m)Q_2$, which is area $B + C$.

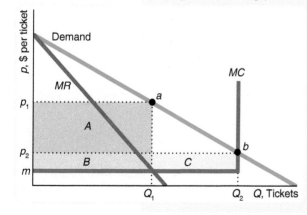

5. *Explain why not selling out the show is profit maximizing.* By charging a higher price and selling fewer tickets, Ms. Swift earns a higher profit: $\pi_1 > \pi_2$. We know that profit is maximized where marginal revenue equals marginal cost. To sell each additional seat, she has to lower the price by enough that the marginal revenue is less than the marginal cost, which reduces profit.

9.2 Market Power

A monopoly has **market power**, which is the ability to significantly affect the market price. In contrast, no single competitive firm can significantly affect the market price.

A profit-maximizing monopoly charges a price that exceeds its marginal cost. The extent to which the monopoly price exceeds marginal cost depends on the shape of the demand curve.

Many people falsely believe that the biggest monopolies have the most power over prices:

Common Confusion The larger the monopoly, the more it can mark up its price over its cost.

Size doesn't matter. Rather, a profit-maximizing monopoly marks up price over marginal cost more if consumers are less sensitive to price (the demand curve is less elastic). For example, some of the drugs mentioned in the Managerial Problem at the beginning of the chapter do not have a large volume of sales but have extremely high prices because they are crucial for a small segment of the population.

Market Power and the Shape of the Demand Curve

If the monopoly faces a highly elastic—nearly flat—demand curve at the profit-maximizing quantity, it would lose substantial sales if it raised its price by even a small amount. Conversely, if the demand curve is not very elastic (if it is relatively steep) at that quantity, the monopoly would lose fewer sales from raising its price by the same amount.

We can derive the relationship between the markup of price over marginal cost and the elasticity of demand at the profit-maximizing quantity using the expression for marginal revenue in Equation 9.5 and the firm's profit-maximizing condition that marginal revenue equals marginal cost:

$$MR = p\left(1 + \frac{1}{\varepsilon}\right) = MC. \tag{9.8}$$

By rearranging terms, we see that a profit-maximizing manager chooses quantity such that

$$\frac{p}{MC} = \frac{1}{1 + (1/\varepsilon)}. \tag{9.9}$$

TABLE 9.2 Elasticity of Demand, Price, and Marginal Cost

	Elasticity of Demand, ε	Price/Marginal Cost Ratio, $p/MC = 1/[1 + (1/\varepsilon)]$	Lerner Index, $(p - MC)/p = -1/\varepsilon$
↑ less elastic	−1.01	101	0.99
	−1.1	11	0.91
	−2	2	0.5
	−3	1.5	0.33
	−5	1.25	0.2
more elastic	−10	1.11	0.1
	−100	1.01	0.01
↓	−∞	1	0

In our linear demand example in panel a of Figure 9.3, the elasticity of demand is $\varepsilon = -3$ at the monopoly optimum where $Q = 6$. As a result, the ratio of price to marginal cost is $p/MC = 1/[1 + 1/(-3)] = 1.5$, or $p = 1.5MC$. The profit-maximizing price, $18, in panel a is 1.5 times the marginal cost of $12.

Table 9.2 illustrates how the ratio of price to marginal cost varies with the elasticity of demand. When the elasticity is −1.01, only slightly elastic, the monopoly's profit-maximizing price is 101 times larger than its marginal cost: $p/MC = 1/[1 + 1/(-1.01)] \approx 101$. As the elasticity of demand approaches negative infinity (becomes perfectly elastic), the ratio of price to marginal cost shrinks to $p/MC = 1$.[9] Thus, even in the absence of rivals, the shape of the demand curve constrains the monopolist's ability to exercise market power.

A manager can use this last result to determine whether the firm is maximizing its profit. Typically, a monopoly knows its costs accurately, but is somewhat uncertain about the demand curve it faces and hence what price (or quantity) to set. Many private firms—such as ACNielsen, IRI, and IMS Health—and industry groups collect data on quantities and prices in a wide variety of industries including automobiles, foods and beverages, drugs, and many services. Firms can use these data to estimate the firm's demand curve (Chapter 3). More commonly, firms hire consulting firms (often the same firms that collect data) to estimate the elasticity of demand for their products.

A manager can use the estimated elasticity of demand to check whether the firm is maximizing profit. If the p/MC ratio does not approximately equal $1/(1 + 1/\varepsilon)$, as required by Equation 9.9, then the manager knows that the firm is not setting its price to maximize its profit. Of course, the manager can also check whether the firm is maximizing profit by varying its price or quantity. However, often such experiments may be more costly than using statistical techniques to estimate the elasticity of demand.

---

[9]As the elasticity approaches negative infinity, $1/\varepsilon$ approaches zero, so $1/(1 + 1/\varepsilon)$ approaches $1/1 = 1$.

The Lerner Index

Another way to show how the elasticity of demand affects a monopoly's price relative to its marginal cost is to look at the firm's **Lerner Index** (or *price markup*)—the ratio of the difference between price and marginal cost to the price: $(p - MC)/p$. This index can be calculated for any firm, regardless of whether the firm is a monopoly. The Lerner Index is zero for a competitive firm because a competitive firm produces where marginal cost equals price. The Lerner Index measures a firm's market power: The larger the difference between price and marginal cost, the larger the Lerner Index and the firm's market power.

If the firm is maximizing its profit, we can express the Lerner Index in terms of the elasticity of demand by rearranging Equation 9.9:[10]

$$\frac{p - MC}{p} = -\frac{1}{\varepsilon}. \tag{9.10}$$

The Lerner Index ranges between 0 and 1 for a profit-maximizing monopoly.[11] Equation 9.10 confirms that a competitive firm has a Lerner Index of zero because its demand curve is perfectly elastic.[12]

As Table 9.2 illustrates, the monopoly's Lerner Index is greater, the less elastic is the demand curve. If $\varepsilon = -5$, the monopoly's markup (Lerner Index) is $1/5 = 0.2$; if $\varepsilon = -2$, the markup is $1/2 = 0.5$; and if $\varepsilon = -1.01$, the markup is 0.99. Monopolies that face demand curves that are only slightly elastic set prices that are multiples of their marginal cost and have Lerner Indexes close to 1.

Q&A 9.5

The EpiPen is a small portable device that can quickly deliver the drug epinephrine to stop a potentially life-threatening allergic reaction. The manufacturer of the EpiPen faces virtually no competition from other firms. The price for a pair of EpiPens is $630 for people without insurance, while two industry experts estimate that its marginal cost is $30.[13] What is its Lerner Index? If the firm is maximizing its short-run profit, what is its elasticity of demand?

Answer

1. *Determine the Lerner Index by substituting the price and marginal cost into the Lerner definition.* The EpiPen's Lerner Index is

$$\frac{p - MC}{p} = \frac{630 - 30}{630} \approx 0.952.$$

2. *Use Equation 9.10 to infer the elasticity.* According to that equation, a profit-maximizing monopoly operates where $(p - MC)/p = -1/\varepsilon$. Combining that equation with the Lerner Index from the previous step, we learn that $0.952 = -1/\varepsilon$, or $\varepsilon \approx -1.05$.

---

[10]Equation 9.9 can be rewritten as $p(1 + 1/\varepsilon) = MC$ or $p - MC = -p/\varepsilon$. Dividing both sides of this equation by p produces Equation 9.10.

[11]For the Lerner Index to be above 1 in Equation 9.10, ε would have to be a negative fraction, indicating that the demand curve was inelastic at the monopoly's output choice. However, as we've already seen, a profit-maximizing monopoly never operates in the inelastic portion of its demand curve.

[12]As the elasticity of demand approaches negative infinity, the Lerner Index, $-1/\varepsilon$, approaches zero.

[13]**www.nbcnews.com/business/consumer/industry-insiders-estimate-epipen-costs-no-more -30-n642091**.

Sources of Market Power

What factors cause a monopoly to face a relatively elastic demand curve and hence have little market power? Ultimately, the elasticity of demand of the market demand curve depends on consumers' tastes and options. The more consumers want a good—the more willing they are to pay "virtually anything" for it—the less elastic is the demand curve.

Other things equal, the demand curve a firm (not necessarily a monopoly) faces becomes more elastic as (1) *better substitutes* for the firm's product are introduced, (2) *more firms* enter the market selling the same product, or (3) firms that provide the same service *locate closer* to this firm. The demand curves for Xerox, the U.S. Postal Service, and McDonald's have become more elastic in recent decades for these three reasons.

When Xerox started selling its plain-paper copier, no other firm sold a close substitute. Other companies' machines produced copies on special heat-sensitive paper that yellowed quickly. As other firms developed plain-paper copiers, the demand curve that Xerox faced became more elastic.

The U.S. Postal Service (USPS) has a legal monopoly in its core business of first-class mail delivery. However, FedEx, United Parcel Service, and many other courier firms are allowed to deliver urgent mail, and internet communication has also become an important alternative to regular mail. Because of increasing competition from courier services and the internet, the demand curve for first-class mail has shifted downward and become flatter. USPS delivers much less mail now than in the past, down from 104 billion pieces of first-class mail in 2001, to only about 59 billion pieces in 2017.[14]

As you drive down a highway, you may notice that McDonald's restaurants are located miles apart. The purpose of this spacing is to reduce the likelihood that two McDonald's outlets will compete for the same customer. Although McDonald's can prevent its own restaurants from competing with each other, it cannot prevent Wendy's or Burger King from locating near its restaurants. As other fast-food restaurants open near a McDonald's, that restaurant faces a more elastic demand. What happens as a profit-maximizing monopoly faces more elastic demand? It has to lower its price.

Of course you could get it done for less if I weren't the only plumber in town.

9.3 Market Failure Due to Monopoly Pricing

A profit-maximizing monopoly is economically inefficient because it wastes potential surplus, resulting in a deadweight loss. In contrast, perfect competition achieves *economic efficiency* because it maximizes total surplus, *TS* (= consumer surplus + producer surplus = *CS* + *PS*). The inefficiency of monopoly pricing is an example of a **market failure**: a non-optimal allocation of goods and services such that a market does not achieve economic efficiency. Market failure

---

[14]**about.usps.com/who-we-are/postal-history/first-class-mail-since-1926.htm.**

often occurs because the price differs from the marginal cost, as with a monopoly. This economic inefficiency creates a rationale for governments to intervene, which we discuss in Chapter 16.

Total surplus (Chapter 8) is lower under monopoly than under competition. That is, monopoly destroys some of the potential gains from trade. Chapter 8 showed that competition maximizes total surplus because price equals marginal cost. By setting its price above its marginal cost, a monopoly causes consumers to buy less than the competitive level of the good, so society suffers a deadweight loss.

If the monopoly were to act like a competitive market, it would produce where the marginal cost curve cuts the demand curve—the output where price equals marginal cost. For example, using the demand curve given by Equation 9.2 and the marginal cost curve given by Equation 9.7,

$$p = 24 - Q = 2Q = MC.$$

Solving this equation, we find that the competitive quantity, Q_c, would be 8 units and the price would be $16, as Figure 9.5 shows. At this competitive price, consumer surplus is area $A + B + C$ and producer surplus is $D + E$.

FIGURE 9.5 Deadweight Loss of Monopoly

A competitive market would produce $Q_c = 8$ at $p_c = \$16$, where the demand curve intersects the marginal cost (supply) curve. A monopoly produces only $Q_m = 6$ at $p_m = \$18$, where the marginal revenue curve intersects the marginal cost curve. Under monopoly, consumer surplus is A, producer surplus is $B + D$, and the inefficiency or deadweight loss of monopoly is $C + E$.

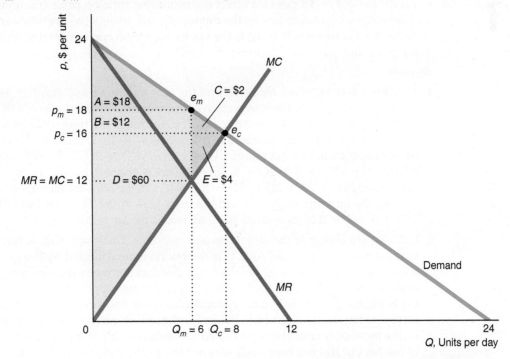

	Competition	Monopoly	Change
Consumer Surplus, CS	$A + B + C$	A	$-B - C = \Delta CS$
Producer Surplus, PS	$D + E$	$B + D$	$B - E = \Delta PS$
Total Surplus, TS = CS + PS	$A + B + C + D + E$	$A + B + D$	$-C - E = \Delta TS = -DWL$

If instead the firm acts like a profit-maximizing monopoly and operates where its marginal revenue equals its marginal cost, the monopoly output, Q_m, is only 6 units and the monopoly price is $18. Consumer surplus is only A. Part of the lost consumer surplus, B, goes to the monopoly, but the rest, C, is lost. The benefit of being a monopoly is that it allows the firm to extract some consumer surplus from consumers and convert it to profit.

By charging the monopoly price of $18 instead of the competitive price of $16, the monopoly receives $2 more per unit and earns extra profit (and extra producer surplus) of area $B = $12 on the $Q_m = 6$ units it sells. The monopoly loses area E, however, because it sells less than the competitive output. Consequently, the monopoly's producer surplus increases by $B - E$ over the competitive level. Monopoly pricing increases producer surplus relative to competition.

Total surplus is less under monopoly than under competition. The change in total surplus is $-C - E$. Thus, the deadweight loss of monopoly is $C + E$, which represents the potential surplus that is wasted because less than the competitive output is produced. The deadweight loss is due to the gap between price and marginal cost at the monopoly output. At $Q_m = 6$, the price, $18, is above the marginal cost, $12, so consumers are willing to pay more for the last unit of output than it costs to produce it.

| **Q&A 9.6** | In the linear example in panel a of Figure 9.3, how does charging the monopoly a specific tax of $t = $8 per unit affect the profit-maximizing price and quantity and the well-being of consumers, the monopoly, and society (where total surplus includes the tax revenue)? What is the tax incidence on consumers (the increase in the price they pay as a fraction of the tax)? |

Answer

1. *Determine how imposing the tax affects the monopoly price and quantity.* In the accompanying graph, the intersection of the marginal revenue curve, MR, and the before-tax marginal cost curve, MC^1, determines the monopoly quantity, $Q_1 = 6$. At the before-tax solution, e_1, the price is $p_1 = 18$. The specific tax causes the monopoly's before-tax marginal cost curve, $MC^1 = 2Q$, to shift upward by 8 to $MC^2 = MC^1 + 8 = 2Q + 8$. After the tax is applied, the monopoly operates where $MR = 24 - 2Q = 2Q + 8 = MC^2$. In the after-tax monopoly solution, e_2, the quantity is $Q_2 = 4$ and the price is $p_2 = 20$. Thus, output falls by $\Delta Q = 6 - 4 = 2$ units and the price increases by $\Delta p = 20 - 18 = 2$.

2. *Calculate the change in the various surplus measures.* The graph shows how the surplus measures change. Area G is the tax revenue collected by the government, $tQ = 32$, because its height is the distance between the two marginal cost curves, $t = 8$, and its width is the output the monopoly produces after the tax is imposed, $Q = 4$. The tax reduces consumer and producer surplus and increases the deadweight loss. We know that producer surplus falls because (a) the monopoly could have produced this reduced output level in the absence of the tax but did not because it was not the profit-maximizing output, so its before-tax profit falls, and (b) the monopoly must now pay taxes. Before the tax, the change in total surplus due to monopoly is $-F$, so the deadweight loss is F. After the tax, the deadweight loss is $C + E + F$. Thus, the increase in deadweight loss due to the tax is $C + E$. The table below the graph shows that consumer surplus changes by $-B - C$ and producer surplus by $B - E - G$.

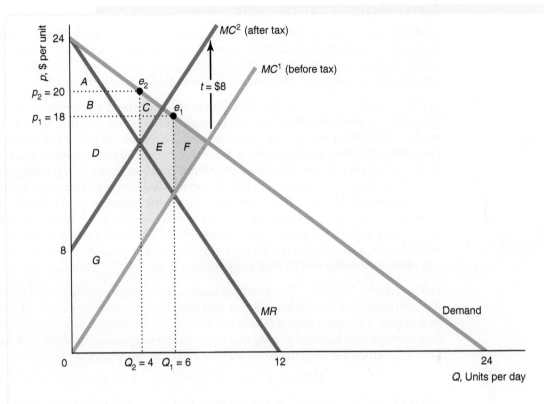

	Monopoly Before Tax	Monopoly After Tax	Change
Consumer Surplus, CS	$A + B + C$	A	$-B - C = \Delta CS$
Producer Surplus, PS	$D + E + G$	$B + D$	$B - E - G = \Delta PS$
Tax Revenues, $T = tQ$	0	G	$G = \Delta T$
Total Surplus, $TS = CS + PS + T$	$A + B + C + D + E + G$	$A + B + D + G$	$-C - E = \Delta TS$
Deadweight Loss, DWL	F	$C + E + F$	$C + E = \Delta DWL$

3. *Calculate the incidence of the tax on consumers.* Because the tax goes from 0 to 8, the change in the tax is $\Delta t = 8$. Because the change in the price that the consumer pays is $\Delta p = 2$, the share of the tax paid by consumers is $\Delta p / \Delta t = 2/8 = \frac{1}{4}$. Thus, the monopoly absorbs $6 of the tax and passes on only $2.

9.4 Causes of Monopoly

Why are some markets monopolized? The two most important reasons are cost considerations and government policy.[15]

---

[15]In later chapters, we discuss other means by which monopolies are created. One method is the merger of several firms into a single firm. This method creates a monopoly if new firms fail to enter the market. A second method is for a monopoly to use strategies that discourage other firms from entering the market. A third possibility is that firms coordinate their activities and set their prices as a monopoly would. Firms that act collectively in this way are called a *cartel* rather than a monopoly.

Cost-Based Monopoly

Certain cost structures may facilitate the creation of a monopoly. One possibility is that a firm may have substantially lower costs than potential rivals. A second possibility is that the firms in an industry have cost functions such that one firm can produce any given output at a lower cost than two or more firms can.

Cost Advantages. If a low-cost firm profitably sells at a price so low that other potential competitors with higher costs would lose money, no other firms enter the market. Thus, the low-cost firm is a monopoly. A firm can have a cost advantage over potential rivals for several reasons. It may have a superior technology or a better way of organizing production.[16] For example, Henry Ford's methods of organizing production using assembly lines and standardization allowed him to produce cars at substantially lower cost than rival firms until they copied his organizational techniques.

If a firm controls an essential facility or a scarce resource that is needed to produce a particular output, no other firm can produce at all—at least not at a reasonable cost. For example, a firm that owns the only gravel quarry in a region is the only firm that can profitably sell gravel to local construction firms.

Natural Monopoly. A market has a **natural monopoly** if one firm can produce the total output of the market at lower cost than two or more firms could. A firm can be a natural monopoly even if it does not have a cost advantage over rivals, provided that average cost is lower if only one firm operates. Specifically, if the cost for any firm to produce q is $C(q)$, the condition for a natural monopoly is

$$C(Q) < C(q_1) + C(q_2) + \cdots + C(q_n), \tag{9.11}$$

where $Q = q_1 + q_2 + \cdots + q_n$ is the sum of the output of any n firms where $n \geq 2$.

If a firm has economies of scale at all levels of output, its average cost curve falls as output increases for any observed level of output. If all potential firms have the same strictly declining average cost curve, this market is a natural monopoly, as we now illustrate.[17]

A company that supplies water to homes incurs a high fixed cost, F, to build a plant and connect houses to the plant. The firm's marginal cost, m, of supplying water is constant, so its marginal cost curve is horizontal and its average cost, $AC = m + F/Q$, declines as output rises. (This cost curve is similar to that of the iPad example in Q&A 9.2.)

Figure 9.6 shows such marginal and average cost curves where $m = 10$ and $F = 60$. If the market output is 12 units per day, one firm produces that output at an average cost of 15, or a total cost of 180 ($= 15 \times 12$). If two firms each produce 6 units, the average cost is 20 and the cost of producing the market output is 240 ($= 20 \times 12$), which is greater than the cost with a single firm.

If the two firms divided total production in any other way, their cost of production would still exceed the cost of a single firm (as the following Q&A asks you to prove).

---

[16]When a firm develops a better production method that provides it with a cost advantage, it is important for the firm to either keep the information secret or obtain a patent, so that it can legally prevent anyone from imitating the firm's innovation. Thus, both secrecy and patents facilitate cost-based monopolies.

[17]A firm may be a natural monopoly even if its cost curve does not fall at all levels of output. If a U-shaped average cost curve reaches its minimum at 100 units of output, it may be less costly for only one firm to produce an output of 101 units even though average cost is rising at that output. Thus, a cost function with economies of scale everywhere is a sufficient but not a necessary condition for a natural monopoly.

FIGURE 9.6 Natural Monopoly

This natural monopoly has a strictly declining average cost, $AC = 10 + 60/Q$.

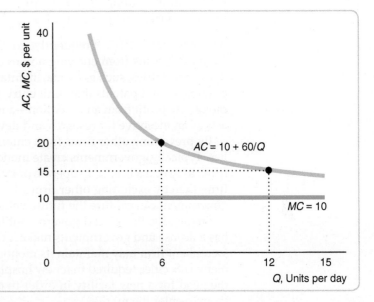

The reason is that the marginal cost per unit is the same no matter how many firms produce, but each additional firm adds a fixed cost, which raises the cost of producing a given quantity. If only one firm provides water, the cost of building a second plant and a second set of pipes is avoided.

In an industry with a natural monopoly cost structure, having just one firm is the cheapest way to produce any given output level. Governments often use a natural monopoly argument to justify their granting monopoly rights to *public utilities*, which provide essential goods or services such as water, gas, electric power, or mail delivery.

Q&A 9.7

A firm that delivers Q units of water to households has a total cost of $C(Q) = mQ + F$. If any entrant would have the same cost, does this market have a natural monopoly?

Answer

Determine whether costs rise if two firms produce a given quantity. Let q_1 be the output of Firm 1 and q_2 be the output of Firm 2. The combined cost of these two firms producing $Q = q_1 + q_2$ is

$$C(q_1) + C(q_2) = (mq_1 + F) + (mq_2 + F) = m(q_1 + q_2) + 2F = mQ + 2F.$$

If a single firm produces Q, its cost is $C(Q) = mQ + F$. Thus, the cost of producing any given Q is greater with two firms than with one firm (the condition in Equation 9.11), so this market is a natural monopoly.

Government Creation of Monopoly

Governments have created many monopolies. Sometimes governments own and manage such monopolies. In the United States, as in most countries, first-class mail delivery is a government monopoly. Many local governments own and operate public utility monopolies that provide garbage collection, electricity, water, gas, phone services, and other utilities.

Barriers to Entry. Frequently, governments create monopolies by preventing competing firms from entering a market occupied by an existing incumbent firm. Several countries, such as China, maintain a tobacco monopoly. Similarly, most governments grant patents that limit entry and allow the patent-holding firm to earn a monopoly profit from an invention—a reward for developing the new product that acts as an incentive for research and development.

By preventing other firms from entering a market, governments create monopolies. Typically, governments create monopolies either by making it difficult for new firms to obtain a license to operate or by explicitly granting a monopoly right to one firm, thereby excluding other firms. By auctioning a monopoly to a private firm, a government can capture the future value of monopoly earnings.[18]

Frequently, firms need government licenses to operate. If one initial incumbent has a license and governments make it difficult for new firms to obtain licenses, the incumbent firm may maintain its monopoly for a substantial period. Until recently, many U.S. cities required that new hospitals or other inpatient facilities demonstrate the need for a new facility in order to obtain a certificate of need, which allowed them to enter the market.

Government grants of monopoly rights have been common for public utilities. Instead of running a public utility itself, a government might give a private sector company the monopoly rights to operate the utility. A government may capture some of the monopoly profits by charging the firm in some way for its monopoly rights. In many countries or other political jurisdictions, such a system is an inducement to corruption, as firms seeking monopoly privileges may bribe public officials to obtain the monopoly rights.

Governments around the world have privatized many state-owned monopolies in the past several decades. By selling cable television, garbage collection, phone service, towing, and other monopolies to private firms, a government can capture the value of future monopoly earnings today. However, for political or other reasons, governments frequently sell at a lower price that does not capture all future profits.

| **Mini-Case** | The Canadian government created a medical marijuana monopoly by issuing only one license allowing a firm to operate. For 13 years, Prairie Plant Systems Inc. was the sole supplier of medical marijuana to Health Canada, which is the Canadian government agency that oversees the program. |

The Canadian Medical Marijuana Market

The government then eliminated the monopoly, creating a competitive market. The licensing law changed in 2014, when other firms could receive licenses and start providing medical marijuana. By early 2015, Health Canada had received more than 1,200 applications for licenses. While many applications were unsuccessful, significant entry occurred rapidly. The industry changed from being a monopoly to being competitive within a year. By early 2018, more than 100 licensed producers of medical marijuana had entered the market. Additional producers of marijuana were poised to enter after the Canadian government passed legislation to legalize recreational marijuana in 2018.

---

[18]Alternatively, a government could auction the rights to the firm that offers to charge the lowest price, so as to maximize total surplus.

Patents. If an innovating firm cannot prevent imitation by keeping its discoveries secret, it may try to obtain government protection to prevent other firms from duplicating its innovations and entering the market. Most countries provide such protection through patents. A **patent** is an exclusive right granted to the inventor of a new and useful product, process, substance, or design for a specified length of time. Most patents in the United States and other major jurisdictions last for up to 20 years from the application date.

This right allows the patent holder to be the exclusive seller or user of the new invention.[19] Patents often give rise to monopoly, but not always. For example, although a patent may grant a firm the exclusive right to use a particular process in making a product, other firms may be able to make the same product using different processes. In Chapter 16, we discuss the reasons why governments grant patents.

Mini-Case **Botox** 	Ophthalmologist Dr. Alan Scott turned the deadly poison botulinum toxin into a miracle drug to treat two eye conditions: strabismus, a condition in which the eyes are not properly aligned, and blepharospasm, an uncontrollable closure of the eyes. Strabismus affects about 4% of children and blepharospasm left about 25,000 Americans functionally blind before Scott's discovery. His patented drug for treating these condition, Botox, is sold by Allergan, Inc.

Dr. Scott has been amused to see several of the unintended beneficiaries of his research at the Academy Awards. Even before it was explicitly approved for cosmetic use, many doctors were injecting Botox into the facial muscles of actors, models, and others to smooth out their wrinkles. (The drug paralyzes the muscles, so those injected with it also lose the ability to frown or smile—and, some would say, act.) The treatment is only temporary, lasting up to 120 days, so repeated injections are necessary.

Allergan has a near-monopoly in the treatment of wrinkles, although plastic surgery and collagen, Restylane, hyaluronic acids, and other filler injections provide limited competition. However, 54% of Botox sales are now for other uses, including as a treatment for chronic migraine and overactive bladder.

Allergan had Botox sales of $800 million in 2004 and about $2.8 billion in 2016. Indeed, Botox's value continues to increase as Allergan finds new uses for Botox. According to one forecast, Botox's global sales will reach $3.2 billion by the end of 2018 and $4.3 billion by 2022.

Dr. Scott can produce a vial of Botox in his lab for about $25. Allergan sells the potion to doctors for about $400. Assuming that the firm is setting its price to maximize its short-run profit, we can rearrange Equation 9.10 to determine the elasticity of demand for Botox:

$$\varepsilon = -\frac{p}{p - MC} = -\frac{400}{400 - 25} \approx -1.067.$$

Thus, the demand that Allergan faces is only slightly elastic: A 1% increase in price causes quantity to fall by slightly more than 1%.

---

[19]Owners of patents may sell or grant the right to use a patented process or produce a patented product to other firms. This practice is called *licensing*.

If the demand curve is linear and the elasticity of demand is -1.067 at the 2002 monopoly optimum, e_m (1 million vials sold at \$400 each, producing revenue of \$400 million), then Allergan's inverse demand function is[20]

$$p = 775 - 375Q.$$

This demand curve (see the graph) has a slope of -375 and hits the price axis at \$775 and the quantity axis at about 2.07 million vials per year. Thus, its revenue is $R = 775Q - 375Q^2$, so its marginal revenue curve is

$$MR = dR/dQ = 775 - 750Q.$$

The MR curve strikes the price axis at \$775 and has twice the slope, -750, of the demand curve.

The intersection of the marginal revenue and marginal cost curves,

$$MR = 775 - 750Q = 25 = MC,$$

determines the monopoly equilibrium at the profit-maximizing quantity of 1 million vials per year and a price of \$400 per vial.

Were the company to sell Botox at a price equal to its marginal cost of \$25 (as a competitive industry would), consumer surplus would equal area $A + B + C$. The height of triangle $A + B + C$ is $\$750 = \$775 - \$25$, and its length is 2 million vials, so its area is \$750 $\left(= \frac{1}{2} \times 750 \times 2\right)$ million. At the higher monopoly price of \$400, the consumer surplus is $A = \$187.5$ million. Compared to the competitive solution, e_c, buyers lose consumer surplus of $B + C = \$562.5$ million per year. Part of this loss, $B = \$375$ million per year, is transferred from consumers to Allergan. The rest, $C = \$187.5$ million per year, is the deadweight loss from monopoly pricing. Allergan's profit is its producer surplus, B, minus its fixed costs.

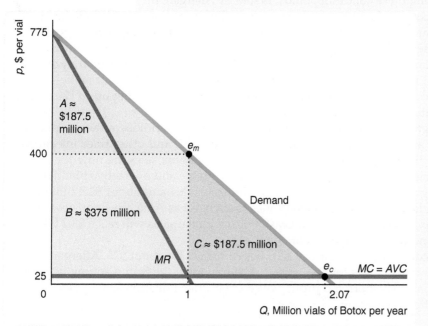

[20]The graph shows a linear demand curve with algebraic form $p = a - bQ$. Such a linear demand curve has an elasticity of $\varepsilon = -(1/b)(p/Q)$. Given that the elasticity of demand is $-400/375 = -(1/b)(400/1)$, where Q is measured in millions of vials, then $b = 375$. Solving $p = 400 = a - 375$, we find that $a = 775$.

9.5 Advertising

> *You can fool all the people all the time if you have a big enough advertising budget.*

In addition to setting prices or quantities and choosing investments, firms engage in many other strategic actions to boost their profits. One of the most important is advertising.[21] By advertising, a monopoly can shift its demand curve, which may allow it to sell more units at a higher price. In contrast, a competitive firm has no incentive to advertise, as it can sell as many units as it wants at the going price without advertising.

Advertising is only one way to promote a product. Other promotional activities include providing free samples and using sales agents. Some promotional tactics are subtle. For example, grocery stores place sugary breakfast cereals on lower shelves so that they are at children's eye level. According to a survey of 27 supermarkets nationwide by the Center for Science in the Public Interest, the average position of 10 child-appealing brands (44% sugar) was on the next-to-bottom shelf, while the average position of 10 adult brands (10% sugar) was on the next-to-top shelf.

A firm advertises to raise its profit. A successful advertising campaign shifts the market demand curve by changing consumers' tastes or informing them about new products. The firm may be able to change the tastes of some consumers by telling them that a famous athlete or performer uses the product. Children and teenagers are frequently the targets of such advertising. If the advertising convinces some consumers that they can't live without the product, the monopoly's demand curve may shift outward and become less elastic at the new equilibrium, at which the firm charges a higher price for its product.

If a firm informs potential consumers about a new use for the product, the demand curve shifts to the right. For example, a 1927 Heinz advertisement suggested that putting its baked beans on toast was a good way to eat beans for breakfast as well as dinner. By so doing, it created a British national dish and shifted the demand curve for its product to the right.

Deciding Whether to Advertise

Japanese space startup, iSpace Technologies, raised $90 million to launch a spacecraft into lunar orbit so that it can offer a "projection mapping service" to advertise on the moon's surface.[22]

Even if advertising succeeds in shifting demand, it may not pay for the firm to advertise. If advertising shifts demand outward or makes it less elastic, the firm's *gross profit*, ignoring the cost of advertising, must rise. The firm undertakes this advertising campaign, however, only if it expects its *net profit* (gross profit minus the cost of advertising) to increase.

We illustrate a monopoly's decision making about advertising in Figure 9.7. If the monopoly does not advertise, it faces the demand curve D^1. If it advertises, its demand curve shifts from D^1 to D^2.

---

[21]For example, Ford spends more on advertising, $4.1 billion in 2017, than anything except R&D (John D. Stoll, "Behind Ford's New Approach to Advertising," *Wall Street Journal*, May 21, 2018).

[22]**www.slate.com/articles/health_and_science/science/2017/12/ispace_wants_to_advertise_on_the_moon_is_that_legal.html**.

FIGURE 9.7 **Advertising**

If the monopoly does not advertise, its demand curve is D^1. At its actual level of advertising, its demand curve is D^2. Advertising increases the monopoly's gross profit (ignoring the cost of advertising) from π_1 to $\pi_2 = \pi_1 + B$. Thus, if the cost of advertising is less than the benefits from advertising, B, the monopoly's net profit (gross profit minus the cost of advertising) rises.

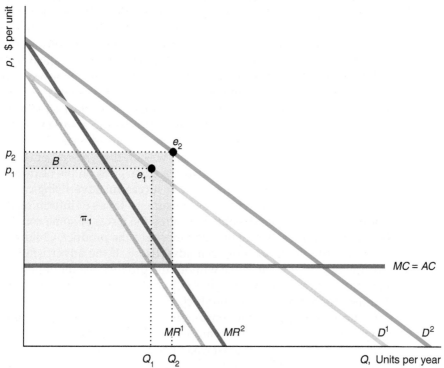

The monopoly's marginal cost, MC, is constant and equals its average cost, AC. Before advertising, the monopoly chooses its output, Q_1, where its marginal cost curve intersects its marginal revenue curve, MR^1, which corresponds to demand curve, D^1. The profit-maximizing equilibrium is e_1, and the monopoly charges a price of p_1. The monopoly's profit, π_1, is a box whose height is the difference between the price and the average cost and whose length is the quantity, Q_1.

After its advertising campaign shifts its demand curve to D^2, the monopoly chooses a higher quantity, $Q_2 (> Q_1)$, where the MR^2 and MC curves intersect. In this new equilibrium, e_2, the monopoly charges p_2. Despite this higher price, the monopoly sells more units after advertising because of the outward shift of its demand curve.

As a consequence, the monopoly's gross profit rises. Its new gross profit is the rectangle $\pi_1 + B$, where the height of the rectangle is the new price minus the average cost, and the length is the quantity, Q_2. Thus, the benefit, B, to the monopoly from advertising at this level is the increase in its gross profit. If its cost of advertising is less than B, its net profit rises, and it pays for the monopoly to advertise at this level rather than not to advertise at all.

How Much to Advertise

The firm that stops advertising to save money is like the person who stops the clock to save time.

How much should a monopoly advertise to maximize its net profit? The rule for setting the profit-maximizing amount of advertising is the same as that for setting the profit-maximizing amount of output: Set advertising or quantity where the marginal benefit (the extra gross profit from one more unit of advertising or the marginal revenue from one more unit of output) equals its marginal cost.

Consider what happens if the monopoly raises or lowers its advertising expenditures by $1, which is its marginal cost of an additional unit of advertising. If a monopoly spends one more dollar on advertising—its marginal cost of advertising—and its gross profit rises by more than $1, its net profit rises, so the extra advertising pays. A profit-maximizing monopoly keeps increasing its advertising until the last dollar of advertising raises its gross profit by exactly $1. If it were to advertise more, its profit would fall.

Using Calculus

Optimal Advertising

We can derive this marginal rule for optimal advertising using calculus. A monopoly's inverse demand function is $p = p(Q, A)$, which says that the price it must charge to clear the market depends on the number of units it chooses to sell, Q, and on the level of its advertising, A. As a result, the firm's revenue function is $R(Q, A) = p(Q, A)Q$. The firm's cost function is $C(Q) + A$, where $C(Q)$ is the cost of manufacturing Q units and A is the cost of advertising, because each unit of advertising costs $1 (by choosing the units of measure appropriately). The monopoly's profit is

$$\pi(Q, A) = R(Q, A) - C(Q) - A. \tag{9.12}$$

The monopoly maximizes its profit by choosing Q and A. Its first-order conditions to maximize its profit are found by partially differentiating the profit function in Equation 9.12 with respect to Q and A in turn:

$$\frac{\partial \pi(Q, A)}{\partial Q} = \frac{\partial R(Q, A)}{\partial Q} - \frac{dC(Q)}{dQ} = 0, \tag{9.13}$$

$$\frac{\partial \pi(Q, A)}{\partial A} = \frac{\partial R(Q, A)}{\partial A} - 1 = 0. \tag{9.14}$$

The profit-maximizing output and advertising levels are the Q and A that simultaneously satisfy Equations 9.13 and 9.14. Equation 9.13 says that the monopoly should set its output so that the marginal revenue from one more unit of output, $\partial R/\partial Q$, equals the marginal cost, dC/dQ, which is the same condition that we previously derived before considering advertising. According to Equation 9.14, the monopoly should advertise to the point where its marginal revenue or marginal benefit from the last unit of advertising, $\partial R/\partial A$, equals the marginal cost of the last unit of advertising, $1.

Q&A 9.8

A monopoly's inverse demand function is $p = 800 - 4Q + 0.2A^{0.5}$, where Q is its quantity, p is its price, and A is the level of advertising. Its marginal cost of production is 2, and its cost of a unit of advertising is 1. What are the firm's profit-maximizing price, quantity, and level of advertising?

Answer

1. *Write the firm's profit function using its inverse demand function.* The monopoly's profit is

$$\pi = (800 - 4Q + 0.2A^{0.5})Q - 2Q - A$$
$$= 798Q - 4Q^2 + 0.2A^{0.5}Q - A. \qquad (9.15)$$

2. *Set the partial derivatives of the profit function in Equation 9.15 with respect to Q and A to zero to obtain the equations that determine the profit-maximizing levels, as in Equations 9.13 and 9.14.* The first-order conditions are

$$\frac{\partial \pi}{\partial Q} = 798 - 8Q + 0.2A^{0.5} = 0, \qquad (9.16)$$

$$\frac{\partial \pi}{\partial A} = 0.1A^{-0.5}Q - 1 = 0. \qquad (9.17)$$

3. *Solve Equations 9.16 and 9.17 for the profit-maximizing levels of Q and A.* We can rearrange Equation 9.17 to show that $A^{0.5} = 0.1Q$. Substituting this expression into Equation 9.16, we find that $798 - 8Q + 0.02Q = 0$, or $Q = 100$. As a result, $A^{0.5} = 0.1Q = 10$. Squaring both sides of this equation, we find that $A = 100$.

Mini-Case

Super Bowl Commercials

Super Bowl commercials are the most expensive commercials on U.S. television. A 30-second spot during the Super Bowl averaged more than $5 million in 2018. A high price for these commercials is not surprising because the cost of commercials generally increases with the number of viewers (*eyeballs* in industry jargon), and the Super Bowl is the most widely watched show, with 103 million viewers in 2018. Super Bowl advertising costs 2.5 times as much per viewer as other TV commercials.

However, a Super Bowl commercial is much more likely to influence viewers than commercials on other shows. The Super Bowl is not only a premier sports event; it also showcases the most memorable commercials of the year, such as Apple's classic 1984 Macintosh ad, which is still discussed today. Indeed, many Super Bowl viewers are not even football fans—they watch to see these superior ads. Moreover, Super Bowl commercials receive extra exposure because these ads often *go viral* on the internet.

Given that Super Bowl ads are more likely to be remembered by viewers, are these commercials worth the extra price? Obviously, many advertisers believe so, as their demand for these ads has bid up the price. Kim, Freling, and Grisaffe (2013) found that immediately after a Super Bowl commercial airs, the advertising firm's stock value rises. Thus, investors apparently believe that Super Bowl commercials raise a firm's profits despite the high cost of the commercial. Ho,

Dhar, and Weinberg (2009) found that for the typical movie with a substantial advertising budget, a Super Bowl commercial advertising the movie raises theater revenues by more than the same expenditure on other television advertising. They also concluded that movie firms' advertising during the Super Bowl was at (or close to) the profit-maximizing amount.

9.6 Internet Monopolies: Network Effects and Scale Economies

A number of technology giants, such as Facebook (95% of young adults on the internet use one of its services), Google (89% of internet searches), and Amazon (75% of electronic book sales), have such large shares of their markets that they are nearly monopolies.[23] Why are they dominant? Two important reasons concern *networks* and natural monopoly.

The demand for many goods and services depends on who else consumes them. In such cases, consumers form a **network**: an interconnected group of people or things. Facebook, LinkedIn, and Twitter users form networks, as no one would be interested in such internet social media services unless others also used them.

Another characteristic that is more common on the internet than elsewhere in the economy is a cost structure with low or zero marginal cost and high fixed cost. For example, your online search using the Google search engine has a negligible marginal cost for Google. However, to provide this service, Google incurs a large fixed cost for programmers and infrastructure. As a result, its average cost curve is downward sloping, which is a condition that can lead to natural monopoly.

Network Externalities

A good has a **network externality** if one person's demand depends on the consumption of a good by others.[24] If a good has a *positive* network externality, its value to a consumer grows as the number of units sold increases. Network externalities are an important source of monopoly power. They arise in many parts of the economy but are particularly important on the internet.

When a firm introduces a new good with a network externality, it faces a chicken-and-egg problem: Ali won't buy the good unless Shan buys it, and Shan won't buy it unless Ali does. The firm wants its customers to coordinate or to make their purchase decisions simultaneously.

The telephone provides a classic example of a positive network externality. When the phone was introduced, potential adopters had no reason to subscribe for phone service unless their family and friends did. Why pay for phone service if you have no one to call? For Bell's phone network to succeed, it had to achieve a *critical mass* of users—enough adopters so that others wanted to join. Had it failed to achieve this critical mass, demand would have withered and the network would have died.

---

[23]www.wsj.com/articles/the-antitrust-case-against-facebook-google-amazon-and-apple-1516121561.

[24] In Chapter 16, we discuss the more general case of an *externality*, which occurs when a person's well-being or a firm's production capability is directly affected by the actions of other consumers or firms rather than indirectly through changes in prices.

Managerial
Implication

Introductory
Prices

Managers of firms that want to sell goods and services with network externalities often initially sell them at a low introductory price to obtain a critical mass. By doing so, the manager maximizes long-run profit but not short-run profit.

Suppose that a monopoly sells its good—root-beer-scented sandals—for only two periods (after that, the demand goes to zero as a new craze hits the market). If the monopoly sells less than a critical quantity of output, Q, in the first period, then its second-period demand curve lies close to the price axis. However, if the good is a success in the first period—at least Q units are sold—the second-period demand curve shifts substantially to the right.

If the monopoly maximizes its short-run profit in the first period, it charges p^* and sells Q^* units, which is fewer than Q. To sell Q units, it would have to lower its first-period price below p^*, which would reduce its first-period profit from π^* to π.

In the second period, the monopoly maximizes its profit given its second-period demand curve. If the monopoly sold only Q^* units in the first period, it earns a relatively low second-period profit of π_l. However, if it sells Q units in the first period, it makes a relatively high second-period profit, π_h.

Should the monopoly charge a low introductory price in the first period? Its objective is to maximize its long-run profit: the sum of its profit in the two periods.[25] If the firm has a critical mass in the second period, its extra profit is $\pi_h - \pi_l$. To obtain this critical mass by charging a low introductory price in the first period, it lowers its first-period profit by $\pi^* - \pi$. Thus, a manager should charge a low introductory price in the first period if the reduction in first-period profit is less than the extra profit in the second period.

This policy is profitable for many firms. A 2018 Google search found over a million web pages touting an introductory price.

A closely related strategy used for many internet services is to start by offering a free version, then, after creating a large enough user base, offer a premium version at a positive (and profitable) price, like Yahoo! mail.

Behavioral Network Externalities

Network externalities depend on the size of the network because customers want to interact with each other. However, sometimes consumers' behavior depends on beliefs or tastes that can be explained by psychological and sociological theories, which economists study in *behavioral economics* (Chapter 4).

One such explanation for a network externality effect is based on consumer attitudes toward other consumers. Harvey Leibenstein (1950) suggested that consumers sometimes want a good because "everyone else has it." A fad or other popularity-based explanation for a positive network externality is called a **bandwagon effect**: A person places greater value on a good as more and more people possess it.[26] The continued dominance of the iPad today may be partially due to its early popularity.

---

[25]Firms place lower value on profit in the future than profit today (Chapter 7). However, for simplicity, we assume that the monopoly places equal value on profit in either period.

[26]*Jargon alert*: Some economists use *bandwagon effect* to mean any positive network externality—not just those that are based on popularity.

The opposite, negative network externality is called a **snob effect**: A person places greater value on a good as fewer and fewer people possess it. Some people prefer an original painting by an unknown artist to a lithograph by a star because no one else can possess that painting. (As Yogi Berra is reported to have said, "Nobody goes there anymore; it's too crowded.")

Two-Sided Markets

A **two-sided market** or **two-sided network** is an economic platform that has two or more user groups that provide each other with network externalities. Two common types of *economic platforms* are online matchmakers and innovation platforms.

Economic platforms such as Airbnb (short-term rentals), Lyft (driver service), and Monster.com (an employment site) match sellers with buyers. If more drivers are available on Lyft, more customers will want to use the service, which is a network externality. Similarly, if more customers use Lyft, more drivers will want to drive for it.

An innovation platform provides a technology upon which other firms can build and customers use. Google's Android operating system for cell phones is an innovation platform. Developers produce apps that function on this operating system. The more apps, the more users. The more users, the more developers producing apps.

The internet itself is an innovation platform. In the early days of the internet, connecting to it over phone lines was slow and costly. Because the internet had relatively little content, many people found that the cost of connecting to the internet and using it exceeded the benefit. But, once a large enough number of customers had internet service, more suppliers found it profitable to provide internet content such as news media and downloadable music, movies, and computer software. As content increased, more people used the internet. And, with more customers, more firms started selling on the internet.

Many non-internet industries also have two-sided networks. Both cardholders and merchants use credit cards. Gamers and game developers link using video-game consoles. Doctors and patients connect through health maintenance organizations and hospitals.

Natural Monopoly on the Internet

Many internet services require a large up-front fixed cost—primarily for development and promotion—but have a low marginal cost, sometimes nearly zero. As a result, such firms have downward-sloping average cost curves, reflecting economies of scale. Under such a cost structure, a monopoly or near-monopoly may emerge after a brief period of internet competition.[27]

---

[27]If internet sites provide differentiated products, then several sites may coexist even though average costs are strictly decreasing. In 2007, commentators were predicting the emergence of monopolies in social networks such as MySpace, an early social networking site. MySpace lost dominance to Facebook. In turn, Facebook may eventually lose ground to a similar site; to newer variants, such as Twitter, Snapchat, and Instagram; or to sites that cater to specialized audiences such as LinkedIn.

Google is an example of such a natural monopoly. It has high fixed costs, but it incurs virtually zero marginal cost when someone uses its search engine. It can therefore easily accommodate more users. And because Google offers this service free to users, a potential competitor providing an identical service cannot undercut Google, short of offering a subsidy, and would struggle to cover its fixed costs. Google is able to cover its fixed costs because its large user base is attractive to advertisers. It earns large advertising revenues and has substantial profits even after covering its fixed costs.

Some firms, such as Facebook, benefit from both a natural monopoly cost structure and network externalities. Like Google, Facebook has high fixed costs and can add users at negligible marginal cost. It continuously expands its user base by offering free use of its service. In addition, because of network externalities, users increasingly want to join Facebook as its network becomes larger, further enhancing the value of Facebook to advertisers.

Mini-Case

Critical Mass and eBay

In the early years of the internet, eBay's online auction site, which started in 1995, faced competition from a variety of other internet sites including Yahoo! Auctions that the then mighty Yahoo! created in 1998. At the time, many commentators correctly predicted that whichever auction site first achieved a critical mass of users would drive the other sites out of business. Indeed, most of these alternative sites died or faded into obscurity. For example, Yahoo! Auctions closed its U.S. and Canada sections of the site in 2007 (although its Hong Kong, Taiwanese, and Japanese sites continue to operate).

Sellers value having a reputation system, based on feedback from many buyers, and one site where virtually all buyers and sellers congregate, which lowers buyers' search costs (Brown and Morgan, 2006). Apparently, these advantages more than compensate sellers for the lack of competition in sellers' fees. Brown and Morgan (2009) found that, prior to the demise of the Yahoo! Auction site, the same type of items attracted an average of two additional bidders on eBay and, consequently, the prices on eBay were consistently 20% to 70% percent higher than Yahoo! Auction prices.

Disruptive Technologies

The internet facilitates the introduction of disruptive technologies (see Disruptive Innovations and the Evolution of Market Structure in Chapter 7) with strong network externalities and economies of scale. Because these new internet technologies have network externalities, low marginal costs, and decreasing average cost curves, they often can drive out existing technologies.

Amazon started by selling books over the internet. The ease of finding and purchasing books that way attracted many consumers. Moreover, Amazon has much lower marginal and average costs than traditional brick-and-mortar bookstores. Its Kindle reader provides a two-sided market for online books. For all these reasons, Amazon is driving many traditional bookstores out of business.

Online news is driving print newspapers out of business. Streaming movies killed off most of the movie videotape/CD/Blu-ray rental stores. Streaming music has largely eliminated record-CD sales.

**Managerial
Solution**

**Brand-Name and
Generic Drugs**

When generic drugs enter the market after the patent on a brand-name drug expires, the demand curve facing the brand-name firm shifts to the left. Why do many brand-name drug companies raise their prices after generic rivals enter the market? The reason is that the demand curve not only shifts to the left but also rotates so that it is less elastic at the original price.

The price the brand-name firm sets depends on the elasticity of demand. When the firm has a patent monopoly, it faces the linear demand curve D^1 in the figure. The intersection of the corresponding marginal revenue curve MR^1 and the marginal cost curve determines the monopoly optimum, e_1. (Because MR^1 is twice as steeply sloped as D^1, it intersects the MC curve at Q_1, while the demand curve D^1 intersects the MC curve at $2Q_1$.) The monopoly sells the Q_1 units at a price of p_1.

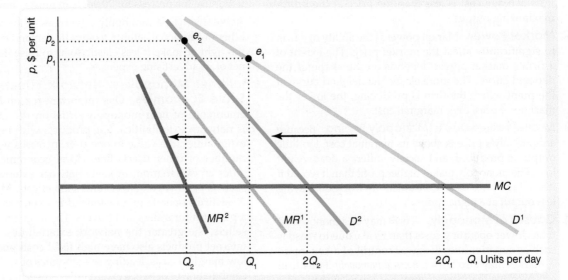

After the generic drugs enter the market, the linear demand curve facing the original patent holder shifts leftward to D^2 and becomes steeper and less elastic at the original price. The firm now maximizes its profit at e_2, where the quantity, Q_2, is smaller than Q_1 because D^2 lies to the left of D^1. However, the new price, p_2, is higher than the initial price, p_1, because the D^2 demand curve is less elastic at the new optimum quantity Q_2 than is the D^1 curve at Q_1.

Why might the demand curve rotate and become less elastic at the initial price? One explanation is that the brand-name firm has two types of consumers with different elasticities of demand who differ in their willingness to switch to a generic. One group of consumers is relatively price sensitive and switches to the lower-priced generics. However, the brand-name drug continues to be the monopoly supplier to the remaining brand-loyal customers whose demand is less elastic than that of the price-sensitive consumers. These loyal customers prefer the brand-name drug because they are more comfortable with a familiar product, worry that new products may be substandard, or fear that differences in the inactive ingredients might affect them.

Older customers are less likely to switch brands than younger people. A survey by the American Association of Retired Persons found that people aged 65 and older were 15% less likely than people aged 45 to 64 to request generic versions of a drug from their doctor or pharmacist. Similarly, patients with generous insurance plans may be more likely to pay for expensive drugs (if their insurer permits) than customers with more limited insurance policies.

SUMMARY

1. **Monopoly Profit Maximization.** Like any firm, a monopoly—a single seller—maximizes its profit by setting its output so that its marginal revenue equals its marginal cost. The monopoly makes a positive profit if its average cost is less than the price at the profit-maximizing output.

2. **Market Power.** Market power is the ability of a firm to significantly affect the market price. The extent of a firm's market power depends on the shape of the demand curve. The more elastic the demand curve at the point where the firm is producing, the lower the markup of price over marginal cost.

3. **Market Failure Due to Monopoly Pricing.** Because a monopoly's price is above its marginal cost, too little output is produced, and society suffers a deadweight loss. The monopoly makes higher profit than it would if it acted as a price taker. Consumers are worse off, buying less output at a higher price.

4. **Causes of Monopoly.** A firm may be a monopoly if it has lower operating costs than rivals, due to reasons such as superior knowledge or control of a key input. A market may also have a *natural monopoly* if one firm can produce the market output at lower average cost than can a larger number of firms (even if all firms have the same cost function). Many, if not most, monopolies

are created by governments, which prevent other firms from entering the markets. One important barrier to entry is a patent, which gives the inventor of a new product or process the exclusive right to sell the product or use the process for 20 years in most countries.

5. **Advertising.** A monopoly advertises or engages in other promotional activity to shift its demand curve to the right or make it less elastic so as to raise its profit net of its advertising expenses.

6. **Internet Monopolies: Network Effects and Scale Economies.** One important reason for the emergence of near-monopoly firms on the internet is network externalities. For products with network externalities, the value to one user increases with the number of other users. Behavioral economics provides an explanation for some network externalities, such as bandwagon effects and snob effects. Many of these firms operate in a two-sided market, serving as a platform for sellers and buyers. The more buyers or sellers, the greater the network externalities. Many internet products also have high fixed costs and very low marginal costs, leading to economies of scale. The combination of network externalities and economies of scale may allow a firm that first establishes critical mass to become a monopoly.

QUESTIONS

All exercises are available on **MyLab Economics;** * = *answer at the back of this book;* **C** = *use of calculus may be necessary;* **✗** = *this exercise is available in Excel Grader in* **MyLab Economics.**

1. Monopoly Profit Maximization

1.1 If the inverse demand function is $p = 800 - 4Q$, what is the marginal revenue function? Draw the demand and marginal revenue curves. At what quantities do the demand and marginal revenue curves hit the quantity axis? (*Hint*: See Q&A 9.1.)

1.2 If the inverse demand function a monopoly faces is $p = 50Q^{-0.5}$, what is the firm's marginal revenue function? (*Hint*: See Q&A 9.1.) **C**

*1.3 If the inverse demand function is $p = 500 - 10Q$, what is the revenue and the elasticity of demand at $Q = 10$?

1.4 Is a monopoly's profit affected by whether it chooses price or quantity (assuming it chooses them optimally)? Why can't a monopoly choose both price *and* quantity?

1.5 For the monopoly in Figure 9.3, at what quantity is its revenue maximized? (*Hint*: At the quantity where the revenue function reaches its peak, the slope of the revenue function is zero. That is, $MR = 0$. See Q&A 9.3.) Why is revenue maximized at a larger quantity than profit? Modify panel b of Figure 9.3 to show the revenue curve.

1.6 Are Major League Baseball clubs profit-maximizing monopolies? Some observers of this market have contended that baseball club owners want to maximize attendance or revenue. Alexander (2001) says that one test of whether a firm is a profit-maximizing monopoly is to check whether the firm is operating in the elastic portion of its demand curve (which he finds is true). Why is that a relevant test? What would the elasticity be if a baseball club were maximizing revenue? (*Hint*: See Q&A 9.3.)

1.7 Using a graph, show under what condition the monopoly operates—does not shut down—in the long run. Discuss your result in terms of the demand curve and the average cost curve at the profit-maximizing quantity.

1.8 Why might a monopoly operate in any part (downward sloping, flat, upward sloping) of its long-run average cost curve, but a competitive firm will operate only at the bottom or in the upward-sloping section?

1.9 AT&T Inc., the large U.S. phone company and the one-time monopoly, left the payphone business at the beginning of 2009 because people were switching to wireless phones. U.S. consumers owning cellphones reached 80% by 2007 and 95% by 2018 according to the Pew Research Center. Consequently, the number of payphones fell from 2.6 million at the peak in 1998 to only about 100,000 in 2018 (**money. cnn.com/2018/03/19/news/companies/pay-phones/ index.html**). Use graphs to explain why a monopoly may exit a market when its demand curve shifts to the left.

*1.10 The inverse demand function a monopoly faces is $p = 100 - Q$. The firm's cost curve is $C(Q) = 10 + 5Q$. What is the profit-maximizing solution? How does your answer change if $C(Q) = 100 + 5Q$? (*Hint*: See "Using Calculus: Solving for the Profit-Maximizing Output" and Q&A 9.2.) **C**

1.11 The inverse demand function a monopoly faces is $p = 50Q^{-0.5}$ (*Hint*: See Question 1.2). The firm's cost curve is $C(Q) = 5Q$. What is the profit-maximizing solution? (*Hint*: See "Using Calculus: Solving for the Profit-Maximizing Output" and Q&A 9.2.) **C**

1.12 Show that after a shift in the demand curve, a monopoly's price may remain constant but its output may rise.

2. Market Power

2.1 Why is the ratio of the monopoly's price to its marginal cost, p/MC, larger if the demand curve is less elastic at the optimum quantity? Can the demand curve be inelastic at that quantity?

2.2 When will a monopoly set its price equal to its marginal cost?

2.3 The U.S. Postal Service (USPS) has a constitutionally guaranteed monopoly on first-class mail. In 2018, it charged 50¢ for a stamp, which was not the profit-maximizing price–the USPS goal, allegedly, is to break even rather than to turn a profit. Following the postal services in Australia, Britain, Canada, Switzerland, and Ireland, the USPS allowed **Stamps.com** to sell a sheet of twenty 50¢ stamps with a photo of your dog, your mommy, or whatever image you want for $23.99 (that's $1.20 per stamp, or a 240% markup). **Stamps.com** keeps the extra beyond the 50¢ it pays the USPS. What is the firm's Lerner Index? If **Stamps.com** is a profit-maximizing monopoly, what elasticity of demand does it face for a customized stamp? (*Hint*: See Q&A 9.5.)

2.4 According to the California Nurses Association, Tenet Healthcare hospitals marked up drugs substantially. At Tenet's Sierra Vista Regional Medical Center, drug prices were 1,840.80% of the hospital's costs (Chuck Squatriglia and Tyche Hendricks, "Tenet Hiked Drug Prices, Study Finds More Than Double U.S. Average," *San Francisco Chronicle*, November 24, 2002: A1, A10). Assuming Tenet was maximizing its profit, what was the elasticity of demand that Tenet believed it faced? What was its Lerner Index for drugs? (*Hint*: See Q&A 9.5.) **C**

2.5 In 2015, Apple introduced the Apple Watch. According to market research firm IHS, the cost of producing the 38 mm Apple Watch Sport was $84. The price was $349. What was Apple's price/marginal cost ratio? What was its Lerner Index? If Apple is a short-run profit-maximizing monopoly, what elasticity of demand did Apple believe it faced? (*Hint*: See Q&A 9.5.) **C**

*2.6 In 2009, the price of Amazon's Kindle 2 was $359, while iSuppli estimated that its marginal cost was $159. What was Amazon's Lerner Index? What elasticity of demand did it face if it was engaging in short-run profit maximization? (*Hint*: See Q&A 9.5.) **C**

2.7 When Apple introduced its first portable media player, the iPod, its constant marginal cost of producing the top-of-the-line model was $200 (iSuppli), its fixed cost was approximately $736 million, and we estimate that its inverse demand function was $p = 600 - 25Q$, where Q is units measured in millions. What was Apple's average cost function? Assuming that Apple was maximizing its short-run monopoly profit, what was its marginal revenue function? What were its profit-maximizing price and quantity, profit, and Lerner Index? What was the elasticity of demand at the profit-maximizing level? Show Apple's profit-maximizing solution in a figure. (*Hint*: See Q&A 9.2 and Q&A 9.5.) **C**

2.8 Xerox, the U.S. Postal Service, and McDonald's have enjoyed significant market power in the past. List and explain three major factors that have eroded this market power.

2.9 Q&A 9.4 shows that a concert's profit-maximizing price may exceed the price that allows the concert to sell out. Redraw the figure if the concert requires a large fixed cost (lighting, the stage's appearance, and so forth). Indicate the profit areas if Ms. Swift sets a price such that (a) marginal revenue equals marginal cost or (b) the concert sells out. How do we know that the first profit area is greater than the second one?

3. Market Failure Due to Monopoly Pricing

3.1 A monopoly has a constant marginal cost of production of $1 per unit and a fixed cost of $10. Draw the firm's *MC*, *AVC*, and *AC* curves. Add a downward-sloping demand curve, and show the profit-maximizing quantity and price. Indicate the profit as an area on your diagram. Show the deadweight loss.

3.2 A monopoly has an inverse demand function given by $p = 480 - 4Q$ and a constant marginal cost of 40. Calculate the deadweight loss if the monopoly charges the profit-maximizing price.

3.3 A monopoly's inverse demand function is $p = 160 - 2Q$, and it has no fixed cost. Initially, its marginal cost is 12. Now, the firm makes a process innovation that reduces its marginal cost to 4. Determine the price, quantity, consumer surplus, profit, total surplus, and deadweight loss before and after the innovation. What share of the increased total surplus goes to consumers?

3.4 What is the effect of a lump-sum tax (which is like an additional fixed cost) on a monopoly? (*Hint*: Consider the possibility that the firm may shut down, and see Q&A 9.6.)

3.5 If the inverse demand function is $p = 200 - 2Q$ and the marginal cost is constant at $20, how does charging the monopoly a specific tax of $t = 20 per unit affect price and quantity and the surplus of consumers, the monopoly, and society (where society's surplus includes the tax revenue)? What is the incidence of the tax on consumers? (*Hint*: See Q&A 9.6.)

*3.6 Show mathematically that a monopoly may raise the price to consumers by more than a specific tax imposed on it. (*Hint*: Consider a monopoly facing a constant-elasticity demand function $Q = Ap^\varepsilon$ where ε is a negative constant greater than 1 in absolute value, and with a constant marginal cost, *m*.) **C**

3.7 Q&A 9.6 illustrates the effect of imposing a specific tax of $8 per unit of a monopoly's output. Suppose that instead of charging a specific tax, the government

charges a profit tax of 10%. How does this profit tax affect the equilibrium price and quantity, consumer surplus, producer surplus, and total surplus?

4. Causes of Monopoly

*4.1 Can a firm be a natural monopoly if it has a U-shaped average cost curve? Why or why not? (*Hint*: See Q&A 9.7.)

*4.2 Can a firm operating in the upward-sloping portion of its average cost curve be a natural monopoly? Explain. (*Hint*: See Q&A 9.7.)

4.3 Figure 9.6 shows that two firms producing 6 units each have a higher total cost than one firm producing 12 units. Given the cost function underlying Figure 9.6, would two firms each producing output $Q(>0)$ always incur more total cost than one firm producing $2Q$? (*Hint*: See Q&A 9.7.)

4.4 Once the copyright runs out on a book or a piece of music, it can legally be placed on the internet for anyone to download. In 1998 the U.S. Congress extended the copyright law to 95 years after the original publication. But the copyright holds for only 50 years in Australia and 70 years in the European Union. Thus, an Australian website could post *Gone with the Wind*, a 1936 novel, or Elvis Presley's 1954 single "That's All Right," while a U.S. site could not. Obviously, this legal nicety won't stop U.S. fans from downloading from Australian or European sites. Discuss how limiting the length of a copyright would affect the pricing used by the publisher of a novel.

4.5 In the Mini-Case "Botox," consumer surplus, triangle *A*, equals the deadweight loss, triangle *C*. Show that this equality is a result of the linear demand and constant marginal cost assumptions.

5. Advertising

5.1 Using a graph, explain why a firm might not want to spend money on advertising, even if such an expenditure would shift the firm's demand curve to the right.

*5.2 A monopoly's inverse demand function is $p = 100 - Q + (5A - A^2)/Q$, where Q is its quantity, p is its price, and A is the level of advertising. Its marginal cost of production is constant at 10, and its cost of a unit of advertising is 1. What are the firm's profit-maximizing price, quantity, and level of advertising? (*Hint*: See Q&A 9.8.) **C**

5.3 A monopoly's inverse demand function is $p = Q^{-0.25}A^{0.5}$, where Q is its quantity, p is its price, and A is the level of advertising. Its constant marginal and average cost of production is 6, and its cost of a unit of advertising is 0.25. What are the firm's profit-maximizing price, quantity, and level of advertising? (*Hint*: See Q&A 9.8.) **C**

5.4 Canada subsidizes Canadian magazines to offset the invasion of foreign (primarily U.S.) magazines, which take 90% of the country's sales. The Canada Magazine Fund provides a lump-sum subsidy to various magazines to "maintain a Canadian presence against the overwhelming presence of foreign magazines." Eligibility is based on high levels of investment in Canadian editorial content and reliance on advertising revenues. What effect will a lump-sum subsidy have on the number of subscriptions sold?

5.5 Use a diagram similar to Figure 9.7 to illustrate the effect of social media on the demand for Super Bowl commercials. (*Hint*: See the Mini-Case "Super Bowl Commercials.")

6. Internet Monopolies: Network Effects and Scale Economies

6.1 A monopoly chocolate manufacturer faces two types of consumers. The larger group, the hoi polloi, loves desserts and has a relatively flat, linear demand curve for chocolate. The smaller group, the snobs, is interested in buying chocolate only if the hoi polloi do not buy it. Given that the hoi polloi do not buy the chocolate, the snobs have a relatively steep, linear demand curve. Show the monopoly's possible outcomes—high price, low quantity; low price, high quantity—and explain the condition under which the monopoly chooses to cater to the snobs rather than to the hoi polloi.

*6.2 A monopoly produces a good with a network externality at a constant marginal and average cost of 2. In the first period, its inverse demand function is $p = 10 - Q$. In the second period, its demand is $p = 10 - Q$ unless it sells at least $Q = 8$ units in the first period. If it meets or exceeds this target, then the demand curve rotates out by v (it sells v times as many units for any given price), so that its inverse demand function is $p = 10 - Q/v$. The monopoly knows that it can sell no output after the second period. The monopoly's objective is to maximize the sum of its profits over the two periods. In the first period, should the monopoly set the output that maximizes its profit in that period? How does your answer depend on v? **C** (*Hint*: See the Managerial Implication "Introductory Prices".)

6.3 What are the main factors that have created positive network externalities for eBay? (*Hint*: See the Mini-Case "eBay's Critical Mass.")

6.4 In the past, Games Unlimited sold copies of its trademark computer game on DVD. It faced inverse demand function $p = 60 - Q$ and had cost function $C = 100 + 20Q$. It recently switched to selling its game online via the internet. Demand was unchanged, but its cost function changed as fixed costs rose to 500 but marginal cost dropped to zero: $C = 500$. Assuming that Games Unlimited maximizes profit, what effect did moving from DVD to internet distribution have on price, quantity, consumer surplus, and profit?

7. Managerial Problem

7.1 Under what circumstances will a drug company charge more for its drug after its patent expires?

7.2 Does the Managerial Solution change if the entry of the generic causes a parallel shift to the left of the patent monopoly's linear demand curve?

7.3 Some people propose reducing the number of years that a drug patent lasts, but their critics argue that such a change would result in even higher prices during the patent period as companies would need to recover drug development costs more quickly. Is this argument valid if drug companies maximize profit?

8. MyLab Economics Spreadsheet Exercises[28]

8.1 A monopoly faces the inverse demand function: $p = 100 - 2Q$, with the corresponding marginal revenue function, $MR = 100 - 4Q$. The firm's total cost of production is $C = 50 + 10Q + 3Q^2$, with a corresponding marginal cost of $MC = 10 + 6Q$.

   a. Create a spreadsheet for $Q = 1, 2, 3, \ldots, 15$. Using the $MR = MC$ rule, determine the profit-maximizing output and price for the firm and the consequent level of profit.

   b. Calculate the Lerner Index of monopoly power for each output level and verify its relationship with the value of the price elasticity of demand (ε) at the profit-maximizing level of output.

   c. Now suppose that a specific tax of 5 per unit is imposed on the monopoly. What is the effect on the monopoly's profit-maximizing price?

8.2 A monopoly faces the demand function $Q = 30 - p$. Its inverse demand function is therefore $p = 30 - Q$, so its marginal revenue function is $MR = 30 - 2Q$. The firm's cost function is $C = 6Q + Q^2$, so its marginal cost is $MC = 6 + 2Q$. The monopoly sets its price. Its quantity is determined by the demand function.

---

[28]The spreadsheet exercises in this chapter are based largely on the work of Satyajit Ghosh, in cooperation with the authors. The answers are available on MyLab Economics.

a. Create a spreadsheet with headings Price, Quantity, Revenue, Cost, Profit, Marginal Revenue, and Marginal Cost. Enter prices ranging from 15 to 30 in increments of one in Column A (the price column). Enter the appropriate formulas in the other cells in the spreadsheet to calculate the values of the other variables for each price. For example, the price of 15 goes in cell A2, the quantity demanded at that price goes in cell B2, the resulting revenue at that price and quantity goes in cell C2, and so on. Find the price that maximizes profit and verify that $MR = MC$ at this price. (*Hint*: See Q&A 9.3.)

b. Add columns for consumer surplus and total surplus in your spreadsheet. The formula for consumer surplus is $CS = 0.5(30 - p)Q$. The firm's producer surplus equals its profit because it has no fixed cost. Total surplus is the sum of the consumer surplus and the producer surplus. Find the price that maximizes total surplus and verify that $p = MC$ at this price. If the profit-maximizing monopoly price is charged instead of the price that maximizes total surplus, what is the deadweight loss?

c. In addition to using the method described in parts a and b, use Excel's *Solver* tool to find the price that maximizes profit and the price that maximizes consumer surplus. (*Hint*: See the instructions for using *Solver* in Question 6.2 of Chapter 8 or use Excel's *Help* feature.)

8.3 A firm's demand function is $Q = 110 - p + 2A^{0.5}$, where A is the amount of advertising undertaken by the firm and the price of advertising is one. The firm's cost of production is $C = 50 + 10Q + 2Q^2$. The government imposes a binding price control at $135. Use Excel to determine the profit-maximizing level of advertising. (*Hint*: Try advertising levels that vary in hundreds from 0 to $1,000. Select the most profitable range and try smaller increments within that range.)

Pricing with Market Power

Everything is worth what its purchaser will pay for it.

—Publilius Syrus (first century B.C.)

Managerial Problem

Sale Prices

Because many retail managers use *sales*—temporarily setting the price below the usual price—some customers pay lower prices than others over time. Grocery stores are particularly likely to put products on sale frequently. In large U.S. supermarkets, a soft drink brand is on sale 94% of the time. Either Coke or Pepsi is on sale half the weeks in a year.

Heinz ketchup controls about 60% of the U.S. ketchup market, 70% of the Canadian market and 80% of the market in the U.K. The Kraft Heinz company sells hundreds of millions of bottles of Heinz ketchup per year in more than 140 countries. Approximately 200 million U.S. consumers used Heinz ketchup in 2018. When Heinz ketchup goes on sale, *switchers*—ketchup customers who normally buy whichever brand is least expensive—purchase Heinz rather than the low-price generic ketchup. How can Heinz's managers design a pattern of sales that maximizes profit by obtaining extra sales from switchers without losing substantial sums by selling to its loyal customers at a discount price? Under what conditions does it pay for Heinz to have a policy of periodic sales?

Sales are not the only means that firms use to charge customers different prices. Why are airline fares often substantially less if you book in advance? Why do the spiritualists who live at the Wonewoc Spiritualist Camp give readings for $60 for half an hour, but charge seniors only $50 on Wednesdays?[1] Why are some goods, including computers and software, combined and sold as a bundle? To answer these questions, we need to examine how monopolies and other noncompetitive firms set prices.

In Chapter 9, we examined how a monopoly maximizes its profit when it uses **uniform pricing**: charging the same price for every unit sold of a particular good. However, a monopoly can increase its profit if it can use **nonuniform pricing**, charging consumers different prices for the same product or charging a single customer a price that depends on the number of units the customer buys. In this chapter, we analyze nonuniform pricing for monopolies, but similar principles apply to any firm with market power.

---

[1]**www.campwonewoc.org/index.html**, July 24, 2018.

As we saw in Chapter 9, a monopoly that sets a uniform price sells only to customers who value the good enough to buy it at the monopoly price, and those customers receive some consumer surplus. The monopoly does not sell the good to other customers who value the good at less than the single price, even if those consumers would be willing to pay more than the marginal cost of production. These lost sales cause *deadweight loss*, which is the foregone value of these potential sales in excess of the cost of producing the good.

A firm with market power can earn a higher profit using nonuniform pricing than by setting a uniform price for two reasons. First, the firm captures some or all of the single-price consumer surplus. Second, the firm converts at least some of the single-price deadweight loss into profit by charging a price below the uniform price (but above the firm's marginal cost) to some customers who would not purchase at the single-price level. A monopoly that uses nonuniform pricing can lower the price to these otherwise excluded consumers without lowering the price to consumers who are willing to pay higher prices.

In this chapter, we examine several types of nonuniform pricing including price discrimination, two-part pricing, bundling, and peak-load pricing. The most common form of nonuniform pricing is **price discrimination**: charging consumers different prices for the same good based on individual characteristics of consumers, on membership in an identifiable subgroup of consumers, or on the quantity purchased by the consumers. For example, regular subscribers to the *Wall Street Journal* Classic package of print and online access pay $222 annually, while students, who are price sensitive, are offered the same product for only about 22% of that price, $49 for the year.

Some firms with market power use other forms of nonuniform pricing to increase profits. A firm may use *two-part pricing*, charging a customer one fee for the right to buy the good and an additional fee for each unit purchased. For example, members of health or golf clubs typically pay an annual fee to belong to the club and then pay an additional amount each time they use the facilities. Similarly, cable television companies often charge a monthly fee for basic service and an additional fee (pay-per-view) for certain shows.

Another type of nonuniform pricing is called *bundling*, where several products are sold together as a package. For example, many restaurants provide full-course dinners for a fixed price that is less than the sum of the prices charged if the items (appetizer, main dish, and dessert) are ordered separately (à la carte).

Finally, some firms use *peak-load pricing*: charging higher prices in periods of peak demand than at other times. For example, ticket prices for flights from cold northern cities to Hawaii are higher in the winter months, when demand is higher than in the summer.

Learning Objectives

1. List the conditions necessary to price discriminate.
2. Show how perfect price discrimination extracts all surplus from consumers.
3. Describe how a firm sets different prices for various consumer groups to raise its profit.
4. Demonstrate how a firm can increase its profit by charging prices based on the quantities consumers buy.
5. Illustrate how a firm may raise its profit by charging an access fee and a per-unit price.
6. Determine when a firm can increase its profit by selling related products in a bundle.
7. Explain why firms charge higher prices in periods of peak demand.

10.1 Conditions for Price Discrimination

We start by studying the most common form of nonuniform pricing, *price discrimination*, where a firm charges various consumers different prices for a good.[2] Many people complain that price discrimination is irrational:

> **Common Confusion** It can't pay for a firm to charge some consumers a different price than others.

However, many (but not all) firms can profit by price discriminating.

Why Price Discrimination Pays

For almost any good or service, some consumers are willing to pay more than others. A firm that sets a single price faces a trade-off between charging consumers with a high willingness to pay a high price and charging a low enough price to sell to other customers with a lower willingness to pay. As a result, a single-price firm sets an intermediate price. By price discriminating, a firm can partially or entirely avoid this trade-off.

As with any kind of nonuniform pricing, price discrimination increases profit above the uniform pricing level through two channels. Price discrimination can extract additional consumer surplus from consumers who place a high value on the good and can simultaneously sell to new customers who would not be willing to pay the profit-maximizing uniform price. We use a pair of extreme examples to illustrate these two benefits of price discrimination to firms—capturing more of the consumer surplus and selling to more customers.

Suppose that the only movie theater in town has two types of patrons: college students and senior citizens. College students see the Saturday night movie if the price is $20 or less, and senior citizens attend if the price is $10 or less. Thus, college students have a willingness to pay $20 and senior citizens have a willingness to pay $10. For simplicity, we assume that the theater incurs no cost when showing the movie, so profit is the same as revenue. We also assume that the theater is large enough to hold all potential customers, so the marginal cost of admitting one more customer is zero. Table 10.1 shows how pricing affects the theater's profit.

In panel a, the theater potentially has 10 college student and 20 senior citizen customers. If the theater charges everyone $10, its profit is $300 because all 30 potential customers buy a ticket. If it charges $20, the senior citizens do not go to the movie, so the theater makes only $200, receiving $20 each from the 10 college students. Thus, if the theater charges everyone the same price, it maximizes its profit by setting the price at $10. The theater does not want to charge less than $10 because the same number of people go to the movie as when $10 is charged. Charging between $10 and $20 is less profitable than charging $20 because no extra seniors go and the college students are willing to pay $20. Charging more than $20 results in no customers.

---

[2]Price discrimination is generally legal in the United States unless it harms competition between firms, as specified in the Robinson-Patman Act of 1936.

TABLE 10.1 Theater Profits Based on the Pricing Method Used

(a) No Extra Customers from Price Discrimination

Pricing	Profit from 10 College Students	Profit from 20 Senior Citizens	Total Profit
Uniform, $10	$100	$200	$300
Uniform, $20	$200	$0	$200
Price discrimination*	$200	$200	$400

(b) Extra Customers from Price Discrimination

Pricing	Profit from 10 College Students	Profit from 5 Senior Citizens	Total Profit
Uniform, $10	$100	$50	$150
Uniform, $20	$200	$0	$200
Price discrimination*	$200	$50	$250

*The theater price discriminates by charging college students $20 and senior citizens $10.
Notes: College students go to the theater if they are charged no more than $20. Senior citizens are willing to pay up to $10. The theater's marginal cost for an extra customer is zero.

If the price is $10, the seniors have no consumer surplus: They pay exactly what seeing the movie is worth to them. Seeing the movie is worth $20 to the college students so, if the price is only $10, each has a consumer surplus of $10, and their combined consumer surplus is $100.

If the theater can price discriminate by charging senior citizens $10 and college students $20, its profit increases to $400. Its profit rises because the theater makes $200 from the seniors (the same amount as when it was selling all tickets for $10) but gets an extra $100 from the college students ($10 more from each of the 10 students). By price discriminating, the theater sells the same number of seats but makes more money from the college students, capturing all the consumer surplus they had under uniform pricing. Neither group of customers has any consumer surplus if the theater price discriminates.

In panel b, the theater potentially has 10 college student and 5 senior citizen customers. If the theater must charge a single price, it charges $20. Only college students see the movie, so the theater's profit is $200. (If it charges $10, both students and seniors go to the theater, but its profit is only $150.) If the theater can price discriminate and charge seniors $10 and college students $20, its profit increases to $250. Here the gain from price discrimination comes from selling more tickets (those sold to seniors) and not from making more money on the same number of tickets, as in panel a. With price discrimination the theater earns as much from the students as without price discrimination, and makes more from the seniors. Neither customer group enjoys any consumer surplus.

These examples illustrate the two channels through which price discrimination can increase profit: charging some existing customers more or selling extra units. Leslie (1997) found that Broadway theaters in New York increase their profits 5% by price discriminating rather than using uniform prices.

In the examples just considered, the movie theater's ability to increase its profits by price discrimination arises from its ability to segment the market into two groups, students and senior citizens, with different levels of willingness to pay.

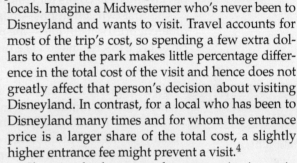

Mini-Case

Disneyland Pricing

Disneyland, in southern California, is a well-run operation that rarely misses a trick when it comes to increasing its profit. (Indeed, Disneyland prints its own money: When you enter the park, you can exchange U.S. currency for Disney dollars, which can be spent only in the park.)[3]

For part of 2018, Disneyland offered local, Southern Californians two-day and three-day theme park tickets at a 25% discount. This policy of charging locals a discounted price makes sense if out-of-town visitors are willing to pay more than locals and if Disneyland can prevent locals from selling discounted tickets to non-

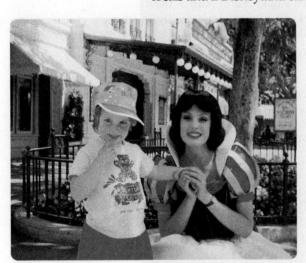

locals. Imagine a Midwesterner who's never been to Disneyland and wants to visit. Travel accounts for most of the trip's cost, so spending a few extra dollars to enter the park makes little percentage difference in the total cost of the visit and hence does not greatly affect that person's decision about visiting Disneyland. In contrast, for a local who has been to Disneyland many times and for whom the entrance price is a larger share of the total cost, a slightly higher entrance fee might prevent a visit.[4]

Charging both groups the same price is not in Disney's best interest. If Disney were to charge the higher price to everyone, many locals wouldn't visit the park. If Disney were to use the lower price for everyone, it would be charging nonresidents much less than they are willing to pay.

Which Firms Can Price Discriminate

For a firm to price discriminate profitably, it must meet three conditions.

First, a firm must have market power to price discriminate profitably. Without market power, a firm cannot charge any consumer more than the competitive price. A monopoly, an oligopoly firm, or a monopolistically competitive firm might be able to price discriminate. However, a perfectly competitive firm cannot price discriminate because it must sell its product at the given market price.

Second, for a firm to price discriminate profitably, groups of consumers or individual consumers must have demand curves that differ, and the firm must be able to identify how its consumers' demand curves differ. The movie theater knows that college students and senior citizens differ in their willingness to pay for a ticket, and Disneyland knows that tourists and local residents differ in their willingness to pay for admission. In both cases, the firms can identify members of these two groups by using driver's licenses or other forms of identification. Similarly, if a firm knows that each individual's demand curve slopes downward, it may charge each customer a higher price for the first unit of a good than for subsequent units.

---

[3]According to **www.babycenter.com/cost-of-raising-child-calculator**, it costs an average U.S. family $334,860 to raise a child from cradle through college. Parents can cut that total in half, however: They don't *have* to take their kids to Disneyland.

[4]In 2012, a Southern Californian couple, Jeff Reitz and Tonya Mickesh, were out of work, so they decided to cheer themselves up by using their annual passes to visit Disneyland 366 days that year (a leap year).

Third, a firm must be able to prevent or limit resale to price discriminate. The price-discriminating firm must be able to prevent consumers who buy the good at low prices from reselling the good to customers who would otherwise pay high prices. Price discrimination doesn't work if resale is easy because the firm would be able to make only low-price sales. A movie theater can charge different prices for different groups of customers because those customers normally enter the theater as soon as they buy their tickets, and therefore they do not have time to resell them. For events that sell tickets in advance, other methods can be used to prevent resale, such as having different colors for children's tickets and adults' tickets.

The first two conditions—market power and the ability to identify groups with different price sensitivities—are present in many markets. Usually, the biggest obstacle to price discrimination is a firm's inability to prevent resale.

Managerial Implication
Preventing Resale

Preventing resale is easier in certain industries than in others. In industries where resale is initially easy, managers can act to make resale more costly.

Resale is difficult or impossible for most services. If a plumber charges you less than your neighbor for fixing a clogged water pipe, you cannot make a deal with your neighbor to resell this service. Even for physical goods, resale is difficult when transaction costs are high. The higher the transaction costs a consumer must incur to resell a good, the less likely resale becomes. Suppose that you are able to buy a 50-pound bag of cement (which, in addition to being heavy, is also dusty) for $1 less than the usual price. Would you take the time and trouble to buy the cement and seek a buyer willing to pay an extra dollar, or would the transaction costs be prohibitive? The more valuable and widely consumed a product is, the more likely it is that transaction costs are low enough to allow resale.

Some firms act to raise transaction costs or otherwise make resale difficult. If your college requires that someone with a student ticket to a sporting event show a student identification card containing a photo, it will be difficult to resell your low-price tickets to nonstudents, who pay higher prices. When students at some universities buy computers at lower-than-usual prices, they must sign a contract that forbids resale of the computer. Disney prevents resale by locals, who can buy a ticket at a lower price, by checking driver's licenses and requiring that the ticket be used for same-day entrance.

Governments frequently aid price discrimination by preventing resale. Government *tariffs* (taxes on imports) limit resale by making it expensive to buy a branded good in a low-price country and resell it in a high-price country. Under U.S. trade laws, certain brand-name perfumes may not be sold in the United States except by their manufacturers. Similarly, if the countries have very different safety rules, a product sold in one country might not be legally sold in another.

However, resale is legal for many products. Imported goods that go through legal but unofficial channels that are unauthorized by the original manufacturer are said to sell in a *gray market* or *parallel market*. To make such a transaction unattractive, Nikon provides a warranty on its cameras that is only applicable in the country in which the good is supposed to be sold.

Mini-Case
Preventing Resale of Designer Bags

During the holiday season, stores often limit how many of the hottest items—such as this year's best-selling toy—a customer can buy. But it may surprise you that websites of luxury-goods retailers such as Saks Fifth Avenue, Neiman Marcus, and Bergdorf Goodman limit how many designer handbags one can buy. For example, the Bergdorf Goodman site won't let you order more than one Prada Lizard Trimmed Nylon Shoulder Bag at $4,190 (darn!).

Some websites explain that they impose limits due to "popular demand." The more plausible explanation is that the restriction facilitates international price discrimination. The handbag manufacturers force U.S. retailers to limit the number one person can buy to prevent people from buying large numbers of bags and reselling them in Europe or Asia where the same items in Prada and Gucci stores often cost 20% to 40% more. By purchasing from Prada's U.S. online site, one must agree that the purchase is solely for private household use, that commercial resale or sale outside the United States is not authorized, and that the company reserves the right to reject orders and to limit order quantities.

Not All Price Differences Are Price Discrimination

Not every seller who charges consumers different prices is price discriminating. A seller price discriminates by charging different prices for units of a good that cost the same to produce. In contrast, e-book and hardcopy versions of the same book sell for different prices in large part because these different versions have different costs.

The Andrew Sean Greer novel *Less*, the winner of the 2018 Pulitzer Prize for fiction, sold on Amazon in July 2018 for $9.88 as a Kindle e-book and for $17.68 in hardcover. This price difference reflects the lower marginal cost of selling an e-book and is therefore not due purely to price discrimination by the publisher.

Types of Price Discrimination

Traditionally, economists focus on three types of price discrimination: perfect price discrimination, group price discrimination, and nonlinear price discrimination. With **perfect price discrimination**—also called *first-degree price discrimination*—the firm sells each unit at the maximum amount any customer is willing to pay. Under perfect price discrimination, the price differs across consumers and a given consumer may pay higher prices for some units than for others.

With **group price discrimination**—also called *third-degree price discrimination*—the firm charges each group of customers a different price, but it does not charge different prices within the group. The price that a firm charges a consumer depends on that consumer's membership in a particular group. Thus, not all customers pay different prices: The firm sets different prices only for a few groups of customers. Group price discrimination is the most common type of price discrimination.

A firm engages in **nonlinear price discrimination** (also called *second-degree price discrimination*) when it charges a different price for large purchases than for small quantities, so that the price paid varies according to the quantity purchased. With pure nonlinear price discrimination, all customers who buy a given quantity pay the same price; however, firms can combine nonlinear price discrimination with group price discrimination, setting different nonlinear price schedules for different groups of consumers.

10.2 Perfect Price Discrimination

A firm with market power that knows exactly how much each customer is willing to pay for each unit of its good and is able to prevent resale can charge each person his or her **reservation price**: the maximum amount a person is willing to pay for a unit of output. Such an all-knowing firm can *perfectly price discriminate*. By selling each unit of its output to the customer who values it the most at the maximum price that person is willing to pay, the perfectly price-discriminating monopoly captures all possible consumer surplus.

Perfect price discrimination is rare because firms do not have perfect information about their customers. Nevertheless, it is useful to examine perfect price discrimination because it is the most efficient form of price discrimination and provides a benchmark against which we can compare other types of nonuniform pricing.

We now show how a firm with full information about consumer reservation prices can use that information to perfectly price discriminate. Next, we compare the market outcomes (price, quantity, surplus) of a perfectly price-discriminating monopoly to those of perfectly competitive and uniform-price monopoly firms.

How a Firm Perfectly Price Discriminates

A firm with market power that can prevent resale and has full information about its customers' willingness-to-pay price discriminates by selling each unit at its reservation price—the maximum amount any consumer would pay for it. The maximum price for any unit of output is given by the height of the demand curve at that output level. In the demand curve facing a monopoly in Figure 10.1, the first customer is willing to pay $6 for a unit, the next is willing to pay $5, and so forth. A perfectly price-discriminating firm sells its first unit of output for $6. Having sold the first unit, the firm can get at most $5 for its second unit. The firm must drop its price by $1 for each successive unit it sells.

FIGURE 10.1 Perfect Price Discrimination

The monopoly can charge $6 for the first unit, $5 for the second, and $4 for the third, as the demand curve shows. Its marginal revenue is $MR_1 = \$6$ for the first unit, $MR_2 = \$5$ for the second unit, and $MR_3 = \$4$ for the third unit. Thus, the demand curve is also the marginal revenue curve. Because the firm's marginal and average cost is $3 per unit, it is unwilling to sell at a price below $3, so it sells 4 units, point e, and breaks even on the last unit.

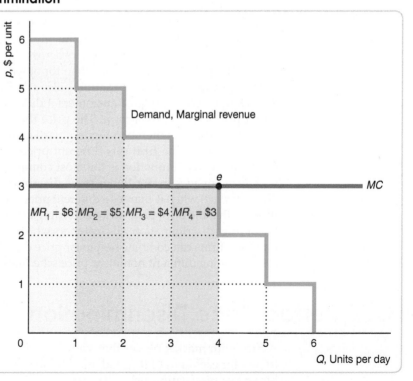

A perfectly price-discriminating firm's marginal revenue is the same as its price. As the figure shows, the firm's marginal revenue is $MR_1 = \$6$ on the first unit, $MR_2 = \$5$ on the second unit, and $MR_3 = \$4$ on the third unit. As a result, *if it can perfectly price discriminate, a firm's marginal revenue curve is the same as its demand curve.*

This firm has a constant marginal cost of $3 per unit. It pays for the firm to produce the first unit because the firm sells that unit for $6, so its marginal revenue exceeds its marginal cost by $3. Similarly, the firm sells the second unit for $5 and the third unit for $4. The firm breaks even when it sells the fourth unit for $3. The firm is unwilling to sell more than four units because its marginal cost would exceed its marginal revenue on all successive units. Thus, like any profit-maximizing firm, a perfectly price-discriminating firm produces at point *e*, where its marginal revenue curve intersects its marginal cost curve.

A firm's revenue is the sum of the marginal revenues for each unit sold. Therefore, this perfectly price-discriminating firm's revenue is $MR_1 + MR_2 + MR_3 + MR_4 = \$6 + \$5 + \$4 + \$3 = \$18$, which is the area under its marginal revenue curve up to the number of units, four, it sells. If the firm has no fixed cost, its cost of producing four units is $12 = \$3 \times 4$, so its profit is $6.

Perfect Price Discrimination Is Efficient but Harms Some Consumers

Perfect price discrimination is efficient: It maximizes the sum of consumer surplus and producer surplus. Therefore, both perfect competition and perfect price discrimination maximize total surplus. However, *the entire surplus goes to the firm with perfect price discrimination, whereas consumers obtain some surplus under competition.*

If the market illustrated in Figure 10.2 is competitive, the intersection of the demand curve and the marginal cost curve, *MC*, determines the competitive equilibrium at e_c, where price is p_c and quantity is Q_c. Consumer surplus is $A + B + C$, producer surplus is $D + E$, and society suffers no deadweight loss. The market is efficient because the price, p_c, equals the marginal cost, MC_c. With a single-price monopoly (which charges all its customers the same price), the intersection of the *MC* curve and the single-price monopoly's marginal revenue curve, MR_s, determines the output, Q_s.[5] The monopoly operates at e_s, where it charges p_s. The deadweight loss from monopoly is $C + E$. This efficiency loss is due to charging a price, p_s, above marginal cost, MC_s, so less is sold than in a competitive market.

A perfectly price-discriminating firm sells each unit at its reservation price, which is the height of the demand curve. As a result, the firm's price-discrimination marginal revenue curve, MR_d, is the same as its demand curve. It sells the Q_d unit for p_c, where its marginal revenue curve, MR_d, intersects the marginal cost curve, *MC*, so it just covers its marginal cost on the last unit. The firm is unwilling to sell additional units because its marginal revenue would be less than the marginal cost of producing them.

A perfectly price-discriminating firm's producer surplus from the Q_d units it sells is the area below its demand curve and above its marginal cost curve, $A + B + C + D + E$. Its profit is the producer surplus minus its fixed cost, if any. Consumers receive no consumer surplus because each consumer pays his or her reservation price. The perfectly price-discriminating firm's profit-maximizing solution

---

[5]We assume that if we convert a monopoly into a competitive industry, the industry's marginal cost curve—the lowest cost at which an additional unit can be produced by any firm—is the same as the monopoly *MC* curve. The industry *MC* curve is the industry supply curve (Chapter 8).

FIGURE 10.2 **Competitive, Single-Price, and Perfect Price Discrimination Outcomes**

In the competitive market equilibrium, e_c, price is p_c, quantity is Q_c, consumer surplus is $A + B + C$, producer surplus is $D + E$, and society has no deadweight loss. In the single-price monopoly equilibrium, e_s, price is p_s, quantity is Q_s, consumer surplus falls to A, producer surplus is $B + D$, and deadweight loss is $C + E$. In the perfect price discrimination equilibrium, the monopoly sells each unit at the customer's reservation price on the demand curve. It sells Q_d ($= Q_c$) units, where the last unit is sold at its marginal cost. Customers have no consumer surplus, but society has no deadweight loss.

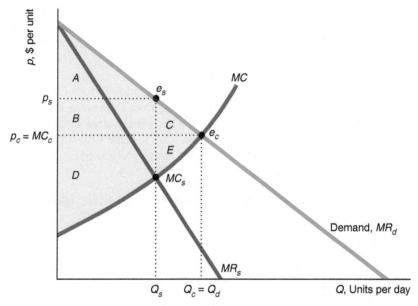

	Competition	Monopoly	
		Single Price	**Perfect Price Discrimination**
Consumer Surplus, CS	$A + B + C$	A	0
Producer Surplus, PS	$D + E$	$B + D$	$A + B + C + D + E$
Total Surplus, $TS = CS + PS$	$A + B + C + D + E$	$A + B + D$	$A + B + C + D + E$
Deadweight Loss	0	$C + E$	0

has *no deadweight loss* because the last unit is sold at a price, p_c, that equals the marginal cost, MC_c, as in a competitive market. Thus, both a perfect price discrimination outcome and a competitive equilibrium are efficient.

The perfect price discrimination solution differs from the competitive equilibrium in two important ways. First, in the competitive equilibrium, everyone is charged a price equal to the equilibrium marginal cost, $p_c = MC_c$; however, in the perfect price discrimination equilibrium, only the last unit is sold at that price. The other units are sold at customers' reservation prices, which are greater than p_c. Second, consumers receive some net benefit (consumer surplus, $A + B + C$) in a competitive market, whereas a perfectly price-discriminating monopoly captures all the surplus or potential gains from trade. Thus, perfect price discrimination does not reduce efficiency—both output and total surplus are the same as under competition—but it does redistribute income away from consumers. Consumers are much better off under competition.

Is a single-price or a perfectly price-discriminating monopoly better for consumers? The perfect price discrimination equilibrium is more efficient than the single-price monopoly equilibrium because more output is produced. A single-price monopoly, however, takes less consumer surplus from consumers than a perfectly price-discriminating monopoly. Consumers who put a relatively high value on the good are better off under single-price monopoly, where they have consumer surplus, than with perfect price discrimination, where they have none. Consumers with lower reservation prices who purchase from the perfectly price-discriminating monopoly but not from the single-price monopoly have no consumer surplus in either case. All the social gain from the extra output goes to the seller under perfect price discrimination. Consumer surplus is greatest with competition, lower with single-price monopoly, and eliminated by perfect price discrimination.

Mini-Case

Botox Revisited

To show how perfect price discrimination differs from competition and single-price monopoly, we revisit the Mini-Case on Allergan's Botox from Chapter 9. The graph shows our estimated linear demand curve for Botox and a constant marginal cost (and average variable cost) of $25 per vial. If the market were competitive (so that price equals marginal cost at e_c), consumer surplus would be the triangle $A + B + C = \$750$ million per year, and there would have been

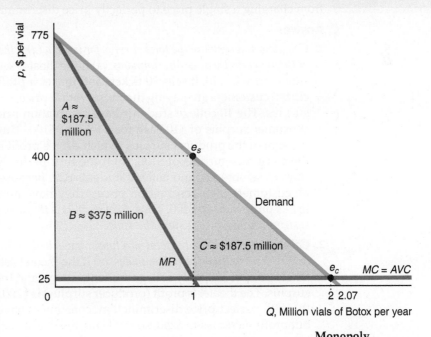

	Competition	Monopoly Single Price	Monopoly Perfect Price Discrimination
Consumer Surplus, CS	$A + B + C$	A	0
Producer Surplus, PS	0	B	$A + B + C$
Total Surplus, $TS = CS + PS$	$A + B + C$	$A + B$	$A + B + C$
Deadweight Loss	0	C	0

no producer surplus or deadweight loss. In the (actual) single-price monopoly equilibrium, e_s, the Botox vials sell for $400 each, and one million vials are sold. The corresponding consumer surplus is triangle A = $187.5 million per year, producer surplus is rectangle B = $375 million, and the deadweight loss is triangle C = $187.5 million.

If Allergan could perfectly price discriminate, its producer surplus would double to $A + B + C$ = $750 million per year, and consumers would obtain no consumer surplus. The marginal consumer would pay a price equal to the marginal cost of $25, just as in a competitive market.

Allergan's inability to perfectly price discriminate costs the company dearly. Its producer surplus as a single-price monopoly is $375 million per year, which is lower than what it could earn if it perfectly price discriminated, $A + B + C$ = $750 million per year. Society's total surplus under single-price monopoly is lower than under perfect price discrimination by the deadweight loss, C, of $187.5 million per year, whereas consumers have no surplus with perfect price discrimination.

Q&A 10.1

How does total surplus change if the movie theater described in Table 10.1 goes from charging a single price to perfectly price discriminating?

Answer

1. *Calculate and compare the total surplus for panel a (a) if the theater sets a single price or (b) if it perfectly price discriminates.* (a) If the theater sets the profit-maximizing single price of $10, it sells 30 tickets and makes a profit of $300. The 20 senior citizen customers are paying their reservation price, so they have no consumer surplus. The 10 college students have reservation prices of $20, so they have consumer surplus of $10 each for a total of $100. Thus, total surplus is $400: the sum of the producer surplus (which equals profit in this case) of $300, and the consumer surplus of $100. (b) If the firm perfectly price discriminates, it charges seniors $10 and college students $20. Because the theater is charging all customers their reservation prices, they have no consumer surplus. The firm's profit rises to $400. Thus, *total surplus is the same ($400) under both pricing systems because output stays the same.*

2. *Calculate and compare the total surplus for panel b (a) if the theater sets a single price or (b) if it perfectly price discriminates.* (a) If the theater sets the profit-maximizing single price of $20, only college students attend and they receive no consumer surplus. The theater's profit (producer surplus) is $200, so total surplus is $200. (b) With perfect price discrimination, consumers have no consumer surplus, but profit increases to $250, so total surplus rises to $250. Thus, *total surplus is greater with perfect price discrimination and output is greater.* (The result that total surplus increases if and only if output rises holds generally.)

Individual Price Discrimination

Perfect price discrimination is rarely fully achieved in practice because firms lack full information about individuals' reservation prices. For example, a coffee shop would have to know that Yi Lin is willing to pay $4 for her first cup of coffee, $3 for her second, and so on and then actually charge these amounts. We use the term *individual price discrimination* to refer to a situation in which a firm charges individual-specific prices to different consumers, which may or may not exactly equal consumers' reservation prices. Even if firms cannot achieve perfect price discrimination, imperfect individual price discrimination can increase their profits significantly.

Some firms do a good job of estimating each person's reservation price. At most car dealerships, a salesperson negotiates with potential buyers. During the discussions, the salesperson tries to determine each individual's reservation price from the buyer's comments and appearance. Is the potential buyer a local? Is the buyer wearing expensive clothing? Does the buyer claim to own other expensive cars? The salesperson uses this information to estimate the buyer's reservation price and offers to sell the car at that price. As a result, prices vary across consumers for a given car. Similarly, the managers of the Suez Canal set tolls on an individual ship-by-ship basis, taking into account many factors such as weather and each ship's alternative routes.

Private colleges request and receive financial information from students, which allows the schools to apply individual price discrimination. The schools give partial scholarships as a means of reducing the tuition for relatively poor students, who presumably have lower willingness to pay than wealthier students. Epple et al. (2017) estimated that private schools raise tuition by an average of $210 to $510 for every $10,000 increase in family income.

Transaction costs are a major reason why these firms do not perfectly price discriminate: It is often too difficult or too costly to gather information about each customer's reservation price for each unit of the product. However, recent advances in computer technologies have lowered these transaction costs, causing hotels, car and truck rental companies, cruise lines, airlines, and other firms to increasingly use individual price discrimination, as the following Mini-Case illustrates.

Mini-Case

Google Uses Bidding for Ads to Price Discriminate

The ads that appear next to your Google search results depend on the terms in your search. That is, Google allows advertisers to *contextually target* people who search for particular phrases (Goldfarb, 2014). By making searches easy and fast with targeted ads, Google helps advertisers reach hard-to-find potential customers. For example, a lawyer specializing in toxic mold lawsuits can place an ad that appears only when someone searches for "toxic mold lawyer."

Google uses auctions to price ads. Advertisers place higher bids for the first listing on Google's search page. Goldfarb and Tucker (2011) found that the amount lawyers are willing to pay for context-based ads depends on the difficulty of making a match. The fewer the number of self-identified potential customers (the fewer people searching for a particular topic), the more lawyers are willing to pay per search request to advertise.

They also found that lawyers bid more when other methods of reaching potential clients are limited. Some states have anti-ambulance-chaser regulations, which prohibit personal injury lawyers from directly contacting potential clients by snail mail, phone, or e-mail for a few months after an accident. Search engine advertising prices per click are 5%–7% higher in those states than in others.

By taking advantage of advertisers' desire to reach small, targeted segments of the population and varying the price according to advertisers' willingness to pay using auctions, Google is achieving the equivalent of individual price discrimination.

10.3 Group Price Discrimination

Most firms have no practical way to estimate the reservation price for each of their customers. But many of these firms know which groups of customers are likely to have higher reservation prices on average than others. A firm engages in *group price discrimination* by dividing potential customers into two or more groups and setting different prices for each group. Consumer groups may differ by age (such as adults and children), by location (such as by country), or in other ways. All units of the good sold to customers within a group are sold at a single price. As with individual price discrimination, to engage in group price discrimination, a firm must have market power, be able to identify groups with different reservation prices, and prevent resale.

For example, first-run movie theaters with market power charge seniors a lower ticket price than they charge younger adults because typically older adults are unwilling to pay as much to see a movie. By admitting seniors immediately after they prove their age and buy tickets, the theater prevents resale.

Group Price Discrimination with Two Groups

How does a firm set its prices if it sells to two (or more) groups of consumers with different demand curves and if resale between the two groups is impossible? We explain the process in the following example, which looks at a firm that sells to groups of consumers in different areas.

A patent gives Tesla the legal monopoly to produce and sell the Tesla S electric car. When Tesla started selling the Model S in 2012, it was the only luxury electric car. Even by 2018, it faced little competition from all-electric luxury cars. Tesla engages in group price discrimination by charging different prices in various countries. Resale is not a problem because Tesla honors its warranty only in the region or country where the car is sold.

A Graphical Approach. How should Tesla set its prices or equivalently its quantities in the United States and in Europe to maximize its total profit? Because Tesla currently manufactures in a single plant, its marginal cost is the same for all customers. A group price-discriminating monopoly with a constant marginal cost maximizes its total profit by maximizing its profit from each group separately, as a single-price monopoly would. Tesla sets its quantities so that the marginal revenue for each group equals the common marginal cost, m, which is about \$30,000 per car.[6] In 2017, American consumers bought about $Q_A = 30$ thousand cars at $p_A = \$80$ thousand. Europeans bought $Q_E = 16$ thousand cars at $p_E = \$130$ thousand (€110,000).[7]

Figure 10.3 shows our estimates of the linear demand curves in the two areas. In panel a, Tesla maximizes its U.S. profit by selling $Q_A = 30$ thousand cars, where its

---

[6]Reportedly according to Elon Musk, the **CEO** of Tesla: **www.inverse.com/article/31597-tesla-secret-profit**. The shipping cost to Europe is sufficiently low that including it would not change our calculations.

[7]The source of the price information for the Tesla Model S D100 is **www.tesla.com**. Prices vary somewhat across European countries. We are using the price for the Netherlands. We are not including government subsidies or taxes. The 2017 quantity data (rounded) come from **http://europe .autonews.com/article/20180220/ANE/180219831/tesla-model-s-outsells-german-luxury-flagships-in-europe** (viewed July 6, 2018). We estimated the linear demand curves using these data based on the assumption that Tesla is maximizing its profit.

FIGURE 10.3 Group Pricing of the Tesla S Car

Tesla, the monopoly producer of the Model S all-electric car, charges more in Europe, $p_E = \$130$ thousand (€110,000), than in the United States, $p_A = \$80$ thousand, because demand is more elastic in the United States. Tesla sets the quantity independently in each country. It maximizes profit by operating where its marginal revenue for each area equals its common, constant marginal cost, $m = \$30$ thousand. Consequently, the marginal revenues in the two countries are equal: $MR^A = m = MR^E$.

(a) United States

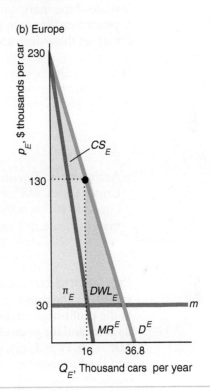
(b) Europe

marginal revenue equals its marginal cost $MR^A = m = \$30$ thousand (Chapter 9), and charging $p_A = \$80$ thousand. Similarly, in panel b, Tesla maximizes its European profit by selling $Q_E = 16$ thousand cars, where $MR^E = m = \$30,000$, at $p_B = \$130$ thousand.

Because the price-discriminating firm maximizes its profit by operating where its marginal revenue for each country equals its common marginal cost, $m = \$30$ thousand, the marginal revenues in the two countries are equal:

$$MR^A = m = MR^E. \tag{10.1}$$

Using Calculus

Maximizing Profit for a Group Discriminating Monopoly

We can also derive these results using calculus. The group discriminating monopoly's total profit, π, is the sum of its American profit, π_A, and its European profit, π_E:

$$\pi(Q_A, Q_E) = \pi_A(Q_A) + \pi_E(Q_E) = [R_A(Q_A) - mQ_A] + [R_E(Q_E) - mQ_E],$$

where $R_A(Q_A) = p_A(Q_A)Q_A$ is the revenue function in the United States, $p_A(Q_A)$ is the U.S. inverse demand function, and $R_E(Q_E)$ and $p_E(Q_E)$ are similarly defined for Europe. Again, because of the constant marginal cost of production, the firm's profit in either country depends only on the quantity that it sells in that country.[8]

To find the Q_A and Q_E that maximize Tesla's total profit, we can maximize its profit in each country separately, as we did in the graphical approach. However, here we solve for the optimal quantities simultaneously (which we would have to do if the marginal cost were not constant). We differentiate the monopoly's profit function with respect to each quantity, holding the other quantity fixed, and set these derivatives equal to zero:

$$\frac{\partial \pi(Q_A, Q_E)}{\partial Q_A} = \frac{dR_A(Q_A)}{dQ_A} - m = 0, \tag{10.2}$$

$$\frac{\partial \pi(Q_A, Q_E)}{\partial Q_E} = \frac{dR_E(Q_E)}{dQ_E} - m = 0. \tag{10.3}$$

According to Equation 10.2, the monopoly sets the marginal revenue in the United States, $MR^A = dR_A/dQ_A$, equal to its constant marginal cost, m. Similarly, Equation 10.3 says the marginal revenue in Europe, $MR^E = dR_E/dQ_E$, equals the marginal cost, m. Consequently, Equation 10.1 holds: $MR^A = m = MR^E$.

Prices and Elasticities. We can use Equation 10.1, $MR^A = m = MR^E$, to determine how the prices in the two countries vary with the price elasticities of demand at the profit-maximizing outputs. Each country's marginal revenue is a function of its price and the price elasticity of demand (Chapter 9). The U.S. marginal revenue is $MR^A = p_A(1 + 1/\varepsilon_A)$, where ε_A is the price elasticity of demand for U.S. consumers, and the European marginal revenue is $MR^E = p_E(1 + 1/\varepsilon_E)$, where ε_E is the price elasticity of demand for European consumers.

Rewriting Equation 10.1 using these expressions for marginal revenue, we find that

$$MR^A = p_A\left(1 + \frac{1}{\varepsilon_A}\right) = m = p_E\left(1 + \frac{1}{\varepsilon_E}\right) = MR^E. \tag{10.4}$$

Equation 10.4 implies that $\varepsilon_A = p_A/(m - p_A)$.[9] As $m =$ \$30 thousand, $p_A =$ \$80 thousand, and $p_E =$ \$130 thousand, Tesla must believe that $\varepsilon_A = p_A/[m - p_A] = 80/[30 - 80] = -1.6$. Similarly, it believes that $\varepsilon_E = p_E/[m - p_E] = 130/[30 - 130] = -1.3$.

We can rearrange Equation 10.4 to show that the ratio of prices in the two countries is a function solely of the demand elasticities in those countries:

$$\frac{p_E}{p_A} = \frac{1 + 1/\varepsilon_A}{1 + 1/\varepsilon_E}. \tag{10.5}$$

---

[8]For a more general cost function, $C(Q_A, Q_B)$, Tesla's profit in each country would depend on the amount it sold in both countries.

[9]We can rewrite the equality $p_A(1 + (1/\varepsilon_A)) = m$ (Equation 10.4) as $p_A + p_A/\varepsilon_A = m$, which implies that $p_A/\varepsilon_A = m - p_A$ or $\varepsilon_A = p_A/(m - p_A)$.

Substituting the prices and the demand elasticities into Equation 10.5, we determine that

$$\frac{p_E}{p_A} = \frac{\$130}{\$80} = 1.625 = \frac{1 + 1/(-1.6)}{1 + 1/(-1.3)} = \frac{1 + 1/\varepsilon_A}{1 + 1/\varepsilon_E}.$$

Thus, Tesla apparently believes that the European demand curve is less elastic at its profit-maximizing price than is the U.S. demand curve. Specifically, $\varepsilon_E = -1.3$ is closer to zero than is $\varepsilon_A = -1.6$. Consequently, Tesla charges European consumers 62.5% more than it charges U.S. customers.

Mini-Case

Age Discrimination

Under U.S. federal law, firms may price discriminate between people except if based on race, religion, nationality, or gender. Firms often discriminate based on age.

You've probably noticed that movie theaters offer discount admission to children and senior citizens. Thus, it was probably a large shock to Tinder, an online dating app, when it was sued for price discriminating based on age.

Allan Candelore filed a class-action lawsuit on behalf of himself and others over the age of 30 who had to pay $19.99 a month to use the app's premium service, Tinder Plus, while those under 30 paid only $9.99 to $14.99. In a ruling that, under California state law, Tinder was unlawfully discriminating against users over 30, a California state appeals court said that "we swipe left, and reverse," using Tinder's terminology to express disapproval.[10]

Q&A 10.2

Greyhound Lines is the monopoly long-distance bus line on many routes in North America, especially those connecting small towns. Greyhound offers a senior discount to passengers aged 62 or older. Suppose that for a particular route Greyhound faces an hourly linear inverse demand function of $p_1 = 60 - 5Q_1$ for seniors and $p_2 = 90 - 10Q_2$ for other passengers ("adults"). The marginal cost of an extra passenger is 10. What price would a profit-maximizing monopoly charge for each age group if it is allowed to price discriminate? What price would it charge if price discrimination by age is prohibited?

---

[10] Individual states may impose stricter restrictions on price discrimination than under federal law.

Answer

If price discrimination by age is legal:

1. *Determine the profit-maximizing quantity and price that the bus line sets for each age group by setting the relevant marginal revenue equal to the marginal cost.* If Greyhound can price discriminate, it sets a monopoly price independently for each group. The marginal revenue curve is twice as steeply sloped as is the linear inverse demand function (see Q&A 9.1), so the marginal revenue function for seniors is $MR_1 = 60 - 10Q_1$, as panel a of the figure shows. Greyhound maximizes its profit where its marginal revenue function equals its marginal cost, $MR_1 = 60 - 10Q_1 = 10 = MC$. Solving this equation, we find that its profit-maximizing output is $Q_1 = 5$. Substituting this expression back into the inverse demand function, we learn that the profit-maximizing price is $p_1 = 60 - 25 = 35$, as panel a illustrates.

   Because the inverse demand function for adults is $p_2 = 90 - 10Q_2$, the bus line chooses Q_2 such that $MR_2 = 90 - 20Q_2 = 10 = MC$. Thus, it maximizes its profit where $Q_2 = 4$ and $p_2 = 50$, as panel b shows.

If price discrimination by age is not legal:

2. *Derive the total demand curve.* If Greyhound cannot price discriminate, it charges the same price, p, to all users. The company faces the total demand curve in panel c, which is the horizontal sum of the demand curves for each of the two age groups in panels a and b (Chapter 2). If the price is between 60 and 90, the quantity demanded is positive only for the adults, so the total demand curve (panel c) is the just the adults' demand curve (panel b). If the price is less than 60, then both groups demand a positive quantity, and the total demand curve in panel c is the horizontal sum of the two age groups' demand curves (panels a and b).[11] As panel c shows, the total demand curve has a kink at $p = 60$, because the quantity demanded by seniors is positive only at lower prices.

3. *Determine the marginal revenue curve corresponding to the total demand curve.* Because the total demand curve has a kink at $p = 60$, the corresponding marginal revenue curve has two sections. At prices greater than 60, the marginal revenue curve is that of the adult group. At prices less than 60, the inverse total demand function is $p = 70 - (1/0.3)Q$, so the marginal revenue function has twice the slope: $MR = 70 - (2/0.3)Q$. Panel c shows that the marginal revenue curve *jumps*—is discontinuous—at the quantity where the total demand curve has a kink.

4. *Solve for the single-price monopoly solution.* Greyhound maximizes its profit where its marginal revenue equals its marginal cost. From inspecting panel c, we learn that the intersection occurs in the section where both age groups have positive demand, so that $MR = 70 - (2/0.3)Q = 10 = MC$. Solving this equation, we find that the profit-maximizing output is $Q = 9$. Substituting that quantity into the inverse total demand function, we learn that Greyhound charges $p = 40$. Thus, a single-price monopoly would charge a price of 40, which lies between the two prices it would charge if it could price discriminate: $35 < 40 < 50$.

---

[11]Rearranging the inverse demand functions, we find that the seniors' demand function is $Q_1 = 12 - 0.2p_1$ and the adults' demand function is $Q_2 = 90 - 0.1p_2$. As a result for a price less than 60, the total demand function is $Q = (12 - 0.2p) + (9 - 0.1p) = 21 - 0.3p$, where $Q = Q_1 + Q_2$ is the total quantity that the monopoly sells and p is the common price. Therefore the inverse demand function is $p = 70 - (\frac{1}{0.3})Q$ for prices less than 60.

Identifying Groups

Firms use two main approaches to divide customers into groups. One method is to divide buyers into groups based on *observable characteristics* of consumers that the firm believes are associated with unusually high or low reservation prices or demand elasticities. For example, age is often used as a basis for price discrimination and is often easy to check, as at a movie theater or buying a ticket from Greyhound. Similarly, as with Tesla, some firms charge customers higher prices in one country than another.

The second approach is to identify and divide consumers on the basis of their *actions*: The firm allows consumers to self-select the group to which they belong. For example, customers may be identified by their willingness to spend time to buy a good at a lower price or to order goods and services in advance of delivery.

Firms use differences in the value customers place on their time to discriminate by using queues (making people wait in line) and other time-intensive methods of selling goods. Store managers who believe that high-wage people are unwilling to "waste their time shopping" may have sales that require consumers to visit the store and pick up the good themselves, while consumers who order over the phone or online pay a higher price. This type of price discrimination increases profit if people who put a high value on their time also have less elastic demand for the good.

Early adopters of a new product are often very enthusiastic and will pay premium prices. Firms can take advantage of early adopters by charging a high initial price for a new product and then lowering the price after the initial sales are made.

Managerial Implication

Discounts

To make sure that price discrimination pays, managers should not offer discounts to all their customers. Rather, they should only give discounts to those consumers who are willing to incur a cost, such as their time, to obtain the discount. Consumers willing to spend extra time to obtain a discount are typically more price sensitive than others. Skilled managers use a variety of methods to induce customers to self-identify as being price sensitive by incurring a cost.

You've got to prove you really want a discount!

Coupons

Many firms use discount coupons to group price discriminate. Through this device, firms divide customers into two groups, charging coupon clippers less than nonclippers. Offering coupons makes sense if the people who do not clip coupons are less price sensitive on average than those who do. People who are willing to spend their time clipping coupons buy cereals and other goods at lower prices than those who value their time more. In the first half of 2018, firms distributed 143 billion print and digital coupons for packaged goods, of which 925 million (about 0.6%) were redeemed. The introduction of digital coupons (for example, **EverSave.com**) has made it easier for firms to target appropriate groups, but has lowered consumers' costs of using them.

Airline Tickets

By choosing between two different types of tickets, airline customers indicate whether they are likely to be business travelers or vacationers. Airlines give customers a choice between high-price tickets with no strings attached and low-price fares that must be purchased long in advance.

Airlines know that many business travelers have little advance warning before they book a flight and have relatively inelastic demand curves. In contrast, vacation travelers can usually plan in advance and have relatively high elasticities of demand for air travel. The airlines' rules ensure that vacationers with relatively elastic demand obtain low fares, while most business travelers with relatively inelastic demand buy high-price tickets (often more than four times higher than the plan-ahead rate).

Reverse Auctions

Priceline.com and other online merchants use a name-your-own-price or "reverse" auction to identify price-sensitive customers. A customer enters a relatively low-price bid for a good or service, such as an airline ticket. Merchants decide whether or not to accept that bid. To prevent their less price-sensitive customers from using these methods, airlines force successful Priceline bidders to be flexible: to fly at off hours, to make one or more connections, and to accept any type of aircraft. Similarly, when bidding on groceries, a customer must list "one or two brands you like." As Jay Walker, Priceline's founder explained, "The manufacturers would rather not give you a discount, of course, but if you prove that you're willing to switch brands, they're willing to pay to keep you."

Rebates

Why do many firms offer a rebate of, say, $5 instead of reducing the price on their product by $5? The reason is that a consumer must incur an extra, time-consuming step to receive the rebate. Thus, only those consumers who are very price sensitive and place a low value on their time will actually apply for the rebate. According to a *Consumer Reports* survey, 47% of customers always or often apply for a rebate, 23% sometimes apply, 25% never apply, and 5% responded that the question was not applicable to them.

Effects of Group Price Discrimination on Total Surplus

Group price discrimination results in inefficient production and consumption. As a result, total surplus under group price discrimination is lower than that under competition or perfect price discrimination. However, total surplus may be lower or higher with group price discrimination than with a single-price monopoly.

Group Price Discrimination Versus Competition. Consumer surplus is greater and more output is produced with perfect competition than with group price discrimination. In Figure 10.3, consumer surplus with group price discrimination is CS_A for American consumers, shown in panel a, and CS_E for European consumers, shown in panel b. Under competition, consumer surplus is the area below the demand curve and above the marginal cost curve: $CS_A + \pi_A + DWL_A$ in panel a and $CS_E + \pi_E + DWL_E$ in panel b.

Thus, group price discrimination transfers some of the competitive consumer surplus, π_A and π_E, to the firm as additional profit and causes deadweight loss, DWL_A and DWL_E, which is reduced consumer surplus that is simply lost or wasted. The deadweight loss is due to the price-discriminating firm charging prices above marginal cost, which results in reduced production from the optimal competitive level.

Group Price Discrimination Versus Single-Price Monopoly. From theory alone, we cannot tell whether total surplus is higher if the monopoly uses group price discrimination or if it sets a single price. Both approaches include a price above marginal cost, so too little is produced relative to competition. If a firm changes from uniform pricing to group price discrimination, it may attract additional price-sensitive customers by charging them low prices, which may cause its total sales to increase.

The closer the firm comes to perfect price discrimination using group price discrimination (by, for example, dividing its customers into many groups rather than just two), the more output it produces, and the less production inefficiency—the greater the total surplus. However, total surplus falls if the firm switches to group price discrimination and total output falls.[12]

10.4 Nonlinear Price Discrimination

Many firms are unable to determine which of their customers have the highest reservation prices. However, such firms may know that most customers are willing to pay more for the first unit than for successive units—that is, a typical customer's demand curve is downward sloping. Such a firm can price discriminate by letting the price each customer pays vary with the number of units the customer buys. That is, the firm uses *nonlinear price discrimination* (second-degree price discrimination). Here, the price varies with quantity, but each customer faces the same nonlinear pricing schedule.[13] To use nonlinear pricing, a firm must have market power and be able to prevent customers who buy at a low price from reselling to those who would otherwise pay a high price.

In 2018, a package of 48 Duracell Energizer AA batteries cost $18.98 (40¢ per battery). A 24-pack of the same battery cost $12.34 (51¢ per battery). The difference in the price per battery is nonlinear price discrimination unless the price difference is due to cost differences. This quantity discount results in customers who make large purchases paying less per unit than those who make small purchases.

Another nonlinear pricing strategy is *block pricing*. Many utilities use block pricing schedules, by which they charge one price per unit for the first few units (a *block*) purchased and a different price per unit for subsequent blocks. Both declining-block and increasing-block pricing are commonly used by gas, electric, water, and other utilities.

---

[12]An additional source of inefficiency is time spent by consumers trying to resell the product to high-willingness-to-pay customers or searching for low prices. These activities do not occur if everyone knows the firm sets a uniform price.

[13]The term *nonlinear* is used because a consumer's expenditure is a nonlinear function of the quantity purchased. A consumer's expenditure, E, is a linear function of quantity, q, only if the price, p, is constant: $E = pq$. If the price varies with quantity, then the expenditure is not linear in quantity.

The block-pricing monopoly in Figure 10.4 faces a linear demand curve for each identical customer. The demand curve hits the vertical axis at $90 and the horizontal axis at 90 units. The monopoly has a constant marginal and average cost of $m = \$30$. Panel a shows how this monopoly maximizes its profit if it can engage in nonlinear price discrimination by setting two prices. The firm uses declining block prices to maximize its profit. The firm charges a price of $70 on any quantity between 1 and 20—the first block—and $50 on any units beyond the first 20—the second block. (The points that determine the blocks, $70 and 20 units and $50 and 40 units, lie on the demand curve.) Given each consumer's demand curve, a consumer decides to buy 40 units and pays $1,400 ($= \$70 \times 20$) for the first block and $1,000 ($= \$50 \times 20$) for the second block. The consumer gains consumer surplus equal to A on the first block and C on the second block, for a total of $A + C$. The discriminating monopoly's

FIGURE 10.4 Block Pricing

If this monopoly engages in block pricing with quantity discounting, it makes a larger profit than it does if it sets a single price, and total surplus is greater. (a) With block pricing, its profit is $B = \$1,200$, total surplus is $A + B + C = \$1,600$, and the deadweight loss is $D = \$200$.

(b) If the monopoly sets a single price (so that its marginal revenue equals its marginal cost), the monopoly's profit is $F = \$900$, total surplus is $E + F = \$1,350$, and the deadweight loss is $G = \$450$.

(a) Quantity Discrimination

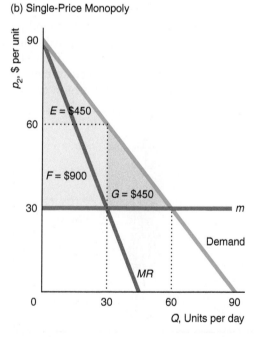

(b) Single-Price Monopoly

	Block Pricing	Single Price
Consumer Surplus, CS	$A + C = \$400$	$E = \$450$
Producer Surplus or Profit, $PS = \pi$	$B = \$1,200$	$F = \$900$
Total Surplus, $TS = CS + PS$	$A + B + C = \$1,600$	$E + F = \$1,350$
Deadweight Loss, DWL	$D = \$200$	$G = \$450$

profit or producer surplus is area B. Society suffers a deadweight loss of D because price, $50, is above marginal cost, $30, on the last unit purchased.

In panel b, the firm can set only a single price. It produces where its marginal revenue equals its marginal cost, and sells 30 units at $60 per unit. By using nonlinear price discrimination instead of setting a single price, the utility sells more units, 40 instead of 30, and makes a larger profit, $B = \$1,200$ instead of $F = \$900$. With quantity discounting, consumer surplus is lower, $A + C = \$400$ instead of $E = \$450$; total surplus (consumer surplus plus producer surplus) is higher, $A + B + C = \$1,600$ instead of $E + F = \$1,350$; and deadweight loss is lower, $D = \$200$ instead of $G = \$450$. Thus, in this example, the firm is better off with nonlinear price discrimination, but consumers as a group suffer. Society benefits.

However, many consumers draw a false inference about these benefits.

Common Confusion Quantity discounts help consumers.

Charging lower prices for high volume purchases allows firms to charge higher prices for low volume purchases than they otherwise would. Changing from uniform monopoly pricing to nonlinear price discrimination often reduces consumer surplus, as in Figure 10.4.

The more block prices that a firm can set, the closer the firm gets to perfect price discrimination, where it captures all the potential consumer surplus, and its profit or producer surplus equals total surplus. If the last unit is sold at a price equal to marginal cost, total surplus is maximized and society suffers no deadweight loss.

10.5 Two-Part Pricing

We now turn to another form of nonuniform pricing, *two-part pricing*. It is similar to nonlinear price discrimination in that the average price per unit paid by a consumer varies with the number of units purchased by that consumer.

With **two-part pricing**, the firm charges each consumer a lump-sum *access fee* for the right to buy as many units of the good as the consumer wants at a per-unit *price*.[14] Thus, a consumer's overall expenditure for amount q consists of two parts: an access fee, A, and a per-unit price, p. Therefore, expenditure is $E = A + pq$.[15] Because of the access fee, the average amount per unit that consumers pay is greater if they buy a small number of units than if they buy a larger number.

Two-part pricing is commonly used.[16] Many fitness clubs charge a yearly access fee and a price per session. Many warehouse stores require that customers buy an

---

[14]The prices used in two-part pricing are often referred to as *two-part tariffs*.

[15]The average price varies with quantity with two-part pricing and nonlinear price discrimination. However, the expenditure in two-part pricing, $E = A + pq$, is linear in quantity, unlike with nonlinear price discrimination.

[16]For example, *venting* stores are springing up in shopping malls in China. Customers pay to enter, and then pay for each second-hand mobile phone, television set, or other product that they smash. (**en.people.cn/90001/90782/90872/6915069.html**, viewed August 16, 2015.)

annual membership before being allowed to buy goods at relatively low prices. Some car rental firms charge a rental or access fee for the day and an additional price per mile driven. To buy season tickets to the Dallas Cowboys football games, a fan first must buy a *personal seat license* (PSL), giving the fan the right to buy season tickets for the next 30 years. Most PSLs sell for between $10,000 and $125,000.

To profit from two-part pricing, a firm must have market power and must successfully prevent resale. In addition, a firm must know how individual demand curves vary across its customers. We start by examining a firm's two-part pricing problem in the extreme case in which all customers have the same demand curve. We then consider what happens when the demand curves of individual customers differ.

Two-Part Pricing with Identical Consumers

If all customers are identical, a firm that knows the customers' demand curve can set a two-part price that has the same two important properties that perfect price discrimination has. First, the efficient quantity is sold because the price of the last unit equals marginal cost. Second, all potential consumer surplus is transferred from consumers to the firm.

To illustrate these points, we consider a monopoly that has a constant marginal cost of $MC = 10$ and no fixed cost, so its average cost is also constant at 10. All of the monopoly's customers have the same demand curve, $Q = 80 - p$. Panel a of Figure 10.5 shows the demand curve, D^1, of one such customer, Valerie.

Total surplus is maximized if the monopoly sets its price, p, equal to its constant marginal cost of 10. The firm breaks even on each unit sold and has no producer surplus. Valerie buys $q = 70$ units. Her consumer surplus is area $A = 2,450$ ($= \frac{1}{2} \times [80 - 10] \times 70$).

However, if the firm also charges an access fee of 2,450, it captures this 2,450 as its producer surplus or its profit per customer, and leaves Valerie with no consumer surplus. The firm's total profit is 2,450 times the number of identical customers.

The firm maximizes its profit by setting its price equal to its marginal cost and charging an access fee that captures the entire potential consumer surplus. If the firm were to charge a price above its marginal cost of 10, it would sell fewer units and make a smaller profit. In panel b of Figure 10.5, the firm charges $p = 20$. At that higher price, Valerie buys only 60 units, which is less than the 70 units that she buys at a price of 10 in panel a. The firm's profit from selling these 60 units is $B_1 = (20 - 10) \times 60 = 600$. For Valerie to agree to buy any units, the monopoly has to lower its access fee to 1,800 ($= \frac{1}{2} \times 60 \times 60$), the new potential consumer surplus, area A_1. The firm's total profit from Valerie is $A_1 + B_1 = 1,800 + 600 = 2,400$. This amount is less than the 2,450 ($= A$ in panel a) profit the firm earns if it sets price equal to marginal cost, 10, and charges the higher access fee. Area A in panel a equals $A_1 + B_1 + C_1$ in panel b. By charging a price above marginal cost, the firm loses C_1, which is the deadweight loss due to selling fewer units.

Similarly, if the firm were to charge a price below its marginal cost, it would also earn less profit. It would sell too many units and make a loss on each unit that it could not fully recapture by charging a higher access fee.

FIGURE 10.5 Two-Part Pricing with Identical Consumers

(a) Because all customers have the same individual demand curve as Valerie, D^1, the monopoly captures the entire potential consumer surplus using two-part pricing. The monopoly charges a per-unit fee price, p, equal to the marginal cost of 10, and an access fee, $A = 2,450$, which is the blue triangle under the demand curve and above the per-unit price of $p = 10$. (b) If the monopoly sets its price at 20, which is above its marginal cost of 10, it would earn less. It makes a profit of $B_1 = 600$ from earning $10 = 20 - 10$ on each of the 60 units that Valerie buys at this higher price. However, the largest access fee the firm can charge is $A_1 = 1,800$, so its total profit is 2,400, which is less than the 2,450 it makes if it sets its price equal to marginal cost. The difference is a deadweight loss of $C_1 = 50$, which is due to fewer units being sold at the higher price.

(a) Price Equals Marginal Cost

(b) Price Is Above Marginal Cost

Two-Part Pricing with Differing Consumers

Two-part pricing is more complex if consumers have different demand curves. Suppose that the monopoly has two customers, Valerie, Consumer 1, and Neal, Consumer 2. Valerie's demand curve, $Q_1 = 80 - p$, is D^1 in panel a of Figure 10.6 (which is the same as panel b of Figure 10.5), and Neal's demand curve, $Q_2 = 100 - p$, is D^2 in panel b. The monopoly's marginal cost, MC, and average cost are constant at 10 per unit.

If the firm knows each customer's demand curve, can prevent resale, and can charge its customers different prices and access fees, it can capture all the potential consumer surplus. The monopoly sets its price for both customers at $p = MC = 10$ and sets its access fee equal to each customer's potential consumer surplus. At $p = 10$, Valerie buys 70 units (panel a) and Neal buys 90 units (panel b). If no access fees were charged, Valerie's consumer surplus would equal the triangle below her demand curve and above the 10 price line, $A_1 + B_1 + C_1$, which is 2,450 ($= \frac{1}{2} \times 70 \times 70$). Similarly, Neal's consumer surplus would be 4,050 ($= \frac{1}{2} \times 90 \times 90$), which is the triangle $A_2 + B_2 + C_2$. Thus, the monopoly charges an access fee of 2,450 to Valerie and 4,050 to Neal, so that the customers receive no consumer surplus. The firm's total profit is $2,450 + 4,050 = 6,500$. The monopoly maximizes its total profit by capturing the maximum potential consumer surplus from both customers.

Now suppose that the firm cannot charge its customers different prices or different access fees. The firm maximizes its profit by setting a price of 20, which exceeds its marginal cost, and collecting an access fee equal to Valerie's potential consumer

FIGURE 10.6 Two-Part Pricing with Different Consumers

The monopoly faces two consumers. Valerie's demand curve is D^1 in panel a, and Neal's demand curve is D^2 in panel b. If the monopoly can set different prices and access fees for its two customers, it charges both a per-unit price of $p = 10$, which equals its marginal cost, and it charges an access fee of 2,450 ($= A_1 + B_1 + C_1$) to Valerie and 4,050 ($= A_2 + B_2 + C_2$) to Neal. If the monopoly cannot charge its customers different prices, it sets its per-unit price at $p = 20$, where Valerie purchases 60 and Neal buys 80 units. The firm charges both the same access fee of 1,800 $= A_1$, which is Valerie's potential consumer surplus. The highest access fee that the firm could charge and have Neal buy is 3,200, but at that level, Valerie would not buy. By charging a price above its marginal cost, the firm captures $B_1 = 600$ from Valerie and $B_2 = 800$ from Neal. Thus, its total profit is 5,000 ($= [2 \times 1,800] + 600 + 800$), which is less than the 6,500 ($= 2,450 + 4,050$) it makes if it can charge separate access fees to each customer.

(a) Valerie

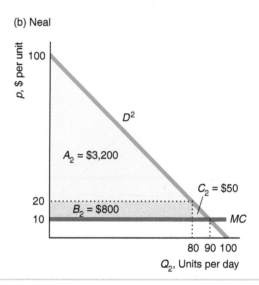

(b) Neal

surplus, $A_1 = 1,800$.[17] Although this access fee captures all of Valerie's potential consumer surplus, it is less than Neal's potential consumer surplus, $3,200 = A_2$. Were the firm to charge an access fee of 3,200, it would sell only to Neal and make less money.

At $p = 20$, Valerie buys 60 units, and Neal buys 80 units. Because the firm's average cost is 10, the firm makes $20 - 10 = 10$ per unit, so it earns $B_1 = 600$ ($= 10 \times 60$) from Valerie and $B_2 = 800$ ($= 10 \times 80$) from Neal for a total $= 1,400$. Adding that to what it makes from the access fees, 3,600, the monopoly's total profit is 5,000 ($= [2 \times 1,800] + 600 + 800$). Valerie receives no consumer surplus, but Neal enjoys a consumer surplus of 1,400 ($= 3,200 - 1,800$).

This 5,000 profit obtained from pure two-part pricing is less than the 6,500 it could obtain if it could set different access fees for each customer. In contrast, its profit from

---

[17]If the firm charges both customers the same access fee, A, and price, p, its profit is $\pi = R - C = p(Q_1 + Q_2) + 2A - 10(Q_1 + Q_2) = pQ + 2A - 10Q$, where $Q = Q_1 + Q_2$. Provided p is less than 80, $Q = (80 - p) + (100 - p) = 180 - 2p$. The access fee, A, is Valerie's potential consumer surplus at a price of p, $\frac{1}{2}(80 - p)^2$, which is the largest fee Valerie is willing to pay. Therefore, $\pi = p(180 - 2p) + (80 - p)^2 - 10(180 - 2p) = 4600 + 40p - p^2$. Maximizing profit by setting $d\pi/dp = 0$, we find that $p = 20$.

pure two-part pricing exceeds the 3,200 profit that the firm could earn from uniform monopoly pricing.[18]

Why does the firm charge a price above marginal cost when using pure two-part pricing? By raising the price, the firm lowers the amount it can earn from the access fee but increases the amount it can earn from the per-unit price. The amount the firm earns from Valerie because of the higher price (600) is less than the amount it loses from her reduced access fee (650 = 2,450 − 1,800). However, the situation with Neal is reversed. The gain the firm gets from charging Neal the higher price (800) exceeds the loss from Neal's smaller access fee (650). Further, the net gain the firm obtains from Neal exceeds the net loss it makes on Valerie (100 = 160 − 50), so it is better off overall.[19] Thus, a price above marginal cost increases profit in this case.

Mini-Case Available for a Song	Prior to 2009, Apple's iTunes music store, the giant of music downloading, used *uniform pricing*, selling songs for 99¢ each. However, some of its competitors, such as Amazon MP3, did not use uniform pricing. Some record labels told Apple that they would not renew their contracts if Apple continued to use uniform pricing. Apparently responding to this pressure and the success of some of its competitors, Apple switched in 2009 to selling each song at one of three prices. Did Apple's one-price-for-all-songs policy cost it substantial potential profit? How do consumer surplus and deadweight loss vary with pricing methods such as a single price, song-specific prices, price discrimination, and two-part pricing? To answer such questions, Shiller and Waldfogel (2011) surveyed nearly 1,000 students and determined each person's willingness to pay for each of 50 popular songs. Then they used this information to calculate optimal pricing under various pricing schemes. First, under uniform pricing, Apple charges the same price for every song. Second, under variable pricing, each song sells at its individual profit-maximizing price. Third, Apple could use two-part pricing, charging a monthly or annual fee for access and then a fixed price for each download. If we know the demand curve and the marginal cost, we can determine the consumer surplus (*CS*), the producer surplus (*PS*), or profit, and the deadweight loss (*DWL*) from each pricing regime. By dividing each of these surplus measures by the total available surplus—the area under the demand curve and above the marginal cost curve—we can determine the shares of *CS*, *PS*, and *DWL*. The following table shows Shiller and Waldfogel's estimates of the percentage shares of *CS*, *PS*, and *DWL* under each of the three pricing methods:

[18]A single-price monopoly faces an aggregate demand function of the sum of the two individual demand functions: $Q = Q_1 + Q_2 = (80 - p) + (100 - p)$ or $Q = 180 - 2p$, for p less than 80, where both consumers demand a positive quantity. Its inverse demand function is $p(Q) = 90 - \frac{1}{2}Q$. Its revenue function is $R(Q) = p(Q) \times Q = 90Q - \frac{1}{2}Q^2$, so its marginal revenue function is $MR = dR(Q)/dQ = 90 - Q$. To maximize its profit given that it sets a uniform price, the monopoly equates its MR and its MC, so that $90 - Q = 10$, or $Q = 80$. At that quantity, the price is $p = 90 - (80/2) = 50$. The firm's profit is $\pi = (p - AC)Q = (50 - 10) \times 80 = 3,200$.

[19]If the monopoly charges a price of $10 per unit, this price just covers its costs. Its profit-maximizing access fee is $2,450, which is the sum of areas A_1, B_1, and C_1 in panel a of Figure 10.6. Both Valerie and Neal pay this access fee, so the firm earns a profit of $4,900, which is less than the $5,000 it earns by raising its per-unit price to $20 and charging an access fee of $1,800.

Pricing	PS	CS	DWL
Uniform	28	42	29
Variable	29	45	26
Two-part pricing	37	43	20

If these students have tastes similar to those of the general market, then the deadweight loss is smaller under either of the alternatives to uniform pricing.

Apple raised its profit by switching from uniform pricing to variable pricing (see the *PS* column in the table). However, these results suggest that it could do even better using two-part pricing. Perhaps in response to this opportunity, Apple added iTunes Match (2011) and Apple Music (2015), which effectively use two-part pricing.

10.6 Bundling

Firms with market power often pursue a pricing strategy called **bundling**: selling multiple goods or services for a single price. Indeed, most goods are bundles of many separate parts. Cars come assembled. Left and right shoes are sold together as a pair and include laces. Usually this bundling is done for efficiency because combining goods in a bundle reduces the transaction costs incurred by consumers or the production costs associated with the product. For example, we buy shirts with buttons already attached. Rather than buying shirts without buttons, and then buying buttons, consumers prefer to buy assembled shirts, eliminating the need to make two separate purchases and then sew on buttons. It is also cheaper for the firm to sew on buttons in the factory rather than to distribute two separate products (shirts and buttons) to the marketplace.

However, firms sometimes bundle even when they gain no production advantages and transaction costs are small. Bundling of such products allows firms to increase their profit by taking advantage of differences in consumers' willingness to pay. For example, a computer firm may sell a package including a computer and a printer for a single price even if it has no cost savings from selling these products together.

There are two common types of bundling. Some firms engage in *pure bundling*, in which only a package deal is offered, as when a cable company sells a bundle of internet, phone, and television services for a single price but does not allow customers to purchase the individual services separately. Other firms use *mixed bundling*, in which the goods are available on a stand-alone basis in addition to being available as part of a bundle, such as a cable company that allows consumers to buy either the bundle or the individual services they want.

Pure Bundling

The two major component programs in Microsoft Office, Word and Excel, were originally sold as stand-alone products. A consumer who wanted both had to buy both separately. Later, Microsoft bundled both Word and Excel into Microsoft Office and also sold the products on a stand-alone basis. At present, if you try to purchase Word or Excel from Microsoft, you are directed only to the bundled product, MS Office.[20]

Whether it pays Microsoft to sell a bundle or sell the programs separately depends on how reservation prices for the components vary across customers. We use an example to show that a firm that sells word processing and spreadsheet programs bundles them if doing so results in a higher profit than if it sells the programs separately.

The marginal cost of producing an extra copy of either type of software is essentially zero. We assume the fixed cost is negligible, so that the firm's revenue equals its profit. The firm must charge all customers the same price—it cannot price discriminate.

The firm has two customers, Alisha and Bob. The first two columns of Table 10.2 show the reservation prices for each consumer for the two products. Alisha's reservation price for the word processing program, $120, is greater than Bob's, $90; however, Alisha's reservation price for the spreadsheet program, $50, is less than Bob's, $70. The reservation prices are *negatively correlated*: The customer who has the higher reservation price for one product has the lower reservation price for the other product. The third column of the table shows each consumer's reservation price for the bundle, which is the sum of the reservation prices for the two underlying products.

If the firm sells the two products separately, it maximizes its profit by charging $90 for the word processor and selling to both consumers, so that its profit is $180, rather than charging $120 and selling only to Alisha. If it charges between $90 and $120, it still only sells to Alisha and earns less than if it charges $120. Similarly, the firm maximizes its profit by selling the spreadsheet program for $50 to both consumers, earning $100, rather than charging $70 and selling to only Bob. The firm's total profit from selling the programs separately is $280 (= $180 + $100).

If the firm sells the two products in a bundle, it maximizes its profit by charging $160, selling to both customers, and earning $320. This is a better outcome than charging $170 and selling only to Alisha. Pure bundling is more profitable for the firm because it earns $320 from selling the bundle and only $280 from selling the programs separately.

Pure bundling is more profitable because the firm captures more of the consumers' potential consumer surplus—their reservation prices. With separate prices, Alisha has consumer surplus of $30 (= $120 − $90) from the word processing program and none from the spreadsheet program. Bob receives no consumer surplus from the word processing program and $20 from the spreadsheet program. Thus, the total consumer surplus is $50. With pure bundling, Alisha gets $10 of consumer surplus and Bob gets none, so the total is only $10. Thus, the pure bundling approach captures $40 more potential consumer surplus than does pricing separately.

TABLE 10.2 Negatively Correlated Reservation Prices

	Word Processor	Spreadsheet	Bundle
Alisha	$120	$50	$170
Bob	$90	$70	$160
Profit-maximizing price	$90	$50	$160
Units sold	2	2	2

---

[20]Microsoft includes additional software in this bundle, which it sells or leases.

TABLE 10.3 Positively Correlated Reservation Prices

	Word Processor	Spreadsheet	Bundle
Carol	$100	$90	$190
Dmitri	$90	$40	$130
Profit-maximizing price	$90	$90	$130
Units sold	2	1	2

Whether pure bundling increases the firm's profit depends on the reservation prices. Table 10.3 shows the reservation prices for two different consumers, Carol and Dmitri. Carol has higher reservation prices for both products than does Dmitri. These reservation prices are *positively correlated*: A higher reservation price for one product is associated with a higher reservation price for the other product.

If the programs are sold separately, the firm charges $90 for the word processor, sells to both consumers, and earns $180. However, it makes more charging $90 for the spreadsheet program and selling only to Carol than it does charging $40 for the spreadsheet, selling to both consumers, and earning $80. The firm's total profit if it prices separately is $270 (= $180 + $90).

If the firm uses pure bundling, it maximizes its profit by charging $130 for the bundle, selling to both customers, and making $260. Because the firm earns more selling the programs separately, $270, than when it bundles them, $260, pure bundling is not profitable in this example. Even if Dmitri placed a higher value on the spreadsheet, as long as reservation prices are positively correlated, pure bundling cannot increase the profit.

Mixed Bundling

Restaurants, computer software firms, and many other companies commonly use mixed bundling—allowing consumers to buy the pure bundle or to buy any of the bundle's components separately. The following example illustrates that mixed bundling may be more profitable than pure bundling or only selling components separately because it may capture more of the potential consumer surplus.

A firm that sells word processing and spreadsheet programs has four potential customers with the reservation prices in Table 10.4. Again, the firm's cost of production is zero, so maximizing its profit is equivalent to maximizing its revenue.

Aaron, a writer, places high value on the word processing program but has relatively little use for a spreadsheet program. Dorothy, an accountant, has the opposite pattern of preferences—placing a high value on having the spreadsheet program but

TABLE 10.4 Reservation Prices and Mixed Bundling

	Word Processor	Spreadsheet	Bundle
Aaron	$120	$30	$150
Brigitte	$110	$90	$200
Charles	$90	$110	$200
Dorothy	$30	$120	$150

little value on a word processing program. Brigitte and Charles have intermediate reservation prices. These reservation prices are negatively correlated: Customers with a relatively high reservation price for one product have relatively low reservation prices for the other program. To determine its best pricing strategy, the firm calculates its profit by pricing the components separately, using pure bundling, and engaging in mixed bundling.

If the firm prices each program separately, it maximizes its profit by charging $90 for each product and selling each to three out of the four potential customers. It sells the word processing program to Aaron, Brigitte, and Charles. It sells the spreadsheet program to Brigitte, Charles, and Dorothy. Thus, it makes $270 (= 3 × $90) from each program or $540 total, which exceeds what it could earn by setting any other price per program.[21]

However, the firm can make a higher profit by engaging in pure bundling. It can charge $150 for the bundle, sell to all four consumers, and earn $600, which is $60 more than the $540 it makes from selling the programs separately.

With mixed bundling, the firm obtains an even larger profit. It charges $200 for the bundle and $120 for each product separately. The firm earns $400 from Brigitte and Charles, who buy the bundle. Aaron buys only the word processing program for $120, and Dorothy buys only the spreadsheet for another $120, so that the firm makes $240 from its individual program sales. Thus, its profit is $640 (= $400 + $240) from mixed bundling, which exceeds the $600 from pure bundling, and the $540 from individual sales. We could construct other examples with different numbers where selling the programs separately would dominate (such as where reservation prices are positively correlated, as in Table 10.3) or where the pure bundle does best (as in Table 10.2).

Q&A 10.3

Package deals are common in vacation travel. Online travel services such as Expedia, Orbitz, and Travelocity offer travelers many attractive package deals that combine a round-trip airfare and a hotel stay or allow booking of airline flights and hotels individually. At some locations, the package price is much less than the sum of the prices for a flight and a hotel room, whereas at other locations, the package provides little savings. Paradise Vacations has two destinations, Hawaii and Cleveland, to which it sends its customers who live in Seattle. The table shows reservation prices for a weekend holiday for the two destinations for three customers. We assume that both hotels and aircraft have excess capacity so that the marginal cost of one more customers is zero.

	Hawaii			Cleveland		
	Flight	**Hotel**	**Bundle**	**Flight**	**Hotel**	**Bundle**
Allen	$400	$50	$450	$400	$50	$450
Barbara	$350	$350	$700	$300	$300	$600
Colin	$50	$400	$450	$50	$400	$450

---

[21]If it sets a price of a program as low as $30, it sells both programs to all four customers, but makes only $240. If it charges $110, it sells each program to two customers and earns $440. If it charges $120, it makes a single sale of each program, so it earns $240.

What are the profit-maximizing pricing strategies for the two destinations? Which destination yields the bigger package deal discount under mixed bundling?

Answer

1. *Determine the best stand-alone prices, bundle price, and mixed bundling prices for Hawaii.* If the firm prices the flight and the hotel separately, its profit-maximizing prices are $350 for each. The firm sells two units of each product (Allen and Barbara buy flights, and Barbara and Colin rent hotel rooms) and earns $1,400. The best bundle price is $450, which, although all three customers buy, generates a profit of only $1,350. Therefore, pricing the components separately produces a higher profit than does the bundle. However, mixed bundling produces the highest profit. The firm charges $700 for the bundle and $400 for each stand-alone product, earning a total of $1,500 by selling one bundle to Barbara, one flight to Allen, and one hotel stay to Colin.

2. *Determine the best stand-alone prices, bundle price, and mixed bundling prices for Cleveland.* With individual pricing, the firm charges $300 for each product, selling two units of each, and makes a profit of $1,200. Bundling is more profitable. At a bundle price of $450, all customers buy the bundle, generating a profit of $1,350. Mixed bundling is better still. By charging $600 for the bundle and $400 for each item, the firm's profit is $1,400.

3. *Under mixed bundling, compare the bundle price and combined individual prices for Hawaii and Cleveland.* For Hawaii with mixed bundling pricing, the cost of a flight and a hotel stay is $800 if purchased separately, while the bundle price is $700, for a $100 saving. In Cleveland, the sum of the individual prices is $800 and the bundle price is only $600, for a $200 savings.

Comments: Hawaii has a relatively low bundling discount because Barbara places a very high value on the bundle compared to other customers who are primarily interested in just one of the products. The firm can charge almost as much for the bundle as for the individual prices and still sell to Barbara. For the Cleveland market, Barbara requires a bigger discount for the bundle compared to the sum of the individual prices.

Requirement Tie-In Sales

One form of bundling—called a *requirement tie-in*—requires customers who buy one product from a firm to make all concurrent and subsequent purchases of a related product from that firm. This requirement allows the firm to identify heavier users and charge them more per unit. For example, if a printer manufacturer can require that consumers buy their ink cartridges only from the manufacturer, then that firm can capture most of the consumers' surplus. Heavy users of the printer, who presumably have a less elastic demand for it, pay the firm more than light users because of the high cost of the ink cartridges.

Unfortunately for such a printer manufacturer, the Magnuson-Moss Warranty Improvement Act of 1975 forbids them from requiring consumers to use their ink cartridges as a condition of the warranty. More broadly, the act prevents any manufacturer from using such tie-in provisions as a condition of warranty.

Managerial Implication

Ties That Bind

Managers can increase profit by promoting consumer loyalty. Despite the Magnuson-Moss Act, such loyalty can be induced through warranty provisions. Printer firms such as Hewlett-Packard (HP) write their warranties to strongly encourage consumers to use only their cartridges and not to refill them:

> . . . [I]f printer failure or damage is attributable to the use of a non-HP or refilled cartridge or an expired ink cartridge, HP will charge its standard time and materials charges to service the printer for the particular failure or damage.

Moreover, the company's literature stresses that

> HP recommends that you use original HP cartridges. Original HP cartridges are designed and tested with HP printers to help you easily produce great results, time after time.

Are these warranty restrictions and advertising claims sufficient to induce most consumers to buy cartridges only from HP? Apparently so. In 2018 HP sold its Deskjet 1112 printer for only $29.99. That is, HP is virtually giving away an impressive machine that will print up to 7.5 pages per minute in black and white and 5.5 pages per minute in color in up to 4800×1200 optimized dots per inch (dpi) in color. HP charges $37.99 for its tri-color ink cartridge. If most customers bought inexpensive cartridges or refills from other firms, HP would not sell its printer at a rock-bottom price. Thus, HP demonstrates that the benefits of requirement tie-in sales can be achieved through careful wording of warranties and advertising.

10.7 Peak-Load Pricing

Rooms in Florida's resort hotels that rent for $100 to $200 per night in the hot, humid summer months often rent for twice as much in the winter months of January and February, when snowbirds from northern states and Canada flock to Florida's warm, sunny beaches. Similarly, in many areas, electricity costs more during business hours than at night. Such pricing strategies are examples of **peak-load pricing**: charging higher prices during periods of peak demand than in other periods.

The popular Whistler Blackcomb ski resort (Whistler) near Vancouver, British Columbia, makes extensive use of peak-load pricing. Early in the season (late November), demand is relatively low. Demand is higher in December and very high in the holiday period at the end of December, when lifts run at capacity most of the time. January and February are busy months, and demand falls off in March and April. Skiers can buy online tickets in advance for any day of the season. For 2018–2019, the adult price for a one-day ticket (on a Saturday) was C$104 (Canadian dollars) on November 24, C$118 on December 15, C$147 on December 29, C$126 on January 12, and C$104 on April 6.

Firms can combine peak-load pricing with other pricing tools such as price discrimination, nonlinear pricing, and bundling. Whistler uses all these tools. For example, Whistler price discriminates by age. For lift tickets on December 12, 2018, children paid C$59, teens paid C$100, and seniors (65+) paid $106. Whistler uses nonlinear price discrimination, offering multiday passes at lower prices per day than single-day passes and offering tickets to large groups at discount prices. Whistler bundles skiing with other products, offering, for example, a daily pass, a lesson, and rental equipment as a package deal for considerably less than the combined stand-alone prices.

Peak-Load Pricing with a Capacity Constraint

Firms commonly use peak-load pricing when they face a production capacity constraint. For example, a hotel's capacity constraint is the maximum number of rooms, $\overline{Q}$, that it can rent. As Figure 10.7 illustrates, the hotel's marginal cost—primarily the cost of cleaning and maintaining the room—is constant at m up to capacity, where no additional room can be provided at any finite cost in the short run. That is, the marginal cost curve is horizontal at m up to capacity $\overline{Q}$, where it becomes vertical.

During the low season, the hotel's demand curve is D^L and its marginal revenue curve is MR^L. The hotel maximizes its profit by operating where its marginal revenue equals its marginal cost. Its marginal revenue curve hits the marginal cost curve in its horizontal section at Q_L. The corresponding price is p_L. Thus, during the off-season, the hotel's price is above its marginal cost, and it does not rent all available rooms, so the hotel has excess capacity.

The high- or peak-season demand curve D^H lies to the right of the low-season demand curve, D^L. The peak-season marginal revenue curve, MR^H, hits the marginal cost curve where it is vertical at $\overline{Q}$. Here, the firm maximizes its profit by charging a price p_H such that the quantity demanded, Q_H, equals the available capacity, $\overline{Q}$. Thus, in the peak period, the hotel charges a price, p_H, that limits the quantity demanded to the available capacity.

FIGURE 10.7 Peak-Load Pricing.

A resort has $\overline{Q}$ rooms, which is its capacity constraint. Its marginal cost of providing a room is m up to $\overline{Q}$ and then becomes infinite because the hotel cannot provide more than $\overline{Q}$ rooms. During the low season, the demand curve is D^L and the associated marginal revenue curve is MR^L. The firm maximizes its profit by renting the number of rooms where its marginal revenue curve crosses its marginal cost curve in the horizontal region and sets its price at p_L and rents Q_L rooms as shown by point e_L. The hotel has excess capacity because $Q_L < \overline{Q}$. During the peak season, the demand curve is D^H. The firm maximizes its profit by setting price, p_H, so that the quantity demanded is just equal to the available capacity, because its marginal revenue curve, MR^H, crosses the marginal cost curve in the vertical section. The price is p_H, and the hotel has no excess capacity.

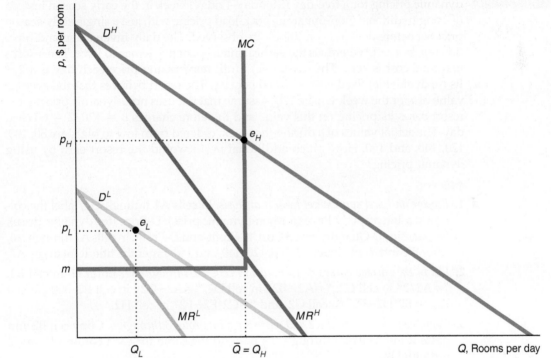

Dynamic Pricing

An important variant of peak-load pricing is **dynamic pricing** (or **surge pricing**), in which sellers frequently change prices based on current market conditions. Dynamic pricing is based on the same principle as traditional peak-load pricing—charging more in times of high demand. The difference is that instead of committing to a set pattern of pricing (as Whistler does for a season's ski tickets), a seller using dynamic pricing changes its price often, quickly responding to changing market conditions in "real time."

The term *surge pricing* has come into common use partly because of Uber. On its website Uber states: "Bad weather, rush hour, and special events, for instance, may cause unusually large numbers of people to want to ride Uber."[22] The website goes on to say that during these high-demand situations, "fares may increase to help ensure those who need a ride can get one." The Uber mobile app reports a surge multiplier when surge pricing is in effect. Riders see a surge multiplier such as 1.8×, indicating that prices are 1.8 times the normal rate.

---

[22]www.uber.com/drive/partner-app/how-surge-works/.

Some highway toll authorities use dynamic pricing for special express lanes. They vary the toll to ensure that the express lane remains uncongested.

A ski resort such as Whistler could use dynamic pricing instead of traditional peak-load pricing. Rather than setting just one pre-specified early-season price for adults based on some expected average early-season level of demand, the ski resort could change the price on a daily basis.

Q&A 10.4

A ski resort wants to determine how much additional profit it would earn if it used dynamic pricing for a five-day (Monday–Friday) week in the early season instead of using traditional (non-dynamic) peak-load pricing with just a single early-season price set before demand conditions are observed. The daily inverse demand function is $p = a - Q$ where a is the vertical intercept of the demand curve. The resort's marginal cost is zero. The (dynamic) profit-maximizing price each day is $a/2$.[23] Its (unavoidable) fixed cost is $3,000 per day. The resort believes that the average value of a for the week will be 120. Assume that if it uses non-dynamic pricing, the resort bases its pricing on this value and therefore charges $p = 120/2 = 60$ each day. The actual values of a during the week, ordered from low to high, are 80, 100, 120, 140, and 160. How much additional profit would the resort earn by using dynamic pricing?

Answer

1. *Prepare an Excel spreadsheet for this analysis.* In cells A1 through H1, label the columns: a-Intercept, N-Price (for non-dynamic price), D-Price (for dynamic price), N-Quantity, D-Quantity, Fixed Cost, N-Profit, and D-Profit. In cells A2 through A6, enter the intercept values 80, 100, 120, 140, and 160. Enter the title Total in cell A7.

2. *Fill in the correct values or formulas in cells B2 through H2.* Enter 60 in cell B2, "=A2/2" in cell C2, "=A2−B2" in cell D2, "=A2−C2" in cell E2, 3000 in cell F2, "=B2*D2−F2" in cell G2, and "=C2*E2−F2" in cell H2.

3. *Copy the formulas in row 2 and paste them into rows 3 through 6.* Copy cell B2 and paste it into cells B3 through B6, then do the same for each column from C2 through H2.

4. *Calculate the total profit under traditional and dynamic pricing and compare the two profit levels.* Enter "=sum(G2:G6)" in cell G7 and "=sum(H2:H6)" in cell H7. In the screenshot, both these total profit cells are highlighted in yellow. Observe that the profit of 4000 under dynamic pricing exceeds the profit of 3000 under traditional pricing.

	A	B	C	D	E	F	G	H
1	a-Intercept	N-Price	D-Price	N-Quantity	D-Quantity	Fixed Cost	N-Profit	D-Profit
2	80	60	40	20	40	3000	-1800	-1400
3	100	60	50	40	50	3000	-600	-500
4	120	60	60	60	60	3000	600	600
5	140	60	70	80	70	3000	1800	1900
6	160	60	80	100	80	3000	3000	3400
7	Total						3000	4000

[23]The marginal revenue curve is twice as steep as the demand curve, so the marginal revenue function is $MR = a - 2Q$. To maximize its daily profit, the resort sets $MR = a - 2Q = 0$, so $Q = a/2$.

Managerial Solution

Sale Prices

By putting Heinz ketchup on sale periodically, Heinz's managers can price discriminate and earn a higher profit for the Kraft Heinz Co. How often should Heinz put its ketchup on sale? Under what conditions does it pay for the firm to have sales? To answer these questions, we study a simplified market in which Heinz ketchup competes with one other ketchup brand, which we refer to as generic ketchup.[24] Every n days, the typical consumer buys either Heinz or generic ketchup. (The number of days between purchases is determined by the storage space in consumers' homes and how frequently they use ketchup.)

Switchers are price sensitive and buy the least expensive ketchup. They pay attention to price information and always know when Heinz ketchup is on sale.

Heinz's managers consider holding periodic sales to capture switchers' purchases. The generic is sold at a competitive price equal to its marginal cost of production of $2.01 per unit. Suppose that Heinz's marginal cost is $MC = \$1$ per unit (due to its large scale) and that, if it only sold to its loyal customers, it would charge a monopoly price of $p = \$3$. Heinz's managers face a trade-off. If Heinz is infrequently on sale for less than the generic price, Heinz sells little to switchers. However, if Heinz is frequently on sale, it loses money on its sales to loyal customers.

We start by supposing that Heinz's managers decide to charge a low sales price, $2, once every n days. For the other $n - 1$ days, Heinz sells at the regular, nonsale (monopoly) price of $3, which is the monopoly price given the demand curve of the loyal customers. During a sale, the switchers buy enough Heinz to last them for n days until it's on sale again. Consequently, the switchers never buy the generic product. (Some other customers are loyal to the generic, so they buy it even when Heinz is on sale.)

If the loyal customers find that Heinz is on sale, which happens $1/n$ of all days, they buy n days' worth at the sale price. Otherwise, they are willing to pay the regular (monopoly) price. If the other loyal customers were aware of this promotion pattern, they could get on a schedule such that they always bought on sale, too, thereby making this strategy non–profit maximizing. However, their shopping schedules are determined independently: They buy many goods and are not willing to distort their shopping patterns solely to buy this one good on sale.[25]

Could Heinz make more money by altering its promotion pattern? It does not want to place its good on sale more frequently because it would earn less from its loyal customers without making more sales to switchers. If it pays to hold sales at all, it does not want to have a sale less frequently because it would sell fewer units to switchers. During a promotion, Heinz wants to charge the highest price it can and yet still attract switchers, which is $2. If it sets a lower price, the quantity sold is unchanged, so its profit falls. If Heinz sets a sale price higher than $2, it loses all switchers.

---

[24]The rest of the U.S. market consists primarily of Hunt's Ketchup (15%) and generic or house brands (22%). In the following discussion, we assume that customers who are loyal to Hunt's or generic ketchup are unaffected by Heinz sales, and hence ignore those customers.

[25]We make this assumption for simplicity. In the real world, firms achieve a similar result by having random sales or by placing ads announcing sales where the ads are seen by primarily the switchers.

Does it pay for the firm to have sales? Whether it pays depends on the number of switchers, S, relative to the number of brand-loyal customers, B. If each customer buys one unit per day, then the firm's profit per day if it sells only to loyals is $\pi = (p - MC)B = (3 - 1)B = 2B$, where $p = 3$ is Heinz's regular price and $MC = 1$ is its marginal and average cost. If Heinz uses the sale pricing scheme, its average profit per day is

$$\pi^* = 2B(n - 1)/n + (B + S)/n.$$

The first term is the profit it makes, $2 per unit, selling B units to loyal customers for the fraction of days that Heinz ketchup is not on sale, $(n - 1)/n$. The second term is the profit it makes, $1 per unit, from selling $B + S$ units on the fraction of days, $1/n$, that Heinz ketchup is on sale.

Thus, it pays to put Heinz ketchup on sale if $\pi < \pi^*$, or $2B < 2B(n - 1)/n + (B + S)/n$. Using algebra, we can simplify this expression to $B < S$. Thus, if switchers outnumber loyal customers, then having sales is more profitable than selling at a uniform price to only loyal customers.

SUMMARY

1. **Conditions for Price Discrimination.** A firm can price discriminate if it has market power, knows which consumers or groups of consumers are willing to pay more than others for the product, and can prevent customers who pay low prices from reselling to those who are willing to pay high prices. A firm earns a higher profit from price discrimination than from uniform pricing because (a) the firm captures additional consumer surplus from customers who are willing to pay more than the uniform price and (b) the firm sells to some people who would not buy at the uniform price.

2. **Perfect Price Discrimination.** To perfectly price discriminate, a firm charges each customer the maximum each is willing to pay for each unit of output. The firm captures all potential consumer surplus and sells the efficient (competitive) level of output. Compared to perfect competition, total surplus is the same, consumers as a whole are worse off, and firms are better off under perfect price discrimination. Perfect price discrimination is rare, but seeking to approach perfect price discrimination using individual-specific prices is quite common.

3. **Group Price Discrimination.** A firm that is not able to perfectly price discriminate can still increase its profit relative to uniform pricing if it can identify different subgroups of consumers with different demand curves. At the profit-maximizing prices, the firm charges groups of consumers prices in proportion to

their elasticities of demand, with the group of consumers having the least elastic demand paying the highest price. Total surplus is less under group price discrimination than under competition or perfect price discrimination but may be greater or less than that under uniform monopoly pricing.

4. **Nonlinear Price Discrimination.** Some firms charge customers different prices depending on how many units they purchase. A common pattern of such prices involves quantity discounts, so that the per-unit price for consumers who buy larger quantities would be less than the per-unit price for consumers who buy smaller quantities.

5. **Two-Part Pricing.** By charging consumers an access fee for the right to buy a good and a separate fee per unit, firms may earn higher profits than from uniform pricing. In an extreme case, a firm that knew its customers' demand curves and could charge a different access fee to every customer could use two-part prices to capture all potential consumer surplus. More realistically, even a firm that does not know each customer's demand curve or that cannot vary the access fee across customers can still use two-part pricing to earn a higher profit than it could earn using a single (uniform) price.

6. **Bundling.** Some firms increase their profits by selling products as bundles, often called package deals. Some firms use pure bundling, in which only the bundle is offered for sale. Others use mixed bundling, in

which both the bundle and the individual goods are offered for sale. Bundling is likely to be a profitable pricing strategy when consumers have reservation prices that are negatively correlated—when consumers who have a relatively high willingness to pay for one good have a relatively low willingness to pay for the other good.

7. Peak-Load Pricing. Some firms charge higher prices during periods of high demand than during periods of low demand. Such pricing strategies are commonly used by firms that have capacity constraints. During the peak period, the firm sets a high price to limit demand to its available capacity. During the off-peak period, the firm's profit-maximizing price leaves excess capacity.

QUESTIONS

All exercises are available on **MyLab Economics**; * = *answer at the back of this book;* **C** = *use of calculus may be necessary;* ✗ = *this exercise is available in Excel Grader in* **MyLab Economics**.

1. Conditions for Price Discrimination

1.1 In the examples in Table 10.1, if the movie theater does not price discriminate, it charges either the highest price the college students are willing to pay or the one that the senior citizens are willing to pay. Why doesn't it charge an intermediate price? (*Hint*: Discuss how the demand curves of these two groups are unusual.)

1.2 Many pharmaceutical companies provide low-income older people with a card guaranteeing them discounts on prescription medicines. As of 2017, such companies included GlaxsoSmithKline, Merck, Pfizer, and Roche, along with many others. Why would these firms provide discount drug cards?

1.3 A monopoly currently sells its product at a single price. What conditions must be met so that it can profitably price discriminate?

*1.4 Many colleges provide students from low-income families with scholarships, subsidized loans, and other programs so that they pay lower tuitions than students from high-income families. Explain why universities behave this way.

*1.5 Disneyland price discriminates by charging lower entry fees for children than adults and for local residents than for other visitors. Why does it not have a resale problem? (*Hint*: See the Mini-Case "Disneyland Pricing.")

1.6 A jean manufacturer would find it profitable to charge higher prices in Europe than in the United States if it could prevent resale between the two countries. What techniques can it use to discourage resale? (*Hint*: See the Managerial Implication "Preventing Resale.")

1.7 Hertz and other car rental companies charge much more to rent luxury cars such as Ferraris and Bentleys than to rent compact cars such as the Toyota Yaris or Chevrolet Sonic. Is this price discrimination? Explain.

1.8 The European Commission charged six U.S. studios and a U.K. pay television company, Sky UK, with unfairly blocking access to films and other content. The charges challenge the studios' requirement under contracts that Sky UK block access for consumers outside Britain and Ireland. The studios have separate contracts with broadcasters in other countries. Why do the studios want such restrictions?

2. Perfect Price Discrimination

2.1 Using the information in the Mini-Case "Botox Revisited," determine how much Allergan loses by being a single-price monopoly rather than a perfectly price-discriminating monopoly. Explain your answer.

*2.2 If a monopoly faces an inverse demand function of $p = 90 - Q$, has a constant marginal and average cost of 30, and can perfectly price discriminate, what is its profit? What are the consumer surplus, total surplus, and deadweight loss? How would these results change if the firm were a single-price monopoly?

2.3 How would the answers to Q&A 10.1 and Table 10.1 change if seniors' reservation price were $5?

2.4 As described in the Mini-Case "Google Uses Bidding for Ads to Price Discriminate," Google uses auctions to charge advertisers according to how much they are willing to pay to reach a target audience. What type of price discrimination is this?

2.5 To promote her platinum-selling CD *Feels Like Home* in 2005, singer Norah Jones toured the country for live performances. However, she sold an average of only two-thirds of the tickets available for each show, T^* (Robert Levine, "The Trick of Making a Hot Ticket Pay," *New York Times*, June 6, 2005, C1, C4).

  a. Suppose that the local promoter is the monopoly provider of each concert. Each concert hall has a fixed number of seats. Assume that the promoter's cost is independent of the number of people who attend the concert (Ms. Jones received a guaranteed payment). Graph the promoter's marginal cost curve for the concert hall, where the number of tickets sold is on the horizontal axis (be sure to show T^*).

b. If the monopoly can charge a single market price, does the concert's failure to sell out prove that the monopoly set too high a price? Explain.

c. Would your answer in part b be the same if the monopoly can perfectly price discriminate? Use a graph to explain.

2.6 A firm is a natural monopoly (Chapter 9). Its marginal cost curve is flat, and its average cost curve is downward sloping (because it has a fixed cost). The firm can perfectly price discriminate.

a. In a graph, show how much the monopoly produces, Q^*.

b. Can it profitably produce where its price equals its marginal cost?

c. Show that a monopoly might shut down if it can only set a single price but will operate if it can perfectly price discriminate.

3. Group Price Discrimination

3.1 A firm charges different prices to two groups. Would the firm ever operate where it was suffering a loss from its sales to the low-price group? Explain.

*3.2 A monopoly sells its good in the U.S. and Japanese markets. The American inverse demand function is $p_A = 100 - Q_A$, and the Japanese inverse demand function is $p_J = 80 - 2Q_J$, where both prices, p_A and p_J, are measured in dollars. The firm's marginal cost of production is $m = 20$ in both countries. If the firm can prevent resale, what price will it charge in both markets? (*Hint*: The monopoly determines its optimal (monopoly) price in each country separately because customers cannot resell the good.)

*3.3 A patent gave Sony a legal monopoly to produce a robot dog called Aibo ("eye-BO"). The Chihuahua-size pooch robot can sit, beg, chase balls, dance, and play an electronic tune. When Sony started selling the toy, it announced that it would sell 3,000 Aibo robots in Japan for about $2,000 each and a limited litter of 2,000 in the United States for $2,500 each. Suppose that Sony's marginal cost of producing Aibo robots was $500. Its inverse demand function was $p_J = 3,500 - \frac{1}{2}Q_J$ in Japan and $p_A = 4,500 - 4,500Q_A$ in the United States. Solve for the equilibrium prices and quantities (assuming that U.S. customers cannot buy robots from Japan). Show how the profit-maximizing price ratio depends on the elasticities of demand in the two countries. What were the deadweight losses in each country, and in which was the loss from monopoly pricing greater? **C** (*Hint*: See Using Calculus: Maximizing Profit for a Group Discriminating Monopoly.)

3.4 A monopoly sells its good in the United States, where the elasticity of demand is -2, and in Japan, where the elasticity of demand is -5. Its marginal cost is $10. At what price does the monopoly sell its good in each country if resale is impossible?

3.5 Why are electronic textbooks likely to facilitate price discrimination by making it easier for textbook publishers to charge different prices in various countries?

3.6 In Q&A 10.2, calculate the firm's profit with and without a ban against price discrimination by age.

3.7 How would the analysis in Q&A 10.2 change if $MC = 7$?

3.8 Does a monopoly's ability to price discriminate between two groups of consumers depend on its marginal cost curve? Why or why not? [Consider two cases: (a) the marginal cost is so high that the monopoly is uninterested in selling to one group; and (b) the marginal cost is low enough that the monopoly wants to sell to both groups.]

3.9 A monopoly has a marginal cost of zero and faces two groups of consumers. At first, the monopoly could not prevent resale, so it maximized its profit by charging everyone the same price, $p = 5. No one from the first group chose to purchase. Now the monopoly can prevent resale, so it decides to price discriminate. Will total output expand? Why or why not? What happens to profit and consumer surplus?

3.10 Provide at least three examples illustrating how firms can use discounts while avoiding giving rebates to consumers with a high willingness to pay. (*Hint*: See the Managerial Implication "Discounts.")

*3.11 Spenser's Superior Stoves advertises a one-day sale on electric stoves. The ad specifies that no phone orders are accepted and that the purchaser must transport the stove. Why does the firm include these restrictions?

3.12 According to a report from the Foundation for Taxpayer and Consumer Rights, gasoline costs twice as much in Europe as in the United States because taxes are higher in Europe. However, the amount per gallon net of taxes that U.S. consumers pay is higher than that paid by Europeans (24¢ per gallon net of taxes). The report concludes that "U.S. motorists are essentially subsidizing European drivers, who pay more for taxes but substantially less into oil company profits" (Tom Doggett, "US Drivers Subsidize European Pump Prices," *Reuters*, August 31, 2006). Given that oil companies have market power and can price discriminate across countries, is it reasonable to conclude that U.S. consumers are subsidizing Europeans? Explain your answer.

4. Nonlinear Price Discrimination

*4.1 Are all the (identical) customers of the nonlinear price-discriminating monopoly in panel a of Figure 10.4 worse off than they would be if the firm set a single (uniform) price (panel b)? What if the consumers were not identical?

4.2 In panel b of Figure 10.4, the single-price monopoly faces a demand curve of $p = 90 - Q$ and a constant marginal (and average) cost of $m = 30$. Find the profit-maximizing quantity (or price) using math (Chapter 9). Determine the profit, consumer surplus, total surplus, and deadweight loss.

4.3 Assume that the quantity-discriminating monopoly in panel a of Figure 10.4 can set three prices, depending on the quantity a consumer purchases. The firm's profit is

$$\pi = p_1 Q_1 + p_2(Q_2 - Q_1) + p_3(Q_3 - Q_2) - mQ_3,$$

where p_1 is the high price charged on the first Q_1 units (first block), p_2 is a lower price charged on the next $Q_2 - Q_1$ units, p_3 is the lowest price charged on the $Q_3 - Q_2$ remaining units, Q_3 is the total number of units actually purchased, and $m = \$30$ is the firm's constant marginal and average cost. Use calculus to determine the profit-maximizing p_1, p_2, and p_3. **C**

4.4 In the nonlinear price discrimination analysis in panel a of Figure 10.4, suppose that the monopoly can make consumers a take-it-or-leave-it offer.

    a. Suppose the monopoly sets a price, p^*, and a minimum quantity, Q^*, that a consumer must pay to be able to purchase any units at all. What price and minimum quantity should it set to achieve the same outcome as it would if it perfectly price discriminated?

    b. Now suppose the monopolist charges a price of \$90 for the first 30 units and a price of \$30 for all subsequent units, but requires that a consumer must buy at least 30 units to be allowed to buy any. Compare this outcome to the one in part a and to the perfectly price-discriminating outcome.

4.5 Grocery store chains often set consumer-specific prices by issuing frequent-buyer cards to willing customers and collecting information about their purchases. Grocery chains can use those data to offer customized discount coupons to individuals. How should a grocery store use past-purchase data to set individualized prices to maximize its profit? (*Hint*: Refer to a customer's price elasticity of demand.)

4.6 Would it pay a seller to use group price discrimination and nonlinear price discrimination at the same time? Can you think of some examples? (*Hint*: See the Mini-Case "Downhill Pricing.")

5. Two-Part Pricing

5.1 Using math, show why, under two-part pricing, customers who purchase fewer units pay more on average per unit than do customers who buy more units.

5.2 Knoebels Amusement Park in Elysburg, Pennsylvania, charges an access fee, A, to enter its Crystal Pool. It also charges p per trip down the pool's water slides. Suppose that 400 teenagers visit the park, each of whom has a demand function of $q_1 = 5 - p$, and that 400 seniors also visit, each of whom has a demand function of $q_2 = 4 - p$. Knoebels' objective is to set A and p so as to maximize its profit given that it has no (non-sunk) cost and must charge both groups the same prices. What are the optimal A and p?

*5.3 Joe has just moved to a small town with only one golf course, the Northlands Golf Club. His inverse demand function is $p = 120 - 2q$, where q is the number of rounds of golf that he plays per year. The manager of the Northlands Club negotiates separately with each person who joins the club and can therefore charge individual prices. This manager has a good idea of what Joe's demand curve is and offers Joe a special deal whereby Joe pays an annual membership fee and can play as many rounds as he wants at \$20, which is the marginal cost his round imposes on the club. What membership fee would maximize profit for the club? The manager could have charged Joe a single price per round. How much extra profit does the club earn by using two-part pricing?

5.4 Joe in Question 5.3 marries Susan, who is also an enthusiastic golfer. Susan wants to join the Northlands Club. The manager believes that Susan's inverse demand function is $p = 100 - 2q$. The manager has a policy of offering each member of a married couple the same two-part prices, so he offers them both a new deal. What two-part pricing deal maximizes the club's profit? Will this new pricing have a higher or lower access fee and per-unit fee than in Joe's original deal? How much more would the club make if it charged Susan and Joe separate prices?

5.5 As described in the Mini-Case "Available for a Song," Shiller and Waldfogel (2011) estimated that if iTunes used two-part pricing charging an annual access fee and a low price per song, it would raise its profit by about 30% relative to what it would earn using uniform pricing or variable pricing. Assume that iTunes uses two-part pricing and assume that the marginal cost of an additional download is zero. How should iTunes set its profit-maximizing price per song if all consumers are identical? Illustrate profit-maximizing two-part pricing in a diagram for the identical consumer case. Explain why the actual profit-maximizing price per song is positive.

6. Bundling

6.1 A monopoly sells two products, of which any given consumer wants to buy only one (and places no value on the other good). If the monopoly can prevent resale, can it increase its profit by bundling the goods, forcing consumers to buy both goods?

*6.2 A computer hardware firm sells both laptop computers and printers. It has a large inventory of laptops and printers that it wants to sell, so it has no variable production cost. Through the magic of focus groups, their pricing team determines that they have an equal number of three types of customers, and that these customers' reservation prices are shown in the table:

	Laptop	Printer	Bundle
Customer Type A	$800	$100	$900
Customer Type B	$1,000	$50	$1,050
Customer Type C	$600	$150	$750

  a. If the firm were to charge only individual prices (not use the bundle price), what prices should it set for its laptops and printers to maximize profit? Assuming for simplicity that the firm has only one customer of each type, how much does it earn in total?

  b. After conducting a costly study, an outside consultant suggests that the company could make more money from its customers if it sold laptops and printers together as a bundle instead of separately. Is the consultant right? Assuming again that the firm has one customer of each type, how much does the firm earn in total from pure bundling?

  c. Why does bundling pay or not pay? (*Hint*: See Q&A 10.3.)

6.3 Initially, Microsoft sold its programs Word and Excel separately. Now, it only sells them as a bundle. Assuming that Microsoft was always trying to maximize profit, what does this change in pricing suggest about how demand for the two products changed over time? (*Hint*: See Table 10.2 and Table 10.3.)

6.4 Why do Honda service departments emphasize to customers the importance of using "genuine Honda parts" when servicing and tuning Honda cars and motorcycles? (*Hint*: See the Managerial Implication "Ties That Bind").

7. Peak-Load Pricing

7.1 The inverse demand function facing a resort hotel is $p = 300 - Q$ during the high season and $p = 100 - Q$ during the low season. The resort's marginal cost is $50 per night in cleaning costs for the room and general maintenance and administration. The resort has 100 rooms. What is the resort's profit-maximizing peak-load pricing strategy? Illustrate the solution in a diagram.

*7.2 Paradise Cruises has a monopoly in renting luxury yachts for sailing in the Caribbean Sea. In winter its monthly inverse demand function is $p = 200 - q$. In summer the inverse demand function is $p = 200 - 2q$. Paradise has a total of 50 yachts available for rental on a monthly basis.

  a. Which season is the peak season? Why?

  b. What are the profit-maximizing prices in both seasons?

7.3 Based on the information in Question 7.2, determine the profit-maximizing uniform price. Does Paradise Cruises earn a higher profit under peak-load pricing or uniform pricing? Compare consumer surplus under these two pricing methods.

7.4 As in Q&A 10.4, a ski resort faces daily demand given by $p = a - Q$, where a varies from day to day. Over a three-day period, a takes on the values 80, 100, and 120. The marginal cost is zero. The fixed cost for the three-day period is $2,500. If the firm uses dynamic pricing, it changes its price every day to maximize profit. If it uses non-dynamic pricing, it sets the same price for all three days, assuming that a takes on its average value of 100 each day. Use math to calculate the consumer surplus and the firm's profit over the three-day period under each pricing approach.

7.5 Uber makes the following statement on its website: "In . . . cases of very high demand, fares may increase to help ensure those who need a ride can get one. This system is called surge pricing, and it lets us continue to be a reliable choice." Does surge pricing help "ensure that those who need a ride can get one" and allow Uber to be more "reliable" in the sense that a driver will show up quickly? Assume that Uber has a capacity constraint. Use a diagram to illustrate your reasoning.

8. Managerial Problem

8.1 Each week, a department store places a different item of clothing on sale. Give an explanation based on price discrimination for why the store conducts such regular sales.

9. MyLab Economics Spreadsheet Exercises[26]

9.1 The Jam Factory makes boutique jams that it sells in specialty stores in two different cities. In City 1, the daily inverse demand function is $p_1 = 12 - 0.5Q_1$ and the marginal revenue function is $MR_1 = 12 - Q_1$. In City 2, the inverse demand and marginal revenue functions are $p_2 = 20 - Q_2$ and $MR_2 = 20 - 2Q_2$. The firm's cost function is $C(Q) = 10 + 6Q$, where $Q = Q_1 + Q_2$. Thus, the firm's marginal cost of production is 6 per unit.

   a. Create a spreadsheet with columns for Q_1, Q_2, p_1, p_2, MR_1, MR_2, and MC. Put the values 1 to 12 in increments of 1 in the Q_1 column and put the same values in the Q_2 column. Fill in the appropriate formulas in the other cells, noting that the MC column has the value 6 for each quantity. The Jam Factory price discriminates by charging a different price in each city. Find the profit-maximizing quantities and prices. Verify that the marginal revenues are the same in each city at the profit-maximizing quantities. Determine the firm's profit.

   b. Add two columns to your spreadsheet showing the price elasticity of demand in each city for each price-quantity combination. Verify that your results are consistent with Equation 10.5. (*Hint*: The price elasticity of demand for City 1 is $\varepsilon_1 = -2p_1/Q_1$ and for City 2 is $\varepsilon_2 = -p_2/Q_2$.)

9.2 Anil is planning a birthday party at an amusement park for his young daughter and her friends. The manager of the park is considering whether to use uniform pricing or two-part pricing. Anil's willingness to pay for rides for the party is $p = 25 - 0.5Q$, where p is the ticket price per ride and Q is the number of rides. The amusement park has a marginal cost of $5 for each additional ride. Its fixed cost for handling the party is $20.

   a. Create a spreadsheet with quantity, price, consumer surplus, revenue, marginal revenue, cost, marginal cost, and profit as column headings. Fill in the spreadsheet's cells for $Q = 5$ to $Q = 50$ in increments of 5 units. If the manager uses uniform pricing, what is the profit-maximizing ticket price per ride, the number of rides, and the profit earned by the park?

   b. Suppose that the manager uses two-part pricing: an entry fee for the entire party of young girls and a price per ride. Calculate the profit-maximizing entry fee if the price per ride is the same as the monopoly price that you determined in part a. Calculate the total profit earned by the park.

   c. Now suppose the manager uses two-part pricing with a per-ride price equal to marginal cost and a profit-maximizing entry fee. Determine the price per ride, the number of rides, and the total profit (including profit from ticket sales and the entry fee) in this case.

9.3 A restaurant faces very high demand for its signature mousse desserts in the evening but is less busy during the day. Its manager estimates that inverse demand functions are $p_e = 20 - Q_e$ in the evening and $p_d = 11 - Q_d$ during the day, where e and d denote evening and daytime. The marginal cost of producing its dessert, MC_1, is $3. Any morning, the restaurant can bring in additional tables and convert its storage space to seating to increase capacity for that day. Creating enough extra capacity to provide one more dessert in the evening or the day costs $5, which is the restaurant's marginal capacity cost, MC_2.

   a. Create a spreadsheet with the column headings Q_e, p_e, MR_e, Q_d, p_d, MR_d, MC_1, MC_2, and $MC_T = MC_1 + MC_2$.

   b. Determine the optimal prices for the dessert that the restaurant should charge during the evening hours and during the day, the associated quantities sold, and the total daily profit.

---

[26]The spreadsheet exercises in this chapter are based on the work of Satyajit Ghosh in cooperation with the authors. The answers are available on **MyLab Economics**.

11 Oligopoly and Monopolistic Competition

Anyone can win unless there happens to be a second entry.

—George Ade

Managerial Problem

Gaining an Edge from Government Aircraft Subsidies

A manager can use a cost advantage over a rival firm to increase profit. Consequently, managers of aircraft manufacturing firms lobby their governments for subsidies and then use these subsidies to increase their profit.

Airbus SAS, based in Europe, and the Boeing Co., based in the United States, are the only two major manufacturers of large commercial jet aircraft. France, Germany, Spain, and the United Kingdom subsidize Airbus, which competes in the wide-body aircraft market with Boeing. The U.S. government decries the European subsidies to Airbus despite giving lucrative military contracts to Boeing, which the Europeans view as implicit subsidies.

This government largess does not magically appear. Managers at both Boeing and Airbus lobby strenuously for this support. For example, in 2017–2018, Boeing spent over $24 million on lobbying and was represented by 105 lobbyists, 76 of whom previously held government jobs.

Washington and the European Union have repeatedly charged each other before the World Trade Organization (WTO) with illegally subsidizing their respective aircraft manufacturers. In 2018, the WTO concluded that the European Union and members France, Germany, Spain, and the United Kingdom "failed to comply with an earlier WTO panel ruling by maintaining illegal subsidies" for Airbus. In 2012, the WTO ruled that Boeing and Airbus both received improper subsidies. In 2015, the WTO agreed to investigate a complaint about Washington State subsidies to Boeing, and Boeing questioned government loans to Airbus. In 2018, the WTO concluded that the European Union and members France, Germany, Spain, and the United Kingdom maintained illegal Airbus subsidies. Thus, the cycle of subsidies, charges, agreements, and new subsidies continues. . . .

If only Boeing or Airbus receives a government subsidy, how should its managers use the subsidy to gain a competitive advantage? What effect does that subsidy have on prices and quantities? What happens if both governments subsidize their firms? Do Boeing and Airbus managers benefit from lobbying for government subsidies if that results in a subsidy war?

I n Chapter 7, we discussed the common market structures: perfect competition, monopoly, oligopoly, and monopolistic competition. In this chapter, we focus on oligopolistic and monopolistically competitive markets, which have more than the single firm of a monopoly but fewer firms than in a perfectly competitive market.

An **oligopoly** has few sellers and barriers to entry. Because relatively few firms compete in such a market, each can influence the market price, and hence its actions affect rival firms. As with a monopoly, an oligopolistic firm has market power and is therefore able to set a price above marginal cost profitably.

Many manufacturing, transportation, financial, and other markets with relatively few firms are either oligopolistic or monopolistically competitive. For example, the worldwide video game market is oligopolistic and is dominated by three firms: Nintendo, Microsoft, and Sony. When one of these three firms changes its price or its product's features, the other firms must either respond or lose a substantial amount of business.

The need to consider the behavior of rivals makes the profit-maximization decision for an oligopolistic firm more difficult than for a competitive firm or a monopoly. A competitive firm ignores the behavior of individual rivals and considers only the market price and its own costs in choosing its profit-maximizing output (Chapter 8). A monopoly has no rivals (Chapter 9) and considers only how its choice of quantity or price affects its profit.

Oligopolistic firms may act independently or may coordinate their actions. In this chapter, we focus primarily on independent or *noncooperative* oligopolies. However, a group of firms in the same industry may seek to cooperate. If they coordinate setting prices or quantities, they are said to *collude* and the group of firms is often called a **cartel**. If the colluding firms can cooperate and behave like a monopoly, the members of the cartel collectively earn the monopoly profit. Even if the cartel cannot achieve the full monopoly outcome, it can often collude sufficiently to provide its members with higher profits than the firms could earn through independent actions. In the United States, Canada, the European Union, and most other economies, such cartels are generally illegal.

If oligopolistic firms do not collude, they normally earn less profit than a monopoly could. However, because oligopolistic markets have relatively few firms, oligopolistic firms that act independently may earn positive economic profits in the long run, unlike competitive firms.

In an oligopolistic market, limitations on entry keep the number of firms small. In a market with no limits on entry, firms enter the market until the profit of the marginal firm falls to zero. In perfectly competitive markets, enough entry occurs that each firm faces a horizontal demand curve and is a price taker.

However, free entry does not necessarily lead to perfect competition. Even if the entry of many firms drives the last firm's economic profit to zero (Chapter 7), each firm's demand curve may be downward sloping, particularly if each firm differentiates its product from those of its rivals. Given that firms face downward-sloping demand curves, they charge a price above their marginal costs. Such a market is not perfectly competitive and is monopolistically competitive.

Monopolistic competition is a market structure in which firms have market power, but free entry occurs in the long run until no additional firm can enter and earn a positive long-run profit. If all firms have identical costs and produce identical products, all firms earn zero long-run economic profits.

As we saw in Chapter 9, the monopoly outcome is the same whether a monopoly sets price or quantity. In contrast, under oligopoly or monopolistic competition, outcomes can differ depending on whether firms choose to set prices or quantities.

Learning Objectives

1. Describe how firms in a cartel raise their profits by coordinating their actions.
2. Model how firms independently choose their output levels to determine the Nash-Cournot equilibrium.
3. Show how firms independently choose their prices to determine the Nash-Bertrand equilibrium.
4. Explain how two conditions determine the monopolistic competition equilibrium.

11.1 Cartels

People of the same trade seldom meet together, even for merriment and diversion, but the conversation ends in a conspiracy against the public, or some contrivance to raise prices.

—Adam Smith (1776)

Oligopolistic firms have an incentive to form cartels in which they collude in setting prices or quantities so as to increase their profits. The Organization of Petroleum Exporting Countries (OPEC) is a well-known example of an international cartel; however, many cartels operate within a single country.

Why Cartels Succeed or Fail

Typically, each member of a cartel agrees to reduce its output from the level it would produce if it acted independently. As a result, the market price rises and the firms earn higher profits. If the firms reduce market output to the monopoly level, they achieve the highest possible collective profit.

Luckily for consumers, cartels often fail because of government policies that forbid cartels or because members of the cartel "cheat" on the cartel agreement. Each member has an incentive to cheat because it can raise its profit if it increases its output while other cartel members stick to the agreement.

Why Cartels Form. A cartel forms if members of the cartel believe that they can raise their profits by coordinating their actions. But, if a firm maximizes its profit when acting independently, why should joining a cartel increase its profit? The answer involves a subtle argument. When a firm acts independently, it considers how increasing its output affects its own profit only. The firm does not care that when it increases its output, it lowers the profits of other firms. A cartel, in contrast, takes into account how changes in any one firm's output affect the profits of all members of the cartel. Therefore, the aggregate profit of a cartel can exceed the combined profits of the same firms acting independently.

Although cartels are most common in oligopolistic markets, occasionally we see cartels formed in what would otherwise be highly competitive markets with many firms. If a competitive firm lowers its output, it raises the market price very slightly—so slightly that the firm ignores the effect not only on other firms' profits but also on its own. If all the identical competitive firms in an industry lower their output by this same amount, however, the market price will change noticeably. Recognizing this effect of collective action, a cartel chooses to produce a smaller market output than is produced by a competitive market.

Figure 11.1 illustrates the difference between a competitive market and a cartel. This oligopolistic market has *n* firms, and no further entry is possible. Panel a shows

FIGURE 11.1 Comparing Competition with a Cartel

(a) The figure shows the marginal cost and average cost of one of the n firms in the market. A competitive firm produces q_c units of output, whereas a cartel member produces $q_m < q_c$. At the cartel price, p_m, each cartel member has an incentive to increase its output from q_m to q^* (where the dotted line at p_m intersects the MC curve).
(b) The competitive equilibrium, e_c, has more output and a lower price than the cartel equilibrium, e_m.

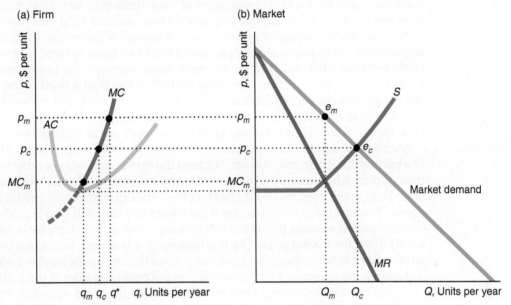

the marginal and average cost curves of a typical perfectly competitive firm. If all firms are price takers, the market supply curve, S in panel b, is the horizontal sum of the individual marginal cost curves above minimum average cost. At the competitive price, p_c, each price-taking firm produces q_c units of output (which is determined by the intersection in panel a of MC and the dotted line at p_c).[1] The market output is $Q_c = nq_c$ (where S intersects the market demand curve in panel b).

Now suppose that the firms form a cartel. Should they reduce their output? At the competitive output, the cartel's marginal cost in panel b (which is S, the sum of the individual firms' marginal cost curves) is greater than its marginal revenue, so the cartel's profit rises if it reduces output. The cartel's collective profit rises until output is reduced enough that its marginal revenue equals its marginal cost, which occurs at Q_m, the monopoly output. If the profit of the cartel increases, the profit of each of the n members of the cartel also increases. To achieve the cartel output level, each firm must reduce its output to $q_m = Q_m/n$, as panel a shows.

Why must the firms form a cartel to achieve these higher profits? A competitive firm produces q_c, where its marginal cost equals the market price. If only one firm reduces its output, it loses profit because it sells fewer units at essentially the same price. By getting all the firms to lower their output together, the cartel raises the market price and hence individual firms' profits. The less elastic the market demand curve that the potential cartel faces, holding everything else constant, the higher the price the cartel sets and the greater the benefit from forming a cartel. In

---

[1]To compare the competitive and cartel outcomes, we hold the number of firms fixed. Without free entry, the competitive price can exceed the minimum average cost, and competitive firms can earn a profit, as in the figure.

regimes where cartels are legal, such possibilities are attractive to producers. Even where cartels are not legal, if the penalty for forming an illegal cartel is relatively low, producers still face an incentive to succumb to the lure of extra profits and join.

Why Cartels Fail. In most countries, cartels are generally illegal, although enforcement levels vary. As we discuss at greater length in Chapter 16, firms in the cartel may incur fines, and the owners or managers of these firms may be subject to individual fines and jail terms.[2] Further, many cartels fail even without legal intervention.

Some cartels fail because they do not control enough of the market to raise the price significantly. For example, copper producers tried four times to form an international cartel between 1918 and 1988. In the most recent attempt, the Intergovernmental Council of Copper Exporting Countries controlled less than a third of the noncommunist world's copper production and faced additional competition from firms that recycle copper from scrap materials. Because of this competition from noncartel members, the cartel could not successfully increase copper prices and dissolved in 1988.

Members of a cartel have incentives to cheat on the cartel agreement. The owner of a participating firm may reason, "I joined the cartel to encourage others to reduce their output, which raises the market price and increases profits for everyone. However, I can make even more if I cheat on the cartel agreement by producing extra output. I can get away with cheating if the other firms can't tell who is producing the extra output because my firm is just one of many firms and my increase in output will hardly affect the market price." By this reasoning, it is in each firm's best interest for all *other* firms to honor the cartel agreement—thus driving up the market price—while it cheats on the agreement and makes additional profitable sales at the high price.

Figure 11.1 illustrates why firms want to cheat. At the cartel output, q_m in panel a, each cartel member's marginal cost is MC_m. A firm that does not restrict its output to the cartel level can increase its profit. It can earn the market price, p_m, on each extra unit it sells because each individual firm's output has little effect on the market price. That is, the firm can act like a price taker, so its marginal revenue equals the market price. The firm maximizes its profit by selling q^* units, which is determined by the intersection of its marginal cost curve and the dotted line at p_m. Because its marginal revenue is above its marginal cost for all the extra units it sells (those between q_m and q^*), it makes extra money by violating the cartel agreement. As more and more firms leave the cartel, the cartel price falls. Eventually, if enough firms quit, the cartel collapses.

Mini-Case Employer "No-Poaching" Cartels	How would you get a higher wage than your current employer is paying? Probably you'd seek a job offer from another firm in the same field. But, if that other firm agrees not to hire anyone employed by your current firm, you're out of luck. That's what happened to many skilled engineers. Such an employer conspiracy is an example of a buyers' cartel, which is similar to the sellers' cartels we've been discussing. In 2005, when demand for Silicon Valley engineers was skyrocketing, Apple's Steve Jobs agreed on a secret, illegal "no-poaching" deal with Google's Eric Schmidt (who was also on Apple's board of directors) to keep their employees' wages low by agreeing not to recruit each other's workers, by sharing wage information, and by punishing a firm that violated the agreement. Intuit, Pixar,

---

[2]With rare exceptions, it is illegal for firms to collude over prices, quantities, market areas, or the equivalent. However, in most jurisdictions, firms may coordinate R&D efforts or technical standards.

and Lucasfilm joined the cartel. It is alleged that many other major tech firms also joined, affecting over a million employees.

In 2014, Intuit, Pixar, and Lucasfilm agreed to a $20 million settlement of a class-action lawsuit alleging that they conspired to suppress wages. In 2015, Apple, Google, Intel, and Adobe agreed to pay $415 million to settle a similar lawsuit.

A similar cartel affected animation workers. In 2017, these workers obtained a $100 million settlement with the Walt Disney Company, Pixar, and Lucasfilm from a class-action lawsuit concerning wage fixing using non-poaching agreements.

Krueger and Ashenfelter (2017) found no-poaching agreements in 58% of major franchisors' contracts across a wide range of industries including firms such as Jiffy Lube and H&R Block, as well as fast-food restaurants. Starr, Prescott, and Bishara (2018) concluded that nearly one in five U.S. workers was bound by noncompete clauses that limit the other firms for which they can work, and that nearly 40% had signed at least one noncompete clause in the past.

In 2018, seven fast-food chains—including Arby's, Cinnabon, and McDonald's—agreed to end no-poaching rules. These rules prevented employees from moving between franchises within a restaurant chain, affecting an estimated 25,000 U.S. restaurants. By settling these lawsuits rather than risk losing in a trial, these companies avoid the costs of a trial and the risk of larger fines.

Maintaining Cartels

To keep firms from violating a cartel agreement, it is important for the cartel to be able to detect cheating and punish violators. Further, the members of the cartel need to keep their illegal behavior sufficiently hidden from customers and government agencies to avoid prosecution.

Detection and Enforcement. Cartels use various techniques to detect cheating. Some cartels, for example, give members the right to inspect each other's accounts. Cartels may also divide the market by region or by customer group, making it more likely that the cartel will know if a firm steals another firm's customers, as in the two-country mercury cartel (1928–1972) that allocated the Americas to Spain and Europe to Italy. Another option is for a cartel to turn to industry organizations that collect data on market share by firm. A cheating cartel's market share would rise, tipping off the other firms that it had cheated.

You perhaps have seen "low price" ads in which local retail stores guarantee to meet or beat the prices of any competitors. These ads may in fact be a way for the firm to induce its customers to report cheating by other firms on an explicit or implicit cartel agreement (Salop, 1986).

Cartels use various methods to enforce their agreements. For example, GE and Westinghouse, the two major sellers of large steam-turbine generators, included "most-favored-customer" clauses in their contracts. These contracts stated that the seller would not offer a lower price to any other current or future buyer without offering the same price decrease to the firms that signed these contracts. This type of rebate clause creates a penalty for cheating on the cartel: If either company cheats by cutting prices, it has to lower prices to all previous buyers as well. Threats of violence are another means of enforcing a cartel agreement.

Governments often enable cartels indirectly:

> **Common Confusion** Requiring government agencies to report which company had the lowest bid for a government contract and the level of the bid is good for the public.

Although society benefits in many ways from government transparency, disclosing this type of information can help a cartel enforce its agreement. If the government reports that the "wrong" cartel member submitted the low bid and won the contract, then the other cartel members know immediately that a firm cheated on the cartel agreement. Electric equipment and heavy construction cartels have made use of such government information.

Government Support. Sometimes governments help create and enforce cartels, exempting them from antitrust and competition laws. By successfully lobbying the U.S. Congress for a special exemption, professional baseball teams have been exempt from most U.S. antitrust laws since 1922. As a result, they can use the courts to help enforce certain aspects of their cartel agreement.

The international airline market provides an example in which governments first created a cartel and then later acted to end it. In 1944, 52 countries signed the Convention on International Civil Aviation, which established rules ("freedoms") that enabled airlines to fly between countries. Rather than having the market determine international airfares, bilateral governmental agreements determined them. These countries exempted airlines from their cartel laws, which allowed the firms to discuss prices through the International Air Transport Association (IATA). In the late 1970s, the United States deregulated its airline industry. Soon thereafter, European countries started to deregulate, allowing nongovernment-owned airlines to enter the market. Countries negotiated bilateral *open skies* agreements that weakened IATA's price-fixing role.[3]

Mini-Case

Cheating on the Maple Syrup Cartel

Most maple syrup comes from Quebec—not Vermont (as many Americans assume). Quebec has many, many trees and about 13,500 maple syrup producers. How could they band together and effectively run a cartel? The provincial government passed a law creating the cartel: the Federation of Quebec Maple Syrup Producers. Simon Trépanier, the federation's executive director, has referred to the federation as the OPEC of maple syrup.

The federation is half a century old. However, technological change, such as the use of plastic pipes, caused a large increase in supply and a drop in price. Since 1990, the federation has been the province's only wholesale seller of syrup. A majority of the federation's members voted to establish mandatory production quotas starting in 2004, which limit how much farmers can sell in a year. Moreover, farmers have to sell all their syrup through the federation. Thus, the federation restricts supply to raise the price of maple syrup.

So, are all the farmers happy? According to Mr. Trépanier, "Three-quarters of our members are happy or very happy with what we are doing." And the rest? Some of them are "cheating" on the cartel.

---

[3]The European Court of Justice struck down the central provisions of aviation treaties among the United States and eight other countries in 2002.

If the federation suspects a farmer is producing and selling outside the federation, it posts guards on the farmer's property. Then it seeks fines, or, in extreme circumstances, it seizes production. In other words, it has powers that illegal cartels can only envy.

But does the federation stop all cheating? It is in a battle with farmers like Robert Hodge who break the law by not participating in the federation's system. The federation did not catch Mr. Hodge from 2004 through 2008. In 2009, the federation demanded C$278,000 from Mr. Hodge for not joining and for selling outside the system, which exceeded his annual sales of about C$50,000 by more than five-fold.

In 2015, the federation hired guards to keep watch over Mr. Hodge's sugar farm. After watching the farm for several weeks, they seized his entire annual production of 20,400 pounds of maple syrup, worth about C$60,000. He remains intransigent, contending that he should be free to choose how much to produce and to whom he sells his product regardless of the law. He says, "They call us rebels, say we're in a sugar war or something." His 20-year-old daughter observed, "A war over maple syrup, like how pathetic can you get?"

Similarly, in 2018, the Sûreté du Québec seized the maple syrup of producers Nathalie Bombardier and Daniel Gaudreau because they refused to sell through the federation.

Barriers to Entry. Barriers to entry that limit the number of firms help the cartel detect and punish cheating. The fewer the firms in a market, the more likely it is that other firms will know if a given firm cheats and the easier it is to impose penalties. Cartels with a large number of firms are relatively rare, except those involving professional associations.

When new firms enter their market, cartels frequently fail. For example, when only Italy and Spain sold mercury, they were able to establish and maintain a stable cartel. When a larger group of countries joined them, their attempts to cartelize the world mercury market repeatedly failed (MacKie-Mason and Pindyck, 1986).

11.2 Cournot Oligopoly

Most oligopolistic firms act independently rather than collude. How do they take their rivals' actions into account? Although economists have only one model of perfect competition and one model of monopoly, they have many models of noncooperative oligopolistic behavior with many possible equilibrium prices and quantities.

Which oligopoly model is appropriate in a particular market depends on the characteristics of the market, including the type of *actions* firms take (such as whether firms set prices or quantities), whether firms act simultaneously or sequentially, and the number of periods over which firms compete. In this chapter and in Chapter 12, we examine oligopoly models in which firms act simultaneously and compete in a single period. In Chapter 13, we examine oligopoly models in which firms may act sequentially and compete over many periods. In this chapter, we assume that firms set only prices or quantities, whereas in Chapters 12 and 13, we consider other decisions by firms, such as how much to advertise and whether to enter a market. To keep the analysis as clear as possible, we initially assume that firms produce identical products, but we later show how these models can incorporate product differentiation.

We begin our study of oligopoly models with the two best-known oligopoly models, the *Cournot model* and the *Bertrand model*. In both models, firms act simultaneously and independently. In the Cournot model, firms choose quantities: how much they produce. In contrast, in the Bertrand model firms set prices. Because each firm acts independently and before it knows how its rivals will act, each firm must choose its output level or price based on how it expects its rivals to behave. In Chapter 13, we examine another well-known oligopoly model, the Stackelberg model, in which one firm is able to act before the others can.

To compare market outcomes under the various oligopoly models, we need to be able to characterize the oligopoly equilibrium. In Chapter 2, we defined an *equilibrium* for the supply-demand model as a situation in which neither firms nor consumers want to change their behavior. John Nash, a Nobel Prize–winning economist and mathematician, defined a related equilibrium concept (Nash, 1951) that has wide applicability to oligopolistic markets and many other situations.

We give a general definition of a Nash equilibrium in Chapter 12. In this chapter we use a special case of a Nash equilibrium that is appropriate for the Cournot model, in which the firm's strategy is the quantity it produces, and for the Bertrand model, in which the firm's strategy is its price. A set of strategies chosen by the oligopolistic firms is a *Nash equilibrium* if, holding the strategies of all other firms constant, no firm can obtain a higher profit by choosing a different strategy. For example, in a Cournot oligopoly, a Nash equilibrium is a set of quantities chosen by the firms such that no firm wants to change its quantity if its rivals' quantities remain constant.

Introduced by the French economist and mathematician Antoine-Augustin Cournot in 1838, the Cournot model is the oldest oligopoly model and is still one of the most widely used models. The simplest version of the Cournot model relies on four assumptions.

1. The market has a small number of firms, and no other firms can enter;

2. the firms set their quantities independently and simultaneously;

3. the firms have identical costs; and

4. the firms sell identical products.

All of these assumptions are relaxed either later in this chapter or in the next two chapters.

Because the firms set quantities, the price adjusts as needed until the market clears in the sense that the amount purchased by consumers equals the amount offered for sale by sellers. Each firm's quantity decision affects the profit of the other firm, because an increase in one firm's quantity drives down market price, reducing the revenues received by the other firm. Thus, the firms' profits are interdependent.

Airlines

To illustrate the basic idea of the Cournot model, we examine a real market in which American Airlines and United Airlines compete for customers on flights between Chicago and Los Angeles.[4] An oligopoly with two firms is referred to as a *duopoly*. The total number of passengers flown by these two firms, Q, is the sum of the number of passengers flown on American, q_A, and those flown on United, q_U.

How many passengers does each airline choose to carry? To answer this question, we determine the Nash equilibrium for this model in which the firms choose quantities. It is called a **Nash-Cournot equilibrium** (or **Cournot-Nash equilibrium** or **Cournot equilibrium**): a set of quantities chosen by the firms such that, holding the quantities of all other firms constant, no firm can obtain a higher profit by choosing a different quantity.

A Graphical Approach. The strategy that each firm uses depends on the demand curve it faces and its marginal cost. American Airlines' profit-maximizing output depends on how many passengers it believes United will fly. Figure 11.2 illustrates two possibilities.

If American were a monopoly, it wouldn't have to worry about United's strategy. American's demand would be the market demand curve, D, in panel a.

FIGURE 11.2 American Airlines' Profit-Maximizing Output

(a) If American is a monopoly, it picks its profit-maximizing output, $q_A = 96$ units (thousand passengers) per quarter, so that its marginal revenue, MR, equals its marginal cost, MC.

(b) If American believes that United will fly $q_U = 64$ units per quarter, its residual demand curve, D^r, is the market demand curve, D, minus q_U. American maximizes its profit at $q_A = 64$, where its marginal revenue, MR^r, equals MC.

---

[4]This example is based on Brander and Zhang (1990). In calculating the airlines' profits, we assume that Brander and Zhang's estimate of the firms' constant marginal cost is the same as the firms' relevant long-run average cost. As Weiher, Sickles, and Perloff (2002) show, duopoly airline routes are common.

The figure illustrates the estimated total demand function for the Chicago–Los Angeles route,

$$Q = 339 - p, \tag{11.1}$$

where price, p, is the dollar cost of a one-way flight, and the total quantity of the two airlines combined, Q, is measured in thousands of passengers flying one way per quarter.

To maximize its profit, American would set its output so that its marginal revenue curve, MR, intersected its marginal cost curve, MC, which is constant at \$147 per passenger. Panel a shows that the monopoly output is 96 units (thousands of passengers) per quarter and the monopoly price is \$243 per passenger (one way).

Because American competes with United, American must consider United's behavior when choosing its profit-maximizing output. American's demand is not the entire market demand. Rather, American is concerned with its *residual demand curve*: the market demand that is not met by other sellers at any given price. In general, if the market demand function is $D(p)$, and the quantity produced by the other firms is Q^o, then the residual demand function, $D^r(p)$, is

$$D^r(p) = D(p) - Q^o.$$

Thus, if United flies q_U passengers regardless of the price, American transports only the residual demand, $Q = D(p)$ minus the q_U passengers, so $q_A = Q - q_U$.

Suppose that American believes that United will fly $q_U = 64$. Panel b shows that American's residual demand curve, D^r, is the market demand curve, D, moved to the left by $q_U = 64$. For example, if the price is \$211, the total number of passengers who want to fly can be determined from market demand Equation 11.1 as $Q = 339 - 211 = 128$. If United transports $q_U = 64$, American flies $Q - q_U = 128 - 64 = 64 = q_A$.

What is American's *best response* (its profit-maximizing output) if its managers believe that United will fly q_U passengers? American can think of itself as having a monopoly with respect to the people who don't fly on United, which its residual demand curve, D^r, shows. To maximize its profit, American sets its output so that its marginal revenue corresponding to this residual demand, MR^r, equals its marginal cost. Panel b shows that if $q_U = 64$, American's best response is $q_A = 64$.

By shifting its residual demand curve appropriately, American can calculate its best response to any given q_U using this type of analysis. Figure 11.3 plots American Airlines' *best-response curve*, which shows how many passengers American flies for each possible q_U.[5] In the figure, the horizontal axis shows American's quantity, q_A, and the vertical axis shows United's quantity, q_U. As the best-response curve shows, American sells the monopoly number of tickets, $q_A = 96$, if American thinks United will fly no passengers, $q_U = 0$. The negative slope of the best-response curve shows that American chooses to sell fewer tickets, the more passengers that it thinks United will fly. American sells $q_A = 64$ if it thinks q_U will be 64. American shuts down, $q_A = 0$, if it thinks q_U will be 192 or more, because operating wouldn't be profitable.

Similarly, United's best-response curve shows how many tickets United sells if it thinks American will sell q_A. For example, United sells $q_U = 0$ if it thinks American will sell $q_A = 192$, $q_U = 48$ if $q_A = 96$, $q_U = 64$ if $q_A = 64$, and $q_U = 96$ if $q_A = 0$.

A firm wants to change its behavior if it is selling a quantity that is not on its best-response curve. The only pair of outputs where both firms are on their best-response curves, $q_A = q_U = 64$, is determined by the intersection of the firms' best-response curves. If American expects United to sell $q_U = 64$, American wants to sell $q_A = 64$.

---

[5]Some economists call the *best-response curve* a *reaction curve*.

FIGURE 11.3 Best-Response Curves for American and United Airlines

The best-response curves show the output each firm picks to maximize its profit, given its belief about its rival's output. The Nash-Cournot equilibrium occurs at the intersection of the best-response curves.

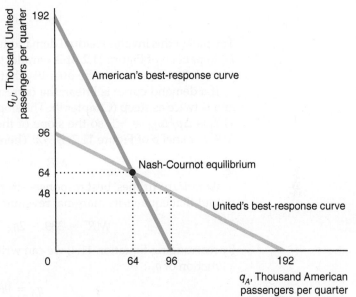

Because this point is on its best-response curve, American doesn't want to change its output from 64. Similarly, if United expects American to sell $q_A = 64$, United doesn't want to change q_U from 64. Thus, this pair of outputs is a Nash-Cournot equilibrium: Given its correct belief about its rival's output, each firm is maximizing its profit, and neither firm wants to change its output because neither firm regrets the choice it has made.

Any pair of outputs other than the pair at an intersection of the best-response functions is *not* a Nash-Cournot equilibrium. If either firm is producing an output level that is not on its best-response curve, it could increase its profit by changing its output. For example, the output pair $q_A = 96$ and $q_U = 0$ is not a Nash-Cournot equilibrium. American is perfectly happy producing the monopoly output if United doesn't operate at all: American is on its best-response curve. However, United would not be happy with this outcome because it is not on United's best-response curve. As its best-response curve shows, if it knows that American will sell $q_A = 96$, United wants to sell $q_U = 48$. Only at $q_A = q_U = 64$ does neither firm want to change its behavior.

An Algebraic Approach. We can also use algebra to solve for the Nash-Cournot equilibrium for these two airlines. We use estimates of the market demand and firms' marginal costs to determine the equilibrium.

Our estimate of the market demand function, Equation 11.1, is $Q = 339 - p$. Panels a and b of Figure 11.2 show that this market demand curve, D, is a straight line that hits the price axis at $339 and the quantity axis at 339 units (thousands of passengers) per quarter. Each airline has a constant marginal cost, MC, and average cost, AC, of $147 per passenger per flight. Using only this information and our economic model, we can find the Nash-Cournot equilibrium for the two airlines.

If American believes that United will fly q_U passengers, American expects to fly only the total market demand minus q_U passengers. At a price of p, the total number of passengers, $Q(p)$, is given by the market demand function, Equation 11.1. Thus, the residual demand American faces is

$$q_A = Q(p) - q_U = (339 - p) - q_U.$$

Using algebra, we can rewrite this residual demand function as the inverse residual demand function:

$$p = 339 - q_A - q_U. \tag{11.2}$$

The plot of this inverse residual demand function is the linear residual demand curve D^r in panel b of Figure 11.2. It is parallel to the market demand, D, and lies 64 units to the left of D, which is the quantity that United sells, $q_U = 64$.

If a demand curve is linear, the corresponding marginal revenue curve is linear and is twice as steep (Chapter 9). The slope of the residual demand curve, Equation 11.2, is $\Delta p / \Delta q_A = -1$, so the slope of the corresponding marginal revenue curve, MR^r in panel b of Figure 11.2, is -2. Therefore, the marginal revenue function is

$$MR^r = 339 - 2q_A - q_U. \tag{11.3}$$

American Airlines' best response—its profit-maximizing output, given q_U—is the output that equates its marginal revenue, Equation 11.3, and its marginal cost:

$$MR^r = 339 - 2q_A - q_U = 147 = MC. \tag{11.4}$$

By rearranging Equation 11.4, we can write American's best-response output, q_A, as a function of q_U:

$$q_A = 96 - \tfrac{1}{2}q_U. \tag{11.5}$$

Figure 11.3 shows American's best-response function, Equation 11.5. According to this best-response function, $q_A = 96$ if $q_U = 0$ and $q_A = 64$ if $q_U = 64$. By the same reasoning, United's best-response function is

$$q_U = 96 - \tfrac{1}{2}q_A. \tag{11.6}$$

A Nash-Cournot equilibrium is a pair of quantities, q_A and q_U, such that Equations 11.5 and 11.6 both hold: Each firm is on its best-response curve. This statement is equivalent to saying that the Nash-Cournot equilibrium is a point at which the best-response curves cross.

One way to determine the Nash-Cournot equilibrium is to substitute Equation 11.6 into Equation 11.5,

$$q_A = 96 - \tfrac{1}{2}(96 - \tfrac{1}{2}q_A), \tag{11.7}$$

and solve Equation 11.7 for q_A. Doing so, we find that $q_A = 64$ is the Nash-Cournot equilibrium quantity for American. Substituting $q_A = 64$ into Equation 11.6, we find that $q_U = 64$ is the Nash-Cournot equilibrium quantity for United. As a result, the total output in the Nash-Cournot equilibrium is $Q = q_A + q_U = 128$. Setting $Q = 128$ in the market demand Equation 11.1, we learn that the Nash-Cournot equilibrium price is $211.

Using Calculus

Deriving
the Cournot
Equilibrium

We derive the Nash-Cournot duopoly equilibrium for a general linear inverse market demand function,

$$p = a - bQ = a - b(q_1 + q_2). \tag{11.8}$$

In the airline example, $a = 339$ and $b = 1$.

Using Equation 11.8, we know that Firm 1's revenue function is $R_1 = pq_1 = (a - b[q_1 + q_2])q_1 = aq_1 - bq_1^2 - bq_2q_1$. Because both firms set their output independently and simultaneously, Firm 1 chooses its output treating Firm 2's output as given. By differentiating the revenue function with respect to q_1 while holding q_2 constant, we obtain Firm 1's marginal revenue function:

$$MR_1 = \partial R_1 / \partial q_1 = a - 2bq_1 - bq_2. \qquad (11.9)$$

We assume that Firm 1 and Firm 2 each face a constant marginal cost, m. In the airline example, $m = \$147$. To determine Firm 1's profit-maximizing output, we set MR_1 equal to m. Solving that expression for q_1, we obtain the best-response function for Firm 1:

$$q_1 = \frac{a - m}{2b} - \frac{q_2}{2}. \qquad (11.10)$$

Equation 11.10 shows how much output Firm 1 produces to maximize its profit given Firm 2's output.

Following the same steps for Firm 2, we obtain its best-response function:

$$q_2 = \frac{a - m}{2b} - \frac{q_1}{2}. \qquad (11.11)$$

The intersection of the two best-response functions, Equations 11.10 and 11.11, determines the market equilibrium, as Figure 11.3 illustrates. We can solve this pair of best-response functions for the equilibrium quantities, q_1 and q_2, by substituting the best-response function for Firm 2 into Firm 1's best-response function:

$$q_1 = \frac{a - m}{2b} - \frac{(a - m)/2b - q_1/2}{2}.$$

Simplifying this equation, we find that Firm 1's equilibrium quantity is

$$q_1 = \frac{a - m}{3b}. \qquad (11.12)$$

Analogously, Firm 2's equilibrium quantity is

$$q_2 = \frac{a - m}{3b}. \qquad (11.13)$$

The market equilibrium quantity is the sum of Equations 11.12 and 11.13:

$$Q = q_1 + q_2 = \frac{2(a - m)}{3b}. \qquad (11.14)$$

By substituting the market quantity, Equation 11.14, into the demand function, Equation 11.8, we learn that the equilibrium price is

$$p = \frac{(a + 2m)}{3}. \qquad (11.15)$$

The Number of Firms

Our airlines example illustrates that if two Cournot firms set output independently, the price to consumers is lower than the monopoly (or cartel) price. The price to consumers is even lower if more than two Cournot firms produce independently.

TABLE 11.1 Nash-Cournot Equilibrium Varies with the Number of Firms

Number of Firms, n	Firm Output, q	Market Output, Q	Price, p	Profit per firm, π ($ thousands)
1 (monopoly)	96	96	243	9,216
2 (duopoly)	64	128	211	4,096
3	48	144	195	2,304
4	38	154	185	1,475
5	32	160	179	1,024
10	18	175	164	305
50	4	188	151	14
100 (nearly competitive)	2	190	149	4

Note: The numbers in this table are rounded.

Table 11.1 illustrates how each firm's output, q, the market quantity, Q, and the price vary with the number of firms in our airlines example.[6] With one firm, the monopoly market price is $243 and $q = Q = 96$ (thousand passengers per quarter). As we've already seen, with two firms, the duopoly price is $211 and market output increases to 128.

As the number of firms grows, the market price approaches the competitive price, $p = MC = \$147$, and the market quantity approaches the competitive quantity, $Q = 192$. As Table 11.1 shows, with 100 firms, the price is only 1.4% above the competitive price and output is only 10% below the competitive quantity. Indeed, even with just 10 firms, the price is only 12% above the competitive level.

Mini-Case

Mobile Phone Number Portability

When mobile phones were introduced in most European countries, a monopoly provided the service. After governments opened their markets to new entrants, customers were slow to switch firms because of large switching costs such as having to obtain a new phone number and get new handsets. Preventing customers from transferring their phone number if they switch carriers makes the demand curve facing a given firm less elastic.

To reduce switching costs and increase competition by new firms, many governments require mobile number portability (MNP), which allows consumers to move their phone number to another mobile phone carrier.[7] Cho, Ferreira, and Telang (2016) estimated that the introduction of MNP in European countries— and the increase in effective competitors—decreased phone service prices by 7.9% and increased consumer surplus by 2.86€ ($3.86) per person per quarter.

---

[6]The generalization of the Cournot duopoly equilibrium quantity, Equation 11.14, for n firms is $Q = n(a - m)/[(n + 1)b]$. The generalization of the duopoly price, Equation 11.15, is $p = (a + nm)/(n + 1)$. The profit calculations in the table assume that the firm has no fixed costs, so average cost is constant at $AC = MC = \$147$.

[7]The United States has required wireless local number portability nationwide since 2003, and Canada has done so since 2007. In 2002, the European Commission mandated that MNP be enacted in each European Community country. At least 78 countries have MNP as of 2018.

Nonidentical Firms

We initially assumed that the firms are identical in the sense that they face the same cost functions and produce identical products. However, costs often vary across firms, and firms often differentiate the products they produce from those of their rivals. We'll now investigate how these differences affect the Nash-Cournot equilibrium output of firms.

Unequal Costs. As we've seen, in the Cournot model, a firm determines its best-response function by equating its marginal revenue to its marginal cost. If one firm's marginal cost rises or falls, then the firm's best-response function shifts. In the new Nash-Cournot equilibrium, the relatively low-cost firm produces more and each higher-cost firm produces less. However, as long as their products are identical, all firms in the market charge the same price.

We can illustrate the effect of unequal costs using our earlier duopoly airlines example. Suppose that American Airlines' marginal cost remains at $147, but United's marginal cost drops to $99. The Cournot model still applies, but we have relaxed the assumption that the firms have identical costs. How does the Nash-Cournot equilibrium change? Your intuition probably tells you that United's output increases relative to that of American. We can show this result in a diagram.

Nothing changes for American, so its best-response function is unchanged. United's best response to any given American output is the output at which its marginal revenue corresponding to its residual demand, MR^r, equals its new, lower marginal cost. Because United's marginal cost curve falls, United wants to produce more than before for any given level of American's output.

Panel a of Figure 11.4 illustrates this reasoning. United's MR^r curve is unaffected, but its marginal cost curve shifts down from MC^1 to MC^2. Suppose we fix American's output at 64 units. Consequently, United's residual demand, D^r, lies 64 units to the left of the market demand, D. United's corresponding MR^r curve intersects its original marginal cost curve, $MC^1 = \$147$, at 64 and its new marginal cost, $MC^2 = \$99$, at 88. Thus, if we hold American's output constant at 64, United produces more as its marginal cost falls.

Because this reasoning applies for any level of output American picks, United's best-response function in panel b shifts outward as its marginal cost falls. United's best response to any given quantity that American sells is to sell more than at its previous, higher cost. As a result, the Nash-Cournot equilibrium shifts from the original e_1, at which both firms sold 64, to e_2, at which United sells 96 and American sells 48.

Using the market demand function, Equation 11.1, we find that the market price falls from $211 to $195, benefiting consumers. United's profit increases from $4.1 million to $9.2 million, while American's profit falls to $2.3 million.[8] Thus, United gains and American loses from the fall in United's marginal cost. As price falls, consumers also benefit from this cost reduction.

---

[8]In the original case with identical costs, each firm's profit per passenger is price minus average cost, $p - AC$, so the firm's profit is $\pi = (p - AC)q$, where q is the number of passengers the firm flies. The price is $211 and the average cost is $147, so the Cournot profit per firm is $\pi = (211 - 147) \times 64$ units per quarter = $4.1 million per quarter in the original symmetric case.

FIGURE 11.4 **Effect of a Drop in One Firm's Marginal Cost on a Nash-Cournot Equilibrium**

(a) United's marginal cost falls from $MC^1 = \$147$ to $MC^2 = \$99$. If American produces $q_a = 64$, United's best response is to increase its output from $q_U = 64$ to 88 given its lower marginal cost. (b) If both airlines' marginal cost is \$147, the Nash-Cournot equilibrium is e_1. After United's marginal cost falls to \$99,

its best-response function shifts outward. It now sells more tickets in response to any given American output than previously. At the new Nash-Cournot equilibrium, e_2, United sells $q_U = 96$, while American sells only $q_A = 48$.

(a) United's Residual Demand

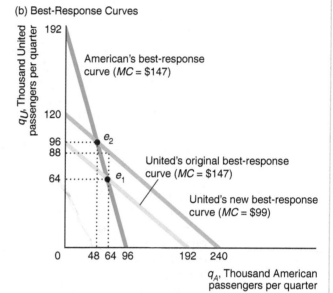

(b) Best-Response Curves

Q&A 11.1

Derive United Airlines' best-response function if its marginal cost falls to \$99 per unit. Given that American's marginal cost does not change, what is the new Nash-Cournot equilibrium?

Answer

1. *Determine United's marginal revenue function corresponding to its residual demand curve.* Luckily, we already know that. The shift in its marginal cost curve does not affect United's residual demand curve; hence its marginal revenue function is the same as before: $MR^r = 339 - 2q_U - q_A$. (This equation for American's marginal revenue is the same as Equation 11.3, with the A and U subscripts reversed.)

2. *Equate United's marginal revenue function and its marginal cost to determine its best-response function.* For a given level of American's output, q_A, United chooses its output, q_U, to equate its marginal revenue and its marginal cost:

$$MR^r = 339 - 2q_U - q_A = 99 = MC.$$

We can use algebra to rearrange this expression for its best-response function to express q_U as a function of q_A:

$$q_U = 120 - \tfrac{1}{2}q_A. \qquad (11.16)$$

This equation corresponds to the darker green best-response curve in panel b of Figure 11.4.

3. *Find the new Nash-Cournot equilibrium pair of quantities by solving the two best-response functions for q_A and q_U.* Because American Airlines' marginal cost is unchanged, its best-response function is the same as in Equation 11.5, $q_A = 96 - \frac{1}{2}q_U$. The intersection of the two best-response functions, Equations 11.16 and 11.5, is that pair of quantities such that both of the best-response functions are true. We can solve for that pair by substituting the expression for q_A from American's best-response function into United's best-response function:

$$q_U = 120 - \tfrac{1}{2}q_A = 120 - \tfrac{1}{2}(96 - \tfrac{1}{2}q_U).$$

Solving, we find that $q_U = 96$. Substituting $q_U = 96$ into either best-response function, we find that $q_A = 48$.

Differentiated Products. By differentiating its product from that of a rival, an oligopolistic firm can shift its demand curve to the right and make it less elastic. The less elastic the demand curve, the more the firm can charge. Loosely speaking, consumers are willing to pay more for a product that they perceive as being superior.

One way to differentiate a product is to give it unique, desirable attributes, such as the Lexus car that was the first to park itself. Many firms differentiate their snack bars to appeal to niche audiences. The Exo protein bar uses flour made from ground crickets, and the Epic Bar has one that is beef liver flavored. Campbell Soup Co. developed slightly more than 100 varieties of soup in its first 90 years, but four times that number in the most recent 30 years.

When Kimberly-Clark introduced a new Huggies disposable diaper with a printed denim pattern, including seams and back pockets, their sales shot up 15%. Alternatively, a firm can differentiate its product by advertising, using colorful labels, and engaging in other promotional activities to convince consumers that its product is superior in some (possibly unspecified) way even if it is virtually identical to its rivals' products physically or chemically. Bayer can charge more for its aspirin, which is chemically identical to other brands, because Bayer has convinced consumers that its product is safer or superior in some other way to its rivals. It is easier to pour from Clorox's bottles than those of its rivals, but the bleach inside is chemically identical to that from rival brands costing much less.

Because differentiation makes demand curves less elastic, price markups over marginal cost are usually higher when products are differentiated than when they're identical. We know that consumer surplus falls as the gap between price and marginal cost rises for a given good. Does it follow that differentiating products lowers total surplus? Not necessarily. Although differentiation leads to higher prices, which harm consumers, differentiation is desirable in its own right. Consumers value having a choice, and some may greatly prefer a new brand to existing ones.

If consumers think products differ, the Cournot quantities and prices may differ across firms. Each firm faces a different inverse demand function and hence charges a different price. For example, suppose that Firm 1's inverse demand function is $p_1 = a - b_1 q_1 - b_2 q_2$, where $b_1 > b_2$ if consumers believe that Good 1 is different from Good 2 and $b_1 = b_2 = b$ if the goods are identical. Given that consumers view the products as differentiated and Firm 2 faces a similar inverse demand function, we replace the single market demand with these individual demand functions in the Cournot model. Q&A 11.2 shows how to solve for the Nash-Cournot equilibrium in an actual market with differentiated products.

Q&A 11.2   Assume that Intel and Advanced Micro Devices (AMD) are the only two firms that produce central processing units (CPUs), which are the brains of personal computers. Both because the products differ physically and because Intel's advertising "Intel Inside" campaign has convinced some consumers of its superiority, consumers view the CPUs as imperfect substitutes.[9] Consequently, the two firms' estimated inverse demand functions differ:

$$p_A = 197 - 15.1q_A - 0.3q_I, \tag{11.17}$$

$$p_I = 490 - 10q_I - 6q_A, \tag{11.18}$$

where price is dollars per CPU, quantity is in millions of CPUs, the subscript I indicates Intel, and the subscript A represents AMD.[10] We assume that each firm faces a constant marginal cost of $40 per unit and has no fixed cost. Solve for the Nash-Cournot equilibrium quantities and prices. Illustrate your answer in a figure.

Answer

1. *Using our rules for determining the marginal revenue for linear demand functions, calculate each firm's marginal revenue function.* For a linear demand curve, we know that the marginal revenue curve is twice as steeply sloped as is the demand curve. Thus, the marginal revenue functions that correspond to the inverse demand Equations 11.17 and 11.18 are:

$$MR^A = 197 - 30.2q_A - 0.3q_I, \tag{11.19}$$

$$MR^I = 490 - 20q_I - 6q_A. \tag{11.20}$$

2. *Equate the marginal revenue functions to the marginal cost to determine the best-response functions.* We determine AMD's best-response function by equating MR^A from Equation 11.19 to its marginal cost of $40,

$$MR^A = 197 - 30.2q_A - 0.3q_I = 40 = MC,$$

and solving for q_A to obtain AMD's best-response function:

$$q_A = \frac{157 - 0.3\,q_I}{30.2}. \tag{11.21}$$

Similarly, Intel's best-response function is

$$q_I = \frac{450 - 6q_A}{20}. \tag{11.22}$$

---

[9]When Intel launched the Intel Inside® marketing and branding campaign, it offered to share costs for any manufacturer's PC print ads if it included the Intel logo. Not only did these funds reduce the computer manufacturers' costs, but also the logo assured consumers that their computers ran on the latest technology. Within six months, 300 computer manufacturers had agreed to support the campaign. After the manufacturers' ads started to appear, Intel advertised globally to explain the significance of the logo to consumers. The Intel Inside campaign was one of the first successful attempts at *ingredient branding*.

[10]We thank Hugo Salgado for estimating these inverse demand functions for us and for providing evidence that this market is well described by a Nash-Cournot equilibrium.

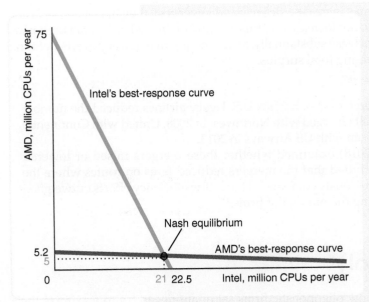

AMD's best-response curve

Intel's best-response curve

Nash equilibrium

AMD, million CPUs per year

Intel, million CPUs per year

3. *Use the best-response functions to solve for the Nash-Cournot equilibrium.* By simultaneously solving the system of best-response functions 11.21 and 11.22, we find that the Nash-Cournot equilibrium quantities are $q_A = 15{,}025/3{,}011 \approx 5$ million CPUs, and $q_I = 63{,}240/3{,}011 \approx 21$ million CPUs. Substituting these values into the inverse demand functions 11.17 and 11.18, we obtain the corresponding prices: $p_A = \$115.20$ and $p_I = \$250$ per CPU.

4. *Use a figure to illustrate the Nash equilibrium.* The figure shows the two firms' best-response curves (Equations 11.21 and 11.22). The Nash equilibrium occurs at their intersection.

Mergers

By merging, two or more firms combine their assets and operations into one firm. Mergers and acquisitions are very common.[11]

Firms typically merge to reduce costs or to increase market power. A merger may provide cost advantages by allowing the new firm to realize increased economies of scale, lowering average cost by operating at a larger scale (Chapter 6). Or, a merger may produce economies of scope (Chapter 6), whereby the new firm achieves a reduction in cost from producing goods jointly rather than separately. Mergers between vertically related firms, such as between a firm and a supplier, may lower cost by allowing for a more efficient organization of the supply chain.

Another important reason for mergers is to reduce competition. If the only two rivals in an industry combine forces through a merger, they become a monopoly and gain market power, which raises the total market profit. Even when only some firms in a market merge, their market power—their ability to set price above marginal cost profitably—may increase.[12] We call mergers between competitors *horizontal mergers*. If such mergers increase market power, raising prices, they harm consumers and lower total welfare.

Because of concerns about concentrating market power, most countries have antitrust or competition laws that subject mergers and acquisitions to legal scrutiny to ensure that competition is not substantially reduced by such combinations (see Chapter 16). These authorities are particularly wary of mergers that create a monopoly. Competition authorities are more likely to approve a merger if the expected market power of the resulting merged firm is small.

---

[11]Many business people use the terms *acquisition* and *merger* interchangeably, because they have no legal distinction. However, some people use the term *acquisition* when a relatively large pre-existing firm (the *acquirer*) buys a smaller firm (the *target*). They use the term *merger* when the combining firms are relatively similar in size or prominence.

[12]Mergers do not always increase market power and profit for the merged firm. In a Cournot oligopoly, if two of three identical firms merge, the merged firms make less profit than does the other firm.

Because mergers may increase efficiency and lower cost, they may increase firms' profits even if they do not increase their market power. Indeed, if cost falls and market power does not increase substantially, then a merger may lower price, benefitting consumers and increasing total surplus.

Mini-Case	In recent years, mergers involving six U.S. legacy airlines reduced the number of firms to three. Delta merged with Northwest in 2008, United with Continental in 2010, and American with US Airways in 2013.
Airline Mergers	Carlton et al. (2018) examined whether these mergers raised or lowered airfares. They concluded that the mergers reduced fares on routes where the merger partners previously competed. That is, the efficiency effects outweighed the effect of reducing the number of firms.

11.3 Bertrand Oligopoly

We have examined how oligopolistic firms set quantities to try to maximize their profits. However, many oligopolistic firms set prices instead of quantities and then allow consumers to decide how much to buy at those prices. The market equilibrium in an oligopoly may be different if firms set prices rather than quantities.

In monopolistic and competitive markets, the issue of whether firms set quantities or prices does not arise. Competitive firms have no choice: They cannot affect price and hence can choose only quantity (Chapter 8). A monopoly can choose either price or quantity, but it cannot set both independently. If it sets one, the other is determined from the demand curve. The monopoly equilibrium is the same whether the monopoly sets price or quantity (Chapter 9).

In 1883, the French mathematician Joseph Bertrand argued that oligopolies often set prices and then consumers decide how many units to buy. The resulting Nash equilibrium is called a **Nash-Bertrand equilibrium** (or **Bertrand-Nash equilibrium** or **Bertrand equilibrium**): a set of prices such that, holding the prices of all other firms constant, no firm can obtain a higher profit by choosing a different price.

Our analysis in this section shows that the price and quantity in a Nash-Bertrand equilibrium are different from those in a Nash-Cournot equilibrium. In addition, the properties of the Nash-Bertrand equilibrium depend on whether firms are producing identical or differentiated products.

Identical Products

We start by examining a price-setting oligopoly in which firms have identical costs and produce identical goods. Because the goods are identical, in any Nash-Bertrand equilibrium, the firms must charge the same price, or no one will buy from the high-price firm. The surprising result of this analysis is that the Nash-Bertrand equilibrium price equals the marginal cost, as in the price-taking equilibrium.

Best-Response Curves. Suppose that each of the two price-setting oligopolistic firms in a market produces an identical product and faces a constant marginal and average cost of $5 per unit. What is Firm 1's best response—what price should it set—if Firm 2 sets a price of $p_2 = \$10$? If Firm 1 charges more than $10, it makes no sales because consumers will buy from Firm 2. Firm 1 makes a profit of $5 on each unit it sells if it also charges $10 per unit. If the market demand is 200 units and both firms charge the same price, we would expect Firm 1 to make half the sales, so its profit is $500.

If Firm 1 slightly undercuts its rival's price by charging $9.99, Firm 1 captures the entire market because the products are identical. Firm 1 makes a profit of $4.99 per unit and a total profit of $998. Thus, Firm 1's profit is higher if it slightly undercuts its rival's price. By similar reasoning, if Firm 2 charges $8, Firm 1 again maximizes its profit by charging slightly less than $8.

Now imagine that Firm 2 charges $p_2 = \$5$. If Firm 1 charges more than $5, it makes no sales. The firms split the market and make zero profit if Firm 1 charges $5. If Firm 1 undercuts its rival, it captures the entire market, but it makes a loss on each unit. Thus, Firm 1 will undercut only if its rival's price is higher than Firm 1's marginal and average cost of $5. By similar reasoning, if Firm 2 charges less than $5, Firm 1 chooses not to produce.

Figure 11.5 shows that Firm 1 will not participate in the market if Firm 2 charges less than $5. Firm 1's best response is $5 if Firm 2 charges $5. If Firm 2 charges prices above $5, Firm 1's best response is to undercut Firm 2's price slightly. Above $5, Firm 1's best-response curve is above the 45° line by the smallest amount possible. (The figure exaggerates the distance of the best-response curve from the 45° line for clarity.) By the same reasoning, Firm 2's best-response curve starts at $5 and lies slightly below the 45° line.

FIGURE 11.5 Nash-Bertrand Equilibrium with Identical Products

With identical products and constant marginal and average costs of $5, Firm 1's best-response curve starts at $5 and then lies slightly above the 45° line. That is, Firm 1 undercuts its rival's price as long as its price remains above $5. The best-response curves intersect at e, the Bertrand or Nash equilibrium, where both firms charge $5.

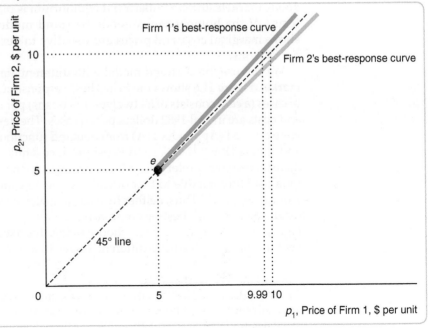

The two best-response curves intersect only at *e*, where each firm charges $5. It does not pay for either firm to change its price as long as the other charges $5, so *e* is a Nash-Bertrand equilibrium. In this equilibrium, each firm makes zero profit. Thus, *the Nash-Bertrand equilibrium when firms produce identical products is the same as the price-taking, competitive equilibrium.*

Bertrand Versus Cournot.   This Nash-Bertrand equilibrium differs substantially from the Nash-Cournot equilibrium. When firms produce identical products and have a constant marginal cost, firms receive positive profits and the price is above marginal cost in the Nash-Cournot equilibrium, whereas firms earn zero profits and price equals marginal cost in the Nash-Bertrand equilibrium.

When firms' products are identical, the Bertrand model seems unrealistic in two major ways. First, we rarely, if ever, observe a market that has only a few firms in which the firms compete so vigorously that they consistently make no profit, as in the Nash-Bertrand equilibrium.

Second, the Nash-Bertrand equilibrium price, which depends only on cost, is insensitive to demand conditions and to the number of firms. In contrast, the Nash-Cournot equilibrium price with a small number of firms lies between the competitive price and the monopoly price and changes as the number of firms or demand conditions change, as is consistent with what we observe. Thus, with identical products, the Cournot model seems more empirically relevant than the Bertrand model. Consequently, economists are much more likely to use the Cournot model than the Bertrand model to study homogeneous goods markets.

Differentiated Products

If firms in most markets produced homogeneous goods, the Bertrand model would probably have been forgotten. However, markets with differentiated goods—automobiles, stereos, computers, toothpastes, and spaghetti sauces—are extremely common, as is price setting by firms in such markets. In differentiated-goods markets, the Nash-Bertrand equilibrium is plausible because the two "problems" of the homogeneous-goods Bertrand model disappear: Firms set prices above marginal cost, and prices are sensitive to demand conditions and the number of firms.

We can use the Bertrand model with differentiated products to analyze the cola market. Figure 11.6 shows the firms' best-response curves. Quantities are in millions of cases (a case consists of 24 twelve-ounce cans) per quarter, and prices (to retailers) and costs are in real 1982 dollars per 10 cases. The best-response curves in the figure were derived (Appendix 11A) from demand functions estimated by Gasmi, Laffont, and Vuong (1992).[13] Coke and Pepsi produce similar but not identical products, so many consumers prefer one of these products to the other. If the price of Pepsi were to fall slightly relative to that of Coke, some consumers who prefer Coke to Pepsi would not switch. Thus, neither firm has to match exactly a price cut by its rival. As a result, neither firm's best-response curve lies along a 45° line through the origin (as in Figure 11.5). Because the firms choose prices, the axes measure prices. The Bertrand best-response curves have different slopes than the Cournot best-response curves

---

[13]Their estimated model allows the firms to set both prices and advertising. We assume that the firms' advertising is held constant. The Coke equations are the authors' estimates (with slight rounding). The Pepsi equation is rescaled so that the equilibrium prices of Coke and Pepsi are equal.

FIGURE 11.6 Nash-Bertrand Equilibrium with Differentiated Products

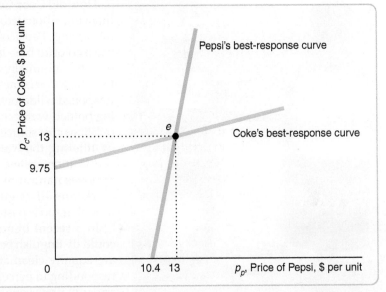

Both Coke and Pepsi, which set prices, have upward-sloping best-response curves. These best-response curves of Coke and Pepsi intersect at e, the Nash-Bertrand equilibrium, where each sets a price of $13 per unit.

in Figure 11.3. The Cournot curves—which plot relationships between quantities—slope downward, showing that a firm produces less the more its rival produces.

The Nash-Bertrand equilibrium, *e* in Figure 11.6, occurs where each firm's price is $13 per unit. In this Nash equilibrium, each firm sets its best-response price *given the price the other firm is charging*. Neither firm wants to change its price because neither firm can increase its profit by so doing.

Bertrand firms may earn positive profits in equilibrium if they differentiate their products. They cannot earn positive profits in equilibrium if they produce identical products. Should a Bertrand firm differentiate its product? Differentiating a product is costly—consider the extensive marketing campaigns Dasani and Aquafina used to convince consumers that their brands differ from other bottled water brands. However, if the alternative is earning zero profit in a Bertrand homogeneous-good equilibrium, it is worth the cost. In contrast, Cournot firms can be profitable even when producing identical products. Thus, Bertrand firms have a stronger incentive to invest in product differentiation than do Cournot firms.[14]

Managerial Implication

Differentiating a Product Through Marketing

A manager can often increase a firm's profit by differentiating its product so that it can charge a higher price. A skillful manager may find it easier and less expensive to differentiate a product using marketing rather than by physically differentiating the product.

One product that is difficult to differentiate is water. Capehart and Berg (2018) found that in a blind taste test, consumers cannot distinguish bottled waters or tap water. Water can be carbonated or flavored, but doing so caters to only a subset of the $16 billion U.S. bottled water market, which grew rapidly from 2010 through 2018.

---

[14]See Brander and Spencer (2015).

How did Coca-Cola and Pepsico's managers differentiate their uncarbonated, unflavored water? Primarily through marketing. Pepsico's top-selling bottled water, Aquafina, has a colorful blue label and a logo showing the sun rising over the mountains. From that logo, consumers may infer that the water comes from some bubbling spring high in an unspoiled wilderness. If so, they're wrong. Pepsi's best-selling bottled water comes from the same place as tap water: public-water sources. Pepsi also claims that it adds value by filtering the water using a state-of-the-art "HydRO-7 purification system," implying that such filtering (which removes natural minerals) is desirable. Similarly, Coke's marketing distinguishes its Dasani bottled water, even though it too is basically bottled public water.

In a recent blind taste test reported in *Slate*, no one could distinguish between Aquafina and Dasani, and both are equally clean and safe. However, many consumers, responding to perceived differences created by marketing, strongly prefer one or the other of these brands and pay a premium for these products.

Having succeeded in differentiating water, Coca-Cola turned to milk. It now sells Fairlife "super milk." Coca-Cola claims that with its special filtration process, Fairlife retains more "natural" protein and calcium and has less sugar. Sandy Douglas, President of Coca-Cola North America, said, "It's basically the premiumization of milk. . . . We'll charge twice as much for it as the milk we're used to buying in a jug."

Mini-Case

Rising Market Power

Cournot, Bertrand, and other oligopoly models predict that price exceeds marginal cost. How large are these markups?

Hall (2018) examined U.S. firms' markups, which he defined as the ratio of price to marginal cost, across all sectors of the economy. He found that the markup ratio grew from 1.12 in 1988 to 1.38 in 2015. The growth rate was particularly fast in the finance and insurance and the utilities sectors.

De Loecker and Eeckhout (2018) examined the same markup for 70,000 firms in 134 countries. They estimated that the average global markup increased from about 1.1 in 1980 to around 1.6 in 2016. The markup increased the most in North America and Europe and the least in Latin America and Asia.

11.4 Monopolistic Competition

We now turn to monopolistic competition, which is a market structure that has the price-setting characteristics of monopoly or oligopoly and the free-entry characteristic of perfect competition. Monopolistically competitive firms have market power because they face downward-sloping demand curves, as do oligopolistic firms, but the firms earn zero long-run economic profit due to free entry, as do perfectly competitive firms.

We have seen that each oligopolistic firm may earn an economic profit because the number of firms is limited due to entry barriers. What would happen without a barrier to entry? Firms seeking profits would enter the market until the last firm to enter earns zero long-run economic profit. The resulting market structure may be either perfectly competitive or monopolistically competitive. In both perfect competition and monopolistic competition, firms earn zero profits. The key difference is that each perfectly competitive firm faces a horizontal residual demand curve and charges a price equal to marginal cost, whereas each monopolistically competitive firm faces a downward-sloping demand curve and can charge a price above marginal cost without losing all of its customers.

Monopolistically competitive firms face downward-sloping demand curves because the market is small or because the firms differentiate their products. Even if the firms produce identical products, if the market demand curve is close to the origin, the market may be able to support only a few firms, so the residual demand curve facing a single firm is downward sloping. For example, in a small town the market may be large enough to support only a few plumbing firms, each of which provides a similar service.

If firms differentiate their products, each firm can retain those customers who particularly like that firm's product even if its price is higher than those of its rivals. Gourmet food trucks serve differentiated food in monopolistically competitive markets. Nouveau food trucks like Chairman Bao, Curry Up Now, and Liba Falafel sell high-quality lunches in San Francisco's blighted mid-Market area, which has few traditional, high-quality lunch restaurants. Because some customers prefer Chinese food to Indian food, Chairman Bao could raise its price without losing all its customers to Curry Up Now. Consequently, each of these trucks faces a downward-sloping demand curve.

Managerial Implication

Managing in the Monopolistically Competitive Food Truck Market

Young entrepreneurs who want to own their own businesses should consider monopolistically competitive markets, as entry costs are often low and a cleverly differentiated product can often succeed. One of the hottest food phenomena in the United States is gourmet food trucks, which started in major West Coast cities such as Los Angeles, Portland, and Seattle. Now, flocks of food trucks ply their business in previously underserved areas of cities across the country. The mobile restaurant business has been exploding. As William Bender, a food service consultant in Santa Clara, California, said, "The limited menu approach, high quality, and low operating costs have opened up an entirely new sector."

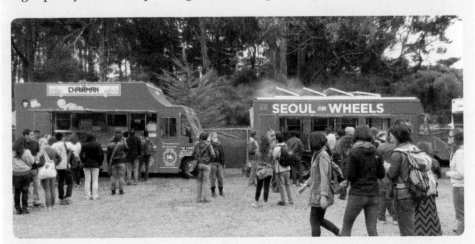

Even top restaurant chefs have entered this business. Celebrity Los Angeles chef Ludovic Lefebvre created LudoTruck, a mobile fried chicken outlet. San Francisco's Chez Spencer has a "French takeaway," Spencer on the Go, that serves bistro food such as foie gras torchon and toast for $12.

The cost of entry is very low, ranging from $50,000 to lease the equipment and pay ancillary expenses, to $250,000 or more for a deluxe truck and top-of-the-line cooking and refrigeration facilities. Potential entrants can learn about the business at **mobilefoodnews.com**, which reports on local laws, where to buy equipment and obtain insurance, and a host of other topics.

Opening a new restaurant is very risky. If demand is less than anticipated, the firm loses its (large) fixed cost. However, if the manager of a food truck makes a bad first guess about where to locate, it is easy to drive to another neighborhood.

How do firms identify profit opportunities? "Lunch is our consistent bread-and-butter market," said Matthew Cohen, proprietor of Off the Grid, a food truck promoter and location finder in the San Francisco Bay Area. When lines in front of his trucks grow longer at lunch time, he sets up additional trucks. Having started with about a dozen trucks in June 2010, Cohen now has over 200.

Rather than drive around the city searching for customers, managers should use internet sites and social media to attract customers to their locations. Fans can find the location of trucks in cities around the country at **Mobimunch.com**. In 2018, Off the Grid had more than 38,400 followers on Twitter and more than 118,000 likes on Facebook. According to Cohen, "It's our primary means of marketing. It tells customers where trucks are going to be and when. You can't underestimate what social media has done for the business." He usually charges his clients a base fee of $55 and 10% of event sales revenue for his help in successfully locating and attracting customers.

Equilibrium

To examine the monopolistically competitive equilibrium, we initially assume that firms have identical cost functions and produce identical products. Two conditions hold in a long-run monopolistically competitive equilibrium: *marginal revenue equals marginal cost* because firms set output to maximize profit, and *price equals average cost*—that is, profit is zero—because firms enter until no further profitable entry is possible.

Figure 11.7 shows a long-run monopolistically competitive market equilibrium for a representative firm, which faces firm-specific demand curve D. To maximize its profit, the firm sets its output, q, where its marginal revenue curve corresponding to D intersects its marginal cost curve: $MR = MC$. At that quantity, the firm's average cost curve, AC, is tangent to its demand curve. Because the height of the demand curve is the price, at the tangency point price equals average cost, $p = AC$, and the firm makes zero profit.

Why do we know that $p = AC$ in the monopolistically competitive equilibrium? The entry and exit responses of firms ensure this result. If the average cost is less than price at the quantity where $MR = MC$, firms in the market make positive profits and new firms enter. If average cost is above price, firms lose money, and firms exit until the marginal firm breaks even, which occurs where $p = AC$.

In most cities, fast-food restaurants are an example of such a monopolistically competitive industry. These restaurants differentiate their food, so each may face a downward-sloping demand curve. However, restaurants can easily enter and exit

FIGURE 11.7 Monopolistic Competition

A monopolistically competitive firm, facing the firm-specific demand curve D, sets its output where its marginal revenue equals its marginal cost: $MR = MC$. Entry by other identical firms drives the profit of each firm to zero, so the price equals the firm's average cost: $p = AC$.

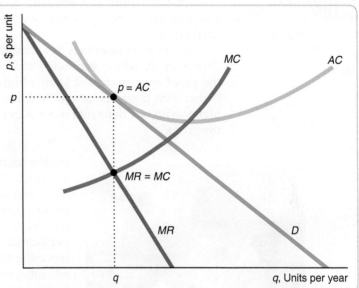

the market, so the marginal firm earns zero economic profit. As you've probably observed, most restaurants have empty seats much of the time and hence are operating below full capacity. Q&A 11.3 provides an explanation for this phenomenon.

Q&A 11.3

Show that a monopolistically competitive firm maximizes its profit where it is operating at less than *full capacity* or *minimum efficient scale*, which is the smallest quantity at which the average cost curve reaches its minimum (the bottom of a U-shaped average cost curve). The firm's minimum efficient scale is the quantity at which the firm no longer benefits from economies of scale.

Answer

Use the properties of the demand curve to show that a monopolistically competitive firm operates in the increasing-returns to scale section of its average cost curve (the downward-sloping section) in the long-run equilibrium. In the long-run equilibrium, a monopolistically competitive firm operates where its downward-sloping demand curve is tangent to its average cost curve, as Figure 11.7 illustrates. Because its demand curve is downward sloping, its average cost curve must also be downward sloping in the equilibrium, where the two curves are tangent. Thus, the firm chooses to operate at less than full capacity in equilibrium.

Profitable Monopolistically Competitive Firms

If all firms in a monopolistically competitive market produce identical products and have identical costs, then each firm earns zero economic profit in the long run. Thus, all firms in the industry are on the margin of exiting the market because even a slight decline in profitability would generate losses. However, it is possible—indeed, likely—that monopolistically competitive firms differ from each other in their profitability because they have different cost functions or because they produce differentiated products. If so, low-cost firms or firms with superior products may earn positive economic profits in the long run.

Markets for dentists are normally monopolistically competitive. Dentists provide similar services. As the number of dentists in a local market increases, dentists' profits fall.

In areas with relatively few dentists, the price for their services is high. Dunne et al. (2013) estimated that relative to an area with five dentists, the profit of each dentist is 10% higher in a market with four dentists, 36% higher with three dentists, 47% higher with two dentists (a duopoly), and 69% higher with one dentist (a monopoly). Thus, the fewer the dentists, the higher the profit.

The U.S. Health Resource and Services Administration identifies underserved areas, called Health Professional Shortage Areas (HPSAs). The government subsidizes the entry costs of primary care physicians, dentists, and mental health professionals in HPSAs. Subsidies range from $30,000 to $200,000 per dentist, depending on how long they commit to serve the HPSA. A typical subsidy is $60,000 for a full-time, two-year commitment.

To enter a market, a dentist incurs fixed costs for equipment and office construction. An entrant must construct a new office that has multiple treatment rooms with specialized electrical, plumbing, and X-ray equipment. The study estimates that on average, the mean entry cost is 11% lower in these subsidized markets, which leads to an average of one-half an additional dentist per market.

If only Boeing or Airbus receives a government subsidy, how should its managers use the subsidy to gain a competitive advantage? What effect does that subsidy have on prices and quantities? What happens if both firms receive subsidies? Do Boeing and Airbus managers benefit from lobbying for government subsidies if that results in a subsidy war?

To keep our answers to these questions as simple as possible, we assume that Airbus and Boeing compete in a Cournot model in which they produce identical products with identical costs and they face a linear demand curve.[15] A government per-unit subsidy to only one firm would cause its marginal cost to be lower than its rival's.

To maximize profit, a firm in a Cournot market should respond by increasing its output for any expected output level by its rival. That is, its best-response curve shifts out. In panel a of Figure 11.4, we saw how the equilibrium changes if United Airline's marginal cost falls while American's remains the same. As its marginal cost drops, United wants to produce more for any given output of its rival, so that its best-response function shifts out, away from the origin in panel b.

---

[15]We would reach the same qualitative conclusions were we to use a Cournot or Bertrand model with differentiated products.

The market equilibrium shifts from e_1 to e_2 in panel b, so that United's Nash-Cournot equilibrium output increases and American's falls. Because total output rises, the equilibrium price falls. United benefits at the expense of American. Indeed, United's profit rises by \$5.1 million, which exceeds the actual cost saving of \$4.6 million. That is, United's managers used the cost savings to gain a competitive advantage.

The same analysis applies to the aircraft market. If Airbus is subsidized and Boeing is not, Airbus should produce more given any expected output from Boeing. Its equilibrium quantity and profit rise, while Boeing's quantity and profit fall. The gain in profit to Airbus exceeds the subsidy from the government.

Now suppose that both firms receive subsidies. The figure here shows an initial Nash-Cournot equilibrium, e_1, where both firms produce q_1 units of output. If both governments give identical subsidies that lower the marginal costs of both firms, then both firms' best-response functions shift out. In the new, subsidized equilibrium, e_2, both firms produce $q_2 > q_1$ units of output, so total equilibrium output increases, which causes the equilibrium price to fall.

The market equilibrium moves further away from the maximum profit (monopoly) equilibrium toward the competitive price and quantity. Therefore, the subsidies lead to lower profits (excluding the subsidies), though the firms benefit from the subsidies directly. Each government is essentially subsidizing final consumers in other countries without giving its own firm a strategic advantage over its rival. Thus, both governments lose. It would be in both countries' best interests not to engage in a subsidy war.

Indeed, in 1992, the various involved governments signed a U.S.–EU agreement on trade in civil aircraft that limited government subsidies, including a maximum direct subsidy limit of 33% of development costs and various limits on variable costs.[16]

Does it follow that the managers at these firms should stop lobbying for subsidies? No. These firms still benefit from subsidies. Moreover, either firm would be at a competitive disadvantage if its rival received a subsidy and it did not.

---

[16]Irwin and Pavcnik (2004) found that aircraft prices increased by about 3.7% after the 1992 agreement. This price hike is consistent with a 5% increase in firms' marginal costs after the subsidy cuts.

SUMMARY

1. **Cartels.** If firms successfully collude, they can seek to produce the monopoly output and collectively earn the monopoly level of profit. Although their collective profits rise if all firms collude, each individual firm has an incentive to cheat on the cartel arrangement so as to raise its own profit even higher. For cartel prices to remain high, cartel members must be able to detect and prevent cheating, and noncartel firms must not be able to supply very much output. When antitrust laws or competition policies prevent firms from colluding, firms may try to merge.

2. **Cournot Oligopoly.** If oligopolistic firms act independently, market output and firms' profits lie between the competitive and monopoly levels. In a Cournot model, each oligopolistic firm sets its output at the same time. In the Nash-Cournot equilibrium, each firm produces its best-response output—the output that maximizes its profit—given the output its rival produces. As the number of Cournot firms increases, the Nash-Cournot equilibrium price, quantity, and profits approach the price-taking (perfectly competitive) levels.

3. **Bertrand Oligopoly.** In many oligopolies, firms set prices instead of quantities. If the product is homogeneous and firms set prices, the Nash-Bertrand equilibrium price equals marginal cost and is therefore lower than the Nash-Cournot equilibrium price. With differentiated products, the Nash-Bertrand equilibrium price is above marginal cost, and the more differentiated the goods, the larger are the firms' markups of price over marginal cost.

4. **Monopolistic Competition.** In monopolistic competition, free entry drives profits to zero for the marginal firm. If firms have identical costs and produce a homogeneous good, all firms earn zero profits. However, even with free entry, firms face downward-sloping demand curves and are therefore able to charge prices that exceed marginal cost. One important reason why demand curves slope downward is that firms may sell differentiated products. However, it is possible that even with homogeneous products the number of firms is small enough that firms face downward-sloping firm-specific demand curves.

QUESTIONS

All exercises are available on **MyLab Economics**; * = *answer at the back of this book;* C = *use of calculus may be necessary;* ✖ = *this exercise is available in Excel Grader in* **MyLab Economics**.

1. Cartels

1.1 In most "normal" years (years in which the market has not been disrupted by Middle East wars), at each Organization of Petroleum Exporting Countries (OPEC) meeting, Saudi Arabia, the largest oil producer, argues that the cartel should cut production. The Saudis complain that most OPEC countries (including Saudi Arabia) produce more oil than they are allotted under their cartel agreement. Use a graph and words to explain why cartel members would produce more than the allotted amount despite their understanding that overproduction will drive down the price of their product.

1.2 Many retail stores offer to match or beat the price offered by a rival store. Explain why firms that belong to a cartel might make this offer.

1.3 What are the main factors that increase the likelihood of a cartel being successful?

*1.4 A market has an inverse demand function $p = 100 - 2Q$ and four firms, each of which has a constant marginal cost of $MC = 20$. If the firms form a profit-maximizing cartel and agree to operate subject to the constraint that each firm will produce the same output level, how much does each firm produce?

1.5 In 2013 and 2014, a federal judge ruled that Apple colluded with five major U.S. publishers to drive up the prices of e-books (which could be read on Apple's iPad). Apple collects a 30% commission on the price of a book from the publisher. Why would Apple want to help publishers raise their price? Given Apple's commission, what price would a book cartel want to set? (*Hint*: The marginal cost of an e-book is virtually zero.)

1.6 Most discussion of cartels addresses seller or producer cartels. Is it possible for *buyers* to gain an advantage by acting as a cartel? Explain, using at least two examples. (*Hint:* See the Mini-Case "Employer 'No-Poaching' Cartels.")

1.7 Based on the Mini-Case "Cheating on the Maple Syrup Cartel," what methods does the cartel use to discourage cheating? Using a graph similar to Figure 11.1 explain why some maple syrup producers cheat on the cartel despite efforts to prevent such actions.

2. Cournot Oligopoly

2.1 According to Robert Guy Matthews, "Fixed Costs Chafe at Steel Mills," *Wall Street Journal*, June 10, 2009, stainless steel manufacturers increased prices even though the market demand curve had shifted to the left. In a letter to its customers, one of these companies announced that "Unlike mill increases announced in recent years, this is obviously not driven by increasing global demand, but rather by fixed costs being proportioned across significantly lower demand." If the firms are oligopolistic, produce a homogeneous good, face a linear market demand curve and have linear costs, and the market outcome is a Nash-Cournot equilibrium, does the firm's explanation as to why the market equilibrium price is rising make sense? What is a better explanation?

*2.2 What is the homogeneous-good duopoly's Nash-Cournot equilibrium if the market demand function is $Q = 1{,}000 - 1{,}000p$ and each firm's marginal cost is $0.28 per unit? (*Hint*: Start by determining the inverse market demand function.)

2.3 Duopoly quantity-setting firms face the inverse market demand function $p = 150 - q_1 - q_2$. Each firm has a marginal cost of $60 per unit. What is the Nash-Cournot equilibrium?

*2.4 Your college is considering renting space in the student union to one or two commercial textbook stores. The rent the college can charge per square foot of space depends on the firms' profit (excluding rent) and hence on whether the market has a monopoly or a Cournot duopoly. Which number of stores is better for the college in terms of rent? Which is better for students? Why?

2.5 The state of Connecticut sets a maximum fee that bail-bond businesses can charge for posting a given-size bond (Ayres and Waldfogel, 1994). The bail-bond fee is set at virtually the maximum amount allowed by law in cities with only one active firm (Plainville, 99% of the maximum; Stamford, 99%; and Wallingford, 99%). The price is as high in cities with a duopoly (Ansonia, 99.6%; Meriden, 98%; and New London, 98%). In cities with 3 or more firms, however, the price falls well below the maximum permitted price. The fees are only 54% of the maximum in Norwalk with 3 firms, 64% in New Haven with 8 firms, and 78% in Bridgeport with 10 firms. Give possible explanations based on the Cournot model for this pattern.

2.6 In 2018, Chinese authorities announced continued efforts to reduce capacity in the cement industry, often forcing producers to close plants.[17] As cement is costly to transport and has significant economies of scale in production, each urban area is a distinct oligopolistic market. If the Cournot model applies, what effect will a reduction in the number of producers have on cement prices? Would the effect be more significant in smaller or larger cities?

2.7 In 2015, Spirit Airlines reported that its "average cost per available seat mile excluding special items and fuel" was 5.7¢ compared to 8.5¢ for Southwest. Assuming that Spirit and Southwest compete on a single route, use a graph to show that their equilibrium quantities differ. (*Hint*: See Q&A 11.1 and Figure 11.4.)

2.8 In a homogeneous-good Cournot duopoly where both firms have a constant marginal cost m and the inverse market demand function is $p = a - bQ$, the Nash-Cournot equilibrium output of a typical firm is $q = (a - m)/3b$ and the price is $p = (a + 2m)/3$. ("Using Calculus: Deriving the Cournot Equilibrium") What is the corresponding equilibrium profit for each firm?

2.9 How does the Nash-Cournot equilibrium change in the airline example if United Airlines' marginal cost is $100 and American's is $200? (*Hint*: See Q&A 11.1.)

2.10 A homogeneous-good duopoly faces an inverse market demand function of $p = 120 - Q$. Firm 1 has a constant marginal cost of $MC^1 = 20$. Firm 2's constant marginal cost is $MC^2 = 30$. Calculate the output of each firm, market output, and price for (a) a Nash-Cournot equilibrium and (b) a collusive equilibrium at the monopoly price.

2.11 In 2018, Delta Air Lines said that it was increasing its fares by 4% because its fuel bill jumped by 33% from the previous year. Other airlines also announced fare increases. Assuming that these firms are oligopolistic and the outcome is a Nash-Cournot equilibrium, why did the prices rise less than in proportion to the firms' cost?

*2.12 Why does differentiating its product allow an oligopoly firm to charge a higher price?

2.13 Firms 1 and 2 produce differentiated goods. Firm 1's inverse demand function is $p_1 = 260 - 2q_1 - q_2$, while Firm 2's inverse demand function is $p_2 = 260 - 2q_2 - q_1$. Each firm has a constant marginal cost of 20. What is the Nash-Cournot equilibrium in this market? (*Hint*: See Q&A 11.2.)

*2.14 If the firms in a Cournot duopoly merge forming a monopoly, the effect on price, profit, and other variables depends on the trade-off between efficiency and market power. The firms produce identical products. Firm 1 has a constant marginal cost of 1, and Firm 2 has a constant marginal cost of 2. The inverse market demand function is $p = 15 - Q$.

   a. Solve for the Nash-Cournot equilibrium price, quantities, profits, consumer surplus, and deadweight loss.

---

b. If the firms merge and produce at the lower marginal cost of 1, how do the equilibrium values change?

c. Discuss the change in efficiency (average cost of producing the output) and total surplus—consumer surplus, producer surplus (or profit), and deadweight loss.

3. Bertrand Oligopoly

3.1 If firms produce identical products and have the same constant marginal cost, explain why the Nash-Bertrand equilibrium price and market quantity are the same regardless of the number of firms.

*3.2 Will price be lower if duopoly firms set price or if they set quantity? Under what conditions can you give a definitive answer to this question?

3.3 In an initial Nash-Bertrand equilibrium, two firms with differentiated products charge the same equilibrium prices. A consumer-testing agency praises the product of one firm, causing its demand curve to shift to the right as new customers start buying the product. (The demand curve of the other product is not substantially affected.) Use a graph to illustrate how this new information affects the Nash-Bertrand equilibrium. What happens to the equilibrium prices of the two firms?

*3.4 Suppose that identical duopoly firms have constant marginal costs of $10 per unit. Firm 1 faces a demand function of $q_1 = 100 - 2p_1 + p_2$, where q_1 is Firm 1's output, p_1 is Firm 1's price, and p_2 is Firm 2's price. Similarly, the demand function Firm 2 faces is $q_2 = 100 - 2p_2 + p_1$. Solve for the Nash-Bertrand equilibrium. (*Hint:* See Appendix 11A.) **C**

3.5 Solve for the Nash-Bertrand equilibrium for the firms described in Question 3.4 if Firm 1's marginal cost is $30 per unit and Firm 2's marginal cost is $10 per unit. **C**

3.6 Water taken from the public water supply and put in bottles would seem to be a homogeneous good. Yet Coke and Pepsi have spent large amounts on advertising to convince consumers that their bottled water products, Dasani and Aquafina, are highly distinctive. Why would these firms undertake such expenditures if the bottled water market is a Bertrand market?

3.7 All the firms in a competitive industry have the same constant marginal cost. All the firms merge into a single firm.

a. If the merged firm's marginal cost does not change, what happens to total surplus? (*Hint:* You may be able to answer this question without having to use a formal analysis.)

b. Use a graph to show that if the merged firm's marginal cost falls, total surplus may rise.

3.8 In 2013, the U.S. Federal Trade Commission (FTC) allowed the number two and number three office supply companies, OfficeMax Inc. and Office Depot, to merge. Office Depot's market value was $1.3 billion and OfficeMax's was $933 million. Reportedly, the efficiency gains from merging would save the new company between $400 and $500 million. However, in 2015, the FTC opposed a proposed merger valued at $6.3 billion between Office Depot and Staples, the largest office supply company, ultimately causing the merger attempt to be abandoned. Why might the FTC permit the earlier merger attempt but not the Staples–Office Depot merger?

4. Monopolistic Competition

4.1 In a monopolistically competitive market, the government applies a specific tax of $1 per unit of output. What happens to the profit of a typical firm in this market? Does the number of firms in the market rise or fall? Why?

*4.2 What is the effect on prices and the number of firms under monopolistic competition if a government provides a subsidy that reduces the fixed cost of each firm in the industry?

4.3 Q&A 11.3 shows that a monopolistically competitive firm maximizes its profit where it is operating at less than full capacity. Does this result depend upon whether firms produce identical or differentiated products? Why?

4.4 Under monopolistic competition with identical firms, is it possible for a firm to produce at the minimum of its average cost curve?

4.5 One of the hottest trends in 2018 was rental scooters. San Francisco capped the number of scooter companies at six. Thus, a market that was going to be monopolistically competitive became, at least in the short run, an oligopoly. What effects does such a barrier to entry create on equilibrium market quantity, price, profits, consumer surplus, and total surplus?

5. Managerial Problem

*5.1 An incumbent firm, Firm 1, faces a potential entrant, Firm 2, that has a lower marginal cost. The market inverse demand function is $p = 120 - q_1 - q_2$. Firm 1 has a constant marginal cost of $20, while Firm 2's is $10, and they have no fixed costs.

a. What are the Nash-Cournot equilibrium price, quantities, and profits without government intervention?

b. To block entry, the incumbent appeals to the government to require that the entrant incur extra costs. What happens to the Nash-Cournot equilibrium if the legal requirement causes the marginal cost of the second firm to rise to that of the first firm, $20?

5.2 Given the demand and cost conditions of Question 5.1, suppose that the legal intervention imposed by the government leaves the marginal cost unchanged but imposes a fixed cost. What is the minimal fixed cost that will prevent entry?

6. MyLab Economics Spreadsheet Exercises[18]

6.1 The inverse market demand curve for a duopoly market is $p = 14 - Q = 14 - q_1 - q_2$, where Q is the market output, and q_1 and q_2 are the outputs of Firms 1 and 2, respectively. Each firm has a constant marginal cost of 2 and a fixed cost of 4. Consequently, the Nash-Cournot best-response curve for Firm 1 is $q_1 = 6 - q_2/2$.

a. Create a spreadsheet with columns titled q_2, BR_1, Q, p, and $Profit_1$. In the first column, list possible quantities for Firm 2, q_2, ranging from 0 to 12 in increments of 2. The column headed BR_1 shows the profit-maximizing output (best response) for Firm 1 given Firm 2's output in the first column. The Q column sums the values in the q_2 and BR_1 columns. The p column lists the price that corresponds to Q. The $Profit_1$ column shows the profit of Firm 1, taking account of its marginal and fixed costs. After filling in the spreadsheet, use the scatterplot option in Excel to draw the best-response curve for Firm 1.

b. What is the monopoly output and profit for Firm 1? (That is, how much does Firm 1 produce if Firm 2 does not produce?) If Firm 1 expects Firm 2 to produce 10 units of output, would it operate in the long run (given that it can avoid incurring its fixed costs by shutting down)? Will it operate in the short run (when its fixed cost cannot be avoided)?

6.2 Use the data from Exercise 6.1. The best-response curve for Firm 2 is $q_2 = 6 - q_1/2$, which can be written as $q_1 = 12 - 2q_2$.

a. Create a spreadsheet with columns denoted BR_2, q_1, Q, p, and $Profit_2$. Set the output of Firm 1 in the second column from 0 to 6 in increments of one unit. Fill in the spreadsheet and use the

scatterplot option to draw the best-response curve for Firm 2.

b. Create a new spreadsheet showing the best-response curves for Firm 1 and Firm 2 on the same diagram, with q_2 on the horizontal axis and q_1 on the vertical axis. What is the Nash-Cournot equilibrium price, quantity (for each firm), and profit (for each firm)?

6.3 Assume that the cola market is a Bertrand oligopoly and that Coke's estimated demand function (based on Gasmi, Laffont, and Vuong, 1992) is $q_c = 58 - 4p_c + 2p_p$, where q_c is the number of cases of Coke, p_c is Coke's price per case, and p_p is Pepsi's price per case. The average and marginal cost of producing a case of Coke or Pepsi is 5.

a. Create a spreadsheet with column A denoted *Pepsi Price*, and with Coke's price, quantity, revenue, cost, and profit in the following columns. Enter the values 10 to 15 in increments of 1 in the Pepsi price column. Leave the *Coke Price* column blank. Enter the formulas for Coke's quantity, revenue, cost, and profit functions. Because the *Coke Price* column is blank, the revenue and profit columns initially show what happens if the Coke price is zero – zero revenue and large losses. Use Excel's *Solver* tool to determine Coke's best price response (the one that maximizes its profit) for each Pepsi price in column A. *Solver* generates a dialog box in which you should select *Keep Solver Solution*, then click on *OK*. *Solver* enters the profit-maximizing Coke price in the *Coke Price* column. You must apply *Solver* in each row of the spreadsheet. (*Hint*: See the instructions for using *Solver* in Question 6.2 of Chapter 8 or use Excel's *Help* feature.)

b. Use the Excel Scatterplot feature to illustrate Coke's best responses to each Pepsi price. Use the Trendline option to determine the equation of Coke's best-response function. (*Hint*: The Trendline option will report the equation if you select *Display Equation on chart* in the Trendline dialog.)

c. Pepsi's demand function is $q_p = 63.2 - 4p_p + 1.6p_c$. Create a new spreadsheet to determine Pepsi's best price response to Coke prices that range from 10 to 15 in increments of 1. Verify that each firm charging a price of 13 is a Nash-Bertrand equilibrium.

[18]The spreadsheet exercises in this chapter are based on the work of Satyajit Ghosh in cooperation with the authors. The answers are available on MyLab Economics.

APPENDIX 11A   Nash-Bertrand Equilibrium

We use math to determine the cola market Nash-Bertrand equilibrium discussed in the text. First, we determine the best-response functions each firm faces. Then, we equate the best-response functions to determine the equilibrium prices for the two firms.

Coke's best-response function tells us which price Coke sets to maximize its profit as a function of the price Pepsi charges. We use the demand function for Coke to derive its best-response function.

The reason Coke's price depends on Pepsi's price is that the quantity of Coke demanded, q_c, depends on the price of Coke, p_c, and the price of Pepsi, p_p. Coke's demand function is

$$q_c = 58 - 4p_c + 2p_p. \tag{11A.1}$$

Partially differentiating Equation 11A.1 with respect to p_c (that is, holding the price of Pepsi fixed), we find that the change in quantity for every dollar change in price is $\partial q_c / \partial p_c = -4$, so an increase of 1 in the price of Coke causes the quantity of Coke demanded to fall by 4 units. Similarly, the demand for Coke rises by 2 units if the price of Pepsi rises by 1 while the price of Coke remains constant: $\partial q_c / \partial p_p = 2$.

If Coke faces a constant marginal and average cost of 5 per unit, its profit is

$$\pi_c = (p_c - 5)q_c = (p_c - 5)(58 - 4p_c + 2p_p), \tag{11A.2}$$

where $p_c - 5$ is Coke's profit per unit, which is its price minus its average cost. To determine Coke's profit-maximizing price for a given p_p, we first set the partial derivative of the profit function, Equation 11A.2 , with respect to the price of Coke equal to zero:

$$\frac{\partial \pi_c}{\partial p_c} = q_c + (p_c - 5)\frac{\partial q_c}{\partial p_c}$$

$$= q_c - 4(p_c - 5) = 0. \tag{11A.3}$$

We then substitute for q_c, using Equation 11A.1, to obtain $58 - 4p_c + 2p_p - 4(p_c - 5) = 0$. Solving this expression for p_c as a function of p_p, we obtain Coke's best-response function:

$$p_c = 9.75 + 0.25p_p. \tag{11A.4}$$

Equation 11A.4 shows that Coke's best-response price is 0.25 (25¢) higher for every extra dollar that Pepsi charges, as Figure 11.6 shows. If $p_p = 13$, then Coke's best response is to set $p_c = 13$.

Pepsi's demand function is

$$q_p = 63.2 - 4p_p + 1.6p_c. \tag{11A.5}$$

Using the same approach, and given that Pepsi also has a constant marginal cost of 5 per unit, we find that Pepsi's best-response function is

$$p_p = 10.4 + 0.2p_c. \tag{11A.6}$$

Solving Coke and Pepsi's best-response functions (Equations 11A.4 and 11A.6) simultaneously determines the Nash equilibrium. By substituting Pepsi's best-response function for p_p from Equation 11A.6 in Coke's best-response function, Equation 11A.4, we find that $p_c = 9.75 + 0.25(10.4 + 0.2p_c)$. Solving this equation for p_c, we determine that the equilibrium price of Coke is $13. Substituting $p_c = \$13$ into Equation 11A.6, we discover that the equilibrium price of Pepsi is also $13.

Game Theory and Business Strategy

12

A camper awakens to the growl of a hungry bear and sees his friend putting on a pair of running shoes. "You can't outrun a bear," scoffs the camper. His friend coolly replies, "I don't have to. I only have to outrun you!"

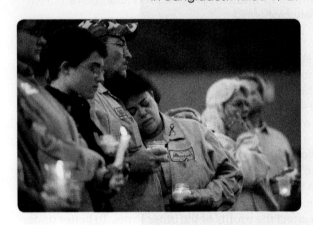

In part because of the differing amounts that firms invest in safety, jobs in some firms are more dangerous than in others. Thousands of U.S. workers are killed on the job every year—5,190 in 2016 or about 14 per day.

Major disasters have occurred in many countries. An apparel factory collapse in Bangladesh killed 1,129 workers in 2013. A warehouse explosion in the port of Tianjin, China, in 2015 killed over 100 workers. In 2017, a power plant explosion in Unchahar, India, killed 38 workers and seriously injured about 100 others. The International Labor Organization estimates that over two million workers die in industrial accidents or due to work-related illnesses every year.

Managers at each firm must decide how much to invest in worker safety. Such investments affect the firm's own reputation for safety, but may also affect how safe workers believe they are at other firms in the industry. Recent U.S. workplace accidents have resulted in renewed calls by unions for greater U.S. government intervention to protect workers, which would affect all firms.

One justification that is often given for government intervention is that firms have more information than workers about job safety at their plants. Prospective employees often do not know the injury rates at individual firms but may know the *average* injury rate over an entire industry from government reports or other sources.

Injury rates vary dramatically by industry. In 2016, the U.S. financial services industry, the safest industry, had a rate of only 0.4 fatal injuries per 100,000 workers. Other safe industries include health care (0.7) and education (1.07—although students risk dying of boredom). Construction (10.1), mining (10.1), agriculture (20.9), and truck driving (25.6) are much more dangerous. The most dangerous industries are fishing, hunting, and trapping (69.1) and logging (100.1).[1]

If people are rational and fear danger, they agree to work in a dangerous job only if that job pays a sufficiently higher wage than less risky alternative jobs. Economists have found that workers receive *compensating wage differentials* in industries and occupations that government statistics show are relatively risky.

---

[1]Government statistics also tell us that males have a fatal accident rate, 5.8, that is an order of magnitude greater than that of females, 0.6. Some of this difference is due to different occupations and some to different attitudes toward risk.

However, if workers are unaware of the greater risks at certain firms within an industry, they may not receive compensating wage differentials from more dangerous employers within that industry. Workers are likely to have a sense of the risks associated with an industry: Everyone knows that mining is relatively risky—but they do not know which mining companies are particularly risky before a major accident occurs. For example, in the decade before Massey Energy was acquired by Alpha Natural Resources in 2011, 54 coal miners were killed in Massey mines, a much higher rate than at other mines, yet there's no evidence that these workers received higher pay than workers at other mining firms.[2]

Because workers do not know which firms are safer than others, each firm bears the full cost of its safety investments but does not get the full benefits. If workers are aware of the average risk in an industry, all firms benefit from one firm's safety investment because that investment improves the industry average. Thus, other firms share the benefit from one firm's investment in safety. Consequently, managers, when making the important strategic decision of how much their firms should invest in safety, must take this spillover effect into account.

Does such a situation cause firms to underinvest in safety? Can government intervention overcome such safety problems?

In deciding how much to invest in safety, firms take into account the safety investments of rivals. In deciding how to price its products or how much to advertise, Procter & Gamble considers the pricing and advertising of its main rivals, Johnson & Johnson and Unilever. When a small number of firms interact, they know that their actions significantly affect each other's profit, so their actions depend on how they think their rivals will act.

An oligopolistic firm that ignores or inaccurately predicts the behavior of rivals is unlikely to do well. If Ford underestimates how many cars Toyota and Honda will produce, Ford may produce too many vehicles and lose money. These firms are aware of this strategic interdependence, recognizing that the plans and decisions of any one firm might significantly affect the profits of the other firms. To better understand managerial decisions within an oligopoly, we employ **game theory**: a set of tools used by economists and others to analyze strategic decision making.

Game theory has many practical applications. It is particularly useful for analyzing how oligopolistic firms set prices, quantities, and advertising levels. Economists also use game theory to analyze bargaining between unions and management or between the buyer and seller of a car, interactions between polluters and those harmed by pollution, transactions between the buyers and sellers of homes, negotiations between parties with different amounts of information (such as between car owners and auto mechanics), bidding in auctions, and many other economic interactions. In addition, political scientists use game theory to analyze electoral politics, military planners apply game theory to military campaigns, biologists employ game theory to analyze evolutionary biology and ecology, and philosophers, computer scientists, and many others use game theory in various other ways.

---

[2]The U.S. Mine Safety and Health Administration issued Massey 124 safety-related citations in 2010 prior to the April 2010 accident at Massey's Upper Big Branch mine in West Virginia that killed 29 workers. Massey had 515 violations in 2009. Mine Safety and Health Administration safety officials concluded in 2011 that the 2010 explosion that took 29 lives could have been prevented by Massey. The former head of security at the mine was prosecuted and convicted of two felonies and ultimately sentenced to 36 months in prison.

In this chapter, we analyze how oligopolistic firms interact within a *game*. A **game** is an interaction between players (such as individuals or firms) in which players use strategies. A **strategy** is a battle plan that specifies the *actions* or *moves* that a player will make. For example, a firm may use a simple business strategy where it produces 100 units of output regardless of what any rival does. In such a case the strategy consists of a single action—producing 100 units of output. However, some strategies consist of a combination of actions or moves, possibly contingent on what a rival does. For example, a firm might decide to produce a small quantity as long as its rival produced a small amount in the previous period, and a large quantity otherwise.

The **payoffs** of a game are the benefits received by players from the game's outcome, such as profits for firms, or incomes or utilities for individuals. A *payoff function* specifies each player's payoff as a function of the strategies chosen by all players. We normally assume that players seek to maximize their payoffs. In essence, this assumption simply defines what we mean by payoffs. Payoffs include all relevant benefits experienced by the players. Therefore, rational players should try to obtain the highest payoffs they can.

The **rules of the game** include the *timing* of players' moves (such as whether one player moves first), the various actions that are possible at a particular point in the game, and possibly other specific aspects of how the game is played. A full description of a game normally includes a statement of the players, the rules of the game (including the possible actions or strategies), and the payoff function, along with a statement regarding the information available to the players.

When analyzing a game, we usually have three objectives: to accurately describe and understand the game, to predict the likely outcome of the game, and to offer advice to managers on how best to play the game.

This chapter focuses on how firms interact strategically in a single period, while the next chapter looks at strategic interactions in games that last for more than one period. The single-period game is called a **static game**, in which each player acts only once and the players act simultaneously (or, at least, each player acts without knowing rivals' actions). For example, each of two rival firms might make simultaneous one-time-only decisions on where to locate its new factory. In the next chapter, we examine *dynamic games*, in which players move either sequentially or repeatedly.

In analyzing a game, it is crucial that we know how much information participants have. We start by assuming that all the relevant information is *common knowledge* to the players and then we relax that assumption. **Common knowledge** is a piece of information known by all players, and it is known by all players to be known by all players, and it is known to be known to be known, and so forth. We initially assume that players have **complete information**, a situation in which the strategies and payoffs of the game are *common knowledge*.

The information possessed by firms affects the outcome of a game. The outcome of a game in which a particular piece of information is known by all firms may differ from the outcome when some firms are uninformed. A firm may suffer a worse outcome if it does not know the potential payoffs of other firms. Similarly, a firm may do worse if it has limited ability to make calculations, as when its cost of making many calculations is prohibitively high or its managers have limited analytical abilities. Such limitations are referred to as *bounded rationality*.

In this chapter, we use game theory to analyze two important mechanisms that frequently determine transaction prices—bargaining and auctions. Both bargaining and auctions may be affected by the nature of the information available to players.

1. Use payoff matrices to analyze oligopoly markets.
2. Describe the different types of Nash equilibria.
3. Explain the role of information and rationality in game theory.
4. Derive the outcome of a bargaining game.
5. Determine the optimal bidding strategy in an auction.

12.1 Oligopoly Games

We start with an example of two firms that can each take one of only two possible actions. Our example is a simplified version of the real-world competition between United and American Airlines that we described in Chapter 11. Later in this chapter, and in Chapter 13, we relax our simplifying assumptions.

The game has the following characteristics. The two *players* or firms are United and American Airlines. They play a *static game*—they compete only once. The *rules* of the game specify the possible actions or strategies that the firms can take and when they can take them. Each firm has only two possible *actions*: Each can fly either 48 thousand or 64 thousand passengers per quarter between Chicago and Los Angeles. Other than announcing their output levels, the firms cannot communicate, so that they cannot make side deals or otherwise coordinate their actions. Each firm's *strategy* is to take one of the two actions, choosing either a low output (48 thousand passengers per quarter) or a high output (64 thousand).[3] The firms announce their actions or strategies *simultaneously*. The firms have *complete information*: They know all the possible strategies and the corresponding payoff (profit) to each firm. However, their information is imperfect in one important respect: Because they choose their output levels simultaneously, neither airline knows what action its rival will take when it makes its output decision.

We summarize this static game using the *payoff matrix* or *profit matrix* in Table 12.1. This payoff matrix shows the profits for each of the four possible strategic (output) combinations that the firms may choose. For example, if American chooses a large quantity, $q_A = 64$ (thousand) per quarter, and United chooses a small quantity, $q_U = 48$, the firms' profits are in the cell in the lower-left corner of the profit matrix. That cell shows that American's profit is 5.1 ($5.1 million) per quarter in the upper-right corner, and United's profit is 3.8 ($3.8 million) per quarter in the lower-left corner. We now have a full description of the game, including a statement of the players, the rules, a list of the allowable strategies, the payoffs, and the available information.

Dominant Strategies

If one is available, a rational player always uses a **dominant strategy**: a strategy that produces a higher payoff than any other strategy the player can use no matter what its rivals do. If American Airlines has a dominant strategy, then no action that United Airlines could take would make American prefer a different strategy. If American

---

[3]A strategy lists what actions to take under various circumstances. In this static game, there is no distinction between an action and a strategy. However, in multiperiod games (Chapter 13), a strategy specifies the set of actions to be taken over time, and an action chosen at a particular time may depend on the actions taken by its rivals in earlier periods.

TABLE 12.1 Dominant Strategies in a Quantity-Setting Game

		American Airlines		
		$q_A = 64$		$q_A = 48$
United Airlines	$q_U = 64$	4.1 / 4.1		3.8 / 5.1
	$q_U = 48$	5.1 / 3.8		4.6 / 4.6

Note: Quantities are in thousands of passengers per quarter; (rounded) profits are in millions of dollars per quarter. The payoff to American Airlines is in the upper-right corner of each cell and the payoff to United Airlines is in the lower left.

and United each have and use a dominant strategy, then those dominant strategies determine the outcome of the game.

Both firms have a dominant strategy in the airline game illustrated in Table 12.1. American's managers can determine its dominant strategy using the following reasoning:

- *If United chooses the high-output strategy* ($q_U = 64$), *American's high-output strategy maximizes its profit*: If United chooses high output, American's profit is $4.1 million (the top-right number in the upper-left cell) if it also chooses high output ($q_A = 64$), but is only $3.8 million (the top-right number in the upper-right cell) if it chooses low output ($q_A = 48$). Thus, American is better off choosing high output if United chooses its high-output strategy.

- *If United chooses the low-output strategy* ($q_U = 48$), *American's high-output strategy maximizes its profit*: If United uses its low-output strategy, American's profit is $5.1 million with its high-output strategy and only $4.6 million with its low-output strategy. Therefore, high output is better for American in this case as well.

- *Thus, the high-output strategy is American's dominant strategy*: Whichever strategy United uses, American's profit is higher if it uses its high-output strategy. The low-output strategy is a *dominated strategy*. We show that American won't use its dominated low-output strategy by drawing a vertical, dark-red line through American's low-output cells in Table 12.1.

By the same type of reasoning, United's high-output strategy is also a dominant strategy. We draw a horizontal, light-red line through United's low-output strategy. Because the high-output strategy is a dominant strategy for both firms, we can predict that the outcome of this game is the pair of high-output strategies, $q_A = q_U = 64$. Because both players have a dominant strategy, we can call the outcome a *dominant strategy solution*.

This game has a surprising feature that is inconsistent with most people's intuition:

Common Confusion Rival firms always choose a set of strategies that benefits all of them.

A striking feature of this game is that the players choose strategies that do not maximize their joint or combined profit. Each firm could earn $4.6 million if each chose low output ($q_A = q_U = 48$) rather than the $4.1 million they actually earn by setting $q_A = q_U = 64$. In this type of game—called a **prisoners' dilemma** game—all players have dominant strategies that lead to a payoff that is inferior to what they could achieve if they cooperated. Given the rules of the game that the players must act independently and simultaneously, their individual incentives cause them to choose strategies that do not maximize their joint profits.

The prisoners' dilemma takes its name from a classic cops-and-robbers example. The police arrest Larry and Duncan and put them in separate rooms so that they cannot talk to each other. An assistant district attorney (DA) tells Larry, "We have enough evidence to convict you both of a minor crime for which you will each serve a year in prison. If you confess and give evidence against your partner while he stays silent, we can convict him of a major crime for which he will serve five years and you will be set free. If you both confess, you will each get two years."

Meanwhile, another assistant DA is making Duncan an identical offer. By the same reasoning as in the airline example, we expect both Larry and Duncan to confess because confessing is a dominant strategy for each of them. From Larry's point of view, confessing is always better no matter what Duncan does. If Duncan confesses, then by confessing also, Larry gets two years instead of five. If Duncan does not confess, then by confessing Larry goes free instead of serving a year. Either way, confessing is better for Larry. The same reasoning applies to Duncan. Therefore, the dominant strategy solution is for both to confess and get two years in jail, even though they would be better off, getting just one year in jail, if they both kept quiet.

Best Responses

Many games do not have a dominant strategy solution. For these games, we use a more general approach. For any given set of strategies chosen by rivals, a player wants to use its **best response**: the strategy that maximizes a player's payoff given its beliefs about its rivals' strategies. We illustrated this idea in Chapter 11 when we derived the best-response curves for an oligopolistic firm.

A dominant strategy is a strategy that is a best response to *all possible* strategies that a rival might use. Thus, a dominant strategy is a best response. However, even if a dominant strategy does not exist, each firm can determine its best response to *any possible* strategies chosen by its rivals.

The idea that players use best responses is the basis for the Nash equilibrium, a solution concept for games formally introduced by John Nash (1951). A set of strategies is a **Nash equilibrium** if, when all other players use these strategies, no player can obtain a higher payoff by choosing a different strategy. An appealing property of the Nash equilibrium is that it is self-enforcing: If each player uses a Nash equilibrium strategy, then no player would want to deviate by choosing another strategy. In other words, no player regrets the strategy choice it made when it finds out the strategies chosen by the other players. Each player would say, "Given the strategies chosen by my rivals, I made the best possible choice—I chose my best response."

The Nash equilibrium is the primary solution concept used by economists in analyzing games. It allows us to find solutions to more games than just those with a dominant strategy solution. If a game has a dominant strategy solution, then that solution must also be a Nash equilibrium. However, a Nash equilibrium can be found for many games that do not have dominant strategy solutions.

To illustrate these points, we examine a more complex simultaneous-move game in which American and United can each produce an output of 96, 64, or 48 (thousand passengers per quarter). This game has nine possible output combinations, as the 3×3 profit matrix in Table 12.2 shows. Neither American nor United has a single, dominant strategy, but we can find a Nash equilibrium by using a two-step procedure. First, we determine each firm's best response to any given strategy of the other firm. Second, we check whether any pairs of strategies (cells in the profit matrix) are best responses for both firms. Each such pair of strategies is a Nash equilibrium.

We start by determining American's best response for each one of United's possible actions. If United chooses $q_U = 96$ (thousand passengers per quarter), the first row of the table, then American's profit is $0 if it sets $q_A = 96$ (the first column), $2.0 million if it chooses $q_A = 64$ (the second column), and $2.3 million if it selects $q_A = 48$ (third column). Thus, American's best response if United sets $q_U = 96$ is to select $q_A = 48$. We indicate American's best response by coloring the upper triangle in the last (third column) cell in this row dark green. Similarly, if United sets $q_U = 64$ (second row), American's best response is to set $q_A = 64$, where it earns $4.1 million, so we color the upper triangle in the middle cell (second column) of the second row dark green. Finally, if United sets $q_U = 48$ (third row), American's best response is $q_A = 64$, where it earns $5.1 million, so we color the upper triangle in the middle cell of the third row dark green.

We can use the same type of reasoning to determine United's best responses to each of American's strategies. If American chooses $q_A = 96$ (first column), then United maximizes its profit at $2.3 million by setting $q_U = 48$, which we indicate by coloring the lower triangle light green in the lower-left cell of the table. Similarly, we show that United's best response is $q_U = 64$, if American sets $q_A = 64$ or 48, which we show by coloring the relevant lower-left triangles light green.

We now look for a Nash equilibrium, which is a pair of strategies where both firms are using a best-response strategy so that neither firm would want to change its strategy. In only one cell are both the upper and lower triangles green: $q_A = q_U = 64$. Given that its rival uses this strategy, neither firm wants to deviate from its strategy.

TABLE 12.2 Best Responses in a Quantity Setting Game

| | | *American Airlines* | |
	$q_A = 96$	$q_A = 64$	$q_A = 48$
$q_U = 96$	0 / 0	2.0 / 3.1	2.3 / 4.6
United Airlines $q_U = 64$	3.1 / 2.0	4.1 / 4.1	3.8 / 5.1
$q_U = 48$	4.6 / 2.3	5.1 / 3.8	4.6 / 4.6

Note: Quantities are in thousands of passengers per quarter; (rounded) profits are in millions of dollars per quarter.

For example, if United continued to set $q_U = 64$, but American raised its quantity to 96, American's profit would fall from $4.1 to $3.1 million. Or, if American lowered its quantity to 48, its profit would fall to $3.8 million. Thus, American does not want to change its strategy.

Because no other cell has a pair of strategies that are best responses (green lower and upper triangles), at least one of the firms would want to change its strategy in each of these other cells. For example, at $q_A = q_U = 48$, either firm could raise its profit from $4.6 to $5.1 million by increasing its output to 64. At $q_A = 48$ and $q_U = 64$, American can raise its profit from $3.8 to $4.1 million by increasing its quantity to $q_A = 64$. Similarly, United would want to increase its output when $q_A = 64$ and $q_U = 48$. None of the other strategy combinations is a Nash equilibrium because at least one firm would want to deviate. Thus, we were able to find the single Nash equilibrium to this game by determining each firm's best responses.

In these airline examples, we have assumed that the firms can only pick between a small number of output levels. However, we can use game theory to find the Nash equilibrium in games in which the firms can choose any output level. We showed such a generalization for the airline example in Chapter 11. In Figure 11.3, we determined the best-response curves for each of these airlines, found that these best-response curves intersected only once, and identified the set of outputs at that intersection as the Nash-Cournot equilibrium. Indeed, that equilibrium is the same as the equilibria in Tables 12.1 and 12.2.

Failure to Maximize Joint Profits

The dominant-strategy analysis in Table 12.1 and the best-response analysis in Table 12.2 show that noncooperative firms may not reach the joint-profit maximizing outcome. Whether players achieve the outcome that maximizes joint profit depends on the profit matrix. We illustrate this idea using an advertising example.

> **Common Confusion** If firms in a market decide to advertise, doing so raises their profits.

We'll show that, for some profit matrices, all the firms would benefit if they could agree not to advertise.

Table 12.3 shows an advertising game in which each firm can choose to advertise or not, with two possible profit matrices. In the first game, where advertising by one firm takes customers from its rival but does not attract new customers, the Nash equilibrium does not maximize the collective profit to the firms. In contrast, in the second game, where advertising by one firm brings in new customers for both firms, the collective profit is maximized in the Nash equilibrium.

In the game in panel a, a firm's advertising does not bring new customers into the market but only has the effect of stealing business from the rival firm. Because each firm must decide whether or not to advertise at the same time, neither firm knows the strategy of its rival when it chooses its strategy.

If neither firm advertises, then each firm makes a profit of 2 (say, $2 million), as the upper-left cell of the profit matrix in panel a shows. If Firm 1 advertises but Firm 2 does not, then Firm 1 takes business from Firm 2 and raises its profit to 3, while the profit of Firm 2 is reduced to 0. The gain to Firm 1 is less than the loss to Firm 2 because the revenue that is transferred from Firm 2 to Firm 1 as customers shift is

TABLE 12.3 Advertising Games: Prisoners' Dilemma or Joint-Profit Maximizing Outcome?

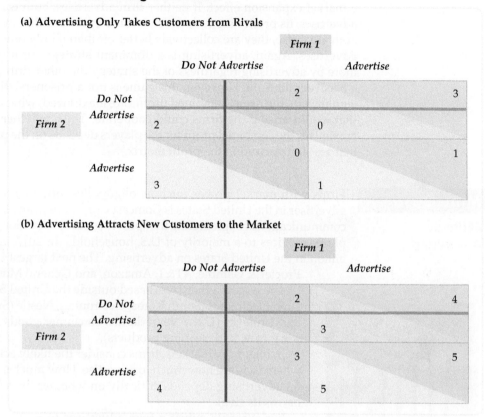

(a) Advertising Only Takes Customers from Rivals

		Firm 1	
		Do Not Advertise	Advertise
Firm 2	Do Not Advertise	2 / 2	3 / 0
	Advertise	0 / 3	1 / 1

(b) Advertising Attracts New Customers to the Market

		Firm 1	
		Do Not Advertise	Advertise
Firm 2	Do Not Advertise	2 / 2	4 / 3
	Advertise	3 / 4	5 / 5

partially offset by the cost of Firm 2's advertising. If both firms advertise, then each firm gets a profit of 1, as the cell on the lower right shows.

Advertising is a dominant strategy for both firms.[4] We use red lines to show that the firms do not use the dominated do-not-advertise strategies. Advertising for both firms is also a Nash equilibrium, because each firm is choosing its best response to the other firm's strategy, as indicated by the green shading in the lower-right cell.

In this Nash equilibrium, each firm earns 1, which is less than the 2 it would make if neither firm advertised. Thus, *the sum of the firms' profits is not maximized in this simultaneous-choice one-period game.*

Many people are surprised the first time they see this result. Why don't the firms cooperate, refrain from advertising, and earn 2 instead of 1? This game is a prisoners' dilemma: The game has a dominant strategy solution in which the players receive lower profits than they would get if the firms could cooperate. Each firm makes more money by advertising than by not advertising regardless of the strategy used by the other firm, even though their joint profit is maximized if neither advertises.

---

[4]Firm 1 goes through the following reasoning. "If my rival does not advertise, I get 2 if I do not advertise and I get 3 if I do advertise, so advertising would be better. If my rival does advertise, I get 0 if I do not advertise and I get 1 if I do advertise, so advertising is still better." Regardless of what Firm 2 does, advertising is better for Firm 1, so advertising is a dominant strategy for Firm 1. Firm 2 faces a symmetric problem and would also conclude that advertising is a dominant strategy.

In the advertising game in panel b, advertising by a firm brings new customers to the market and consequently helps both firms. That is, each firm's advertising has a market expansion effect. If neither firm advertises, both earn 2. If only one firm advertises, its profit rises to 4, which is more than the 3 that the other firm makes. If both advertise, they are collectively better off than if only one advertises or neither advertises. Again, advertising is a dominant strategy for a firm because it earns more by advertising regardless of the strategy the other firm uses and is therefore a Nash equilibrium. However, this game is not a prisoners' dilemma. In this Nash equilibrium, the firms' combined profits are maximized, which is the same outcome that would arise if the firms could cooperate. Thus, whether a Nash equilibrium maximizes the combined profit for the players depends on the properties of the game that are summarized in the profit matrix.

Mini-Case

Strategic Advertising

Firms with market power, such as oligopolies, often advertise.[5] The largest advertiser in the United States is Comcast Corporation, an American global telecommunications conglomerate that provides cable television, internet, and telephone services to a majority of U.S. households. In 2017, Comcast spent $5.7 billion in the United States on advertising. The next largest U.S. advertisers are Procter & Gamble, AT&T, Amazon, and General Motors.

The largest advertisers based outside the United States include Samsung Electronics (South Korea, electronics), Nestlé (Switzerland, foods), and Unilever (U.K./Netherlands, consumer goods such as food, personal care, and cleaning products).

In oligopoly markets, firms consider the likely actions of their rivals when deciding how much to advertise. How much a firm should spend on advertising depends critically on whether the advertising helps or harms its rival.

For example, when a firm advertises to inform consumers about a new use for its product, its advertising may cause the quantity demanded for its own *and* rival brands to rise, as happened with toothpaste ads. Before World War I, only 26% of Americans brushed their teeth. By 1926, in part because of ads like those in Ipana's "pink toothbrush" campaign, which detailed the perils of bleeding gums, the share of Americans who brushed rose to 40%. Ipana's advertising helped all manufacturers of toothbrushes and toothpaste.

Alternatively, a firm's advertising might increase demand for its product by taking customers away from other firms. A firm may use advertising to differentiate its products from those of rivals. The advertising may describe actual physical differences in the products or try to convince customers that essentially identical products differ. If a firm succeeds with this latter type of advertising, the products are described as *spuriously* differentiated.

A firm can raise its profit if it can convince consumers that its product is superior to other brands. From the 1930s through the early 1970s, *secret ingredients* were a mainstay of consumer advertising. These ingredients were given names combining letters and numbers to suggest that they were developed in laboratories rather than by Madison Avenue. Dial soap boasted that it contained

---

[5]Under perfect competition, an individual firm has no incentive to advertise, as it can sell as much as it wants at the market price.

AT-7. Rinso detergent had Solium, Comet included Chlorinol, and Bufferin had Di-Alminate. Among the toothpastes, Colgate had Gardol, Gleem had GL-70, Crest had Fluoristan, and Ipana had hexachlorophene and Durenamel.

Empirical evidence indicates that the impact of a firm's advertising on other firms varies across industries. The cola market is an example of the extreme case in which a firm's advertising brings few new customers into the market and primarily serves to steal business from rivals. Gasmi, Laffont, and Vuong (1992) reported that Coke's or Pepsi's gain from advertising comes at the expense of its rivals; however, cola advertising has almost no effect on total market demand, as in panel a of Table 12.3. Similarly, advertising by one brand of an erectile dysfunction drug increases its share and decreases that of its rivals (David and Markowitz, 2011).

At the other extreme is cigarette and beer advertising. Roberts and Samuelson (1988) found that cigarette advertising increases the size of the market but does not change market shares substantially, as in panel b of Table 12.3.[6] Similarly, Shapiro (2018) finds a positive spillover of a prescription antidepressant manufacturer's advertising on its rivals. Intermediate results include Canadian fast foods, where advertising primarily increases general demand but has a small effect on market share (Richards and Padilla, 2009).

Q&A 12.1

Suppose Procter & Gamble (PG) and Johnson & Johnson (JNJ) are simultaneously considering new advertising campaigns. Each firm may choose a high, medium, or low level of advertising, as the profit matrix shows:

What are each firm's best responses to each of its rival's strategies? Does either firm have a dominant strategy? What is the Nash equilibrium in this game?

Answer

1. *Show JNJ's best response for each possible strategy of PG.* The light green triangles are JNJ's best responses to each action by PG. If PG chooses a high level of advertising (the first column), JNJ's best response is low, because its profit is 1 if it chooses high, 2 if it chooses medium, and 3 if it chooses low, so we color the lower triangle light green in the last cell in this column. Similarly, low is the best response of JNJ to either medium or low advertising by PG, so the lower triangle is light green in every cell in the bottom row.

2. *Show PG's best response for each possible strategy of JNJ.* The dark green triangles are PG's best responses to each action by JNJ. If JNJ chooses a high level of advertising (the first row), JNJ's best response is low so we color the upper triangle dark green in the cell in the last column of this row. Similarly, low is PG's best response if JNJ picks medium, so the upper triangle is dark green in the cell in the last column of the second row. However, if JNJ chooses low, then PG's best response is medium, so the upper triangle is dark green in the middle cell of the last row.

3. *By inspection, determine if either firm has a dominant strategy.* JNJ has a dominant strategy because it chooses low regardless of the strategy that PG selects.

---

[6]However, the Centers for Disease Control and Prevention's evidence suggests that advertising may shift the brand loyalty of youths.

		PG High		PG Medium		PG Low	
JNJ	**High**	1			2		3
		1		3		5	
	Medium	3			4		5
		2		4		6	
	Low	5			6		5
		3		5		7	

However, PG does not have a dominant strategy, as its best response depends on the strategy selected by JNJ.

4. *Use the best responses to determine the Nash equilibrium.* In only one cell are the strategies a best response for both firms (that is, all green). It is the one where JNJ selects low and PG picks medium: the middle cell in the bottom row. Thus, that pair of strategies is the Nash equilibrium. We can also determine the Nash equilibrium another way. PG knows that JNJ has a dominant strategy of low. Given that JNJ chooses low, we know that PG's best response is medium; thus, that pair of strategies is the Nash equilibrium.

Comment: In this game, the lowest combined profit occurs when both firms use a high level of advertising and the highest combined profit corresponds to both firms choosing a low level of advertising. This pattern is consistent with a market in which advertising attracts relatively few new customers, and the business-stealing effect of advertising is more important than the market expansion effect. As a consequence, if firms use advertising to fight over existing consumers, joint profit falls.

Pricing Games in Two-Sided Markets

We can use game theory to analyze strategic rivalry in two-sided markets. A two-sided market is an economic platform that has two or more user groups that provide each other with network externalities (Chapter 9).

A credit card, such as MasterCard or Visa, connects merchants and consumers. The more consumers who use a card, the more attractive accepting that card is to merchants. The more merchants who accept the card, the more likely consumers want to use it.

The strategic rivalry between MasterCard and Visa determines the equilibrium prices they charge the two user groups. We assume that these firms choose one of two possible pricing strategies: balanced pricing, in which both merchants and consumers pay fees, and unbalanced pricing, in which only merchants pay. In Table 12.4, unbalanced pricing is the dominant strategy for each firm, so both use this strategy in the Nash equilibrium. This example is a prisoners' dilemma game. The firms would earn more if they used balanced pricing, 7 each, instead of unbalanced pricing, 4 each.

In contrast, consider a different game between the eHarmony and Match.com dating platforms. Each firm can use a balanced pricing strategy, charging both

TABLE 12.4 Unbalanced Pricing in a Two-Sided Market

		Visa	
		Balanced	Unbalanced
MasterCard	Balanced	7 / 7	9 / 2
	Unbalanced	2 / 9	4 / 4

TABLE 12.5 Balanced Pricing in a Two-Sided Market

		eHarmony	
		Balanced	Unbalanced
Match.com	Balanced	7 / 7	6 / 5
	Unbalanced	5 / 6	4 / 4

men and women, or it can use an unbalanced pricing strategy, charging only one group. The example in Table 12.5 is not a prisoners' dilemma game. Balanced pricing is the dominant strategy for each firm. The solution maximizes the joint payoffs to the firms.

12.2 Types of Nash Equilibria

Each of the games in Tables 12.1 through 12.5 have a unique Nash equilibrium: For only one combination of strategies is each firm's strategy a best response to its rival's strategy. The Cournot and Bertrand models of Chapter 11 are other examples of games with unique Nash equilibria. We now consider two other situations. First, we examine games that have multiple Nash equilibria. Second, we consider games in which the firms' strategies require them to choose randomly between possible actions.

Multiple Equilibria

Many oligopoly games have more than one Nash equilibrium. When a game has multiple Nash equilibria, we may be able to use additional criteria to predict the likely outcome. The scheduling or coordination game between two television networks that is summarized in Table 12.6 has multiple Nash equilibria.

TABLE 12.6 Network Scheduling: A Coordination Game

		Network 1 Wednesday	Network 1 Thursday
Network 2	Wednesday	−10 / −10	10 / 10
	Thursday	10 / 10	−10 / −10

This profit matrix shows that each network's profit depends on whether new reality TV shows—one for each network—air on Wednesday or Thursday. Neither network can change its decision once the networks simultaneously announce their schedules. Thus, each network must choose its schedule before it knows its rival's choice. The number of people who watch reality shows is enough for only one show to be profitable on a given night. If both shows appear on Wednesday or if both appear on Thursday, they share the reality market for that night and each network loses 10 (say, $10 million). However, if the shows appear on different nights, then each network earns a profit of 10.

Neither network has a dominant strategy. The best choice for each network depends on the choice of its rival. If Network 1 opts for Wednesday, then Network 2 prefers Thursday, but if Network 1 chooses Thursday, then Network 2 prefers Wednesday.

To determine the Nash equilibria for this game, we first determine each firm's best responses. If Network 2 were to choose Wednesday, then Network 1 loses 10 if it chooses Wednesday and earns 10 if it chooses Thursday. Thus, Network 1's best response is Thursday, which we indicate by coloring the upper triangle dark green in the upper-right cell. Similarly, Network 1's best response is Wednesday, if Network 2 picks Thursday, which we show by coloring the upper triangle dark green in the lower-left cell. Similarly, we color the lower triangles light green for Network 2's best responses.

The Nash equilibria are the two cells that are entirely green, showing that those pairs of strategies are best responses for both firms. These Nash equilibria have one firm broadcast on Wednesday and the other on Thursday. Neither firm would want to deviate from these Nash equilibria because doing so would cause it to lose money.

Thus, this game has two Nash equilibria. We might reasonably predict that the networks would show the two new shows on different nights, but we do not have any basis for forecasting which night each network chooses.

Cheap Talk. How can the networks avoid a disaster in this scheduling game? One possibility is that a network communicates with its rival before choosing its strategy if doing so is allowed by the rules of the game.

The firms engage in *cheap talk* (or *pre-play communication*) if they communicate before the game starts but the communication does not directly affect the payoffs of the game. Cheap talk does not mean that firms can agree in advance on their strategies. In a real-world, noncooperative game such as this one, firms may not legally make binding agreements of this type. A firm might make a cheap-talk claim, but then do something different. Therefore, in many games, allowing cheap talk has no effect: "Talk is cheap." Managers can say anything, but until decisions are actually made, claims made by firms may lack credibility.

In this game, however, players have an incentive to be truthful, so the cheap talk is credible. Each network wants the other to know its actual choice and therefore has an incentive to truthfully reveal its intentions and follow through accordingly. For example, if Network 1 announces in advance that it will broadcast on Wednesday, Network 2 will choose Thursday and both networks will benefit from communicating. Games with multiple Nash equilibria where players can credibly coordinate to select one of these equilibria are referred to as *coordination games*.

Mini-Case	In addition to auctions, eBay allows a seller to offer to sell a good for a specified price. The seller may allow a potential buyer to respond with a *best offer* of a lower price. The seller may accept the best-offer bid, decline it, or make a counteroffer. The transaction is completed when a buyer or the seller accepts the other side's offer.
Cheap Talk in eBay's Best Offer Market	Backus et al. (forthcoming) suggested that some sellers use cheap talk by posting an initial price that is a multiple of $100. Items listed in multiples of $100 receive offers that are 8% to 12% lower and are 15% to 25% more likely to sell than are items listed at similar "precise" prices such as $109. Thus, these round numbers may provide information that helps both parties: The seller makes a quick sale, and the customer buys at a low price.

The Pareto Criterion. Not all games with multiple Nash equilibria can be resolved with pre-play communication. Cheap talk may be prohibited by antitrust laws. Even where it is allowed, cheap talk lacks credibility if players have an incentive to lie. A variety of other criteria have been suggested to predict a single Nash equilibrium in a game with multiple equilibria. For example, it is possible that one of the Nash equilibria provides a higher payoff to all players than the other Nash equilibria. If so, we expect firms acting independently to choose strategies that lead to that outcome even without communicating.

Table 12.7 shows a different scheduling game with two Nash equilibria in which the networks choose different nights. Given the payoffs in this game, neither network

TABLE 12.7 The Pareto Criterion in a Network Scheduling Coordination Game

		Network 1	
		Wednesday	Thursday
Network 2	Wednesday	−10 −10	10 10
	Thursday	15 15	−10 −10

wants to switch nights and go head-to-head with its rival. However, both firms receive higher profits if Network 1's show airs on Wednesday and Network 2 chooses Thursday because of other programming in place on those nights.

We might expect that, even without cheap talk, the networks would opt for the Nash equilibrium with the higher profits because each network expects its rival to have a similar understanding of the situation. This criterion—selecting a solution that is better for all parties—is called the *Pareto criterion*. Of course, each firm may prefer to engage in cheap talk to make sure that the other network understands the situation. Unfortunately, we cannot always use cheap talk or the Pareto criterion to predict the outcome in a game with multiple equilibria.

Mini-Case

Timing Radio Ads

A contemporary music radio station can time its commercial breaks so that they occur at the same time as those of its rival stations or at different times. If the breaks are not coordinated, many listeners switch stations at a commercial break. This switching behavior lowers the value of commercials to advertisers, so that they pay the stations less.

Sweeting (2006, 2009) found that stations often have commercial breaks at the same time. During commuting hours, "drive time" listeners are likely to switch stations during commercials. Sweeting estimated that the length of time that commercial breaks occur simultaneously across stations increases by 6% during drive time. Such coordination increases the number of commercials heard by in-car listeners, and Sweeting estimates that such coordination raises annual industry advertising revenues by roughly $90 million.

Mixed-Strategy Equilibria

So far, we have assumed that each firm uses a **pure strategy**, which specifies the action that a player will take in every possible situation in a game. We now consider

How business decisions are made.

games in which a firm uses a **mixed strategy**, in which a player chooses among possible pure strategies according to probabilities that the player sets. That is, a pure strategy is a rule telling the player with certainty what action to take at each decision point in a game, whereas a mixed strategy is a rule telling the player which dice to throw, coin to flip, or other method to use to randomly choose among possible pure strategies.

In static games—the focus of this chapter—a strategy is a single action, such as choosing a particular output level. Thus, for example, in our original airlines example of Table 12.1, an airline manager could use a mixed strategy by assigning a 50% probability to both the low output and the high output, as if choosing randomly between them by flipping a coin.[7]

A pure strategy can be viewed as a special case of a mixed strategy in which a player assigns a probability of one to a single pure strategy and a probability of zero to all other possible pure strategies. A mixed strategy that

---

[7]In the more complex dynamic games that we examine in the next chapter, a strategy may be a sequence of actions, so a mixed strategy would apply probabilities to particular alternative action sequences.

assigns positive probabilities to two or more pure strategies is sometimes called a *non-pure* mixed strategy. Unless we state otherwise, from now on, when we refer to a mixed strategy, we mean a non-pure mixed strategy.

Some games have no pure-strategy Nash equilibrium, but have a mixed-strategy Nash equilibrium. Others have both pure-strategy and mixed-strategy Nash equilibria.[8]

Only Mixed-Strategy Equilibria. The following design competition game has no pure-strategy Nash equilibrium, but it has a mixed-strategy Nash equilibrium. A firm that wants a new building conducts a design competition between two architectural firms. The terms of the competition specify the location and size of the structure, the maximum allowable construction budget, and various design requirements. The architectural firms compete for the contract by creating preliminary designs.

An established architectural firm competes with a relatively new, upstart firm. They can use only two possible types of design: a traditional design and a modern design. If both firms adopt the same type of design, then the established firm wins the contract in view of its stronger reputation and longer track record. However, if the firms adopt different designs, the upstart wins the contract.

Table 12.8 is the profit matrix, where the contract winner receives a net benefit of 20 ($20 thousand) and the loser incurs the cost of its initial design, 2 ($2 thousand). As before, we indicate each firm's best response by coloring the appropriate triangle green (dark green for the established firm and light green for the upstart firm). The table shows that the upstart's best response is a modern design if the established firm uses a traditional design, and the upstart's best response is a traditional design if the established firm uses a modern approach.

No cell in the table is a Nash equilibrium because in no cell of this profit matrix are both triangles green. For each cell, one firm or the other says, "I regret my choice. Given the choice made by my rival, I should have made a different choice." If both firms pick the same style, the upstart firm regrets its choice. Similarly, if they pick different styles, the established firm regrets its choice.

Thus, if both firms use pure strategies, this game has no Nash equilibrium. However, this design game has a mixed-strategy Nash equilibrium in which each firm chooses the traditional design with probability $\frac{1}{2}$. The probabilities in a mixed-strategy equilibrium are not always $\frac{1}{2}$ but they are in this case, as we now show.

TABLE 12.8 Mixed Strategies in a Design Competition

		Established Firm	
		Traditional	Modern
Upstart	Traditional	–2 20	20 –2
	Modern	20 –2	–2 20

---

[8]Nash (1950) proved that every game with a finite number of players and strategies has at least one pure-strategy or mixed-strategy Nash equilibrium.

The probability that a firm chooses a given style is $\frac{1}{2}$. Therefore, the probability that both firms independently choose a given pair of styles (a cell) is $\frac{1}{2} \times \frac{1}{2} = \frac{1}{4}$. That is, each of the four cells in Table 12.8 is equally likely to be chosen and hence has a one-fourth chance of being chosen. In two cells (the upper left and lower right), the established firm earns 20, so it has a $\frac{1}{2}$ probability of earning 20. Similarly, it has a $\frac{1}{2}$ probability of losing 2 (lower-left and upper-right cells). Thus, the established firm's expected profit—the firm's profit in each possible outcome times the probability of that outcome—is $\left(20 \times \frac{1}{2} \right) + \left([-2] \times \frac{1}{2} \right) = 9$.

Given that the established firm uses this mixed strategy—in effect flipping a coin to choose between its two possible actions—the upstart firm cannot achieve a higher expected profit by using a pure strategy rather than using the same mixed strategy. If the upstart uses the pure strategy of choosing the traditional style or the pure strategy of choosing the modern style, it has a $\frac{1}{2}$ chance of earning 20 and a $\frac{1}{2}$ probability of losing 2, so it has the same expected profit as if it uses the mixed strategy.[9] If the upstart uses a mixed strategy with a probability of $\frac{1}{2}$ for each possible action, it has no incentive to change its strategy. The same is true of the established firm, so this combination of mixed strategies is a Nash equilibrium.

How do we calculate the probability that each firm uses for its mixed strategy? The key concept behind the mixed-strategy equilibrium is that each firm must be indifferent between choosing either of the two architectural styles. If one style offers a higher expected profit than the other, the firm would choose that style with certainty. Thus, the firm places a positive probability weight on both styles only if both styles yield the same expected profit.

Consider the upstart firm's choice between the two actions if it knows that the probability that the established firm chooses the traditional style is θ. The upstart firm's expected payoff is $[\theta \times (-2)] + [(1 - \theta) \times 20] = 20 - 22\theta$ if it picks the traditional style and $[\theta \times 20] + [(1 - \theta) \times (-2)] = -2 + 22\theta$ if it picks the modern style. The upstart is indifferent between these two pure strategies only if the two expected payoffs are equal: $20 - 22\theta = -2 + 22\theta$, or $22 = 44\theta$, or $\theta = \frac{1}{2}$. Thus, given that the established firm uses the mixed strategy $\theta = \frac{1}{2}$, the upstart is indifferent between using the pure strategy or the same mixed strategy, $\theta = \frac{1}{2}$. The upstart has no incentive to deviate from using a probability of $\frac{1}{2}$ for each style, as no other combination of probabilities would increase its expected payoff. The established firm is in the same position. Therefore, if each firm picks a probability of $\frac{1}{2}$, the result is a Nash equilibrium. Each firm is doing the best it can given its rival's strategy.

If the established firm chooses $\theta > \frac{1}{2}$ so that it is more likely to choose the traditional style, the upstart's best response is to pick the modern style with certainty, as its chance of winning would exceed $\frac{1}{2}$. Similarly, if the established firm is very likely to use the modern style, the upstart's best response is to choose the traditional style with certainty, and win with a probability greater than $\frac{1}{2}$. Only if both firms are using a mixed strategy of $\frac{1}{2}$ is each firm maximizing its expected profit given the strategy of its rival.

---

[9]Some economists don't like stories where managers literally flip coins or use another randomization device to choose strategies, arguing that we rarely see such behavior. Instead, managers almost always come up with some substantive reason to choose one action over another rather than resorting to a coin or a dice or some other device. Regardless, as long as their choice appears to be probabilistic to their rivals, they are effectively using a mixed strategy.

Both Pure- and Mixed-Strategy Equilibria. Some games have both pure-strategy and mixed-strategy Nash equilibria. The following entry game has two pure-strategy Nash equilibria and a mixed-strategy Nash equilibrium.

Two firms are considering opening gas stations at a highway rest stop that currently has no gas station. The rest stop has enough physical space for at most two gas stations. The profit matrix in Table 12.9 shows that only one station can operate profitably. If both firms enter, each loses 2 (say, $200,000). Neither firm has a dominant strategy. Each firm's best action depends on what the other firm does.

The two Nash equilibria in pure strategies are Firm 1 *enters* and Firm 2 *does not enter*, or Firm 2 *enters* and Firm 1 *does not enter*. The equilibrium in which only Firm 1 enters is a Nash equilibrium because neither firm would regret its choice. Given that Firm 2 did not enter, Firm 1 would not regret its decision to enter. If it changed its behavior, it would go from earning 1 to earning nothing. Similarly, given that Firm 1 enters, Firm 2 does not regret staying out because entering would have cost it 2 instead of being able to walk away without any losses. However, the outcome where only Firm 2 enters is also a Nash equilibrium by the same type of reasoning.

How do the players know which outcome will arise? They *don't* know. Without an enforceable collusive agreement, even pre-play communication is unlikely to help. These pure-strategy Nash equilibria might seem unappealing because they call for identical firms to use different strategies.[10]

This entry game also has a mixed-strategy Nash equilibrium in which each firm enters with $\frac{1}{3}$ probability. No firm could raise its expected profit by changing its strategy. The game therefore has three Nash equilibria in total: two pure-strategy Nash equilibria and one additional mixed-strategy Nash equilibrium.

TABLE 12.9 Nash Equilibria in an Entry Game

---

[10]This entry game, in which both firms lose if both enter, is called a *hawk-dove game*, because players choose between an aggressive and a passive strategy. It is also called a *game of chicken*. Movies sometimes show a game of chicken where two drivers race toward each other in the middle of a road. As they approach the impact point, each has the option of continuing to drive down the middle of the road or to swerve. Both believe that if only one driver swerves, that driver loses face and the other gains in self-esteem. If neither swerves, they are maimed or killed. If both swerve, no harm is done to either. Bertrand Russell observed that nuclear brinksmanship is essentially a game of chicken.

A key strategy decision for a manufacturer of an e-book is which format to use. Currently, not all e-book readers use the same format for books.[11] The current best-selling product, Amazon's Kindle (and its applications for the iPhone and for Windows PCs), uses Amazon's proprietary AZW format. Amazon does not support the open-standard EPUB format, which is used by the Kindle's competitors, such as Barnes & Noble's NOOK, Kobo, and Apple's iPad. Amazon provides applications that allow consumers to read AZW books on the iPhone as well as on Windows PCs but not on the other readers. Because e-book readers' formats differ, e-book publishers must incur additional expenses in producing books in the various formats or sell books that can be read on only some readers, which affects consumers' costs and the practicality of using a given reader.

Amazon faces the Other group, which consists of e-book manufacturers other than Amazon, in a game in which the players choose a format, as the profit matrix shows.[12] What are the pure-strategy Nash equilibria if the firms choose their formats simultaneously and are free to choose either format? Determine the mixed-strategy equilibrium, if any.

Answer

1. *Determine the pure-strategy Nash equilibria if the firms decide simultaneously.* We add green triangles to the relevant cells in the profit matrix to indicate each firm's best responses to its rival's strategy. The game has two pure-strategy Nash equilibria in which Amazon and the other manufacturers choose the same format. If both choose the AZW standard, neither Amazon nor the Other group would change its strategy if it knew that its rival was using the AZW format. The Other group's profit falls from 1 to −1 if it changes its strategy from the AZW to the EPUB format, whereas Amazon's profit falls from 3 to −1 if it makes that change. Similarly, no firm would change its strategy from the EPUB format if it believed that its rival would use the EPUB format. Thus, if the firms must choose the formats simultaneously, the only pure-strategy

---

[11]However, all readers can display Adobe PDF files, which are used for documents and books in the public domain.

[12]This game is of the same form as the game called *the battle of the sexes*. In that game, the husband likes to go to the mountains on vacation, and the wife prefers the ocean, but they both prefer to take their vacations together.

Nash equilibria are where they use the same format; however, each prefers its own format, where its profit is 3 rather than 1.

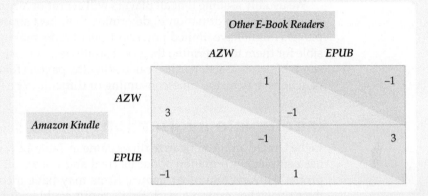

2. *Show that this game has a mixed-strategy Nash equilibrium by calculating the relevant probabilities.* This game has a mixed-strategy equilibrium in which Amazon selects the AZW standard with a probability of $\frac{2}{3}$ and the Other group selects AZW with probability $\frac{1}{3}$. If the Other group chooses the AZW standard with a probability of θ_O, Amazon's expected profit is $(3 \times \theta_O) + (-1 \times [1 - \theta_O]) = 4\theta_O - 1$ if it chooses the AZW standard and $(-1 \times \theta_O) + (1 \times [1 - \theta_O]) = 1 - 2\theta_O$ if it chooses the EPUB standard. For Amazon to be indifferent between these two actions, its expected profits must be equal: $4\theta_O - 1 = 1 - 2\theta_O$. That is, if $\theta_O = \frac{1}{2}$, Amazon is indifferent between choosing either standard. Similarly, if Amazon selects the AZW standard with a probability of $\theta_A = \frac{2}{3}$, the Other group is indifferent between choosing either of the two standards.[13]

12.3 Information and Rationality

"All that I have to say has already crossed your mind," said [Moriarty]. "Then possibly my answer has crossed yours," I replied. —Sherlock Holmes (Sir Arthur Conan Doyle)

Game theory focuses our attention on the crucial role that information plays in a firm's decision-making process. In some situations it makes sense to assume that players have full information about the profits and possible strategies of other players, and that they have full information about how much other players know. For example, our discussion of American and United Airlines assumes that both airlines

---

[13]Depending on the profits in the game, other outcomes are possible: only one format and one group of firms survives in the Nash equilibrium, or the firms adopt a single format (like the universally used MP3 and MP4 standards for digital music players). The real-world competition among e-book reader manufacturers has two additional complications. First, AZW is the proprietary format of Amazon, so the other firms would have to pay Amazon to use it, if Amazon would even permit them to do so. Second, Amazon, which entered the market first, chose its e-book format before other, later entrants into this market. In Chapter 13, we examine how this game changes given that Amazon acted first.

have the same costs and demand functions, so that each knows virtually everything that the other firm knows. In other situations, particularly in relatively complex games, players may not have complete information about their rival.

We usually assume that all players will act rationally in the sense that they use all their available information to determine their best strategies. However, sometimes players might have limited powers of calculation, making it difficult or even impossible for them to determine their best strategies. For example, if all firms have thousands of possible actions, then calculating the payoffs for every possible combination of actions may be too time-consuming or difficult to be feasible.

Incomplete Information

In the United and American Airlines game in Table 12.1, we assume that each airline has complete information about its rival and knows all the possible strategies and profits. However, in other games, firms may have incomplete information about their rivals. For example, each firm's profit could be *private information* rather than *common knowledge*.

To illustrate how having incomplete information affects a game's outcome, we consider an investment game in which two firms are considering investing in complementary products that "go together." For example, Google considered whether to invest in a new operating system, Chrome OS, for laptops and netbooks, while Samsung considered whether to design and build a new laptop, a Chromebook, which would use this operating system. The firms made their decisions simultaneously, announcing the availability of the first Chromebook and the new operating system together.

Table 12.10 illustrates a simplified version of the game Google and Samsung played (with hypothetical profits). If neither firm invests, each earns nothing (upper-left cell). However, the returns are asymmetric if only one firm invests. We assume that the new operating system is of value by itself, even without a new laptop by Samsung, as other firms could produce such a laptop (and soon thereafter several other producers such as Acer, Dell, and Google itself were also producing Chromebooks). Consequently, in our game, Google receives a benefit of 5 (say, $50 million) if Samsung does not invest in a new laptop and Samsung earns 0 (lower-left cell). Because the new, specialized laptop is completely useless without the new operating system, if Samsung invests and Google does not (upper-right cell), Samsung incurs a large loss, −25, and Google earns 0. If both firms invest (lower-right cell), each receives a profit of 20.

TABLE 12.10 Complementary Investment Game

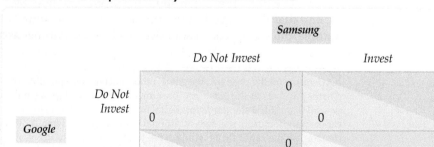

		Samsung	
		Do Not Invest	Invest
Google	Do Not Invest	0 0	−25 0
	Invest	0 5	20 20

We start by assuming that each firm has complete information about each other's profit—the information in the profit matrix in Table 12.10. This game has a unique Nash equilibrium in which both firms invest. For each firm, investment is the best response to the other firm's decision to invest.

However, what happens if the firms' profits are not common knowledge? In particular, if Samsung does not know Google's possible profits it may not realize that it is in Google's best interest to invest regardless of Samsung's action—that investing is a dominant strategy for Google. Consequently, Samsung might worry that Google will not invest. If all goes well and Google decides to invest in developing the Chrome operating system, then Samsung makes a significant profit if it also invests. But, given its limited information, Samsung may worry that Google will fail to invest, causing Samsung to suffer a big loss. Thus, if Samsung thinks it is likely that Google will not invest, Samsung may decide not to invest. In this game, Samsung and Google fail to coordinate their strategies due to incomplete information.

Managerial Implication

Solving Coordination Problems

Managers often worry about whether their products will work with other products. For example, it is important for smartphones to work with headphones, with car audio systems, and with hearing aids produced by other companies. To work together, each of these products must use the same technical standard.

Managers may be reluctant to invest in adopting a particular technical standard unless they are confident other companies will use the same standard. Wi-Fi internet protocols, USB connectivity, HDMI communications, and Bluetooth wireless data exchange are all examples of widely used standards. Smartphones use the Bluetooth standard, as do many car audio systems, headphones, and hearing aids. If you have a Bluetooth-compliant car audio system, you can listen to your iPhone through it.

How did so many different companies agree to coordinate on the Bluetooth standard? This coordination is handled by the Bluetooth Special Interest Group, a not-for-profit standard setting organization (SSO) with over 33,000 member companies who use the Bluetooth standard as of 2018. Antitrust and competition laws allow companies to legally coordinate over technical standards through SSOs. SSOs may agree to incorporate a firm's newly patented technology into a standard if the patent-holder agrees to license the technology on a "fair, reasonable, and non-discriminatory" basis. Managers can often solve coordination problems by joining SSOs.

Rationality

We normally assume that economic agents are rational in the sense that they consistently choose actions that are in their best interests given the information they have. Rational players choose payoff-maximizing strategies. In the game in Table 12.10, if Google is rational, it invests because its profit is higher if it invests, no matter what Samsung does.

Bounded Rationality. Actual business games are usually much more complex than the one in Table 12.10. For example, AT&T, Verizon, and MetroPCS, among other companies, use complicated strategies in the mobile phone market. Each firm's managers set prices on a variety of products, choose how much to advertise, select locations for cell towers, consider mergers with other companies, contract with cell phone manufacturers (such as to be able to carry Apple's iPhone), and decide simultaneously on many other actions.

Perhaps a manager with infinite powers of calculation could consider all possible combinations of actions by all firms and calculate the resulting profit to each firm and select the optimal strategy. However, even the very best managers do not always choose the optimal strategy. It does not seem reasonable to dismiss such managers as irrational just because they cannot find a fully optimal strategy. Instead, managers with limited powers of calculation or logical inference are described as having *bounded rationality*. Such managers try to maximize profits but, due to their cognitive limitations, do not always succeed.

In a wide range of strategic games, especially business strategy games, it is important to consider how sophisticated or rational one's rivals are. The best strategy against a highly sophisticated rival might differ from the best strategy against a rival with a limited ability to obtain and analyze information.

Maximin Strategies. In very complex games, a manager with bounded rationality may use a *rule of thumb* approach, perhaps using a rule that has worked in the past in choosing a strategy. For example, some players with bounded rationality use a **maximin strategy**, which maximizes the lowest possible payoff the player might receive. This approach is designed to ensure the best possible payoff if your rival takes the action that is worst for you.

In Table 12.10, Samsung gets zero if it does not invest. If it does invest, it might lose 25 or earn 20. Thus, Samsung's lowest (or minimum) profit is 0 if it does not invest and is −25 if it does invest. The maximum of these two values is 0, which arises if the firm does not invest. Therefore, not investing is Samsung's maximin strategy in this game. If Samsung fears that Google is subject to bounded rationality and might be unable to determine that it should invest, playing a maximin strategy might be attractive to Samsung. If all players adopt a maximin strategy, then we call the outcome a maximin solution. The maximin solution for the game in Table 12.10 is for Google to invest and for Samsung not to invest.

Managerial Implication

Using Game Theory to Make Business Decisions

While many actual business games are too complex to analyze as completely as we've analyzed the relatively simple games in this chapter, knowledge of these games provides insights that a manager can use in designing business strategies. When making strategic decisions, managers should consider five principles based on game theory:

1. *Dominance.* A manager who has a dominant strategy—a strategy that is always best no matter what rivals do—should use it.
2. *Best Response.* A manager who does not have a dominant strategy should determine the best responses to the strategies that rivals might use.
3. *Point of View.* A manager should consider possible strategies from the rival's vantage point, try to predict which strategy the rival will choose, and select the best response to that strategy.
4. *Coordination.* When doing so increases profit, a manager should coordinate with other firms through pre-play communication (cheap talk) or by using legal contracts.
5. *Randomize.* A manager may be able to earn a higher profit by using a mixed strategy to keep rivals guessing.

12.4 Bargaining

Most consumer items are sold in *posted price* markets. Customers go to a supermarket or a department store, check out the posted prices, and decide what to buy. Rarely do customers in a supermarket bargain over the price of milk or bid on milk in an auction. However, in other markets, bargaining and auctions are used.[14]

Bargaining is common between a manager and employees over wages and working conditions. When workers are represented by a labor union, the bargaining process is referred to as *collective bargaining*. Bargaining between employers and specific employees is common even for many nonunionized workers. Bargaining is also important in the legal system. For example, one party (the plaintiff) might sue another (the defendant) but be willing to bargain with the defendant over the actual payment to avoid the cost and uncertainty of a trial.

Bargaining often arises in vertical business relationships. For example, a manufacturer may bargain with suppliers of specialized inputs to the production process or with downstream distributors or retailers of the produced product. Bargaining is also important in our personal lives. Car buyers bargain with car dealers. Married couples and roommates bargain over responsibility for household chores. Teenagers bargain with their parents over how much time they must spend on homework, how late they can stay out, and when they can drive their parents' cars.

Bargaining Games

Game theory can be used to explain bargaining strategies. We can think of a **bargaining game** as any situation in which two or more parties with different interests or objectives negotiate voluntarily over the terms of some interaction, such as the transfer of a good from one party to another. For example, the owner of a house might negotiate with a potential buyer over the price of the house and over other aspects of the transaction, such as the date when the house changes hands and any repairs to be made by the seller.

To keep our analysis as simple as possible, we focus on bargaining games between two players. John Nash presented the earliest formal analysis of two-person bargaining games. He proposed a solution for bargaining games, which is called the *Nash bargaining solution*. The Nash bargaining solution is not the same as the *Nash equilibrium* that we have previously discussed. The Nash equilibrium is the solution to a noncooperative game, such as the Cournot game, where firms choose output levels. In that game, firms do *not* bargain over output levels, reflecting the legal reality that such bargaining is illegal.

The Nash Bargaining Solution

In two classic papers, Nash (1950, 1953) proposed a solution for two-player cooperative bargaining games. The Nash bargaining solution satisfies several properties. Most importantly, the Nash bargaining solution to a cooperative game is *efficient* in the sense that no alternative outcome is better for both parties or strictly better for

---

[14]An important factor in choosing which market mechanism to use is the size of transaction costs relative to the value of the item being sold. In a supermarket, it is not worth the time it would take for customers to bargain with sales clerks over the price of milk or to participate in an auction.

one party and no worse for the other. Basically, the two parties are trying to reach an agreement to divide profits or some other payoff. For example, two roommates could bargain about how to divide a pie between them.

Some of the noncooperative games that we have studied could be converted to cooperative bargaining games by allowing the players to sign binding agreements. For example, Table 12.1 shows the profit matrix for an oligopoly game between American Airlines and United Airlines, where each firm must produce an output of either 48 or 64 (thousand passengers per quarter). We showed that if the game is a static, noncooperative game, the firms face a prisoners' dilemma in which each produces the higher output and each firm earns 4.1 ($4.1 million) in the noncooperative Nash equilibrium.

Suppose U.S. antitrust laws change so that the rules of the game allow the two firms to bargain over their output levels and to reach a binding agreement. Given that the firms can bargain, we would not expect the firms to choose the high-output outcome because both firms would be better off with an alternative outcome in which each produces the lower output. The Nash bargaining solution, which requires efficiency for the players, rules out the high-output result.

To find the Nash bargaining solution, we first need to determine what happens if the firms cannot reach an agreement. The *disagreement point* or *threat point* is the outcome that arises if no agreement is reached. The profit to a firm at the disagreement point is d. If a proposed agreement is reached, the firm receives a profit of π. Thus, if an agreement is reached, the firm obtains an extra profit or *surplus* that equals the difference between what that player receives under the proposed agreement and what it receives at the disagreement point, $\pi - d$.

The Nash bargaining solution is the outcome in which each firm receives a nonnegative surplus (a firm would not agree to an outcome in which it loses money) and in which the product of the net surplus of the two firms (called the *Nash product, NP*) is maximized. For the airlines, the Nash bargaining solution maximizes

$$NP = (\pi_A - d_A) \times (\pi_U - d_U), \tag{12.1}$$

where the subscript A refers to American Airlines and U to United Airlines.

In this game, the natural disagreement point is the noncooperative outcome: If no agreement is reached, each firm chooses the high output. Thus, $d_A = d_U = 4.1$.

We can evaluate the Nash product for each of the four possible outcomes for this game. In the upper-left cell in Table 12.1, in which each firm produces the large output, the Nash product is zero and each firm has zero net surplus. This cell represents the disagreement point. In the lower-left cell and in the upper-right cell one of the firms earns a negative net surplus—which is less than at the disagreement point—so the Nash product is negative. Only in the lower-right cell, where each firm produces the small output and earns 4.6, is the Nash product positive: Using Equation 12.1, $NP = (4.6 - 4.1) \times (4.6 - 4.1) = 0.25$. Thus, the outcome in the lower-right cell maximizes the Nash product and is the Nash bargaining solution to this bargaining game.

If the firms could bargain about how they set their output levels in an oligopoly game, they could presumably reach an outcome that they view as *efficient* in the sense that it maximizes the Nash product, *NP*. Such an agreement creates a cartel and raises the firms' profits. The gain to firms from such a cartel agreement is more than offset by lost surplus for consumers (Chapter 11). Consequently, such agreements are illegal in most countries under antitrust or competition laws. Although the Nash bargaining solution is not a full theory of bargaining, it is a good predictor in certain situations—especially if contractual obligations arising from bargaining are legally enforceable and if the two parties have full information.

Q&A 12.3

Jane is interested in buying a car from a used car dealer. Her maximum willingness to pay for the car is 12 ($12,000). Bo, the dealer, is willing to sell the car as long as he receives at least 10. Thus, the potential surplus or gain from trade is 2. Jane and the dealer bargain over the transaction price, p. If they cannot agree on a price, then the transaction does not occur, and neither party receives any surplus. Use a spreadsheet to calculate the Nash product for each price from 10 to 12 in increments of 0.2 ($200). What is the Nash bargaining solution to this game?

Answer

1. *Prepare an Excel spreadsheet.* In cells A1 through A4, label the rows: Price, Jane's Payoff, Bo's Payoff, and Nash Product. In cells B1 through L1, enter the values 10.0, 10.2, 10.4, . . . , 12.0.

2. *Fill in the formulas.* Enter "=12−B1" in cell B2, "=B1−10" in cell B3, and "=B2*B3" in cell B4. Copy the formulas in column B and paste them into columns C through L.

3. *By inspection, find the highest value of the Nash product and the associated price.* The highest value of the Nash product is 1 (shaded yellow), and the associated price is 11 (shaded blue). Therefore, the Nash bargaining solution is to agree on a price of 11.

	A	B	C	D	E	F	G	H	I	J	K	L
1	Price	10	10.2	10.4	10.6	10.8	11	11.2	11.4	11.6	11.8	12
2	Jane's Payoff	2	1.8	1.6	1.4	1.2	1	0.8	0.6	0.4	0.2	0
3	Bo's Payoff	0	0.2	0.4	0.6	0.8	1	1.2	1.4	1.6	1.8	2
4	Nash Product	0	0.36	0.64	0.84	0.96	1	0.96	0.84	0.64	0.36	0

Comment: This Nash bargaining solution produces the plausible result that the two parties split the available surplus, which is the sum of their potential gain from trade. Jane values the car at 12, pays 11, and is left with surplus of 1. Bo receives 11, but values the car at 10, so he earns a net surplus of 1. A person's bargaining position is weaker the more that person stands to lose if no agreement is reached.

Using Calculus

Maximizing the Nash Product

We can use calculus to solve for the price, p, that maximizes the Nash product, NP. In our example, $NP = (12 - p)(p - 10) = 22p - p^2 - 120$. To find the maximum, we set the derivative of NP with respect to p equal to zero:

$$\frac{dNP}{dp} = 22 - 2p = 0.$$

Using algebra, we can rewrite this expression as $2p = 22$ or $p = 11$, which is the price that maximizes the NP.

Mini-Case

Nash Bargaining over Coffee

In Britain, France, Germany, the United States, and other developed countries, many managers believe that big-box retail chains such as Walmart and Target are increasingly squeezing manufacturer margins due to the consolidation of the retail sector. To examine this belief, Draganska, Klapper, and Villas-Boas (2010) investigated how grocery store chains and ground coffee manufacturers bargain over the wholesale price that manufacturers charge retailers.[15]

Draganska et al. (2010) considered two ways in which the Nash bargaining solution might vary with the party's characteristics. First, a firm's bargaining position depends on that firm's disagreement point, d_R for the retailer or d_M for the manufacturer. Second, Draganska et al. estimated a commonly used generalization of the Nash product, $NP = (\pi_R - d_R)^a(\pi_M - d_M)^{1-a}$, where a indicates the bargaining power of the parties. The larger a is, the more bargaining power the retailer has and the less the manufacturer has.

They estimated how d_R, d_M, and a vary with the characteristics of the firms, using data from Germany's six largest supermarket chains—Edeka, Markant, Metro, Rewe, Spar, and Tengelmann—which account for 80% of the German grocery market, and its seven largest ground coffee manufacturers—Dallmayr, Eduscho, Idee, Jacobs, Melitta, Onko, and Tchibo—which control more than 95% of the ground coffee market.

They found that bargaining power lies mainly with manufacturers: On average, the manufacturer gets more than half of the profits ($a < 0.5$). The larger the manufacturer's size, the greater the manufacturer's bargaining power and hence the larger the manufacturer's share of profit. Similarly, larger retailers have more bargaining power. In addition, retailers that position their store brands close to national brands reduce the wholesale margins by nearly a quarter (24%).

Inefficiency in Bargaining

The Nash bargaining solution presumes that the parties achieve an efficient outcome whereby neither party could be made better off without harming the other party. However, in the real world, bargaining frequently yields inefficient outcomes. One common type of inefficiency occurs because the bargaining process takes time, which delays the start of the benefit flow and therefore reduces the value of benefits overall. That is, it makes the pie to be divided smaller than it needs to be. An extreme example of a loss due to delay in reaching an agreement is a strike. When a union is on strike, workers do not receive wages from the firm, and the firm cannot produce and sell its product efficiently, if at all.

Strikes may occur because of irrational behavior or limited information. Union-management negotiations may become so acrimonious that the parties act irrationally, leading to a costly strike. More commonly, negotiators fail to quickly reach an agreement due to bounded rationality or incomplete information about the other side's payoffs. The parties are doing the best they can but are unable to determine the best possible strategies, and therefore they make mistakes. A union may strike or the employer may shut down operations to convince the other party that failing to reach an agreement has high costs.

---

[15]Bargaining not only affects how profits are split between manufacturers and retailers—the share of the pie—but it determines the prices paid by consumers and hence total profits—the size of the pie. For example, if a brand's high wholesale price drives up the retail price, consumers may substitute other brands or go to another retailer.

12.5 Auctions

We now turn to another important type of game, called an **auction**: a sale in which a good or service is sold to the highest bidder. In auctions, players normally devise bidding strategies without knowing other players' payoff functions.

A substantial amount of exchange takes place through auctions. Government contracts are typically awarded using procurement auctions. In recent years, governments have auctioned portions of the airwaves for radio stations, mobile phones, and wireless internet access and have used auctions to set up electricity and transport markets. Other goods commonly sold at auction are natural resources such as timber and drilling rights for oil, as well as houses, cars, agricultural produce, horses, antiques, and art. On the internet, many goods can be purchased on auction websites such as eBay. In this section, we first consider the various types of auctions and then investigate how the rules of the auction influence buyers' strategies.

Elements of Auctions

Before deciding which strategy to use when bidding in an auction, a bidder (or player) needs to know the rules of the game. Auctions have three key components: the number of units being sold, the format of the bidding, and the value that potential bidders place on the good.

Number of Units. Auctions can be used to sell one or many units of a good. The U.S. Department of the Treasury holds regular auctions of U.S. government bonds, selling bonds to many different buyers in the same auction. In many other auctions, a single good—such as an original painting—is sold. For simplicity in this discussion, we concentrate on auctions where a single, indivisible item is sold.

Format of Bidding. Virtually all auctions are variants of the *English auction*, the *Dutch auction*, the *sealed-bid auction, or* the *double auction*.

- **English auction**. Most people have seen an *English* or *ascending-bid auction*, at least on TV or in the movies. The auctioneer starts the bidding at the lowest price that is acceptable to the seller and then repeatedly encourages potential buyers to bid more than the previous highest bidder. The auction ends when no one is willing to bid more than the current highest bid: "Going, going, gone!" The good is sold to the last bidder for the highest bid. Sotheby's and Christie's use English auctions to sell art and antiques.

- **Dutch auction**. A *Dutch auction* or *descending-bid auction* ends dramatically with the first bid. The seller starts by asking if anyone wants to buy at a relatively high price. The seller reduces the price by given increments until someone accepts the offered price and buys at that price. Variants of Dutch auctions are often used to sell multiple goods at once, such as in Google's initial public offering auction and the U.S. Treasury's sales of Treasury bills.

- **Sealed-bid auction**. In a *sealed-bid auction,* everyone submits a bid simultaneously without seeing anyone else's bid (for example, by submitting each bid in a sealed envelope), and the highest bidder wins. The price the winner pays depends on whether it is a first-price auction or a second-price auction. In a *first-price auction*, the winner pays its own, highest bid. Governments often use this type of auction. In a *second-price auction*, the winner pays the amount bid by the second-highest bidder. Many computer auction houses use a variant of the second-price auction.

For example, you bid on eBay by specifying the maximum amount you are willing to bid. If your maximum is greater than the maximum bid of other participants, eBay's computer places a bid on your behalf that is a small increment above the maximum bid of the second-highest bidder. This system differs from the traditional sealed-bid auction in that people can continue to bid until the official end-time of the auction, and potential bidders know the current bid price (but not the maximum that the highest bidder is willing to pay). Thus, eBay has some of the characteristics of an English auction.

- **Double Auction.** All potential buyers and sellers in a *double auction* may make public offers stating prices at which they are willing to buy or sell. They may, of course, accept another participant's offer to buy or sell. Traditionally, most financial exchanges in which people trade stocks, options, or other securities were *oral* double auctions. Traders stood in *open pits* and would shout, wave cards in the air, or use hand signals to convey their offers or to signal agreements to trade. In recent years, almost all of these exchanges have switched to *electronic* double auction systems.[16]

Value.   Auctioned goods are normally described as having a *private value* or a *common value*. Typically, this distinction turns on whether the good is unique.

- **Private value.** If each potential bidder places a different personal value on the good, we say that the good has a *private value*. Individual bidders know how much the good is worth to them but not how much other bidders value it. One example is an original work of art about which people differ greatly as to how much they value it.

- **Common value.** Many auctions involve a good that has the same fundamental value to everyone, but no buyer knows exactly what that *common value* is. For example, in a timber auction, firms bid on all the trees in a given area. All firms know what the current price of lumber is; however, they do not know exactly the volume of lumber contained in the trees.

In many actual auctions, both private value and common value are present. For example, in the tree auction, bidding firms may differ not only in their estimates of the amount of lumber in the trees (common value), but also in their costs of harvesting (private value).

Bidding Strategies in Private-Value Auctions

A potential buyer's optimal strategy depends on the number of units, the format, and the type of values in an auction. To be specific, we examine auctions in which each bidder places a different private value on a single, indivisible good.

Second-Price Auction Strategies.   According to eBay, "Automatic bidding is the easiest way to bid on an eBay auction. Simply enter the highest price you're willing to pay for an item, and we do the rest."[17] Is eBay's advice to bid the most you are willing to pay correct?

---

[16]Saefong, Myra P., "Closure of Futures Trading Pits Will Render a Language Extinct," **www.marketwatch.com**, July 1, 2015.

[17]**www.ebay.com/help/buying/bidding/automatic-bidding?id=4014** (viewed August 6, 2018).

In a traditional sealed-bid, second-price auction, bidding your highest value *weakly dominates* (is at least as good as) all other bidding strategies: The strategy of bidding your maximum value leaves you *as well off* as, *or better off* than, bidding any other value. The amount that you bid affects whether you win, but it does not affect how much you pay if you win, which equals the second-highest bid.

Suppose that you value a folk art carving at $100. If the highest amount that any other participant is willing to bid is $85 and you place a bid greater than $85, you will buy the carving for $85 and receive $15 (= $100 − $85) of consumer surplus. Other bidders pay nothing and gain no consumer surplus.

Should you ever bid more than your value? Suppose that you bid $120. There are three possibilities. First, if the highest bid of your rivals is greater than $120, then you do not buy the good and receive no consumer surplus. If you had instead bid your valuation of the carving, $100, you still would have lost the auction and received no consumer surplus. Thus, bidding higher than $100 does not benefit you.

Second, if the highest alternative bid is less than $100, then you win and receive the same consumer surplus that you would have received had you bid $100. Again, bidding higher does not affect the outcome.

Third, if the highest bid by a rival is between $100 and $120—say, $110—then bidding more than your maximum value causes you to win, but you purchase the good for more than you value it, so you receive negative consumer surplus: −$10 (= $100 − $110). In contrast, if you had bid your maximum value, you would not have won, and your consumer surplus would have been zero—which is better than losing $10. Thus, bidding more than your maximum value can never make you better off than bidding your maximum value. Instead, you may actually be worse off.

Should you ever bid less than your maximum value, say, $90? No, because you only lower the odds of winning without affecting the price that you pay if you do win. If the highest alternative bid is less than $90, you win the auction and pay the same price whether you bid $100 or $90. If the alternative bid exceeds $100, you do not win the auction whether you bid $100 or $90. However, if the highest alternative bid lies between $90 and $100, you lose the auction if you bid $90 and give up the positive consumer surplus you would have gained if you had bid your true value of $100 and won the auction. You are therefore worse off by underbidding in this case.

Thus, you do as well or better by bidding your value rather than over- or underbidding. This argument does not turn on whether or not you know other bidders' valuation. If you know your own value but not other bidders' values, bidding your value is your best strategy. If everyone follows this strategy, the person who places the highest value on the good will win and will pay the second-highest value.

Mini-Case

Experienced Bidders

We've seen that bidding one's value is the dominant strategy in a sealed-bid, second-price auction. In experiments in which college students participate in sealed-bid, second-price auctions, the students more commonly overbid—placed bids that exceeded the bidder's value—than underbid.

Why? The students participating in these experiments had little prior experience bidding in auctions. When these experiments are repeated using experienced bidders, systematic overbidding is less likely to occur (Garratt, Walker, and Wooders, 2012, Feng, Fay, and Sivakumar, 2015).

English Auction Strategy. Suppose, instead, that the seller uses an English auction to sell the carving to bidders with various private values. Your best strategy is to raise the current highest bid as long as your bid is less than the value you place on the good, $100. If the current bid is $85, you should increase your bid by the smallest permitted amount, say, $86, which is less than your value. If no one raises the bid further, you win and receive a positive surplus of $14. By the same reasoning, it always pays to increase your bid up to $100, where you receive zero surplus if you win.

However, it never pays to bid more than $100. The best outcome that you can hope for is to lose and receive zero surplus. Were you to win, you would have negative surplus.

If all participants bid up to their value, the winner will pay slightly more than the value of the second-highest bidder. Thus, the outcome is essentially the same as in the sealed-bid, second-price auction.

Equivalence of Auction Outcomes. For Dutch or first-price sealed-bid auctions, one can show that participants *shave* their bids to less than their value. The intuition for this result is based on your lack of knowledge about the values of the other bidders. Reducing your bid decreases the probability that you win but increases your consumer surplus if you win. Your optimal bid, which balances these two effects, is lower than your actual value. Your bid depends on your beliefs about the strategies of your rivals. It can be shown that the best strategy is to bid an amount equal to or slightly greater than what you expect will be the second-highest bid, given that your value is the highest.

Thus, the expected outcome is the same under each format for private-value auctions: The winner is the person with the highest value, and the winner pays roughly the second-highest value. According to the Revenue Equivalence Theorem (Klemperer, 2004), under certain plausible conditions we would expect the same revenue from any English auction, Dutch auction, or sealed-bid auction in which the winner is the person who places the highest value on the good.

The Winner's Curse

Unlike in private-value auctions, in common-value auctions, a phenomenon called **the winner's curse** occurs in which the auction winner's bid exceeds the common-value item's value. The overbidding occurs when bidders are uncertain about the true value of the good.[18]

When the government auctions off timber on a plot of land, potential bidders may differ in their estimates of how many board feet of lumber are available on that land. Typically, bidders' estimates of the value are distributed randomly around the true value. If these people place bids close to their estimates, then the highest bid is likely to be made by a bidder with a very optimistic estimate, and the bid itself is likely to exceed the true value. The "winner" ends up paying too much, which is the winner's curse.

Rational bidders adjust their bids to avoid the winner's curse. Each bidder reasons that, "I can reduce the likelihood of falling prey to the winner's curse by *shading* or reducing my bid below my estimate. I know that if I win without shading my bid, I am probably overestimating the value of the good. The amount by which I should shade my bid depends on the number of other bidders, because the more people who bid, the more likely it is that the winning bid is an overestimate."

---

[18]Mike Shor has a clever website, **www.gametheory.net/mike/applets/winnercurse/**, which demonstrates the winner's curse. You are asked, "How much should you offer for a company of uncertain valuation?" You can try various bidding strategies to see which works best.

Although rational managers should avoid the winner's curse, economists have observed the winner's curse in many situations. An important example is the take-over market: the market for corporate acquisitions.[19]

One possible reason for the winner's curse is that bidders have bounded rationality. It is difficult to calculate the correct adjustment that should be made to a bid to offset the winner's curse. Even if most bidders correctly adjust, all it takes to generate a winner's curse is one optimistic bidder who does not adjust properly.

Managerial Implication

Auction Design

Managers who sell assets using auctions need to understand how an auction's design affects bidders' behavior. Because intelligent bidders shade their bids, sellers of common-value goods can do better with an English auction than with a sealed-bid auction. In an English auction, bidders may revise their views about the object's value as they watch others bid.

Many sellers have learned this lesson. For example, online auction sites such as eBay do not use sealed-bid auctions, choosing modified English auctions or other types of auctions instead. This lesson is one that many governments have failed to learn. They continue to rely heavily on sealed-bid auctions even though it is likely they would earn more money if they used an English auction to sell lumber, rights to airwaves, and other property.

Managerial Solution

Dying to Work

In the Managerial Problem at the beginning of the chapter, we asked whether a firm underinvests in safety if the firm knows how dangerous a job is but potential employees do not. Can the government intervene to improve this situation?

Consider an industry with two firms that are simultaneously deciding whether to make costly safety investments such as sprinkler systems in a plant or escape tunnels in a mine. Unlike the firms, potential employees do not know how safe it is to work at each firm. They only know how risky it is to work in this industry. If only Firm 1 invests, workers in the industry do not know that safety has improved at only Firm 1's plant. Because the government's accident statistics for the industry fall, workers realize that it is safer to work in the industry, so both firms pay lower wages.

The profit matrix shows how the firms' profits depend on their safety investments. Firm 1 has a dominant strategy. If Firm 2 invests (compare profits in the cells in the lower row), Firm 1's *no investment* strategy has a higher profit, 250, than its *investment* strategy, 225. Similarly, if Firm 2 does not invest (compare the cells in the upper row), Firm 1's profit is higher if it doesn't invest, 200, than if it does. Thus, not investing is the dominant strategy and investing is the dominated strategy,

		Firm 1	
		No Investment	Investment
Firm 2	No Investment	200 / 200	100 / 250
	Investment	250 / 100	225 / 225

[19]See Thaler (1994) for many examples of the winner's curse, including a discussion of corporate takeovers.

as is indicated by the horizontal red line through the investing strategy. Because the game is symmetric, the same reasoning shows that not investing is the dominant strategy for Firm 2 as well.

Because both firms have a dominant strategy of not investing, that combination of dominant strategies (the upper-left cell) is the Nash equilibrium. Both firms receive an equilibrium profit of 200. If both firms invest in safety (the lower-right cell), each earns 225, which is more than they earn in the Nash equilibrium. However, both firms making an investment is not a Nash equilibrium, because each firm can increase its profit from 225 to 250 by not investing if the other firm invests.

The firms are engaged in a prisoners' dilemma game. *Because each firm bears the full cost of its safety investments but derives only some of the benefits, the firms underinvest in safety.*

This prisoners' dilemma outcome results because workers cannot tell which firm is safer. If workers know how safe each firm is, only a firm that invests in safety would be able to pay a lower wage, which would change the profits and increase the likelihood that firms invest in safety. Thus, if the government or a union were to collect and provide workers with firm-specific safety information, the firms might opt to invest. However, for the government or a union to provide this information, their cost of gathering the necessary information has to be relatively low.

SUMMARY

1. **Oligopoly Games.** Interactions between firms can often be analyzed and understood using a set of tools known as game theory. Such interactions or games are particularly important in oligopolies, where a small number of firms compete and hence each firm's action affects the profits of other firms. A game in which players act simultaneously and act only once is called a static game. Games with repeated or sequential actions are called dynamic games and are analyzed in the next chapter. A combination of player strategies is a Nash equilibrium if, given that all other players use these strategies, no one player can obtain a higher profit by independently choosing a different strategy. In many games, we can find Nash equilibria by eliminating dominated strategies or by examining all firms' best responses to the actions of other firms.

2. **Types of Nash Equilibria.** If each player has a dominant strategy—a strategy that is best no matter what the rivals do—we expect that strategy to be played. If all players have a dominant strategy and play it, the outcome is called a dominant strategy solution. Such a solution is the only possible Nash equilibrium. A game without dominant strategies may also have a unique Nash equilibrium, but some games have multiple Nash equilibria, in which case additional considerations can sometimes be used to predict the likely outcome. For example, if one Nash equilibrium is better for all players than another, the Pareto criterion selects that preferred equilibrium.

Some games have no Nash equilibria in pure strategies, where each firm chooses a particular strategy with certainty. Games with no pure-strategy Nash equilibria and games with multiple pure-strategy Nash equilibria have mixed-strategy Nash equilibria, where players randomize over two or more pure strategies.

3. **Information and Rationality.** In some games, players have complete information about the payoffs and possible strategies of other players. However, participants in games may sometimes lack important information and, in particular, might be uninformed about their rivals' payoffs or strategies. We typically assume that players are rational and can therefore determine their best strategies based on the information they have. Players that have imperfect powers of calculation and might therefore be unable to calculate optimal strategies are said to have *bounded rationality*.

4. **Bargaining.** An important business activity is bargaining: Buyers and sellers negotiate the price of a good such as a house or a car, and employers and unions engage in collective bargaining over wages and work rules. One possible outcome of bargaining games is the Nash bargaining solution, in which the product of the parties' net surplus from bargaining is maximized.

5. **Auctions.** Auctions are games of incomplete information if bidders do not know the valuation others place on a good. Buyers' optimal strategies depend on the

characteristics of an auction. Under fairly general conditions, if the auction rules result in a win by the person placing the highest value on a good that various bidders value differently, the expected price is the same in all auctions. For example, the expected price in various types of private-value auctions is the value of the good to the person who values it second highest. In auctions where everyone values the good the same, though they may differ in their estimates of that value, the successful bidder may suffer from the winner's curse—paying too much—unless bidders shade their bids to compensate for their overoptimistic estimation of the good's value.

QUESTIONS

*All exercises are available on **MyLab Economics**; * = answer at the back of this book; **C** = use of calculus may be necessary.*

1. Oligopoly Games

*1.1 Show the profit matrix and explain the reasoning in the prisoners' dilemma example where Larry and Duncan, possible criminals, will get one year in prison if neither talks, two years in jail if both talk, and if one talks that one goes free while the other gets five years. (*Note*: The payoffs are negative because they represent years in jail, which is a negative payoff.)

1.2 Two firms compete by advertising. Given the profit matrix for this advertising game, identify each firm's best response to its rival's possible actions. Does either firm have a dominant strategy? What is the Nash equilibrium?

Firm 1

	Do Not Advertise	Advertise
Do Not Advertise	1 / 2	0 / 0
Advertise	2 / 4	1 / 3

Firm 2 (rows)

1.3 How does your answer to Question 1.2 change if Firm 1 gets 3 instead of 1 when both firms advertise? (*Hint*: Start by drawing the new profit matrix.)

1.4 Two firms face the following profit matrix:

Firm 1

	Low Price	High Price
Low Price	0 / 2	2 / 1
High Price	6 / 0	7 / 6

Firm 2 (rows)

Is it true that, given these profits, Firm 2 wants to match Firm 1's price, but Firm 1 does not want to match Firm 2's price? Does either firm have a dominant strategy? What is the Nash equilibrium in this game? Explain.

1.5 How do your answers to Question 1.4 change if Firm 2 gets 3 instead of 1 when Firm 1 charges a high price and Firm 2 charges a low price?

*1.6 Suppose that Toyota and GM are considering entering a market for electric automobiles and that their profits (in millions of dollars) from entering or staying out of the market are

GM

	Enter	Do Not Enter
Enter	−40 / 10	0 / 250
Do Not Enter	200 / 0	0 / 0

Toyota (rows)

If the firms make their decisions simultaneously, do either or both firms enter? How would your answer change if the U.S. government committed to paying GM a lump-sum subsidy of $50 million on the condition that it would produce this new type of car?

1.7 Based on the Mini-Case "Strategic Advertising," would cola advertising or cigarette advertising correspond more closely to a prisoners' dilemma game?

1.8 Firm 1 and Firm 2 manufacture blankets. They compete in quality. Given their payoff matrix, identify each firm's best response to its rival's actions. What is the Nash equilibrium? (*Hint*: See Q&A 12.1.)

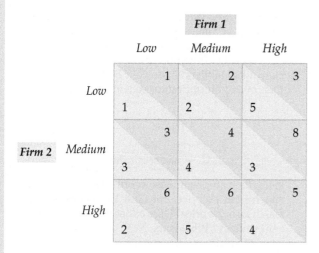

1.9 Modify Question 1.8 so that if Firm 1 chooses High and Firm 2 chooses Low (the upper-right corner), Firm 1 receives 1 rather than 3. How does that change your answer?

1.10 Provide three examples of two-sided markets (other than the examples in the text).

1.11 For the two examples of two-sided markets shown in Tables 12.4 and 12.5, would you expect a change in strategies if the two firms were to merge or collude?

2. Types of Nash Equilibria

2.1 Assume the network scheduling profit matrix is

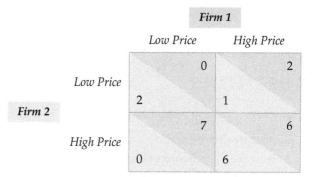

How many pure-strategy Nash equilibria does this game have? Explain.

*2.2 Given the network profit matrix in Question 2.1, can cheap talk (pre-play communication) help the networks settle on a single equilibrium? Why or why not?

2.3 Given the network profit matrix in Question 2.1, can the Pareto criterion help the networks settle on a single equilibrium? Explain.

2.4 Based on the Mini-Case "Timing Radio Ads," would competing radio stations benefit from applying the Pareto criterion (even if they do not use that term) in deciding on timing for radio ads?

2.5 Two firms face the following profit matrix:

Given these profits, Firm 2 wants to match Firm 1's price, but Firm 1 does not want to match Firm 2's price. Does either firm have a dominant strategy? Does this game have a unique, pure-strategy Nash equilibrium? Identify all pure- and mixed-strategy Nash equilibria.

2.6 How would your answers to Question 2.5 change if Firm 2 gets 5 instead of 7 when it chooses a high price and Firm 1 chooses a low price?

2.7 Suppose that you and a friend play a "matching pennies" game in which each of you uncovers a penny. If both pennies show heads or both show tails, you keep both. If one shows heads and the other shows tails, your friend keeps them. Show the payoff matrix. What, if any, is the pure-strategy Nash equilibrium to this game? Does this game have a mixed-strategy Nash equilibrium? If so, what is it?

2.8 Takashi Hashiyama, president of the Japanese electronics firm Maspro Denkoh Corporation, was torn between having Christie's or Sotheby's auction the company's $20 million art collection, which included a van Gogh, a Cézanne, and an early Picasso (Carol Vogel, "Rock, Paper, Payoff," *New York Times*, April 29, 2005, A1, A24). He resolved the issue by having the two auction houses' representatives compete in the playground game of rock-paper-scissors. A rock (fist) breaks scissors (two fingers sticking out), scissors cut paper (flat hand), and paper smothers rock. At stake were several million dollars in commissions. Christie's won: scissors beat paper. Show the profit or payoff matrix for this rock-paper-scissors game where the payoff is −1 if you lose, 0 if you tie, and 1 if you win. What pure or mixed strategy would you have recommended, and why?

2.9 The Great Recession of 2007–2009 hit young people particularly hard, with long-lasting effects. The U.S. unemployment rate for 20- to 24-year-olds went from 8.5% in 2007 to 16% in 2009, stayed above 13% through 2012, but fell to 7% by the first half of 2018. As a result, more adult children moved back to live with their parents or asked for financial help than in previous years. The share of 25- to 34-year-olds living in multigenerational households rose from 11% in 1980 to 15% in 2016. A recent survey finds that 41% of parents provide financial support to their 23- to 28-year-old offspring. Indeed, parents give 10% of their income on average to their adult children. Mimi wants to support her son Jeff if he looks for work but not otherwise. Jeff (unlike most young people) wants to try to find a job only if his mother will not support his life of indolence. Their payoff matrix is

		Jeff	
		Look for Work	Loaf
Mimi	Support	2 / 4	4 / −1
	No Support	1 / −1	0 / 0

If Jeff and Mimi choose actions simultaneously, what are the pure- or mixed-strategy equilibria?

2.10 Lori employs Max. She wants him to work hard rather than to loaf. She considers offering him a bonus or not giving him one. All else the same, Max prefers to loaf.

		Max	
		Work	Loaf
Lori	Bonus	2 / 1	3 / −1
	No Bonus	−1 / 3	0 / 0

If they choose actions simultaneously, what are their strategies? Why does this game have a different type of equilibrium than the game in Question 2.9?

*2.11 Show that the mixed-strategy equilibrium for the game in Table 12.9 has both firms enter with probability $\frac{1}{3}$.

2.12 How would the analysis in Q&A 12.2 change if the payoffs to both firms are 3 in the upper-left corner of the profit matrix (where both firms choose the Amazon standard) and the payoffs to both firms are 2 in the lower-right corner, where both firms use the EPUB standard?

3. Information and Rationality

*3.1 Consider the following payoff matrix for a complementary investment game. The number in the

		Blues Brothers Investments	
		Don't Invest	Invest
Wild and Crazy Guys	Don't Invest	0 / 0	0 / 5
	Invest	−100 / 0	20 / 10

lower-left corner is the payoff to Wild and Crazy Guys (WCG). The other number is the payoff to Blues Brothers Investments (BB).

a. Does either firm have a dominant strategy?

b. What is the Nash equilibrium?

c. What is the maximin solution?

3.2 How do your answers to Question 3.1 change if everything in the profit matrix remains the same except that Blues Brothers loses 5 (payoff is −5) if it invests and WCG doesn't invest (the upper-right cell in the matrix)?

3.3 For the payoffs described in Questions 3.1 and 3.2, would Blues Brothers and Wild and Crazy Guys gain by merging? (*Hint*: See the Managerial Implication "Solving Coordination Problems.")

3.4 Traditionally, the Harrison Resort Hotel sponsors an annual festival, making a significant investment in marketing to attract tourists to its hotel. Julie, the manager of nearby Lakeshore Flowers, normally orders extra merchandise in preparation for the festival. However, Harrison was recently bought by a large chain, so its management has changed. Julie is not sure that the new manager knows that investing in marketing will benefit Harrison.

Harrison Hotel

	Don't Invest	Invest
Lakeshore Gifts Don't Invest	0 / 0	0 / 5
Invest	0 / -20	6 / 10

a. What is the Nash equilibrium in this game?

b. What can Julie do to make sure that Harrison's new manager does what's best for the resort (and also best for her)?

3.5 As described in the Managerial Implication "Solving Coordination Problems," standard setting organizations (SSOs) facilitate agreement over technical standards between the member companies. Incorporating a particular technical standard in a product is costly. By joining an SSO and adopting a technical standard supported by the SSO, a manager ensures that other firms will use the same technical standard. Under what circumstances is this approach valuable to a manager?

4. Bargaining

4.1 In the used car bargaining problem in Q&A 12.3, if Bo can get only 9 elsewhere and therefore has a reservation price of 9, what price is implied by the Nash bargaining solution? (*Hint*: Find the new Nash bargaining solution using a spreadsheet or using calculus.) **C**

*4.2 Oculus and Maxygen are small drug companies. Oculus has obtained a patent on a new antibiotic that is effective against an emerging superbug—a bacterium that is resistant to traditional antibiotics. Unfortunately, the Oculus drug has severe side effects, making the drug unsuitable except for patients who are desperate. Ownership of this drug is worth $10 (million) to Oculus under the current situation. Maxygen has a patent on another drug that is of no therapeutic value in itself, so the drug generates no current income for Maxygen. However, when combined in a particular way with the Oculus drug, it dramatically reduces the negative side effects. The value of the two drugs together is estimated at $50 (million). Maxygen is negotiating to sell its patent to Oculus. What price would be implied by the Nash bargaining solution? (*Hint*: See Q&A 12.3 and Using Calculus: "Maximizing the Nash Product.") **C**

4.3 Situations of the type described in Question 4.2 are fairly common in the drug business and sales

of patent rights are common. However, sometimes negotiations over such sales take a long time and sometimes negotiations are unsuccessful. Why would such wasteful outcomes occur?

4.4 The Mini-Case "Nash Bargaining over Coffee" applies the generalized Nash product, $NP = (\pi_R - d_R)^a (\pi_M - d_M)^{1-a}$, to bargaining between retailers and manufacturers over the price of coffee. Assume that $d_R = d_M = 0$, that $a = 0.5$, and that manufacturers and retailers divide up a potential combined profit of 100 depending on the price so that $\pi_R = 100 - p$ and $\pi_M = p$. What price maximizes the generalized Nash product? What happens if $a = 0$. Explain. (*Hint*: See Using Calculus: "Maximizing the Nash Product.") **C**

5. Auctions

5.1 Charity events often use silent auctions. A donated item, such as a date with a movie star, is put up for bid. (See **www.ecorazzi.com/2008/02/22/ebay-and-oxfam-help-you-win-a-date-with-colin-firth** for a description of auctions for celebrity dates with Colin Firth and Scarlett Johansson.) In a silent auction, bidders write down bids and submit them. Some silent auctions use secret bids, which are submitted in sealed envelopes and kept confidential. Other silent auctions are open: The bidder writes down a bid on a bulletin board that everyone present can see. Which kind of auction would you expect to raise more revenue for the charity?

5.2 At the end of performances of his Broadway play *Cyrano de Bergerac*, Kevin Kline, who starred as Cyrano, the cavalier poet with a huge nose, auctioned his prosthetic proboscis, which he and his co-star, Jennifer Garner, autographed (Dan Mitchell, "This Time, Santa Has Been Too Naughty," *New York Times*, December 9, 2007) to benefit Broadway Cares in its fight against AIDS. An English auction was used. One night, a television producer grabbed the nose for $1,400, while the next night it fetched $1,600. On other nights it sold for $3,000 and $900. Why did the value fluctuate substantially from night to night? Which bidder's bid determined the sales price? How was the auction price affected by the audience's knowledge that the proceeds would go to charity? Why?

5.3 Suppose that Alpha Inc., Richardson Industries, and K-Tek are the only three firms interested in a plot of land on the outskirts of town. The lot is being auctioned by a second-price sealed-bid auction. Alpha values the lot at $1.3 million, Richardson at $1.05 million, and K-Tek at $950,000. Each bidding firm's surplus is $v_i - p$ if it wins the auction and 0 if it loses. The values are private. What is each bidder's optimal bid? Which firm wins the auction, and what price does that firm pay?

6. Managerial Problem

6.1 In the Managerial Solution safety game, could cheap talk lead both firms to invest in safety? Why or why not? What is the minimum fine that the government could levy on firms that do not invest in safety that would lead to a Nash equilibrium in which both firms invest?

7. MyLab Economics Spreadsheet Exercises[20]

7.1 General Mills and Kellogg's, major rivals in the breakfast cereal market, decide simultaneously on their advertising strategies. Each has five options, A through E. The following table shows their net profits (in millions of dollars) for various advertising strategy combinations. In each cell, the first entry is the profit for Kellogg's and the second is the profit for General Mills.

| | | General Mills | | | |
	A	B	C	D	E
A	23, 22	37, 18	42, 11	21, 20	25, 15
B	11, 24	30, 20	27, 29	25, 22	27, 27
Kellogg's C	32, 18	28, 22	30, 20	37, 18	34, 16
D	19, 20	41, 26	38, 24	32, 25	28, 23
E	21, 31	33, 17	25, 22	30, 19	23, 28

a. Use Excel to create a spreadsheet showing only the payoff to Kellogg's arising from each strategy combination. For each possible strategy for General Mills (that is, for each column), determine the best response for Kellogg's. (*Hint*: Use the MAX function to find the maximum value for each column.) Does Kellogg's have a dominant strategy?

b. In the same spreadsheet, create a new block of entries showing the payoff to General Mills for each strategy combination. For each possible strategy of Kellogg's, identify General Mills' highest possible payoff and corresponding best strategy.

c. Determine the Nash equilibrium for this game. Is it a dominant-strategy equilibrium?

7.2 Gray's Gravel and Gravel Depot are duopoly producers of gravel in a small city. Industry output Q is the sum of Gray's output and Gravel Depot's output. The market demand function for truckloads of gravel is $Q = 20p^{-2.0}$ and therefore has a constant price elasticity of -2. The inverse market demand function is $p = (20/Q)^{0.5}$. As in the Cournot model of Chapter 11, the firms decide simultaneously on

their output levels, but each firm has only three possible output choices: 1, 2, or 3 truckloads. Each firm has a constant average cost and marginal cost of 7.

a. In an Excel spreadsheet, create labels at the top of columns A through J, indicating, in order, Gray's output, Gravel Depot's output, industry output, industry price, the revenue for each of the firms, the cost for each of the firms, and each firm's profit. In column A, enter the numbers 1, 2, and 3 in cells A2, A3, and A4, then again in cells A5–A7 and again in cells A8–A10. In column B enter the number 1 in cells B2–B4, the number 2 in cells B5–B7, and the number 3 in cells B8–B10. Fill in the corresponding formulas and determine the values in the other columns for each possible output combination (rounded to one digit after the decimal point).

b. In the same spreadsheet, create the game's profit matrix as follows. Enter the numbers 1, 2, and 3 in cells B16–B18. These numbers are the possible output levels for Gray's Gravel. Enter the numbers 1, 2, and 3 in cells C15–E15, showing the possible output levels for Gravel Depot. Then enter the firms' profit levels in cells C16–E18. Follow the convention illustrated in Question 7.1: For each cell (that is, for each output combination) enter the profit of Gray's, followed by a comma, followed by the profit of Gravel Depot. What is the Nash equilibrium in this game?

c. If firms could produce 4 units of output instead of being limited to a maximum of 3, would that change the Nash equilibrium? (*Hint*: Modify the spreadsheet accordingly and see what happens.)

7.3 Atlas Construction wants to buy some custom equipment from Vulcan Manufacturing. Atlas' maximum willingness to pay for the equipment is $320 (thousand). Vulcan is willing to sell the equipment as long as it gets at least $260 (thousand). The two companies bargain over the price, p. The net benefit to Atlas is $320 - p$ and the net benefit to Vulcan is $p - 260$. The Nash product is the product of these two benefits.

a. Use Excel to create a spreadsheet with columns for the price, the benefit to Atlas, the benefit to Vulcan, and the Nash product. Let the price go from 260 to 320 in increments of 10 and find the price that maximizes the Nash product.

b. Now suppose that Atlas' maximum willingness to pay is only 300. What is the price that arises from Nash bargaining now? Explain why the price would change in this way.

---

[20]The spreadsheet exercises in this chapter are based on the work of Satyajit Ghosh in cooperation with the authors. The answers are available on MyLab Economics.

13 Strategies Over Time

In solving a problem of this sort, the grand thing is to be able to reason backward.
—Sherlock Holmes (Sir Arthur Conan Doyle)

Managerial Problem

Intel and AMD's Advertising Strategies

Intel and Advanced Micro Devices (AMD) dominate the central processing unit (CPU) market for personal computers, with over 99% of total sales in 2018. They also have 82% of sales in the graphic chips market in 2018. Intel uses aggressive advertising—its very successful *Intel Inside®* campaign—and charges relatively high prices, while traditionally AMD used little advertising and relied on the appeal of its lower prices. Intel controls more than 78% of the processor market and 67% of the graphic chips market.

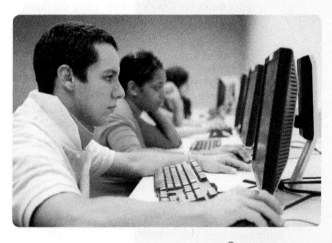

According to Salgado's (2008) estimated demand functions, consumers were willing to pay a large premium for the Intel brand of processors. He found that if Intel increased its advertising by 10% (holding prices constant), the total market demand would increase by 1%, while Intel's relative share would rise by more than 3%. Demand for AMD products would therefore fall. Salgado's work indicates that the two firms' shares would be roughly equal if they advertised equally (regardless of the level).

From the start of the personal computer era, Intel has been the 800-pound gorilla in the CPU market. Intel created the first commercial microprocessor chip in 1971. In 1991, Intel launched the Intel Inside® marketing and branding campaign. Intel offered to share costs for any manufacturer's PC print ads if they included the Intel logo. Not only did these funds reduce the computer manufacturers' costs, but the logo also assured consumers that their computers were powered by the latest technology. Within six months, 300 computer manufacturers had agreed to support the campaign. After the manufacturers' ads started to appear, Intel advertised globally to explain the significance of the logo to consumers. The Intel Inside® campaign was one of the first successful attempts at *ingredient branding*.

Advanced Micro Devices (AMD) entered the microchip market in 1975, when it started selling a reverse-engineered clone of the Intel 8080 microprocessor. In 1982, AMD and Intel signed a contract allowing AMD to be a licensed second-source manufacturer of Intel's 8086 and 8088 processors because IBM would use these chips in its PCs only if it had two microchip sources.

Why have Intel's managers chosen to advertise aggressively while AMD engages in relatively little advertising? At the end of the chapter, we discuss one possible explanation: Intel was able to act first and thereby gain an advantage.

The business strategy games we studied in Chapters 11 and 12 are *static* games, in which firms make simultaneous decisions and in which each firm has just a single action to take, such as producing a particular output level, charging a particular price, or choosing a particular level of advertising. However, many interactions between firms have a *dynamic* character, because firms act at different times. In a **dynamic game**, players move either repeatedly or sequentially. Therefore, dynamic games may be repeated games or sequential games.

In a *repeated game*, a basic component game or *constituent game* is repeated, perhaps many times. Firms choose from the same set of possible actions again and again. An example of a repeated game is a Cournot oligopoly game played period after period.

In a *sequential game*, one player moves before another moves, possibly making alternating moves, as in chess or tic-tac-toe. A game is also sequential if players have a sequence of different decisions to make, even if moves are made simultaneously with a rival. For example, two firms might play a game in which they first simultaneously choose how much capital to invest and then later simultaneously decide how much output to produce.

In this chapter, we start with repeated games. We show that the strategies in these repeated games are more complex than the strategies used when the constituent game is played only once. In a repeated game, moves made in one period can affect choices made in subsequent periods. Consequently, the equilibrium in a given period of a repeated game may differ from the equilibrium of a corresponding static game. In particular, we show that collusive behavior may be more likely in a repeated-game oligopoly than in a "one-shot" or static oligopoly setting.

Next, we turn to sequential games. We analyze an oligopoly model in which one firm (the leader) chooses an output level before its rival (the follower). We also examine sequential games in which managers must decide whether their firm should act to prevent potential rivals from entering the market, and in which managers must decide whether to introduce a new product. We show that the leader may gain an advantage over its rival because moving first allows it to *commit* to a particular output level and force the rival to react. Finally, we consider what happens if players are not fully rational.

Learning Objectives

1. Explain the differences between static games and repeated games.
2. Analyze sequential games in which first one player acts and then another player acts.
3. Use a dynamic game to show how the action of an incumbent firm may deter entry by a rival.
4. Describe the methods an incumbent firm can use to gain a cost advantage over rivals.
5. Discuss why moving first in a sequential game may be disadvantageous.
6. Illustrate the effects of psychological biases in dynamic games.

13.1 Repeated Games

In the previous chapter, we analyzed static games, in which firms compete only once. We now consider how firms change their strategies and how the game's equilibrium changes if a static game is repeated. The static constituent game might be played just once, repeated a finite (and prespecified) number of times, or repeated indefinitely.[1]

Strategies and Actions in Dynamic Games

In both static and dynamic games, managers need to be able to describe and understand the game and predict the likely outcome so they can determine their best strategies. To understand either a static or a dynamic game, a manager needs to know the players, the rules, the information that each firm has, and the payoffs or profits. However, a major difference between static and dynamic games is that dynamic games require us to distinguish between strategies and actions.

An *action* is a single move that a player makes at a specified time, such as choosing an output level or a price. A *strategy* is a battle plan that specifies the full set of actions that a player will make throughout the game and may involve actions that are conditional on prior actions of other players or on additional information available at a given time.

In a static game, an action and a strategy are identical. The game lasts for only one period, so the action taken in that period represents the full battle plan or strategy. For example, if two firms play a static game in which their only two possible actions are to set a high price or a low price, then the firms' only possible strategies are the same as the actions: set either a high price or a low price.

In contrast, in a repeated or sequential game, actions and strategies differ. If a static game—in which the firms choose either a high price or a low price—is played repeatedly period after period, a firm's strategy determines its action in each period. One possible strategy is for the firm to set the low price in each period. However, it could use a more complex strategy, such as one in which its action in a given period depends on its rival's actions in previous periods. For example, a firm could set a high price in the first period and then, in subsequent periods, it could set its price at the same level that its rival chose in the previous period.

Cooperation in a Repeated Prisoners' Dilemma Game

Because firms may use more complex strategies in repeated games than in static games, the outcomes may differ. To illustrate this difference, we return to the real-world competition between American and United Airlines in which they compete for customers on the Chicago–Los Angeles route, which we examined in Chapter 12. Table 13.1 is the profit matrix for the airlines' static, one-period prisoners' dilemma game in which each firm's only possible actions are to produce a large output (fly 64 thousand passengers per quarter) or a small output (fly 48 thousand passengers per quarter).[2]

---

[1]When we say that a game goes on indefinitely, we mean that the players do not anticipate a definite end point. Each period, the players believe that the game may be repeated in the next period.

[2]Table 13.1 reproduces the profit matrix in Table 12.1, and is based on the estimates of Brander and Zhang (1990).

TABLE 13.1 An Airlines Prisoners' Dilemma Game with Two Actions

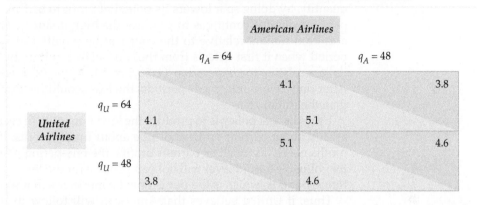

		American Airlines	
		$q_A = 64$	$q_A = 48$
United Airlines	$q_U = 64$	4.1 / 4.1	3.8 / 5.1
	$q_U = 48$	5.1 / 3.8	4.6 / 4.6

Note: Quantities are in thousands of passengers per quarter; (rounded) profits are in millions of dollars per quarter.

In Chapter 12, we noted that in the static game in Table 13.1, each firm has the dominant strategy of selecting the larger output. In the Nash equilibrium in which both firms use their dominant strategy, each firm receives a profit of $4.1 million, which is less than the $4.6 million they would earn if they both produced the smaller output. Thus, our analysis of this static game demonstrates that a firm's best strategy is to pick an action that does not result in the collusive or cartel outcome.

This result is surprising because we know that some real-world firms collude (Chapter 11). Why does our analysis differ from reality? The problem does not lie with the logic behind our analysis of the prisoners' dilemma. Rather, the explanation is that we have been assuming the game is played only once. In real-world markets, interactions between firms are often repeated. We now show that the cooperative or cartel outcome is more likely if the airlines' single-period prisoners' dilemma game in Table 13.1 is repeated indefinitely, quarter after quarter.

In a single-period game, each firm must choose its action *before* observing the rival's action. Therefore, a firm's choice cannot be influenced by its rival's action. It chooses its best response given what it *expects* the rival to do. When the same game is played repeatedly, United may use a strategy in which its action in the current period depends on American's observed actions in previous periods. American may use a similar strategy.

For example, in this repeated game each airline may use a strategy whereby it *threatens to punish* its rival in later periods by producing a high level of output if its rival produces a high level of output in an early period. In particular, suppose that American tells United in a pre-play communication (Chapter 12) that it will produce the smaller collusive or cooperative quantity in the first period, but that it will use the following two-part strategy to determine its output in subsequent periods:

- If United produces the smaller, cooperative quantity in all periods through period t, then American will produce the smaller, cooperative quantity in period $t + 1$.

- However, following the first period t, in which United produces the larger quantity, American will produce the larger quantity in period $t + 1$ and in all subsequent periods.

If United believes that American will follow this strategy, United knows that it will make $4.6 million each period if it produces the smaller quantity. Although

United can make a higher profit, $5.1 million, in period t by producing the larger quantity, by doing so it lowers its potential profit to $4.1 million in each following period even if it continues to produce the high quantity. Thus, United gains half a million dollars relative to the cooperative payoff ($0.5 = $5.1 − $4.6) in the period when it first defects from the cooperative output, but it loses half a million dollars relative to cooperation (−$0.5 = $4.1 − $4.6) in each subsequent period. After only two punishment periods, the loss would be much larger in magnitude than the initial gain.

United's best policy is to produce the lower quantity in each period unless it cares greatly about current profit and little about future profits. If United values future profits nearly as much as current profits, the one-period gain from deviating from the collusive output level will not compensate for the losses from reduced profits in future periods, which is the punishment American will impose.[3]

Thus, if United believes that American will follow its announced strategy, it should produce the lower output level. But should United believe American? While United cannot be certain of American's future strategy, it is at least reasonable for United to take this threat by American seriously because American's best response is to produce the larger quantity if it believes it can't trust United to produce the smaller quantity. Thus, if firms play the same game *indefinitely*, they should find it easier to reach the lower (and more profitable) output level.

American's strategy is an example of a **trigger strategy**, a strategy in which a rival's defection from a collusive outcome triggers a punishment. In this case, the trigger strategy is extreme because a single defection calls for a firm to permanently punish its rival by producing the high output in all subsequent periods. However, if both firms adopt this trigger strategy, the outcome is a Nash equilibrium in which both firms choose the low output and obtain the collusive profit in every period: Defection and punishment need not occur. Less extreme trigger strategies can also be used. For example, a strategy that involved just two periods of punishment for a defection would still be likely to make defection unattractive in this example.

If the low-output strategy is so lucrative for everyone, why don't firms always cooperate when engaging in such indefinitely repeated games? One reason is that the cooperative outcome is not the only possible Nash equilibrium. This game has another Nash equilibrium in which each firm chooses the high output every period. If United believes that American will produce the high output in every period, then its best response is to also produce the high output every period. This same reasoning applies to American as well. Each firm's belief about its rival will be confirmed by experience, and neither firm will have an incentive to change its strategy.

Firms would prefer the cooperative outcome and would probably achieve it in a game as straightforward as this one. However, such cooperation may not be possible in real markets because of antitrust and competition laws or because of limited information. For example, if a firm cannot observe its rival's sales directly, it may try to infer its rival's behavior from observing the demand for its own product. In such a game, the firm may not be able to tell if a dip in the demand for its product is due to its rival producing more or to a reduction in market demand. Appropriate punishments would become more difficult to devise, and implicit agreement among firms would become more difficult to enforce.

---

[3]Presumably, a firm discounts future gains or losses (Chapter 7) because a dollar today is worth more than a dollar in the future. However, the effect of such discounting over a period as short as a few quarters is small.

The trigger strategy that we've been discussing is only one of many possible punishment strategies. Another is the **tit-for-tat strategy**, a strategy for repeated prisoners' dilemma games that involves cooperating in the first round and then copying the rival's previous action in each subsequent round. Thus, producing high output in one period would induce punishment (high output by the rival) in the next. In our airline example, the level of punishment in this tit-for-tat strategy might not be enough to induce cooperation, depending on how much firms discount future gains and losses relative to those in the current period. However, it might work well in other games, as the next Mini-Case illustrates.

Mini-Case

**Tit-for-Tat
Strategies in
Trench Warfare**

Although we focus primarily on business games, game theory is commonly applied in other areas as well, including military situations. One striking example of the tit-for-tat strategy arose in trench warfare in World War I, as Axelrod (2006) described.

No war is pleasant, but the violence in World War I was particularly awful, especially along the 500-mile Western Front in France and Belgium, where Germany and its allies fought against the United Kingdom, France, and their allies. Soldiers on the two sides spent most of their time engaged in trench warfare: hiding in trenches, then occasionally standing up and taking shots at the enemy while hoping not to be shot. However, soldiers were sometimes ordered to charge soldiers in the opposing trenches. These actions usually resulted in a terrible loss of life while moving the front only a short distance.

Newcomers to the front were often surprised to discover that soldiers would apparently shoot over the heads of enemy soldiers, deliberately failing to take shots that had a high probability of killing the enemy. A British staff officer on a tour of the trenches remarked that he was "astonished to observe German soldiers walking about within rifle range behind their own line. Our men appeared to take no notice." The newcomers quickly discovered that a tit-for-tat strategy was being played, often referred to as a "live and let live" strategy.

Axelrod pointed out that the soldiers on the Western Front were engaged in a repeated prisoners' dilemma game. Soldiers needed to shoot their weapons, because the generals and other staff officers behind the lines expected to hear shooting when they approached the front. Given that soldiers had to shoot, they had two possible actions: shoot to kill or shoot to miss.

If the game was played only once—a one-day battle—then shooting to kill was a dominant strategy. Regardless of what the enemy did, preventing enemy soldiers from shooting at you by killing or disabling them offered you a better chance of survival than wasting shots. However, the game was played repeatedly, day after day, month after month, often in the same location. In this repeated game, a strategy that led to cooperation—not shooting to kill—was feasible.

Initially, if one side happened to unleash an unusually intense and damaging barrage of fire, the other side was likely to respond with an intense barrage of its own. Soon it became apparent that the way to avoid an intense barrage was not to initiate one. Adopting a "shoot to miss" strategy could induce the other side to do the same thing. Hence, when an enthusiastic new recruit started shooting aggressively at the enemy, experienced soldiers would yell at him to stop before he got everyone killed, as the enemy would fire back.

Implicit Versus Explicit Collusion

In most modern economies, explicit collusion among the firms in an industry is illegal. Firms are prohibited from meeting and agreeing to restrict their outputs or to set high prices. However, antitrust or competition laws do not strictly prohibit choosing the cooperative (cartel) quantity or price as long as no *explicit* agreement is reached.

Thus, if the firms never meet and openly discuss their behavior, they can produce at the collusive level with little chance of running afoul of the law.[4] Firms may be able to engage in such *implicit collusion* or *tacit collusion* using trigger, tit-for-tat, or other similar strategies. For example, if one firm lowers its output in the current period in the hope that other firms will follow its lead in the next period, it may have stayed within the law as long as it doesn't explicitly communicate with the other firms. Nonetheless, tacit collusion lowers society's total surplus just as explicit collusion does.

<table>
<tr><td>

Mini-Case

Signaling Drug Price Increases

</td><td colspan="2">

In June 2016, Pfizer Inc. raised the list price of its drug Viagra by 13%. Less than a week later, Eli Lilly & Co. increased the price of its similar pill, Cialis, by 13%.

</td></tr>
<tr><td></td><td>

Data sources: Connecture and Rockoff, Jonathan D., "Drugmakers Find Competition Doesn't Keep a Lid on Prices," *Wall Street Journal*, November 27, 2016.

</td><td>

That was not the first time Lilly followed a Pfizer price increase. As the figure shows, these two drugs' prices have been moving in lockstep roughly twice annually for several years. As a result, the list price has more than doubled over the past five years.

The prices of competing insulin, blood-thinner, and other drugs have also moved together. This practice has contributed to the surge in prescription drug spending over recent years.

As a result, legislators have been calling upon the Justice Department and the Federal Trade Commission to investigate possible collusion. However, as long as the firms do not explicitly communicate, such signaling does not violate antitrust laws.

</td></tr>
</table>

Finitely Repeated Games

We have just seen that if firms repeat a prisoners' dilemma game, such as the one in Table 13.1, for an indefinite number of periods, they may achieve a cooperative (low-output) equilibrium. However, if the firms know that the game will be repeated only a finite number of times, *T*, then cooperation (both firms choosing the low output) is not a Nash equilibrium.

In the final period of the game, *T*, the firms know that they're not going to play again, so they are essentially playing a static prisoners' dilemma game in this last period. They know they can "cheat"—produce a large quantity—without fear of

---

[4]U.S. antitrust authorities may prosecute *tacit collusion plus*, where the *plus* indicates some communication occurred that facilitated collusion between firms, even if the communication stopped short of explicit talks about restricting output or setting high prices.

punishment. Thus, producing a large output in the final period is a dominant strategy for both firms.

As a result, the last period in which they might achieve the cooperative outcome is period $T - 1$. In period $T - 1$, each firm reasons that it will get punished in the final period in any case. No additional punishment can be imposed. Nothing the firm does in period $T - 1$ will influence what happens in period T. Therefore, the firms view the game in period $T - 1$ in the same way as they view a static prisoners' dilemma game. They have no incentive to produce the low output in period $T - 1$, because they cannot avoid subsequent punishment in period T. Thus, the dominant strategy for each firm in period $T - 1$ is to produce the large output, because that output maximizes the firm's return in period $T - 1$, regardless of what the rival does. Thus, period $T - 1$ is also a punishment period.

By the same reasoning, the firms will cheat in period $T - 2$ because they know that they will both cheat in period $T - 1$ anyway. Repeating this reasoning, we conclude that they will cheat in periods $T - 3$, $T - 4$, and so forth, all the way back to the first period. That is, any attempt by the firms to cooperate *unravels* at the very start of the game! The only Nash equilibrium is for the static, high-output equilibrium to occur in every period. Thus, maintaining an agreement to produce the small quantity (or to cooperate in any prisoners' dilemma game) will be more difficult if the game has a known stopping point and if players have complete foresight.[5]

13.2 Sequential Games

In a static Cournot game (Chapter 12), before the firms (simultaneously) choose their output levels, Firm 1 could threaten Firm 2 that it will produce a very large output. If Firm 2 believed that threat, it would be in Firm 2's best interest to reduce its output below the Cournot level, ceding an advantage to Firm 1. However, Firm 2 is unlikely to believe this threat, as Firm 1 has not made any commitment to produce the large quantity and therefore might not do it. And Firm 2 could make the same threat, or at least could threaten to produce the Cournot quantity. Firm 1 should not be able to gain a strategic advantage over Firm 2 because they are in symmetric positions.

On the other hand, if Firm 1 produces a large quantity before Firm 2 can act, Firm 1's action is a commitment. The threat to produce a large output acquires credibility once the output is actually produced and observed by the rival. The follower has no choice but to accept that Firm 1 has produced a large output, so the follower chooses to produce less than it otherwise would. Such a game, where one firm moves before the other, is an example of a sequential game.

More generally, a sequential game can have many stages or decision points, such as a game where the players alternate moves indefinitely. In this section, we examine a sequential oligopoly game in which one firm acts before its rival does.

---

[5]However, trigger strategies can potentially support cooperation if the game always has a chance of continuing to the next period. For example, suppose that one firm has a 20% chance of going out of business in any period. Sooner or later the firm will go out of business, but the rival can never be sure that the current period is the firm's last period and must always be concerned about the possibility of being punished in the next period if it deviates from the collusive output this period. As long as the time horizon is indefinite, a cooperative outcome is a possibility for suitable payoff functions.

Stackelberg Oligopoly

In Chapters 11 and 12, we examined oligopoly models, such as the Cournot model, in which firms act simultaneously. Suppose, however, that the rules of the game change so that one of the firms, the *leader*, can set its output in the first stage of the game, but that its rival, the *follower*, cannot choose its output until the second stage of the game. Having one firm act before the other arises naturally if one firm enters the market first. Would the firm that acts first have an advantage?

Heinrich von Stackelberg showed how to modify the Cournot model to answer this question. The Stackelberg model is similar to the Cournot model except that instead of being a static game, it is a sequential game. We examine a duopoly, with one leader and one follower. (A Stackelberg model can also have one leader and several followers.) The leader realizes that once it sets its output, the rival firm will make its best response to the leader's output decision. That is, the leader predicts what the follower will do before the follower acts. Using this knowledge, the leader chooses its output level to manipulate the follower, thereby benefiting at the follower's expense.

We illustrate this two-stage, sequential-move oligopoly game by changing the airline example in Chapters 11 and 12 to allow American Airlines to commit to a quantity before United chooses its quantity. We simplify the problem by assuming initially that each airline has only three actions: to fly 96, 64, or 48 thousand passengers per quarter. Table 13.2 shows the corresponding profits (the same information as is in the profit matrix in Table 12.2). However, this matrix does not show the sequential nature of this new game.

Instead, we can illustrate this sequential game using an *extensive form* diagram (sometimes called a *game tree* or *decision tree*), which is a branched diagram that shows the sequence of moves each player makes. A complete **extensive form** representation shows the players, the sequence of moves, the actions players can take at each move, the information that each player has about previous moves, and the payoff function over all possible strategy combinations. In this section, we assume that players know the payoff function and that, when a player moves, this player knows and can recall the moves each player has made up to that point.

TABLE 13.2 An Airlines Prisoners' Dilemma Game with Three Actions

		American Airlines		
		$q_A = 96$	$q_A = 64$	$q_A = 48$
United Airlines	$q_U = 96$	0 / 0	3.1 / 2.0	4.6 / 2.3
	$q_U = 64$	2.0 / 3.1	4.1 / 4.1	5.1 / 3.8
	$q_U = 48$	2.3 / 4.6	3.8 / 5.1	4.6 / 4.6

Note: Quantities are in thousands of passengers per quarter; (rounded) profits are in millions of dollars per quarter.

The extensive-form diagram in Figure 13.1 shows the order of the airlines' moves, each firm's possible actions at the time of its move, and the resulting profits at the end of the game (using the same profit information as in Table 13.2). In the figure, each box is a point at which the firm named in the box makes a move. The lines extending from the box provide a complete list of the possible actions that the player can make at this particular point in the game. On the left side of the figure, American, the *leader* firm, starts by picking one of the three output levels. In the middle of the figure, United, the *follower* firm, chooses one of the three quantities after learning the output level chosen by American. The right side of the figure shows the profits that American and United earn, given that they sequentially took the actions to reach this final branch. For instance, if American selects 64 and then United chooses 96, American earns $2.0 million profit per quarter and United earns $3.1 million.

Within this game are *subgames*. At a given stage, a **subgame** consists of all the subsequent actions that players can take (given the actions already taken) and the corresponding payoffs. The game in Figure 13.1 has four subgames. Three of these subgames arise in the second stage: United makes a decision given which of the three possible first-stage actions American takes. In addition, the entire game is a subgame because it is the set of subsequent decisions arising at the beginning of the game. Subgames other than the entire game are sometimes referred to as *proper* subgames or *strict* subgames.

To predict the outcome of this sequential game between airlines, we introduce a stronger version of the Nash equilibrium concept—a subgame-perfect Nash equilibrium. A set of strategies forms a **subgame-perfect Nash equilibrium** if the players' strategies form a Nash equilibrium in every subgame (including the overall game).

In Chapter 12, we saw that the static, simultaneous-move version of this game results in a Nash equilibrium in which each firm chooses an output level of 64 thousand passengers per quarter. A static game lacks a strict subgame because players move only once and they move at the same time. The only subgame is the overall game. Therefore, any Nash equilibrium in a static game must be subgame perfect.

FIGURE 13.1 Airlines' Stackelberg Game Tree

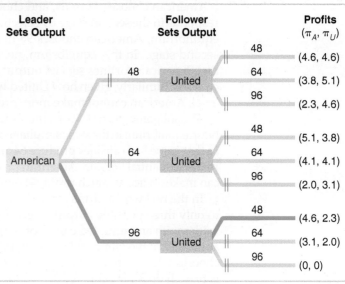

American, the leader firm, chooses its output level first. Given American's choice, United, the follower, picks an output level. The firms' profits that result from these decisions are shown on the right side of the figure. Two red lines through an action line show that the firm rejects that action. The action that each firm chooses is indicated by a dark blue line.

In sequential games, it is possible to have Nash equilibria that are not subgame perfect. However, we focus on only subgame-perfect Nash equilibria because players who rationally plan will reject outcomes that are not subgame perfect. We can solve for a subgame-perfect Nash equilibrium using **backward induction**, in which we first determine the best response by the last player to move, then determine the best response for the player who made the next-to-last move, and so on until we reach the first move of the game. In our example, we work backward from the decision by the follower, United, to the decision by the leader, American, moving from the right to the left side of the game tree.

How should American, the leader, select its output in the first stage? American determines what United, the follower, will do in the second stage, given each possible output choice by American in the first stage. Thus, American anticipates United's reaction to each output level American might choose. Using its conclusions about United's second-stage reaction, American makes its first-stage decision.

In this game, United, the follower, does not have a dominant strategy. The amount it chooses to produce depends on the quantity that American chose in the first stage. If American chooses 96, then United's profit is $2.3 million if it picks 48, $2.0 million if it chooses 64, and $0 if it selects 96. Thus, if American chooses 96, United's best response is 48 with a profit of $2.3 million. The pair of red vertical lines through the other two action lines show that United will not choose those actions.

Using the same reasoning, American determines how United will respond to each of American's possible actions, as the right side of the figure illustrates. American predicts that

- If American chooses 48, United will pick 64, so American's profit will be $3.8 million.

- If American chooses 64, United will pick 64, so American's profit will be $4.1 million.

- If American chooses 96, United will pick 48, so American's profit will be $4.6 million.

Thus, to maximize its profit, American chooses 96 in the first stage. United's strategy is to make its best response to American's first-stage action: United selects 64 if American chooses 48 or 64, and chooses 48 if American chooses 96. Thus, United responds in the second stage by selecting 48. Therefore, in the subgame-perfect Nash equilibrium, American chooses 96 in the first stage and United chooses 48 in the second stage. In this equilibrium, neither firm wants to change its strategy. Given that American Airlines sets its output at 96, United maximizes its profit by setting $q_U = 48$. Similarly, given how United will respond to each possible American output level, American cannot make more profit than if it chooses 96.

The subgame-perfect Nash equilibrium in this sequential game is different from the Nash equilibrium in the static simultaneous-move game based on Table 13.2 (Chapter 12). In that game both airlines produce 64 and both earn the same profit level, $4.1 million. In the sequential version, American produces 96 and United produces 48, and American makes twice as much profit, $4.6 million, as does United, $2.3 million.

In the real world, firms can choose any output they want—they're not restricted to only three possible output levels. As in the limited-choice game, the Stackelberg leader with an unlimited choice of output levels uses backward induction—starting at the end of the game and working toward the beginning. That is, before the leader chooses which action to take, the leader considers what the follower's best response is to each possible action of the leader.

We show how to determine the leader's profit-maximizing output mathematically in Appendix 13A. The following Q&A shows how to use a spreadsheet to determine the leader's profit-maximizing output.

Q&A 13.1

Suppose that American Airlines is the leader. It sets its output, qA, before United sets its output, qU. The industry inverse demand function is $Q = 339 - p$, and both firms have a constant average and marginal cost of $147 per passenger. United's best-response function is $q_U = 96 - \frac{1}{2} q_A$ (Equation 11.6). Use a spreadsheet to determine industry quantity, industry price, and the profit of each firm for each output level that American might choose between 48 and 120 in increments of 8. What is American's maximum profit? In the Stackelberg equilibrium, what quantity is produced by each firm, and what are the industry quantity and price?

Answer

1. *Prepare an Excel spreadsheet.* In cells A1 through F1 enter the following labels: qA, qU, Q, Price, Profit-A, and Profit-U. In cells A2 through A11 enter the quantities 48 through 120 in increments of 8.

2. *Fill in the formulas.* Enter "=96−0.5*A2" in cell B2 and "=A2+B2" in cell C2. As the inverse demand function is $p = 339 - Q$, enter "=339−C2" in cell D2. Also enter "=(D2−147)*A2" in cell E2 and "=(D2−147)*B2" in cell F2. Copy and paste the formula in cell B2 into cells B3 through B11 and do a corresponding copy and paste in columns C through F.

3. *By inspection, find the highest value of American's profit.* The highest profit for American, shown in yellow in the spreadsheet, is $4608 in cell E8.

4. *Determine the Stackelberg equilibrium values based on American's optimal quantity.* Because American's profit reaches a maximum in row 8, the other values in that row are the Stackelberg equilibrium values: American's quantity is 96, United's quantity is 48, the market quantity is 144, and the price is 195.

	A	B	C	D	E	F
1	qA	qU	Q	Price	Profit-A	Profit-U
2	48	72	120	219	3456	5184
3	56	68	124	215	3808	4624
4	64	64	128	211	4096	4096
5	72	60	132	207	4320	3600
6	80	56	136	203	4480	3136
7	88	52	140	199	4576	2704
8	96	48	144	195	4608	2304
9	104	44	148	191	4576	1936
10	112	40	152	187	4480	1600
11	120	36	156	183	4320	1296

Come here! Don't make me run after you!

Credible Threats

Why do the simultaneous-move and sequential-move output games have different outcomes? Given the option to act first, American chooses a large output level to make it in United's best interest to pick a relatively small output level, 48. American benefits from moving first and choosing a large quantity.

In the simultaneous-move game, United will not believe a threat by American that it will produce a large quantity. For a firm's announced strategy to be a **credible threat**, rivals must believe that the firm's strategy is rational in the sense that it is in the firm's best interest to use it.[6] If American produced the leader's level of output and United produced the Cournot level, American's profit would be lower than if it, too, produced the Cournot level. Because American cannot be sure that United will believe its threat and reduce its output in the simultaneous-move game, American produces only the Cournot output level. In contrast, in the sequential-move game, because American moves first, its commitment to produce a large quantity is credible.

The intuition for why commitment makes a threat credible is similar to that of "burning bridges." If a general burns the bridge behind an army so that the troops can only advance and not retreat, the army becomes a more fearsome foe. An army facing a choice of winning a battle or dying is likely to fight more aggressively than one that can retreat if things are not going well. Similarly, by limiting its future options, a firm can make itself stronger.[7]

Q&A 13.2

Consider the game described in the Mini-Case, "Competing E-Book Formats" in Chapter 12 and analyzed in Q&A 12.2 where Amazon and other e-book firms choose between the e-book formats AZW (the Amazon Kindle's standard) and EPUB (a widely used alternative standard). In Q&A 12.2, we assumed that Amazon and the Other group of e-book manufacturers simultaneously chose their formats. However, because it entered the market first, Amazon chose its e-book standard before the Other group did. Using the numbers in Q&A 12.2, which is reproduced here, show the game tree. What is the Nash equilibrium if firms are free to choose whichever standard they want?

---

[6]You may have been in a restaurant where an exasperated parent tries to control a difficult child with extreme threats like "If you don't behave, you'll have to sit in the car while we eat dinner" or "If you don't behave, I'll never let you watch TV again!" The kid, of course, does not view such threats as credible and continues to terrorize the restaurant—proving that the kid is a better game theorist than the parent.

[9]Some psychologists use the idea of commitment to treat behavioral problems. A psychologist may advise an author with writer's block to set up an irreversible procedure whereby if the author's book is not finished by a certain date, the author's check for $10,000 will be sent to a political candidate the author detests. Such an irreversible commitment helps the author get the project done by raising the cost of failure.

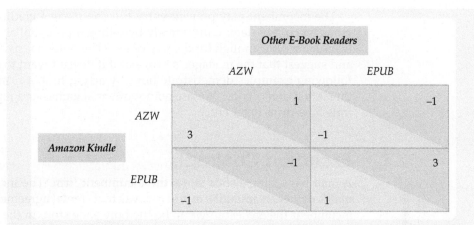

Answer

1. *Draw the extensive-form diagram given that Amazon moves before the Other group of manufacturers using the numbers from the profit matrix.*

2. *Solve backward to determine the Nash equilibrium.* The figure shows that if Amazon initially chooses the AZW format, then the Other group would also choose the AZW format because its profit, $\pi_O = 1$, would be higher than if it chose EPUB, $\pi_O = -1$, as indicated by the red double lines through the EPUB option. Similarly, if Amazon initially chooses the EPUB format, so would the Other group. Because Amazon's profit is greater if it chooses the AZW format, $\pi_A = 3$, than if it picks the EPUB format, $\pi_A = 1$, it prefers the AZW format. Thus, with a first-mover advantage, Amazon chooses the AZW format, which the Other group would accept.

13.3 Deterring Entry

The Stackelberg game demonstrates that the leader firm can benefit from moving before the follower firm. In some markets, by moving first, a manager can act strategically to prevent potential rivals from entering the market. How can an *incumbent*, monopoly firm deter a (potential) *rival* from entering that market? Does it pay for the incumbent to take the actions that will deter entry?

The incumbent may prevent entry if it can make a credible threat. However, a manager cannot deter entry merely by telling a potential rival, "Don't enter! This market ain't big enough for the two of us." The potential rival would merely laugh and suggest that the manager's firm exit if it doesn't want to share the market. The following examples demonstrate how, by acting first, a firm can make a credible threat that deters entry. We use both sequential games and repeated games to illustrate how firms deter entry.

Exclusion Contracts

A mall has a single shoe store, the incumbent firm. The incumbent may pay the mall's owner an amount b to add a clause to its rental agreement that guarantees the incumbent the *exclusive right* to be the only shoe store in the mall. If this payment is made, the landlord agrees to rent the remaining space only to a restaurant, a toy store, or some other business that does not sell shoes. Should the shoe store pay?

The game tree, Figure 13.2, shows the two stages of the game involving the incumbent and its potential rival, another shoe store. In the first stage, the incumbent decides whether to pay b to prevent entry. In the second stage, the potential rival decides whether to enter. If it enters, it incurs a fixed fee of F to build its store in the mall.

The right side of the figure shows the incumbent's and the potential rival's profits (π_i, π_r) for each of the three possible outcomes. The outcome at the top of the figure shows that if the incumbent does not buy exclusivity and the potential rival does not enter, the incumbent earns the "monopoly" profit of $\pi_i = 10$ ($10 thousand) per month and its potential rival earns nothing, $\pi_r = 0$. The middle outcome shows that if the incumbent does not pay the exclusivity fee and the potential rival enters, the incumbent earns a duopoly profit of $\pi_i = 4$ and the rival earns the duopoly profit less its fixed cost, F, of entering, $\pi_r = 4 - F$. In the bottom outcome, the incumbent pays b for the exclusivity right so that it earns the monopoly profit less the exclusivity fee, $\pi_i = 10 - b$, and its potential rival earns nothing, $\pi_r = 0$.

To solve for the subgame-perfect Nash equilibrium, we work backward, starting with the last decision, the potential rival's entry decision. The top portion of the game tree shows what happens if the incumbent does not pay the landlord to prevent entry. The potential rival earns $\pi_r = 4 - F$ if it enters. We assume the rival enters

FIGURE 13.2 **Paying to Prevent Entry**

If the potential rival stays out of the mall, it makes no profit, $\pi_r = 0$, and the incumbent firm makes the monopoly profit, $\pi_i = 10$. If the potential rival enters, the incumbent earns the duopoly profit of 4 and the rival makes $4 - F$, where F is its fixed cost of entry. If the duopoly profit, 4, is less than F, entry does not occur. Otherwise, entry occurs unless the incumbent acts to deter entry by paying for exclusive rights to be the only shoe store in the mall. The incumbent pays the landlord only if $10 - b > 4$.

as long as its profit from entering is at least as much as it earns by staying out of the market, $\pi_r \geq 0$. That is, the potential rival enters if $F \leq 4$. In the bottom portion of the game tree, where the incumbent pays b for an exclusive contract that prevents entry, the potential rival has no possible action.

Which of the three possible outcomes occurs depends on the parameters b (the incumbent's exclusivity fee) and F (the potential rival's fixed cost of entering the market):

- **Blockaded entry** $(F > 4)$: The potential rival chooses not to enter even if the incumbent does not pay to have an exclusive contract, so $\pi_r = 0$. The incumbent avoids spending b and still earns the monopoly profit, $\pi_i = 10$.

- **Deterred entry** $(F \leq 4, b \leq 6)$: Because $F \leq 4$, entry will occur unless the incumbent pays the exclusivity fee. The incumbent chooses to pay the exclusivity fee, b, because its profit from doing so, $\pi_i = 10 - b \geq 4$, is at least as large as what it earns if it permits entry and earns the duopoly profit, $\pi_i = 4$. Because the rival does not enter, it earns nothing: $\pi_r = 0$.

- **Accommodated entry** $(F \leq 4, b > 6)$: Entry will occur unless the incumbent pays the fee because the rival's fixed costs are less than or equal to 4. The incumbent does not pay for an exclusive contract. The exclusivity fee is so high that the incumbent earns more by allowing entry, $\pi_i = 4$, than it earns if it pays for exclusivity, $\pi_i = 10 - b < 4$. Thus, the incumbent earns the duopoly profit, $\pi_i = 4$, and the rival makes $\pi_r = 4 - F$.

In short, the incumbent does not pay for an exclusive contract if the potential rival's cost of entry is prohibitively high $(F > 4)$ or if the cost of the exclusive contract is too high $(b > 6)$.

The next Q&A uses dynamic game theory to reject the following false belief:

Common Confusion A firm invests in new equipment only if the variable cost savings outweigh the fixed cost of the investment.

Mini-Case

Pay-for-Delay Agreements

If managers cannot deter entry, they may try to delay entry. For example, pharmaceutical companies pay large amounts to delay the entry of generic competitors following the expiration of a drug patent.

Every year many drug patents expire. In 2018, drugs worth $31 billion in sales lost U.S. patent protection. After a U.S. pharmaceutical patent expires, the company that was the first to file with the U.S. Food and Drug Administration (FDA) to produce a generic version of the medication has a 180-day exclusivity period during which it is the only new firm that may sell a generic version of the drug. During that period, the former patent holder may also sell its drug under a generic name as well as its original brand name. For a valuable drug, after the six-month period elapses, many generics enter the market, typically siphoning off 90% of sales because generic prices average 30% of brand-name prices. It can be very valuable for a drug company to prevent the first firm from entering during that six-month period so that it can continue to charge a monopoly price.

Drug companies with expired patents have used a variety of *pay-for-delay* schemes to slow the entry of generics. The U.S. Federal Trade Commission (FTC) has charged that some drug makers had either paid generic firms directly or promised not to introduce their own generic versions if a potential rival delayed its entry into the market. The industry contended that these pay-for-delay deals are legal business decisions, but the U.S. Supreme Court ruled that such deals were illegal if they violate antitrust laws. Thus, the FTC could take legal action against the companies on a case-by-case basis. In one subsequent case, the FTC reached a settlement with Teva Ltd. in which the company agreed to pay $1.2 billion to compensate purchasers who overpaid for the drug Provigil (for sleep disorders) due to a pay-for-delay agreement.

Limit Pricing

A firm is **limit pricing** if it sets its price (or, equivalently, its output) so that another firm cannot enter the market profitably. For example, the incumbent could set a price below the potential rival's marginal cost so entry would be unprofitable if that price were maintained after entry. Or the incumbent could produce so much output that the price is very low and too few customers remain for the potential rival to make a profit. However, to successfully limit price, a firm must be able to credibly threaten to choose a price (or output) that will cause an entrant to make losses if entry occurs. Such credibility requires the incumbent to have an advantage over its rivals, as the following example illustrates.

An incumbent could threaten a potential rival that, if entry occurs, it will charge a price so low that the entrant will make a loss. This threat will only work if the threat is credible. It is not credible if the two firms have identical costs and market demand is adequate to support both firms. In that case, if entry occurs, it is in the incumbent's best interest to charge the duopoly price and make a profit rather than charge such a low price that everyone loses money. In this case, the potential rival ignores the threat and enters.

For the threat of limit pricing to be credible, the incumbent must have an advantage over its rival. For example, if the incumbent's costs are lower than those of the potential rival, the incumbent can charge a price so low that the rival would lose money while the incumbent earns a higher profit than if it allows entry.

Another example is an extreme form of the Stackelberg oligopoly example. The Stackelberg leader acts first and produces a large quantity so that the follower produces a smaller quantity. Depending on the demand curve and the firms' costs, it may be even more profitable for the leader to produce such a large quantity that the follower cannot earn a profit. That is, the leader makes limit pricing credible by committing to provide a very large output level.

Mini-Case	On November 30, 2011, the main patent for Lipitor—a drug that treats high cholesterol—expired, allowing generic drug manufacturers to enter this market. That was a tragedy for its manufacturer, Pfizer, because Lipitor was the world's best-selling drug ever, with $106 billion in sales over the previous decade and $10.8 billion in sales in 2010.
Pfizer Uses Limit Pricing to Slow Entry	

Ranbaxy Laboratories of India, as the first firm to file with the FDA to produce generic Lipitor, gained the exclusive rights to produce generic Lipitor from December 2011 through May 2012. Pfizer realized that delaying the entry of firms producing generic Lipitor for even a few months would pay handsomely.

Pfizer used many methods to delay entry, including limit pricing. Pfizer issued a statement saying that "Our intent is to offer Lipitor to payers and patients at or below the cost of the generic during the 180-day period." Pfizer also subsidized patients' private insurance for Lipitor, lowering their out-of-pocket costs to the same level or below what they paid for generic drugs. One top Pfizer official said that the company would adjust its discounts to beat any tit-for-tat reduction in generic pricing during the first six months.

Pfizer ended its extreme discount program after the first six months. Once other firms entered and generic drugs flooded the market, driving down prices, these subsidies would have been more costly. After ending its limit pricing program, Pfizer reverted to high prices for the customers who remain loyal to brand-name Lipitor. (See the Managerial Problem "Brand-Name and Generic Drugs" in Chapter 9.)

Q&A 13.3

In the first stage of a game between an incumbent and a potential rival, the incumbent builds its plant using either an inflexible technology that allows it to produce only a (large) fixed quantity, or a flexible technology that allows it to produce small or large quantities. In the second stage, the potential rival decides whether to enter. With the inflexible technology, the incumbent makes so much output that its threat to limit price is credible, as the following game tree illustrates. What strategy (technology) maximizes the incumbent's profit?

Answer

1. *Work backward by determining the potential rival's best strategy conditional on each possible action by the incumbent.* This game has two proper subgames. The upper-right subgame shows the profits if the potential rival enters or if it does not enter given that the incumbent uses the inflexible technology. The potential rival loses money ($\pi_r = -1$) if it enters, but breaks even ($\pi_r = 0$) if it doesn't, so it does not enter. In the lower-right subgame, the potential rival decides whether to enter given that the incumbent is using the flexible technology. Here, the potential rival prefers to enter and earn a profit of $\pi_r = 5$ rather than stay out and earn nothing.

2. *Given the responses by the potential rival to each of the incumbent's strategies, determine the incumbent's best strategy.* If the incumbent uses the flexible technology, entry occurs, and the incumbent earns $\pi_i = 5$. However, if the incumbent uses the inflexible technology, the other firm does not enter, and the incumbent's profit is $\pi_i = 20$. Thus, the incumbent chooses the inflexible technology.

Comment: If entry is not possible, the incumbent earns a higher profit with the flexible technology than with the inflexible technology. However, the possibility of entry changes the problem facing the incumbent. If the incumbent chooses the flexible technology, its rival enters, so the incumbent is better off committing to the inflexible technology.

Entry Deterrence in a Repeated Game

An entry game can be repeated over time or over space. A successful, profitable firm is likely to face repeated threats of entry by potential rivals over time. A grocery chain with a monopoly in many small towns faces potential entry by other firms in some or all of these towns.

Figure 13.3 shows the constituent entry game—the game in only one town—that the grocery chain faces. If the incumbent retains its monopoly position, its profit is 10 ($10 million). If it accommodates entry, both firms receive 3, and if the incumbent fights by pricing aggressively, it gets only 1, while the rival loses 1. The incumbent must decide whether to engage in a price war with the rival or accommodate the rival by keeping its price high (or its output low) and sharing the market.

Given the profits in this constituent game, if this game is played only once and if the profits are common knowledge, then the only subgame-perfect Nash equilibrium is for entry to occur and for the incumbent to accommodate entry. The potential rival reasons that if it enters, then the incumbent can choose to fight and get 1 or accommodate entry and gain 3. The potential rival realizes that the incumbent maximizes its profit by accommodating entry. Thus, entry occurs, because the rival earns 3 by entering and nothing by staying out of the market.

Does the equilibrium change if the game is repeated many times in different locations and possibly at different times? Suppose the incumbent firm faces a potential rival in one town and knows that other potential rivals may later enter in other towns. Because what it does in the current game may affect future entry, the manager of the chain may conclude that engaging in an unprofitable price war when the first entry occurs is a good idea if doing so is likely to deter many future rivals.

FIGURE 13.3 **A Constituent Game of a Repeated Entry Game**

This game tree shows the constituent game in one town that is repeated in many towns. If the potential rival does not enter, the incumbent grocery chain retains its monopoly. If entry occurs, the incumbent decides whether to fight (price aggressively) or accommodate the rival (set a high price). It does not pay for the incumbent to fight once entry occurs, so its rival enters.

*"Yes, I pay you to keep rivals out of our territory.
But, I don't want to hear all the gory details."*

If the incumbent has the reputation of being a rational profit maximizer and if its profits are common knowledge, the chain will not intimidate future potential rivals merely by fighting once, because the potential rivals realize that fighting each time is not in the chain's best interest.

However, fighting may be a good strategy for the chain if the chain's profits are not common knowledge, so that potential rivals have incomplete information. If the chain fights with the first entrant, potential rivals may (falsely) conclude that the chain's profits are such that fighting is its best strategy even if the game is played only once. If potential rivals conclude that the incumbent will always fight, they won't enter because they know they would lose money in a price war.

In such a repeated game, although fighting the first rival is not profitable, the incumbent does so to develop a reputation for being a tough competitor. Thus, fighting the first rival is part of a rational long-run strategy and can be part of a subgame-perfect Nash equilibrium in which entry is successfully deterred.[8]

13.4 Cost and Innovation Strategies

A firm may be able to gain a cost advantage over a rival by moving first. Our analysis of the Cournot model in Chapter 11 shows that a firm with a lower marginal cost produces more and earns a higher profit than does its high-cost rival. We start by examining two cases where a firm moves first to gain a marginal cost advantage over its rivals by undertaking process innovation or increasing the rate of learning by doing to lower its own marginal cost. Then we consider a firm's strategic action that raises its rivals' marginal cost by more than its own.

Investing to Lower Marginal Cost

A firm should invest in a *process innovation*, which improves the method of production for an existing product, if the resulting reduction in its marginal cost more than offsets the investment of developing and installing the innovation. Also, a firm may invest in a process innovation even if the cost savings do not justify that investment, if the investment deters entry.

For example, an incumbent monopoly considers investing in a process innovation: buying and customizing industrial robots for its assembly line. These robots would replace some workers and lower its marginal cost of production. However, if the incumbent remains a monopoly, this investment does not pay because its cost exceeds the extra profit from the lower marginal cost. Nonetheless, the incumbent may undertake such R&D under certain conditions.

---

[8]This game-theoretic argument is presented formally in Kreps and Wilson (1982) and Milgrom and Roberts (1982).

If the market conditions are such that entry is *blockaded*—no firm will enter even if the incumbent produces the monopoly output—the incumbent does not invest. Now suppose that entry is not blockaded: A new firm will enter the market if the monopoly does not act. However, if the monopoly makes the investment and lowers its marginal cost, the potential rival observes that the incumbent is producing more output than it previously did, flooding the market with extra output and lowering the market price. Faced with this credible threat to produce a lot of output after entry, the potential rival does not enter because it realizes that it will lose money. As a result, the incumbent may invest to discourage entry.

Figure 13.4 shows a game tree that illustrates this reasoning. The incumbent decides whether to invest in the first stage, and the potential rival decides whether to enter in the second stage.

To solve for the subgame-perfect Nash equilibrium, we work backward from the potential rival's entry decision in the second stage of the game. We start by looking at the potential rival's decision in the proper subgame at the top of the tree given that the incumbent does not invest in the first stage. The potential rival's profit is $\pi_r = 0$ if it stays out of the market and $\pi_r = 4$ (million dollars) if it enters. Thus, the rival chooses to enter because $4 > 0$. We draw a pair of red parallel lines on the path labeled "Do not enter" to indicate that the rival rejects that choice given that the incumbent does not invest in the first stage.

Next, we look at the proper subgame in the lower part of the game tree in which the incumbent invests in the first stage. Here, the potential rival chooses not to enter because $\pi_r = -1$ if it enters and 0 if it stays out of the market.

We now turn to the incumbent's decision in the first stage. By working backward, the incumbent knows that if it does not invest, the potential rival enters, so that the incumbent's profit is $\pi_i = 4$. Alternatively, if it invests, the potential rival stays out of the market, and the incumbent's profit is $\pi_i = 8$. Because $8 > 4$, the incumbent makes the investment.

FIGURE 13.4 **Investing to Prevent Entry**

First, the incumbent monopoly decides whether to invest in R&D for a process innovation that reduces its marginal cost of production, which will induce it to produce more, all else the same. Second, the potential rival decides whether to enter the market. If the incumbent does not invest in R&D, it pays for the rival to enter: $\pi_r = 4 > 0$. If the incumbent does invest in R&D, the rival knows entry will be unprofitable: $\pi_r = -1 < 0$. The incumbent chooses to invest in R&D because its profit if it invests, $\pi_i = 8$, is greater than its payoff if it does not invest, $\pi_i = 4$.

The incumbent's profit, $\pi_i = 8$, is lower than the profit, $\pi_i = 10$, that it would have earned if it did not make the investment *and* the potential rival stayed out of the market. Nevertheless, the incumbent benefits from this "unprofitable" investment because it deters the entry that would otherwise occur.

Learning by Doing

What we have to learn to do, we learn by doing. —Aristotle

In aircraft and computer chip manufacturing and in some other industries, the more cumulative output a firm has produced, the lower its marginal cost, as its workers and managers learn by doing (Chapter 6). Consequently, the first firm in a market may want to produce more than the quantity that maximizes its short-run profit, so that its future marginal cost will be lower than that of a late-entering rival.

Indeed, Benkard (2004) demonstrated that an aircraft manufacturer may price below current marginal cost in the short run, because of its steep learning curve. The price of the Lockheed L-1011 was below the static marginal cost for essentially its entire 14-year production run. Salgado (2008) found that AMD's cost of manufacturing computer chips was about 12% higher than Intel's cost because AMD had less learning by doing, as it had produced fewer units.

Raising Rivals' Costs

A firm may benefit from using a strategy that raises its own cost but raises its rivals' costs by more. As the Cournot example in Chapter 11 illustrates, a firm can benefit from being the lower-cost firm.

Firms can use many methods to raise rivals' costs. An incumbent firm may lobby the government for more industry regulations that raise costs, as long as the legislation *grandfathers* existing firms' plants. For example, the incumbent may want all new plants to install expensive pollution-control equipment that raises production costs, provided that its existing plants are exempted.

An incumbent can take many actions that make it costly for its consumers to switch to a rival's product in the future. It may impose a *switching fee*: a charge that customers must pay to take their business elsewhere. By designing software for its computer, phone, or other electronic device so that it won't work on a rival's equipment, an incumbent can raise the cost of switching.

Alternatively, a firm may patent its software, so that it can prevent rivals from using its software on their equipment. Before U.S. legislation prevented this practice, a phone company would prevent customers from transferring their phone numbers to a rival provider, so as to reduce the chance of a consumer switching providers. These practices raise the cost to latecomers of attracting new customers.

Q&A 13.4   In a duopoly market, to produce a given amount of output, Firm 1 uses relatively more capital but less labor than does Firm 2. Both firms hire labor from the same labor union, which sets the same wage for both firms. Firm 1 is about to bargain with the union. Whatever wage it negotiates, Firm 2 has to pay the same wage. Because this industry is suffering from a downturn in demand, the union is willing to accept the current (lower) wage. However, if Firm 1 agrees to a higher wage, its cost of production will rise by less than Firm 2's cost. The game tree shows the profits corresponding to the various actions by the firms. Firm 1's profit is A if it chooses the high wage and Firm 2 chooses the low output level. Under what condition should Firm 1 offer to pay a high wage?

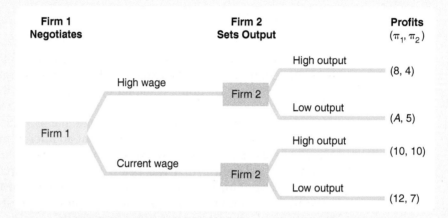

Answer

1. *Determine Firm 2's action conditional on the wage by comparing its profits at each output.* We start by solving backward, as usual. If Firm 1 keeps the current wage (the bottom half of the figure), then Firm 2 will pick a high output level and earn a profit of 10 ($10 million), rather than a low output level and earn only 7. If Firm 1 agrees to the high wage, Firm 2's profit is 5 if it produces the low output level and 4 if produces the high output level. Therefore, Firm 2 produces the low output level.

2. *Determine which wage Firm 1 chooses by comparing the profits from different wage choices.* If Firm 1 chooses the current wage, Firm 2 produces the high output, so Firm 1 earns 10. Alternatively, if Firm 1 agrees to the high wage, Firm 2 produces the low output, so Firm 1 earns A. Consequently, Firm 1 chooses the current wage if $A < 10$ and agrees to the high wage otherwise.

Mini-Case	The United Auto Workers (UAW), the union that provides labor to the U.S. auto industry, negotiates contracts with the Big 3 automakers (General Motors, Ford, and Fiat-Chrysler) when the old contract expires, which occurs roughly every three or four years. Traditionally, the UAW initially negotiates with only one auto firm—the *target* firm—while implicitly threatening that if the parties fail to come to terms, the UAW will strike only that one company, putting it at a competitive disadvantage. Negotiations began in July 2015 on a new UAW contract, and the UAW selected Fiat-Chrysler as the target firm. As of 2018, the UAW has not announced its target for the 2019 contract negotiations.
Auto Union Negotiations	

Other car companies almost always adopt the agreement or *pattern contract* between the target firm and the union to avoid strikes of their own. As a consequence, if the target firm makes large wage concessions, it essentially inflicts those high wages on its rivals.

13.5 Disadvantages of Moving First

Although moving first often benefits a firm, it is important not to overgeneralize.

> **Common Confusion** A firm that moves first always has an advantage.

Moving first is not always an advantage. We discuss two possible drawbacks to moving first: the holdup problem and acting too quickly.

The Holdup Problem

One of the most serious potential problems with moving first is the holdup problem. It arises when two parties want to contract or trade with each other but one must move first by making a *specific* investment: an investment that it can use only in its transaction with the second party. A **holdup problem** arises if two parties agree to work together and the one that acts second takes advantage of a specific investment made by the party that acts first.

Holdup problems may arise between governments and firms or between individuals, but most commonly arise between firms. If the firm that acts first does not anticipate opportunistic behavior by the second firm and it occurs, then the first firm loses part of its investment. Here, the first mover is at a disadvantage by moving first. Alternatively, if the first firm anticipates that such opportunistic behavior is likely, it may not make the specific investment out of fear that the other firm will exploit it, with the result that both firms lose the potential benefits from transacting.

The most famous example concerns negotiations between Fisher Body and General Motors (GM) about a century ago (Klein, Crawford, and Alchian, 1978). Fisher Body was considering whether to produce metal parts for particular GM cars. To do so for each GM part, it needed to create specific dies (molds used to make parts) that a machine press uses to manufacture a part. Fisher worried that these dies were such *specific investments*, with no alternative use, that they would serve as *hostages*—something that Fisher could lose if GM later lowered the amount it would pay for Fisher parts.[9]

We formally analyze a holdup game using a recent example of nationalization, which is government seizure of property owned by a foreign firm. We focus on Venezuela, but many other countries have also nationalized foreign firms.

ExxonMobil, an oil company, is the first mover in a game with the Venezuelan government. It considers making a large investment to obtain rights and build facilities to drill for and refine oil in either Venezuela or some other country. If Venezuela honors their deal, ExxonMobil believes that it can earn 20 ($20 billion) in Venezuela or 10 elsewhere. If the investment is made, the Venezuelan government, the second mover, has a hostage: the oil company's investment, which cannot be moved elsewhere. The government can nationalize part of the oil field operations. The game tree in Figure 13.5 indicates that if the Venezuelan government does not nationalize, ExxonMobil's profit is $\pi_X = 20$. However, with a (partial) nationalization, its profit falls to $\pi_X = 8$. The difference, 12, goes to the Venezuelan government, so π_V increases from 20 to 32.

---

[9]A reverse holdup problem could also have occurred. If GM committed to allowing Fisher to be its only supplier of parts, then Fisher could demand higher prices for these parts and GM would have little recourse in the short run. To keep our formal analysis relatively simple, we concentrate on situations where only the firm that acts first is at risk of being exploited.

FIGURE 13.5 **Venezuela–ExxonMobil Holdup Problem**

If ExxonMobil invests in Venezuela's oil fields, it runs the risk that Venezuela will later partially nationalize the firm. Given that ExxonMobil invests, Venezuela's profit is higher if it nationalizes, $\pi_V = 32$, than if it does not, $\pi_V = 20$. If Exxon realizes that Venezuela will nationalize, it does not invest in Venezuela because, after nationalization, its Venezuelan profit, $\pi_X = 8$, is less than what it can earn elsewhere, $\pi_X = 10$.

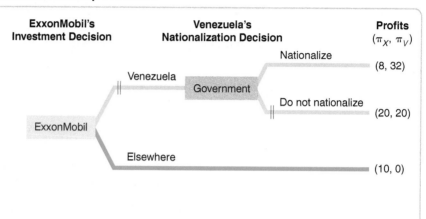

If the company does not expect a nationalization problem, it makes the investment because it prefers a profit of 20 to the 10 it would earn elsewhere. However, if nationalization occurs, the company earns only 8. Therefore, if the oil company anticipates that the Venezuelan government is likely to nationalize its investment, the company invests elsewhere because $\pi_X = 10$ is more than the $\pi_X = 8$ that the company earns after the partial nationalization. Thus, ExxonMobil does not make an investment that would benefit both it and Venezuela.

Mini-Case

Venezuelan Nationalization

In the 1990s, private oil companies were permitted to invest in a joint venture agreement with Venezuela's state-owned oil company Petroleos de Venezuela S.A. (PDVSA), which had a minority share. Mobil (now ExxonMobil), Chevron-Texaco (now Chevron), Statoil, ConocoPhillips, and BP invested in the Orinoco Oil Belt in eastern Venezuela, which is thought to contain the world's largest reserves of extra-heavy oil. Their plants convert the heavy crude to lighter crude oil.

When these companies first invested in Venezuela, they were given various promises about how they would be treated. However, soon thereafter, newly elected President Hugo Chavez started nationalizing investments by oil companies and other businesses. In 2007, President Chavez announced that Venezuela was partially nationalizing the Orinoco Oil Belt, substantially reducing foreign oil companies' ownership shares, with PDVSA gaining a minimum of 60% of the shares and hence majority control. Chavez claimed that foreign oil companies were still welcome in Venezuela, but not as majority stakeholders: "The owner will be PDVSA and the business will be in the hands of Venezuelans."

After complaints from ExxonMobil and ConocoPhillips, the Venezuelan government ultimately agreed to go to the International Centre for Settlement of Investment Disputes (ICSID), an international arbitration panel, to determine the amount of compensation the two oil companies would receive. In 2014, the panel awarded Exxon $1.6 billion in compensation, which was much less than Exxon had demanded. This award was substantially reduced to $188 million on appeal before an ICSID appeal committee in 2017, and even this payment is subject to further legal dispute.

Regardless of whether Venezuela ever pays compensation to Exxon, Venezuela has suffered costs in foregone investment. While some firms have made investments in Venezuelan oil since the partial nationalizations, Exxon has invested heavily in neighboring Guyana and has found large oil deposits there.

Nationalization is a shortsighted policy that can destroy a nation's reputation and prevent foreign direct investment. For example, since Fidel Castro nationalized American-owned companies in Cuba without compensation in 1960, Cuba suffered from 55 years of sanctions and no U.S. foreign investment. In 2017, Tanzania's President Magufuli stated that he "will not hesitate to close down all the mines if companies don't pay us what they owe us" after insisting on greatly increased payments from foreign mining companies. Several companies immediately ceased or scaled back operations.

Managerial Implication
Avoiding Holdups

Managers should seek ways to avoid losing money due to holdups. Five frequently used approaches are contracts, vertical integration, quasi-vertical integration, reputation building, and multiple or open sourcing.

Many managers use contracts to prevent holdup problems. The second-mover firm contractually guarantees the first-mover firm that it will not be exploited. To alleviate the fears of Fisher Body that GM would later drop its price or stop buying from Fisher, GM signed a 10-year exclusive cost-plus contract stipulating that Fisher Body would be the exclusive supplier for GM.

By vertically integrating (Chapter 7)—that is, becoming one firm—two firms can eliminate the possibility of a holdup problem. After a number of years under the contract, unanticipated holdup problems occurred between GM and Fisher Body. To eliminate them, GM bought Fisher Body, vertically integrating with its parts supplier.

A "mild form" of vertical integration is quasi-vertical integration, which is a contracting solution that mimics vertical integration. The biggest danger to Fisher Body was that it would invest in expensive dies and machines whose only use was to produce parts for GM cars. To avoid this danger before the two firms merged, GM partially or *quasi-vertically integrated* with Fisher Body, by paying for and owning the specific physical asset (the dies) rather than buying all of Fisher. Consequently, Fisher and GM were both protected against holdups. If something went wrong in their relationship, Fisher could transfer GM's dies back to GM and both firms could walk away unharmed.[10]

---

[10]Monteverde and Teece (1982) looked at hundreds of parts that GM and Ford bought from suppliers. They found that the more specialized the die (the less likely it produces a part that can be used by another firm), the more likely an automobile company was to own it or to vertically integrate with the supplier.

Establishing a reputation for straight dealing can also prevent holdup problems. If GM goes many years without behaving opportunistically, then new suppliers are unlikely to worry about having their specific investments held as hostages by GM.

Managers use multiple sources or open sources for software to avoid holdup problems. For example, a firm that uses proprietary software may want to upgrade its computer in a few years, but to do so it needs the software firm to modify its code. Thus, the firm using the software is at the mercy of the software firm. By using open-source software, the user firm can modify the code itself if need be and is not subject to a holdup problem. Some firms prefer to use the open-source Linux computer operating system rather than proprietary Windows and Mac operating systems.

Too-Early Product Innovation

Typically, introducing the first product in a new product class gives a firm important advantages. The early innovator may earn substantial profits before competing products enter. In addition, many consumers become loyal to the initial product so that later entrants find it difficult to take market share from the leader firm. However, the disadvantages of entering early are that the cost of entering quickly is higher, the odds of miscalculating demand are greater, and later rivals may build on the pioneer's research to produce a superior product.

For example, as the first of a new class of anti-ulcer drugs, Tagamet was extremely successful when it was introduced. However, the second entrant, Zantac, rapidly took the lion's share of the market. Zantac worked similarly to Tagamet but had fewer side effects, needed to be taken less frequently, and was promoted more effectively when it was introduced.

Mini-Case

Advantages and Disadvantages of Moving First

We have seen how a firm that enters the market first gains an advantage over potential rivals by moving first. The first-mover firm may prevent entry by developing production processes that lower its marginal cost, raising costs to potential rivals, or getting an early start on learning by doing. Denstadli, Lines, and Grønhaug (2005) found that early Norwegian discount supermarket entrants benefited from long-lasting consumer perceptions that they had superior attributes compared with later entrants.

However, first movers do not always gain an advantage. Sony pioneered modern smartwatches with its 2013 Sony Smartwatch but later lost command of the market to the Apple Watch. In 2018, Apple had 80% of the U.S. market and about 60% of the world market. The Apple Watch gained an advantage because it had a large number of apps, most of which were created by third-party developers of iPhone and iPad apps. Other successful late entrants include Microsoft, which was a late entrant in the spreadsheet market, and Amazon, which started its online retail business by selling books several years after online book-selling pioneer Book Stacks Unlimited.

Nonetheless, first movers commonly have an advantage. Urban, Carter, and Gaskin (1986) examined 129 successful consumer products and found that the second entrant gained, on average, only three-quarters of the market share of the pioneer and that later entrants captured even smaller shares. Similarly,

Porath (2018) found that early entrants into pharmaceutical markets benefited by entering early, with the first entrant having the largest market share advantage over later entrants, followed by the second entrant, and so forth through the sixth entrant.

13.6 Behavioral Game Theory

We normally assume that managers are rational in the sense that they optimize using all available information. However, they may be subject to psychological biases and may have limited powers of calculation that cause them to act less than fully rationally. Such possibilities are the domain of behavioral economics (Chapters 4 and 9), which seeks to augment the rational economic model so as to better understand and predict economic decision making.

Ultimatum Games

One example of failing to maximize profit occurs in *ultimatum games*. Businesspeople often face an *ultimatum*, where one person (the *proposer*) makes a "take it or leave it" offer to another (the *responder*). No matter how long the parties have negotiated, once an ultimatum is issued, the responder has to accept or reject the offer with no opportunity to make a counteroffer. An ultimatum can be viewed as a sequential game in which the proposer moves first and the responder moves second.

Mini-Case

GM's Ultimatum

In 2009, General Motors (GM) was struggling financially and planned to shut down about one-fourth of its dealerships in the United States and Canada. Because GM was concerned that dealer opposition could cause delays and impose other costs, it offered dealers slated for closure an ultimatum. They would receive a (small) payment from GM if they did not oppose the restructuring plan.

Dealers could accept the ultimatum and get something, or they could reject the offer, oppose the reorganization, and receive nothing. Although it was irrational, some dealers rejected the ultimatum and loudly complained that GM was "high-handed, oppressive, and patently unfair." In 2011, some terminated Canadian dealerships filed a class-action suit against GM of Canada, which they lost in 2017.

An Experiment. The possibility that someone might turn down an offer even at some personal cost is important in business negotiations. To gain insight into real decisions, researchers have conducted ultimatum experiments.[11]

In a typical experiment, student participants sit in a computer lab. Each person is designated as either a proposer or a responder. A computer anonymously matches each proposer with a responder. The game is usually based on dividing $10. Each proposer makes an ultimatum offer to the responder of a particular amount. A responder who accepts the offer receives the amount offered, and the proposer gets

---

[11]Camerer (2003) describes several of these experiments.

the rest of the $10. If the responder rejects the offer, both players get nothing. Participants play the game only once.

To find the rational, subgame-perfect solution, we use backward induction. In the second stage, the responder should accept any positive offer. Thus in the first stage, the proposer should offer the lowest possible positive amount. For example, if the rules of the game specify that the proposer must offer an integer dollar amount, the proposer should offer $1.

However, such rational behavior is not a good predictor of actual outcomes. The lowest possible offer is almost never made and, when it is made, it is usually rejected. Thus, a proposer who makes the mistake of expecting the responder to be fully rational is likely to receive nothing. The most common range for offers is between $3 and $4—far more than the "rational" minimum offer. Offers of $2 or less are relatively rare and, when they do occur, responders turn them down about half the time.

One concern about such experiments is that the payoffs are small enough that not all participants take the game seriously. However, when the total amount to be divided is increased to $100, the results are essentially unchanged: The typical offer remains between 30% and 40% of the total. If anything, responders are even more likely to turn down lowball offers when the stakes are higher.

Reciprocity. Some responders who reject lowball offers feel the proposer is being greedy and would prefer to make a small sacrifice rather than reward such behavior. Some responders are angered by low offers, some feel insulted, and some feel that they should oppose "unfair" behavior. Most proposers anticipate such feelings and offer a significant amount to the responder, but almost always less than 50%.

Apparently, most people accept that the advantage of moving first should provide some extra benefit to proposers, but not too much. Moreover, they believe in *reciprocity*. If others treat us well, we want to return the favor. If they treat us badly, we want to "get even" and will retaliate if the cost does not seem excessive.[12] Thus, if a proposer makes a low offer, many responders are willing to give up something to punish the proposer.

Analysis of ultimatum games is useful partly because ultimatums arise in real business interactions. More important, however, the behavioral norms illustrated by the ultimatum game are of general significance—even in nonultimatum situations. For example, in dealing with workers, good managers often take account of reciprocity by providing benefits over and above the minimum needed, rather than squeezing every cent they can from workers. Such an approach makes sense if workers who feel exploited might quit or go on strike even when it is against their economic interest. Conversely, workers who feel well treated often develop a sense of loyalty that causes them to work harder than needed—such as staying late to get a job finished—rather than doing only the minimum amount required.

Eckel and Grossman (1996) found that men are more likely than women to punish if the personal cost is high in an ultimatum game. They speculate that this difference may explain gender patterns in wages and unemployment during downturns, where men are more likely to rigidly insist on a given wage than more flexible women. Visser and Roelofs (2011) are able to explain gender effects based on a few personality traits.[13]

---

[12]Reciprocity is central to many ethical systems as with, for example, the Golden Rule: "Do unto others as you would have them do unto you," and the Code of Hammurabi: "An eye for an eye and a tooth for a tooth."

[13]The personality traits considered were "extraversion, agreeableness, conscientiousness, emotional stability, and intellect/imagination." After controlling for these personality traits, they find no other differences between men and women. That is, gender matters only to the extent that these personality attributes differ by gender.

Levels of Reasoning

John Maynard Keynes (1936) observed that investment decisions are often based on "animal spirits" rather than rational calculation. He questioned whether investors are able to rationally assess the value of a stock by recognizing that its value is based primarily on what *other people* think the stock is worth.

Keynes suggested that deciding which stock to buy is like predicting the outcome of a beauty contest. You should not base your prediction on what *you* think of the contestants; you should base it on what you think *other people* will think. Keynes questioned whether most people rationally assess the likely opinions of others—in stock markets, beauty contests, and other situations.

Modern experimental economists have devoted considerable attention to testing whether decision makers do rationally infer the likely assessments and actions of others in strategic games. A game that is often used for such experiments is called the *beauty contest game* in recognition of Keynes's original example.

The *Financial Times* (FT) of London, with the help of economist Richard Thaler, held a relatively straightforward beauty contest game (Bosch-Domènech et al., 2002). The FT invited readers to choose an integer between 0 and 100. The submission closest to two-thirds of the average of all numbers submitted would win. If 10, 20, 30, 40, and 50 are the five numbers submitted, the average is 30. As two-thirds of this average is 20, the person who chose 20 would win. Thus, the objective is to predict the average and pick a number that is two-thirds of that amount.

The Nash equilibrium to this game is for everyone to choose zero! The average would then be 0, and two-thirds of 0 is 0, so everyone would be correct and would share the prize for winning. No one would have an incentive to defect by choosing a higher number, as someone who did so would lose rather than have a winning number.[14] Further, this common choice of zero is the *only* possible Nash equilibrium.[15]

Thus if all players are fully rational, they should choose zero. However, only about 5% of the nearly 1,500 people who participated chose zero. The average in the FT experiment was 18.9, and the winning submission was 13. Some people chose randomly, not thinking about what other people might do. This approach is called *level-0 strategic reasoning*. A more sophisticated participant might expect others to choose randomly so that the average would be roughly 50, and should therefore choose the integer closest to two-thirds of 50, which is 33. In fact, a large group did choose 33, exhibiting level-1 reasoning.

A still more sophisticated person may anticipate that others would use level-1 reasoning to choose 33, and therefore choose two-thirds of this amount, which is 22. Many people did choose 22, exhibiting level-2 reasoning. Similarly, a player who expects others to use level-2 reasoning should expect an average of 22 and should therefore choose 15, which is level-3 reasoning, and so on. The end point of this thought process is to select 0, the (fully rational) Nash equilibrium.

---

[14]Suppose the game has five players. If one person were to defect from the Nash equilibrium and choose 1 instead of 0, then the average would be $\frac{1}{5}$ and two-thirds of the average is $\frac{2}{15}$. Those who chose 0 would be closer to $\frac{2}{15}$ than the defector. The same type of reasoning applies for any positive number and for any number of players greater than two.

[15]If any positive number is submitted, then the average must exceed zero and at least one person must be above two-thirds of the average, as it is impossible for everyone to be below the average. But a choice above two-thirds of the average cannot be a best response, as the person could do better by choosing two-thirds of the average instead.

This experiment has been repeated many times. The overall average is usually about 22, implying a winning number of about 15. Therefore, on average, participants seem to exhibit level-2 reasoning. To win the game, it is therefore usually necessary to go through three layers of reasoning—not more and not less—so as to be one step ahead of most other players.

A manager who underestimates the capability of rivals for strategic thinking (similar to assuming others will use level-0 reasoning in the beauty contest game) will make mistakes. However, a manager who overestimates the strategic sophistication of others will also make mistakes. The best results are obtained by having a good sense of exactly how sophisticated others are and staying one step ahead.

A dramatic example of CEOs anticipating rivals' strategies is provided by the telecommunications industry. The U.S. Telecommunications Act of 1996 allowed new firms to enter local telephone markets. Goldfarb and Xiao (2011) found that some CEOs consistently made the mistake of entering markets that became excessively crowded while others consistently entered markets that did not attract excessive entry, apparently anticipating the behavior of rivals. The more successful CEOs were those who had greater experience, were more likely to have studied economics or business in university, and had stronger records of academic achievement.

Managerial Implication

Taking Advantage of Limited Strategic Thinking

Managers should consider the level of strategic sophistication of customers (and rivals). For example, successful managers of Hollywood movie studios anticipate limited strategic thinking by moviegoers. Normally Hollywood studios release movies for prescreening by critics before general release to generate buzz through positive reviews. This technique works well for good movies, but has the opposite effect for movies that get poor reviews.

If a studio is not confident about a movie's quality it can use a *cold opening*, releasing the movie with no prescreenings for movie critics. A fully rational moviegoer understands this tactic and is less likely to go to movies with cold opens. Thus, if everyone were rational, studios wouldn't use cold openings.

However, Brown, Camerer, and Lovallo (2012) found that while some moviegoers instantly understand the system, some never catch on to this pattern. As a result, cold opens generate more revenue and more profit on average than comparable not-very-good movies that are prescreened. And, on average, moviegoers are disappointed by cold opens relative to other movies. Thus, a manager should not overestimate the reasoning ability of the general movie-going public.

Managerial Solution

Intel and AMD's Advertising Strategies

As we've seen, when one firm in a market acts before another, the first mover may gain an advantage large enough to discourage the second firm from entering the market. In a less extreme case, the original firm may gain a smaller advantage so that the second firm enters, but it produces less than the original firm (as in a Stackelberg model). We can use this insight to provide a possible explanation for the Managerial Problem: In the market for CPUs for personal computers, why does Intel advertise substantially while AMD does not?

The game tree indicates a plausible explanation. Intel decides on how much to invest in its advertising campaign before AMD can act. AMD then decides whether to advertise heavily. We solve for the subgame-perfect Nash equilibrium by working backward. For the profits in this game, if Intel were to have a minimal advertising campaign, AMD makes more if it advertises a lot ($\pi_A = 8$) than if it, too, has a low level of advertising ($\pi_A = 2$). If Intel advertises heavily, AMD makes more with a low-level advertising campaign ($\pi_A = 4$) than with a high-level campaign ($\pi_A = 3$). Given how it expects AMD to behave, Intel intensively advertises because doing so produces a higher profit ($\pi_I = 8$) than does the lower level of advertising ($\pi_I = 4$).

Thus, because Intel acts first and can commit to advertising aggressively, it can place AMD in a position where it makes more with a low-key advertising campaign. Of course, the results might vary if the profits in the game tree differ, but this example provides a plausible explanation for why the firms use different strategies.

SUMMARY

1. **Repeated Games.** In some dynamic games, a constituent game (a static game) is repeated over subsequent periods, such as when firms make price or quantity decisions every quarter. Therefore, a firm may use a strategy in which it makes a particular move contingent on its rival's actions in previous periods. By using contingent strategies, such as a tit-for-tat strategy or another trigger strategy, it is often easier for firms to maximize their joint payoff—achieve a collusive solution—in a repeated game than in a single-period game.

2. **Sequential Games.** In other dynamic games, firms move sequentially, with one player acting before another. By moving first, a firm is able to make a *commitment* or *credible threat*. As a consequence, the first mover may receive a higher profit than if the firms act simultaneously. For example, in the Stackelberg oligopoly model, one firm is a *leader* in a sequential game and therefore chooses its output level before rival firms (followers) choose theirs. Applying backward induction, the leader anticipates a follower's reaction and chooses its best output accordingly in the first stage. This first-stage output is a commitment that allows the leader to gain a first-mover advantage. The leader produces more output and earns higher profits than does a follower firm with the same costs.

3. **Deterring Entry.** An incumbent firm may be able to maintain its monopoly by acting first to deter entry. Some incumbents can sign exclusive contracts that prevent entry, but they do so only if entry is likely and it pays to prevent it. Other incumbents engage in limit pricing where they set a low price or, equivalently, produce a large quantity of output so that a rival cannot profitably enter. The incumbent can feasibly do so only if it has an advantage over the potential rival. If the incumbent can act first, it may be able to commit to producing a large enough output or low enough price after entry that the rival would make losses, thereby deterring entry. If an incumbent faces entry in many markets, it may act to deter the first several entry attempts even if it doesn't pay in those markets so as to gain a reputation for toughness that may deter entry in other markets.

4. **Cost and Innovation Strategies.** A firm that can act first to lower its marginal cost relative to that of its rivals may gain a strategic advantage. This strategic advantage from having a relatively low cost may be large enough that it pays a firm to invest in capital to lower its marginal cost even if the investment cost exceeds the potential production cost savings. Because firms in many industries can lower their marginal cost of production through learning by doing, the first firm

in the industry may produce more than the short-run profit-maximizing output so as to lower its future costs and gain an advantage over latecomers. Similarly, firms sometimes lobby legislators or regulators to impose standards that raise costs throughout the industry if they raise rivals' costs by more than their own.

5. **Disadvantages of Moving First.** Although moving first is usually an advantage, exceptions exist. If one firm must make a specific investment to transact with another firm, the investment may become a hostage. The second firm can hold up the investing firm, for example, by lowering its payment to the investing firm.

When firms fear such holdup problems, some desirable transactions never occur. Early innovators may also suffer first-mover disadvantages if later entrants develop superior products.

6. **Behavioral Game Theory.** Managers in strategic games may not use fully rational strategies because of psychological bias, lack of reasoning ability, or a belief that other managers will not use fully rational strategies. The ultimatum and beauty contest games illustrate that managers should take account of the limited powers of calculation and insight of rivals and should not necessarily assume that all rivals are fully rational.

QUESTIONS

All exercises are available on **MyLab Economics;** * = *answer at the back of this book;* **C** = *use of calculus may be necessary.*

1. Repeated Games

*1.1 Two firms are planning to sell 10 or 20 units of their goods and face the following profit matrix:

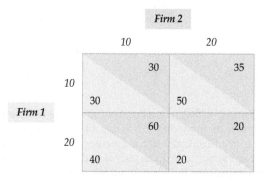

a. What is the Nash equilibrium if both firms make their decisions simultaneously? (*Hint:* See Chapter 12.) What strategy does each firm use?

b. Draw the game tree if Firm 1 can decide first. What is the outcome? Why?

c. Draw the game tree if Firm 2 can decide first. What is the outcome? Why?

*1.2 In the repeated-game airline example illustrated in Table 13.1, what happens if the players know the game will last only five periods? What happens if the game is played forever but the managers of one or both firms care only about current profit?

1.3 In a repeated game, how does the outcome differ if firms know that the game will be (a) repeated indefinitely, (b) repeated a known, finite number of times, and (c) repeated a finite number of times but the firms are always unsure whether the current period will be the last?

1.4 A small tourist town has two Italian restaurants, Romano's and Giardino's. Normally, both restaurants prosper with no advertising. Romano's could take some of Giardino's customers by running radio ads, and Giardino's could do the same thing. The one-month profit matrix (showing payoffs in thousands of dollars) is:

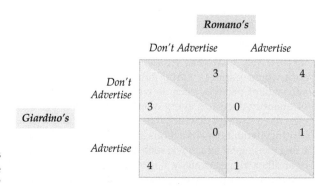

a. What is the Nash equilibrium in the static (one-month) game?

b. If the game is repeated indefinitely, can the use of tit-for-tat strategies result in a Nash equilibrium?

c. Does the game have multiple equilibria if it is repeated indefinitely?

d. Would pre-play communication (Chapter 12) or the Pareto criterion (Chapter 12) have implications for the repeated game equilibrium?

1.5 Change the profit matrix in Question 1.4 so that each firm gets 2 (instead of 4) if it advertises and the other firm does not. How does that change your answers?

1.6 In the Mini-Case "Tit-for-Tat Strategies in Trench Warfare," why did soldiers advise new recruits not to shoot at the enemy?

1.7 In most countries, explicit collusion over prices or quantities between firms in the same industry is illegal. Is it possible that collusive prices can be achieved by tacit collusion? Give an explanation of how such tacit collusion can occur.

2. Sequential Games

2.1 Solve for the Stackelberg subgame-perfect Nash equilibrium for the following game tree. What is the joint-profit maximizing outcome? Why is that not the outcome of this game? (*Hint*: See Q&A 13.2.)

Leader Sets Output		Follower Sets Output		Profits (π_1, π_2)
	180	Firm 2	48	(64.9, 64.8)
			64	(54.0, 72.0)
			96	(32.4, 64.8)
Firm 1	240	Firm 2	48	(72.0, 54.0)
			64	(57.6, 57.6)
			96	(28.8, 43.2)
	360	Firm 2	48	(64.8, 32.4)
			64	(43.2, 28.8)
			96	(0, 0)

*2.2 The market demand function is $Q = 1{,}000 - 1{,}000p$. Each firm has a marginal cost of $m = 0.28$ (28¢ per unit). Firm 1, the leader, acts before Firm 2, the follower. Solve for the Stackelberg equilibrium quantities, prices, and profits. (*Hint*: See Appendix 13A.) Compare your solution to the Nash-Cournot equilibrium. **C**

2.3 Suppose the demand function is $Q = 400 - 10p$. Firm A, the leader, acts before Firm B, the follower. Both firms have a constant marginal cost of 20. Draw a diagram with Firm A's output on the horizontal axis. Show the best-response function of Firm B. On the diagram, identify the Nash-Cournot solution, the Stackelberg solution, and the cartel solution.

2.4 Using the information in the previous question, use a spreadsheet to determine the industry price and quantity in the Stackelberg equilibrium. (*Hint*: See Q&A 13.1.)

2.5 Levi Strauss and Wrangler are planning new-generation jeans and must decide on the colors for their products. The possible colors are white, black, and violet. The payoff to each firm depends on the color it chooses and the color chosen by its rival, as the profit matrix shows:

		Levi Strauss		
		White	Black	Violet
Wrangler	White	10 / 10	30 / 20	40 / 30
	Black	20 / 30	0 / 0	35 / 15
	Violet	15 / 40	20 / 35	0 / 0

a. Given that the firms move simultaneously, identify any dominant strategies in this game and find any Nash equilibria.

b. Now suppose the firms move sequentially, with Wrangler moving first. Draw a game tree and identify any subgame-perfect Nash equilibria in this sequential-move game.

*2.6 In the sequential-move game described in part b of the previous question, Levi Strauss engages in pre-play communication (cheap talk). Levi Strauss tells Wrangler that it will match Wrangler's color choice if Wrangler chooses black and violet, but that if Wrangler opts for white, Levi Strauss will choose violet. Why would Levi Strauss want Wrangler to believe this claim? Should Wrangler believe it?

2.7 In the game described in Question 2.5, a new CEO takes over at Wrangler. It is common knowledge that this CEO hates the color violet and would never produce violet jeans. You can therefore remove the third row from the profit matrix. How do your answers to Question 2.5 change?

2.8 A thug wants the contents of a safe and is threatening the owner, the only person who knows the code, to open the safe. "I will kill you if you don't open the safe, and let you live if you do." Should the owner believe the threat and open the safe? The table shows the value that each person places on the various possible outcomes.

	Thug	Safe's Owner
Open the safe, thug does not kill	4	3
Open the safe, thug kills	2	1
Do not open, thug kills	1	2
Do not open, thug does not kill	3	4

Similar games appear in many films, including *Die Hard*, *Crimson Tide*, and *The Maltese Falcon*.

a. Draw the game tree. Who moves first?

b. What is the equilibrium?

c. Does the safe's owner believe the thug's threat?

d. Does the safe's owner open the safe?

3. Deterring Entry

3.1 Ricardo owns a small gift shop on the pier in a popular summer vacation town. The owner of the pier approaches Ricardo with an offer that would grant him exclusive rights to operate a gift shop on the pier in exchange for $100,000. If entry does not occur, Ricardo would earn $240,000 in profit. With entry, his profit in a duopoly would be $120,000 and the new gift shop would earn $70,000. Will Ricardo pay for exclusivity? Will entry occur? Use a game-tree diagram to answer these questions.

3.2 The Mini-Case "Pay-for-Delay Agreements" states that some incumbent producers of drugs with expiring patents paid potential generic producers to delay entry into the market. Why were incumbents willing to offer enough to potential entrants to make them delay entry? How does the 2013 Supreme Court decision allowing possible legal action against the companies affect this calculation? (*Hint:* The decision creates a potential financial liability.)

3.3 The more an incumbent firm produces in the first period, the lower its marginal cost is in the second period. If a potential rival expects the incumbent to produce a large quantity in the second period, it does not enter. Draw a game tree to illustrate why an incumbent would produce more in the first period than the single-period profit-maximizing level. Now change the payoffs in the tree to show a situation in which the firm does not increase production in the first period.

*3.4 An incumbent can commit to producing a large quantity of output before the potential rival decides whether to enter. The incumbent chooses whether to commit to produce a small quantity, q_i, or a large quantity. The rival then decides whether to enter. If the incumbent commits to the small output level and the rival does not enter, the rival makes $0 and the incumbent makes $900. If it does enter, the rival makes $125 and the incumbent earns $450. If the incumbent commits to producing the large quantity, and the potential rival stays out of the market, the potential rival makes $0 and the incumbent makes $800. If the rival enters, it loses $20, and the incumbent earns only $400. Show the game tree. What is the subgame-perfect Nash equilibrium? (*Hint:* See Q&A 13.3.)

*3.5 Xavier and Ying are partners in a course project. Xavier is the project leader and is the first to decide how many hours, x, to put into the project. After observing the amount of time that Xavier contributes, Ying decides how many hours, y, to devote. The mark obtained by the project is $10(x + y)^{0.5}$. Ying's utility function is $U = 10(x + y)^{0.5} - y$. How many hours does Ying work if Xavier works 15 hours? If Xavier does not want Ying to work on the project at all, how many hours should he work? **C**

3.6 Walmart has a reputation for using a variety of legal means to prevent unionization of its employees by frustrating union organizers (Lichtenstein, 2008). Why would it make sense for Walmart to spend more trying to deter unionization at a given store than it would save by preventing unionization at that one store? (*Hint:* Walmart has thousands of stores in the United States alone and thousands more in other countries. Would the theory of repeated games apply?)

3.7 Suppose that the constituent game shown in Figure 13.3 is played exactly twice instead of many times. Would that change the behavior of the incumbent?

4. Cost and Innovation Strategies

4.1 A monopoly manufacturing plant currently uses many workers to pack its product into boxes. It believes that by investing in installing and customizing robotic arms it can hire fewer workers and lower its marginal cost of production. But given the demand curve it faces, the firm does not sell enough units so that its lower production costs offset its investment cost. Suppose the incumbent does not invest. If its rival does not enter, it earns $0 and the incumbent earns $30,000. If the rival enters, the rival earns $10,000 and the incumbent earns $12,500. Now suppose that the incumbent does invest. If the rival does not enter, it earns $0 and the incumbent earns $16,000. If the rival enters, the rival loses $2,000 and the incumbent makes $6,000. Show the game tree. Should the monopoly invest?

*4.2 Before entry, the incumbent earns a monopoly profit of $\pi_m = \$10$ (million). If entry occurs, the incumbent and rival each earn the duopoly profit, $\pi_d = \$3$. Suppose that the incumbent can induce the government to require all firms to install pollution-control devices that cost each firm $4. Show the game tree. Should the incumbent urge the government to require pollution-control devices? Why or why not?

4.3 Use a game tree to illustrate why an aircraft manufacturer may price below the current marginal cost in the short run if it has a steep learning curve. (*Hint:* Show that learning by doing lowers its cost in the second period.)

4.4 In Q&A 13.4, suppose that $A = 12$ but that profits under the current wage and high output are 14 for Firm 1 and 11 for Firm 2. Which wage would Firm 1 choose?

4.5 Would a labor union gain any advantage related to raising rivals' costs in bargaining over wages in an industry with two or three firms rather than bargaining with a monopoly producer? (*Hint*: See the Mini-Case "Auto Union Negotiations.")

5. Disadvantages of Moving First

5.1 In the Venezuela–ExxonMobil Holdup Problem in Figure 13.5, suppose that the parties could initially agree to a binding contract that Venezuela would pay ExxonMobil x dollars if it nationalizes the oil fields. How large does x have to be for ExxonMobil to invest in Venezuela?

5.2 Based on the Mini-Case "Venezuelan Nationalization," if Venezuela ultimately pays nothing to Exxon in direct compensation, would that mean that Venezuela's partial expropriation of Exxon assets was a success? Explain.

*5.3 Ford invites Clarion to set up a plant at Ford's industrial complex in Brazil, where Clarion will build navigation systems for installation in the Ford cars produced there. If Clarion builds the plant, it would have no buyers for the plant's output except Ford. If Clarion does not build the plant, neither firm benefits. If Clarion does build the plant, Ford considers paying three possible prices for the systems: $p_1 < p_2 < p_3$. Price p_1 is below Clarion's average variable cost, which implies that Clarion would produce nothing. Therefore, Clarion would be out of pocket for the cost of the plant, 100 (million), and Ford would get nothing. If Ford pays price p_2, Clarion would more than cover its variable costs but still lose 90 and Ford would gain 140. At price p_3, both firms would gain 25. Draw the game tree. What is the subgame-perfect Nash equilibrium? Specify a contract that would solve the potential holdup problem. Illustrate your solution in a new game tree and explain why it works.

5.4 Show a game tree where the firm that moves second has a higher profit than the one that moves first in the subgame-perfect Nash equilibrium.

5.5 List at least two major advantages and two major disadvantages of being the first firm in a new product class. (*Hint*: See the Mini-Case "Advantages and Disadvantages of Moving First.")

6. Behavioral Game Theory

6.1 In an ultimatum game, the Proposer moves first, making an offer to the Responder. Once the offer is made, the Responder decides to accept or reject the offer. The total amount available is $100 if the players reach an agreement, but both players get $0 if the responder rejects the offer. The proposer is allowed to make offers of $5, $20, $35, $50, $65, $80, or $95. What is the subgame-perfect Nash equilibrium? What would you expect to happen in practice?

6.2 A prisoners' dilemma game is played for a fixed number of periods. The fully rational solution is for each player to defect in each period. However, in experiments with students, players often cooperate for a significant number of periods if the total number of repetitions is fairly large (such as 10 or 15 periods). Why? (*Hint*: Consider reciprocity and players' limited reasoning ability.)

*6.3 A new government lottery has been announced. Each person who buys a ticket submits an integer number between 0 and 100. The winner is the person whose submission is closest to two-thirds of the average of all submissions. If ties occur, the winners share the prize. If Chloe expects other players to select numbers randomly, what number should she choose? If you expect all other players to exhibit the same depth of reasoning as Chloe, what number would you choose?

6.4 As the familiar adage advises, it is important to "never underestimate a rival." Do the games described in the section "Behavioral Game Theory" suggest that it is also important not to overestimate rivals? Explain.

6.5 Based on the Managerial Implication "Taking Advantage of Limited Strategic Thinking," can a manager ever go wrong by assuming that customers are fully rational?

7. Managerial Problem

7.1 In the game between Intel and AMD in the Managerial Solution, suppose that each firm earns a profit of 9 if both firms advertise. Use a game tree to determine the new subgame-perfect Nash equilibrium outcome.

7.2 What are the Nash equilibria if both Intel and AMD act simultaneously in the game in the Managerial Solution?

8. MyLab Economics Spreadsheet Exercises[16]

8.1 Outreach Explorations and Summit Adventures are the only two vacation adventure companies operating in a national park. The adventure experiences they offer are very similar and they compete using their prices. Each firm can choose a high price (collude) or a low aggressive price (defect). The following profit matrix shows the one-period profits arising from these actions.

---

[16]The spreadsheet exercises in this chapter are based on the work of Satyajit Ghosh in cooperation with the authors. The answers are available on **MyLab Economics**.

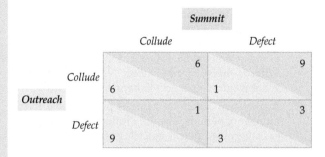

Summit

	Collude	*Defect*
Collude	6 / 6	9 / 1
Defect	1 / 9	3 / 3

Outreach

These firms compete with each other for five periods.

a. Summit follows a tit-for-tat strategy: It chooses the collusive price in the first period and in each later period chooses whichever action (collude or defect) that Outreach chose in the previous period. Create an Excel spreadsheet that shows Outreach's profit on a period-by-period basis as follows. Column A shows the time periods. Enter 1 in cell A2, 2 in cell A3, and so on up to 5 in cell A6. In cells B1 to F1, enter the column titles Strategy 1, ..., Strategy 5. In column B, enter Outreach's profit each period if it chooses the collusive price each period. In column C, assume that Outreach defects in each period. In column D, assume that Outreach defects in the first period, then plays the collusive price in each subsequent period. In column E, assume that Outreach colludes for the first 4 periods, then defects in the last period. In column F, assume that Outreach plays a tit-for-tat strategy. If Outreach wants to maximize its combined profit over all 5 periods, which of the 5 strategies is the best response to Summit's tit-for-tat strategy? Which is the worst?

b. Is the combination of strategies identified in part a (the tit-for-tat strategy by Summit and the best response by Outreach) a Nash equilibrium? (*Hint:* Create a new block of entries in your spreadsheet in which you assume that Outreach chooses the best response determined in part a. Enter the profits earned by Summit if it uses the tit-for-tat strategy and see if you can find a strategy that yields a higher cumulative profit for Summit over the 5 periods.)

c. Is it a Nash equilibrium in this game if each firm defects every period? Would your answer change if the game were repeated indefinitely instead of lasting only 5 periods?

8.2 The local cement market is a duopoly with City Cement and Mountain Cement producing quantities q_c and q_m. Cement is a homogeneous product with the inverse demand function $p = 20 - Q$, where $Q = q_c + q_m$. Each firm has a marginal cost of $4 and a fixed cost of $6. City Cement is a Stackelberg leader that sets output first. Mountain Cement acts as a follower. Mountain's best response to any output of City's is $q_m = 8 - q_c/2$.

a. Create a spreadsheet with columns for q_c, q_m, Q, p, and the revenue and profit of each firm. Let q_c take on the values of 0 to 16 in increments of 2 and use the spreadsheet to determine the other values in the table. Assuming that Mountain cannot avoid its fixed costs by shutting down, what output level will City Cement choose?

b. Now use the spreadsheet to determine the monopoly output by setting $q_m = 0$ no matter what output City produces. What is the monopoly price and output? How do these amounts compare with the industry price and output for the Stackelberg model?

8.3 Using the same data as in Spreadsheet Exercise 8.1, assume that City Cement is an incumbent monopoly and Mountain Cement is a potential entrant. City chooses an output level, and then Mountain decides whether or not to enter the industry. Mountain can avoid paying fixed costs if it decides not to enter. Create a modified version of the spreadsheet used for Exercise 8.1 to determine what output City should produce now to maximize profit. Is entry blockaded, deterred, or accommodated? (*Hint:* Mountain does not enter if it will earn a negative profit. If it does not enter, its output is 0.) How would your answer change if fixed costs were 2 instead of 6?

APPENDIX 13A   A Mathematical Approach to Stackelberg Oligopoly

We derive the Stackelberg duopoly equilibrium for a general linear inverse demand function, $p = a - bQ = a - b(q_1 + q_2)$, where the two firms produce identical products, have identical marginal costs, m, and have no fixed costs. This is the same demand and cost structure as in Appendix 11A for the Cournot model.

Firm 1, the Stackelberg leader, chooses its output first. After observing the output q_1 that the leader chooses, the follower chooses its output q_2 using its best-response function, which is given by Equation 11.11:

$$q_2 = \frac{a - m}{2b} - \frac{1}{2}q_1. \tag{13A.1}$$

How does the leader pick its output level? Firm 1 starts by writing its profit function by expressing q_2 as a function of q_1 using Firm 2's best-response function 13A.1:

$$\pi_1(q_1, q_2(q_1)) = \left[a - b\left(q_1 + \frac{a - m}{2b} - \frac{1}{2}q_1 \right) - m \right]$$

$$q_1 = \left(\frac{a - m - bq_1}{2} \right)q_1. \tag{13A.2}$$

The leader's first-order condition is derived by setting the derivative of its profit (Equation 13A.2) with respect to q_1 equal to zero: $d\pi_1/dq_1 = (a - m - 2bq_1)/2 = 0$. Solving this expression for q_1, we find that

$$q_1 = \frac{a - m}{2b}. \tag{13A.3}$$

Substituting the expression for q_1 in Equation 13A.3 into the follower's best-response function 13A.1 gives us the equilibrium output for the follower:

$$q_2 = \frac{a - m}{4b}. \tag{13A.4}$$

Thus, given a linear demand curve and constant marginal cost, the leader produces twice as much as the follower.

We can use this analysis to ask what would happen in our airline example if American Airlines can act before United Airlines, so that American is a Stackelberg leader and United is a Stackelberg follower. Replacing the parameters in our linear analysis with the specific values for the airlines, $a = 339$, $b = 1$, and $m = 147$, we find that American's output is $q_1 = (339 - 147)/2 = 96$, and United's output is $q_2 = (339 - 147)/4 = 48$. These are the equilibrium values in Figure 13.1.

14 Decision Making Under Uncertainty

In America anyone can be president. That's one of the risks you take. —Adlai Stevenson

On April 20, 2010, in the Gulf of Mexico, a massive explosion occurred on the Transocean Deepwater Horizon oil rig, which was leased by the oil company BP. The explosion itself killed 11 workers and seriously injured 17 others. In addition, many of the 90,000 workers who participated in the cleanup suffered significant health problems from exposure to various toxins. Safeguards to automatically cap the oil well in case of an accident did not work as expected. Consequently, a massive spill of roughly 200 million gallons of oil polluted the Gulf of Mexico before the well was finally capped. This catastrophic oil spill inflicted gigantic costs for cleaning up Louisiana and other Gulf states and imposed very large losses on the Gulf fishing and tourism industries.

This bad outcome, however, does not necessarily imply that BP made bad decisions before the event. BP could have taken reasonable safety precautions and merely been unlucky. However, government agencies concluded that the explosion and the resulting massive oil leak were largely due to a failure on the part of BP

and its subcontractors to take appropriate safety and other precautions.[1] In 2012, BP pled guilty to 11 counts of seaman's manslaughter and was fined a record $4 billion in penalties. In addition, BP was liable for much more due to cleanup costs, civil lawsuits, and other fines and penalties.

BP managers may have acted as they did for two possible reasons. First, they may have ignored or underestimated the chance of these expensive calamities, improperly reasoning that such major disasters had not happened to them before and would therefore never happen in the future (or at least that the chances were minuscule).

---

[1]According to a *New York Times* column, years before its Deepwater Horizon rig blew, BP was developing a reputation as an oil company that took safety risks to save money. Politicians and regulators pointed to a 2005 Texas refinery explosion that killed 15 workers and a corroded pipeline in Alaska that poured oil into Prudhoe Bay in 2006. Congressman Joe Barton chastised BP managers for their "seeming indifference to safety and environmental issues."

Second, they may have assumed that they would not bear the full costs of the catastrophe even if it did occur because governments would either partially bail them out or the courts would limit their liability. They had good reason for making this assumption. In 1990, Congress passed a law that limited liability beyond cleanup costs at $75 million for a rig spill, a tiny fraction of the harm in this case.

In the face of international condemnation for the massive Gulf spill, BP agreed to waive this cap. In 2015, BP struck a $20.8 billion agreement to settle damages with Gulf Coast states and the federal government. By the start of 2018, BP's total costs arising from the disaster were $65.1 billion, about 870 times larger than $75 million. These losses are substantial compared to BP shareholders' equity of $188 billion at the time of the disaster.

BP made a calculated decision that reflected its estimate of the risk of a catastrophic oil spill, presumably taking the $75 million cap on liability into account. How does a cap on liability affect a firm's willingness to make a risky investment or to invest less than the optimal amount in safety? How does a cap affect the amount of risk that the firm and others in society bear? How does a cap affect the amount of insurance that a firm buys against the costs of an oil spill?

L ife is full of uncertainty. Will you get a good summer job? Will you be in a car accident? Will the shares of stock you've bought increase in value? Will you avoid earthquakes and floods? Managers in all types of business confront a wide variety of risks, including the danger of fire and theft, exchange rate fluctuations, economic downturns, and adverse scientific findings about their products. Some managers dread having to make risky decisions, because if the outcome is bad, they may be fired or have their pay cut.

In this chapter, we extend our analyses of decision making by individuals and firms to include uncertainty. We look at how uncertainty affects consumption decisions made by individuals and business decisions made by firms.

When making decisions about investments and other matters, consumers and managers consider the possible *outcomes* under various circumstances, or *states of nature*. For example, a government regulatory authority may approve or reject a pharmaceutical firm's new drug, so the two states of nature are *approve* or *reject*. Associated with each of these states of nature is an outcome: The value of the pharmaceutical firm's stock will be $100 per share if the drug is approved and only $75 if the drug is rejected.

Although we cannot know with certainty what the future outcome will be, we may know which outcomes are more likely. Often, we can quantify an uncertain situation—one in which no single outcome is certain to occur—because we can assign a probability to each possible outcome. For example, if we toss a coin, we can assign a probability of 50% to each of the two possible outcomes: heads or tails. Some people refer to quantifiable uncertainty as *risk*. However, many people do not distinguish between the terms *risk* and *uncertainty*. Henceforth, we use these terms interchangeably. All of the examples in this chapter concern quantifiable uncertainty.[2]

---

[2]Uncertainty is unquantifiable when we do not know enough to assign meaningful probabilities to different outcomes or if we do not even know what the possible outcomes are. If asked "Who will be the U.S. President in 10 years?" most of us do not even know the likely contenders, let alone the probabilities.

Consumers and firms modify their decisions about consumption and investment as the degree of risk varies. Indeed, most people are willing to spend money to reduce risk by buying insurance or taking preventive measures. Moreover, most people will choose a riskier investment over a less risky one only if they expect a higher return from the riskier investment.

Learning Objectives

1. Calculate the expected profit from a risky undertaking.
2. Discuss how attitudes toward risk affect choice under uncertainty.
3. List actions decision makers can take to reduce their risk.
4. Analyze whether to invest in uncertain situations.
5. Describe psychological factors in analyzing decision making under uncertainty.

14.1 Assessing Risk

Gregg, a promoter, is considering whether to schedule an outdoor concert on July 4th. Booking the concert is a gamble: He stands to make a tidy profit if the weather is good, but he'll lose a substantial amount if it rains.

To analyze this decision Gregg needs a way to describe and quantify risk. A particular *event*—such as holding an outdoor concert—has a number of possible *outcomes*—here, either it rains or it does not rain. When deciding whether to schedule the concert, Gregg quantifies how risky each outcome is using a *probability* and then uses these probabilities to determine what he can expect to earn.

Probability

A *probability* is a number between 0 and 1 that indicates the likelihood that a particular outcome will occur. If an outcome cannot occur, it has a probability of 0. If the outcome is sure to happen, it has a probability of 1. If it rains one time in four on July 4th, the probability of rain is $\frac{1}{4}$ or 25%.

These weather outcomes are *mutually exclusive*. Only one of these outcomes can occur: Either it rains or it does not rain. This list of outcomes is also *exhaustive*, as no other outcomes are possible. If outcomes are mutually exclusive and exhaustive, exactly one of these outcomes will occur, and the probabilities must add up to 100%.

How can Gregg estimate the probability of rain on July 4th? Usually the best approach is to use the *frequency*, which tells us how often an uncertain event occurred in the past. Otherwise, one has to use a *subjective probability*, which is an estimate of the probability that may be based on other information, such as informal "best guesses" of experienced weather forecasters.

Frequency. The probability is the actual chance that an outcome will occur. Managers do not know the true probability, so they have to estimate it. Because Gregg (or the weather department) knows how often it rained on July 4th over many years, he can use that information to estimate the probability that it will rain this year. He calculates θ (theta), the frequency that it rained, by dividing n, the number of years that it rained on July 4th, by N, the total number of years for which he has data:

$$\theta = \frac{n}{N}.$$

Gregg then uses θ, the frequency, as his estimate of the true probability that it will rain this year.

Subjective Probability. Unfortunately, often we lack a history of repeated events that allows us to calculate frequencies. For example, the disastrous magnitude-9 earthquake that struck Japan in 2011, with an accompanying tsunami and nuclear reactor crisis, was unprecedented in modern history.

Where events occur very infrequently, we cannot use a frequency calculation to predict a probability. We use whatever information we have to form a *subjective probability*, which is a best estimate of the likelihood that the outcome will occur—that is, our best, informed guess.

The subjective probability can combine frequencies and all other available information—even information that is not based on scientific observation. If Gregg is planning a concert months in advance, his best estimate of the probability of rain is based on the frequency of rain in the past. However, as the event approaches, a weather forecaster can give him a better estimate that takes into account atmospheric conditions and other information in addition to the historical frequency. Because the forecaster's probability estimate uses personal judgment in addition to an observed frequency, it is a subjective probability.

Mini-Case	Cyberattacks—attempts to gain illegal access to computer systems to steal information or harm the system—are one of the newest and largest sources of risk facing major corporations. A cyberattack on Target Corporation exposed personal information of nearly 70 million of their customers. News of the attack resulted in reduced customer traffic and many expenses. Target's earnings before interest and taxes fell by nearly 30%, or $1.58 billion, from the year before the attack. Its breach-related expenses were $292 million, including the settlement of class action lawsuits. After the 2017 announcement of the cyberattack on Equifax, a consumer credit report firm, its stock prices fell by almost one-quarter.
Risk of a Cyberattack	

Which firms should put a high probability on an attack? According to Kamiya et al. (2018), cyberattacks are more likely to afflict large, visible firms; highly valued firms; firms with more intangible assets; and firms whose board pays inadequate attention to risk management. They also found that firms suffer major losses when consumer financial information is stolen, but attacks have relatively little effect otherwise.

Probability Distributions. A *probability distribution* relates the probability of occurrence to each possible outcome. Panel a of Figure 14.1 shows a probability distribution over five possible outcomes: zero to four days of rain per month in a relatively dry city. The probability that it rains no days during the month is 10%, as is the probability of exactly four days of rain. The chance of two rainy days is 40%, and the chance of one or three rainy days is 20% each. The probability that it rains five or more days in a month is 0%. These weather outcomes are mutually exclusive and exhaustive, so exactly one of these outcomes will occur, and the probabilities must

FIGURE 14.1 Probability Distributions

The probability distribution shows the probability of occurrence for each of the mutually exclusive outcomes. Panel a shows five possible mutually exclusive outcomes. The probability that it rains exactly two days per month is 40%. The probability that it rains more than four days per month is 0%.

The probability distributions in panels a and b have the same expected value or mean. The variance is smaller in panel b, where the probability distribution is more concentrated around the mean than the distribution in panel a.

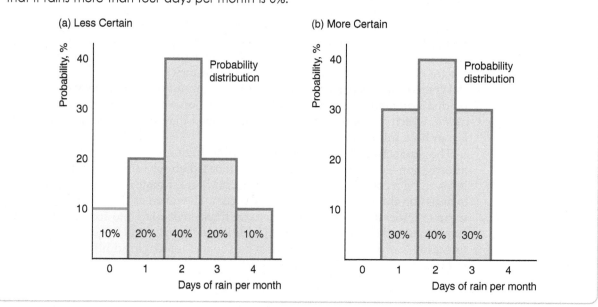

add up to 100%. For simplicity in the following examples, we concentrate mainly on situations with only two possible outcomes.

Expected Value

One of the common denominators I have found is that expectations rise above that which is expected. —George W. Bush

Gregg's earnings from his outdoor concert will depend on the weather. If it doesn't rain, his profit or value from the concert is $V = 15$ ($15,000). If it rains, he'll have to cancel the concert and he will lose the money, $V = -5$ ($5,000), that he must pay the band. Although Gregg does not know with certainty what the weather will be, he knows that the weather department forecasts a 50% chance of rain.

Gregg may use the *mean* or the *average* of the values from both outcomes as a summary statistic of the likely payoff from booking this concert. The amount Gregg expects to earn is called his *expected value* (here, his *expected profit*). The **expected value**, EV, is the weighted average of the values of the outcomes, where each possible outcome is weighted by its probability. That is, the expected value is the sum of the product of the probability and the value of each outcome:[3]

---

[3]The expectation operator, E, tells us to take the weighted average of all possible values, where the weights are the probabilities that a particular value will be observed. With n possible outcomes, the value of outcome i is V_i, and the probability of that outcome is Pr_i; then the expected value is $EV = Pr_1V_1 + Pr_2V_2 + \cdots + Pr_nV_n$.

$$EV = [Pr(\text{no rain}) \times \text{Value}(\text{no rain})] + [Pr(\text{rain}) \times \text{Value}(\text{rain})]$$
$$= \left[\tfrac{1}{2} \times 15\right] + \left[\tfrac{1}{2} \times (-5)\right] = 5,$$

where Pr is the probability of an outcome, so $Pr(\text{rain})$ is the "probability that rain occurs."

The expected value is the amount Gregg would earn, on average, if the event were repeated many times. If he puts on such concerts on the same date over many years and the weather follows historical patterns, he will earn 15 at half of the concerts (those without rain), and he will get soaked for −5 at the other half of the concerts, when it rains. Thus, he'll earn an average of 5 per concert over a long period.

Q&A 14.1

Suppose that Gregg is able to obtain perfect information so that he can accurately predict whether it will rain far enough before the concert that he could book the band only if needed. How much would he expect to earn, knowing that he will eventually have this perfect information? How much does he gain by having this perfect information?

Answer

1. *Determine how much Gregg would earn if he had perfect information in each state of nature.* If Gregg knew with certainty that it would rain at the time of the concert, he would not book the band, so he would make no loss or profit: $V = 0$. If Gregg knew that it would not rain, he would hold the concert and make 15.

2. *Determine how much Gregg would expect to earn before he learns with certainty what the weather will be.* Gregg knows that he'll make 15 with a 50% probability $\left(= \tfrac{1}{2}\right)$ and 0 with a 50% probability, so his expected value, given that he'll receive perfect information in time to act on it, is

$$\left(\tfrac{1}{2} \times 15\right) + \left(\tfrac{1}{2} \times 0\right) = 7.5.$$

3. *Calculate his gain from perfect information as the difference between his expected earnings with perfect information and his expected earnings with imperfect information.* Gregg's gain from perfect information is the difference between the expected earnings with perfect information, 7.5, and the expected earnings without perfect information, 5. Thus, Gregg expects to earn 2.50 (= 7.50 − 5) more with perfect information than with imperfect information.[4]

Variance and Standard Deviation

From the expected value, Gregg knows how much he is likely to earn, on average, if he books many similar concerts. However, he cannot tell from the expected value how risky the concert is.

If Gregg's earnings are the same whether it rains or not, he faces no risk and the actual return he receives is the expected value. If the possible outcomes differ from one another, he faces risk.

We can measure the risk Gregg faces in various ways. The most common approach is to use a measure based on how much the values of the possible outcomes differ from the expected value, EV. If it does not rain, the *difference* between Gregg's actual

---

[4]We can derive this answer directly. Perfect weather information is valuable to Gregg because he can avoid hiring the band when it rains. (The information has no value if it has no use.) The value of this information is his expected savings from not hiring the band when it rains: $\tfrac{1}{2} \times 5 = 2.50$.

earnings, 15, and his expected earnings, 5, is 10. The difference if it does rain is $-5 - 5 = -10$. It is convenient to combine the two differences—one difference for each state of nature (possible outcome)—into a single measure of risk.

One such measure of risk is the *variance*, which measures the spread of the probability distribution. For example, the probability distributions in the two panels in Figure 14.1 have the same mean (two days of rain) but different variances. The variance in panel a, where the probability distribution ranges from zero to four days of rain per month, is greater than the variance in panel b, where the probability distribution ranges from one to three days of rain per month.

Formally, the variance is the probability-weighted average of the squares of the differences between the observed outcome and the expected value.[5] The variance of the value Gregg obtains from the outdoor concert is

$$
\begin{aligned}
\text{Variance} &= \big[Pr(\text{no rain}) \times (\text{Value}(\text{no rain}) - EV)^2\big] \\
&\quad + \big[Pr(\text{rain}) \times (\text{Value}(\text{rain}) - EV)^2\big] \\
&= \big[\tfrac{1}{2} \times (15 - 5)^2\big] + \big[\tfrac{1}{2} \times (-5 - 5)^2\big] \\
&= \big[\tfrac{1}{2} \times (10)^2\big] + \big[\tfrac{1}{2} \times (-10)^2\big] = 100.
\end{aligned}
$$

Table 14.1 shows how to calculate the variance of the profit from this concert step by step. The first column lists the two outcomes: rain and no rain. The next column gives the probability that each outcome will occur. The third column shows the value or profit of each outcome. The next column calculates the difference between the values in the third column and the expected value, $EV = 5$. The following column squares these differences, and the last column multiplies these squared differences by the probabilities in the second column. The sum of these probability-weighted differences, 100, is the variance.

Instead of describing risk using the variance, economists and businesspeople often report the *standard deviation*, which is the square root of the variance. The usual symbol for the standard deviation is σ (sigma), so the symbol for variance is σ^2. For the outdoor concert, the variance is $\sigma^2 = 100$ and the standard deviation is $\sigma = 10$.

TABLE 14.1 Variance and Standard Deviation: Measures of Risk

Outcome	Probability	Value	Deviation = Value − 5	Deviation²	Deviation² × Probability
No rain	$\tfrac{1}{2}$	15	10	100	50
Rain	$\tfrac{1}{2}$	−5	−10	100	50
				Variance	100
				Standard Deviation	10

Note: Deviation = Value − EV.

[5]With n possible outcomes, if the value of outcome i is V_i, the probability of that outcome is Pr_i, and the expected value is EV, then the variance is

$$
Pr_1(V_1 - EV)^2 + Pr_2(V_2 - EV)^2 + \cdots + Pr_n(V_n - EV)^2.
$$

The variance puts more weight on large deviations from the expected value than it does on smaller ones.

<table>
<tr><td>

Managerial Implication

Summarizing Risk

</td><td>

Making managerial decisions in the presence of uncertainty is challenging. Managers can make better decisions by listing the possible outcomes, assigning probabilities to each, and calculating expected values and variances that serve as summary measures of the uncertainty they face. They can use these measures to evaluate the profit potential of risky investments and to determine the degree of risk arising from such investments.

</td></tr>
</table>

14.2 Attitudes Toward Risk

Given the risks Gregg faces if he schedules a concert, will Gregg stage the concert? To answer this question, we need to know Gregg's attitude toward risk.

Expected Utility

If Gregg did not care about risk, then he would promote either an indoor or an outdoor concert based on which option had a higher expected value (profit) regardless of any difference in risk. However, like most people, Gregg cares about risk as well as expected value. Indeed, most people are *risk averse*—they dislike risk. They will choose a riskier option over a less risky option only if the expected value of the riskier option is sufficiently higher than that of the less risky one.

We need a formal means to judge the trade-off between expected value and risk—to determine if the expected value of the riskier option is sufficiently higher to justify the greater risk. The most commonly used method is to extend the model of utility maximization. In Chapter 4, we noted that one can describe an individual's preferences over various bundles of goods by using a utility function. John von Neumann and Oskar Morgenstern (1944) extended the standard utility-maximizing model to include risk. Using this approach can show how people's taste for risk affects their career choices, the types of contracts to accept, where to build plants, whether to buy insurance, and which stocks to buy.

In this reformulation, we assume that the individual knows the value of each possible outcome and the probability that each will occur. A rational person maximizes *expected utility*.[6] Expected utility is the probability-weighted average of the utility from each possible outcome. For example, Gregg's expected utility, EU, from promoting the outdoor concert is

$$EU = [Pr(\text{no rain}) \times U(\text{Value}(\text{no rain}))] + [Pr(\text{rain}) \times U(\text{Value}(\text{rain}))]$$
$$= \left[\tfrac{1}{2} \times U(15)\right] + \left[\tfrac{1}{2} \times U(-5)\right],$$

---

[6]This approach to handling choice under uncertainty, often called the *expected utility hypothesis*, is the most commonly used method. Schoemaker (1982) discusses the logic underlying this approach, the evidence for it, and several variants. Machina (1989) discusses a number of alternative methods. Here we treat utility as a cardinal measure rather than an ordinal measure.

where his utility function, U, is a function of his earnings. For example, $U(15)$ is the amount of utility Gregg gets from earnings or wealth of 15.[7]

In short, the expected utility calculation is similar to the expected value calculation. Both are weighted averages in which the weights are the probabilities that correspond to the various possible outcomes. The mathematical difference is that the expected value is the probability-weighted average of the monetary value, whereas the expected utility is the probability-weighted average of the utility from the monetary value. The key economic difference is that the expected utility captures the trade-off between risk and value, whereas the expected value considers only value.

If we know how an individual's utility increases with wealth, we can determine how that person reacts to risky situations. We refer to a risky situation as a *bet*. Thus, for example, if Gregg schedules his concert outdoors, he is betting that it will not rain. We can classify people based on their willingness to make a **fair bet**: a bet with an expected value of zero. An example of a fair bet is one in which you pay a dollar if a flipped coin comes up heads and receive a dollar if it comes up tails. Because you expect to win half the time and lose half the time, the expected value of this bet is zero:

$$\left[\tfrac{1}{2} \times (-1)\right] + \left[\tfrac{1}{2} \times 1\right] = 0.$$

In contrast, a bet in which you pay \$2 if you lose the coin flip and receive \$4 if you win is an unfair bet that favors you, with an expected value of

$$\left[\tfrac{1}{2} \times (-2)\right] + \left[\tfrac{1}{2} \times 4\right] = 1.$$

Someone who is unwilling to make a fair bet is **risk averse**. A person who is indifferent about making a fair bet is **risk neutral**. A person who is **risk preferring** is always willing to make a fair bet.[8]

Risk Aversion

We can use our expected utility model to examine how Irma, who is risk averse, makes a choice under uncertainty. Figure 14.2 shows Irma's utility function. The utility function is concave to the wealth axis, indicating that Irma's utility rises with wealth but at a diminishing rate. She has *diminishing marginal utility of wealth*: The extra pleasure from each extra dollar of wealth is smaller than the extra pleasure from the previous dollar. An individual whose utility function is concave to the wealth axis is risk averse. More precisely, a person with a concave utility function would be unwilling to take a fair bet, as we now illustrate.

Unwillingness to Take a Fair Bet. Suppose that Irma has an initial wealth of 40 and has two options. One option is to do nothing and keep the 40, so that her utility is $U(40) = 120$ (the height of point d in Figure 14.2) with certainty. Her other option is to buy a share (a unit of stock) in a start-up company. Her wealth will be 70 if the start-up is a big success and 10 otherwise. Irma's subjective probability is 50% that the firm will be a big success. Her expected value of wealth remains

$$40 = \left(\tfrac{1}{2} \times 10\right) + \left(\tfrac{1}{2} \times 70\right).$$

Thus, buying the stock is a fair bet because she has the same expected wealth whether she purchases the stock or not.

---

[7]People have preferences over the goods they consume. However, for simplicity, we'll say that a person receives utility from earnings or wealth, which can be spent on consumption goods.

[8]The terms *risk loving* and *risk seeking* are sometimes used as synonyms for risk preferring.

FIGURE 14.2 Risk Aversion

Initially, Irma's wealth is 40, so her utility is $U(40) = 120$, at point d. If she buys the stock and it's worth 70, her utility is $U(70) = 140$ at point c. If she buys the stock and it's worth only 10, she is at point a, where $U(10) = 70$. If her subjective probability that the stock will be worth 70 is 50%, her expected value of the stock is $40 = (0.5 \times 10) + (0.5 \times 70)$. Her expected utility from buying the stock is $0.5U(10) + 0.5U(70) = 105$, at point b, which is the midpoint of the line between the good outcome,

point c, and the bad outcome, point a. Thus, her expected utility from buying the stock, 105, is less than her utility from having a certain wealth of 40, $U(40) = 120$, so she does not buy the stock. In contrast, if Irma's subjective probability that the stock will be worth 70 is 90%, her expected utility from buying the stock is $0.1U(10) + 0.9U(70) = 133$, point f, which is more than her utility with a certain wealth of 40, $U(40) = 120$, at d, so she buys the stock.

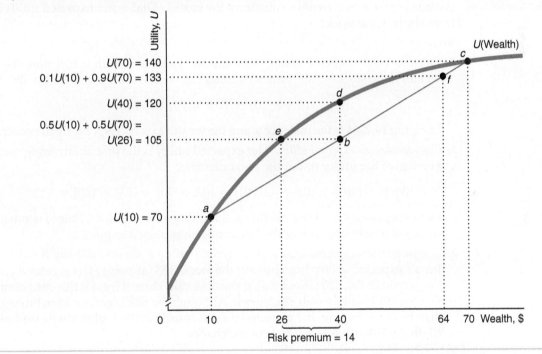

If Irma were risk neutral so that she only cared about her expected value and didn't care about risk, she would be indifferent between buying the stock or not. However, because Irma is risk averse, she prefers not buying the stock because both options have the same expected wealth and buying the stock carries more risk.

We can show that her expected utility is lower if she buys the stock than if she does not. If she buys the stock, her utility if the stock does well is $U(70) = 140$, at point c. If it doesn't do well, her utility is $U(10) = 70$, at point a. Thus, her expected utility from buying the stock is

$$\left[\tfrac{1}{2} \times U(10)\right] + \left[\tfrac{1}{2} \times U(70)\right] = \left[\tfrac{1}{2} \times 70\right] + \left[\tfrac{1}{2} \times 140\right] = 105.$$

Her expected utility is the height of point b, which is the midpoint of a line between points a and c. Because Irma's utility function is concave, her utility from certain wealth, 120 at point d, is greater than her expected utility from the risky activity, 105 at point b. As a result, she does not buy the stock. Buying the stock, which is a fair bet, increases the risk she faces without changing her expected wealth. Thus, Irma, because her utility function is concave, prefers not to take a fair bet and is therefore risk averse. *A person whose utility function is concave picks the less risky choice if both choices have the same expected value.*

> **Common Confusion** A risk-averse person always chooses the least risky option.

A risk-averse person chooses a riskier option only if it has a sufficiently higher expected value. Even though Irma is risk averse, she will buy the risky stock if its expected value is adequately large, as Q&A 14.2 shows.

Q&A 14.2

Suppose that Irma's subjective probability is 90% that the stock will be valuable. What is her expected wealth if she buys the stock? What is her expected utility? Does she buy the stock?

Answer

1. *Calculate Irma's expected wealth.* Her expected value or wealth is 10% times her wealth if the stock bombs plus 90% times her wealth if the stock does well:

$$(0.1 \times 10) + (0.9 \times 70) = 64.$$

In Figure 14.2, 64 is the distance along the wealth axis corresponding to point f.

2. *Calculate Irma's expected utility.* Her expected utility is the probability-weighted average of her utility under the two outcomes:

$$[0.1 \times U(10)] + [0.9 \times U(70)] = [0.1 \times 70] + [0.9 \times 140] = 133.$$

Her expected utility is the height on the utility axis of point f. Point f is nine-tenths of the distance along the line connecting point a to point c.

3. *Compare Irma's expected utility to her certain utility if she does not buy the stock.* Irma's expected utility from buying the stock, 133 (at point f), is greater than her certain utility, 120 (at point d), if she does not. Thus, if Irma is this confident that the stock will do well, she buys it. Although the risk is greater from buying than from not buying, her expected wealth is sufficiently higher (64 instead of 40) that it's worth it to her to take the chance.

Using Calculus

Diminishing
Marginal Utility
of Wealth

Irma's utility from W wealth is $U(W)$. She has positive marginal utility from extra wealth, $dU(W)/dW > 0$. That is, the slope of her utility function is positive.

Because Irma's utility function is concave in Figure 14.2, Irma is risk averse. This concavity is also equivalent to saying that her utility increases with wealth at a diminishing rate: $d^2U(W)/dW^2 < 0$. Therefore, if we know an individual's utility function, we can infer that person is risk averse if the second derivative of the utility function is negative.

The Risk Premium. The **risk premium** is the maximum amount that a decision maker would pay to avoid taking a risk. Equivalently, the risk premium is the minimum extra compensation (premium) that a decision maker would require to incur a risk.

To calculate a risk premium, we can use the **certainty equivalent**: the amount of certain wealth that would yield the same utility as a risky prospect. We can use the information in Figure 14.2, where Irma owns the stock that has a 50% chance of being worth 70 and a 50% chance of being worth 10, to calculate Irma's risk premium. The risk premium is the difference between her expected wealth from the risky stock and her certainty equivalent.

Irma's expected wealth from holding the stock is 40, and the corresponding expected utility is 105. Irma's certainty equivalent wealth is 26, because her utility is 105 if she has 26 with certainty: $U(26) = 105$, which is the same as her expected utility from owning the stock. Thus, she would be indifferent between keeping the stock or selling it for a price of 26. Irma's risk premium, the difference between the expected value of the uncertain prospect and the certainty equivalent, is $40 - 26 = 14$, as the figure shows.

Mini-Case

Stocks' Risk Premium

The value of most stocks is more variable over time than that of bonds. Because stocks are riskier than bonds, for both to sell in the market to risk-averse investors, the anticipated rates of return on investing in stocks must exceed those on bonds over the period that the investor plans to hold these investments. This greater return is an investor's risk premium for stocks.

For example, a U.S. government bond is essentially free of any risk that the U.S. government will default. As Figure 14.2 illustrates, an investor will buy a stock only if it provides a risk premium over a risk-free U.S. government bond. That is, the investor buys the stock only if the expected return on the stock exceeds the rate of return on the bond.

In 2017, the stocks in the Standard and Poor's index of 500 leading stocks, the S&P 500, had a return of 21.6%, which exceeded the 2.8% return on 10-year U.S. Treasury bonds by a large margin. However, stocks do not always outperform safe government bonds. In certain years, such as 2008 and 2011, stocks have performed worse than bonds.

Nonetheless, stocks have had a higher rate of return over the long run. For the 50-year period 1968–2017, the annualized return was 10.0% for S&P 500 stocks and 6.8% on long-term bonds.

Risk Neutrality

Someone who is risk neutral is indifferent about taking a fair bet. Such a person has a constant marginal utility of wealth: Each extra dollar of wealth raises utility by the same amount as the previous dollar. With a constant marginal utility of wealth, the utility function is a straight line in a graph of utility against wealth. Consequently, a risk-neutral person's utility depends only on wealth and not on risk.

Suppose that Irma is risk neutral and has the straight-line utility function in panel a of Figure 14.3. As before, she must either buy a stock at a price of 40 or keep the 40 dollars. She is indifferent between the two alternatives if her subjective probability that the stock will do well is 50%. Her expected utility from buying the stock is the average of her utility at points a (where her wealth is 10) and c (where her wealth is 70):

$$\left[\tfrac{1}{2} \times U(10)\right] + \left[\tfrac{1}{2} \times U(70)\right] = \left[\tfrac{1}{2} \times 70\right] + \left[\tfrac{1}{2} \times 140\right] = 105.$$

This expected utility of 105 from buying the stock exactly equals the utility she obtains from retaining certain wealth of 40, which is also 105, as shown by point b. We know that $U(40) = 105$ because Irma's utility function is the straight line that goes through points a and c, and point b is halfway between those two points. Therefore $U(40)$ must be the average of $U(70)$ and $U(10)$.

Here Irma is indifferent between buying the stock, which is risky, and keeping a certain wealth of 40, which is not risky. Because she is risk neutral she doesn't care how much risk she faces. She cares only about which option has the higher expected wealth. As this expected wealth is 40 in both cases, she is indifferent between them.

FIGURE 14.3 **Risk Neutrality and Risk Preference**

(a) If the plot of Irma's utility function is a straight line, she is risk neutral and is indifferent as to whether or not to make a fair bet. Her expected utility from buying the stock, 105 at *b*, is the same as from a certain wealth of 40 at *b*.

(b) If the plot of Irma's utility function is convex to the horizontal axis, Irma has increasing marginal utility of wealth and is risk preferring. She buys the stock because her expected utility from buying the stock, 105 at *b*, is higher than her utility from a certain wealth of 40, 82 at *d*.

(a) Risk-Neutral Individual

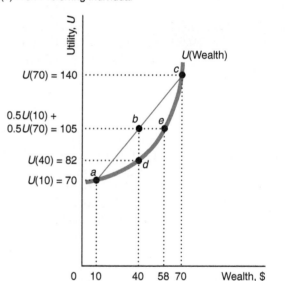

(b) Risk-Preferring Individual

In general, *a risk-neutral person chooses the option with the highest expected value, because maximizing expected value maximizes utility.* A risk-neutral person chooses the riskier option if it has even a slightly higher expected value than the less risky option. Equivalently, the risk premium for a risk-neutral person is zero.

Risk Preference

An individual with an increasing marginal utility of wealth is risk preferring and is happy to take a fair bet. If Irma has the utility function in panel b of Figure 14.3, she is risk preferring. Her expected utility from buying the stock, 105 at *b*, is higher than her certain utility if she does not buy the stock, 82 at *d*. Therefore, she buys the stock.

A risk-preferring person is willing to pay for the right to make a fair bet (a negative risk premium). As the figure shows, Irma's expected utility from buying the stock is the same as the utility from a certain wealth of 58. Given her initial wealth of 40, if you offer her the opportunity to buy the stock or offer to give her 18, she is indifferent. With any payment smaller than 18, she prefers to buy the stock.

Mini-Case

Gambling

Most people say that they don't like bearing risk. Consistent with such statements, most consumers purchase insurance such as car insurance, homeowner's insurance, medical insurance, and other forms of insurance that reduce the risks they face. But many of these same people gamble.

According to one estimate, global gaming revenues were $137.9 billion in 2018. Over half of the countries in the world have lotteries.

Not only do many people gamble, but they also make unfair bets, in which the expected value of the gamble is negative. That is, if they play the game repeatedly, they are likely to lose money in the long run. For example, the British government keeps half of the total amount bet on its lottery, and government-run lotteries in other countries are similar. Legal gambling casinos have a *house edge* that varies from game to game. In U.S. casinos, the house edge for roulette is 5.5%, so players lose 5.5% of all money bet.

According to a *Wall Street Journal* study, internet gamblers win money on 30% of the days they play, but only 11% of these gamblers were in the black over a two-year period. Of the most frequent 10% of bettors, 95% lost money. The big winners in internet gambling are the companies that run the gambling sites.

Why do people take unfair bets? Some people gamble because they are risk preferring or because they have a compulsion to gamble.[9] However, neither of these observations is likely to explain noncompulsive gambling by most people who exhibit risk-averse behavior in the other aspects of their lives (such as buying insurance). Risk-averse people may make unfair bets because they get pleasure from participating in the game or because they falsely believe that the gamble favors them.

The first explanation is that gambling provides entertainment as well as risk. Risk-averse people insure their property, such as their homes, because they do not want to bear the risk of theft, flooding, and fire. However, these same people may play poker or bet on horse races because they get enough pleasure from playing those games to put up with the financial risk and the expected loss.

Many people definitely like games of chance. One survey found that 65% of Americans say that they engage in games of chance even when the games involve no money or only trivial sums. That is, they play because they enjoy the games. The anticipation of possibly winning and the satisfaction and excitement arising from a win generate greater benefits than the negative feelings associated with a loss.

Instead, or in addition, people may gamble because they make mistakes.[10] Either people do not know the true probabilities or they cannot properly calculate expected values, so they do not realize they are participating in an unfair bet. And some gamblers are simply overconfident: They overestimate their likelihood of winning.

---

[9] Friedman and Savage (1948) suggest that some gamblers are risk averse with respect to small gambles but risk preferring for large ones, such as a lottery.

[10] Economists, who know how to calculate expected values and derive most of their excitement from economic models, are apparently less likely to gamble than other people. A number of years ago, an association of economists met in Reno, Nevada. Reno hotels charge low room rates on the assumption that they'll make plenty from guests' gambling losses. However, the economists gambled so little that they were asked pointedly not to return.

Risk Attitudes of Managers

Some shareholders want managers to be risk neutral and to maximize expected profit. However, for a variety of reasons, managers may make either risk-averse or risk-preferring decisions even if shareholders prefer risk-neutral decisions.

First, managers may act in their own interests. (See Chapter 15 for a discussion of the principal-agent problem.) If a manager is risk averse when making personal decisions, the manager may also avoid risk when making decisions for the firm. For example, if a manager is worried about being fired if the firm has large losses, the manager may act to avoid the possibility of such losses, even if doing so lowers the firm's expected profit. That is, the manager is willing for the firm to pay a risk premium (reduced expected profit) to avoid bearing an extreme risk of losing a lot of money. Alternatively, a manager may prefer risk if the manager's compensation is based on the firm's short-run profit and the manager can walk away in the event of a very bad outcome.

It is also possible that shareholders might want managers to behave in a risk-averse manner. For example, if bankruptcy would impose large costs on individual shareholders, they might prefer that managers try to avoid the very bad outcome of bankruptcy even at the expense of reduced expected profit.

Q&A 14.3

The manager of a property development company must choose to pursue one of four possible development projects. Each project will be worth more if its rezoning application is approved. The following Excel spreadsheet shows the probability of approval for each project and the associated payoff conditional on whether approval is granted:

	A	B	C	D	E
1	Project	Rezoned		Not Rezoned	
2		Probability	Payoff	Probability	Payoff
3	A	0.4	9	0.6	5
4	B	0.7	5	0.3	4
5	C	0.5	12	0.5	3
6	D	0.2	11	0.8	4

Augment this spreadsheet to determine the expected value, variance, and standard deviation for each project. Which project would a risk-neutral manager choose? If possible, determine which project a risk-preferring or risk-averse manager would choose if the manager cares only about expected value and variance. If you cannot determine which project would be chosen, can any projects be ruled out?

Answer

1. *Add three columns to the Excel spreadsheet for the expected value, variance, and standard deviation.* Add three columns on the right side of the table: columns F, G, and H. Enter the titles "EV," "VAR," and "SD" in cells F1–H1, respectively.

2. *Fill in the formulas for the expected value, variance, and standard deviation.* Enter "=B3*C3+D3*E3" in cell F3. Enter "=B3*(C3−F3)^2+D3*(E3−F3)^2" in cell G3. Enter "=SQRT(G3)" in cell H3. Copy and paste the formula in cell F3 into cells F4–F6 and fill out columns G and H correspondingly. Format columns G and H to show two positions after the decimal point.

3. *By inspection, find that highest expected value.* Project C has the highest expected value (7.5, which we have highlighted in yellow). Thus, a risk-neutral manager, who cares only about expected value, chooses this project.

4. *Determine which project a risk-preferring manager would choose.* A risk-preferring manager places positive weight on both expected value and variance. As project C has the highest expected value and the highest variance (20.25, highlighted in blue), a risk-preferring manager would choose project C. (Rather than look at the variance, we could look at the standard deviation, which is an alternative measure of risk. The ordering of the variance and the standard deviation is always the same.)

5. *Analyze the decision of a risk-averse manager.* A risk-averse manager values both higher expected value and lower variance. As no project has the highest expected value and lowest variance, we cannot determine which project a risk-averse manager would choose without more information. However, we know the manager would not choose project D, as it has a lower expected value than project A and a higher variance. Therefore, a risk-averse manager would prefer project A to project D.

	A	B	C	D	E	F	G	H
1	Project	Rezoned		Not Rezoned		EV	VAR	SD
2		Probability	Payoff	Probability	Payoff			
3	A	0.4	9	0.6	5	6.6	3.84	1.96
4	B	0.7	5	0.3	4	4.7	0.21	0.46
5	C	0.5	12	0.5	3	7.5	20.25	4.50
6	D	0.2	11	0.8	4	5.4	7.84	2.80

14.3 Reducing Risk

But dear! Flying is safer than driving.

If most accidents occur in the home, why not live elsewhere?

Risk-averse people want to eliminate or reduce the risks they face. Risk-neutral people avoid unfair bets that are stacked against them, and even risk-preferring people avoid very unfair bets. Individuals can avoid optional risky activities, but often they can't escape risk altogether. Property owners, for instance, know that their property may be damaged or stolen. However, they may be able to reduce the probability that bad events (such as earthquakes, tornadoes, fires, floods, and thefts) happen to them.

The simplest way to avoid risk is to abstain from optional risky activities. No one forces you to bet on the lottery, go into a high-risk occupation, or buy stock in a start-up biotech firm. If one brand of a product you use comes with a warranty and an otherwise comparable brand does not, you lower your risk by buying the product with the warranty.

Even when you can't avoid risk altogether, you can take precautions to reduce the probability of bad events or the magnitude of any loss that might occur. For example, by maintaining a car as the manufacturer recommends, you reduce the probability that it will break down. By locking the door to your home, you lower the chance that someone will steal your television. Installing fire alarms and indoor sprinkler systems lessens the likelihood that a house will burn down. By reducing risk, these actions raise the expected value of an asset.

In this section, we look at the three most common ways in which people and firms avoid or limit the risks they face: obtaining information, diversification, and insurance.

Obtaining Information

Collecting accurate information before acting is one of the most important ways people can reduce risk and increase expected value and expected utility, as Q&A 14.1 illustrated. Armed with information, you might avoid a risky choice or be able to take actions that reduce the probability of a disaster or decrease the size of the loss.

Before deciding where to locate a new plant, a prudent manager collects information about various locations concerning local crime rates, fire risks, and other potential hazards. Similarly, a bond fund manager tries to determine risk associated with various bonds before buying them.

Mini-Case

Bond Ratings

Investors obtain information about the riskiness of bonds by checking reports on their riskiness, such as the Moody's and Standard & Poor's ratings in the table. These letter-grade ratings reflect whether a bond's issuer has made timely payments in the past, whether the issuer is in danger of becoming bankrupt, and other problems. *Investment grade* bonds (Moody Baa through Aaa or Standard and Poor's BBB– through AAA) are said to be suitable for purchase by an institutional money manager, such as a pension fund manager, who is legally obligated to be a *prudent investor*—one who does not take great risks. Lower-ranked bonds (Moody's C through Ba and Standard and Poor's D through BB+) are riskier and thus must offer higher rates of return as inducements for people to buy them. The lowest ranked, junk bonds, are generally issued by new firms that have little or no financial history or by established firms that have had their bond ratings downgraded because they've suffered severe financial problems.

Bond Ratings[11]

Moody's		Standard and Poor's	
Descriptor	Grade	Descriptor	Grade
Investment Grade			
Highest quality/minimal credit risk	Aaa	Extremely strong capacity to meet financial commitments	AAA

---

[11]The labels in the table are descriptive. See the companies' websites (**www.moodys.com** and **www .standardandpoors.com**) for more precise definitions.

Moody's		Standard and Poor's	
Descriptor	Grade	Descriptor	Grade
Investment Grade (cont'd)			
High quality/very low credit risk	Aa	Very strong capacity to meet financial commitments	AA
Upper medium quality/low credit risk	A	Strong capacity to meet financial commitments	A
Medium grade/moderate credit risk	Baa	Adequate capacity to meet financial commitments	BBB
		Lowest investment grade	BBB−
High Yield or Junk Bonds			
Speculative elements/subject to substantial credit risk	Ba	Speculative, major ongoing uncertainties	BB+, BB
Speculative/high credit risk	B	Vulnerable but has current capacity to meet commitments	B
Poor quality/very high credit risk	Caa	Vulnerable, dependent on favorable conditions	CCC
Highly speculative/default likely	Ca	Highly vulnerable	CC, C
Lowest quality/in default or default imminent	C	In default	D

Diversification

Although it may sound paradoxical, individuals and firms often reduce their overall risk by making many risky investments instead of only one. This practice is called *risk pooling* or *diversification* and is reflected in this commonly given advice: "Don't put all your eggs in one basket."

Correlation and Diversification. The extent to which diversification reduces risk depends on the degree to which the payoffs of various investments are *correlated*: Their values move in the same direction over time.[12] If two investments are positively correlated, one performs well when the other performs well. If two investments are negatively correlated, when one performs well, the other performs badly. If the performances of two investments move *independently*—do not move together in a predictable way—their payoffs are uncorrelated.

---

[12]A measure of the *correlation* between two random variables x and y is

$$\rho = E\left(\frac{(x - \bar{x})}{\sigma_x} \frac{(y - \bar{y})}{\sigma_y}\right),$$

where the $E(\cdot)$ means "take the expectation" of the term in parentheses, $\bar{x}$ and $\bar{y}$ are the means (expected values), and σ_x and σ_y are the standard deviations of x and y. This correlation can vary between -1 and 1. If $\rho = 1$, these random variables are perfectly positively correlated; if $\rho = -1$, they have a perfect negative correlation; and if $\rho = 0$, they are uncorrelated.

Diversification can eliminate risk if the returns to two investments are perfectly negatively correlated. Suppose that two firms are competing for a government contract and have an equal chance of winning it. Because only one firm can win, if one wins the other must lose. You can buy a share of stock in either firm for $20. The stock of the firm that wins the contract will be worth $40, whereas the stock of the loser will be worth $10. Investments in these stocks have a perfect negative correlation. If one stock turns out to have the high value, 40, the other must have the low value, 10, and vice versa.

If you buy two shares of the same company, your shares are going to be worth either 80 or 20 after the contract is awarded. Thus, their expected value is

$$EV = \left(\tfrac{1}{2} \times 80\right) + \left(\tfrac{1}{2} \times 20\right) = 50$$

with a variance of

$$\sigma^2 = \left[\tfrac{1}{2} \times (80 - 50)^2\right] + \left[\tfrac{1}{2} \times (20 - 50)^2\right] = 900.$$

However, if you buy one share of each, one stock will be worth $40, and the other will be worth $10, so your two shares together will be worth $50 no matter which firm wins, and the variance is zero. Thus, you eliminate all risk by investing in both of these negatively correlated stocks.

For diversification to reduce risk, it is not necessary for the investments to have a perfect negative correlation. Indeed, it is not even necessary for the investments to have any negative correlation. Diversification reduces risk even if the two investments are uncorrelated or imperfectly positively correlated, although the risk is not eliminated as it is with perfectly negatively correlated investments.

Suppose, for example, that each of the two firms has a 50% chance of getting a government contract, but whether one firm gets a contract does *not* affect whether the other firm wins one. Thus, the stock values of the two firms are uncorrelated and each firm's stock price has an equal probability of being 40 or 10. The probability that both firms win contracts and have a stock price of 40 is $\tfrac{1}{4}$, the chance that one is worth 40 and the other is worth 10 is $\tfrac{1}{2}$, and the chance that each is worth 10 is $\tfrac{1}{4}$. If you buy one share of each firm, the expected value of these two shares is

$$EV = \left(\tfrac{1}{4} \times 80\right) + \left(\tfrac{1}{2} \times 50\right) + \left(\tfrac{1}{4} \times 20\right) = 50,$$

and the variance is

$$\sigma^2 = \left[\tfrac{1}{4} \times (80 - 50)^2\right] + \left[\tfrac{1}{2} \times (50 - 50)^2\right] + \left[\tfrac{1}{4} \times (20 - 50)^2\right] = 450.$$

This expected value is the same as from buying two shares of one firm, but the variance is only half as large. Thus, diversification lowers risk when the values are uncorrelated.

Diversification can reduce risk even if the investments are positively correlated, provided that the correlation is not perfect. *Diversification does not reduce risk if two investments have a perfect positive correlation.* For example, risks are perfectly positively correlated if the government awards contracts either to both firms or to neither firm. The expected value of the stocks and the variance are the same whether you buy two shares of one firm or one share of each firm.

Diversification Through Mutual Funds. Because the stock price of any given firm is not perfectly correlated with the stock price of other firms, an investor or a manager can reduce risk by buying the stocks of many companies rather than the stock of just one firm. One way to effectively own shares in a number of companies at once is by buying shares in a *mutual fund* of stocks. A mutual fund share is issued by a company that buys stocks in many other companies.

One well-known type of mutual fund is based on the *Standard & Poor's Composite Index of 500 Stocks* (S&P 500), which is a value-weighted average of 500 large firms' stocks.[13] The S&P 500 companies constitute only about 14% of all the actively publicly traded firms in the United States, but they represent approximately 80% of the total value of U.S. stock markets. The *Wilshire 5000 Index Portfolio* attempts to track all actively traded U.S. stocks.[14] Other mutual funds hold bonds, stocks and bonds, or other types of investments.

Mutual funds allow investors to reduce the risk associated with uncorrelated price movements across stocks. Suppose you believe that two companies are very similar. You have no reason to think that the stock in one firm will increase more in value or be riskier than the stock of the other firm. However, luck may cause one stock to do better than the other. You can reduce this type of random, firm-specific risk by diversifying and buying stock in both firms.

However, a stock mutual fund has a *market-wide risk*, a risk that is common to the overall market, which arises because the prices of almost all stocks tend to rise when the economy is expanding and to fall when the economy is contracting. You cannot avoid the systematic risks associated with shifts in the economy that have a similar effect on most stocks even if you buy a diversified stock mutual fund.

Managerial Implication

Diversify Your Savings

Risk-averse managers and other employees should diversify their own retirement funds and other savings. However, many managers and other employees invest the lion's share of their pension fund savings in their employer's stock. Managers receive company stock from their employers as bonuses or to match their pension contributions and many of them retain that stock instead of selling it to diversify their savings. In addition, some managers invest in company stock as a sign of loyalty.

If the firm fails, these employees lose not only their jobs but much of the value of their retirement portfolio as well, as happened to many of RadioShack's employees when it declared bankruptcy in 2015. Such pension losses arising from a firm's insolvency are common. Duan et al. (2015) analyzed 20 years of data for 729 troubled large, publicly traded companies. They found that employees kept the amounts of money they held in company stock relatively stable during periods of trouble. Pension losses were particularly bad during the Great Recession of 2007–2009.

Many investment advisors recommend investing at most 5% in employer stock—much less than the 26% level found by a 2006 survey of large U.S. pension plans. The good news is that the share of company stock in pension plans has decreased in recent years as participants have become more educated, and both employees and firms have

Stockbrokers at Work

...for a small fee, I can place a bet for you.

---

[13]The weights are the market values of the firms, so larger firms get more weight in the index.

[14]When the index started in 1974, the number of firms was about 5,000. That number peaked at about 7,500 companies in 1998 and fell to about 3,500 as of 2018. See **wilshire.com/indexes/wilshire-5000-family/wilshire-5000-total-market-index**.

taken the lessons of the Great Recession to heart. Many firms now restrict employees' ability to invest their pension savings in company stock. The 2018 *Investment Company Fact Book* reports that younger workers were down to holding only about 5% of their pension savings in company stock.

Insurance

Individuals and organizations can also avoid or reduce risk by purchasing insurance. As we've already seen, a risk-averse person is willing to pay money—a risk premium—to avoid risk. The demand for risk reduction is met by insurance companies, which bear the risk for anyone who buys an insurance policy. Many risk-averse individuals and firms buy insurance, leading to an industry of enormous size. According to the Swiss Re Institute's Insurance Information, global insurance premiums in 2017 were about $4.9 trillion, which is more than 6% of world GDP.[15]

Determining the Amount of Insurance to Buy.   Many individuals and firms buy insurance to shift some or all of the risk they face to an insurance company. A risk-averse person or firm pays a premium to the insurance company, and the insurance company transfers money to the policyholder if a bad outcome occurs, such as becoming ill, having an accident, or suffering a property loss due to theft or fire.

Because Scott is risk averse, he wants to insure his store, which is worth 500. The probability that his store will burn next year is 20%. If a fire occurs, the store will be worth nothing.

With no insurance, the expected value of his store is

$$EV = (0.2 \times 0) + (0.8 \times 500) = 400.$$

Scott faces a good deal of risk. The variance of the value of his store is

$$\sigma^2 = \left[0.2 \times (0 - 400)^2\right] + \left[0.8 \times (500 - 400)^2\right] = 40,000.$$

Suppose that an insurance company offers **fair insurance**: a contract between an insurer and a policyholder in which the expected value of the contract to the policyholder is zero. That is, the insurance is a fair bet. With fair insurance, for every 1 dollar that Scott pays the insurance company, the *insurance premium*, the company will pay Scott $5 to cover the damage if the fire occurs, so that he has $1 less if the fire does not occur, but $4 (= $5 − $1) more if it does occur.[16]

Because Scott is risk averse and the insurance is fair, he wants to *fully insure* by buying enough insurance to eliminate his risk altogether. That is, he wants to buy the amount of fair insurance that will leave him equally well off in both states of nature. He pays a premium of x so that he has $500 - x$ if the fire does not occur, and has $4x$ if the fire occurs, such that $500 - x = 4x$, or $x = 100$.[17] If a fire does not occur, he pays a premium of 100 and has a store worth 500, for a net value of 400. If a fire

---

[15]See **institute.swissre.com/research/overview/sigma/3_2018.html**.

[16]Following standard practice in the insurance industry, we use the term *insurance premium* (or just *premium*) in this section to refer to the amount *actually paid* for insurance. The *insurance premium* is different from a *risk premium*, which is a person's *willingness to pay* to avoid risk.

[17]The expected value of Scott's insurance contract is $[0.8 \times (-100)] + [0.2 \times 400] = 0$, which shows that the insurance is fair.

does occur, Scott pays 100 but receives 500 from the insurance company, for a net value of 400. Thus, Scott's wealth is 400 in either case.

Although Scott's expected value with full and fair insurance is the same as his expected value without insurance, the variance he faces drops from 40,000 without insurance to 0 with insurance. Scott is better off with full fair insurance because he has the same expected value and faces no risk. A risk-averse person always wants full insurance if the insurance is fair.

Sometimes insurance companies put limits on the amount of insurance offered. For example, the insurance company could offer Scott fair insurance but only up to a maximum gross payment of, for example, 400 rather than 500. Given this limit, Scott would buy the maximum amount of fair insurance that he could.

Q&A 14.4

Suppose the local government collects a property tax of 20 on Scott's store. If the tax is collected whether or not the store burns, how much fair insurance does Scott buy? If the tax is collected only if the store does not burn, how much fair insurance does Scott buy?

Answer

1. *Determine the after-tax expected value of the store with and without insurance.* If the tax is always collected, the store is worth $480 = 500 - 20$ if it does not burn and -20 if it does burn. Thus, the expected value of the store is

$$380 = [0.2 \times (-20)] + [0.8 \times 480].$$

If the tax is collected only if the fire does not occur, the expected value of the store is

$$384 = [0.2 \times 0] + [0.8 \times 480].$$

2. *Calculate the amount of fair insurance Scott buys if the tax is always collected.* Because Scott is risk averse, he wants to be fully insured so that the after-tax value of his store is the same in both states of nature. If the tax is always collected and fair insurance is available, Scott pays the insurance company a premium of x such that $500 - x - 20 = 4x - 20$, so $x = 100$. If no fire occurs, his net wealth is $500 - 100 - 20 = 380$. If a fire occurs, the insurance company pays 500, or a net payment of 400 above the cost of the insurance, and Scott pays 20 in taxes, leaving him with 380 once again. That is, he buys the same amount of insurance as he would without any taxes. The tax has no effect on his insurance decision because he owes the tax regardless of the state of nature.

3. *Calculate the amount of fair insurance Scott buys if the tax is collected only if no fire occurs.* If the tax is collected only if no fire occurs, fair insurance implies that Scott pays a premium of y such that $500 - y - 20 = 4y$, so $y = 96$. Thus Scott pays the insurance company 96 and receives 480 if a fire occurs. With no fire, Scott's wealth is $500 - 96 - 20 = 384$. If a fire occurs, the insurance company pays 480, so Scott's wealth is $480 - 96 = 384$. He therefore has the same after-tax wealth in both states of nature.

Comment: Because the tax system is partially insuring Scott by dropping the tax in the bad state of nature, he purchases private insurance coverage of only 480, which is less than the coverage of 500 he buys if the tax is collected in both states of nature.

Fairness and Insurance. We have been examining situations in which the insurance is fair so that the customer's insurance contract has an expected value of zero. However, an insurance company could not stay in business if it offered fair insurance. With fair insurance, the insurance company's expected payments would equal the premiums that the insurance company collects. Because the insurance company has operating expenses—costs of maintaining offices, keeping records, hiring sales agents, and so forth—an insurance firm providing fair insurance would lose money. Insurance companies' rates must be high enough to cover their operating expenses. Thus, we expect that real-world insurance companies offer unfair insurance, charging a premium that exceeds the fair-insurance premium. However, it is important to realize that when we say insurance companies offer unfair insurance, we are not implying that insurance companies are behaving unethically. We only mean that the expected payout to policyholders is less than the premiums paid by policyholders.

In the previous section, we showed that a risk-averse consumer who is offered fair insurance fully insures so that the consumer is equally well off in all states of nature. If insurance companies charge a premium that exceeds the fair-insurance price, these same individuals will buy less insurance so that they are not fully insured.[18]

How much can insurance companies charge for insurance? A monopoly insurance company could charge an amount up to the risk premium a person is willing to pay to avoid risk. For example, in Figure 14.2, Irma's risk premium is 14. She would be willing to pay up to $14 for an insurance policy that would compensate her if her stock did not perform well. The more risk averse an individual is, the more a monopoly insurance company can charge. If many insurance companies compete for business, the price of an insurance policy is less than the maximum that risk-averse individuals are willing to pay—but still high enough that the firms can cover their operating expenses.

Insurance and Diversifiable Risks. Why is an insurance company willing to sell policies and take on risk? By pooling the risks of many people, the insurance company can lower its risk much below that of any individual. If the probability that one car is stolen is independent of whether other cars are stolen, the risk to an insurance company of insuring one person against theft is much greater than the average risk of insuring many people.

Insurance companies generally try to protect themselves from insolvency (going bankrupt) by selling policies only for risks that they can adequately diversify. If the risks from disasters to its policyholders are highly positively correlated, an insurance company is not well diversified just by holding many policies. A war affects all policyholders, so the outcomes that they face are highly positively correlated. Because wars are *nondiversifiable risks*, insurance companies normally do not offer policies insuring against wars.

Mini-Case	Global economic losses from natural disasters in 2017 were $337 billion. About

Mini-Case

Flooded by Insurance Claims

Global economic losses from natural disasters in 2017 were $337 billion. About 43% of these losses, $144 billion, were insured, setting a new annual record for insured natural disaster losses. Hurricanes Harvey, Irma, and Maria and the associated flooding accounted for $92 billion of this loss.

In disaster-prone areas, private flood insurance is generally not available, so homeowners rely on government programs, such as the U.S. National Flood

---

[18]As Q&A 14.4 shows, tax laws may offset the problem of unfair insurance, so that some insurance may be fair or more than fair after tax.

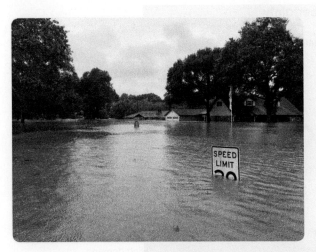

Insurance Program (NFIP). A few insured properties account for a disproportionate share of NFIP claims.

Brian Harman's property in Texas is one of several million insured by NFIP. Shortly after completing major home renovations in 2017, Mr. Harman's property was flooded by Hurricane Harvey. The flood should not have been a surprise. Mr. Harman's house, situated in a flood plain of the San Jacinto River, has flooded 22 times since 1979. Between 1979 and 2015, NFIP paid out almost $2 million—much more than the property is worth—to fix the house multiple times.

Largely because of such "frequent flooders," NFIP has taken in much less in premiums than it has paid out in recent years. Even before the 2017 floods, NFIP owed the U.S. Treasury $24.6 billion. For a combination of political and other reasons, premiums for the high-risk properties are less than the actuarially fair value.

For many of these properties, it would be cheaper for NFIP to buy them and return them to an undeveloped state rather than repeatedly repair flood damage. The U.S. government is trying to do just that, but homeowners often do not want to move, and local governments often oppose losing developed properties from their tax base.

14.4 Investing Under Uncertainty

We now investigate how uncertainty affects investment decisions. In particular, we examine how attitudes toward risk affect willingness to invest and how investors pay to alter their probabilities of success.

We start by examining a monopoly's decision whether to open a new retail outlet. Because the firm is a monopoly, the return from the investment (the profit from the new store) does not depend on the actions of other firms. As a result, the owner of the monopoly faces no strategic considerations. The owner knows the cost of the investment but is unsure about how many people will patronize the new store; hence, the store's future profit is uncertain. Because the investment has an uncertain payoff, the owner should consider risk when deciding to invest in the new store.

We first consider the decision of Chris, a risk-neutral owner. Because she is risk neutral, she invests if the expected value of the firm rises due to the investment. Any action that increases her expected value must also increase her expected utility because she is indifferent to risk. In contrast, in the next example, Ken is risk averse, so he might not make an investment that increases his firm's expected value if the investment is very risky. That is, maximizing expected value does not necessarily maximize his expected utility.

Risk-Neutral Investing

Chris, the risk-neutral owner of the monopoly, uses a *decision tree* (panel a of Figure 14.4) to decide whether to invest. The rectangle, called a *decision node*, indicates that she must make a decision about whether to invest. The circle, a *chance node*, denotes that

FIGURE 14.4 Investment Decision Trees with Uncertainty

Chris and Ken, each the owner of a monopoly, must decide whether to invest in a new store.
(a) The expected value of the investment is 140, so it pays for Chris, who is risk neutral, to invest.
(b) Ken is so risk averse that he does not invest even though the expected value of the investment is positive. His expected utility falls if he makes this risky investment.

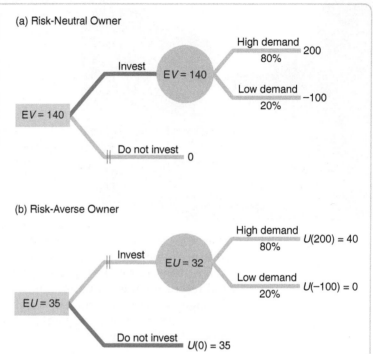

(a) Risk-Neutral Owner

(b) Risk-Averse Owner

a random process determines the outcome (consistent with the given probabilities). If Chris does not open the new store, she makes $0. If she does open the new store, she expects to make $200 (thousand) with 80% probability and to lose $100 (thousand) with 20% probability. The expected value from a new store (see the circle in panel a) is

$$EV = [0.2 \times (-100)] + [0.8 \times 200] = 140.$$

Because Chris is risk neutral, she prefers an expected value of 140 to a certain one of 0, so she invests. Thus, her expected value in the rectangle is 140.

Risk-Averse Investing

Let's compare Chris' decision-making process to that of Ken, a risk-averse owner of a monopoly facing the same investment decision. Ken invests in the new store if his expected utility from investing is greater than his certain utility from not investing. Panel b of Figure 14.4 shows his decision tree, which is based on a particular risk-averse utility function. The circle shows that Ken's expected utility from the investment is

$$EU = [0.2 \times U(-100)] + [0.8 \times U(200)]$$
$$= (0.2 \times 0) + (0.8 \times 40) = 32.$$

Ken's certain utility from not investing is $U(0) = 35$, which is greater than 32. Thus, Ken does not invest. As a result, his expected utility in the rectangle is 35 (his certain utility from not investing).

Q&A 14.5

We have been assuming that nature dictates the probabilities of various possible events. However, sometimes we can alter the probabilities at some expense. Gautam, who is risk neutral, is considering whether to invest in a new store, as Figure 14.5 shows. After investing, he can increase the probability that demand will be high at the new store by advertising at a cost of $50 (thousand). If he makes the investment but does not advertise, he has a 40% probability of making 100 and a 60% probability of losing 100. Should he invest in the new store?

Answer

1. *Calculate the expected value of the investment if Gautam does not advertise.* If Gautam makes the investment but does not advertise, the expected value of his investment is

$$[0.4 \times 100] + [0.6 \times (-100)] = -20.$$

Thus, if he does not advertise, he expects to lose money if he makes this investment.

2. *Calculate the expected value of the investment if Gautam advertises and determine whether he should invest and whether he should advertise.* With advertising, Gautam's expected value before paying for the advertisements is

$$[0.8 \times 100] + [0.2 \times (-100)] = 60.$$

Thus, his expected value after paying for the advertisements is 10 ($= 60 - 50$). Because Gautam is risk neutral, he cares only about expected value. His expected value is higher if he invests *and* advertises than if he does not invest or if he invests without advertising. He should therefore invest and advertise.

FIGURE 14.5 An Investment Decision Tree with Uncertainty and Advertising

By advertising, Gautam, the risk-neutral owner of a monopoly, can alter the probability of high demand. The expected value of the investment is −20 without advertising and 60 with advertising.

Because the cost of advertising is 50, the expected value of investing and advertising is 10 (= 60 − 50). Thus, Gautam invests and advertises.

Oligopolistic R&D Investments Under Uncertainty

Investing under uncertainty is much more challenging for an oligopolistic firm than for a monopoly. In oligopoly markets, firms are affected by uncertainty about the success of both their own investments and those of their rivals.

Uncertainty is particularly important for R&D investments. Oligopolistic firms in an industry often race to be the first to invent a new process, machine, method of manufacturing, or composition of matter. The winner of this race receives a patent, giving it monopoly rights to the invention. Thus, the winner may earn substantial returns to its investment, while the other firms lose their investments. Losing a race for a minor innovation is bad enough. Losing a race for a disruptive innovation (Chapter 7, Chapter 9) is even worse, as losers are likely to be driven out of business.

One of the most famous patent races was to invent the telephone. Alexander Graham Bell won the race in 1876, and received the patent and riches. Elisha Gray, who lost the race, is largely forgotten by history.

14.5 Behavioral Economics and Uncertainty

In the expected utility model, as in the standard utility model, we assume that people make rational choices (Chapter 4). However, many individuals make choices that are inconsistent with the predictions of the expected utility model. Economists and psychologists explain some of these departures from the predictions of the expected utility model using *behavioral economics*: the use of insights from psychology and research on human cognition and emotional biases to augment the rational economic model in an attempt to better predict economic decision making. (We discussed other applications of behavioral economics in Chapters 4, 9, and 13.)

Biased Assessment of Probabilities

People often have mistaken beliefs about the probability that an event will occur. These biases in estimating probabilities come from several sources, including false beliefs about causality and overconfidence.

The Gambler's Fallacy. Many—perhaps most—people subscribe to the *gambler's fallacy*:

> **Common Confusion** Past events affect current, independent outcomes.[19]

For example, suppose that you flip a fair coin and it comes up heads six times in a row. What are the odds that you'll get a tail on the next flip? Because past flips do not affect this one, the chance of a tail remains 50%, yet many people believe that a head is much more likely because they are on a "run." Others hold the opposite but equally false view that the chance of a tail is high because a tail is "due."

Suppose that you have an urn containing three black balls and two red ones. If you draw a ball without looking, your probability of getting a black ball is $\frac{3}{5} = 60\%$. If you replace the ball and draw again, the chance of picking a black ball remains the same. However, if you draw a black ball and do not replace it, the probability of

---

[19]The false belief that one event affects another independent event is captured by the joke about a man who brings a bomb on board a plane whenever he flies because he believes that "The chance of having one bomb on a plane is very small, so the chance of having two bombs on a plane is near zero!"

drawing a black ball again falls to $\frac{2}{4} = 50\%$. Thus, the belief that a tail is due after several heads are tossed in a row is analogous to falsely believing that you are drawing without replacement when you are actually drawing with replacement.

Overconfidence. Another common explanation for why some people make bets that the rest of us avoid is that these gamblers are overconfident. For example, Golec and Tamarkin (1995) found that football bettors tend to make low-probability bets because they greatly overestimate their probabilities of winning certain types of exotic football bets (an *exotic bet* depends on the outcome of more than one game). In one survey, gamblers estimated their chance of winning a particular bet at 45% when the objective probability was 20%.

Few groups exhibit more overconfidence than male high school athletes. Many U.S. high school basketball and football players believe they will get an athletic scholarship to attend college, but less than 5% receive one. Of this elite group, three-quarters believe that it is at least "somewhat" likely that they will play professionally, but only 1.6% of college football players are drafted into the NFL and only 1.2% of college basketball players are drafted into the NBA.[20]

Mini-Case

Biased Estimates

Do newspaper stories, television, and movies cause people to overestimate relatively rare events and underestimate relatively common ones? Newspapers are more likely to publish "man bites dog" stories than the more common "dog bites man" reports.[21]

If you have seen the movie *Jaws*, you can't help but think about sharks before wading into the ocean. In 2018, news media around the world reported shark attacks along the coasts of Florida, New York, Western Australia, Brazil, and Egypt. Do you worry about shark attacks? You really shouldn't.

Only 8 people were killed by sharks in U.S. waters in the decade from 2008 through 2017: fewer than one a year. An American's chance of dying from a shark attack is 1 in 3.7 million, but is 1 in 80 thousand from lightning (about 43 times as likely), 1 in 14 thousand from sun or heat exposure, 1 in 218 from a fall, 1 in 84 from a car accident, 1 in 63 from flu, 1 in 38 from hospital infection, 1 in 24 from a stroke, 1 in 7 from cancer, and 1 in 5 from a heart attack.

Benjamin et al. (2001) reported that when people are asked to estimate the frequency of deaths from various causes for the entire population, they overestimate the number of deaths from infrequent causes and underestimate those from more common causes. In contrast, if asked to estimate the number of deaths among their own age group from a variety of causes, their estimates are almost completely unbiased. That is not to say that people know the true probabilities—only that their mistakes are not systematic.

---

[20]See Rossi and Armstrong (1989), **www.ncaa.org/about/resources/research/probablility-competing-beyond-high-school**, **www.inside highered.com/news/2015/01/27/college-athletes-greatly-overestimate-their-chances-playing-professionally**.

[21]For example, Indian papers reported on a man bites snake story, noting that Neeranjan Bhaskar has eaten more than 4,000 snakes (*Calcutta Telegraph*, August 1, 2005), and the even stranger "Cobra Dies After Biting Priest of Snake Temple!" (*Express India*, July 11, 2005).

Violations of Expected Utility Theory

Economists and psychologists have shown that some people's choices violate the basic assumptions of expected utility theory. One important class of violations arises because people change their choices in response to inessential changes in how choices are described or *framed*, even when the underlying probabilities and events do not change. Another class of violations arises because of a bias toward certainty.

Framing. A widely held view is that people are generally rational:

> **Common Confusion** People react the same way when given equivalent choices no matter how they are posed.

However, experiments show that many people reverse their preferences when a problem is presented, or *framed,* in different but equivalent ways. Tversky and Kahneman (1981) posed the problem that the United States expects an unusual disease (e.g., avian flu) to kill 600 people. The government is considering two alternative programs to combat the disease. The "exact scientific estimates" of the consequences of these programs are as follows:

- If Program A is adopted, 200 out of 600 people will be saved.
- If Program B is adopted, the probabilities are $\frac{1}{3}$ that 600 people will be saved and $\frac{2}{3}$ that no one will be saved.

When college students were asked to choose, 72% opted for the certain gains of Program A over the possibly larger but riskier gains of Program B.

A second group of students was asked to choose between an alternative pair of programs, and were told:

- If Program C is adopted, 400 out of 600 people will die.
- If Program D is adopted, the probabilities are $\frac{1}{3}$ that no one will die, and $\frac{2}{3}$ that 600 people will die.

When faced with this choice, 78% chose the potentially larger but uncertain losses of Program D over the certain losses of Program C. These results are surprising if people maximize their expected utility: Program A is identical to Program C and Program B is the same as Program D in the sense that these pairs have identical expected outcomes. Expected utility theory predicts consistent choices for the two pairs of programs, but many people make inconsistent choices, preferring Programs A and D. (Even after rereading the options and having the inconsistency problem explained, most of us still feel drawn toward Programs A and D.)

In many similar experiments, researchers have repeatedly observed this pattern, called the *reflection effect*: Attitudes toward risk are reversed (reflected) for gains versus losses. People are often risk averse when making choices involving gains, but they are often risk preferring when making choices involving losses.

The Certainty Effect. Many people put excessive weight on outcomes they consider to be certain relative to risky outcomes. This *certainty effect* (or *Allais effect,* after the French economist who first reported it) can be illustrated using an example from Kahneman and Tversky (1979). First, a group of subjects was asked to choose between two options:

- **Option A.** You receive $4,000 with probability 80% and $0 with probability 20%.
- **Option B.** You receive $3,000 with certainty.

The vast majority, 80%, chose the certain outcome, B.

Then, the subjects were given another set of options:

- **Option C.** You receive $4,000 with probability 20% and $0 with probability 80%.
- **Option D.** You receive $3,000 with probability 25% and $0 with probability 75%.

Now, 65% prefer C.

Kahneman and Tversky found that over half the respondents violated expected utility theory by choosing B in the first experiment and C in the second one. If $U(0) = 0$, then choosing B over A implies that the expected utility from B is greater than the expected utility from A, so that $U(3,000) > 0.8U(4,000)$, or $U(3,000)/U(4,000) > 0.8$. Choosing C over D implies that $0.2U(4,000) > 0.25U(3,000)$, or $U(3,000)/U(4,000) < 0.8 \ (= 0.2/0.25)$. Thus, these choices are inconsistent with each other, and hence inconsistent with expected utility theory. The certainty of option B seems to give it extra attractiveness over and above what is implied by expected utility theory.

Expected utility theory is based on gambles with known probabilities, whereas most real-world situations involve unknown or subjective probabilities. Ellsberg (1961) pointed out that expected utility theory cannot account for an ambiguous situation in which many people are reluctant to put substantial decision weight on any outcome. He illustrated the problem in a "paradox." Each of two urns contains 100 balls that are either red or black. You know with certainty that the first urn has 50 red and 50 black balls. You do not know the ratio of red to black balls in the second urn. Most of us would agree that the known probability of drawing a red from the first urn, 50%, equals the subjective probability of drawing a red from the second urn. That is, not knowing how many red and black balls are in the second urn, we have no reason to believe that the probability of drawing a red is greater or less than 50%. Yet, most people would prefer to bet that a red ball will be drawn from the first urn rather than from the second urn.

Prospect Theory

Kahneman and Tversky's (1979) *prospect theory*, an alternative theory of decision making under uncertainty, can explain some of the choices people make that are inconsistent with expected utility theory. According to *prospect theory*, people are concerned about gains and losses—the changes in wealth—rather than the level of wealth, as in expected utility theory. People start with a reference point—a base level of wealth—and think about alternative outcomes as gains or losses relative to that reference level.

Comparing Expected Utility and Prospect Theories.   We can illustrate the differences in the two theories by comparing how people would act under the two theories when facing the same situation. Both Muzhe and Rui have initial wealth W. They may choose a gamble where they get A dollars with probability θ or B dollars with probability $1 - \theta$. For example, A might be negative, reflecting a loss, and B might be positive, indicating a gain.

Muzhe wants to maximize his expected utility. If he does not gamble, his utility is $U(W)$. To calculate his expected utility if he gambles, Muzhe uses the probabilities θ and $1 - \theta$ to weight the utilities from the two possible outcomes:

$$EU = \theta U(W + A) + (1 - \theta)U(W + B),$$

where $U(W + A)$ is the utility he gets from his after-gambling wealth if A occurs and $U(W + B)$ is the utility if he receives B. He chooses to gamble if his expected utility from gambling exceeds his certain utility from his initial wealth: $EU > U(W)$.

In contrast, Rui's decisions are consistent with prospect theory. Rui compares the gamble to her current reference point, which is her initial situation where she has W with certainty. The value she places on her reference point is $V(0)$, where 0 indicates that she has neither a gain nor a loss with this certain outcome. The negative value that she places on losing is $V(A)$, and the positive value from winning is $V(B)$.

To determine the value from taking the gamble, Rui does not calculate the expectation using the probabilities θ and $1 - \theta$, as she would with expected utility theory. Rather, she uses *decision weights* $w(\theta)$ and $w(1 - \theta)$, where the w function assigns a weight that differs from θ. If people assign disproportionately high weights to rare events (see the Mini-Case "Biased Estimates"), the weight $w(\theta)$ exceeds θ for low values of θ and is less than θ for high values of θ.

Rui gambles if the value from not gambling, $V(0)$, is less than her evaluation of the gamble, which is the weighted average of her values in the two cases:

$$V(0) < [w(\theta) \times V(A)] + [w(1 - \theta) \times V(B)].$$

Thus, prospect theory differs from expected utility theory in both how outcomes are valued and weighted.

Properties of Prospect Theory.

To resolve various mysteries about how people choose, prospect theory proposes a value function, V, that has an S-shape, as in Figure 14.6. This curve has three properties. First, the curve passes through the reference point at the origin, because gains and losses are determined relative to the initial situation.

Second, the prospect theory utility function is concave over gains and convex over losses. Because of this shape, Rui is less sensitive to a given change in the outcome for large gains or losses than for small ones. For example, she cares more about whether she has a loss of $1 rather than $2 than she does about a loss of $1,001 rather than $1,002.

FIGURE 14.6 The Prospect Theory Value Function

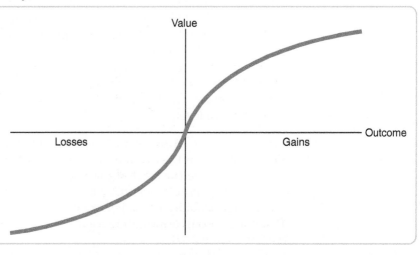

The prospect theory value function has an S-shape. It passes through the reference point at the origin, because gains and losses are measured relative to the reference point. Because the curve is asymmetric with respect to gains and losses, people treat gains and losses differently. This S-curve shows a bigger impact to a loss than to a comparably sized gain, reflecting loss aversion.

Third, the curve is asymmetric with respect to gains and losses. People treat gains and losses differently, in contrast to the predictions of expected utility theory. The S-curve in the figure shows that people suffer more from a loss than they benefit from a comparable size gain. That is, the value function reflects *loss aversion*: People dislike making losses more than they like making gains. Given the subjective weights, valuations based on gains and losses, and the shape of the value curve, prospect theory can resolve some of the behavioral mysteries of choice under uncertainty. The S-shaped curve shows that people treat gains and losses differently: They are risk averse over gains but risk preferring over losses. In the disease experiment described earlier in this section, most people choose the riskier (higher variance) option when considering lives lost but select the less risky option when the identical outcomes are stated in terms of lives saved (gained) instead.

Managerial Implication Loss Aversion Contracts	How can a manager induce employees to work hard? If workers have loss aversion, then employees work harder if offered a loss contract—they lose a bonus if they do not work hard enough—than if offered an equivalent gain contract—they receive a bonus if they work hard. Hossain and List (2012), Fryer et al. (2012), and Imas, Sadoff, and Samek (2015) found that productivity is higher with a loss contract than with a gain contract. However, the firm may not benefit from using a loss contract if they have to pay workers more to start work at the firm because they prefer a gain contract. Luckily, Imas, Sadoff, and Samek (2015) indicate that workers actually prefer loss contracts.

Managerial Solution BP's Risk and Limited Liability	As the Managerial Problem at the beginning of this chapter noted, firms such as BP and Transocean that have deep-water oil rigs may face limited liability for a major spill. Although it is possible that BP and Transocean underestimated the true probabilities of disaster prior to the 2010 spill, a cap on the firms' liability may have also influenced these firms' behavior and led to the disaster. In particular, we now address the three questions raised in the Managerial Problem: How does a cap on liability affect a firm's willingness to make a risky investment or to invest less than the optimal amount in safety? How does a cap affect the amount of risk borne by the firm and by the rest of society? How does a cap affect the amount of insurance that a firm buys?

To illustrate the basic ideas, suppose that an oil rig firm expects to earn \$1 billion in the absence of a spill on its new rig and to lose \$39 billion if a spill occurs. The probability of a spill is θ. We start by considering whether the firm invests in a new rig (the analysis would be similar if it were deciding to invest in a given safety feature for a rig).

If the firm is risk neutral, then it invests in the new rig only if the expected return is positive, $[(1 - \theta) \times 1] + [\theta \times (-39)] > 0$, or if $\theta < 1/40 = 2.5\%$.[22] If the firm is risk averse, this *threshold probability*—the highest probability at which the firm is willing to invest—is less than 2.5%.

Now suppose that the firm's liability is capped at \$19 billion. If the firm is risk neutral, it invests in the new rig if $[(1 - \theta) \times 1] + [\theta \times (-19)] > 0$, or if $\theta < 1/20 = 5\%$. Similarly, if the firm is risk averse, the threshold probability is higher than it would be without the limit on liability.

---

[22]The firm compares the expected return to that of the second-best investment opportunity, which we assume is zero for simplicity.

A limit on liability increases society's total risk if this limited liability causes the drilling company to drill when it would not otherwise do so. Suppose that the probability of a spill is $\theta = 3\%$. If the drilling company is risk neutral and bears the full liability for the damages from a spill, then the company's expected earnings are $[0.97 \times 1] + [0.03 \times (-39)] = -0.2 < 0$, so it chooses not to drill to avoid an expected loss of $0.2 billion. However, if its liability is capped at $19 billion, then its expected gain from drilling is $[0.97 \times 1] + [0.03 \times (-19)] = 0.4 > 0$, so it would drill. Because the firm is more likely to drill because of the liability cap, the cap causes the rest of society's total risk to increase. Moreover, the rest of society bears the risk from the $20 billion ($39 billion − $19 billion) for which it is now responsible if a spill occurs.

If the firm is risk averse, it wants to buy fair insurance to cover its risk. To illustrate the effect of the cap on its decision regarding how much insurance the firm buys, we now assume that the probability of a disaster is $\theta = 1\%$. Without either a liability cap or insurance, the firm's expected gain is $[0.99 \times 1] + [0.01 \times (-39)] = 0.6$. If an insurance company would provide fair insurance, the drilling firm could buy $100 of insurance for each $1 spent. Given that the drilling company is risk averse, it fully insures, so that if a spill occurs, the insurance company pays $39 billion. To buy this much insurance, the drilling company pays $0.39 billion, so that the expected value of the insurance contract is $-0.39 + [0.01 \times 39] = 0$. With the insurance, the company earns $[0.99 \times 1] - 0.39 = 0.6$ whether or not a spill occurs.

If the drilling company's liability is capped at $19 billion, it buys $19 billion worth of insurance for $0.19 billion, so that its expected gain is $[0.99 \times 1] = [0.01 \times (-19)] = \$0.8$ billion. Therefore, the drilling company's expected profit increases by $0.8 - 0.6 = \$0.2$ billion due to the limit on its liability. This amount is a transfer from the rest of society to the firm, because society will be responsible for the extra $20 billion in damages if the spill occurs.[23]

SUMMARY

1. **Assessing Risk.** A probability measures the likelihood that a particular state of nature occurs. People may use historical frequencies, if available, to calculate probabilities. Lacking detailed information, people may form subjective estimates of a probability on the basis of available information. The expected value is the probability-weighted average of the values in each state of nature. One widely used measure of risk is the variance (or the standard deviation, which is the square root of the variance). The variance is the probability-weighted average of the squared difference between the value in each state of nature and the expected value.

2. **Attitudes Toward Risk.** Whether people choose a risky option over a nonrisky one depends on their attitudes toward risk and the expected payoffs of the various options. Most people are *risk averse* and will choose a riskier option only if its expected value is sufficiently higher than that of a less risky option. *Risk-neutral* people choose whichever option has the higher rate of return because they do not care about risk. *Risk-preferring* people may choose the riskier option even if it has a lower rate of return because they like risk and are willing to give up some expected return to take on more risk. An individual's utility function reflects

---

[23]Why would governments adopt such limits on liability? One possible answer is rent seeking, by which firms induce legislatures to pass laws that favor the firms (Chapter 9). However, proponents of the policy argue that oil drilling provides social benefits that are not captured by the companies (including having a secure energy supply) and that private insurance companies would not be large enough to diversify over such large risks. In effect, the government acts as the insurer of last resort.

that person's attitude toward risk. Expected utility is the probability-weighted average of the utility from the outcomes in the various states of nature. According to expected utility theory, decision makers choose the option that provides the highest expected utility.

3. **Reducing Risk.** People try to reduce the risk they face in several ways. They avoid some risks altogether and, when risks cannot be avoided, take actions that lower the probabilities of bad events. They might also take actions that reduce the harm from bad events when they do occur. By collecting information before acting, investors can make better choices. People can further reduce risk by diversifying over a range of investments. Unless returns to the different investments are perfectly positively correlated, diversification reduces risk. Insurance companies offer policies for risks they can diversify by pooling risks across many individuals. Insurance is called fair insurance if the expected return to the policyholder is zero: The expected payout equals the premium paid. Risk-averse people fully insure if they can buy fair insurance. Because insurance companies must earn enough income to cover their full operating costs, including paying salaries to workers, they offer insurance that is less than fair. Risk-averse people often buy some insurance even if it is unfair, but they typically buy less than full insurance. When buying unfair insurance, policyholders exchange the risk of a large loss for the certainty of a smaller loss (paying the premium).

4. **Investing Under Uncertainty.** Whether a person makes an investment depends on the uncertainty of the payoff, the expected return, the individual's attitudes toward risk, the interest rate, and the cost of altering the probabilities of various outcomes. For a risk-neutral person, an investment pays if the expected value is positive. A risk-averse person invests only if that person's expected utility is higher after investing. Thus, risk-averse people make risky investments if the investments pay sufficiently higher rates of return than do safer investments. People pay to alter the probabilities of various outcomes from an investment if doing so raises their expected utility. R&D patent races are an important source of uncertainty for firms in oligopolistic markets.

5. **Behavioral Economics and Uncertainty.** Economists and psychologists have identified behavior under uncertainty that is inconsistent with expected utility theory. These choices may be due to biased estimates of probabilities or different objectives than maximizing expected utility. For example, some people care more about losses than about gains. One alternative theory that is consistent with many of these puzzling choices is prospect theory, which allows individuals to be risk averse over gains but risk preferring over losses.

QUESTIONS

All exercises are available on **MyLab Economics;** * = *answer at the back of this book;* **C** = *use of calculus may be necessary.*

1. Assessing Risk

1.1 Mme. Giselle's boutique in Cleveland, Ohio, is planning to sell Parisian frocks. If the public view them as being the latest style, the frocks will be worth $10,000. However, if the public view them as passé, they will be worth only $2,000. If the probability that they are stylish is 20%, what is the expected value of the frocks?

*1.2 Asa buys a painting. He believes that the artist will become famous and the painting will be worth $1,000 with a 20% probability, the painting will be destroyed by fire or some other disaster with a 10% probability, and otherwise the painting will be worth $500. What is the expected value of the painting?

1.3 The EZ Construction Company is offered a $40,000 contract to build a new deck for a house. The company's profit if it does not have to sink piers (vertical supports) down to bedrock will be $9,000. However, if it does have to sink the piers, it will lose $2,000. The probability it will have to put in the piers is 20%. What is the expected value of this contract? Now, EZ learns that it can obtain a seismic study of the property that would specify whether piers have to be sunk before EZ must accept or reject this contract. By how much would the seismic study increase EZ's expected value? What is the most that it will pay for such a study? (*Hint*: See Q&A 14.1.)

*1.4 By next year, a stock you own has a 25% chance of being worth $400 and a 75% probability of being worth $200. What are the expected value and the variance?

1.5 A drug development company develops a new antiviral medication. It applies for a patent and for Federal Drug Administration (FDA) approval to sell it. The firm estimates that the patent application has a 60% chance of success and that FDA approval has a probability of 50%. If both applications are successful, the drug can be sold to a major drug producer for $10 million. If FDA approval is obtained but the patent application is unsuccessful, the drug can be sold for $4 million. If the drug is not approved by the FDA, it is worth nothing. What are the expected value and variance of this drug? (Work in units of $1 million.)

1.6   What is the difference—if any—between an individual gambling at a casino and gambling by buying a stock? What is the difference for society?

1.7   To discourage people from breaking laws against speeding, society can increase the probability that someone exceeding the speed limit will be caught and punished, or it can increase the size of the fine for speeding. Explain why either method can be used to discourage speeding. Which approach is a government likely to prefer, and why?

2. Attitudes Toward Risk

2.1   Ryan offers to bet Kristin that if a six-sided die comes up with one or two dots showing, he will pay her $5, but if it comes up with any other number of dots, she'll owe him $3. Is that a fair bet for Kristin? If Kristin takes the bet, what is Ryan's expected value?

2.2   Would risk-neutral people ever buy insurance that was not fair (that was biased against them)? Explain.

2.3   Maoyong's utility function with respect to wealth is $U(W) = \ln W$ (where "ln W" means the natural logarithm of W). Plot his utility function and use your figure to determine whether Maoyong is risk averse.

2.4   Use calculus to determine whether the following utility functions imply risk aversion, risk neutrality, or risk preference:

   a. $U(W) = \ln (W)$.

   b. $U(W) = W^{0.4}$.

   c. $U(W) = W^2$.

   d. $U(W) = 2W$.

   (*Hint*: See Using Calculus: "Diminishing Marginal Utility of Wealth.") C

2.5   Suppose that Emily has a utility function of $U(W) = \sqrt{W}$ and an initial wealth of $W = \$900$. How much of a risk premium would she require to participate in a gamble that has a 50% chance of increasing her wealth to $980 and a 50% chance of lowering her wealth to $820?

*2.6   Hugo has a concave utility function of $U(W) = W^{0.5}$. His only asset is shares in an internet start-up company. Tomorrow he will learn the stock's value. He believes that it is worth $144 with probability $\frac{2}{3}$ and $225 with probability $\frac{1}{3}$. What is his expected utility? What risk premium would he pay to avoid bearing this risk? (*Hint*: See Q&A 14.2 and the discussion of the risk premium in Figure 14.2.)

2.7   Given the information in Q&A 14.2, Irma prefers to buy the stock. Show graphically how high her certain wealth would have to be for her to choose not to buy the stock.

2.8   Suppose that an individual is risk averse and has to choose between $100 with certainty and a risky option with two equally likely outcomes: $100 − x$ and $100 + x$. Use a graph (or math) to show that this person's risk premium is smaller, the smaller x is (the less variable the gamble is).

2.9   Based on the information in the Mini-Case "Stocks' Risk Premium," are the comparative returns to 10-year U.S. Treasury bonds and the S&P 500 stock index consistent with risk aversion on the part of investors? Explain.

2.10   Joanna is considering three possible jobs. The following table shows the possible incomes she might get in each job.

	Outcome A		Outcome B	
	Probability	Earnings	Probability	Earnings
Job 1	0.5	20	0.5	40
Job 2	0.3	15	0.7	45
Job 3	1	30		

For each job, calculate the expected value, the variance, and the standard deviation. If Joanna is averse to risk (as measured by variance), what can you predict about her job choice? What if she is risk neutral?

2.11   Catalina just inherited a vineyard from a distant relative. In good years (those without rain and frost during harvest season), she earns $150,000 from the sale of grapes from the vineyard. If the weather is poor, she loses $30,000. Catalina's estimate of the probability of good weather is 60%.

   a. Calculate the expected value and the variance of Catalina's income from the vineyard.

   b. Catalina is risk averse. Ethan, a grape buyer, offers Catalina a guaranteed payment of $70,000 each year in exchange for her entire harvest. Will she accept this offer? Explain.

   c. Why might Ethan make such an offer?

2.12   Based on the information in the Mini-Case "Gambling," provide at least three reasons why many risk-averse people gamble in casinos.

2.13   Joachim's utility function is $U(W) = \ln (W)$, where ln (W) is the natural logarithm of W. Cindy's utility function is $U(W) = W^{0.5}$ (the square root function). Which of the projects described in Q&A 14.3 would be chosen by Joachim? Show that Cindy would favor a different project. (*Hint*: Answer this question using the spreadsheet specified in the question. Add a column for the expected utility of Joachim and one for the expected utility of Cindy.)

2.14   Using the information in the preceding question, show that both Joachim and Cindy are risk averse. Explain why they favor different projects even though they are both risk averse. (*Hint*: Plot both utility functions and recall that a concave utility function implies risk aversion.)

3. Reducing Risk

3.1 Malee, who is risk averse, has two pieces of jewelry, each worth $1,000. She plans to send them to her sister's firm in Thailand to be sold there. She is concerned about the safety of shipping them. She believes that the probability that any box shipped will not reach its destination is θ. Is her expected utility higher if she sends the articles together or in two separate shipments?

3.2 Why do many investment advisors recommend that managers invest only a small share of their savings in the stock of companies they work for? (*Hint*: See the Managerial Implication "Diversify Your Savings.")

3.3 Lucy, the manager of a medical test firm, Dubrow Labs, worries about the firm being sued for botched results from blood tests. If it isn't sued, the firm expects to earn a profit of 100, but if it is successfully sued, its profit will be only 10. Lucy believes the probability of a successful suit is 5%. If fair insurance is available and Lucy is risk averse, how much insurance will she buy?

*3.4 Consider a household that possesses $160,000 worth of valuables such as jewelry. This household faces a 0.2 probability of burglary, in which case it loses $70,000 worth of the valuables. Suppose it can buy an insurance policy for $15,000 that would fully reimburse the amount of loss from burglary. The household's utility is given by $U(X) = 4X^{0.5}$

a. Should the household buy this insurance policy?

b. What is the actuarially fair price for the insurance policy?

c. What is the most the household is willing to pay for this insurance policy that fully covers it against the loss?

3.5 An insurance agent (interviewed in Jonathan Clements, "Dare to Live Dangerously: Passing on Some Insurance Can Pay Off," *Wall Street Journal*, July 23, 2005, D1) states, "On paper, it never makes sense to have a policy with low deductibles or carry collision on an old car." But the agent notes that raising deductibles and dropping collision coverage can be a tough decision for people with a low income or little savings. (Collision insurance is the coverage on a policyholder's own car for accidents in which another driver is not at fault.)

a. Suppose that the loss is $4,000 if an old car is in an accident. During the six-month coverage period, the probability that a court finds the insured person at fault in an accident is $\frac{1}{36}$. Suppose that the price of the coverage is $150. Should a wealthy person purchase the coverage? Should a poor person purchase the coverage? Do your answers depend on the policyholder's degree of risk aversion? Does the policyholder's degree of risk aversion depend on his or her wealth?

b. The agent advises wealthy people not to purchase insurance to protect against possible small losses. Why?

3.6 After Superstorm Sandy in 2012, the government offered subsidies to people whose houses were destroyed. How does the expectation that subsidies will be offered again for future major disasters affect the probability that risk-averse people will buy insurance as well as the amount they buy? (*Hint*: Use a utility function for a risk-averse person to illustrate your answer. See Q&A 14.4.)

3.7 In 2015, Lloyd's of London, a major global insurer, concluded that a chain reaction of floods, drought, and related diseases could cripple the world's food supply. What actions can firms and individuals take to mitigate the risks they face?

3.8 In 2015, San Francisco's Lazy Bear restaurant and a variety of other restaurants around the country started using a reservation system in which diners pay for their meal in advance. No refunds are possible, though diners can give their tickets to others. Previously, these restaurants used traditional reservations, in which diners suffered no loss if they canceled, even at the last minute. How does this new system affect restaurants' risks? What are some of the potential costs of this new system?

4. Investing Under Uncertainty

*4.1 Andy and Kim live together. Andy may invest $10,000 (possibly by taking on an extra job to earn the additional money) in Kim's MBA education this year. This investment will raise the current value of Kim's earnings by $24,000. If they stay together, they will share the benefit from the additional earnings. However, the probability is $\frac{1}{2}$ that they will split up in the future. If they were married and then split, Andy would get half of Kim's additional earnings. If they were living together without any legal ties and they split, then Andy would get nothing. Suppose that Andy is risk neutral. Will Andy invest in Kim's education? Does your answer depend on the couple's legal status?

4.2 A risk-neutral plaintiff in a lawsuit must decide whether to settle a claim or go to trial. The defendants offer $140,000 to settle now. If the plaintiff does not settle, the plaintiff believes that the probability of winning at trial is 70%. If the plaintiff wins, the amount awarded to the plaintiff is X. Will the plaintiff settle if X is $170,000? What if $X = $250,000? What is the critical value of X that would make the plaintiff indifferent between settling and going to trial? If the plaintiff were risk averse instead of risk neutral, would this critical value of X be higher or lower?

4.3 DVD retailers choose how many copies of a movie to purchase from a studio and to stock. The retailers have the right to return all unsold copies to the studio for a full refund, but the retailer pays the shipping costs for returned copies. A small mom-and-pop retailer will sell 1, 2, 3, or 4 copies with probabilities 0.2, 0.3, 0.3, and 0.2, respectively. Suppose that the retail market price of the DVD is $15 and that the retailer must pay the studio $8 for each copy. The studio's marginal cost is $1. The retailer's marginal profit is $7 for selling each copy, and the studio's marginal profit is $7 for each nonreturned copy sold to the retailer. The cost of shipping each DVD back to the studio is $2. The studio and retailer are risk neutral.

   a. How many copies of the DVD will the retailer order from the studio? What is the studio's expected profit-maximizing number of copies for the retailer to order?

   b. Alternatively, suppose that the studio pays the shipping costs to return unsold DVDs. How many copies would the retailer order?

   c. Does the number of copies the retailer orders depend on which party pays the shipping costs? Why?

4.4 Use a decision tree to illustrate how a risk-averse kidney patient would make a decision about whether to have a transplant operation. The patient currently uses a dialysis machine, which lowers her utility. If the operation is successful, her utility will return to its level before the onset of her kidney problems. However, she faces a 5% probability that she will die if she has the operation. (If it will help, make up utility numbers to illustrate your answer.)

4.5 Robert Green repeatedly and painstakingly applied herbicides to kill weeds that would harm his sugar beet crops in 2007. However, in 2008, he planted beets genetically engineered to withstand Monsanto's Roundup herbicide. Roundup destroys weeds but leaves the crop unharmed, thereby saving a farmer thousands of dollars in tractor fuel and labor. This policy was risky. In the past when beet breeders announced they were going to use Roundup-resistant seeds, sugar-using food companies like Hershey and Mars objected, fearing consumer resistance. Now, though, sensing that consumer concerns have subsided, many processors have cleared their growers to plant the Roundup-resistant beets. A Kellogg spokeswoman said her company was willing to use such beets, but Hershey and Mars declined to comment. Thus, a farmer like Mr. Green faces risks by switching to Roundup Ready beets. Use a decision tree to illustrate the analysis that a farmer in this situation needs to do.

4.6 In Q&A 14.5, advertising increases the probability of high demand to 80%. If all the other information in the Q&A stays the same, what is the minimum probability of high demand resulting from advertising such that Gautam decides to invest and advertise?

4.7 During the Great Recession, many homeowners around the world owed more on their houses than they were worth. Often, U.S. borrowers who cannot meet their mortgage payments can give their houses to the banks that hold their mortgage without declaring bankruptcy or being held accountable for any unpaid balance. However, Europeans, who face tougher bankruptcy laws, are responsible for unpaid mortgage balances even after losing their homes (Gabriele Steinhauser and Matthew Dalton, "Lingering Bad Debts Stifle Europe Recovery," *Wall Street Journal*, January 31, 2013). Using a decision tree, show that Americans are more likely to buy houses than Europeans, all else the same.

4.8 A risk-neutral firm believes that the probability of a harmful cyberattack (see the Mini-Case "Risk of a Cyberattack") is 25%. It expects to make a profit of $200 million if no attack occurs and $120 million if it is attacked. The firm can spend $5 million to increase its electronic defenses, which reduces the probability of a successful cyberattack to 10%. Use a decision tree similar to Figure 14.4 to assess whether the firm should make this investment.

4.9 R&D investments are a major source of business uncertainty. Do all risk-averse managers fail to invest in R&D? Why or why not?

5. Behavioral Economics and Uncertainty

5.1 First, answer the following two questions about your preferences:

   a. You receive $5,000 and are offered a choice between receiving an extra $2,500 with certainty or flipping a coin and getting $5,000 more if heads or $0 if tails. Which option do you prefer?

   b. You receive $10,000 conditional on making the following choice: Return $2,500 or flip a coin and return $5,000 if heads and $0 if tails. Which option do you prefer?

Most people choose the certain $2,500 in the first case but flip the coin in the second. Explain why this behavior is not consistent. What do you conclude about how people make decisions concerning uncertain events?

5.2 Evan is risk preferring with respect to gains and risk averse with respect to losses. Louisa is risk preferring with respect to losses and risk averse with respect to gains. Illustrate both utility functions. Which person's attitudes toward risk are consistent with prospect theory? Which of these people would you expect to be susceptible to framing effects?

*5.3 Joe lost a substantial amount gambling at a racetrack today. On the last race of the day, he decides to make a large enough bet on a longshot so that, if he wins, he will make up for his earlier losses and break even on the day. His friend Sue, who won more than she lost on the day, makes just a small final bet so that she will end up ahead for the day even if she loses the last race. Would you explain this behavior using overconfidence bias, prospect theory, or some other principle of behavioral economics?

6. Managerial Problem

6.1 Global Gas International offers to subcontract the Halidurton Heavy Construction Corporation to build an oil pipeline from Canada to New Orleans for $500 million. The probability that the oil pipeline will leak, causing environmental damage, is θ. If so, the legal liabilities will be $600 million.

    a. If Halidurton is risk neutral and liable for the damages from a leak, what is the θ such that it is indifferent between accepting or rejecting the contract?

    b. If Halidurton is risk averse and fair insurance is offered, how much insurance would it buy?

    c. If Global Gas International will partially indemnify Halidurton so that the largest damages that Halidurton would have to pay is $200 million, what is the θ that leaves it indifferent about accepting the contract?

    d. If partially indemnified, how much fair insurance will Halidurton buy?

7. MyLab Economics Spreadsheet Exercises[24]

7.1 Aman, Bo, and Celia are considering an investment opportunity such that each person's final wealth (the return net of the investment) will be $W_1 = \$25$ thousand with probability 0.6 or $W_2 = \$100$ thousand with probability 0.4.

    a. Calculate the expected value of wealth $E(W)$.

    b. Aman's utility function is $U(W) = W$, while Bo's is $U(W) = W^{0.5}$ and Celia's is $U(W) = W^2$. For each person, calculate the expected utility of wealth, $EU(W)$, the certainty equivalent wealth, CE, and the risk premium, RP. (*Hint*: If an individual's utility function is, say, $U = W^x$, then the wealth corresponding to that utility level is $W = U^{1/x}$, so the certainty equivalent wealth is $CE = EU^{1/x}$.)

    c. Determine each person's attitude toward risk from his or her risk premium.

7.2 An investor is considering five possible investment strategies. The investor cares only about the expected payoff and possibly the variance of each strategy. The following table shows the payoffs under bad luck and good luck and the associated probabilities.

Strategy	Bad Luck Payoff	Probability of Bad Luck	Good Luck Payoff	Probability of Good Luck
A	4	0.6	9	0.4
B	5	0.3	5	0.7
C	2	0.5	12	0.5
D	4	0.8	11	0.2
E	3	0.7	10	0.3

    a. Using a spreadsheet, determine the expected value and variance for each strategy.

    b. Which strategy would be chosen by a risk-neutral investor? A risk-preferring investor?

    c. If we know only that the investor is risk averse, can we rule out any strategies?

7.3 Samantha's utility function over this year's net income, Y, is $U(Y) = Y^{0.5}$. She owns a car for business that she will have to replace if it is stolen. If her car is not stolen, her net income is $122,500. If the car is stolen, her net income is reduced by the car's replacement cost of $20,100. The probability that the car will be stolen this year is 20%.

    a. Use Excel to calculate Samantha's expected utility and to calculate the price of fair insurance that would cover the full replacement cost of the car.

    b. An insurance company is considering four possible prices for full insurance for Samantha's car: $4,020, $4,090, $4,851, and $4,164. Assume Samantha buys full insurance and use Excel to determine Samantha's income and utility for each of these prices if the car is stolen and if it is not stolen. Then calculate Samantha's expected income and expected utility for each of these prices. Would she buy full insurance at these prices? What is the maximum price Samantha would pay for full insurance?

    c. Suppose the insurance company offers an insurance policy with a $1,000 deductible: If the car is stolen, Samantha will absorb the first $1,000 of the loss and the company will pay the remaining $19,100. Use Excel to calculate Samantha's expected utility if the price for this policy is $3,820. What if the price is $3,970? Would Samantha buy the policy at either of these prices?

15 Asymmetric Information

The contracts of at least 33 major league baseball players had incentive clauses providing a bonus if that player was named the Most Valuable Player in a Division Series. Unfortunately, no such award is given for a Division Series.[1]

Managerial Problem

Clawing Back Bonuses

Many managers receive an annual bonus based on their firms' performance in the current year. Such managers may take actions that increase this year's profit, even if these actions will reduce future profits.

For example, Wells Fargo managers had employees engage in outrageous behavior, such as opening as many as 1.5 million bank accounts and 565,000 credit card accounts without the authorization of customers. Managers who encouraged and permitted this risky and unethical behavior were rewarded based on the increased (short-run) profits. The manager in charge of the relevant division received stock grants of about $19 million. The chief executive received at least $41 million in equity awards.

When this behavior became widely known, the bank paid dearly. Its reputation was damaged, and some customers took their money elsewhere. For fraudulently opening accounts, Wells Fargo was fined $185 million. For a variety of bad actions dating back to before the Great Recession, Wells Fargo has paid fines of $12.6 billion between 2000 and 2018.

One response to bad managerial behavior was the 2010 Dodd-Frank Consumer Protection Act. That act instructed the Security and Exchange Commission (SEC) to develop rules requiring firms to institute *clawback* provisions that would allow firms to claw back, or reclaim, some earlier bonus payments to managers if their past actions resulted in later losses. Many firms instituted such provisions voluntarily. While only 18% of Fortune 100 companies reported having a clawback policy in 1986, almost 90% had such a provision by 2013. In 2015, the SEC proposed a rule that would require all U.S. publicly traded corporations to have clawback provisions, but it still has not finalized these rules as of 2018.

Three years after its accounts scandal, Wells Fargo's directors acted to claw back $60 million in stock grants from two top executives. However, such clawbacks remain relatively rare.

We're now tying annual executive bonuses to performance. You owe us $100,000.

---

[1]Tom FitzGerald, "Top of the Sixth," *San Francisco Chronicle*, January 31, 1997, C6.

500

An alternative policy to a clawback is for a firm to withhold bonuses and other compensation for an extended period (often several years) so that managers are rewarded only for the long-run success arising from their decisions. Does evaluating a manager's performance over a longer period, using delayed compensation or clawback provisions, lead to better management?

In previous chapters, we focused on situations in which all firms and consumers have *symmetric information*: Everyone is equally knowledgeable or equally ignorant about prices, product quality, and other factors relevant to a transaction. In perfectly competitive markets, everyone knows all the relevant facts about a potential transaction. In the insurance examples discussed in Chapter 14, the companies that sell insurance and the people who buy it are equally uncertain about future events. In contrast, in this chapter, we consider situations in which people have **asymmetric information**: One party to a transaction has relevant information that another party does not have.

We concentrate on two types of asymmetric information: *hidden characteristics* and *hidden actions*. A **hidden characteristic** is an attribute of a person or thing that is known to one party but unknown to others. For example, the owner of a property may possess extensive information about the mineral composition of the land that is unknown to a mining company that is considering buying the land.

Another type of informational asymmetry, a **hidden action**, occurs when one party to a transaction cannot observe important *actions* taken by another party. For example, senior managers may take actions that shareholders do not observe, such as commandeering the company jet for personal use or making hidden financial decisions that create excessive risk for shareholders.

A more informed party may exploit the less informed party, engaging in *opportunistic behavior*: taking economic advantage of someone when circumstances permit. Two problems of opportunistic behavior arise from asymmetric information. One—*adverse selection*—is due to hidden characteristics, while the other—*moral hazard*—is associated with hidden actions.

The problem of **adverse selection** arises when one party to a transaction possesses information about a hidden characteristic that is unknown to other parties and takes economic advantage of this information. For example, if a roadside vendor sells a box of oranges to a passing motorist and only the vendor knows that the oranges are of low quality, the vendor may allege that the oranges are of high quality and charge a premium price for them. That is, the seller seeks to benefit from an informational asymmetry due to a hidden characteristic, the quality of the oranges. If potential buyers worry about such opportunistic behavior, they may be willing to pay only low prices or may forego purchasing the oranges entirely.

The primary problem arising from hidden action is **moral hazard**, which occurs when an informed party takes an action that the other party cannot observe and that harms the less informed party. If you pay a mechanic by the hour to fix your car and you do not watch the repairs, then the actual time spent by the mechanic on your car is a hidden action.[2] A moral hazard occurs if the mechanic bills you for excessive hours.

---

[2]A lawyer dies in an accident and goes to heaven. A host of angels greet him with a banner that reads, "Welcome Oldest Man!" The lawyer is puzzled: "Why do you think I'm the oldest man who ever lived? I was only 47 when I died." One of the angels replied, "You can't fool us; you were at least 152 when you died. We saw how many hours you billed!"

This chapter concentrates on identifying the various problems that arise due to asymmetric information. In particular, adverse selection often leads to markets in which some desirable transactions do not take place or even the market as a whole cannot exist. Moral hazard often results from contracts that give one party an incentive to take actions that reduce joint profits or cause the relatively risk-averse party to bear excessive risk. We discuss how to reduce or eliminate these problems by government actions, properly designed contracts, outside firms that provide information, and other means.

Learning Objectives

1. Explain how adverse selection prevents desirable transactions.
2. Describe the methods used to reduce adverse selection.
3. Show how moral hazard distorts economic transactions.
4. Construct contracts that reduce moral hazard.
5. Demonstrate how monitoring can solve moral hazard problems.

15.1 Adverse Selection

One of the most important problems associated with adverse selection is that if consumers lack relevant information, they may not engage in transactions to avoid being exploited by better-informed sellers. As a result, not all desirable transactions occur, and potential consumer and producer surplus is lost. Indeed, in the extreme case, adverse selection may prevent a market from operating at all. We illustrate this idea using two important examples of adverse selection problems: insurance and products of varying quality.

Adverse Selection in Insurance Markets

Hidden characteristics and adverse selection are very important in the insurance industry. If a health insurance company provided fair insurance by charging everyone a rate for insurance equal to the average cost of health care for the entire population, then the company would lose money due to adverse selection. Unhealthy people—people who expect to incur health care costs that are higher than average—would view this insurance as a good deal and many would buy it. In contrast, unless they were very risk averse, healthy people would not buy it because the premiums would exceed their expected health care costs. Given that a disproportionately large share of unhealthy people would buy the insurance, the market for health insurance would exhibit adverse selection, and the insurance company's average cost of medical care for covered people would exceed the population's average.

Adverse selection results in an inefficient market outcome, which reduces total surplus. The loss of potential total surplus occurs because some potentially beneficial sales of insurance to relatively healthy individuals do not occur. These consumers would be willing to buy insurance at a lower rate that was closer to the fair rate for them given their superior health. The insurance company would be willing to offer such low rates only if it could be sure that these individuals were relatively healthy.

Products of Unknown Quality

Anagram for General Motors: Or Great Lemons

Adverse selection often arises because sellers of a product have better information about the product's quality—a hidden characteristic—than do buyers. Cars that

appear to be identical on the outside often differ substantially in the number of repairs they will need. Some cars, often called *lemons,* have a variety of problems that become apparent to the owner only after buying the car and driving it for a while. The seller of a used car usually knows whether a car is a lemon.

If buyers have the same information as sellers, no adverse selection problem arises. However, if sellers have more information than buyers, adverse selection may drive high-quality products out of the market (Akerlof, 1970). Why? Potential buyers worry that a used car might be a lemon. As a result, they will not pay as high a price as they would if they knew the car was of good quality. They will only buy if the price is low enough to reflect the possibility of getting a lemon. Given that sellers of excellent used cars do not want to sell their cars for that low a price, they do not enter the market. Adverse selection has driven the high-quality cars out of the market, leaving only the lemons.

In the following example, we assume that sellers cannot alter the quality of their used cars and that the number of potential used car buyers is large. All are willing to pay $4,000 for a lemon and $8,000 for a good used car: The demand curve for lemons, D^L, is horizontal at $4,000 in panel a of Figure 15.1, and the demand curve for good cars, D^G, is horizontal at $8,000 in panel b.

Although the number of potential buyers is virtually unlimited, only 1,000 owners of lemons and 1,000 owners of good cars are willing to sell. The *reservation price* of lemon owners—the lowest price at which they will sell their cars—is $3,000. Consequently, the supply curve for lemons, S^L in panel a, is horizontal at $3,000 up to 1,000 cars, where it becomes vertical (no more cars are for sale at any price). The reservation price of owners of high-quality used cars is v, which is less than $8,000. Panel b shows two possible values of v. If $v = \$5,000$, the supply curve for good cars, S^1, is horizontal at $5,000 up to 1,000 cars and then becomes vertical. If $v = \$7,000$, the supply curve is S^2.

Symmetric Information Market Equilibrium. If both sellers and buyers know the quality of all the used cars before any sales take place (they have full, symmetric information), all 2,000 cars are sold, and the good cars sell for more than the lemons. In panel a of Figure 15.1, the intersection of the lemons demand curve D^L and the lemons supply curve S^L determines the equilibrium at e in the lemons market, where 1,000 lemons sell for $4,000 each. Regardless of whether the supply curve for good cars is S^1 or S^2 in panel b, the equilibrium in the good-car market is E, where 1,000 good cars sell for $8,000 each.

This market is efficient because the goods go to the people who value them the most. All current owners, who value the cars less than the potential buyers, sell their cars. It does not matter whether all buyers and sellers have full information or all lack information—it's the equality (or symmetry) of information that matters. However, *the amount of information they have affects the price at which the cars sell.* With full information, good cars sell for $8,000 and lemons for $4,000.

If information is symmetric and buyers and sellers are equally ignorant (they don't know if a car is good or a lemon), both types of cars sell for the same price.

FIGURE 15.1 **Markets for Lemons and Good Cars**

If everyone has full information, the equilibrium in the lemons market is e (1,000 cars sold for $4,000 each), and the equilibrium in the good-car market is E (1,000 cars sold for $8,000 each). If buyers can't tell quality before buying but assume that equal numbers of the two types of cars are for sale, their demand in both markets is D*, which is horizontal at $6,000. If the good-car owners' reservation price is $5,000, the supply curve for good cars is S¹, and 1,000 good cars (point F) and 1,000 lemons (point f) sell for $6,000 each. If their reservation price is $7,000, the supply curve is S². No good cars are sold; 1,000 lemons sell for $4,000 each (point e).

(a) Market for Lemons

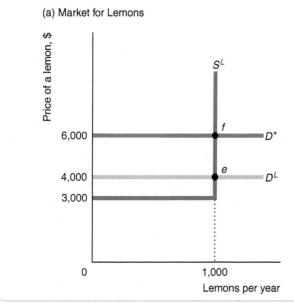

(b) Market for Good Cars

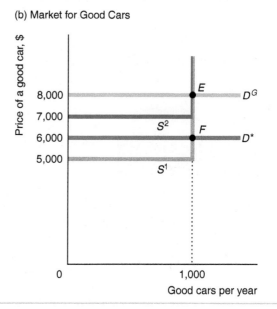

A buyer has an equal chance of buying a lemon or a good car. The expected value of a used car is

$$\$6{,}000 = \left(\tfrac{1}{2} \times \$4{,}000\right) + \left(\tfrac{1}{2} \times \$8{,}000\right).$$

A risk-neutral buyer would pay $6,000 for a car of unknown quality.[3] Because sellers cannot distinguish between the cars either, sellers accept this amount and sell all the cars.[4] Thus, this market is efficient because the cars go to people who value them more than their original owners.

If the only cars sold were lemons, they would sell for $4,000. The presence of good-quality cars raises the price received by sellers of lemons to $6,000. Similarly, if only good cars were sold, they would sell for $8,000. The presence of lemons lowers the price that sellers of good cars receive to $6,000. Thus, effectively, sellers of good-quality cars are subsidizing sellers of lemons.

Asymmetric Information Market Equilibrium. If sellers know the quality but buyers do not, this market may be inefficient: The better-quality cars may not be sold even though buyers value good cars more than sellers do. The equilibrium in this market depends on whether the value that the owners of good cars place on their cars, v, is greater or less than the expected value of buyers, $6,000. The two possible

---

[3]A risk-neutral person cares about only the expected value and does not worry about uncertainty (Chapter 14).

[4]Risk-neutral sellers place an expected value of $\left(\tfrac{1}{2} \times \$3{,}000\right) + \tfrac{1}{2}v = \$1{,}500 + \tfrac{1}{2}v$ on a car of unknown quality. If $v = \$7{,}000$, this expected value is $\$1{,}500 + \$3{,}500 = \$5{,}000$. If $v = \$5{,}000$, the expected value is only $4,000. In either case, sellers would be happy to sell their cars for $6,000.

equilibria are: (1) All cars sell at the average price, or (2) only lemons sell at a price equal to the value that buyers place on lemons.

Initially, we assume that the sellers of good cars value their cars at $v = \$5,000$, which is less than the buyers' expected value of the cars ($6,000), so that transactions occur. The equilibrium in the good-car market is determined by the intersection of S^1 and D^* at F in panel b of Figure 15.1, where 1,000 good cars sell at $6,000. Similarly, owners of lemons, who value their cars at only $3,000, are happy to sell them for $6,000 each. The new equilibrium in the lemons market is f.

Thus, all cars sell at the same price. In this case, *asymmetric information does not cause an efficiency problem, but it does have equity implications.* Sellers of lemons benefit and sellers of good cars suffer from consumers' inability to distinguish quality. Consumers who buy the good cars get a bargain, and buyers of lemons are left with a sour taste in their mouths.

Now suppose that the sellers of good cars place a value of $v = \$7,000$ on their cars and thus are unwilling to sell them for $6,000. As a result, the *lemons drive good cars out of the market.* Buyers realize that they can buy only lemons at any price less than $7,000. Consequently, in equilibrium, the 1,000 lemons sell for the expected (and actual) price of $4,000, and no good cars change hands. This equilibrium is inefficient because high-quality cars remain in the hands of people who value them less than potential buyers do.

In summary, if buyers have less information about product quality than sellers do, the result might be a lemons problem in which high-quality cars do not sell even though potential buyers value the cars more than their current owners do[5]. If so, asymmetric information causes an otherwise perfectly competitive market to lose its desirable efficiency properties. The lemons problem does not occur if the information is symmetric. If buyers and sellers of used cars know the quality of the cars, each car sells for its true value in a perfectly competitive market. If, as with new cars, neither buyers nor sellers can identify lemons, both good cars and lemons sell at a price equal to the expected value rather than at their (unknown) true values.

Q&A 15.1

Suppose that everyone in our used car example is risk neutral, and potential car buyers value lemons at $4,000 and good used cars at $8,000. The reservation price of lemon owners is $3,000 and the reservation price of owners of high-quality used cars is $7,000. The share of current owners who have lemons is $\frac{1}{5}$ (in contrast to our previous example, where the share was $\frac{1}{2}$). Describe the equilibrium.

Answer

1. *Determine how much buyers are willing to pay if all cars are sold.* Because buyers are risk neutral, if they believe that the probability of getting a lemon is $\frac{1}{5}$, the most they are willing to pay for a car of unknown quality is

$$p = \left[\$8,000 \times \left(1 - \tfrac{1}{5}\right)\right] + \left(4,000 \times \tfrac{1}{5}\right) = \$7,200. \tag{15.1}$$

2. *Determine whether sellers will sell their cars and describe the equilibrium.* The owners of lemons will sell if the price equals or exceeds their reservation price of $3,000. The owners of high-quality used cars will sell if the market price equals or exceeds $7,000. Using Equation 15.1, we know that the market (equilibrium) price is $7,200 if all cars are sold. Thus, all sellers will choose to sell their cars and the equilibrium price will be $7,200.

---

[5]"MyLab Economics has a *Lemons Market Experiment* that illustrates adverse selection. To participate, go to the MyLab Economics Multimedia Library, Single Player Experiment, and set the Chapter field to "All Chapters.""

Varying Quality Under Asymmetric Information. Most firms can adjust their product's quality. If consumers cannot identify high-quality goods before purchase, they pay the same for all goods regardless of quality. Because the price that firms receive for top-quality goods is the same as the price they receive for low-quality items, they do not produce top-quality goods. Such an outcome is inefficient if consumers are willing to pay sufficiently more for top-quality goods.

Q&A 15.2	

It costs $10 to produce a low-quality wallet and $20 to produce a high-quality wallet. Consumers cannot distinguish between the products before purchase, they do not make repeat purchases, and they value the wallets at the cost of production. The five firms in the market produce 100 wallets each. Each firm produces only high-quality or only low-quality wallets. Consumers pay the expected value of a wallet. If all five firms initially produce low-quality wallets, could any one firm increase its profit by producing high-quality wallets instead?

Answer

Show that it does not pay for one firm to make high-quality wallets if the other firms make low-quality wallets due to asymmetric information. If all five firms make a low-quality wallet, consumers pay $10 per wallet. If one firm makes a high-quality wallet and all the others make low-quality wallets (so the probability that a consumer buys a high-quality wallet is $\frac{1}{5}$), the expected value per wallet to consumers is

$$\left(\$10 \times \tfrac{4}{5} \right) + \left(\$20 \times \tfrac{1}{5} \right) = \$12.$$

Thus, if one firm raises the quality of its product, all firms benefit because the wallets sell for $12 instead of $10. The high-quality firm receives only a fraction of the total benefit from raising quality. It gets $2 extra per high-quality wallet sold, which is less than the extra $10 it costs to make the better wallet. The other $8 is shared by the other firms. The high-quality firm would incur all the expenses of raising quality, $10 extra per wallet, and reap only a fraction, $2, of the benefits. Therefore, it opts not to produce the high-quality wallets. *Due to asymmetric information, the firms do not produce high-quality goods even though consumers are willing to pay for the extra quality.*

Mini-Case	
Reducing Consumers' Information	

By selling the same product under more than one brand name, firms can charge poorly-informed consumers higher prices. For decades, Amana, Caloric, GE, Gibson, Jenn-Air, Toshiba, and Whirlpool manufactured products that Sears, Roebuck & Company sold under its house (private label) brand names—Kenmore, DieHard, and Craftsman.

Frequently, the Kenmore product was identical to or even superior to the brand-name product and cost less. Knowledgeable consumers realizing that the two brands were identical except for the label bought the Sears brand at the lower price. But customers who falsely believed that the name brand is better than the Kenmore product pay more for the name brand. Amazon is currently following this approach with its Amazon Basic and many other private-label brands.

Over time, as consumers have become familiar with private-label brands and recognized their quality, private-label products have rapidly gained market share. According to the Nielsen Company's 2018 report, the private-label value share was 16.7% globally, 31.4% in the European Union, and 17.7% in North America. As consumers gain more knowledge about the quality of private-label brands, the advantage from maintaining multiple brands diminishes, which partially explains why Sears sold its Craftsman brand in 2017 and put the Kenmore brand up for sale in 2018.

15.2 Reducing Adverse Selection

Because adverse selection results from one party exploiting asymmetric information about a hidden characteristic, the two main methods for solving adverse selection problems are to *restrict the ability of the informed party to take advantage of hidden information* and to *equalize information* among the parties. Responses to adverse selection problems increase welfare in some markets, but may do more harm than good in others.

Restricting Opportunistic Behavior

Which type of restriction works best to curb opportunistic behavior depends on the nature of the adverse selection problem. The government can prevent adverse selection insurance problems by mandating universal insurance coverage. The government uses a variety of other laws to prevent opportunism associated with varying product quality.

Universal Coverage. Health insurance markets have adverse selection because low-risk consumers do not buy insurance at prices that reflect the average risk. The government can eliminate such adverse selection by providing insurance to everyone or by mandating that everyone buy insurance. Canada, the United Kingdom, and many other countries provide basic health insurance to all residents, financed by a combination of mandatory premiums and taxes. In the United States, the 2010 Patient Protection and Affordable Care Act required virtually all Americans to have health care coverage, although that aspect of the act was subsequently weakened by 2017 legislation.

Similarly, firms often provide mandatory health insurance to all employees as a benefit, rather than paying a higher wage and letting employees decide whether to buy such insurance on their own. By doing so, firms reduce adverse selection problems for their insurance carriers: Both healthy and unhealthy people are covered. As a result, firms can buy medical insurance for their workers at a lower cost per person than workers could obtain on their own.

Laws to Prevent Opportunism. Product quality and product safety are often hidden characteristics that are known to manufacturers but are not observed by consumers. Manufacturers have an incentive to behave opportunistically by selling low-quality or unsafe products to consumers at excessive prices. However, product liability laws protect consumers from being stuck with nonfunctional or dangerous products.

Moreover, many U.S. state supreme courts have concluded that products are sold with an implicit understanding that they will safely perform their intended function. If they do not, consumers can sue the seller even in the absence of product liability laws. If consumers can rely on explicit or implicit product liability laws to force a manufacturer to make good on defective products, they need not worry about adverse selection. Similarly, truth-in-advertising laws and food labeling requirements are both efforts to discourage opportunistic behavior by preventing misleading claims about product characteristics.

Equalizing Information

Providing information to all parties eliminates adverse selection problems. Either informed or uninformed parties can act to eliminate or reduce informational asymmetries. Three methods for reducing informational asymmetries are as follows:

1. An uninformed party (such as an insurance company) can use **screening** to infer the information possessed by informed parties.

2. An informed party (such as a person seeking to buy health insurance) can use **signaling** to send information to a less informed party.

3. A third party (such as a firm or a government agency) not directly involved in the transaction may collect information and sell it or give it to the uninformed party.

Screening. Insurance companies reduce adverse selection problems by screening potential customers based on their health records or requiring them to undergo medical exams. A life insurance company uses such information to better estimate the probability that it will have to pay off on a policy. The firm can then decide not to insure high-risk individuals or it can charge high-risk people higher premiums.

It is costly to collect information on the health of a person or to investigate whether that individual has dangerous habits such as smoking, drinking, or skydiving. As a result, insurance companies collect information only up to the point at which the marginal benefit from the extra information they gather equals the marginal cost of obtaining it. Over time, insurance companies have increasingly concluded that it pays to collect information about whether individuals exercise, have a family history of dying young, or engage in potentially life-threatening activities. If the individuals, but not the insurance companies, know about these characteristics, adverse selection occurs.

Consumers can use screening techniques, too. For example, they can screen used cars by test-driving them or by having an objective, trustworthy mechanic examine the car. They can also pay a company such as CARFAX to check the history of the repairs on a vehicle they are considering purchasing.

As long as the consumers' costs of securing information are less than the private benefits, they obtain the information, transactions occur, and markets function smoothly. However, if the costs exceed the benefits, consumers do not gather the information, which prevents some mutually beneficial transactions from occurring, so the market is inefficient.

In some markets, consumers rely on a firm's *reputation*, which they learn from other consumers or from observation. Consumers can avoid the adverse selection problem by buying only from firms that have reputations for providing high-quality goods. For example, consumers know that a used car dealer that expects repeat customers has a strong incentive not to sell defective products.

Generally, in markets in which the same consumers and firms trade regularly, a reputation is easy to establish. In markets in which consumers buy a good only once, such as in tourist areas, firms cannot establish reputations as

Congratulations! You qualify for our auto insurance.

easily and we might expect adverse selection to be a more significant problem. Remember this warning the next time you are tempted to buy an "authentic, genuine designer" watch or purse from a street vendor.

Signaling. An informed party may signal the uninformed party to eliminate adverse selection. However, signals solve the adverse selection problem only when the recipients view them as credible. Smart consumers may place little confidence in a firm's unsubstantiated claims. Would you believe that a used car runs well just because an ad tells you so?

If only high-quality firms find it worthwhile to send a signal, then a signal is credible. Producers of high-quality goods often try to signal to consumers that their products are of better quality than those of their rivals. If consumers believe their signals, these firms can charge higher prices for their goods. But if the signals are to be effective, they must be credible. For example, a firm may distribute a favorable report on its product by an independent testing agency to try to convince buyers that its product is of high quality. Because low-quality firms cannot obtain such a report from a reliable independent testing agency, consumers believe this signal.

An applicant for life insurance could have a physical examination and then present an insurance company with a written statement from the doctor as a signal of good health. If the only people who want to send a signal are those who believe they are healthier than others, insurance companies may rely upon this signal. However, an insurance company may not trust such a signal if it is easy for people to find unscrupulous doctors who will report falsely that their patients are in good health. Screening by the insurance company using its own doctors may work better because the information is more credible.

Education can also serve as a signal. No doubt you've been told that one good reason to go to college is to get a good job. Going to college may get you a better job because you obtain valuable training. However, another possibility is that a college degree may land you a good job because it serves as a signal to employers about your ability. If high-ability people are more likely to go to college than low-ability people, schooling signals ability to employers.

Managerial Implication

Using Brand Names and Warranties as Signals

Honesty is the best policy—when there is money in it. —Mark Twain

Managers can often sell more if they successfully send potential customers a signal that the quality of their product is high. Some agricultural firms brand their produce (such as Dole pineapples and Chiquita bananas), while rivals sell their produce without labels. Many shoppers assume that branding makes sense for a firm only if its product quality is superior to that of unbranded products.

A warranty may serve as both a signal and a guarantee. It is less expensive for the manufacturer of a reliable product to offer a warranty than it is for a firm that produces low-quality products. Consequently, if one firm offers a warranty and another does not, then a consumer may infer that the firm with the warranty produces a superior product. Of course, sleazy firms may try to imitate high-quality firms by offering a warranty that they do not intend to honor.

Top manufacturers of consumer durables such as cars and refrigerators usually offer warranties. In recent years, to signal quality, some leading auto manufacturers have started offering warranties on their pre-owned cars that are comparable to those of new cars.

Are you healthy? Your insurance company wants to know. And it wants to keep you healthy. Life insurance companies in Australia, Europe, Singapore, and South Africa use the internet to allow customers to signal that they're healthy.

When Andrew Thomas swipes his membership card upon arriving at his gym, his South African life insurance company, Vitality, receives instant information. The company checks whether he's still there 30 minutes later by tracking his location using his smartphone. In return for sharing medical and exercise information with his insurance company, Mr. Thomas earns points, which reduce his insurance premium by 9%.

In 2015, John Hancock became the first U.S. life insurance company to introduce a similar program. The company provides customers with Fitbit monitors that automatically upload their activity levels. The most active customers will earn a discount of up to 15% on their life insurance premium, Amazon gift cards, and half-price stays at Hyatt hotels. In 2017, Humana launched a similar program for health insurance after doing a three-year study suggesting that health care costs for study participants fell by about 10%.

Thus, insurance companies are helping their customers signal that they're healthy, reducing the adverse selection problem. In addition, the companies are using this information to provide incentives for the insured to lead healthier lives so that their families have to wait longer to collect on their life insurance.

Third-Party Information.   In some markets, consumer groups, nonprofit organizations, and government agencies provide buyers with information about the quality of different goods and services. If this information is credible, it can reduce adverse selection by enabling consumers to avoid buying low-quality goods or to lower the price of poorer-quality products.

For an outside organization to provide believable information, it must convince consumers that it is trustworthy. Consumers Union, which publishes the product evaluation guide *Consumer Reports*, tries to establish its trustworthiness by refusing to accept advertising or other payments from firms.

Auditing is another important example of third-party assessment, in which an independent accounting firm evaluates the financial statements of a firm or other organization. Sometimes a firm obtains an audit voluntarily to enhance its reputation (a signal). Sometimes audits are required as a condition of being listed on a particular exchange or of participating in a particular transaction (screening), and sometimes laws require that audits be performed.

Many local governments require that home sellers disclose all relevant facts about the home to potential buyers, such as the age of the home and any known defects in the electrical work or plumbing. By doing so, these governments protect buyers against adverse selection due to undisclosed defects.

Governments, consumer groups, industry groups, and others also provide information by establishing *standards*, which are metrics or scales for evaluating the quality of a particular product. For example, the R-value of insulation tells how effectively insulation works. Consumers learn about a brand's quality through **certification**: a report that a particular product meets or exceeds a given standard.

Many industry groups set their own standards and get an outside group or firm, such as Underwriters Laboratories (UL) or Factory Mutual Engineering Corporation (FMEC), to certify that their products meet specified standard levels. For example, by setting standards for the size of the thread on a screw, we ensure that screws work in products regardless of brand.

When standard and certification programs inexpensively and completely inform consumers about the relative quality of all goods in a market and do not restrict the goods available, the programs are socially desirable. However, some of these programs have harmful effects for two reasons.

First, standard and certification programs that provide imprecise information may mislead consumers. Some standards use only a high- versus low-quality rating even though quality varies continuously. Such standards encourage the manufacture of products that either have the minimum quality level necessary to obtain the top rating or, if the producer forgoes the high rating, have the lowest cost of production and therefore the lowest possible quality.

Second, if standard and certification programs restrict salable goods and services to those that are certified, such programs may also have anticompetitive effects. Many governments license only professionals and craftspeople who meet some minimum standards. A licensing law forbids people without a license to practice their profession or craft. In most states, dozens, if not hundreds, of categories of professionals, craftspeople, and others are licensed, including public school teachers, electricians, plumbers, dentists, psychologists, contractors, and beauticians. (See the Mini-Case "Occupational Licensing" in Chapter 2.)

Licenses or certifications that restrict entry raise the average quality in the industry by eliminating low-quality goods and services. They drive up prices to consumers for two reasons. First, the number of people providing services is reduced because the restrictions eliminate some potential suppliers. Second, consumers are unable to obtain lower-quality and less expensive goods or services. As a result, welfare may go up or down, depending on whether the increased-quality effect or the higher-price effect dominates. Whether such restrictions can be set properly and cost effectively by government agencies is widely debated.

Mini-Case

Adverse Selection and Remanufactured Goods

Because consumers can't see a good before buying it over the internet, it's easy for a shady seller to misrepresent its quality. In the worst-case lemons-market scenario, low-quality goods drive out high-quality goods.

Adverse selection concerns are particularly strong for electronic goods sold on eBay, as consumers cannot "squeeze the orange" (try the product) before purchase. That this market exists on eBay indicates sellers have found ways to signal quality. Consumers know that selling on eBay creates an enforceable contract, so sellers' signals reduce adverse selection on eBay. A sleazy seller will have a bad reputation score (the percentage of positive ratings by past customers). Some sellers offer money back guarantees or warranties. Some pay extra to eBay to post photos.

One important signal is whether the good is new, remanufactured, or used. For years, manufacturers of cameras, computers, mobile phones, MP3 players, and other consumer durables have refurbished or upgraded such equipment before trying to sell it again. Even though these remanufactured products may be comparable to new ones, consumers do not perceive them that way, so they are willing to pay a premium for new items.

Neto, Bloemhof, and Corbett (2015) studied sales on eBay of three types of iPods: the Classic, the Touch, and the Nano. They found, for example, that the average price of a used iPod Nano was 65% of a new one, while a remanufactured Nano was 82% of a new one. Thus, the signal of the good's type affects the price.

What about other signals, such as positive descriptions? Consumers view used goods as varying more in quality than remanufactured or new products: The prices of used goods have greater variance than those of new goods. As a result, quality claims may be more likely to affect the price of used goods than those of new and remanufactured goods. Neto et al. found that positive descriptions affected the price of most types of used iPods, but not new and remanufactured iPods.

Subramanian and Subramanyam (2012) studied the sales of electronic goods on eBay. They found that a higher seller feedback score reduced the price differential between new and remanufactured goods. They also discovered that consumers pay higher prices for products remanufactured by the original manufacturer or their authorized factories than for those remanufactured by third parties.

Thus, a variety of signals helps reduce the adverse selection problem for used and remanufactured goods.

15.3 Moral Hazard

We now turn from adverse selection problems caused by hidden characteristics to moral hazard problems that result from hidden actions. Examples include individuals driving rental cars off-road, workers loafing when the boss is not watching, and lawyers acting in their own interests instead of those of their clients.

Moral Hazard in Insurance Markets

The insurance industry introduced the term *moral hazard* into common usage. Many types of insurance are highly vulnerable to hidden actions by insured parties that result in moral hazard problems.

For example, Ralph, the owner of a clothing store, purchased a large quantity of designer jeans and stored the jeans in a warehouse. Following standard practice, he insured the merchandise for its original purchase price against such hazards as fire or theft. Unfortunately for Ralph, these jeans have become unfashionable and are not selling. Because he faces a significant financial loss, he burns down the warehouse and makes an insurance claim.[6] The hidden action is that of setting the warehouse on fire. Such an action is called a *moral* hazard because most people view it as unethical or *immoral* (as well as illegal).

A less extreme example of moral hazard arises when medical insurance covers the expense of doctor visits. If one of the benefits of the medical insurance is that insured people do not have to pay for visits to their doctors, some insured people make "excessive" visits to the doctor—more than if they had to pay for the visits themselves. Some people visit a doctor in part because they are hypochondriacs or are lonely and want some company.

Such behavior is not illegal and may not seem unethical. However, because it is costly, insurance companies take actions to reduce the

---

[6]Insurance frauds are common. A wide range of examples are described by the Coalition Against Insurance Fraud at **www.insurancefraud.org/**.

number of visits. For example, they may cap the number of visits to, say, three per year. Or the insurance company may require its customers to make a copayment, which is part of the cost of each visit to a doctor, often about $20 to $30 per visit.[7]

Moral Hazard in Principal-Agent Relationships

In a **principal-agent relationship,** a principal contracts with an agent to take an action on behalf of the principal. Moral hazard problems are frequent in principal-agent relationships. Moral hazard in a principal-agent relationship is referred to as a **principal-agent problem** or **agency problem**.

Principal-agent relationships arise in many situations. The relationship between an employer (principal) and employee (agent) is an important example. Doctors, lawyers, real estate agents, and financial planners are all agents who act on behalf of principals (their clients). A taxi driver is an agent whom a passenger (the principal) relies on to take the best route to a desired location.

If information is symmetric so that no actions are hidden, principal-agent relationships do not give rise to moral hazard. When a building contractor (the principal) subcontracts with a house painter (the agent) and both work on the same building site, the contractor can directly observe how hard and how well the painter is working. Due to this close monitoring, the painter cannot engage in any hidden action, such as taking an hour-long coffee break or running personal errands during work hours. Consequently, no inefficiency arises from this principal-agent relationship.

However, if the principal does not observe the agents' actions, moral hazard may result. If the contractor hires a painter to work at a remote site that cannot be observed, then the painter may *shirk* by taking long breaks or not providing all the agreed-upon services.

Moral hazard problems are extremely important. According to the Association of Certified Fraud Examiners (2018), companies lose about 5% of their annual revenues to various forms of internal fraud alone. They suffer additional losses due to shirking.

Mini-Case	You arrive in a strange city and get in a cab. Will the driver take you to your destination by the shortest route, or will you get ripped off?
Honest Cabbies?	To find out, Balafoutas, Kerschbamer, and Sutter (2017) ran an experiment in Athens. Four native-speaking Greeks took 400 taxi trips. For each trip, they said, "I would like to get to [name of a destination]. Do you know where it is? I am not from Athens." A few seconds after the ride began, the passenger said either, "Can I get a receipt at the end of the ride?" or "Can I get a receipt at the end of the ride? I need it to have my expenses reimbursed by my employer."

The experimenters expected that fraudulent behavior would be less likely in the former (control) case than in the latter ("moral hazard") case, where passengers would have weaker incentives to control or report a longer than necessary trip or overcharging. Overcharging (mostly bonus surcharges) occurred 36.5% of the time for the moral hazard rides compared to 19.5% for the control rides. Overall, the fare for the moral hazard trips averaged 17% more than for the control trips.

---

[7]The lower the copayment, the more likely a patient visits a doctor, which increases the chance of early detection and treatment of health problems. Because early detection reduces the long-run cost, the insurance company has to balance this advantage against the moral hazard problem of excessive visits.

The Owner-Manager Relationship

Except for the smallest of firms, one person cannot perform all the tasks necessary to run a firm. In most firms, the owners of the firm (principals) have to delegate tasks to managers (agents). A conflict may arise between an owner who wants to maximize profit and a manager who is interested in pursuing other goals, such as maximizing personal income. If an owner cannot observe the actions of a manager, this conflict may give rise to moral hazard that imposes costs on the firm—agency costs—resulting in lower profit for the firm.

In an extreme case, a manager who is solely interested in personal gain may steal from a firm, but we hope that relatively few managers are that dishonest. Nonetheless, many managers believe it is appropriate to treat themselves to a variety of *perquisites* (*perks*)—benefits beyond their salary—of dubious value to the firm, such as using a company jet for personal travel.

It is perfectly appropriate for a corporation to provide a manager with health or various other benefits. If the firm reduces the manager's salary by the cost of such benefits, then these benefits do not harm the firm's bottom line. A firm might want to provide a flashy perk such as a luxurious office to impress clients or a chauffeured limo that saves a manager's time and increases profit. However, shareholders and boards of directors are typically less well informed about the extent and value of such perks than managers. This informational asymmetry causes potential moral hazard, as some managers may unilaterally grant themselves perks that come out of the firm's profit with little or no tangible advantage to the firm.

Mini-Case

Company Jets

Some corporations allow the chief executive officer (CEO) to make personal use of the company's plane—for example, to play golf at a distant course. The *Wall Street Journal* reported that, based on a review of the flight records of dozens of corporate jets over a four-year period, more than half of their trips were to or from resort destinations, and usually to locations where executives owned homes. Friends, family, and even pets may benefit from corporate jets. Former RJR Nabisco CEO Ross Johnson flew his dog (under the name "G. Shepherd") on a company jet. Barry Diller, the billionaire media mogul, took more than $12 million of personal flights on a company-owned private jet from 2005 through 2014, including $1.7 million, or about $4,500 a day, in 2014.

If the corporation reduces the CEO's earnings so that the CEO is effectively paying for this privilege, then providing the aircraft should have no effect on the firm's bottom line or the value of its stock. However, if the managers do not pay for using the jet for personal purposes, this perk lowers the firm's profit and reduces its stock value. Moreover, if workers react adversely to managers' perks, morale may fall and shirking and unethical behavior may increase. If so, we would expect the firm's profit and stock value to fall even more.

According to Yermack (2006), when firms first disclose a CEO's jet plane perquisites, shareholders react very negatively, causing the firm's stock price to fall by 1.1% on average. Moreover, the long-run effect of such disclosures is to reduce average shareholder returns by more than 4% below market benchmarks annually—a large gap that greatly exceeds the cost of resources consumed. Nonetheless in 2015, of the 95 public Fortune 100 companies, 65 either provided or offered to provide a jet perk to their CEOs.

Although perks may be given to reward excellent work by managers, large perks often indicate weak governance by boards. Companies disclosing a plane perk are more likely to take extraordinary accounting write-offs and to report quarterly earnings per share significantly below analyst estimates. According to Lee et al. (2018), the use of corporate jets for "internal" flights, such as to corporate subsidiaries, increases the operating performance of corporations, unlike flights to resort destinations.

Reducing Moral Hazard Using Efficient Contracts. The cost of moral hazard can often be reduced through the use of well-designed contracts. We consider a principal-agent example in which the payoffs to the owner of a firm (the principal) and the manager (the agent) depend on the agent's actions and the *state of nature*, such as weather (which affects demand) or input prices (which affect costs). The principal and the agent care about how payoffs are allocated and how the risk is shared.

Ideally, the principal and agent agree to an **efficient contract**: an agreement in which neither party can be made better off without harming the other party. If the parties to the contract are risk neutral, efficiency requires that the combined profit of the principal and the agent be maximized. If one party is more risk averse than the other, efficiency requires that the less risk-averse party bear more of the risk (Chapter 14). In our example, the outcome is efficient if the agent works extra hard so that the total profit that the parties share is as large as possible and if the agent, who is the only risk-averse party, bears none of the risk.

Paul, the principal, owns many ice cream parlors across North America. He contracts with Amy, the agent, to manage his Miami shop. Her duties include supervising workers, purchasing supplies, and performing other necessary actions.

The shop's daily earnings depend on the local demand conditions and on how hard Amy works. Demand for ice cream varies with the weather, and is high half the time, and low otherwise.

Amy puts forth either normal or extra effort. She views herself as an honest person and would never steal from Paul. She is always at the shop during regular business hours and puts in at least a normal amount of effort, even if Paul cannot check on her. She politely, but impersonally, asks everyone who enters the shop, "May I help you?"

Nonetheless, Amy might not be working as hard as possible. She could put forth extra effort by enthusiastically greeting regular customers by name, serving customers rapidly, spending extra hours checking with nearby businesses to see if they would be interested in joint promotions, and improving the appearance of the shop. However, extra work is tiring and prevents Amy from spending time at the beach with friends, reading novels, watching her favorite TV shows on Netflix, and engaging in other activities that she enjoys. She values her personal cost of this extra effort at $40 per day.

For any given level of demand, the shop sells more ice cream if Amy puts forth extra effort. The shop also sells more for a given level of Amy's effort if demand is high. Table 15.1 shows the profit of the ice cream shop before Amy is paid—the combined payoff to Paul and Amy—for the four possible combinations of effort and demand. If demand is high and Amy puts in normal effort, or if demand is low and

TABLE 15.1 Ice Cream Shop Profits

		Demand	
		Low	High
Amy's Effort	Normal	100	300
	Extra	300	500

she provides extra effort, the firm's daily profit is 300. The profit is 500 if demand is high and Amy works extra hard but is only 100 if demand is low and she applies only normal effort.

Because Paul owns many ice cream parlors across North America, he can pool the returns from all these stores and is risk neutral. Amy, like most people, is risk averse. Thus, risk bearing is efficient if Paul bears all of the risk and Amy bears none of it (Chapter 14).

Symmetric Information. Moral hazard is not a problem if Paul lives in Miami and can directly supervise Amy. They could agree to a contract that specifies Amy receives 200 per day if she works extra hard, but loses her job if she doesn't. Because Amy's cost of working extra hard is 40, she nets 160 (= 200 − 40) if she works hard, which is better than being fired and getting nothing. Even though the shop's profit varies with demand, Amy bears no risk: She receives 200 regardless of demand conditions.

Paul is the *residual claimant*: He receives the *residual profit*, which is the amount left over from the store's profit after Amy's wage is paid. Because Amy works hard (as she does not want to get fired), Paul's residual profit varies only with demand. If demand is low, the shop earns 300, he pays Amy 200, and he retains 100. If demand is high, the shop earns 500, so Paul keeps 300, after paying Amy 200. Paul's expected profit is the probability of low demand, 50% (or $\frac{1}{2}$) times 100, plus the probability of high demand, 50% times 300, or

$$\left(\tfrac{1}{2} \times 100\right) + \left(\tfrac{1}{2} \times 300\right) = 200.$$

Under this contract, Paul bears all the risk from the shop's uncertain earnings. The variance of Paul's earnings is large relative to his expected profit: $\frac{1}{2}(100 - 200)^2 + \frac{1}{2}(300 - 200)^2 = 10{,}000$.[8]

The first row of Table 15.2 summarizes this result, which is labeled *perfect monitoring*. Is this contract efficient? The last two columns show that it is because Paul, the risk-neutral party, bears all the risk, and their combined earnings are as high as possible because Amy works extra hard.

---

[8]The variance (Chapter 14) is the probability of low demand, 50%, times the square of the difference between the payoff under low demand, 100, and the expected payoff, 200, plus the probability of high demand, 50%, times the square of the difference between the payoff under high demand, 300, and the expected payoff.

TABLE 15.2 **Ice Cream Shop Outcomes**

| Contract | Expected Payoffs | | | Amy's Variance | Efficiency | |
	Paul	Amy[a]	Paul + Amy		Risk Bearing[b]	Joint Payoff[c]
Symmetric Information						
Perfect monitoring	200	160	360	0	yes	yes
Asymmetric Information						
Fixed wage of 100	100	100	200	0	yes	no
Licensing fee of 200	200	160	360	10,000	no	yes
State-contingent fee of 100 or 300	200	160	360	0	yes	yes
50% profit share	200	160	360	2,500	no	yes
Wage and bonus of 200; Amy is risk neutral	200	160	360	10,000	yes	yes
Wage and bonus of 200; Amy is very risk averse	100	100	200	0	yes	no

[a]If Amy puts in extra work, her payoff is net of 40, which is the value she places on having to work harder.

[b]When Paul is risk neutral and Amy is risk averse (all rows except the second to last row), risk bearing is efficient only if Paul bears all the risk, so that Amy's variance is zero. In the second to last row Amy is risk neutral and risk bearing is therefore efficient even though Amy bears risk.

[c]Production is efficient if Amy puts in extra effort, so that the shop's expected earnings are 400 rather than 200 and the joint payoff is 360 after deducting Amy's cost of extra effort.

Asymmetric Information. Paul grows tired of warm weather and moves from Miami to Toronto, Canada, where he can no longer observe Amy's effort. Because Amy's effort is now a hidden action to Paul, he faces a moral hazard problem.

When Paul could monitor Amy's effort, he could make her wage contingent on hard work. Now, as he can no longer observe her effort, Paul pays Amy a wage that does not vary with her (hidden) effort. Initially, let's assume that Paul and Amy's contract specifies that Paul pays Amy a daily wage of 100 regardless of how much profit the shop earns. Such a contract is called a *fixed-fee contract*, because one party pays the other a constant payment or fee.

Because Amy receives the same amount no matter how hard she works, Amy chooses not to work hard, which is a moral hazard problem. If she works normally, she incurs no additional personal cost from extra effort and receives 100. On the other hand, if she provides extra effort, she receives a wage of 100 but incurs a personal cost of 40, so her net return is only 60.

Because Amy provides normal effort, the shop earns 100 with low demand, which is just enough to pay Amy with nothing left over for Paul, and the shop earns 300 with high demand, so Paul nets 200. Thus Paul faces an uncertain profit with an expected value of $\left(\frac{1}{2} \times 0\right) + \left(\frac{1}{2} \times 200\right) = 100$. The variance of Paul's earnings remains high: $\frac{1}{2}(0 - 100)^2 + \frac{1}{2}(200 - 100)^2 = 10,000$.

The second row of Table 15.2 summarizes this situation, which is labeled *fixed wage*. Paul bears all the risk, so risk bearing is again efficient. However, their combined earnings are less than in the previous example with symmetric information. Amy now makes 100. Paul has an expected value of 100, which is all he cares about because he is risk neutral. Both were better off with symmetric information: Amy netted 160 and Paul expected to earn 200. Because the moral hazard substantially reduces the shop's expected earnings, having Paul pay Amy a fixed wage is not the best way to compensate her. In the next section, we examine how well-designed contracts can reduce inefficiency due to moral hazard.

Q&A 15.3

Traditionally, the Las Vegas Home Bank made only *prime* loans—providing mortgages just to people who were very likely to repay the loans. However, Leonardo, a senior executive at the bank, is considering offering *subprime* loans—mortgages to speculators and other less creditworthy borrowers. If he makes only prime loans, the bank will earn $160 million. If he also makes subprime loans, the bank will make a very high profit, $800 million, if the economy is good so that few people default. However, if the economy is bad, the large number of defaults will cause the bank to lose $320 million.

The probability that the economy is bad is 75%. Leonardo will receive 1% of the bank's profit if it is positive. He believes that if the bank loses money, he can walk away from his job without repercussions but with no compensation. Leonardo and the bank's shareholders are risk neutral. Does Leonardo provide subprime loans if all he cares about is maximizing his personal expected earnings? What would the bank's stockholders prefer that Leonardo do (given that they know the risks involved)?

Answer

1. *Compare the bank's expected return on the two types of mortgages.* If the bank makes both prime and subprime loans, its expected return is $(0.25 \times 800) + (0.75 \times [-320]) = -40$ million dollars, an expected loss. That is substantially less than the certain profit of $160 million the bank makes if it provides only prime mortgages.

2. *Compare the manager's expected profits on the two investments.* Leonardo earns 1% of $160 million, or $1.6 million, if he provides only prime loans. If he makes prime and subprime loans, he earns 1% of $800 million, or $8 million, with a probability of 25%, and gets no compensation with a probability of 75%. Thus, he expects to earn $(0.25 \times 8) + (0.75 \times 0) = 2$ million dollars. Because Leonardo is risk neutral and does not care about the shareholders' returns, he makes both types of loans.

3. *Compare the shareholders' expected profits on the two types of mortgages.* If the bank provides only prime mortgages, the bank's shareholders earn 99% of the profit from the prime mortgages, or $0.99 \times \$160$ million $= \$158.4$ million. If the bank makes both prime and subprime loans, shareholders earn 99% of the $800 million, $792 million, if the economy is good. But in a bad economy, the shareholders bear the full loss, $320 million. The expected return to shareholders is $(0.25 \times 792) + (0.75 \times [-320]) = -42$ million dollars, an expected loss. Thus, the shareholders would prefer that the bank make only prime loans.

Comment: Given that Leonardo has the wrong incentives (and ignores his responsibility to shareholders), he takes a hidden action—choosing to provide subprime loans—that is not in the shareholders' best interest. This type of moral hazard was one of the major causes of the 2007–2009 financial crisis. One possible solution to the problem of managers' and shareholders' diverging interests is to change the manager's compensation scheme, as we discuss in the Managerial Solution.

15.4 Using Contracts to Reduce Moral Hazard

A verbal contract isn't worth the paper it's written on.

Many people share the belief that

> **Common Confusion** It doesn't matter whether someone is paid a lump-sum, by the hour, a percentage of the revenue, or in other ways.

On the contrary, in many situations the way someone is paid has a major effect on the outcome. For example, in principal-agent settings, a skillfully designed payment contract may reduce or eliminate moral hazard problems. In this section, we illustrate how several types of contracts can increase efficiency in the Paul and Amy ice cream shop example. These contracts provide greater incentives for Amy, the agent, to work hard, but often require her to bear some risk even though she is more risk averse than Paul, the principal.

Fixed-Fee Contracts

We initially considered a fixed-fee contract in which Paul (the principal) pays Amy (the agent) a fixed wage, with the result that Paul bears all of the risk and Amy bears none. Alternatively, Amy could pay Paul a fixed amount so that she receives the residual profit: the profit left over after Paul is paid his fixed return. Effectively, Amy is paying a *license fee* to operate Paul's ice cream shop.[9] With such a contract, Paul bears no risk as he receives a fixed fee, while Amy bears all the risk.[10]

As Amy receives the residual profit under such a licensing contract, she gets all the increase in expected profit from her extra effort. She is therefore motivated to work hard.

To illustrate why, we suppose that Amy pays Paul a fixed licensing fee of 200 per day and keeps any residual profit. (Our analysis depends *only* on Amy paying Paul a fixed fee and *not* on the exact amount that she pays.) If she does not work hard, she makes 100 ($= 300 - 200$) with high demand, but suffers a loss, -100 ($= 100 - 200$), if demand is low. Her expected gain if she does not work hard is $0 = \left(\frac{1}{2} \times [-100]\right) + \left(\frac{1}{2} \times 100\right)$. If she works hard, she nets 60 ($= 300 - 200 - 40$) with low demand and 260 ($= 500 - 200 - 40$) with high demand, so that her expected net payoff is $160 = \left(\frac{1}{2} \times 60\right) + \left(\frac{1}{2} \times 260\right)$. Thus, her expected gain from working hard is 160.

Her variance in earnings is $10,000 = \frac{1}{2}(-100 - 0)^2 + \frac{1}{2}(100 - 0)^2$ with low demand, which is the same as the variance with high demand, $10,000 = \frac{1}{2}(60 - 160)^2 + \frac{1}{2}(260 - 160)^2$. Thus, because her risk is the same with both levels of effort but her

[9]In the Sherlock Holmes mystery *A Study in Scarlet*, Jefferson Hope says, "I applied at a cab-owner's office, and soon got employment. I was to bring a certain sum a week to the owner, and whatever was over that I might keep for myself."

[10]In some businesses, both types of fixed-fee contracts are used. For example, in some hair salons, hairdressers rent a chair from the owner for a fixed fee and bear all the risk associated with variations in demand, while other hairdressers are paid an hourly rate, with the owner getting the residual profit from their activities.

expected net earnings are higher if she puts forth high effort, it is in her best interest to work hard.

Consequently, Amy's and Paul's total expected earnings are higher if Amy pays a fixed fee to Paul than if Paul pays a fixed fee to Amy, because Amy works harder if she is the residual claimant and therefore reaps all the benefits of working harder. As the third row (*licensing fee*) of Table 15.2 shows, when Amy pays Paul a license fee, the shop's expected earnings are 400 because Amy works hard. Paul makes 200 with certainty, and Amy expects a net gain of 160 after deducting her cost, 40, of providing high effort. Therefore, the sum of their expected payoffs is 360. In contrast, if Paul pays Amy a fixed wage (second row), Amy earns 100 and Paul expects to earn 100 for an expected total payoff of 200.

Although Amy paying Paul rather than the other way around increases their total earnings, it makes the risk-averse person, Amy, bear all the risk, while Paul, the risk-neutral person, bears no risk. Therefore, although this contract maximizes combined expected earnings, it does not provide for efficient risk bearing.

Which contract is better depends on how risk averse Amy is. If Amy is nearly risk neutral, the fixed payment to Paul is superior, because both parties have higher expected earnings and Amy is not very concerned about the risk. However, if Amy is extremely risk averse, she may prefer receiving a fixed wage even if that means giving up significant expected earnings.[11]

Contingent Contracts

Many contracts specify that the parties receive payoffs that are contingent on some other variable, such as the action taken by the agent, the state of nature, or the firm's profit, output, or revenue. For example, if Paul can monitor Amy's effort, he offers her a contract such that her payoff is contingent on her effort. She is paid only if she provides extra effort, and loses her job otherwise. Such a contract would be efficient, but is not feasible if Paul cannot monitor Amy's effort. Principals use other types of contingent contracts when monitoring is not feasible.

State-Contingent Contracts.   In a *state-contingent contract*, one party's payoff is contingent on *only* the state of nature. For example, suppose Amy pays Paul a license fee of 100 if demand is low and a license fee of 300 if demand is high and keeps any additional earnings. As the residual claimant, Amy has an incentive to provide high effort. With low demand the shop earns 300, Amy pays Paul 100, and Amy's residual profit is $160 = 300 - 100 - 40$, where 40 is the cost of her extra effort. With high demand, the shop earns 500, Amy pays Paul 300, and Amy's residual profit is $160 = 500 - 300 - 40$.

Paul's expected payoff is $200 = \left(\frac{1}{2} \times 100\right) + \left(\frac{1}{2} \times 300\right)$, as the fourth row of Table 15.2 shows. Because Amy earns 160 in both states of nature, she bears no risk, while Paul bears all the risk. This result is efficient because Paul is risk neutral and Amy is risk averse. This state-contingent contract is fully efficient even if Paul cannot monitor Amy's effort. However, it does require that both parties observe and agree on the state of nature, which may not be possible.

---

[11]Amy might be more risk averse if, for example, she has no savings and would find it difficult to support herself during periods of low demand if she were the residual claimant.

Profit-Sharing Contracts. Even if the principal cannot observe the state of nature or the agent's actions, the principal may be able to design a contingent contract that reduces the moral hazard problem by making payments contingent on an outcome, such as profit or output. One common contingent contract is a *profit-sharing contract*, in which the payoff to each party is a fraction of the observable total profit.

Suppose that Paul and Amy agree to split the earnings of the ice cream shop equally. Does making Amy's pay contingent on the firm's earnings induce Amy to work hard?

If Amy works normally, the shop earns 100 if demand is low and Amy receives half, or 50. If demand is high, the shop earns 300, so Amy's share is 150 $\left(= \frac{1}{2} \times 300 \right)$. Thus, Amy's expected value from normal effort is $100 = \left(\frac{1}{2} \times 50 \right) + \left(\frac{1}{2} \times 150 \right)$. The variance of her earnings is $2,500 = \frac{1}{2}(50 - 100)^2 + \frac{1}{2}(150 - 100)^2$.

If Amy provides extra effort, the shop earns 300 if the demand is low, and Amy receives 150, but she incurs a personal cost of 40 for providing high effort, so her net return is 110. If the demand is high, the shop's profit is 500, so that Amy nets 210 (= 250 − 40). Thus, her expected return from high effort is $160 = \left(\frac{1}{2} \times 110 \right) + \left(\frac{1}{2} \times 210 \right)$. The variance of her earnings is $2,500 = \frac{1}{2}(110 - 160)^2 + \frac{1}{2}(210 - 160)^2$, which is the same as with normal effort. Because extra effort provides Amy with higher expected earnings without increasing her risk, she provides extra effort.

Given that Amy works hard, Paul makes 150 $\left(= \frac{1}{2} \times 300 \right)$ if demand is low and 250 $\left(= \frac{1}{2} \times 500 \right)$ if demand is high. Because Amy and Paul split the shop's earnings, Paul's expected profit is $200 = \left(\frac{1}{2} \times 150 \right) + \left(\frac{1}{2} \times 250 \right)$, as the profit-sharing row of Table 15.2 shows. Paul prefers this profit-sharing contract to a fixed-fee contract by which he pays Amy a fixed wage of 100 and makes an expected profit of 100.

However, Amy chooses to work harder only if she gets a large enough share of the profit to offset her personal cost from doing the extra work. If Amy gets less than 20% of the profit, she chooses not to work hard and earns less than she would from the wage of 100.[12] Thus, profit sharing may reduce or eliminate the moral hazard problem, especially if the agent's share of the profit is large, but it may not do so if the agent's share is small.

Q&A 15.4

Paul wants to hire Amy to manage a shop he owns. He is considering three different payment contracts: a fixed wage of 100, a 25% profit share, and a 30% profit share. If Amy provides normal effort, the shop earns 200 with bad luck and 600 with good luck. If Amy provides high effort, the shop earns 600 with bad luck and 900 with good luck. The chance of bad luck is 40% and of good luck is 60%. Amy incurs a personal cost of 90 if she provides high effort but incurs no personal cost for normal effort. Assume that both Paul and Amy are risk neutral and therefore

	A	B	C	D	E	F	G	H	I
1	Effort Level	Bad Luck	Good Luck	EV	Effort Cost	Payoffs	Fixed Wage	25% share	30% share
2	Normal	200	600		0	Amy			
3	High	600	900		90	Amy			
4						Paul			

---

[12]If θ is Amy's share, then her expected return with normal effort is $\left(\frac{1}{2} \times 100\theta \right) + \left(\frac{1}{2} \times 300\theta \right) = 200\theta$, and her expected return from extra effort is $\left(\frac{1}{2} \times 300\theta \right) + \left(\frac{1}{2} \times 500\theta \right) - 40 = 400\theta - 40$. She chooses not to put in extra effort if her expected return from normal effort exceeds that from extra effort: $200\theta > 400\theta - 40$, or $\theta < 20\%$.

want to maximize their expected payoffs. Set up a spreadsheet as shown and use it to determine which contract would maximize Paul's expected payoff.

Answer

1. *In an Excel spreadsheet (as shown) enter the relevant formulas for columns D, G, H, and I for rows 2 and 3.* Column D shows the expected value (EV) of the shop's profit. Enter "=0.4*B2+0.6*C2" in cell D2. Copy cell D2 into cell D3. Column G shows Amy's expected payoff under a fixed-wage contract, which is the fixed wage of 100 minus her cost of effort. Enter "=100−E2" in cell G2 and copy cell G2 into cell G3. Columns H and I show Amy's expected payoff under the two profit-sharing contracts. Enter "=(0.25*D2)−E2" in cell H2 and copy cell H2 into cell H3. Enter "=(0.3*D2)−E2" in cell I2 and copy cell I2 into cell I3.

2. *Based on inspection, enter the formula for Paul's payoff if he offers a fixed wage into cell G4.* Paul's payoff depends on Amy's choice, which can be determined from the spreadsheet. If Amy gets a fixed wage of 100, in the following spreadsheet, we see that she would choose normal effort because the value in cell G2 (which we shaded yellow) exceeds that in cell G3. Therefore, the shop's expected value of its profit is that in D2. Paul receives that expected value of its profit minus the wage of 100 paid to Amy. Thus, enter "=D2−100" into cell G4.

3. *Based on inspection, enter the formulas for Paul's payoffs under profit sharing into cells H4 and I4.* We see that with a 25% profit share, Amy would choose normal effort. Therefore, enter "=0.75*D2" (or "D2−H2") in cell H4. With a 30% profit share Amy would choose high effort. Enter "=0.7*D3" in cell I4.

4. *Find Paul's highest expected value.* Paul's highest expected value is 546, which is in cell I4 (which we shaded blue). Therefore, Paul can maximize his expected value by offering Amy a 30% profit share.

	A	B	C	D	E	F	G	H	I
1	Effort Level	Bad Luck	Good Luck	EV	Effort Cost	Payoffs	Fixed Wage	25% share	30% share
2	Normal	200	600	440	0	Amy	100	110	132
3	High	600	900	780	90	Amy	10	105	144
4						Paul	340	330	546

Comments: Paul earns more by offering Amy a 30% rather than a 25% profit share, because the higher profit share provides better incentives than the lower share. Owners do not always prefer profit sharing to fixed wages. If Paul had to choose between offering a fixed wage and a 25% profit share, he would choose the fixed wage.

Bonuses and Options. To induce an agent to work hard, a principal may offer the agent a *bonus*: an extra payment if the agent hits a performance target. For example, Paul could offer Amy a base wage of 100 and a bonus of 200 if the shop's earnings (before paying Amy) exceed 300.

If Amy provides normal effort, the shop does not earn enough to trigger the bonus, so Amy receives 100 in both states of nature. If Amy provides extra effort but the demand is low, the shop earns 300, so Amy receives her wage of 100 and incurs a cost of 40, so her net benefit is 60. However, if she works hard and the demand is high, the shop earns 500, the bonus is triggered, and Amy gets her wage of 100 plus the bonus of 200. After subtracting her cost of extra effort, 40, she nets 260. Thus, Amy's expected return with extra effort is $160 = \left(\frac{1}{2} \times 60\right) + \left(\frac{1}{2} \times 260\right)$, which exceeds the 100 she earns with normal effort.

However, the variance in her net earnings with extra effort is $10{,}000 = \frac{1}{2}(60 - 160)^2 + \frac{1}{2}(260 - 160)^2$. Thus, whether Amy chooses to work extra hard depends on how risk averse she is. If she is nearly risk neutral, she works extra hard. However, if she is very risk averse, she puts in only normal effort, receives a modest but predictable wage, and avoids the risk of sometimes earning very little.

The next to last row of Table 15.2 shows the outcome of a bonus contract if Amy is risk neutral. If Amy is risk neutral or nearly risk neutral, she chooses to work hard. If demand is low, the bonus is not triggered, so Paul pays Amy only her base salary of 100 and keeps the residual amount of 200. With high demand, Paul pays Amy 300—the base of 100 plus the bonus of 200—and keeps the residual of 200 ($= 500 - 300$). Paul expects to earn $200 = \left(\frac{1}{2} \times 200\right) + \left(\frac{1}{2} \times 200\right)$. Indeed, he earns 200 regardless of demand conditions, so he bears no risk. Thus, if Amy is risk neutral, the bonus leads to efficient payoffs and efficient risk bearing even though Amy bears all the risk. (If Amy were nearly but not quite risk neutral, she would still choose to work hard, but would dislike bearing all the risk.)

The last row in Table 15.2 shows the outcome of a bonus contract if Amy is extremely risk averse. Now, she'd rather have 100 with certainty than take a chance on sometimes netting only 60 after incurring the cost of high effort, so she works only normal hours. Consequently, the total payoffs are low and hence not efficient, but risk is shared efficiently, with Paul bearing all the risk. Thus, this bonus may—but does not necessarily—induce Amy to work hard.

Many senior executives receive part of their salary in the form of an *option*, which is a type of bonus (Chapter 7). An option gives the holder the right to buy up to a certain number of shares of the company at a given price (the *exercise price*) during a specified time interval. An option provides a benefit to the executive if the firm's stock price exceeds the exercise price and is therefore a bonus based on the stock price.

Piece Rates and Commissions. Another common type of contingent contract is a *piece-rate contract*, in which the agent receives a payment for each unit of output the agent produces. Under such a contract, Paul pays Amy for every serving of ice cream she sells rather than by the hour, which gives her an incentive to work hard, but she bears the risk from fluctuations in demand, which she does not control.

Similarly, under a revenue-sharing contract, the agent receives some share of revenues earned. For people who work in sales, such payments are called *commissions*. For example, a salesperson in a clothing store might receive a commission of 5% of the revenue for each item sold. As with profit sharing, piece rates and commissions provide an incentive for agents to provide more effort than they would with a fixed-rate contract. As with a bonus, this incentive is not necessarily strong enough to offset the agent's cost of extra effort and the agent bears some risk.

Mini-Case

Sing for Your Supper

The concert producer of one of the world's largest music festivals, Outside Lands Music & Arts Festival, negotiates with dozens of food and drink vendors to sell goods at his annual event. According to his contract with them, they owe him a share of their revenues.

He worries that the vendors might underreport their revenues, as he cannot easily monitor them. In the past, to minimize this problem, he took two actions. First, they owe him the larger of a minimum amount (the "guarantee") and his percentage of the revenues.

Second, he compared reported revenues across vendors and found that the vast majority of vendors reported comparable revenues within their categories. He did not invite the 10% of vendors who reported substantially smaller amounts back the next year. Thus, substantial cheating by vendors cost them the opportunity to participate in the event in the future.

However, in 2015, he tried something new. Concertgoers could buy wine only by using an electronic payment system, which kept track of sales. He estimated that revenues increased by over 30% from the previous year due to more accurate reporting.

Q&A 15.5

Gary's demand for doctor visits depends on his health. Half the time his health is good and his demand is D^1 in the figure. When his health is poor, his demand is D^2. Gary is risk averse. Without medical insurance, he pays $50 a visit. With full insurance, he pays a fixed fee at the beginning of the year, and the insurance company pays the full cost of any visit. Alternatively, with a contingent contract, Gary pays a smaller premium at the beginning of the year, and the insurance company covers only $20 per visit, with Gary paying the remaining $30. How likely is a moral hazard problem to occur with each of these contracts? What is Gary's risk (the variance of his medical costs) with no insurance and with each of the two types of insurance? Compare the contracts in terms of the trade-offs between risk and moral hazard.

Answer

1. *Describe the moral hazard for each demand curve for each contract.* Given that Gary's health is good, if he does not have insurance, Gary pays the doctor $50 a visit and goes to the doctor once, at point a_1 in the figure. In contrast, with full insurance, where he pays nothing per visit, he visits the doctor six times, at c_1. Similarly, if his health is poor, he goes to the doctor five times, a_2, without insurance, and 10 times, c_2, with full insurance. Thus, regardless of his health, he makes five extra visits a year with full insurance. These extra visits are the moral hazard.

    With a contingent contract, Gary pays $30 a visit. He makes three visits if his health is good (at point b_1)—only two more than at a_1. If his health is poor, he makes seven visits, once again two more than if he were paying the full fee (at a_1). Thus, with a contingent contract, he makes only two extra visits, so the moral hazard problem is reduced.

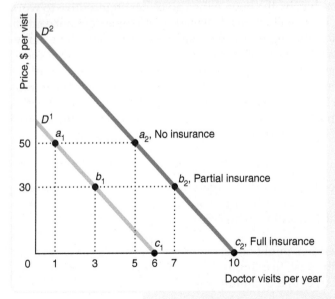

2. *Calculate the variance of Gary's medical expenses for no insurance and for the two insurance contracts.* Without insurance, his average number of visits is $3 = \left(\frac{1}{2} \times 1\right) + \left(\frac{1}{2} \times 5\right)$, so his average annual medical cost is \$150. Thus, the variance of his medical expenses without insurance is

$$\sigma_n^2 = \tfrac{1}{2}[(1 \times \$50) - \$150]^2 + \tfrac{1}{2}[(5 \times 50) - \$150]^2$$
$$= \tfrac{1}{2}(\$50 - \$150)^2 + \tfrac{1}{2}(\$250 - \$150)^2$$
$$= \$10,000.$$

If he has full insurance, he makes a single fixed payment each year, so his payments do not vary with his health: His variance is $\sigma_f^2 = 0$. Finally, with partial insurance, he averages five visits with an average cost of \$150, so his variance is

$$\sigma_p^2 = \tfrac{1}{2}(\$90 - \$150)^2 + \tfrac{1}{2}(\$210 - \$150)^2 = \$3,600.$$

Thus, $\sigma_n^2 > \sigma_p^2 > \sigma_f^2$.

3. *Discuss the trade-offs.* Because Gary is risk averse, efficiency in risk bearing requires the insurance company to bear all the risk, as with full insurance. However, full insurance results in the largest moral hazard. Removing insurance eliminates moral hazard, but Gary bears all the risk. This contingent contract is a compromise in which both the moral hazard and the degree of risk lie between the extremes.

15.5 Using Monitoring to Reduce Moral Hazard

Often when a firm cannot use piece rates or reward workers contingent on the firm's success, the employer pays fixed-fee salaries or hourly wages. As we've seen, employees who are paid a fixed salary have little incentive to work hard if the employer cannot observe shirking. And if an employer pays employees by the hour but cannot observe how many hours they work, employees may inflate the number of hours they report working. A firm can reduce such shirking by intensively supervising or monitoring its workers. Monitoring eliminates or at least reduces the asymmetric information problem: Both the employee and the employer know how hard the employee works. If the cost of monitoring workers is low enough, it pays to prevent shirking by carefully monitoring and firing employees who do not work hard.

Firms have experimented with various means of lowering the cost of monitoring. Requiring employees to punch a time clock and installing video cameras to record employee work effort are examples of firms' attempts to use capital to monitor job performance. Similarly, by installing assembly lines that force employees to work at a pace dictated by the firm, employers can control employees' work rate.

According to a survey by the American Management Association, nearly two-thirds of employers record employees' voice mail, e-mail, or phone calls; review their computer files; or videotape workers. A quarter of the firms that use surveillance don't tell their employees. The most common types of surveillance are tallying phone numbers called and recording the duration of the calls (37%), videotaping employees' work (16%), storing and reviewing e-mail (15%), storing and reviewing computer files (14%), and taping and reviewing phone conversations (10%). Monitoring and surveillance are most common in the financial sector, in which 81% of firms use these techniques. Rather than watching all employees all the time, companies usually monitor selected workers using spot checks.

For some jobs, however, monitoring is counterproductive or not cost effective. Monitoring may lower employees' morale, which in turn reduces productivity. Many years ago, Northwest Airlines took the doors off bathroom stalls to prevent workers from staying too long in the stalls. When new management eliminated this policy (and made many other changes as well), productivity increased.

It is usually impractical for firms to monitor how hard salespeople work if they spend most of their time away from the main office. As telecommuting increases, monitoring workers may become increasingly difficult.

A firm's board of directors is supposed to represent shareholders (principals) by monitoring senior executives (agents) to ensure that executive decisions are made in the shareholders' interests. Bad executives may try to hide their actions from directors or select directors who won't "rat" on them. González, Schmid, and Yermack (2013) studied firms in which senior executives were engaging in illegal price fixing, exposing the firm and its shareholders to significant legal liability. They found that senior executives in such firms were more inclined to recruit directors who were likely to be inattentive monitors.

Hostages

When direct monitoring is very costly, firms often use contracts containing various financial incentives to reduce the amount of monitoring that is necessary. Each of these incentives—bonding, deferred payments, and efficiency wages (unusually high wages)—acts as a *hostage* for good behavior (Williamson, 1983). Workers caught shirking or engaging in other undesirable acts not only lose their jobs but give up the hostage, too. The more valuable the hostage, the less monitoring the firm needs to use to deter bad behavior.

Bonding. One way to ensure agents behave well is to require them to deposit funds guaranteeing their good behavior, just as a landlord requires tenants to post security deposits to ensure that they will not damage an apartment. For example, an employer (principal) may require an employee (agent) to provide a *performance bond*, an amount of money that the principal receives if the agent fails to complete certain duties or achieve certain goals. Typically, the agent posts (leaves) this bond with the principal or another party, such as an insurance company, before starting the job.

Many couriers who transport valuable shipments (such as jewels) or guards who watch over them have to post bonds against theft and other forms of moral hazard. Similarly, employers use bonds to keep employees from quitting immediately after receiving costly training. Two major problems are inherent in posting bonds. First, to capture a bond, an unscrupulous employer might falsely accuse an employee of stealing or of failing to meet the required performance standard. An employee who fears such employer opportunism might be unwilling to post a bond. One possible solution to this problem is for the firm to develop a reputation for not behaving in this manner. Another possible approach is for the firm to make the grounds for forfeiture of the bond objective and thus verifiable by others.

A second problem with bonds is that workers may not have enough wealth to post them. Because of such problems, bonds are more common in contracts between firms than in those between an employer and employees. Moreover, firms have fewer problems than typical employees do in raising funds to post bonds.

Construction contractors frequently post bonds to guarantee that they will satisfactorily finish their work by a given date. It is easy to verify whether the agent completes the project on time, so the principal is unlikely to engage in opportunistic behavior.

Why are most onshore gas and oil producers small firms? A major reason is to avoid liability. Being small allows them to produce as much as they can, and if they cause environmental damages—water pollution, toxic gas releases, or explosions—greater than their assets, they avoid liability by declaring bankruptcy. They are "judgment proof." A large firm with substantial assets would pay the damages and stay in business.

Texas has roughly 5,000 oil- and gas-producing firms. Most of these have less than two million dollars in annual revenue—much less than their liability exposure. However, as of 2001, Texas required these firms to post a *surety bond*, which is an insurance contract that obligates the insurer to compensate the state for environmental damages by the insured oil or gas producer. Insurance companies set a high premium for a firm with a bad safety record or one with little incentive to act prudently because it is financially weak. In contrast, a large, financially secure firm is less likely to act irresponsibly and hence pays a lower premium.

Boomhower (forthcoming) showed that the bond requirement improves firms' safety incentives. As soon as the bond mandate went into effect, 6% of firms exited the market (twice the usual rate). These firms were primarily small firms with poor environmental records. These exiting firms transferred 88% of their oil and gas leases to larger firms. The smallest 80% of the remaining firms reduced oil production, while the large firms' production was unaffected. That is, the ability to avoid responsibility prior to bonding inflated the number of small firms and their production.

The amount of environmental damage fell after the bond mandate went into effect. At the end of production, many fewer firms left their wells unplugged, which causes a serious risk of groundwater pollution. Well blowouts and water protection violations also fell substantially.

Deferred Payments. Effectively, firms can post bonds for their employees using deferred payments. For example, a firm pays new workers a low wage for some initial period of employment. Then, over time, the firm fires workers caught shirking, and those good workers who remain receive higher wages. In another form of deferred wages, the firm provides a retirement pension that rewards only workers who stay with the firm for a sufficiently long period (or who reach a certain age). Fired workers forfeit this benefit, so they have an incentive to work hard to avoid early termination. Deferred payments serve the same function as bonds. They raise the cost of being fired, so less monitoring is necessary to deter shirking.

Reduced shirking leads to greater output. If the employer and the employee share the extra output in the form of higher profit and lifetime earnings, both the firm and workers prefer the deferred-payment scheme that lowers incentives to shirk.

A drawback of the deferred-payment approach is that, like posting bonds, it can encourage employers to engage in opportunistic behavior. For example, an employer might fire nonshirking senior workers to avoid paying their higher wages or pensions and then replace them with less expensive junior workers. However, if the firm can establish a reputation for not unjustifiably firing senior workers, the deferred-payment system can help prevent shirking.

Managers can often reduce employee shirking by paying an *efficiency wage*: an unusually high wage above the worker's opportunity cost (the amount the worker can get elsewhere). If a worker who is fired for shirking can immediately go to another firm and earn the same wage, the worker risks nothing by shirking.

But an efficiency wage acts as a hostage. A high wage raises the cost of getting fired, so it discourages shirking.[13] Also, some economists (Akerlof, 1982) and management experts contend that the higher wage acts like a gift, making workers feel beholden or loyal to the firm, so less (or no) monitoring is needed.[14] If the saving from reducing shirking exceeds the cost of the higher wage, then paying an efficiency wage is profitable.

After-the-Fact Monitoring

So far we've concentrated on monitoring by employers looking for undesirable behavior as it occurs. However, it is often easier to detect the effects of shirking or other undesirable actions after the actions occur. For example, an employer can check the amount that an employee produces or the quality of the work after it is completed. If the employer detects shirking or other unwanted behavior after the fact, the offending employee may be fired or otherwise disciplined. This punishment discourages shirking in the future.

If an insurance company determines after the fact that an insurance claim resulted from intentional behavior rather than chance, the firm may deny payment. Insurance companies may refuse to pay damages for a traffic accident if the insured driver was drunk at the time. House insurance companies disallow claims due to explosions resulting from illegal activities such as making methamphetamine and claims by arsonists who torch their own homes or businesses. Life insurance companies may refuse to pay benefits to the family of someone who commits suicide soon after buying the policy (as in the play *Death of a Salesman*).

Managerial Solution	Does evaluating a manager's performance over a longer time period, using delayed compensation or clawback provisions, lead to better management? The answer depends on whether the reward a manager receives in the short run induces the manager to sacrifice long-run profit for short-run gains.
Clawing Back Bonuses	Managers prefer to be paid sooner rather than later because money today is worth more than the same amount later. Thus, if a manager can move a major sale from January of next year to December of this year, the firm's total profits over the two years are unchanged, but the manager's performance-based bonus is paid this year rather than next year. Most boards are probably not very concerned with such shifts over time, as they are unlikely to lower long-run profits.
	Of more concern are managers who increase this year's profit even though doing so lowers profit in later years. Many firms pay a bonus on a positive profit

---

[13]See Yellen (1984), Stiglitz (1987), and Shapiro and Stiglitz (1984). Economists have posited other explanations for why efficiency wages lead to higher productivity. Some economists claim that in less developed countries, employers pay an efficiency wage—more than they need to hire workers—to ensure that workers can afford to eat well enough so that they can work hard.

[14]The extent of moral hazard may depend on how workers feel about their work. Using an online experiment, List and Momeni (2017) found evidence supporting a "moral license" effect: More workers shirked if their "firm" provided socially responsible contributions to nonprofits. Apparently the workers felt less constrained to act morally in other dimensions.

but do not impose fines or penalties (negative bonuses) for a loss (negative profit). Suppose that a particular policy results in a large profit this year but a larger loss next year. If the manager gets a bonus based on each year's profit, the manager receives a large bonus this year and no bonus next year. However, if the bonus is calculated over two years, the manager would receive no bonus in either year. A firm could achieve a similar effect by allowing for a bonus given in one year to be *clawed back* if the firm does badly in the subsequent year. Without such clawbacks, the manager has a greater incentive to adopt this policy of increasing profit in one year at the cost of lower profit the next.

In an extreme case, a manager engages in reckless behavior that increases this year's profit but bankrupts the firm next year. The manager plans to grab this year's bonus and then disappear. Many mortgage and financial instrument managers engaged in such reckless and irresponsible behavior leading up to the 2007–2009 financial meltdown. Bad decisions at Merrill Lynch, a wealth management firm, cost shareholders billions of dollars, but senior managers kept bonuses despite the negative effects of their decisions on shareholders.

One solution to bad managerial incentives is to base bonuses on more than one year. Starting in 2012, Morgan Stanley paid bonuses to high-income employees over a three-year period.

To illustrate why paying over time provides a better incentive structure, we examine the case of Angelo, who is an executive in a company that provides auto loans for a two-year period. Initially, he receives 10% of the amount of the loans he makes in the first year. He can loan to two groups of customers. Customers in one group have excellent financial histories and repay their loans on time. Loans to this group produce revenue of $10 million this year, so that over the two-year period, the firm nets $9 million after paying Angelo. Customers in the other group are much more likely to default. That group produces $30 million in revenue this year, but their defaults in the second year cost the firm $40 million. After paying Angelo $3 million in the first year, the firm suffers a $13 million loss over the two years (ignoring discounting).

Because Angelo prefers receiving $4 million by loaning to both groups to $1 million from loaning to only the good risks, he may expose the firm to devastating losses in the second year. He may be happy earning a gigantic amount in the first year even if he's fired in the second year. This management problem can be avoided if his compensation is based on profit over a two-year period, so that he has less incentive to make loans to the bad risks.

SUMMARY

1. **Adverse Selection.** Adverse selection arises when one party to a transaction possesses information about a hidden characteristic that is unknown to other parties and the informed party exploits this advantage. Due to adverse selection, not all desirable transactions take place. As a result, low-quality items tend to be overrepresented in transactions, as with the lemons problem associated with used cars and many other products. Bad products may drive good products out of the market. Adverse selection creates problems in insurance markets because people with low risk do not buy insurance, which drives up the price for high-risk people.

2. **Reducing Adverse Selection.** Methods of dealing with the adverse selection problem include laws limiting the ability of informed parties to exploit their private information, consumer screening (such as by using experts or relying on firms' reputations), the provision of information by third parties such as government agencies or consumer groups, and signaling by firms (including establishing brand names and providing guarantees or warranties).

3. **Moral Hazard.** If one party to a transaction can act in a way that is unobserved by the other party, a moral hazard problem may occur in which the informed person exploits the ignorance of the other by means of this hidden action. Moral hazard problems are common in insurance markets and in principal-agent relationships when the agent, such as an employee, takes actions that the principal, such as the manager, cannot observe. For example, if the manager cannot observe how hard an employee works, the employee may shirk. Ideally, a contract or agreement between the parties is efficient, maximizing the total profit of the parties and sharing risk optimally.

4. **Using Contracts to Reduce Moral Hazard.** Appropriately designed contracts that align parties' interests reduce or eliminate moral hazard problems. Often such contracts reflect a trade-off between maximizing total profit and efficient risk bearing. Many of these contracts incorporate outcome-based contingent rewards, such as profit sharing, bonuses, commissions, and piece-rate payments.

5. **Using Monitoring to Reduce Moral Hazard.** A direct approach to limiting moral hazard problems is for a principal to monitor the agent. Monitoring coupled with a contract that penalizes bad behavior may reduce or eliminate moral hazard problems. For example, employers can reduce monitoring as the employee's interest in keeping the job increases. Thus, an employer may require an employee to post a large bond that the employee forfeits if caught shirking, stealing, or otherwise misbehaving. If an employee cannot afford to post a bond, the employer may use deferred payments or efficiency wages—unusually high wages—to make it worthwhile for the employee to keep the job.

QUESTIONS

All exercises are available on **MyLab Economics;** * = *answer at the back of this book;* C = *use of calculus may be necessary.*

1. Adverse Selection

1.1 According to the Federal Trade Commission, millions of U.S. consumers have been victims of weight-loss frauds, ranging from a tea that promised to help you shed the pounds to fraudulent clinical trials and fat-dissolving injections. Do these frauds illustrate adverse selection or moral hazard?

*1.2 The state of California set up its own earthquake insurance program for homeowners. The rates vary by ZIP code, depending on the proximity of the nearest fault line. However, critics claim that the people who set the rates ignored soil type. Some houses rest on bedrock; others sit on unstable soil. What are the implications of such rate setting for possible adverse selection?

*1.3 A firm spends a great deal of money on advertising to inform consumers of the brand name of its mushrooms. Should consumers conclude that its mushrooms are likely to be of higher quality than unbranded mushrooms? Why or why not?

1.4 You want to determine whether the market for single-engine airplanes has a lemons problem. Can you use any of the following information to help answer this question? If so, how?

a. Repair rates for original-owner planes versus resold planes.

b. The fraction of planes resold in each year after purchase.

1.5 Akerlof (1970) observed that if you buy a new car and try to sell it in the first year—indeed, in the first few weeks after you buy it—the price that you get is substantially less than the original price. His *lemons model* shows how adverse selection can cause such an effect. Use your knowledge of adverse selection to explain why a car's price falls soon after it leaves the showroom.

1.6 Use Akerlof's lemons model to explain why restaurants that cater to tourists are likely to serve low-quality meals. Tourists will not return to this area, and they have no information about the relative quality of the food at various restaurants, but they can determine the relative price by looking at menus posted outside each restaurant.

1.7 Suppose that everyone in the used car example in the text is risk neutral, potential car buyers value lemons at \$5,000 and good used cars at \$11,000, the reservation price of lemon owners is \$3,500, and the reservation price of owners of high-quality used cars is \$8,000. The share of current owners who have lemons is θ [in the example in the text, $\theta = \frac{1}{2} = 1{,}000/(1{,}000 + 1{,}000)$]. For what values of θ do all the potential sellers sell their used cars? Describe the equilibrium. (*Hint:* See Q&A 15.1.)

*1.8 Many buyers value high-quality used cars at the full-information market price of p_1 and lemons at p_2. A limited number of potential sellers value high-quality cars at $v_1 \leq p_1$ and lemons at $v_2 \leq p_2$. Everyone is risk neutral. The share of lemons among all the used cars that might potentially be sold is θ. Under what conditions are all cars sold? When are only lemons sold? Under what, if any, conditions are no cars sold?

1.9 It costs $18 to produce a low-quality stapler and $24 to produce a high-quality stapler. Consumers cannot distinguish good staplers from poor staplers when they make their purchases. Consumers value staplers at their cost of production and are risk neutral. The three firms in the market produce low-quality staplers at a price of $18. A fourth firm is considering entering the market. Given that each firm produces and sells the same quantity of staplers, will the fourth firm be able to produce high-quality staplers without making losses? How does your answer change if consumers are willing to pay $60 for high-quality staplers? (*Hint*: See Q&A 15.2.)

1.10 Suppose that half the population is healthy and the other half is unhealthy. If an insured healthy person gets sick, the full cost to the insurance company is $2,000. If an insured unhealthy person gets sick, the cost to the insurance company is $11,000. In a given year, any one person (healthy or unhealthy) has a 35% chance of getting sick. People know whether they are healthy, but the insurance company does not. The insurance company offers complete, actuarially fair insurance at the same price to everyone. The insurance company covers all medical expenses of its policyholders, and its expected profit is zero.

   a. If everyone purchases insurance, what is the price of the insurance?

   b. If only unhealthy people purchase insurance, what is the price of the insurance?

   c. If each person has the option of buying insurance, explain why adverse selection might be expected unless healthy people are highly risk averse.

2. Reducing Adverse Selection

2.1 In the world of French high cuisine, a three-star rating from the Michelin Red Guide is a widely accepted indicator of gastronomic excellence. French consumers consider Gault Milleau, another restaurant guide, not as authoritative as the Michelin guide because Gault Milleau, unlike Michelin, accepts advertising and its critics accept free meals.

   a. Why are guides' ratings important to restaurant owners and chefs? Discuss the effect of a restaurant's rating on the demand for the restaurant.

   b. Why do advertising and free meals taint the credibility of Gault Milleau? Discuss the moral hazard problem of Gault Milleau's ratings.

   c. If advertising and free meals taint the credibility of Gault Milleau, why does the guide accept advertising and free meals?

2.2 Certain universities give written evaluations of student performance rather than letter grades. One rationale is that eliminating the letter-grade system reduces the pressure on students, thus enabling them to do better in school. Why might this policy help or hurt students?

*2.3 Employers often have a hard time predicting the quality of job applicants. Can workers use education as a signal to indicate that they have high ability?

2.4 Some sellers offer to buy back a good later at some prespecified price. Why would a firm make such a commitment?

2.5 How does John Hancock Life Insurance use modern communications technology to reduce adverse selection? (*Hint*: See the Mini-Case "Discounts for Data.")

2.6 According to Edelman (2011), the widely used online "trust" authorities issue certifications without adequate verification, giving rise to adverse selection. Edelman finds that TRUST e-certified sites are more than twice as likely to be untrustworthy as uncertified sites. Explain why.

2.7 The Mini-Case "Adverse Selection and Remanufactured Goods" reports that, for electronic goods sold on eBay, higher seller feedback scores reduce the price differential between new goods and remanufactured goods. Explain why this pattern is consistent with the theory of adverse selection. Would you also expect higher seller feedback to reduce the price differential between new goods and used (but not remanufactured) goods?

3. Moral Hazard

*3.1 Sometimes a group of hungry students will go to a restaurant and agree to share the bill at the end regardless of who orders what. What is the implication of this fee-sharing arrangement for the size of the overall bill? Why?

3.2 In 2012, a California environmental group found that 14 plum and ginger candies imported from Asia contained 4 to 96 times the level of lead allowed under California law (Stephanie M. Lee, "Lead Found in Asian Candies," *San Francisco Chronicle*, August 14, 2012). Some observers predicted that U.S. consumers would face significant price increases if U.S. law were changed to require third-party testing by manufacturers and sellers. Suppose instead that candies could be reliably labeled "tested" or "untested," and untested candy sold at a discount. Would consumers buy cheaper, untested goods, or would they fear a moral hazard problem? Discuss.

3.3 Suppose that the expected value (see Chapter 14) of daily profits for an ice cream shop, before paying the manager, Amy, is $E\pi = 1000 + 20e$, where e is Amy's daily overtime hours. Amy is risk neutral but incurs a cost $C(e) = 4e^2$ from working overtime. Thus, total expected surplus is $ES = E\pi - C(e)$. What level of effort maximizes total expected surplus? **C**

3.4 In Question 3.3, will Amy choose the surplus-maximizing level of effort if she pays the owner a fixed fee and keeps the residual profit from the shop? Alternatively, what happens if Amy earns a fixed wage and the owner gets the residual profit?

*3.5 A promoter arranges for many different restaurants to set up booths to sell Cajun-Creole food at a fair. The promoter provides appropriate music and other entertainment. Restaurants agree to pay a share of their earnings to the promoter, but the promoter cannot monitor how much business each restaurant does. However, the promoter requires that customers can buy food using only "Cajun Cash," which is scrip with the same denominations as actual cash sold by the promoter at the fair. How does Cajun Cash solve a potential moral hazard problem that might arise between the promoter and the restaurants? (*Hint*: See the Mini-Case "Sing for Your Supper.")

3.6 Topside Tiles, which produces roofing tiles, is a local monopoly. Its inverse demand function is $p = 50 - 2Q$, and its constant marginal cost is 10. The owner has delegated the decision of how much output to produce to the plant manager. The manager's income, Y, is 10% of revenue: $Y = 0.1R$. Show that a manager who wishes to maximize income, Y, will choose an output that exceeds the profit-maximizing level. Is there a conflict of interest between the owner and manager? Is this situation an agency problem? **C** (*Hint*: This problem can be solved using a graph, by using calculus, or by using the rule that the MR curve has twice the slope of the demand curve.)

3.7 Now suppose that the owner of Topside Tiles in the previous question changes the manager's compensation to a fixed share (15%) of profit: $Y = 0.15\pi$. The situation is otherwise the same as in Question 3.6. Are the interests of the owner and manager aligned or in conflict? Is there an agency problem in this case?

3.8 The state of California set up its own earthquake insurance program. Because the state agency in charge has few staff members, it pays private insurance carriers to handle claims for earthquake damage. These insurance firms receive 9% of each approved claim. Is this compensation scheme likely to lead to opportunistic behavior by insurance companies? What would be a better way to handle the compensation?

3.9 A bank can make one of two types of loans. It can loan money to local firms, and have an 80% probability of earning $140 million and a 20% probability

of earning $90 million. Alternatively, it can loan money to oil speculators, and have a 30% probability of earning $450 million and a 70% probability of losing $200 million (due to loan defaults by the speculators). Sarah, the manager of the bank, makes the lending decisions, and receives 1% of the bank's earnings. She believes that if the bank loses money, she can walk away from her job without repercussions, although she will not receive any compensation. Sarah and the bank's shareholders are risk neutral. How does Sarah invest the bank's money if all she cares about is maximizing her personal expected earnings? How would the stockholders prefer that Sarah invest the bank's money? (See Q&A 15.3.)

3.10 A study found that urologists in group practices that profit from tests for prostate cancer order more of them than doctors who send samples to independent laboratories. Doctors' groups that perform their own lab work bill Medicare for analyzing 72% more prostate tissue samples per biopsy and detect fewer cases of cancer than doctors who use outside labs (Christopher Weaver, "Prostate-Test Fees Challenged," *Wall Street Journal*, April 9, 2012). Explain these results. Do these results necessarily demonstrate moral hazard, or can you explain them in another way?

3.11 The U.S. government provides home insurance for floods (see Chapter 14's Mini-Case "Flooded by Insurance Claims"). The government will pay no matter how many times floods destroy a home. Does this policy create a moral hazard problem? Explain.

4. Using Contracts to Reduce Moral Hazard

4.1 Traditionally, doctors were paid on a fee-for-service basis. Now, increasingly, doctors are paid on a capitated basis (they get paid for treating a patient for a year, regardless of how much treatment is required), though a patient may still have to pay a small fee each visit. In this arrangement, doctors form a group and sign a capitation contract whereby they take turns seeing a given patient. What are the implications of this change in compensation for moral hazard and for risk bearing?

4.2 According to a flyer from a well-known broker, "Most personal investment managers base their fees on a percentage of assets managed. We believe this is in your best interest because your manager is paid for investment management, not solely on the basis of trading commissions charged to your account. You can be assured your manager's investment decisions are guided by one primary goal—increasing your assets." Is this policy in a customer's best interest? Why?

*4.3 Zhihua and Pu are partners in a store in which they do all the work. They split the store's *business profit* equally (ignoring the opportunity cost of their own time in calculating this profit). Does their business profit-sharing contract give them an incentive to maximize their joint economic profit if neither can force the other to work? (*Hint*: Imagine Zhihua's thought process late one Saturday night when he is alone in the store, debating whether to keep the store open a little later or to go out on the town.)

*4.4 Priscilla hires Arnie to manage her store. Arnie's effort is given in the left column of the table. Each cell shows the net profit to Priscilla (ignoring Arnie's cost of effort).

	Low Demand	High Demand
Low Effort	20	40
Medium Effort	40	80
High Effort	80	100

Arnie's personal cost of effort is 0 at low effort, 10 at medium effort, and 30 at high effort. It is equally likely that demand will be low or high. Arnie and Priscilla are risk neutral. They consider two possible contracts: (1) *fixed fee*: Arnie receives a fixed wage of 10; and (2) *profit sharing*: Arnie receives 50% of the firm's net income but no wage.

a. What happens if they use the fixed-fee contract?

b. What happens if they use the profit-sharing contract?

c. Which contract does each prefer?

4.5 In the situation described in Question 4.4, how do your answers change if Arnie's first contract changes so that he receives a basic fixed wage of 10 and, in addition, a bonus equal to 80% of any net income?

4.6 Determine which contract Paul would prefer if Amy's cost of normal effort is 10 instead of 0 in the spreadsheet in Q&A 15.4.

4.7 Suppose that an author of popular science fiction novels is paid a royalty share v of the revenue from sales, where the revenue is $R = pq$, p is the competitive market price for such novels, and q is the number of copies of this novel sold. The publisher's cost of printing and distributing the book is $C(q)$. Determine the output level that maximizes the publisher's profit. Compare it to the outcome that maximizes the sum of the payment to the author plus the firm's profit. Answer using both math and a graph. **C**

4.8 Suppose now that the publisher in Question 4.7 faces a downward-sloping demand curve. The revenue is $R(Q)$, and the publisher's cost of printing and distributing the book is $C(Q)$. Compare the equilibria

for the following compensation methods in which the author receives the same total compensation from each method:

a. The author is paid a lump sum.

b. The author is paid a share of the revenue.

c. The author receives a lump-sum payment and a share of the revenue.

Why do you think that publishers pay authors a share of revenue?

4.9 A health insurance company tries to prevent the moral hazard of "excessive" dentist visits by limiting the visits per person per year to a specific number. How does such a restriction affect moral hazard and risk bearing? (*Hint*: See Q&A 15.5.)

4.10 Louisa is an avid cyclist who is currently working on her business degree. She normally rides an $800 bike to class. If Louisa locks her bike carefully—locks both wheels—the chance of theft for the term is 5%, but this careful locking procedure is time consuming. If she is less careful—just quickly locks the frame to a bike rack—the chance of theft is 20%. Louisa is risk averse and is considering buying theft insurance for her bike. Louisa may purchase one of two types of insurance. With full insurance, Louisa pays the premium and gets the full, $800 value of the bike if it is stolen. Alternatively, with partial insurance, Louisa receives only 75% of the bike's value, $600, if the bike is stolen. Which contract is more likely to induce moral hazard problems? To break even on consumers like Louisa, what price would the risk-neutral insurance company have to charge for full insurance? If we observe Louisa buying partial insurance, what can we say about the trade-off between moral hazard and efficient risk bearing? (*Hint*: See Q&A 15.3.)

5. Using Monitoring to Reduce Moral Hazard

5.1 Many law firms consist of partners who share profits. On being made a partner, a lawyer must post a bond, a large payment to the firm that will be forfeited on bad behavior. How would such an arrangement reduce moral hazard problems?

5.2 Substandard condo developments have often been built by small corporations that declare bankruptcy or go out of business when legal actions are started against them by condo buyers. What legal remedies might reduce this moral hazard problem? If you were considering buying a condo in a new building, what characteristics of the builder would make you more likely to buy? Explain. (*Hint*: See the Mini-Case "Capping Oil and Gas Bankruptcies.")

*5.3 Explain why full employment may be inconsistent with no shirking based on the efficiency wage model.

5.4 Starting in 2008, Medicare would not cover the cost of certain surgical mistakes, certain types of hospital-acquired infections, or other "preventable" mistakes (Liz Marlantes, "Medicare Won't Cover Hospital Mistakes: New Rules Aimed at Promoting Better Hospital Care and Safety," *ABC News*, August 19, 2007). Hospitals have to cover these costs and cannot bill the patient. These changes were designed to provide hospitals with a stronger incentive to prevent those mistakes, particularly infections. The Centers for Disease Control and Prevention estimates that 2 million patients are annually infected in hospitals, costing society more than $27 billion. Nearly 100,000 of those infections are fatal. Hospitals could prevent many of these infections if they more rigorously followed basic infection control procedures, including having doctors and nurses wash their hands between visiting patients. Is Medicare's policy designed to deal with adverse selection or moral hazard? Is it likely to help? Explain.

5.5 Rental cars sold on the used car market receive lower prices than cars of the same model and year that were owned by individual owners. Does this price difference reflect adverse selection or moral hazard? Could car rental companies reduce this problem by carefully inspecting rental cars for damage when renters return such cars? Why do car companies normally perform only a cursory inspection?

5.6 Many firms pay bonuses or make contributions to an employee's pension fund on an annual basis but require a *vesting period*—often eight to ten years—during which the employee must stay with the company to obtain ownership of these assets. An employee who leaves the company before the vesting period loses any claim to the assets. How does *vesting* reduce moral hazard in employment relationships?

5.7 In 2018, Amazon received a pair of patents for a wristband that can locate warehouse employees and track their hand movements in real time and an inventory management system using trackers and receivers to monitor workers' movements and breaks. Can Amazon use these innovations to address moral hazard problems? How do they help?

6. Managerial Problem

6.1 In the Managerial Solution, show that shareholders' expected earnings are higher with the new compensation scheme than with the original one.

6.2 Curtis manages an electronics store in Wichita, Kansas. He considers carrying either cameras from Nikon Americas that come with a U.S. warranty or *gray market* Nikon cameras from a European supplier, which are the same cameras but their warranties are only good in Europe. The gray market cameras have a lower wholesale price. Curtis earns 10% of the store's profit (and no wage). If the store loses money, he leaves with nothing. He believes that if he sells the Nikon Americas cameras, the store's profit will be $400,000. The profit on the gray market cameras is more uncertain—will locals be willing to buy a less expensive camera without a warranty? If he sells the gray market cameras, he believes that he has a 50% chance that the store's profit will be $1,000,000 and a 50% probability that the store will lose $300,000. Curtis and the store's owner are both risk neutral. Which camera does Curtis choose to sell? What choice would the owner prefer (if she were fully informed)? Construct an alternative compensation plan involving a salary such that Curtis will earn as much from selling Nikon Americas cameras as from selling gray market cameras, and that will dissuade him from selling gray market cameras if doing so lowers the owner's expected earnings.

6.3 In 2012, Hewlett-Packard Co. announced that its new chief executive, Meg Whitman, would receive a salary of $1 and about $16.1 million in stock options, which are valuable if the stock does well (**marketwatch.com**, February 3, 2012). How would you feel about this compensation package if you were a shareholder? What are the implications for moral hazard, efficiency, and risk sharing?

7. MyLab Economics Spreadsheet Exercises[15]

7.1 In a used car market, all potential buyers and sellers are risk neutral. The buyers value the good-quality used cars at $10,000 and the lemons at $4,000, while the reservation price of the lemon owners is $2,000. The probability that a car potentially available for sale in the market is a lemon is θ.

a. For $\theta = 0.1$ to $\theta = 0.9$ in increments of 0.1, calculate the price that the buyers will be willing to pay if all cars are sold. (*Hint*: Put the values of z in column A and put the associated buyers' expected value of a car in column B, assuming that all cars are sold.)

b. For which values of θ will all cars be sold if sellers of good-quality cars have a reservation price of $7,600?

c. How does your answer to part b change if sellers of good used cars have a reservation price of $8,500?

[15]The spreadsheet exercises in this chapter are based on the work of Satyajit Ghosh in cooperation with the authors. The answers are available on **MyLab Economics**.

7.2 Anika is hired by the owner of a kitchen supply store to manage the store. Anika and the owner are both risk neutral. The probability of weak demand is 0.2, and the probability of strong demand is 0.8. Each cell in the following table shows the store's profit from a specific combination of demand and Anika's managerial effort. Anika's cost of effort is *not* subtracted from these profits. This effort cost is 2 for low effort, 10 for medium, and 32 for high.

	Weak Demand	Strong Demand
Low Effort	40	60
Medium Effort	60	100
High Effort	100	140

Create a spreadsheet containing this information. Add a column showing Anika's cost of effort and also add columns for the expected payoff to Anika and the owner.

a. Fill in the expected payoffs to both parties if Anika is compensated with a profit-sharing contract providing her with 50% of the profits (and the owner gets the other 50%). Which effort level does Anika choose?

b. Now suppose that Anika's contract provides her with a base salary of 30 and 100% of any profits exceeding 100. Which effort level does she choose?

c. Which of the two contracts in parts a and b would Anika prefer? Which would the owner prefer?

7.3 As in Question 7.3 of Chapter 14, Samantha's utility function is $U(Y) = Y^{0.5}$. She tries to maximize her expected utility. She owns a car for business that she will have to replace if it is stolen. If her car is not stolen, her net income will be $122,500. If the car is stolen, her net income will be reduced by the car's replacement cost of $20,100. The probability that the car will be stolen is 20%. Use Excel to answer the following questions.

a. Samantha learns that she can purchase an anti-theft device that will lower the probability the car will be stolen to 10%. Would Samantha purchase the device at prices of $1,900, $2,000, or $2,100?

b. Samantha can buy insurance that will pay the full replacement cost of the car if it is stolen. The price of this insurance is $4,090. For each of the prices of the anti-theft device given in part a, determine whether Samantha would buy insurance, buy the anti-theft device, or buy neither. Explain why she would not buy both.

c. If Samantha buys insurance, how much would the insurance company gain in expected value if the anti-theft device was installed in Samantha's car?

d. The insurance company is willing to offer a rebate to Samantha if she purchases the anti-theft device. However, the company would need to incur a monitoring cost to insure that Samantha installs and retains the device (to avoid moral hazard). If the price of the device is $2,000, determine the largest monitoring cost the company would be willing to incur while still offering a large enough rebate to cover the cost of the device. How would your answer change if the price of the anti-theft device were $2,100?

16 Government and Business

If it moves, tax it. If it still moves, regulate it. If it stops moving, subsidize it. —Ronald Reagan

Managerial Problem

Licensing Inventions

Government patents grant *intellectual property* rights to inventors of new products or processes. The owner of such a property right has an exclusive right to produce the new product or use the new process covered by the patent for up to 20 years, but may sell the patent or license its use to others. Selling and licensing patents and other forms of intellectual property is big business. Global payments for cross-border use of intellectual property exceeded $400 billion in 2017.

Each patent applies only to the countries where it is granted, so innovators often apply for patents in multiple jurisdictions. Firms from all over the world seeking patent protection for major innovations usually apply for U.S. patents, and may also apply to the European Patent Office and elsewhere. In 2017, the United States granted 320,000 patents, of which over half (54%) were from applicants outside the United States. IBM is more active in patenting than any other firm and received a record 9,043 new U.S. patents in 2017 alone—nearly 25 a day. IBM earned $1.2 billion in 2017 from licensing its patents to other firms. However, IBM and other successful innovators keep many of their patents to themselves and do not license them. U.S. firms typically license less than 10% of their patents to other firms.

Consider a competitive market in which all firms use the same technology, but one firm invents a new, lower-cost process. Should that firm patent its invention or keep it a trade secret? If the innovating firm also manufactures the good, under what conditions can it charge the monopoly price? If the innovating firm obtains a patent, will the firm earn more if it produces the good itself or if it licenses its new process to other firms?

Surprisingly, those robo-arms increase productivity substantially.

Because governments intervene in markets in many ways, almost all managers have to respond to a range of government policies. In our earlier chapters, we often touched on various government interventions in the economy, such as taxes and price ceilings and floors. In this chapter, we examine many additional government policies that affect business, especially those designed to address a *market failure*, which is a non-optimal allocation of goods and services such that a market does not achieve economic efficiency.

We start by discussing rules that a government might use to decide whether to intervene in a market. This discussion is *normative* or *prescriptive* because it suggests or prescribes what governments *should do* (a value judgment). Then we examine *positive* questions concerning what governments *actually do* and how managers respond, issues that we can examine objectively or scientifically.

We examine government responses to market failures from noncompetitive market structures and those that arise when the rights to a resource are not clearly defined. We describe two basic approaches to dealing with market failures due to *noncompetitive market structures*. A preventative approach is to regulate the behavior of firms with market power to avoid a market failure. A remedial approach is to correct serious market power problems *after* they emerge and to punish firms that fail to obey legal requirements regarding the creation and exploitation of market power.

We then look at market failures that arise due to *incomplete property rights*, which lead to such problems as pollution. We consider government policies that directly regulate the related problem and those that assign and enforce property rights.

Learning Objectives

1. Explain why a government may act to eliminate a market inefficiency.
2. Illustrate the effects of price regulation in imperfectly competitive markets.
3. Describe how antitrust laws and competition policies reduce market failures.
4. Demonstrate how government policies can reduce harms from externalities.
5. Show why open-access, club, and public goods cause market failures.
6. Discuss why granting intellectual property rights may promote innovation.

16.1 Market Failure and Government Policy

A perfectly competitive market—which does not suffer from externalities or other market failures—achieves economic efficiency: It maximizes total surplus, the sum of consumer and producer surplus (Chapter 8). This property is one of the strongest arguments for relying on competitive markets without government intervention. However, most markets fall short of perfect competition, and some exhibit a significant market failure, which substantially reduces economic efficiency and results in deadweight losses. Thus, one important rationale for government policy is to reduce or eliminate market failure. By eliminating a market failure, society can recapture the deadweight loss.

In addition to wanting to reduce deadweight loss, society may care about who benefits and who loses from a government policy. However, for some policies, no one loses.

The Pareto Principle

Economist Vilfredo Pareto argued that society should favor a change that benefits some people without harming anyone else, a belief called the **Pareto principle**. According to this principle, if everyone shares in the extra surplus when a government policy eliminates a market failure, then this change is socially desirable. Even if only some people gain, as long as no one is harmed, the Pareto principle is satisfied.

A **Pareto improvement** is a change, such as a reallocation of goods or productive inputs, that helps at least one person without harming anyone else. When two collectors of baseball cards trade cards, both benefit and the exchange harms no one else. Thus, this exchange is a Pareto improvement.

We cannot always use the Pareto principle to compare allocations. Some changes that eliminate a market failure benefit one group while harming another. For example, a monopoly creates a market failure by charging a price above marginal cost, causing a deadweight loss to society (Chapter 9). If the government breaks up the monopoly and replaces it with a competitive industry, the price falls to eliminate the deadweight loss from monopoly. For example, during World War II, the U.S. government ended Alcoa's aluminum monopoly to aid the war effort by increasing production. This change benefited consumers but harmed the owners of the monopoly.

However, the government could modify such a policy to create a Pareto improvement by compensating the former owners. Because consumers gain more than the owners of the monopoly lose (Chapter 9), the government could tax away some of the gain to consumers and use it to fully compensate the owners of the former monopoly. This redistribution of income might be difficult to achieve politically, but this example illustrates that Pareto improvements are possible in principle when a market failure creates a deadweight loss.

Once all possible Pareto improvements have occurred, the outcome is **Pareto efficient**: Any possible change would harm at least one person. A perfectly competitive market is Pareto efficient. Any possible reallocation that benefits someone without harming others occurs through voluntary exchange in a competitive market, so any additional reallocation must harm someone. When assessing market transactions, Pareto efficiency implies economic efficiency: the maximization of surplus.[1]

Cost-Benefit Analysis

When a policy benefits some people while harming others, we cannot use the Pareto principle to evaluate its desirability. Instead, we can evaluate a policy using an alternative value judgment based on the **cost-benefit principle**: A change is desirable if its benefits exceed the costs. To do so, we may need to make interpersonal comparisons in which a gain of one dollar of surplus to one person has the same weight as a loss of one dollar of surplus to anyone else. That is, if one person gains $1,000 in surplus and another loses $500, society has a net gain of $500 and the cost-benefit test is satisfied. Thus, the cost-benefit principle supports policies that increase total surplus. Policies that pass the cost-benefit test are *potential Pareto improvements* as the winners could fully compensate the losers and still have gains left over.

Any policy that generates a Pareto improvement satisfies the cost-benefit principle. If some people gain from a policy and no one suffers a loss, then the aggregate benefit is positive. However, the converse is not true. Many policies that pass the cost-benefit test by generating net benefits are not Pareto improvements because they produce both winners and losers.

While the vast majority of people would probably support eliminating a monopoly even though the monopoly's owners suffer a loss, other policies that create winners and losers are more contentious. Consider a new tax policy that reduces the tax burden on people with incomes over $1 million a year by $50 billion, while increasing the tax burden on those earning less than $50,000 per year by $49 billion. In addition to producing a relatively small net benefit, this policy would have a large effect on the distribution of after-tax income, generating large gains for people who are

---

[1]Pareto efficiency is a more general concept than economic efficiency, which is based on maximization of total surplus. If a market exhibits Pareto efficiency, the market is efficient: It maximizes total surplus. Unlike the surplus concept, the Pareto concept can also be used in nonmarket situations. For example, if two people are happier after they marry, and no one else is harmed, then that marriage is a Pareto improvement, even if we cannot reasonably define a related price or measure of consumer and producer surplus.

already very well off and imposing a very large burden on people of modest means. Many people would oppose such a change, viewing it as unfair and inequitable.

As a practical matter, policies that have large net benefits and only small distributional effects tend to generate broad support. Policies whose distributional effects are large relative to the net benefits are likely to be more contentious, especially if the distributional effect is *regressive*, making the distribution of income less equal.

16.2 Regulation of Imperfectly Competitive Markets

Some government policies create market power, such as monopolies (Chapter 9). However, other government policies reduce market power. A government can take one of three approaches to eliminating a market failure caused by noncompetitive pricing, such as by a monopoly. The most direct approach is for the government to own the monopoly and set relatively low prices. For example, many governments own and operate electric power and water utilities.

A second approach is to change the market structure, as when the U.S. government increased the number of aluminum manufacturers during World War II, ending Alcoa's monopoly. We address other attempts to change the nature of competition in a market using antitrust or competition laws in the next section.

A third approach is to regulate the industry to prevent firms from setting excessively high prices, which we examine now. We show how regulations can correct market structure problems and then discuss why some regulators do not regulate effectively.

Regulating to Correct a Market Failure

Today, the most commonly used approach to regulating monopoly pricing is to impose a price ceiling, called a *price cap*. For example, price cap regulation is used for telecommunications monopolies in 33 U.S. states and in many other countries, including Australia, Canada, Denmark, France, Germany, Mexico, Sweden, and the United Kingdom (Sappington and Weisman, 2010).[2]

Optimal Price Regulation. A government can eliminate the deadweight loss of monopoly by imposing a price cap equal to the price that would prevail in a competitive market, as we now illustrate. Given the demand and marginal cost curves in Figure 16.1, an unregulated monopoly maximizes its profit at e_m, where marginal revenue equals marginal cost: $MR = MC$. The monopoly sells 6 units at a price of $18 per unit, and society suffers a deadweight loss, $C + E$ (Chapter 9). The optimal price cap is $16, which is the competitive price.

Because the price cap prevents the monopoly from charging a price greater than $16, the monopoly's regulated demand curve is horizontal at $16 up to 8 units. At larger output levels, the monopoly's regulated demand curve is the market demand curve: The monopoly can lower its price to sell extra units because it charges less than the maximum price of $16. The regulated marginal revenue curve, MR^r, corresponding to the regulated demand curve, is horizontal where the regulated demand curve is horizontal up to 8 units and equals the original marginal revenue curve, MR, at larger quantities.

To maximize its profit, the regulated monopoly sets its output at 8 units, where MR^r equals its marginal cost, MC, and charges the maximum permitted price, $16. The regulated firm still makes a profit provided that its average cost is less than $16

---

[2]Governments also use price regulation in some oligopolistic markets. Although we concentrate here on regulating a monopoly, similar principles apply to markets with oligopolistic firms.

FIGURE 16.1 **Optimal Price Regulation**

If the government sets a price ceiling at $16, where the monopoly's marginal cost curve hits the demand curve, the new demand curve the monopoly faces has a kink at 8 units, and the corresponding marginal revenue curve, MR^r, "jumps" at that quantity. The regulated monopoly sets its output where $MR^r = MC$, selling the same quantity, 8 units, at the same price, $16, as a competitive industry would. The regulation eliminates the monopoly deadweight loss, $C + E$. Consumer surplus, $A + B + C$, and producer surplus, $D + E$, are the same as under competition.

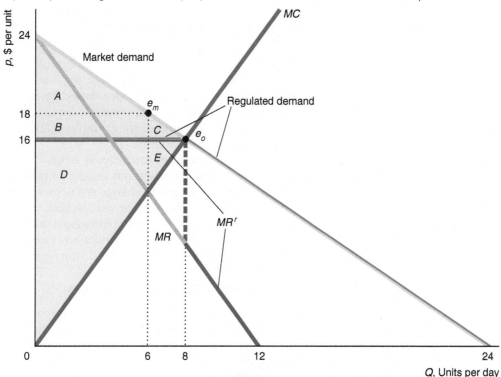

	Monopoly without Regulation	Monopoly with Optimal Regulation	Change
Consumer Surplus, CS	A	$A + B + C$	$B + C$
Producer Surplus, PS	$B + D$	$D + E$	$E - B$
Total Surplus, $TS = CS + PS$	$A + B + D$	$A + B + C + D + E$	$C + E$
Deadweight Loss, DWL	$C + E$	0	$-C - E$

at an output of 8 units. The regulated monopoly optimum, e_o, occurs where the MC curve intersects the market demand curve. Thus, setting a price ceiling where the MC curve and market demand curve intersect eliminates the deadweight loss of monopoly.

We know this outcome is economically efficient because it is the same as the competitive market equilibrium. It occurs where the marginal cost equals price so that total surplus is maximized (Chapter 8). As the table accompanying Figure 16.1 shows, efficient regulation eliminates the deadweight loss from unregulated monopoly, $C + E$.

Non-Optimal Price Regulation Due to Poor Information. Well-intentioned government regulators often fail to regulate monopolies optimally because of limited information about the monopoly's demand and cost curves. Consequently, the regulators may mistakenly set the price cap above or below the competitive level.

If regulators rely on the monopoly or on industry experts for information, they may be misled. For example, a regulated monopoly might deliberately overstate its costs so that regulators impose an excessively high price cap.

If the government sets the price ceiling below the optimal price but high enough that the firm does not shut down, a different deadweight loss results. The regulated firm chooses to sell less than consumers want at the regulated price, creating excess demand. Consumers who are lucky enough to buy the good are better off because they can buy goods at a lower price than with optimal regulation. However, other potential customers are frustrated because the monopoly will not sell them the good. Some of those frustrated consumers are willing to pay more than marginal cost, and their inability to buy the good is a loss of potential surplus or inefficiency, as Q&A 16.1 shows.

Q&A 16.1

Suppose that a government regulates a monopoly by setting a maximum price, p_2, that is below the economically efficient level, which is p_1 in the figure, but above the monopoly's minimum average cost. How do the price, quantity sold, quantity demanded, and total surplus under this regulation compare to those under optimal regulation?

	Monopoly with Optimal Regulation	Monopoly with a Low Regulated Price	Change
Consumer Surplus, CS	$A + B$	$A + C$	$C - B$
Producer Surplus, PS	$C + D + E$	E	$-C - D$
Total Surplus, $TS = CS + PS$	$A + B + C + D + E$	$A + C + E$	$-B - D = -DWL$

Answer

1. *Describe the optimally regulated outcome.* With optimal regulation, e_1, the price is set at p_1, where the market demand curve intersects the monopoly's marginal cost curve on the accompanying graph. The optimally regulated monopoly sells Q_1 units.

2. *Describe the outcome when the government regulates the price at p_2.* Where the market demand is above p_2, the regulated demand curve for the monopoly is horizontal at p_2 (up to Q_d). The corresponding regulated marginal revenue curve, MR^r, is horizontal where the regulated demand curve is horizontal. At the kink in the regulated demand curve where it starts sloping down, the MR^r drops, as the dashed line shows, to the original, downward-sloping marginal revenue line, MR. The monopoly maximizes its profit by selling Q_2 units at p_2. The new regulated monopoly optimum is e_2, where MR^r intersects MC. The firm does not shut down when regulated as long as its average variable cost at Q_2 is less than p_2.

3. *Compare the outcomes.* The quantity that the monopoly sells falls from Q_1 to Q_2 when the government lowers its price ceiling from p_1 to p_2. At that low price, consumers want to buy Q_d, so excess demand equals $Q_d - Q_2$. Compared to optimal regulation, total surplus is lower by at least $B + D$.

Comment: The total surplus loss is even greater if unlucky consumers waste time trying to buy the good unsuccessfully or if the good is allocated non-optimally among consumers. A consumer who values the good at only p_2 may be lucky enough to buy it, while a consumer who values the good at p_1 or more may not be able to obtain it.

Non-Optimal Price Regulation Due to Inability to Subsidize. Because regulators generally cannot subsidize a monopoly, they cannot set the price as low as the marginal cost if the firm would lose money at that price and choose to shut down. For example, if the production process exhibits economies of scale over all relevant levels of output, average cost falls with output and exceeds marginal cost everywhere (Chapter 9). As a result, if the regulator sets the price equal to marginal cost, the price is less than average cost, so the firm cannot profitably produce and shuts down. Unless the regulators are willing to subsidize the firm, the regulators must raise the price to a level where the firm at least breaks even or society loses the product altogether. If the firm shuts down, society's deadweight loss is the loss in total (potential) surplus.

This example illustrates the well-known saying that "the perfect is the enemy of the good." Here, attempting to achieve perfection—using efficient marginal cost pricing—causes a problem by forcing the firm to shut down. A better regulation is to set the price cap equal to the average cost so that the firm continues to operate. Here, average-cost pricing is a Pareto improvement over (unsubsidized) marginal cost pricing. Both consumers and producers are better off under average cost pricing than if the firm is forced out of business even though deadweight loss is not eliminated.

Mini-Case

Natural Gas Regulation

Because U.S. natural gas monopolies usually have significant economies of scale and regulators generally cannot subsidize them, the regulated price is set above marginal cost, creating a deadweight loss. The figure uses the estimates of Davis and Muehlegger (2010).[3] If unregulated, this monopoly would sell 12.1 trillion cubic feet of natural gas per year, where its marginal revenue and marginal cost curves intersect. It would charge the corresponding price on the demand curve at point *a*. Its profit is the rectangle labeled *A*, with a length equal to the quantity, 12.1 trillion cubic feet, and a height equal to the difference between the price at *a* and the corresponding average cost.

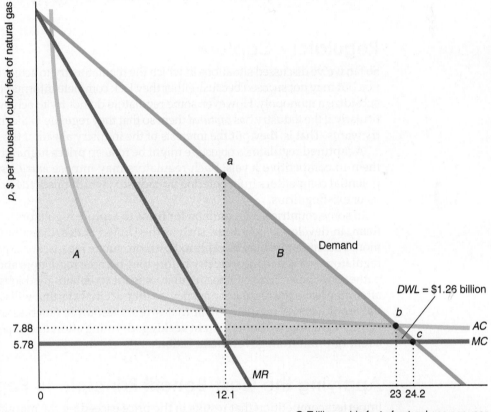

To eliminate deadweight loss, the government should set the price ceiling equal to the marginal cost of $5.78 per thousand cubic feet of natural gas so that the monopoly behaves like a price taker. The price ceiling or marginal cost curve hits the demand curve at *c*, where the quantity is 24.2 trillion cubic feet per year—double the unregulated quantity. At that quantity, the regulated utility would lose money. The average cost at that quantity is $7.78 (slightly less than the average cost of $7.88 at a quantity of 23 trillion cubic feet). The regulated

---

[3]We use their most conservative estimate: the one that produces the smallest deadweight loss. We approximate their demand curve with a linear one that has the same price elasticity of demand of −0.2 at point *b*. This figure represents the aggregation of state-level monopolies to the national level.

price, $5.78, is less than the average cost at that quantity of $7.78, so it would lose $2 on each thousand cubic feet it sells, or $48.4 billion in total. Thus, it would be willing to sell this quantity at this price only if the government subsidizes it.

Typically, it is politically infeasible for a government regulatory agency to subsidize a monopoly. On average, the natural gas regulatory agencies set the price at $7.88 per thousand cubic feet, where the demand curve intersects the average cost curve and the monopoly breaks even, point *b*. The monopoly sells 23 trillion cubic feet per year. The corresponding price, $7.88, is 36% above marginal cost, $5.78. The deadweight loss is $1.26 billion annually, which is the small, dark gray triangle labeled *DWL*. Without regulation, the deadweight loss would be much greater: this area plus area *B*.

Regulatory Capture

So far, we've discussed situations in which the regulators try to achieve efficient regulation but may not succeed because either they lack complete information or they cannot subsidize a monopoly. However, some regulators do not try to achieve efficiency, particularly if the industry has *captured* them so that they regulate in the manner the industry wants. That is, they put the interests of the industry ahead of the public interest.

A captured regulator's objective might be to keep prices high rather than to lower them to competitive levels. Such regulators may impose *entry restrictions* to keep potential competitors from entering an industry, which raises the price and the profits of existing firms.

In some countries, it is common for firms to capture regulators by directly bribing them. In developed countries, such as the United States, direct bribery is not common, but regulators may be captured by more subtle means. For example, many U.S. regulators worked in the industry before they became regulators and hence are sympathetic to those firms.[4] Other regulators want to obtain good jobs in the industry after they leave the regulatory agency, so they act in ways that will not offend potential employers. A regulated firm that invests resources (such as explicit bribes or taking regulators to dinner) is **rent seeking**: devoting effort and expenditures to gain a rent or profit from government actions.

Applying the Cost-Benefit Principle to Regulation

Imperfect competition that results in the price exceeding the marginal cost causes a market failure. Therefore, most imperfectly competitive markets—everything from restaurants to jet aircraft—suffer from market failure.

Would regulating each of these markets increase total surplus? No, because a regulation would not pass a cost-benefit test in some markets. Regulation has its own costs. It may be difficult or costly for regulators to gather the information they need, regulators may make honest mistakes, or the industry may capture regulators. Firms in the industry may engage in costly rent-seeking activities. Price regulation, or regulation of any type, passes a cost-benefit test only when the market failure is large enough that the benefits from significantly reducing it exceed the cost associated with regulation.

---

[4]Overall, 40% of state oil and gas regulators have industry connections. Indeed, five of nine members of the Arkansas regulatory commission own drilling companies and two others are officers of such companies (Mike Soraghan, "40% of State Drilling Regulators Have Industry Ties," *Greenwire*, December 19, 2011.)

16.3 Antitrust Law and Competition Policy

Rather than regulate firms that set high prices, a government may forbid firms from collectively setting high prices—that is, acting like a cartel (Chapter 11). These laws are called *antitrust laws* in the United States and *competition policies* in many other countries.

In the late nineteenth century, cartels, then called *trusts*, were legal and were common in the United States. Oil, railroad, sugar, and tobacco trusts raised prices substantially above competitive levels.[5] In response to the trusts' high prices, the U.S. Congress passed the Sherman Antitrust Act in 1890 and the Federal Trade Commission Act of 1914, which prohibited firms from *explicitly* agreeing to take actions that reduce competition.[6] In particular, cartels that jointly set prices are strictly prohibited. In legal jargon, price fixing is a *per se* violation: It is strictly against the law, and firms have no possible mitigating justifications. By imposing penalties on firms caught colluding, government agencies seek to discourage cartels from forming.

The Antitrust Division of the Department of Justice (DOJ) and the Federal Trade Commission (FTC) divide the responsibility for U.S. antitrust policy. The Antitrust Division states that its mission is "to promote economic competition through . . . promoting free and fair competition in the marketplace." The FTC's objective is "to prevent unfair methods of competition in commerce" and "to administer . . . other consumer protection laws." Both U.S. agencies can use criminal and civil law to attack cartels, price fixing, and other anticompetitive actions.

Recently, the U.S. Department of Justice, quoting the Supreme Court that collusion is the "supreme evil of antitrust," stated that prosecuting cartels was its "top enforcement priority." However, cartels persist despite these laws, for three reasons. First, some international cartels and cartels within certain countries operate legally. In 1960, five major oil-exporting countries—Iran, Iraq, Kuwait, Saudi Arabia, and Venezuela—created the Organization of Petroleum Exporting Countries (OPEC), which is an international cartel.[7] In 1971, OPEC members agreed to take an active role in setting oil prices.

Second, some illegal cartels believe that they can avoid detection or that the punishment will be insignificant. At least until recently, they were often correct. For example, in a cartel case involving the $9 billion U.S. carpet industry, a firm with $150 million in annual sales agreed with the DOJ to plead guilty and pay a fine of $150,000. It is difficult to imagine that a fine of one-tenth of 1% of annual sales significantly deters cartel behavior.

However, starting in the 1990s, U.S. authorities greatly increased the size of fines for price-fixing. For example, in 1996, Archer Daniels Midland (ADM) agreed to

---

[5]Nineteenth-century and early twentieth-century *robber barons* who made fortunes from these cartels include John Jacob Astor (real estate, fur), Andrew Carnegie (railroads, steel), Henry Clay Frick (steel), Jay Gould (finance, railroads), Mark Hopkins (railroads), J. P. Morgan (banking), John D. Rockefeller (oil), Leland Stanford (railroads), and Cornelius Vanderbilt (railroads, shipping).

[6]U.S. law does not prohibit all cartels. For example, a bizarre Supreme Court decision largely exempted Major League Baseball from antitrust laws (**www.slate.com/articles/news_and_politics/ history_lesson/2002/07/baseballs_con_game.html**). Unions are explicitly exempt from antitrust laws. Workers may act collectively to raise wages. A historical justification for exempting labor unions was that the workers faced employers that could exercise monopsony power.

[7]As of 2018, OPEC had 15 member countries, including the 5 original members. The newest members are Equatorial Guinea (2017) and Congo (2018).

pay what was then a record U.S. antitrust fine of $100 million for price-fixing of citric acid (used in many consumer products) and lysine (an animal feed additive). In 2004, ADM agreed to pay a much larger amount, $400 million, to settle a price-fixing lawsuit brought by purchasers of its high-fructose corn syrup (used mainly to sweeten soft drinks).

We can't legally discuss price. However, look at how many sugar cubes I can stack!

Third, some firms are able to coordinate their activities without explicitly colluding and thereby running afoul of competition laws. To determine guilt, U.S. antitrust laws require evidence of conspiracy (such as explicit agreements) rather than the economic effect of the suspected cartel. Charging monopoly-level prices is not necessarily illegal—only the "bad behavior" of explicitly agreeing to raise prices is against the law. As a result, some groups of firms charge monopoly-level prices without violating competition laws. These firms may *tacitly collude* without meeting by signaling to each other through their actions. If one firm raises its price and keeps it high only if other firms follow its lead, it is not necessarily violating the law if the firms did not explicitly communicate.

For example, shortly before Thanksgiving in 2012, United Airlines announced a fare increase. However, when rivals failed to match this increase, United rolled back its fares the next day. Shortly thereafter, the president of US Airways observed that if Southwest Airlines, the firm that carries the most passengers, fails to match an increase by other airlines, rivals cancel their increase.[8]

Canada enacted the world's first antitrust statute in 1889, one year before the U.S. Sherman Act. Canada's current Competition Act regulates most business conduct. It contains both criminal and civil provisions that prohibit anticompetitive practices and that are enforced by the Competition Bureau. As under U.S. law, price-fixing cartels are *per se* illegal and are subject to civil and criminal punishment. Australia and New Zealand have laws on cartels that are similar to those in Canada and the United States.

In the past, the German, Japanese, and British governments permitted some cartels to operate because these governments felt doing so would promote economic efficiency. However, in recent years, most developed countries have followed Canada and the United States in strictly prohibiting cartels. The European Union's competition policy under the Treaty of the European Community (EC Treaty or Treaty of Rome) in 1957 gives the European Union and member states substantial civil powers to prevent actions that hinder competition, including formation of cartels. Price fixing is *per se* illegal.

The DOJ, the FTC, the Canadian Competition Bureau, and the European Union authorities have become increasingly aggressive, prosecuting many more cases and increasing fines dramatically. Following the lead of the United States, which imposes both civil and criminal penalties, the British government introduced legislation in

---

[8]Charisse Jones, "United Airlines Hikes Fares; Will Rivals Follow?" *USA Today*, October 11, 2012; "US Airways President Talks About Southwest Fares," *Businessweek*, October 24, 2012.

2002 to criminalize certain cartel-related conduct. In 2004, Japan started pursuing antitrust cases more aggressively.

In 1993, the DOJ introduced the Corporate Leniency Program, guaranteeing that cartel whistle-blowers will receive immunity from federal prosecution. Consequently, the DOJ has caught, prosecuted, and fined several gigantic cartels. In 2002, European authorities adopted a similar policy.

In addition to making price fixing strictly illegal, these competition laws restrict mergers between firms and ban abusive behavior by firms that dominate a market. In addition, such laws limit various vertical relationships between firms (relationships governing how firms deal with their suppliers and their customers in the supply chain).[9]

Increasingly, antitrust authorities from around the world are coordinating activities. Cooperation agreements exist between authorities in Canada, Mexico, Europe, Australia, New Zealand, and the United States, among others. Such government collaboration is critical given the increasingly global scope of the firms engaged in collusion and other anticompetitive activities.

U.S. authorities cooperated with competition authorities in Canada, Europe, and Japan over price fixing of auto parts, the largest price-fixing case in U.S. legal history. By 2018, the accused companies had paid nearly $3 billion in U.S. fines and an additional $1.3 billion in private lawsuits, and several executives had received jail sentences.[10]

Mergers

If antitrust or competition laws prevent firms from colluding, firms could try to achieve the same end by merging to form a monopoly. To prevent this potential problem, most antitrust and competition laws restrict the ability of firms to merge if the net effect is to harm society.

Large U.S. firms that want to merge must submit their proposed merger to either the DOJ or the FTC for approval. These agencies block mergers they believe would harm society. However, firms can appeal such a decision to the federal courts. Most other developed countries have similar merger review procedures.

Would banning all mergers increase economic efficiency? No, because some mergers reduce production costs substantially. Formerly separate firms may become more efficient because of greater scale, the sharing of trade secrets, or the closure of duplicative retail outlets. For example, when Chase and Chemical banks merged, they closed or combined seven Manhattan branches that were located within two blocks of other branches.

Whether a merger helps or harms society depends on which of its two offsetting effects—reducing competition and increasing efficiency—is larger. Consider two extreme cases. In one, the merger of the only two firms in the market does not lower costs, but it increases monopoly power, so the newly merged firm substantially raises prices to consumers. Here, the merger hurts society. At the other extreme, two of a large number of firms in the market merge, with substantial cost savings, but with no noticeable increase in market power or market price. Here, the merger benefits society.

---

[9]The FTC has a broader range of other responsibilities that include *consumer protection*, such as preventing misleading advertising, which we do not discuss here.

[10]See **www.rubbernews.com/article/20180521/NEWS/180529991/price-fixing-payouts-top-4-billion**.

The contentious cases lie in the middle, where market power increases significantly *and* costs decrease. However, if the price falls after the merger because the cost reduction effect dominates the increased market power effect, the merger is desirable.

| Mini-Case | Why should governments worry about mergers that create monopolies? Won't the resulting higher price and profit attract new firms into the market? That |

Mini-Case

Are Monopoly Mergers Harmful?

Why should governments worry about mergers that create monopolies? Won't the resulting higher price and profit attract new firms into the market? That argument makes sense if firms do not have to incur substantial sunk costs to enter and the market has no other entry barriers. But, if new firms are unlikely to enter, then governments should worry about mergers. Thus, in judging whether to permit a merger, governments consider the difficulty of entry.

Collard-Wexler (2014) provided an example of why entry is important in the ready-mix concrete industry. Although the United States has about 5,000 ready-mix concrete plants, few of them directly compete. Given high shipping costs, the country has at least 449 small, local markets. New plants must incur substantial, sunk entry costs. He found that it takes nine to ten years for a new firm to enter the market following a merger to monopoly. Thus, if the only two firms in a local market merge, the resulting firm can earn monopoly profits for the better part of a decade, generating damages nearly eight times those from one year of monopoly.

Q&A 16.2

A1 Concrete and Apex Concrete are Cournot duopoly producers of ready-mix concrete. The market inverse demand function is $p = a - bQ = 80 - 0.5Q$. Each firm has a constant marginal cost $m = 20$ and no fixed costs. The firms are considering a merger. Such a move may reduce their marginal cost. Use a spreadsheet to show the quantity, price, consumer surplus, profit, and total surplus under Cournot duopoly and a (merged) monopoly. Remember that a Cournot duopoly facing a linear inverse demand function $p = a - bQ$ and with constant marginal cost m produces market output $Q = 2(a - m)/3b$ (see Chapter 11) and a profit-maximizing monopoly produces $Q = (a - m)/2b$ (see Chapter 9). Is total surplus after the merger higher or lower than under duopoly if the marginal cost falls to 16 or to 12? How much would marginal cost have to fall to avoid a reduction in consumer surplus?

Augment the following spreadsheet to calculate the quantity, price, consumer surplus (*CS*), profit, and total surplus (*TS*) if the two firms merge to form a monopoly for values of marginal cost ranging from 0 to 20 in increments of 4.

Answer

1. *In the Excel spreadsheet enter the relevant formulas in cells B3 through B7.* Using the formula for the duopoly quantity, enter "=2*(80−B2)/(3*0.5)" in cell B3. Using the inverse demand function, enter "=80−0.5*B3" for the price in cell B4. Using standard formulas for consumer surplus, profit, and total surplus, enter "=0.5*(80−B4)*B3" in cell B5, "=(B4−B2)*B3 in cell B6, and "=B5+B6" in cell B7.[11]

---

[11]Chapter 8 discusses surplus measures and how to calculate them. Consumer surplus is the area under the demand curve and above the price, which is 0.5 (80 − *p*)*Q* in this case.

	A	B	C	D	E	F	G	H
1		Duopoly			Monopoly			
2	m	20	0	4	8	12	16	20
3	Q							
4	p							
5	CS							
6	Profit							
7	TS							

2. *Enter the relevant formulas in columns C through H. Enter* "=(80−C2)/(2*0.5) in cell C3. Copy cells B4 through B7 and paste them into cells C4 through C7. Copy cells C3 through C7 and paste them into columns D through H.*

3. *Compare total surplus under duopoly to that under monopoly for m = 16 and m = 12.* We have highlighted cell B7 in blue, showing that total surplus is 3,200 under duopoly. We have highlighted cell G7 in pink, showing total surplus is less under monopoly if marginal cost m falls to 16. Cell F7, highlighted in green, shows that total surplus is higher under monopoly if m falls to 12.

4. *Compare consumer surplus under duopoly and monopoly by examining row 5.* We have highlighted cell B5 showing that consumer surplus is 1,600 under duopoly. As long as marginal cost is positive, the merger always reduces consumer surplus. Only if marginal cost drops to zero (shown in the yellow highlighted cell C5) is consumer surplus as high as under duopoly.

	A	B	C	D	E	F	G	H
1		Duopoly			Monopoly			
2	m	20	0	4	8	12	16	20
3	Q	80	80	76	72	68	64	60
4	p	40	40	42	44	46	48	50
5	CS	1600	1600	1444	1296	1156	1024	900
6	Profit	1600	3200	2888	2592	2312	2048	1800
7	TS	3200	4800	4332	3888	3468	3072	2700

Predatory Actions

Antitrust policy also seeks to prevent other actions that harm society, such as predatory pricing. A firm engages in *predatory pricing* if it charges a price below marginal cost (or average cost in some jurisdictions) so as to drive its rivals out of business and then raise its price.

Presumably, if the firm that engages in predation has deep pockets and its rivals do not, it can absorb short-run losses until its rivals leave the market. However, the firm does not benefit from predatory behavior if its rivals or other firms reenter the market as soon as it raises its price. Thus, for a firm to benefit from engaging in predation, something must prevent firms from reentering the market when the predatory firm eventually raises its price. In 1993, the U.S. Supreme Court agreed with this reasoning in *Brooke Group Ltd. v. Brown and Williamson Tobacco Corp.* Since then, the federal government has brought few predation cases and has won none.

Vertical Relationships

Laws that forbid price fixing and predatory practices and limit mergers are directed at *horizontal* interactions between firms that compete directly in a given industry. Antitrust policy also addresses vertical interactions between a firm and its customers or suppliers. Vertical actions that competition authorities investigate include resale price maintenance, refusal to deal, exclusive dealing, and price discrimination.

Resale Price Maintenance.
A manufacturer engages in *resale price maintenance* (RPM) if it requires the retailers that sell its product to charge a price no lower than a price it specifies. (Price ceilings are also possible, but not frequently observed.) The rule on RPM does not apply if the manufacturer only *suggests* a price and does not require it.

At one time, RPM was *per se* illegal in the United States. That is, this practice was strictly banned with no appeal to mitigating circumstances. However, in 2007, the U.S. Supreme Court changed to a *rule of reason* (or cost-benefit) approach where an RPM rule is illegal only if it has a net negative effect on competition.

This legal decision is consistent with an argument made by many economists. Usually, a manufacturer wants its dealers to add as small a markup as possible to its wholesale price to keep the price low to final consumers so that they buy many units. That is, both the manufacturer and consumers prefer low markups by dealers. However, for some products, the amount sold depends on promotional or informational activities by retailers as well as price, as when a camera store salesperson demonstrates a camera's features to potential customers. If discounters such as internet firms can sell the camera at lower prices without providing such services, few camera stores can afford to provide these services. A store owner who tried to provide this service would find that many customers would come into the store to learn about the product but then would purchase the camera from a discount store. Therefore, the manufacturer wants all dealers to charge a relatively high price to encourage the provision of these valuable information services.

Today, restrictions on dealers' prices or other activities are usually legal if the manufacturer acts unilaterally. However, if the manufacturer tries to coordinate its actions with other manufacturers, then RPM and related restrictions are an attempt to create a cartel.

Refusal to Deal.
Some firms *integrate*, selling both the final product in the *downstream market* and the key input to this product in the *upstream market*. An integrated aluminum firm not only produces and sells aluminum, but also produces bauxite, the main input required to make aluminum. If such a firm is *dominant*—has a very large share—in both markets, and it refuses to sell the input to other downstream rivals, it may be charged with a *refusal to deal*. The law is still evolving in this area. In general, a firm does not have an obligation to sell to another firm. However, if a dominant firm such as a monopoly refuses to sell to one firm what it sells to others, it needs to provide a sound business reason for its actions other than an attempt to destroy competition.

U.S. courts are more likely to find a firm (or a group of firms) guilty of illegally refusing to deal if the firm has an **essential facility**: a scarce resource that a rival needs to use to survive. The classic example is a century-old case in which all the railroad bridges into St. Louis were owned by a group of railroads. The U.S. Supreme Court was concerned that these railroad companies could keep rivals from serving St. Louis. The Court ruled that the owning group had to provide access to rival railroads on reasonable terms.

Exclusive Dealing. A concept similar to refusal to deal is *exclusive dealing*, which arises when a firm will sell its product only to customers who agree to buy from that firm and not from its rivals. Or the relationship can be reversed: An upstream firm could be forced to sell to only one buyer and not to the buyer's rivals. (Chapter 13 discusses the theory of exclusive dealing.)

Exclusive contracts can promote efficiency and competition in the market by guaranteeing a source of supply, lowering transaction costs, or creating dealer loyalty. The courts have found that exclusive dealing contracts between a manufacturer and its dealers are lawful if they increase competition between this manufacturer and its rivals. However, exclusive contracts are illegal if a monopoly uses them to prevent new firms from entering the market and, more generally, if competition is significantly damaged.

Mini-Case

Piping Up About Exclusive Dealing

As of 2016, McWane, Inc., the dominant U.S. producer of pipe fittings, was forced to end its exclusive dealing practices after exhausting legal appeals to a Federal Trade Commission ruling. The primary purchasers of pipe fittings, which join pipes and direct the flow of water, are municipal water authorities and their contractors.

McWane was the only domestic supplier of pipe fittings until Star Pipe Products entered the market. McWane responded by informing customers that it was implementing a "Full Support Program." Essentially, if the customers did not buy exclusively from McWane, they could be cut off for 12 weeks and lose unpaid rebates. McWane's internal documents showed that the purpose was to raise Star's cost and prevent it from becoming a viable competitor. This policy kept Star's market share small, prevented another firm from entering the market, and allowed McWane to repeatedly increase its prices. The Court held that the program had no procompetitive benefits.

McWane claimed that because its policy was nonbinding and of short duration, the law did not apply. They were wrong.

Price Discrimination. Under the U.S. Robinson-Patman Act of 1936, *price discrimination* (Chapter 10) is legal unless it harms competition. For example, price discrimination is probably illegal if a manufacturer sells a good at a lower price to only one of several downstream firms, which may allow the favored customer to drive its rivals out of business.

A firm accused of a Robinson-Patman Act violation has two possible defenses. A price concession offered to one firm but not to its rivals can be justified if it is due to cost differences, such as a volume discount to a larger firm, or because it is offered in good faith to meet a competitor's price.

16.4 Externalities

An **externality** occurs when a person's well-being or a firm's production capability is directly affected by the actions of other consumers or firms rather than indirectly through changes in prices. The effect is *external* in the sense that it occurs outside a market and hence has no associated price. A firm whose production process lets off fumes that harm its neighbors is creating an externality for which no market exists. In contrast, the firm is not causing an externality when it harms a rival by selling extra output that lowers the market price.

Externalities may either help or harm others. An externality that harms someone is a *negative externality*. You are harmed if your neighbors keep you awake by playing loud music late at night. A chemical plant creates a negative externality when it dumps its waste into the water, reducing the profits of a firm that rents boats on the lake and the utility of visitors to the lake. A *positive externality* benefits others. By installing attractive shrubs and outdoor sculpture around its building, a firm provides a positive externality to its neighbors.

A single action may confer positive externalities on some people and negative externalities on others. The smell of perfume pleases some people, but causes an unpleasant allergic reaction in others. Some people think that their wind chimes please their neighbors, whereas anyone with an ounce of sense would realize that those chimes drive us crazy! It was reported that efforts to clean up the air in Los Angeles, while helping people breathe more easily, caused harmful ultraviolet (UV) radiation levels to increase more rapidly as cleaner air filtered out less of the sun's UV emissions.

Managerial Implication Disney Internalizes an Externality	A firm may be missing an opportunity if it creates positive externalities for another company. Walt Disney made relatively few mistakes. But one that he greatly regretted concerned the positive externalities from his highly successful theme park, Disneyland. When he built Disneyland in Anaheim, California, in the early 1950s, this little town was surrounded by acres of orange groves. Disney purchased 160 acres of orange groves and built his Magic Kingdom. Eventually, it grew to 300 acres. Soon after the park opened, it was surrounded by hotels, gift shops, restaurants, and other businesses that benefited from the crowds that Disneyland attracted. Not only was Disney losing that business, but he worried that the tackiness of the surrounding businesses could harm his theme park. He vowed that he'd never make that mistake again. Early in the 1960s, he set up dozens of dummy corporations (with names like "M. T. Lott") to buy land southwest of Orlando. The Walt Disney Company acquired 30,000 acres, or 47 square miles, of land, which is the size of San Francisco, California, and twice as big as Manhattan. Eventually, the company built four theme parks including Walt Disney World, but they occupied only 7,100 acres. Because Disney owns all the surrounding land, a visitor to Walt Disney World who wants to stay at a hotel, eat at a restaurant, or buy a souvenir now deals directly with Disney, and no one else. That is, Disney *internalized the externality* by capturing the potential externality for itself.

The Inefficiency of Competition with Externalities

Competitive firms and consumers do not have to pay for the harm caused by negative externalities, so they create excessive amounts. Similarly, if producers are not compensated for the benefits of a positive externality, too little of such externalities is produced.

Externalities create a market failure, causing economic inefficiency. To illustrate why externalities cause such inefficiency, we examine a competitive market in which firms produce paper and emit by-products of the production process—such as air and water pollution—that harm people who live near paper mills. (The paper industry is a major industrial source of water pollution.)

To make the point as clearly as possible, we assume initially that each additional ton of paper produced increases these harmful emissions and that the only way to decrease the volume of emissions is to reduce the amount of paper manufactured. No alternative technologies that reduce pollution are available, and it is not possible to locate plants where the emissions harm no one.

Paper firms do not have to pay for the harm their emissions cause. As a result, each firm's **private cost** includes its direct costs of production (such as the cost of inputs), but does not include costs imposed on others. The true **social cost** consists of all the costs incurred by society, including the private costs of firms and individuals and the harm from externalities.

We use a supply-and-demand diagram for the paper market in Figure 16.2 to illustrate that *a competitive market produces excessive pollution because the firms' private cost is less than the social cost.* In the competitive equilibrium, the firms consider only their private costs in making decisions and ignore the harm of the pollution externality they inflict on others. The market supply curve is the aggregate *private marginal cost* curve, MC^p, which is the horizontal sum of the private marginal cost curves of each of the paper manufacturing firms.

The intersection of the market supply curve and the market demand curve for paper determines the competitive equilibrium, e_c. The competitive equilibrium quantity is $Q_c = 105$ tons per day, and the competitive equilibrium price is $p_c = \$240$ per ton.

The firms' *private producer surplus* is the producer surplus of the paper mills based on their *private marginal cost* curve: the area $F + G + H$, which is below the market price and above MC^p up to the competitive equilibrium quantity, 105. The competitive equilibrium maximizes the sum of consumer surplus and private producer surplus. In the absence of an externality, the sum of consumer surplus and private producer surplus equals total surplus, so competition maximizes total surplus.

When we introduced surplus measures in Chapter 8, we considered examples in which the total surplus associated with a particular market consisted of the sum of producer surplus and consumer surplus. However, externalities impose additional costs that are not captured by total surplus if the producer surplus is calculated using the supply curves based only on firms' private costs. To properly measure total surplus, we need to calculate producer surplus based on the full social costs.

Because the paper market produces pollution, the competitive equilibrium does *not* maximize the correct measure of total surplus, which takes into account the harm from the externality. Competitive firms produce too much pollution because they do not have to pay for the harm caused by the externality. This market failure results from competitive forces that equalize the price and *private marginal cost* rather than the *social marginal cost*, which includes both the private costs of production and the external damage.

FIGURE 16.2 Welfare Effects of Pollution in a Competitive Market

The competitive equilibrium, e_c, is determined by the intersection of the demand curve and the competitive supply or private marginal cost curve, MC^P, which ignores the cost of pollution. The social optimum, e_s, is at the intersection of the demand curve and the social marginal cost curve, $MC^S = MC^P + MC^X$, where MC^X is the marginal cost of the pollution. Private producer surplus is based on the MC^P curve, and social producer surplus is based on the MC^S curve.

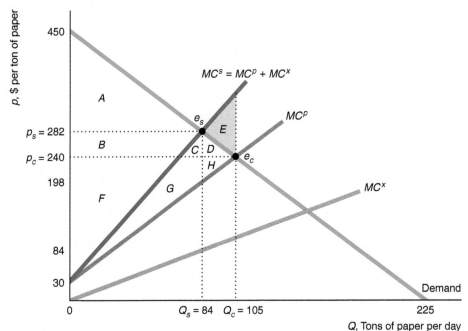

	Private	Social Optimum	Change
Consumer Surplus, CS	$A + B + C + D$	A	$-B - C - D$
Private Producer Surplus, PS_p	$F + G + H$	$B + C + F + G$	$B + C - H$
Externality Cost, C_x	$C + D + E + G + H$	$C + G$	$-D - E - H$
Social Producer Surplus, $PS_s = PS_p - C_x$	$F - C - D - E$	$B + F$	$B + C + D + E$
Total Surplus, $TS = CS + PS_s$	$A + B + F - E$	$A + B + F$	$E = DWL$

For a given amount of paper production, the full cost of one more ton of paper to society, the *social marginal cost* (MC^s), is the cost of manufacturing one more ton of paper to the paper firms plus the additional external damage to people in the community from producing this last ton of paper. Thus, the height of the social marginal cost curve, MC^s, at any given quantity equals the vertical sum of the height of the MC^p curve (the private marginal cost of producing another ton of paper) plus the height of the MC^x curve (the marginal external damage) at that quantity.

The social marginal cost curve intersects the demand curve at the socially efficient quantity, $Q_s = 84$. At smaller quantities, the price—the value consumers place on the last unit of the good sold—is higher than the full social marginal cost. The gain to consumers of paper exceeds the cost of producing an extra unit of output (and hence an extra unit of pollution). At larger quantities, the price is below the social marginal cost, so the gain to consumers is less than the cost of producing an extra unit.

Total surplus is maximized where price equals social marginal cost. At this output level no deadweight loss occurs, so the result is Pareto efficient. Total surplus equals $A + B + F$: the area between the demand curve and the MC^s curve up to the optimal quantity, 84 tons of paper.

Total surplus at the competitive equilibrium, e_c, is lower: $A + B + F - E$, the areas between the demand curve and the MC^s curve up to 105 tons of paper. The area between these curves from 84 to 105, E, is a deadweight loss because the social cost exceeds the value that consumers place on these last 21 tons of paper. *A deadweight loss results because the competitive market equates price with private marginal cost instead of with social marginal cost.*

Total surplus is higher at the efficient output level than at the competitive equilibrium because the gain from reducing pollution from the competitive to the efficient level more than offsets the loss to consumers and producers of the paper. The cost of the pollution to people who live near the factories is the area under the MC^x curve between zero and the quantity produced. By construction, this area is the same as the area between the MC^p and the MC^s curves. The total damage from the pollution is $C + D + E + G + H$ at the competitive equilibrium and only $C + G$ at the efficient outcome. Consequently, the extra pollution damage from producing the competitive output rather than the efficient quantity is $D + E + H$. The main beneficiaries from producing at the competitive output level rather than at the efficient level are the paper buyers, who pay $240 rather than $282 for a ton of paper. Their consumer surplus rises from A to $A + B + C + D$.

The figure illustrates two main results with respect to negative externalities. First, *if production generates negative externalities, then a competitive market produces excessive negative externalities*. Because the price of the pollution to the firms is zero, which is less than the marginal cost that the last unit of pollution imposes on society, an unregulated competitive market produces more pollution than is socially optimal.

Second, *the optimal amount of pollution is greater than zero*. Even though pollution is harmful and we'd like to have none of it, we cannot wipe it out without eliminating virtually all production and consumption. Making paper, dishwashers, and televisions creates air and water pollution. Fertilizers used in farming pollute the water supply. Delivery people pollute the air by driving to your home.

Good news. Production's up 13%!

Reducing Externalities

Because competitive markets produce excessive negative externalities, government intervention may provide a social gain. More than 60 years ago, in 1952, London suffered from a particularly thick "peasouper" fog—pollution so dense that people had trouble finding their way home—for five days. This pollution-based fog killed an estimated 4,000 to 12,000 people and caused perhaps 100,000 more to experience significant illness. Those dark days prompted the British government to pass its first Clean Air Act, in 1956. Both the United States and Canada passed a Clean Air Act in 1970.

The Clean Air Act (CAA) of 1970 and the Clean Air Act Amendments of 1990 greatly improved U.S. air quality. Between 1980 and 2017, the national average atmospheric concentration of sulfur dioxide (SO_2) plummeted 90%, carbon monoxide (CO) fell 84%, nitrogen dioxide (NO_2) tumbled 60%, and ozone dropped 32%. From 1990 to 2017, particulate matter (PM10) in the air decreased by 34%.[12]

The Environmental Protection Agency (EPA, 2011) estimated that the CAA saved over 160,000 lives in 2010 and forecast that it will be responsible for saving over 230,000 lives per year by 2020. The main benefits come from reducing respiratory problems and heart disease, avoiding millions of lost workdays and over 100,000 hospital visits every year. Using data from the pre-2011 period and forecasts up to 2020, the EPA estimated the costs of complying with the Clean Air Act at $65 billion for the 1990–2020 period, but estimated the benefits at $2 trillion, implying a benefit-to-cost ratio of more than 30 to 1.

Politicians around the world disagree about how and whether to control pollution. In 2012 at the United Nations (U.N.) Rio+20 meeting, 120 heads of state and 50,000 environmentalists, social activists, and business leaders met to encourage sustainable, green growth in poor countries. They argued and accomplished little. The one bright spot is the 2015 Paris Agreement. Each U.N. member country that signed agreed to implement national goals to restrict greenhouse emissions. By the end of 2016, almost the entire U.N. membership had ratified the agreement, including the United States. Russia and Iran were the notable holdouts. However, President Donald Trump gave formal notice in 2017 that the United States would withdraw from the agreement at the first legal opportunity in 2020.

If a government has sufficient knowledge about pollution damage, the demand curve, costs, and the production technology, it can force a competitive market to produce at the social optimum. The government can control pollution directly by restricting the amount of pollution that firms may produce or by taxing them for the pollution they create. A governmental limit on the amount of air pollution that may be released is called an *emissions standard* and a limit on discharges into waterways is an *effluent standard*. Correspondingly, a tax on air pollution is an *emissions fee*, and a tax on water pollution is an *effluent charge*.

Frequently, however, a government controls pollution indirectly, through quantity restrictions or taxes on outputs or inputs. Whether the government restricts or taxes outputs or inputs may depend on the nature of the production process. It is generally more efficient to regulate pollution directly rather than to regulate output. Direct regulation of pollution encourages firms to adopt efficient new technologies to control pollution (a possibility we ignore in our paper mill example).

One alternative to direct government taxation or regulation is for the government or the courts to clearly assign property rights, giving one party the right to pollute or the other party the right to be free from pollution. With clear property rights, pollution can be priced and the externality problem can be reduced or eliminated.

Pollution Standards.   In Figure 16.2 the government can maximize total surplus by forcing the paper mills to produce no more than 84 units of paper per day. Thus, the government can use an output restriction to regulate pollution. Alternatively, the government could impose a *pollution standard*, which limits the amount of pollution released. Because output and pollution move together in this example, regulating either reduces pollution in the same way.

Unfortunately, the government usually does not know enough to regulate optimally. For example, to set quantity restrictions on output optimally, the government must know how the marginal social cost curve, the demand for paper curve, and pollution

---

[12]According to **www.epa.gov/air-trends** (viewed August 31, 2018).

vary with output. The ease with which the government can monitor output and pollution may determine whether it sets an output restriction or a pollution standard.

Even if the government knows enough to set the optimal regulation, it must enforce this regulation to achieve the desired outcome. Though the EPA sets federal pollution standards for major air and water pollutants, obtaining compliance is not easy. The EPA posts online a (long) list of areas that do not meet regulatory standards. For example, in 2018, the large Los Angeles–South Coast Air Basin was in "extreme" noncompliance with the ground-level ozone standard and in the "serious" category for carbon monoxide.[13]

Mini-Case

Pulp and Paper Mill Pollution and Regulation

Pulp and paper mills are major sources of air and water pollution. Air pollution is generated primarily during the pulping process, in which the plant separates the wood fibers from the rest of the tree using various chemical and mechanical methods. Additional pollution occurs during the paper-making process if the paper is chemically treated to produce smoother surfaces.

For simplicity in our example, we assumed that the amount of pollution emitted varied with only output. However, in reality, firms may use less-polluting production technologies (such as pollution-abatement equipment) or may change the input mix to lower the amount of pollution for a given level of output.

Gray and Shimshack (2011) and Alm and Shimshack (2014) summarized many studies on regulating paper mill pollution and concluded that effective regulation can reduce pollution markedly. A 10% increase in pollution-reducing capital lowers emissions for a given amount of paper by 6.9% (Shadbegian and Gray, 2003). Each dollar spent on extra capital stock provides an annual return of about 75¢ in pollution reduction benefits. An additional fine for violating pollution laws induces about a two-thirds reduction in the statewide water pollution violation rate of pulp and paper mills in the year following the fine (Shimshack and Ward, 2005). Inclusion on a public list of noncompliant pulp and paper mills in British Columbia, Canada, produced incentives for pollution control that were similar to a regulatory fine (Foulon, Lanoie, and Laplante, 2002).

Emission Fees. The government may impose costs on polluters by taxing their output or the amount of pollution produced. (Similarly, a law could make a polluter liable for damages in a court.) In our paper mill example, taxing output works as well as taxing the pollution directly because the relationship between output and pollution is fixed. However, if firms can vary the output-pollution relationship by varying inputs or adding pollution-control devices, then it may be more efficient for the government to tax pollution instead of output.

---

[13]See **www3.epa.gov/airquality/greenbook/hnc.html/** and **www3.epa.gov/airquality/greenbook/cmc.html** for details on noncompliance with EPA standards, and go to **scorecard.goodguide.com** to learn about environmental risks in your area.

In our paper mill example, if the government knows the marginal cost of the emissions, MC^x, it can set the output tax, $t(Q)$, which varies with output, Q, equal to this marginal cost curve: $t(Q) = MC^x$. Figure 16.3 illustrates the manufacturers' after-tax marginal cost, $MC^s = MC^p + t(Q)$.

The output tax causes a manufacturer to *internalize the externality*—to bear the cost of the harm that the firm inflicts on others. The after-tax private marginal cost or supply curve is the same as the social marginal cost curve. As a result, the after-tax competitive equilibrium is efficient.

Usually, the government sets a specific tax rather than a tax that varies with the amount of pollution, as MC^x does. As Q&A 16.3 shows, applying an appropriate specific tax results in the socially efficient level of production.

Q&A 16.3

For the market with pollution in Figure 16.3, what constant, specific tax, t, on output could the government set to maximize total surplus?

Answer

Set the specific tax equal to the marginal harm of pollution at the optimal quantity. At the optimal quantity, $Q_s = 84$, the marginal harm from the emissions is $84, as Figure 16.3 shows. If the specific tax is $t = \$84$, the after-tax private marginal cost (after-tax competitive supply curve), $MC^p + t$, equals the social marginal cost at the optimal quantity, where total surplus is maximized. Consequently, the after-tax competitive supply curve intersects the demand curve at the optimal quantity. By paying this specific tax, the firms internalize the cost of the externality at the optimum quantity. All that is required for optimal production is that the tax equal the marginal cost of pollution at the optimum quantity; it need not equal the marginal cost of pollution at other quantities.

FIGURE 16.3 Using Taxes to Control Pollution

Placing a tax on the firms equal to the harm from the pollution, $t(Q) = MC^x$, causes them to internalize the externality, so their private marginal cost is the same as the social marginal cost, MC^x. As a result, the competitive after-tax equilibrium is the same as the social optimum, e_s. Alternatively, applying a specific tax of $t = \$84$ per ton of paper, which is the marginal harm at $Q_s = 84$, also results in the social optimum.

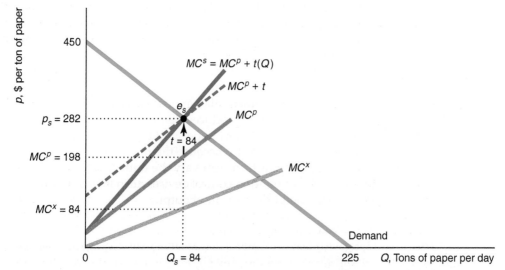

Driving causes many externalities, including pollution, congestion, and accidents. Taking account of pollution from producing fuel and driving, Hill et al. (2009) estimated that burning one gallon of gasoline (including all downstream effects) causes a carbon dioxide–related climate change cost of 37¢ and a health-related cost of conventional pollutants associated with fine particulate matter of 34¢.

A driver imposes delays on other drivers during congested periods. Parry, Walls, and Harrington (2007) estimated that this cost was $1.05 per gallon of gas, on average, across the United States.

Edlin and Karaca-Mandic (2006) measured the accident externality from additional cars by the increase in the cost of insurance. These externalities are big in states with a high concentration of traffic but not in states with low densities. In California, with many cars per mile, an extra driver raises the total statewide insurance costs of other drivers by between $1,725 and $3,239 per year, and a 1% increase in driving raises insurance costs 3.3% to 5.4%.

Vehicles such as SUVs are inefficiently heavy because owners of these tank-like vehicles ignore the greater risk of death they impose on other drivers and pedestrians in accidents (Anderson and Auffhammer, 2014). Raising the weight of a vehicle that hits you by 1,000 pounds increases your chance of dying by 47%. The higher externality risk due to the greater weight of vehicles since 1989 is 26¢ per gallon of gasoline, and the total fatality externality roughly equals a gas tax of between 97¢ and $2.17 per gallon. Taking account of both carbon dioxide emissions and accidents, Sheehan-Connor (2015) estimated that the optimal flat tax is $1.14 per gallon.

Traditionally, governments have relied mainly on gasoline taxes to address driving externalities and to pay for roads. Vehicle taxes and carbon taxes have also been used. However, such taxes have been much lower than the marginal cost of the externalities and have not been adequately sensitive to vehicle weight or the time of day when the vehicle is driven. In California, a tax equal to the marginal externality cost of accidents would raise $66 billion annually—more than the $57 billion raised by all existing state taxes—and over $220 billion nationally.

Gasoline taxes target consumption of gasoline, but gasoline use is not the only problem. Even electric vehicles contribute to congestion and accidents but do not pay a gasoline tax. Some governments have adopted a *vehicle miles traveled tax* (VMT) to either supplement or replace gasoline taxes. Such a tax can be linked to vehicle weight or time of day. As of 2018, Germany, Austria, Slovakia, the Czech Republic, Poland, Hungary, and Switzerland had some form of a VMT. The state of Oregon has a voluntary VMT system in place and several other U.S. states are considering a similar approach.

Assigning Property Rights. Instead of controlling externalities directly through emission fees, effluent charges, or standards, the government may take an indirect approach by assigning a property right. If no one holds a property right for a good or a bad, the good or bad is unlikely to have a price. If you had a property right to be free from air pollution, you could get the courts to prevent a factory next door from emitting smoke. Or you could sell your right, permitting the factory to emit. If you did not have this property right, no one would be willing to pay you a positive price for this right.

Environmental Corporate Social Responsibility. Most major corporations have active corporate social responsibility (CSR) policies, particularly relating to the environment. Ninety-five percent of the 250 largest global companies report their CSR activities (de Bettignies and Robinson, 2015). Many companies assert that they are voluntarily reducing negative externalities. A visit to the website of major oil producer BP shows that *sustainability* is on its top menu, getting equal billing with *customers* and *investors*. In 2015, food giant General Mills announced a planned 28% cut in greenhouse gas emissions and a commitment to use clean energy. CEO Ken Powell stated that "we must do our part to protect and conserve natural resources."[14]

How much does environmental CSR reduce externality problems? CSR activities may be *altruistic*, or they may be *strategic*—that is, intended to increase profit in the long run by creating a positive image for the firm (Chapter 7). Either type of CSR could affect a firm's environmental performance.

Altruistic CSR includes actions firms undertake to help society even though these actions reduce both profit and the value of the firm. In a study of agribusiness firms, Detre and Gunderson (2011) found that a firm's stock price typically falls in the short run when its CSR performance is strong enough for it to join the Dow Jones Sustainability World Index. Such an effect is consistent with altruistic CSR.

It is also possible that publicizing positive environmental practices could be strategic—raising profit and stock prices in the long run, especially given the growth of social media. Twenty years ago many small oil spills and other problems would go largely unnoticed. Now, many Twitter messages cover topics such as "oil spills" and "pollution" and the problems of specific companies on a daily basis.[15] As a result, companies have stronger incentives to minimize environmental harm and pursue (apparently) environment-friendly policies. In effect, internet-based scrutiny induces companies to internalize some of the formerly external costs of their activities.

However, many companies with environmental CSR policies quietly lobby governments to weaken environmental regulation. Such lobbying works to offset the environmental benefits arising from CSR activities (de Bettignies and Robinson, 2018).

The Coase Theorem

Before Ronald Coase published his classic paper in 1960, economists, like other people, suffered from a

Common Confusion A polluter will necessarily pollute more if the government grants it the right to pollute than if the government grants the victim of pollution the right to be free from pollution.

According to the Coase Theorem (Coase, 1960), regardless of which party gets clearly defined property rights, a polluter and its victim may achieve the optimal levels of pollution if they can bargain costlessly.

The Coase Theorem is not a practical solution to most pollution problems. Rather, it demonstrates that a lack of clearly defined property rights is the root of the externality problem.

---

[14]See "General Mills Pledges to Slash Emissions, Spend $100M on Clean Energy," September 8, 2015, **www.eenews.net/**.

[15]For example, like many other companies, ExxonMobil provides its own Twitter feed, and claimed it had 282,000 followers as of September 2018.

To illustrate the Coase Theorem, we consider two adjacent firms, the Fixit Auto Body Shop and the Secret Garden Tea House. Fixit causes noise pollution, which hurts business at the Secret Garden, as Table 16.1 illustrates. If the auto body shop works on more cars per hour, its profit increases, but the resulting extra noise reduces the tea house's profit. The last column shows the total profit of the two firms. Having the auto body shop work on one car per hour maximizes their joint profit. Anything else is inefficient.

Initially, because property rights are not clearly defined, Fixit won't negotiate with the Secret Garden. After all, why would Fixit reduce its output and the associated noise if the Secret Garden has no legal right to be free of noise? Thus, Fixit works on two cars per hour, which maximizes its profit at 400. The resulting excessive noise drives the Secret Garden out of business, so the joint profit is 400.

Now, suppose that the courts grant the Secret Garden the right to silence. If it forces Fixit Auto Body to shut down, the Secret Garden makes 400 and their joint profit is 400. However, if Fixit works on one car at a time, its gain is 300, while the Secret Garden earns 200, which is only 200 less than before. The firms should be able to reach an agreement whereby Fixit pays the tea house between 200 and 300 for the right to work on one car. Under such an agreement, their joint profit is maximized at 500.

Why doesn't Fixit buy the rights to work on two cars instead of one? Its gain of 100 from working on a second car is less than the tea house's loss of 200, so the firms cannot rationally reach a deal to let Fixit work on the second car.

Alternatively, suppose that the court says that Fixit has the right to make as much noise as it wants. Unless the tea house pays Fixit to reduce the noise, it has to shut down. The gain to the tea house of 200 from Fixit working on only one car rather than two is greater than the 100 loss to Fixit. They should be able to reach a deal whereby the tea house pays Fixit between 100 and 200, Fixit works on only one car, and the two firms maximize their joint profit at 500.

This example illustrates the three key implications of the Coase Theorem:

1. Without clearly assigned property rights, one firm pollutes excessively and the firms earn less than the maximum possible joint profit.

2. Clearly assigning the property rights maximizes joint profit, regardless of who gets the rights.

3. However, who gets the property rights affects how they split the joint profit. The property rights are valuable. The party without property rights compensates the party with property rights.

To achieve the efficient outcome, the two sides must bargain successfully with each other. However, the parties may not be able to bargain successfully if transaction costs are so high that it doesn't pay for the two sides to meet or if either side lacks information about the costs or benefits of reducing pollution. Because these impediments are common, Coasian bargaining is likely to occur in relatively few situations. However, even if bargaining is not feasible, the allocation of property

TABLE 16.1 Daily Profits Vary with Production and Noise

Fixit's Output, Cars per Hour	Profit, $		
	Auto Body Shop	Tea House	Total
0	0	400	400
1	300	200	500
2	400	0	400

rights may affect the amount of pollution. For example, if the tea house has the right to be free of noise pollution, it can shut down the auto body shop.

When the EPA stated that the James Gavin American Electric Power plant was violating the Clean Air Act by polluting Cheshire, Ohio, the EPA effectively gave the residents the right to be free from pollution. To avoid the higher cost of litigation and installing new equipment and other actions to reduce pollution at its plant, the company bought the town for $20 million, inducing the residents to pack up and leave. As of 2018, only 129 people still live in Cheshire.

Thus, once clear property rights are established, a manager may find it less expensive to purchase those rights from others rather than incur endless litigation and pollution-reduction costs.

16.5 Open-Access, Club, and Public Goods

Previous chapters focused on *private goods*, which have the properties of rivalry and exclusion. A **rival good** is used up as it is consumed. If Jane eats an orange, that orange is gone so no one else can consume it. **Exclusion** means that others can be prevented from consuming the good. If Jane owns an orange, she can easily prevent others from consuming that orange. Thus, an orange is subject to rivalry and exclusion.

If a good lacks rivalry, everyone can consume the same good, such as clean air or national defense or the light from a streetlight. If a market charges a positive price for that good, a market failure occurs because the marginal cost of providing the good to one more person is zero.

If the good lacks exclusion, such as clean air—you can't stop anyone else from breathing the clean air—then no one has a property right to the good. Consequently, a market failure may occur if people who don't have to pay for the good exploit it excessively, as when they pollute the air. If the market failure is severe, as it often is for open-access common property and for public goods, governments may play an important role in provision or control of the good. For example, local governments normally provide streetlights.

We can classify goods by whether they exhibit rivalry and exclusion. Table 16.2 outlines the four possibilities: private good (rivalry and exclusion), open-access common property (rivalry, no exclusion), club good (no rivalry, exclusion), and public good (no rivalry, no exclusion).

TABLE 16.2 Rivalry and Exclusion

	Exclusion	No Exclusion
Rivalry	*Private good*: apple, pencil, computer, car	*Open-access common property good*: fishery, freeway
No Rivalry	*Club good*: cable television, concert, tennis club	*Public good*: national defense, clean air, lighthouse

Open-Access Common Property

An **open-access common property** is a resource that is nonexclusive but rival, such as an open-access fishery. Anyone can fish in an open-access fishery so it is nonexclusive, but a fish is rival. If one person catches a fish, that fish (and its future offspring) are not available for anyone else.

Open-access common property leads to the overexploitation of the resource due to incomplete property rights. In an open-access ocean fishery, everyone has equal rights to a fish until it is caught, at which point it becomes private property. Each fisher wants to catch a given fish before others to gain the property right to that fish, even if that means catching fish while they are still young and small. The lack of clearly defined property rights leads to overfishing.

Like polluting manufacturers, fishing boat owners look at only their private costs. In calculating these costs, they include the cost of boats, other equipment, a crew, and supplies. They do not include the cost they impose on future generations by decreasing the stock of fish today, which reduces the number of fish in the sea next year. The fewer fish in the sea, the harder it is to catch any, so reducing the population today raises the cost of catching fish for others, both now and in the future.

The social cost of catching a fish is the private cost plus the *externality cost* from reduced current and future populations of fish. Thus, the market failure arising from open-access common property is a negative externality.

Other important examples of open-access common property are petroleum, water, and other fluids and gases that firms extract from a *common pool*. Owners of wells drawing from a common pool compete to remove the substance most rapidly, thereby gaining ownership of the good. This competition creates an externality by lowering fluid pressure, which makes further pumping more difficult. Iraq justified its invasion of Kuwait, which led to the Persian Gulf War in 1991, partly on the grounds that Kuwait was overexploiting common pools of oil underlying both countries. In 2011, the State of Alaska proposed leasing land next to the Arctic National Wildlife Refuge (ANWR), which would allow the leasing companies to drill and potentially drain oil from ANWR.[16]

If you own a car, you have a property right to drive that car, but public roads and freeways are common property. Because you lack an exclusive property right to the highway on which you drive, you cannot exclude others from also driving on the highway and you must share it with them. Each driver, however, claims a temporary property right to a portion of the highway by occupying it, thereby preventing others from occupying the same space. Competition for space on the highway leads to congestion, a negative externality that slows down every driver.

---

[16]The U.S. Congress passed legislation lifting the ANWR drilling ban in 2017, although various regulatory requirements that will delay and possibly prevent drilling remain in place. In 2018, Alaska's governor asked the legislature for funds for seismic testing to attract more oil companies to bid on possible ANWR lease sales. Opening ANWR to drilling reduces the attraction of the state's earlier plan to drill nearby.

If many people try to access a single website at one time, congestion may slow traffic to a crawl. In addition, you can send e-mail messages freely, because the internet allows open access, even though each message imposes a handling cost on its recipients. This negative externality leads to excessive amounts of unwanted or "junk" e-mail.

Spam—unsolicited bulk e-mail messages—inflicts a major negative externality on businesses and individuals around the world by forcing people to waste time removing it, by inducing people to reveal private information unintentionally, and by infecting computers with malicious software. Spammers take advantage of the open-access nature of e-mail. A spammer targets people who might be interested in the information provided in the spam message. This target group is relatively small compared to the vast majority of recipients who do not want the message and who incur the costs of reading and removing it. (Moreover, many spam messages are scams.) In 2018, 14.5 billion spam messages were sent daily, constituting 45% of global e-mail traffic according to **www.spamlaws.com.**

The worldwide cost of spam is enormous. Firms incur large costs to delete spam by installing spam filters and using employees' labor. A study at a German university found that the working time losses caused by spam were approximately 1,200 minutes, or $2\frac{1}{2}$ days, per employee per year (Caliendo et al., 2012). The Radicati research group estimated that the annual cost of spam to business grew almost 13-fold between 2012 and 2018 (from $20.5 billion to $257 billion). Various estimates of the cost range from $20 billion to $50 billion per year. Yahoo! researchers Rao and Reiley (2012) concluded that society loses $100 for every $1 of profit to a spammer, a rate that is "at least 100 times higher than that of automobile pollution."

Government Regulation of Common Property. Overuse of an open-access common resource occurs because individuals do not bear the full social cost: They ignore the externality they impose on other users. The government can restrict access to these common areas. A typical approach is to grant access on a first-come, first-served basis, such as at some popular national parks.

Alternatively, the government can impose a tax or fee to use the resource so that only those users who value the resource more than that fee gain access. Governments often charge an entrance fee to a park or a museum and collect tolls on highways and bridges. By applying a tax or fee equal to the externality harm that each individual imposes on others (such as the value of increased congestion on a highway), a government forces each person to internalize the externality. Unfortunately, park entrance fees are often just token amounts, toll booths are often bottlenecks, and many governments subsidize fishing efforts rather than taxing or restricting fishing, which leads to even more fishing.

Assigning Property Rights. An alternative approach to resolving the commons problem is to assign private property rights. Converting open-access common property to private property removes the incentive to overuse it.

Not all fisheries are open access. The owners of fish farms and privately owned lakes have clearly defined property rights and therefore do not face an externality. These owners are careful not to overfish their private property, maintaining adequate numbers of fish to breed for the future. Similarly, in many developing countries, common agricultural land has been broken up into smaller private farms to avoid excess exploitation of the resource.

Club Goods

A **club good** is a good that is nonrival but is subject to exclusion. True clubs, such as swimming clubs and golf clubs, provide club goods. These clubs exclude people who do not pay membership fees, but the services they provide, swimming or golfing, are nonrival: An extra person can swim or golf without reducing the enjoyment of others until these facilities become congested as capacity is reached.

However, the most significant club goods are not offered through actual clubs. An important example is cable television. The cable company can provide any available channels to additional consumers at almost no extra cost to the cable company once the cable is in place. The service lacks rivalry, as adding one more viewer for a given channel in no way impairs the viewing experience of others. However, the company can easily exclude people. Only customers who pay for the service receive the signal and can view the channel. Unlike with swimming pools or golf courses, extra consumers can subscribe to cable television channels almost without limit.

A cable company causes a market failure by charging a positive price, which exceeds the near-zero marginal cost of providing cable service. If some cable subscribers are willing to pay a positive amount for the channel, but less than the current price, then failure to provide the channel to those people is a deadweight loss to society.

Although club goods create a market failure, government intervention is rare because it is difficult for the government to help. As with regulation, an attempt to eliminate deadweight loss by forcing a cable television company to charge a price equal to its near-zero marginal cost would be self-defeating. The company would not produce the service, and even more total surplus would be lost. A government could cap the cable TV price at average cost, which would reduce, but not eliminate, the deadweight loss.

Mini-Case

Piracy

One of the most important examples of a good that is not rival but does allow for exclusion is computer software, such as Microsoft Word. Software is nonrival. At almost no extra cost, Microsoft can provide a copy of the software program to another consumer. Because Microsoft charges a (high) positive price, a market failure results in which too few units are sold.

However, if Microsoft cannot enforce its property right by preventing *pirating* of its software (use of software without paying for it), an even greater market failure may result: It may stop producing the product altogether. In countries where the cost of excluding nonpaying users is high, computer software is pirated and widely shared, which reduces the profitability of producing and selling software. In its 2018 report, the Business Software Alliance (BSA) estimated that 37% of software installed on personal computers globally was pirated. Their estimate of the unlicensed share was 15% in the United States, 16% in Japan, and 26% in Western Europe, but much higher in lower-income countries such as India, 56%, Russia, 62%, and China, 66%.

Public Goods

A **public good** is nonrival and nonexclusive. Clean air is a public good. One person's enjoyment of clean air does not stop other people from enjoying clean air as well, so clean air is nonrival. In addition, if we clean up the air, we cannot prevent others who live nearby from benefiting, so clean air is nonexclusive.

A public good reflects a special type of externality. If a firm reduces the amount of pollution it produces, thereby cleaning the air, it provides a nonpriced benefit to its neighbors: a positive externality.

Free Riding. Unfortunately, public goods tend to be undersupplied by markets. As with other externality problems, the underprovision of a public good is due to a lack of clearly defined property rights. Because people who do not pay for the good cannot be excluded from consuming it, the provider of a public good cannot exercise property rights over the services provided by the public good. This **free-rider problem** is a situation in which people benefit from the actions of others without paying. That is, they benefit from a positive externality. Consequently, it is very difficult for firms to provide a public good profitably because few people want to pay for the good no matter how much they value it.

To illustrate why public goods are underprovided by markets, we first examine why the demand curve for a public good is different from that for a private good. The social marginal benefit of a private good is the same as the marginal benefit to the individual who consumes that good. The market demand or social marginal benefit curve for private goods is the *horizontal* sum of the demand curves of each individual (Chapter 2).

In contrast, the social marginal benefit of a public good is the sum of the marginal benefit to each person who consumes the good. Because a public good lacks rivalry, many people can get pleasure from the same unit of output. Consequently, the *social demand curve* or *willingness-to-pay curve* for a public good is the *vertical* sum of the demand curves of each individual.

We illustrate this vertical summing by deriving the demand for guard services by stores in a mall that want to discourage theft. Guards who patrol the mall provide a service that is nonrival. By regularly walking through the mall, they protect all the stores. Each store's demand for guards reflects its marginal benefit from a reduction in thefts due to the guards. The television store stands to lose a lot if thieves strike. Its demand curve for guards is D^1 in Figure 16.4. The ice-cream parlor, which has less to lose than the television store if a theft occurs, demands fewer guards at any given price, as D^2 shows.

Because a guard patrolling the mall protects both stores at once, the marginal benefit to society of an additional guard is the sum of the benefit to each store. The social marginal benefit of a fifth guard, $20, is the sum of the marginal benefit to the television store, $16 (the height of D^1 at five guards per hour), and the marginal

FIGURE 16.4 Inadequate Provision of a Public Good

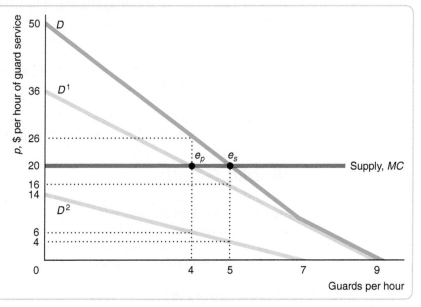

Security guards protect both tenants of the mall. If each guard costs $20 per hour, the television store, with demand D^1, is willing to hire four guards per hour. The ice-cream parlor, with demand D^2, is not willing to hire any guards. Thus, if everyone acts independently, the equilibrium is e_p. The social demand for this public good is the vertical sum of the individual demand curves, D. Thus, the social optimum is e_s, at which five guards are hired.

benefit to the ice-cream store, $4 (the height of D^2 at five guards per hour). Thus, the social demand curve, D, is the *vertical* sum of the individual demand curves.

A competitive market supplies as many guards as the stores want at $20 per hour per guard. At that price, the ice-cream store would not hire any guards on its own. The television store would hire four. If the stores act independently, they hire four guards at the private equilibrium, e_p. The sum of the marginal benefit to the two stores from four guards is $26, which is greater than the $20 marginal cost of an additional guard. If a fifth guard is hired, the social marginal benefit, $20, equals the marginal cost of the last guard. Therefore, the social equilibrium, e_s, has five guards.

The ice-cream store can get guard services without paying because the guard service is a public good. Acting alone, the television store hires fewer guards than are socially optimal because it ignores the positive externality provided to the ice-cream store, which the television store does not capture. Thus, the competitive market for guard services provides too little of this public good. In more extreme cases, the competitive market fails to provide any of the public good.

Reducing Free Riding. One solution to the underprovision of a public good due to free riding is for the government to provide it. Societies rely on governments to provide public defense, roads, and many other common goods. In addition, governmental or other collective actions can reduce free riding. Methods that may be used include social pressure, mergers, contracts, privatization, and compulsion.

Social pressure may reduce or eliminate free riding, especially for a small group. Such pressure may cause most firms in a mall to contribute "voluntarily" to hire security guards.

A direct way to eliminate free riding by firms is for them to *merge* into a single firm and thereby internalize the positive externality. The sum of the benefits to the individual stores equals the benefit to the single firm, so it hires the optimal number of guards.

If the independent stores sign a contract that commits them to share the cost of the guards, they achieve the practical advantage from a merger. However, the question remains why they would agree to sign the contract, given the prisoners' dilemma problem (Chapter 12). One explanation is that firms are more likely to cooperate in a repeated prisoners' dilemma game (Chapter 13).

Privatization—exclusion—eliminates free riding. A good that would be a public good if anyone could use it becomes a private good if access to it is restricted. An example is clean water provided by a water utility, which monitors water usage and charges people using individual meters at each home or apartment.

Another way to overcome free riding is through *mandates*. Some outside entity such as the government may mandate (dictate) a solution to a free-riding problem. For example, the management of a mall with many firms may require tenants to sign a rental contract committing them to pay fees to hire security guards that are determined through tenants' votes. If the majority votes to hire guards, all must share the cost. Although a firm might be unwilling to pay for the guard service if it has no guarantee that others will also pay, it may vote to assess everyone—including itself—fees to pay for the service.[17]

---

[17]**MyLab Economics** has a *Public Goods Experiment* that illustrates that the provision of a public good suffers from a free-rider problem. To participate go to the **MyLab Economics** Multimedia Library, Single Player Experiment, and set the Chapter field to "All Chapters."

16.6 Intellectual Property

Inventions, music, art, literature, and even textbooks make our lives better. The rate of innovation has been much more rapid in the past two centuries than at any other time in human history. One major reason for the increased rate of invention is that society developed mechanisms to assign property rights to knowledge, making it *intellectual property*. Without property rights, potential innovators have weaker incentives to innovate due to the public good nature of knowledge.

For example, when a chip manufacturer develops a new microchip, one particular chip is rival and exclusive. However, without intellectual property rights, the knowledge of how to make the chip is a public good. This knowledge is nonrival: If one person uses that knowledge, it does not prevent others from also using it. Moreover, it is nonexclusive if another company can buy a chip, reverse engineer it, and copy it.

Almost all of the cost of producing a new drug is the development cost of discovering the new medicine and verifying its efficacy and safety. If other firms can free ride on this knowledge and produce the same medicine, the innovator would have little chance of recovering its development cost. The free riders only have to pay the small production cost of the pills. Thus, this free-rider problem would greatly reduce private-sector incentives to develop new drugs.

The innovation problem, as with other public good and externality problems, is due to a failure of property rights. If an innovator is able to treat the new knowledge embodied in an invention or other innovation as *intellectual property* and can prevent others from using it, then the ability of potential users to free ride is greatly diminished and the incentive to innovate is enhanced. Governments provide protection for intellectual property in several ways, including by patents (which cover inventions) and copyrights (which protect original works such as books and music).[18]

Patents

The inventor of a new product can apply for a patent, which provides the intellectual property right underlying a new invention. The patent grants the inventor or the inventor's designate—often a firm—exclusive rights over the invention for 20 years in the United States and in most other countries.[19] Inventors can obtain patents for new and useful machines, new compositions of material (such as pharmaceuticals), new production processes, and improvements in any of these areas.

---

[18]A firm can also protect its trademarks, which allows the firm to protect its investment in building a favorable reputation for its brand.

[19]This 20-year period is based on the international agreement on Trade-Related Aspects of Intellectual Property Rights (TRIPs) that went into effect in 1995. Strongly supported by the United States, the TRIPs agreement largely harmonized the treatment of patents in much of the world. Before TRIPs, U.S. patents lasted 17 years from the date they were *granted*. Under the new rules, patents last for 20 years from the date the inventor *files* for patent protection. The length of protection can be shorter under these new rules, because it sometimes takes more than three years after filing to obtain final approval of a patent. According to the U.S. Patent and Trademark Office, the average time between the date a successful patent application is filed and the date the patent is granted is about two years (**www.uspto.gov**).

The owner of a patent may choose to be the sole producer of the product, license others to produce the good for a fee, or sell the patent. In essence, the owner of a patent can treat the covered intellectual property like any other type of property.

Advantages and Disadvantages of Patents. The patent system greatly reduces the free-rider problem. Because of the patent system, other companies cannot legally free ride on the drug discovery process or on other innovative activities that receive patent protection. Supporters of the patent system argue that firms would not have invented most new drugs developed in the past 50 years without patent protection. As those drugs have provided enormous and frequently life-saving benefits to many people, the loss of total surplus from such a market failure would have been very large.

Patents apply to a wide range of potential innovations in all areas of the economy. In the United States, the U.S. Patent and Trademark Office (USPTO) administers the patent process. Other countries have similar patent agencies, many of which cooperate closely with the USPTO under the terms of an international patent treaty called the Patent Cooperation Treaty. Inventors can apply for patents in many jurisdictions relatively easily using a common application process.

The key disadvantage of the patent system is that a patent creates monopoly power. As the Botox example in Chapter 9 illustrates, the holder of a patent on a new drug may have considerable monopoly power and may charge a monopoly price that is substantially greater than its marginal cost. Thus, in implementing a patent system, society reduces the social cost from reduced innovation due to the free-rider problem but incurs the deadweight loss of monopoly pricing. Patent policy also causes other problems, such as patent holders using methods like litigation, for example, to block others from building on their discoveries to create new inventions.

Alternatives to Patents. Some alternatives to patents encourage research while avoiding the creation of monopoly power by making the knowledge from the discoveries public or *open source*. One important alternative is for the government to fund

---

Q&A 16.4

In a competitive market with identical firms, the inverse demand function is $p = 100 - Q$. The supply curve is horizontal at a price of 70, which implies that each firm has a marginal cost of 70. However, one firm believes that if it invests 1,000 in research and development, it can develop a new production process that will lower its marginal cost from 70 to 20, and that it will be able to obtain a patent for its invention. Would this profit-maximizing firm undertake the innovation (assuming that the market lasts one period)? Does consumer surplus increase? Would consumers be better off or worse off if this firm could not obtain patent protection?

Answer

1. *Solve for the monopoly outcome and show that this monopoly pricing is feasible because no competitive firm can afford to undercut its price.* If the firm is a monopoly, its marginal revenue function is $MR = 100 - 2Q$ (Chapter 9).[20] It would produce where $MR = MC$ or $100 - 2Q = 20$, or $Q = 40$. The price at that quantity is

---

[20]Its revenue is $R = pQ = (100 - Q)Q = 100Q - Q^2$. Differentiating, we find that the marginal revenue is $MR = dR/dQ = 100 - 2Q$. See Chapter 9 for a non-calculus approach to finding the marginal revenue of a linear demand curve.

$p = 100 - 40 = 60$. This outcome is feasible because the monopoly price is less than the price of 70 that any other firm would need to charge.

2. *Calculate the firm's profit net of its investment to determine if the investment is profitable.* The firm's profit including the investment cost is $\pi = pQ - 20Q - 1{,}000 = (60 \times 40) - (20 \times 40) - 1{,}000 = 2{,}400 - 800 - 1{,}000 = 600$. Thus, it pays to innovate and become a monopoly.

3. *Determine if consumer surplus increases by comparing price before and after the invention.* The competitive price is 70, while the patent monopoly price is 60, so consumers benefit from the invention despite the exercise of monopoly power because the cost of production has fallen substantially. That is, the consumer surplus increases.[21]

research by firms and universities. In 2009, the U.S. Congress allocated $2.4 billion to encourage development of plug-in vehicles and advanced batteries. Between 2004 and 2011, the U.S. Energy Department along with state agencies granted $348 million in loans, grants, and tax exemptions to research centers, fuel producers, and refiners to develop biofuels for jetliners.

Another method is to offer a prize for a discovery. Napoleon's prize for finding a way that the army could safely transport food great distances led to the invention of canning. More recent prizes have been offered to develop new lightweight batteries for military use (U.S. government), energy-saving refrigerators (industry organization), new rockets capable of moon exploration (Google), and new meat substitutes (People for the Ethical Treatment of Animals).

Managerial Implication

Trade Secrets

Managers do not necessarily patent new inventions to prevent free riding. Sometimes the best way to protect intellectual property is to keep it secret. A *trade secret* is a form of intellectual property, though it remains the exclusive property of the inventor only as long as it remains secret.

In the United States, the United Kingdom, and many other countries, government policy supports trade secrets by allowing firms to enter into enforceable contracts with employees that prevent employees from revealing trade secrets to others. Coca-Cola's formula is one of the world's most famous trade secrets. Not only has Coca-Cola kept the formula secret, but it has used the existence of the secret formula as a marketing tool.

Cohen and Gutterman (2000) surveyed 1,478 R&D labs at U.S. manufacturing firms. Firms reported protecting their inventions using patents, secrecy, lead time advantages, and other mechanisms. When asked whether a method was effective in protecting a product innovation, 51% mentioned secrecy compared to only 35% for patents. Secrecy was most frequently mentioned in miscellaneous chemicals (71%), textiles (64%), and petroleum (62%). Thus, many managers believe that secrecy is one of the best ways to protect intellectual property. In Britain, only 22% of firms use formal intellectual property protection such as patents, while 32% use trade secrets (Hall et al., 2012).

---

[21]At the competitive equilibrium where $p = 70$ and $Q = 30$, the consumer surplus is a triangle with a height of $30 = 100 - p = 100 - 70$ and a base of $Q = 30$, so $CS = \frac{1}{2} \times 30 \times 30 = 450$. Under the patent monopoly, the consumer surplus is the triangle with a height of $40 = 100 - 60$ and a base of 40, so $CS = \frac{1}{2} \times 40 \times 40 = 800$.

Copyright Protection

Copyrights provide intellectual property rights to creative arts, such as music, literature, and visual images. The principles underlying copyright protection are generally the same as for patents. For example, the composer of a popular song faces the same free-rider problem that the inventor of a new drug faces. The song is essentially a public good: One person can listen to it without preventing others from also listening, and it is very difficult to stop people from copying songs.

The owner of the copyright to a song has an intellectual property right. According to U.S. law, the owner can prevent anyone else from playing or listening to that song without paying for that right. Without such protection, it would be difficult for an artist to earn a return from songwriting efforts. It is true that many people would produce music anyway "for love, not money." However, the incentive for highly talented artists to produce music would be much reduced, and they might be diverted to areas where they could expect compensation, such as creating advertising jingles.

Managerial Solution Licensing Inventions	We now return to the three questions we posed at the beginning of the chapter. Should a firm patent its invention or keep it a trade secret? If the innovating firm produces the product itself, under what conditions can it charge the monopoly price for its product? Given that it obtains a patent, will the innovating firm earn more if it produces the good itself or licenses its new process to other firms?

A firm may use trade secrets instead of patenting for at least three reasons. First, it is costly to apply for a patent. Second, patents have a finite life, whereas a firm may be able to maintain a secret indefinitely (as Coca-Cola has done with its famous formula). Third, another firm may use the information in a patent to invent around the patent and create another invention that is sufficiently different that it does not violate the patent. Nonetheless, many firms opt for a patent because of the extra protection it provides, especially if the firm wants to license its invention.

We illustrate the answer to the next two questions using an example. Initially, a competitive market has many firms that produce at a constant marginal and average cost m, so that the competitive market supply curve is horizontal at m. As the figure shows, at the competitive equilibrium, e_c, the market price, p^*, equals m, and the quantity is Q^*.

A firm invents a new process that lowers the cost of production by 20% to $0.8m$. If the firm manufactures the good itself, under what conditions can it charge the monopoly price for its product?

If it were an unconstrained monopoly, the innovating firm would sell Q_m units at price p_m. The intersection of its red marginal cost line at $0.8m$ and the light purple marginal revenue curve (which corresponds to the light blue market demand curve) determines this outcome. However, the competitive supply curve at m constrains the monopoly exactly as would a government price cap set at m: It prevents the innovating firm from charging a price above m. Thus, the innovating firm can charge the unconstrained monopoly price only if p_m is less than m. Because m is less than p_m in the figure, this firm charges a price less than p_m.

Given that the competitive supply curve is horizontal at m, the residual demand curve facing the innovating firm is the dark blue line that is horizontal at m until

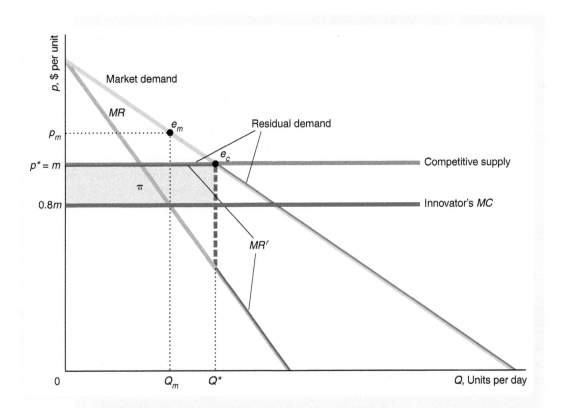

it hits the market demand curve, and then it equals the market demand curve at prices below m. Consequently, the firm's dark purple residual marginal revenue curve, MR^r, is horizontal at m up to Q^*, and then, at larger quantities, it equals the light purple marginal revenue curve that corresponds to the downward-sloping market demand curve.

The innovating firm's marginal cost curve at $0.8m$ cuts MR^r in the (dashed) vertical section at Q^*. Thus, the firm's profit-maximizing output is Q^*. The firm charges a price that is slightly less than m so that it undercuts the competitive firms and makes all the sales. Thus, this equilibrium has (virtually) the same price and quantity as the competitive equilibrium. However, one firm sells the entire quantity and makes a profit virtually equal to $\pi = (m - 0.8m)Q^* = 0.2mQ^*$, which equals the gold rectangle in the figure.

Should the firm manufacture the good itself or license its process? The competitive firms are willing to pay a license fee up to $0.2m$ for the ability to produce at a marginal cost of $0.8m$. If they had to pay more than that, their costs would rise above their current cost of m. Given that the innovating firm sets this maximum possible license fee at $0.2m$, the competitive firms' supply curve is unchanged and the competitive equilibrium remains the same. The licensing firm's total license payments equal $\pi = 0.2mQ^*$. That is, the firm makes the same profit whether it produces itself or licenses its process.

SUMMARY

1. **Market Failure and Government Policy.** A perfectly competitive market achieves economic efficiency—it maximizes total surplus—so government intervention can only reduce total surplus. In contrast, in markets that are not perfectly competitive, market failures occur—total surplus is not maximized—which provides an important rationale for government action. Ideally, the government intervenes to make a Pareto improvement: a change that helps some people without harming anyone. An alternative approach to choosing government policies is the cost-benefit principle: The government imposes a policy if it results in a net benefit to society because the winners gain more than others lose. If the government can require that gainers compensate losers, then such policies provide a Pareto improvement.

2. **Regulation of Imperfectly Competitive Markets.** Governments often use direct controls on price or other variables to eliminate or reduce market failures arising from monopoly power or other sources. For example, to prevent a profit-maximizing monopoly from charging a price above marginal cost, which creates a market failure, the government can set a price ceiling. If the government sets the maximum allowed price equal to the marginal cost, it eliminates the market failure and associated deadweight loss, provided the firm stays in business. If it sets the price ceiling at a higher level, but below the unregulated monopoly price, it reduces the harm of the market failure but does not eliminate it. Well-intentioned regulators do not achieve economic efficiency if they have inadequate information about demand or marginal cost. However, the regulated industry captures other regulators—for example, they might be bribed—who work to enrich the industry rather than benefit society.

3. **Antitrust Law and Competition Policy.** Rather than regulate a noncompetitive market, governments may use antitrust laws or competition policy to promote competition and to prevent a market failure from occurring. The most important competition policies are those that forbid price fixing and other cartel behavior. Merger policies try to prevent harmful mergers, such as those that increase market power by more than any offsetting benefits from lower costs. Other policies seek to prevent predatory actions where a dominant firm drops its price to drive out other firms and then raises the price. Several policies limit certain vertical interactions such as resale price maintenance, refusal to deal, and certain types of price discrimination that have the effect of reducing competition.

4. **Externalities.** An externality occurs when a consumer's well-being or a firm's production capabilities are directly affected by the actions of other consumers or firms rather than being affected only through changes in prices. Maintaining a beautiful garden provides a positive externality to your neighbors. Pollution is a negative externality that harms others. Because manufacturers do not pay for the externalities they create by producing pollution, their private costs of production are less than the full social cost, which includes the private costs and the externality cost. Consequently, competitive markets produce more than the efficient output due to a negative externality, causing a market failure. If the government has sufficient information about demand, production cost, and the harm from the externality, it can use taxes or quotas to reduce or even eliminate the associated inefficiency or deadweight loss. Alternatively, assigning property rights sometimes leads to the optimal reduction in an externality.

5. **Open-Access, Club, and Public Goods.** Private goods are subject to rivalry—when one person consumes a unit of the good, no one else can consume it—and to exclusion—the owner can prevent others from consuming the good. Some goods lack one or both of these properties. Open-access common property, such as a fishery, is nonexclusive, but is subject to rivalry. This lack of exclusion causes overfishing because users of the fishery do not take into account the costs they impose on others (foregone fish) when they go fishing. A club good is nonrival but exclusive. For example, a swimming club lacks rivalry up to capacity but can exclude nonmembers. If a firm charges a positive price for such a good despite having extra capacity, a market failure results because the marginal cost of providing the good to one more person is zero, which is less than the price. A public good such as public defense is both nonrival and nonexclusive. The lack of exclusion causes a free-rider problem in a market: People use the good without paying for it. As a result, potential suppliers of such goods are inadequately compensated so they underprovide the good. Because private markets tend to underprovide nonprivate goods, governments often produce or subsidize such goods.

6. **Intellectual Property.** In the absence of government intervention, innovation is a public good. The resulting knowledge is nonrival and lacks exclusion. The information about the new invention has a free-rider problem: People who did not pay to develop the new product can copy the product and produce it. Thus, people may put little effort into inventing because they are not fully compensated. To avoid this problem, governments provide patents (and copyrights for the arts) that give the creator intellectual property rights to the invention for 20 years. While patents encourage invention, they create monopoly power. Alternatively, governments can subsidize research or provide other incentives to promote research. Some innovators rely on trade secrets rather than patents to protect their intellectual property.

QUESTIONS

All exercises are available on **MyLab Economics**; * = *answer at the back of this book;* **C** = *use of calculus may be necessary.*

1. Market Failure and Government Policy

*1.1 If a policy change causes a Pareto improvement, is the outcome necessarily Pareto efficient? If a situation is Pareto efficient, are Pareto improvements possible? If a change occurs that causes a Pareto efficient outcome, is the change necessarily a Pareto improvement? Explain.

1.2 Does a Pareto improvement necessarily pass the cost-benefit test? Is the converse true? Explain.

1.3 A town council is considering building a new bridge over a small river that runs through the town to reduce congestion on the existing bridge and decrease commuting times. Each of 1,000 commuters who must cross the bridge would experience a benefit of $15 per day from the reduction in commuting time. The government would finance the bridge through increased property taxes that amount to $1 per day for each of the 10,000 households in the town. Would the bridge pass a cost-benefit test? Would building the bridge be a Pareto improvement (relative to not having a bridge)?

1.4 In Question 1.3, could using tolls instead of taxes to finance the bridge yield a Pareto improvement? (*Hint*: Consider the effects on commuters who would be willing to pay the toll on the new bridge, on commuters who would use the old bridge, and on non-commuters.) Would using tolls be Pareto efficient? (Assume that the marginal cost of using the new bridge for an extra trip is zero and assume that the demand for trips across the bridge is downward sloping.)

2. Regulation of Imperfectly Competitive Markets

2.1 Illustrate and describe the effects on output and welfare if the government regulates a monopoly so that it may not charge a price above $\bar{p}$, which lies between the unregulated monopoly price and the economically efficient price (determined by the intersection of the firm's marginal cost and the market demand curve). In Figure 16.1, what effect would the regulation have if the regulated price ceiling was set at 18? (*Hint*: See Q&A 16.1.)

*2.2 A monopoly drug company produces a life-saving medicine at a constant cost of $10 per dose. The demand for this medicine is perfectly inelastic at prices less than or equal to the $100 (per day) income of the 100 patients who need to take this drug daily. At a higher price, consumers buy nothing. Show the equilibrium price and quantity, and the consumer

and producer surplus, in a diagram. Now the government imposes a price ceiling of $30. Show how the equilibrium, consumer surplus, and producer surplus change. What is the deadweight loss, if any, from this price control?

2.3 The price of wholesale milk dropped by 30.3% when the Pennsylvania Milk Marketing Board lowered the regulated price. The price to consumers fell by substantially less than 30.3% in Philadelphia. Why? (*Hint*: Show that a monopoly will not necessarily lower its price by the same percentage as its constant marginal cost drops.)

2.4 Using the figure in the Mini-Case "Natural Gas Regulation," show how much consumer surplus increases if regulators require the producer to change from average cost pricing to marginal cost pricing. Explain why, despite this difference in consumer surplus, regulators generally prefer average cost pricing to marginal cost pricing.

2.5 Q&A 16.1 shows that a regulated price ceiling set below the optimal regulated price causes a loss in total surplus compared with optimal regulation. The diagram illustrates only a lower bound for the loss of surplus. Explain why the loss in consumer surplus is likely to be even greater than $B + D$.

3. Antitrust Law and Competition Policy

*3.1 Suppose that the only two firms in an industry face the market (inverse) demand curve $p = 100 - Q$. Each has constant marginal cost equal to 10 and no fixed costs. Initially, the two firms compete as Cournot rivals (Chapter 11) and each produces an output of 30. Why might these firms want to merge to form a monopoly? What reason would antitrust authorities have for opposing the merger? (*Hint*: Calculate price, profits, and total surplus before and after the merger.) **C**

3.2 Modify Question 3.1 so that each firm has a fixed cost, F, of 500. Merging would imply that the monopoly firm would pay fixed costs of 500. How would your answer change?

3.3 Q&A 16.2 shows that a merger may increase total surplus if the merger reduces marginal cost. Give examples of how a merger could reduce marginal cost.

3.4 In Q&A 16.2, under what conditions (if any) would a cost-reducing merger that converts a duopoly into a monopoly cause a Pareto improvement? Would a cost-reducing merger always increase total surplus? Explain briefly.

3.5 The Mini-Case "Are Monopoly Mergers Harmful?" states that there are about 5,000 ready-mix concrete plants in the United States. With so many plants in operation, why should we worry that mergers may create monopoly power? Explain why the speed of entry is important in assessing the cost of mergers that create a monopoly.

3.6 Aloha Coffee is a coffee roasting and blending company that supplies a unique coffee bean grown only in a very particular part of the Hawaiian island of Kauai to the only two coffee shops in a small town. The producer sells the coffee to the shops at the marginal cost of production, $9 per pound, and receives 20% of the profit earned when the retailers sell the coffee to customers. Would Aloha prefer that the retailers compete with each other on price or would Aloha rather set the retail price of the coffee for both shops?

3.7 Why would an upstream producer of some product ever refuse to sell to downstream buyers who wish to buy the product at the going price?

4. Externalities

4.1. According to a study in the *New England Journal of Medicine*, your friendships or "social networks" are more likely than your genes to make you overweight (Jennifer Levitz, "Can Your Friends Make You Fat?" *Wall Street Journal*, July 26, 2007, D1). If it is true that people who have overweight friends are more likely to be overweight, is that an example of a negative externality? Why? (*Hints*: Is this relationship a causal one, or do heavier people choose heavier friends?)

4.2 When *Star Wars Episode III: Revenge of the Sith* opened at 12:01 a.m., Thursday, May 19, 2005, the most fanatical *Star Wars* fans paid $50 million for tickets to stay up until 3:00 to 4:00 a.m. Businesses around the country, especially those tied to high-tech industries, suffered reduced productivity due to absent (suffering from Darth Vader flu) or groggy workers on Thursday and Friday. By one estimate, fan loyalty cost U.S. employers as much as $627 million (Josie Roberts, *Pittsburgh Tribune-Review*, May 19, 2005). In contrast, this sum is chicken feed compared to the estimated $890 million loss during NCAA March Madness: 16 days of virtually nonstop college basketball games (James Paton, "Hooky and Hoops— March Rituals," *Rocky Mountain News*, March 19, 2005, 3C). Are these examples of a negative externality? Explain.

*4.3 Why is zero pollution not the best solution for society? Can we have too little pollution? Why or why not?

4.4 A number of countries have either banned incandescent light bulbs already or have begun phasing out such lighting in favor of more fuel-efficient compact fluorescent bulbs. These restrictions are intended to promote energy conservation and therefore to reduce greenhouse gas emissions and global warming. What alternative approaches could a government use to achieve the same goals? What are the advantages and disadvantages of a ban relative to the alternatives?

4.5 The State of Connecticut announced that commercial fleet operators would get a tax break if they converted vehicles from ozone-producing gasoline to what the state said were cleaner fuels, such as natural gas and electricity. For every dollar spent on the conversion of their fleets or on building alternative fueling stations, operators could deduct 50¢ from their corporate tax. Is this approach likely to be a cost-effective way to control pollution?

4.6 Let $H = \bar{E} - E$ be the amount that emissions, E, are reduced from the competitive level, $\bar{E}$. The benefit of reducing emissions is $B(H) = AH^\alpha$. The cost is $C(H) = H^\beta$. If the benefit is increasing but at a diminishing rate in H, and the cost is rising at an increasing rate, what are the possible ranges of values for A, α, and B? **C**

4.7 In the model in Question 4.6, use calculus to determine the optimal level of H. **C**

*4.8 Suppose that the inverse demand function for paper is $p = 200 - Q$, the private marginal cost (unregulated competitive market supply) is $MC^p = 80 + Q$, and the marginal external harm from emissions is $MC^x = Q$. Determine the unregulated competitive equilibrium and the social optimum (where total surplus is maximized). What specific tax (per unit of output) would achieve the social optimum? (*Hint*: See Q&A 16.2.)

4.9 In the model in Question 4.8, what is the unregulated monopoly equilibrium? How would you optimally regulate the monopoly to maximize total surplus? What is the resulting equilibrium? **C**

4.10 Suppose that the only way to reduce pollution from paper production is to reduce output. The government imposes a tax equal to the marginal harm from the pollution on the monopoly producer. Show that the tax may or may not raise welfare.

4.11 Aaron is traveling to Europe for vacation and is seated in a first-class airline seat holding his infant daughter in his arms. He values being in first class instead of coach at $600. Samantha, a CEO of a major multinational corporation, is sitting in the adjacent seat and is considering offering to pay Aaron to move to one of the empty seats in coach.

  a. Samantha values quiet at $1,100. Can Aaron and Samantha reach a mutually agreeable price for Aaron to move to coach?

b. If instead Samantha values quiet at $400, can Aaron and Samantha reach a mutually agreeable price for Aaron to move to coach?

c. Assuming efficient bargaining, for what range of Samantha's value of quiet will Aaron move to coach?

4.12 Many jurisdictions strictly limit sales of hard liquor (liquor with a significantly higher alcohol content than wine) in an effort to limit the associated negative externalities. (De Melo, Mejia, and Suarez, 2013). One approach is to impose a high tax on sales of such products. Another approach is to require sellers to obtain licenses and to limit the number of licenses to the socially desirable number. Sometimes these licenses are sold to the highest bidder. Frequently, however, the price of such licenses is set at a low enough level that extensive excess demand for licenses occurs at that price.

a. Under what circumstances would auctioning licenses be equivalent to a tax?

b. Why might regulators or politicians favor underpricing of liquor licenses? (*Hint*: Such licenses often end up in the hands of political donors or of friends and associates of donors.)

4.13 Alyakoob and Rahman (2018) found that if activity on home-sharing platform Airbnb increases by 2%, restaurant employment in that neighborhood rises by 3%. This effect demonstrates which economic concept? (*Hint*: See the Managerial Implication "Disney Internalizes an Externality.")

5. Open-Access, Club, and Public Goods

5.1 Are heavily used bridges, such as the Brooklyn Bridge and the Golden Gate Bridge, commons? If so, what can a government do to mitigate congestion problems?

5.2 To prevent overfishing, could regulators set a tax on fish or on boats? Explain and illustrate with a graph.

5.3 Spam imposes significant negative externalities on e-mail users (see the Mini-Case "Spam"). If a small charge were applied to every e-mail message, would the extent and impact of this negative externality decline? What effect would such a charge have on the net benefits arising from non-spam messages? How would the charge affect the proportion of spam in overall e-mail traffic?

*5.4 Are broadcast television and cable television public goods? Is exclusion possible? If either is a public good, why is it privately provided?

5.5 Do publishers sell the socially optimal number of managerial economics textbooks? Discuss in terms of public goods, rivalry, and exclusion.

5.6 Guards patrolling a mall protect the mall's two stores. The television store's demand curve for guards is strictly greater at all prices than that of the ice-cream parlor. The marginal cost of a guard is $20 per hour. Use a diagram to show the equilibrium, and compare that to the socially optimal equilibrium. Now suppose that the mall's owner will provide a $s per hour subsidy per guard. Show in your graph the optimal s that leads to the socially optimal outcome for the two stores.

5.7 In 2009, when the world was worried about the danger of the H1N1 influenza virus (swine flu), Representative Rosa DeLauro and Senator Edward Kennedy proposed the Healthy Families Act in Congress to guarantee paid sick days to all workers (Ellen Wu and Rajiv Bhatia, "A Case for Paid Sick Days," *San Francisco Chronicle*, May 15, 2009). Although the Centers for Disease Control and Prevention urges ill people to stay home from work or school to keep from infecting others, many workers—especially those who do not receive paid sick days—ignore this advice. Evaluate the efficiency and welfare implications of the proposed law, taking account of externalities.

5.8 Receiving flu shots provides private benefits to recipients. However, pandemic influenza spreads between cities through the international airline network and between cities and rural areas through ground transport. Thus, it may be in the self-interest of rich countries to pay for flu shots in poor countries (Bobashev et al., 2011). Discuss this issue using the concepts of externalities, public goods, and free riders.

5.9 You and your roommate have a stack of dirty dishes in the sink. Either of you would wash the dishes if you were the only one who could wash the dishes; however, neither will do it in the expectation (hope?) that the other will deal with the mess. Explain how this example illustrates the problem of public goods and free riding.

5.10 Under certain U.S. laws, all the firms in some agricultural industries must contribute to collective activities, such as industry advertising, if the majority agrees. Under the Beef Promotion and Research Act, all beef producers must pay a $1-per-head fee on cattle sold in the United States as of 2018. This fee raises $80 million annually, which finances research; educational programs on mad cow disease; and collective advertising, such as the 2012 campaign, "Stay Home. Grill Out," and its 2018 campaign, "Beef. It's What's For Dinner." Explain the logic of this law, using the concepts of free riding and public goods. Supporters of this collective advertising estimate that producers receive $5.67 in additional marginal revenue for every dollar they contribute. If so, does this result suggest that the producers had a public good problem? Is the industry advertising optimally? (Chapter 9)

5.11 In 2018, the U.S. Centers for Disease Control and Prevention (CDC) is cutting 80% of its epidemic prevention activities overseas. The former chief of the CDC says that this decision "would significantly increase the chance an epidemic will spread without our knowledge and endanger lives in our country and around the world."[22] What economic concepts does this story reflect?

6. Intellectual Property

6.1 Woz Enterprises specializes in electrical components. The market for one particular component is perfectly competitive and in long-run equilibrium. Marginal cost is constant at 30. Woz can develop a much cheaper process for producing this component, lowering its marginal cost to 10. The R&D cost of developing the new process would be F, and Woz would be able to obtain a patent for it and become a monopoly supplier of this component. Demand for the product over the relevant period is given by $p = 50 - 2Q$. Show that the R&D investment would be worthwhile (raise profit) for Woz if $F = 150$ but not if $F = 250$. What is the critical value for F that determines whether R&D is worthwhile for Woz? (*Hint*: See Q&A 16.3.)

*6.2 In Question 6.1, assume that the R&D cost is 150. Are consumers made better off by the action taken by Woz? Does total surplus rise?

6.3 In Question 6.1 with an R&D cost of 150, suppose that the government waits until Woz works out the new process and then changes patent rules, requiring Woz to charge a price no greater than 12. Does Woz stay in business? What happens to consumer surplus and to total surplus? Why don't governments impose such price controls on patented processes and products?

6.4 For trade secrets to effectively protect intellectual property, it is important that the innovation cannot be easily *reverse engineered*, a process by which a firm can take a rival's product and determine how it was produced. Patents are important when reverse engineering is easy. In the chemical business, firms often develop lower-cost processes for producing chemical products, but the chemical product itself does not change. Examining the product does not reveal the new process, so reverse engineering is not feasible. With a computer chip, on the other hand, the innovation is embodied in the chip, so rivals can copy the chip. Which industry would you expect to rely more on trade secrets? Explain briefly.

6.5 Explain why the innovation process may give rise to market failure. (*Hint*: Consider the free-rider problem.) How do patents reduce this market failure? Could government-funded prizes or R&D subsidies be partial substitutes for patent protection in some cases?

7. Managerial Problem

7.1 In the Managerial Solution example, who benefits and who loses from the invention? Does the innovating firm capture the full value of its innovation?

8. MyLab Economics Spreadsheet Exercises[23]

8.1 A monopolist's inverse demand function is $p = 100 - 2Q$, so its marginal revenue is $MR = 100 - 4Q$. Its cost function is $C = 25 + 4Q + 2Q^2$ and its marginal cost is therefore $MC = 4 + 4Q$.

a. Create a spreadsheet with column headings Q, p, MR, MC, R, C, profit, and CS (consumer surplus). Enter the values 1 to 25 in one-unit increments in the quantity column and enter the appropriate formulas in all the other cells. Determine the profit maximizing output and price for an unregulated monopoly. What is the monopoly's profit and the consumer surplus at this output and price?

b. Now use your spreadsheet to determine the price, quantity, profit, and consumer surplus if the regulator imposes a price cap (ceiling) of 70.

c. Which of the two pricing structures yields the highest total surplus? If the regulator wants to use price cap regulation *and* wants to maximize total surplus, what price cap should the regulator choose?

8.2 A competitive fertilizer market has many small firms. The inverse demand function for fertilizer is $p = 40 - 2Q$, where Q is a ton of fertilizer and p is the price per ton of fertilizer. The market supply curve—the sum of the private marginal cost curves of all the firms—is $MC^p = Q + 4$. The fertilizer industry is a major source of water pollution, and the marginal external damage, MC^x, caused by the industry to the communities near the fertilizer firms is $6 per ton of fertilizer produced.

[22]www.cnn.com/2018/02/03/health/cdc-slashes-global-epidemic-programs-outrage/index.html.

[23]The spreadsheet exercises in this chapter are based on the work of Satyajit Ghosh in cooperation with the authors. The answers are available on MyLab Economics.

a. Create a spreadsheet with column headings for output Q, price p, private marginal cost MC^p, marginal cost of pollution MC^x, and social marginal cost $MC^s = MC^p + MC^x$. Fill in the spreadsheet for $Q = 1, 2, 3, \ldots, 20$.

b. Determine the equilibrium output and price in the competitive fertilizer market if firms do not have to pay for the pollution they create.

c. Determine the socially optimal amount of fertilizer.

d. What per-unit tax can the government impose to generate the socially optimal amount of output?

8.3 In a perfectly competitive market, the inverse demand function is $p = 50 - Q$. Market supply, Q^s, is perfectly elastic at a price of 40, because each firm has a constant marginal cost $MC = 40$.

a. Create a spreadsheet with column headings Q, p, MC, and CS (consumer surplus). Fill in the spreadsheet for $Q = 1, 2, 3, \ldots, 25$. Calculate the competitive market's equilibrium output and price.

b. One firm invests 200 in a successful R&D project that allows it to lower its marginal cost of production from 40 to 10. The firm gets a patent for its new process. Create a new spreadsheet showing the situation under this patent monopoly, with no competitive firms. The column headings are Q, p, MR, MC, CS, and Profit (including the investment of 200). Calculate the patent monopoly's profit-maximizing output, price, and profit. Did the R&D investment pay?

c. How does consumer surplus change if the market changes from competition to a patent monopoly?

Global Business 17

Traditionally, most imports come from other countries.

Business is now global. Virtually every country in the world exports and imports goods and services and invests in assets in other countries. Both competitive firms and major corporations with market power actively trade internationally.

The United States is the world's largest exporter of wheat in the highly competitive global market. In 2018, its exports were 15.7% of world exports even though U.S. production was only about 7% of the world's total.

Trade also plays an important role in oligopolistic and other less competitive markets. Rolls-Royce Motors, the maker of the world's most famous luxury cars, sold 3,362 of its British-built cars worldwide in 2017 in over 50 countries, with most sold in the Americas. Although Rolls-Royce sells far fewer cars than General Motors, Toyota, and other large producers, its revenue is large because it charges astronomical prices. A 2018 Rolls-Royce Phantom VIII without many options cost about half a million dollars.

Managers of firms must make crucial pricing decisions when an exchange rate changes. An *exchange rate* is the number of units of one currency it takes to buy a unit of another currency. For example, in mid-2018 the exchange rate between the U.S. dollar ($) and the Japanese yen (¥) as about 110, so that it took 110 yen to buy one dollar.

How do firms' prices change around the world when exchange rates change? In particular, is the responsiveness of prices to exchange rates greater for highly competitive wheat or for Rolls-Royce automobiles, which are not sold in a competitive market?

Not long ago international business issues were of only modest significance in countries such as the United States, China, and India, each of which had large domestic markets and engaged in little trade. However, **globalization**—the increasing integration or interconnectedness of the global economy—has resulted in a substantial rise in international trade in recent years. From 1990 to 2017, exports rose from 19% of the world's total output, as measured by gross domestic product (GDP), to 29%.[1] The growth was particularly dramatic for India, as exports increased by almost three-fold, going from 7% of GDP in 1990 to 19% in 2015. For China, exports grew from 14% to 20% of GDP, and U.S exports grew from 9% to 12% of GDP.

---

[1]Data in this paragraph and the next are from the World Bank Development Indicators **data.worldbank.org/products/wdi** and the United States Census Bureau: **www.census.gov/foreign-trade/balance/c5700.html**.

Simply quoting exports as a share of GDP fails to adequately portray the remarkable increase in trade that has occurred in much of the world, especially in countries where GDP has been growing rapidly. The real value of U.S. imports from China rose from $8.8 billion (measured in 2017 U.S. dollars) in 1985 to $505 billion in 2017. That is, for every freighter taking goods from China to the United States in 1985, 57 freighters made the trip in 2017!

Effectively, the world has grown smaller, with countries becoming more interconnected and more interdependent than ever. This increasing integration of the world economy is due in large part to improvements in communications technology, which have reduced the effect of distance, and to policy changes that have allowed for freer trade and investment flows between countries.

The greater integration of the world economy creates both opportunities and challenges for businesses. Gaining increased access to foreign markets is an important means of expanding demand for many firms. A more integrated global economy also provides managers with the opportunity to use an international supply chain, obtaining materials, components, and other inputs to production from many countries. For example, IBM uses inputs from over 13,000 suppliers in over 100 different countries in producing its products and sells its output in almost all of the world's more than 190 countries.[2] However, increasing competition from foreign rivals is a potential problem for managers, as is the difficulty of dealing with a range of different legal and policy environments from country to country.

In this chapter, we start by considering why countries and firms engage in international trade by exporting and importing goods and services, and then address the role of exchange rates in international trade. Next, we examine how international trade policy affects managerial decisions regarding trade flows. We then turn to trade and investment by *multinational enterprises* (MNEs), which are firms that control productive assets in more than one country. We show how managers of an MNE must take into account international differences in law and in economic policy. For example, we show how an MNE reacts to differential corporate tax rates in the countries where it operates. Finally, we discuss a very contentious issue: international outsourcing. In many developed countries, labor unions and other groups have protested when a firm lays off domestic employees and shifts production to foreign countries where labor costs are lower

Learning Objectives

1. Use the concept of comparative advantage to explain why countries trade.
2. Describe the effects of a change in an exchange rate on international trade.
3. Analyze the effects of tariffs, quotas, and subsidies on international markets.
4. Explain how multinational enterprises take advantage of international tax rate differences to raise profits.
5. Discuss the causes and effects of outsourcing.

---

[2]See **www.ibm.com/ibm/responsibility/2017/assets/downloads/IBM-2017-CRR-SupplyChain.pdf** (viewed August 24, 2017).

17.1 Reasons for International Trade

Everyone consumes many imported products. A typical American breakfast might include bread made from Canadian wheat, jam imported from England, fruit from Mexico, and tea from India or coffee from Brazil—along with perhaps some corn flakes produced in the United States.

Why do we rely on other countries for the goods that we consume? Why doesn't each country produce everything it needs domestically?

Trade between countries occurs for many reasons. The most important is that international trade allows countries to specialize in producing goods and services for which they have a **comparative advantage**: the ability to produce a good or service at lower opportunity cost than other countries.

Comparative Advantage

I inherited a painting and a violin which turned out to be a Rembrandt and a Stradivarius. Unfortunately, Rembrandt made lousy violins and Stradivarius was a terrible painter. —Tommy Cooper

According to the principle of comparative advantage, a country exports goods it can produce at relatively low cost and imports goods that are relatively costly to produce domestically. For example, Sweden and Spain benefit from such trade. Sweden has a climate and geography that enable it to produce forest products such as timber, pulp, and paper. Spain has a climate well suited to producing many types of fruit. Neither country is good at producing the other country's product. Thus, it is not surprising that Sweden exports forest products to Spain while Spain exports fruit to Sweden and that both countries benefit from such trade.

Gains from Trade Between Countries. We use an example to illustrate why participants gain from trade. Suppose that the United States and Japan initially do not trade and each country is in competitive equilibrium, in which the prices of goods equal their marginal costs of production. The United States produces and sells a bag of rice for $1 and a silk scarf for $10. That is, the value of ten bags of rice is equal to that of one silk scarf. Japan produces and sells a bag of rice for ¥200 and a silk scarf for ¥1,000: The value of five bags of rice equals that of one silk scarf. If the United States were to reduce the number of silk scarves it produces by one, it could afford to produce 10 extra bags of rice. In contrast, Japan could produce one more scarf at the cost of only five bags of rice. Therefore, the two countries could produce the same number of scarves and have five extra bags of rice if they reallocated their resources. In the absence of transportation costs, both countries could gain if the United States shipped rice to Japan and Japan shipped scarves to the United States.

The reason for this gain is that the United States has a comparative advantage in producing rice and Japan has a comparative advantage in producing scarves. The cost of producing a scarf is 10 bags of rice in the United States and only 5 in Japan, so it is relatively inexpensive to produce a scarf in Japan. Similarly, the cost of producing a bag of rice is one-tenth of a scarf in the United States and one-fifth of a scarf in Japan, so it is relatively inexpensive to produce a bag of rice in the United States.

Gains from Intra-Firm Trade. This basic idea of comparative advantage also works for *intra-firm trade*—where a single firm is on both sides of an international transaction—exporting the output from its operation in one country to an affiliated business unit in another country. For example, Bombardier, which manufactures small jets such as the Learjet, has production and engineering sites in 26 countries. It produces composite parts in Mexico, flight controls in Morocco, and engine housings in the United Kingdom, then exports those components and others to assembly plants in Canada and the United States. Such intra-firm trade is about 40% of U.S. trade according to the World Bank (2017).

We illustrate the gains from intra-firm trade with an example concerning General Electric (GE), a major producer of kitchen appliances and many other products, which has production facilities in many countries, including Hungary and Romania. Suppose that GE is considering how to organize its production of refrigerators in Eastern Europe. To produce a refrigerator, GE must manufacture the basic parts or components and assemble those components into a finished product. A production employee might work in either component production or assembly.

We assume that Hungarian workers are more productive at both component production and assembly than workers in Romania. (This difference in productivity might reflect factors such as the quality of equipment and training.) That is, a Hungarian worker has *absolute advantage* over a Romanian worker: With the same amount of effort, the Hungarian worker can produce more of both outputs than can the Romanian. As Table 17.1 shows, a Hungarian worker can produce enough components (parts) for four refrigerators per day or can assemble four refrigerators in a day. A Romanian worker can produce enough parts for two refrigerators per day or can assemble one refrigerator per day.

TABLE 17.1 Output per Worker per Day

	Components	Assembly
Hungary	4	4
Romania	2	1

However, both plants have a comparative advantage. If a Romanian worker assembles one refrigerator, that worker does not have the time to produce two sets of parts, so the opportunity cost of assembling a refrigerator is the value of the two sets of parts. In contrast, if a Hungarian assembles one refrigerator, the opportunity cost is the value of only one set of parts. Thus, the cost to GE of having a Romanian working in assembly is twice that of a Hungarian. Therefore, the Hungarian plant should specialize in assembling refrigerators. Similarly, it is more efficient to have the Romanian plant produce parts, because producing a set of parts has an opportunity cost of assembling one refrigerator in Hungary, but only half a refrigerator in Romania.

Suppose that GE has 120 workers in its Hungarian plant and 240 in its Romanian plant. If GE cannot lay off any workers in the short run, how should GE allocate activities in Hungary and Romania to maximize total output?

One approach is for each plant to act independently, producing complete refrigerators by manufacturing the parts and then assembling them. Under this plan, the Hungarian plant allocates 60 workers to parts and 60 to assembly. Because a component worker produces 4 sets of parts per day, these workers produce $4 \times 60 = 240$ sets of parts. The 60 Hungarian assembly workers can assemble all 240 sets of parts because each worker can assemble 4 refrigerators per day. This allocation of workers to tasks yields 240 refrigerators per day in Hungary. Any other allocation would yield less output.

In Romania, 80 workers work on parts and 160 on assembly, yielding an output of 160 refrigerators per day. Thus, the two plants working independently can produce

400 refrigerators per day—240 in Hungary and 160 in Romania—as the first row of Table 17.2 shows.

TABLE 17.2 Total Production of Refrigerators

	Refrigerators per day
No trade: Plants work independently	400
Trade: Plants specialize	
Romania specializes in components, Hungary in assembly	480
Romania specializes in assembly, Hungary in components	360

A better alternative is to have Romania specialize in producing parts and Hungary specialize in production. If all 240 workers in Romania produced parts, they could manufacture enough for 480 refrigerators each day. If these parts were then sent to Hungary, the 120 Hungarian workers could assemble all 480 refrigerators in a day, as the second line of Table 17.2 shows.[3] This allocation of labor, involving specialization and trade, maximizes output. The gain from trade is 80 refrigerators.

If, instead, GE has its Romanian plant specialize in assembly, only 360 refrigerators would be produced (third row of Table 17.2), as Q&A 17.1 explains. Such an outcome is worse than no trade, as 40 fewer refrigerators are produced. As summarized in Table 17.2, the best outcome is for the Romanian plant to produce parts and for the Hungarian plant to assemble these parts into refrigerators. This allocation of resources produces the most output because each plant specializes in the activity in which it has a comparative advantage.

Q&A 17.1

In our GE example, if the Romanian plant specializes in assembly and the Hungarian plant in producing components, what is the largest number of refrigerators that GE can produce per day?

Answer

1. *Determine how many Hungarian workers must produce components to keep the 240 Romanian workers fully occupied assembling refrigerators and how many refrigerators are produced.* The Romanian workers can assemble 240 refrigerators a day. To keep all the Romanian workers busy, only 60 Hungarian workers are needed to make 240 sets of parts each day.

2. *Explain how the remaining 60 Hungarian workers must be allocated to produce the most additional refrigerators and determine how many refrigerators they make.* The remaining 60 Hungarian workers can produce the largest number of refrigerators by having 30 workers each producing 4 sets of components a day and 30 assembling 4 refrigerators per day, thereby producing an additional 120 refrigerators.

3. *Determine GE's total production with this allocation of workers and compare it to GE's other two options.* Because 240 refrigerators are assembled in the Romanian plant and 120 more refrigerators are completely produced in the Hungarian plant, this approach yields a total of only 360 refrigerators. This quantity is less than the 400 GE produces if the plants do not trade or the 480 they produce if they trade and the Romanian plant specializes in components and the Hungarian plant in assembly.

---

[3]We assume the cost of transporting components or assembled products is small enough so that we do not need to consider it explicitly.

The principle of comparative advantage is important in making decisions, even in the rock music business. Brian May had completed most of his PhD in astrophysics at Imperial College in London by 1974. In that year, his band, Queen, launched its second album, *Queen II*, which became internationally successful. Discovering that his comparative advantage was in rock music, he stopped working on his PhD and toured the world with Queen. After the death of its lead singer, Freddie Mercury, in 1991, the band became less active. Its last major world tour as Queen + Paul Rodgers ended in 2006.

In 2007, as the opportunity cost of spending his time in studying dropped, May returned to complete his PhD, as implied by the principle of comparative advantage. Since then, he's worked at least part time as an astrophysicist, including collaborating on NASA's New Horizons space probe in 2015, working with the European Space Agency in 2016, and creating a stereo image of the Ryugu asteroid discovered by the Japan Aerospace Exploration Agency in 2018. (He also still finds time to perform at the occasional concert.)

Increasing Returns to Scale

Trade occurs for many reasons in addition to comparative advantage. One of the other major motives for trade is to take advantage of increasing returns to scale (Chapter 5). With an increasing returns to scale (IRS) production function, doubling all the inputs more than doubles output. Thus, all else the same, having one IRS plant produce a given amount of output is less costly than spreading the production over two IRS plants.

In our GE refrigerator example, the production process exhibits constant returns to scale. Production involves only one input, labor. Doubling the number of workers doubles the output. We showed that with constant returns to scale, GE benefits from trade due to comparative advantage.

Suppose instead that GE's production function exhibits increasing returns to scale, so that doubling labor triples output. Initially, GE has two plants in Hungary, each with 50 workers. The workers in both plants are equally productive in all activities. Operating independently, each plant can produce 200 refrigerators, so total production is 400 refrigerators. GE could increase its output by closing one plant and shifting all its workers to the remaining plant, where the 100 workers could produce 600 refrigerators due to increasing returns to scale.

Indeed, if GE increases its labor force at this one plant even more, its production will grow more than in proportion, so that its cost per refrigerator would drop further. If GE can sell its refrigerators only in Hungary, the limited demand for refrigerators there would cap the number of refrigerators GE wants to produce at this plant. However, if GE can export refrigerators to other countries, it can increase production at this one plant and lower its cost of production. Thus, increasing returns to scale provides an incentive to trade by selling in other countries.

Country Size. Relatively small countries in particular may benefit from taking advantage of returns to scale. Consider Canada, whose population and gross domestic product (GDP) are about one-tenth that of the United States. If Canada were unable to trade with other countries, its relatively small market would prevent it from cost-effectively producing and consuming commercial jet aircraft, which are produced with substantial increasing returns to scale.

However, if a Canadian producer can export its products all over the world, it can take advantage of increasing returns to scale by producing a large quantity of jet aircraft. For example, by taking advantage of international trade, Bombardier Aerospace, a Canadian firm, has become the world's third-largest commercial jet producer, specializing in light jets, including the business jets favored by senior executives and rock stars. Canada exports these light commercial jets and imports large commercial jets manufactured by the two major producers, the United States' Boeing Company and Europe's Airbus S.A.S. All the countries involved gain from trade due to increasing returns to scale.

Product Variety. Increasing returns to scale play an even greater role in a market with substantial product variety, such as toys, than in a market with a homogeneous product, such as DRAM memory chips for computers. The more varieties in a market, the fewer units of any one variety a firm can sell. Thus, without international trade, it is very difficult for the manufacturer of a highly differentiated product to benefit from returns to scale.

The toy industry produces an incredible variety of products, and adds new varieties every year (usually in time for the winter holiday season). Toy producers could lower their average cost by producing fewer toy varieties and using longer production runs for the toys they do produce, so that they could spread the design, setup, and marketing fixed costs over more units of output. However, children love variety and new toys. Even a single category of toys, such as dolls or trucks, has hundreds of different varieties. Because children demand variety, a manufacturer that decides to sell only one product year after year so as to lower its average cost will quickly find that it can sell very few units and will likely go out of business.

How can a toy manufacturer produce differentiated toys and yet take advantage of increasing returns to scale? The only practical way is to sell its product to children in many countries instead of only in its home country.

| Mini-Case | Barbie, produced by the U.S.-based Mattel, Inc., is perhaps the world's best-known toy. While other toy fads come and go, Barbie has had remarkable staying power. She was introduced in 1959 and is still a popular product. Although Barbie was invented and first produced in the United States, Mattel has produced Barbie dolls in many other countries, including Indonesia, China, Malaysia, Thailand, and Mexico. |

Barbie Doll Varieties

One key to Barbie's success is product variety. In 2018, Mattel's Barbie website listed over 100 versions of Barbie, along with multiple versions of many other characters in Barbie's world, including Ken, her on-again, off-again boyfriend.[4]

Barbie dolls come in several different price categories, ranging from entry-level pink label dolls to expensive platinum label varieties. Every year new versions are introduced. A featured new variant for 2018 was a robotics engineer version of Barbie.

---

[4]In 2004, Mattel sent out a news release indicating that Barbie and Ken had decided to "spend some time apart" after being together for 43 years, although they would "remain the best of friends." In 2011, they got back together.

International trade facilitates Barbie's success through constantly introducing new varieties. Each variety requires a significant fixed cost in product design and manufacturing setup, so Mattel must produce a large number of each variety to benefit from increasing returns to scale. Thus, global trade, by increasing sales, results in more varieties.

17.2 Exchange Rates

How willing people are to trade one type of currency for another affects trade in goods and services. An **exchange rate** is the price of one currency (such as the euro) in terms of another currency (such as the dollar). Most countries or groups of countries have a unique currency, which can be traded or exchanged for the currencies of other countries. The euro (€) is the currency of 19 European countries that belong to the Eurozone.[5] It can be traded for U.S. dollars ($), Japanese yen (¥), British pounds (£), or many other currencies. In August 2018, one euro could be exchanged for $1.17 in U.S. currency. That is, the exchange rate between the dollar and the euro was $1.17. Equivalently, the exchange rate denominated in euros was €0.85: One dollar could buy 85 euro cents.

Determining the Exchange Rate

Because currency is exchanged in a competitive market, we can use a supply-and-demand model to determine the exchange rate or price of one currency in terms of another. In Figure 17.1, the quantity on the horizontal axis is the number of euros that Americans want to buy using dollars. The price on the vertical axis is the exchange rate, X, which is the number of dollars it takes to buy one euro. As X increases, the price of a euro in terms of dollars increases, or equivalently, the price of the dollar in terms of euros falls.

FIGURE 17.1 Supply and Demand Curves Determine the Exchange Rate

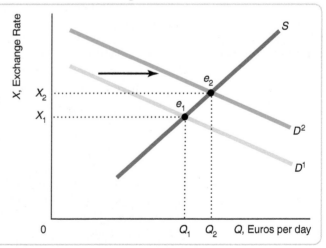

The interaction between supply and demand curves determines the exchange rate or price of one currency in terms of another. If U.S. consumers and firms want more euros at any given exchange rate so that the U.S. demand curve for euros shifts to the right from D^1 to D^2 while the supply curve of euros remains unchanged, then the equilibrium exchange rate specified as the number of dollars it takes to buy one euro rises from X_1 to X_2.

---

[5]The euro was created by the European Union (EU). As of 2018, it was the currency of 19 of 28 EU countries, including France, Germany, and Italy. Non-EU sovereign states using the euro include Andorra, Kosovo, Monaco, Montenegro, San Marino, and the Vatican City.

The initial demand curve for euros in the United States is D^1. The demand curve slopes down because the quantity of euros demanded by Americans increases as the exchange rate falls: The euro costs fewer dollars. The supply curve of euros, S, slopes up because Europeans are willing to trade more euros as the exchange rate increases.

The intersection of the supply and demand curves determines the initial equilibrium: the number of euros exchanged, Q_1, and the exchange rate, X_1, which was 1.16 in late 2018. If U.S. consumers and firms want more euros at any given exchange rate, so that the demand curve for euros shifts to the right to D^2, then the equilibrium quantity increases to Q_2 and the equilibrium exchange rate rises to X_2. That is, the price of a euro in U.S. dollars increases.

Many factors affect the supply and demand for a particular currency, including financial and macroeconomic conditions. For example, if investment opportunities increase in the United States relative to those in Europe, the exchange rate for the euro falls.

Exchange Rates and the Pattern of Trade

If the exchange rate for the euro falls, U.S. consumers and firms increase their demand for European goods, as they can now buy more goods for a given number of dollars. Similarly, the demand of European consumers and firms for U.S. goods falls. Thus, a change in exchange rates affects the incentives to trade between countries.

The Brazilian currency is the real, denoted BRL. Suppose that initially one U.S. dollar is worth four Brazilian reals. A volleyball sells for $10 in the United States or 40 BRL in Brazil. Now suppose that the exchange rate changes so that $1 is worth 5 BRL. If transaction and shipping costs are negligible, Brazilian retailers can increase their profits by selling the product in the United States for $10 (now worth 50 BRL), rather than in Brazil for 40 BRL. As the quantity sold in the United States increases, the U.S. price of the ball falls because the U.S. demand curve slopes down. Similarly, as the number of balls sold in Brazil falls, the price in Brazil rises.

This process, called *arbitrage*, equates the prices of the ball in the two countries in the absence of transaction costs. If the transaction cost is t, arbitrage moves the price in one country to within t of the price in the other country because further arbitrage is unprofitable.

Managerial Implication Limiting Arbitrage and Gray Markets	Managers can often increase profits by engaging in international price discrimination (Chapter 10): charging higher prices in countries where consumers have a greater willingness to pay. However, for international price discrimination to be profitable, firms must limit resale or arbitrage across countries. Managers have to be particularly concerned about increased arbitrage opportunities as exchange rates change.

If arbitrageurs can buy the good in the low-price country and sell it at a higher price in other countries without incurring transaction costs, their actions eliminate the price differential. Arbitrage will not completely eliminate price differentials if arbitrageurs incur transaction costs. If the price differential between countries for some product is $5 while the transaction cost (including transportation) is $10 per unit, then no arbitrage occurs. Thus, a price difference of $10 or less could persist.

For many goods, the internet has greatly facilitated arbitrage. A student in the United States can save money by buying textbooks from Amazon's sites in lower-price countries. People around the world use eBay to trade a wide variety of goods from one country to another. The internet has reduced, but not eliminated, international price differences in such products.

One way that a firm's managers try to prevent arbitrage is to permit only authorized dealers to handle their products. Any authorized dealer that imports the product from another country instead of buying it from the manufacturer could lose its authorization.

Foreign goods shipped to the high-price country and sold outside authorized channels of distribution are called *gray market* goods. Costco and Swiss watchmaker Omega fought a long legal battle over gray market sales. Costco, which is not an authorized dealer of Omega watches, purchased watches from dealers in Paraguay and elsewhere. It sold the watches in the United States for prices above those charged in Paraguay but below the prices charged by authorized U.S. dealers. Omega sued to block Costco's action, but a court decided in Costco's favor. However, for some other products, the courts have blocked gray market sales.

In addition to litigation, managers use a variety of techniques to prevent gray markets. One technique that most camera and electronic equipment manufacturers use to limit arbitrage is to provide a country-specific warranty. A gray market camera purchased in the United States that was imported from Europe comes with a warranty that is good only in Europe and hence is less attractive to U.S. customers. Of course, arbitrageurs responded. Today, many stores offer third-party insurance on gray market cameras and electronic equipment. The main lesson for managers in firms selling branded products internationally is that investments in preventing or reducing arbitrage are often profitable.

Managing Exchange Rate Risk

Managing risk (Chapter 14) is particularly important for firms doing business in multiple countries because exchange rate movements increase risk, as we now illustrate. Martin, the manager of a small U.S. producer of medical equipment, signs a contract to provide custom equipment to a hospital in India for 84 million Indian rupees (INR), to be paid in 6 months when the equipment is delivered. At the current exchange rate, 70 rupees can be exchanged for one U.S. dollar, so Martin's firm would earn $1.2 (= 84/70) million if it received payment in INR today.

Martin is very worried about the risk from a change in the exchange rate. Martin's firm is going to incur $1.1 million in expenses to build and ship the equipment. Thus, at the current exchange rate, his firm stands to make a profit of $100,000. However, if the exchange rate falls to 84 rupees per dollar in 6 months, Martin's firm will receive only $1 (= 84/84) million and suffer a loss of $100,000, which may be enough to bankrupt the firm.

Of course, if the exchange rate moves in the other direction, Martin's firm will earn additional profit. If the rupee appreciates to INR 60 per dollar, Martin's firm will earn $1.4 (= 84/60) million, and make a profit of $300,000. Nonetheless, this exchange rate risk, which may lead to bankruptcy, is unacceptable to Martin.

Martin has a couple of options. First, he could try to insist that payment be made in U.S. dollars so that the Indian firm bears the exchange rate risk.

Second, Martin can *hedge* the risk by purchasing a *forward contract* or a *futures contract*. Such a contract is an agreement to exchange one currency for another in the future at a specified rate. For example, Martin could contract to exchange INR 84 million for $1.2 million in 6 months. Such a contract is called a forward contract if it is a private agreement with another party, such as a bank. The bank would charge a fee for the contract, say, $10,000. Effectively, the bank is selling Martin an insurance policy for $10,000.

Futures contracts are similar, except that they are standardized contracts that sell on organized exchanges. The Chicago Mercantile Exchange is the major trading venue for such contracts in the United States.

17.3 International Trade Policies

Although firms and consumers in one country want to trade with people in other countries, governments often prevent free trade between nations. A government may prevent trade to protect domestic suppliers from competition by foreign firms. For example, a government may ban trade or set a *quota* that limits the amount of a good that can be imported. Alternatively, a government may tax imports or exports to raise government revenue. Commonly, governments collect an import *tariff* (sometimes called a *duty*), which is a tax on only imported items.

Historically, governments have concentrated on restricting imports rather than limiting or encouraging exports. Consequently, we focus on the effects on prices, government revenue, and total surplus of import-restricting trade policies.

Quotas and Tariffs in Competitive Markets

Quotas and tariffs are usually applied to imports by the government of the importing country. A government chooses one of four import policies:

- **Allow free trade**: Foreign firms may sell in the importing country without restrictions.
- **Ban all imports**: The government sets a quota of zero on imports.
- **Set a tariff**: The government imposes a tariff on imported goods.
- **Set a positive quota**: The government limits imports to $\overline{Q}$.

To illustrate the effects of these various policies, we examine the U.S. market for crude oil. For simplicity, we assume that transportation costs are zero and that the United States is small enough to be a price taker in world markets. We further assume that the supply curve of oil is horizontal at the *world price*, which is the market clearing price in the world market. Given these assumptions, the importing country, the United States, can buy as much crude oil as it wants at the world price.

Free Trade Versus a Ban on Imports. Preventing imports into the domestic market raises the price. In Figure 17.2, the estimated U.S. domestic supply curve, S^a, is upward sloping and the foreign supply curve is horizontal at the world price, which is $60 per barrel (the price in early 2018).[6] The total U.S. supply curve, S^1, is the horizontal sum of the domestic supply curve and the foreign supply curve. Thus, S^1 is the same as the upward-sloping domestic supply curve for prices below $60 and is horizontal at $60. With free trade, the United States imports crude oil if its domestic price in the absence of imports exceeds the world price.

The free-trade equilibrium, e_1, is determined by the intersection of S^1 and the demand curve, where the U.S. price equals the world price, $60, and the quantity

---

[6]The figures are based on Baumeister and Peersman (2013).

FIGURE 17.2 **The Loss from Eliminating Free Trade**

Because the world supply curve is horizontal at the world price of $60, the total U.S. supply curve of crude oil is S^1 with free trade. The free-trade equilibrium is e_1. With a ban on imports, the equilibrium e_2 occurs where the domestic supply curve, $S^a = S^2$, intersects D. The ban increases producer surplus by $B \approx$ $1.606 billion per day and decreases consumer surplus by $B + C \approx$ $2.045 billion per day, so the deadweight loss is $C =$ $439 million per day or $160 billion per year.

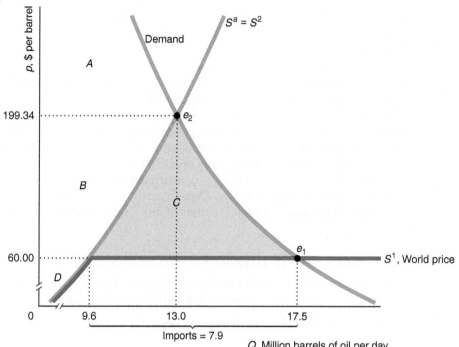

U.S.	Free Trade	U.S.Import Ban	Change ($ millions)
Consumer Surplus, CS	$A + B + C$	A	$-B - C = -2,045 = \Delta CS$
Producer Surplus, PS	D	$B + D$	$B = 1,606 = \Delta PS$
Total Surplus, $TS = CS + PS$	$A + B + C + D$	$A + B + D$	$-C = -439 = \Delta TS = -DWL$

is 17.5 million barrels per day. At the equilibrium price, domestic supply is 9.6 on S^2. Imports are therefore $17.5 - 9.6 = 7.9$ million barrels. U.S. consumer surplus is $A + B + C$, U.S. producer surplus is D, and the U.S. total surplus is $A + B + C + D$. (Throughout our discussion of trade, we ignore welfare effects in other countries.)

If imports are banned, the total U.S. supply curve, S^2, is the American domestic supply curve, S^a. The equilibrium is at e_2, where S^2 intersects the demand curve. The new equilibrium price is $199.34, and the new equilibrium quantity, 13 million barrels per day, is produced domestically. Consumer surplus is A, producer surplus is $B + D$, and total surplus is $A + B + D$.

The ban helps U.S. crude oil producers but harms consumers. Because of the higher price, domestic firms gain producer surplus of $\Delta PS = B \approx$ $1.606 billion per day.[7] The change in consumers' surplus is $\Delta CS = -B - C \approx -2.045 billion per day. Consumers lose $1.27 ($= 2.045/1.606$) for every $1 that producers gain from a ban.

---

[7]Because the demand and supply curves are nonlinear, we calculated the surplus measures using areas of shapes other than rectangles and triangles.

Does the ban help the United States? No. The change in total surplus, ΔTS, is the sum of the gain to producers and the loss to consumers: $\Delta TS = \Delta PS + \Delta CS = -C \approx -\$439$ million per day. The reduction in total surplus of \$439 million per day (about \$160 billion per year) is the deadweight loss from the ban.

Mini-Case

Russian Food Ban

Starting in 2014, many Western nations imposed a variety of sanctions on Russia because of its military activities in Ukraine. In retaliation, Russia banned imports of many agricultural products from the United States, the European Union, Australia, Canada, and Norway.

Russians, particularly in prosperous cities such as Moscow, depend heavily on imported foods from the West. The previous year, 2013, Russian agricultural imports were about \$1 billion from the United States and 11.8 billion euros (\$15.7 billion) from the European Union. In 2017, the Agriculture Ministry said that over the previous three years, food imports fell from \$42 billion to \$25 billion, while Russian agricultural production rose by 11%.

The ban imposes substantial costs on Russian consumers. In 2014, food prices soared 11.5%, which was 5.8 percentage points higher than the overall inflation rate. Prices for some types of food increased even more. Meat and poultry prices rose 18% over the previous year, while the price of butter shot up by 17%. In early 2015, the Russian Finance Minister said that Russia's losses from the Western sanctions were \$50 billion.

The ban had less effect on firms in exporting nations, which could sell their products elsewhere. Russian food-producing firms benefited. For example, in the first quarter after the ban went into effect, the profit of Cherkizovo, a Russian producer of meat, rose eight-fold from the previous year.

The ban is scheduled to stay in effect at least through 2019.

Free Trade Versus a Tariff. Two common types of tariffs are *specific tariffs*—*t* dollars per unit—and *ad valorem tariffs*—a percentage of the sales price. In the modern era, tariffs have been applied throughout the world, most commonly to agricultural products.[8] For most of the post–World War II period, the United States has had a tariff on oil to raise government revenue or to reduce U.S. dependence on foreign oil.

You may be asking yourself, "Why should we study tariffs if we've already looked at taxes (Chapter 2)? Isn't a tariff just another tax?" Good point! Tariffs are just taxes. If the only goods sold were imported, the effect of a tariff in the importing country would be the same as we showed for a sales tax. We study tariffs separately because a tariff is applied only to imported goods, so it affects domestic and foreign producers differently.

---

[8]After World War II, most trading nations signed the General Agreement on Tariffs and Trade (GATT), which limited their ability to subsidize exports or limit imports using quotas and tariffs. The rules prohibited most export subsidies and import quotas, except when imports threatened "market disruption" (a term that was left undefined). Modifications of the GATT and agreements negotiated by its successor, the World Trade Organization, have reduced or eliminated many tariffs.

Because tariffs are applied to only imported goods, they do not raise as much tax revenue or affect equilibrium quantities as much as taxes applied to all goods in a market. For example, De Melo and Tarr (1992) calculated that almost five times more tax revenue would be generated by a 15% additional *ad valorem* tax on petroleum products than by a 25% additional import tariff on oil and gas.

To illustrate the effect of a tariff, suppose that the government imposes a specific tariff of $t = \$40$ per barrel of crude oil. Given this tariff, firms will not import oil into the United States unless the U.S. price is at least $40 above the $60 world price. The tariff creates a wedge between the world price and the U.S. price. This tariff causes the total supply curve to shift from S^1 to S^3 in Figure 17.3. As the world supply curve for oil is horizontal at $60, adding a $40 tariff shifts this supply curve upward so that it is horizontal at $100. That is, the rest of the world will supply an unlimited amount of oil at $100 inclusive of the tariff. As a result, the total U.S. supply curve with the tariff, S^3, equals the domestic supply curve for prices below $100 and is horizontal at $100.

The new equilibrium, e_3, occurs where S^3 intersects the demand curve. At this equilibrium, price is $100 and quantity is 15.4 million barrels of oil per day. At this higher price, domestic firms supply 10.9 million barrels of oil per day, so imports are $15.4 - 10.9 = 4.5$ million barrels of oil per day.

The tariff *protects* American producers from foreign competition. The larger the tariff is, the less crude oil is imported; hence the higher is the price that domestic firms charge. (With a large enough tariff, nothing is imported, and the price rises to the no-trade level, $199.34.) With a tariff of $40, domestic firms' producer surplus increases by area $B \approx \$412$ million per day.

Because the U.S. price rises from $60 to $100, consumer surplus falls by $B + C + D + E \approx \$654$ million per day. The government receives tariff revenues, T, equal to area $D \approx \$180$ million per day, which is $t = \$40$ times the quantity imported, 4.5 million.

The deadweight loss is the loss of consumer surplus, $B + C + D + E$, minus the tax revenue, D, minus the producer surplus gain, B. That is, the deadweight loss is $C + E = \$62$ million per day, or $22.6 billion per year. This deadweight loss is 15% of the gain to producers. Consumers lose $1.59 for each $1 that domestic producers gain. Because the tariff doesn't completely eliminate imports, the loss of total surplus is smaller than it is if all imports are banned.

This deadweight loss has two components. First, C is a *production distortion lost* from U.S. firms producing 10.9 million barrels per day instead of 9.6 million barrels per day. Domestic firms produce this extra output because the tariff drives up the price from $60 to $100. The cost of producing these extra 1.3 million barrels of oil per day domestically is $C + G$, the area under the domestic supply curve, S^a, between 9.6 and 10.9. Had Americans bought this oil at the world price, the cost would have been only G. Thus, C is the additional cost of producing the extra 1.3 million barrels of oil per day domestically instead of importing it.

Second, E is a *consumption distortion loss* from U.S. consumers' buying too little oil, 15.4 instead of 17.5 million barrels, because the tariff increases the price from $60 to $100.[9] U.S. consumers place a value on this extra output of $E + H$, the area under their demand curve between 15.4 and 17.5. The cost of buying this extra oil from the world market is only H, the area below the line at $60 between 15.4 and 17.5. Thus, E is the difference between the value at the world price and the value U.S. consumers place on this extra 1.3 million barrels per day.

---

[9]This analysis ignores the effect of oil consumption on the environment.

FIGURE 17.3 Effects of a Tariff or a Quota

A tariff of $t = \$40$ per barrel of oil imported or a quota of 4.5 million barrels per day drives the U.S. price of crude oil to $100, which is $40 more than the world price. Under the tariff, the equilibrium, e_3, is determined by the intersection of the S^3 total U.S. supply curve and the D demand curve. Under the quota, e_3 is determined by a quantity wedge of 4.5 million barrels per day between the quantity demanded, 15.4 million barrels per day, and the quantity supplied by domestic firms, 10.9 million barrels per day, at a price of $100 per barrel. Compared to free trade, domestic producers gain area B and consumers lose areas $B + C + D + E$ from either a tariff or a quota. If the government gives the quota rights to foreign producers, the deadweight loss is $C + D + E$. With a tariff, the government's tariff revenue increases by D, so the deadweight loss is only $C + E$.

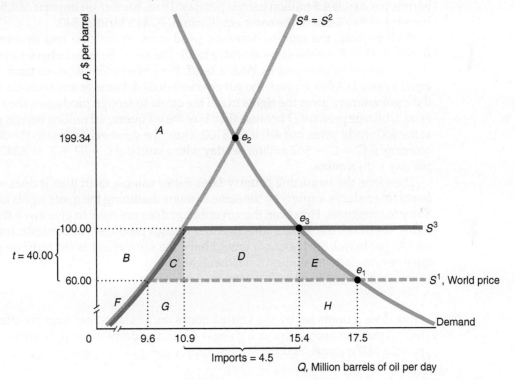

U.S.	Free Trade	U.S. Tariff or Quota	Change ($ millions)
Consumer Surplus, CS	$A + B + C + D + E$	A	$- B - C - D - E = -654$
Producer Surplus, PS	F	$B + F$	$B = 412$
TariRevenues, T	0	D (tariff)	$D = 180$ (tariff)
		0 (quota)	0 (quota)
Total Surplus from a Tariff $TS = CS + PS + T$	$A + B + C + D + E + F$	$A + B + D + F$	$- C - E = -62 = -DWL$
Total Surplus from a Quota, $TS = CS + PS$	$A + B + C + D + E + F$	$A + B + F$	$- C - D - E = -242 = -DWL$

Free Trade Versus a Quota. Many countries use quotas instead of tariffs, which may lead to a false belief:

Common Confusion Quotas are preferable to tariffs.

Although politicians have a variety of reasons to prefer quotas, countries usually benefit from employing a tariff rather than an equivalent quota—one that reduces imports by the same amount—because only the tariff produces revenue for the government. Of course, countries would generally be better off using neither.

The market effects of a quota are similar to those of a tariff. In Figure 17.3, if the government limits oil imports to 4.5 million barrels per day, the quota is binding because 7.9 million barrels per day were imported under free trade (see Figure 17.2). In Figure 17.3, if the price equals $100, the gap between the quantity demanded, 15.4 million barrels per day, and the quantity supplied by domestic firms, 10.9 million barrels per day, is 4.5 million barrels per day. Thus, a quota on imports of 4.5 million barrels per day leads to the same equilibrium, e_3, as a tariff of $40.

With a quota, the gain to domestic producers, B, and the loss to consumers, $B + C + D + E$, are the same as with a tariff. The key difference between a tariff and a quota concerns who gets D. With a tariff, the government receives tariff revenue equal to area D. With a quota, the government does not receive any revenue. Instead, if the government gives the rights to sell the quota to foreign producers, they earn an extra arbitrage profit of D because they buy the oil quota, 4.5 million barrels per day, at the $60 world price, but sell it for $100. Thus, the deadweight loss to the domestic economy is $C + E = \$62$ million per day with a tariff but $C + D + E = \$242$ million per day with a quota.

Therefore, the importing country fares better using a tariff than it does setting a quota that reduces imports by the same amount, assuming the quota rights are given away to foreigners. However, the government does not have to give away the quota rights. It can sell the quota rights to either foreign producers or domestic importers for $40 per barrel. Such a quota would have the same effect as the tariff on government revenue and on domestic deadweight loss.

Q&A 17.2   How does a quota set by the United States on foreign sugar imports affect the total American supply curve for sugar given the domestic supply curve, S^d, in panel a of the graph, and the foreign supply curve, S^f, in panel b?

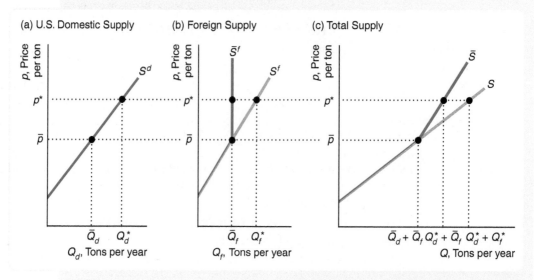

Answer

1. *Determine the U.S. supply curve without the quota.* The *no-quota* total supply curve, S, in panel c, is the horizontal sum of the U.S. domestic supply curve, S^d, and the no-quota foreign supply curve, S^f.

2. *Show the effect of the quota on foreign supply.* At prices below $\bar{p}$, foreign suppliers want to supply quantities less than the quota, $\overline{Q}_f$, as panel b shows. As a result, the foreign supply curve under the quota, $\overline{S}^f$, is the same as the no-quota foreign supply curve, S^f, for prices less than $\bar{p}$. At prices above $\bar{p}$, foreign suppliers want to supply more but are limited to $\overline{Q}_f$. Thus, the foreign supply curve with a quota, $\overline{S}^f$, is vertical at $\overline{Q}_f$ for prices above $\bar{p}$.

3. *Determine the U.S. total supply curve with the quota.* The total supply curve with the quota, $\overline{S}$, is the horizontal sum of S^d and $\overline{S}^f$. At any price above $\bar{p}$, the total supply equals the quota plus the domestic supply. For example, at p^*, the domestic supply is Q^*_d and the foreign supply is $\overline{Q}_f$, so the total supply is $Q^*_d + \overline{Q}_f$. Above $\bar{p}$, $\overline{S}$ is the domestic supply curve shifted $\overline{Q}_f$ units to the right. As a result, the portion of $\overline{S}$ above $\bar{p}$ has the same slope as S^d.

4. *Compare the U.S. total supply curves with and without the quota.* At prices less than or equal to $\bar{p}$, the same quantity is supplied with and without the quota, so $\overline{S}$ is the same as S. At prices above $\bar{p}$, less is supplied with the quota than without it, so $\overline{S}$ is steeper than S, indicating that a given increase in price raises the quantity supplied by less with a quota than without one.

Rent Seeking

Given that tariffs and quotas hurt the importing country, why do the Japanese, U.S., and other governments impose tariffs, quotas, or other trade barriers? One reason is that domestic producers stand to make large gains from such government actions; hence, it pays for them to organize and lobby the government to enact these trade policies. Although consumers as a whole suffer large losses, the loss to any one consumer is usually small. Moreover, consumers rarely organize to lobby the government about trade issues. Thus in most countries, producers are often able to convince (cajole, influence, or bribe) legislators or government officials to aid them, even though consumers suffer more-than-offsetting losses.

If domestic producers can talk the government into a tariff, quota, or other policy that reduces imports, they gain extra producer surplus, such as area B in Figures 17.2 and 17.3. Economists call efforts and expenditures to gain a rent or a profit from government actions rent seeking. If producers or other interest groups bribe legislators to influence policy, the bribe is a transfer of income and hence does not directly increase deadweight loss. However, if this rent-seeking behavior—such as hiring lobbyists and engaging in advertising to influence legislators—uses up resources, the deadweight loss from tariffs and quotas understates the true loss to society. The domestic producers may spend an amount up to the gain in producer surplus to influence the government.[10]

---

[10]Tullock (1967) and Posner (1975) made this argument. Fisher (1985) and Varian (1989) contended that the expenditure is typically less than the producer surplus.

Lopez and Pagoulatos (1994) estimated the deadweight loss and the additional losses due to rent-seeking activities in the United States in food and tobacco products. They estimated that the deadweight loss was $19.3 billion (in 2018 dollars), which was 2.6% of the domestic consumption expenditure on these products. The largest deadweight losses were in dairy products and sugar manufacturing, which primarily use import quotas to raise domestic prices. The overall gain in producer surplus was $69.9 billion. In addition, the government gained $2.8 billion in tariff revenues. If all of producer surplus and government revenues were expended in rent-seeking behavior and other wasteful activities, the total loss was $72.7 billion, or 12.5% of consumption, which is 4.77 times larger than the deadweight loss alone. In other words, the loss to society is somewhere between the deadweight loss of $19.3 billion and $72.7 + $19.3 = $92 billion.

Noncompetitive Reasons for Trade Policy

A government intervenes in international trade for many reasons beyond raising revenues from tariffs or from selling quotas. Often, trade policy is used to create or eliminate market failures that result from noncompetitive markets. First, the government may use trade policy to create market power and capture some of the extra profit. Second, the government may use strategic trade policies to help its domestic industry compete more effectively with foreign firms when selling in a world market. Third, it may use contingent protection policies to prevent predation by foreign firms or to protect domestic firms from foreign competition.

Creating Market Power.   A government can exploit monopoly power by using tariffs or quotas, even if the underlying industry is highly competitive. By restricting supply in a competitive market, the government can drive the price to the monopoly level.

The Philippines supplied four-fifths of the world's coconut oil, so it was large enough to affect the world price of coconut oil. However, because its growers, refiners, and exporters operated in competitive markets, the world price was a competitive price. To create market power, the government imposed a tariff or tax on copra (the part of the coconut used to create coconut oil). Doing so not only increased the world price but also allowed the government to capture the increased profit as tariff revenue. The government could have achieved the same outcome by limiting exports using quotas that it would sell to the highest bidder.

Strategic Trade Policy.[11]   A government's trade policy can increase the share of the profits in imperfectly competitive industries that goes to its domestic industry. To illustrate this idea, we consider a vaccine market that is large enough to support one producer but not two—a market with a natural monopoly. Each disease requires a different vaccine, and each vaccine is costly to develop. Many vaccines in a given region are produced and sold by a monopoly supplier (Danzon and Pereira, 2011).

Ajinomoto (a major Japanese vaccine producer) and Novartis (a Swiss producer) choose whether to enter and produce a particular vaccine for the U.S. market. Table 17.3 shows their profits from the resulting entry game (Chapter 12).

If both firms enter, both lose, making a profit of −5. Therefore, if its rival enters, a firm prefers to stay out of the market. If Novartis enters and Ajinomoto does not,

---

[11]This section uses game theory (Chapter 12); however, the rest of this chapter does not assume knowledge of this material. The following analysis is based on Brander and Spencer (1985) and Krugman (1987).

TABLE 17.3 Drug Entry Game

		Novartis	
		Enter	Do Not Enter
Ajinomoto	Enter	−5 −5	0 90
	Do Not Enter	90 0	0 0

then Novartis earns 90 and Ajinomoto earns nothing. If Ajinomoto also enters, its profit is −5, so it regrets entering. Similarly, if Ajinomoto enters, then Novartis prefers not to enter. Neither firm has a dominant strategy. However, using the game theory analysis from Chapter 12, we see that this game has two pure strategy Nash equilibria: Novartis enters while Ajinomoto stays out, or Ajinomoto enters and Novartis stays out.[12]

Can a government act to increase the profit of its domestic firm? If only the Japanese government acts by offering a subsidy of 10 to Ajinomoto if it enters, then the profit matrix changes to Table 17.4. This subsidy makes entering a dominant strategy for Ajinomoto. If Novartis enters, Ajinomoto earns 5, which is greater than the zero profit it earns if it does not enter. If Novartis does not enter, Ajinomoto's profit is 100 if it enters and 0 otherwise. Thus, Ajinomoto should enter regardless of what Novartis does. Knowing that Ajinomoto wants to enter, Novartis decides not to enter, because to do so would cause it to lose 5. Thus, the subsidy results in a Nash equilibrium in which Ajinomoto enters and earns 100, and Novartis stays out.

As a consequence, Japan obtains a net surplus of 90 (= Ajinomoto's profit of 100 minus the subsidy of 10). This surplus is much more than Japan gets if Novartis enters and Ajinomoto does not, or if both firms enter—both of which are possibilities without a subsidy. Using this strategic trade policy, Japan has shifted an uncertain situation in its favor.

TABLE 17.4 Drug Entry Game with a Subsidy of 10 to Ajinomoto

		Novartis	
		Enter	Do Not Enter
Ajinomoto	Enter	−5 5	0 100
	Do Not Enter	90 0	0 0

---

[12]The game also has a mixed-strategy equilibrium, in which each firm chooses to enter with a positive probability less than one (Chapter 12).

Both strategic trade policy tools and the trade policies that create market power are *beggar-thy-neighbor* policies. One country gains at the expense of other countries. Therefore, an important component of international trade agreements is to prevent or limit the use of such trade policies. Consequently, the trade agreements underlying the World Trade Organization specify that signatory countries agree not to use export subsidies.

Contingent Protection. *Contingent protection* is a trade policy that protects domestic producers by responding to certain actions by foreign firms or governments. The World Trade Organization allows member countries to impose contingent protection using antidumping laws and countervailing duty policies.

Many countries have contingent protection laws against *dumping*, which occurs if a foreign producer sells a product at a price that is below the price that it sets in its home country or at a price that is lower than its cost of production. Under its antidumping law, the United States imposes a tariff (or *duty*) on the dumped good.

A common justification for this law is to prevent a foreign firm from engaging in predation (Chapter 16), keeping its U.S. price low until it drives U.S. firms out of the industry and then raising its U.S. price. However, such a story is implausible unless something prevents firms from entering the market after the price rises. Apparently the primary use of antidumping laws is to protect domestic industries from lower-price foreign competition and to prevent foreign firms from price discriminating when such discrimination would favor domestic consumers.

Under a *countervailing duty policy*, a government may impose a duty if an imported good is subsidized by a foreign government through direct cash payments, credits against taxes, below-market rate loans, or in other ways. For example, in 2016, the U.S. Department of Commerce imposed both antidumping and countervailing duties on imports of corrosive-resistant steel from China and other countries. The antidumping duty imposed on imports from China was 210% and the countervailing duty varied across suppliers from 38% to 241%. These duties resulted from a legal determination that the price of the Chinese firms' steel was low due to dumping and subsidies, thereby materially injuring, or threatening material injury to, the U.S. domestic industry.[13]

Mini-Case Protection of U.S. Steel, Aluminum, and Washing Machines	The United States has, on several occasions, used antidumping and countervailing duties against steel imports from China and other countries. In 2018, the Trump administration invoked a rarely used aspect of U.S. law to impose tariffs on almost all U.S. imports of steel and aluminum. The stated rationale for the tariffs of 25% on steel and 10% on aluminum was national security.[14] Many affected countries, including Canada, China, and the EU countries, responded with retaliatory tariffs. In 2018, the United States also imposed a 20% tariff on washing machine imports. Rather than claiming that a robust washing machine industry is necessary for national security, the Trump administration used another little-used

[13]One response of Chinese suppliers was to export steel to Vietnam instead, then re-export steel from Vietnam to the United States to avoid the duties. In 2018, the United States imposed antidumping and countervailing duties on these re-exports from Vietnam. This case and others are described on U.S. Department of Commerce websites at **www.commerce.gov/tags/antidumping** and **www.commerce.gov/tags/countervailing-duty**.

[14]Canada, the largest supplier of both steel and aluminum exports to the United States, criticized the national security rationale as "insulting" given Canada's long record of support for U.S. military actions. Canada also argued that the tariffs are illegal under the World Trade Organization (WTO) and launched a WTO complaint, as did the European Union (EU).

aspect of U.S. and international trade law called the *safeguard provision*, which allows for "emergency actions" to protect an industry threatened with serious injury due to an increase in imports.

Trade Liberalization and the World Trading System

The World Trade Organization (WTO), an organization comprising most of the world's trading nations, coordinates international trade and limits trade policies that produce distortions, such as tariffs and quotas used to create market power. The WTO was formed by several international agreements. The most important of these agreements is the General Agreement on Tariffs and Trade (GATT). The GATT was originally drafted and signed in 1947, partly in reaction to the costly trade wars of the 1930s and partly to re-establish commercial relations among the nations that were disrupted during World War II. The WTO was established in 1995, although it was, in essence, a formalization of the administrative structure that had developed around the GATT.

The most important aspect of the GATT and the WTO has been to promote trade liberalization, which allows firms and consumers to benefit from trade. The WTO imposes various requirements on member countries that facilitate international trade, including limits on tariffs and quotas. Over time, countries gradually accepted the WTO free-trade principles. Only 23 nations signed the first GATT agreement in 1947. At present, over 160 countries are members of the WTO and signatories to the GATT. These countries are responsible for almost all of the world's trade. Most of the other countries in the world have *observer* status in the WTO and hope to become full members.

Reducing trade barriers, particularly tariffs and quotas, has been the most significant achievement of the GATT and the WTO. When the GATT was first created, many countries had prohibitive trade barriers, which prevented any trade with a wide range of potential trading partners. The immediate contribution of the GATT during its early years was to enable any trade at all between many countries. However, even as late as the 1980s, tariffs, quotas, and other trade barriers were still significant impediments to trade. Since then, trade barriers have continued to fall. By 2015, the world trade-weighted average tariff rate had fallen to only 2%.[15]

However, recent actions by the Trump administration may cause this downward trend in tariff rates to reverse. In particular, in 2018, President Trump imposed tariffs on a broad range of Chinese imports, which resulted in retaliatory Chinese tariffs, with threats of further escalation by both sides

Countries that belong to the WTO are allowed to establish *preferential trading arrangements* between groups of WTO member countries, including free trade agreements that eliminate tariffs and quotas altogether. The United States participates in the Dominican Republic-Central America-United States Free Trade Agreement (CAFTA-DR) with Costa Rica, El Salvador, Guatemala, Honduras, Nicaragua, and Dominican Republic and the North American Free Trade Agreement (NAFTA) with Canada and Mexico.[16] In addition, the United States has bilateral free trade

---

[15]See Thomson Reuters, **blogs.thomsonreuters.com/financial-risk/investment-management/america-first-means-global-economy/**.

[16]In 2018, representatives of Canada, Mexico, and the United States renegotiated NAFTA, reaching agreement on some small changes and on a name change to the United States Mexico Canada Agreement (USMCA). Before the revisions and name change take effect they must be approved ("ratified") by domestic legislatures in all three countries (the U.S. Congress, the Mexican General Congress, and the Canadian Parliament).

agreements with Australia, Bahrain, Chile, Colombia, Israel, Jordan, Morocco, Oman, Panama, Peru, Singapore, and South Korea. In 2017, President Trump refused to join 11 other Pacific-rim countries in a free trade agreement negotiated by President Obama. However, in 2018, he talked about joining that agreement.

Not surprisingly, trade liberalization has increased the amount of international trade. Perhaps less obviously, trade liberalization has made it easier for firms to use inputs from many different countries to produce their final products. General Motors, Westinghouse, Sony, and other companies can manufacture parts in one country and assemble them in another because tariffs and other trade barriers are low or nonexistent. High tariffs would make such supply chain arrangements much less attractive. Thus, a major effect of trade liberalization has been to increase the globalization of supply chains. Many efforts have been made to assess the costs and benefits of trade liberalization. Virtually all such studies find that these trading nations gain significantly from liberalization (Feenstra, 2010). Trade liberalization has been a major driving force behind the recent dramatic improvements in the standard of living in China, India, and other rapidly developing economies.

Trade Liberalization Problems

Critics of freer trade raise concerns about a variety of negative effects, particularly relating to environmental standards and to wages and labor standards. Freer trade might exacerbate environmental problems caused by environmental externalities or open-access common property (Chapter 16). Because most developing countries have weaker environmental laws than do the United States and other high-income countries, critics predict that freer trade will cause these developing countries to become *pollution havens*: Firms based in developed countries will move their manufacturing to these developing countries, save money by avoiding the cost of environmental regulation, and then export their products to their home countries. Such issues were important when Mexico joined Canada and the United States in the North American Free Trade Agreement (NAFTA) in 1994, which removed tariffs on goods traded by these countries. Many U.S. companies moved operations across the Mexican border, including major auto producers such as Ford and General Motors and major producers of electrical equipment such as Honeywell and General Electric.[17]

Analysis of the Mexican experience following its entry into NAFTA indicates neither a notable increase in environmental problems nor a notable decrease (Gallagher, 2004; Lipford and Yandle, 2011). Some areas close to the U.S. border experienced an increase in pollution problems, but improvements occurred in other areas.

Critics of freer trade similarly argue that U.S. firms might move operations to developing countries with low wages and weak labor standards. However, these cases differ in a critical manner. The pollution haven problem is based on market failure, and liberalizing trade and investment can make this market failure worse— reducing total surplus in the global economy. Low wages do not, in themselves, imply a market failure. Freer trade should be faulted only if it results in lower wages or labor standards in developing nations. So far, little evidence exists showing such a negative effect (Salem and Rozental, 2012).

---

[17]Proponents of NAFTA noted that it incorporated specific agreements on environmental regulation that were intended to improve environmental policy in Mexico. They also argued that because NAFTA would raise incomes in Mexico, Mexico would be more likely to institute greater environmental protections.

17.4 Multinational Enterprises

The managers of companies that produce in many countries must decide how much to trade and what prices to use when trading internationally between their units. These decisions turn critically on differences in tax laws across countries.

Most of the world's largest companies are *multinational enterprises* (MNEs): enterprises that control productive assets in more than one country.[18] MNEs play a dominant role in world trade flows, accounting for approximately 90% of U.S. exports and imports (Antràs and Yeaple, 2014).

Multinationals normally have a parent company and a number of foreign affiliates. According to the definitions used by international agencies including the United Nations Conference on Trade and Development (UNCTAD) and the International Monetary Fund (IMF), any company in which the parent has an ownership share of 10% or more is regarded as an *affiliate*. An affiliate in which the parent has an ownership share of 50% or more is called a *subsidiary*. Many subsidiaries are wholly owned by the parent.

Toyota is one of the world's largest MNEs. The parent Toyota Motor Corporation is based in Japan and has subsidiaries throughout the world, including in the United States. Typically, a multinational enterprise is not a single corporation. Rather, the parent company is a corporation and each subsidiary is itself a corporation, with its own CEO and senior managers. The only shareholder of a wholly owned subsidiary is the parent corporation. Thus, a multinational enterprise, such as Toyota, is an interlocking network of corporations connected through ownership.

The management of each subsidiary normally has discretion over business decisions such as how much to produce, what prices to charge, and how much and where to advertise. Each subsidiary is normally treated as an independent profit center: The managers of each subsidiary seek to maximize the profits of their subsidiary and do not consider the profits of other subsidiaries. However, the parent corporation may intervene in business decisions of subsidiaries to achieve better performance for its bottom line, even if that imposes costs on particular subsidiaries.

Very few firms start as multinational enterprises. A start-up firm typically initially focuses only on its domestic market. After it is well established, it may export its products. After its exports become numerous enough, the firm may decide that it is more cost-effective to produce its good or services in another country, and it becomes a multinational enterprise.

Becoming a Multinational

A firm becomes a multinational through foreign direct investment (FDI). The two types of FDI are *greenfield investments* and the purchase of foreign assets.

A *greenfield investment* creates a new production facility in a foreign country, such as in an undeveloped green field. For example, in 2018, German auto producer BMW announced a greenfield investment in Hungary, building a state-of-the-art auto plant to produce both conventional and electronic vehicles.

The other type of FDI is the acquisition of existing productive assets such as a plant or a firm. When a foreign firm acquires 10% or more of a domestic company's voting stock, the purchase is categorized as a direct investment, and is sufficient to

---

[18]MNEs are sometimes called transnational corporations (TNCs) or multinational corporations (MNCs).

classify the parent company as a multinational in official statistics. For example, in 2018, Switzerland's Nestlé, the world's largest food company, purchased a majority interest in Ecuadorian organic food company Terrafertil, expanding Nestlé's footprint in Latin America.

Traditionally, a major motive for a firm to acquire or build foreign productive assets is to lower its cost of supplying that foreign market by producing in that market rather than exporting to it. Toyota originally built plants in the United States to produce for the American market largely because it was less expensive than shipping cars from Japan. Producing locally allows the company to reduce transport costs and avoid tariffs or quotas on imported goods.

However, as tariffs and transportation costs have fallen in recent years, and international communication has become easier, a second motive has become relatively more important: comparative advantage in the supply chain. Increasingly, multinationals have found it efficient to produce various components or other inputs to production around the world, selecting the best location for each component.

Mini-Case

What's an American Car?

U.S. car manufacturers and labor unions regularly lobby the U.S. government for trade policies that favor their cars over imports. However, one might ask, which firms are the true all-American manufacturers?

No car is entirely built in the United States using only U.S. parts. In 2018, Japan's Honda Corporation produced the cars that ranked second and third in American content. The car with the most American content was the Jeep Cherokee produced by Fiat-Chrysler, a company created by the 2014 merger of Italy's Fiat and the U.S-based Chrysler Corporation. (It moved its financial headquarters to London after the merger.) Several cars made by U.S.-based producers Ford and General Motors appear lower in the top ten, with the iconic Ford F-150 pickup truck and GM's Chevrolet Corvette in ninth and tenth place, respectively.

For all manufacturers, the share of U.S. parts in their vehicles varies annually in response to changes in relative prices, disruption of supply lines due to natural disasters, and other factors. The combined U.S. and Canadian content of the Ford F-150 was 70% in 2015 and 2016, 85% in 2017, and 65% in 2018. Many of the main U.S. auto manufacturers' models are assembled in Canada or Mexico, due in large part to the trade liberalization incorporated in the North American Free Trade Agreement.

International Transfer Pricing

An MNE can gain many tax and other advantages by having its subsidiary in one country sell its goods or services to a subsidiary in another country. Typically, an MNE lets its subsidiaries make most decisions independently. However, the parent firm may lose profit if it lets one subsidiary set a very high **transfer price**: the price used for an intra-firm transfer of goods or services.

Toyota provides an example of such intra-firm transfers. Toyota Motor Engineering & Manufacturing North America (TEMA), a subsidiary of the parent firm, Toyota Motor Corporation, produces most of the Toyota motor vehicles sold in the United States. The cars are marketed and sold primarily by Toyota Motor Sales, U.S.A., Inc. (TMS), another subsidiary of the parent Toyota Motor Corporation. TEMA sells cars to TMS, which in turn sells and distributes them to Toyota dealerships. The price at which TEMA sells cars to TMS is a domestic transfer price.

Toyota subsidiaries also engage in international transfer pricing. For example, Toyota Motor Manufacturing Canada Inc. (TMMC) is another Toyota subsidiary, based in Canada, which sells vehicles to TMS for sale in the United States using an international transfer price.

We illustrate the key issues in international transfer pricing by examining how TMMC sets its transfer price to TMS for a Toyota RAV4 SUV, which is produced by TMMC. For simplicity, we assume that the RAV4 is essentially a monopoly product (the only such vehicle in its class).

Profit-Maximizing Transfer Pricing. How should TMMC set its transfer price? We consider two possibilities. First, we ask how TMS would set its monopoly price if it were a vertically integrated firm (Chapter 7) that both manufactured and sold cars. Second, we examine how TMS would price the car if TMMC sets a monopoly transfer price to TMS, which then sets a monopoly price to final consumers.

If TMS were vertically integrated—if it produced the RAV4 instead of obtaining it from TMMC—it would apply a monopoly markup M based on the demand curve of its U.S. customers to its marginal cost of producing a car, m, to obtain its profit-maximizing monopoly price, $p_1 = M \times m$.[19] We know that the markup M exceeds 1 because a profit-maximizing monopoly sets its price above its marginal cost.

However, the two subsidiaries are not vertically integrated. If TMMC maximizes its profit independently, it sets a monopoly transfer price for the cars it manufactures and sells to TMS. TMMC applies a markup of M^* to its marginal cost, m, setting its transfer price to TMS at $p^* = M^* \times m$. TMS views this transfer price, p^*, as its marginal cost (rather than m). TMS applies its markup, M, to its marginal cost p^* to determine the final price to consumers: $p_2 = M \times p^* = M \times M^* \times m$. Thus, the final price reflects a double markup, $M \times M^*$, instead of the single markup, M, if the companies were vertically integrated. Because both markups are larger than one, the double markup price, p_2, is greater than the price of the vertically integrated company with a single markup, p_1. As a result, TMS sells fewer cars at a higher price than if it were a vertically integrated firm. Because p_1 is the profit-maximizing monopoly price, charging a higher-than-monopoly price reduces the parent company's total profit.

For this reason, the parent company would not want TMMC to set a monopoly transfer price. The transfer price that maximizes combined profits of TMMC and TMS equals TMMC's marginal cost of production. This price maximizes the combined returns to the two subsidiaries.

However, Toyota might have a tax-based incentive to use a different transfer price—one that does not equal marginal cost. Using an alternative transfer price can help Toyota avoid taxes.[20]

---

[19]Equation 9.5 shows that the monopoly's marginal revenue is $MR = p(1 + 1/\varepsilon)$, where ε is the elasticity of demand. Thus, as Equation 9.8 shows, the monopoly sets $MR = p(1 + 1/\varepsilon) = m$. Therefore, its profit-maximizing monopoly price is $p = m/(1 + 1/\varepsilon)$. That is, its markup is $M = 1/(1 + 1/\varepsilon)$. For simplicity in this section, we assume that ε is constant, so that M is a constant. It does not change even if a change in m causes the firm to move to a different point on its demand curve. If ε is not constant (such as with a linear demand curve), M varies as m varies. We use a linear demand curve in Q&A 17.3.

[20]Toyota might also want to make sure that TMMC does not incur a loss, which occurs if TMMC incurs fixed costs such that a transfer price equal to marginal cost does not cover its total costs. Car production has high fixed costs (plant, equipment, and managerial staff).

Q&A 17.3

Reebok Vietnam (RV) is a subsidiary of the German multinational corporation Adidas. RV makes shoes in Vietnam and sells some of these shoes to Adidas Japan (AJ), another Adidas subsidiary, at the transfer price p^*. AJ sells the shoes to Japanese consumers. For simplicity, we assume AJ has a monopoly in Japan. Suppose that the inverse demand function in Japan for Reebok shoes is $p = 100 - Q$, where Q is measured in tens of thousands of pairs per month and p is the price per pair of shoes. RV's cost of production is $C^R = 20Q$, so its marginal cost of producing shoes is $20 per pair in Vietnam. If the parent Adidas Corporation directs RV and AJ to maximize their combined profit, what are the price, quantity, and resulting profit? What happens if, instead, RV sets its transfer price at $p^* = 60$?

Answer

1. *Determine the profit-maximizing quantity and price for shoes if RV and AJ act like a single profit-maximizing firm, and calculate the profit.* Because the demand curve is linear, the marginal revenue curve has the same intercept and twice the slope of the inverse demand function: $MR = 100 - 2Q$. To maximize its profit, Adidas operates where its marginal cost, 20, equals its MR:

$$MR = 100 - 2Q = 20 = MC.$$

By solving this equation for Q, we find that the firm's optimal $Q = 40$. Substituting that quantity into the inverse demand function, we learn that Adidas sets a price in Japan of $p = 100 - 40 = 60$. Its profit, π, is the difference between its revenue and cost: $\pi = R - C = (60 \times 40) - (20 \times 40) = 1,600$.

2. *Determine AJ's profit-maximizing quantity and price for shoes and the profits of RV and AJ if RV sets a transfer price of $p^* = 60$.* The transfer price is AJ's new marginal cost. It operates where its marginal revenue equals its marginal cost: $MR = 100 - 2Q = 60$. Thus, the quantity that maximizes AJ's profit is $Q = 20$. Substituting that quantity into the inverse demand function, we find that AJ's price is $p = 80$. AJ's profit is $\pi^J = R^J - C^J = pQ - (p^* \times Q) = (p - p^*)Q = (80 - 60) \times 20 = 400$. RV's profit is $\pi^R = R^R - C^R = (p^* \times Q) - 20Q = (60 \times 20) - (20 \times 20) = 800$. The sum of the profits of AJ and RV is $400 + 800 = 1,200$. This sum is considerably less than the profit of 1,600 that they earn if they act like a single firm.

Comment: The transfer price $p^* = 60$ maximizes RV's profit given that the subsidiaries act independently.[21]

Tax Avoidance. If corporate tax rates differ across countries, Toyota prefers to earn most of its profit in the low-tax country. The transfer price determines the allocation of profits between TMMC and TMS. As the price increases from marginal cost toward the monopoly price, TMMC's profit rises and TMS's profit falls.

---

[21]Because AJ views the transfer price p^* as its marginal cost, it sets its marginal revenue equal to p^*: $MR = 100 - 2Q = p^*$ or $Q = 50 - 0.5p^*$. That is, for any transfer price p^*, AJ will purchase $Q = 50 - 0.5p^*$ from RV. This relationship is the demand function facing RV. It is referred to as a *derived demand* because it is derived from the downstream consumer demand for shoes. RV's corresponding marginal revenue function is $MR = 100 - 4Q$, which it equates to its marginal cost of 20: $100 - 4Q = 20$. Thus, it maximizes its profit when $Q = 20$. Substituting this quantity into RV's derived demand function, we know that $20 = 50 - 0.5p^*$, so $p^* = (50 - 20)/0.5 = 60$. Thus, RV's profit-maximizing transfer price is $p^* = 60$.

If the Canadian corporate income tax, which is paid by TMMC, is 20%, while the U.S. corporate tax rate, which is paid by TMS, is 30%, then Toyota prefers to earn its profits in Canada rather than in the United States.[22] Accordingly, the Toyota parent prefers a relatively high transfer price.

Suppose that TMMC initially produces a vehicle at a marginal cost of $30,000 and transfers that vehicle to TMS at a transfer price of $30,000, so that TMMC earns no profit in Canada. TMS resells the vehicle to an independent locally owned American dealership at a (wholesale) price of $32,000, so that its before-tax profit margin on this car is $2,000. Given that the U.S. corporate tax rate is 30%, TMS pays 30% of its profit on the vehicle—$600 to the U.S. tax authorities—yielding an after-tax profit of $1,400 (= $2,000 − $600), which goes to the parent, Toyota.

Now suppose that the transfer price on the vehicle is raised to $32,000. TMMC earns a before-tax profit of $2,000, on which it pays taxes of $400 at the Canadian rate of 20% per vehicle, yielding a net profit of $1,600. TMS earns no profit and therefore pays no U.S. corporate income tax on this vehicle. Toyota now earns an after-tax profit of $1,600 on this vehicle instead of the $1,400 it earned with the lower transfer price in place.

Thus, the higher transfer price has the effect of shifting profit from the U.S. to the Canadian subsidiary, where the profit is taxed at a lower rate. As the parent Toyota Motor Corporation is the owner of both TMMC and TMS, it benefits from this increased transfer price, other things equal.

But other things are not equal. A trade-off exists between the tax advantage of high transfer prices and the inefficiency of having a transfer price above marginal cost. The after-tax profit per vehicle transferred rises with the higher transfer price, but TMS imports fewer vehicles. If the marginal benefit of raising the transfer price from avoiding taxes exceeds the marginal cost from a non-optimal price signal to a subsidiary, the firm should raise the transfer price. The profit-maximizing transfer price would be where the marginal cost and marginal benefit of increases in the transfer price were just equal.

An MNE might be able to avoid this distortion. For example, it could use a marginal cost transfer price as the *real* price between the subsidiaries, but tell the tax authorities that the price was higher to reduce its tax liability. However, such a practice is not legal.

Tax authorities pay careful attention to transfer pricing to restrain the ability of companies to reduce tax liabilities. Specific rules vary from country to country, but the general rule is that transfer prices must reflect normal pricing practices that apply in the absence of tax incentives. Presumably because of an inability to determine a single "correct" transfer price, tax authorities set a reasonable range. Within that range, companies have some ability to use transfer price variations to reduce taxes. Such a practice is called *tax avoidance*: a legal way of reducing taxes. Illegal methods of reducing tax payments, such as keeping fraudulent financial records, are called *tax evasion*.

---

[22]The U.S. federal corporate income tax rate was reduced to 21% as of 2018. However, state governments also tax corporations, so the combined corporate tax rate varies from state to state. Similarly, in Canada the rate varies from province to province. In both countries, the actual amount paid also depends on a host of special deductions and other tax code provisions. Firms often locate offices in low-tax jurisdictions to reduce taxes. For example, although Apple has its corporate headquarters in California, it set up a small office in Nevada to collect and invest its profits because California's corporate tax is 8.84% and Nevada's is zero.

Until the Tax Cuts and Jobs Act of 2017 went into effect in 2018, a U.S. parent firm that used transfer pricing to avoid paying taxes in the United States faced incentives to keep the money in foreign countries. Unlike most other countries, the United States taxed its multinational corporations on their repatriated foreign earnings (earnings brought back to the United States). U.S. companies could avoid these taxes as long as the profits remained overseas.

Sophisticated managers used transfer pricing to shift profits to low-tax countries and then invested these profits offshore. Goldman Sachs estimated that U.S. corporations held $3.1 trillion outside the United States as of 2017. Apple had had the largest overseas cash hoard ($246 billion), followed by Microsoft ($132 billion) and Cisco Systems ($68 billion).

Periodically, large U.S. corporations would lobby for a repatriation holiday—paying a low federal tax rate such as 5% or 6% on repatriated earnings instead of the much higher normal corporate rate. These firms argued that the tax break would stimulate the economy by inducing multinational corporations to invest repatriated earnings in the United States, creating hundreds of thousands of jobs.

However, the American Jobs Creation Act of 2004 provided a temporary repatriated profits tax rate of 5.25% but did not result in significant domestic investment. In 2005, 800 firms repatriated $312 billion back to the United States, paid $16 billion in taxes, but returned 92% of the repatriated money to shareholders in dividends and stock buybacks rather than use this money to expand domestic operations.

The U.S. tax law that went into effect in 2018 includes a retroactive tax rate of 15.5% on most corporate earnings held overseas and 8% on some (less a credit for taxes paid in the foreign country). The tax applies whether earnings are repatriated or not. Corporations get the benefit of a reduced corporate tax rate but can no longer avoid paying U.S. taxes by keeping earnings abroad. In the first quarter of 2018, about $300 billion (10% of the outstanding stock) was repatriated. Going forward, U.S. corporations will not have to pay U.S. corporate tax on most foreign earnings.

17.5 Outsourcing

Probably no international trade issue has been more controversial in recent years than *international outsourcing*, whereby a firm buys goods and services from foreign suppliers that the firm would otherwise provide internally. In extreme cases, a manager who outsources abroad to reduce costs may face a boycott by consumers, which can hurt the firm's bottom line.

Less controversial and more common is domestic outsourcing. For example, a restaurant may outsource its cleaning needs to a company that provides janitorial services rather than hire its own cleaning staff. No firm produces all its own inputs and provides all the necessary services to sell its product. All firms outsource to some degree.

International outsourcing used to be rare. However, trade liberalization under the World Trade Organization and other international agreements has made it much easier for firms to outsource internationally. Manufacturing firms import inputs rather than producing them in their home countries, and call centers in India and other nations provide phone support service for many U.S. firms.

Multinational enterprises often engage in foreign outsourcing by shifting production of a needed input from a subsidiary in one country to one in another country. For example, Toyota's wholly owned U.S. production subsidiary imports some parts from Toyota affiliates in China rather than produce them domestically. However, a firm does not need to be a multinational enterprise to engage in foreign outsourcing. Some firms with purely domestic production operations import inputs that they previously produced themselves. Deloitte's 2016 survey of large corporations found that 72% of U.S. information technology units outsourced work, as did 47% of human resource units and 42% of finance units.[23]

The increased use of outsourcing triggered a major debate in the United States about the social desirability of permitting outsourcing. When a firm starts outsourcing abroad, it lays off domestic workers who produced a needed input and instead imports that input from another country, where new workers are hired. Many U.S. groups are upset by this outsourcing of U.S. jobs, particularly workers in the service sector. By some reports, U.S. financial services firms save $2 billion per year by outsourcing to India, giving this sector a strong incentive to outsource.

Brown, Sturgeon, and Cole (2013), who surveyed U.S. full-time workers, concluded that the debate on the desirability of outsourcing exaggerates the degree of outsourcing. Half the surveyed employees worked in organizations that have some domestic outsourcing for a major business function, and almost one-quarter work at organizations that outsource internationally. However, the share of business costs from domestic outsourcing and offshoring is small: Nearly all (93%) of the costs for major business functions continue to be within the firm's or organization's operations in the United States.

While the debate rages in the United States about jobs moving to India and other foreign countries, Europeans are protesting that high-paying European R&D jobs are being outsourced to the United States. Moreover, foreign companies increasingly buy U.S. services—particularly legal services. Ultimately, outsourcing is a consequence of comparative advantage—particular tasks get shifted to locations where they have the lowest opportunity cost.

Virtually all economists argue that international trade, including outsourcing, leads to more efficient market outcomes due to comparative advantage. Does it follow that people who attack free trade and outsourcing are simply ignorant or venal?

---

[23]www2.deloitte.com/content/dam/Deloitte/nl/Documents/operations/deloitte-nl-s&o-global-outsourcing-survey.pdf

No. Once a nation starts trading, it reduces the production of some goods and services so that it can concentrate on those for which it has a comparative advantage. As a consequence, some people gain and some people lose from free trade. Domestic firms driven out of business by foreign firms lose their sunk capital. Their workers may suffer from at least temporary unemployment. The gains in the other sectors are large enough to compensate the losers. However, because society fails to compensate the losers, they are adamantly (and reasonably) opposed to free trade.

As the cartoon illustrates, we can see the gains from trade in services by imagining that domestic workers rather than firms outsource. Suppose that you are hired to design web pages for $30 an hour. You know that Ivan, a very competent, reliable web designer in Russia, can do the job as well as you can, and he is willing to work for $10 an hour. You can subcontract with Ivan, pocket $20 an hour, and, with your free time, take on an additional job or enjoy your extra leisure. Clearly, you would favor this plan. However, if your firm fired you and outsourced your job to Ivan, you would be outraged over your loss. This example illustrates that much of the debate on outsourcing jobs concerns who reaps the benefits and who suffers the losses rather than whether or not society has a net gain. As with any desirable trade, the winners can in principle compensate the losers so that everyone benefits, although such compensation often does not take place.[24]

Rather than giving up the benefits of free trade, both domestic proponents and opponents of free trade often call for more compensation for the losers. The U.S. Trade Adjustment Assistance program provides relatively small amounts for training and other benefits for workers who lose their jobs due to foreign competition.[25] In addition, displaced workers may receive unemployment insurance. Even so, total support for displaced U.S. workers does not come close to compensating them for their losses.

Managerial Solution

Responding to Exchange Rates

How does the price of wheat or a Rolls-Royce change in response to a change in exchange rates? Does the change depend on the competitiveness of the market?

Earlier in the chapter, we discussed why arbitrage causes a price to react completely to changes in exchange rates. Wheat is a perfectly competitive market, and less than 5% of U.S. wheat output is exported to Japan. If the U.S. supply curve of wheat is horizontal at a dollar price of p in the United States and the exchange rate is 110 yen per dollar, then arbitrage forces the yen price in Japan to be $110p$. If the exchange rate goes to 125 yen to the dollar, the U.S. price remains constant and the Japanese price shifts to $125p$. Consequently, the yen-denominated price and the dollar-denominated price are equivalent.

It is not much of a stretch to think of Rolls-Royce as a monopoly. Obviously no one "needs" a Rolls-Royce, but it is perhaps the world's best-known luxury product and is a must for people who want "the best of everything."

New vehicles are sold in Britain and the United States at only a handful of authorized dealers. Given the desire for warranty protection among customers and the high cost of shipping a Rolls across the Atlantic Ocean, the company does not worry excessively about resale or international arbitrage. As a consequence, the U.S. and the U.K. prices may differ.

---

[24]An Amazon employee, Dina Vaccari, reported that she used her own money to pay a freelancer in India to enter data so that she could get more done. Kantor, Jodi, and David Streitfeld, "Inside Amazon: Wrestling Big Ideas in a Bruising Workplace," *New York Times*, August 15, 2015.

[25]See Collins (2016).

The figure shows the U.S. demand curve for a Phantom Coupé. Rolls-Royce acts like a monopoly, equating its marginal revenue, MR, to its marginal cost, $MC^1 = \$150$ thousand, to determine its profit-maximizing quantity, Q_1. At that quantity, the dollar-denominated price is $500 thousand.[26] This price is equivalent to about £333.3 thousand if the exchange rate is 1.5 dollars to a pound.

Now suppose that the dollar becomes less valuable relative to the pound so that the exchange rate depreciates to 2 dollars to a pound. The change in the exchange rate causes the U.S. dollar marginal cost to rise by a third (= [2 − 1.5]/1.5) to $MC^2 = \$200$ thousand. In the figure, this increase in the marginal cost causes the profit-maximizing U.S. price to rise to $525 thousand, or £262.5 thousand.[27] Thus, when the exchange rate increases by a third, the dollar-denominated price increases by only 5% ($\approx$ [525 − 500]/500) and the pound-denominated price falls by 21.2% ($\approx$ [262.5 − 333.3]/333.3).

In the competitive wheat example and in the Rolls-Royce example, the price in the exporting country remains constant in response to a change in the exchange rate. In the wheat market, the foreign (Japanese) price adjusted fully to a change in the exchange rate. In contrast, in the noncompetitive Rolls-Royce example, the foreign, U.S. price only partially adjusted to a change in the exchange rate. Indeed, if the Rolls were manufactured in the United States as well as in Britain (as is the case for a Rolls-Royce jet engine), then the exchange rate change would have no effect on the U.S. price.

SUMMARY

1. **Reasons for International Trade.** One key reason for international trade is comparative advantage. If Country A can produce Good 1 at a lower opportunity cost than Country B, and has a higher opportunity cost for producing Good 2, both countries can benefit from trading these goods. A second important reason for trade is increasing returns to scale. Rather than producing everything at a small scale in a single country, producers can take advantage of increasing returns to scale by producing a large quantity of some good in one country and exporting much of the output to other countries. Increasing returns to scale are particularly important in industries where product variety is important. Allowing each country to produce and export a few varieties while its consumers enjoy a wide range of variety based on production in many countries underlies much of the trade we see.

---

[26]This figure is based on the assumption that the U.S. inverse demand function (in thousands of dollars) is $p = 850 - Q$. Thus, the marginal revenue function is $MR = 850 - 2Q$. Given that the marginal cost is $MC = 150$, then profit is maximized where $MR = 850 - 2Q = 150 = MC$, or $Q = 350$. Substituting this quantity into the inverse demand function, we find that the price is $p = \$500$ thousand. At the exchange rate $R_1 = 1.5$, the price in pounds is $p^* \approx$ £333.3 thousand.

[27]Continuing our example from the last footnote, if the exchange rate increases to 2 dollars to the pound, the dollar-denominated marginal cost increases to $MC = 200$. Thus, the profit-maximizing solution is determined by $MR = 850 - 2Q = 200 = MC$, so $Q = 325$ and $p = \$525$ thousand.

2. **Exchange Rates.** An exchange rate is the price of one currency, such as the euro, in terms of another currency, such as the dollar. A change in an exchange rate can cause large changes in which goods and services are traded and at what prices. After an exchange rate changes, arbitrage causes the prices across countries for a given good to move closer together. The possibility of exchange rate fluctuations creates additional risk for firms engaged in international trade and investment. Such risks can be reduced by using forward or futures contracts.

3. **International Trade Policies.** Governments intervene in the movement of goods across borders. The most important types of intervention are tariffs—taxes on imports (or, rarely, on exports)—and quotas, which limit the quantity of a good that can be imported (or exported). Tariffs produce government revenue, as do quotas if the government sells them to importers or exporters. Governments sometimes intervene to create market power for domestic exporters or to help domestic firms compete with foreign firms in world markets. Trade policy is also often used to protect domestic firms from certain contingencies, such

as dumping (selling at unreasonably low prices) by foreign firms.

4. **Multinational Enterprises.** Multinational enterprises are firms that own production facilities in more than one country. Such enterprises are responsible for the majority of the world's international trade and investment flows. Most firms that become multinationals initially produce in a single country and then expand into other countries by purchasing productive assets in those countries or by building new production facilities in those countries (greenfield investments). Trade between units of a multinational enterprise is significantly affected by variations in tax rates across nations. These firms may reduce their taxes by adjusting the transfer price that one unit charges another for a good shipped internationally.

5. **Outsourcing.** A firm outsources if it buys an input from another firm rather than producing it internally. Although most outsourcing occurs within a single country, global outsourcing is increasing and is controversial. Critics complain that sending work overseas causes a loss of domestic jobs. Firms outsource to lower their production costs. International outsourcing reflects comparative advantage.

QUESTIONS

All exercises are available on **MyLab Economics;** * = *answer at the back of this book.*

1. Reasons for International Trade

*1.1 Suppose that auto workers in South Korea can produce components used to make cars at the rate of six sets of components per worker per day and can assemble cars at the rate of four cars per worker per day. In North Korea, auto workers can produce components at the rate of one set of components per day and can assemble cars at the rate of three cars per worker per day. What is the opportunity cost of car assembly in terms of component production in each country? If one economy exports components and the other exports assembled cars, which economy will export cars according to the theory of comparative advantage?

1.2 Trade between North and South Korea was legalized in 1988, but is currently very limited. Assume, however, that Hyundai has 200 workers in a plant in North Korea just across the boundary with South Korea, where a "partner" plant with 200 workers is located. Using the numbers from Question 1.1, how much output can be produced if each plant carries out component production and assembly independently and no trade occurs? How much output can be produced if specialization according to comparative advantage occurs and how should labor be allocated in each plant? (*Hint*: See Q&A 17.1.)

1.3 ABC Software, a small software producer, decides to renovate its premises. Instead of hiring an outside contractor and tradespeople, the firm decides to use its employees—secretaries, programmers, sales staff, and others—to do most of the work. The firm makes all its employees try painting and carpentry and other tasks needed for the renovation, and selects the people with the strongest skills in those areas to take time off from their regular tasks and work on the renovation. Is this strategy a good one? Why or why not?

1.4 Paul Allen co-founded Microsoft with Bill Gates. In the early years he spent his time programming, but as time went on he became more involved in management and stopped programming. Suppose Allen was the best programmer in the company. Does it follow that shifting to management was a mistake? (*Hint*: See the Managerial Implication "Brian May's Comparative Advantage.")

1.5 Celery Patch Dolls, a small Malaysian doll producer, is considering producing a new doll variety. Production of this doll type requires an initial setup cost, followed by constant variable cost. The cost function of producing variety i is $C = 12{,}000 + 2Q_i$, where Q_i is the quantity of variety i. The demand function for this particular variety in Malaysia is

$Q_i = 4000 - 1000p$. Celery Patch seeks to maximize its profit and will not produce the doll if it would make a loss ($p < AC$) by doing so. If Celery Patch cannot sell the doll outside Malaysia, does it pay to produce this variety? What decision does Celery Patch make if it is able to sell the doll in Singapore as well as Malaysia, where the demand curve is exactly the same as in Malaysia?

1.6 Has international trade had an effect on the size of Barbie doll collections? (*Hint*: See the Mini-Case "Barbie Doll Varieties.")

2. Exchange Rates

2.1 Suppose that one euro can be exchanged for 1.2 U.S. dollars and that one U.S. dollar can be exchanged for 110 Japanese yen. If these currencies can be traded freely with low transaction costs, what exchange rate would you expect between euros and the Japanese yen? Describe the transactions that would occur if the euro-yen exchange rate is higher than this amount (more yen per euro). (*Hint*: Is arbitrage relevant?)

*2.2 Figure 17.1 shows the effect on the exchange rate (U.S. dollars per euro) of the demand for euros by U.S. residents. What would happen if the U.S. government tried to establish a fixed exchange rate at X_2 after demand shifted out to D^2?

2.3 Explain why gray markets reduce the ability of multinational firms to price discriminate. (*Hint:* See the Managerial Implication "Limiting Arbitrage and Gray Markets.")

2.4 Arvind runs a small electronics company in India and has just sold some equipment to a U.S. company for $1.5 million to be paid in 90 days. His cost in Indian rupees (INR) is 90 million. The current exchange rate is 66 INR per dollar. How much profit in INR would Arvind earn if the exchange rate is unchanged in 90 days? What happens to his profit if the exchange rate goes to 70 INR per dollar in 90 days? At what exchange rate would Arvind just break even?

2.5 In Question 2.4, suppose that Arvind is not worried about risk provided that he can cover his costs. If he thinks that the exchange rate will change to 50 INR in 90 days, explain how he could use a forward contract to hedge his risk. Would Arvind want to hedge if he thinks that the exchange rate might rise above 60 but will not fall below 60?

3. International Trade Policies

3.1 Based on the Mini-Case "Russian Food Ban," who were the main winners and losers from the ban imposed by Russia on imports of agricultural products from the United States, the European Union, and various other countries?

3.2 In August 2018, the world price for raw sugar, 11¢ per pound, was less than half of the U.S. price, 27¢ per pound, because of quotas and tariffs on sugar imports. As a consequence, a larger quantity of American-made corn sweeteners can be profitably sold domestically. Use graphs to show the effects of a quota on sugar on prices and quantities in both the sugar and corn sweetener markets. (*Hint*: See Figure 17.3. You may assume there are no imports of corn sweeteners.)

3.3 How would the shape of the total supply curve in Q&A 17.2 change if the U.S. domestic supply curve hit the vertical axis at a price above $\bar{p}$?

3.4 Canada has 20% of the world's known freshwater resources, yet many Canadians believe that the country has little or none to spare. Over the years, U.S. and Canadian firms have struck deals to export bulk shipments of water to drought-afflicted U.S. cities and towns. Provincial leaders have blocked these deals in British Columbia and Ontario. Use graphs to show the likely outcome of such an export ban on the price and quantity of water used in Canada and in the United States if markets for water are competitive. Show the effects on consumer and producer surplus in both countries. Show that if the importing country faces an upward-sloping foreign supply curve (excess supply curve), a tariff may raise welfare in the importing country.

3.5 If the world supply curve is horizontal at the world price for a particular good, can a subsidy on imports raise welfare in the importing country? Explain your answer.

3.6 After Mexico signed the North American Free Trade Agreement (NAFTA) in 1994, corn imports from the United States doubled within a year, and today U.S. imports make up nearly one-third of the corn consumed in Mexico. According to the charity Oxfam in 2003, the price of Mexican corn fell more than 70% after NAFTA took effect. Part of the reason for this flow south of the border is that the U.S. government subsidizes corn production to the tune of $10 billion a year. According to Oxfam, the 2002 U.S. cost of production was $3.08 per bushel, but the export price was $2.69 per bushel, with the difference reflecting an export subsidy of 39¢ per bushel. The United States exported 5.3 metric tons. Use graphs to show the effect of such a subsidy on the welfare of various groups and on government expenditures in the United States and Mexico.

3.7 During the Napoleonic Wars, Britain blockaded North America, seizing U.S. vessels and cargo and impressing sailors. At President Thomas Jefferson's request, Congress imposed a nearly complete—perhaps 80%—embargo on international commerce from December 1807 to March 1809. Just before the embargo, exports were about 13% of the U.S. gross national product (GNP). Due to the embargo, U.S. consumers could not find acceptable substitutes for manufactured goods from Europe, and producers could not sell farm produce and other goods for as much as in Europe. According to Irwin (2005), the welfare cost of the embargo was at least 8% of the GNP in 1807. Use graphs to show the effects of the embargo on a market for an exported good and one for an imported good. Show the change in equilibria and the welfare effects on consumers and firms.

3.8 A government is considering a quota and a tariff, both of which will reduce imports by the same amount. Why might the government prefer one of these policies to the other?

*3.9 In Table 17.3, suppose that the payoff if both firms enter is positive, 5 rather than −5, while the other payoffs remain the same. Now, what is the effect of a subsidy of 10 to Novartis?

3.10 Why do antidumping policies limit the ability of firms to carry out international price discrimination? (*Hint*: See the Mini-Case "Protection of U.S. Steel, Aluminum, and Washing Machines.")

4. Multinational Enterprises

4.1 As a result of international trade agreements, many iconic "American" cars are not assembled in the United States. Explain why. (*Hint*: See the Mini-Case "What's an American Car?")

*4.2 The Timex Group, a large multinational watchmaker, has its headquarters in the Netherlands. It has subsidiaries in many countries, including the Timex Group USA and TMX Philippines, Inc. One particular type of specialty watch is produced in the Philippines for export to the Timex Group USA. Suppose the inverse demand function for this watch in the United States is $p = 90 − 2Q$, where p is measured in dollars and Q is measured in thousands of watches per week. These watches are produced at a constant marginal cost of $10 per watch by TMX Philippines. Timex USA treats the transfer price charged by TMX Philippines as its marginal cost. If these two subsidiaries are instructed to maximize combined profits, what are the price, quantity, and transfer price? Could TMX Philippines raise its own profit by charging a higher price? (*Hint*: See Q&A 17.3.)

4.3 In Question 4.2, what transfer price would maximize the profit of TMX Philippines? (*Hint*: For any given transfer price, the Timex Group USA will demand some quantity of watches. This relationship determines the demand facing TMX Philippines.)

4.4 In Question 4.2, suppose that the Philippines has a lower corporate tax rate than the United States. How would that lower tax rate affect the transfer price that maximizes the overall profit of the Timex Group?

4.5 Based on the Mini-Case "Profit Repatriation," how would you expect the Tax Cuts and Jobs Act of 2017 to affect the stock of foreign-earned income held outside the United States by U.S. firms?

4.6 The Tax Cuts and Jobs Act of 2017 reduced the standard U.S. federal corporate income tax rate from 35% to 21%. How would this change affect incentives for U.S. multinational firms to shift profits from the United States to other countries, using transfer pricing?

5. Outsourcing

5.1 Outsourcing of services by American firms has contributed significantly to wage growth in India. Explain why, using a graph of the Indian labor market.

5.2 Suppose Hewlett-Packard is considering outsourcing its telephone-based technical support functions for its printers to India. The hourly cost of a tech support person in the United States is $50 per hour. In India workers are paid in rupees but, at the current exchange rate, cost the equivalent of $20 per hour. However, calls serviced in India require paying for long-distance telephone service. Initially, the telephone costs were about $35 per hour. However, a switch to voice over internet protocol (VOIP) technology reduced the telephone cost to $25 per hour. Explain how the technological change affects the decision of where to base service.

5.3 In Question 5.2, how much would the Indian currency (the rupee) have to rise in value (in percentage terms) for Hewlett-Packard to keep the service activity in the United States even after telephone time falls in price?

6. Managerial Problem

6.1 Chanel perfume is sold in France and in the United States. Assume initially that one euro is worth $1.30 and that a 100 ml bottle of perfume sells for $80 in the United States. If Chanel does not price discriminate internationally, what is the price that would be paid for this perfume in France? Now suppose that Chanel decides to price discriminate and finds that it would maximize its profit by lowering its price in the United States to $70 and raising its price by 25% in France. Explain why. Next, explain what happens if the value of the euro rises by 25% in terms of the dollar.

7. MyLab Economics Spreadsheet Exercises[28]

7.1 Suppose the demand function for U.S. dollars by holders of Japanese yen is $Q_{d1} = 1000 - 5x$, where Q is the amount of U.S. dollars per day and x is the exchange rate (yen per dollar). The supply function of U.S. dollars available to be exchanged into Japanese yen is $Q_{s1} = 100 + 4x$.

    a. Create a spreadsheet with columns for the exchange rate, x, the quantity demanded, and the quantity supplied. Let the exchange rate range from 50 to 150 in increments of 10. Determine the equilibrium exchange rate using the spreadsheet.

    b. Now suppose that the U.S. Federal Reserve announces a long-run low-interest-rate policy that causes the foreign demand for U.S. dollars to fall. The new demand function is $Q_{d2} = 850 - 4x$. The Japanese investors begin to liquidate their holdings of U.S. assets, increasing the supply of U.S. dollars to $Q_{s2} = 130 + 4x$. Add additional columns for Q_{d2} and Q_{s2} to the spreadsheet from part a and determine the new dollar-yen exchange rate.

    c. Use the Excel charting tool to draw the graphs of the demand and supply curves for U.S. dollars to illustrate the change in the equilibrium exchange rate.

7.2 The domestic demand and supply functions for a particular type of latex paint are $Q_d = 14 - 0.5p$ and $Q_s = -4 + p$, respectively. The price is measured in dollars per gallon, and the quantities are measured in millions of gallons. The world price for the paint is $p^* = \$8$, at which the foreign producers are willing to sell unlimited quantities.

    a. Suppose paint is freely traded. Create a spreadsheet with columns for price (p), domestic demand (D), domestic supply (S), imports (M), consumer surplus (CS), producer surplus (PS), and total surplus (TS). Let the price go from $4 to $28 in increments of $1. Fill in the spreadsheet.

    b. Determine the domestic price, domestic consumption, domestic production, and the amount of imports in the free-trade equilibrium. Also calculate the consumer surplus, producer surplus, and the total surplus using the spreadsheet.

    c. Now, the government bans importing paint. Determine the domestic price, domestic consumption, domestic production, consumer surplus, producer surplus, total surplus, and the deadweight loss.

    d. Next, instead of banning imports, the domestic government imposes an import quota of 3 million gallons. Determine the domestic price, domestic consumption, domestic production, consumer surplus, producer surplus, total surplus, and the deadweight loss under such a quota.

7.3 Consider the market for paint as described in Question 7.2. As before, the world price for paint is $8. This question examines the effect of introducing a tariff.

    a. Create a spreadsheet as in Question 7.2 with columns for price (p), domestic quantity demanded (D), domestic quantity supplied (S), imports (M), consumer surplus (CS), producer surplus (PS), and total surplus (TS). Let the price increase from $4 to $28 in increments of $1. Fill in the spreadsheet.

    b. Suppose the domestic government imposes a tariff of $2 per gallon on any imported paint. Use your spreadsheet to identify the domestic price, domestic consumption, domestic production, and the amount of imports. Also determine the consumer surplus, producer surplus, total surplus, and deadweight loss. How does this equilibrium differ from the equilibrium in part d of Question 17.2, where there is a quota of 3 and no tariff?

    c. Suppose now that the domestic government raises the tariff from $2 to $3 per gallon. Determine the domestic price, consumption, production, amount of imports, consumer surplus, producer surplus, and deadweight loss in this case.

---

[28]The spreadsheet exercises in this chapter are based on the work of Satyajit Ghosh in cooperation with the authors. The answers are available on MyLab Economics.

Answers to Selected Questions

I know the answer! The answer lies within the heart of all mankind! The answer is twelve? I think I'm in the wrong building. —Charles Schultz

Chapter 2

1.1 Draw the graph with quantity on the horizontal axis and price on the vertical axis. The coffee demand function (Equation 2.2) shows that, for any given price, quantity demanded increases as income increases. Therefore, an increase in income causes the demand curve to shift to the right. A movement along the demand curve is caused by a change in price, holding income and other relevant variables constant.

1.5 (a) The inverse demand function for town residents is $p = 200 - 0.5Q_r$. (b) At a price of $300, college students will buy some firewood, but other town residents will not. Other town residents will demand a quantity of zero at any price of $200 or more. (c) The total demand curve has a price intercept of $400 and coincides with the college students' demand curve for prices from $400 to $200. At a price of $200 it has a kink, and for prices of $200 or below it is the horizontal sum of student demand and other town residents' demand and follows the equation $Q = 600 - 2p$.

2.2 A movement along the supply curve occurs only when the price of the good changes. Therefore, a change in the price of fertilizer would not cause a movement along the supply curve. A change in a variable that affects quantity demanded other than the good's own price would cause the entire supply curve to shift. In this example, fertilizer is such a variable. For any given price of avocados, the quantity supplied would be lower if the price of fertilizer is higher. Thus, a change in the price of fertilizer shifts the entire supply curve.

2.3 The supply function for avocados is $Q = 58 + 15p - 20p_f$. The change in quantity supplied is therefore $\Delta Q = Q_2 - Q_1 = (50 + 15p_2) -$

$(50 + 15p_1) = 15(p_2 - p_1) = 15\Delta p$. It follows that the change in price needed to cause $\Delta Q = 60$ is $\Delta p = 60/15 = 4$.

3.1 When the graph is drawn, the intercept of the supply curve on the vertical axis is 6 and the curve slopes up from there. The demand curve has a vertical axis intercept at 4 and slopes down from there. Therefore, the demand and supply curves do not intersect each other at any positive price and quantity. The equilibrium in this case is at a quantity of 0. There is no market price for this good, as no trades take place.

3.4 If $Y = \$55,000$, $p_s = 0.20$, $p_c = \$5$, and $p = 4$, the quantity demanded is $Q = 8.56 - 4 - 0.3(0.2) + 0.1(55) = 10$. The quantity supplied is $Q = 9.6 + 0.5(4) - 0.2(5) = 10.6$. There is an excess supply equal to $10.6 - 10.0 = 0.6$ in this case. Because of the excess supply, firms unable to sell at the price of $4 would lower their prices, forcing the market price down. Price would fall until the equilibrium price was reached.

4.3 Outsourcing of skilled jobs to India increases the demand for skilled workers in India. Therefore, the (downward-sloping) demand curve for skilled workers in India shifts outward. If the supply curve is upward sloping and stays in the same place, the shift in demand will cause the equilibrium price—the wage—to increase.

4.6 A freeze that damages the orange crop in Florida would increase the price and reduce the quantity of frozen orange juice sold in the United States. As grapefruit juice is a substitute for orange juice, the demand curve for grapefruit juice would shift out and the price of grapefruit juice would rise.

4.10 If the price of petroleum rises, the cost of producing plastic rises, causing the supply curve for plastic to shift in and its price to rise. As plastic is a substitute for aluminum, the demand for aluminum shifts out. An increase in the price of petroleum also increases the cost of producing electricity, which in turn increases the cost of producing aluminum, causing the supply curve for aluminum to shift in. Therefore, the demand for aluminum shifts out and the supply shifts in. The price of aluminum must rise and the quantity sold could rise, fall, or remain unchanged depending upon the relative size of the shifts in the demand curve and the supply curve.

5.2 If the law had passed, a price ceiling would have been imposed, presumably at a level below the intersection of the supply and demand curves. At this price there would be an excess demand for gasoline, resulting in a shortage of gasoline and likely giving rise to lines at gas stations.

Chapter 3

1.3 The point price elasticity ε is given by $\varepsilon = (\Delta Q/\Delta p)(p/Q) = -2p/Q = -2(10/80) = -0.25$.

1.4 Differentiating the demand function $Q = Ap^\varepsilon$, we find that $dQ/dp = \varepsilon Ap^{\varepsilon-1}$. Substituting that expression into the point elasticity definition, Equation 3.8, we learn that the elasticity is

$$\frac{dQ}{dp}\frac{p}{Q} = \varepsilon Ap^{\varepsilon-1}\frac{p}{Q} = \varepsilon Ap^{\varepsilon-1}\frac{p}{Ap^\varepsilon} = \varepsilon.$$

Because the elasticity is a constant, it does not depend on a particular value of p or Q and is therefore the same at every point along the demand curve.

1.7 The price elasticity of demand ε is the percentage change in quantity demanded divided by the percentage change in price, which in this case is $-3.8/10 = -0.38$. As this elasticity has an absolute value of less than one, demand is inelastic.

1.9 The elasticity of demand $\varepsilon = (\Delta Q/\Delta p)(p/Q) = (-9.5)(45)/1,275 \approx -0.34$. That is, for every 1% fall in the price, a third of a percent more coconut oil is demanded. The cross-price elasticity of demand for coconut oil with respect to the price of palm oil is $(\Delta Q/\Delta p_p)(p_p/Q) = (16.2)(31)/1,275 \approx 0.39$.

2.3 The predicted quantity is $Q = 130 - 3.5p = 130 - 3.5(2.0) = 123$. The residual is $129 - 123 = 6$. There are several possible relevant unobserved variables, including the temperature and the price of substitute goods (such as ice cream).

3.3 The estimated demand function is $Q = 53.857 - 1.438p$, where p is measured in thousands

of dollars. If p rises by $1 (thousand), then Q falls by 1.438. At a price of $20 (thousand), the predicted demand from the focus group is $Q = 53.857 - 1.438(20) = 25.097$. The elasticity of demand at this price is $-(1.438)(20/25.097) \approx -1.146$.

4.3 Linear demand has the form $Q = a - bp$. Revenue, which is price times quantity, has the form $R = pQ = p(a - bp) = ap - bp^2$. Thus, revenue is a *quadratic* function of price, *not* a linear function. Using a linear functional form for the regression would be a mistake. A quadratic functional form should be used.

6.2 The R^2 is 0.96 (rounded to two decimal places). The coefficient estimates are 1,024 and -413 (rounded to whole numbers), the standard errors are 33.8 and 32.7 (rounded to one decimal place), and the t-statistics are 30.3 and -12.6 (rounded to one decimal place). Thus, using the 95% confidence criterion, we would reject the hypothesis that the price coefficient is zero.

Chapter 4

1.2 With the neutral product (bread) on the vertical axis, the indifference curves are parallel, vertical lines.

2.1 William's indifference curves are right angles (as in panel b of Figure 4.4). His utility function is $U = \min(H, W)$, where *min* means the minimum of the two arguments, H is the number of units of hot dogs, and W is the number of units of mustard.

2.4 If Sanghoon prefers consumption Bundle b to consumption Bundle c, it must be the case that the value of his utility function is higher at b than at c. It follows that the square of his utility at b must exceed the square of his utility at c. Therefore, Linh's utility, which is the square of Sanghoon's utility, must also be higher at b than at c. For any two consumption bundles, the one preferred by Sanghoon is also preferred by Linh. As they have exactly the same ordering of consumption bundles, Sanghoon and Linh have the same ordinal preferences.

2.5 Andy's marginal utility of apples per dollar is $\frac{3}{2} = 1.5$. The marginal utility per dollar for kumquats is $\frac{5}{4} = 1.2$. That is, a dollar spent on apples gives Andy more extra utility than a dollar spent on kumquats. He therefore maximizes his utility by spending all his money on apples and buying $\frac{40}{2} = 20$ pounds of apples.

3.4 Suppose that Dale purchases opera and ice hockey tickets at prices p_1 and p_2. If her original income is

Y_1, the intercept of the budget line on the opera axis (where she buys only opera tickets) is Y_1/p_1. Similarly, the intercept is Y_1/p_2 on the hockey axis. A 25% income tax lowers after-tax income to 75% of its original level, $0.75Y_1$. As a result, the budget line shifts inward toward the origin. The intercepts on the opera and hockey axes are $0.75Y_1/p_1$ and $0.75Y_1/p_2$, respectively. The slope is unchanged. The opportunity set is reduced by the area between the original budget line and the new budget line.

4.2 (a) Setting $MU_R/p_R = MU_C/p_C$ yields $20RC/10 = 10R^2/5$ or $2C = 2R$. Therefore, $R = C$. We then substitute $R = C$ into the budget equation to obtain $10C + 5C = 90$ or $C = 6$ (and $R = 6$). The diagram looks like Figure 4.8 with only the middle indifference curve shown and with R and C on the axes. (b) Using the same method as in part a, the new solution is $R = 6$, $C = 3$. In this case the budget line from part a has the same intercept on the R axis but the intercept on the C axis falls by half, so the budget line pivots inward.

4.4 If the U.S. price of gasoline changes from being below the Canadian price to going above it, then a utility-maximizing Canadian who lives equally close to gas stations on both sides of the border would shift from buying gas in the United States to buying gas in Canada. In the diagram, the two goods on the axes are Canadian gas and U.S. gas. They are perfect substitutes, so the indifference curves are straight lines. The consumer will consume on one axis or the other, depending on which price is lower.

6.1 Suppose that the restaurant always offers two specials chosen from three possibilities: a chicken special, a fish special, and a vegetarian special. Initially, the menu ordering is chicken, then fish. As Professor Cerf always picks the second item, he picks the fish special. Later the restaurant changes its offerings to fish (listed first) and vegetarian. In this case, Professor Cerf again chooses the second special, vegetarian. As Professor Cerf chooses fish over chicken and vegetarian over fish, transitivity of preferences would imply that he would choose vegetarian over chicken. But if the restaurant later lists vegetarian and chicken in that order as its two specials, Professor Cerf chooses chicken over vegetarian, as chicken is the second item. Thus his choices are not transitive.

6.3 The answer relates to *salience* and *bounded rationality*. A consumer's demand for a product might change when the product price is quoted inclusive of taxes because the taxes and the associated higher price become more salient (more obvious) to the consumer. Some consumers might therefore ignore a tax that is not quoted in the price but would take the tax into account if it is quoted, or they might not calculate the effect of the tax if doing calculations is difficult for them (bounded rationality). These *salience* and *bounded rationality* effects would imply that a job would attract fewer applicants if the salary were quoted after deducting income tax.

Chapter 5

1.2 No, it is not possible for $q = 10$, $L = 3$, and $K = 6$ to be a point on this production function. Holding output and other inputs fixed, a production function shows the minimum amount needed of a given factor. As only 5 units of capital are needed to produce 10 units of output given that 3 units of labor are used, using 6 units of capital would imply excess capital. Such an input combination cannot be on the production function.

2.1 One worker produces one unit of output, two workers produce two units of output, and n workers produce n units of output. Thus, the total product of labor equals the number of workers: $q = L$. The total product of labor curve is a straight line with a slope of 1. Because we are told that each extra worker produces one more unit of output, we know that the marginal product of labor, $\Delta q/\Delta L$, is 1. By dividing both sides of the production function, $q = L$, by L, we find that the average product of labor, q/L, is 1.

2.3 The production function is $q = L^{0.75}K^{0.25}$. (a) As a result, the average product of labor, holding capital fixed at $\overline{K}$, is $AP_L = q/L = L^{-0.25}\overline{K}^{0.25} = (\overline{K}/L)^{0.25}$. (b) The marginal product of labor is $MP_L = dq/dL = \frac{3}{4}(\overline{K}/L)^{0.25}$. (c) The marginal product curve intersects the average product at the maximum of the average product curve. If the marginal product exceeds the average product, the average product curve must be rising. If the marginal product is less than the average product, the marginal product curve must be falling.

2.6 There are three main factors that may increase undernourishment even if agricultural output per acre (yield) rises. First, a decrease in the total amount of land used for food production may partially offset increases in yield. Second, population growth may exceed the increase in food production. Third, political failures, particularly those resulting in wars and other violent conflicts, may disrupt food distribution systems. This third factor was by far the most important reason for increasing undernourishment in the 2014–2016 period.

3.5 (a) The isoquants are right angles, as the firm must have one disk and one hour of recording time (capital) to make a recording. Increasing one input without increasing the other results in no increase in output. (b) The *MRTS* is 0 along the horizontal portion of an isoquant and is negative infinity along the vertical portion. It is undefined at the corner point. (c) If labor is less than capital, then the total product curve is increasing in the labor input up to the point where labor equals capital, after which it is constant. The average product of labor is positive and constant if labor is less than capital and declining if labor exceeds capital. The marginal product of labor is one if labor is less than capital and drops to zero if labor exceeds or equals capital.

3.8 The isoquants are straight lines. The marginal product of B is one. If we put B on the vertical axis, the *MRTS* (the slope of the isoquant) is $-\frac{1}{2}$.

3.9 Using Equation 5.3, we know that the marginal rate of technical substitution is $MRTS = -MP_L/MP_K = -\frac{2}{3}$.

3.10 The production function is $q = 10L^{0.5}K^{0.5}$. The marginal product of labor is $\partial q/\partial L = (0.5)(10)L^{-0.5}K^{0.5}$. At $L = 16$ and $K = 25$, the marginal product is $(0.5)(10)(5)/4 = 6.25$. The marginal product of capital is $\partial q/\partial K = 0.5(10)L^{0.5}K^{-0.5} = 0.5(10)(4)/5 = 4.0$.

4.2 This production function is Cobb-Douglas. Even though it has three inputs instead of two, the same logic applies. Thus, we can calculate the returns to scale as the sum of the exponents: $0.27 + 0.16 + 0.61 = 1.04$. Therefore, this production function has nearly constant but slightly increasing returns to scale. The marginal product of materials is $\partial q/\partial M = 0.61L^{0.27}K^{0.16}M^{-0.39} \approx 0.61q/M$.

4.5 Diminishing marginal returns to each factor imply convex isoquants—isoquants that are bowed in toward the origin. Constant returns to scale imply that the distance between isoquants is proportional to the amount of input used. Thus, diminishing marginal returns relate to the shape of a single isoquant, and returns to scale relate to the distance between isoquants.

4.7 We can determine returns to scale for Cobb-Douglas production functions by adding the exponents. If the sum exceeds one, there are increasing returns to scale. If the sum equals one, there are constant returns; if the sum is less than one, there are decreasing returns. In this case Crocs

production has increasing returns to scale, U.S. housing has constant returns to scale, and U.K. supermarkets have slightly decreasing but almost constant returns to scale.

5.2 If the two firms have the same input levels, Firm 2 has a higher marginal product of labor and of capital. For Firm 1, $MP_L = \partial q_1/\partial L = 0.9\partial q_2/\partial L$. Thus, the marginal product of labor for Firm 1 is 90% that of Firm 2 if input levels are the same.

6.2 Not enough information is given to fully answer this question. However, if we assume that Japanese and American firms have identical production functions, produce using the same ratio of factors during good times, and experience recessions of the same duration, we can answer the question. Japanese firms would have a lower average product of labor during recessions because they are less likely to lay off workers and therefore would have more labor than necessary to produce the (reduced) recessionary output at minimum cost. In good times, average product would be the same in both countries. Over the entire business cycle (good times and recessions), average labor productivity would be lower in Japan.

Chapter 6

1.4 The opportunity cost of each pipe is $9. The sunk cost is $1 per pipe.

2.1 Once Nicolas has paid his monthly fee for the audio service, that cost is sunk and should not affect his decision about how much time he should spend listening to music that month. Nicolas should listen to an additional song only if the benefit he gets exceeds the opportunity cost of his time. If he has other activities that have higher value (such as studying managerial economics), giving up those activities to listen to more music would be a mistake. Therefore, Nicolas should not maximize the time spent listening to music.

2.7 The total cost of building a 1-cubic-foot crate is $6. It costs four times as much to build an 8-cubic-foot crate, $24. In general, as the height of a cube increases, the total cost of building it rises with the square of the height, but the volume increases with the cube of the height. Thus, the cost per unit of volume falls.

3.2 To minimize costs, the firm should set the marginal product per dollar equal for each factor. For labor, $MP_L/w = 50/200 = 0.25$. For capital, $MP_K/r = 200/1000 = 0.2$. In this case, the firm is not minimizing the cost of Sludge because these ratios are not equal. The firm should use more capital and less labor. (This assumes that the isoquants are smooth, which means the firm can make small adjustments to capital.)

3.4 From the information given and assuming that there are no economies of scale in shipping baseballs, it appears that balls are produced using a constant returns to scale, fixed-proportion production function. The corresponding cost function is $C(q) = [w + s + m]q$, where w is the wage for the time period it takes to stitch one ball, s is the cost of shipping one ball, and m is the price of all material to produce a ball. As the cost of all inputs other than labor and transportation are the same everywhere, the cost difference between Georgia and Costa Rica depends on $w + s$ in both locations. As firms choose to produce in Costa Rica, the extra shipping cost must be less than the labor savings in Costa Rica.

3.8 Let w be the cost of a unit of L and r be the cost of a unit of K. The cost function for the fixed-proportions production function is $C(q) = (2w + K)q$. For the other (linear) production function, the two inputs are perfect substitutes in the production process so the firm uses only the less expensive of the two inputs. Therefore, the long-run cost function is $C(q) = wq$ if $w \leq r$; otherwise, it is $C(q) = rq$.

4.2 (a) If $r = 0$, the average cost (AC) of producing one unit is $a + b$ (regardless of the value of N). There is no learning by doing in this case. (b) If $r > 0$, then average cost falls as N rises, so learning by doing does occur. As N gets very large, AC approaches a. Therefore, a is the lower limit for average cost—no matter how much learning is done, AC can never fall below a.

5.3 This firm has significant economies of scope, as producing gasoline and heating oil separately would cost approximately twice as much as producing them together. In this case, the measure of economies of scope, SC, is a positive number.

6.1 The firm will be indifferent between using the wafer-handling stepper technology and the basic stepper technology if $-w/r$ is the same as the slope of a line segment connecting the two technologies. The C^2 isocost line is steeper than this line segment and therefore has a higher wage/rental ratio. The C^3 isocost line is flatter than the line segment and therefore has a lower wage/rental ratio.

Chapter 7

1.2 One important consequence of going public is that the firm is able to raise money by issuing stock

and selling it on a public stock exchange. Another important consequence is that ownership of the firm becomes more broadly distributed as investors purchase the stock. A third frequent consequence is that the original owners lose control over the firm.

2.2 To maximize profit we set $MR = MC$, where $MR = dR/dq = 100 - 6q$ and $MC = dC/dq = 10$. Setting $MR = MC$ yields $100 - 6q = 10$ or $q = 15$.

2.4 Only $200 of the fixed cost is sunk. The firm should shut down if its revenue is less than the avoidable cost. Avoidable cost in this case is $500 + $600 = $1,100 and revenue is $1,000. As revenue is less than the avoidable cost, the firm should shut down. Shutdown rule 1: The firm shuts down only if it can reduce its loss by doing so.

4.1 Campbell gains produce and savings worth $85 million per year. Using an interest rate of 5% and applying Equation 7A.4 implies that the present value of this flow is $85/0.05 million = $1,700 million, or $1.7 billion. The cost of the acquisition is $1.55 billion plus the one-time transaction cost of $50 million, or $0.05 billion, yielding a total cost of $1.6 billion. The overall gain in value to Campbell is $1.7 - $1.6 = $0.1 billion, or $100 million.

Chapter 8

1.2 If the transaction costs of switching to a different seller are high, then some consumers would continue to buy from a seller even if that seller raised its price. The seller would therefore not be a price taker, as it would not lose all its sales by raising its price above the going market level. Also, if buyers do not know the prices available in the market (imperfect information), then a seller might be able to raise prices without losing all its customers, so it would not be a price taker in this case either.

2.2 Suppose that a U-shaped marginal cost curve cuts a competitive firm's demand curve (price line) from above at q_1 and from below at q_2. By increasing output to $q_1 + 1$, the firm earns extra profit because the last unit sells for price p, which is greater than the marginal cost of that last unit. Indeed, the price exceeds the marginal cost for all units between q_1 and q_2, so it is more profitable to produce q_2 than q_1. Thus, the firm should either produce q_2 or shut down (if it is making a loss at q_2).

2.5 Average cost is $AC = C(q)/q = 10/q + 10 + q$. Similarly, average variable cost is $AVC = VC/q = 10 + q$. If the market price is p, the firm maximizes profit by setting $MC = 10 + 2q = p$. Therefore, $q = p/2 - 5$. If $p = 50$, then $q = 50/2 - 5 = 20$.

3.2 This law has no effect on the long-run equilibrium. However, in the short run—within the six-month worker notification period—the cost of labor would be an unavoidable fixed cost instead of an avoidable variable cost. Even if the firm did not earn enough to pay its labor cost, it would stay in business in the short run, whereas without the notification law, it would shut down in the short run. The effect of the law in the short run is to make quantity larger and price lower than it would otherwise be and to impose additional losses on the firm that it would otherwise avoid.

4.2 The consumer surplus at a price of 30 is $\frac{1}{2}(30 \times 30) = 450$.

4.5 We can draw a diagram with a downward-sloping industry demand curve and an upward-sloping industry marginal cost curve (which is the industry supply curve). The competitive output occurs where the industry marginal cost curve intersects the demand curve. If output rises above this level, the marginal cost of the extra output exceeds its marginal benefit as given by the demand curve. The area between the marginal cost curve and the demand curve at output levels beyond the competitive level is a deadweight loss that must be subtracted in calculating the total surplus provided by this market. Thus, total surplus falls as output rises above the competitive level.

Chapter 9

1.3 At $Q = 10$, $p = 500 - 10(10) = 400$. The demand function is $Q = 50 - 0.1p$. The price elasticity of demand is $\varepsilon = -0.1p/Q = -0.1(400)/10 = -4$. Revenue $R = pQ = 10(400) = \$4,000$.

1.10 To obtain the profit-maximizing output, we set $MR = MC$. As $MR = 100 - 2Q$ and $MC = 5$, it follows that $100 - 2Q = 5$ or $Q = 47.5$. If the cost function changes to $C = 100 + 5Q$, there is no change in the profit-maximizing output, as the marginal cost function does not change. Also, the firm continues to earn positive profits even with the higher level of fixed costs and therefore does not shut down.

2.6 The Lerner Index was $(p - MC)/p = (359 - 159)/359 \approx 0.557$. If the firm was profit maximizing, it follows that $0.557 = -1/\varepsilon$ or $\varepsilon = -1/0.557 = -1.795$.

3.6 Suppose that the monopoly faces a constant elasticity demand function $Q = Ap^\varepsilon$ where elasticity

ε is a constant that is greater than 1 in absolute value. Marginal cost m is constant and the government imposes specific tax t. Therefore, profit is $R - C = [p - (m + t)]Q = [p - (m + t)]Ap^\varepsilon$. Taking the derivative of profit with respect to p and setting it to zero yields $p = (m + t)/(1 + 1/\varepsilon)$. Thus $dp/dt = 1/(1 + 1/\varepsilon) > 1$.

4.1 Yes. If the demand curve intersects the downward-sloping part of the AC curve, then AC is downward sloping over the relevant range and the firm is a natural monopoly.

4.2 A firm may be able to produce the market quantity more cheaply than the aggregation of separate firms' production and therefore be a natural monopoly even if the demand curve intersects the upward-sloping portion of its AC cost curve, provided this intersection occurs sufficiently close to the minimum of the AC curve.

5.2 To maximize profit, the monopoly must set marginal revenue $MR(=\partial R/\partial Q)$ equal to marginal cost, MC, and must set the marginal revenue of advertising, $MR_A(=\partial Q/\partial A)$, equal to the marginal cost of advertising, which is 1. $R = pQ = 100Q - Q^2 + 5A - A^2$. Setting $MR = MC$ yields $100 - 2Q = 10$ or $Q = 45$. Setting $MR_A = 1$ yields $5 - 2A = 1$ or $A = 2$. The profit-maximizing price is $p = 100 - 45 + (5(2) - 2^2)/(45) = 55.13$.

6.2 If the inverse demand function is given by $p = 10 - Q$, the marginal revenue function is $MR = 10 - 2Q$. Thus, the output that maximizes the monopoly's profit is determined by $MR = MC$ or $10 - 2Q = 2$. Therefore, $Q = 4$. At that output level, its price is $p = 6$ and its profit is $\pi = 16$. If the monopoly chooses to sell 8 units in the first period (it has no incentive to sell more), its price is 2 and it makes no profit. Given that the firm sells 8 units in the first period, its demand curve in the second period is $p = 10 - Q/v$, so its marginal revenue function is $MR = 10 - 2Q/v$. The output that leads to its maximum profit is determined by $MR = 10 - 2Q/v = 2 = MC$, so its output is $4v$. Thus, its price is 6 and its profit is $16v$. It pays for the firm to set a low price in the first period if the lost profit, 16, is less than the extra profit in the second period, which is $16(v - 1)$. Thus, it pays to set a low price in the first period if $16 < 16(v - 1)$, or $2 < v$.

Chapter 10

1.4 The colleges may be providing scholarships as a form of charity, or they may be price discriminating by lowering the final price to less wealthy families (with presumably higher elasticities of demand). Because wealthier families have lower elasticities (and higher willingness to pay) than poor families, they pay higher prices.

1.5 A Disneyland ticket clearly identifies whether it is a child's ticket or an adult's ticket. Thus, only children are allowed to enter using a child's ticket. Similarly, local residents are required to show identification (such as a driver's license) before being allowed to enter using a local resident ticket. Using these methods prevents resale across groups.

2.2 Under perfect price discrimination, the firm's profit is the area below the demand curve and above marginal cost. This area is $\frac{1}{2}(60)(60) = 1,800$. The consumer surplus is zero, as all surplus is extracted by the monopoly. The total surplus is therefore 1,800. The deadweight loss is zero as the monopoly produces up to the point where marginal cost cuts the demand curve. For a single-price monopoly, $Q = 30$, $p = 60$, profit is $(p - AC)\,Q = (60 - 30)\,30 = 900$, consumer surplus is 450, total surplus is 1,350, and the deadweight loss is 450.

3.2 The marginal revenue function corresponding to a linear inverse demand function has the same intercept and a slope that is twice as steep. Thus, the American marginal revenue function is $MR_A = 100 - 2Q_A$, and the Japanese one is $MR_J = 80 - 4Q_J$. To determine how many units to sell in the United States, the monopoly sets its American marginal revenue equal to its marginal cost, $MR_A = 100 - 2Q_A = 20$, and solves for the optimal quantity, $Q_A = 40$ units. Similarly, because $MR_J = 80 - 4Q_J = 20$, the optimal quantity is $Q_J = 15$ units in Japan. Substituting $Q_A = 40$ into the American demand function, we find that $p_A = 100 - 40 = \$60$. Similarly, substituting $Q_J = 15$ units into the Japanese demand function, we learn that $p_J = 80 - (2 \times 15) = \$50$. Thus, the price-discriminating monopoly charges 20% more in the United States than in Japan.

We can also show this result using elasticities. From Equation 3.6, we know that the elasticity of demand is $\varepsilon_A = -p_A/Q_A$ in the United States and $\varepsilon_J = -\frac{1}{2}p_J/Q_J$ in Japan. In the equilibrium, $\varepsilon_A = -60/40 = -\frac{3}{2}$ and $\varepsilon_J = -50/(2 \times 15) = -\frac{5}{3}$. As Equation 10.5 shows, the ratio of the prices depends on the relative elasticities of demand: $p_A/p_J = 60/50 = (1 + 1/\varepsilon_J)/(1 + 1/\varepsilon_A) = \left(1 - \frac{3}{5}\right)/\left(1 - \frac{2}{3}\right) = \frac{6}{5}$.

3.3 The two marginal revenue curves are $MR_J = 3,500 - Q_J$ and $MR_A = 4,500 - 2Q_A$. Equating the marginal revenues with the marginal cost of 500, we find that $Q_J = 3,000$ and $Q_A = 2,000$. Substituting these quantities into the demand

curve equations, we learn that $p_J = \$2,000$ and $p_A = \$2,500$. We can use Equation 9.10 to determine the elasticities of demand

$$\varepsilon_J = p/(MC - p) = 2,000/(500 - 2,000) = -4/3,$$
$$\varepsilon_A = 2,500/(500 - 2,500) = -5/4.$$

Thus, using Equation 10.3, we find that

$$\frac{p_J}{p_A} = \frac{2,000}{2,500} = 0.8 = \frac{1 + 1/(-5/4)}{1 + 1/(-4/3)} = \frac{1 + 1/\varepsilon_A}{1 + 1/\varepsilon_J}.$$

The profit in Japan is $(p_J - m)Q_J = (\$2,000 - \$500) \times 3,000 = \$4.5$ million, and the U.S. profit is $\$4$ million. The deadweight loss is greater in Japan, $\$2.25$ million $\left(\frac{1}{2} \times \$1,500 \times 3,000\right)$, than in the United States, $\$2$ million $\left(\frac{1}{2} \times \$2,000 \times 2,000\right)$.

3.11 This policy allows the firm to maximize its profit by price discriminating if people who put a lower value on their time (and are therefore willing to drive to the store and move their purchases themselves) have a higher elasticity of demand than people who want to order over the phone and have the goods delivered.

4.1 Figure 10.4 depicts a situation with identical consumers. Each consumer purchases the same fraction of the total output and gets the same fraction of the consumer surplus. As consumer surplus is lower in panel a than in panel b, it follows that all consumers are made worse off by nonlinear price discrimination in this case. However, if consumers were different, it is possible that some consumers would gain under nonlinear price discrimination. Specifically, consumers who purchase a large volume at the lower price might be better off under nonlinear price discrimination than under uniform monopoly pricing.

5.3 Under two-part pricing, the Club would charge a fee per round of $\$20$ and Joe would purchase 50 rounds. In the absence of a membership fee, his consumer surplus would be $\$2,500\,(=0.5(100)(50))$. The Club can charge this amount as an annual membership fee and thereby convert this consumer surplus to profit. Therefore, the profit-maximizing membership fee is $\$2,500$. Under standard (uniform) monopoly pricing, the Club would charge a price of $\$70$ and Joe would purchase 25 rounds, generating a profit of only $\$1,250$ for the Club. The Club therefore earns an additional $\$1,250$ from two-part pricing.

6.2 (a) If the firm uses individual pricing, the best it can do is to charge $\$600$ for the laptop and $\$100$ for the printer. It will sell laptops to all consumer types and will sell printers only to *Type A* and *Type B* consumers. Assuming just one consumer of each type, the revenue (and profit) would be $\$1,800$ for laptops and $\$200$ for printers, or $\$2,000$ in total.

(b) If the firm bundles the two products, it would maximize profit by charging a bundle price of $750 and selling to all three customers for a profit of $2,250, which is $250 more than it earns from pricing the products individually. (c) Bundling pays in this case and in Q&A 10.3 because reservation prices are negatively correlated.

7.2 (a) Winter is the peak season. Write the equations for the demand curves with q on the left side. Then we have $q^W = 200 - p$ in winter and $q^S = 100 - p/2$ in the summer. The difference is $100 - p/2$, which is strictly positive for any price at which output can be sold ($p < 200$). Thus, demand is higher in winter than in summer for any feasible price. (b) In the winter, setting $MR = MC = 0$ yields $q = 100$, but the firm has only 50 yachts. It will therefore maximize profit by choosing the price at which demand is exactly 50, which is given by $p = 200 - 50 = 150$. In the summer, the firm's profit-maximizing output is also 50, but the price needed to sell this output level is $200 - (2 \times 50) = 100$.

Chapter 11

1.4 The profit-maximizing cartel output is the monopoly output. Setting $MR = MC$ yields $100 - 4Q = 20$, so $Q = 20$. There are four firms, so each firm produces $20/4 = 5$.

2.2 The inverse demand function is $p = 1 - 0.001Q$. The first firm's profit is $\pi_1 = [1 - 0.001(q_1 + q_2)]q_1 - 0.28q_1$. Its first-order condition is $d\pi_1/dq_1 = 1 - 0.001(2q_1 + q_2) - 0.28 = 0$. If we rearrange the terms, the first firm's best-response function is $q_1 = 360 - \frac{1}{2}q_2$. Similarly, the second firm's best-response function is $q_2 = 360 - \frac{1}{2}q_1$. By substituting one of these best-response functions into the other, we learn that the Nash-Cournot equilibrium occurs at $q_1 = q_2 = 240$, and the equilibrium price is 52¢.

2.4 The monopoly will make more profit than the duopoly will, so the monopoly is willing to pay the college more rent. Although granting monopoly rights may be attractive to the college because of the higher rent that can be earned, students will suffer (lose consumer surplus) because of the higher prices.

2.12 By differentiating its product, a firm makes the residual demand curve it faces less elastic everywhere. For example, no consumer will buy from a firm if its rival charges less and the goods are homogeneous. In contrast, some consumers who prefer a firm's product to that of its rival will still buy from this firm even if its rival charges less. As implied by Equation 9.10,

the profit-maximizing price is higher if the equilibrium elasticity of demand is smaller in magnitude.

2.14 (a) At the Nash-Cournot duopoly equilibrium, $q_1 = 5$, $q_2 = (15 - 4 + 1)/3 = 4$, $p_d = 6$, $\pi_1 = (6 - 1)5 = 25$, and $\pi_2 = (6 - 2)4 = 16$. Total output is $Q_d = 5 + 4 = 9$. Total profit is $\pi_d = 25 + 16 = 41$. Consumer surplus is $CS_d = \frac{1}{2}(15 - 6)9 = 40.5$. At the efficient price (equal to the marginal cost of 1), the output is 14. The deadweight loss is $DWL_d = \frac{1}{2}(6 - 1)(14 - 9) = 12.5$. (b) A monopoly equates its marginal revenue and marginal cost: $MR = 15 - 2Q_m = 1 = MC$. Thus, $Q_m = 7$, $p_m = 8$, and $\pi_m = (8 - 1)7 = 49$. Consumer surplus is $CS_m = \frac{1}{2}(15 - 8)7 = 24.5$. The deadweight loss is $DWL_m = \frac{1}{2}(8 - 1)(14 - 7) = 24.5$. (c) The average cost of production for the duopoly is $[(5 \times 1) + (4 \times 2)]/(5 + 4) = 1.44$, whereas the average cost of production for the monopoly is 1. The increase in market power effect swamps the efficiency gain, so consumer surplus falls while deadweight loss nearly doubles.

3.2 If duopoly firms produce identical goods, the equilibrium price is lower if the firms set price rather than quantity. If the goods are differentiated, we cannot answer this question definitively.

3.4 Firm 1 wants to maximize its profit: $\pi_1 = (p_1 - 10)q_1 = (p_1 - 10)(100 - 2p_1 + p_2)$. Its first-order condition is $d\pi_1/dp_1 = 100 - 4p_1 + p_2 + 20 = 0$, so its best-response function is $p_1 = 30 + \frac{1}{4}p_2$. Similarly, Firm 2's best-response function is $p_2 = 30 + \frac{1}{4}p_1$. Solving for the Nash-Bertrand equilibrium prices yields $p_1 = p_2 = 40$. Each firm produces 60 units.

4.2 Initially, in the short run, the subsidy will lower fixed costs and increase profits for firms in the industry. However, above-normal profits will attract entry into the industry in the long run and the increased competition will force prices down until a new equilibrium is re-established in which marginal firms again earn zero profit. In the new equilibrium, there will be more firms and lower prices.

5.1 (a) The Nash-Cournot equilibrium in the absence of a government intervention is $q_1 = 30$, $q_2 = 40$, $p = 50$, $\pi_1 = 900$, and $\pi_2 = 1,600$. (b) The Nash-Cournot equilibrium is now $q_1 = 33.3$, $q_2 = 33.3$, $p = 53.3$, $\pi_1 = 1,108.9$, and $\pi_2 = 1,108.9$.

Chapter 12

1.1 If Duncan stays silent, Larry gets 0 if he talks and −1 (a year in jail) if he stays silent. If Duncan confesses, Larry gets −2 if he talks and −5 if he does not. Thus, Larry is better off talking in either case, so talking is his dominant strategy. By the same reasoning, talking is also Duncan's dominant strategy. As a result, the Nash equilibrium is for both to confess.

1.6 We start by checking for dominant strategies. Given the payoff matrix, Toyota always does at least as well by entering the market. If GM enters, Toyota earns 10 by entering and 0 by staying out of the market. If GM does not enter, Toyota earns 250 if it enters and 0 otherwise. Thus, entering is Toyota's dominant strategy. GM does not have a dominant strategy. It wants to enter if Toyota does not enter (earning 200 rather than 0), and it wants to stay out if Toyota enters (earning 0 rather than −40). Because GM knows that Toyota will enter (given that entering is Toyota's dominant strategy), GM stays out of the market. Toyota's entering and GM's not entering is a Nash equilibrium. Given the other firm's strategy, neither firm wants to change its strategy.

Next we examine how the subsidy affects the payoff matrix and dominant strategies. The subsidy does not affect Toyota's payoff, so Toyota still has a dominant strategy: It enters the market. With the subsidy, GM's payoffs if it enters increase by 50: GM earns 10 if both enter and 250 if it enters and Toyota does not. With the subsidy, entering is a dominant strategy for GM. Thus, both firms' entering is a Nash equilibrium.

2.2 If the firms can engage in cheap talk (pre-play communication) they can presumably avoid a scheduling conflict in which they both choose the same night. However, cheap talk cannot identify a unique Nash equilibrium. Network 2 would prefer the Nash equilibrium in which it schedules the show on Thursday and can indicate its intent to choose Thursday. However, Network 1 prefers the Nash equilibrium in which it schedules the show on Thursday so it can announce the same intention. These announcements are not consistent and would not determine a unique equilibrium.

2.11 We can see whether this outcome is a mixed-strategy equilibrium by checking whether either firm wishes to change its strategy given its rival's strategy. Consider the situation from Firm 1's point of view. If both firms enter with probability $\frac{1}{3}$, then Firm 1 will stay out $\frac{2}{3}$ of the time and get nothing. Both firms will enter $\left(\frac{1}{3}\right)\left(\frac{1}{3}\right) = \frac{1}{9}$ of the time and Firm 1 will get −2. Firm 1 will enter alone $\left(\frac{1}{3}\right)\left(\frac{2}{3}\right) = \frac{2}{9}$ of the time and get 1. The expected payoff to Firm 1 is therefore $\left(\frac{2}{3}\right)(0) + \left(\frac{1}{9}\right)(-2) + \left(\frac{2}{9}\right)(1) = 0$. Firm 1 can do no better by adopting any other strategy, including entering with certainty or staying out with certainty. It therefore has no incentive to

change its strategy. The same is true of Firm 2. Therefore, this combination of mixed strategies is a mixed-strategy equilibrium.

3.1 (a) WCG does not have a dominant strategy. BB does have a dominant strategy. Investing is better for BB no matter what WCG does. (b) The Nash equilibrium is for BB and WCG to both invest. At this outcome each is doing the best it can given the other's strategy. (c) The maximin solution is for BB to invest and WCG not to invest.

4.2 If the two firms reach agreement, Maxygen sells the patent to Oculus for a price of p. Oculus has a net value of $50 − p$ and Maxygen gets p. If they do not agree, Oculus' value is 10, and Maxygen gets nothing. Therefore, the Nash product is $N = (50 − p − 10)(p − 0) = 40p − p^2$. To maximize the Nash product, we set the derivative of the product with respect to p equal to zero: $dN/dp = 60 − 2p = 0$ or $p = 20$. In the Nash bargaining solution, Maxygen sells the patent for 20 and gets a net gain of 20 relative to the disagreement point. Oculus also gains $20(= 50 − 20 − 10)$ relative to the disagreement point.

Chapter 13

1.1 (a) In the simultaneous move game there are two Nash equilibria (in pure strategies). One Nash equilibrium is for Firm 1 to sell 10 and Firm 2 to sell 20. The other is for Firm 1 to sell 20 while Firm 2 sells 10. (b) After drawing the game tree, you can use backward induction to see that if Firm 1 sells 10, then Firm 2 will choose 20, while if Firm 1 sells 20, then Firm 1 will sell 10. The first of these possibilities is better for Firm 1. Since Firm 1, the leader, can choose first, it therefore sells 10. Thus, the subgame-perfect Nash equilibrium is for Firm 1 to sell 10 and Firm 2 to sell 20. (c) If Firm 2 is the leader, the subgame-perfect Nash equilibrium is that Firm 2 sells 10 and Firm 1 sells 20.

1.2 In a game that is repeated a finite number of times, the outcome will yield the noncooperative solution if the players are fully rational. This solution is $q_u = 64$ and $q_a = 64$ in each period. Similarly, if one firm cares only about current period profits (and both firms know this), then the same thing happens.

2.2 First we determine the Nash-Cournot equilibrium. The inverse demand function is $p = 1 − 0.001Q$. Firm 1's profit is $\pi_1 = [1 − 0.001(q_1 + q_2)]q_1 − 0.28q_1$. Its first-order condition is $d\pi_1/dq_1 = 1 − 0.001(2q_1 + q_2) − 0.28 = 0$. If we rearrange the terms, the Firm 1's best-response function is $q_1 = 360 - \frac{1}{2}q_2$. Similarly, Firm 2's best-response function is $q_2 = 360 - \frac{1}{2}q_1$. By substituting one of these best-response functions into the other, we learn that the Nash-Cournot equilibrium occurs at $q_1 = q_2 = 240$, so the total output is 480 and the equilibrium price is 52¢.

Next we determine the Stackelberg equilibrium. In this case Firm 1 substitutes the best-response function of Firm 2 into Firm 1's profit function: $\pi_1 = [1 - 0.001(q_1 + 360 - \frac{1}{2}q_1)]q_1 - 0.28q_1$. Taking the derivative of this profit function and setting it to zero yields $d\pi_1/dq_1 = 0.36 - 0.001q_1 = 0$ or $q_1 = 360$. Therefore, $q_2 = 360 - \frac{1}{2}(360) = 180$. The total Stackelberg output is $360 + 180 = 540$, which exceeds the Nash-Cournot output of 480. The Stackelberg price is $1 - 0.001(540) = \$0.46$ or 46¢, which is lower than the Nash-Cournot price. Relative to the Nash-Cournot case, profit is higher for the leader and lower for the follower, and aggregate profits are lower in the Stackelberg case.

2.6 Levi Strauss would want Wrangler to believe this claim because, if it did, Wrangler would choose white and Levi Strauss would choose violet and earn a profit of 40, the highest possible profit. However, Wrangler should not believe this claim. If, for example, Wrangler chooses violet, then Levi would be better off choosing black rather than also choosing violet. Levi's claim that it would choose violet in this case is not credible.

3.4 Draw the game tree and analyze the game using backward induction (moving from right to left in the diagram). If the incumbent commits to the small quantity, its rival enters and the incumbent earns $450. If the incumbent commits to the larger quantity, its rival does not enter and the incumbent earns $800. Clearly, the incumbent should commit to the larger quantity because it earns a larger profit and the potential entrant chooses to stay out of the market. In the subgame-perfect Nash equilibrium, the incumbent produces the large quantity and the potential rival stays out.

3.5 Ying takes x as fixed and maximizes utility with respect to y: $dU/dy = 5(x + y)^{(-0.5)} - 1$. Therefore, $5 = (x + y)^{0.5}$, so $y = 25 - x$. If $x = 15$, it follows that $y = 10$. Ying will work for 10 hours. Xavier can keep Ying from doing any work by working for 25 hours or more.

4.2 Draw the game tree. It is worth more to the monopoly to keep the potential entrant out than it is worth to the potential entrant to enter, as the figure shows. Before the pollution-control device requirement, the entrant would pay up to $3 to enter, whereas the incumbent would pay up to $\pi_m - \pi_d = \$7$ to exclude the potential entrant. With the device, the incumbent's profit is $6 if entry does not occur, and it loses $1 if entry occurs. Because the new firm would lose $1 if it enters, it does not enter. Thus, the incumbent has an incentive to raise costs by $4 to both firms. The incumbent's profit is $6 if it raises costs and only $3 if it does not.

5.3 The subgame-perfect Nash equilibrium is that Clarion would not build the plant. The problem is that if it did, then Ford would have an incentive to pay only p_2 and Clarion would lose money, an example of the hold-up problem. One possible solution is for Ford to make a contractual commitment before Clarion invests to pay p_3.

6.3 If Chloe expects other players to choose randomly, then she would expect the average among those players to be about 50. Her own bid will lower the average slightly, but we will assume that there are enough players so that her effect on the average is too small to affect her optimal bid. She should therefore pick the integer closest to $\frac{2}{3}$ of 50, which is 33. If you are playing and you think everyone else is like Chloe, then you should bid $\frac{2}{3}$ of 33, which is 22.

Chapter 14

1.2 Assuming that the painting is not insured against fire, its expected value is $(0.2 \times \$1,000) + (0.1 \times \$0) + (0.7 \times \$500) = \$550$.

1.4 The expected value of the stock is $(0.25 \times 400) + (0.75 \times 200) = 250$. The variance is $0.25(400 - 250)^2 + 0.75(200 - 250)^2 = 0.25(150)^2 + 0.75(-50)^2 = 5,625 + 1,875 = 7,500$. The standard deviation is 86.6.

2.6 Hugo's expected wealth is $EW = \left(\frac{2}{3} \times 144\right) + \left(\frac{1}{3} \times 225\right) = 96 + 75 = 171$. His expected utility is $EU = \left[\frac{2}{3} \times U(144)\right] + \left[\frac{1}{3} \times U(225)\right] = \left[\frac{2}{3} \times \sqrt{144}\right] + \left[\frac{1}{3} \times \sqrt{225}\right] = \left[\frac{2}{3} \times 12\right] + \left[\frac{1}{3} \times 15\right] = 13$.

Hugo's certainty equivalent, CE, is the certain wealth that would give him the same utility as this risky prospect. Therefore, $13 = \sqrt{CE}$, so $CE = 13^2 = 169$. The risk premium, RP, is the difference between expected wealth and the certainty equivalent: $RP = 171 - 169 = 2$. That is, Hugo would accept an offer for his stock today of $169 (or more), which reflects his risk premium of $2.

3.4 (a) $EU(\text{No Insurance}) = (0.2)U(90,000) + (0.8)U(160,000) = 240 + 1,280 = 1,520$. $U(\text{Insurance}) = U(160,000 - 15,000) = 1,523.15$. Because

U(Insurance) $> EU$(No Insurance), this household should buy the insurance. (b) The actuarially fair price is the expected value of the payout, which is $(0.2)(70,000) = 14,000$. (c) The maximum the household would pay for this insurance is the price that would give it the same utility as not buying the insurance. If this price is p, then $U(160,000 - p) = EU$(No Insurance) $= 1,520$. Therefore, $(4)(160,000 - p)^{0.5} = 1,520$ or $160,000 - p = (1,520/4)^2 = 144,400$. It follows that $p = 15,600$.

4.1 If they were married, Andy would receive half the potential earnings whether they stayed married or not. As a result, Andy will receive $12,000 in present-value terms from Kim's additional earnings. Because the returns to the investment exceed the cost, Andy will make this investment (unless a better investment is available). However, if they stay unmarried and split, Andy's expected return on the investment is the probability of staying together, $\frac{1}{2}$, times Kim's half of the returns if they stay together, $12,000. Thus, Andy's expected return on the investment, $6,000, is less than the cost of the education, so Andy is unwilling to make that investment (regardless of other investment opportunities).

5.3 Either Joe or Sue might be overconfident, but there is no information in the question to indicate that would be the reason for their different behavior. However, prospect theory would be a good explanation. Under prospect theory, people are risk seeking in the domain of losses, so Joe is willing to take a substantial risk on the last race. Sue is in the domain of gains and is therefore fundamentally risk averse. A small gamble is still fun for her (see the Mini-Case, "Gambling"), but she does not want to take a large risk.

Chapter 15

1.2 Because insurance costs do not vary with soil type, buying insurance is unattractive for houses on good soil and relatively attractive for houses on bad soil. Relatively more homeowners with houses on poor soil buy insurance, so the state insurance agency will have a higher payout rate in the next major earthquake than it would if everyone bought earthquake insurance. This is a form of adverse selection—high-risk consumers will buy the insurance.

1.3 Brand names allow consumers to identify a particular company's product in the future. If a mushroom company expects to remain in business over time, it would be foolish to brand its product if its mushrooms are of inferior quality. Thus, all else the same, we would expect branded mushrooms to be of higher quality than unbranded ones.

1.8 Because buyers are risk neutral, if they believe that the probability of getting a lemon is θ, the most they are willing to pay for a car of unknown quality is $p = p_1(1 - \theta) + p_2\theta$. If p is greater than both v_1 and v_2, all cars are sold. If $v_1 > p > v_2$, only lemons are sold. If p were less than both v_1 and v_2, no cars would be sold. However, we know that $v_2 < p_2$ and $p_2 < p$, so owners of lemons are certainly willing to sell them. (If sellers bear a transaction cost of c and $p < v_2 + c$, no cars are sold.)

2.3 If education is easier to obtain for high-quality workers than for low-quality workers, then high-quality workers may signal their quality to prospective employers by getting higher levels of education than lower-quality workers.

3.1 This arrangement would likely increase the size of the overall bill. If there are n students, then each student will incur a cost of only $1/n$ times the cost of any additional item that the student orders. Because the student placing the order will get the entire marginal benefit but will bear only a small part of the marginal cost, an excessive amount would be ordered.

3.5 Presumably, the promoter collects a percentage of the revenue at each restaurant. If customers can pay cash, the restaurants may lie to the promoter as to the amount of food they sold. The scrip (Cajun Cash) makes such opportunistic behavior difficult.

4.3 A partner who works an extra hour bears the full opportunity cost of this extra hour but gets only half the marginal benefit from the extra business profit. The opportunity cost of extra time spent at the store is the partner's best alternative use of time. A partner could earn money working for someone else or use the time to have fun. Because a partner bears the full marginal cost but gets only half the marginal benefit (the extra business profit) from an extra hour of work, each partner works only up to the point at which the marginal cost equals half the marginal benefit. Thus, each has an incentive to put in less effort than the level that maximizes their joint profit, where the marginal cost equals the marginal benefit.

4.4 (a) If Arnie is paid a fixed wage of 10, then Arnie would provide low effort. Any additional effort would be costly to him and would not increase his wage and therefore be a net loss. (b) Under a 50-50 profit-sharing contract, Arnie would choose medium effort. With medium effort the expected profit is $0.5(40) + 0.5(80) = 60$. Arnie gets 50%, or 30, and subtracts the cost of effort, 10, yielding a net gain of 20. With either low effort or high effort,

Arnie's net gain is only 15. (c) Arnie gets 20 under the profit-sharing contract and 10 with a fixed wage, so he prefers profit sharing. Priscilla has an expected value of $30 - 10 = 20$ with a fixed wage and $0.5(60) = 30$ under profit sharing, so she prefers profit sharing also.

5.3 One important factor that deters shirking is that employees may lose their jobs if they are caught shirking. This possibility is a stronger deterrent to shirking if the employee anticipates a period of unemployment after being fired. If the worker can easily move to a new job, as occurs under full employment, then the incentive to avoid shirking is weaker.

Chapter 16

1.1 A Pareto improvement does not necessarily yield a Pareto-efficient outcome, as further Pareto improvements may be possible. If a situation is Pareto efficient, no further Pareto improvements are possible. A change that leads to Pareto efficiency does not necessarily cause a Pareto improvement, as there may be losers as well as winners.

2.2 As demand is perfectly inelastic up to a price of $100 per day, the profit-maximizing monopoly price is $100 and all 100 consumers will purchase a daily dose at this price. There is no consumer surplus. The daily producer surplus (and profit) is $(100 - 10)100 = 9,000$. If a price ceiling of $30 is imposed, the price falls to $30, quantity remains unchanged at 100, consumer surplus rises to $(100 - 30)100 = 7,000$, and producer surplus falls to $(30 - 10)100 = 2,000$. In this case, the price control imposes no deadweight loss.

3.1 Under duopoly each firm produces 30, so total industry output is 60, price is 40, and total profit for the two firms combined is $(40 - 10)60 = 1,800$. If the two firms merge to form a monopoly, industry quantity falls to 45, price rises to 55, and profit rises to $(55 - 10)45 = 2,025$. Thus, merging increases the combined profit of the firms. Antitrust authorities might oppose the merger because consumer surplus falls by more than profit rises, so deadweight loss rises as a result of the merger.

4.3 Zero pollution is not the optimal level of pollution for society. The optimal level of pollution is where the marginal social cost of pollution is equal to the marginal social benefit of pollution. At zero pollution, the marginal social benefit of a little pollution is high, while the marginal social cost is low. We can have "too little" pollution.

4.8 The competitive outcome occurs where the supply and demand curves cross, which is where price (inverse demand) equals marginal cost. Therefore, $200 - Q = 80 + Q$ or $Q = 60$. The social optimum occurs where the social marginal benefit given by the inverse demand function equals the social marginal cost, which is the sum of the private marginal cost and the marginal external damage. Therefore, $200 - Q = 80 + 2Q$ and the optimal output level is $Q = 40$. The market will produce this amount of output if a specific tax is set equal to the amount of the external damage at the optimal output level. In this case, the tax should therefore be 40.

5.4 A public good is both nonrival and nonexclusive. Cable television is nonrival but it is exclusive, as potential users can be easily excluded. Therefore, cable television is not a public good. (It is a club good.) Broadcast television is both nonrival and nonexclusive—anyone with a TV and appropriate antenna can receive and view the signals. Therefore, broadcast TV is a public good. However, broadcast TV is provided by private firms because those firms do not need to collect revenue from viewers. Instead, the revenue comes from advertisers who hope to sell products to the viewers. Even so, in the days before cable TV became common, broadcast TV probably was underprovided by private sources and, in many countries, broadcasting was (and is) either provided by government or subsidized by government.

6.2 In this case, price is 30 and output is 10 whether or not Woz develops the new process. Therefore, consumer surplus does not change. However, Woz earns positive producer surplus (and positive profit) from the innovation and total surplus rises.

Chapter 17

1.1 In South Korea, the opportunity cost of car assembly is 1.5 sets of components per assembled car. In North Korea, the opportunity cost of car assembly is only one-third of a set of components. The theory of comparative advantage implies that North Korea would export assembled cars, as it has a lower opportunity cost of assembly.

2.2 Figure 17.1 shows the supply and demand for euros per day. The exchange rate is the price in U.S. dollars of a euro. If the U.S. government tries to fix the exchange rate at X_1 even after demand for euros shifts out to D^2, there will be an excess demand for euros at that price. Supply and demand would come into balance only if the exchange rate were allowed to rise to the new equilibrium level at X_2.

3.9 If the payoff to each firm is 5 (rather than −5) if both enter, then entering becomes a dominant strategy for each firm, even without a subsidy to Novartis. If a subsidy of 10 is provided to Novartis, both firms enter, Ajinomoto earns 5, and Novartis earns 15.

4.2 To maximize combined profits, TMX Philippines should charge a transfer price equal to the marginal cost of $10. The Timex Group USA then sets its marginal revenue of $90 - 4Q$ equal to the transfer price (its marginal cost) of 10, which yields $90 - 4Q = 10$ or $Q = 20$. Price will be $90 - 40 = 50$. TMX Philippines makes no profit in this case, but it could make positive profits if it raised the transfer price. However, the profit of the Timex Group USA would fall by more than the profit of TMX Philippines would rise.

Definitions

adverse selection: when one party to a transaction possesses information about a hidden characteristic that is unknown to other parties and takes economic advantage of this information, causing low-quality items to be overrepresented in transactions. (15)

arc price elasticity: an elasticity that uses the average price and average quantity as the denominator for percentage calculations. (3)

asymmetric information: a situation in which one party to a transaction has relevant information that another party does not have. (15)

auction: a sale in which a good or service is sold to the highest bidder. (12)

average cost (or _average total cost_) (_AC_): the total cost divided by the units of output produced: $AC = C/q$. (6)

average fixed cost (_AFC_): the fixed cost divided by the units of output produced: $AFC = F/q$. (6)

average product of labor (_AP_$_L$): the ratio of output, q, to the amount of labor, L, used to produce that output: $AP_L = q/L$. (5)

average variable cost (or _variable cost per unit of output_) (_AVC_): the variable cost divided by the units of output produced: $AVC = VC/q$. (6)

backward induction (in a game): first determine the best response by the last player to move, next determine the best response for the player who made the next-to-last move, and then repeat the process back to the first move of the game. (13)

bad: something for which less is preferred to more, such as pollution. (4)

bandwagon effect: the situation in which a person places greater value on a good as more and more other people possess it. (9)

bargaining game: any situation in which two or more parties with different interests or objectives negotiate voluntarily over the terms of some interaction, such as the transfer of a good from one party to another. (12)

behavioral economics: the use of insights from psychology and research on human cognition and emotional biases to augment the rational economic model to better predict economic decision making. (4)

Bertrand equilibrium (or _Nash-Bertrand_ or _Bertrand-Nash equilibrium_): a Nash equilibrium in prices; a set of prices such that, holding the prices of all other firms constant, no firm can obtain a higher profit by choosing a different price. (11)

best response (in a game): the strategy that maximizes a player's payoff given its beliefs about its rivals' strategies. (12)

bounded rationality: a situation in which people have a limited capacity to anticipate, solve complex problems, or enumerate all options. (4)

budget line (or _budget constraint_): the bundles of goods that can be bought if the entire budget is spent on those goods at given prices. (4)

bundling (or _package deal_): a type of sale in which two or more goods or services are combined and offered at a single price. (10)

cartel: a group of firms that explicitly agree (collude) to coordinate setting prices or quantities. (11)

certification: a report that a particular product meets or exceeds a given standard. (15)

club good: a good that is nonrival but is subject to exclusion. (16)

common knowledge (in a game): a piece of information known by all players, and is known by all players to be known, and is known to be known to be known, etc. (12)

common property, open-access: resources to which everyone has free access and equal rights to exploit. (16)

comparative advantage (in international trade): the ability to produce a good or service at lower opportunity cost than other countries. (17)

complements: a pair of goods or services for which an increase in the price of one causes a consumer to demand a smaller quantity of the other. (2)

complete information (in a game): a situation in which the strategies and payoffs of the game are common knowledge. (12)

constant returns to scale (_CRS_): the property of a production function whereby when all inputs are increased by the same proportion, output increases by that same proportion. (5)

consumer surplus (_CS_): the monetary difference between what a consumer is willing to pay for the quantity of the good purchased and what the good actually costs. (8)

cost (or _total cost_, _C_): the sum of a firm's variable cost and fixed cost: $C = VC + F$. (6)

cost-benefit principle: a change is desirable if its benefits exceed the costs. (16)

Cournot equilibrium (or _Nash-Cournot_ or _Cournot-Nash equilibrium_): a set of quantities chosen by firms such that, holding the quantities of all other firms constant, no firm can obtain a higher profit by choosing a different quantity. (11)

credible threat: a claim or threat that a player will, under particular circumstances, use a strategy harmful to its rival, and the threat is believable because it is in the player's best interest to use it if those circumstances arise. (13)

cross-price elasticity of demand: the percentage change in the quantity demanded divided by the percentage change in the price of another good. (3)

deadweight loss (*DWL*): the net reduction in total surplus from a loss of surplus by one group that is not offset by a gain to another group from an action that alters a market equilibrium. (8)

decreasing returns to scale (*DRS*): the property of a production function whereby output rises less than in proportion to an equal proportional increase in all inputs. (5)

demand curve: a curve showing the quantity of a good demanded at each possible price, holding constant the other factors that influence purchases. (2)

dependent variable: the variable whose variation is to be explained. (3)

diminishing marginal returns (law of): if a firm keeps increasing an input, holding all other inputs and technology constant, the corresponding increases in output will eventually become smaller (diminish). (5)

diseconomies of scale: the property of a cost function whereby the average cost of production rises when output increases. (6)

dominant strategy: a strategy that produces a higher payoff than any other strategy the player can use no matter what its rivals do. (12)

duopoly: an oligopoly with two firms. (11)

durable good: a product that is usable for a long period, perhaps for many years. (6)

dynamic game: a game in which players move either sequentially or repeatedly. (13)

economically efficient (for a producer): minimizing the cost of producing a specified output level. (6)

economic profit: revenue minus opportunity cost (7)

economics: the study of decision making in the presence of scarcity. (1)

economies of scale: the property of a cost function whereby the average cost of production falls as output expands. (6)

economies of scope: the situation in which it is less expensive to produce goods jointly than separately. (6)

efficient contract: an agreement in which neither party can be made better off without harming the other party. (15)

efficient production (or *technological efficiency*): the situation in which the current level of output cannot be produced with fewer inputs, given existing knowledge about technology and the organization of production. (5)

elasticity: the percentage change in one variable divided by the associated percentage change in the other variable. (3)

endowment effect: people place a higher value on a good if they own it than if they are considering buying it. (4)

equilibrium: a situation in which no participant wants to change his or her behavior. (2)

essential facility: a scarce resource that a rival needs to use to survive. (16)

excess demand: the amount by which the quantity demanded exceeds the quantity supplied at a specified price. (2)

excess supply: the amount by which the quantity supplied exceeds the quantity demanded at a specified price. (2)

exchange rate: the price of one currency (such as the euro) in terms of another currency (such as the U.S. dollar). (17)

exclusion: the property that others can be prevented from consuming a good. (16)

expected value: is derived by taking the value of each possible outcome times the probability of that outcome and adding up those values. (14)

explanatory variables: the factors that are thought to affect the value of a dependent variable. (3)

extensive form (of a game): specifies the n players, the sequence in which they make their moves, the actions they can take at each move, the information that each player has about players' previous moves, and the payoff function over all possible strategies. (13)

externality: a person's well-being or a firm's production capability is directly affected by the actions of other consumers or firms rather than indirectly through changes in prices. (16)

fair bet: a bet with an expected value of zero. (14)

fair insurance: a contract between an insurer and a policyholder in which the expected value of the contract to the policyholder is zero. (14)

fixed cost (*F*): a production expense that does not vary with output. (6)

fixed input: a factor of production that cannot be varied in the short run. (5)

free-rider problem: a situation in which people benefit from the actions of others without paying. (16)

game: any interaction between players (such as individuals or firms) in which strategic interdependence plays a major role. (12)

game theory: a set of tools used by economists and others to analyze decision making in situations of strategic interdependence. (12)

good: a commodity for which more is preferred to less, at least at some levels of consumption. (4)

group price discrimination (or *third-degree price discrimination*): a situation in which a firm charges each group of customers a different price. (10)

hidden action: an act by one party to a transaction that is not observed by the other party. (15)

hidden characteristic: an attribute of a person or thing that is known to one party but unknown to others. (15)

holdup problem: two firms agree to work together and the firm that acts second takes advantage of a specific investment made by the firm that acts first. (13)

income elasticity of demand (or *income elasticity*): the percentage change in the quantity demanded divided by the given percentage change in income. (3)

increasing returns to scale (*IRS*): the property of a production function whereby output rises more than in proportion to an equal proportional increase in all inputs. (5)

indifference curve: the set of all bundles of goods that a consumer views as being equally desirable. (4)

indifference map (or *preference map*): a complete set of indifference curves that summarize a consumer's tastes or preferences. (4)

inferior good: a good for which the quantity demanded falls as income rises. (3)

innovation: a new idea, device, or method. (5)

interest rate: the percentage more that must be repaid to borrow money for a fixed period of time. (7)

isocost line: all the combinations of inputs that require the same (*iso-*) total expenditure (*cost*). (6)

isoquant: a curve that shows the efficient combinations of labor and capital that can produce a single (*iso-*) level of output (*quant*ity). (5)

Law of Demand: consumers demand more of a good if its price is lower, holding constant the prices of other goods, tastes, and other factors that influence the amount they want to consume. (2)

learning by doing: the productive skills and knowledge that workers and managers gain from experience. (6)

learning curve: the relationship between average cost and cumulative output. (6)

Lerner Index: the ratio of the difference between price and marginal cost to the price: $(p - MC)/p$. (9)

limit pricing: when a firm sets its price (or, equivalently, its output) so that another firm cannot enter the market profitably. (13)

limited liability (for a corporation): the condition whereby the personal assets of the corporate owners cannot be taken to pay a corporation's debts even if it goes into bankruptcy. (7)

long run: a lengthy enough period of time that all relevant inputs can be varied. (5)

managerial economics: the application of economic analysis to managerial decision making. (1)

marginal cost (*MC*): the amount by which a firm's cost changes if the firm produces one more unit of output. (6)

marginal product of labor (*MP_L*): the change in total output resulting from using an extra unit of labor, holding other factors constant. (5)

marginal profit: the change in profit a firm gets from selling one more unit of output. (7)

marginal rate of substitution (*MRS*): the rate at which a consumer can substitute one good for another while remaining on the same indifference curve. (4)

marginal rate of technical substitution (of capital for labor) (*MRTS*): the units of capital the firm can replace with an extra unit of labor while holding output constant. (5)

marginal rate of transformation (*MRT*): the trade-off the market imposes on the consumer in terms of the amount of one good the consumer must give up to purchase more of the other good. (4)

marginal revenue (*MR*): the change in revenue a firm gets from selling one more unit of output. (7)

marginal utility: the extra utility that a consumer gets from consuming one more unit of a good. (4)

market: an exchange mechanism that allows buyers to trade with sellers. (1)

market failure: a non-optimal allocation of resources such that total surplus in a market is not maximized. (9)

market power: the ability of a firm to significantly affect the market price. (9)

market structure: the number of firms in the market, the ease with which firms can enter and leave the market, and the ability of firms to differentiate their products from those of their rivals. (7)

maximin strategy (in a game): a strategy that maximizes the lowest possible payoff the player might receive. (12)

mixed strategy: a player in a game chooses among possible pure strategies according to probabilities it assigns. (12)

model: a description of the relationship between two or more variables. (1)

monopolistic competition: a market structure in which firms have market power, but free entry occurs in the long run until no additional firm can enter and earn a positive long-run profit. (11)

monopoly: the sole supplier of a good that has no close substitute. (9)

moral hazard: an informed party takes an action that another party cannot observe and that harms the less-informed party. (15)

multivariate regression (or *multiple regression*): regression with two or more explanatory variables. (3)

Nash equilibrium: a set of strategies such that, holding the strategies of all other players constant, no player can obtain a higher payoff by choosing a different strategy. (12)

Nash-Bertrand equilibrium (or *Bertrand* or *Bertrand-Nash equilibrium*): a set of prices such that, holding the prices of all other firms constant, no firm can obtain a higher profit by choosing a different price. (11)

Nash-Cournot equilibrium (or *Cournot* or *Cournot-Nash equilibrium*): a set of quantities chosen by firms such that, holding the quantities of all other firms constant, no firm can obtain a higher profit by choosing a different quantity. (11)

natural monopoly: the situation in which one firm can produce the total output of the market at lower cost than two or more firms could. (9)

network externality: the situation in which one person's demand for a good depends on the consumption of the good by others. (9)

nonlinear price discrimination (or *second-degree price discrimination*): a firm charges a different price for large quantities than for small quantities, with the result that the price paid varies according to the quantity purchased. (10)

nonuniform pricing: charging consumers different prices for the same product, or charging a single customer a price that depends on the number of units the customer buys. (10)

normal good: a good for which the quantity demanded increases as income rises. (3)

normative statement: a belief about whether something is good or bad. (1)

oligopoly: a market structure with only a few firms and limited entry. (11)

open-access common property: resources to which everyone has free access and equal rights to exploit. (16)

opportunistic behavior: taking advantage of someone when circumstances permit. (7)

opportunity cost (or *economic cost*): the value of the best alternative use of a resource. (6)

opportunity set: all the bundles a consumer can buy, including all the bundles inside the budget constraint and on the budget constraint. (4)

Pareto efficient: an outcome with the property that any change would harm at least one person. (16)

Pareto improvement: a change, such as a reallocation of goods and services between people, that helps at least one person without harming anyone else. (16)

Pareto principle: society should favor any change that benefits some people without harming anyone else. (16)

patent: an exclusive right granted to the inventor of a new and useful product, process, substance, or design for a specified length of time. (9)

payoffs (of a game): players' valuations of the outcome of the game, such as profits for firms or income or utilities for individuals. (12)

peak-load pricing: charging higher prices during periods of peak demand than in other periods. (10)

perfect complements: goods that a consumer wants to consume only in fixed proportions. (4)

perfect price discrimination (or *first-degree price discrimination*): a situation in which a firm sells each unit at the maximum amount any customer is willing to pay for it. (10)

perfect substitutes: goods that are essentially equivalent from the consumer's point of view. (4)

positive statement: a testable hypothesis about matters of fact such as cause-and-effect relationships. (1)

price discrimination: charging consumers different prices for the same good based on individual characteristics of consumers, on membership in an identifiable subgroup of consumers, or on the quantity purchased. (10)

price elasticity of demand (or *elasticity of demand*, *demand elasticity*, ε): the percentage change in the quantity demanded, Q, divided by the percentage change in the price, p. (3)

price elasticity of supply (or *elasticity of supply*): the percentage change in the quantity supplied divided by the percentage in price. (3)

prisoners' dilemma: a game in which all players have dominant strategies that lead to a payoff that is inferior to what they could achieve if they cooperated. (12)

private cost: a firm's direct costs of production (such as the cost of inputs), but not including any costs imposed on others. (16)

producer surplus (*PS*): the difference between the amount for which a good sells and the minimum amount necessary for the producers to be willing to produce the good. (8)

production function: the relationship between the quantities of inputs used and the maximum quantity of output that can be produced, given current knowledge about technology and organization. (5)

profit (π): revenue minus opportunity cost. (7)

public good: a commodity or service that is both nonrival and nonexclusive. (16)

pure strategy: a specification of the action that a player will take in every possible situation in a game. (12)

quantity demanded: the amount of a good that consumers are *willing* to buy at a given price, holding constant the other factors that influence purchases. (2)

quantity supplied: the amount of a good that firms *want* to sell at a given price, holding constant other factors that influence firms' supply decisions, such as costs and government actions. (2)

random error term (in a regression equation): a term that captures the effects of unobserved influences on the dependent variable that are not included as explanatory variables. (3)

regression analysis: a statistical technique used to estimate the mathematical relationship between a dependent variable, such as quantity demanded, and one or more explanatory variables, such as price and income. (3)

regression specification: includes the choice of the dependent variable, the explanatory variables, and the functional relationship between them (such as linear, quadratic, or exponential). (3)

rent seeking: devoting effort and expenditures to gain a rent or a profit from government actions. (16)

reservation price: the maximum amount a person is willing to pay for a unit of output. (10)

risk averse: unwilling to make a fair bet. (14)

risk neutral: indifferent about making a fair bet. (14)

risk preferring: always willing to make a fair bet. (14)

risk premium: the maximum amount that a decision maker would pay to avoid taking a risk. (Equivalently, the risk premium is the minimum extra compensation (premium) that a decision maker would require to incur a risk.) (14)

rival good: a good that is used up as it is consumed. (16)

rules of the game: regulations that determine the timing of players' moves and the actions that players can make at each move, and possibly other specific aspects of how the game is played. (12)

screening: an action taken by an uninformed party to determine the information possessed by informed parties. (15)

short run: a period of time so brief that at least one factor of production cannot be varied practically. (5)

shortage: a persistent excess demand. (2)

signaling: an action taken by an informed party to send information to an uninformed party. (15)

snob effect: the situation in which a person places greater value on a good as fewer and fewer other people possess it. (9)

social cost: all the costs incurred by society, including the private costs of firms and individuals and the harm from externalities. (16)

static game: a game in which each player acts only once and the players act simultaneously (or, at least, each player acts without knowing rivals' actions). (12)

strategy: a battle plan that specifies the actions or moves that a player will make conditional on the information available at each move and for any possible contingency. (12)

subgame: all the subsequent actions that players can take given the actions already taken and the corresponding payoffs. (13)

subgame-perfect Nash equilibrium: players' strategies are a Nash equilibrium in every subgame (including the overall game). (13)

substitutes: a pair of goods or services for which an increase in the price of one causes a consumer to demand a larger quantity of the other. (2)

sunk cost: a past expenditure that cannot be recovered. (6)

supply curve: the quantity supplied at each possible price, holding constant the other factors that influence firms' supply decisions. (2)

technical progress: an advance in knowledge that allows more output to be produced with the same level of inputs. (5)

technological efficiency (or *efficient production*): the property of a production function such that the current level of output cannot be produced with fewer inputs, given existing knowledge about technology and the organization of production. (5)

tit-for-tat strategy: in a game, a strategy for repeated prisoners' dilemma games that involves cooperation in the first round and then copying the rival's previous action in each subsequent round. (13)

total cost (or *cost*, *C*): the sum of a firm's variable cost and fixed cost: $C = VC + F$. (6)

total surplus: the sum of consumer surplus and producer surplus, $TS = CS + PS$. (8)

transaction costs: the expenses, over and above the price of the product, of finding a trading partner and making a trade for the product. (2)

transfer price: the price used for an intra-firm transfer of goods or services. (17)

trigger strategy (in a game): a strategy in which a rival's defection from a collusive outcome triggers a punishment. (13)

two-part pricing: a pricing system in which the firm charges each consumer a lump-sum access fee for the right to buy as many units of the good as the consumer wants at a per-unit price. (10)

unbiased: an estimation method that produces an estimated coefficient, $\hat{b}$ that equals the true coefficient, b, on average. (3)

uniform pricing: charging the same price for every unit sold of a particular good. (10)

utility: a set of numerical values that reflect a consumer's relative rankings of various bundles of goods. (4)

utility function: the relationship between a utility measure and every possible bundle of goods. (4)

variable cost (*VC*): a cost that changes as the quantity of output changes. (6)

variable input: a factor of production whose quantity can be changed readily by the firm during the relevant time period. (5)

vertically integrated: describing a firm that participates in more than one successive stage of the production or distribution of goods or services. (7)

winner's curse: in an auction, the phenomenon that a winner's bid exceeds a common-value item's value. (12)

References

Akerlof, George A., "The Market for 'Lemons': Quality Uncertainty and the Market Mechanism," *Quarterly Journal of Economics*, 84(3), August 1970:488–500.

Akerlof, George A., "Labor Contacts as Partial Gift Exchanges," *Quarterly Journal of Economics*, 97(4), November 1982:543–569.

Alexander, Donald L., "Major League Baseball," *Journal of Sports Economics*, 2(4), November 2001:341–355.

Alm, James, and Jay Shimshack, "Environmental Enforcement and Compliance: Lessons from Pollution, Safety, and Tax Settings," *Foundations and Trends in Microeconomics*, 10(4), 2014:209–274.

Alyakoob, Mohammed, and Mohammed Rahman, "Shared Prosperity (or Lack Thereof) in the Sharing Economy," Working Paper, 2018. Available at https://cdn.questromworld.bu.edu/platformstrategy/files/2018/07/Airbnb_Employment.pdf

Anderson, Michael, and Maximilian Auffhammer, "Pounds That Kill: The External Costs of Vehicle Weight," *Review of Economics Studies*, 81(2), April 2014:535–571.

Antràs, Pol, and Stephen R. Yeaple, "Multinational Firms and the Structure of International Trade," in Gita Gopinath, Elhanan Helpman, and Kenneth Rogoff, eds., *Handbook of International Economics* 4. Amsterdam: Elsevier, 2014.

Association of Certified Fraud Examiners, *Report to the Nations: 2018 Global Study on Occupational Fraud and Abuse*, 2018, www.acfe.com/report-to-the-nations/2018/

Axelrod, Robert, *The Evolution of Cooperation* (Revised ed.). Cambridge, MA: Perseus Books Group, 2006.

Ayres, Ian, and Joel Waldfogel, "A Market Test for Race Discrimination in Bail Setting," *Stanford Law Review*, 46(5), May 1994:987–1047.

Bab, Andrew L., and Sean P. Neenan, "Poison Pills in 2011," *Director Notes Series*, 3(5), March 2011.

Backus, Matthew, Tom Blake, and Steven Tadelis, "The Empirical Content of Cheap-Talk Signaling: An Application to Bargaining," *Journal of Political Economy* 2018: forthcoming.

Balafoutas, Loukas, Rudolf Kerschbamer, and Matthias Sutter, "Second-Degree Moral Hazard in a Real-World Credence Goods Market," *Economic Journal*, 127(599), February, 2017:1–18.

Ball, Casey, and Courtney Moran, "Penny Lane, Literally: Funding Roads One Vehicle Mile at a Time," *Williamette Environmental Law Journal*, 5, Fall 2016:1–36.

Bapna, Ravi, Wolfgang Jank, and Galit Shmueli, "Consumer Surplus in Online Auctions," *Information Systems Research*, 19(4), December 2008:400–416.

Basker, Emek, "Raising the Barcode Scanner: Technology and Productivity in the Retail Sector," NBER Working Paper 17825, 2012.

Bauer, Thomas K., and Christoph M. Schmidt, "WTP vs. WTA: Christmas Presents and the Endowment Effect," Institute for the Study of Labor Working Paper, 2008.

Baumeister, Christiane, and Gert Peersman, "The Role of Time-Varying Price Elasticities in Accounting for Volatility Changes in the Crude Oil Market," *Journal of Applied Econometrics*, 28(7), November/December 2013:1087–1109.

Benjamin, Daniel K., William R. Dougan, and David Buschena, "Individuals' Estimates of the Risks of Death: Part II—New Evidence," *Journal of Risk and Uncertainty*, 22(1), January 2001:35–57.

Benkard, C. Lanier, "A Dynamic Analysis of the Market for Wide-Bodied Commercial Aircraft," *Review of Economic Studies*, 71(3), July 2004:581–611.

Bobashev, Georgiy, Maureen L. Cropper, Joshua M. Epstein, D. Michael Goedecke, Stephen Hutton, and Mead Over, "Policy Response to Pandemic Influenza: The Value of Collective Action," NBER Working Paper 17195, July 2011.

Boomhower, Judson, "Drilling Like There's No Tomorrow: Bankruptcy, Insurance, and Environmental Risk," *American Economic Review*, forthcoming.

Borenstein, Severin, "The Private Net Benefits of Residential Solar PV: And Who Gets Them," Energy Institute at Haas Working Paper, May 2015.

Borenstein, Severin, and Nancy L. Rose, "Competition and Price Dispersion in the U.S. Airline Industry," *Journal of Political Economy*, 102(4), August 1994:653–683.

Borjas, George J., "The Labor Demand Curve Is Downward Sloping: Reexamining the Impact of Immigration on the Labor Market," *Quarterly Journal of Economics*, 118(4), November 2003:1335–1374.

Bosch-Domènech, Antoni, José G. Montalvo, Rosemarie Nagel, and Albert Satorra, "One, Two, (Three), Infinity, . . . : Newspaper and Lab Beauty-Contest Experiments," *American Economic Review*, 92(5), December 2002:1687–1701.

Brander, James A., and Barbara J. Spencer, "Export Subsidies and International Market Share Rivalry," *Journal of International Economics*, 18(2), 1985:83–100.

Brander, James A., and Barbara J. Spencer, "Intra-Industry Trade with Bertrand and Cournot Oligopoly: The Role of Endogenous Horizontal Product Differentiation," *Research in Economics*, 69(2), June 2015:157–165.

Brander, James A., and M. Scott Taylor, "The Simple Economics of Easter Island: A Ricardo-Malthus Model of Renewable Resource Use," *American Economic Review*, 88(1), March 1998:119–138.

Brander, James A., and Anming Zhang, "Market Conduct in the Airline Industry: An Empirical Investigation," *RAND Journal of Economics*, 21(4), Winter 1990:567–583.

Bray, Jeremy W., and Albert N. Link, "Dynamic Entrepreneurship: On the Performance of US Research Joint Ventures," *Small Business Economics* 49(4), 2017:785–797.

Brown, Alexander L., Colin F. Camerer, and Dan Lovallo, "To Review or Not to Review? Limited Strategic Thinking at the Movie Box Office," *American Economic Journal: Microeconomics* 4(2), May 2012:1–26.

Brown, Clair, Timothy Sturgeon, and Connor Cole, "The 2010 National Organizations Survey: Examining the Relationships Between Job Quality and the Domestic and International Sourcing of Business Functions by United States Organizations," IRLE Working Paper, 2013.

Brown, Jennifer, and John Morgan, "Reputation in Online Auctions: The Market for Trust," *California Management Review*, 49(1), Fall 2006:61–81.

Brown, Jennifer, and John Morgan, "How Much Is a Dollar Worth? Tipping versus Equilibrium Coexistence on Competing Online Auction Sites," *Journal of Political Economy*, 117(4), August 2009:668–700.

Brunk, Gregory G., "A Test of the Friedman-Savage Gambling Model," *Quarterly Journal of Economics*, 96(2), May 1981:341–348.

Brynjolfsson, Erik, Felix Eggers, and Avinash Gannamaneni, "Using Massive Online Choice Experiments to Measure Changes in Well-being," NBER Working Paper 24514, 2018.

Buschena, David E., and Jeffrey M. Perloff, "The Creation of Dominant Firm Market Power in the Coconut Oil Export Market," *American Journal of Agricultural Economics*, 73(4), November 1991:1000–1008.

Caliendo, Marco, Michel Clement, Dominik Papies, and Sabine Scheel-Kopeinig, "The Cost Impact of Spam Filters: Measuring the Effect of Information System Technologies in Organizations," *Information Systems Research*, 23, September 2012:1068–1080.

Camerer, Colin F., *Behavioral Game Theory: Experiments in Strategic Interaction*. New York: Russell Sage Foundation, 2003.

Camerer, Colin F., George Lowenstein, and Matthew Rabin, eds., *Advances in Behavioral Economics*. New York: Russell Sage Foundation, 2004.

Capehart, Kevin, and Elena C. Berg, "Fine Water: A Blind Taste Test," *Journal of Wine Economics*, 13(1), 2018:20–40.

Card, David, and Alan B. Krueger, *Myth and Measurement: The New Economics of the Minimum Wage*. Princeton, NJ: Princeton University Press, 1995.

Carey, Kathleen, James F. Burgess Jr., and Gary J. Young, "Economies of Scale and Scope: The Case of Specialty Hospitals," *Contemporary Economic Policy*, 33(1), January 2015:104–117.

Carlton, Dennis, Mark Israel, Ian MacSwain, and Eugene Orlov, "Are Legacy Airline Mergers Pro- or Anti-competitive? Evidence from Recent U.S. Airline Mergers," *International Journal of Industrial Organization*, 2018 forthcoming.

Carlton, Dennis W., and Jeffrey M. Perloff, *Modern Industrial Organization*, 4th ed. Boston: Addison-Wesley, 2005.

Chandra, Ambarish, and Matthew Weinberg, "How Does Advertising Depend on Competition? Evidence from U.S. Brewing," University of Toronto manuscript, 2015.

Chakravorti, Sujit, and Roberto Roson, "Platform Competition in Two-Sided Markets: The Case of Payment Networks," *Review of Network Economics* 5(1), 2006:118–142.

Chandrasekaran, Deepa, Raji Srinivasan, and Debika Sihi, "Effects of Offline Ad Content on Online Brand Search: Insights from Super Bowl Advertising," *Journal of the Academy of Marketing Science* 46(3), 2018:403–430.

Chaudry, Ajay, Christopher Wimer, Suzanne Macartney, Lauren Frohlich, Colin Campbell, Kendall Swenson, Don Oellerich, and Susan Hauan, "Poverty in the United States: 50-Year Trends and Safety Net Impacts," U.S. Department of Health and Human Services, March 2016. Available at https://aspe.hhs.gov/system/files/pdf/154286/50YearTrends.pdf

Chetty, Raj, Adam Looney, and Kory Kroft, "Salience and Taxation: Theory and Evidence," NBER Working Paper 13330, 2007.

Cho, Daegon, Pedro Ferreira, and Rahul Telang, "The Impact of Mobile Number Portability on Price and Consumer Welfare," Carnegie Mellon University Working Paper, 2016.

Chouinard, Hayley H., and Jeffrey M. Perloff, "Gasoline Price Differences: Taxes, Pollution Regulations, Mergers, Market Power, and Market Conditions." *BE Journal of Economic Analysis & Policy* 7(1:8), 2007.

Chouinard, Hayley H., David Davis, Jeffrey T. LaFrance, and Jeffrey M. Perloff, "Fat Taxes: Big Money for Small Change," *Forum for Health Economics & Policy*, 10(2), 2007.

Coase, Ronald H., "The Nature of the Firm," *Economica*, 4(16), November 1937:386–405.

Coase, Ronald H., "The Problem of Social Cost," *Journal of Law and Economics*, 3, October 1960:1–44.

Cohen, Jeffrey P., and Catherine Morrison Paul, "Scale and Scope Economies for Drug Abuse Treatment Costs: Evidence for Washington State," *Applied Economics*, 43(30), 2011:4827–4834.

Cohen, Jerry, and Allan S. Gutterman, *Trade Secret Protection and Exploitation 2000 Supplement Edition*, BNA Books, 2000.

Collard-Wexler, Allan, "Mergers and Sunk Costs: An Application to the Ready-Mix Concrete Industry," *American Economic Journal: Microeconomics*, 6(4), November 2014:407–447.

Collins, Benjamin, *Trade Adjustment Assistance for Workers and the TAA Reauthorization Act of 2015* (CRS Report R44153). Washington, DC: Congressional Research Service, 2016.

Conyon, Martin J., Nuno Fernandes, Miguel Ferreira, Pedro Matos, and Kevin Murphy, "The Executive Compensation Controversy: A Transatlantic Analysis," Institute for Compensation Studies, Cornell University ILR School, 2011.

Christensen, Clayton M., *The Innovator's Dilemma: When New Technologies Cause Great Firms to Fail*, Harvard Business School Press, 1997.

Cruz, Marcio, James Foster, Bryce Quillin, and Philip Schellekens, "Ending Extreme Poverty and Sharing Prosperity: Progress and Policies," World Bank Group Policy Research Note, October 2015. available at http://pubdocs.worldbank.org/en/109701443800596288/PRN03Oct2015TwinGoals.pdf

Danzon, Patricia, and Nuno Pereira, "Vaccine Supply: Effects of Regulation and Competition," NBER Working Paper 17205, July 2011.

David, Guy, and Sara Markowitz, "Side Effects of Competition: The Role of Advertising and Promotion in Pharmaceutical Markets," NBER Working Paper, 2011.

Davis, Lucas W., and Alex Chun, "A Deeper Look into the Fragmented Residential Solar Market," energyathaas.wordpress.com/2015/06/08/a-deeper-look-into-the-fragmented-residential-solar-market, June 8, 2015.

Davis, Lucas W., and Erich Muehlegger, "Do Americans Consume Too Little Natural Gas? An Empirical Test of Marginal Cost Pricing," *RAND Journal of Economics*, 41(4), Winter 2010:791–810.

de Bettignies, Jean-Etienne, and David T. Robinson, "When Is Social Responsibility Socially Desirable?" *Journal of Labor Economics*, 36(4), October 2018:1023–1072.

De Loechker, Jan, and Jan Eeckhout, "Global Market Power," NBER Working Paper, 2018.

de Mello, Joao, Daniel Mejia, and Lucia Suarez, "The Pharmacological Channel Revisited: Alcohol Sales Restrictions and Crime in Bogotá," March 6, 2013, Documento CEDE No. 2013-20. ssrn.com/abstract=2262335.

de Melo, Jaime, and David Tarr, *A General Equilibrium Analysis of U.S. Foreign Trade Policy*. Cambridge, MA: MIT Press, 1992.

De Pelsmacker, Patrick, Liesbeth Driesen, and Glenn Rayp, "Do Consumers Care About Ethics? Willingness to Pay for Fair-Trade Coffee," *Journal of Consumer Affairs*, 39(2), 2005:363–385.

Deacon, Robert T., and Jon Sonstelie, "The Welfare Costs of Rationing by Waiting," *Economic Inquiry*, 27(2), April 1989:179–196.

DellaVigna, Stefano, "Psychology and Economics: Evidence from the Field," *Journal of Economic Literature*, 47(2), June 2009:315–372.

Denstadli, Jon Martin, Rune Lines, and Kjell Grønhaug, "First Mover Advantages in the Discount Grocery Industry," *European Journal of Marketing*, 39(7–8), 2005:872–884.

Detre, Joshua, and Michael A. Gunderson, "The Triple Bottom Line: What Is the Impact on Returns to Agribusiness?" *International Food and Agribusiness Management Review*, 14(4), 2011:165–178.

Devine, Hilary, Tinh Doan, and Philip Stevens, "Explaining Productivity Distribution in New Zealand Industries: The Effects of Input Quality on Firm Productivity Differences," New Zealand Ministry of Economic Development, 2012.

Draganska, Michaela, Daniel Klapper, and Sofia B. Villas-Boas, "A Larger Slice or a Larger Pie? An Empirical Investigation of Bargaining Power in the Distribution Channel," *Marketing Science*, 29(1), January-February 2010:57–74.

Duan, Ying, Edith S. Hotchkiss, and Yawen Jiao, "Corporate Pensions and Financial Distress," SSRN Working Paper, January 2015.

Duffy-Deno, Kevin T., "Business Demand for Broadband Access Capacity," *Journal of Regulatory Economics*, 24(3), 2003:359–372.

Dunne, Timothy, Shawn D. Klimek, Mark J. Roberts, and Daniel Yi Xu, "Entry, Exit, and the Determinants of Market Structure," *Rand Journal of Economics*, 44(3), Fall 2013:462–487.

Eastlack, Joseph, and Ambar G. Rao, "Advertising Experiments at the Campbell Soup Company," *Marketing Science*, 8(1), Winter 1989:57–71.

Eckel, Catherine C., and Philip J. Grossman, "Altruism in Anonymous Dictator Games, *Games and Economic Behavior*, 16, 1996:181–191.

Economides, Nicholas, "The Economics of Networks," *International Journal of Industrial Organization*, 14(6), October 1996:673–699.

Edelman, Benjamin, "Adverse Selection in Online 'Trust' Certifications and Search Results," *Electronic Commerce Research and Applications*, 10(1), January-February, 2011:17–25.

Edlin, Aaron S., and Pinar Karaca-Mandic, "The Accident Externality from Driving," *Journal of Political Economy*, 114(5), October 2006:931–955.

Ellsberg, Daniel, "Risk, Ambiguity, and the Savage Axioms," *Quarterly Journal of Economics*, 75(4), November 1961:643–669.

Elshurafa, Amro M., Shahad R. Albardi, Simona Bigerna, and Carlo Andrea Bollino, "Estimating the Learning Curve of Solar PV Balance–of–System for over 20 Countries: Implications and Policy Recommendations," *Journal of Cleaner Production*, 196, September 2018:122–134.

Environmental Protection Agency, "The Benefits and Costs of the Clean Air Act from 1990 to 2020," www2.epa.gov/clean-air-act-overview/benefits-and-costs-clean-air-act-1990-2020-second-prospective-study.

Epple, Dennis, Brett Gordon, and Holger Sieg, "A New Approach to Estimating the Production Function for Housing," *American Economic Review*, 100(3), June 2010:905–924.

Epple, Dennis, Richard Romano, Sinan Sarpça, Holger Sieg, and Melanie Zaber, "Market Power and Price Discrimination in the US Market for Higher Education", NBER Working Paper, 2017.

Exxon Company, U.S.A., *Competition in the Petroleum Industry*. Submission to the U.S. Senate Judiciary Subcommittee on Antitrust and Monopoly, January 21, 1975.

Farrell, Diana, "U.S. Offshoring: Small Steps to Make It Win-Win," *Economists' Voice*, 3(3), March 2006:1–5.

Feenstra, Robert, *Product Variety and the Gains from International Trade*. Cambridge, MA: MIT Press, 2010.

Feenstra, Robert C., Robert Inklaar, and Marcel P. Timmer (2015), "The Next Generation of the Penn World Table," *American Economic Review*, 105(10), October 2015:3150–3182, available for download at www.ggdc.net/pwt.

Feng, Cong, Scott Fay, K. Sivakumar, "Overbidding in Electronic Auctions: Factors Influencing the Propensity to Overbid and the Magnitude of Overbidding," *Journal of the Academy of Marketing Science*, June 2015.

Fisher, Franklin M., "The Social Cost of Monopoly and Regulation: Posner Reconsidered," *Journal of Political Economy*, 93(2), April 1985:410–416.

Flath, David, "Industrial Concentration, Price-Cost Margins, and Innovation," *Japan and the World Economy*, 23(2), March 2011:129–139.

Foulon, Jerome, Paul Lanoie, and Benoit Laplante, "Incentives for Pollution Control: Regulation or Information?" *Journal of Environmental Economics and Management*, 44(1), July 2002:169–187.

Fowlie, Meredith, Catherine Wolfram, C. Anna Spurlock, Annika Todd, Patrick Baylis, and Peter Cappers, "Default Effects and Follow-On Behavior: Evidence from An Electricity Pricing Program," Energy Institute at Haas, 2017.

Freeman, Michael, Nicos Savva, and Stefan Scholtes, "Economies of Scale and Scope in Hospitals" Working Paper, Judge Business School, Cambridge University, 2018.

Freeman, R. Edward, *Strategic Management: A Stakeholder Approach*. Boston: Pitman, 1984.

Friedman, Milton, and Leonard J. Savage, "The Utility Analysis of Choices Involving Risk," *Journal of Political Economy*, 56(4), August 1948:279–304.

Frydman, Carola, and R. E. Saks, "Executive Compensation: A New View from a Long-Term Perspective, 1936–2005," *Review of Financial Studies*, 23(5), 2010:2099–2138.

Fryer, Roland G., Jr., Steven D. Levitt, John A. List, and Sally Sadoff, "Enhancing the Efficacy of Teacher Incentives Through Loss Aversion: A Field Experiment," NBER Working Paper, 2012.

Furnham, Adrian, "Understanding the Meaning of Tax: Young Peoples' Knowledge of the Principles of Taxation," *Journal of Socio-Economics*, 34(5), October 2005:703–713.

Gallagher, Kevin, *Free Trade and the Environment: Mexico, NAFTA, and Beyond*. Stanford, CA: Stanford University Press, 2004.

Garratt, Rod, Mark Walker, and John Wooders, "Behavior in Second-Price Auctions by Highly Experienced eBay Buyers and Sellers," *Experimental Economics*, 15(1), March 2012:44–57.

Garrett, Thomas A., "An International Comparison and Analysis of Lotteries and the Distribution of Lottery Expenditures," *International Review of Applied Economics*, 15(20), April 2001:213–227.

Gasmi, Farid, D. Mark Kennet, Jean-Jacques Laffont, and William W. Sharkey, *Cost Proxy Models and Telecommunications Policy.* Cambridge, MA: MIT Press, 2002.

Gasmi, Farid, Jean-Jacques Laffont, and Quang H. Vuong, "Econometric Analysis of Collusive Behavior in a Soft-Drink Market," *Journal of Economics and Management Strategy*, 1(2), Summer 1992:277–311.

Gere, Judith, and Ulrich Schimmack. "Benefits of Income: Associations with Life Satisfaction Among Earners and Homemakers," *Personality and Individual Differences* 119(1), December 2017:92–95.

Ghose, Anindya, and Sang Pil Han, "Estimating Demand for Mobile Applications in the New Economy," *Management Science*, 60(6), June 2014:1470–1488.

Gittleman, Maury, Mark A. Klee, and Morris M. Kleiner, "Analyzing the Labor Market Outcomes of Occupational Licensing," *Industrial Relations*, 57(1), January 2018:57–100.

Goldfarb, Avi, "What Is Different About Online Advertising?" *Review of Industrial Organization*, 44(2), March 2014:115–129.

Goldfarb, Avi, and Catherine Tucker, "Search Engine Advertising: Channel Substitution When Pricing Ads to Context," *Management Science*, 57(3), March 2011:458–470.

Goldfarb, Avi, and Mo Xiao, "Who Thinks About Competition? Managerial Ability and Strategic Entry in U.S. Telephone Markets," *American Economic Review*, 10(1), December 2011:3130–3161.

Golec, Joseph, and Maurry Tamarkin, "Do Bettors Prefer Long Shots Because They Are Risk Lovers, or Are They Just Overconfident?" *Journal of Risk and Uncertainty*, 11(1), July 1995:51–64.

Gonçalves, Ricardo, and Pedro Pita Barros, "Economies of Scale and Scope in the Provision of Diagnostic Techniques and Therapeutic Services in Portuguese Hospitals," *Applied Economics*, 45(4), February 2013:415–433.

González, Tanja, Markus Schmid, and David Yermack, "Smokescreen: How Managers Behave When They Have Something to Hide," NBER Working Paper 18886, March 2013.

Gray, Wayne B., and Jay P. Shimshack, "The Effectiveness of Environmental Monitoring and Enforcement: A Review of the Empirical Evidence," *Review of Environmental Economics and Policy*, 5(1), Winter 2011:1–23.

Hall, Bronwyn H., Christian Helmers, Mark Rogers, and Vania Sena, "The Choice Between Formal and Informal Intellectual Property: A Review," *Journal of Economic Literature*, 52(2), 2014:375–423.

Hall, Robert E., "New Evidence on the Markup of Prices over Marginal Costs and the Role of Mega-Firms in the US Economy," NBER Working Paper, 2018.

Hartmann, Wesley R., and Daniel Klapper, "Super Bowl Ads," *Marketing Science* 37(1), 2017:78–96.

Haskel, Jonathan, and Raffaella Sadun, "Regulation and UK Retailing Productivity: Evidence from Micro Data," *Economica*, 79, July 2012:425–448.

Hasker, Kevin, Bibo Jiang, and Robin C. Sickles, "Estimating Consumer Surplus in eBay Computer Monitor Auctions," in Robin C. Sickles and William C. Horrace, eds., *Festschrift in Honor of Peter Schmidt*. New York: Springer, 2014, pp. 83–102.

Helliwell, John, Richard Layard, and Jeffrey D. Sachs, eds., *World Happiness Report*. New York: The Earth Institute, Columbia University, 2012. www.earth.columbia.edu/articles/view/2960.

Hendel, Igal, and Aviv Nevo, "Intertemporal Price Discrimination in Storable Goods Markets," *American Economic Review*, 103(7), December 2013:2722–2751.

Herod, Roger, "Analyzing the Metrics of Global Mobility Programs," *International HR Journal*, Summer 2008:9–15.

Hill, Jason, Stephen Polasky, Erik Nelson, David Tilman, Hong Huo, Lindsay Ludwig, James Neumann, Haochi Zheng, and Deigo Bonta, "Climate Change and Health Costs of Air Emissions from Biofuels and Gasoline," *Proceedings of the National Academy of Sciences*, 106(6), February 2009:2077–2082.

Ho, Jason, Tirtha Dhar, and Charles Weinberg, "Playoff Payoff: Super Bowl Advertising for Movies," *International Journal of Research in Marketing*, 26(3), September 2009:168–179.

Hossain, Tanjim, and John A. List, "The Behavioralist Visits the Factory: Increasing Productivity Using Simple Framing Manipulations," *Management Science* 58(12), December 2012:2151–2167.

Hsieh, Wen-Jen, "Test of Variable Output and Scale Elasticities for 20 U.S. Manufacturing Industries," *Applied Economics Letters*, 2(8), August 1995:284–287.

Imas, Alex, Sally Sadoff, and Anya Samek, "Do People Anticipate Loss Aversion," CESIFO Working Paper, 2015.

Irwin, Douglas A., "The Welfare Cost of Autarky: Evidence from the Jeffersonian Trade Embargo, 1807–09," *Review of International Economics*, 13(4), September 2005:631–645.

Irwin, Douglas A., and Nina Pavcnik, "Airbus Versus Boeing Revisited: International Competition in the Aircraft Market," *Journal of International Economics*, 64(2), December 2004:223–245.

Kahneman, Daniel, Jack L. Knetsch, and Richard H. Thaler, "Experimental Tests of the Endowment Effect and the Coase Theorem," *Journal of Political Economy*, 98(6), December 1990:1325–1348.

Kahneman, Daniel, and Amos Tversky, "Prospect Theory: An Analysis of Decisions under Risk," *Econometrica*, 47(2), March 1979:313–327.

Kamiya, Shinichi, Jun-Koo Kang, Jungmin Kim, Andreas Milidonis, and René M. Stulzet, "What Is the Impact of Successful Cyberattacks on Target Firms?" NBER Working Paper w204409, 2018.

Katchova, Ani L., and Mary Clare Ahearn, "Farm Entry and Exit from US Agriculture," *Agricultural Finance Review* 77(1), 2017:50–63.

Katz, Michael L., and Carl Shapiro, "Systems Competition and Network Effects," *Journal of Economic Perspectives*, 8(2), 1994:93–115.

Kellogg, Ryan, "Learning by Drilling: Inter-Firm Learning and Relationship Persistence in the Texas Oilpatch," *Quarterly Journal of Economics*, 126(4), 2011:1961–2004.

Keynes, John Maynard, *The General Theory of Employment, Interest and Money*. Basingstoke, Hampshire, United Kingdom: Palgrave Macmillan, 1936.

Kim, Jin-Woo, Traci H. Freling, and Douglas B. Grisaffe, "The Secret Sauce for Super Bowl Advertising: What Makes Marketing Work in the World's Most Watched Event?" *Journal of Advertising Research* 53(2), June 2013:134–149.

Klein, Benjamin, Robert G. Crawford, and Armen A. Alchian, "Vertical Integration, Appropriable Rents, and the Competitive Contracting Process," *Journal of Law and Economics*, 21(2), October 1978:297–326.

Klein, Lawrence R., "The Use of the Input-Output Tables to Estimate the Productivity of IT," *Journal of Policy Modeling*, 25(5), July 2003:471–475.

Kleiner, Morris M., "Reforming Occupational Licensing Policies," The Hamilton Project, Brookings Institution, Discussion Paper 2015-01, 2015.

Kleiner, Morris M., and Alan B. Krueger, "Analyzing the Extent and Influence of Occupational Licensing on the Labor Market," *Journal of Labor Economics*, April 2013, 31(2):S173–S202.

Kleiner, Morris M., and Kyoung Won Park, "Life, Limbs, and Licensing: Occupational Regulation, Wages, and Workplace Safety of Electricians, 1992–2007," *Monthly Labor Review*, 137, January 2014:1.

Kleiner, Morris M., and Evgeny Vorotnikov, "Analyzing Occupational Licensing Among the States," *Journal of Regulatory Economics*, 52(2), 2017:132–158.

Klemperer, Paul, *Auctions: Theory and Practice*. Princeton, NJ: Princeton University Press, 2004.

Knetsch, Jack L., "Preferences and Nonreversibility of Indifference Curves," *Journal of Economic Behavior and Organization*, 17(1), 1992:131–139.

Koumenta, Maria, and Mario Pagliero, "Occupational Licensing in the European Union: Coverage and Wage Effects," Centre for Economic Policy Research Working Paper, 2018.

Krauss, Melissa J., Patricia Cavazos-Rehg, Andrew Plunk, Laura Bierut, and Richard Grucza, "Effects of State Cigarette Excise Taxes and Smoke-Free Air Policies on State Per Capita Alcohol Consumption in the United States, 1980 to 2009," *Alcoholism: Clinical and Experimental Research*, 38(10), October 2014:2630–2638.

Kreps, David M., and Robert Wilson, "Reputation and Imperfect Information," *Journal of Economic Theory*, 27(2), August 1982:253–279.

Krueger, Alan B., "Where Have All the Workers Gone? An Inquiry into the Decline of the U.S. Labor Force Participation Rate," *Brookings Paper on Economic Activity*, Fall 2017:1–59.

Krueger, Alan B., and Orley Ashenfelter, "Theory and Evidence on Employer Collusion in the Franchise Sector," Princeton University Working Paper, 2017.

Krugman, Paul R., "Is Free Trade Passé?" *Journal of Economic Perspectives*, 1, 1987:131–144.

Langer, Ashley, Vikram Maheshri, and Clifford Winston, "From gallons to miles: A disaggregate analysis of automobile travel and externality taxes," *Journal of Public Economics* 152, 2017:34–46.

Lanz, Ranier, and Sébastien Miroudot, "Intra-Firm Trade: Patterns, Determinants and Policy Implications," *OECD Trade Policy Papers*, No. 114, OECD Publishing, 2011. dx.doi.org/10.1787/5kg9p391rwnn-en.

LaPlante, Benoit, and Paul Rilstone, "Environmental Inspections and Emissions of the Pulp and Paper Industry in Quebec," *Journal of Environmental Economics and Management*, 31(1), July 1996:19–36.

Lazear, Edward P., Kathryn L. Shaw, and Christopher T. Stanton, "Making Do with Less: Working Harder During Recessions," *Journal of Labor Economics*, 34(S1), January 2016:S333–S360.

Lazear, Edward P., Kathryn L. Shaw, and Christopher T. Stanton, "The Value of Bosses," *Journal of Labor Economics*, 33(4), October 2015:823–861.

Lee, Lian Fen, Michelle Lowry, and Susan Shu, "Are All Perks Solely Perks? Evidence from Corporate Jets," *Journal of Corporate Finance* 48, February 2018:460–473.

Lehecka, Georg V., Xiaoyang Wang, and Philip Garcia, "Gone in Ten Minutes: Intraday Evidence of Announcement Effects in the Electronic Corn Futures Market," *Applied Economic Perspectives and Policy*, 36(3), 2014:504–526.

Leibenstein, Harvey, "Bandwagon, Snob, and Veblen Effects in the Theory of Consumers' Demand," *Quarterly Journal of Economics*, 64(2), May 1950:183–207.

Leslie, Phillip J., "A Structural Econometric Analysis of Price Discrimination in Broadway Theatre," Working Paper, University of California, Los Angeles, November 15, 1997.

Levy, Douglas E., and Ellen Meara, "The Effect of the 1998 Master Settlement Agreement on Prenatal Smoking," NBER Working Paper 11176, March 2005.

Lichtenstein, Nelson, "How Walmart Fights Unions," *Minnesota Law Review*, 92(5), May 2008:1462–1501.

Liddle, Brantley, "The Systemic, Long-Run Relation among Gasoline Demand, Gasoline Price, Income, and Vehicle Ownership In OECD Countries: Evidence from Panel Cointegration and Causality Modeling," *Transportation Research Part D: Transport and Environment*, 17(4), June 2012:237–331.

Lipford, Jody W., and Bruce Yandle, "NAFTA, Environmental Kuznets Curves, and Mexico's Progress," *Global Economy Journal*, 10(4), January 2011.

List, John A., "Does Market Experience Eliminate Market Anomalies?" *Quarterly Journal of Economics*, 118(1), February 2003:41–71.

List, John A., and Fatemeh Momeni, "When Corporate Social Responsibility Backfires: Theory and Evidence from a Natural Field Experiment," NBER Working Paper 24169, 2017.

Lopez, Rigoberto A., and Emilio Pagoulatos, "Rent Seeking and the Welfare Cost of Trade Barriers," *Public Choice*, 79(1–2), April 1994:149–160.

Lu, Fangwen, "Insurance Coverage and Agency Problems in Doctor Prescriptions: Evidence from a Field Experiment in China," *Journal of Development Economics*, 106(1), January 2014:156–167.

Luchansky, Matthew S., and James Monks, "Supply and Demand Elasticities in the U.S. Ethanol Fuel Market," *Energy Economics*, 31(3), 2009:403–410.

MacCrimmon, Kenneth R., and M. Toda, "The Experimental Determination of Indifference Curves," *Review of Economic Studies*, 56(3), July 1969:433–451.

Machina, Mark, "Dynamic Consistency and Non-Expected Utility Models of Choice Under Uncertainty," *Journal of Economic Literature*, 27(4), December 1989:1622–1668.

MacKie-Mason, Jeffrey K., and Robert S. Pindyck, "Cartel Theory and Cartel Experience in International Minerals Markets," in R. L. Gordon, H. D. Jacoby, and M. B. Zimmerman, eds., *Energy: Markets and Regulation: Essays in Honor of M. A. Adelman*. Cambridge, MA: MIT Press, 1986.

Madrian, Brigitte C., and Dennis F. Shea, "The Power of Suggestion: Inertia in 401(k) Participation and Savings Behavior," *Quarterly Journal of Economics*, 116(4), November 2001:1149–1187.

Madrian, Brigitte C., and Dennis F. Shea, "The Power of Suggestion: Inertia in 401(k) Participation and Savings Behavior: Erratum," *Quarterly Journal of Economics*, 117(1), February 2002:377.

Mankiw, Gregory N., and Phillip Swagel, "The Politics and Economics of Offshore Outsourcing," *Journal of Monetary Economics*, 53(5), July 2006:1027–1056.

Manzi, Jim, *Uncontrolled: The Surprising Payoff of Trial-and-Error for Business, Politics, and Society*. New York: Basic Books, 2012.

Martinez, Steve W., "Vertical Coordination in the Pork and Broiler Industries: Implications for Pork and Chicken Products," Food and Rural Economics Division, Economic Research Service, U.S. Department of Agriculture, Agricultural Economic Report No. 777, 1999.

McPhail, Lihong Lu, and Bruce A. Babcock. "Impact of US biofuel policy on US corn and gasoline price variability." *Energy* 37(1), 2012:505–513.

Milgrom, Paul, and John Roberts, "Predation, Reputation, and Entry Deterrence," *Journal of Economic Theory*, 27(2), August 1982:280–312.

Monteverde, Kirk, and David J. Teece, "Appropriable Rents and Quasi-Vertical Integration," *Journal of Law and Economics*, 25(2), October 1982:403–418.

Nash, John F., "Equilibrium Points in *n*-Person Games," *Proceedings of the National Academy of Sciences*, 36, 1950:48–49.

Nash, John F., "Non-Cooperative Games," *Annals of Mathematics*, 54(2), July 1951:286–295.

Nash, John F., "Two-Person Cooperative Games," *Econometrica*, 21(1), April 1953:128–140.

Nenci, Silvia, "Tariff liberalisation and the growth of world trade: A comparative historical analysis of the multilateral trading system." *The World Economy* 34, no. 10 (2011):1809–1835.

Neto, João Quariguasi Frota, Jacqueline Bloemhof, and Charles Corbett, "Market Prices of Remanufactured, Used and New Items: Evidence from eBay," *International Journal of Production Economics*, 2015.

Neumark, David, and William L. Wascher, *Minimum Wages*. Cambridge, MA: MIT Press, 2008.

Nordhaus, William D., "Schumpeterian Profits and the Alchemist Fallacy," Yale Economic Applications and Policy Discussion Paper No. 6, April 2005.

Panzar, John C., and Robert D. Willig, "Economies of Scale in Multi-Output Production," *Quarterly Journal of Economics*, 91(3), August 1977:481–493.

Panzar, John C., and Robert D. Willig, "Economies of Scope," *American Economic Review*, 71(2), May 1981:268–272.

Parry, Ian W. H., Margaret Walls, and Winston Harrington, "Automobile Externalities and Policies," *Journal of Economic Literature*, 45(2), June 2007:373–399.

Perloff, Jeffrey M., and Ximing Wu, "Tax Incidence Varies Across the Price Distribution," *Economics Letters*, 96(1), July 2007:116–119.

Perry, Martin K., "Vertical Integration: Determinants and Effects," in Richard Schmalensee and Robert D. Willig, eds., *Handbook of Industrial Organization*. New York: North Holland, 1989.

Pielke, Roger A., Jr., Joel Gratz, Christopher W. Landsea, Douglas Collins, Mark A. Saunders, and Rade Musulin, "Normalized Hurricane Damages in the United States: 1900–2005." *Natural Hazards Review*, 9(1), February 2008:29–42.

Plott, Charles R., and Kathryn Zeiler, "The Willingness to Pay—Willingness to Accept Gap, the 'Endowment Effect,' Subject Misconceptions, and Experimental Procedures for Eliciting Values," *American Economic Review*, 95(3), June 2005: 530–545.

Porath, Daniel, "Size and Dynamics of Order-of-Entry Effects in Pharmaceutical Markets," *International Journal of Market Research*, 60(1), 2018:50–66.

Posner, Richard A., "The Social Cost of Monopoly and Regulation," *Journal of Political Economy*, 83(4), August 1975:807–827.

Rao, Justin M., and David H. Reiley, "The Economics of Spam," *Journal of Economic Perspectives*, 26(3), Fall 2012:87–110.

Regan, Tracy L., "Generic Entry, Price Competition, and Market Segmentation in the Prescription Drug Market," *International Journal of Industrial Organization*, 26(4), July 2008:930–948.

Reinstein, David A., and Christopher M. Snyder, "The Influence of Expert Reviews on Consumer Demand for Experience Goods: A Case Study of Movie Critics," *Journal of Industrial Economics*, 53(1), March 2005:27–51.

Richards, Timothy J., and Luis Padilla, "Promotion and Fast Food Demand," *American Journal of Agricultural Economics*, 91(1), February 2009:168–183.

Rifkin, Jeremy, *The Zero Marginal Cost Society: The Internet of Things, the Collaborative Commons, and the Eclipse of Capitalism*. New York: St Martin's Press, 2014.

Roberts, Mark J., and Larry Samuelson, "An Empirical Analysis of Dynamic Nonprice Competition in an Oligopolistic Industry," *RAND Journal of Economics*, 19(2), Summer 1988:200–220.

Roberts, Michael J., and Wolfram Schlenker, "Identifying Supply and Demand Elasticities of Agricultural Commodities: Implications for the US Ethanol Mandate," *American Economic Review*, 103(6), October 2013:2265–2295.

Robidoux, Benoît, and John Lester, "Econometric Estimates of Scale Economies in Canadian Manufacturing," Working Paper No. 88-4, Canadian Dept. of Finance, 1988.

Roelofs, Matthew R., Stein E. Østbye, and Eirik E. Heen, "Asymmetric Firms, Technology Sharing and R&D Investment," *Experimental Economics*, 20(3), 2017:574–600.

Rohlfs, Jeffrey H., "A Theory of Interdependent Demand for a Communications Service," *Bell Journal of Economics and Management Science*, 5(1), Spring 1974:16–37.

Rohlfs, Jeffrey H., *Bandwagon Effects in High-Technology Industries*. Cambridge, MA: MIT Press, 2001.

Rosenberg, Howard R., "Many Fewer Steps for Pickers—A Leap for Harvestkind? Emerging Change in Strawberry Harvest Technology," *Choices*, 1st Quarter 2004:5–11.

Rossi, R. J., and T. Armstrong, "Studies of Intercollegiate Athletics: Summary Results from the 1987–88 National Study of Intercollegiate Athletes" (Report No. 1), Palo Alto, CA: Center for the Study of Athletics, American Institutes for Research, 1989.

Rousseas, S. W., and A. G. Hart, "Experimental Verification of a Composite Indifference Map," *Journal of Political Economy*, 59(4), August 1951:288–318.

Salem, Samira, and Faina Rozental, "Labor Standards and Trade: A Review of Recent Empirical Evidence," *Journal of International Commerce and Economics*, 4(2), November 2012:63–98.

Salgado, Hugo, "A Dynamic Duopoly Model under Learning by Doing in the Computer CPU Industry," University of California, Berkeley, Ph.D. dissertation, 2008.

Salop, Steven C., "The Noisy Monopolist: Imperfect Information, Price Dispersion, and Price Discrimination," *Review of Economic Studies*, 44(3), October 1977:393–406.

Salop, Steven C., "Practices That (Credibly) Facilitate Oligopoly Coordination," in Joseph E. Stiglitz and G. Frank Mathewson, eds., *New Developments in the Analysis of Market Structure*. Cambridge, MA: MIT Press, 1986.

Sappington, David E. M., and Dennis L. Weisman, "Price Cap Regulation: What Have We Learned from 25 Years of Experience in the Telecommunications Industry?" *Journal of Regulatory Economics*, 38(3), 2010:227–257.

Scherer, F. M., "An Early Application of the Average Total Cost Concept," *Journal of Economic Literature*, 39(3), September 2001:897–901.

Schoemaker, Paul J. H., "The Expected Utility Model: Its Variants, Purposes, Evidence and Limitation," *Journal of Economic Literature*, 20(2), June 1982:529–563.

Schumpeter, Joseph A., *Capitalism, Socialism, and Democracy*. New York: Harper and Brothers, 1942.

Sexton, Stephen, "The Economics of Agricultural Biotechnology: Implications for Biofuel Sustainability," University of California, Berkeley, Working Paper, 2010.

Shadbegian, Ronald J., and Wayne B. Gray, "What Determines Environmental Performance at Paper Mills? The Roles of Abatement Spending, Regulation and Efficiency," *Topics in Economic Analysis and Policy*, 3(1), 2003.

Shapiro, Bradley T., "Positive Spillovers and Free Riding in Advertising of Prescription Pharmaceuticals: The Case of Antidepressants," *Journal of Political Economy*, 126(1), February, 2018:381–437.

Shapiro, Carl, and Joseph E. Stiglitz, "Equilibrium Unemployment as a Worker Discipline Device," *American Economic Review*, 74(3), June 1984:434–444.

Shapiro, Carl, and Hal R. Varian, *Information Rules: A Strategic Guide to the Network Economy*. Boston: Harvard Business School Press, 1999.

Sheehan-Connor, Damien, "Environmental Policy and Vehicle Safety: The Impact of Gasoline Taxes," *Economic Inquiry*, 53(3), July 2015:1606–1629.

Shiller, Ben, and Joel Waldfogel, "Music for a Song: An Empirical Look at Uniform Pricing and Its Alternatives," *The Journal of Industrial Economics*, 59(4), December 2011:630–660.

Shimshack, Jay, and Michael B. Ward, "Regulator Reputation, Enforcement, and Environmental Compliance," *Journal of Environmental Economics and Management*, 50(3), November 2005:519–540.

Slade, Margaret E., "Product Rivalry with Multiple Strategic Weapons: An Analysis of Price and Advertising Competition," *Journal of Economics and Management Strategy*," 4(3), Fall 1995:224–276.

Starr, Evan, J. J. Prescott, and Norma Bishara, "Noncompetes in the U.S. Labor Force," University of Michigan Law & Economics Research Paper, 2018.

Stephens-Davidowitz, Seth, Hal Varian, and Michael D. Smith, "Super returns to Super Bowl ads?" *Quantitative Marketing and Economics* 15(1), 2017:1–28.

Stevenson, Betsey, and Justin Wolfers, "Subjective Well-Being and Income: Is There Any Evidence of Satiation?" *American Economic Review: Papers and Proceedings*, 103(3), May 2013:598–604.

Stigler, George J., "The Division of Labor Is Limited by the Extent of the Market," *Journal of Political Economy*, 59(3), June 1951:185–193.

Stiglitz, Joseph E., "The Causes and Consequences of the Dependence of Quality on Price," *Journal of Economic Literature*, 25(1), March 1987:1–48.

Subramanian, Ravi, and Ramanath Subramanyam, "Key Factors in the Market for Remanufactured Products," *Manufacturing & Service Operations Management*, 14(2), Spring 2012: 315–326.

Suzuki, Junichi, "Land Use Regulation as a Barrier to Entry: Evidence from the Texas Lodging Industry," *International Economic Review*, 54(2), 2013:495–523.

Sweeting, Andrew, "Coordination, Differentiation and the Timing of Radio Commercials," *Journal of Economics and Management Strategy*, 15(4), Winter 2006:909–942.

Sweeting, Andrew, "The Strategic Timing of Radio Commercials: An Empirical Analysis Using Multiple Equilibria," *RAND Journal of Economics*, 40(4), Winter 2009, 710–742.

Thaler, Richard H., *The Winner's Curse: Paradoxes and Anomalies of Economic Life*. Princeton, NJ: Princeton University Press, 1994.

Tullock, G., "The Welfare Cost of Tariffs, Monopolies, and Theft," *Western Economic Journal*, 5(3), June 1967:224–232.

Tversky, Amos, and Daniel Kahneman, "The Framing of Decisions and the Psychology of Choice," *Science*, 211(4481), January 1981:453–458.

Urban, Glen L., Theresa Carter, and Steven Gaskin, "Market Share Rewards to Pioneering Brands: An Empirical Analysis and Strategic Implications," *Management Science*, 32(6), June 1986:645–659.

U.S. Census Bureau, *Statistical Abstract of the United States: 2012* (131st Edition), Washington, DC.

U.S. Environmental Protection Agency, *The Green Book Nonattainment Areas for Criteria Pollutants*, 2012. www.epa.gov/airquality/greenbook/

Usero, B., and Z. Fernández. "First Come, First Served: How Market and Non-Market Actions Influence Pioneer Market Share," *Journal of Business Research*, 62, 2009:1139–1145.

Varian, Hal R., "Measuring the Deadweight Cost of DUP and Rent-Seeking Activities," *Economics and Politics*, 1(1), Spring 1989:81–95.

Veracietro, Marcelo Luis, "Firing Costs and Business Cycle Fluctuations," *International Economic Review*, 49(1), 2008:1–39.

Visser, Michael S., and Matthew Roelofs, "Heterogeneous Preferences for Altruism: Gender and Personality, Social Status, Giving and Taking," *Experimental Economics*, 14, 2011:490–506.

von Neumann, John, and Oskar Morgenstern, *Theory of Games and Economic Behavior*. Princeton, NJ: Princeton University Press, 1944.

Waldfogel, Joel, "The Deadweight Loss of Christmas," *American Economic Review*, 83(5), December 1993:1328–1336.

Waldfogel, Joel, "Does Consumer Irrationality Trump Consumer Sovereignty?" *Review of Economics and Statistics*, 87(4), November 2005:691–696.

Waldfogel, Joel, *Scroogenomics*. Princeton, NJ: Princeton University Press, 2009.

Weiher, Jesse C., Robin C. Sickles, and Jeffrey M. Perloff, "Market Power in the U.S. Airline Industry," in D. J. Slottje, ed., *Economic Issues in Measuring Market Power, Contributions to Economic Analysis*, Volume 255, Elsevier 2002.

Weinstein, Arnold A., "Transitivity of Preferences: A Comparison Among Age Groups," *Journal of Political Economy*, 76(2), March/April 1968:307–311.

Williamson, Oliver E., *Markets and Hierarchies: Analysis and Antitrust Implications*. New York: Free Press, 1975.

Williamson, Oliver E., "Credible Commitments: Using Hostages to Support Exchange," *American Economic Review*, 73(4), September 1983:519–540.

World Bank, *Global Economic Prospects Special Focus 2: Arms-Length Trade*, Washington, D.C., June, 2017.

Wyatt, Edward, "Supreme Court Lets Regulators Sue over Generic Deals," *New York Times*, June 17, 2013.

Yellen, Janet L., "Efficiency Wage Models of Unemployment," *American Economic Review*, 74(2), May 1984:200–205.

Yermack, David, "Flights of Fancy: Corporate Jets, CEO Perquisites, and Inferior Shareholder Returns," *Journal of Financial Economics*, 80(1), April 2006:211–242.

Sources for Managerial Problems, Mini-Cases, and Managerial Implications

Chapter 1

Mini-Case *Using an Income Threshold Model in China*: "Next in Line: Chinese Consumers," *Economist*, 326 (7795), January 23, 1993:66–67. Jeff Pelline, "U.S. Businesses Pour into China," *San Francisco Chronicle*, May 17, 1994:B1–B2. *China Statistical Yearbook* (Beijing: China Statistical Publishing House, 2000). www.uschina.org/info/forecast/2007/foreign-investment .html. Jiang Wei, "FDI Doubles Despite Tax Concerns," *China Daily*, February 19, 2008. Keith Bradsher, "With First Car, a New Life in China," *New York Times*, April 24, 2008. www .worldometers.info/cars (viewed on May 6, 2012). "China January FDI Grows at Strongest Pace in Four Years," Reuters, February 15, 2015, CAAM. Production of Cars in China from 2008 to 2018 (in 1,000 units). www.statista.com/statistics/281133/car-production-in-china/ (accessed March 26, 2018). www.acea.be/statistics/article/top-10-car-producing-countries-worldwide-and-eu (viewed on September 8, 2018).

Chapter 2

Managerial Problem: Carbon Taxes Soren Amelang, "Renewables Cover About 100% of German Power Use for First Time Ever," Clean Energy Wire, January 5, 2018, www.cleanenergywire.org/news/renewables-cover-about-100-german-power-use-first-time-ever. Kaavya Chandrasekaran, "SECI Invites Bids for 2000MW Hybrid Projects," *Economic Times*, April 27, 2018, https://economictimes.indiatimes.com/industry/energy/power/seci-invites-bids-for-2000mw-hybrid-projects/articleshow/63943554.cms. Chouinard and Perloff (2007). Charles Herman, "Pain in the Gas: Refinery Troubles Push Gas Prices Higher," ABC News, May 15, 2007, www.abcnews.go.com/print?id=3176143. Tom Krisher, "Why Honda Is Growing as Detroit Falls Behind," *San Francisco Chronicle*, July 3, 2008. "Cedar Balls and Rum," *Economist*, June 7, 2011. Chris Isidore, "GM Set to Reclaim No. 1 Spot from Toyota," June 13, 2011, www.money .cnn.com. Mike Ramsey, "GM's 2011 Auto Sales Spark Feud Over Count," *Wall Street Journal*, January 20, 2012. Daniel Cusick, The Carbon Tax Center, www.carbontax.org (viewed on May 1, 2018). Leslie Hook, "Alphabet Becomes Biggest Corporate Renewable Energy Buyer in US," *Financial Times*, April 4, 2018, www.ft.com/content/3f259ae2-381a-11e8-8eee-e06bde01c544. Sammy Roth, "Warren Buffett Is Rushing to Build Hundreds of Wind Turbines to Power the West," *The Desert Sun*, April 5, 2017, www.desertsun.com/story/tech/science/energy/2017/04/05/warren-buffett-wind-turbines-wyoming-donald-trump-coal/304642001/. Joanna Slater, "Germany Recharged: EU Powerhouse Goes All in on Alternative Energy," *The Globe and Mail*, April 10, 2015, www .theglobeandmail.com.

Mini-Cases *Summing Corn Demand Curves*: Roberts and Schlenker (2013). McPhail and Babcock (2012). www.ncga .com/worldofcorn.

Speed of Adjustment to New Information: Lehecka, Wang, and Garcia (2014).

The Opioid Epidemic Reduces Labor Market Participation: www.drugabuse.gov/drugs-abuse/opioids. www.bls. gov/webapps/legacy/cpsatab1.htm. Krueger (2017). Sarah Chaney, "Why U.S. Prime-Age Workforce Participation Is Lagging Behind Other Nations," *Wall Street Journal*, June 6, 2018.

Occupational Licensing: Kleiner and Krueger (2013). Kleiner and Park (2014). Kleiner (2015). Kleiner and Vorotnikov (2017). Koumenta and Pagliero (2018). www.calbar. ca.gov/About-Us/News-Events/News-Releases/state-bar-of-california-releases-results-of-the-february-2018-bar-exam.

Venezuelan Price Ceilings and Shortages: William Neuman, "With Venezuelan Food Shortages, Some Blame Price Controls," *New York Times*, April 20, 2012 (source of the quote). William Neuman, "Protests Swell in Venezuela as Places to Rally Disappear," *New York Times*, February 20, 2014. Linette Lopez, "This Is a Food Line in Venezuela," *Business Insider*, February 28, 2014, www.businessinsider.com. Francisco Toro, "How Venezuela Turns Butter Vendors into Currency Manipulators," *New Republic*, March 4, 2014. S. B., "The Dividing

Line, *Economist*, March 10, 2014. Rafael Romo, "Fistfights Amid Long Bread Lines in Venezuela," May 2014, www.cnn.com, www.customstoday.com.pk/smugglers-turn-venezuelan-crisis-into-colombian-cash-out-2 (viewed on March 31, 2015). Rafael Romo, "$755 for a Box of Condoms? No Protection from Shortages in Venezuela," February 6, 2015, www.cnn.com. Joshua Keating, "Venezuela Is Running Out of Toilet Paper," February 25, 2015, www.slate.com. "Venezuelans are Starving Amid Economic Crisis, Food Shortages," *New York Post*, February 22, 2018. Emma Graham-Harrison and Mariana Zuniga, "Over Half of Young Venezuelans Want to Flee as Economy Collapses, Poll Finds," *The Guardian*, March 6, 2018.

Managerial Implication *Taking Advantage of Future Shocks*: http://sharedvalue.org/examples/sustainable-cocoa-initiative-creating-cocoa-clusters-and-increasing-production-west-africa. David Kaplan, "Mars Incorporated: A Pretty Sweet Place to Work," *Fortune*, January 17, 2013.

Chapter 3

Managerial Problem: Estimating the Effect of an iTunes Price Change "Changes Coming to the iTunes Store," Apple Press Info, January 6, 2009, www.apple.com. John Paczkowski, "25 Million iPads, 14 Billion Apps: WWDC 2011 by the Numbers," All Things D, June 7, 2011, http://allthingsd.com/20110607/25-million-ipads-1-billion-tweets-wwdc-2011-by-the-numbers/. www.apple.com/ca/itunes/.

Mini-Cases *Demand Elasticities for Google Play and Apple Apps*: Ghose and Han (2014). Sam Costello, "How Many Apps Are in the App Store?" *Lifewire*, April 7, 2018, www.lifewire.com/how-many-apps-in-app-store-2000252. AppBrain, www.appbrain.com/stats/number-of-android-apps.

Anti-Smoking Policies May Reduce Drunk Driving: Wang Hongyi, "Shanghai's New Smoking Ban Takes Effect," *China Daily*, March 2, 2017, www.chinadaily.com.cn/china/2017-03/02/content_28402208.htm. Krauss et al. (2014). Alan Mozes, "Anti-Smoking Policies May Also Curtail Drinking," Healthday, Tuesday, Sept. 23, 2014, www.consumer.healthday.com. Reuters Staff, "Austrian Lawmakers Vote to Hinder Smoking Ban in Restaurants and Bars," Reuters, March 22, 2018.

The Portland Fish Exchange: "Portland Fish Exchange," www.pfex.org/ .

Determinants of CEO Compensation: Standard & Poor's Execucomp (viewed on May 9, 2018) through http://whartonwrds.com/.

Managerial Implication *Experiments*: Jim Manzi, "What Social Science Does—and Doesn't—Know," *City Journal*, Summer 2010, Vol. 20, No. 3, www.city-journal.org. Lizzy Van Alstine and Jon Vaver, "Measuring Ad Effectiveness Using Geo Experiments," Google Research Blogspot, December 9, 2011, http://googleresearch.blogspot.ca. Jon Vaver and Jim Koehler, "Measuring Ad Effectiveness Using Geo Experiments," Google Inc., December 9, 2011, http://services.google.com/fh/files/blogs/geo_experiments_final_version.pdf. Manzi (2012). Barry Schwartz, "Just Testing: Google Users May See Up to a Dozen Experiments," Search Engine Land, December 2012, www.searchengineland.com.http://support.google.com/analytics/

answer/1745147?hl=en (viewed on September 1, 2015). Ben Clarke, "Why These Tech Companies Keep Running Thousands of Failed Experiments," *Fast Company*, September 21, 2016, www.fastcompany.com/3063846/why-these-tech-companies-keep-running-thousands-of-failed. Ron Kohavi and Stefan Thomke, "The Surprising Power of Online Experiments," *Harvard Business Review*, September-October 2017, pp. 74-82, https://hbr.org/2017/09/the-surprising-power-of-online-experiments.

Chapter 4

Managerial Problem: Paying Employees to Relocate Katherine Rosman, "Expat Life Gets Less Cushy," *Wall Street Journal*, October 26, 2007. Barbara Worthington, "FYI: Relocation," *Human Resource Executive Online*, February 1, 2008, www.hreonline.com. Grace W. Weinstein, "The Good and Bad of Moving Overseas," *Financial Times*, May 24, 2008, www.ft.com. www.mercer.com/newsroom/cost-of-living-survey.html (viewed on November 8, 2015). "The Most Expensive and Richest Cities in the World," *City Mayors Economics*, August 15, 2012, www.citymayors.com/economics/richest_cities.html (viewed on November 8, 2015). "Cost of Living Comparison between London (United Kingdom) and Seattle (United States)," *Expatistan*, 2012, www.expatistan.com/cost-of-living/comparison/seattle/london (viewed on April 22, 2015). KPMG Global Mobility Services, Global Assignment Policies and Practices Survey 2015, www.kpmg.com/Global/en/services/Tax/Global-Mobility-Services/Pages/default.aspx .

Mini-Cases *You Can't Have Too Much Money*: *Businessweek*, February 28, 2005, p. 13. Stevenson and Wolfers (2013). www.digitaljournal.com. Emily Alpert, "Happiness Tops in Denmark, Lowest in Togo, Study Says," *Los Angeles Times*, April 2, 2012. World Happiness Report 2018 http://worldhappiness.report/ed/2018/ . Helliwell, Layard, and Sachs (2013). Stevenson and Wolfers (2013). Gere and Schimmack (2017).

Rationing: Rawlings Otini, "Dams Full, but Water Rationing Goes On," *Business Daily*, May 17, 2010, www.businessdailyafrica.com. "Egypt PM Reassures About Water Quota," Kuwait News Agency, May 24, 2010, www.kuna.net.kw. "Water Rationing in Pindi from June 1," *Daily Times*, May 28, 2010. Joe Carroll, "Worst Drought in More Than a Century Strikes Texas Oil Boom," Bloomberg News, June 13, 2011, www.bloomberg.com. Marussia Whately and Rebeca Lerer, "Brazil Drought: Water Rationing Alone Won't Save Sao Paulo," *The Guardian*, February 11, 2015, www.theguardian.com. www.usatoday.com/picture-gallery/news/world/2018/01/19/cape-town-suffers-major-water-rationing/109619834/.

Why Americans Buy More E-Books Than Do Germans: http://authorearnings.com/report/dbw2017/. Michael Koslowski, "The State of the European eBook Market, *GoodEReader*, March 16, 2017, https://goodereader.com/blog/e-book-news/the-state-of-the-european-ebook-market. Aaron Wiener, "We Read Best on Paper, Cultural Resistance Hobbles German E-Book Market," *Der Spiegel*, April 13, 2012, www.spiegel.de. Caroline Winter, "The Story Behind Germany's Scant E-Book Sales,"

Bloomberg Businessweek, April 19, 2012, www.bloomberg .com. Rüdiger Wischenbart et al., *The Global ebook Market*, O'Reilly: 2014.

   How You Ask the Question Matters: Fowlie et al. (2017).

Chapter 5

Managerial Problem: Labor Productivity During Recessions Lazear, Shaw, and Stanton (2016).

Mini-Cases *Malthus and the Green Revolution*: Norman Borlaug, "Nobel Lecture," December 11, 1970, www .nobelprize.org. Gregg Easterbrook, "Forgotten Benefactor of Humanity," *Atlantic Monthly*, February 1997, www .theatlantic.com. Brander and Taylor (1998). Alan Barkema, "Ag Biotech," *The Main Street Economist*, October 2000, www .kansascityfed.org/Publicat/mse/MSE_1000.pdf. "Biotechnology and the Green Revolution: Interview with Norman Borlaug," November 2002, www.actionBioscience.org. United Nations, *Millennium Development Goals Report*, New York, 2008. www.ers.usda.gov/data-products/agricultural-productivity-in-the-us/. www.fao.org/NEWS/2000/000704-e.htm (viewed on May 17, 2012). Food and Agriculture Organization of the United Nations, *The State of Food Insecurity in the World*, 2017, www.fao.org/state-of-food-security-nutrition. Max Roser and Esteban Ortiz-Ospina (2018), "World Population Growth," published online at OurWorldInData. org, retrieved from: https://ourworldindata.org/world-population-growth [Online Resource].

   Self-Driving Trucks: David H. Freedman, "Self-Driving Trucks," *MIT Technology Review*, March/April 2017. Conor Dougherty, "Self-Driving Trucks May Be Closer Than They Appear," *New York Times*, November 13, 2017. Alex Davies, "Self-Driving Trucks Are Now Delivering Refrigerators," wired.com, November 13, 2017. Aarian Marshall, "What Does Tesla's Automated Truck Mean for Truckers?" wired.com, November 17, 2017. Madrigal, Alexis C., "Could Self-Driving Trucks Be Good for Truckers?" *The Atlantic*, February 1, 2018.

   Returns to Scale for Crocs: www.company.crocs.com .(annual reports from various years.)

   Robots and the Food You Eat: Ken Teh, "Robot Waiters in China Never Lose Patience," Associated Press, December 22, 2010, www.washingtontimes.com. Ilan Brat, "Robots Step Into New Planting, Harvesting Roles," *Wall Street Journal*, April 23, 2015. Aviva Rutkin, "Harvey, the Robot Farmer Fixing the US Labour Shortage," *New Scientist*, June 18, 2014. Jesse McKinley, "With Farm Robotics, the Cows Decide When It's Milking Time," *New York Times*, April 22, 2014. www.cnbc.com/2018/03/08/wave-of-agriculture-robotics-holds-potential-to-ease-farm-labor-crunch.html.

   A Good Boss Raises Productivity: Lazear, Shaw, and Stanton (2015).

Managerial Implication *Small Is Beautiful*: "Print Me a Stradivarius," economist.com, February 10, 2011. Lucas Mearian, "3D Printing Moves from Prototypes to Production," *Computerworld*, April 30, 2014. Lucas Mearian, "Is Apple Planning a 3D Printer?" *Computerworld*, May 21, 2015. Brian Deagon, "3D Printers Gaining Traction with Nike, Boeing, HP Inc.," *Investor's Business Daily*, March 24, 2016. http://phys

.org/news/2016-06-airbus-3d-printed-mini-aircraft.html. Lucas Mearian, "Boeing Turns to 3D-Printed Parts to Save Millions on Its 787 Dreamliner," *Computerworld*, April 11, 2017.

Chapter 6

Managerial Problem: Technology Choice at Home Versus Abroad *Semiconductor Industry Association*, www.sia-online .org (viewed on February 10, 2013). www.semiconductors. org/industry_statistics/historical_billing_reports/ (viewed on June 20, 2018).

Mini-Cases *The Opportunity Cost of an MBA*: Profile of GMAT Candidates, Five Year Summary, GMAT, www.gmac .com, various years (most recently, June 27, 2018). John Byrne, "Where MBA Apps Are Way Up—And Down," *Poets & Quants*, September 18, 2017, https://poetsandquants.com/.

   Costs of Building a Guitar: Chris McMahon, "Guitaronomics: How Much Does It Actually Cost to Build a Guitar?" https:// reverb.com/news/guitaronomics-how-much-does-it-actually-cost-to-build-a-guitar, April 8, 2016. www.shopbottools.com/ mApplications/instruments.htm (viewed on April 16, 2018).

   Short Run vs. Long Run in the Sharing Economy: James R. Hagerty, "Startup Matches Heavy Equipment Owners and Renters," *Wall Street Journal*, May 28, 2015. www.gminsights .com/industry-analysis/construction-equipment-rental-market/ (viewed on June 16, 2018).

   The Internet and Outsourcing: Matt Richtel, "Outsourced All the Way," *New York Times*, June 21, 2005. *Economies of Scale at Google*: http://googleforwork.blogspot.ca/ "2010/04/google-apps-and-cloud-maximum-economies .html (viewed on November 8, 2015). Charles Babcock, "Microsoft: 'Incredible Economies of Scale' Await Cloud Users," *InformationWeek*, May 11, 2011, www.informationweek .com.

   Solar Power Learning Curves: Elshurafa et al. (2018).

   Medical Economies of Scope: Gonçalves and Barros (2013), Carey, Burgess, and Young (2015), Freeman, Savva, and Scholtes (2018).

Chapter 7

Managerial Problem: Amazon's Delivery Services Laura Stevens, "Amazon to Launch Delivery Service That Would Vie with FedEx, UPS," *Wall Street Journal*, February 9, 2018. Courtney Reagan, "Amazon Reveals a New Plan to Deliver More Packages," www.cnbc.com/2018/06/27/amazon-is-recruiting-entrepreneurs-to-start-delivery-networks.html. Laura Stevens, "Amazon Drives Deeper Into Package Delivery," *Wall Street Journal*, June 28, 2018. Dan Gallagher, "Why Amazon Needs to Do Everything," *Wall Street Journal*, June 30, 2018. https://money.cnn.com/2018/09/06/technology/ amazon-van-mercedes/index.html.

Mini-Cases *Chinese State-Owned Enterprises*: Gao Xu, "State-Owned Enterprises in China: How Big Are They?" January 19, 2010, http://blogs.worldbank.org/

eastasiapacific/state-owned-enterprises-in-china-how-big-are-they (viewed on November 8, 2015). National Bureau of Statistics of China, *China Statistical Yearbook*, 2014. www.export.gov/article?id=China-State-Owned-Enterprises, July 25, 2017. Carlos Tejada, "China's Online Giants Back $12 Billion Deal to Shake Up State Firm." *New York Times*, August 16, 2017. https://chinadashboard.asiasociety.org/winter-2018/page/state-owned-enterprise.

Trends in Social Responsibility: www.susanjfowler.com/blog/2017/2/19/reflecting-on-one-very-strange-year-at-uber.www.forbes.com/sites/susanmcpherson/2018/01/12/8-corporate-social-responsibility-csr-trends-to-look-for-in-2018/#45c521e540ce.www.vox.com/2015/7/23/9025975/toms-shoes-poverty-giving.

NetFlix: Where Netflix Sees Potential—and Risks, *Wall Street Journal*, October 30, 2016. Annabelle Gauberti, "Netflix Vertical Integration Strategy: I Was Right on the Money," Crefovi, April 1, 2018, http://crefovi.com/articles/entertainment-media/netflix-vertical-integration-strategy-i-was-right-on-the-money-crefovi/.

The Gig Economy: www.cnbc.com/2018/02/12/gig-economy-workers-lose-certain-employee-perks.html. Ben Casselman, "Maybe the Gig Economy Isn't Reshaping Work After All," *New York Times*, June 7, 2018.

Chapter 8

Managerial Problem: The Rising Cost of Keeping on Truckin' Nicholas Katers, "About Interstate Trucking Authority," eHow, www.ehow.com/about_4739672_interstate-trucking-authority.html (viewed on June 16, 2012). "Rules & Regulations," U.S. Department of Transportation, www.fmcsa.dot.gov/rules-regulations/rules-regulations.htm (viewed on June 16, 2012). "Unified Carrier Registration," www.dotauthority.com/ucr.htm?gclid=CKma5tebnqQCFSFZiAodN2bunA (viewed on June 16, 2012). James L. Gattuso, "Truckers Don't Need Mandated Recorders," *Freemont Tribune*, May 29, 2012, www.fremonttribune.com. James Jaillet, "Logging Device Mandate Could Come in 2016, Outlines Hardware Spec's, Harassment Provisions," *Overdrive* March 13, 2014, www.overdriveonline.com/eld-mandate-specifics-on-harassment-and-devices-industry-groups-split-on-rules-support/. William Cassidy, "US Regulators Add Some Flexibility to Trucker ELD Work Rules," *Journal of Commerce*, May 31, 2018, www.joc.com. www.fmcsa.dot.gov/regulations/title49/b/5/3 (viewed on June 30, 2018).

Mini-Cases *Fracking and Shutdowns*: Agis Salpukas, "Low Prices Have Sapped Little Oil Producers," *New York Times*, April 3, 1999: B1, B4. Robert Collier, "Oil's Dirty Future," *San Francisco Chronicle*, May 22, 2005: A1, A14, A15. Jon Birger, "Oil Shale May Finally Have Its Moment," *Fortune*, November 1, 2007, www.fortune.com. Judith Kohler, "Energy Firms Cautious on Oil Shale," *OCRegister*, November 3, 2007, www.ocregister.com. Steve Austin, "Falling Oil Prices Slows US Fracking," December 8, 2014, www.oil-price.net. Shaw Tully, "The Shale Oil Revolution Is in Danger," January 9, 2015, www.fortune.com. Reuters, "All Drill, No Pump: Oil Producers Are Leaving Thousands of U.S. Wells Unfinished," *Fortune*, March 24, 2017, http://fortune.com/2017/03/24/drill-pump-unfinished-wells-oil/. www.macrotrends.net/2516/wti-crude-oil-prices-10-year-daily-chart. Bradley Olson, "Frackers Could Make More Money Than Ever in 2018, if They Don't Blow It," *Wall Street Journal*, January, 22, 2018.

The Size of Ethanol Processing Plants: "Statistics," Renewable Fuels Association, www.ethanolrfa.org/pages/statistics (viewed on June 6, 2015). www.neo.ne.gov/statshtml/122.htm (viewed on June 6, 2015). www.tradingeconomics.com/commodity/ethanol (viewed on June 6, 2015). www.eia.gov/petroleum/ethanolcapacity/ (viewed on June 20, 2016). www.tradingeconomics.com/commodity/ethanol (viewed on June 18, 2018). www.eia.gov/petroleum/ethanolcapacity/ (viewed June 18, 2018). "Statistics," Renewable Fuels Association, www.ethanolrfa.org/resources/industry/statistics/ (viewed on June 20, 2016).

Industries with High Entry and Exit Rates https://energyathaas.wordpress.com/2015/06/08/a-deeper-look-into-the-fragmented-residential-solar-market/. Katchova and Ahearn (2017). www.census.gov/ces/data-products/bds/data.html/ (viewed on July 1, 2018). www.choicesmagazine.org/choices-magazine/theme-articles/theme-overview-addressing-the-challenges-of-entry-into-farming/theme-overview-addressing-the-challenges-of-entry-into-farming. www.seia.org/state-solar-policy/california-solar (viewed on July 5, 2018).

An Upward-Sloping Long-Run Supply Curve for Cotton: International Cotton Advisory Committee, *Survey of the Cost of Production of Raw Cotton*, September 1992:5. *Cotton: World Statistics*, April 1993:4–5.

Digital Surplus: Nordhaus (2005). Brynjolfsson, Eggers, and Gannamaneni (2018). www.bea.gov/iTable/iTable.cfm?ReqID=51&step=1#reqid=51&step=51&isuri=1&5114=a&5102=5 (viewed on July 2, 2018). www.statista.com/statistics/408971/number-of-us-facebook-users/ (viewed on July 2, 2018).

The Deadweight Loss of Holiday Gifts: Waldfogel (1993, 2005, 2009). Bauer and Schmidt (2008). Eve Mitchell, "Cashing In," *Oakland Tribune*, June 12, 2011, C1. Barbara Farfan, "2011 U.S. Christmas Holiday Retail Data, Statistics, Results, Numbers Roundup Complete U.S. Retail Industry Christmas Holiday Shopping Year-Over-Year Results," *About Money*, December 29, 2011, http://retailindustry.about.com/od/statisticsresearch/a/2011-Us-Christmas-Holiday-Shopping-Sales-Data-Statistics-Results-And-Numbers.htm. Miguel Helft, "Meet the Anti-Groupon," CNN Money, April 30, 2012, www.money.cnn.com. http://tech.fortune.cnn.com/2012/04/30/wrapp/. Matt Brownell, "Gift Cards," *Forbes*, December 12, 2012, www.forbes.com. Jason Russell, "Christmas Gift Fraud Costs Billions," *Washington Examiner*, December 26, 2014, www.washingtonexaminer.com. www.cardhub.com/edu/gift-card-market-size (viewed on June 27, 2015).

Managerial Implication *Willingness to Pay on eBay*: Bapna, Jank, and Shmueli (2008). Hasker, Jiang, and Sickles (2014). www.eBay.com (2015).

Chapter 9

Managerial Problem: Brand-Name and Generic Drugs "Thailand Imports Generic Plavix from India," PMLiVE Intelligence Online, August 24, 2007, www.pmlive.com. Richard

G. Frank, "The Ongoing Regulation of Generic Drugs," *New England Journal of Medicine*, November 15, 2007, www.nejm.org. Regan (2008). Milt Freudenheim, "Benefit Managers Profit by Specialty Drug Rights," *New York Times*, April 19, 2008. "Canada Generics Set for Double Digit Growth," Email-Wire, August 26, 2009, www.emailwire.com/release/printPR.php?prID=26411. Ken MacQueen, "The Case for a National Drug Plan," *Maclean's*, June 8, 2011, www.macleans.ca. www.fiercepharma.com/special-reports/top-10-patent-expirations-2015 (viewed on December 17, 2014). Trefis Team, "Why Are Generic Drug Prices Shooting Up?" *Forbes*, February 27, 2015, www.forbes.com. "Pricey Hep C Successor Overtakes Solvadi," *Health News Florida*, July 13, 2015, http://health.wusf.usf.edu. www.huffingtonpost.com/entry/martin-shkreli-aids-drug-price-the-same_us_5aa3117fe4b07047bec694cb, March 9, 2018. www.cnbc.com/2018/05/07/mallinckrodt-shares-rebound-after-60-minutes-report-on-drug-prices.html. www.pharmacytimes.com/resource-centers/hepatitisc/will-hepatitis-c-virus-medicaton-costs-drop-in-the-years-ahead (viewed on July 9, 2018). www.infoholicresearch.com/market-updates/pharmaceutical-drugs-going-off-patent-in-2018/ (viewed on July 9, 2018). www.pti-nps.com/nps/wp-content/uploads/2017/04/NPS_Drugs-Coming-Off-Patent-by-2022-Web.pdf (viewed on July 9, 2018).

Mini-Cases *Apple's iPad*: Chloe Albanesius, "iSuppli: iPad Could Produce Profits for Apple," *PC Magazine*, February 10, 2010, www.pcmag.com. Arik Hesseldahl, "Apple iPad Components Cost at Least $259," *Businessweek*, April 7, 2010, www.businessweek.com. Don Reisinger, "IDC: Apple iPad Secures 87 Percent Market Share," CNET News, January 18, 2011, www.cnet.com. Don Reisinger, "Study: iPad Tallies 89 Percent of Table Traffic," CNET News, January 24, 2011, www.cnet.com. Jenna Wortham, "So Far Rivals Can't Beat iPad's Price," *New York Times*, March 6, 2011. "iPad Remains Dominant in 1Q 2012 While Kindle Fire Fizzles," ABI Research, www.abiresearch.com/press/ipad-remains-dominant-in-1q2012-while-kindle-fire. "Apple iPad Shipments Down 23% as Tablet Market Continues to Lose Steam," *Forbes*, April 30, 2015, www.forbes.com. In Q&A 9.2, the marginal cost estimate (slightly rounded) is from iSuppli. Seth Fiegerman, "Apple Vs. Samsung: Everything You Need to Know About the (Patent) Trial of the Century," *Business Insider*, June 30, 2012, www.businessinsider.com. www.statista.com/statistics/268711/global-market-share-of-the-apple-ipad-since-2010/ (viewed on July 11, 2018).

We assumed that the company's gross profit margin for 2010 of about 40% (http://forbes.com) held for the iPad and used that to calculate the fixed cost. We derived the linear demand curve by assuming Apple maximizes short-run profit using the information on price, marginal cost, and quantity. The marginal cost estimate is based on iSuppli.

Taylor Swift Concert Pricing: Randy Lewis, "Taylor Swift's '1989' is 2015's Highest Grossing Concert Tour by Far," *Los Angeles Times*, December 30, 2015. Anne Steele, "Why Empty Seats at Taylor Swift's Concerts Are Good for Business," *Wall Street Journal*, May 15, 2018.

The Canadian Medical Marijuana Market: Will Connors, "Investors Jump In After Canada Changes Marijuana Rules," *Wall Street Journal*, April 17, 2014. Geordon Omand, "Canada's Medical Marijuana Industry Competes for Scarce Investment Dollars," May 1, 2015, www.huffingtonpost.com.ca/. www.prairieplant.com/news.html (viewed on July 18, 2015). www.canada.ca/en/health-canada/services/drugs-medication/cannabis/licensed-producers/authorized-licensed-producers-medical-purposes.html (viewed on July 11, 2018).

Botox: Mike Weiss, "For S.F. Doctor, Drug Botox Becomes a Real Eye-Opener," *San Francisco Chronicle*, April 14, 2002. Reed Abelson, "F.D.A. Approves Allergan Drug for Fighting Wrinkles," *New York Times*, April 16. Harriet Tramer, "Docs Detecting How to Boost Botox Profitability," *Crain's Cleveland Business*, March 7, 2005, www.crainscleveland.com. Natasha Singer, "Botox Plus: New Mixes for Plumping and Padding," *New York Times*, July 14, 2005. Lisa Rapaport, "Allergan Profit Rises on Sales of Botox," Bloomberg News, August 1, 2007, www.bloomberg.com. www.forums.pharma-mkting.com/showthread.php?t=921. Natasha Singer, "So Botox Isn't Just Skin Deep," *New York Times*, April 12, 2009. "Nice News for Allergan—Analyst Blog," NASDAQ, June 29, 2012, www.nasdaq.com. "Botox Itself Aims Not to Age," *Wall Street Journal*, May 18, 2014. Ryan Sachetta and Cynthia Koons, "Worried About Wrinkles, Guys? Allergan Bets You'll Want 'Brotox,'" June 17, 2015, www.bloomberg.com. www.statista.com/statistics/737477/global-sales-of-allergan-s-botox/ (viewed on July 11, 2018).

Super Bowl Commercials: Ho, Dhar, and Weinberg et al. (2009). Kim, Freling, and Grisaffe (2013). Yinka Adegoke, "Super Bowl Advertisers Seek Buzz on Social Media," Reuters, January 29, 2012. Sharon Terlep and Suzanne Vranica, "GM to Forgo Pricey Super Bowl Ads," *Wall Street Journal*, May 18, 2012. Frank Pallotta, "Super Bowl XLIX Posts the Largest Audience in TV History," CNN Money, February 2, 2015, www.money.cnn.com. Steven Perlberg and Willa Plank, "Super Bowl Spending Since 2000: The Big Game Ad-Tracker," *Wall Street Journal*, January 28, 2015. http://blogs.wsj.com/cmo/2015/01/28/super-bowl-ad-spending-graphic/?mod=e2tw. Stephens-Davidowitz, Varian, and Smith (2017). Hartmann and Klapper (2017). Chandrasekaran, Srinivasan, and Sihi (2018). www.si.com/nfl/2018/01/11/super-bowl-lii-ad-cost (viewed on July 12, 2018).

Critical Mass and eBay: Ina Steiner, "Yahoo Closes Australian Auction Site," August 7, 2003, www.auctionbytes.com/cab/abn/y03/m08/i07/s03. Brown and Morgan (2006, 2009). John Barrett, "MySpace Is a Natural Monopoly," January 17, 2007, www.ecommercetimes.com/story/55185.html?welcome=1218648444&wlc=1251740474. Carol Xiaojuan Ou and Robert M. Davison, "Why eBay Lost to TaoBao in China: The Global Advantage," *Communications of the ACM*, 52(1), January 2009, www.cacm.acm.org.

Chapter 10

Managerial Problem: Sale Prices Perloff and Wu (2007). Karen Datko, "My Ketchup Taste Test: It's an Upset!" January 14, 2011, www.msn.com. Rebecca Smithers, "Heinz Left Playing Tomato Catch-Up after Ketchup Tasting Trouncing," *The Guardian*, May 25, 2011, www.theguardian.com. Andrew Adam Newman, "Ketchup Moves Upmarket, with a Balsamic Tinge," *New York Times*, October 25, 2011. Hendel and Nevo (2013). Whitney Filloon, "Heinz and French's Are Embroiled in a Ketchup and Mustard War," April 23, 2015, www.eater.com. www.heinz.com/our-company/

press-room/trivia.aspx (viewed on August 1, 2015). www
.mordorintelligence.com/industry-reports/ketchup-
market (viewed on November 5, 2018). /www.statista.com/
statistics/278061/us-households-most-used-brands-of-cat-
sup--ketchup/ (viewed on November 5, 2018).

Mini-Cases *Disneyland Pricing*: "Couple Tries for Year of
Daily Disneyland Visits," *San Francisco Chronicle*, July 3, 2012.
Joseph Pimentel, "Disney Announces Discounted Tickets
for SoCal Residents," January 23, 2015, www.ocregister.com
.Disneyland Resort, 2015, www.Disneyland.com (viewed on
August 2, 2015).

Preventing Resale of Designer Bags: Eric Wilson, "Retailers Limit Purchases of Designer Handbags," *New York Times*,
January 10, 2008. www.prada.com, www.gucci.com, www
.saksfifthavenue.com (viewed on August 2, 2015).

Botox Revisited: See Chapter 9, "Botox."

Google Uses Bidding for Ads to Price Discriminate: Goldfarb and Tucker (2011). Goldfarb (2014).

Age Discrimination: Luis Gomez, "Why a California
Judge Swiped Left on Tinder's 30-or-Older Fees," *San Diego
Union Tribune*, January 30, 2018.

Available for a Song: "iTunes Store Tops 10 Billion Songs
Sold," Apple Press Info, February 25, 2010, www.apple.com/pr/
library/2010/02/25itunes.html. Shiller and Waldfogel (2011).

Downhill Pricing: www.whistlerblackcomb.com/plan-
your-trip/lift-access/tickets.aspx (viewed on July 26, 2018).

Managerial Implication *Discounts*: Borenstein and Rose
(1994). Jenna Wortham, "Coupons You Don't Clip, Sent
to Your Cellphone," *New York Times*, August 29, 2009.
"Up Front," *Consumer Reports*, September 2009:7. Carmen
Musick, "Computer Technology Fueling Coupon Trend,"
Times News, October 31, 2009, http://e-edition.timesnews
.net/article/9018027/computer-technology-fueling-
coupon-trend. "Groupon and the Online Deal Revolution,"
eMarketer, June 7, 2011, www.emarketer.com/Article/Shop-
pers-Turn-Smartphones-Tablets-Cash-Coupons/1011582.
"Coupon Trends," *JPS*, March 2, 2012, www.santella.com/
Trends.htm. "NCH Annual Coupon Facts," NCH Marketing,
2012, www.nchmarketing.com/. www.forbes.com/sites/
bryanpearson/2017/03/15/research-reveals-how-retailers-
can-maximize-the-power-of-coupons/#74c3fe882f01. www
.statista.com/statistics/630086/total-number-of-coupons-
distributed-in-the-us/ (viewed on July 25, 2018). www
.statista.com/statistics/630123/total-number-of-coupons-
redeemed-in-the-us/ (viewed on July 25, 2018). *NCH
Mid-Year 2018 Coupon Facts*, www.nchmarketing.com/
couponindustrytrends.aspx (viewed on August 19, 2018).

Ties That Bind: www.hp.com (viewed on July 15, 2013). www
.consumerchoice.info/warranty.htm (viewed on August
19, 2018.). www.mlmlaw.com/library/guides/ftc/warranties/
undermag.htm (viewed on August 19, 2018).
https://store.hp.com/us/en/pdp/hp-deskjet-1112-printer

Chapter 11

**Managerial Problem: Gaining an Edge from Government
Aircraft Subsidies** Irwin and Pavcnik (2004). John Heilpin,
"WTO: Boeing Got $5B in Illegal Subsidies," March 12, 2012,
www.manufacturing.net/news/2012/03/wto-boeing-got-5b-in-

illegal-subsidies.www.opensecrets.org/lobby/clientlbs.php?
id=D000000100&year=2015 (viewed on November 8, 2015).
www.opensecrets.org/lobby/clientlbs.php?id=
D000000100&year=2015 (viewed on November 8, 2015). Paul
Ausick, "WTO to Examine Boeing 777X Subsidies," 24/7
Wall St., February 27, 2015, http://247wallst.com. Tim Hep-
her and James Regan, "Boeing Says Government Loans for
Airbus A380neo Would Go Against WTO Rulings," Reuters,
June 16, 2015. www.opensecrets.org/orgs/summary
.php?id=d000000100 (viewed on July 12, 2018). Robert Wall
and Emre Peker, "WTO Ruling Advances U.S. and Boeing in
Case Against Airbus," *Wall Street Journal*, July 13, 2018.

Mini-Cases *Employer "No-Poaching" Cartels*: Mark Ames,
"The Techtopus: How Silicon Valley's Most Celebrated CEOs
Conspired to Drive Down 100,000 Tech Engineers' Wages,"
January 23, 2014, www.pando.com. Mark Ames, "Revealed:
Apple and Google's Wage-Fixing Cartel Involved Dozens
More Companies, Over One Million Employees," March 22,
2014, www.pando.com. Michael Liedtke, "Apple, Google,
Other Tech Firms to Pay $415M in Wage Case," January 15,
2015, www.seattletimes.com. Ted Johnson, "Animation Work-
ers Reach $100 Million Settlement with Disney in Wage-
Fixing Suit," January 17, 2017, http://variety.com/2017/
biz/news/disney-settlement-wage-fixing-anti-poaching-
animation-1201975084/. Krueger and Ashenfelter (2017).
Jackie Wattles, "7 Fast Food Chains Agree to End 'No-poach'
Rules," money.cnn.com/2018/07/12/news/companies/no-
poach-fast-food-industry-wages-attorneys-general/index.
html, July12, 2018. Rachel Abrams, "7 Fast-Food Chains to End
'No Poach' Deals That Lock Down Low-Wage Workers," *New
York Times*, July 12, 2018. Starr, Prescott, and Bishara (2018).

Cheating on the Maple Syrup Cartel: Bertrand Marotte,
"Quebec Losing Hold Over Maple Syrup Industry to U.S.
Competition," *Globe and Mail*, April 6, 2015. Ian Austen,
"The Maple Syrup Mavericks," *New York Times*, August
23, 2015. www.siropderable.ca/home.aspx Jen Skerritt,
"Maple Syrup Cartel Battles a Black Market Rebellion,"
Bloomberg, August 9, 2016, www.bloomberg.com/news/
features/2016-08-10/maple-syrup-cartel-battles-a-black-
market-rebellion. Michael Moynihan, Syrup Wars, Vice
News, April 19, 2017, news.vice.com/en_us/article/ywnjkv/
inside-quebecs-maple-syrup-black-market. Marie-Ève Dumont,
"Trois Autos de la SQ Pour Saisir Leur Sirop d'Erable," *Le
Journal de Montréal* (in French), Retrieved February 2, 2018.
Giuseppe Valiante, "Quebec's Maple Syrup Industry Losing
Ground as U.S. Imports Rise: Report," *The Star*, March 8, 2018.
Jake Edminston and Graeme Hamilton, "The Last Days of
Quebec's Maple Syrup Rebellion," *National Post*, April 6, 2018.
ycharts.com/indicators/us_maple_syrup_price_received
(viewed on August 2, 2018).

Mobile Number Portability: Cho, Ferreira, and Telang
(2016). https://telqtele.com/countries-with-mnp-map/
(viewed on July 14, 2018).

Airline Mergers: Carlton et al. (2018).

Rising Market Power: Hall (2018). De Loecker and Eeckhout (2018).

Subsidizing the Entry Cost of Dentists: Dunne et al.
(2013).

Managerial Implications *Differentiating a Product
Through Marketing*: Julia Felsenthal, "Water, Water Everywhere: What's the Best-Tasting Kind of Water?" Slate, October

12, 2011 www.slate.com. Trefis Team, "Bottled Water Is a Potential Growth Category That Can't Be Ignored," *Forbes*, June 26, 2015, www.forbes.com. Vanessa Wong, "Coca-Cola Wants to Buy the World a Milk," December 1, 2014, www.businessweek.com. Khushbu Shah, "Coca-Cola's New 'Super Milk' Fairlife Is Super Weird," Eater, February 16, 2015, www.eater.com. Dan Nosowitz,"Coca-Cola to Sell Sexy Lactose-Free Milk Product of Some Kind," December 2, 2014, www.modernfarmer.com. Capehart and Berg (2018). www.prnewswire.com/news-releases/us-bottled-water-market-will-net-us-222-bn-revenues-by-end-of-2024---persistence-market-research-report-616324704.html (viewed on July 12, 2018). www.statista.com/outlook/20010000/109/bottled-water/united-states#marketStudy (viewed on July 28, 2018).

Managing in the Monopolistically Competitive Food Truck Market: Andrew S. Ross, "San Francisco Food Truck Empire Expanding," *San Francisco Chronicle*, February 18, 2011. www.mobilefoodnews.com (viewed on June 17, 2012). http://offthegridsf.com/about-3 (viewed on March 29, 2013). http://offthegridsf.com/vendors#food (viewed on November 8, 2015). https://offthegrid.com/ (viewed on July 28, 2018).

Chapter 12

Managerial Problem: Dying to Work "Mining: Probe Faults Massey, Regulators in Upper Big Branch Disaster," Greenwire, May 19, 2011, www.eenews.net/gw. Kris Maher, "Agency Blames Massey for Fatal Mine Disaster," *Wall Street Journal*, June 29, 2011. Lateef Mungin and Farid Ahmed, "Report: 8 Arrested After Deadly Bangladesh Building Collapse," CNN, April 27, 2013, www.cnn.com. http://world.time.com/2013/06/10/bangladesh-factory-collapse-uncertain-future-for-rana-plaza-survivors, June 10, 2013. www.bls.gov/iif/oshcfoi1.htm. Ceylan Yeginsu, "Anger and Grief Simmer in Turkey a Year After Soma Mine Disaster," *New York Times*, June 2, 2015. Andrew Jones, "In Tianjin Blasts, a Heavy Toll for Unsuspecting Firefighters," *New York Times*, August 17, 2015. Christopher Bodeen, "Final Death Toll Set at 173 in China Warehouse Explosion," Associated Press, September 11, 2015, www.ap.org. Omar Rashid, 32 Dead, Many Injured as Boiler Explodes in NTPC's Unchahar Plant in Rae Bareli, *The Hindu*, Nov. 3, 2017, www.thehindu.com/news/national/other-states/boiler-explodes-in-ntpc-unchahar-plant/article19961812.ece. www.osha.gov/oshstats/commonstats.html (viewed on July 30, 2018). www.bls.gov/news.release/cfoi.t04.htm (viewed on July 30, 2018). www.ilo.org/global/topics/safety-and-health-at-work/lang--de/index.htm, (viewed on July 30, 2018). www.bls.gov/iif/oshcfoi1.htm#rates, 2016.

Mini-Cases *Strategic Advertising*: Roberts and Samuelson (1988). Slade (1995). Gasmi et al. (2002). Salgado (2008). Richards and Padilla (2009). Chandra and Weinberg (2015). http://adage.com/article/advertising/big-spenders-facts-stats-top-200-u-s-advertisers/299270 (viewed on July 5, 2015). www.statista.com/topics/1625/procter-and-gamble (viewed on August 7, 2015). http://adage.com/trend-reports/report.php?id=136 (viewed on July 11, 2018). http://prcouncil.net/wp-content/uploads/2018/01/Marketing-Fact-Pack-2018.pdf (viewed on August 4, 2018). Shapiro (2018).

Cheap Talk in eBay's Best Offer Market: Backus, Blake, and Tadelis (2018).

Timing Radio Ads: Sweeting (2006, 2009).

Competing E-Book Formats: http://wiki.mobileread.com/wiki/AZW (viewed on September 3, 2015). http://wiki.mobileread.com/wiki/EPUB (viewed on September 3, 2015). http://ebook-reader-review.toptenreviews.com (viewed on September 3, 2015).

Nash Bargaining over Coffee: Draganska, Klapper, and Villas-Boas (2010).

Experienced Bidders: Garratt, Walker, and Wooders (2012). Feng, Fay, and Sivakumar (2015).

Managerial Implication *Solving Coordination Problems*: David Goldman, "Google Seats $13 Billion Motorola Buy," CNN Money, May 22, 2012, www.money.cnn.com.

Chapter 13

Managerial Problem: Intel and AMD's Advertising Strategies Salgado (2008). www.kitguru.net/desktop-pc/anton-shilov/amds-x86-processor-market-share-rises-thanks-to-game-consoles/. http://jonpeddie.com/publications/market_watch. www.cpubenchmark.net/market_share.html (viewed on August 7, 2018). www.jonpeddie.com/store/market-watch (viewed on August 7, 2018).

Mini-Cases *Tit-for-Tat Strategies in Trench Warfare*: Axelrod (2006).

Signaling Drug Price Increases: Jonathan D. Rockoff, "Drugmakers Find Competition Doesn't Keep a Lid on Prices," *Wall Street Journal*, November 27, 2016.

Pay-for-Delay Agreements: Matthew Herper, "The Best-Selling Drugs in America," *Forbes*, April 19, 2011, www.forbes.com. Duff Wilson, "F.T.C.: 28 'Pay-for-Delay' Generic Drug Deals," *New York Times*, October 25, 2011. Edward Wyatt, "Justices to Take Up Generic Drug Case," *New York Times*, December 7, 2012. Katie Thomas and Barry Meier, "Drug Makers Losing a Bid to Foil Generic Painkillers," *New York Times*, January 1, 2013. Edward Wyatt, "Supreme Court Lets Regulators Sue over Generic Deals," *New York Times*, June 17, 2013. www.drugs.com/article/patent-expirations.html (viewed on July 18, 2015). www.ftc.gov/news-events/press-releases/2015/05/ftc-settlement-cephalon-pay-delay-case-ensures-12-billion-ill. www.ftc.gov/news-events/press-releases/2015/05/ftc-settlement-cephalon-pay-delay-case-ensures-12-billion-ill (viewed on August 8, 2018).

www.pharmamanufacturing.com/articles/2018/10-major-drugs-losing-patent-protections-in-2018 (viewed on August 8, 2018).

Pfizer Uses Limit Pricing to Slow Entry: Melly Alazraki, "The 10 Biggest-Selling Drugs That Are About to Lose Their Patent," *Daily Finance*, February 27, 2011, www.dailyfinance.com. Duff Wilson, "Facing Generic Lipitor Rivals, Pfizer Battles to Protect Its Cash Cow," *New York Times*, November 29, 2011. Anna Edney and Adi Narayan, "Ranbaxy's Lipitor Copy in U.S. Stores Threatens Pfizer Sales," *Bloomberg Businessweek*, December 1, 2011, www.bloomberg.com. Duff Wilson, "Senators Question Deals to Block Generic Lipitor," *New York Times*, December 1, 2011. Drew Armstrong, "Pfizer After Lipitor

Slims Down to Push Mini-Blockbusters," *Bloomberg Businessweek*, December 5, 2011, www.bloomberg.com. Anna Edney, Adi Narayan, and Drew Armstrong, "Pfizer Lipitor Sales Are Threatened by Ranbaxy Generic Copy," *Bloomberg Businessweek*, December 6, 2011, www.bloomberg.com. Jonathan Rockoff, "Goodbye, Lipitor. Pfizer Bids a Farewell," *Wall Street Journal*, May 9, 2012. www.therubins.com/legal/patext2.htm. "U.S. Pharmaceutical Sales 2012," www.drugs.com/stats/top100/2012/sales (viewed on November 8, 2015).

Auto Union Negotiations: Alisa Priddle, "Ford Wants to Lead UAW Talks to Address Wage Disparity," *Detroit Free Press*, June 15, 2015, www.freep.com. David Barkholz, "UAW to Press for 'Pattern' Labor Deals in Detroit 3 Talks, Williams Says," *Automotive News*, March 25, 2015, www.autonews.com. Bernie Woodall, "UAW Picks Fiat Chrysler as Target Company in Labor Talks," Reuters, September 13, 2005. www.reuters.com/article/us-autos-uaw/uaw-elects-new-leader-to-face-contract-talks-federal-probe-idUSKBN1J91C6.

Venezuelan Nationalization: Gregory Wilpert, "Venezuela Decrees Nationalization of Last Foreign Controlled Oil Fields," February 27, 2007, http://venezuelanalysis.com/news/2245. "Venezuela," U.S. Energy Information Administration, March 2011, www.eia.gov/countries/cab.cfm?fips=VE (viewed on November 8, 2015). Patrick MacLeod, "U.S. Energy Information Administration Assessment of the Venezuelan Oil Industry," *Blogspot*, April 4, 2011, http://venezuelanoil.blogspot.com/2011/04/us-energy-information-administration.html. Marianna Parraga and Daniel Wallis, "PDVSA Says Debt Rose 55 Percent to $10.9 Billion at the End of 2010," Reuters, July 27, 2011. www.petroleumworld.com/storyt11072701.htm. Marianna Parraga, "Venezuela Sees Exxon, Conoco Arbitration Rules in Late 2013," Reuters, November 8, 2012. Alexandra Ulmer, "Tribunal Denies Venezuela Review Request of $1.6 Billion Exxon Award," Reuters, June 18, 2015. http://fuelfix.com/blog/2015/08/13/exxons-40-billion-oil-discovery-sparks-venezuelan-feud-with-guyana/#28248101=0. www.cnbc.com/2017/03/10/order-for-venezuela-to-pay-exxon-14-bln-in-damages-overturned--lawyer.html (viewed on August 8, 2018).Nicholas Bariyo and Jacquie McNish, "Tanzania's Tougher Mining Laws Rattle Companies," *Wall Street Journal*, August 2, 2017.

Advantages and Disadvantages of Moving First: Urban, Carter, and Gaskin (1986). Denstadli, Lines, and Grønhaug (2005). Dylan McGrath, "'Teardown' Finds Toshiba Taking a Loss on HD DVD Player," *EE Times*, June 23, 2006, www.eetimes.com. Dylan McGrath, "Analyst Predicts Stalemate in Next-Gen DVD War," *EE Times*, June 23, 2006, www.eetimes.com. Usero and Fernández (2009). Rex Santus, "Apple Watch Seized 75% of Smartwatch Market Last Quarter, According to Report." *Forbes*, July 23, 2015, www.forbes.com.https://9to5mac.com/2018/05/23/apple-watch-lte-defining-wearable-market (viewed on July 16, 2018). Porath (2018).

GM's Ultimatum: Robert Schoenberger, "GM Sends Ultimatums to All Its 6000 US Dealers," *Cleveland Plain Dealer*, June 2, 2009, www.cleveland.com/plaindealer, and "GM Dealers Sue to Keep Doors Open," *Toronto Star*, November 27, 2009, www.thestar.com. Janet Kurnovich, Greg Keenan, "Judge Dismisses Class Action by GM Canada Dealers, Upholds Claim Against Law Firm," *The Globe and Mail*, July 9, 2015, www.theglobeandmail.com. Jackson Hayes, "Trillium's $750M-Class Action Against GM Will Not Proceed to Supreme Court of Canada," *Canadian Autoworld*, January 24, 2018.

Managerial Implication ***Taking Advantage of Limited Strategic Thinking:*** Brown, Camerer, and Lovallo (2012).

Chapter 14

Managerial Problem: BP's Risk and Limited Liability Mark Long and Angel Gonzalez, "Transocean Seeks Limit on Liability," *Wall Street Journal*, May 13, 2010. David Leonhardt, "Spillonomics: Underestimating Risk," *New York Times*, May 21, 2010. Andrew Ross Sorkin, "Imagining the Worst in BP's Future," *New York Times*, June 7, 2010. James Quinn and Rowena Mason, "BP Oil Spill: Billions Wiped off Value BP as Share Price Plummets," *The Telegraph*, June 10, 2010. "BP Reports $4.9bn Annual Loss after Oil Spill Costs," BBC News, February 1, 2011, www.bbc.com/news/business. Sabrina Canfield, "BP, Transocean Wrangle over Insurance," Courthouse News Service, February 28, 2011, www.courthousenews.com. Jef Feeley and Allen Johnson Jr., "BP Wins Final Approval of Guilty Plea over Gulf Oil Spill," Bloomberg News, January 29, 2013, www.bloomberg.com. Kathy Finn, "Gulf Oil Spill Payouts," www.huffingtonpost.com. www.bp.com/sectiongenericarticle800.do?categoryId=9048917&contentId=7082602 (viewed on April 12, 2013). Coral Davenport and Johyn Schwartz, "BP Settlement in Gulf Oil Spill Is Raised to $20.8 Billion," *New York Times*, October 5, 2015. Ron Rousso, "BP Deepwater Horizon Costs Balloon to $65 Billion," Reuters, January 15, 2018.

Mini-Cases ***Stocks' Risk Premium:*** "The Cost of Looking," *Economist*, 328(7828), September 11, 1993:74. Leslie Eaton, "Assessing a Fund's Risk Is Part Math, Part Art," *New York Times*, April 2, 1995. http://pages.stern.nyu.edu/~adamodar/New_Home_Page/datafile/histretSP.html (viewed on August 12, 2018).

Gambling: Friedman and Savage (1948). Brunk (1981). Steve Coll, "Chances Are Brits Have Bet on It," *San Francisco Examiner*, July 10, 1994:4. Meghan Cox Gurdon, "British Accuse Their Lottery of Robbing the Poor to Give to the Rich," *San Francisco Chronicle*, November 25, 1995. Andrew Pollack, "In the Gaming Industry, the House Can Have Bad Luck, Too," *New York Times*, July 25, 1999. Garrett (2001). Marsha Walton, "The Business of Gambling," CNN, July 6, 2005, www.cnn.com. www.elottery.com/markets.html (viewed on June 26, 2012).

www.reportlinker.com/p0157384-summary/Global-Online-Gaming-Report.html (viewed on April 8, 2013). Mark Maremont and Alexandra Berzon, "How Often Do Gamblers Really Win?" *Wall Street Journal*, October 11, 2013. http://vegasclick.com/gambling/houseedge (viewed on November 8, 2015). https://newzoo.com/insights/articles/global-games-market-reaches-137-9-billion-in-2018-mobile-games-take-half/ (viewed on August 12, 2018).

Bond Ratings: "Standard and Poor's Ratings Definitions," 2018, Standard and Poor's, www.standardandpoors.com//en_US/web/guest/article/-/view/sourceId/504352 (viewed on August 12, 2018). "Rating Symbols and

Definitions," Moody's Investors Services, www.moodys.com/researchdocumentcontentpage.aspx?docid=PBC_79004 (viewed on August 12, 2018).

Flooded by Insurance Claims: Ruth Simon, "One House, 22 Floods, Repeated Claims Drain Federal Insurance Program," *Wall Street Journal*, September 15, 2017. Jen Schwartz, "National Flood Insurance Is Underwater Because of Outdated Science," *Scientific American*, March 23, 2018. www.swissre.com/media/news_releases/nr20180410_sigma_global_insured_losses_highest_ever.html (viewed August 13, 2018).

Biased Estimates: Benjamin, Dougan, and Buschena (2001). Sophie Tedmanson, "Fisherman Dean Brougham Tells of Lucky Escape After Shark Attack," *The Times*, November 9, 2009. Arthur Hu, "Death Spectrum," April 11, 2011, www.arthurhu.com/index/health/death.htm#deathrank. International Shark Attack File, *Ichthyology*, www.flmnh.ufl.edu/fish/sharks/isaf/graphs.htm (viewed on June 26, 2012). www.propertycasualty360.com/2015/07/27/first-half-of-2015-recorded-below-average-global-n. www.flmnh.ufl.edu/fish/sharks/statistics/statsus.htm (viewed on August 14, 2015).

Managerial Implications *Diversify Your Savings:* Paul J. Lim, "Don't Paint Nest Eggs in Company Colors," *New York Times*, March 30, 2008. Jilian Mincer, "Company-Stock Ownership Down Amid Fears," Financial Advisor, August 9, 2010, http://financialadviserblog.dowjones.com/blog/stay-ahead-of-your-clients/company-stock-ownership-down-amid-fears. Michael J. Moore, "Wall Streeters Lose $2 Billion in 401(k) Bet on Own Firms," Bloomberg News, July 9, 2012, www.bloomberg.com/news/2012-07-09/wall-streeters-lose-2-billion-in-401-k-bet-on-own-firms.html. Duan, Hotchkiss, and Jiao (2015). Ron Lieber, "A Scary Movie: Filling Your 401(k) with Company Stock," *New York Times*, March 21, 2015. Robert Steyer, "Company Stock Option Fading from 401(k) Plans," www.pionline.com, February 23, 2015, www.pionline.com/article/20150223/PRINT/302239977/company-stock-option-fading-from-401k-plans. www.icifactbook.org/ch8/18_fb_ch8 (viewed on August 12, 2018).

Loss Aversion Contracts: Hossain and List (2012). Fryer et al. (2012). Imas, Sadoff, and Samek (2015).

Chapter 15

Managerial Problem: Clawing Back Bonuses Jake Bernstein and Jesse Eisinger, "How Merrill Lynch Bankers Helped Blow Up Their Firm," NBC News, December 24, 2010, www.nbcnews.com/id/40795080/ns/business/t/how-merrill-lynch-bankers-helped-blow-their-firm/. "Morgan Stanley Defers Bonuses for High-Earners," *Chicago Tribune*, January 15, 2013. Elizabeth G. Olson, "Executive Pay Clawbacks: Just a Shareholder Pacifier?" CNN Money, August 16, 2012. www.execcomp.org/News/NewsStories/nearly-90-pct-of-fortune-100-companies-now-disclose-clawback-policies-according-to-equilar-survey. Andrew Ackerman, "SEC Proposes Broadened Corporate Clawback Rules," *Wall Street Journal*, July 1, 2015. Michael Corkery, "Wells Fargo Fined $185 Million for Fraudulently Opening Accounts," *New York*

Times, September 8, 2016. Gretchen Morgenson, "Executive Pay Clawbacks Are Gratifying, but Not Particularly Effective," *New York Times*, September 30, 2016. https://violationtracker.goodjobsfirst.org/parent/wells-fargo. www.shearman.com/perspectives/2018/04/embracing-the-quasi-clawback.

Mini-Cases *Reducing Consumers' Information:* Salop (1977). Nielsen Company, *The Rise and Rise Again of Private Label*, 2018. www.forbes.com/sites/pamdanziger/2018/05/06/how-amazon-plans-to-dominate-the-private-label-market/ (viewed on September 6, 2018). money.cnn.com/2018/04/23/news/companies/sears-ceo-offers-buy-kenmore/index.html.

Discounts for Data: Tara Siegel Bernard, "Giving Out Private Data for Discount in Insurance," *New York Times*, April 8, 2015. https://rootsrated.media/blog/these-health-insurance-companies-will-pay-you-to-exercise/ (viewed on August 17, 2018).

Adverse Selection and Remanufactured Goods: Neto, Bloemhof, and Corbett (2015). Subramanian and Subramanyam (2012).

Honest Cabbies: Balafoutas, Kerschbamer, and Sutter (2017).

Company Jets: Yermack (2006). Kim Peterson, "Should CEOs Vacation with the Corporate Jet?" MSN Money, June 16, 2011, www.msn.com/en-us/money. Paul Hodgson, "Come Fly with Them: These CEOs Spend the Most on the Corporate Jet," *Fortune*, January 27, 2015, www.fortune.com. Rik Myslewski, "Zuckerberg's 2012 Personal Income Tax Bill: $1.5 Billion," The Register, February 4, 2012, www.theregister.co.uk. https://ig.ft.com/sites/business-jets/. Lee (2018). www.americanbanker.com/slideshow/jets-drivers-champagne-checkups-perks-for-bank-ceos (viewed on August 17, 2018). www.wsj.com/articles/ceos-enjoy-richer-perks-1481036403, (viewed on August 17, 2018).

Sing for Your Supper: Personal communication (2015).

Capping Oil and Gas Bankruptcies: Boomhower (forthcoming). "Goin' for Broke in Texas . . . Protecting the Environment Without Slowing Economic Growth," http://energyathaas.wordpress.com/2014/12/01/goin-for-broke-in-texas-protecting-the-environment-without-slowing-economic-growth.

Managerial Implication *Efficiency Wages:* Yellen (1984). Stiglitz (1987). Shapiro and Stiglitz (1984).

Chapter 16

Managerial Problem: Licensing Inventions www.wipo.int/ipstats/en/wipi/ (viewed on November 8, 2015). Steve Lohr, "The 2012 Patent Ranks," *New York Times*, January 10, 2013. www.progressive-economy.org/trade_facts/u-s-share-of-world-intellectual-property-revenue-39-percent/ (viewed on November 8, 2015). WIPO IP Facts and Figures, 2014, www.wipo.int/edocs/pubdocs/en/wipo_pub_943_2014.pdf. http://venturebeat.com/2015/01/12/ibm-sets-patent-record-in-2014-with-7534/. 2014 IBM Annual Report, www.ibm.com/annualreport/. www.uspto.gov/web/offices/ac/ido/oeip/taf/us_stat.htm. Samuel Stebbins, "The World's 50 Most Innovative Companies," *USA Today*, January 12, 2018.

Jan Wolfe, "IBM Wins $83 Million from Groupon in Internet Patent Fight," Reuters, July 27, 2018. https://data.world-bank.org/indicator/BM.GSR.ROYL.CD (viewed on August 21, 2018).

Mini-Cases *Natural Gas Regulation*: Davis and Muehleg-ger (2009).

Are Monopoly Mergers Harmful?: Collard-Wexler (2014).

Piping Up About Exclusive Dealing: http://blogs.orrick .com/antitrust/2015/04/24/11th-circuit-affirms-ftc-ruling-that-exclusive-dealing-arrangements-violated-section-5-of-the-ftc-act. Bruce D. Sokler, Helen J. Kim, and Timothy J. Slattery, "FTC Flushes McWane in a Big Eleventh Circuit Exclusive Dealing Win," *National Law Review*, April 22, 2015, www.natlawreview.com. Diane Bartz, "Supreme Court Declines to hear McWane Case; a Win for the FTC," Reuters, March 21, 2016.

Pulp and Paper Mill Pollution and Regulation: LaPlante and Rilstone (1996). Foulon, Lanoie, and Laplante (2002). Shimshack and Ward (2005). Gray and Shimshack (2011). Alm and Shimshack (2014).

Why Tax Drivers: Edlin and Karaca-Mandic (2006). Parry, Walls, and Harrington (2007). Hill et. al. (2009). Anderson and Auffhammer (2014). Sheehan-Connor (2015).

Spam: Marc Caliendo et al. (2013). "Email Attacks: This Time It's Personal," Cisco, June 2011, www.cisco.com. Nicole Henderson, "Symantec Report Finds Spam Accounts for 73 Percent of June Email," *Web Host Industry Review*, June 28, 2011, www.thewhir.com. Rao and Reiley (2012). Dino Grandoni, "Spam Costs You a Lot More Than You'd Think," www .huffingtonpost.com. Lance Whitney, "Targeted Cyberattacks Jump 42 Percent in 2012, Symantec Says," www.cnet.com. www.propellercrm.com/blog/email-spam-statistics (viewed on August 6, 2018). www.spamlaws.com/spam-stats.html (viewed on August 21, 2018).

Piracy: Business Software Alliance, *Software Management: Security Imperative, Business Opportunity—BSA Global Software Survey*, June 2018. Available at www.bsa.org/studies.

Managerial Implications *Disney Internalizes an External-ity*: Lou Mongello, "Walt Disney World History 101—'How to Buy 27,000 Acres of Land and Have No One Notice," www .wdwradio.com/2005/02/wdw-history-101-how-to-buy-27000-acres-of-land-and-no-one-notice/, February 11, 2005. "The Secret Florida Land Deal That Became Walt Disney World," www.miamiherald.com/news/state/florida/article 150733437.html, May 16, 2017.

Buying a Town: Katharine Q. Seelye, "Utility Buys Town It Choked, Lock, Stock and Blue Plume," *New York Times*, May 13, 2002. "Cheshire Ohio," Abandoned, www.abandonedonline.net/ neighborhoods/cheshire-ohio. http://worldpopulationreview .com/us-cities/cheshire-oh-population/ (viewed on August 31, 2018).

Trade Secrets: Hall et al. (2014).

Chapter 17

Managerial Problem: Responding to Exchange Rates
https://apps.fas.usda.gov/psdonline/circulars/grain-wheat.

pdf (viewed on August 23, 2018). www.press.rolls-roycemotorcars .com/rolls-royce-motor-cars-pressclub/article/detail/ T0277884EN/rolls-royce-motor-cars-delivers-outstanding-result-in-2017?language=en (viewed on August 23, 2018). www .businessinsider.com/new-rolls-royce-phantom-vii-pri-vate-jet-road-2017-7 (viewed on August 23, 2018). www .bloomberg.com/quote/USDJPY:CUR (viewed on August 23, 2018).

Mini-Cases *Barbie Doll Varieties*: "The Storybook Romance Comes to an End for Barbie and Ken," Mattel, February 12, 2004, www.mattel.com. Venessa Wong, "Barbie Wins Contest for No. 1 Holiday Import," *Bloomberg Businessweek*, December 13, 2011, www.bloomberg.com/businessweek. Neil Unger-leider, December 17, 2014, www.fastcolabs.com/3039986/ the-most-popular-toys-of-the-holidays-according-to-shipping-containers. http://time.com/3089384/influential-toys/ (viewed on August 27, 2018). https://money.cnn.com/ 2018/03/13/news/companies/barbie-mattel-toys-r-us/index. html (viewed on August 27, 2018). https://mashable.com/ 2018/06/26/barbie-careers-stem-robotics-engineer/ #Di0OSpxj1Oqx (viewed on August 27, 2018).

Russian Food Ban: "Inflation Soars Above 8% as Food Bans and Ruble Bite," *Moscow Times*, November 5, 2014, www .moscowtimes.com. Alexey Eremenko, "Russia's Sanctions War Against the West Explained," NBC News, August 22, 2015, www. nbcnews.com. Polina Devitt, Reuters, "Russia Looks Set to Extend Import Ban on Western Food," April 30, 2015. www.usnews .com/news/best-countries/articles/2017-08-18/3-years-of-sanctions-changes-russias-food-market (viewed August 18, 2017). http://sputniknews.com/world/201808071067013027-food-russia-embargo-eu-losses/ (viewed August 8, 2018).

Mini-Case: Protection of U.S. Steel, Aluminum, and Washing Machines: www.wto.org/english/news_e/news18_e/ds548_ 550rfc_06jun18_e.htm (viewed on August 28, 2018). www .heritage.org/trade/report/steel-imports-do-not-threaten-national-security (viewed on August 28, 2018). Kimberly Janeway, "What the New Tariff on Washing Machines Means for Consumers," *Consumer Reports*, January 23, 2018, www. consumerreports.org/washing-machines/what-the-new-tariff-on-washing-machines-means-for-consumers/.

What's an American Car?: www.cars.com/go/advice/Story .jsp?section=top&subject=ami&story=amMade0712 (viewed on December 3, 2012). www.nhtsa.gov/Laws+&+Regulations/ Part+583+American+Automobile+Labeling+Act+(AALA)+ Reports (viewed on August 22, 2015). Kelsey Mays, "The Cars. com American-Made Index," 2018, www.cars.com/articles/ carscom-2018-american-made-index-whats-the-most-american-car-1420700348632/ /. www.forbes.com/pictures/ 593acc11a7ea434078d4eed5/2-ford-f-150/#4f4cfd5075da (viewed on August 24, 2018). www.nhtsa.gov/part-583-american-automobile-labeling-act-reports (viewed on September 1, 2018).

Profit Repatriation: John Aloysius Farrell, "Senate Com-mittee Finds Most 'Trapped' Offshore Income Is Already in U.S.," The Cutting Edge News, December 18, 2011. Jeff Cox, "Why Bringing Corporate Cash Home Won't Help," March 5, 2015, http://cnbc.com. Philip Elmer-DeWitt, "Congress Has Its Eye on Apple's $158 Billion in Offshore Cash. UPDATE: So Does Obama," *Fortune*, January 31, 2015, www.fortune .com. www.money.cnn.com. Matthew Townsend and Lau-rie Meisler, "These Are the Biggest Overseas Cash Hoards

Congress Wants to Tax," Bloomberg, November 2017. Lynnley Browning, "Apple's $38 Billion Tax Bill? The Company Has Eight Years to Pay," Bloomberg, January 25, 2018. Ritvik Carvalho and Sujata Rao, "Falling Offshore T-Bond Holdings Highlight U.S. Cash Repatriation," Reuters, August 16, 2018.

Managerial Implications *Brian May's Comparative Advantage*: http://astro.ic.ac.uk/bmay/home. Stuart Clark, "European Space Agency to join Brian May's Asteroid Day," *The Guardian*, February 9, 2016. www.smithsonian-mag.com/smart-news/new-horizons-team-got-little-help-queen-guitarist-brian-may-180956073. https://mainichi.jp/english/articles/20180627/p2a/00m/0na/020000c (viewed on August 27, 2018).

Limiting Arbitrage and Gray Markets: Peter Sayer, "EU Court Says eBay Must Comply with Trademark Rules," *PC World Australia*, July 13, 2011, www.pcworld.idg.com.au. David Needle, "Unauthorized iPads Make Up Half of All Sales in China," Tab Times, October 11, 2011, http://tabtimes.com/news/ittech-other/2011/10/11/unauthorized-ipads-make-half-all-sales-china. www.ipbrief.net/2015/02/25/buying-the-real-thing-for-less-copyright-and-first-sale-doctrine-implications-of-omega-s-a-v-costco-wholesale-corp/. Susanna Kim, "Costco's Deep Discount Ticks Off a Luxury Watchmaker," ABC News, January 22, 2015, https://abcnews.go.com/Business/costcos-deep-discounts-ticks-off-luxury-watchmaker/story?id=28399405

Index

Credits

p. 5, cartoon (top): Pearson Education

p. 5, cartoon (bottom): www.speedbump.com.

p. 9, epigraph: Mason, John. (2010). *Believe You Can— The Power of a Positive Attitude*. Revel.

p. 9, photo: Tatiana Grozetskaya/Shutterstock

p. 12, photo: Lev/Fotolia

p. 23, photo: Americanspirit/Visions Of America LLC/123RF GB Ltd

p. 25, cartoon: Pearson Education, Inc.

p. 29, photo: National Archives and Records Administration

p. 31, photo: Carlos Garcia Rawlins/Thompson Reuters

p. 44, photo: Pingpao/Fotolia

p. 57, photo: Jeffrey M. Perloff

p. 64, epigraph: Banksy

p. 65, epigraph: "Quest for the Best," (1979), by Stanley Marcus

p. 67, epigraph: Enrico Fermi, from Jevremovic, Tatjana. *Nuclear Principles in Engineering*. Springer: 2005, p. 397.

p. 68, epigraph: John Tukey, from Institute of Mathematical Statistics

p. 69, epigraph: Malcolm Forbes, from *The Sayings of Chairman Malcolm*, 1978, by Malcolm S. Forbes, Harpercollins

p. 71, cartoon: Pearson Education, Inc.

p. 73, epigraph: John McPhee, from *In Suspect Terrain* (1984)

p. 76, photo: Pearson Education, Inc.

p. 87, epigraph: 1840 January 18, *Madison Courier* (Short untitled item), Quote Page 1, Column 6, Madison, Indiana.

p. 87, photo: John Foxx/Getty Images

p. 88, epigraph: Marcel Duchamp, from Harriet & Sidney Janis in "Marchel Duchamp: Anti-Artist" in *View* magazine 3/21/45; reprinted in Robert Motherwell, *Dada Painters and Poets* (1951).

p. 89, epigraph: George Bernard Shaw, from Shaw, B. (1907). *Man and Superman. A Comedy and a Philosophy*, The Floating Press.

p. 90, cartoon: Pearson Education, Inc.

p. 95, cartoon: Pearson Education, Inc.

p. 104, photo: Benjamin Goode/123RF GB Ltd

p. 105, epigraph: Errol Flynn, quoted in Jane Mercer, *Great Lover of the Movies*, "Errol Flynn," 1975.

p. 110, photo: nikd90/123RF GB Ltd

p. 124, epigraph: quoted in Goldman, Todd Harris (2001) *Teachers: Jokes, Quotes, and Anecdotes*. Andrews McMeel Publishing, p. 136.

p. 124, photo: vario images GmbH & Co.KG/Alamy Stock Photo

p. 131, photo: Big Cheese Photo/Getty Images

p. 133, photo (top): Pearson Education, Inc.

p. 133, photo (bottom): Micheline Pelletier Decaux/Getty Images

p. 142. cartoon: Pearson Education, Inc.

p. 143, photo: teabum/Fotolia

p. 147, photo: Wang Jianwei/Newscom

p. 153, epigraph: Samuel Goldwyn, from *The Great Goldwyn*, Alva Johnston, Random House, 1937, p. 34.

p. 153, photo: Photodisc/Getty Images

p. 159, photo: nobilior/123RF

p. 159, cartoon: Pearson Education, Inc.

p. 168, photo: Dmitry Kalinovsky/Shutterstock

p. 172, photo: TONY MCNICOL/Alamy Stock Photo

p. 181, photo: 123RF

p. 191, epigraph: Telegram to the Friar's Club of Beverly Hills to which he belonged, as recounted in *Groucho and Me* (1959), p. 32.

p. 191, photo: Interim Archives/Getty Images

p. 192, epigraph: George Carlin

p. 205, photo: poosan/Fotolia

p. 212, epigraph: Carl Sagan from Sagan, C., Tyson, N. D., & Druyan, A. (1980). *Cosmos*. New York: The Random House Publishing Group.

p. 214, quotation: Reed Hastings talks with WSJ Financial Editor Dennis Berman at the WSJDLive conference.

p. 214, photo: Oshchepkov Konstantin/Shutterstock

pp. 216–217, excerpts: Adam Smith, from Smith, A. (1776). *An Inquiry into the Nature and Causes of the Wealth of Nations*. Scotland, Kingdom of Great Britain: Strahan.

p. 225, epigraph: George Bernard Shaw, from Shaw, B. (1901). *Man and Superman*. Mattituck, NY: Amereon House.

p. 225, photo: Konstantin Sutyagin/Fotolia

p. 235, photo: Jaddingt/Fotolia

p. 241, epigraph: Howard H. Aiken, from Cohen, I. B. (1999). *Howard Aiken: Portrait of a Computer Pioneer* (History of computing). MIT Press.

p. 244, photo: Brocreative/Shutterstock

p. 250, photo: Jeffrey M. Perloff

p. 258, cartoon: Pearson Education, Inc.

p. 266, photo: Jeffrey M. Perloff

p. 276, photo: Utah/Shutterstock

p. 284, cartoon: Pearson Education, Inc.

p. 291, photo: Philadelphia Inquirer/KRT/Newscom

p. 293, epigraph: Joseph E. Levine, quoted in Halliwell's Filmgoer's Companion, 1984

p. 293, extract: Patel, N. V. (2017, December 18). *A Japanese Startup Wants to Put Advertising on the Moon. Is That Legal?* Retrieved from http://www.slate.com/articles/health_and_science/science/2017/12/ispace_wants_to_advertise_on_the_moon_is_that_legal.html

p. 295, epigraph: *An advertisement in Brick and Clay Record, Volumes 52–53.* Kenfield-Leach, 1918.

p. 307, epigraph: Syrus, P. (1856). *The Moral Sayings of Publius Syrus: A Roman Slave. From the Latin* (D. Lyman, Trans.). New York: L.E. Bernard & Company.

p. 307, photo: Jeffrey M. Perloff

p. 311, photo: Jeffrey M. Perloff

p. 323, excerpt: California Second District Court of Appeal said in a unanimous Jan. 29, 2018 ruling against Tinder's age-based pricing for its premium subscription service.

p. 325, cartoon: Pearson Education, Inc.

p. 326, quotation: SLATALLA, M. (2000, January 5). *To Boldly Go to the Supermarket With Captain Kirk.* Retrieved August 16, 2018, from https://archive.nytimes.com/www.nytimes.com/library/tech/00/01/circuits/articles/06shop.html

p. 339, excerpts: HP LaserJet - HP Print Cartridges and Imaging Drums Limited Warranty Statement | HP® Customer Support. (n.d.). Retrieved from https://support.hp.com/ph-en/document/c01848047

p. 340, photo: Radius Images/Corbis

p. 341, excerpts: *How surge pricing works* | Uber. (n.d.). Retrieved from https://www.uber.com/en-PH/drive/partner-app/how-surge-works/

p. 350, epigraph: George Ade, from E. Esar and N. Bentley, *Treasury of Humorous Quotations*

p. 350, photo: MarchCattle/Shutterstock

p. 352, epigraph: Adam Smith, from Smith, A., & McCulloch, J. R. (1870). *An inquiry into the nature and causes of the wealth of nations*. Glasgow: Grand Colosseum Warehouse.

pp. 356–357, excerpt: Austen, I. (2015, August 20). *Canadian Maple Syrup 'Rebels' Clash With Law*. Retrieved from https://www.nytimes.com/2015/08/23/business/international/canadian-maple-syrup-producers-clash-with-law.html

p. 357, photo: Sweet Memento Photography/Shutterstock

p. 367, photo: Jeffrey M. Perloff

p. 371, cartoon: Pearson Education, Inc.

p. 374, photo: Jeffrey M. Perloff

p. 375, photo: Jeffrey M. Perloff

p. 378, photo: Pearson Education, Inc.

p. 385, photo: Davis Turner/Newscom

p. 394, photo: Trevor Smith/Alamy Stock Photo

p. 400, cartoon: Pearson Education, Inc.

p. 404, photo: Jeffrey M. Perloff

p. 405, epigraph: Doyle, A. C. (1892). *The Adventures of Sherlock Holmes*. United Kingdom: George Newnes.

p. 424, epigraph: Doyle, A. C. (1892). The Adventures of Sherlock Holmes. United Kingdom: George Newnes.

p. 424, photo: sirtravelalot/Shutterstock

p. 429, excerpt: Axelrod, R. (n.d.). *The Evolution of Cooperation*. Retrieved August 17, 2018, from http://www.heretical.com/games/trenches.html

p. 436, cartoon: Pearson Education, Inc.

p. 443, cartoon: Pearson Education, Inc.

p. 445, epigraph: Aristotle (2004). *The Nicomachean ethics* (J. A. Thomson, H. Tredennick, & J. Barnes, Trans.). London: Penguin Books.

p. 448, photo: Aaron Sosa/Picture Alliance/DPA/Newscom

p. 462, Adlai Stevenson speech, Indianapolis (26 September 1952)

p. 462, photo: US Coast Guard

p. 466, epigraph: Personal quote of George W. Bush

p. 469, photo: Jeffrey M. Perloff

p. 475, photo: Jeffrey M. Perloff

p. 477, cartoon: Pearson Education, Inc.

p. 481, cartoon: Pearson Education, Inc.

p. 485, photo: MDay Photography/Shutterstock

p. 489, photo: Cathy Keifer/123 RF

p. 500, cartoon: Pearson Education, Inc.

p. 503, photo: Pearson Education, Inc.

p. 508, cartoon: Pearson Education, Inc.

p. 509, epigraph: Mark Twain—Honesty Is The Best Policy. (2015, November 18). Retrieved from https://due.com/blog/mark-twain-honesty-is-the-best-policy/

p. 512, photo: ALEXEY FILATOV/Shutterstock

p. 514, photo: MO_SES Premium/Shutterstock

p. 519, epigraph: Boller, P. F., Jr., & George, J. (1990). *They Never Said It: A Book of Fake Quotes, Misquotes, and Misleading Attributions.* Oxford University Press.

p. 524, photo: Damian Dovarganes/AP Images

p. 536, epigraph: Ronald Reagan: "Remarks to State Chairpersons of the National White House Conference on Small Business," August 15, 1986. Online by Gerhard Peters and John T. Woolley, The American Presidency Project. http://www.presidency.ucsb.edu/ws/?pid=37767

p. 536, cartoon: Pearson Education, Inc.

p. 545, extract: *Mission.* (2015, July 20). Retrieved September 8, 2018, from https://www.justice.gov/atr/mission

p. 545, extracts: *About the FTC.* (2018, July 17). Retrieved September 8, 2018, from https://www.ftc.gov/about-ftc

p. 546, cartoon: Pearson Education, Inc.

p. 555, cartoon: Pearson Education, Inc.

p. 557, photo: Solares/Shutterstock

p. 562, photo: Doral Chenoweth III/The Columbus Dispatch/AP Images

p. 568, photo: Jeffrey Coolidge/Stone/Getty Images

p. 579, epigraph: Former Australian cabinet minister Keppel Enderbery

p. 579, photo: iStockphoto/Thinkstock/Getty Images

p. 581, epigraph: Tommy Cooper. The Duck Trick. https://www.youtube.com/watch?v=Po8lywTWrJA

p. 584, photo: Deposit Photos/Glow Images

p. 591, photo: JackF/Fotolia

p. 607, cartoon: Pearson Education, Inc.

Featured Mini-Cases in This Book